THE RENAISSANCE:
An Illustrated Encyclopedia

The Virgin and St. Ann with St. John the Baptist, *drawing by Leonardo*

THE RENAISSANCE:
An Illustrated Encyclopedia

Ilan Rachum

[c1979]

Designed by: A. Yuval.

Published in the United States by Mayflower Books Inc.,
575 Lexington Avenue, New York City 10022. Originally published
in England by Octopus Books Limited, 59 Grosvenor Street,
London Wl.

Printed in U.S.A.

Rachum, Ilan, 1937–
The Renaissance, an illustrated encyclopedia.
Bibliography: p.
Includes index.
1. Renaissance–Dictionaries. I. Title.
CB361.R26 909.'4'03 79-13631
ISBN 0-7064-0857-8

Page 1: Late secular Gothic architecture in Italy: the Doges' Palace in Venice

Contents

Foreword

The Renaissance: An Illustrated Encyclopedia is one of a series of encyclopedias designed to give a comprehensive view of Western civilization, beginning with Classical Greece and ending with the world of the Twentieth Century. The geographical scope of each volume is determined by its period, the centres of its civilization and historical events. Thus, the first volume naturally concentrates on the countries of the Mediterranean basin, and succeeding volumes cover a larger area, to include, in the one on the Middle Ages, all the countries of Europe and some of North Africa and Asia, while the present Encyclopedia deals also with the New World, and other regions explored and colonized by Europeans. The civilization of medieval and Renaissance Europe was built on the cultural heritage of the ancient Graeco-Roman world, combined with Judaeo-Christian ethos. The Europeans carried it with them wherever they went, and transmitted it to some extent to the indigenous populations of America and Africa. For the intelligent reader, who wishes to trace and understand the development of this great heritage, these encyclopedias are designed.

The period covered by the present volume, the Renaissance, is traditionally described as the cultural link connecting antiquity with the modern world. Spanning the so-called Dark Ages of medieval Europe, it was an intellectual bridge between the summit of human creativity in Classical Greece and Rome, and the Age of Enlightenment. The humanists of the 14th, 15th and 16th centuries sought to advance and revitalize the intellectual and cultural life in their societies by recovering the ancient heritage, of which they had scant but tantalizing knowledge. They searched for old manuscripts and translations of the works of Greek and Roman authors, and collected ancient art. This was not, of course, their sole concern – they were also deeply rooted in the soil of Christendom, which determined their manner of thinking even in secular matters. Yet, manifest in every enterprise in Renaissance Europe was a sense of individualism and human destiny. It gave rise to a proliferation of new discoveries and concepts, new approaches to the natural world, a fresh view of Man and of his cherished values and beliefs. It also provided the impetus for the great geographical discoveries, which expanded the world of European man to include America, Africa and Asia. Against this background of seething social and intellectual ferment, the great inventions and developments seem almost inevitable. It is as if European civilization, arrested with the decline of the Graeco-Roman world, was eagerly making up for lost time. It is the age when Copernicus, Kepler and Galileo dislodged, as it were, the earth from its traditional place in the centre of the universe and placed it with its sister planets in orbit around the sun – a cosmological development that would not have surprised the ancients. The voyages of Columbus, Magellan, Vasco da Gama and Vespucci played a similar role in showing the narrow world of Europe and the Mediterranean its proper

Victory, ***marble statue by Michelangelo***

place on the globe. It is the age when social and political change put an end to the vestiges of feudalism and saw the emergence of the centrally-governed state, with such outstanding rulers as Emperor Charles V, Francis I of France and Elizabeth I of England stamping the institution of monarchy with their personal imprint that would last for generations. It is also the age of Machiavelli and Thomas More and many other, less renowned social theorists, whose thought shaped the world to come. It is the age of the Reformation, of Martin Luther, John Calvin and John Knox, who tore whole countries from the bosom of the Church of Rome, and established new concepts of the relationship between Man and God. The Counter-Reformation, which gave birth to such figures as Ignatius of Loyola and Theresa of Avila, restored some countries to the Church and revitalized its spiritual message. The Renaissance saw inventions that were to change the face of the world, including printing, artillery, the galleon and the caravel, and the telescope. Medical science made its first advances since Classical times, with the beginning of modern anatomy and empirical pharmacology. Above all, it was the age when learning was taken out the monasteries and stripped of its Latin shroud, and education became a major concern of the humanist scholars. The rise of vernacular prose and poetry gave the world the works of Shakespeare, Rabelais, Cervantes and Boccaccio, and the Authorized Version of the Bible. But it was in the visual arts that the Renaissance made its most memorable contribution to civilization – Leonardo da Vinci, Raphael, Michelangelo, Jan van Eyck, Albrecht Dürer, Botticelli, Alberti and Brunelleschi are but some of the names that come to mind, leaving no doubt that the aesthetic values of the modern world are firmly rooted in their age. A similar development took place in music, with the birth of the opera and the appearance of musical forms and instruments familiar to this day. It is therefore a proper and legitimate statement, that the modern world has grown out of the Renaissance.

Significantly, the modern use of the word "encyclopedia", meaning a reference work containing comprehensive information either on one or on all branches of human knowledge, was first used in the Renaissance. The humanists' ideal of a civilized person was one who was educated in all the fields of cultural and scientific knowledge, particularly the seven Liberal Arts – the *trivium* (grammar, logic and rhetoric) and the *quadrivium* (geometry, arithmetic, astronomy and music). These were also considered the principal components of an encyclopedia.

Nowadays, an encyclopedia is a much broader and more comprehensive work. We live in a world of infinitely great complexity than did the first encyclopedists, and our analysis of events and developments takes in aspects they never dreamed of. This affects our historical comprehension, too, so that our view of a past period is far more complex than that of its contemporaries. We are conscious of the tremendous influence of economics upon the social fabric and, indirectly, upon cultural and political developments. We take into consideration such factors as population density, technology, climate, diet and communications, and we are aware of their interdependence. Inevitably, then, our view of the Renaissance is both deeper and wider than that of the people who were living then, even though they were aware, to a unique degree, of living in a new age, and of pioneering a greater conception of humanity and its place in the world. Thus, in setting out to compile an encyclopedia of the Renaissance, the editor must be guided by two broad considerations: one is the nature of the period itself, and the other – the requirements of the modern reader.

Regarding the first consideration, nothing we can say here will add to the clear and comprehensive picture that emerges from the pages of the Encyclopedia itself. Regarding the second, the author, Dr Ilan Rachum, a modern historian with wide fields of interest, designed the volume to serve both the intelligent general reader and the college student seeking information on more specialized areas and aspects of the Renaissance. This dual purpose determined the structure of the Encyclopedia. There are many long articles on general subjects, each of which includes many cross-references to shorter entries, of which there are over two thousand. The longer articles and most of the short entries have bibliographies appended to them, of great help to the student. In addition, there is a general bibliography, arranged by subject, at the end of the Encyclopedia, which will no doubt be an invaluable aid to students and layman alike.

Some of the major subjects covered by long articles in this volume are:

The Arts. There are articles on Painting, Sculpture, Music and Architecture, as well as biographies of some four hundred of the most important artists, architects and composers of the age. There are also articles on Drama, Philosophy, and the rise of Vernacular Literature in Europe, as well as biographies of the outstanding contributors in these fields.

Religion. There are articles on the Reformation and Counter-Reformation; biographies of the major leaders and theologians of the Roman Catholic and Protestant camps, including all the popes of the period; entries on the contemporary religious sects, orders and national churches; articles on Bible Translations and Scholarship, and on Mysticism.

The intellectual world of the Renaissance. There are articles on Humanism and on the revival of Greek learning; Historiography, Political Theory, Education, Philosophy and Cosmology, as well as biographies of outstanding figures in these fields.

Exploration. In addition to a long article on this subject, there are also long articles on Navigation, Ships and Ship-building, and Cartography, with many short entries and biographies of all the main persons in these fields.

Science and Technology. There are articles on Anatomy, Astronomy, Mechanics, Mathematics, Medicine and their development during the Renaissance. There is an important long article on Printing, tracing its technical development and diffusion throughout Europe, and biographies of the prominent printers and publishers. There are also articles on Mining and Metallurgy.

Military History and International Relations. There are articles on Arms, Armies, Artillery and Diplomacy, as well as individual entries on major treaties and battles, military conflicts and famous soldiers.

Political History. There are articles on each of the major European countries and on each of the great rulers of the period; the evolution and development of the principal political institutions including Monarchy and Parliaments; legal and administrative systems; revolutions and social upheavals.

Economic History. There are articles on Agriculture, Commerce and Banking.

For the reader's convenience, the Encyclopedia is provided with a comprehensive Index to the terms, personalities, places and subjects which do not have separate entries, but which are mentioned in the major entries. The Index is an indispensable component of the Encyclopedia and greatly increases its usefulness.

No effort has been spared to illustrate the extraordinary artistic achievements of the Renaissance with a wealth of colour and black-and-white plates. In the Publishers' view the function of the pictorial material is not only to attract the eye and provide aesthetic pleasure – it is an integral part of the information contained in the Encyclopedia, without which the reader's general picture of the Renaissance would be greatly limited. There is also a considerable number of maps, which help the reader to gain a visual image of the political and geographical developments of the period.

The Editor and the Publishers believe that this Encyclopedia will further the understanding and study of the period, whose manifold achievements and cultural contributions are an integral part of the civilization that we know today.

Cross-references are marked by an asterisk (*) and bibliographical information is added in italics at the end of most entries. Articles by the two contributors, Dr Miriam Eliav and Ms Nava Dekalo are signed with their initials.

The Publishers

The Spanish Armada, by an anonymous painter

Late Gothic religious architecture in England: the great cathedral of York (c. 1220-c. 1470)

ABBATE (ABATE), NICCOLO DELL' (c. 1512-71) Italian painter. A. began his career in his birthplace, Modena, but his mature style developed in Bologna (1548-52) under the influence of *Correggio and *Parmigianino. There he painted stucco-surface landscapes in the Palazzo Poggi (now Palazzo dell' Università). In 1552 he was invited to the court of *Henry II at *Fontainebleau and remained in France for the rest of his life. Together with Francesco *Primaticcio he painted large murals depicting lyrical landscapes with pagan mythological themes. Most of these were later lost. A series of his latest paintings, done for *Charles IX, had a direct influence on the French painters of the 17th century such as Claude Lorrain and Nicolas Poussin. Some of his designs for tapestries were used in the industry of painted enamel of Limoges. A. is recognized as one of the early contributors to the Fontainebleau school.

ABRABANEL, ISAAC (1437-1508) Jewish banker, statesman, philosopher and biblical commentator. Born in Lisbon to a noble family which claimed descent from the house of David, A. acquired a general education, which included rabbinical literature as well as the Christian concepts of Renaissance humanism. Upon the death of his father Judah (1471), he succeeded him as treasurer to *Afonso V, but when *John II ascended the throne, A. lost his place at court and went to Spain. There he entered the service of *Ferdinand and *Isabella, to whom he lent money for the war against *Granada. When the Jews were expelled from Spain in 1492 A. went to Naples, where he was employed by kings *Ferrante and *Alfonso II. When the French invaded he moved to Corfu but returned in 1496 and in 1503 settled in *Venice, where he negotiated with Portugal in matters relating to the spice trade. He did much of his writing during these years of wandering after the expulsion from Spain, his response to it taking the form of messianic speculations, which contributed to the persistence of this theme in Jewish thought during the next two centuries.

B.-Z. Netanyahu, *Don Isaac Abravanel: Statesman and Philosopher* (1972);
A. J. Raines, *Maimonides and Abrabanel on Prophecy* (1970).

ABRABANEL, JUDAH (Leone Ebreo; c. 1460-1525) Son of Isaac, a physician, poet and philosopher. Born in Lisbon, where he studied and practiced medicine, he followed his father first to Spain and then to Naples. In Italy he continued practicing and teaching medicine, and treated the Spanish viceroy of Naples, Gonzalo de *Cordoba. At that time he read the writings of *Pico and *Ficino. His main work *Dialoghi di Amore* investigates the nature of love. It was first published in 1535, and there were numerous editions and translations throughout the 16th century.

Leone Ebreo, *The Philosophy of Love* (1937);
S. Damiens, *Amour et intellect chez Léon l'Hébreu* (1971).

ACADEMIES The development of humanist studies in the 15th century brought forward the A. as a new type of institution of learning. The early A., however, were not much more than occasional gatherings of intimate circles of scholars, joined together by common intellectual interests. The earliest was *Ficino's Platonic Academy of Florence (1442), which Cosimo de' *Medici encouraged and maintained. To this was soon added a Roman academy, dedicated to the study of history and archaeology. Later, A. appeared all over Italy, and by the late 16th century their number approached 700. The best known was the Accademia della Crusca of Florence, which was founded in 1582. In 1612 it published the first major dictionary of the Italian language. In Germany, where a number of humanist sodalities were formed during the late 15th century, they were never more than loose associations. Most of the early A. had literary scopes. Those of the 16th century were either literary, philosophical or scientific; although a number of institutions for the study of fine arts and music were also coming into existence. The earliest attempt to create an A. of fine arts was made by Baccio *Bandinelli in 1531, but the first, properly speaking, institution of that kind was founded by *Vasari in Florence only in 1563. In England, France and other countries national A. of sciences were not established until the 17th century.

M. Maylender, *Storia delle accademie d'Italia*, 5 vols. (1926-30);

Manuscript illustration of The Proportions of Man *by Leonardo (*c. *1509).*

F. A. Yates, *The French Academies of the Sixteenth Century* (1947).

ACCIAIUOLI, DONATO (1428-78) Florentine humanist scholar. He studied under John *Argyropoulos and was famous for his knowledge of Greece and for his Aristotelian tendency, which contradicted the Neoplatonic one current in Florence. Besides writing commentaries to Aristotle's *Ethics* and *Politics*, A. translated Plutarch and took part in the government of his city.

ACONTIUS, GIACOMO (1492-1566) An Italian spokesman for religious toleration. A. left Italy because of the rising tide of persecution against unorthodoxy and spent years in Switzerland and *Strassburg. His *De methodo* came out in *Basle in 1558, setting down rules for a critical investigation of the *Bible. Shortly afterwards he went to England where he published a second work, *Stratagemata satanae* (1565), which sought to find a common doctrinal base for all Christian churches. His ideas, which consciously tried to minimize the differences between the various creeds, were obviously beyond the comprehension of his intolerant contemporaries. In England A. returned to his profession, engineering, and drained marshes.

P. Rossi, *Giacomo Aconcio* (1952).

ACOSTA, JOSÉ DE (1540-1600) Spanish author. In 1570 A. went to Peru as a missionary of the *Jesuit order. He spent 17 years there, studying the Indian languages, all the while advancing in the hierarchy of his order. After his return to Spain, A. was involved in fierce factional struggle inside the Jesuit order, which led to his imprisonment (1592-93), but eventually regained his standing and became the head of the order's college in Salamanca. His most famous work, *Historia natural y moral de las Indias*, came out in *Seville in 1590 and was quickly translated into other languages. It dealt with the physical geography, plant life, agriculture and mining in the New World, as well as with the political and social institutions of the ruined Indian empires.

ACQUAVIVA, CLAUDIUS (1543-1615) Fifth general of the *Jesuit order. Born to an important Neapolitan family, which produced several prominent ecclesiastics, A. entered the order in 1567. He became provincial of Naples, then of Rome, and in 1581 was elected general. His tenure of office, which lasted for 34 years, was characterized by a tremendous expansion of Jesuit activity in Europe, as well as by the growth of missionary work in *Asia and America. But his administration saw also many internal controversies, the most serious of which was an attempt by the Spanish Jesuits to establish a separate organization. Although A. incurred the enmity of Pope *Sixtus V, and had other powerful opponents, he brought the order out of the struggles more cohesive and regimented than before. The number of members, 5,000 when he became general, stood at 13,000 at the time of his death.

ADIAPHORA A Greek term, meaning 'indifferent things'. It was employed by Protestant theologians in the 16th century to describe Roman Catholic doctrines that might be acceptable because they were 'morally indifferent'. The adiaphorist argument was first put forward by *Melanchthon in 1548, for the sake of accomodation with the then victorious imperial forces. He claimed that certain Catholic rites could be admitted by Protestants as *adiaphora*. This created a controversy in which *Flacius Illyricus accused Melanchthon of doctrinal surrender. The controversy ended only with the *Formula of Concord (1577), which forbade concessions, but left much room for individual decisions by the churches.

ADMONITION TO PARLIAMENT A pamphlet presented to the English parliament in 1572, calling for the replacement of the episcopacy by a *presbyterian system. Although the government reacted strongly, the subsequent flood of pamphlets revealed a growing strength of the *Puritans.

ADRIAN VI (Adrian Florents of Utrecht; 1459-1523) Pope from 1522 to 1523. A. studied under the *Brethren of the Common Life and then at the university of Louvain, where he became doctor of theology (1492) and chancellor and rector of the university. In 1507 he was entrusted with the education of the future *Charles V. He exercised a formative influence on the religious and intellectual development of the future Holy Roman Emperor and remained his spiritual guide throughout his life. Charles V entrusted him with the highest offices. In 1516 A. became bishop of Tortosa; in 1517 he was created cardinal and grand inquisitor of Aragon and Navarre. On the death of *Leo X, A. was unanimously elected pope (January 1522) – he was the last non-Italian and the only Dutch pope. With great zeal he took up the task of reforming the Church, beginning with the Roman Curia, in an attempt to check the spread of *Protestantism. But his reign was too brief to accomplish such radical reforms. (ME)

ADVERTISEMENTS, BOOK OF A work by Archbishop *Parker published in 1566, which meant to establish strict observance of the Act of *Uniformity. The archbishop published the book on his own authority, attempting, among other things, to enforce conformity of the priestly garment. This aroused the opposition of the *Puritan clergy, who denounced even the simpler garment. Eventually the controversy over ritual matters which resulted from the publication of the *Book of Advertisements* came to encompass questions related to the constitution of the Anglican church as well.

AERSCHOT, PHILIPPE DE CROY, DUKE OF (1526-95) Leader of the Roman Catholic nobility in the *Netherlands. He belonged to one of the wealthiest families and took part in the wars against France (1557-58). When many of the nobles began to oppose *Granvelle, A. supported him. In 1565 *Philip II made him head of the council of state. From then on he became the opponent of *William the Silent, backing the Spanish attempts to recover their hold over the Netherlands. A., however, did not condone the extreme measures of the duke of *Alba, and in 1576 played an important role in framing the Pacification of *Ghent. In 1577 he championed the invitation of Archduke *Matthias as governor-general of the Netherlands, only to find that the latter preferred to work with his rival, the Prince of Orange. He subsequently gravitated back to the side of Spain.

AFONSO V (1432-81) King of Portugal; known as 'the African'. He was declared king after the death of his father in 1438, but until 1448 the actual government was in the hands of a regent, his uncle and father-in-law, Dom Pedro. In May 1449, the enmity which had grown between the young king and his uncle, culminated in a battle at Alfarrobeira, at which Dom Pedro lost his life. In 1458, responding to the papal call for a crusade, A. undertook his first expedition to northern Africa. In

1471 he gained his greatest victory there when he captured Tangier. Four years later he involved himself in the affairs of Castile, with the design of placing his niece, *Juana la Beltraneja, on the throne. His first wife having died, he decided to marry his niece, but the project had to be postponed when he lost the battle of Toro (1476) to *Ferdinand and *Isabella. Still hoping to realize his ambition to the Castilian throne, A. undertook a mission to *Louis XI, but returned from France empty-handed. In 1477 he almost abdicated in favour of his son. In 1479 he accepted his failure with regard to Castile and signed the Treaty of *Alcaçovas. During his reign the Portuguese interest in further maritime explorations declined somewhat, and the higher nobility amassed much power.

AFRICA Until the early 15th century, European knowledge of A. was confined to its northern Mediterranean littoral, long ruled by the Arabs. The exploration of coastal contours of the rest of A. was largely the work of *Portugal. In 1415 the Portuguese captured Ceuta, on the African side of the Straits of Gibraltar, and began to explore southwards along the coast. Under *Henry the Navigator, who led the initial phase, the Portuguese reached Cape Bojador (1434), the Senegal River (1444) and Cape Verde (1445). This brought them into contact with the black population of the Coast of Guinea. A trade in slaves, spices, ivory and gold began to develop and, in 1455-57, *Cadamosto, an Italian in the service of Portugal, explored the Senegal and Gambia Rivers and discovered Cape Verde Islands. Portuguese exploration continued slowly during the next two decades, but was intensified after Diogo *Cão reached the mouth of the Congo River in 1482. Six years later Bartolomeu *Dias was blown by storms away from the southern coast of A., and when he reached shore again discovered that he had rounded the Cape of Good Hope (1488). This proved the feasibility of a maritime route to *India, a project that was accomplished by Vasco da *Gama. On his way he stopped at Quilimane, in Mozambique (March 1498), and Mombasa, thus completing the first encirclement of the shores of A.

During the next half century or so, the Portuguese had the trade of A. practically to themselves. They established **feitorias* along the coast, especially in Guinea, where they developed the slave trade, now intended for the Transatlantic territories. In East Africa, Mozambique became the centre of Portuguese activity, and, in 1541, a military expedition under Cristoforo da Gama established relations with the Christian rulers of Ethiopia. But, apart from a number of expeditions inland in search of gold, the Portuguese limited themselves to the coastal lands. Further attempts inland were made, however, during the latter part of the 16th century, when *Jesuit missionaries tried to convert the inhabitants of Congo and Angola. But by that time the Portuguese were hard-pressed by English, Spanish, Dutch and French sailors, who competed in the slave trade and in the search for gold.

J. W. Blake, *European Beginnings in West Africa, 1454-1578* (1937);
E. Prestage, *The Portuguese Pioneers* (1933);
Ch. Boxer, *Four Centuries of Portuguese Expansion* (1961).

AGINCOURT, BATTLE OF (25 October 1415) A major English victory in the *Hundred Years' War against the French, and one which reestablished England's military ascendancy, first proved at Crecy (1346). Agincourt may be described the last great mediaeval battle, where firearms and infantry as such were not yet employed. *Henry V of England with some 10,000 men, many of them longbow archers, defeated over twice that number of Frenchmen, including a large contingent of feudal cavalry. The French knights, who dismounted during the course of battle, were almost immobilized in the soft muddy terrain, and offered little resistance to the English soldiers. The French lost about 7,000 men, or about a third of their force; the English less than a quarter that number. The battle led to the English reconquest of Normandy (1415-17) and to the Treaty of Troyes (1420), in which Henry V was betrothed to Catherine, daughter of Charles VI of France, and was acknowledged heir to the French throne.

AGOSTINO DI DUCCIO (1413-81) Italian sculptor. Born in Florence, he was a mercenary soldier in his youth and led a rather turbulent life. His earliest work of significance was done in Rimini (1449-57), where he decorated the interior of the Tempio Malatestiano, which was then being built by *Alberti. He executed strikingly beautiful works, mainly in low relief, at the oratory of S. Bernardino in Perugia (1457-60), and in 1462 returned to Florence, where he completed a huge statue, which was lost later, for the cathedral. In his last years he worked again in Perugia.

J. Pope-Hennessy, *The Virgin and Child by Agostino di Duccio* (1952).

AGRICOLA, GEORG BAUER (1494-1555) A German mineralogist and humanist scholar. He studied philosophy and medicine at Leipzig and then in Bologna, Padua and Venice. After returning to his own country he was first town physician in Joachimstal and later the burgomaster of Chemnitz and began an intensive study of the techniques of mining, under the patronage of the elector of Saxony. In good Latin prose, using many classical quotations, he wrote a number of books on minerals and mining methods. The first was the *Bermannus* (1530), on the minerals of Saxony; the second, *Natura Fossilium* (1546), was a systematic classification of minerals. But he is best renowned for *De re metallica* which became a textbook for the chemistry of metals. The twelve parts of this work deal with the extraction of metals, the assaying and smelting of ores and the chemical technology of his day. The book was first published in Basle in 1556 (An English edition appeared in 1912, annotated by Herbert C. Hoover, who became president of the USA). A. was one of the first scholars who founded a natural science upon observation rather than speculation and, although he was not an important innovator, his work was a major contribution to the emergence of *chemistry as a science. (ME)

H. Hartmann, *Georg Agricola* 1494-1555 (1953);
J. R. Partington, *A History of Chemistry*, Vol. II (1961).

AGRICOLA, JOHANNES (1494-1566) German Protestant reformer. A. was one of the earliest followers of *Luther. He propagated the Reformation in Wittenberg, *Frankfurt, and in his own native town of Eisleben, but in 1536 entered into a bitter dispute with Luther over the question of repentance. A. maintained that faith alone, rather than the observance of moral laws, was the key to repentance. This was the only controversy among

Luther's followers during his lifetime. In 1540 A. left Wittenberg for Berlin. There he became court preacher of the elector *Joachim II, and exercised considerable influence until his death.

AGRICOLA, MICHAEL (c. 1510-57) Protestant reformer, leader of the *Reformation in Finland. A. came to Wittenberg as a student, sent by his bishop who was in sympathy with *Luther's ideas. Upon his return to Finland he began to spread a conservative version of Lutheranism. His writings include a manual for pastors (1545) and a Finish translation of the New Testament (1548).

AGRICOLA, RUDOLF (1444-85) Promoter of *humanism in Germany. Born in Groningen, Frisia, A. studied in Erfurt and Louvain, and after residing some time in Paris, spent almost ten years in Italy (1469-79). He attended the lectures of *Theodore of Gaza in *Ferrara and wrote a book on the life of *Petrarch. In 1482 he was invited to Heidelberg, where he lectured on classical literature, and encouraged the work of a new generation of German humanists. A.'s main work, *De inventione dialectica*, attempted to combat scholastic philosophy in the name of straight thinking and the new humanist approach. However, his influence was personal and not noticed in his writings. His value as a transmitter of humanism from Italy to Germany was already acknowledged by his contemporaries.

H. E. J. van der Velden, *Rudolphus Agricola* (1911).

AGRICULTURE The outbreak of the Black Death in the middle of the 14th century signalled a prolonged decline in European agriculture. A series of plagues combined with famines resulted in a sharp reduction (over a third) of the peasant population and of agricultural produce. Because of wars and the deficient level of nourishment of the general population, which made it an easy victim of the recurrent epidemics, the depression continued for about a 100 years, and only about 1450 did agricultural production begin to increase. The disappearance of many villages and the return of much arable land back to pasture, which had taken place during the recession, was continued after the end of the 15th century with the rise of sheep farming. In northern Italy, in Spain, where the *Mesta became an important economic factor, and in England, the persistent pressures of the sheep-growers resulted in social unrest. Especially in the last country, the *enclosure movement, prompted by the demand for wool, caused the peasant uprisings.

European agricultural methods remained more or less the same as they had been. The open-field system of long narrow strips of land, with a third of the arable land lying fallow each year, still held, especially in England and France. An exception to this conservative uniformity of European A. was the Netherlands, where, since the 15th century, a continuous field rotation without fallow intervals was practiced. The Dutch also became known for their cattle breeding and their method of draining land for agricultural purposes, and they experimented with alternating pulses (legumes) and grain crops, to conserve the fertility of the land. These early experiments eventually led to the 'Norfolk four-course system', which did away with unproductive fallow land; but this did not happen until the end of the 17th century.

In the 16th century agricultural produce enjoyed comparatively high prices and supplied the demands of the urban markets. It was not, however, the producer who always reaped the profits. Agricultural expertise began to be disseminated in print, as, for example, in the *Book of Husbandry* (1523) by Anthony Fitzherbert, which was the first of its kind in English. Another well-known work, by the German Konrad von Heresbach, was translated into English in 1577. But for all their interest in agriculture, the Europeans did not hurry to take advantage of the new food plants that had been discovered in America. The potato, which had been introduced into Ireland by the returning colonists from *Virginia (1586), was cultivated by Sir Walter *Raleigh on his estate, but not until the 18th century was it planted on a large scale.

B. H. Slicher van Bath, *Agrarian History of Western Europe, 1500-1850* (1963);

G. E. Fussel, *Farming Technique from Prehistoric to Modern Times* (1966).

AGRIPPA, CORNELIUS (1486-1533) Scholar, international adventurer and occultist. He was born in *Cologne and studied there, as well as in Paris and Pavia, then served for some time as a soldier in Spain. In 1509 he lectured on the *Kabbalah at Dole, but had to leave the following year, having been charged with heresy. A. spent seven years in Italy (1511-18), where he served *Maximilian I both as a soldier and as a theologian; in the latter capacity he attended the schismitical Council of Pisa. Later he was employed as a physician in *Geneva and Fribourg, but lasted only a short time as a physician to Louise of Savoy, the French king's mother. He then lived in *Antwerp, served *Margaret of Austria and, subsequently, the Archbishop of Cologne, and died in Grenoble, France. His first major work, *De occulta philosophia*, was written in 1510, though published only in 1533. It attempted to establish the secret of interrelationship between things, based on a mystical interpretation of nature, as well as on textual sources. A second work, *De incertitudine et vanitate scientiarum et artium*, was published in 1530 and rejected all sciences and scholarship. Persecuted for his views and fiercely anticlerical, A. showed sympathy for *Luther, but did not break with Roman Catholicism.

C. G. Nauert, *Agrippa and the Crisis of Renaissance Thought* (1965).

ALAMANNI, LUIGI (1495-1556) Italian poet and humanist. A native of *Florence, he had to leave the city after the return of the *Medici, and found shelter in France, where he became a protegé of *Francis I. Of his many written works, the most important are *La coltivazione* (1546), a didactic poem on rustic life, and *Girone il cortese* (1548), a poem in the style of the mediaeval heroic epos. He also wrote a tragedy, *Antigone*, and a mediocre comedy, *Flora*. His works exercised some influence on the *Pléiade.

H. Hauvette, *Un exilé florentin à la cour de la France au XVI*^{e} *siècle* (1903).

ALBA, FERNANDO ALVAREZ DE TOLEDO, DUKE OF (1508-82) Spanish military commander and statesman. Of a noble Castilian family, he had an energetic and powerful personality and distinguished himself as a soldier from an early age. His first great victory was over the Protestant *Schmalkaldic League in Mühlberg (1547). This earned him the command of the Spanish troops in Italy, and, after the accession of *Philip II to the throne of Spain, the position of viceroy of *Naples

(1556). In this capacity he took part in the final battles of the long Italian wars, which ended with the Treaty of *Cateau-Cambrésis in 1559. In 1567 he was sent at the head of a large army to suppress the revolt in the *Netherlands. A. arrested and executed the two leaders of the revolt, the Counts of *Egmont and Horn, and set up a tribunal with extraordinary powers which condemned thousands to death. This reign of terror, and the victories which A. scored over *William of Orange, seemed to have reestablished Spanish rule in the Netherlands. But rebellion broke out again in 1572, and this time A. failed to take the northern provinces, in spite of a hard-fought campaign and numerous atrocities. This failure led to his fall. In 1573 he went back to Spain and for the next few years was denied military command. However, in 1580, when Philip II set out to conquer Portugal, he was recalled, and it was he who captured Lisbon in 1581. His rule over Portugal, where he died, was also characterized by tough repressive measures. A devout Catholic, a believer in hierarchy and absolute monarchy, A. became a symbol of the repressive aspect of the *Counter Reformation. In Protestant Europe his name was associated with terror and religious fanaticism.

H. Schubart, *Arias Montano y el Duque de Alba en los Países Bajos* (1962);
P. Geyl, *The Revolt of the Netherlands, 1555-1609*, 2nd ed. (1958).

ALBERT ACHILLES (1414-86) Elector of *Brandenburg and champion of the rights of his family, the *Hohenzollern. In 1440 he became the ruler of Ansbach, which was in the possession of his family, and in 1464 added Bayreuth. In 1470, with the abdication of his elder brother, Friedrich, A. became the Elector of Brandenburg, to which he soon added Pomerania (1472). In February 1473 he issued his famous decree, the *Dispositio Achillea*, which determined that Brandenburg would be inherited by his eldest son, while his younger sons would be entitled to Ansbach and Bayreuth. A year later he left his eldest son Johann to rule Brandenburg, while he moved to the southern territories. But in 1478 he had to return to Brandenburg in order to confront an invasion from outside and an internal revolt. This struggle he eventually won, though not without difficulties.

ALBERT ALCIBIADES (1522-57) Margrave of Brandenburg-Kulmbach. Member of the *Hohenzollern family, he began a military career as a partisan of *Charles V. After the battle of Mühlberg (1547), he abandoned the emperor and during the next few years alternated his allegiance between one side and the other. In 1553 his rapacious campaign in Franconia prompted the organization of a league of princes against him, led by *Maurice of Saxony. Defeated, A. fled to France and entered the service of *Henry II. He died three years after his return to Germany.

ALBERT OF HABSBURG (1559-1621) Archduke and governor of the Spanish Netherlands. The younger son of *Maximilian II, he was first destined for the church, becoming a cardinal at 18, and was made archbishop of Toledo by his uncle, *Philip II. He later served as governor of Portugal and, in 1596, was sent to the Netherlands. However, by the Peace of Vervins (May 1598), it was agreed that Philip II would transfer his possessions in the Netherlands to his daughter Isabella. A. then received permission to renounce his clerical orders and married her. As an independent ruler A. continued the war against *Maurice of Nassau and the Dutch, finally recognizing their independence. He nevertheless campaigned relentlessly against Protestants in his own territories. His widow continued to rule after his death. She died in 1633.

ALBERT OF MAINZ (1490-1545) German cardinal, generous patron of the arts and letters and an opponent of the *Reformation. As the younger son of the elector of Brandenburg, A. rose quickly in his ecclesiastical career, becoming archbishop of Magdeburg in 1513, of Mainz in 1514 and a cardinal in 1518. To pay for his benefices, A. took a large loan from the *Fuggers, intending to pay it back with money from the sale of *indulgences; *Tetzel worked on his behalf. At first, A. espoused a liberal attitude towards *Luther, but, after the *Peasants' War of 1525, adopted a hostile position. Although he granted the citizens of Magdeburg religious liberty – in return for an appropriate sum of money – he became increasingly intolerant later. Among the scholars he patronized were *Erasmus and Ulrich von *Hutten.

ALBERT OF PRUSSIA (1490-1568) Last grand master of the *Teutonic order and first duke of Prussia. As third son of the prince of Brandenburg-Ansbach, A. was intended for the church, but instead chose a military career. In 1511 he joined the Teutonic order and was elected as its head, a choice inspired by the hope that, his mother being a daughter of a Polish king, he would settle the long-standing disputes between the order and Poland. A., however, began almost immediately to prepare for the conversion of East Prussia into a secular duchy, a move which, in 1519, led to an open war which lasted two years. The conflict with Poland was finally settled in 1525, when A. acknowledged the suzerainty of *Sigismund I and, in turn, was recognized by the latter as the ruler of a hereditary duchy. Together with these political changes, A. introduced the *Reformation into Prussia, an outcome of his meeting with *Luther in 1522. From then on he was one of the chief German Protestant princes, although he did not play a prominent part in the military activities of the period. Andreas *Osiander, the reformer, was particularly favoured by A. who, in 1549, appointed him professor at the new Protestant university of Königsberg. The Duke also supported Osiander in his theological controversies with *Melanchthon. A.'s last few years were characterized by a growing opposition. In 1566 this was settled with the mediation of *Sigismund II, but in the process the Duke lost much power to the nobility and the estates.

P. G. Thielen, *Die Kultur am Hofe Herzog Albrechts von Preussen* (1953).

ALBERT V (1528-79) Duke of *Bavaria from 1550. Wavering between Protestantism and the Roman Catholic faith, A. was persuaded by his father-in-law, Emperor *Ferdinand I, to back Catholicism. In 1556 he allowed the *Jesuits to establish themselves in Bavaria, thus signalling the beginning of the reconquest of the area by the *Counter Reformation. In 1564 he supressed a Lutheran "conspiracy", a move that actually amounted to a subjugation of the Bavarian estates. A. was a patron of the arts; he founded a state library and employed the composer Orlando di *Lasso.

ALBERTI, LEONE BATTISTA (1404-72) Italian architect and art theoretician, also musician, playwright and social commentator. A. was born in *Genoa to a wealthy Florentine exile. He studied law in Bologna and came to *Florence when his family was allowed to return in 1428. In 1431 he went to Rome and, while in the service of the papal court, explored ancient ruins and studied classical forms. His first major work was the Rucellai palace in Florence (1446-51). In 1450 he was commissioned by Sigismondo *Malatesta of Rimini to transform a Gothic church into a memorial; he covered the building with marble, giving its front the look of a Roman triumphal arch; but the work was not completed. Other architectural works of Alberti include the façade of S. Maria Novella in Florence (1456-70), and churches in Mantua. Regarding himself as a creative artist rather than a builder, A. limited himself to design and would have nothing to do with the actual building. He passed the last years of his life in Florence, remaining a lifelong bachelor.

Of his theoretical works, the earliest, *De pictura* (1435), dealt with the new Florentine art, which saw painting as nature reproduced in an idealized and harmonious form. It also analyzed such problems as perspective, proportions and the colour spectrum. *De statua* (1464), which dealt with sculpture, was less influential. His great treatise on architecture, *De re aedificatoria*, was completed in 1452 and published in 1485. It reflected the influence of Vitruvius, the ancient Roman architect, and emphasized the value of the classical form. A. wrote also on social problems and considered architecture to be a socially-relevant art, concerned with overall planning of an urban setting, with health and recreation. His wide-ranging intellectual interests characterized him as an embodiment of the humanist ideal of a universal man.

L. B. Alberti, *On Painting*, trans. with an introduction by J. R. Spencer (1965);
P. H. Michel, *Un idéal humain au 15° siècle. La pensée de L. B. Alberti, 1404-1472* (1930).

ALBIZZI A family that dominated *Florence from the middle of the 14th century, until it was displaced by the *Medici in 1434. Maso degli Albizzi became the most influential political personality of the republic in 1382, in the wake of the Ciompi revolt. He consolidated his position in 1393 by exiling his enemies, among them the *Albertis, and practically ruled the city until his death (1417). His son, Rinaldo (1370-1442) took over his father's position, but was opposed first by Giovanni de' Medici and then by the latter's son, Cosimo the Elder. In 1434 Rinaldo found himself without support and was exiled. He plotted for some years to reverse the fortunes of his family, but did not succeed.

ALBUQUERQUE, AFONSO DE (c. 1462-1515) A major figure in the Portuguese colonization in *Asia. A. first went to *India in 1503, where he fought the rulers of Culicut and built a fortress in Cochin. He returned to Portugal in 1504, but was sent to the East again in 1506 and spent two years in the Persian Gulf, conquering the ports of Oman and Ormuz. He then went to India where, after some difficulties, he succeeded Francisco de *Almeida as governor. In 1510 he captured Goa, and the next year he sailed to the Far East and took *Malacca. Returning to India, he sailed in 1513 to the Straits of Bab-el-Mandeb. Though he failed to conquer Aden, he did penetrate into the Red Sea. The last two years of his life were dedicated to the consolidation of Portuguese rule in the Indian Ocean. He died at sea near Goa.

E. Prestage, *Afonso de Albuquerque* (1929).

ALCAÇOVAS, TREATY OF (1479) The first European treaty to deal with overseas possessions. The T.o.A. between Portugal and Spain ended the war of succession to the throne of Castile. Since the quarrel between the two kingdoms involved intermittent fighting at sea, the treaty also defined the right of each one in the Atlantic Ocean. Portugal, on her part, abandoned all claims to the Canary Islands, while Spain recognized Portuguese domination over the Azores, Cape Verde and the Madeira Islands, as well as the Portuguese monopoly of trade in West Africa.

ALCHEMY A name given in 12th-century Europe to a mystical philosophy which attempted to reveal the relationship of man to the cosmos and to command nature in order to attain wealth, longevity and immortality. The history of A. in Europe goes back to the Hellenistic period, but during the Middle Ages it began to be concerned almost exclusively with discovering methods for the transmutation of baser metals into gold. There was then no separate science of matter, and it was in the laboratories of the alchemists that alcohol (*aqua vitae*, 'the water of life') and the mineral acids were discovered. A. apparently contributed also some industrial techniques of distillation, of dissolving and recovering of metals. With the developments in industrial and medical chemistry in the 16th century A. ceased to contribute to the chemical arts, but it was not totally discredited and, to some extent, continued to inhibit the formation of new scientific theories. The 16th and early 17th centuries were, in fact, a period of vigorous alchemical activity. Many new tracts were published, and spurious works were attributed to the great philosophers of the Middle Ages (a collection of such works is the *Artis auriferae quam chemiam vocant*, published in Basle in 1572). The alchemists in their published reminiscences rarely claimed to have discovered the secret of gold-making through personal experimentation, but rather that it was revealed to them by other adepts who had discovered it in texts of ancient wisdom. Sovereigns often gave their patronage to gold-making alchemists – notably the Holy Roman Emperors, *Maximilian II and *Rudolf II, who turned Prague into 'the metropolis of alchemy'. *Paracelsus and his follow-

The Alchemist's Shop, *a drawing by Pieter Breughel*

ers, who advocated iatrochemistry and combined it with mystic and esoteric creeds, gave a considerable impetus to alchemy. In the early 17th century, the Rosicrucian brotherhood continued the tradition of linking alchemy to Egyptian magic and to the Jewish mystic writings of the *Kabbalah. Modern historiography regards most alchemists of the Renaissance period as outright charlatans and the developments in chemistry in that period are attributed not to alchemy, but to the metallurgists and to the nascent science of medical therapy by chemical drugs.

Robert P. Multhauf, *The Origins of Chemistry* (1967); Francis Yates, *The Rosicrucian Enlightenment* (1972); E. J. Holmyard, *Alchemy* (1975). (ME)

ALCIATI, ANDREA (1492-1550) Italian jurist. Born in Como, he studied at Pavia and Bologna and, in 1518, went to teach law in France, making a name for himself in Avignon and in Bourges, where he was the teacher of *Cujas. Later, he returned to Italy and taught at several places. He died in Pavia. A. introduced into the study of the law a new critical attitude which he adopted from the methods of humanist learning. Nevertheless, he was a great continuator of an old tradition of jurisprudence, rather than an innovator.

ALDEGREVER, HEINRICH (1502-58) German painter and engraver. A. is known especially for his numerous engravings, which were done in the style of *Dürer. He left only a few paintings. He liked working on a small scale, and is usually grouped among the so-called Little Masters.

ALDINE PRESS The Venice printing shop founded around 1490 by Aldus *Manutius. It successfully printed, what was considered at that time, large editions of the classics, especially Greek authors. It was famous for its typographical designs of *italics*, and is accredited with setting the design of Greek type.

ALDROVANDI, ULISSI (1522-1605) Italian naturalist. A. was born and spent most of his life in Bologna, where he learned medicine and became a lecturer on *botany in 1554. At his urging, the city founded in 1568 a botanical garden. It also supported A. in publishing his researches. His two great works were a manual of drugs and medicines published in 1574, and a monumental, multi-volume Natural History, which included many illustrations. Only the first four volumes (1599-1602), which dealt with birds and insects, appeared during the author's lifetime. A. was a great collector of information, but rather uncritical in his scientific judgement.

G. Sarton, *The Appreciation of Ancient and Medieval Science During the Renaissance* (1953).

ALEANDRO, GIROLAMO (1480-1542) Italian churchman and *Luther's adversary at the Diet of *Worms. A. began his career as a typical Renaissance humanist. He studied in Venice where he came to know *Erasmus and Aldus *Manutius and in 1508 went to Paris, where he became a famous teacher at the Sorbonne. In 1519 he was invited by *Leo X to serve as papal librarian. It was as a papal ambassador that he went to Worms in 1521, where he urged *Charles V to declare Luther a heretic, and composed the edict which was issued by the Emperor. From here on A. was engaged in a fight against the Reformation. He is said to have been responsible for the first burning at the stake of suspected Protestants, which took place in Antwerp. Later on he went on diplomatic missions to France and returned to Germany, again as a papal legate, charged with the task of opposing the progress of Lutheranism. In 1524 he was made archbishop of Brindisi and in 1538 a cardinal.

E. Jovy, *François Tissard et Jérôme Aléandre* (1913; reprinted 1971).

ALEMAN, MATEO (1547-1614) Spanish novelist. Born at *Seville, he was educated at the universities of Salamanca and Alcalá, but led an unsettled existence, ending his life in Mexico. His reputation as an author is based on the long and immensely successful *picaresque novel *Guzmán de Alfarache* (1599-1604). It describes the adventures and moral decay of a young vagrant, and offers a pessimistic view of Spanish society and of humanity in general. Within a few years the book was translated into all the major European languages.

ALESIUS, ALEXANDER (1500-65) Scottish-born Lutheran reformer. Educated at St. Andrews University, he was won over to the Reformation by witnessing the experience of Patrick *Hamilton. In 1532 he fled to Germany, joining *Luther at Wittenberg and, in 1535, went to England carrying a letter of recommendation from *Melanchthon. He was received warmly by *Cromwell, who employed him as a sort of official disputant, but in 1539 returned to Germany, becoming a professor at Frankfurt on the Oder. A. wrote several theological works. In later years, he undertook more missions for the Reformation, including a second visit to England during the reign of Edward VI.

ALESSI, GALEAZZO (1512-72) Italian architect. Born in Perugia; it is not certain under whom he studied, but he was evidently influenced by *Michelangelo while on a visit to Rome. In 1548 he settled in *Genoa and became famous for his churches and, especially, his resi-

The entrance to the Palazzo Pubblico of Bologna, by Galeazzo Alessi

dential palaces. Later he also worked in Milan, where he built the Palazzo Marino (1558-60). His beautiful mansions in Genoa, such as the Villa Cambiaso and Palazzo Parodi, made his name known beyond the borders of Italy. His beautiful *Mannerist style was widely copied.

E. de Negri, *Galeazzo Alessi; architetto a Genova* (1957).

ALEXANDER VI (Rodrigo Borgia, 1431-1503) Pope from 1492. Born near Valencia, Spain, A. studied law in Bologna and was made cardinal by his uncle, *Calixtus III, in 1455. He then served several popes as administrator leading the life of a secular Renaissance magnate. He had a number of mistresses, the most important of whom, Vanozza dei Catanei, bore him four children. His long experience at the papal court and his relations with Italian princes, helped him to influence the electoral college of cardinals in his favour. As pope, A. ignored religious issues and devoted himself principally to political affairs. He first allied himself with *Naples, the *Holy Roman Empire and Spain against the French, who invaded Italy under *Charles VIII. At Charles's death, A. entered an alliance with his successor, *Louis XII, and supported the second French invasion, hoping in the process to win Romagna for his son Cesare *Borgia. He had almost succeeded in doing this when he died.

A. was the pope who excommunicated *Savonarola, and who, in 1493, issued the famous bull which divided the right of possession of the new trans-Atlantic territories between Spain and Portugal. He was a patron of humanist scholars and commissioned artists, especially *Pinturicchio to work in the Vatican. However, his political preoccupations and personal conduct, and his misuse of the spiritual papal powers, ultimately undermined the authority of the church.

P. de Roo, *Material for the History of Pope Alexander VI*, 5 vols. (1924);

G. Soranzo, *Il tempo di Alessandro VI e di Girolamo Savonarola* (1960).

ALFONSO II (1448-95) King of Naples. Son of *Ferrante I, he was created duke of Calabria and, while his father reigned, devoted most of his attention to military campaigns. A. led the Neapolitan armies in Tuscany (1478-79), his victories there forcing Lorenzo de' *Medici to go submissively to Naples. He repelled a Turkish invasion of Otranto in 1481 and, in 1484, fought *Venice. In 1486 he suppressed a revolt by the Neapolitan barons. The cruelty which characterized him resulted in increased opposition to himself and his father. Upon his father's death in 1494, A. ascended the throne but did not have the loyal support of the nobility and, after the first defeats of the Neapolitan armies by the French invaders, found himself isolated. In January 1495, after a reign of only one year, he abdicated in favour of his son *Ferrante II. Retiring to Sicily, he died at the end of that year.

ALFONSO V OF ARAGON (1396-1458) King of *Aragon, Catalonia and *Naples; known as 'the Magnanimous'. He ascended to the throne of Aragon in 1416 and immediately dedicated himself to a policy of territorial expansion, envisioning the effective incorporation of Sicily, Sardinia and Corsica to his possessions. He was defeated by the Genoese navy near Corsica in 1421, but shortly afterwards Queen *Joanna of Naples, besieged by the forces of Louis III of Anjou, asked for his help, offering to adopt him as her son and heir. After a series of military engagements, involving the forces of *Genoa and *Milan as well, A. had to return to Aragon. He came back to Sicily in 1432. This time he was defeated at sea by the Genoese in the Battle of Ponza (1435) and taken prisoner, but was released after signing a secret treaty with his captor, Filippo Maria *Visconti of Milan. In 1442 he succeeded in conquering Naples, which he now made the capital of his Mediterranean empire. Even after securing Naples, A. continued his aggressive policy and his military engagements in Italy. He also contemplated a crusade against the Turks and to this end made peace with the sultan of Egypt (1454). His endless military exploits made him an almost legendary figure in the eyes of his Italian subjects. But his absence from Aragon produced a feeling of despair there. If his aim was to consolidate a multi-national empire, it came to nought at his death. His Spanish and Italian dominions were severed, his illegitimate son *Ferrante becoming the king of Naples. A. was a patron of artists and humanists, and was famous for the splendour of his court.

A. F. C. Ryder, *The Kingdom of Naples under Alfonso the Magnanimous* (1976).

ALGIERS A harbour of minor commercial significance, A. acquired importance in the early 16th century, when the Spaniards, inspired by the successful completion of the **reconquista*, attempted to conquer territories in North Africa. In 1505 they besieged Mars-al-Kabir and, in 1510, following the conquest of Oran, began to apply military pressure on A. itself. The local emir then invited Kair-ed-Din *Barbarossa, who in 1530 drove the Spaniards from their position near the harbour. Converted into a strong Turkish naval base, A. was attacked in 1541 by an expedition led by *Charles V in person. However, the invasion failed, and the Emperor lost many of his ships in a storm and was defeated on land. Thereafter, A. became the safe harbour of North African pirates who harassed Christian shipping.

ALLEN, WILLIAM (1532-94) Cardinal and leader of the campaign of the *Counter Reformation with regard to England. A. began his career as churchman and defender of Roman Catholicism during the Marian Reaction (1553-58). He left England after the second break with Rome under *Elizabeth I. In 1568 he founded a seminary for priests in Douai which, in 1578, he moved to Rheims. At the same time he cooperated with the *Jesuits in sending secret agents to England, with the aim of inciting a Catholic revolt. A. also wrote extensively, denouncing royal supremacy over the church as 'monstrous and unnatural'. His most virulent attack came in 1588 in *An Admonition to the People of England*, wherein he supported a Spanish invasion as the proper way to implement the papal excommunication of Elizabeth I. A year before he wrote this tract A. had been made a cardinal. He was made archbishop of Malines in 1591, but passed the last years of his life in Rome.

R. Paul, *The British Church from the Days of Cardinal Allen* (1929).

ALMAGRO, DIEGO DE (1475-1538) Spanish **conquistador*. Son of a Castilian peasant, A. went to the New World in 1514 where he joined *Pizarro. In 1525 they set out from Panama and reached the northern shores of Peru. A. was Pizarro's second in command during the conquest of Cuzco, capital of the Inca Empire

(1533), but in 1535 he led an expedition of his own into Chile. Finding no riches there, he returned in 1537 and captured the government of Cuzco, thus causing an open breach with his former captain. Defeated in the battle of Las Salinas on 6 April 1538, A. was captured and executed by order of Pizarro's brother Hernando. Three years later A.'s son by an Indian woman, Diego (1520-42) avenged his father by organizing the assassination of Pizarro, but was himself captured and put to death.

ALMEIDA, FRANCISCO DE (c. 1450-1510) First Portuguese governor in *India. A. left Portugal in 1505 at the head of an expeditionary force of 91 ships and about 1500 men, to secure for Portugal strategic positions on the route to India. He conquered Mombasa in East Africa, built a fortress in Cananor and then fortified the Portuguese positions in Cochin. On 2 February 1509, he destroyed at Diu the fleet sent against him by the sultan of Egypt, thus ensuring Portuguese supremacy in the Indian Ocean. He refused to cede his place to Afonso de *Albuquerque, who had been sent to replace him, but resigned after receiving a royal command (October 1509). He was killed on his way back, in a skirmish with Hottentots on the coast of Africa near present day Cape Town.

ALTDORFER, ALBRECHT (c. 1480-1538) German artist; considered one of the earliest landscape painters. A. worked in Regensburg, where he was the city architect and a member of the Council. A few years younger than *Dürer and *Cranach, he was influenced by them and acquired the *Italianate style. His romantic treatment of nature and his emphasis of landscape over the human figure places him ahead of his time. On the other hand, he was not as successful in depicting nature in his numerous engravings. A. was employed by *Maximilian I, and painted the monumental *Battle of Issus* (1529) for the duke of Bavaria. Among his many other works, the altarpiece for S. Florian near Linz (1518) is outstanding. A. is usually regarded as one of the most prominent members of the so-called Danube School, and is thought to have developed his interest in nature during an early journey through Austria.

O. Benesch, *Der Maler Albrecht Altdorfer* (1939);
F. Winzinger, *Albrecht Altdorfer: Graphik* (1963).

Portrait of a Lady *by Albrecht Altdorfer*

ALTHUSIUS, JOHANNES (1557-1638) German jurist; proponent of civil and religious liberty. In 1590 he became professor of civil law in Herborn, and published several works, the most important of which was *Politica methodice digesta* (1603). A. championed the idea of popular sovereignty and viewed the monarchy as a subordinated office. He is important as one of the early liberal voices, which were to become widely heard during the 17th century.

ALUMBRADOS (Illuminati) A Spanish religious movement which stressed devotional feelings and mystical contemplation as means of direct communication with God. The movement became influential in the early 16th century. Led by a Franciscan sister, Isabel de la Cruz, and Pedro Ruiz de Alcaraz, it became popular in Toledo and other cities of New Castile. In 1524 the *Inquisition arrested the leaders for heresy and condemned their practices. The A. were mainly supported by the lower classes and, therefore, easily suppressed. The Inquisition later searched for a link between the A. and Protestantism, but it seems that no direct connection ever existed.

ALVARADO, PEDRO DE (c. 1485-1541) Spanish **conquistador*. Alvarado was *Cortes' second in command during the conquest of Mexico and was left in charge of the city when Cortes returned to the coast to confront Panfilo Narvaez (May 1520). Fearing a conspiracy, A. massacred several hundred members of the Aztec nobility, which led to a general uprising, eventually forcing the Spaniards to evacuate and then reconquer the city. In 1523 A. led a successful expedition to Guatemala and El Salvador, and, in 1534, set out on his own initiative to conquer Quito, but was intercepted by *Almagro and sold his soldiers to him for 100,000 gold pesos. Settling in Guatemala, A. was confirmed as its governor when he visited Spain. A few years later he consented to lead another expedition to the legendary 'Seven Cities of Cibola'. He was killed by Indian rebels in Jalisco, Mexico, on his way north.

J. E. Kelly, *Pedro de Alvarado, Conquistador* (1932).

AMADEO, GIOVANNI ANTONIO (1447-1522) Italian architect and sculptor. Born in Pavia, he lived in Milan, where he became a follower of *Filarete. His buildings are characterized by profuse outward embellishments. The Colleoni chapel at Bergamo (1470-76) is considered his major work, but he also worked on the duomo of Milan and on the lower part of the façade of the Certosa di Pavia (1491-98).

AMADIS DE GAULA The hero of the tremendously popular prose romance, *Los quatro libros del virtuoso caballero Amadis de Gaula.* Written in Portugal in the 14th century, it was rewritten by the Spanish author Garci Rodríguez de Montalvo, published in 1508. The work was subsequently translated, and other authors added to it or wrote continuations. Extolling the ideals of *chivalry, the book described the adventures of the son of the king of Wales (Gaula) and a princess of Brittany, who fell in love with Oriana, daughter of the King of Greece. The fantastic world projected by the work was ridiculed by *Cervantes in his *Don Quixote*.

AMASEO, ROMULO (1489-1552) Italian humanist scholar. Born in Udine to a family known for its tradition of learning, he studied in Padua, and from 1513 to 1544 was mostly in Bologna. He was especially esteemed for his mastery of classical *Latin and *Greek and considered among the leading *Ciceronians. He had numerous students, many of them non-Italians. One of his most memorable achievements was an oral dissertation which he delivered in 1529 before *Charles V and *Clement VII, against the vernacular and in support of polished Latin. It lasted two days.

AMBOISE, GEORGES D' (1460-1510) French cardinal and statesman. Born to a noble family that had long served the crown, A. was made bishop of Montauban and then archbishop of Narbonne and Rouen (1493). He was more active, however, in his secular functions as aide to the Duke of Orleans. When the latter ascended to the throne, in 1498, as *Louis XII, A. was appointed prime minister and was made a cardinal. His first task was to help organize the 1499 campaign for the conquest of *Milan. He went with the army to Italy and administered the territories which fell under French rule. After the death of Pope *Alexander VI, A. made a lukewarm bid for the papacy, but accepted the election of *Pius III and, a month later, of *Julius II. In 1504 he participated in the negotiations which led to the French evacuation of *Naples, and in 1508 took part in forming the League of *Cambrai. He died in *Lyons and was buried in the Cathedral of Rouen.

AMBOISE, PEACE OF A French royal edict issued in 1563 at the chateau of Amboise in the Loire valley, which granted *Huguenot nobles the right to hold Protestant services in their castles. Three years earlier (March 1560), A. gave its name to a Huguenot conspiracy to capture *Francis II, in order to free him from the domination of the *Guises. The discovery of the plot led to a massacre of over one thousand Huguenots, and to the beginning of the French *Religious Wars in 1562. The P.o.A. was an attempt to conciliate between the two religious camps, but it did not last long.

AMBROSIANA A library founded in *Milan by Archbishop Federico Borromeo (1564-1631). Begun in 1609, it became the first major library to be opened to the general public. In addition to printed works, it had a fine collection of manuscripts; more were added later, as well as a number of important works of art.

AMERBACH, JOHANNES (1443-1513) A printer and humanist of *Basle. A. studied in Paris under Jean Heynlen. In 1477 he founded a press in Basle, which he developed into a centre for the publication of Christian humanist works. Heynlen later joined him in Basle, and together they looked after the textual accuracy and the design of the printed books. A. also employed other scholars as proofreaders. His most famous achievement was an 11-volume edition of the works of St. Augustine.

AMERICA A term, derived from the name of Amerigo *Vespucci, which was adopted early in the 16th century for the new continent discovered by *Columbus. That Columbus was not honoured by having the new territories named after him was probably due to his insistence that he had reached the eastern islands of *Asia. He always referred to the newly discovered lands as 'las Indias', a term which was used in Spain and which has, in fact, remained in partial use. Amerigo Vespucci's letter, which carried the title *Mundus novus*, was first published in Paris in 1504. During the next four years it was reprinted in about 20 other places throughout Europe, and consolidated the recognition that a formerly unknown continent had been discovered. *Waldseemüller's map of 1507 already designates the new territories as A.

AMMAN, JOST (1539-91) German engraver. Born in *Zurich, he spent most of his active years in *Nuremberg, where he settled in 1560. He was probably the most industrious and prolific engraver of his time, and his biblical scenes were in great demand. His woodcuts, greatly superior to his copper plates, reflect contemporary culture, especially his series of 115 prints on arts and trades (1568).

AMMANNATI, BARTOLOMMEO (1511-92) Florentine architect and sculptor. Influenced primarily by *Michelangelo, A. was a sculptor and accomplished *Mannerist. He was perhaps more important as an architect. His most famous architectural work during his lifetime was the extension of the Pitti Palace in Florence (1558-70). But his bridge over the Arno, the Ponte S. Trinità, has subsequently received greater appreciation. A. also executed works in Rome and Lucca. Of his many sculptural works, the *Neptune* fountain (1563-75) in Florence's Piazza della Signoria is best known. It has in its centre a gigantic, awkward statue of Neptune, known as *Biancone*, meaning the big white one.

AMMIRATO, SCIPIONE (1531-1601) Italian courtier and historian. A. was born near Naples, but eventually settled in Florence, where he was supported by Duke *Cosimo I. His main work, *Istorie Fiorentine* (1600), carried an official character. Although it was informative and erudite, it displayed little of the originality of Florentine historiography during the early part of the 16th century.

AMSDORF, NIKOLAUS VON (1483-1565) German Protestant reformer. A. studied at the University of Wittenberg, where he became professor of theology in 1511. This placed him in direct contact with *Luther, who also taught at Wittenberg, and he became one of Luther's early followers. He accompanied Luther to the disputation at Leipzig (1519), to the Diet of *Worms (1521), assisted him in the translation of the *Bible, and after 1524 led the reform at Magdeburg. An outspoken person, he continued to support Luther on most issues until the latter's death (1546). In 1548 he cooperated in founding the University of Jena, where he took charge of the publication of Luther's works. During the last years of his life he championed orthodox Lutheranism in opposition to *Melanchthon.

AMSTERDAM Although it had grown during the 15th century into a commercial town of some importance, A.'s rise and prosperity did not begin until the revolt of the *Netherlands against Spain separated the north from the south, and brought about the decline of *Antwerp. Joining the rebels only in 1578, the city soon became the storehouse of the United Provinces. It took in many refugees from Flanders and France and gave shelter to Jewish **marranos* from Portugal. In the 17th century A. was the capital of the farflung Dutch empire, and one of the principal European centres of artistic and intellectual life.

V. Barbour, *Capitalism in Amsterdam in the 17th Century* (1963).

AMYOT, JACQUES (1513-93) French translator. The gifted son of a tanner from Melun, he obtained a good education, including Greek, attracting the attention and patronage of *Marguerite d'Angoulême. From 1536 to about 1546 he taught Greek at the University of Bourges. Later. he visited Italy and, in 1554, was made tutor of the sons of *Henry II, the future *Charles IX and *Henry III, who afterwards supported him. He became bishop of Auxerre in 1570, but his last years were marred by the political persecutions of the *League. A.'s major achievement was the translation into French of Plutarch's *Lives* (1559), a work commissioned by *Francis I, which had a significant influence on the development of French prose. Its English translation (1579) supplied *Shakespeare with the sources for his Roman plays. A. also translated Longus' *Daphnis and Chloe* (1559), and the works of Diodorus Siculus and Heliodorus, which he had found in Italy.

A. Cioranescu, *Vie de Jacques Amyot* (1941).

ANABAPTISTS (so called by their enemies, from the Greek words meaning 're baptizers'). The term is employed in reference to a broad movement of the Reformation, contemporary with those led by *Luther, *Zwingli and *Calvin, but of different social and religious orientation. The A. were more radical in their insistence upon a literal implementation of biblical models, e.g., refusing to allow infant baptism, preferring adult, or believers' baptism. Essentially, however, their movement was more than an attempt to return to primitive Christianity; it was an endeavour of moral liberation and a quest for redemption through a collective religious experience. The movement was characterized by chiliastic tendencies as well as by antinomian concepts and behaviour. It embodied many qualities of social protest and combined an elitist intellectual leadership with a large following of simple social background. These features, seemingly contradictory but actually of a complementary nature and belonging to the same context, may account for both the ecstatic and violent nature of the A. experience, and for the elements of pacifism, nonresistance and social withdrawal.

Although the A. sprang up more or less simultaneously in Switzerland, Germany and the Netherlands, it was a group of young supporters of Zwingli at *Zurich which set the precedent, when they performed the first ceremony of adult rebaptism on 21 January 1525. Denounced as moral and religious transgressors, they were forced to leave the city, but began to spread the movement in the Tyrolean valleys and the Rhineland. The first doctrinal statement of the movement, the *Schleitheim Confession, was published in 1527.

The role played by Thomas *Münzer in the development of the A. was at most inconclusive. Direct responsibility for the spread of the movement rests with the early leaders, such as Conrad *Grebel and Georg *Blaurock, and a number of successful itinerant preachers, Balthasar *Hübmaier, Hans *Denck, Hans *Hut and Michael *Sattler. Melchior *Hoffmann and David *Joris exercised a great influence in the Netherlands, and Jacob *Hutter was the founder of the communistic settlements in Moravia. Many of these leaders and

The "Anabaptist Uproar" in Amsterdam (1535): A crowd watching the executions

The "Anabaptist Uproar" in Amsterdam (1535): men and women running naked to indicate that they spoke the "naked" truth of God

other Anabaptists were persecuted and some executed by Protestants and Roman Catholics alike. The fanatic cruelties and the practice of polygamy by the A. during their rule in *Münster (1534-35), were exploited by their enemies as evidence of the immorality of the movement. But immediately afterwards, Menno *Simons began his patient work among the persecuted communities of Holland and Friesland, which resulted in the removal of excessive eschatological enthusiasm in favour of pacific voluntarism.

R. J. Smithson, *The Anabaptists* (1953);
G. H. Williams, *The Radical Reformation* (1962);
B. Bax, *The Rise and Fall of the Anabaptists* (1903);
H. Hillerbrand, *A Bibliography of Anabaptism, 1520-1630* (1962).

ANATOMY Dissections of human bodies for purposes of medical learning were practiced in the late mediaeval *universities. In 1315 the most famous mediaeval anatomist, Luigi Mondino of Bologna, published a small work called *Anathomia*, which was for over two centuries the authorized text in many European schools. But mediaeval A. merely followed the ancient works of Galen. The lecturer, seated high above his audiences, read aloud from the ancient authority, while his assistants illustrated it to the students, using the corpse of an executed criminal. However, A. was destined to develop into one of the most typical branches of science during the *Renaissance, and a subject which aroused popular interest, controversy and even enthusiasm. The reasons for this seem to have been outside the realm of pure scientific development; indeed it is quite clear that the first to show a new interest in the workings of the human body were the artists in the second half of the 15th century. Antonio *Pollaiuolo is known to have dissected corpses to improve his depiction of the human body in action. *Leonardo was a great anatomist, besides being an artistic genius. He dissected many bodies which he studied objectively, and left over a hundred anatomical notebooks and hundreds of drawings. *Dürer too, was interested in the human body and wrote about it, while sculptors such as *Michelangelo and *Cellini were bound to acquire anatomical knowledge.

Jacopo Berengario da Carpi of Bologna, who died in 1530, was responsible for renewing the study of A. at university level. But a real change came about with the publication of *Vesalius' *De humani corporis fabrica* (1543). The bitter criticism, which initially accompanied the work, testified to the public interest, and the superb woodcuts by Stephen de Calcar proved again the connection between the Renaissance artists and anatomists.

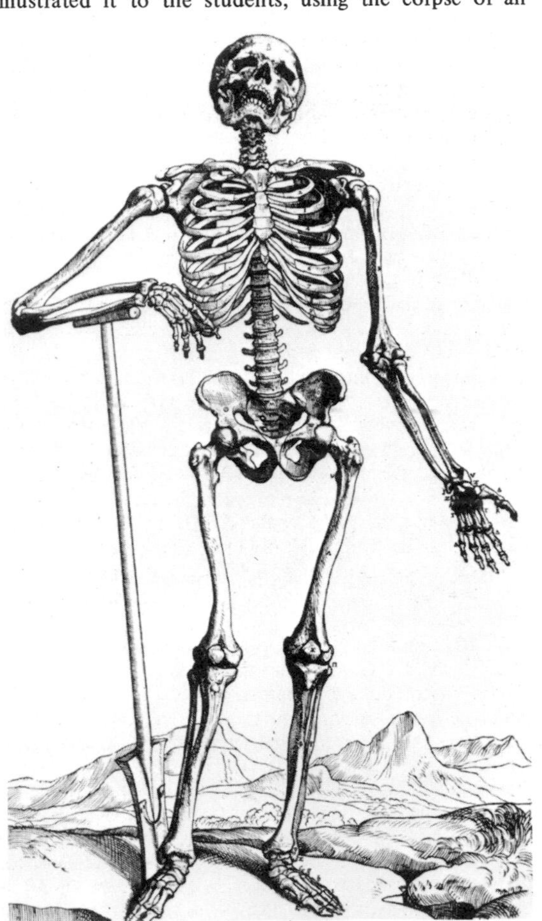

An illustration from Vesalius' De humani corporis fabrica *(1543), by Stephen de Calcar*

An illustration from Vesalius' De humani corporis fabrica *(1543), by Stephen de Calcar*

Vesalius was the first and greatest representative of the school of Padua, which led the study of anatomy throughout the 16th century. He was followed there by, among others, *Fallopio and Girolamo Fabrici (*c.* 1533-1619). The latter also dealt with embryology and biology and taught the future discoverer of blood circulation, William Harvey. Other outstanding 16th-century anatomists were Bartolomeo Eustachio (1524-74) of Rome and Jacques Dubois (1478-1555), Vesalius' teacher and later his opponent from Paris.
C. J. Singer, *A Short History of Anatomy from the Greeks to Harvey*, 2nd ed. (1957).

ANCHIETA, JOSÉ DE (c. 1533-97) Portuguese *Jesuit missionary. In 1553 he wento to Brazil, where he founded a school near present-day São Paulo. He dedicated much of his efforts to educate Indian children, and campaigned against the enslavement of the Indians. He also wrote extensively on Brazil and on the Tupi language.

ANDELOT, FRANÇOIS D' (1531-69) French *Huguenot leader. The younger brother of Admiral *Coligny, he distinguished himself in military service in Italy, but in 1551 was taken prisoner by the imperial forces near *Milan. Held in captivity until 1556, he became interested in the teachings of *Calvin, thus becoming the first of his family to join the *Huguenot camp. A. never attempted to hide his conversion, and led the most assertive wing of the Huguenots. In 1562, he took command of the mercenaries brought into France with the help of the German *Protestant princes. He continued to play an important military role in the religious wars until his sudden death.

ANDREA DEL SARTO (1486-1531) Florentine painter. Born to a father who was a tailor (*sarto*), A. showed exceptional talent for drawing from childhood and studied under Piero di Cosimo. He began to work on his own at an early age, and became famous around 1510, when he began the execution of a series of *frescoes in the Annunziata. In contrast to other famous contemporaries, he had no ambition to move beyond the social milieu from which he had come, and he lived and worked in Florence. Once, in 1518, he accepted an invitation to the French court, but returned to Florence shortly after, urged, it was said, by his domineering wife. A. was a master of the art of frescoes, which he executed with precision and with no need of correction. He was also an innovator in his use of colours, light-and-shade and toning. As such, his work is significant to the emergence of *Mannerism. Among his students were *Pontormo and *Vasari.
J. K. G. Shearman, *Andrea del Sarto*, 2 vols. (1965);
S. J. Freedberg, *Andrea del Sarto* (1963).

Christ and St. John, a detail from The Last Supper, *by Andrea del Sarto*

ANDREAE, JACOB (1528-90) German Lutheran leader and theologist. In 1561 he became a professor at the university of Tübingen, and later headed that institution. Although he was a prolific writer, A.'s principal contribution was his ceaseless effort to reunite the divided Lutheran factions in Germany. He was the moving spirit behind the *Formula of Concord (1577).

ANDREAE, LAURENTIUS (Lars Andersson; 1470-1552) Swedish reformer and counsellor of *Gustavus Vasa. A man of great political ability who had studied abroad, A. became archdeacon of Strängnäs and already in 1524 interceded with the King on behalf of the Lutheran reformer Olavus *Petri. After the Diet of Västeras (1527), he was the King's chief adviser on religious matters, but gradually lost his influence. In 1540 he was condemned to death, together with Olavus Petri, because of their criticism of the King, but the sentence was not carried out.

ANDREWS, LANCELOT (1555-1626) English bishop of Winchester; scholar, theologian and preacher. Educated at Cambridge, he first attracted the attention of *Elizabeth I by his preaching abilities, but rose to a position of influence only under *James I, becoming in succession, bishop of Chichester (1605), Ely (1609) and Winchester (1619). A. took part in the *Hampton Court Conference. He was charged with preparing important portions of the Authorized Version of the *Bible, and conducted a written debate with Cardinal *Bellarmine on the issue of royal authority. Notwithstanding his opposition to Roman Catholicism, he objected to the Calvinist interpretations of the *Puritans, and influenced the formation of established Anglican doctrine and ceremony.

ANGELICO, FRA (1387-1455) The name given to the Italian painter Giovanni da Fiesole, known also as Il Beato Angelico. A Dominican friar, A.'s earliest works were done in Cortona, but his career as a painter really began when he moved to Florence. There he executed, at the convent of S. Marco, a series of about 50 *frescoes; his earliest datable work, the *Linaiuoli Madonna*, is of 1433. About 1445 he was invited to Rome by *Eugenius IV and decorated a chapel in the Vatican. In 1447 he executed two frescoes in Orvieto. A. returned to Rome around 1452 to work on the decorations of the Chapel of the Sacrament at the Vatican (later demolished), and died there. Compared to his Florentine contemporaries, *Masaccio and Filippo

The Deposition *by Fra Angelico, at the convent of S. Marco, Florence*

*Lippi, A. had a more conservative style. His paintings had a didactic purpose and intended to recreate a pietistic atmosphere of devotion and religious reverence.
J. Pope-Hennessy, *Fra Angelico* (1952);
M. Salmi, *Il beato Angelico* (1958).

ANGHIERA, PIETRO MARTIRE DI (1459-1526) Italian-Spanish historian and humanist. Born and educated in Italy, A. moved to Spain where he eventually became a priest and confidant of Queen *Isabella. He went on a diplomatic mission to Egypt (1501) and was made a member of the *Consejo de Indias. He met many of the great Spanish explorers, a fact that helped him in writing the *Decadas de Orbe Novo*, the first major work on the newly discovered American continent.

ANJOU, FRANCIS DUKE OF (1554-84) Fifth son of *Henry II of France and *Catherine de Médicis; known until 1576 as Duke of Alençon. Adventurous by nature, he took part in the *Religious Wars as one of the leaders of the **politiques*, and actually came to support the *Huguenots. But in 1576 he reached an agreement with his brother *Henry III, who conferred on him the title of Anjou. In 1578 he accepted the invitation of a faction of the rebels in the Netherlands and assumed the title of 'defender', although he was recognized only in Brabant. His involvement in the Netherlands was encouraged by England, and he was spoken about as a likely husband for *Elizabeth I. He actually came to London in 1579 to ask for the hand of the Queen, and tried his chance again in 1581. On his second visit to England, A. was spoken of as the new sovereign who would replace *Philip II in the Netherlands. The plan was favoured by *William of Orange himself, and in February 1582 A. came to *Antwerp as Duke of Brabant. But in January 1583 his French soldiers failed in their attempt to take the city by force, and their discredited leader finally left the Netherlands later that year. He died of an illness in France in June 1584.

ANNE BOLEYN (1507-36) Queen of England, second wife of *Henry VIII, mother of *Elizabeth I. In her youth, A. spent some years in France. She caught Henry's eye when she came to the English court. In 1529 the King asked *Catherine of Aragon for a divorce so as to marry A. The relationship between them became public knowledge, but remained unofficial for over five years, until they were married by *Cranmer on 25 January 1533. The archbishop pronounced Henry's divorce from Catherine at the same time. A. was crowned in June and gave birth to Elizabeth in September 1533. Early in 1536 she gave birth to a stillborn boy which greatly disappointed Henry who wished for a male heir. On 2 May she was arrested and charged with infidelity and treason, and condemned to death by special court. It is almost certain that the charges against her were false. The marriage was annulled by Cranmer and A. was publicly beheaded on 19 May 1536.

H. W. Trovillion, ed., *The Love Letters of Henry VIII to Anne Boleyn* (1945).

ANNE OF BRITTANY (1477-1514) Duchess of Brittany and queen of France. A. succeeded to the Duchy of Brittany at the age of 12 and thus became a coveted prize for European rulers who wished to enlarge their political power. She was first married by proxy to *Maximilian of Austria (1489), but in the face of French military threat this alliance was annulled, and A. was betrothed to *Charles VIII (1491). When he died in 1498, she married his successor, *Louis XII, for whom she bore a daughter, Claude of France. In her marriage contracts with the two French kings A. took care to include provisions ensuring the relative independence of Brittany, and she continued to deal personally with the administration of the duchy. However, since her daughter, Claude, was married to the duke of Angoulême, who in 1515 became king of France as *Francis I, the union of Brittany with the possessions of the French crown was settled.

H. A. Butler, *Twice Queen of France: Anne of Brittany* (1967).

ANNE OF CLEVES (1515-57) Queen of England, fourth wife of *Henry VIII. The marriage was *Cromwell's idea as a means of allying England with the *Schmalkaldic League. Henry had been impressed by her portrait (which had been painted by Hans *Holbein the Younger) but was disappointed when they met. The wedding was celebrated on 6 January 1540, but the King soon got rid of Cromwell and asked for a divorce. This was granted by Parliament, among other reasons, on the grounds that the marriage had not been consumated. A. remained in England and was awarded a yearly pension and honours compatible with her status.

ANNE OF FRANCE (1460-1522) Called Dame de Beaujeu, eldest daughter of *Louis XI and Regent of France. A. married Pierre de Beaujeu, brother of the Duke of Bourbon. She was highly esteemed by her father, who, before dying, entrusted her and her husband with the care of *Charles VIII, at the time a 13-year old boy, and with the regency of France. She exercised her role as Regent from 1483 to 1491, and succeeded in strengthening royal authority in the face of feudal opposition. However, after Charles VIII took over the control of the government, A., as a member of the house of *Bourbon, often opposed the royal power.

P. Pélicier, *Essai sur le gouvernement de la dame de Beaujeu, 1483-91* (1882, reprinted 1970).

ANTOINE DE BOURBON (1518-62) King of Navarre. A scion of the junior branch of the *Bourbons, bearing the title of Duke of Vendôme, he married, in 1548, *Jeanne d'Albret, who two years later became queen of Navarre. Probably influenced by his wife, A. became an adherent of Protestantism, but he tended to be inconstant and reaffirmed his attachment to the Catholic Church when political circumstances dictated. In 1561, after the death of *Francis II, A. tried to gain the regency of France, but lost the bid to *Catherine de Medici and was given the title of Lieutenant-General of the kingdom. He was the father of *Henry IV. He died of wounds incurred in a battle at the beginning of the *Religious Wars in France.

Anne of Cleves, *by Hans Holbein the Younger*

ANTONELLO DA MESSINA (1430-79) Italian painter. A. was born and probably also died in Messina, and studied in Naples where he was probably influenced by the work of Jan van *Eyck. This would explain his Flemish style and his care for minute details; there is no evidence that he ever visited the Netherlands. He worked in Venice from 1472 to 1475 and had a noticeable influence on his contemporary Giovanni *Bellini. Less than two dozen of his works have survived, mostly religious. A. was the only outstanding Italian painter of the 15th century who came from the south.

S. Bottari, *Antonello da Messina* (1955).

ANTONINO, ST. (1389-1459) Italian archbishop of *Florence. Joining the Dominicans in his youth, he gradually rose to a position of influence inside the Order. In 1436 he established the famous convent of S. Marco in Florence, which was decorated by Fra *Angelico and, in 1446, became the city's archbishop. A. was known for his affection for the poor, his wisdom and moderation. However, he was helped in his career by his association with Cosimo de' *Medici the Elder. Their connection reflected in A.'s moral and theological treatises, wherein he departed from the mediaeval prohibition on the charging of interest, allowing it in the case of money invested in business. He also wrote a chronicle of world history.

ANTONIO DE CRATO (1531-95) Illegitimate son of the Infante Dom Luis and nephew of *John III of Portugal. A. was destined for an ecclesiastic career, and was made prior of Crato, but after his father's death in 1555, he left the church and led a secular life. He participated in the Portuguese campaigns in North Africa, including the disastrous Battle of Alcacerquivir, where *Sebastian I lost his life, and was taken prisoner. Once released, he tried to legitimize his status and strengthen his claims to the Portuguese throne. Although his uncle Cardinal *Henrique, who became king after the death of Sebastian, had no children, he thwarted A.'s ambitions, as he had not forgiven him for leaving the church. After Henrique's death in 1580, A. was proclaimed king by his followers, but was defeated by the Spanish troops of the duke of *Alba and had to leave the country. He went to France, and in 1585 to England. When Queen *Elizabeth I sent *Drake in 1589 to invade Portugal, A. went with him, hoping to promote national uprising against Spain. The expedition was unsuccessful and A. returned to England. He spent the last three years of his life at the court of *Henry IV of France.

ANTWERP (Antwerpen in Flemish and Anvers in French). A city situated on the Schelde river, 55 miles from the North Sea. The first half of the 16th century is described as the 'golden age' of A., when it became the greatest economic centre of Europe. The geographical discoveries of the Portuguese and the Spaniards, the beginnings of the colonial trade, and the inclusion of the Netherlands through dynastic ties in the vast *Habsburg Empire all benefited this Brabant town. The rise of A. is attributed in part to its geographical position: the deepening of the Schelde provided easier access from the sea, while the waterways and convenient landroutes to the East and South made it a natural local point for trade from the hinterland. Its remarkable degree of autonomy and the liberal attitude to foreign merchants constituted a further attraction. It first began to gain ascendancy over *Bruges when the Portuguese chose A. as their spice trade centre. The English made it a mart-town for their cloth trade; the South Germans came to trade in metals and cloth. Soon merchants of other nations began to congregate there too. A. quickly became the biggest financial centre (the Stock Exchange was inaugurated in 1531), and it was there that the leading financiers of Europe conducted their business with governments, lending huge sums of money to kings and emperors. It was also an industrial town specializing in cloth-finishing and in luxury products. At the same time it was a cultural centre with many printing houses and a school of painting. From a population of 50,000 at the beginning of the century, it grew to be one of the biggest towns in Europe with approximately 100,000 inhabitants in 1550. The decline began when Spain and Portugal declared themselves bankrupt, thus causing a major catastrophe in the world of high finance. The removal of the royal Portuguese factory and the slump in the English cloth trade were further disasters. Later

Antwerp surrenders to Alexander Farnese, Duke of Parma (1585). *An early 17th-century print*

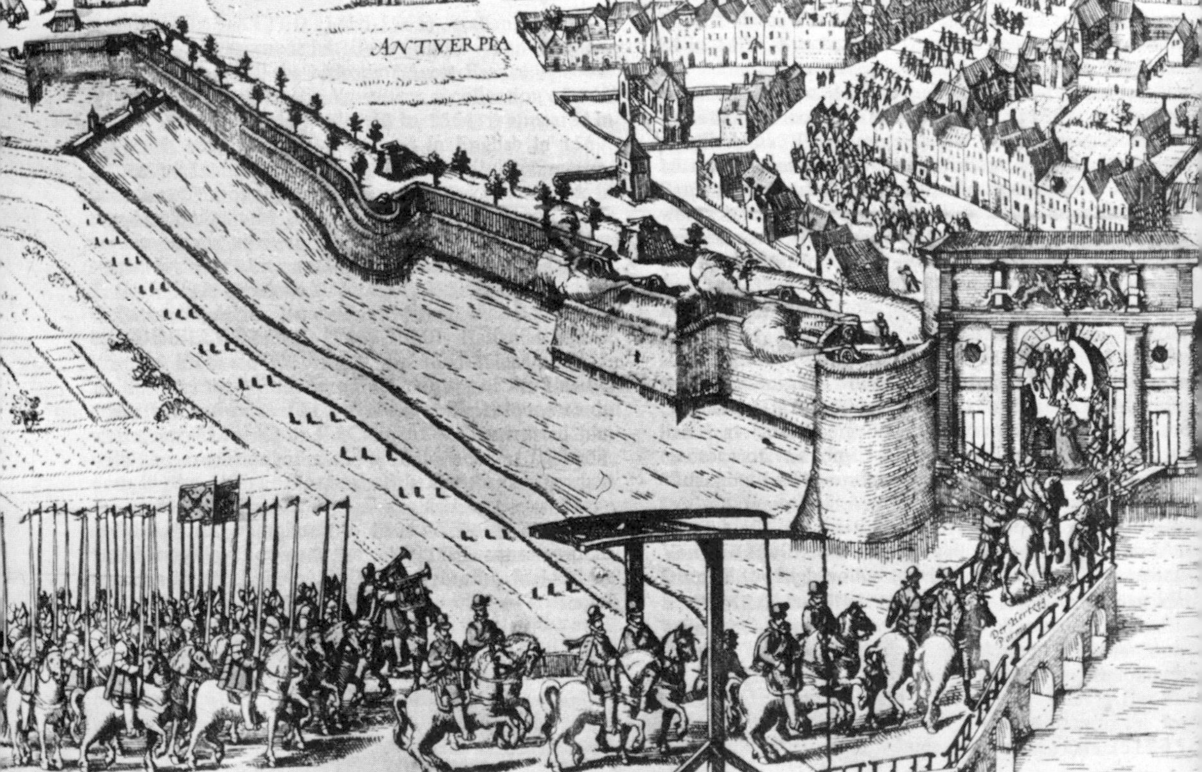

A. was involved in the revolt of the Netherlands: it was sacked by Spanish troops (1576), was besieged by the French army, which was repulsed by *William of Orange (1583), and was finally captured, after another long siege, by Alexander *Farnese in 1585. The Schelde was closed, the financiers and the merchants left, the population diminished, and before long *Amsterdam inherited the place of A. as the leading commercial centre.
T. S. Bindoff, 'The Greatness of Antwerp' in the *The New Cambridge Modern History*, vol. II (1958). (ME)

ANTWERP MANNERISTS Unidentified artists who painted in Antwerp and in other Flemish towns during the first three decades of the 16th century. Their style is an attempt to combine Gothic and Renaissance, Flemish and Italian. The most popular themes of this school were the Nativity and the Adoration of the Magi. Names associated with the group are Jan de Beer, Jan van Dormicke, Jan Gossaert (*Mabuse) and Adriaen Ysenbrandt. (ME)

APIANUS, PETRUS (Peter Bienewitz; 1495-1552) German geographer and astronomer. Born in Leisnig, Saxony, he studied at Leipzig and, in 1527, became a professor of mathematics at Ingolstadt, where he spent the rest of his life. His main work, frequently reissued, was the *Cosmographia* (1520, 1522, 1530), which included a general map of the world, combining the ancient views of Ptolemy with contemporary information.

ARAGON In the late Middle Ages and early Renaissance this kingdom in the north-eastern part of the Iberian peninsula grew into a Mediterranean empire. Since the 14th century it had dominated *Sicily and Sardinia, and for a period also controlled the duchy of Athens in Greece. The Aragonese played an important role in the commercial life of the Levant. Their Catalonian seaboard, with its dynamic industrial and maritime centres, principally the port of Barcelona, competed with *Genoa and *Venice in the Eastern spice trade. In 1409, A. formally incorporated Sicily under its crown, and shortly after the accession of *Alfonso V (1416), began a prolonged effort to gain the kingdom of *Naples. The conquest of Naples finally accomplished (1442), the King became more interested in his Italian possessions, and tended to neglect his Spanish territories. After his death, the Aragonese empire was divided between his son *Ferrante, who took Naples, and his brother John II (1458-79). The latter then shifted the political orientation of A. Wishing to strengthen his kingdom, especially against the French threat, he sought unification with Castile and, in 1469, accomplished this goal by marrying his son *Ferdinand to *Isabella, sister of Henry IV of Castile. Thus in 1479, A. became part of a united Spanish monarchy, while conserving its local institutions and its traditions of political representation and limited power of the monarchy. Resentment against the predominance of Castile was not lacking, however, and in 1591 there was an attempted uprising in Saragossa, in defence of Aragonese traditional liberties. Following the revolt, *Philip II imposed some limitations on the privileges of A.
H. J. Chaytor, *A History of Aragon and Catalonia* (1933); J. L. Shneidman, *The Rise of the Aragonese-Catalan Empire, 1200-1350*, 2 vols. (1970).

ARCHAEOLOGY No systematic survey and excavation of past civilizations was ever undertaken during the Renaissance. What took place was mostly a search for ancient objects and works of art, mainly in Italy and particularly in *Rome. The originator of this interest in the physical evidence of classical antiquity was Flavio *Biondo, whose *Roma instaurata* (1446) attempted a topographical reconstruction of ancient Rome. Pomponius *Laetus further stimulated the interest in archaeological remains, and by the end of the 15th century the cult of unearthing of old treasures spread throughout Italy. The two most famous ancient sculptures excavated were the *Apollo Belvedere* and the *Laocoön*, the first some time in the 1480s, the second in 1506. High Renaissance painters frequently used ancient ruins for the background of their pictures, and a few, like *Raphael and *Michelangelo, either took part in excavations or worked out plans for conducting them. *Bosio in the late 16th century, enlarged the knowledge of ancient Rome by his survey of the catacombs.

ARCHITECTURE In this most socially-oriented medium of the arts the vision of the Renaissance achieved its greatest degree of diffusion, influence and endurance. The Renaissance gave birth to the modern conceptions of A. as the 'art of building' and as an intellectual pursuit of multiple aesthetic and practical considerations. Its great theoreticians, who followed the ancient Vitruvius, reaffirmed the ideals of architectural synthesis, which were defined by *Palladio as *comoditá, perpetuitá, belleza*, i.e. spatial usefulness, structural firmness and an attractive appearance. Although Renaissance architects stressed values of proportional harmony and equilibrium, they did not for these reasons neglect to pay attention to social considerations. The notion that Renaissance architecture was interested only in pure form is a misconception and arose from the fact that this style remained in existence for almost 500 years.

Renaissance A. began in the 1420s with the work of *Brunelleschi in Florence. In the rest of Europe, however, the architecture remained predominantly Gothic for most of the 15th century. Combining high rib vaults, external flying buttresses and large glazed windows from pier to pier, Gothic architecture had, from the late 12th century, endowed Europe with huge cathedrals, whose high pointed towers and immense interiors meant to evoke a spiritually uplifting emotion. Although the *Hundred Years' War halted the building of Gothic cathedrals in the north of France, where the style had originated, it continued to proliferate in other parts of the Continent. The town-halls of the southern Netherlands, such as those of *Bruges, Brussels, Louvain and *Ghent, all designed in the 15th century, are superb examples of the ornate style of secular late-Gothic architecture; the 14th-century Cloth Hall of Ypres was the greatest building of this kind in Europe. Spain, where the Gothic had arrived two hundred years earlier, produced in the 15th century the famous towers of the cathedral of Burgos and the huge cathedral of *Seville (begun in 1402). In England Gothic church architecture remained the established style during the reign of the early Tudors, producing such fine examples as the chapel of Henry VII at Westminster Abbey. In Germany a distinctive Gothic style is exemplified in the cathedral of Ulm, with its single tower, the highest of all mediaeval structures. Another form of the German late-Gothic was the clean-surface brick church, like the Munich Frauenkirche (begun in 1468). Finally, in Italy itself, the Gothic style revealed itself in the lavishly decorated

Courtyard of the Palace of Charles V in Granada

masonry of the Milan cathedral (begun 1386) and distinctive Venetian civic buildings, such as the Doge's Palace and the Ca d'Oro. However, Italian Gothic, especially as practised in Tuscany, was always marked by wider spaces between the columns, round arches and horizontal instead of vertical stress in the general form of the building.

The stylistic revolution ushered in by Brunelleschi began as a conscious movement in favour of the architectural forms of classical antiquity; although not everything that distinguished the new style was borrowed indiscriminately from the ancients. Brunelleschi himself was responsible for the most important innovations: the ponderous central dome, which was to be the Renaissance heir of the Gothic tower, and the trend of constructing arcades supported by delicate Corinthian columns. To him, too, is due the characteristic heavy rustication on the walls of Florentine palaces, and the experimentation with barrel vaults. Renaissance architecture thus became the art of the modelling of mass, instead of the Gothic encompassment of space. The exciting disproportion of the Gothic was replaced with symmetry, concise geometric forms and serene regularity. The centrally-planned structure created a sense of ease and confidence, as if man were in complete command of his universe.

Early Renaissance architecture, the work of Brunelleschi, *Alberti, *Michelozzo and Giuliano da *Sangallo, was for a comparatively long embryonic period centred in Florence, before it spread to other parts of Italy in the third quarter of the 15th century. With *Bramante's move to Rome (1499) the centre shifted. During the short, but intense period which ended with the Sack of *Rome (1527), the High Renaissance style of monumentality and solid mass found its expression in the works of Bramante himself, and a small group which included *Raphael, Antonio da *Sangallo, *Peruzzi and the early *Giulio Romano. *Michelangelo, who influenced the course of Renaissance sculpture and painting, also took the lead in introducing *Mannerism in architecture, stressing the motif as a self-justifying element. In this he was followed by lesser architects, such as *Ammannati and *Vasari, and notably, by the inventive and elegant *Vignola. But while Mannerism was making itself felt in the centre of Italy, *Venice, Verona, Vicenza and other northern cities remained faithful to the heritage of Bramante. The structures erected by *Alessi, *Sanmicheli and *Sansovino, around the middle of the 16th century, display further experimentation with the mainstream Renaissance ideas of classical harmony. The trend reached its highest point in the work of *Palladio, who excelled in recreating the splendour of antiquity, and was the greatest Italian architect before the transition to the *Baroque.

Outside Italy, Renaissance principles were first applied in France, particularly in secular architecture. This was a rather unusual development, since France, as may be perceived from the famous house of Jacques *Coeur in Bourges (begun 1443), had a strong tradition of Gothic in its fashionable residential structures. The Gothic still dominated the parts of the Chateau de Blois built by *Louis XII, but the wing added by *Francis I had much of the Renaissance motif, and the impressive Chateau de Chambord on the Loire (begun 1519) may already qualify as a High Renaissance building. Even if one considers *Fontainebleau as a case apart, it is still possible to argue that by the middle of the 16th century France had developed her own style; less monumental than the Italian, highly decorative and preserving some elements of Gothic form. One of the foremost examples was the joint elegance of *Lescot and *Goujon in the Louvre, to which should be added the more massive works of *Delorme and *Bullant. In *Ducerceau the Elder France gained both a popularizer of Renaissance architectural principles and the founder of an architectural dynasty.

The situation was different in other parts of Europe. In Spain, where the *Plateresque became a sort of 16th-century obsession, the High Renaissance concept of harmony was early represented in the Palace of *Charles V in Granada (begun 1526). But only with the work of Juan de *Herrera, about half a century later, did the Italianate style attain a significant degree of diffusion. In England, Germany and the Netherlands, for most of the 16th century occasional structures went up which employed Renaissance principles of architecture, but in many buildings the Renaissance motif was espoused for purposes of decoration, or an eclectic admixture of elements and styles was casually employed. Cornelis *Floris was the principal mid-16th-century Renaissance architect in the southern Netherlands. In England old Somerset House in London (1547-52) is frequently cited as the first Renaissance type of residence, while John *Shute is referred to as the first Englishman who wrote on Renaissance principles of architecture. However, it was not until Inigo *Jones, a conscious practitioner of Palladian architecture, that England found her first true Renaissance builder. In Germany the same role is assigned to Elias *Holl.

R. Wittkower, *Architectural Principles in the Age of Humanism* (1949);
P. Frankl, *Gothic Architecture* (1962);
P. Murray, *The Architecture of the Italian Renaissance* (1963);
A. Blunt, *Art and Architecture in France, 1500-1700* (1953);
N. Pevsner, *An Outline of European Architecture* (1948).

ARCIMBOLDO, GIUSEPPE (1530-93) Italian painter. Born in Milan, his career began to flourish in 1562 when he became a court painter to the Habsburg emperors, three of whom – *Ferdinand I, *Maximilian II and *Rudolf II – he served until 1587, working mostly in Vienna and Prague. A. carried to the extreme the latent Renaissance penchant for the bizarre and fantastic, painting heads modelled from fruits, vegetables, flowers and other objects. Only about twenty oil paintings of his are known, although there is a good number of coloured drawings. A comparison of his work with 20th century Surrealists is unavoidable, and his *Librarian*, an image of a person made up of books, resembles a cubist painting.

Late secular Gothic architecture; the belfry in Bruges

Winter *by Giuseppe Arcimboldo*

F. C. Legrand and F. Sluys, *Archimboldo et les Archimboldesques* (1955).

ARETINO, PIETRO (1492-1556) Italian writer. Born in Arezzo, whence his name, A. displayed from youth unusual literary talents. Because of his known disrespect for religion he was compelled to leave his home town. He spent a few years in Perugia, but his fame was established when he moved to Rome in 1517. A. endeared himself to some personages by praising them profusely, and was hated by others whom he ridiculed. He was first supported by *Leo X, then by Giovanni de' *Medici. When the latter died (1526), he settled in Venice where he befriended *Titian and continued his literary work. His best known work, *I Ragionamenti*, stands out as an example of the urbane cynicism and licentious spirit of his time. His letters, which he began publishing in 1538, have the same qualities. Aretino wrote five comedies – which are now considered the best part of his work, sonnets, and toward the latter part of his life, treatises on religious themes. He was known, however, as the most scandalous author in Italy and, with the coming of the Counter Reformation, his writings were prohibited by the Church.

E. Hutton, *Pietro Aretino: The Scourge of Princes* (1922);
G. Petrocchi, *Pietro Aretino, tra Rinascimento e Contrariforma* (1948).

ARGYROPOULOS, JOHN (c. 1416-86) Greek scholar; one of the influential promoters of Greek studies in

Italy. Born in Constantinople, A. went to Europe twice – once before the fall of his native city to the Turks, and again as a refugee. In 1456 Cosimo de' *Medici the Elder appointed him professor of Greek in Florence. He lectured there for many years, mainly on Aristotle, and had many students who became known in their own right. He died in Rome.

ARIAS DE AVILA, PEDRO (c. 1440-1530) Spanish **conquistador*, known commonly as Pedrarias Davila. Born in Old Castile, he was for many years a soldier, taking part in the last battles of the **reconquista*. In 1514 he left Spain to assume the governorship of Panamá, accompanied by his family and a considerable number of troops. Taking over from *Balboa, he later had him executed on a spurious charge of treason (1519). A vigorous man in spite of his old age, he was able to overcome the difficult conditions in Central America and explored the area of present-day Costa Rica and conquered Nicaragua. However, his treatment of Balboa and other subordinates gave him a reputation as one of the cruellest of the early *conquistadors*.

ARIAS MONTANO, BENITO (1527-98) Spanish theologian and orientalist. In 1562 he distinguished himself as theological adviser to the Council of *Trent. In 1568 *Philip II put him in charge of the Polyglot Bible, which was published in *Antwerp (1572) in eight volumes. The suspicion then fell on him that he had tampered with the authorized text of the Vulgate, but, retaining the support of his king, he was cleared and made head of the *Escorial library. A. was an authority on oriental languages and his Bible included a Syriac text as well as Hebrew. In 1575 he edited a Latin translation of the 12th-century Jewish traveller Benjamin of Tudela. He also published biblical commentaries.

ARIOSTO, LUDOVICO (1474-1533) Italian poet. Born in Reggio, Emilia, to a family which belonged to the minor nobility, he first studied law but later decided to dedicate himself to literature. However, the death of his father (1500) changed the circumstances of the family and A. spent the next 25 years mostly as an administrator, first for Cardinal Ippolito d'Este, then for his brother Alfonso d'Este, duke of Ferrara. In 1525 he finally settled in *Ferrara where he supervised the construction of the theatre and the performance of his own comedies. He married Alessandra Benucci, a widow, with whom he had been in love for many years. A. wrote five comedies and other works, but his fame rests on the epic poem *Orlando furioso*, considered second only to the work of *Dante. It was first published in 1516, but A. continued to revise the work practically until the end of his life. A sequel to *Boiardo's *Orlando innamorato*, the poem is set in the time of Charlemagne. A., however, is not a simple admirer of the world of chivalry; he tells his stories of love and adventure in a distinctly Renaissance language of wit and romance.

E. G. Gardner, *The King of Court Poets* (1906);
R. Ramat, *La critica ariotesca dal secolo XVI ad oggi* (1954).

ARMADA, THE INVINCIBLE The name given in Spain to the great naval expedition which *Philip II sent against England in 1588. The decision to invade England came after years of intensifying hostility between the two nations. Philip II helped the Irish rebels against *Elizabeth I. For her part, the Queen aided the Netherlands revolt against Spain, and encouraged *Drake to plunder Spanish ports in the Carribean. In 1587 Drake attacked the harbour of Càdiz, while the preparations for the A. were going on. The A., which left Lisbon on 28 May 1588, consisted of 132 ships carrying about 30,000 sailors and soldiers. The Spanish planned to stop in Flanders and join forces with Alexander *Farnese before crossing the Channel to England. But the two Spanish forces never met. Under continuous attack by the English from the moment he entered the Channel, the Spanish commander, the duke of *Medina Sidonia, reached only the vicinity of Calais. On the night of 7 August, the English broke the tight Spanish formation with six fire-ships, and in the ensuing battle inflicted heavy damages on the Spanish fleet. The A. now sailed north towards Scotland on her long and tragic journey home. Lacking food, water and supplies, with diseases breaking out among its crews, the A. suffered more losses on her way back than in battle. Only 66 ships and about 10,000 men reached Spain. The destruction of the A. was one of the major naval encounters of all times: while it did not immediately establish English domination of the seas, it did demonstrate that the combination of speed, ability to manoeuvre and long-range guns, was the essence of naval power.

G. Mattingly, *Armada* (1959);
M. Lewis, *The Spanish Armada* (1906).

ARMAGNACS AND BURGUNDIANS The two factions of the higher nobility of France, whose bitter struggle weakened the country and facilitated a series of English conquests. The factions emerged in 1407, when John the Fearless (1404-19), duke of *Burgundy, arranged the assassination of Louis of Orléans, brother of the mad king, Charles VI (1380-1422). Louis' successor as head of the anti-Burgundian faction was the count of Armagnac, who gave his name to his supporters. The Armagnacs, as the war-party, led France to her defeat at *Agincourt (1415) and lost their leader in 1418 during a massacre in Paris. They got even in 1419, when John the Fearless was assassinated at a meeting with the dauphin (the future *Charles VII) on the bridge of Montereau. *Philip the Good of Burgundy then joined the English, and influenced the king of France to repudiate the dauphin and recognize *Henry V of England as his heir (Treaty of Troyes, 1420). The dauphin, backed by the Armagnacs, continued to hold out south of the Loire, his military situation improving only with the moral resurgence led by *Joan of Arc. The rift with Burgundians was ended in 1435, by the Peace of Arras.

J. d'Avont, *La querelle des Armagnacs et des Bourguignons* (1943).

ARMIES The development of European armies between the battle of *Agincourt (1415) and the onset of the Thirty Years' War (1618-48), was characterized by structural experimentations and incomplete attempts to find solutions to the development of firearms. At Agincourt the longbow, which had helped the English to win victories since Crécy (1346), was still decisive. But by the end of the 15th century, when great military engagements were resumed, the capabilities of the *arquebus were perfected to a degree that it could replace both the English longbow and the Continental crossbow. However, at the same time an old-fashioned and simple weapon, the infantry-wielded pike, became for some five decades the real master of the battlefield.

An imaginary battle between Alexander the Great and the Persians – Renaissance style – by Altdorfer (1529)

It postponed for a while the integration of firearms; although in the final analysis both the old pike and the new firearms combined to bring about the same result: the superiority of infantry over the heavily-armoured feudal cavalry.

Military developments and the composition of armies during the Renaissance responded to changing social and political circumstances. Whereas the employment of mercenaries was not uncommon during the Middle Ages, the main force of the army, made up of knights, archers and foot soldiers, was usually recruited either by emergency levies or by the enforcement of feudal duties. The constant warring of the Italian city-states in the 14th and 15th centuries introduced a novelty, the famous armies of the **condottieri*, consisting of small mercenary bands whose leaders were expected to provide professional military services. The *Swiss mercenaries, however, were a phenomenon of a different kind. They first proved their worth on the battelfield when they destroyed the feudal army of *Charles the Bold. By the last quarter of the 15th century they were sought after by foreign rulers, who employed them in massive infantry units. The **Landsknechte*, the mercenary German infantry who succeeded the Swiss, continued the general trend, especially during the *Italian Wars, of using large armies made up of hired infantry. Usually organized in free companies and having their own leaders, these mercenaries now and then became unruly and threatened their own masters. To save money, it was customary to discharge them at the end of the fighting season, hiring them again the following year. This frequently resulted in the unleashing of thousands of armed men, desperate for food and shelter, upon a helpless civilian population. In some instances, the mercenaries turned overnight into furiously undisciplined and destructive hordes, as during the Sack of *Rome (1527), or in a similar misfortune which befell *Antwerp (1576). Renaissance authors, with their yearning for the norms of the ancient Greek and Romans, never tired denouncing the extensive use of mercenaries, who were devoid of civic virtues and lasting morale. They were accused of faking long, inconclusive campaigns and lacking the determination to make decisive moves.

Spain, the strongest European power in the 16th century, was also most innovative in military tactics and organization. This was principally the work of four generals, Gonzalo de *Córdoba and Fernando de *Avalos early in the *Italian Wars, and the duke of *Alba and Alexander *Farnese during the long wars of the revolt in the Netherlands. The Spanish innovations began as variations on the solid mass of the Swiss phalanx. The Spanish square consisted of a tactical unit 50 lines deep, with 50 men in each line, bearing pikes and swords as well as light firearms. This unit became known as the *tercio*. It was supposed to include 12 companies of 250 men each, although normally the number was considerably smaller. To deploy such a unit and take full advantage of its *musket fire, lengthy exercises were necessary. *Maurice of Nassau, who borrowed many of the techniques of the Spanish armies, subsequently surpassed them in producing trained infantry.

Renaissance armies were comparatively small. Except for some of the great battles of the Italian Wars, the average size of the armies fluctuated between 11,000 and 15,000 men. These numbers apply particularly to the battles of the *Religious Wars of France and the long campaigns in the Netherlands. Although some efforts to create standing national armies were made as early as the 15th century, the expense was onerous even for a wealthy monarch. However, the cost of making war was nevertheless on the increase. The use of *artillery, and the corresponding attention given to fortifications, meant that total expenditure for military purposes was escalating. Since the ratio of cavalry to infantry changed constantly in favour of the latter, it meant that tactical mobility in the battlefield was a secondary consideration. Consequently, by the end of the 16th century European methods of waging war were overdue for revision. This took place during the *Thirty Years' War with the appearance of a great military innovator, Gustavus Adolphus of Sweden.

F. L. Taylor, *The Art of War in Italy, 1494-1529* (1921);
O. L. Spaulding et al., *Warfare: A Study of Military Methods from the Earliest Times* (1925);
C. Oman, *The Art of War in the Sixteenth Century*, 2 vols. (1937).

ARMINIUS, JACOBUS (1560-1609) Dutch theologian. Although orphaned at an early age, A. was able to receive proper education. He studied at Utrecht, Leiden, *Geneva and *Basle and, in 1586, spent some time in Rome. Upon his return to Amsterdam in 1588 he was ordained as minister, but found himself embroiled in controversies because of his criticism of the Dutch Calvinist doctrine of *predestination. A. denied the rigid determinism implicit in the notion that God had decreed the election of the individual before the fall of Adam, and claimed that predestination might be compatible with free will. His supporters gained for him the chair of theology at the University of Leiden (1603), which he held until his death. After his death his followers reasserted his views in a more insistent form (1610), and were attacked on both theological and political grounds for harbouring pro-Spanish sentiments. The Arminians were condemned by the Synod of *Dort (1618), and persecuted, but their ideas gained acceptance in other countries, especially in England during the anti-Calvinist trend under *James I.

A. W. Harrison, *Arminianism* (1937).

ARMOUR Body armour, an essential component of mediaeval warfare, devised to protect the mounted feudal knight, was bound to disappear with the advent of firearms and the effective use of pike-wielding infantry against cavalry. But the process lasted through the 15th and 16th centuries, and for most of this period the use of armour continued and its production underwent technical perfection and improved design. In the second half of the 14th century the iron and steel-plate armour replaced the coat-of-mail, and in the early 15th century it was designed to follow the contours of the human body, so as to give the warrior a greater freedom of movement. Several European centres of industry competed in the production of fine armour, *Augsburg and *Nuremberg in Germany being the most famous, followed by the workshops of Northern Italy. The final product of Renaissance armour industry was an attractive-looking suit of steel, which provided complete cover for the body, but was also vulnerable to musket fire and, therefore, quickly fell into disuse. Early examples of Renaissance armour-suits are distinguished by their combination of mail and plate, and by their 'Gothic pattern' of pointed endings. After 1500 the design became more 'sculptural' and the plates were often etched or gilded, making the final product a true work of art. Late 16th-century armour was sometimes embellished to such a degree that its real function was to indicate the commanding officer. In the early 17th century cavalry gradually joined infantry in using a protection limited to a helmet and breast- and back-plates for the upper part of the body.

G. Laking, *A Record of European Armour and Arms Through Seven Centuries*, 5 vols. (1922);
F. M. Kelly and R. Schwabe, *A Short History of Costume and Armour*, 2 vols. (1931).

ARNDT, JOHANN (1555-1621) German Lutheran mystic. A pastor who had been educated at *Wittenberg, *Strassburg and *Basle, he expressed dissatisfaction with the dry doctrinaire character of late 16th-century Lutheran theology. His *Vier Bücher von wahren Christentum* (1606) emphasized Christ's continued influence on the heart of man. This book later influenced the thought of German Pietists.

ARNOLFO DI CAMBIO Italian architect. Active in the second half of the 13th century (his date of death is believed to be 1302), A.'s relation to Renaissance *architecture parallels that of *Cimabue's to *painting. In 1296 he began the building of the cathedral of *Florence, on a plan which showed strong French Gothic influence. Several other buildings in Florence are also attributed to him, as well as important sculptural works.

ARQUEBUS A term of German origin which came to denote several types of light firearms of the 15th and 16th centuries. The A. weighed about eight pounds, was four feet long and was used mainly by infantry, although it could also be used by cavalry. It had an effective range of about 200 yards. Further developed and used in comparatively large numbers by the Spaniards, it decided the Battle of Pavia in their favour. The A. remained the standard infantry weapon of Europe until the introduction of the much heavier *musket late in the 16th century.

Late Renaissance cavalry carrying arquebuses

ARRAS, UNION OF (January 1579) A treaty concluded by five of the southern provinces of the *Netherlands, which outdid the Pacification of *Ghent and paved the way for the separation of the Spanish-dominated south from the north. In May 1579 this was followed by an agreement of the signatories with Alexander *Farnese, in which *Philip II was recognized as sole ruler and Roman Catholicism as the exclusive faith of the Netherlands.

ARRIGHI, LUDOVICO (?-1527) Italian writing-master, type designer and printer. A professional copyist at the papal chancery in Rome, he wrote the first printed manual on calligraphy, *Operina da imparare di scrivere littera cancellaresca* (1522). His typeface, modelled on the letters of the papal chancery, influenced the style of italics. By teaching all laymen the art of drawing beautiful letters, he is said to have undermined the trade of the scribe.

ARRUDA, DIOGO AND FRANCISCO DE Two Portuguese brothers and architects; among the foremost exponents of the Orientalist ornamental style characteristic of Portugal's golden age. Diogo, active between 1508 and 1531, made important additions to the church of the Templars in Tomar, distinguished by complex decorations. Francisco, active from 1510 to 1547, is considered the principal designer of the exotic tower of Belem at Lisbon.

R. C. Smith, *The Art of Portugal, 1500-1800* (1968).

ARTICLES OF RELIGION Following *Henry VIII's break with Rome, it became necessary to define the religious doctrine of the *Church of England. This was done first in 1536 in the *Book of Articles* which limited the sacraments to three: Baptism, Penance and the Eucharist, and inclined to the teachings of *Luther with respect to the worship of saints and the saying of mass for the dead. The principles reflected the king's personal religious beliefs, as did the more conservative *Six Articles*, which were appended in 1539. They reaffirmed transubstantiation and celibacy of the clergy. However, immediately after the death of Henry VIII, the *Six Articles* were repealed and work began on what is known as the *Forty-Two Articles* of 1553. While these went further towards Protestantism, they were published only a few weeks before the ascension of the Queen *Mary, and became ineffectual. In 1563, under Queen *Elizabeth I, were published the *Thirty-Nine Articles*, the work of archbishop *Parker. These were approved by a general church assembly in 1571, and are still the official doctrine of the Church of England. Although the 1571 principles again came close to Protestantism, they failed at the time to satisfy the growing number of *Puritans.

ARTILLERY The use of gunpowder for propelling projectiles was a development of the 14th century. The earliest mention of cannons dates from the 3rd decade of that century. The first famous battle in which A. was used was at Crécy, France, in 1346, where the English are said to have fired three cannons – chiefly, however, for the noise effect rather than to inflict actual damage. In the 15th century cannon was used as a weapon of fixed position, particularly in besieging walled cities and fortified castles, thus hastening the end of the crumbling feudal system. The most impressive deployment of A. in this respect was in the siege of Constantinople (1453). *Mehemmed II used numerous cannons of different calibres, including two monstrous mortars which fired stone-balls weighing over half a ton each. Other famous cannons of that time were the 'bombard of Ghent', known as 'Dulle Griete', weighing 13 tons, and the 'Mons Meg', built in Edinburgh in 1460, which weighed 5 tons and could propel a 350 lb. stoneball nearly a mile.

The *Italian Wars opened a new age of A., introducing the element of mobility. *Charles VIII carried with him to Italy, in 1495, a siege train of guns that could advance at the same pace as the main body of his army. This was an important departure from the mainly stationary character of A. until then. It allowed the French not only to attack effectively any walled city, but also to use their guns on the battlefield. Field guns, mounted on wheeled carriages drawn by horses, played a major role in the Battle of Fornovo (1495), as well as in Ravenna (1512), Marignano (1515) and Pavia (1525). The French were also the first to improve the quality of their guns and to construct them according to classified types, sizes and weights. Indeed, standardization, without which battlefield deployment could not have been achieved, was a characteristic development in the 16th century. In 1544 Charles V limited Spanish guns to seven types only, ranging from a 40-pounder to a 3-pounder known as 'falcon'. In 1551 the French established six standard models, ranging from a cannon shooting a ball of 33 lb., to a 'falconet' which shot a one-pound ball. To appreciate the difficulties which beset field artillery in the 16th century, it will be recalled that the heavy pieces averaged 4 tons in weight and needed more than 20 horses each to be moved.

Until the 16th century the cannon was considered a risky weapon, and the status of the gunner and his chosen assistants was much lower than the mercenary soldier's. But as the weapon improved, European rulers began giving more attention to A. One famous example is that of Ercole d'Este, duke of Ferrara, who supervised in person the production of tremendous cannons. Henry VIII also took a great interest in A., importing foreign cannon founders and experimenting with crude forms of explosive shells. In 1537 Niccolo *Tartaglia published what may be the first work on ballistics. He demonstrated the curving trajectory of the ball, and that a shot would reach maximum range when the cannon is at an angle of 45°. Until then it had been thought that the

The Cannon *by Albrecht Dürer*

ball flew in a straight line until it lost its velocity and fell down suddenly.

The development of wheeled guncarriages and guns cast with trunnions made possible the appearance of true naval A. in the late 16th century. The guns were placed on the broadside of the ship, the heaviest on the lower decks. Big warships carried up to 50 heavy guns, becoming veritable floating platforms of A. Guns played a major role in the encounter of the English fleet with the Spanish *Armada in 1588, although in this case the English employed medium-size guns of long range, as opposed to the heavy Spanish guns.

C. Oman, *The Art of War in the Sixteenth Century*, 2 vols. (1937);
A. Manucy, *Artillery Through the Ages* (1955);
W. Y. Carman, *History of Firearms* (1955).

ARTISTS, THE SOCIAL POSITION OF Periods marked by intense artistic activity usually correspond with a rise in the social status of artists. In the Middle Ages artists were considered craftsmen and held in low esteem. In the 15th century painters and sculptors became publicly-recognized figures, and they began to claim admission to the liberal professions, and oppose classification as mechanics or craftsmen. *Alberti, *Ghiberti and *Leonardo all argued that painters were learned men, and Leonardo claimed equality for painters with poets and philosophers. These arguments demonstrate the resistance which artists encountered in the social strata to which they sought to belong. It must be remembered, however, that the *guilds were also reluctant to have artists become independent professionals. Nevertheless this is what happened during the second half of the 16th century, and the trend was further emphasized by the appearance of the first painting *academies in Italy.

A. Blunt, *Artistic Theory in Italy: 1450-1600* (1962), 48-57.

ASCHAM, ROGER (1515-68) English scholar. In his lifetime Ascham's reputation rested on his mastery of Greek, which he taught at Cambridge. He also tutored the young *Elizabeth I and Lady Jane *Grey in this language, and later served *Eduard VI, *Mary and *Elizabeth I as Latin secretary. In a book he wrote on archery and in his *Schoolmaster* (published 1570), which dealt with education, he advocated a less rigid approach by teachers and encouraged physical activity.

E. M. Nugent, *The Thought and Culture of the English Renaissance* (1956).

ASIA In the Far East as in *Africa, early European penetration was mainly the work of Portugal. The first Asian outpost of the Portuguese was in *India, which Vasco da *Gama reached in 1498. Soon after they had established themselves on the Indian coast of Malabar, the Portuguese continued to advance eastwards in pursuit of the spice trade. *Malacca, the strategic harbour in the straits between the Malayan peninsula and Sumatra, was captured by Afonso de *Albuquerque in 1511 and, in 1514, the *Moluccas were visited by Portuguese ships. A year earlier the first Portuguese ship had arrived at the port of Canton, and in time they secured the right to settle in Macao, which became the centre of their activities in *China. Direct relations with

*Japan had to wait a few more years. It was not until 1543 that the first Portuguese ship went there from China, to be followed in 1549 by the arrival of the *Jesuit missionary St. Francis *Xavier. During the first three-quarters of the 16th century, the Portuguese had Asia practically to themselves. The presence of Spain in the *Philippines was the only exception, and almost no other European shipping had reached the continent. This situation ended in the 1590s, when the English and, even more, the Dutch began to send trading expeditions to the Far East. In the course of the first half of the 17th century, the Dutch dislodged the Portuguese from a number of key posts, and supplanted them as the leading European power in Asia.

K. M. Pannikar, *Asia and Western Dominance* (1953);
M. Edwards, *Asia in the European Age, 1498-1955* (1962);
R. W. Whiteway, *The Rise of Portuguese Power in India 1497-1550* (1967).

ASTROLABE An instrument, first developed in ancient Greece, consisting of a disc of metal or wood and a rotating diametral rule for measuring the position of the sun and stars. On this basis both time and geographical latitude could be calculated. During the second half of the 15th century Portuguese seamen adopted the use of the A., together with tables of the sun's declination, for finding their latitude. The development is usually ascribed to the German Martin *Behaim.

ASTROLOGY Judicial A., or the belief that the fate of human beings could be determined by the positions of the stars, was a cultural feature inherited by the Renaissance from the mediaeval and ancient civilisations. However, there are many indications that, during the Renaissance, the belief in astral influence over the destiny of man actually increased. This may be due to the fact that Renaissance culture sought inspiration in the mores and lifestyle of ancient Greece and Rome, where A. had been particularly widespread.

The flourishing of A. in the 15th and 16th centuries may also have been related to the general inquietude of the age, the great religious convulsions and the need for definite answers in times of moral uncertainty. Whatever the reason, A. coexisted side by side with *astronomy, in spite of the advances made by the latter. Poets, who had long been accustomed to astrological ideas and metaphors, were joined by philosophers, like the *Neoplatonist *Ficino, who expounded metaphysics with an obvious astrological influence. Many Italian rulers, as well as kings and emperors like Charles V and *Francis I, used to consult astrologers before making important political or military decisions. Comets, periodic stars and eclipses were interpreted as portents of crucial events. Theologians might declare the second coming of Christ on the evidence of the appearance of a shiny new star, and the great astronomers of the 16th century were themselves prone to make astrological interpretations from time to time. For example, Tycho *Brahe believed in A. for most of his life, and interpreted the comet of 1577 both in astronomical terms and as a sign of political events in the future. The almanacs printed in the 16th century usually included astrological predictions about the coming year and were, therefore, named 'prognostications'. The cult of A. apparently declined at the beginning of the 17th century, when the heliocentric theory finally gained general acceptance.

Lynn Thorndyke, *A History of Magic and Experimental Science*, 6 vols. (1923-41);
L. MacNeice, *Astrology* (1964).

ASTRONOMY AND COSMOGRAPHY Throughout the Middle Ages, the Ptolemaic system, a survival from the Hellenistic age, persisted as the unchallenged configuration of the universe. Based on the conception of a stationary earth at the centre of the cosmos, this model remained intact, and actually acquired additional confirmation in the famous planetary tables of 1252, drawn for Alfonso X of Castile. *Regiomontanus, the most important astronomer of the 15th century, also accepted Ptolemy. Indeed, well into the 16th century, the sole aim of astronomers was not to disprove the great assumption of antiquity, but to elaborate on it and add new stellar constellations to the old planeray charts.

The cosmographic revolution of the Renaissance was born in the mind of a theoretician, rather than a result of improved astronomical observations. In fact, so well-aware was *Copernicus of the impact of his theories, that he postponed the publication of his work for many years, until shortly before his death. His main proposition, that the earth orbits around the sun and rotates daily on its axis, aroused the angry reactions of Protestants and Roman Catholics alike. Heliocentrism conflicted with the conception of the universe which underlays the European religious traditions. But the opposition was not confined to the simple champions of Biblical authority: even Tycho *Brahe, the last great naked-eye astronomer, refused to accept the Copernican theory on the grounds that, although the earth was supposed to be moving in orbit around the sun, he could not perceive any shift in the positions of the stars.

Brahe's contribution to A. were accurate measurements of planetary motions, for which he used large-scale instruments. His younger associate, Johann *Kepler, was consequently in a better position to accept the heliocentric theory, eliminating at the same time some of the discrepancies which Copernicus had inherited from Ptolemy. Kepler, therefore, did away with the old epicycles of Ptolemy, and established an elliptical, rather than a circular planeraty orbit. Galileo *Galilei, Kepler's contemporary, was the last great figure of the Renaissance A., as well as the founder of modern astronomical observation. A champion of the Copernican theory, he disproved Aristotle's physics, thus opening the way to Isaac Newton's explanation of celestial motions by the force of gravity. His initiation of *telescopic A. in 1609, led to the immediate discovery of much new data, and brought to an end the age in which man's physical limitations restricted his knowledge of the universe.

J. L. E. Dreyer, *A History of Astronomy from Thales to Kepler* (1952);
A. Pannkock, *A History of Astronomy* (1961).

AUGSBURG Situated on the route to Italy, this city, dominated by a commercially-minded oligarchy, became in the 15th century one of the foremost centres of industry, trade and banking in southern Germany. A. also played an important role as a place through which humanist learning was transmitted to the north, and as the location of important printers and artists, including *Holbein the Elder and *Burgkmair. The city was host to several German Imperial Diets. In the 1520s, in spite of the fact that its two most powerful banking houses,

the *Fuggers and *Welsers, remained Roman Catholic, A. was agitated by the Reformation. Supporters of *Luther and *Zwingli, and even some *Anabaptist leaders, preached there with some measure of success. The opposition to the old faith reached a climax in 1537, when images were forbidden in the churches. But *Charles V's victory over the *Schmalkaldic League (1547) changed the situation. The exiled Catholic clergy were allowed to return, and the religious peace of 1555 established an uneasy parity between Lutherans and Catholics.
W. Zorn, *Augsburg: Geschichte einer Stadt* (1955).

AUGSBURG, CONFESSION OF (1530) The confession of faith, composed largely by *Melanchthon with *Luther's approval, and presented to *Charles V at the Diet of Augsburg. The C.o.A. attempted to minimize the differences between Luther's views and Roman Catholicism, but its moderate language did not make it more acceptable to the emperor, who rejected it after consulting his own theological advisors. However, the C.o.A. gained authority as an official Lutheran document, although slight variations were later introduced.
E. Schlink, *Theology of the Lutheran Confessions* (1961); C. Bergendoff, *The Church of the Lutheran Reformation* (1967).

AUGSBURG INTERIM, THE (1548) A provisional doctrinal formula prepared by Roman Catholic and Protestant theologians, and approved by *Charles V and the Diet of Augsburg as a basis for truce. Although the formula conceded some points to the Protestants on religious matters, and guaranteed secularized church property to Protestant princes, it was rejected by many leaders in the Lutheran camp. *Melanchthon, who was ready to support it, was attacked by *Amsdorf and by *Flacius Illyricus. In Saxony, an edict known as the 'Leipzig Interim' was proclaimed by the Protestant elector *Maurice (1549), but it too was criticized by Lutheran leaders.

AUGSBURG, RELIGIOUS PEACE OF (1555) An agreement made between *Ferdinand I and the German electors, to settle the religious-political affairs of the empire, at Augsburg on 25 September 1555. The settlement was based on the principle that a subject should follow the religion of his ruler (*cuius regio eius religio*). The agreement was not an act of religious toleration; it did not recognize Calvinism. But it meant an advance for the Lutheran churches which were given imperial recognition. The agreement regulated the religious and territorial *status quo* in Germany until the Peace of Westphalia (1648).

AUGUSTUS I (1526-86) Elector of Saxony from 1553. Succeeding to the electoral dignity following the death of his brother, *Maurice of Saxony, he put an end to the expansionist policy of his predecessor, preferring a peaceful accomodation with the *Habsburgs. In 1554 he ended the conflict with *John Frederick I of Saxony with the Treaty of Naumburg. A. was a strict supporter of Lutheranism, and solicited the support of other Protestant German princes to the *Formula of Concord (1577). Saxony's economy improved under his peaceful rule.

AURISPA, GIOVANNI (1376-1459) Italian humanist. A native of Sicily, he studied at Naples and about 1413 went as a commercial agent to the East, where he first began to collect Greek manuscripts. From 1414 to 1419 he taught at Savona, and after about two years in the service of *Martin V, made another voyage to the East, this time as a diplomatic emissary of the *Gonzagas to Constantinople (1421-1423). A. then taught Greek at Bologna and Florence but, in 1427, settled in *Ferrara, where he held a position as tutor and sometimes as ambassador of the *Estes. While he was not himself an author of significance, A. introduced into Italy the Greek manuscripts of the *Iliad* and the works of Aristophanes, Sophocles, Aeschylus, Plato and others. Between 1433 and 1443 he attended the Council of *Basle and worked at the papal court, and later in Florence.

AUSTRIA The growth of A. in the 15th and 16th centuries, from an unimportant German duchy into a European power of the first order, did not lack accidental factors. First and foremost, however, the development was due to the policy of unremitting territorial expansion pursued by the ruling ducal house, the *Habsburgs. In 1438 Duke Albert V (1404-39) was elected German king and from here on the rulers of A. were also the ruling dynasty of the *Holy Roman Empire. Under the even longer rule of Emperor *Frederick III (1440-93), which hardly left an imprint on the Empire, A. was continuously troubled by revolts of the nobility and the estates, but gradually the different Habsburg possession of A. proper, Styria, Carinthia, Carniola and Tyrol were brought together under a central government. Attempts at further organizational and territorial consolidation were made by *Maximiliam I (1493-1519), though with varying measures of success. The rich Tyrolean silver and copper mines provided this monarch with resources for his great territorial schemes elsewhere in Europe, and the position of A., between Italy, Germany and Poland, made her the beneficiary of expanding commercial activities. In the 16th century A. was mainly concerned with the military threat of the *Ottoman Turkish Empire. The problem was anticipated by *Charles V, who upon his election as emperor, transferred the Austrian territories to his brother *Ferdinand (1521-64). But in 1529 Vienna almost succumbed to the armies of *Suleiman I, and a massive military effort was necessary to maintain parts of Hungary as a buffer zone between A. and the Ottoman Empire. Ferdinand's involvement in *Hungary and *Bohemia and his claim to the thrones of these countries, laid the foundations for the multinational Austrian Empire, which was destined to last until 1918. But, in the meantime, he had to deal with the social and religious problems caused by the Reformation. Peasant unrest (1525) was followed by Anabaptist activities and the spread of Lutheranism among the nobility. Therefore, Ferdinand, late in his reign, allowed the *Jesuits to enter A., thereby starting the process of winning the population back to Roman Catholicism. His decision to divide his patrimony among his three sons inevitably led to intense rivalries under his successors, *Maximilian II (1546-76), *Rudolf II (1576-1611) and *Matthias (1611-19). A. was by then a conglomeration of Germans, Bohemians, Moravians and Hungarians, and was able to deal adequately with the Turkish menace, but could not find a solution to the religious problem. Outright repression, as in the case of the peasant uprising of 1594-97, worked well only in the German territories. The Bohemians and the rebellious Hungarians took advantage of the bitter conflict between two brothers,

Rudolf II and Matthias, to secure far-reaching political liberties. At the eve of the *Thirty Years' War, A. was indeed a territorial empire, but lacking a unified governmental machinery and beset by internal cleavages.

A. W. A. Leeper, *A History of Mediaeval Austria* (1941); R. A. Kann, *A History of the Hapsburg Empire, 1526-1818* (1974).

AVALOS, FERNANDO DE (1490-1525) Italian military commander in the service of Spain. He was born to a family of Spanish descent which had settled in Italy in the 15th century, becoming the Marquises of Pescara, and was married to Vittoria *Colonna. In 1512 he participated in the battle of Ravenna and was taken prisoner, but during the next few years distinguished himself in military engagements against Venice, Milan and Genoa. His greatest feat was leading the imperial army to victory at the battle of Pavia (1525), where he successfully employed infantry armed with *arquebuses against the heavy French cavalry.

AVENTINUS (Johann Turmair, 1477-1534) German historian; the name A. derived from the Latin version of Turmair's native town. A. studied in Ingolstadt, Cracow and Paris, and in 1509 became the tutor of the two younger sons of the duke of Bavaria. In 1517 he began to write the *Annals of the Dukes of Bavaria*, which he completed in 1521. The work was coloured by an anti-papal sentiment and by German, or rather Bavarian, nationalism. Although it was informative, it lacked a critical spirit. However, A. supplied a vivid description of the manners and customs of the peoples he studied and had a clear style. Late in his life he showed sympathy for the Reformation and left Ingolstadt for Regensburg, where he died.

G. Strauss, *Historian in an Age of Crisis: The Life and Work of Johannes Aventinus, 1477-1534* (1963).

B

BACCHIACCA (1494-1557) The name given to the Italian painter Francesco Ubertini. A pupil of *Perugino in Florence, he went to Rome in 1525 and there painted the famous portrait *La Maddalena*. He returned to Florence in 1527, and was employed in several decorative works by various patrons, including Grand Duke *Cosimo I. Borrowing frequently from the works of others, B. was essentially a *Mannerist and was overshadowed by his friends, *Pontormo, *Andrea del Sarto and *Vasari.

BACCIO DA MONTELUPO (1469-1535) Italian sculptor and architect. Raised in Florence, he became a follower of *Savonarola, who inspired the religious intensity of his terra-cotta busts. In 1498 he fled to Venice, returning to Florence in 1504. Afterwards he worked in various Florentine churches, including S. Lorenzo and Orsanmichele. He spent his last years in Lucca, where he added architecture to sculpture, building a church in a simple traditional design. A High Renaissance realist, B.'s fame declined with the passage of time.

BACON, FRANCIS (1561-1626) English philosopher, essayist and lawyer. The youngest son of the Lord Keeper to *Elizabeth I, he demonstrated from his early youth high intellectual abilities. He attended Cambridge University (1573-76), studied law and spent some years in France. Returning to England after his father's death (1579), B. tried to use his connections at court to secure himself a suitable office, but was several times rebuffed by William Cecil, the husband of his mother's sister. Even his friendship with the Earl of *Essex failed to bring him an appointment and, in 1593, he lost to Edward *Coke a bid for the office of Attorney-General, which started a life-long enmity between the two. In 1601 B. took part in the condemnation of his former friend Essex and wrote a pamphlet justifying his execution. *James I's accession brought a change in his fortune. Having defended the King's rights in Parliament (1604), B. was given the office of Solicitor-General (1607). In the next few years he became, in succession, clerk of the *Star-Chamber (1608), Attorney-General (1613), Lord Keeper (1617) and Lord Chancellor (1618). However, he never had a real influence in the government and was dependent on the King's young favourite, the Duke of Buckingham. In 1621, B. was accused of receiving bribes, a charge which emerged in a confrontation between the House of Commons and the King on the issue of the crown's right to award trade monopolies. Coke, whose downfall B. had assisted in 1616, led the assault. Convicted by the Lords, he was deprived of his office and retired to private life.

B.'s literary fame was established with the *Essays* (1597), a work which reflected his practical wisdom and

Francis Bacon

The court of Burgundy in a 15th century illuminated manuscript

was reissued, greatly enlarged, twice more in his lifetime. More ambitious, philosophically, was his *On the Advancement of Learning* (1605), which analyzed the shortcomings of human knowledge, but argued man's power to control nature. Here B. proposed the method of induction, namely, the way to attain practical results by the application of general rules, discovered through observation and experience of the simplest facts. This philosophic experimentalism was further developed in the *Novum organum* (1620), where in a famous section he describes the four false attitudes which lead man's thought astray. A violent opponent of reasoning from authority, he restated his position in *De augmentis scientiarum* (1623), an expanded Latin version of his book of 1605. His *New Atlantis* (1627), describes an ideal state where true science would be encouraged by the government for the benefit of all.

B.'s dual career as a courtier and as an innovative philosopher may appear inconsistent today, but was in harmony with the temper of the Renaissance. He was not, as sometimes presented, the father of the experimental method of modern science, nor did he make any efforts to discover scientific truths. Rather, in his writings, which were popular in his own age, he reflected the growing awareness of the potential of science.

F. H. Anderson, *The Philosophy of Francis Bacon* (1948);
P. Rossi, *Francis Bacon; From Magic to Science* (1968);
C. W. S. Williams, *Bacon* (1933).

BADIUS, JODOCUS ASCENSIUS (1462-1535) Humanist and printer at Paris. Born in *Ghent, he studied in Italy and later taught at *Lyons where he published an edition of Terence (1493). In 1499, he moved to Paris where, in 1503, he opened his printing shop, whose emblem, showing the inside of a printing establishment, is famous. He exercised a great influence on the development of French publishing, and issued many of the early works of *Erasmus and of Guillaume *Budé. Robert *Estienne was his son-in-law.

Badius' press

BAFFIN, WILLIAM (1584-1622) English navigator. Born probably in London, he sailed in 1612 with an expedition which searched for a *northwest passage and was later in the service of the *Muscovy Company. In 1616 he discovered the bay which bears his name, located north of *Davis Strait and separating Greenland from Baffin Island. In 1617 he sailed to the East for the English *East India Company, returning in 1619 after he had conducted surveys at the Persian Gulf. He sailed to the East again in 1620, and died in military action near Ormuz.

BAGLIONI The family which dominated Perugia until its conquest in 1540 by Pope *Paul III. The B. rose to prominence in the 14th century as **condottieri* and leaders of one of the main political factions of Perugia. They gained control of the city following the death of *Braccio da Montone in 1424, and ruled supreme throughout the 15th century. Giampaolo B., who gained power in 1500 after a fratricidal struggle among members of the family, supported Pope *Julius II, but was beheaded in Rome by his successor *Leo X in 1520. The power of the family then declined. Between 1527 and 1530 they supported the republic of Florence against the *Medici.

BAÏF, JEAN ANTOINE DE (1532-89) French poet. Born in Venice, the son of the French ambassador Lazare de Baïf and an Italian mother, he was provided by his scholarly father with the best education, and studied at the Collège de Cocqueret at Paris together with *Ronsard and *Du Bellay. An active member of the *Pléiade, B. produced a considerable number of literary works, but never found a definitive style of hiw own and tended to follow alternative models. Between 1552 and 1555 he published a series of sonnet cycles in imitation of *Petrarch, dedicated to real or imaginary mistresses. His *Mimes, enseignements et proverbes*, first published in 1576, included poetic satires, as well as allegorical pieces, and earned him fame. The work was reprinted twice during his lifetime. B. also translated and adapted classical plays. His comedy, *Le brave*, modelled after Plautus' *Miles gloriosus*, was performed in 1567; in 1573 he completed a translation of Sophocles' *Antigone*.

M. Auge-Chiquet, *La vie, les idées et l'oeuvre de Jean Antoine de Baïf* (1909; reprinted 1969).

BALBI, GIROLAMO (c. 1450-1535) Italian humanist. Born in Venice, he became a member of the Roman Academy of Pomponius *Laetus and, in 1489, went to Paris. There he was accused of heresy and immoral conduct and, in 1496, fled to England. Later he went to Vienna and Prague and finally Hungary. Important as one of the wandering promoters of *humanism outside Italy, he ended his life as bishop of Pressburg.

BALBOA, VASCO NUÑEZ DE (1475-1517) Spanish **conquistador* and discoverer of the Pacific. Born to an impoverished noble family of Estremadura, B. went to the New World in 1500 and settled in Hispaniola. In 1510 he escaped his creditors by embarking as a stowaway on a ship which was sent to rescue the settlement of San Sebastian on the mainland. After landing, B. managed to take command of the ship's force, led an expedition to the banks of a river on the isthmus of Panama, where he founded a new town, Darien. He began to explore and conquer the adjoining territory and on 25 September 1513 reached the Pacific. When his report of the discovery reached Spain, *Ferdinand the Catholic gave him the title *adelantado* (governor) of the South Sea, but at the same time sent Pedro *Arias de Avila to substitute him in the governorship of Panama. B. then dedicated his efforts to the construction of a small fleet in the Pacific, in order to continue the explorations to the south. This aroused the jealousy of Arias de Avila, who accused him of insubordination and had him arrested and executed after a summary trial.

C. L. G. Anderson, *Life and Letters of Vasco Nuñez de Balboa* (1941).

BALDOVINETTI, ALESSIO (1425-99) Italian painter. A native of Florence, B. is known for his *Annunciation*, now in the Uffizi, and for a beautiful *Madonna*, now at the Louvre. A disciple of Fra *Angelico, his style has both similarities and contrasts with that of *Piero della Francesca. B. also designed mosaics, and left an important document on the social aspects of the life of 15th-century artists in the diary of his commissions.

R. W. Kennedy, *Alessio Baldovinetti: a Critical and Historical Study* (1938).

BALDUNG, HANS (called Grien, 1484-1545) German painter and engraver. B. was for several years *Dürer's assistant in Nuremberg, but most of his identified work was done later, in Strassburg. The theme of the female nude, usually in an unreal setting, recurs in his paintings, while his woodcuts often display extreme anguish in nightmarish scenes of Christ's passion and ascent to heaven.

G. Bussmann, *Manierismus im Spätwerk Hans Baldung Griens* (1966).

BALE, JOHN (1495-1563) English Protestant reformer and author. Joining the Carmelite order as a boy, B. studied at Cambridge, where he caught the spirit of the *Reformation. But, after graduating in 1529, he relinquished his monastic vows and married. He then became an aid to Thomas *Cromwell, who protected him, and wrote derisively about the monastic institution. When Cromwell fell in 1540, B. fled to the Continent, but returned in 1547 upon the accession of *Edward VI. He was given an ecclesiastical position and in 1552 made bishop of the Irish diocese of Ossory. He had to leave England again on the accession of *Mary, finding shelter in Holland, then in Frankfurt and Basle. He came back after *Elizabeth I ascended the throne, and in 1560 was given a prebend at Canterbury. B. was a prolific writer. His *morality plays, which contained harsh attacks on Roman Catholicism, foreshadowed the Elizabethan historical drama. However, his most important work was a chronological catalogue of British authors, which was first published in 1549.

BAMBAIA (c. 1480-1548) The name given to the Italian sculptor Agostino Busti. He was born near Milan and was trained in Pavia. In 1513 he completed in Milan the tomb of the poet Lancino Curzio and, in 1515, undertook the execution of the tomb of Gaston de *Foix, also in Milan. Other works by B. were the Bua monument in Treviso and the tombs of Caracciolo and Vimercati in the *Duomo* of Milan. Individual figures from these works were later removed. His style is elegant and emphasizes ornamentation.

The Three Ages of Woman *by Hans Baldung*

BANCROFT, RICHARD (1544-1610) English churchman; archbishop of Canterbury and a fierce opponent of the *Puritans. Educated at Cambridge, he became famous as a preacher and gradually rose in the ranks of the church. He was made treasurer of St. Paul's cathedral in 1585, and bishop of London in 1597. At that time Archbishop Whitgift, who was old and incapacitated, entrusted him with the management of ecclesiastical affairs, and his election as Whitgift's successor in 1604 was merely a confirmation of his actual role. B. attacked the Puritans, both in public sermons and in numerous ecclesiastical lawsuits. His rigid and uncompromising attitude at the *Hampton Court Conference of 1604 led to the subsequent ejection of about 300 Puritan clergymen from the ranks, and helped to make Puritanism into a political force. In the following years B. fought to make the ecclesiastical courts more independent, but was unsuccessful, and continued his campaign for discipline within the church. In 1608 he became chancellor of Oxford University, and shortly before his death consulted *James I on a plan for a Scottish episcopal church.

Hercules and Cacus *by Bandinelli*

BANDELLO, MATTEO (1485-1561) Italian author. A witty person who spent his life as a diplomat-churchman, he became in 1550 the bishop of Agen, France, and was a friend of *Scaliger. His *Novelliere*, a collection of over 200 short stories, was published in 1554; it appeared in a French adaptation in 1565 and in English in 1567. The stories, modelled after *Boccaccio's *Decameron*, became very popular and are considered a landmark in the development of the novel. *Shakespeare and other contemporary authors borrowed themes from these stories for their plots, as, for example, *Romeo and Juliet*.

T. G. Griffith, *Bandello's Fiction* (1955);
G. Petrocchi, *Mateo Bandello* (1949).

BANDINELLI, BACCIO (1488-1560) Italian sculptor. Born in Florence to one of the town's leading goldsmiths, he became the favoured sculptor of the *Medici after their return in 1512. He was commissioned to do works for *Leo X, and *Clement VII entrusted him with the execution of a copy of the ancient *Laocoön*, now in the Uffizi, Florence. B.'s best-known work is the statue of *Hercules and Cacus* at Florence's Piazza della Signoria, completed in 1534. A would-be rival to *Michelangelo, he was the object of contemptuous remarks by *Cellini in his *Autobiography*. In 1531 he founded in the Vatican a formal gathering of artists for the purpose of artistic studies. This was one of the earliest attempts to establish an *academy of fine arts.

BANKING The great intensification of international commerce, which had made possible the development of mediaeval b., also favoured the growth of banks during the Renaissance. However, Renaissance and mediaeval b. were separated by the long economic recession of the second half of the 14th century. The mighty Florentine banks, Bardi, Peruzzi and Frescobaldi, had suffered great losses even before the deterioration of the economic conditions; the Bardi receiving its final blow about 1350, when Edward III of England repudiated all his debts. The *Medici, whose rise in the second quarter of the 15th century coincided with the improvement of international commerce, learned from the experience of their Florentine predecessors and took care to broaden and decentralize their operations, and to have their agents invest in the local European branches of the bank, so as to make them responsible junior partners. Long years of mismanagement, as well as the French invasion of Italy, caused the fall of the Medici bank in 1494. By then a new b. family, the *Fugger, was rising to power, followed by another *Augsburg house, the *Welser. In contrast with the Medici, the Fuggers maintained central control and advanced large loans to the *Habsburgs. B. houses which belonged to the patrician class of autonomous cities survived longer during the Renaissance than individual ones, which were dependent on a particular ruler. The career of Jacques *Coeur in the 15th century illustrates the vulnerability of the individual banker-merchant, although Agostino *Chigi, the banker of *Leo X and *Clement VII, fared better.

B. operations in the 15th century were concerned not so much with loans and the collections of interest, as with the conversion of bills of exchange. As time went on, it became necessary to find formal solutions to this problem. The two oldest public banks were, not surprisingly, located in the traditional commercial centres; these were the bank founded at Barcelona in 1401 and the Casa di San Giorgio of *Genoa, established in 1407. But in view of the tremendous transition in the economic activity, which took place in the 16th century, it would be more correct to consider the Venetian Banco della Piazza di Rialto (1587) as the first public bank. Concerned mainly with management of bills of exchange, it was soon followed by the Exchange Bank of Amsterdam (1609), and signalled the shift towards more modern b. methods in the 17th century.

R. de Roover, *The Rise and Decline of the Medici Bank, 1397-1494* (1963);
R. Eherenberg, *Capital and Finance in the Age of Renaissance* (1963).

BARBARI, JACOPO DE' (1440-1516) Italian painter and engraver. Born in Venice and influenced by the style of Giovanni *Bellini, he left Italy about 1500 for Germany. Until 1504 he worked for Emperor *Maximilian I at Nuremberg; later he was court painter to the elector of Saxony, *Frederick the Wise, and to *Joachim I of Brandenburg. In 1509 he went to work for *Margaret of Austria in the Netherlands. Of his engravings, the best known is a large aerial view of Venice (1500), the first overall view of a city, as seen from all the high points to which the artist had access.

BARBARO, DANIEL (1513-70) Italian historian and humanist. Born to the well-known Venetian family, he pursued an ecclesiastical career, taking part in the Council of *Trent. But he was also involved in diplomacy, going in 1548 to England on behalf of Venice. After the death of *Bembo, he was appointed historian of the Republic; his history of Venice covers the years 1512-15.

He translated Vitruvius' essay on architecture to Italian (1556), wrote *La prattica della perspettiva* (1568) on the rules of *perspective, and other works.

BARBARO, ERMOLAO (1453-93) Italian humanist and diplomat. Born in Venice, he studied in Rome under Pomponius *Laetus, and in 1477 was appointed to a chair of philosophy at the University of Padua. B. was chiefly a translator and editor of classical works, among which were Aristotle's *Rhetoric* and Pliny's *Natural History*. As a diplomat he went on several missions on behalf of the Venetian government. Two years before his death he was made the patriarch of Aquileia by *Innocent VIII. But, since he accepted his nomination without obtaining prior approval from his government, he was ordered to resign this post. B. found it wise not to return to Venetian territory. He died in Rome.

BARBARO, GIOSAFAT (1413-94) Venetian merchant and traveller. In 1436 he left for the ports of the Black Sea and subsequently visited southern Russia, Georgia and the Caucasus. After his return in 1451 he filled several public offices of the Republic and, in 1473, was sent as ambassador to the Shah of Persia with the aim of promoting an alliance against the *Ottoman Turks. He returned in 1477 following an eventful voyage during which he familiarized himself with Persia, its customs and languages. B. left in manuscript form an account of his travels, *Viaggi fatti da Venetia*, first published in 1543.

BARBAROSSA The name given in Christian Europe to the Turkish admiral Khair-ed-Din. Of Albanian descent, he established himself early in the 16th century in bases on the north coast of Africa, from which he attacked Christian shipping. In 1515 he took possession of *Algiers and was confirmed as its ruler by *Selim I. In 1534 he conquered Tunis in the name of *Suleiman II. This brought about the North African expedition of *Charles V, who drove B. out, destroying his fleet. The Emperor then attacked B.'s base in Algiers (1541), which was countered by the Admiral's plundering of the coasts of Italy. B. also commanded the fleet which Suleiman sent in 1543 to help his ally *Francis I of France.

BARCLAY, ALEXANDER (1476-1552) English poet and translator. Not much is known about his early life, but it seems that he attended either Oxford or Cambridge, and probably spent some time on the Continent. He then became a chaplain and later a Benedictine monk. His best-known work is an English adaptation of Sebastian *Brant's *Ship of Fools*, which was printed in 1509. Some years later his *Eclogues* appeared, which are among the earliest examples of English pastoral poetry, inspired, however, by foreign examples. His other works included translations of Sallust, a life of St. George and a book on the French language.

A. Pompen, *The English Versions of the 'Ship of Fools'* (1928).

BARCLAY, WILLIAM (1546-1608) Scottish political philosopher. Educated at the University of Aberdeen, he left Scotland forever in 1573 and settled in France, where he studied and later taught civil law. In 1600 his *De regno et regali potestate* was published in Paris, an extreme statement on the divine right of kings. With this work as his letter of recommendation, he went in 1603 to England and was well received by *James I. Shortly before his death he returned to France. Although a devout Roman Catholic, B. denied the temporal power of the pope over kings. His views on this subject, written in answer to *Bellarmine, were stated in his *De potestate Papae*, published a year after his death.

BARENTS, WILLEM (1550-97) Dutch explorer. In 1594 he sailed from *Amsterdam with two ships to search for a *northeast passage to India. Reaching Novaya Zemlya, he explored the area before returning to Holland. He came back at the head of a larger expedition in 1595. In 1596 he sighted Bear Island and Spitzbergen, but was trapped by the ice and was forced to spend the winter in Novaya Zemlya. He died the following spring while trying to escape; most of his men came back. The sea between Spitzbergen, Novaya Zemlya and Scandinavia was named after him.

BARILI (Antonio di Neri; 1453-1517) Italian architect, engraver and inlay designer. Born in *Siena he began as an architect and civil engineer, repairing bridges and planning fortifications. Between 1483 and 1502 he executed a great work of carving and inlay in the chapel of S. Giovanni of the cathedral of Siena, of which only fragments remain. Among his other works, distinguished by their exquisite style and grace, are the benches for the Piccolomini library of the cathedral (1496), and the organ in the chantry (1510). He was assisted by his nephew Giovanni B., who later in Rome executed wood works according to the instructions of *Raphael.

Selfportrait of Barili at work, signed 1502

BARNABITES The popular name of a small religious order, founded in Milan in 1530 by St. Antonio Maria Zaccaria. Officially known as the Clerks Regular of St. Paul, the B. wore black cassocks and dedicated themselves to preaching and catechizing. Although a small group, they are significant as an expression of the fervour of reform within the Catholic church in the 16th century.

BARNES, ROBERT (1495-1540) English religious reformer. Educated at Cambridge, B. joined the group of humanists which, under the influence of *Erasmus, became interested in theological questions. In 1526 he was charged with spreading heresy, but under the threat of a death sentence recanted and then left England. Between 1528 and 1531 he was in Antwerp and also visited Germany, where he met and became a follower of *Luther. Following *Henry VIII's break with Rome he returned to England, where Thomas *Cromwell aided him, making use of his connections with the Protestants on the Continent. Cromwell's fall in July 1540 was also the end for B., who was charged with heresy. He was burned at the stake together with five other persons charged with similar offenses.

BAROCCI (Federico Fiori; 1528-1612) Italian painter. Born in Urbino, he was the pupil of Taddeo *Zuccari in Rome, where together with other artists he painted frescoes in the *casino* of *Pius IV (1561-63). Later he returned to Urbino, and for the rest of his life worked there and in nearby towns. Suffering from frequent bouts of ill health, he nevertheless had a long and very productive artistic career, painting hundreds of pictures which included numerous religious subjects and portraits. B.'s style was influenced by the soft luminosity of *Correggio, and he did not belong to the mainstream *Mannerism of his time.

BARONCELLI, NICCOLO (?-1453) Italian sculptor. Believed to have been born in Florence, he was a pupil of *Brunelleschi, but executed his first works in Padua (1436-42). In Ferrara, where he spent the rest of his life, B. contributed the horse to the monument honouring Niccolo III d'Este, thus earning his sobriquet, Niccolo del Cavallo. His principal extant work is *Christ Crucified Between Mary and St. John* in the cathedral of Ferrara. A bronze sculpture in a realistic style, it is marked by the influence of *Donatello. B.'s son, Giovanni, continued to work in Ferrara as sculptor and wood carver.

BARONIUS, CAESAR (1538-1607) Cardinal and historian. Born in Sora, Italy, B. was influenced by the reformatory movement under St. Philip *Neri. In 1597 he was made chief librarian at the Vatican. But his preparations for the writing of a general history of the Church began much earlier. He is said to have devoted some 30 years, from 1559 on, to the study. His *Annales Ecclesiastici*, which covered church history from the beginning to 1198, appeared in 12 volumes between 1588 and 1607. This was intended as a Roman Catholic reply to the *Magdeburg Centuries*, the famous work which put forward the Protestant point of view. B. supplied in his work many hitherto unknown documents and, though apologetic, was reliable with regard to his sources.

BAROQUE A term of Spanish origin used in references to stylistic tendencies in the visual arts from about the last quarter of the 16th century. The B. was an outcome of stylistic developments in the arts, as well as a response to a cultural and ideological climate originated by the *Counter Reformation. It is characterized by movement, richness of colour, grand and even extravagant dimensions, all of which combined to produce an emotional appeal. In architecture the B. tended towards curved forms, large but complex spaces and exuberant decoration. In painting it favoured simple iconography and clarity of composition, combined with the emotive effects of the play of light and shade, and a preference for religious scenes. Rome, where *Caravaggio and Annibale *Carracci worked during the last decade of the 16th century, became the centre of the emerging style. The greatest figure, however, of the Roman B. was the architect, sculptor, painter and poet Gianlorenzo Bernini, (1598-1680). The greatest representative of the B. in northern Europe was *Rubens. The B. influence was also felt in 17th-century music and literature.

H. Wölfflin, *Renaissance and Baroque* (1964);
W. Sypher, *Four Stages of Renaissance Style: Transformations in Art and Literature, 1400-1700* (1955).

BARROS, JOÃO DE (1496-1570) Portuguese historian and royal administrator. B. was educated at the royal palace in Lisbon and put in charge of Portugal's commerce with its overseas possessions. In 1539 he organized a colonizing expedition to Maranhão in northern Brazil, but the attempt ended in failure. Shortly afterwards he began to work on a history of Portuguese exploration and conquest. Though entitled *Da Asia*, the work also dealt with the discovery of Brazil. B. based his narrative on authentic documents and wrote in a clear, straightforward style. The first part of this work was published in 1552, the fourth and last part in 1615, after the author's death.

C. Boxer, *Three Historians of Portuguese Asia* (1948).

BARROWISTS One of the earliest English sects of *Puritans. Henry Barrow (*c.* 1550-93) was imprisoned in 1587 for attacking the ecclesiastical hierarchy of the English episcopal church. He was executed in 1593, and his followers, called B., were subjected to severe prosecution. The B. regarded the official church as idolatrous and the government as heretical. Like the *Brownists, they fled to Holland, and eventually emigrated to America.

F. J. Powicke, *Henry Barrow, Separatist, and the Exiled Church in Amsterdam* (1900).

BAROZZI, FRANCESCO (?-c. 1587) Italian mathematician and translator. A native of Venice, he translated into Italian Proclus' commentary on Euclid (1560) and Hero of Alexandria (1572). In 1586 he published his principal mathematical work, *Quel mirabile problema geometrico*. The following year he was accused of sorcery and imprisoned. He probably died in jail.

BARTOLOMEO DELLA PORTA, FRA (1474-1517) Florentine painter. Born near Florence, he studied under Cosimo Rosselli. He was influenced by the powerful personality of *Savonarola, and after witnessing the latter's imprisonment and execution decided to become a monk (1500). In 1504 he became the head of a painters' workshop at the Convent of S. Marco, and from 1508 to 1511 worked there in partnership with his friend Mariotto Albertinelli. Fra Bartolomeo seems to have influenced the early development of *Raphael, and in turn, was seized with admiration when he saw the masterpieces of Raphael and *Michelangelo in Rome, during a visit to that city a year before his death. His main contribution was the introduction of elements of simplicity and balance to early 16th-century painting. The majority of his works were altarpieces, but he also left a great number of drawings.

BARTON, ELIZABETH (c. 1506-34) An English preacher, by popular acclaim believed to be divinely-inspired, or a prophetess; also known as the Nun of Kent. B. became an object of admiration around 1526 when, during states of trance, probably caused by epilepsy, she uttered a stream of prophecies and religious exhortations. Becoming a nun, she continued her prophecies, attracting many pilgrims to her convent. When *Henry VIII's intention to divorce *Catherine of Aragon became known, she spoke against it and, in 1532, did so in the presence of the king himself. When again she attacked the king's divorce and his marriage to *Anne Boleyn after the latter was crowned in June 1533, she was examined by Archbishop *Cranmer and brought before the court of the *Star Chamber. Under torture she confessed to being an impostor, was made to read a public recantation, and on 20 April 1534 was executed together with several accomplices.

BASINIO (1424-57) Italian humanist poet. A pupil of *Vittorino da Feltre and *Theodore of Gaza, he was welcomed to the court of *Ferrara but, in 1451, went to Rimini, where Sigismondo *Malatesta became his patron. B. wrote poems in Latin which imitated the style and imagery of the ancient Greek and Roman poets. Some of his poems described scenes from the life of his patron. Of these *Hesperis* is considered the most original neo-Latin poem of the 15th century.

BASLE This Swiss city, sitting astride the Rhine, was of great importance during the Renaissance. It appeared on the European political stage in the early 15th century, when it was the site of the long rebellious church council, which bore its name (1431-47). The years of the Council coincided with the flourishing of trade and a general economic prosperity. At the same time, the *guilds and the commercial corporations gathered strength which, by 1450, gave them complete control of the city government, over the nobility and the bishop. The city's new status was recognized by *Pius II in 1460, when he allowed the founding of a *university, thereby making it an important cultural centre. At the end of the 15th century B. was the place where important humanists, such as *Reuchlin and *Erasmus, studied and taught, boasting also a successful *printing industry. Finally, in 1501, B. became the 11th canton of the *Swiss Confederation. B. espoused the *Reformation in 1529 under the leadership of *Oecolampadius. But in the ensuing period it gradually declined in influence as a cultural centre. During the French *Religious Wars, the city gave shelter to many *Huguenots.

P. Burckhardt, *Geschichte der Stadt Basel von der Reformation bis zur Gegenwart* (1942).

BASLE, COUNCIL OF (1431-49) A general council of the church, convoked by *Martin V and at first presided over by Cardinal Giuliano *Cesarini. *Eugenius IV, who succeeded to the papacy in 1431, tried to dissolve the council later that year, but it refused to disband, maintaining that its authority was superior to the Pope's. Although the original number of prelates of Basle was small, they had the support of the Emperor and of important German princes, and in 1433 the Pope accepted it. Friction continued, however, especially over the question of the Bohemian *Hussites and the union

Pastoral scene by Jacopo da Bassano

with the Eastern Church. In 1437 the break became final, when the papal party left Basle to attend the Council of *Ferrara-Florence. In 1439 the council declared Eugenius deposed, electing in his stead Amadeus VIII, duke of Savoy, as *Felix V. But the renewal of the schism caused the number of its supporters to dwindle, and in 1448 it was forced to move from Basle to Lausanne. A year later its anti-pope resigned and the council recognized the legitimacy of *Nicholas V. Its submission signalled the failure of the *Conciliar Movement.

BASSANO, JACOPO DA (c. 1517-92) Italian painter. The son of the painter Francesco da Ponte, born in the town of Bassano in northern Italy, he was influenced by the Venetian painter *Bonifazio Veronese and through him by *Titian. B., who spent most of his working life in his native town, excelled in the painting of landscapes and pastoral scenes, and was particularly interested in the depiction of animals. He developed a strong personal style, characterized by thick figures and dark tones. His many biblical scenes display a sense of drama and movement. The Holy Family and the saints are frequently presented as poor peasant types, as revealed in one of his best-known paintings, *The Adoration of the Kings*, now in the National Gallery, Edinburgh. A contemporary of Tintoretto, his human figures remind one of those in the paintings of Caravaggio. In many respects his work anticipated the 17th-century treatment of genre scenes. Much of his work was done in collaboration with his four sons, who were important painters in their own right.

E. Arslan, *I Bassano*, 2 vols. (1960).

BATTISTA DA CREMA (1460-1537) Italian religious leader. Born in Crema, he became a Dominican friar and took part in the early stages of the *Theatine order. In 1529 he became the confessor of countess Ludovica *Torelli, whom he persuaded to devote herself to religion. B. is also remembered for his spiritual writings which were quite popular at the time, and through his life and writings exercised a profound influence on his generation. He advocated rigorous forms of asceticism. He was the mentor of Antonio Maria *Zaccaria, founder of the *Barnabites.

BAVARIA Ruled since the late 12th century by the *Wittelsbach dynasty, this large agricultural and politically important German duchy gradually lost much of its influence as a result of successive partitions among members of the ruling house. The struggles between branches of the family continued to affect the history of B. in the first half of the 15th century. The reunification was largely the work of Duke Albert IV (1467-1508). During his long reign he consolidated Munich's position as capital, founded the first university at Ingolstadt (1472), and, in 1506, established the principle of primogeniture with the aim of forestalling further divisions. Although after his death his younger son Louis X (1516-45) forced the elder brother, William IV (1508-50), to give him a part of the duchy, the latter reunified it when Louis died.

B. rejected the *Reformation, William being repaid by Rome with greater rights over the church. In his German politics, he took an interest in the *Schmalkaldic League, but from 1546 gave his entire support to the *Habsburgs. His son, *Albert V (1550-79), not only continued the same policy, but eventually made B. a strictly Roman Catholic area. Under him, however, Munich began to develop into a cultural centre, especially for *music and *architecture. William V (1579-97), who had to abdicate at the end of an extravagant administration, was followed by the extremely long reign of Maximilian I (1597-1651). In the early stages of the *Thirty Years War this ambitious prince made B. the vanguard of the German Catholic forces, thus securing for himself the electoral dignity (1623). But during the later stages of the war, B. was ravaged by the Swedish and French forces.

M. Spindler, *Handbuch der bayerischen Geschichte*, 4 vols. (1967).

BAYARD, PIERRE TERRAIL, SEIGNEUR DE (1473-1524) A French soldier; one of the last great figures of idealized chivalry, known as *le chevalier sans peur et sans reproche*. Born to a noble family, B. accompanied *Charles VIII on his invasion of Italy (1494), and quickly distinguished himself by his daring exploits in combat. He fought in the *Italian Wars also under *Louis XII and *Francis I, becoming a skillful commander and military organizer. His fame, however, was based on his one-man heroic exploits and on his gallantry in fighting fellow officers. In Italy he once led thirteen French knights into battle with an equal number of Germans. He was twice taken prisoner, once in Milan and again by the English during the Battle of the *Spurs, but in both instances he was released without ransom, thanks to the impression he left on Ludovico *Sforza and *Henry VIII. B. was also famous for his low opinion of infantry and of the new firearms. Appropriately, he was killed in Sesia, Italy, by a shot fired from an *arquebus.

M. Brion, *Bayard* (1952).

BAYEZID I (1347-1403) Sultan of the *Ottoman Turks from 1389, known as *Yilderim*, 'The Thunderbolt'. The son of Murad I, he served with distinction as governor of Anatolia, and succeeded his father when he died at the Battle of Kossovo. To assure his government, he at once ordered the excution of his brother Yakub. He expanded the Turkish-held territories in the Balkans. This prompted a west European *crusade which B. decisively routed at Nicopolis (1396). The appearance of the Mongol invader Tamerlane in Asia Minor diverted his attention from the Balkans. In 1402 he was defeated and taken prisoner by Tamerlane near Ankara, dying in captivity the following year. His defeat was followed by an Ottoman interregnum and internal disorders were ended only by *Mehemmed I in 1413.

BAYEZID II (1447-1512) Sultan of the *Ottoman Empire from 1481. When his father, *Mehemmed II, died B. was engaged in a struggle with his brother *Djem, and in order to secure the throne had to bribe the *Janissaries. After Djem took shelter in Rhodes, B. payed the Knights of *St. John, and later the papacy, an annual stipend for keeping his brother in custody. This may have been the reason for his relatively non-aggressive policy towards Christian Europe. Nevertheless, he made efforts to consolidate the Ottoman possessions in the Danube valley and in 1499, after the death of Djem, opened a three-year campaign against *Venice and made some gains in the Morea and along the Dalmatian coast. B.'s fall from power matched the way he ascended the throne. *Selim, his youngest son, revolted against him and, although defeated in 1511, he was able in March 1512 to bring the Janissaries over to his side and

The Chevalier Bayard

force his father to abdicate. B. died a few days later.

S. N. Fisher, *The Foreign Relations of Turkey, 1481-1512* (1948).

BEATON, DAVID (1494-1546) Scottish cardinal and archbishop of St. Andrews. Educated in Paris, he was made Scottish ambassador to France in 1519 and employed in various diplomatic missions. In 1538 *Paul III made him cardinal and a year later he succeeded his uncle as archbishop. When *James V died (1542), he tried to obtain the regency, but failed. In 1546 he became chancellor of Scotland, a post in which he distinguished himself by his uncompromising persecution of Protestant reformers and by his strong opposition to the English designs regarding Scotland. On 29 May 1546 he was assassinated by conspirators who were motivated by political and religious reasons.

BEAUFORT An aristocratic English family which exercised considerable influence during the reign of *Henry VI and throughout the Wars of the *Roses. The B.s were the natural sons, later legitimized, of John of Gaunt (1340-99), duke of Lancaster and son of Edward III. In 1424 Cardinal Henry B. (1377-1447) was made a member of the council of regency and for the next two decades was known as the head of the party that sought a peaceful accomodation with France. The Wars of the Roses decimated the B.s and brought an end to the royal line of Lancaster. *Henry VII, who came to the throne in 1485, was a descendant of the B.s through his mother *Margaret, the great-granddaughter of John of Gaunt. This established the hereditary claim of the *Tudors to the throne.

BEAUFORT, HENRY (1377-1447) English statesman and cardinal. The illegitimate son of John of Gaunt, he was destined for the Church and was educated at Cambridge, Oxford and Aachen, where he studied civil and canon law. He became bishop of Lincoln in 1398 and, in 1404, succeeded to the diocese of Winchester. Upon the accession of *Henry V in 1413 he was appointed Chancellor of England, but left the post in 1417, when he went to the Council of *Constance; there he was instrumental in bringing about the election of *Martin V. The Pope repaid him with a cardinalship, naming him also a papal legate. In 1421 he assumed a strong influence over the government as guardian of the infant *Henry VI, and in 1424 became again chancellor. But in 1426 he resigned and led a military crusade against the Hussites of *Bohemia, which was unsuccessful. B. had frequent clashes with his nephew the Duke of *Gloucester, who attempted to dominate the government. He succeeded in bringing the downfall of the latter in 1441, but afterwards declined to take a leading role in the government. As a leader of the peace party, he attempted to find an accommodation with France. More a statesman than a clergyman, he amassed a great fortune, and lent money to the monarchy at high interest. Together with the Duke of *Bedford, B. helped to maintain political stability during the minority of Henry VI.

L. B. Radford, *Henry Beaufort; Bishop, Chancellor, Cardinal* (1908).

BEAUMONT, FRANCIS (1584-1616) and JOHN FLETCHER (1579-1625) English playwrights who collaborated. The number of plays written jointly by these authors was once believed to be about fifty, but in fact was probably no more than nine. These were mostly facile tragedies and tragi-comedies, which failed to make an impression on English drama, although they were very popular with 17th-century audiences. After Beaumont's death, Fletcher collaborated on a number of plays with Philip Massinger (1583-1640).

W. W. Appleton, *Beaumont and Fletcher* (1956).

BEBEL, HEINRICH (c. 1475-1518) German humanist. Born to a peasant family in Württemberg, he studied in Cracow and Basle, and in 1497 became a lecturer of rhetorics at Tübingen. In 1501 he was honoured by *Maximilian I with the title of Imperial Poet-Laureate. B. wrote books on Latin grammar, and translated into Latin a collection of German popular anecdotes and fables. His *Triumphus Veneris* (1509) is a satirical poem which, in the secular style of the time, makes fun of the clergy.

BECCAFUMI, DOMENICO (c. 1486-1551) Italian painter. Born near *Siena, he came in 1510 to Rome, where he absorbed influences of *Michelangelo and *Raphael. He returned to Siena about 1512 and, except for a few working visits to Pisa and Genoa, resided continuously in his native city. His works have an exceptional quality of luminosity, and his figures tend towards monumentality, a combination which anticipated the development of *Mannerism. He painted allegorical frescoes for Siena's *Palazzo Pubblico* (1529-35) and designed the marble pavement of the cathedral. Late in his life he also did some works in sculpture and engraving.

BECON, THOMAS (c. 1513-67) English Protestant reformer. Educated at Cambridge, he became a priest in 1533, but soon revealed a strong inclination to reformist ideas and was forced to recant. His opportunity came at the reign of *Edward VI, when he was appointed chaplain to the Lord Protector *Somerset and, with the support of *Cranmer, did much to propagate in England the Lutheran point of view. After the accession of *Mary (1553) he fled to the Continent, but returned to England when *Elizabeth I mounted the throne, and was named canon of Canterbury Cathedral. B. was a prolific author of homilies, which were widely popular.

D. S. Bailey, *Thomas Becon and the Reformation of the Church in England* (1952).

BEDFORD, JOHN, DUKE OF (1389-1435) English statesman and military commander. The third son of Henry IV (1399-1413) and brother of *Henry V, he was appointed, upon the latter's death, regent of the English possessions in France (1422). Cementing the alliance with *Burgundy by his own marriage to the sister of *Philip the Good, he won, in 1424, a great victory over the French at Verneuil. His military ascendency came to an end when the French recovered their morale following the appearance of *Joan of Arc. After her capture by the English forces B. caused her to be burned as a witch (1431). His administration in France was hampered by the quarrels between his brother *Gloucester, regent of England, and Cardinal Henry *Beaufort, between whom he tried mediate. In 1434 he lost the alliance with Burgundy, but died before the subsequent French victories.

BEHAIM, MARTIN (1436-1507) German geographer, navigator and constructor of the first terrestrial globe. Born in *Nuremberg, he settled in Portugal, where he became a member of the council called by *John II to supervise the progress of maritime exploration. He accompanied Diogo *Cão in his expedition to the coast of Guinea, and on his return to Portugal in 1486 receiv-

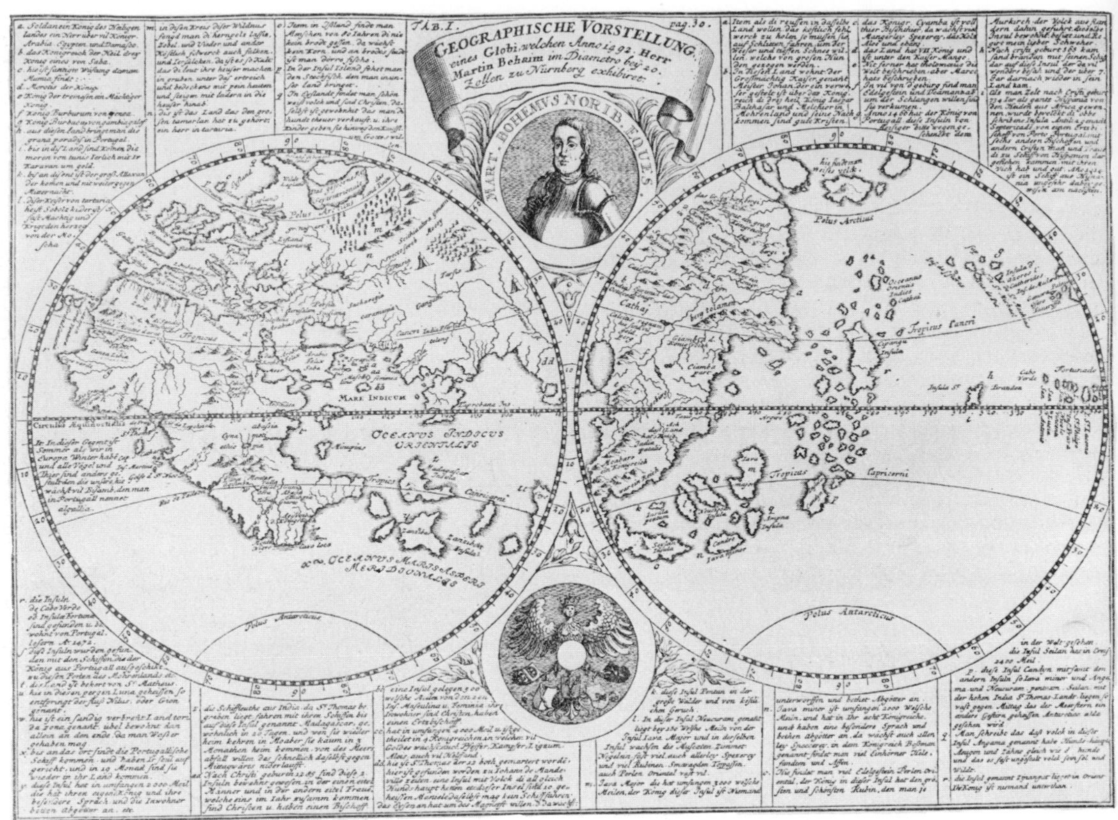

The geography of the world according to Behaim's globe of 1492

ed a title of nobility. His famous globe was constructed in 1492 while on a visit to his native city of Nuremberg. Although it had many errors, it served to illustrate his belief that every part of the world might be reached by ships. B. died in Lisbon.

E. G. Ravenstein, *Martin Behaim: His Life and His Globe* (1908).

BEHAM, BARTEL (1502-40) and HANS SEBALD (1500-50) Two German artists, brothers, counted among the post-*Dürer "Little Masters". The two B. brothers were born and grew up in *Nuremberg, where they became known as excellent engravers. Their small copperplates and woodcuts displayed a delicate style and a very fine technique. In 1525 both were expelled from their native city after having been charged with heretical ideas. Hans, the older, resided later in *Frankfurt. He left hundreds of engravings on religious and mythological themes, as well as genre scenes. Bartel, the younger, went to Italy, where he died. In addition to prints he left a number of paintings.

E. Waldmann, *Die Nürnberger Kleinmeister* (1911).

BELALCAZAR, SEBASTIAN DE (c. 1495-1551) Spanish **conquistador*. The son of a peasant, he took part in the conquest of Nicaragua (1524-27), then joined *Pizarro in his expedition to Peru. Appointed by the latter to command the town of Piura on the Pacific coast, he undertook the conquest of Quito (1534), and, in 1536, continued north towards Popayán, Cali and Bogotá. Reaching Bogotá (1539), he encountered Gonzalo *Jimenez de Quesada and Nikolaus *Federmann, and had to be satisfied with the governorship of Popayán. He died en route to Spain.

BELLANO, BARTOLOMEO (c. 1435-97) Italian sculptor and architect. Born in Padua, he studied under *Donatello, whom he followed to Florence. In 1464 he went to Rome at the invitation of Pope *Paul II but, in 1469, returned to Padua, where he produced his best work, a marble receptacle for relics at the church of S. Antonio. In 1479 he and the painter Gentile *Bellini were sent by the republic of Venice to Constantinople. His last completed work was the bronze reliefs for S. Antonio, Padua, depicting biblical scenes. A skilful artist, B. remained generally faithful to the style of Donatello.

BELLARMINE, ST. ROBERTO (1542-1621) Cardinal and Roman Catholic theologian. Italian by birth, B. entered the *Jesuit order in 1560, studied theology in Padua and was ordained in Louvain in 1570. There he lectured on theology at the university, and made a study of the Protestant arguments regarding free will, predestination and grace. After he returned to Rome in 1576, B. began writing a theological work which contained a refutation of the Protestant doctrines from the Catholic point of view. It was published in three volumes between 1581 and 1593 and established his name in Protestant Europe as the chief spokesman for the papacy. Another work, published in 1610, reasserted the pope's authority to depose secular rulers. B. was sent by the Vatican on a mission to France in 1589, was made cardinal in 1599 and archbishop of Capua in 1601. As theological advisor to the *Inquisition, he took part in the first hearing of *Galileo, and told him that he was forbidden by the pope to teach his scientific ideas, although he himself did not see them as religiously harmful.

J. Brodrick, *The Life and Work of Robert Francis Bellarmin* (1928).

BELLEAU, REMI (1528-77) French poet. The brilliant child of a poor family, B. had the good fortune to attract the support of patrons who helped him to receive a good education. At the Collège de Boncourt of Paris, where he studied, he took part in the performance of the first French tragedy by *Jodelle (1553), and joined the circle of the *Pléiade. He then served under the Marquis d'Elbeuf in Italy (1557), and later tutored that nobleman's son (1563-66). He became a welcome figure at the courts of *Charles IX and *Henry III. His reputation as a poet was established early, with the publication of his translation of *Anacreon* (1556), to which was appended his own original verses. In 1565 he published *La Bergerie*, an imitation of *Sannazaro's *Arcadia*, in a blend of verse and prose. His *Les amours et nouveaux échanges des pierres précieuses* (1576) utilized mythological references to describe the properties of gems. His friends, *Ronsard, *Baïf and *Desportes, who buried him, published a complete edition of his works in 1578.

The Standard Bearer *by Hans Sebald Beham*

Roberto Bellarmine *by Pietro da Cortona*

BELLINI, GENTILE (1429-1507) Venetian painter; son of Jacopo and brother of Giovanni. His early work was done at the father's workshop but he began to work independently before the latter's death. In 1474, he was commissioned by the Venetian senate to decorate the hall of the Great Council in the ducal palace. In 1479 he was sent to Constantinople by the government of Venice at the request of *Mehemmed II. There he painted a portrait of the Sultan and other works which are extant. Upon returning to Venice he continued his work in the ducal palace, which, unfortunately was destroyed by fire in 1577. B. was famous as a portrait painter and also did many paintings whose subject was religious processions. One large picture on this subject, *St. Mark Preaching at Alexandria*, was completed by his brother after his death.

BELLINI, GIOVANNI (1430-1516) Venetian painter; son of Jacopo and younger brother of Gentile. Like his brother, B. worked in his father's shop but became independent in his father's lifetime. In his early work there are clear influence of *Mantegna, who married his sister Nicolosia in 1454. Later, his style became more open and worldly and his colours bright and sensuous. B. excelled in the painting of altarpiece Madonnas, combining religious feeling, iconographic inventiveness and a human quality. He also did portraits of Venetian politi-

Madonna and Child *by Giovanni Bellini*

Madonna and Child *by Jacopo Bellini*

cal figures. In 1479, when his brother Gentile went to Constantinople, B. took his place as Venice's official painter and continued the work at the ducal palace, which was destroyed in the fire of 1577. In the last years of his life his name was known throughout northern Italy, and he received more commissions than he could handle. Some of the works, signed *Op. Ioh. Bell*, were actually painted by his assistants. B. had many students and followers. Among his immediate pupils were *Titian and *Giorgione.

P. Hendy and L. Goldscheider, *Giovanni Bellini* (1945); F. Heinemann, *Giovanni Bellini e i Belliniani*, 2 vols. (1962).

BELLINI, JACOPO (1400-71) Venetian painter; father of Gentile and Giovanni. Born in Venice, Jacopo followed his teacher, *Gentile de Fabriano to Florence. There he was involved, in 1423, in a lawsuit as a result of the overzealous manner in which he tackled a youth who stoned the works of his master. In spite of his familiarity with the evolving Florentine realism he remained attached to the more static style, known as *International Gothic, which was practiced by his teacher. In 1429 he returned to Venice and worked there as well as in other places in northern Italy. Only four paintings are unquestionably identified as his. B.'s two sketchbooks, which survived, contained many drawings which are freer in style than his paintings.

BEMBO, PIETRO (1470-1547) Italian humanist scholar. Born in Venice, studied in several places, including two years under the Greek scholar *Lascaris at Messina. Although he took religious orders, his main interests were literary. He earned a name for himself as a linguistic purist and as one of the foremost supporters of *Ciceronianism. *Leo X, who sought the company of scholars and artists, made him his secretary and after his death (1521) B. left Rome for Padua, where he returned to his literary pursuits. In 1529 he undertook the writing of the history of his native city, Venice, and in 1539 returned to Rome where *Paul III made him cardinal. His last years were marked by a gradual withdrawal from non-Christian cultural preoccupations. The work which first made B.'s reputation was *Gli Asolani* (1505), a dialogue in prose on love and other themes that was reminiscent of *Boccaccio and *Petrarch. But he left a vast literary output including essays, poems and translations, in addition to his *History of Venice*. His failure to produce a significant contribution was due to the fact that he sacrificed originality and creativity for the sake of exact imitation of the ancients.

M. Santoro, *Pietro Bembo* (1937);
G. Santangelo, *Il Bembo critico* (1950).

BENEDETTO DA MAJANO (1442-97) Italian sculptor and architect. The leading Florentine sculptor after *Donatello, he excelled in portrait busts, though he also worked as a painter. His best known work as architect is the Strozzi palace at Florence, which he began in 1489. This elegant structure, with rusticated external walls and a superb arcaded courtyard, was completed after B.'s death by Simone del Pollaiuolo (1454-1508), known as *Cronaca. It is an architectural masterpiece of the Renaissance.

BENTIVOGLIO, GIOVANNI (1443-1508) Ruler of Bologna. Born to a family with a long tradition in Bolognese politics, B. became the influential force in the republic in 1462. Later, he not only curtailed the power

Feast of the Gods *by Giovanni Bellini*

La Primavera *by Botticelli*

Earthly Paradise *by Bosch*

Two portraits of Bembo *by Titian*

Giovanni Bentivoglio

of the papal legate, who was supposed to share the government of Bologna, but also aided other independent rulers in the Papal States. The test of his long rule came with the French invasion of 1500, which coincided with Cesare *Borgia's attempt to unseat the independent rulers in Romagna. B. withstood the threat of Borgia, but had to leave Bologna in 1506, after *Julius II convinced the French to attack him.

BENVENUTO DA IMOLA (1336-90) Italian humanist. A native of Imola, he taught at Bologna and Ferrara and was a friend of *Petrarch and *Boccaccio. In 1373 he wrote the first commentary on *Dante's *Divine Comedy*, containing much information on the customs and beliefs of his own time. Other works of his dealt with classical literature and the history of ancient Rome.

BENZI, UGO (1360-1439) Italian physician. A native of Spain, he taught at Bologna, Pavia and Ferrara, where he served as physician of Nicolò III d'*Este. His fame brought him an invitation to Paris, where he treated *Charles VII. His treatise, *Trattato utilissimo circa la conservazione della sanitate*, was printed posthumously in 1481. It was one of the first medical texts in the vernacular, and saw several editions.

BENZONI, GEROLAMO (1519-c. 72) Italian traveller and historian. The son of a Milanese merchant, he travelled on business to Germany and Spain and, in 1542, went to the New World, where he joined Spanish expeditions of discovery. He visited Peru and the West Indies, returning to Spain in 1556. His *Historia del nuovo mundo* is very autobiographical; it utilizes previous sources, but also contains many valuable personal observations.

BERLICHINGEN, GOETZ VON (1480-1562) A German knight; a *condottiere* and robber baron. Born to

Goetz von Berlichingen and his iron hand

a declining noble family. B. became a professional soldier and sold his services as a mercenary. In 1505 he lost his right hand, replacing it with one made of iron. He was twice put under the ban of the empire by *Maximilian I because of his plundering raids. In 1525, during the *Peasants' War, he was recruited by the rebels and served as leader of one of their groups, but only for a short time, and at the Diet of Speier in 1526 he was acquitted of the charges that were brought against him. He was imprisoned in 1528 on other charges, and after his release in 1530 refrained from participating in private wars. *Charles V later gave him a command in his army, and in 1544 he accompanied the emperor on his invasion of France. B. left an autobiography, first published in 1731, but his fame endures due to Goethe's play of 1773, which bears his name.

R. Weimann, *Götz von Berlichingen* (1930).

BERNARDES, DIOGO (1530-1605) Portuguese poet. The son of a notary from the province of Minho, he is known to have spent some of his early years at the court in Lisbon, returning later to his native town to take up his father's post. In 1576 he went as secretary with a Portuguese mission to Madrid and, in 1578, joined King *Sebastian on his ill-fated expedition to Morocco. He was taken prisoner and released only in 1581, serving afterwards in a minor capacity under *Philip II. B.'s poems, which appeared in three volumes, included the *Varias rimas ao bom Jesus* (1594), *Rimas varias; flores do Lima* (1596), and *O Lima* (1596). His style alternated between the old verse form and the new Italianate style of *Sa de Miranda. He excelled in descriptions of bucolic scenes which reflected a true feeling for nature. His experience in captivity induced him to write also on religious themes.

BERNARDINO OF SIENA, ST. (1380-1444) Italian Franciscan friar and preacher. Joining the Franciscans in his youth, he was in 1438 elected head of the Observants' branch of the order, and a year afterwards participated prominently in the Council of *Ferrara-Florence. In the main, however, he was known as a preacher, and after 1408 would address great crowds in the cities of Italy. In 1424 he inaugurated the cult of devotion to the name of Jesus, a practice which in 1427 brought him under suspicion of heresy. His friend and disciple, *Capistrano, helped him to convince *Martin V of his doctrinal integrity.

BERNI, FRANCESCO (1497-1535) Italian poet. A contemporary of *Aretino, with whom he exchanged bitter invectives, he cultivated a style of burlesque poetry, employing elements of parody and satire, which was later termed 'bernesque' after him. His best work, however, was not his original poetry but his version (*rifacimento*) of *Boiardo's *Orlando innamorato*, which he rewrote in polished Italian.

BEROALDO, FILIPPO (1453-1505) Italian humanist. Born in Bologna, he was educated there; he taught in Parma and Paris. In 1478 he returned to his native city, where he taught and held certain public offices. He wrote commentaries on classical authors, interspersed with remarks on contemporary society. His son, by the same name (1472-1518), was also active in Bologna, but subsequently went to Rome at the invitation of *Leo X, and issued the first edition of Tacitus' *Annales* (1515).

BERRUGUETE Two Spanish painters, father and son, who took the lead in introducing the *Italianate and *Mannerist styles to their country. Pedro, the father, worked at Toledo from 1483 as court painter to *Ferdinand and *Isabella. He may have visited Italy; Italian influences can be discerned even in his early work for the cathedral of Avila. He died *c.* 1503. Alonso (*c.* 1485-1561), the son, spent several years in Italy, where he studied *Michelangelo's work and befriended *Andrea del Sarto. By 1518 he was back in Spain and became a court painter of *Charles V. Besides painting he undertook such projects as monuments and carved reliefs in a combined setting. These works can be found mainly in Toledo and Valladolid. He was patronized by *Philip II.

R. Lainez Alcala, *Pedro Berruguete, pintor de Castilla* (1943).

BERTOLDO DI GIOVANNI (c. 1420-91) Italian sculptor. A former assistant of *Donatello, with whom he worked during the latter's last years, he was patronized by Lorenzo de' *Medici, who made him head of the school in the S. Marco gardens. There he counted *Michelangelo among his pupils. B. continued the realist style of Donatello. His works included reliefs in marble and bronze, as well as bronze statuettes and *medals. Some of his secular works, inspired by classical models, show a flare for stylized expression and movement.

BESSARION, JOHANNES (1403-72) Metropolitan of Nicea, cardinal and humanist scholar. B. was born near Trebizond and educated at Constantinople. His admiration for the philosophy of Plato was a product of his studies with *Gemistus Pletho. In 1437 John VII Palaeologue elevated him to the office of metropolitan,

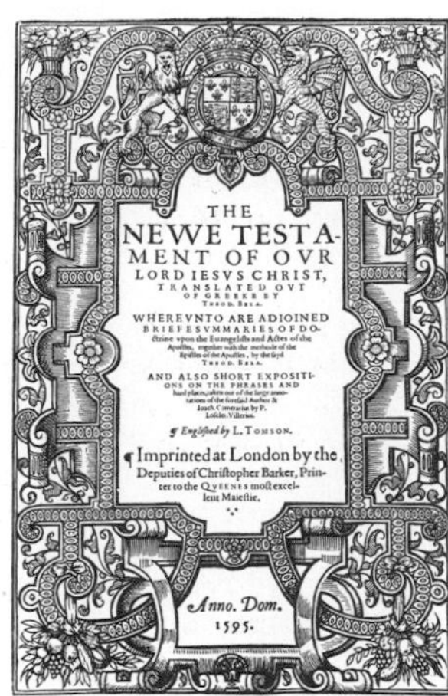

Titlepage of Beza's English Translation of the Bible (1595)

and the next year took him on a trip to Italy to raise help against the Turks at the Council of *Ferrara-Florence. B. remained in the West and in 1439 was made cardinal by *Eugenius IV. In 1463 he was named titular Latin patriarch of Constantinople. He was employed by the papacy in various missions and became, in spite of his Greek background, a distinguished member of the Roman hierarchy. He also contributed to the development of Greek studies in Italy, collected many manuscripts, which he bequeathed to Venice, and wrote on Platonic philosophy and on Greek patristic literature.

J. Gill, *The Council of Florence* (1959).

BEZA, THEODORE (1519-1605) French theologian and scholar; one of *Calvin's foremost aids. Born to a family with some standing in the royal French bureaucracy, B. studied Greek at Orléans with Melchior Wolmar and in 1539 completed his training in law. He then practiced law for some years in Paris, but in 1548, after a severe illness and a spiritual crisis, joined Calvin in *Geneva. B. supported Calvin, and wrote in defence of his conduct during the crisis connected with the burning of *Servetus (1554). In 1559 Calvin appointed him rector of the Geneva Theological Academy, where Latin, Greek and Hebrew were taught. In 1561 B. went to France and represented the *Huguenots in the religious debate known as the Colloquy of Poissy. After Calvin's death (1564) he became his successor and biographer. Among his other writings was the *Histoire ecclésiastique des églises réformées au royaume de France* (1580), which, although it had appeared without his name, is considered to be his. Outlining the rise of Calvinism in France, it did not possess a high scholarly standard. He also wrote a biblical tragedy, *Abraham sacrifiant*, a very early example of this genre which was performed at the University of Lausanne. B. completed the French translation of the Psalms by *Marot (1562). He prepared a new Latin translation of the New Testament (1556), and in 1565 brought out a famous critical edition of the Greek New Testament. He resigned his posts in 1600, five years before his death.

H. M. Baird, *Theodore Beza, Counsellor of the French Reform* (1900);
P. F. Geisendorf, *Théodore de Bèze* (1949).

BIBBIENA The name by which Bernardo Dovizi (1470-1520), an Italian cardinal and author, is known. Born in the town of B., he entered the service of the *Medici as a youth. When Giovanni de' Medici became pope as *Leo X (1513), he at once raised B. to the dignity of cardinal. He then became the Pope's chief adviser and was sent by him on important diplomatic missions. B. wrote a successful comedy, *Calandria*, which was first performed in 1513. He was a patron of the letters and arts, especially favouring *Raphael, who painted his portrait.

BIBLE, Study, Translation and Printed Editions of the In the Middle Ages the Bible was known to Christian Europe mainly through the Vulgate, a *Latin translation, the work of St. Jerome (347-420), which had been recognized since the 7th century as the official version. Moreover, from the 13th century, after dissenting movements like the Albigenses and Waldenses had demonstrated the theological confusion that can ensue from independent interpretations of biblical passages, the Church pursued a deliberate restrictive policy, to discourage the diffusion of the text in the vernacular. *Wycliffe, whose English translation (1382) had a dicisive influence on the *Lollards, was later denounced by the ecclesiastical hierarchy especially for this reason. In Germany also there were repeated attempts in the 15th century to forbid the translation of the B., or portions of it, into the vernacular, although in general the Church preferred to overlook the matter, so long as there was no suspicion of heresy.

The great expansion of the diffusion of the B. resulted from the advent of *printing. The B. in its authorized Latin version was the first book to be printed by *Gutenberg (1456), and numerous other editions soon

A page from the Complutensian Polyglot Bible

The Bible in the vernacular; woodcut illustrations in a Czech translation of the Bible published in Kuttenberg (1489)

followed. The first printed Italian translation appeared in *Venice in 1471; the first French edition *c.* 1498, and the first German one in *Strassburg as early as 1466. All these early printed translations were based on existing manuscripts, which followed the Vulgate. The printing of the complete Old Testament in *Hebrew at *Soncino, Italy, in 1488 is also of historical importance. However, the change was marked not only by greater diffusion. By the end of the 15th century the tools of humanist scholarship were increasingly applied to the study of the B., and by their critical approach and emphasis on familiarity with the original texts, scholars began to undermine the traditional interpretations. The parallel publication of the text in Hebrew, *Greek and Latin was undertaken in Spain by a team working for Cardinal *Jiménez de Cisneros (1502). But this *Complutensian Polyglot*, as it is called, was put into circulation only in 1522, and in the meantime *Erasmus, cooperating with the printer *Froben in *Basle, published the first Greek New Testament (1516).

At the beginning of the *Reformation, the printed B., in the original languages or in translation, was easily available to scholars and laymen. This may explain why the calls of *Luther and *Calvin to abide by the authority of the Scripture alone were met with such affirmative response. Luther himself was responsible for the famous new translation of the B. into German from the Hebrew and Greek, a work which was first published in its entirety in 1534. Other well known editions of the B. by Protestant scholars were: Robert *Estienne's Latin edition, a Hebrew edition of the Old Testament, and Greek editions of the New Testament (1546; 1549; 1550); *Beza's ten Greek editions of the New Testament, published between 1565 and 1611, and the editions based on Beza which the *Elzevir brothers published in Leiden in 1624 and 1633. On the Roman Catholic side, the Council of *Trent reconfirmed in 1546 the authencity of the text of the Vulgate. Between 1569 and 1572 the printer *Plantin issued at *Antwerp a famous polyglot Bible, sponsored by *Philip II, the work of *Arias Montano.

Because of the particular nature of the *Reformation in England and the long-standing prohibition stemming from Wycliffe's time, the translation of the B. into English became a problematic issue. When, in 1525 *Tyndale published the New Testament in English at

Cologne and Worms, copies of it were apprehended in England and burned by the authorities. In 1535 *Coverdale published at Cologne a full English translation. Having in mind Henry VIII's quarrel with Rome, he dedicated it to the king. This translation, and the version printed by Tyndale's friend John *Rogers, known as Matthew's Bible (1537), were actually given the royal licence. In 1539 *Cranmer sponsored the publication of the Great Bible, also the work of Coverdale, which became the authorized version for the next generation. However, in the 1560s the B. published in Geneva by English Protestant refugees from *Mary's persecutions, quickly gained popularity in England. Since this edition was particularly liked by the *Puritans, Archbishop *Parker caused the publication of a new authorized version, known as the Bishop's Bible (1568). Between 1582 and 1609 Roman Catholic refugee scholars from Oxford published at Douai and Reims a translation based on the Vulgate. Finally, on the accession of *James I, work began on a revised English translation in which some fifty scholars took part. This project, which made use of most of the earlier translations, was completed in 1611 with the appearance of what is since known as King James', or the Authorized Version of the B.

T. L. Leishman, *Our Ageless Bible: From Early Manuscripts to Modern Versions* (1960);
H. W. Robinson, *The Bible in its Ancient and English Versions* (1954);
S. L. Greenslade, ed., *Cambridge History of the Bible: The West from the Reformation to the Present Day* (1963).

BIEL, GABRIEL (c. 1420-85) German philosopher. Although his life spanned much of the 15th century, B. was a mediaeval thinker rather than a man of the Renaissance. He was the last great adherent to the nominalism of William of Ockham; he also wrote a treatise on money, which showed willingness to sanction morally some of the economic realities of his age. He took a leading part in the founding of the University of Tübingen (1477), where he taught theology.

BILNEY, THOMAS (c. 1495-1531) English martyr of the *Reformation. Educated at Cambridge and influenced by the teachings of *Erasmus, B. belonged to a small group of people who were impressed early by the ideas of *Luther. In 1527 he was arrested after preaching against relics and the cult of the saints. He recanted ostensibly and was released, but four years later was again arrested on charges of heresy and subsequently burnt at the stake in Norwich.

BIONDO, FLAVIO (1392-1463) Italian humanist, historian and pioneer of modern archaeology. Born in Forli, B. served several Italian rulers as secretary. In 1433 he became a notary for the papal court, but was also employed by *Eugenius IV as a diplomatic secretary. During the last 20 years of his life he dedicated himself to research and writing on the history of Rome and Italy, and produced a number of great works. His *Historiarum ab inclinatione Romanorum decades* dealt with the history of Europe from 412 on and showed his skill in using mediaeval sources. *Roma instaurata* (1446) attempted to reconstruct the topography of ancient Rome. *Italia illustrata* (1453) described the geography and historical formation of Italy, and *Roma triumphans*, his last work, depicted the private customs and public institutions of ancient Rome. His works contain abundant information and served as a source for other writers.

A. Campana, *Flavio Biondo* (1928).

BIRINGUCCIO, VANNOCCIO (1480-c.1539) Italian expert in metallurgy. Born in *Siena, he became a leading expert on the subjects of mining and the production of metals. In 1526 he had to leave Siena because of his association with a certain political faction, and went to *Florence where he cast a famous piece of *artillery. About 1538 he was invited to Rome by *Paul III, but died soon afterwards. His book, *De la pirotechnia*, was published in Venice in 1540. It dealt with almost everything connected with the smelting of metals. In contrast with *Agricola, B. emphasized the practical aspects of metallurgy and describes processes and techniques of which he appears to have had direct experimental knowledge.

The Pirotechnia of Vannoccio Biringuccio, trans. with an Introduction by C. Stanley and M. T. Gnudi (1959).

BIRÓ, MATTHIAS (c. 1500-45) Hungarian Protestant reformer. Member of the Franciscan order, B. became an adherent of the teachings of *Luther while he was a student at Wittenberg (1529-30). He returned to Hungary, where he devoted himself to spreading the new ideas, but some time after 1541 he apparently became a follower of *Calvin, especially with regard to his views on the Eucharist. This merited him the censure of Luther in 1544.

BISTICCI, VESPASIANO DA (1421-98) Italian dealer in books and manuscripts and an author. An uneducated person of humble social background, he opened in Florence, in 1440, a famous business which supplied books to many of the Italian and European rulers of his time. His shop became a meeting ground for leading humanists, as Leonardo *Bruni and *Ficino. In 1480, being in difficulties competing with the printed book, B. closed his business and retired. He then wrote the *Vite*, a collection of biographic sketches of the famous men he had known during his active years. Although written in a simple language, the work is a lively presentation of the personalities and a valuable historical source.

The Vespasiano Memoirs, trans. by W. G. and E. Waters (1926).

BLACK LEGEND, THE (Spanish, *La Leyenda Negra*) A series of polemical arguments which present the

A print illustrating Spanish atrocities against the Indians

Spaniards as a greedy, intolerant and cruel people. The B.L. arose during the second half of the 16th century particularly through the efforts of Dutch and English authors. While they meant to attack the practises and policies of *Philip II and the duke of *Alba in Europe, the critics also emphasized the brutalities perpetrated by the Spaniards on the Indians during the conquest of America. To prove their contentions, they resorted to the work of Bartolomé de *las Casas, *A Brief Relation of the Destruction of the Indies*. First published in Spanish in Seville in 1552, it was translated from 1578 on to other European languages. An edition adorned with gruesome engravings by Theodore de Bry was particularly effective as anti-Spanish propaganda.

S. Arnoldsson, *La leyenda negra* (1960);
Ch. Gibson, ed., *The Black Legend: Anti-Spanish Attitudes in the Old World and the New* (1971).

BLACKWELL, GEORGE (c. 1545-1613) English Roman Catholic leader. Educated at Oxford, he subsequently converted, and in 1574 joined William *Allen's college at Douai, where he was ordained priest. He served under Allen until the latter's death (1594), and was then given by *Clement VIII the title of archpriest and put in charge of the Roman Catholic secular clergy in England (1598). At first he pursued a militant pro-*Jesuit policy, which brough him into conflict with some of his English constituents, but changed his course following a period of imprisonment in 1607, and took the oath of allegiance to *James I.

BLADO, ANTONIO (1490-1567) Italian printer. Born at Asola, he went to Rome about 1516, and from 1546 on was a printer for the papal court. Among the famous works which he issued were *Il principe* of *Machiavelli (1532), and *Palladio's *Antichità di Roma* (1553). The printing firm was continued by his sons, retaining its reputation throughout the 16th century.

BLAURER, AMBROSIUS (1492-1564) German Protestant reformer. Born in Constance, he became a monk and from 1510 to 1513 studied at Tübingen, where he met *Melanchthon. Influenced by the teachings of *Luther, he returned to his native city in 1522 and became the spokesman for reform in Constance. After 1528 he worked for the dissemination of Protestantism throughout southern Germany. In 1534 he returned to Tübingen at the invitation of Duke *Ulrich to work for the consolidation of the Reformation in Württemberg, alongside *Brenz. However, he was dismissed in 1538. Ten years later he also had to leave Constance, when it was taken by imperial forces, and ended his life as a preacher in towns of lesser significance. B. was more important as a religious organizer than an author or ideologist.

BLAUROCK, GEORG Swiss *Anabaptist leader. A former monk, he became a follower of *Zwingli in Zurich; but looking for more radical forms of religious expression, joined the original group of Anabaptists which, in January 1525, performed the ritual of rebaptism, thus launching a new movement. Following the death of Conrad *Grebel (1526), he became the main leader of the Anabaptists in the Tyrolean area, but was arrested and burned at the stake in 1529.

BLOEMAERT, ABRAHAM (1564-1651) Dutch painter and engraver. After studying at Paris (1580-83) and elsewhere, this painter of historical subjects, mythology, allegory and landscapes was all his life open to outside

Juno, *an etching by Abraham Bloemart*

influences. In Utrecht, where he spent most of his active years, he taught a group of young artists including his own four sons. With his students, some of whom later visited Italy, B. was responsible for the formation of the Utrecht School, which introduced to 17th-century Dutch painting the pictorial ideas of *Caravaggio.

G. Delbanco, *Der Maler Abraham Bloemaert* (1928).

BOBADILLA, FRANCISCO DE Spanish colonial governor. A former official in the military order of Calatrava, he was known for his arbitrary conduct, but succeeded in getting himself nominated, in 1499, as the governor of the newly-discovered American territories, replacing *Columbus. Reaching Santo Domingo in August 1500, B. imprisoned Columbus and his brothers in a humiliating manner, and in October sent them to Spain. Although *Ferdinand and *Isabella freed Columbus upon his arrival, they kept B. in his post until 1502, when *Ovando was sent to replace him. He died in a storm while on his way back to Spain.

BOBADILLA, NICOLAS (1511-90) Spanish churchman. Born at Valencia, he was studying in Paris when he joined, in August 1534, Ignatius of *Loyola and six others to form the original membership of the *Jesuits. During the 1540's he was active in Germany, rallying the Catholic forces against the rising tide of Protestantism. However, he opposed the *Augsburg Interim of 1548, as conceding too much to the other side, and was ordered by the imperial court to leave Germany. B. was, in the main, a preacher and propagandist. Late in his life he remained the only survivor of the original nucleus of the Jesuits, but did not become a general of the Order.

BOCCACCINO (c. 1467-1524) Italian painter. Born in Ferrara, he studied under Ercole de' *Roberti, and was later much influenced by the Venetian painters. He had a stormy career, frequently changing his patrons and residences but, in 1510, he settled permanently in Cremona. There he decorated the cathedral with his frescoes (1515-19), depicting scenes from the New Testament.

BOCCACCIO, GIOVANNI (1313-75) Italian poet, novelist and humanist. The illegitimate son of a Florentine merchant, he was born in Paris, taken by his father to *Florence, and in 1325 sent to *Naples to learn commerce. After a few years, however, he began to study law and developed an interest in classical Latin poetry. In Naples, about 1336, B. fell in love with "Fiammetta", identified as the king's natural daughter, Maria d'Aquino. She inspired his first work – and appears in almost all his Italian works – but left him after a stormy romance. By 1340 B. was back in Florence, and in the next few years wrote *Ameto* (1341), a pastoral romance; the *Amorosa visione* (1342), a poem dedicated to his former love, and a work in prose about a lady abandoned by her lover, called *Fiammetta* (1343). The best of these early works was the *Ninfale fiesolano* (1346), a pastoral poem about youthful love interwoven with a legend about the foundation of Florence. He began working on his masterpiece, the *Decameron*, immediately after the plague of 1348, completing it in 1353. This collection of a 100 tales, told by a group of young men and women who had taken refuge from the plague in a villa near Florence, was destined to remain one of the greatest works of literature. It also influenced the development of the Renaissance novel. Characterized by a joyous eroticism, it celebrated human senses and passions and addressed itself realistically to contemporary society.

Boccaccio *by Andrea del Castagno*

In 1350, B. met *Petrarch, with whom he had corresponded before and remained later on the closest terms. In 1355 he completed his last Italian work, *Corbaccio*, an old lover's invective against the failings of women. From then on he wrote in Latin and, following a spiritual crisis in 1362, was at the point of burning his early Italian works. Of his later works, *De casibus virorum illustrium* was a collection of biographies of great men, and *De claris mulieribus*, a similar work about women. Also important was *De genealogiis Deorum*, a repertory of ancient mythology, completed in 1366.

B. spent his mature years in filling occasional diplomatic and administrative posts. For some time he lived in Certaldo, his father's native town, but, in 1373, Florence invited him to inaugurate the *Lectura Dantis*, public lectures on the *Divine Comedy*, of which he gave about 60, before retiring to Certaldo to die. B. also wrote a biography of Dante. As a humanist, he promoted especially the study of the Greek language in Florence, and himself acquired a good knowledge of it. His contribution to the development of Renaissance culture is second only to his friend Petrarch's.

V. Branca, *Boccaccio medievale*, 4th ed. (1975);
T. C. Chubb, *The Life of Giovanni Boccaccio* (1930);
D. Thompson, ed., *The Three Crowns of Florence; Humanist Assessments of Dante, Petrarch and Boccaccio* (1972).

BOCCALINI, TRAIANO (1556-1613) Italian author of political satires. Born at Loreto, he studied in Perugia and spent many years as judge and administrator in the papal service. In 1612 he went to Venice, where he published the *Ragguagli di Parnaso*, a description of an imaginary kingdom, which, however, contained criticisms of the mores of his age. Written in a vigorous style marked by a mordant irony, this work was continued with *Pietra del paragone politico*, published posthumously (1615), which attacked the Spanish domination of *Italy. Other works attributed to B. also dealt with political questions.

E. G. Gardner, *Traiano Boccalini: Satire and History in the Counter-Reformation* (1926);
R. H. Williams, *Boccalini in Spain: A Study of his Influence* (1946).

BOCKELSON, JAN (John of Leiden; 1508-36) *Anabaptist extremist leader and millenarian visionary. An illegitimate son of a Dutch peasant woman, he travelled widely as a journeyman tailor, before joining in 1533 the Anabaptist faction of Jan Matthys. B. came to *Münster from Holland in January 1534, where he began to lead rallies of religious ecstasy, thus hastening the complete domination of the city by the Anabaptists. After the death of Matthys on 5 April 1534, B. himself became the chief personage and virtual dictator of the besieged city. In August 1534 he proclaimed himself king and instituted a theocratic regime, characterized by the establishment of polygamy and a cruel repression of those who doubted his divine revelations. He married Divora the beautiful young widow of Matthys', and later fifteen women more, and encouraged his lieutenants to collect similar harems. On 24 June 1535, when Münster fell, he was captured by the enemy, tortured, and spent

John of Leiden, King of the Anabaptists *by Aldegrever*

months chained in a cage before being put to death in January 1536. B.'s apocalyptic tyranny and his violation of conventional sexual mores, brought enduring disrepute on the Anabaptist movement as a whole.

N. Cohn, *The Pursuit of the Millennium* (1962), pp. 282-306.

BODIN, JEAN (1530-96) French author and political theorist. The son of a well-to-do tailor of Angers, he entered the Carmelite order, but later relinquished his vows and studied law at Toulouse. In 1561 he went to Paris, becoming a royal legal councilor. His years of work in this capacity brought him into contact with influential courtiers at a time of rising civil and religious strife. B. was a deputy of the Third Estate to the Estates-General of Blois in 1576, but did not participate further in direct political activity. He had to leave the court in 1583, following the death of his patron, the duke of Alençon, and moved to nearby Laon, where he died.

B. was an intellectual of varied interests, as may be judged from the range of his works. His first major work was the *Methodus ad facilem historiarum cognitionem*, published in 1566, which dealt with the laws that govern history. Another work, *Démonomanie des sorciers* (1580), dealt with witchcraft and showed that he was not exempt from the superstitions of his day. A third work, the *Heptaplomeres*, written in 1588, but published only in 1841, was a colloquy between spokesmen for different religious denominations in search of a universal moral creed. B.'s most important work is the *Six livres de la République*, published in 1576. It was quickly translated into all the principal European languages and appeared in several French editions in the author's lifetime. In this work, trying to address the problems of his times, he dealt with the issue of political stability. B's answer was the principle of absolute government, formulating the concept of the sovereign state. Although he agreed that under normal conditions the powers of governments to command should be exercised with consideration for the subjects' fundamental rights to property and freedom, he claimed that, in principle, the sovereign power of the state was not limited by obligations or legal constraints. The work contained other themes, including a discussion on the influence of climates on laws and institutions, but it was the support of royal power which interested the author's contemporaries. In another work, *Responsio ad paradoxa Melestretti* (1588), B. dealt with the price revolution of his day and advocated principles of mercantilism. A final work, *Universale Theatrum naturae* (1596), dealt with cosmology.

P. T. King, *The Ideology of Order: A Comparative Analysis of Jean Bodin and Thomas Hobbes* (1974);
J. H. Franklin, *Jean Bodin and the Sixteenth-Century Revolution in the Methodology of Law and History* (1963).

BODLEY, SIR THOMAS (1545-1613) English diplomat and founder of the Bodleian libray at Oxford. Educated in Geneva, whither his father had fled during *Mary's reign, and at Oxford, he served *Elizabeth I for many years in diplomatic assignments in Germany, France and the Netherlands. After his retirement in 1596, he decided to aid the enlargement of the Oxford University library, which was reopened in 1602 with some 2,000 books. B. continued his sponsorship of the libray until his death, and bequeathed to it much of his wealth.

BOECE, HECTOR (c. 1465-c. 1536) Scottish humanist scholar. Born in Dundee, he was educated in Paris, where he befriended *Erasmus. Returning to Scotland, he became the first principal of the University of Aberdeen (1498). He is chiefly remembered for his history of Scotland in 17 books, written in Latin and first published in 1527. Here, in accordance with humanist *historiography, he incorporated many Scottish popular legends.

BOEHME, JACOB (1575-1624) German Protestant mystic thinker. A shoemaker of peasant stock, he settled in 1599 in Görlitz, where he achieved a moderate measure of affluence. He seems to have had visionary experience from an early age, and was acquainted with the works of *Paracelsus. In 1612, encouraged by a local nobleman, he let his manuscript, *Aurora*, be published and circulated among friends. This aroused the fury of the local minister, who had him brought before the town council which made him promise to write no more. B., however, resumed his writings after a few years, and in consequence, had to leave Görlitz in 1624. He went to Dresden, where he was cleared of suspicion and encouraged to return to his home. He died in Gorlitz shortly aftet his return. B.'s most famous tract, *Der Weg zu Christo*, as well as his other writings, are devoted to the questions of good versus evil, and the relationship of man to God and Nature. He claimed to write what was revealed to him in visions and, while holding orthodox views, discussed complicated theological matters in the simplest language. His works appeared in numerous editions and are part of the existentialist current in Western philosophy.

Brunelleschi's cathedral of Florence, S. Maria del Fiore

Madonna and Chil
Enthroned
with Donor
by Carlo Crivelli

J. J. Stoudt, *Sunrise to Eternity: A Study of Jacob Boehme's Life* (1957);
M. L. Bailey, *Milton and Jakob Boehme: A Study of German Mysticism in Seventeenth-Century England* (1964);
W. Elert, *Die voluntaristische Mystik Jacob Böhmes* (1973).

BOHEMIA The history of the Czech people in the 15th and 16th centuries was marked by two major issues: religious strife and foreign domination. The Luxembourg dynasty, under which B. enjoyed relative prosperity in the 14th century, kept an uneasy balance between the Czechs and the German element, but began to lose control as a result of the growing movement of religious reform. Led by Jan *Hus, this movement reacted with a sense of national indignation when its leader was burnt at the stake in *Constance (1415). Within a short time, B. was plunged into a period of external and internal strife, commonly known as the *Hussite Wars. Only the religious concessions made by the Council of *Basle (1436) restored a semblance of unity between the Czech Hussite majority and the Church. Then the death of Emperor *Sigismund (1437), who had been accepted as king of B., prolonged the political crisis. Internal conflict continued during the regency and reign of the young Ladislas Posthumus (1453-57). After his death, the leader of the *Utraquist party, *George of Podebrady, was elected by the Bohemian estates, and gave the country a taste of a national monarchy for a few years. But by the time he died (1471), the kingdom had become divided again, largely as a result of Catholic revolts in Silesia and Moravia. Internal rifts and a sharp decline of royal authority characterized the reigns of the *Jagiello kings, *Ladislas II and his son *Louis II. During that time, the nobility, through the provincial diets, actually took charge of the government, and the tradition of religious plurality was kept alive.

When Louis was killed at the Battle of *Mohacs (1526), B. elected *Ferdinand, brother of Emperor *Charles V, as its king. With this began the 400-year long domination of B. by the *Habsburgs. Taking advantage of the internal divisions between B. itself and "the incorporated provinces" of Moravia, Silesia and Lusatia, Ferdinand persuaded the estates in 1547 to acknowledge the hereditary rights of the crown. At the same time, he had to deal with the resurgent religious question, which, with the impact of the Reformation, became an acute issue also in the German parts of the kingdom. Persecution, especially of the *Unity of the Brothers, alternated with concessions, and in 1561 the *Jesuits were allowed to enter. Under *Maximilian II there was greater religious liberty, and by the time he died (1576), probably three-quarters of the population was no longer Roman Catholic. Established religious plurality was strengthened by the famous charter, the *Majestätsbrief* of 1609, which the estates had persuaded Emperor *Rudolf to grant, exploiting the struggle between him and his brother *Matthias. However, the latter, who became king of B. in 1611, brought matters to a crisis when, in 1617, he sponsored his orthodox Roman Catholic nephew Ferdinand as his successor. In May 1618 the *Defenestration of Prague, signalling a Czech national revolt, opened the *Thirty Years War. In 1619 B. invited the Calvinist elector palatine Frederick V to assume the crown. But then came the decisive defeat of the insurgents at the Battle of the White Mountain (8 November 1620). Reconquered by the *Habsburgs, the country was stripped of its autonomous institutions and underwent a forced process of re-Catholization.

R. W. Seton-Watson, *A History of the Czechs and Slovaks* (1943);
S. H. Thomson, *Czechoslovakia in European History* (1943).

BÖHM, HANS (?-1476) German rebel, a forerunner of the leaders of the *Peasants' War, known as "the Piper of Niklashausen". A young shepherd, who was also known as the village entertainer, he began preaching in March 1476, attacking the clergy and the nobility and proclaiming the coming of an egalitarian Kingdom of Heaven. He attracted crowds of peasants and artisans with their families and, in July, was arrested by order of the bishop of Würzburg, who feared the movement would turn into an outright revolt. B.'s followers then marched to Würzburg in an attempt to free him, but were dispersed by force. Their "prophet" was quickly tried and burnt at the stake as a sorcerer and heretic.

W. E. Peuckert, *Die grosse Wende. Das apokalyptische Saeculum und Luther* (1948).

BOIARDO, MATTEO MARIA (1441-94) Italian poet. Born to a noble family of *Ferrara, B. attached himself to the rulers of the duchy, Borso *d'Este and his successor Ercole, under whom he served as governor of Reggio. His literary works, designed to please the Ferraran court, included a comedy, a collection of sonnets, an Italian translation of Apuleius' *The Golden Ass*, and a translation of Herodotus. His fame as an author, however, stems from his long unfinished poem *Orlando innamorato*, which was printed in 1495, shortly after B.'s death. The

Boiardo

work is an epic romance of adventures recreating the heroic days of chivalry during the wars of Charlemagne against Saracen invaders. Although the language and style of the work were crude, it was continued by Niccolo degli Agostini, and recast into a more polished Italian by Francesco *Berni. This *rifacimento* was first published in 1541 and became the standard version, substituting the original text. The work also inspired other poems, the most important of which was *Ariosto's *Orlando furioso*.

V. Procacci, *La vita e l'opera di Matteo Maria Boiardo* (1931).

BOLOGNA Situated in the plain of Emilia, at the crossroads between *Milan, *Florence and *Ferrara, B. enjoyed, since the 12th century, a European renown for its school of law which attracted many foreign students. Formally, the city was ruled from 1300 onwards by a papal legate but, in 1401, Giovanni *Bentivoglio made himself the real ruler of B., and his descendants continued to hold power there until 1512. *Julius II restored the papal domination of B., and so it remained until the 19th century. B. was where *Charles V was crowned emperor by *Clement VII, and where the political settlement of Italy was agreed (1530). Late in the 16th century a distinctive school of art evolved in the city, of which the most important representatives were the *Caracci.

BOLOGNA, CONCORDAT OF (1516) An agreement between Pope *Leo X and *Francis I of France, in which the latter repudiated the *Pragmatic Sanction of Bourges (1438), but in return was granted by the papacy the right to appoint French bishops and priors. Under normal circumstances, papal confirmation of the nominations was not to be denied.

BOLSEC, HERMES French theologian. A Carmelite friar, he became influenced by Protestant teachings and after spending some years in Italy, came to *Geneva. Here he attacked *Calvin's doctrine of predestination, and for a time caused Calvin serious difficulties. In 1551, he was imprisoned and finally banished. Later, B. rejoined the Roman Catholic Church. He never ceased his attacks on Calvin and in 1577 published a scurrilous account of his life. He died in 1585.

BOLTRAFFIO, GIOVANNI ANTONIO (1467-1516) Italian painter. Born in Milan, he became a disciple of *Leonardo's, whose Milanese workshop he joined in 1491. When Leonardo left the city, B. did so too. He later worked in Bologna, where he produced one of his masterpieces, the *Casio Madonna* (1500) and, in 1514, painted in Rome. Although his style is closely modelled on Leonardo's, B. was a master in his own right. A technical virtuoso of refined taste, he left many beautiful pictures and drawings.

BOMBERG, DANIEL (?-1549) A Flemish Christian printer of *Hebrew books. Born in *Antwerp, he went to Venice in 1516, and began to publish Hebrew *Bibles, with and without commentaries. He was the first printer of the Talmud (1520-23), and employed Jewish scholars to edit these and other works of Jewish religious literature. B., who was wealthy and well educated, knew Hebrew himself and was admired by the *Jews. In 1539 he was forced to go back to Antwerp where he died.

BONFINI, ANTONIO (c. 1427-c. 1502) Italian humanist. In 1486 he left his native land and went to the court of *Matthias Corvinus of Hungary. There, at Buda, he wrote a history of the Magyar people, *Rerum Hungaricarum decades*, for which *Ladislas II rewarded him with a title of nobility. An author of lesser works and translations, B. had a great influence on the growth of Hungarian humanism.

BONIFAZIO VERONESE (1487-1553) Italian painter. A native of Verona he settled in Venice, where he assimilated the style of *Giorgione and *Titian. His large output created some problems of identification, as many of his paintings were attributed to those masters. B. excelled in the handling of colour.

BONNER, EDMUND (1496-1569) English bishop of London. A former chaplain of *Wolsey's, he managed to retain his position with Thomas *Cromwell, and in 1539 was given the diocese of London. In the last years of the reign of *Henry VIII he was one of the leading conservatives; under *Edward VI he was deprived of his see (1549), accused of adhering to the doctrine of transubstantiation, and imprisoned. B.'s hour came when *Mary acceeded to the throne. Restored to his see of London, he persecuted relentlessly the reform leaders with the result that a number of persons were burnt at the stake. *Elizabeth I, to whom he refused the oath of supremacy, committed him to the Marshalsea prison (1559), where he languished a decade until his death.

BONSIGNORI, FRANCESCO (c. 1455-1519) Italian painter. Born in Verona, he was influenced by his Venetian contemporaries, especially *Vivarini and the *Bellini, but also by *Mantegna. His style is distinguished for clear forms and keen realism. He was employed by the *Gonzagas at Mantua, but mostly resided in Verona, of which he is considered the most significant 15th-century painter.

BOOK OF HOURS A prayerbook of small size and richly illustrated, containing a varying number of prayers of the canonical hours, and psalms. The B.s were intended for use by members of the higher classes. Known since the 12th century, they became highly fashionable in the late 14th century, when courtiers, nobles and ecclesiastical dignitaries commissioned some of the best artists to execute them. The most splendid B.s were created just before and after 1400 by Northern painters working in the style of *International Gothic, e.g., the *Limbourg Brothers. With the advent of *printing, publishers responded to the desire of the less affluent by issuing a great number of handy little prayer books for families. The centre of this industry was Paris where, between 1480 and 1540, more than 1,500 editions of B.s were printed. The first promoter of this industry was Jean *Dupré, followed by Antoine *Verard. Later, Geoffroy *Tory published beautifully decorated B.s, which were greatly admired. By mid-16th century the art and the demand for the illustrated prayerbook went into decline.

V. Leroquais, *Les livres d'heures*, 3 vols. (1927-43).

BORDONE, PARIS (1500-71) Italian painter. A pupil of *Titian, he quarrelled with his master, and at the age of 20 began to work on his own, decorating many churches in Venice, Vicenza, Treviso and elsewhere. In 1538 he was invited to work in France and, in 1540, went to *Augsburg where he decorated the *Fugger house. Like his early master, B. excelled in his colour scheme and the monumental proportions of his figures. His works were much sought by European leaders of his age, who filled his workshop in Venice with commissions.

BORGHESE A noble Italian family. Of Sienese origin, the B. family settled in Rome when Marcantonio B. (1507-74) became legal adviser to the papal court. His son Camillo was made cardinal and later Pope *Paul V (1605-21). The term 'nepotism' originated from his way of bestowing favours on members of his family.

BORGIA A noble family of Spanish origin. The family's influence began to grow when Alonso B., bishop of Valencia, became cardinal and then Pope *Calixtus III (1455-57). He brought several of his relatives to Rome. One of them, Rodrigo B., became Pope *Alexander VI (1492-1503). During his reign the power of the B. was at its zenith. Several members of the family were made cardinals and others exercised tremendous political influence, especially in the centre of Italy. The death of Alexander VI, which in turn brought about the imprisonment of his son Cesare, signalled the downfall of the B.

C. Fusero, *The Borgias* (1972);
J. Lucas-Dubreton, *The Borgias* (1954);
M. E. Mallett, *The Borgias: the Rise and Fall of a Renaissance Dynasty* (1969).

BORGIA, CESARE (1475-1507) Son of *Alexander VI by his mistress Vanozza Catanei. Destined for a career in the church, he was made cardinal in 1493, shortly after his father had become pope. But his violent temper, as well as his political and military ambitions, interfered. In 1497, the corpse of his brother Giovanni was found in the Tiber. The murder was attributed to B., and suspicions did not abate when his father suspended the investigation of the case. Now his father's favourite, B. was allowed to renounce the priesthood in 1498 to enable him to marry in accordance with his father's political designs. Failing to win the hand of Carlotta, daughter of the king of Naples, he married the sister of the king of Navarre in 1499. The marriage was celebrated in France, where B. acted as papal legate, bringing *Louis XII the pope's permission to divorce his wife. In return, the French king bestowed on him the title of Duke of Valentinois. In the same year he set out to conquer Romagna, a region which was only nominally under papal domination. With the aid of French troops he took Imola and Forli, and, early in 1500, returned to Rome, where he arranged the murder of his brother-in-law, the duke of Bisceglie, to forestall a rapprochement between Rome and Naples. B.'s military campaign in Romagna continued in 1501, his aim being to create a unified principality which he could continue to rule even after the death of his father. He soon went further, helping France invade Naples, participating in the sack of Capua and capturing Urbino. Some of the rulers whom he deposed attempted to join forces against him, but, although he suffered several military setbacks, he outwitted his enemies and succeeded in dividing them. His famous cunning was displayed in the town of Senigallia on 31 December 1502, when he arrested a group of rebels who had come to renew their allegiance to him, and had two of them, Oliverotto da Fermo and Vitellozzo Vitelli, strangled.

The question whether B. was growing into something more than a successful *condottiere* is still open. It should be remembered that the papal treasury financed his army, and though the French supported him, they also controlled his activities. It was inevitable, therefore,

Cesare Borgia *by Giorgione*

that with the defeat of the French army by Spain in early 1503, and the death of his father in August of the same year, B. would be unable to stand up to his enemies. He was assured of the papal intention to recognize his claim to Romagna until the end of October 1503, during the papacy of old *Pius III. But with the accession of *Julius II on 1 November, this policy changed: B. quickly lost his hold over Romagna, was arrested, allowed to depart for Naples, but was there arrested again by the Spanish viceroy. In August 1504 he was sent to Spain, but, in November 1506, he fled and found shelter with his brother-in-law in Navarre. He died in action with the army of Navarre on 12 March 1507.

B. served as a model for the new type of ruler described by *Machiavelli in *The Prince*. The Florentine writer saw in B. treachery and cruelty, necessary qualities for the achievement of a unified Italian monarchy.

C. Yriarte, *Cesare Borgia* (1947);
G. Sasso, *Macchiavelli e Cesare Borgia: storia di un giudizio* (1966).

BORGIA, LUCREZIA (1480-1519) Daughter of *Alexander VI and sister of Cesare *Borgia. She was used by her father to further his personal ambitions and political schemes. In February 1493, he married her to Giovanni *Sforza, vicar of Pesaro. But when his policies changed he annulled the marriage (1497), and gave her to Alfonso of Aragon, duke of Bisceglie, who was related to the king of Naples. This second husband was murdered by order of Cesare in 1500, whereupon a third

Lucrezia Borgia

marriage was arranged with Alfonso *d'Este, heir to the duchy of *Ferrara (September 1501). Even after her family lost its power in Rome, she led a peaceful life, bearing her third husband four children and becoming an influential patron of the arts in Ferrara. Her reputation as the beautiful incestuous daughter, who actively cooperated in the cruel machinations of her father and brother, proves the persistence of popular slander.

J. Haslip, *Lucrezia Borgia* (1953);
S. Harcourt-Smith, *The Marriage at Ferrara* (1952);
M. Bellonci, *The Life and Times of Lucrezia Borgia* (1953).

BORGIA, ST. FRANCIS (1510-72) Spanish *Jesuit, promotor of education and author of works on ascetism. The heir of the third duke of Gandia, near Valencia, he was educated at Saragossa and, in 1529, married Eleanor de Castro, a friend of the Empress. In 1539 *Charles V made him viceroy of Catalonia, a post he held until 1543, when he succeeded his father to the title. After his wife's death (1546), he entered the Jesuit order, and soon distinguished himself by establishing new schools. He became a close friend of *Loyola, whom he met at Rome in 1550, and also befriended *Teresa de Avila. In 1554 he was made the general commissary of the Jesuits in Spain and, in 1565, following the death of *Lainez, was elected the third general of the Order. During tenure of office the Jesuits expanded their activity in Europe and established missions in the New World. He was canonized in 1671.

BORGOGNONE, AMBROGIO (c. 1455-1524) Italian painter. Born in Milan, he is considered one of the best representatives of the local School in a style conveying a calm devotional mood. Little is known about his life. His early important works were executed on the walls of the Certosa di Pavia (1488-95), but he also worked in Lodi and Bergamo. In his later works one can perceive traces of the influence of *Leonardo.

BORROMEO, ST. CARLO (1538-84) Cardinal and a leading Roman Catholic reformer. Born to a noble Milanese family, B. at the age of twenty-two reached a very influential position in the ecclesiastical hierarchy, after his uncle became pope as *Pius IV. He was made cardinal, as well as archbishop of Milan, and was actually his uncle's principal aid. In this capacity he contributed to the conclusion of the Council of *Trent and to the writing of the new Roman Catechism. After the death of Pius IV (1565), B. dedicated his efforts to the implementation of the Tridentine reforms in his diocese of Milan. He cleared superfluous ornaments from the churches, established several colleges and religious schools, disciplined priests who were found negligent in their duties and curtailed the freedoms of some religious orders. These reforms aroused opposition inside the church and among the civil authorities, who thought that his actions encroached on their own jurisdictions. But B. persevered and found a way to neutralize his opponents. He was canonized in 1610.

M. Yeo, *A Prince of Pastors: St. Charles Borromeo* (1938);
A. Deroo, *Saint Charles Borromée, cardinal reformateur, docteur de la pastorale* (1963).

BOSCAN, JUAN (1490-1542) Spanish poet. B. is known chiefly for his introduction of the Renaissance Italian lyrical style into the Spanish language. He was influenced by the Italian poet Andrea Navagero (1483-1529), the Venetian ambassador to Spain, whom he met in 1525. While his poetry, besides being stylistically innovative, was undistinguished, B. produced an excellent Spanish translation of *Il cortegiano* by *Castiglione. A friend of *Garcilaso de la Vega, the verses of both poets were published by B.'s widow in 1543.

BOSCH, HIERONYMUS (c. 1450-1516) A Dutch painter, considered one of the greatest masters of pictorial fantasy. B.'s name derives from his birth place, Hertogenbosch, where he worked and died. His pictures, painted in a style which was unmarked by Italian influences, portrayed deformed creatures and cruel or bizarre scenes, recreating a haunted, nightmarish world. His paintings were not entirely a product of his imagination: they were inspired by certain mediaeval allegories, but it is difficult to establish the exact sources. His interpretation of the castigation of sinners in hell impressed his contemporaries. *Philip II of Spain admired his works. In the 20th century interest in B. reawakened and attention was drawn to the weird, obscure or sexual images in his work. Little is known about B.'s life. In the history of painting in the Netherlands he may belong to a trend which began before him by Roger van der *Weyden and was followed by *Breughel.

L. von Baldass, *Hieronymus Bosch* (1960);
C. Linfert, ed., *Hieronymus Bosch: The Paintings* (1959).

BOSIO, ANTONIO (1575-1629) Italian archaeologist. A native of Malta, he came to Rome as a boy, and dedicated his life to the discovery and study of the Roman catacombs. He first descended to the Catacomb of Domitilla in 1593 in order to demonstrate his daring.

However, what began as youth bravado turned into a lifetime preoccupation. His discoveries were described in his book *Roma sotterranea*, which was published in 1632, shortly after his death.

BOTANY The knowledge of the world of plants, studied in ancient times by Dioscorides and Pliny the Elder, went into complete decline during the Middle Ages. In the 15th century, the discovery of the works of the two classical scholars which raised them to the rank of authorities, signalled a new period in the development of botanical studies. As in the past, Renaissance botanists were chiefly interested in the medical properties of plants; this is in the famous commentary of the Italian Pierandrea Mattioli (1544) on the work of Dioscorides. But new works constantly expanded the available knowledge. Otto Brunfels (1530) described the flora of the Rhine, Hieronymus Bock (1539), added accurate drawings of the plants he studied, and Leonhard *Fuchs offered a new terminology. Outstanding botanists of the second half of the 16th century were Robert Dodoens and Charles de l'Ecluse, both of the Netherlands, and the Italian Andrea Cesalpino (1519-1603), whose *De plantis* (1583) applied methods of classification. The most impressive achievement of Renaissance b. was the work of two French Huguenot brothers, Jean and Gaspard Bauhin, who had settled in *Basle. In their *Historia plantarum generalis* (1619) and *Pinax theatri botanici* (1594;1619), over 5,000 plants were described, most of them with illustrations. In these works they attempted to compile everything that had been written on plants since antiquity.

The ability to reproduce the illustrations of plants in woodcuts no doubt increased the interest in b. and raised the standards of accurate description. Another important factor was the contact with the exciting new discoveries in America. Only a few of these plants were actually brought over to Europe, but by the second half of the 16th century there were attempts to grow some exemplars in what became the first European botanical gardens. The potato and pineapple especially attracted attention.

Woodcut illustration from the Herbarius latinus

H. S. Reed, *A Short History of the Plant Sciences* (1942);

A. Arber, *Herbals, Their Origin and Evolution, 1470-1670* (1938).

BOTERO, GIOVANNI (1544-1617) Italian political writer. Born in Piedmont, he was educated by the *Jesuits and taught in the colleges, although he did not become a full member of the Order. In 1579 he was dismissed, because of a sermon in which he criticized papal secular power, but was helped by Archbishop Carlo *Borromeo, who made him his secretary (1582). In 1598 he became a tutor to the son of the Duke of Savoy, with whom he travelled to Spain. His main work, *Della ragione di stato*, was published in 1589. In it he refuted *Machiavelli's view of political morality, and argued for a state based on Christian principles; nevertheless, he admitted that "reasons of state" as an end justified the means. Of his other works, *Relazioni universali* (1596), contained historical descriptions and interesting views on population. *Cause della grandezza e magnificenza delle città* (1589) dealt with the factors underlaying the growth of cities.

BOTHWELL, JAMES HEPBURN, EARL OF (1536-78) Scottish royal consort. Belonging to a noble Scotch family, whose lands were situated near the English border, B. succeeded in 1556 his father's titles, including the office of Lord High Admiral of Scotland. Of a violent temper, he soon became embroiled in political rivalries in Scotland and incurred the enmity of Queen *Elizabeth I of England. His political support of Queen *Mary began in 1560, when he met the young queen while on a mission to France, but their relationship became close only in 1566, after the murder of *Rizzio, Mary's secretary and confidant. B. now became the queen's chief protector against the rebellious lords and, in February 1567, arranged the murder of her hated husband, *Darnley. In April he was acquitted of charges related to the murder, mainly because the accuser did not dare to come to the trial, and on the 24th of the same month seized the queen and carried her, with her consent, to his castle at Dunbar. B. then divorced his wife and, on 15 May, married the queen, but found himself facing powerful opposition from both Protestant and Catholic nobles. By the end of June he was forced to leave the queen and flee north. He then left Scotland, but was captured by a Danish ship, and spent the rest of his life as a prisoner in Denmark.

BOTTICELLI, SANDRO (1445-1510) Italian painter. B.'s real name was Alessandro Filipepi. The youngest son of a tanner, he was born in Florence, where he lived and worked for most of his life. He showed a talent for painting from early childhood and at the age of 13 became an apprentice of Fra Filippo *Lippi, in whose shop he served as an assistant for 10 years. His earliest independent works date from about 1470 and display traces of *Pollaiuolo's influence. By the mid-1470s he was personally commissioned to carry out works for

Madonna of the Magnificat *by Botticelli*

members of the *Medici family, the ruling power in Florence. Some of his best pictures were painted at that time. In 1481 he went to Rome, where he painted frescoes in the Sistine Chapel, alongside *Ghirlandaio's and *Perugino's. Back in Florence, he decorated a villa belonging to Lorenzo the Magnificent with frescoes, and created many altarpieces with exquisitely beautiful Madonnas. Lorenzo's heirs commissioned B. to do a series of drawings illustrating *Dante's *Divine Comedy*; many of these have survived. But his relations with the Medicis seem to have come to an end in 1497 during the *Savonarola affair. While Savonarola dominated Florence, or immediately after his execution, B.'s works became intensely religious. His major work of this period, the *Mystic Nativity* of 1500, discarded the rules of perspective and proportion to create an air of religious devotion. B.'s most famous pictures are the *Primavera* (*Spring*), and the *Birth of Venus*, inspired by classical mythological themes and painted during his association with the Medicis. These works, influenced by Neoplatonic ideas of beauty, are superb examples of Florentine notions of refined grace and delicacy.

H. P. Horne, *Alessandro Filipepi Commonly Called Sandro Botticelli* (1908);
G. C. Argan, *Botticelli* (1957);
R. Salvini, *All the Paintings of Botticelli* (1965).

BOTTICINI, FRANCESCO (1446-97) Italian painter. Born in Florence, where he worked during most of his life, B. imitated the style of several of his contemporary great Florentine masters, especially *Botticelli. As most of the paintings are attributed to him on stylistic grounds, the procedure is made all the more difficult by his dependence on the styles of others.

BOURBON A French noble family which, beginning with *Henry IV, became the ruling dynasty of France and, eventually, also of Spain. Holders of one of the largest baronies in France, the B.s became related to the *Valois royal family when Pierre, lord of Beaujeu and husband of *Anne, daughter of *Louis XI, inherited the title (1488). His daughter, Suzanne, married Charles of the Montpensier branch of the B.s, the famous Constable of France. After the latter's death the title fell to the Vendôme branch of the family and, in 1548, *Antoine de Bourbon married *Jeanne d'Albret, heiress to the kingdom of Navarre and daughter of *Marguerite, sister of *Francis I. Their son Henry ascended the throne in 1589.

BOURBON, CHARLES, DUKE OF (1490-1527) Constable of France; one of the outstanding military figures of his age. Son of one of the wealthiest French families and related by marriage to the royal house, he dedicated himself early to a military career and took part in the Italian campaigns of *Louis XII (1507-12). The title and office of constable, which at the time connoted a military rank, was given to him by *Francis I in 1515, the year in which he distinguished himself at the Battle of Marignano. Later, however, his relations with the king deteriorated and led to the confiscation of B.'s properties in 1521 and, finally, to his defection and acceptance of a command in the imperial army. In 1525 he led the imperial troops who dealt the French a crushing defeat at Pavia, the battle in which Francis I was taken prisoner. Two years later he led German and Spanish troops against Rome in an attempt to force *Clement VII into complete surrender. He was killed by an *arquebus shot, fired, according to his own claim, by Benvenuto *Cellini. Upon his death the mercenary soldiers savagely sacked the city.

C. Hare, *Charles de Bourbon* (1924).

BOURDICHON, JEAN (1457-1521) French painter and illuminator of manuscripts. He executed works for *Louis XI, *Charles VIII and *Louis XII, though only a few of these survived. His fame derives mainly from the *Book of Hours of *Anne of Brittany*, a manuscript illuminated in a style reminiscent of *Fouquet. B. was one of the major artists of the early French Renaissance and the head of the School of Tours. However, his talents lay in technique, rather than innovative ideas.

BOUTS, DIERIC (c. 1415-75) Dutch painter. Born in Haarlem, his active years were spent in the southern Netherlands at Louvain, where he executed works for the municipality. In 1464 he was commissioned to make an altarpiece for the church of St. Pierre, considered to be his major work, and about 1468 he completed two large pictures for the Louvain Town Hall. His style resembles in some respects that of Roger van der *Weiden. B. was an accomplished master who excelled especially in the detail of costume and landscape. His sons, Dieric and Aelbrecht, were also well-known painters.

BRACCIO DA MONTONE, ANDREA (1368-1424) Italian **condottiere*. The son of a noble Perugian family which had been exiled, he became a military commander for Pope *John XXIII and, in 1416, took Perugia. In 1417 he reached the zenith of his power when he occu-

St. Martin *a miniature by Jean Bourdichon in The Book of Hours of Anne of Brittany*

St. Christopher *by Dieric Bouts*

pied Rome for over two months. Later he was attacked by *Martin V and the *Sforzas, whom he fought back successfully. He died in a battle before the walls of Aquila. Known for his audacity and cruelty, B. made Perugia for a short time a significant independent factor in the politics of central Italy.

BRAHE, TYCHO (1546-1601) Danish astronomer. Born to a noble family, B. went in 1562 to Leipzig as a law student, but devoted most of his time to the study of *astronomy. In 1565, aided by his uncle, he constructed his first observatory, and in 1572 discovered the 'new star' in the Cassiopeia constellation. His observations, published in *De nova stella*, brought him fame. Estranged from his family, because he had married a simple peasant girl, B. was supported after 1574 by Frederick II, who gave him the island of Hveen, near Copenhagen. Here he founded Uraniborg, an observatory on a grand scale, which he furnished with the most precise instruments then available, and where he pursued his plans for a star catalogue. The death of his patron in 1596 brought an end to the support of the Danish crown. In 1597 he left Denmark and, in 1599, came to Prague, and enjoyed the patronage of Emperor *Rudolf II. He was joined there by *Kepler, who worked as his assistant, and resumed his observations. However, he died the following year.

B.'s contribution to astronomy was based principally on the precision of his observations, made before the invention of the *telescope. His principal work, *Astronomiae instauratae progymnasmata*, published in two volumes by Kepler in 1602-03, established the location of 777 fixed stars, and analyzed the comet of the year 1577. B., however, retained many of the old beliefs about the structure of the universe. He believed in *alchemy and *astrology, and in the Ptolemaic geocentric system. This meant that he could not accept the Copernican system, though he espoused views which were a partial acknowledgement of heliocentrism.

J. L. E. Dreyer, *Tycho Brahe: A Picture of Scientific Life in the Sixteenth Century* (1890; reprinted 1963);
J. A. Gade, *The Life and Times of Tycho Brahe* (1947).

BRAMANTE, DONATO (1444-1514) Italian architect. Born near Urbino, B. first showed an aptitude for drawing and for some years earned his living as a painter. In about 1476, he went to Milan, where he remained for over 20 years. Here, under the patronage of Duke

Tycho Brahe in his observatory, *a 17th-century print*

In 1499, when the French invasion caused the downfall of the Sforzas, B. went to Rome. Here he was commissioned to design the cloister of S. Maria della Pace (1500). The impressive Roman aspects of this building, and the fact that it was completed in a very short time, made his name known to Pope *Alexander VI, who comissioned him to design the church of S. Pietro in Montorio, a circular building which is a superb example of the indebtedness of Renaissance architecture to classical forms. Under *Julius II (1503-13), B. became the regular architect for the papal court. The reigning pope commissioned him to design a group of buildings around the Cortile di S. Damaso, and subsequently, an even more ambitious project around the Cortile del Belvedere, a huge courtyard which B. flanked with arcaded buildings. During these years B. also designed the choir for the Roman church of S. Maria del Popolo, began the building of Palazzo Caprini and planned smaller works in Rome and Bologna. His most important task was the rebuilding of *St. Peter's Cathedral. B. conceived a huge building with its base a cross with four equal arms. By the time he died he had built the four great piers with their connecting arches. After his death the design was much altered, chiefly by *Michelangelo. B.'s immediate successor as the leading architect of Rome was *Raphael.

O. H. Förster, *Bramante* (1956).

BRAMANTINO (Bartolomeo Suardi; c. 1466-1530) Italian painter and architect. He was born in Milan, where he did most of his work; he got his nickname from the fact that he had been the pupil of *Bramante. His style was influenced by *Foppa but, following a Ludovico *Sforza, he began to design architectural works, while continuing to produce decorative paintings. His first buildings, mostly churches, showed the influence of *Alberti, especially in the design of the façade.

Cortile del Belvedere in the Vatican, Rome, designed by Bramante

The Tempietto in the cloister of S. Pietro in Montorio, Rome, by Bramante

visit to Rome in 1508, it became freer and closer to the High Renaissance form of monumentality. Of his architectural works the best known is the chapel of the church of S. Nazaro Maggiore in Milan, designed for the *Trivulzio family (1519), in a simple classical style.

BRANDENBURG In 1415 Emperor *Sigismund invested Frederick of *Hohenzollern with this margraviate of northeastern *Germany, to which was attached an electorate of the *Holy Roman Empire. The first task of the new rulers was to assert their power over the strong local nobility and the semi-independent towns, among them Berlin. In fact, it was not until the end of the reign of Frederick II "the Iron" (1470), so called for the style of his government, that the new dynasty secured its hold over B. *Albert Achilles (1470-86) was already in position to expand the territory, acquiring parts of Pomerania. His son, John Cicero (1486-99), and his grandson, *Joachim I (1499-1535), were preoccupied chiefly with organizing their administration. In 1506 the first university of B. was founded at Frankfurt on the Oder. It was during this period of relative calm that the now docile nobility became interested in grain production and the export trade, for which purpose the great landowners, the *Junkers*, reduced the peasantry to serfdom.

After the death of Joachim I, B. was divided between his sons, *Joachim II (1535-71) and John (1535-71), and guided cautiously by its rulers towards the Lutheran *Reformation. However, it was spared the devastations of war thanks to Joachim II's decision not to join the *Schmalkaldic League and his good relations with the emperor. This margrave paved the way, in 1569, to the future greatness of B., when he reached an agreement with the duke of Prussia, envisioning the joining of the two territories under one rule, when the Prussian ducal family line would end. John George (1571-98) reunited B. and gave her more years of peaceful government, abstaining from intervention in the fierce religious conflicts that tore western Europe. His son, Joachim Frederick (1598-1608), pursued similar policies and consolidated Lutheranism as the official state religion, reaffirming the *Formula of Concord. John Sigismund (1608-20), however, broke with the stability-conscious policies of his predecessors. By marrying the daughter of Duke Albert Frederick of Prussia, he ensured the fulfilment of the 1569 agreement, but at the same time claimed on his wife's behalf the duchies *Jülich and Cleve in the lower Rhine valley. This involved him in a long political and military struggle, which was very costly and caused disaffection among his subjects in B. As a result, the elector had to make concessions to the local nobility in B., but consoled himself with the final incorporation of Prussia in 1618.

S. B. Fay, *The Rise of Brandenburg-Prussia to 1786* (1964).

BRANKOVICH, GEORGE (?-1456) Serbian ruler. The son of the ruling family of Serbia, long attached to the Byzantine emperors, he assumed the government in 1427. B. shifted his support from one of the contending powers in the Balkan to another. He first fought against *Venice, then joined the *crusade of *Vladislav III against the *Ottoman Turks (1443), but afterwards recognized the suzerainty of *Murad II, to whom he gave his daughter in marriage. *Mehemmed II who, in 1454, advanced against Belgrade, made him renew his alliance with the Hungarians and their leader Janos *Hunyadi. After his death Serbia was conquered by the Turks (1459).

BRANT, SEBASTIAN (1457-1521) German humanist author. Born in *Strassburg, B. studied law in *Basle, but returned to his native town where he later held public office. He produced literary as well as legal works, but is known primarily for his popular satire *Das Narrenschiff* (*The Ship of Fools*), published in 1494. The work is an allegory describing the sailing of fools to a fools' paradise, but under this amusing cover B. dealt with many social issues and criticized the failures of the church. The work had an immediate success, both in German and in translation, as well as several imitations. It certainly helped prepare a climate of opinion favourable to the Reformation.

U. Gaier, *Studien zu Brants Narrenschiff* (1966);
F. A. Pompen, *The English Versions of the 'Ship of Fools'* (1925).

BRANTOME, PIERRE DE BOURDEILLES DE (c. 1540-1614) French author of historical biographies. The son of an aristocratic family, he became a courtier and soldier and travelled widely, visiting Italy, Scotland, Spain and Portugal. Later he participated in the French *Religious Wars, but a fall from a horse in 1584 crippled him and it was then that he took to writing. His voluminous *Vies des hommes illustres et des grandes capitaines* and the *Vies des dames galantes et des dames illustres* were published only in 1665. They give a vivid portrayal of the courtly life in his time and contain an abundance of historically useful gossip.

A. Grimaldi, *Brantôme et le sens de l'histoire* (1971);
R. D. Cottrell, *Brantôme; The writer as Portraitist of his Age* (1970).

BRAY, GUIDO DE (Guy de Brès; 1522-67) Protestant reformer in the Netherlands. Born at Mons, he went to England in 1548 to avoid persecution for his Protestant beliefs. In 1552 he returned to the Continent, serving as a preacher in Liège and *Ghent, and later at Tournai and Valenciennes. His Calvinist-inspired confession of faith, *Confession de foi des églises des Pays Bas* (1562) roused the authorities against him, especially since it gained popular approval and went through many edi-

An illustration to Brant's Ship of Fools, *published in Strassburg in 1502*

tions. B. visited Brussels and *Antwerp and made efforts to bring about unity between the various forms of Protestantism in the Netherlands. In August 1566 his presence at Valenciennes led to a disturbance by his followers, which later developed into an outright revolt, B. taking the spiritual leadership of the movement. After the surrender of the city in March 1567, he was caught and sentenced to be hanged.

BREDERO, GERBRAND ADRIAANSZ (1585-1618) Dutch poet and playwright. A shoemaker's son, who first intended to become a painter, he began to write melancholic love songs in his youth. His dramas, for which he was known in his lifetime, fall under two categories. The first follows the romantic tradition of love and adventure; the other includes a number of farces and comedies that are full of popular expressions and scenes from daily life. His *Den Spaansche Brabander* (1617) was inspired by the famous *picaresque novel **Lazarillo de Tormes*.

BREGNO, ANDREA (1421-1506) Italian sculptor. Born near Lake Lugano, he was trained in the traditional ornate Lombard style, but after he moved to Rome adopted the classically-oriented forms. Heading a flourishing workshop, B. produced many tombs and altars. His sepulchres generally have figures of saints in niches, and are decorated with carefully-designed ornamentation. B. was the leading Roman sculptor in the second half of the 15th century.

BRENZ, JOHANNES (1499-1570) German Protestant reformer. A native of Württemberg, B. went in 1514 to the University of Heidelberg where he heard the lectures of *Oecolampadius and, in 1518, met *Luther. He was ordained in 1520 and, in 1522, became the promoter of the Reformation in Swäbischen Hall. B. remained a faithful follower of Luther, whom he accompanied in 1529 to the debate in Marburg. Earlier, in 1525, he had compiled the *Syngramma Suevicum*, which defended Luther's views on the Lord's Supper against those of Oecolampadius. B. enjoyed the support of Duke *Ulrich, who encouraged him to reform the school and church systems of Württemberg. During the *Schmalkaldic War (1546-48) he had to go into hiding, and refused to accept the *Augsburg Interim. But in 1551 he attended the Council of *Trent as a representative of the duke of Württemberg, though he was not allowed to participate. For the latter part of his life he headed the Protestant church in Stuttgart. His treatise on heretics, published in 1554, displayed a relatively tolerant attitude towards the *Anabaptists.

BRETHREN OF THE COMMON LIFE A religious association founded at the end of the 14th century by Geert de *Groote at Deventer in the Netherlands. Some of de Groote's disciples became Augustinian canons and established the Windesheim Congregation. The Brethren, however, did not take monastic vows but remained a lay community. Both groups were exponents of the new pietist movement known as **Devotio Moderna*, which put the emphasis on the inner life and on meditation as opposed to formal scholastic speculation. The best expression of the spirit of the 'new devotion' is to be found in *Thomas à Kempis' *Imitatio Christi* (The Imitation of Christ). Piety and character were valued more than strict observation of rites; they did not seek individual mystic experiences, but fortification through the reading of the Scriptures and through moral actions. During the 15th century the Brethren and the Sisters of the Common Life spread throughout the Netherlands, in Germany and in Switzerland. They lived in common houses, renouncing private property, leading a life of chastity and sober piety according to a prescribed schedule of devotion and labour. They were industrious copyists of manuscripts and, when printing began, they set up printing presses which published many books of devotion, grammars and writings of classic and humanist authors suitable for school curricula. The most important contribution of the B. was in the sphere of education. At first they founded and supervised dormitories for pupils, but later they established schools of their own, the most famous of which being the school in Deventer that attained its prestige through the work of Alexander *Hegius, a scholar and an excellent administrator. The school became a model for many others in Northern Europe. Although not humanistic in spirit, these schools combined the most advanced methods of teachings with the scholarship of the Italian Renaissance, and a strong emphasis on *Bible study. Some of the leading humanists of Germany and the Netherlands attended these schools. The association of the B. ceased to exist in the early 17th century, after the great upheavals of the Reformation.

A. Hyma, *The Christian Renaissance* (2nd ed. 1965);
id., *Brethren of the Common Life* (1950);
R. R. Post, *The Modern Devotion* (1968). (ME)

BRETHREN OF THE FREE SPIRIT A general designation for various religious sects which sprang up during the latter part of the Middle Ages, especially in Germany, Switzerland and the Netherlands. These groups, among them the Beghards and Beguines, were not under direct ecclesiastical authority, and were frequently accused of professing pantheistic ideas and of transgressing against conventional morality. They may have influenced the rise of *Anabaptism.

BREUGHEL, JAN (1568-1625) Flemish painter; known as "Velvet Breughel", younger son of (Pieter) *Breughel the Elder. Greatly admired by his contemporaries, he worked for some time with *Rubens, and excelled in landscapes and still-life. Born in Brussels, he resided for a time in Germany, and also travelled to Italy. He left a great number of works.

BREUGHEL, PIETER (1528-69) Flemish painter; also referred to as the Elder, to distinguish him from his son. B. became a master in the guild of Antwerp in 1551. He then travelled to Italy and in 1553 visited Rome. After his return he settled in Brussels, where he lived until his death. Most of his oil paintings were done during the last ten years of his life. Like *Bosch before him, B. had an eye for the weird and grotesque, but he aimed at satire and moral statement, rather than fantasy. His famous portrayals of village scenes and peasants' life show sympathy mingled with irony for his subject, and were probably meant to depict universal human faults; gluttony and drunkenness are two recurrent themes. B.'s other great pictorial achievement is his series of five landscapes entitled *Months*, which were done in 1565. With great sensitivity, they do not merely reproduce nature, but recreate an atmospheric unity and show man as part of his surroundings. Yet B. himself was certainly not a peasant, but a condescending townsman. He enjoyed the patronage of Cardinal *Granvelle and received commissions from the wealthy.

The Parable of the Seven Blind Men *by Pieter Breughel the Elder*

V. Denis, *All the Paintings of Pieter Breughel* (1961); F. G. Grossman, *Breughel: The Paintings* (1966).

BREUGHEL, PIETER (1564-1637) Flemish painter; known as "Hell Breughel", son of *Breughel the Elder. He was born in Brussels and died in Antwerp. Much of his work derives from his father.

BRIÇONNET, GUILLAUME (1470-1534) French churchman, reformer and sponsor of humanist learning. The son of an important statesman and prelate, B. succeeded his father in 1507 as abbot of St. Germain des-Prés. He enjoyed the confidence of *Louis XII, who entrusted him with a mission to Rome, and was equally favoured by *Francis I, who made him bishop of Meaux. B. tried to introduce reforms in his diocese, and invited preachers and humanists to undertake the translation of the Gospels. However, before long, the reforming zeal turned some of his protegés, as *Lefèvre, *Roussel and *Farel against basic Catholic doctrine and, after 1524, B. had to restrain the movement which he himself had launched. Nevertheless, at the Parlement of Paris (1526), he was accused of sympathizing with Lutheranism, and two of the Meaux reformers were convicted of heresy and burnt at the stake. The Bishop, supported by the king, was made to write a letter of submission to the Parlement. B. wrote a number of theological works, and corresponded with *Marguerite d'Angoulême, queen of Navarre.

A. Renandet, *Préreforme et humanisme à Paris pendant les premières guerres d'Italie* (1953).

BRIL Two brothers. Flemish painters, natives of *Antwerp, who attained success in Italy. Mattheus (1548-83), the older, went to Rome around 1575 and was employed by *Gregory XIII at the Vatican, where he executed fresco landscapes. Paul (1556-1626) followed his brother to Rome, and became his assistant. He inherited his brother's position at the Vatican, and was particularly favoured by *Sixtus V. His landscapes were praised by Annibale *Carracci; he also excelled in the execution of etched sceneries.

BRIOSCO, ANDREA (c. 1471-1532) Italian sculptor, known as Il Riccio, "the curly-haired". Born in Padua, he was the student of *Bellano. His best-known work is the great candlestick in the basilica of S. Antonio, Padua, depicting biblical and pagan scenes (1507-16). In the same church is his monument of Antonio Trombetta (1521-24). B. followed the classical style of the ancients, and cast many small bronzes. Another great work of his was the Della Torre monument in the church of S. Fermo Maggiore of Verona (1516-21), with eight reliefs in bronze.

BROEDERLAM, MELCHIOR Flemish painter. Active mainly in Ypres during the last two decades of the 14th century, he is known especially for the two wood panels of an altarpiece which he completed in 1399. These are considered the first examples of the *International Gothic style. B. was the court painter of Philip the Bold, duke of Burgundy, but the works he executed for him are lost. He is believed to have died in 1409.

BRONZINO, IL (1503-72) The name under which the Florentine painter Angelo Allori is known. He was a student of Jacopo da *Pontormo, whose style and colour technique he imitated, but was also influenced by *Michelangelo. B. became court painter to *Cosimo I, the first Grand Duke of Tuscany, and painted many

The Annunciation
by Broederlam

portraits of his patron, his family and courtiers. The faces in his portraits are distinguished by their impassive stony looks, while his most famous picture, *Venus, Cupid, Folly and Time*, has an air of cold eroticism. B. is considered one of the leading Italian Mannerists.

A. K. McComb, *Bronzino: His Life and Works* (1928).

BROSSE, SALOMON DE (1571-1626) French architect. A son of the *Ducerceau family, he was educated as an architect and later left his native town of Verneuil and moved to Paris. Here he became a leader of his profession, building several great *chateaux*, most prominently the monumental palace of Luxembourg (1615-24). It was built for *Marie de Medicis, and had rusticated walls, in imitation of the Queen's early home, the Pitti palace at Florence. B. successfully adopted Italian architectural ideas, and was a true precursor of the great French architects of the 17th century. François Mansart (1598-1666) was his pupil.

BROWNISTS One of the earliest extreme *Puritan sects in England. They owed their name to Robert Browne, (*c.* 1550-1633), a Cambridge-educated relative of William *Cecil, who began preaching around 1580. The B. criticized the *Church of England. They rejected the episcopelian authority, favouring a purely congregational system. Their persecution by the bishops compelled many of them to seek shelter in Holland. Their first leader, who between 1582 and 1584 published several polemical tracts, quarrelled with his congregation, and in 1586 made a formal submission to the Church of England. But his name had already become synonymous with early Puritanism.

BRUGES A city in western *Flanders; a centre of international commercial and financial activity at the end of the Middle Ages and in the early Renaissance. In the 15th century B. had a resident community of commercial representatives from Germany, England, Spain, Portugal and the Italian city-states. The movement of merchandise was regulated by a well-supervised system, and B. was the first European town to establish a *bourse*, or centre for the exchange of staples and money. The city enjoyed a brilliant period under the dukes of *Burgundy, who held their court there. In 1484 she revolted against *Maximilian of Austria, and as a result of the destruction caused in the suppression of the rebellion, lost her commercial preeminence and was largely superseded by *Antwerp. B. was also an important centre of art. Adorned by buildings in the Gothic style of architecture, she was the home of Jan van *Eyck and possessed paintings by Hans *Memling, Hugo van der *Goes and Gerard *David.

R. de Roover, *Money, Banking and Credit in Medieval Bruges* (1948);

J. A. van Houtte, *Bruges; Essai d'histoire urbaine* (1967).

BRUNELLESCHI, FILIPPO (1377-1446) The first great Renaissance architect who revived in Italy the ancient Roman style. The son of a notary, B. was born in

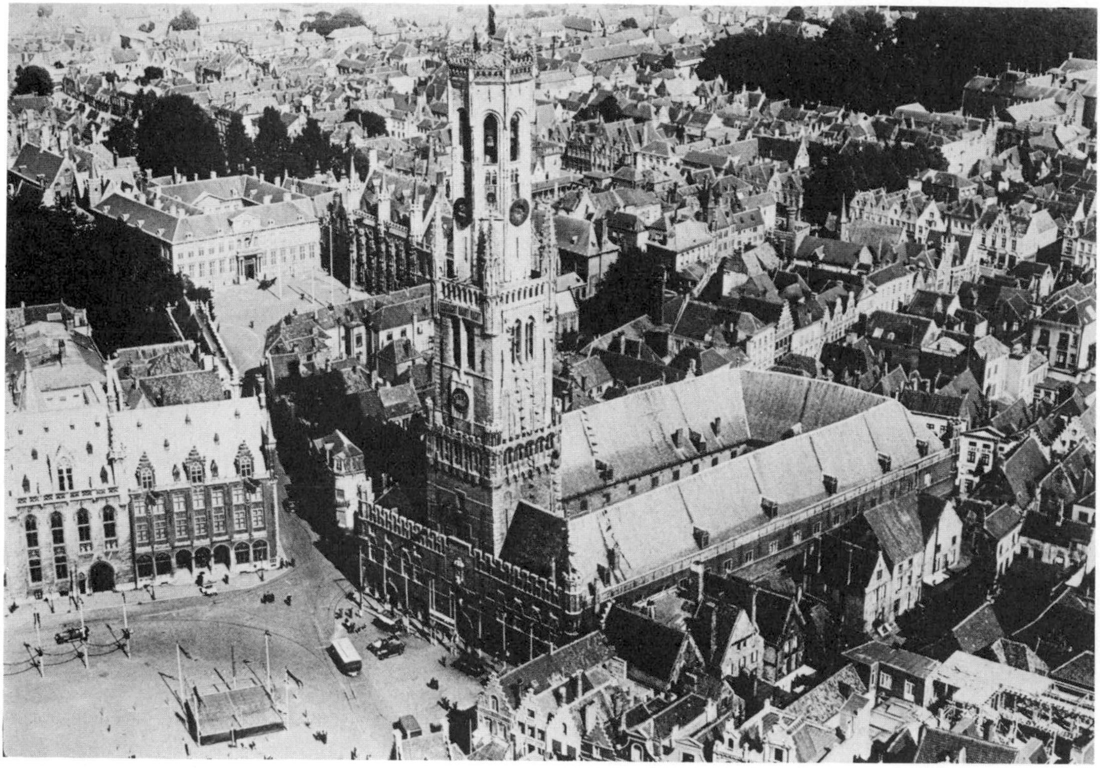

Bruges

Interior of the Church of S. Lorenzo, Florence, by Brunelleschi

Giordano Bruno

Florence and became a goldsmith. In 1401 he lost to *Ghiberti the competition for the second bronze door of the Florence Baptistery. In *c*. 1402 he went to Rome, where he studied with *Donatello ancient sculpture and structures. It was here that he formed his ideas about linear perspective which characterize his architecture. He returned to Florence in 1407 and immediately won approval of his plan for the completion of the Florence cathedral, S. Maria del Fiore, but it was not until 1420 that construction actually began. It was completed after his death, not entirely according to his instructions. The great cupola, a masterpiece of Renaissance architecture, is in some respects even more impressive than that of *St. Peter's in Rome. In 1421 B. began to build the Hospital of the Innocents, an edifice distinguished for its arcade of Corinthian columns and widely-spaced arches. Another major work was the palace he planned, in 1435, for Luca Pitti. It was completed after his death and many 15th-century Tuscan *palazzi* were influenced by it. Other works of B. included the Florentine churches of S. Lorenzo and S. Spirito, and the Pazzi Chapel in the cloister S. Croce begun, in 1429 – a complex structure, it is considered to be the first church built entirely in Renaissance style. Although an innovator and the first great architect who consciously emulated classical forms, B. was not dogmatic like his immediate followers; beside the questions of form, he was concerned with the practical problems of construction and internal space. He was, in fact, rather eclectic, borrowing ideas from Gothic architecture, as well as from ancient archaeological remains. The result, however, was a style distinguished for its elegance and proportion.

G. C. Argan, *Brunelleschi* (1955).

BRUNI, LEONARDO (1370-1444) Florentine statesman and humanist. Born in Arezzo, B. studied in Florence where he learned Greek and became a tutor in the house of the *Medici. In 1405 he became a secretary to Innocent VII and also served *John XXIII, whom he accompanied to the Council of *Constance (1414). In 1415, he returned to Florence, where he served in the council of government. He held the office of chancellor of the republic from 1427 until his death. A leading humanist of his age, B. furthered the expansion of the new learning into the spheres of education, history and civic virtues. His main work, *History of the Florentine People*, was a product of almost three decades of work. It followed the example of the great ancient Greek and Roman historians, and argued that the Florentine republic was based on a republican tradition of liberty and patriotism.

D. J. Wilcox, *The Development of Florentine Humanist Historiography in the Fifteenth Century* (1969);
H. Baron, *From Petrarch to Leonardo Bruni: Studies in Humanistic Political Literature* (1968).

BRUNO, GIORDANO (1548-1600) Italian philosopher, known as the foremost martyr of the Renaissance. Born Filippo, B. changed his name to Giordano at the age of 15, when he entered the Dominican order. The decade or so that he spent as a friar led him to question the fundamental doctrines of the Church, and in 1576 he left Italy. He was in *Geneva in 1579, and from 1581 to 1583 lectured on logic at the University of Paris. The next two years were spent with the French ambassador to England, Michel de *Castelnau, and there he wrote some of his best work. He returned to Paris, and then went to Germany. He stayed at Marburg and Wittenberg, Prague and Frankfurt. In 1592 he accepted an invitation to go to Venice, but shortly after returning to Italy was denounced to the *Inquisition. B. was imprisoned for seven years before he was declared guilty of heresy, and burned at the stake in Rome on 17 February 1600.

B.'s vast philosophical work embraces logic, metaphysics, morality and religion. He was a staunch critic of the Aristotelian system and the first great philosopher who gave the Copernican theory a metaphysical interpretation. His views of the infinity of the universe and his enthusiasm for Nature led him to a pantheistic conception of God. This idea, according to which God is present in every stone, plant and animal, was particularly developed in his two works, *Della causa, principio ed uno* and *Del'infinito, universo e mondi*, both published in 1584. Persecuted during his lifetime by both Catholics and Protestants, B. is often thought of as a symbol of free thought and opposition to narrow-minded clericalism.

D. Singer, *Giordano Bruno; His Life and Thought* (1950);
P. H. Michel, *The Cosmology of Giordano Bruno* (1973);
F. A. Yates, *Giordano Bruno and the Hermetic Tradition* (1964);

A. M. Paterson, *The Infinite Worlds of Giordano Bruno* (1970).

BRUYN, BARTHEL (c. 1493-1555) German painter. Born in *Cologne, he began to paint in the style of the Flemish school, but later in his life showed a distinct tendency towards the *Italianate style. His best-known work is the wings of a shrine in the church of Xanten, completed in 1536. He also painted numerous portraits and historical scenes.

BRY, THEODORE DE (1528-98) Flemish engraver. Born in Liege, he settled in 1570 in *Frankfurt, where he established a thriving workshop together with his two sons. They published illustrated books, chiefly on travel and overseas voyages, which B. adorned with his clearly-executed human figures. With his engravings for *Las Casas' *Brief Account of the Destruction of the Indies* B. contributed to the *Black Legend.

BUCER, MARTIN (1491-1551) German Protestant reformer. Born in Schlettstadt in Alsace, he entered the Dominican order as a boy and was influenced by the ideas of *Erasmus. In 1518, while studying at Heidelberg, he heard *Luther debating his theses with Augustinian friars and was converted to the ideas of reform. In 1521 he abandoned his order and married a former nun; he then travelled in Germany propagating the new ideas and, for a time, joined the *Knights' War as a chaplain of Franz von *Sickingen. In 1523 B. came to *Strassburg and was soon the principal leader of the reform movement in that city. His leadership was distinguished by moderation, religious tolerance and an attempt to promote unity among the various reform groups. B.'s inclination to follow the sacramentarian ideas of *Zwingli was evident in the *Confessio tetrapolitana* which he wrote in *Augsburg in 1530. In 1536 he found common grounds with Luther at Wittenberg and, a few years later, also cooperated with *Calvin during a debate with Catholic theologians. In spite of his moderate inclinations, B. refused to subscribe to the *Augsburg Interim of 1548 and, in order to escape the victorious imperial armies, accepted the invitation of Thomas *Cranmer and, in 1549, went to England. There he was received with great respect, appointed regius professor of divinity at Cambridge by *Edward VI, and consulted on various theological questions. B. wrote numerous religious tracts of which *De regno christi*, a vision of Christ's kingdom on earth, is the most important. He died and was buried at Cambridge. His tomb was desecrated in *Mary's reign, but it was later rebuilt by order of *Elizabeth I.

C. Hopf, *Martin Bucer and the English Reformation* (1946).

BUCHANAN, GEORGE (1506-82) Scottish author, political theorist and poet. Studying first at the University of St. Andrews, then in Paris, he was away from Scotland for many years, undergoing his intellectual development under the influence of French humanism. Between 1547 and 1552 he was in Portugal, where he was imprisoned on suspicion of Protestant sympathies. Released, he returned to France and, in 1561, to Scotland as a Latin tutor to Queen *Mary. By 1567, B. had become deeply involved with the party which opposed the Queen, and after she took refuge in England, attacked her violently in his *De Maria Scotorum Regina* (1571). B. wrote poetry in Latin, in which he had a distinctive style which was much admired at the time.

Theodore de Bry's engraved self-portrait

But his most important work was *De jure regni apud Scotos*, a dialogue between himself and another person on the nature of political authority. First published in 1578, the work is notable for the limitations it would put on royal power, without, however, resorting to theological arguments based on the Scriptures. B. also served as tutor to the future *James I, for whose instruction the book was written.

H. R. Trevor-Roper, *George Buchanan and the Ancient Scottish Constitution* (1966);

D. Macmillan, *George Buchanan: A Biography* (1906).

BUDÉ, GUILLAUME (1468-1540) French humanist. Born in Paris, he studied law in Orléans, but later decided to dedicate himself to the studying of the ancient languages and culture. B. was patronised by *Francis I who appointed him to public office. The king also helped him found the *Collegium Trilingue* (1530), which later became the *Collège de France, and established a library at Fontainebleau, according to B.'s advice. It is the original floor of the Bibliothèque Nationale. B. excelled in his knowledge of the Greek language, and his chief work, *Commentarii linguae Graecae* (1529), was an extensive analysis of grammatical and textual problems of Greek. An earlier work which had earned him a reputation was *De asse* (1514) on ancient coins. Earlier, in 1508, he had published a commentary on the Digest of Roman Law. After his death his wife moved to Geneva and followed the teachings of Calvin, which may suggest that B. himself had secretly sympathized with Protestantism.

J. Plattard, *Guillaume Budé et les origines de l'humanisme français* (1923).

BUGENHAGEN, JOHANNES (1485-1558) German Protestant reformer and preacher. Born near Stettin, B. prepared for an ecclesiastical career, becoming a priest

The petit Château at Chantilly by Bullant

in 1509. However, in 1520 he was converted to the Reformation by *Luther's writings. He joined Luther in *Wittenberg, where he preached at the university, and also helped Luther with the translation of the *Bible. Soon his talents as an itinerant Protestant missionary and organizer became known. In 1528 he preached in Brunswick and Hamburg, and in 1530 helped spread Reformation through Pomerania. In 1537 B. went to Denmark at the invitation of *Christian III. He remained there for about five years, in which time a new Lutheran church structure was adopted. The last years of his life were spent in Wittenberg.

BULLANT, JEAN (c. 1520-1578) French architect. B. learnt his craft at Rome, where he spent a few years, returning to France about 1545. Like his slightly older contemporary *Delorme, he tended towards a monumental conception of design, as shown in his additions to the chateau of Ecouen, which belonged to *Montmorency. Later his style displayed Mannerist tendencies, e.g., the castle of Chantilly. He published the *Reigle générale d'architecture* (1563) and a book on geometry. Few of his structures have survived to this day.

BULLINGER, HEINRICH (1504-75) Swiss Protestant reformer. Born in Bremgarten, B. studied at Emmerich and *Cologne, where he was inspired by the ideas of *Luther. Back in Switzerland, he was appointed a teacher at the cloister school of Cappel, and in 1527 joined *Zwingli in *Zurich. Destined to become Zwingli's successor and biographer, he accompanied him to the 1528 Disputation at Bern. For some time he served as a pastor of his native town, Bremgarten, but, immediately after Zwingli's death in 1531, went to Zurich and was chosen to be its chief pastor. As leader of an important current of the Reformation, B. had contacts with reformers all over Europe, and generally assumed a conciliatory stand aiming at unity and understanding. In this spirit he authored the Helvetic Confession of 1536, subscribed by *Basle and Zurich, as well as the *Consensus Tigurinus* of 1549, which he concluded with *Calvin. His second Helvetic Confession of 1566 was adopted by most reformers in Switzerland, and also in Hungary and Bohemia. His writings consist chiefly of polemics and sermons and seem to have influenced some of the English reformers.

A. Bouvier, *Henri Bullinger* (1940);
G. W. Bromiley, ed., *Zwingli and Bullinger* (1953).

BUNDSCHUH A type of simple shoe, made of a single piece of leather and fastened to the ankles with long straps, which was in common use in Germany. During the early 16th century it became the emblem of the rebellious peasants in southern Germany, who painted it on their banners. It then became a popular name for the rebels themselves.

BUON, BARTOLOMMEO (1374-1467) Venetian sculptor and architect. With his father Giovanni, he headed a successful workshop. He worked on the Ca d'Oro (1422) and on the Porta della Carta of the Doge's palace (1438-42). His architectural style is not yet touched by Renaissance ideas, and his sculpture reflects strong traces of German influences.

BUONACCORSI, FILIPPO (1437-96) Italian-Polish humanist and statesman. Born to a noble family, he studied in Rome, where he joined the circle of Pomponius *Laetus, but in 1468 had to leave the city, having been accused of conspirational activities. In 1470 he came to Poland and in a very short time rose to an influential position. He served as secretary to *Casimir IV and John Albert, undertook diplomatic missions to Constantinople, Venice and Rome, and introduced humanist learning into the university of Cracow. B. wrote a number of historical works and composed poetry in Latin.

BURCHIELLO, DOMENICO DA GIOVANNI (1404-49) Italian poet. Born in Florence, he was a barber by profession, but became known as the author of many poems, especially sonnets, distinguished for their humorous-satirical style. Because many of them were directed against the *Medici, he had to go into exile in 1434 and moved to Siena. He died in Rome. His verses, full of bizarre phrases and obscure allusions, gave rise to a type of poetry known as *maniera burchiellesca*, which later found followers in *Doni and others.

D. Guerri, *La corrente popolare nel Rinascimento* (1931).

BURCKHARDT, JACOB (1818-97) Swiss historian. In the new historiography of the *Renaissance the work of B. is of unique significance. Born in Basle, B. studied under Leopold von Ranke and Johann Droysen at the University of Berlin (1839-43), then returned to Basle where he taught until his retirement in 1893. His first work related to the Renaissance was *Der Cicerone*

The Flight to Egypt *by Caravaggio*

The Arnolfini *by Jan van Eyck*

(1855), a guide and study of the artistic treasures of Italy. *Die Kultur der Renaissance in Italien* (*The Civilization of the Renaissance in Italy*) was published in 1860. The book had a phenomenal success and influenced both the scholarly study and the present-day popular conception of the Renaissance. B. saw the Renaissance as a turning point in world history and the beginning of what we associate with the "modern" statecraft and culture. Although 20th-century research takes issue with many of his interpretations, the broad vision of the Renaissance which he had outlined endures.

W. K. Ferguson, *The Renaissance in Historical Thought* (1948).

BURGKMAIR, HANS (1473-1531) German painter and engraver. B. resided and worked in *Augsburg. His works show that he was influenced by the contemporary Italian style, and he may have visited Venice, although there is no proof of that. He was more important as an engraver than as a painter, and from 1510 executed hundreds of prints for *Maximilian I. The illustrations which he prepared for the emperor's political autobiography were not printed at the time, as Maximilian abandoned the project, but the blocks have survived.

BURGUNDY In 1363 King John II of France bestowed the duchy of B. upon his youngest son, Philip the Bold. Six years later the latter married Margaret, heiress of *Flanders, Artois and the county of Burgundy, (Franche-Comté). By the time of his death (1404), Philip had also incorporated into his possessions Brabant, Hainault, Zeeland, *Holland and Luxembourg, thus creating a formidable state between France and Germany. Although these territories lacked a common institutional framework, being united only in the person of their ruler, they possessed potential force and great resources, combining the agricultural richness of B. with the commercial and industrial power of the *Netherlands.

The next duke of B., John the Fearless (1404-19), behaved more like a troublesome French feudal noble than an independent prince, but his son *Philip the Good gave much of his attention to consolidating the different territories, with notable success. The apogee of B.'s history, in the second and third quarters of the 15th century, was accompanied by impressive cultural achievements, especially in the fields of *painting, *architecture and *literature. Politically, the rise of B. was facilitated by the prolonged weakness of the French monarchy. However, by the time *Louis XI inherited the throne of France (1461), conditions had changed and a final confrontation with B., still considered a part of France, became unavoidable. The conflict was exacerbated by the agressive policies of Duke *Charles the Bold, who entertained the idea of making B. a separate kingdom. Upon the death of Charles (1477), Louis seized the duchy of B., uniting it to the French crown. He later had to return the county of B., and was thwarted in his attempt to take Flanders. But the Burgundian menace to France had come to an end.

J. Calmette, *The Golden Age of Burgundy* (1962);
O. Cartellieri, *The Court of Burgundy* (1929).

BURLAMACCHI CONSPIRACY, THE An abortive revolt in Tuscany against the *Medici and Spain, led by Francesco Burlamacchi (1498-1548). The latter, a member of a rich merchant family from Lucca, was in contact with conspirators in other towns, among them Florentine exiles. Their aim was to demolish the government imposed on Tuscany by Duke *Cosimo I, and revive republican freedom and government in its cities. The conspiracy was discovered (1546) and Burlamacchi delivered to the Spanish imperial governor in Milan and executed.

BUSCH, JAN (1399-1480) German priest and religious reformer. Born in Zwolle, he joined the school of the *Brethren of the Common Life at Windesheim, where he taught. Following his ordination as priest (1424), he was active in the reforming of the monasteries in Germany and the Netherlands. In this he cooperated for some years with *Nicholas of Cusa.

BUSLEIDEN, JEROME (c. 1470-1517) Churchman, diplomat and humanist. A native of the southern Netherlands, he studied at Louvain and Bologna, and after his return from Italy became the leader of the governing council of Brabant (1503). *Maximilian I employed him as his emissary and showered on him ecclesiastical benefices. He also served as councillor to the young *Charles V. B. was the author of Latin poetry and letters and a patron of artists and humanists. In his will he bequeathed funds for the establishment of the *Collegium Trilingue* at Louvain, a school for the teaching of Latin, Greek and Hebrew.

H. de Vocht, *Jerome de Busleiden, Founder of the Louvain Collegium Trilingue* (1950).

BUSSI, GIOVANNI ANDREA (1417-75) Italian prelate and humanist. In 1451 he entered the service of *Nicholas V. Afterwards he served Cardinal *Nicholas of Cusa, was made a bishop, and during the final years of his life was the papal secretary. B. edited classical Latin authors, among them Livy (1469), and enriched the Vatican library with many classical manuscripts.

BUXTORF, JOHANNES (1564-1629) German scholar of the Hebrew language and rabbinic literature. The son

William Byrd, *from an engraving by Van der Gucht*

of a minister, he studied at the University of Herborn and then moved to *Basle, where he was given the chair of Hebraic Studies (1591) and where he remained until his death. B. devoted his endeavours to publishing a Hebrew *Bible with a compilation of the most important Jewish commentaries. For this purpose he obtained permission for two Jews, whom he employed, to reside in Basle. He corresponded extensively with Jewish scholars in Germany, Holland and Constantinople, wrote a Hebrew grammar textbook (1605), and several dictionaries. His attitude toward Judaism marks the beginning of a shift towards increased tolerance, after a long period of rigid discrimination. B. left a large collection of letters which are an important source on the spiritual life of his time.

BYRD, WILLIAM (1543-1623) English composer and organist. Born in Lincolnshire, he studied music with Thomas *Tallis. In 1563 he became the organist at Lincoln Cathedral and, in 1572, went to London where he was a Gentleman of the Royal Chapel. With his teacher Tallis he was awarded, in 1575, the sole right to print music sheets in England. Although his music was favoured by Queen Elizabeth I, B. preferred to live away from the court on account of his Roman Catholic faith, and resided mostly in the country. His religion notwithstanding, he wrote superb Masses and services for the *Church of England, and composed a great number of motets, madrigals and other forms of choral music. Many of his works were published during his lifetime. B. is held to be the originator of the solo song with string accompaniment. His reputation was so great that his contemporaries styled him the "Father of Music".

E. H. Fellowers, *William Byrd*, 2nd ed. (1948).

C

CABEZA DE VACA, ALVAR NUÑEZ (c. 1490-1557) Spanish explorer. Born in Jerez de la Frontera, he fought in Italy and took part in the suppression of the revolt of the **comuneros* in Spain. In 1527 he joined, as treasurer, the expedition of Panfilo de *Narváez, which landed in Florida and fell prey to Indian attacks. He returned to Mexico by raft and over land with only three other survivors, after enduring several years of captivity with the Indians of Texas (1536). Of these experiences he left a written account. He then went to Spain (1537) and, in 1540, was appointed to succeed Pedro de *Mendoza as governor of Río de la Plata and Paraguay. There he entered into a bitter feud with the powerful Domingo Martínez de Irala who, in 1545, sent him to Spain as a prisoner, charging him with exceeding his authority. He was convicted on the evidence of his enemies, imprisoned for several years, and died old and poor.
C. Hallenbeck, *Álvar Nuñez Cabeza de Vaca: The Journey and Route of the First European to Cross the Continent of North America, 1534-36* (1940; rep. 1971).

CABOT, JOHN (1450-98) Italian-English navigator. Born in Genoa, C. grew up in Venice, and acquired some experience in the sea trade of the eastern Mediterranean. During his visits to the Near East he began, like *Columbus, to think of a westward route to Asia. For this reason he went to England, where he sought the cooperation of merchants in Bristol. When news reached England that Columbus had discovered islands which were believed to be part of Asia, C. decided to repeat the voyage through a northern route, and was authorized to do so by *Henry VII. He set out of Bristol in a small ship on 2 May 1497 and, on 24 June arrived at Cape Breton Island. From there he sailed along the coasts of Newfoundland, at one point touching the American mainland. Convinced that he had discovered the northern reaches of Asia, C. hastened to return to Bristol, which he reached on 6 August, and began to gather a larger expedition. He sailed again in May 1498. He reached Greenland, but, failing to find a northwest passage, again visited Newfoundland and the coast of New England. He died shortly after his return.
C. R. Beazley, *John and Sebastian Cabot* (1898);
F. A. Ober, *John and Sebastian Cabot* (1908).

CABOT, SEBASTIAN (1476-1557) English navigator; son of John *C. He accompanied his father on his voyages. In 1512 *Ferdinand the Catholic asked him to enter the services of Spain and command an expedition to North America. C. went to Spain, but the king's death in 1516 prevented his sailing. During the next decade he was employed by England as well as Spain. His main exploration was made as *piloto mayor* of Spain in 1526. He was about to cross the Straits of Magellan on his way to Asia, but instead decided to enter the La Plata Estuary and the Paraná River, and returned to Spain only in 1530. His failure to reach Asia did not seem to harm his reputation, and after he returned to England in 1548, *Charles V still wanted his services. During the last years of his life, C. was governor of the English branch of the *Merchants Adventurers. In this capacity he was responsible for sending the expedition which, in 1553, set out to find the *northeast passage to Asia and which reached the Russian port of Archangel.
C. R. Beazley, *John and Sebastian Cabot* (1898);
F. A. Ober, *John and Sebastian Cabot* (1908).

CABRAL, PEDRO ALVARES (1460-1526) Portuguese navigator; discoverer of Brazil. After the return of Vasco da *Gama from his successful voyage to India, C. was sent there at the head of a fleet of 13 ships by *Manoel I. During his journey southward in the Atlantic, he strayed west and, on 22 April 1500, landed on the coast of Brazil, not far from present-day Salvador. Before continuing his voyage to India he took possession of the territory in the name of his king, and sent a vessel back to Portugal to announce the discovery. It is still not clear whether C. knew about Brazil and went there intentionally, or whether his discovery was accidental. He lost four of his ships in storms on his way to India, but reached Calicut. His expedition was the beginning of regular trade between Portugal and India.
E. Metzner Leone, *Pedro Alvares Cabral* (1968).

CADAMOSTO, ALVISE (1432-88) Italian navigator in the service of Portugal. A native of *Venice, he sailed in 1454 to Flanders, but instead was persuaded to remain in Portugal, and joined an expedition to the coast of Senegal. In 1456 he sailed again, together with the Genoese Antoniotto Uso di Mare, and reached the islands of Cape Verde and the River Gambia. Returning to Portugal, he remained there until 1463, engaging chiefly in commerce. He then returned to Venice where he wrote the *Navigazioni*, a description of Portuguese voyages, which was published in 1507. C. was one of the foremost navigators employed by Prince *Henry the Navigator.

CADE'S REBELLION (1450) A revolt in southeastern England led by Jack Cade, a former soldier-adventurer and the son-in-law of a small landowner in Kent. The rebels, numbering over 20,000, protested against material oppression, government incompetence and the defeats in France. They also demanded the restoration of Duke Richard of *York. They occupied London for three days (2-5 July 1450), but following a bloody clash with the inhabitants, accepted a pardon and dispersed. Cade himself was afterwards captured and killed.

CAJETAN (Tommaso de Vio; 1469-1534) Cardinal, theologian and general of the Dominican order (1508-18). Dubbed C. after his birthplace Gaeta, he entered the Dominican order in 1484 and, between 1493 and 1507, taught at the universities of Padua, Pavia and Rome. In 1511 he defended the principle of papal supremacy at the Council of Pisa and, in 1517, was created cardinal by *Leo X. He was sent as a papal legate to Germany, where he argued theological matters with *Luther at Augsburg (1518), and worked for the election of *Charles V as emperor (1519). In 1522 he strongly supported the election of the reformist *Adrian VI, but during the reign of *Clement VII lost much of his former influence. A prolific writer on theological matters, C. is considered the reviver of Thomistic philosophy in the 16th century. He also wrote biblical exegeses.

CALCAR, STEPHEN DE (1499-c. 1546) Dutch painter and engraver. A native of the upper valley of the Rhine, he is believed to have eloped with a young woman and gone to Venice, where he became a pupil of *Titian. His works came to resemble Titian's to such an extent that it was hard to distinguish between master and pupil. C. later spent several years at Naples and died there. His most renowned works were the beautiful anatomical figures which he contributed to *Vesalius' *De humanis corporis fabrica* (1543).

CALEPINO, AMBROGIO (1435-1511) Italian lexicographer. Born in Calepio, near Bergamo, he was the author of a Latin-Italian dictionary, the *Cornucopiae*, first published in 1502. The work, which was several times revised and enlarged, eventually became a multi-lingual dictionary. It became so well known that in Italy the word *calepino* came to signify dictionary. The 1590 edition included eleven languages: Latin, Hebrew, Greek, French, Italian, German, Flemish, Spanish, Polish, Hungarian and English.

CALIXTUS III (1378-1458) Pope from 1455 to 1458. Born Alonso Borgia in Jativa near Valencia, Spain, he entered the services of the king of Aragon, and in 1429 became bishop of Valencia. His successful mediation between *Alfonso V and the papacy brought him a cardinalship in 1444, and led to his succeeding *Nicholas V to the papal throne. As pope, C. did not hesitate to clash with his former benefactor, Alfonso V of Aragon, who had by then become king of Naples too, and refused to recognize his illegitimate son *Ferrante. He promoted the interests of his own family, in particular his young nephew Rodrigo Borgia, the future *Alexander VI, whom he made cardinal.

CALMO, ANDREA (1510-71) Italian actor and playwright. Born in Venice, he won fame with his comedies, some of which, e.g., *Rodiana* (1540) and *Travaglia* (1546), were based on classical models; others, such as *La Spagnola* (1549) and *Saltuzza* (1551), were original and in a realistic manner. C. had some of his characters express themselves in elegant language, but made others use popular north Italian dialects. His collection of letters in versified dialect, dealing with diverse subjects, became immensely popular. A follower of *Ruzzante, he was a forerunner of the *Commedia dell'Arte.

CALVAERT, DENYS (c. 1540-1619) Flemish-Italian artist, called also Dionisio Fiammingo. A native of Antwerp, he went to Italy and, in 1572, opened in Bologna a painting *academy that became very influential. Among his famous pupils were *Domenichino and Guido *Reni.

CALVIN, JOHN (1509-64) French theologian and religious leader, the second great leader of the *Reformation, after *Luther. Born in Noyon, northeast of Paris, to a father who was an apostolic notary, he was destined for an ecclesiastical career, and at eleven was given a small church benefice and received the tonsure. In 1523 he was sent to study theology in Paris. Although not ordained, he seemed to be on the way to become a priest, but in 1528, at his father's suggestion, began to study law at Orleans. Moving to Bourges (1529), where he heard lectures by *Alciati, C. became influenced by Protestant ideas at a local circle of students which was dominated by the German Melchior *Wolmar. However, he did not yet break with Roman Catholicism, and his first published work, a Latin commentary of Seneca's *De clementia* (1532), which displayed a great deal of humanist erudition, had little to do with the religious issue.

C.'s espousal of the Reformation took place late in 1533 while he was on a visit to Paris. Forced to flee persecution, he found refuge in Angoulême, where he met the old *Lefèvre d'Etaples. He then returned to Noyon (1534), resigned his benefices and was briefly imprisoned. The Affair of the *Placards, which signalled a wider wave of persecution, and in which his brother was executed, forced him to go to *Basle (1535). It was there that the first edition of his *Christianae religionis institutio* (*Institutes of the Christian Religion*) first appeared (March 1536). Later this exposition of C.'s religious doctrine was twice enlarged, and masterfully translated into French by the author (1541; 1560). But already in its first form it revealed a superb quality of intellectual clarity and systematic thought. Proceeding from the assumption that mankind was in a state of wickedness, the consequence of Adam's fall, and that man had no free will of his own, C. concluded that salvation was predestined and the result of God's grace alone. The *Institutes* reduced the sacraments to two, baptism and the Lord's supper, and gave them a largely symbolic meaning. While denying that transubstantiation took place at the Eucharist, C. contended that Christ was spiritually present and communicated his virtue to the faithful.

While passing through *Geneva in July 1536, C. accepted the invitation of Guillaume *Farel and stayed on as a preacher and professor of theology. He soon be-

Calvin

came the leading personality in the city, and persuaded the Council of government to adopt severe regulations with regard to admission to the Lord's supper. But his attempt to establish control over morals aroused opposition and, in 1538, he was ordered to leave. For the next three years he headed a French congregation at *Strassburg, where he befriended *Bucer. There he wrote a number of theological tracts and his famous reply to Cardinal *Sadoleto (1539), in which he defended the Reformation. In 1541 he represented Strassburg at the Diet of Regensburg, where he met *Melanchthon. That year he married Idelette de Bure, a widow with three children, who died eight years later.

A change of government in Geneva brought C. an invitation to return (September 1541). This time his plans for a theocratic regime were carried through, and by a series of periodically-approved ordinances, he established a church government that increasingly tightened the supervision over the private lives of the citizens. C.'s complicated system, which included four classes of officers – pastors, doctors, elders and deacons – was assisted by laymen informers who admonished and reported the sinners, and by the Consistory, a tribunal of morals, which wielded the right of excommunication. Resistance to this system periodically flared up. In addition to many prosecutions of persons convicted for heresy, adultery and blasphemy, in which confession was frequently extorted by torture, there was a good number of cases which ended with death sentences and public executions, notably the burning of *Servetus (1553). Other forms of punishment were public recantation and exile. Nevertheless, in the last ten years of his life, C. became the supreme authority in Geneva, and imposed a moralistic code of behaviour, which prohibited loud singing and dancing, indecent dress and drunkenness.

At the same time, C. made Geneva the most important European Protestant centre of his time. He gave shelter to English refugees and inspired the spreading of his doctrines in France and the Netherlands. He continuously preached and wrote and, in 1559, founded the Geneva Theological Academy, which was headed by his closest supporter, Theodore *Beza. A strong personality, leading a simple and austere life, C. emphasized the values of discipline, hard work, thrift and strict morality. Carried to the New World by the English *Puritans, his teachings had a bearing on the consolidation of the national ethics of the mightiest modern capitalistic state. But from the vantage point of the present, and despite his many qualities as theologian, educator and leader of a religious community, C. seems more relevant to the past century than to our own.

W. F. Graham, *Calvin and his City* (1970);
J. Cadier, *The Man God Mastered; A New Biography of John Calvin* (1960);
F. Wendel, *Calvin* (1963).

CAMBIASO, LUCA (1527-85) Italian painter. Born near Genoa, he became famous as a superb draftsman, and was given many commissions to decorate Genoese palaces. His murals are in a monumental style showing the influence of *Michelangelo, but later changed to *Mannerist elegance. In 1583 he left Genoa for Spain at the invitation of *Philip II, and died at the *Escorial while completing a fresco on a church ceiling. C. is especially remembered for his hundreds of drawings, in which he frequently utilized geometrical forms, making some of them look like 20th-century Cubist experiments.

CAMBRAI, LEAGUE OF An alliance signed at C. on 10 December 1508 between *Louis XII of France and Emperor *Maximilian I, and joined by the kings of England and Hungary, Pope *Julius II and *Ferdinand of Aragon. Officially the League was designed to campaign against the *Ottoman Turks, but in reality it aimed against *Venice, which was to be divested of territories in northern and southern Italy. However, following an initial victory of the French over the Venetians, the allies turned against each other and the League was dissolved (1510).

CAMBRAI, PEACE OF A treaty, sometimes referred to as the *Paix des Dames*, signed on 3 August 1529 between *Louise of Savoy, representing her son *Francis I, and *Margaret of Austria, acting for her nephew *Charles V. By the terms of the peace, Francis was to marry the Emperor's sister, Eleanor, and renounce his claims to Flanders, Artois and Naples. However, he retained the French possession of Burgundy. As a result of the treaty the French princes, held as hostages by *Charles V, were released.

CAMDEN, WILLIAM (1551-1623) English antiquarian and promoter of historical studies. Born in London, C. studied at Oxford and, in 1575, became second master of Westminster School; he became headmaster in 1593. In his spare time C. pursued his antiquarian studies, the most important outcome of which was *Britannia*, a handbook on the chronology and geography of England, Scotland and Ireland. This storehouse of information was first published in 1586 and reached its ninth edition in 1594. In a second work, *Annals of English and Irish History in the Reign of Elizabeth* (1615), C. treated politics as well as ecclesiastical questions, but espoused a conservative attitude in support of the monarchy and the established church. A year before his death, he provided the means for creating a lectureship in history at Oxford, and appointed the first occupant of the post.

F. Smith Fussner, *The Historical Revolution; English Historical Writing and Thought, 1580-1640* (1962), 230-53.

CAMERARIUS, JOACHIM (1500-74) German classical scholar. A native of Bamberg, he became a close friend of *Melanchthon's. In 1526 he became professor of classical studies at *Nuremberg. In 1530 he was a deputy to the Diet of *Augsburg, taking part in the writing of the Confession, and in 1535 moved to Tübingen. From 1541 until his death he taught at Leipzig. C. edited the works of many Greek authors, among them Homer, Sophocles, Thucydides, Herodotus, Ptolemy, Aristotle and Galen. He also translated from Greek into Latin, and wrote a biography of his friend Melanchthon.

CAMILLO DE LELLIS, ST. (1550-1614) Italian founder of the "Fathers of a Good Death", also known as "Camillians". A former soldier in the Venetian army, he suffered from the consequences of a wound in his thigh. In 1575 he experienced religious conversion and decided to devote his life to the nursing of the sick and the dying. In 1584 he was ordained and, in 1586, *Sixtus V approved his congregation, which *Gregory XIV later raised to the status of an order. C. introduced many reforms in the field of nursing the sick and in giving spiritual aid to the dying. By the time he died the order had spread to 16 Italian towns. Shortly afterwards the Camillians also expanded to other European countries.

CAMÕES, LUIS VAZ DE (1524-80) Portuguese poet; author of *Os Lusiadas*, considered the national epic poem of Portugal. Born in Lisbon, he was educated at the University of Coimbra and, in 1547, went with the Portuguese forces to North Africa, where he lost an eye in battle. In 1553 he sailed to India and remained there for almost 17 years. He resided mainly in Goa, but went on expeditions to other Portuguese possessions in the East, and also visited China. It was during his service in Asia that he began to compose his long poem, which he brought back with him and published in 1572. The last years of his life were spent in Lisbon, maintained by a royal pension.

Os Lusiadas describes the heroic period in the history of the Portuguese people, namely the exploration of the coasts of *Africa and the discovery of the route to India by Vasco da *Gama. But although C. glorified the achievements of his people in terms of a victory of Christianity over paganism, he pictured the ocean which they sailed as ruled by Greek gods. This underscores his tendency to use classical allusion and construction. It also facilitated his intention to portray modern heroes as superior to the ancient. C. also wrote dramatic works and sonnets, which were collected and published after his death.

L. de Camões, *The Lusiads*, trans. by W. C. Atkinson (1953);
A. F. Bell, *Luis de Camões* (1923);
R. Bismut, *La lyrique de Camões* (1970).

CAMPAGNOLA, DOMENICO (c. 1500-1562) Italian painter. Born in Padua, he was adopted by the Paduan engraver Giulio Campagnola (1482-1514), whose name he took. Later he was influenced by *Titian, whom he assisted in several works. Aside from his *frescoes in Padua, he is known for his series of exquisite drawings and engravings.

CAMPANELLA, TOMMASO (1568-1639) Italian philosopher. Born in Calabria, he joined the Dominican order in Naples, but left when his ideas brought him into conflict with his superiors. In 1599, being back in Calabria, he was imprisoned by the Spanish authorities on suspicion of conspirational activities. Although he was allowed certain freedoms, he did not gain complete liberty until 1629. In 1634 he went to France, where he was favourably received by Richelieu. As a philosopher C. belonged to the individualistic current which held that perception and personal consciousness were the true foundations of man's faith and moral outlook. This basic thought brought him into disfavour in ecclesiastical circles, although he never challenged the Church on specific dogmas. C. is best known for his contributions in the realm of political thought. In his *Civitas solis* (1623) he pictured an ideal communist state where property, as well as wives, were to be shared in a tightly supervised system.

H. Morley, ed., *Ideal Commonwealths* (1901; rep. 1968).

CAMPEGGIO, LORENZO (1464-1539) Italian cardinal. Of a noble Bolognese family, C. became a prominent authority on civil and canon law. Although he entered the service of the Church in middle age (1510), he was immediately given important diplomatic assignments and created cardinal in 1517. His first legation to England was in 1518, and concerned church reform and soliciting *Henry VIII's aid in a *crusade against the Turks. In 1528 he went to England again, this time to deal with the king's request to divorce *Catherine of Aragon. C.'s policy, dictated by the uneasy political circumstances of the papacy, was to prolong the matter without passing sentence. By the time he left England, late in 1529, still undecided, relations between Henry VIII and Rome were substantially strained. C. continued as a prominent member of the Church's hierarchy until his death. His son, born before he had joined the Church, also became a cardinal.

CAMPIN, ROBERT (c. 1378-1444) Flemish painter. About 1406 he settled in Tournai, where he eventually became head of the painters' guild (1423) and took an active part in the life of the community. The history of his thriving workshop is well documented; from 1427 to 1432 it included C.'s most famous pupil, Roger van der *Weyden. However, there are no works that are directly attributed to C. Of late, it has become customary to

Portrait of a Man *by Campin*

ascribe to him the considerable *oeuvre* formerly believed to have been done by a certain Master of Flémalle. It includes the triptych of the *Annunciation* (the *Mérode Altar*), the *Were Altar* of 1438, and a few other paintings. The works are characterized by a somewhat plebeian, but extremely realistic setting and atmosphere.
E. Panofsky, *Early Netherlandish Painting* (1954).

CAMPION, EDMUND (1540-81) English *Jesuit. The brilliant son of a London bookseller, he was educated at Oxford and, in 1569, ordained deacon in the *Church of England. In 1571, however, he joined William *Allen at Douai, and in 1573 entered the Jesuit order in *Rome. Following several years in Bohemia, he undertook, together with Robert Parsons, the first Jesuit mission to England (1580). They preached successfully in London, causing much apprehension, which resulted in the passing of repressive laws against the sheltering Roman Catholic missionaries. C. was arrested in July 1581. Rejecting an offer to save himself by renouncing his faith, he was tortured and executed.
E. Waugh, *Edmund Campion* (1935).

CAMPION, THOMAS (1576-1620) English poet and musician. A physician by profession, C.'s literary originality was revealed in his *A Booke of Ayres, Set Foorth to be Sung to the Lute, Orpherian and Base Violl* (1601), *Two Bookes of Ayres* (*c*. 1613), and *The Third and Fourth Booke of Ayres* (*c*. 1617), where the lyrics were accompanied by music composed by the author. Earlier C. had argued for the use of classical metres in

Madonna and Child *by Robert Campin*

English verse, in his *Observations in the Art of English Poesie* (1602), to which Samuel *Daniel published a response. He also wrote a textbook on music.

CANISIUS, ST. PETER (1521-97) German *Jesuit theologian; leader of the Catholic *Counter Reformation in Germany. C. studied in *Cologne and was the first German to join the new Jesuit order (1543). In 1549, *Loyola sent him to Ingolstadt, which he made into a centre of anti-Protestant teaching. He later moved to Austria, Bohemia and Poland. In 1556 he became the Jesuit provincial of Upper Germany, and shortly afterwards papal legate to Germany, charged with implementing the decisions of the Council of *Trent. C. composed the very successful *Summa Doctrinae Christianae* (1554), a catechism containing 211 questions-and-answers on the Roman Catholic faith. He also published theological polemical works, and is considered the most important figure of the Catholic resurgence in southern Germany during the latter part of the 16th century. In 1925 he was canonized and declared Doctor of the Church.

J. Brodrick, *Saint Peter Canisius* (1935).

CANO, MELCHOR (1525-60) Spanish theologian. A member of the Dominican order, he studied at the university of Salamanca, where he began to lecture on theology at a very early age. His intellectual abilities were so well appreciated that in 1545 he assisted at the opening session of the Council of *Trent. He was later made bishop and advised *Philip II about church matters and on his relations with Rome. His most important work, *De locis theologicis* (1562), is an attempt to treat the essential Catholic doctrines in a manner compatible with humanist learning, freed from the cumbersome scholastic methods.

CÃO, DIOGO A Portuguese navigator. In 1483 he went up the Zaire River and reached the Congo. He returned to Portugal, carrying with him black slaves, and in the following year (1485) went back to the Congo and established relations with its native king. The date of his death is unknown.

CAPECE, SCIPIONE (c. 1490-1551) Italian jurist and humanist. A native of Naples, he lectured on civil law, and joined the humanist circle of *Pontano's academy. In 1543 he was banished from Naples because of his association with the group of Juan de *Valdés, and spent most of his final years in Salerno. Besides works on jurisprudence, he wrote Latin poetry modelled on the classics.

CAPELLO, BIANCA (1548-87) Grand-duchess of Tuscany. Born to a prominent Venetian family, she ran away from home at 15 with a Florentine lover. In Florence she became the mistress of Francesco, the son of *Cosimo de' Medici, who then arranged to have her lover murdered. In 1574 Francesco became the grand-duke of Tuscany and, in 1579, following the death of his legal wife, he married C. The marriage was celebrated with pomp; C.'s parents made peace with their renegade daughter on this occasion, and the Venetian government gave her a title of honour. In Florence, however, the union gave rise to opposition. In 1587 the grand-duke and his wife died suddenly, within a day of each other, probably as a result of poisoning. Rumours implicated the grand-duke's brother, Cardinal Ferdinando, in their death.

P. Gauthiez, *Vie de Bianca Capello* (1929).

CAPGRAVE, JOHN (1396-1464) English chronicler. A native of Norfolk, he was educated at Oxford and then joined the Augustinian hermits. Most of his works were written at the house of his Order at Lynn. He wrote biblical commentaries and sermons, but is especially remembered for his *Chronicle of England*, in English,

Bianca Capello *by Bronzino*

which ended at 1417. The collection of lives of saints attributed to him, *Nova legenda Angliae*, was not entirely his own work. It was first printed in 1516.

CAPISTRANO, GIOVANNI DI (1386-1456) Italian friar and preacher. C. joined the Franciscan order at a mature age and became an ardent defender of orthodoxy. He served as inquisitor against heretics in Italy, and was sent as a papal legate to Bohemia, Hungary and Poland, where he vehemently combatted the *Hussites and preached against the *Jews. After the fall of *Constantinople, he was instrumental in gathering the troops which raised the Turkish siege of Belgrade.

J. Hofer, *Johannes von Capistrano* (1936).

CAPITO, WOLFGANG (1478-1541) German Protestant reformer. Educated at Freiburg, he was ordained as priest and, after living for some time in Basle, became in 1519 chaplain to the archbishop of Mainz. He was influenced by the ideas of *Erasmus on church reform and corresponded with *Luther and *Zwingli. In 1523 he came to *Strassburg and took the lead in the reform activities in this city, until he was supplanted in the leadership by *Bucer. C. was known for his moderation and his willingness to bridge over the differences of the Protestant camps. He collaborated with Bucer on the *Tetrapolitan Confession* (1530), a work that was presented to *Charles V at Augsburg in the name of four German cities, but never formally sanctioned.

J. M. Kittelson, *Wolfgang Capito; From Humanist to Reformer* (1975).

CAPITULATIONS The concessions given by the *Ottoman Turks to some European nations, conferring trading rights and privileges of extraterritorial jurisdiction. The 16th-century C. were based on precedents set by the Byzantine emperors. The first and most important were granted in 1535 to France by *Suleiman I. These included a commercial agreement and the right to appoint consuls, who could judge cases affecting French subjects according to French law. Venice was given similar privileges in 1540, England in 1583 and Holland in 1613. However, the French were recognized as representing all European subjects whose nations did not have ambassadors at Constantinople. Granted originally from a position of strength, the C. turned, in the 18th century, into a means by which the European nations further weakened the Turkish government.

CAPORALI, BARTOLOMEO (c. 1420-c. 1503) Italian painter. A native of Perugia, he was considered the greatest Umbrian painter of his time. His mature style bears a resemblance to that of *Piero della Francesca. He also illuminated manuscripts.

CAPPONI A Florentine political family which played an important role in the affairs of the Republic, both for and against the *Medici. Gino C. (*c.* 1350-1421) was a devoted supporter of the *Albizzi, but his son, Neri (1388-1457), was responsible for recalling Cosimo de' Medici from exile in 1434, and represented him on diplomatic missions. Piero Capponi (1446-96) served Lorenzo de' Medici, and became the head of the Republic in 1494 after the fall of Lorenzo's son. A certain C. wrote a history of the republic. The family gradually lost influence in the 16th century.

CAPRANICA, DOMENICO (1400-58) Italian cardinal. Educated at Padua and at the University of Bologna, he was made apostolic secretary by *Martin V and created cardinal at the tender age of 23. In 1430 *Eugenius IV deprived him of his benefices. C. then went to join the anti-papal Council of *Basle, accompanied by Enea Silvio Piccolomini – the future *Pius II – as secretary. But in 1434 he was reconciled with Eugenius V, and resumed his position as one of the most influential papal aides. He continued to wield power also under *Nicholas V and *Calixtus III.

CAPUCHINS A Roman Catholic order of friars, founded by Matteo de *Bascio around 1520. The C. represented the quest for a return to the simplicity of St. Francis, their founder having belonged to the Franciscan order before his decision to launch a new order. In 1528 *Clement VII recognized the new movement – though at first only as a congregation within the Franciscan order. The name C. is of popular origin, referring to the pointed hood worn by the friars. The C. sought to re-establish extreme austerity and poverty, to obtain their necessities by begging and live in small communities of no more than 12 friars. They dedicated themselves to preaching among the poor. They underwent a critical period, their founder eventually leaving them and returning to the Franciscans, and their third vicar, Bernardino *Ochino, becoming a Protestant in 1542. These developments almost led to the suppression of the order. But by the mid-16th century, as the tide of the *Counter Reformation rose, the C. began to prove their worth as catechizers, helping to restore the credibility of Roman Catholicism among the masses. Permission to preach, which had been suspended for a time, was restored to them, and their small congregations began to spread all over Europe. They became a fully independent order in 1619. The C. also sent missions to work among the indigenous people of America, Asia and Africa. A female order of C. nuns was founded in Naples in 1538.

Father Cuthbert, *The Capuchins* (1928; rep. 1971).

CARACCIOLI, GALEAZZO (1517-86) Italian Protestant. Of an aristocratic Neapolitan family, C. was related to the *Caraffas, through both his mother, a sister of *Paul IV, and his wife. His early links with Protestantism began in his contact with the circle of Juan de *Valdes in Naples. In 1544 he went to Germany, but after his return did not dare divulge his new faith. Finally, in 1551, he left Italy for *Geneva, leaving his wife and son behind. After his accession to the papacy his uncle, Paul IV, tried to bring him back, but to no avail.

CARACCIOLO, GIOVANNI (?-1431) Italian statesman, known as Sergianni. Belonging to an old aristocratic family of *Naples, he served King Ladislas against the house of Anjou. In 1414 he became the lover and trusted councillor of Queen *Joanna II. As grand seneschal he virtually ruled the kingdom. In 1418 he had to leave Naples because of a quarrel with Muzio Attendolo *Sforza, but returned in 1419 after Sforza had left, and regained his influence with the Queen. It was at his suggestion that the Queen adopted as heirs first *Alfonso of Aragon (1420) and later, in opposition, *René of Anjou. Gradually, however, his relations with the Queen worsened. He was assassinated by political enemies, probably with the connivance of his royal mistress.

CARADOSSO (c. 1452-1527) Italian goldsmith and medalist. He worked at Rome in 1477 but, in 1480, entered the service of the Duke of Milan, who also employed him to purchase works of art. He returned to Rome in 1505, and concentrated in his final years, in casting *medals and coins. His works are strongly inspired by classical motifs.

CARAFFA A Neapolitan family which, during the 15th and 16th centuries, took an active part in the political life of Italy and in the internal affairs of the Catholic Church. The peak of their influence was reached when Giampietro C. became pope as *Paul IV. His nephew, Cardinal Carlo C. (1518-61), who had been a military man, was made very powerful by his uncle. But the family lost its influence when *Pius IV ascended the papal throne in 1559.

CARAVAGGIO, MICHELANGELO MERISI DA (1573-1610) Italian painter. Born in a village of the same name near Milan, C. started out as a mason, but later went to Rome and became an artist. Between 1597 and 1606 he decorated and made altarpieces for a number of Roman churches; his paintings included many scenes from the New Testament. Both his subject-matter and the technique conformed well with the cultural climate of his time. His use of contrasting light and shade, his rich coloration and wealth of detail, endowed his paintings with an emotional content that corresponded to the religious ideals of the *Counter Reformation. It makes him one of the leading precursors of the *Baroque. On the other hand, his naturalist tendencies as, for example, his manner of portraying the apostles in the likeness of contemporary old labourers and peasants, gave rise to strong opposition among academic purists. But the opposition was also due to C.'s violent character, and his life in Rome was punctuated by many quarrels.

In 1606 C. stabbed a man to death during a game and had to leave Rome. He went to Naples and, in 1607, to Malta, where he was received well and commissioned

Young Bacchus *by Caravaggio*

to do works for the Order of *St. John. But in 1608 he was again involved in a bloody quarrel and fled to Sicily; a year later he was almost killed in Naples by the agents of the Order who had pursued him. He died of fever the following year, while on his way to Rome, where he was about to be pardoned for his crime.

An intrepid individual who introduced social significance into his art, C. was also a revolutionary in technique, driven by an urge to shock his public. It was only fitting that, although his work was criticized at the time, he readily found buyers for his paintings among churchmen and nobles.

R. P. Hinks, *Caravaggio; His Life, His Legend, His Works* (1953);
W. Friedlaender, *Caravaggio Studies* (1955).

CARAVEL A type of small sailing vessel of the 15th and 16th centuries which was used primarily by the people of the Iberian Peninsula and adapted to ocean voyages. Borrowing from the Arab sail and hull design, the builders of caravels introduced the three-cornered lateen sail, in place of the older European square rig, or combined the two. They also adopted high narrow poops and broad bows and increased the number of masts to three. Weighing from 50 to 100 tons, the C. was usually fully-decked, but had no raised forecastle, lacked sleeping accomodations and most other facilities. It could carry, however, some light artillery. Most discovery voyages of the early 16th century, including Columbus', were made in this type of vessel.

CARDANO, GIROLAMO (1501-76) Italian mathematician, physician and astrologer. An illegitimate son of a Milanese jurist, C. became a physician, but attained eminence as a mathematician when he published his *Practica arithmeticae generalis* (1539). In 1547 he became a professor of medicine at Pavia and, in 1551, when his prestige was at its peak, accepted invitations to Scotland, England and France. The latter part of his life, however, was full of hardships. In 1562 he came to teach in Bologna, where he was arrested on suspicion of heresy. Released, he was not allowed to teach and ended his life in Rome.

C. also wrote on astrology, natural phenomena and medicine. He possessed an unusually inquisitive mind and a non-dogmatic approach to scientific questions. His writings are replete with intelligent speculations on different subjects, but his interests spread too widely for him to become a great scientist in a particular field. His autobiography, *De vita propria*, is an extremely valuable document of its time.

O. Ore, *Cardano, the Gambling Scholar* (1965);
G. Cardano, *The Book of My Life*, Trans. by J. Stoner (1962).

CARLOS, DON (1545-68) Son of Philip II and heir to the Spanish throne. C. was Philip II's son by his first marriage, to Maria of Portugal. An unstable youth, he was unfit for the tasks of government and hated his rigid father. In January 1568 the King himself, at the head of members of his council, arrested the Prince and placed him under permanent custody. There was no real

A late 15th-century caravel; a model of Columbus' Niña

HIERONYMI CAR
DANI, PRÆSTANTISSIMI MATHE-
MATICI, PHILOSOPHI, AC MEDICI,
ARTIS MAGNÆ,
SIVE DE REGVLIS ALGEBRAICIS,
Lib. unus. Qui & totius operis de Arithmetica, quod
OPVS PERFECTVM
inscripsit, est in ordine Decimus.

HAbes in hoc libro, studiose Lector, Regulas Algebraicas (Itali, de la Cossa uocant) nouis adinuentionibus, ac demonstrationibus ab Authore ita locupletatas, ut pro pauculis antea uulgò tritis, iam septuaginta euaserint. Neque solum, ubi unus numerus alteri, aut duo uni, uerum etiam, ubi duo duobus, aut tres uni æquales fuerint, nodum explicant. Hunc aūt librum ideo seorsim edere placuit, ut hoc abstrusissimo, & planè inexhausto totius Arithmeticæ thesauro in lucem eruto, & quasi in theatro quodam omnibus ad spectandum exposito, Lectores incitarētur, ut reliquos Operis Perfecti libros, qui per Tomos edentur, tanto auidius amplectantur, ac minore fastidio perdiscant.

Titlepage of a work on mathematics by Cardano (Nuremberg, 1545)

explanation to this act, beyond the statement that it was a matter of state; and, although everyone knew of the Prince's unruly character, the King was criticized for his action by his enemies and by his own subjects. C.'s death six months later, while in confinement, caused a wave of rumours, and even open accusations charging Philip with his son's murder. The story of Philip and his son was treated by a number of modern poets and novelists.

F. W. C. Lieder, *The Don Carlos Theme* (1930).

CARLSTADT The birthplace and assumed name of the German Protestant reformer Andreas Rudolf Bodenstein (1480-1541). He studied at the University of Erfurt (1499-1503), and after a short stay in *Cologne came to *Wittenberg, where he began to teach philosophy in 1505. A firm advocate of Thomistic scholasticism, C. changed his views as a result of a visit to Rome in 1515, where he witnessed the secular character of the papal court. On his return to Wittenberg he attacked Aristotelianism and anticipated *Luther in his assertion that redemption was exclusively the work of divine grace. C. was the first opponent of *Eck in the Disputation of Leipzig (1519), until Luther himself took his place. He became recognized as the most extreme of the Wittenberg reformers, and in 1521, when Luther was hiding in Wartburg, performed the Mass service in secular cloth, giving his followers communion under both kinds into their hands. C. also abolished auricular confession, took the pictures out of churches and attacked clerical celibacy. When Luther returned to Wittenberg in March 1522, he reversed some of these reforms and C.'s leadership came to an end. In 1524 he had to leave Wittenberg, having been bitterly attacked by Luther. He was allowed to return in 1525, but subsequently left again, and passed several years in poverty. In 1530 he went to *Zurich, where he was kindly received by *Zwingli, and in 1534 became professor of theology at the University of *Basle. In the last years of his life he became more conciliatory, attempting in some instances to achieve a theological compromise with the Lutherans.

E. Hertzsch, *Karlstadts Schriften aus den Jahren 1523-25*, 2 vols. (1956-57).

CARMAGNOLA, FRANCESCO BUSSONE DA (1380-1432) Italian **condottiere*. An officer in the army of Filippo Maria *Visconti, he regained for him several cities which had broken away from the duchy of Milan. His master later deprived him of his command, and C. went on to serve the Republic of Venice (1425). In 1427 he defeated Sforza's army at Maclodio, but the Venetians began to suspect him of dealing with Sforza behind their backs. In 1431 they arrested him, had him tortured, and executed as a traitor.

CARNESECCHI, PIETRO (1508-67) Leader of the Italian current of unorthodox Catholics. Son of a Florentine merchant, connected with the *Medici, he rose rapidly at the papal court becoming in 1533 a secretary of *Clement VII. Here he first met Juan de *Valdes, whom he followed to Naples in 1536, and from whom he took the idea of *Justification by Faith. After Valdes' death, C. left Naples. In 1547 he was in France and in 1522 in Venice. Suspected of propagating Protestant ideas, he was called to Rome in 1558 and condemned for heresy, but subsequently pardoned, his case having been annulled. However, in 1566 *Cosimo de' Medici caused him to be arrested again and delivered to the Roman *Inquisition. This time C. underwent a long judicial process, condemned to death and beheaded.

CARO, ANNIBALE (1507-66) Italian author. Born near Ancona, he studied at Florence, and became the secretary of a cardinal. Subsequently he entered the service of a *Farnese, the son of *Paul III (1542). C. wrote a comedy in prose, *Gli straccioni* (1544), composed the *Rime* (1557), and earned fame for his interesting *Lettere familiari*, which he wrote in emulation of *Petrarch. His posthumously-published translation of the *Aeneid* (1581) was likewise popular. C. is also remembered for the controversy between him and the literary critic *Castelvetro, who he accused of unorthodox religious leanings.

A. Greco, *Annibale Caro* (1950).

CARON, ANTOINE (c. 1527-99) French painter. A pupil of *Primaticcio at *Fontainebleau, he developed into one of the foremost French *Mannerists. C.'s paintings have a courtly atmosphere and are characterized by their architectural background. Another group of works was politically inspired, reflecting his leanings towards the *Guise family and the *League. He was for some years in the service of *Catherine de Medicis. C. also arranged festivals and was a close friend of members of the *Pléiade. A series of his drawings were later transformed into a 28-piece tapestry.

J. Ehrmann, *Antoine Caron* (1955).

CARPACCIO, VITTORE (c. 1465-1523) Italian painter. Born in Venice, he was probably a student of the *Bellinis and was influenced by *Giorgione. His best known work, a series of large paintings depicting the legend of St. Ursula, was begun in 1490. His paintings were distinguished for their luminous colours and careful detail.

J. Lauts, *Carpaccio; Paintings and Drawings* (1962).

CARRACCI Three Bolognese painters who influenced the transition from *Mannerism to the rich style of the *Baroque. The C., Ludovico (1555-1619) and his two younger cousins, the brothers Agostino (1557-1602) and Annibale (1560-1609), founded in 1582 an academy in Bologna which became an important training centre for young artists. For several years they worked together; most of their early work is in Bologna. Later Agostino and Annibale increasingly accepted commissions elsewhere. Agostino worked with his brother in Rome and died in Parma. Annibale, who was the most influential of the three, excelled as a landscape painter and is also considered one of the earliest designers of caricatures. His greatest project was the decoration of the *Farnese palace in Rome (1595-1604). There he executed frescoes and oil paintings on classical themes and allegories. Although in other instances he followed the High Renaissance style of *Raphael, this project was an original creation and is probably the most impressive scheme of decoration of the early Baroque.

A. W. A. Boschloo, *Annibale Carracci in Bologna*, 2 vols. (1974);
J. R. Martin, *The Farnese Gallery* (1965);
D. Posner, *Annibale Carracci* (1971).

The Old Clothes Pedlar, *etching by Annibale Carracci*

CARRANZA, BARTOLOME DE (1503-76) Spanish theologian. He studied in Alcalá and Valladolid, entered the Dominican order and participated in the early sessions of the Council of *Trent. *Philip II then sent him to fight Protestantism in the Netherlands, and in 1557 made him archbishop of Toledo. In 1559, however, C. was imprisoned by the *Inquisition as a suspected Lutheran. His trial lasted practically until his death. He was brought to Rome in 1566, but the Spanish church and Philip II opposed his acquittal. A few days before his death *Gregory XIII made him concede that some of his doctrines were theologically unsound.

The Three Maries *by Annibale Carracci*

J. I. Tellechea Idiogoras, *El arzobispo Carranza y su tiempo* (1968).

CARTIER, JACQUES (1491-1557) French explorer. A native of St. Malo in Brittany, C. undertook, between 1534 and 1541, three voyages to the Northern Atlantic in search of a northwest passage to Asia. On his second voyage he penetrated the Bay of St. Lawrence, which was thus named by him, discovered the Rock of Quebec and proceeded to the site of present-day Montreal, also named by him; he designated the whole region 'Canada', a word meaning 'village' in the local Indian language. C. carried some Indians with him to France, and convinced *Francis I to furnish him with a fleet for a third voyage, with the aim of reaching the mythical rich kingdom of Saguenay. This third voyage was a fiasco, C. returning with a load of iron pyrites which only looked like gold.

J. A. Neret, *Capitaine Jacques Cartier* (1949).

CARTOGRAPHY Throughout the Middle Ages the cartographic description of the world pictured the three continents – *Europe, *Asia and *Africa – clustered together and surrounded by a circular ocean. These 'T and O' maps, as they are known, placed the Mediterranean at the joint of the 'T' and put Jerusalem in the centre of the world. These were the expression of a static view of the universe, which followed the early Greek

Cartier lands in Canada, *engraving from the Vallard Atlas (1546)*

configuration of the earth as a disc floating in an ocean, and repeated the Roman conception of the *Orbis Terrarum*. From the late 13th century, Italian navigators began to draw Portolan Charts, so called after the *portolano*, the pilot's book which listed sailing courses, ports and anchorages. Based on data gathered from practical experience, and with the aid of the recently-developed *compass, these charts of the Mediterranean and the Black Sea furnished relatively accurate information on the coastlines. They are recognized by the

The Triumph of St. George *by Carpaccio in S. Giorgio de' Schiavoni, Venice*

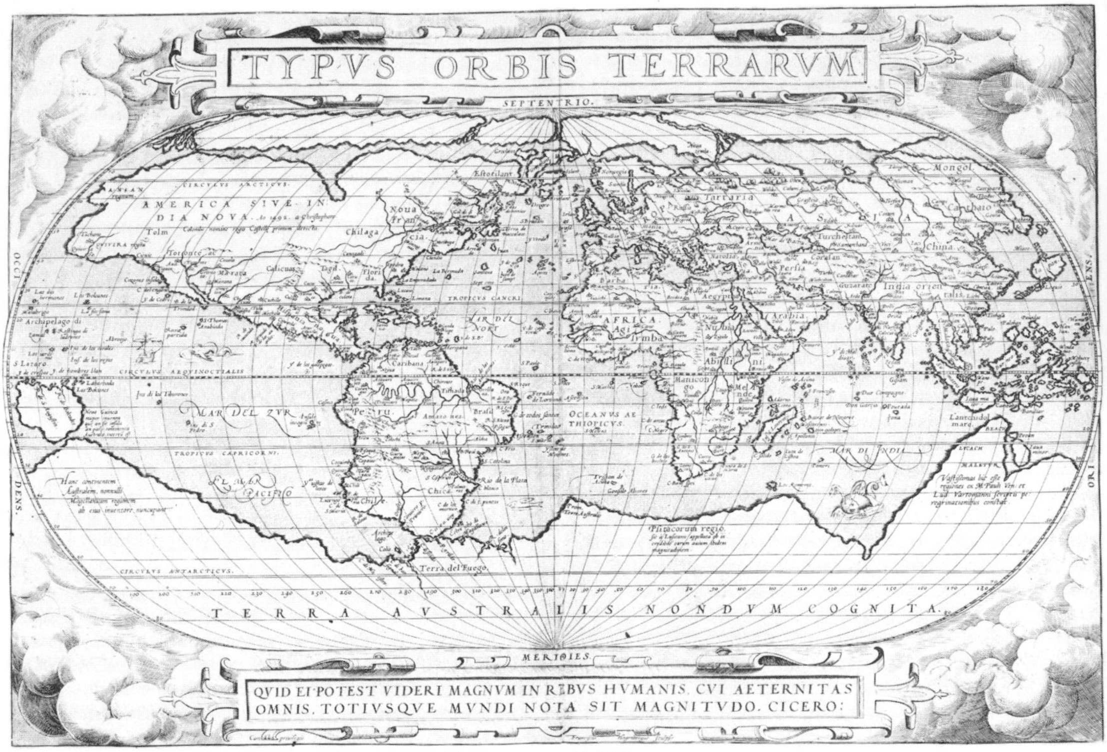

Map of the World from Ortelius' Theatrum Orbis Terrarum *(1575)*

The Eastern Mediterranean *in Mercator's map of 1569*

network of radiating lines which crisscrossed the map, showing directions from one point to another. Although the Portolan Charts covered only the Mediterranean Basin and the navigated parts of the Atlantic, they greatly promoted cartographic accuracy. This is evident in the Catalan Map of the World of 1375, which also incorporated the information supplied by contemporary travellers to the East. What is generally regarded as the last outstanding example of mediaeval cartography, the circular Venetian Map of the World by Fra Mauro (1457), added much accurate content into an otherwise obsolete conception of the shape of the earth. A Genoese map of the same year included some information drawn from the Portuguese exploration of the west coast of Africa.

The second half of the 15th century, the time of the invention of printing and of a growing interest in geographic discoveries, necessarily brought great advances in the art, science and technique of making maps. However, to understand these development one must take into account the influence of Ptolemy's *Geography*. Translated into Latin about 1407 and printed in 1477, it supplied map-makers with a model which was far superior to the mediaeval one and reestablished the concept of the spherical earth. The impact of Ptolemy was best expressed in the construction of the first terrestrial globe by Martin *Behaim. Produced in the year in which *Columbus went on his first voyage, it followed the classical geographer even where 15th-century data had already showed him to be wrong. By the end of the 16th century over 30 editions of Ptolemy had been printed, giving widespread promotion to methods of projection, more accurate techniques of surveying, systems of map graduation and the use of co-ordinates. Indeed, early 16th-century publishers used to reissue the Ptolemaic atlas and merely added new maps.

The great challenge of Renaissance C., the pictorial representation of the newly discovered territories and oceans, was appropriately first tackled by a Spaniard. Juan de la *Cosa's Portolan Chart of 1500 depicted Europe, Africa, the West Indies and portions of the South American coast with surprising accuracy. The maps of Alberto Cantino (1502) and Nicolaus de Canerio (1504) described the recent Portuguese discoveries in the East, and added more detail to the coastline of South America. In his huge map of the world of 1507, *Waldseemüller was the first to separate America and Asia by a wide ocean, but a map published by John Ruysch in 1508 still reflected *Columbus' belief that he had reached the vicinity of 'Cathay', and showed Greenland as an extension of eastern Asia. It was only after *Magellans's voyage that cartographers had a clearer idea of the magnitude of the Americas and the breadth of the Pacific. In the map of Diogo Ribeiro (1527), a Portuguese in the service of Spain, the New World was already delineated with reasonable precision, and placed in its true relationship to West and East.

The great numbers of hastily-issued maps and terrestrial globes which were produced during the first quarter of the 16th century, were designed partly to satisfy the public's wish to share in the epoch-making voyages of exploration. However, standards gradually improved. The mapping of particular regions of Europe had begun in the late 15th century, and within the next hundred years the technique of survey by triangulation was applied to map-making. Centres of C. were established and later shifted from one place to another. At the beginning of the 16th century Italian and German map-makers seemed to dominate the art, but about the end of the century the lead was taken by *Antwerp and *Amsterdam, where it was to remain for a long time. The second half of the 16th century was marked by the work of two men in particular. The first was Gerhard Kremer, better known as *Mercator, whose marine chart of the world (1569) became the forerunner of the modern map; the second, Abraham *Ortelius, was the great map publisher who was the pioneer of the modern atlas. These two were responsible for several changes: Mercator, for instance, solved the technical problems connected with the engraving of maps on copper plates, thus bringing an end to the coarsely-impressed maps printed from cheaper woodcuts. As well as being more accurate, late 16th-century maps were also pleasing to the eye. They were expertly coloured, adopted the ornamental *cartouche* in a corner of the map, and enlivened the cartographic data with pictures of sailing ships, sea monsters, images of the inhabitants of faraway lands, and other fanciful details. The ultimate product of Renaissance C. was a map which combined scientific accuracy with a feeling for art and fantasy.

L. Bagrow, *History of Cartography*, reissued and enlarged by R. A. Skelton (1964);
C. Bricker and R. V. Tooley, *A History of Cartography: 2500 years of Maps and Mapmakers* (1969);
W. W. Ristow and C. E. Egear, *A Guide to Historical Cartography* (1970);
R. A. Skelton, *Decorative Printed Maps of the 15th to 18th Centuries* (1952).

CARTWRIGHT, THOMAS (1535-1603) English leader of the *Presbyterian *Puritans. Having been forced to leave Cambridge during the reign of *Mary Tudor, C. was able to return to his theological studies after the accession of *Elizabeth I. He remained in Cambridge as a lecturer and became a well-known controversialist and a critic of the episcopalian structure of the *Church of England. In 1571 John *Whitgift, the future archbishop of Canterbury, forced him out of Cambridge. C. then visited *Geneva and, upon returning to England in 1572, became involved in the publication of the **Admonition to Parliament*. To avoid arrest, he again went to the Continent, and became the minister of English exiles in Antwerp. He returned to London in 1584 and was twice imprisoned, but released thanks to the intercession of highly placed supporters. In his writings C. advocated a church made up of self-governing consistories, headed by elected ministers and elders. While this plan broke with the established structure, it did not go so far as the extreme form of Puritanism advocated by the *Barrowists and *Brownists.

A. F. Scott Pearson, *Thomas Cartwright and Elizabethan Puritanism* (1925).

CARVAJAL, JUAN (c. 1400-1469) Spanish cardinal. Born in Trujillo, Estremadura, he is known to have studied canon and civil law. In 1440 he was made governor of the city of Rome, and shortly afterwards went on the first of his numerous diplomatic missions to Germany. Pope *Eugenius IV, whom he did a great service by rallying the German princes to the papal side against the Council of *Basle, created him cardinal in

1446. In 1455 he went with Giovanni *Capistrano to Hungary to preach a *crusade against the *Ottoman Turks, returning to Rome only in 1461. C. enjoyed a great reputation for his integrity and tireless efforts on behalf of the Church. His last legation was to Venice (1466), which he attempted to mobilize for a crusade. He left in manuscript a description of his missions and treaties in defence of the papacy.

CASA DA INDIA The official establishment created by the Portuguese government to deal with the commerce of *India and the Far East. It grew out of the *Casa da Guiné e Mina*, a smaller establishment that had supervised the commerce with *Africa, but grew tremendously following Vasco da *Gama's return from Calicut. It was through the C.d.I. that imposts were paid to the government, ships inspected and sails certified. At a later date it employed a huge staff and dealt with many foreign merchants, mainly from the Netherlands, who took part in the European end of the oriental spice commerce.

CASA DE CONTRATACION The earliest Spanish institution created in 1503 to regulate and govern trade with America. The C.d.C. was located in *Seville until 1718. All ships carrying goods and persons to and from America had to be inspected and pay the appropriate taxes. The C.d.C. received the 'royal fifth', the Crown's share of the precious metals mined in America. It also established a court of law to deal with commercial cases.

H. and P. Chaunu, *Seville et l'Antlantique*, 8 vols. (1955);

C. H. Haring, *Trade and Navigation between Spain and the Indies in the Time of the Hapsburgs* (1918).

CASAUBON, ISAAC (1559-1614) French classical scholar. Born to a *Huguenot father in *Geneva, he returned to that city in 1578, remaining there for 18 years as a professor of Greek. In 1586 he married the daughter of the printer Henry *Estienne. In 1596, he moved to Montpellier, where there was a great interest in the classics, and, in 1599, accepted the invitation of *Henry IV and went to Paris. In 1604 he became the sub-librarian of the royal library. After the assassination of the King (1610), C. decided, because of his religious views, to leave France. He came to England, where he was supported by *James I during the last years of his life. C.'s numerous works in the field of classical studies included editions of Suetonius, Polybius, and a complete edition of Aristotle. He was also involved in religious polemics, and in 1614 published a refutation of *Baronius' annals.

M. Pattison, *Isaac Casaubon* (1892);

L. J. Nazelle, *Isaac Casaubon* (1897; rep. 1970).

CASIMIR IV (1427-92) King of Poland. Crowned at Cracow in 1447, C. reigned for 45 years, during which he successfully conserved the stormy Polish-Lithuanian union. He also involved himself in the affairs of Prussia, *Bohemia and *Hungary. In 1453 the Prussian nobility and cities asked for his help against the government of the *Teutonic Knights. This led to a 13-year war, which came to an end only in 1466 with the second Peace of Thorn. Under the terms of the treaty, the knights recognized C. as their suzerain and furnished Poland with an outlet to the Baltic Sea. After the death of *George of Podebrady, in 1471, C. quarrelled with *Matthias Corvinus of Hungary over the crown of Bohemia. By 1478 he had secured Bohemia for his son *Ladislas. Two years before his death the influence of Poland reached an apex, when the Magyar nobility elected Ladislas king of Hungary. During his long reign the gentry, or *szlachta*, acquired important privileges, while the power of the Polish magnates was considerably reduced.

CASSANDER, GEORG (1513-66) German theologian. Born near *Bruges, he studied at Louvain, and from about 1549 lived and taught at Cologne. A prolific writer, he tried to minimize the differences between Roman Catholics and Protestants, arguing that old abuses should be corrected, rather than be used as reasons for division. His principal works, published in the last years of his life, were immediately criticized by both camps, but in 1564 Emperor *Ferdinand I consulted him about a possible theological basis for an attempted reunion.

CASTAGNO, ANDREA DEL (1423-57) Italian painter. His earliest known artistic activity are some *frescoes he did in Venice in 1442, but most of his work was done in Florence. C. continued the realistic tradition of *Masaccio. He was a somewhat deficient colourist but a

Young David *by Andrea del Castagno*

superb draughtsman, as may be seen in his *Last Supper*. In later years he was especially influenced by the sculptor *Donatello. His frescoes of *Famous Men and Women* is a series of single figures of deliberate statuesque qualities.
A. M. Fortuna, *Andrea del Castagno* (1957).

CASTANHEDA, FERNÃO LOPES DE (?-1559) Portuguese historian. The illegitimate son of a royal administrator, he accompanied his father to *India in 1528 and served in Goa and the *Moluccas. Upon his return (1538), C. began to collect data for his great history, which was based on both written and oral sources. The first book of his *Historia do descobrimento e conquista da India pelos portugueses* appeared in 1551; six more volumes were published in his lifetime and three more posthumously. The work was soon translated into the major European languages.

CASTELLIO, SEBASTIANUS (1515-63) French reformer and advocate of religious toleration. Born near *Geneva, C. met *Calvin in 1540 in *Strassburg, and accompanied him to Geneva. Disagreement over doctrinal matters soon strained their relations, and in 1544 C. left for *Basle, where he lived in poverty until his nomination to the chair of Greek language (1552). He produced a number of works, including a complete French translation of the Bible, and a Latin Bible with critical annotations (1551). In 1554 he published *De hereticis*, a criticism of the burning of *Servetus by Calvin, and a plea for religious tolerance and mutual understanding.
S. Zweig, *The Right to Heresy; Castellio Against Calvin* (1936).

CASTELLO, GIAMBATTISTA (c. 1509-1569) Italian architect, known as Bergamasco. He began his career as a painter at Genoa, where he befriended Luca *Cambiaso, but later turned to architecture. Basically practitioner of the High Renaissance style of classical serenity, he designed a number of palaces and churches, including S. Matteo, a church in the Gothic style, which he completed in 1554. In 1567 he went to Spain at the invitation of *Philip II, but died before he accomplished much in that country.

CASTELNAU, MICHEL DE (1520-91) French diplomat, author and soldier. Born to a noble family, C. first embarked on a soldier's career, but after some years of service was assigned diplomatic duties. His first notable success was an agreement with *Elizabeth I for the continued occupation of Calais by the French (1559), which cleared the way for the general settlement of *Cateau-Cambresis. He also tried, in vain, to reconcile Elizabeth I with *Mary Queen of Scots, who had returned to Scotland. In 1562 he went back to France, where he participated on the Catholic side in the early phases of the religious wars. Following several diplomatic missions on the Continent, C. went back to England in 1574 and remained for ten years. This time he tried to cement an alliance with England by proposing a suitable French match for the Queen, but Elizabeth's tactics of deliberate procrastination undermined his efforts. In the last years of his life, he was entrusted with a military command by *Henry IV. C. wrote his *Memoires* on the years 1559-70, which were published after his death.
G. Hubault, *Michel de Castelnau ambassadeur en Angleterre* (1856; rep. 1970).

CASTELVETRO, LUDOVICO (1505-71) Italian poet and theorist of literature. A native of Modena, where he spent most of his life, he is believed to be the author of a comedy, *Gli ingannati*, which was produced in 1531. Other works by him include commentaries on the poetry of *Dante and *Petrarch, and on works of *Bembo's. Following a fierce controversy with Annibale *Caro, he was accused of Lutheran leanings and, in 1560, left Modena in order to escape torture. He spent the rest of his life in exile. Shortly before his death he published in Vienna a translation of Aristotle's *Poetics*, to which he added his own commentary. This work came to have a considerable impact on French literature. C. argued that the poet should aim at giving pleasure to the masses, although not without gaining fame for himself.
H. B. Charlton, *Castelvetro's Theory of Poetry* (1913).

CASTIGLIONE, BALDASSARE (1478-1529) Italian author. Born to a prominent family in Mantua, C. entered, in 1496, the services of Duke *Ludovico Moro of Milan. Following the latter's fall, C. moved on to Urbino (1504), serving as an adviser and diplomatic emissary of Duke Guidobaldo and his successor. In 1513, still in the service of the dukes of Urbino, he went to Rome, where he was in close contact with the papal court. After the death of his wife, he decided to be ordained and, in 1524, was sent by *Clement VII to Spain as a papal legate. Although he worked hard to smooth relations between the Pope and *Charles V, it was during his mission that the imperial forces sacked Rome. He died in Toledo, Spain.

C. produced several minor works, but is primarily known for *Il cortegiano*, a work which dealt with the correct manners of the courtier. It was composed when he was serving in Urbino, but published only in 1528. The book was favourably received at the time, and remains one of the foremost literary documents of the Renaissance. The work reflects the form, style and ideals of personal relations in the Italian courts. It also treated the subject of the status of women with sympathy.
B. Castiglione, *The Book of the Courtier* (1944);
R. Roeder, *The Men of the Renaissance; Four Lawgivers: Savonarola; Machiavelli, Castiglione, Aretino* (1958).

CASTILLEJO, CRISTOBAL DE (c. 1490-1550) Spanish author. A native of Ciudad Rodrigo, he became, *c.* 1506, an aide to *Ferdinand, the brother of *Charles V and future emperor who was educated in Spain. Afterwards, C. was for a number of years a Cistercian monk but, following his master's assumption of the government of Austria, joined him in Vienna, where he died. C. championed the old tradition of poetry, although he himself introduced much of the new style, which he was reluctant to admit. His best-known work was an attack on "those Spanish poets who write Italian verses", aimed especially against *Boscán and *Garcilaso. He also wrote treatises on moral and religious themes. His *Dialogo de mujeres* (1544) contained a satire on women, while his *Aula de cortesanos* on court life, displayed an attitude in which mediaeval and Renaissance notions were mixed.
C. L. Nicolay, *The Life and Work of Cristobal de Castillejo* (1910).

CASTRO, GUILLEN DE (1569-1631) Spanish playwright. The scion of a noble family of Valencia, he began to write in his native town and became famous locally. However, it was only after he returned from a long period of military and administrative service in *Naples (1606-16) and settled in Madrid (1618), that he acquired a national reputation. His best plays were inspired by old national legends and ballads. He also dramatized the works of *Cervantes, and was the first to adapt parts of *Don Quixote* for the theatre. Other plays dealt with classical mythological subjects. C.'s most successful work, *Las mocedades del Cid*, transferred to the stage a story of love and vengeance from the life of the mediaeval national hero. An intimate friend of *Lope de Vega, his collected plays were published in two volumes (1618-25).

Las mocedades del Cid, Prologo y notas de Idelfonso Manuel Gil (1964).

CATEAU-CAMBRÉSIS, TREATY OF (1-3 April 1559) A series of agreements concluded between Spain, France and England, ending over 50 years of the *Habsburg-*Valois struggle in Europe. The treaty reaffirmed the Spanish possession of Franche-Comté and left Spain in control of the duchy of *Milan and the kingdom of *Naples, ensuring her domination of Italy. *Flanders remained part of the Spanish Netherlands, but *Philip II renounced his claim to *Burgundy. France restored *Savoy and Piedmont to their rulers, but was to retain Calais, an English possession which had been captured by the duke of *Guise in 1558, for eight years. England, which had been Spain's ally in the last war, and France agreed to abstain from intervening in Scotland. The treaty included a marriage between Philip II and the young daughter of *Henry II of France, and the two monarchs agreed to combat heresy at home.

CATENA, VINCENZO (c. 1480-1531) Italian painter. Born to a wealthy Venetian family, he was given a humanist education, but gradually turned to painting and befriended *Giorgione. His early works are in a stiff archaic style, but those made after 1510 are softer, showing the influence of Giovanni *Bellini, Giorgione and *Titian. Though not a great master, C. eventually achieved high technical ability, a feeling for light and colour and stylized grace. His masterpiece is the *Martyrdom of St. Christina* (1520) at S. Maria Materdomini, Venice.

G. Robertson, *Vincenzo Catena* (1954).

CATHERINE DE MÉDICIS (1519-89) Queen of France; wife of one French king and mother of three, she was a dominant figure in French politics for almost 20 years. A daughter of Lorenzo II de' Medici, she was orphaned at an early age and was educated in a convent. Her marriage at 14 to the future *Henry II (1533) came as a result of a political manoeuvre between *Clement VII and *Francis I. During her husband's reign C. did not take part in politics. She bore him nine children. She also kept in the background during the one-year reign of her son *Francis II (1559-60). However, with the accession of her second son, the ten-year old *Charles IX (1560-74), she became regent of France, and retained her hold of the government even after the king attained maturity. C. pursued a moderate policy at the beginning, backing the conciliatory Michel de *L'Hôpital. Her attempt to keep a delicate balance in French religious life was evident in the Edict of January (1562), which, for the first time, gave the *Huguenots a legal recognition, allowing them to gather for prayer outside walled cities. But this policy failed with the massacre of Vassy (1562), which opened the first of the *Religious Wars. Caught between the two warring parties, C. adopted an opportunistic policy aimed at preserving her own position and that of her children. In 1567, following the attempt of the Huguenots to capture the King at Meaux, she went over to the Catholic side, but, in 1570, when she suspected the *Guises of dealing with *Philip II of Spain, she issued the Edict of St. Germain, which again granted the Huguenots freedom of worship. Then came her clash with the Huguenot leader *Coligny, who had returned to the court, and which she tried to solve by

Catherine de Médicis

arranging his assassination. When this failed, she entered into a conspiracy with the Guises, the outcome of which was the Massacre of *St. Bartholomew (August 1572). This was, without doubt, a political blunder, since it eliminated the advantage C. had as a third party, representing royal authority. She continued to be involved in politics during the reign of her third son, *Henry III (1574-89), who, in his turn, contributed political mistakes of his own. She died a few months before his assassination, which ended the rule of the house of *Valois and thus destroyed the goals which C. had striven for.

J. E. Neale, *The Age of Catherine de Medici* (1943);
N. M. Sutherland, *Catherine de Medici and the Ancien Regime* (1966);
P. Van Dyke, *Catherine de Medici*, 2 vols. (1927).

CATHERINE DE' RICCI (1522-90) Italian visionary. Born in Florence, she was 13 when she entered the Convent of the Dominican nuns at Prato, where she eventually became prioress and spent the rest of her life. In 1542 she began to experience ecstatic visions every week. Her growing fame for sanctity turned her convent into a place of pilgrimage, and she was also consulted by dignitaries of the Church. She was canonized in 1746.

F. M. Capes, *St. Catherine de' Ricci* (1905).

CATHERINE HOWARD (1522-42) Queen of England; fifth wife of *Henry VIII. C. was the pretty and frivolous niece of Thomas Howard, the third duke of *Norfolk and one of the king's chief ministers. Henry VIII, who was 30 years older, married her on 28 July 1540, but soon became suspicious of her conduct and, in November 1541, ordered her arrest on a charge of adultery; she was accused of renewing a romantic affair with a former lover. Her supposed lover was quickly beheaded, while C. languished in the Tower for another two months, before meeting the same fate on 12 February 1542.

CATHERINE OF ARAGON (1485-1536) Queen of England; first wife of *Henry VIII. The youngest daughter of *Ferdinand and *Isabella of Spain, she went to England in 1501 to marry Arthur, *Henry VII's eldest son, but her 15-year old husband died within four months of their marriage. C. remained in England, waiting for Arthur's brother, Henry, to come of age and marry her. The marriage took place when Henry ascended to the throne in 1509. C., who was six years older than her husband, bore him six children, but only one daughter, *Mary, survived. Henry's decision to divorce C. had several causes: she was unable to give him a male heir and politically she became expendable after his relations with Spain had become strained. But the personal reason, his love for *Anne Boleyn, was probably the major cause. The King's efforts to obtain a divorce began in 1527, and lasted through several years of complicated negotiations with Rome, culminating in an open clash with the papacy. C., who objected to the divorce, was under constant pressure to accept it, but obstinately refused. In 1531 Henry ordered her removal from the court, and her daughter was taken away from her. From then on she was more or less a prisoner; unable to judge the extent of the sympathy which her fate elicited from the common people, she still resolutely opposed the divorce. In May 1533 Archbishop *Cranmer decreed her marriage null and void from the beginning, on the grounds of her former marriage to Henry's brother. The Archbishop had earlier secretly married Henry to Anne Boleyn. *Clement VII's order in 1534 that the King take back C., since she was his legal wife, only hastened the final break with Rome. C., now designated Dowager Princess of Wales, lived in seclusion until her death in January 1536. Before her death she wrote her former husband a letter of forgiveness.

J. A. Froude, *The Divorce of Catherine of Aragon* (1891);
G. Mattingly, *Catherine of Aragon* (1941).

CATHERINE OF GENOA (1447-1510) Italian mystic. Born to the noble Genoese family of *Fieschi, she was inclined to religiosity from an early age but made to marry by her family at 16. In 1463 she experienced a spiritual crisis and decided to dedicate her life to the care of the sick. Later her pleasure-loving husband joined her, becoming a Franciscan tertiary, and from 1479 on they resided in a hospital in Genoa. C.'s spiritual doctrine was written down by her confessor and published in 1551 as *Vita e dottrina*. Her dedicated work at the hospital aroused great admiration, and soon after her death her tomb became a popular shrine. She was canonized in 1737.

The "Treatise of Purgatory" and "The Dialogue" of St. Catherine of Genoa, Translated by C. Balfour and H. Douglas Irvine (1946);
F. von Hügel, *The Mystical Element of Religion as Studied in St. Catherine of Genoa and Her Friends* (1908).

CATHERINE PAAR (1512-48) Queen of England; sixth wife of *Henry VIII. Born to a noble family, C. was married twice and left a widow for the second time in 1542. An intelligent woman, in possession of a great estate and still beautiful, she was courted by many prospective husbands. In July 1543 she married Henry VIII, and lived with him in the last three years of his life. It seems that even her restrained personality aroused the King's suspicions, because of her learning and her sympathy for Protestant reformers. He may have been considering a charge of treason against her when he died in January 1547. C. immediately married Thomas Seymour whom she had apparently favoured before her marriage to the King. She died in childbirth in August 1548.

CATTANEO, DANESE (1509-73) Italian sculptor and architect. A pupil of Jacopo *Sansovino in Rome, he followed his master to Venice, where he spent his entire creative career. He made sculptures for Sansovino's buildings, and later also undertook architectural design, although he remained for a long time in the shadow of his master. A friend of many contemporary artists, he wrote an epic poem and other works, some of which were published during his lifetime.

CAVALIERE D'ARPINO (c. 1560-1640) The name given to the Italian painter Giuseppe Cesari. Assisting painters at work in the Vatican, he impressed Pope Gregory XIII with his facile hand, and was awarded important commissions. Later he was supported also by *Clement VIII. C.'s elegant but old-fashioned style was rejected by the new generation represented by *Carracci and *Caravaggio, the latter having been briefly employed by C. when he came to Rome. But C. managed to keep his popularity for a long time, before losing favour to the new style of the *Baroque.

CAVALIERI, EMILIO DE' (c. 1550-1602) Italian composer. Although he was born in Rome and died there, C.

spent most of his life in Florence in the service of the *Medici. He was a member of the group of musicians and poets who experimented with the combination of *drama and *music which resulted in the *opera. C. himself is credited with the composition of the first oratorio, *La rappresentazione di anima e di corpo*, and was among the first to use figured bass.

CAVENDISH, THOMAS (1555-92) English navigator. Being of an adventurous spirit, C. turned to the sea with the idea of making a fortune through *privateering. In 1586 he sailed to South America and, crossing the Straits of Magellan, plundered Spanish towns and ships along the coasts of Peru, Mexico and California. He returned to England in 1588, through the Philippines and round the Cape of Good Hope, becoming, the third circumnavigator of the globe after *Magellan and *Drake. A second voyage, which he undertook together with John *Davis in 1591, was much less successful, and C. died at sea.

CAVICEO, JACOPO (1443-1511) Italian author. Born in Parma, he became a priest, but during his early manhood was embroiled in scandals in his native city and had to flee abroad, spending some time in Constantinople. Later he returned to Parma and, in the last years of his life, also lived in *Ferrara, where he wrote his best-known work, a romance on love and adventure, *Il peregrino*. With its licentious scenes and irreverence for the Church, it enjoyed wide popularity and was many times reprinted and translated.

E. Carrara, ed., *Saggi dell'Hypnerotomachia Poliphili' di Francesco Colonna e del 'Peregrino' di Jacopo Caviceo* (1952).

CAXTON, WILLIAM (1422-91) The first English printer. Born in Kent and apprenticed to a London trader in silks, C. spent over 30 years in *Bruges, rising eventually to the position of governor of the guild of the *Merchant Adventurers. In 1471 he completed the translation into English of a popular French romance on the subject of the Trojan Wars, which he dedicated to Margaret, sister of *Edward IV and duchess of Burgundy. He then went to *Cologne to learn the printing craft and, in 1474, published in Bruges the *Recuyell of the Histories of Troye*. In 1476 he returned to England and opened a printing press in Westminster. By the time he died he had published about 90 books, most of them in English. These included romances of chivalry, histories, handbooks of morals and education, and classical writings. His was also the first publication of *Chaucer's *Canterbury Tales* (1478). C. was supported by *Edward IV, *Richard III and and *Henry VII, and his books sold well among the English gentry.

N. S. Aurner, *Caxton: Mirror of Fifteenth-Century Letters* (1926);
H. R. Plomer, *William Caxton* (1925, rep. 1968).

CECIL, SIR WILLIAM (1520-98) English statesman. Born to a family of Lincolnshire gentry, C.'s capacity for administrative work was recognized at an early stage. He was promoted by the Protector *Somerset to the position of Secretary of State, and retained a post in the court even when his benefactor fell from grace, in 1550, and was succeeded by *Northumberland. In the same adaptable manner, C. passed the reign of *Mary, and when *Elizabeth I came to the throne (1558) his influence grew. He was reappointed Secretary of State and continued to serve as the Queen's chief adviser and policy-maker during most of her reign. In foreign affairs C. from the beginning espoused an anti-Spanish policy, preferring a possible alliance with Protestant rulers on the Continent and with the French *Huguenots. In domestic matters he was particularly noted for his campaign against the Catholics and for the network of informers which he established and which, more than once, prevented an attempt on the queen's life. C. advocated to Elizabeth to have *Mary, Queen of Scots, executed; he supported the harassment of the Spanish settlements in America by *Drake, but did not satisfactorily prepare England to meet the challenge of the *Armada. From 1571 on he was also known by his title of Lord Burghley.

C. Read, *Lord Burghley and Queen Elizabeth* (1960).

CELLINI, BENVENUTO (1500-71) Italian goldsmith and sculptor. Having learned his craft in his birthplace, Florence, C. had to leave the city in 1519, and again in 1523, after taking part in bloody brawls. He lived in Rome intermittently until 1540, working for prominent patrons, among them Pope *Clement VII. During the Sack of *Rome of 1527, he distinguished himself in the defence of Castello St. Angelo, the papal stronghold, and, according to his own account, shot the Constable of *Bourbon. He also received commissions and the protection of *Paul III. He went to France at the invitation of *Francis I, and stayed there until 1543, producing bronze sculptures and small pieces in gold, including a famous saltcellar (today in Vienna), which amazed his patron. C. moved back to Florence in 1545, where he began to work on his most important statue, *Perseus*, which was completed in 1554. Although he never quite outgrew the tendency to violence which had marked his youth and early manhood, C. seems to have mellowed later in life. Besides being the greatest Florentine sculptor of his time, he wrote a famous autobiography which he began in 1558, and which was first published in 1728. Written in a free style and full of exaggerations, it gives a lively portrait of the artist's personality. A unique Renaissance document, it never lost its popularity among readers. C. also wrote treatises on sculpture and architecture.

C. Antoniade, *Trois figures de la Renaissance; Pierre Arétin, Guichardin, Benvenuto Cellini* (1937).

CELTIS, CONRAD (1459-1508) German poet and humanist. The son of a peasant, C. studied at *Cologne, at Heidelberg under Rudolf *Agricola, and later at Rostock and Leipzig. By 1487 his fame as a poet was so well established that *Frederick III bestowed special honours upon him. In that same year C. travelled to Italy, and later went to Cracow, where he studied mathematics. Subsequently he taught rhetoric in *Nuremberg and Ingolstadt and, from 1497 until his death, lectured at the University of Vienna, where he had been invited by *Maximilian I. His Latin poetry, like his style of life, verged on immorality and is well represented by his *Amores* of 1502. His encouragement of humanist letters was probably more important than his poetry. He organized local associations of humanists, with the aim of producing a great collective work, *Germania illustrata*, on the history of Germany. C. himself wrote on Nuremberg, but the project was never completed. He also published Tacitus' *Germania*, and works of the 10th-century German nun Roswitha. Although he wrote poetry in Latin, C. actively promoted a German cultural

Cellini's salt cellar for Francis I now in Vienna

identity, which would differ from the Italian.

L. W. Spitz, *Conrad Celtis, the German Arch-Humanist* (1957).

CENNINI, CENNINO (c. 1370-?) Italian author of the first technical treatise on painting. Born near Florence, C. settled in Padua where he probably spent the rest of his life. He was a painter, but there are no known works by him in existence. His contribution to the world of art was *Il libro dell'arte*, a widely used manual describing in detail techniques and processes of painting, written early in the 15th century. Although he compared painting to poetry, C. still viewed the artist as a craftsman.

C. Cennini, *The Craftsman's Handbook* (1933).

CENSORSHIP With the advent of *printing, established authorities, both secular and spiritual, found that the problem of suppressing objectionable literature assumed new dimensions. In addition to the sensitivity of the Church with regard to the publication of the *Bible in the vernacular and the circulation of heretical ideas, there existed a more general anxiety that the new medium would be used for the dissemination of pornography. The first instance of state C. of printed books occurred in Mainz, where printing had begun, and in *Frankfurt. In 1486 a joint C. office was established in these cities. Papal efforts to impose universal C. throughout Christendom were made already by *Alexander VI, but only after the beginning of the *Reformation was there a serious effort to establish a coordinated machinery, which finally took the form of the **Index*. C. was much less effective in Protestant areas, although in some places, such as *Calvin's *Geneva, it was absolute. European printers resorted to a variety of means to evade C., the commonest being a title page giving a false name of the printer and place of publication. By the late 16th century there was a clear connection between the relative absence of C. and printing on a large scale. Leiden and *Amsterdam, where religious tolerance prevailed, became the centres of European printing.

F. S. Siebert, *Freedom of the Press in England, 1476-1776* (1952).

CERVANTES SAAVEDRA, MIGUEL DE (1547-1616) Spanish novelist, poet and playwright; considered with *Shakespeare the two outstanding literary geniuses of their age. The fourth son of an unsuccessful surgeon, he was born in Alcalá de Henares and studied at Valladolid, *Seville and Madrid. In 1569 he went to Italy, where he served briefly in the household of Cardinal *Acquaviva and, in 1570, enlisted as a soldier. In the great victory at *Lepanto (1571), C. was maimed in his left hand which was rendered useless, but later he participated in other engagements in Corfu, Navarino and Tunis. On his return voyage to Spain in 1575 his ship was seized by corsairs, and he was taken with his brother Rodrigo to *Algiers, where he spent five years as a slave. He made several vain attempts to escape and was released in 1580, being ransomed by the friar Juan Gil. He returned to Spain to lead a precarious existence as a minor government official, mainly as tax collector and purchasing agent for the *Armada. In 1584 he married the 19-year old Catalina de Salazar, a union which proved childless and unhappy. Shortly before his marriage, however, C. fathered an illegitimate daughter, Isabel, the offspring of an amorous liaison. Moving periodically from town to town, he was several times charged with illegal requisitioning and mishandling of accounts. The most serious case (1596) involved a sum of money due to the royal treasury, which he had entrusted to a Seville banker who absconded. As a result, C. spent three months in jail. In 1605 he was again arrested with his family in Valladolid, when his daughter became involved in a stabbing incident. Financial difficulties and legal embroilments troubled his life even after he attained literary fame.

C. began his literary career as a poet, his earliest poems being published in 1568. But his natural talent lay in prose. His first and unfinished novel, *La Galatea*, published in Alcalá (1585), was replete with pastoral scenes, which he was to use again in other works. About that time he also wrote many plays, which were staged (1581-87), though with only moderate success. In 1615, when he was already famous, a collection of these plays was published as *Ocho comedias y ocho entremeses*, but only the short, one-act comic pieces, ironic and satirical, show superior literary qualities. In the last years of his life he also published the *Novelas ejemplares* (1613), a group of 12 stories on themes of adventure and love, including some that displayed a penetrating observation of social and moral issues. The *Viaje del Parnaso* (1614) was a long allegorical poem. His last work, *Los trabajos de Persiles y Sigismunda* (1617), was published soon after his death. A huge novel of unreal adventures in an idealized setting, it was a resounding success with 17th-century European readers.

C.'s major work, *El ingenioso hidalgo Don Quixote de la Mancha*, is in a category by itself. It was written in two parts: the first published in Madrid in 1605, the second in 1615. Describing the wanderings of Don Quixote, a dreamy elderly knight-errant, and his earthy faithful squire, Sancho Panza, the book satirized the novels of *chivalry and was thus received and acclaimed by the public. Hugely successful, the first part of *Don Quixote* was translated into English in 1612 and into French in 1614. Later generations, especially since the 18th century, have continued to admire the work for its superb treatment of the eternal duality in human life – that of realism *versus* idealism, truth and illusion, faith and disenchantment.

S. J. Arbo, *Cervantes: Adventurer, Idealist and Destiny's Fool* (1955);
A. F. Bell, *Cervantes* (1947; 1961);
W. J. Entwistle, *Cervantes* (1965).

CESALPINO, ANDREA (1519-1603) Italian *botanist. Born in Arezzo, he studied medicine at Pisa where, in 1555, he became the director of the botanical garden.

Cervantes

In 1592 he went to Rome as physician of Pope *Clement VIII. He wrote on various subjects, including philosophy, biology and mineralogy, but especially on botany. His *De plantis*, published in 1583 in Florence, introduced a scheme of plant classification according to fruits.

CESARINI, GIULIANO (1398-1444) Italian cardinal. Of a prominent Roman family, he entered the papal service and advanced quickly as a trusted diplomatic envoy. Made cardinal by *Martin V in 1426, he was sent by him in 1431 against the *Hussites in Bohemia, a mission that was quickly changed to an appointment to preside at the Council of *Basle. When this body broke with *Eugenius IV, C. decided to support the pope and took part in the deliberations that led to the union with the Eastern Church at the Council of *Ferrara-Florence. In 1442 he went to *Hungary to organize a *crusade against the *Ottoman Turks. But his insistence on continuing the fight, in spite of a truce signed with *Murad II at Szegedin, led to a complete defeat of the crusaders at Varna (November 1444), where he lost his life.

CESPEDES, PABLO DE (1538-1608) Spanish painter, sculptor and architect. Born in Córdoba, he began to paint while on a visit to Rome, where he had gone with the intention of furthering his knowledge of oriental languages. He was then nicknamed 'The Spanish Raphael'. In 1575 he returned to Córdoba, where he spent most of his later years. His best-known painting, *The Last Supper*, is plainly influenced by the Italian *Mannerism, but possesses expressive power. He wrote a poem on the art of painting and had many pupils.

CHALCONDYLAS, DEMETRIUS (1424-1511) A Byzantine scholar. He was born in Athens and emigrated to Italy a few years before the fall of *Constantinople. Between 1479 and 1492 he taught Greek letters in Florence, where he was invited by Lorenzo de' *Medici. Afterwards he resided in Milan, where he also died. C.

was a friend of Marsilio *Ficino and other famous humanists of the day, had many students and supervised the first printing of a number of Greek classical texts. His brother, Laonicas C., about whom there is only scant information, was the author of a history on the long struggle between the *Ottoman Turks and the decaying Byzantine empire.

CHAMPLAIN, SAMUEL DE (1567-1635) French explorer and founder of French Canada. The son of a sea captain, C. was permitted in 1599 to visit the Spanish possessions in America. Returning to France two years later, he undertook his first voyage to Canada in 1603 and, in 1608, founded a settlement in Quebec. He took care to cultivate the friendship of the Algonquin and Huron Indians and, in 1611, expanded the French settlement and established the trading post of Montreal. He busied himself constantly with the exploration of the territory, pushing east as far as Lake Ontario. In 1629 the English took Quebec and sent Champlain to England as prisoner, but he was later released and returned to Canada, where he died two years later. C. wrote accounts of his exploratory expeditions and a description of his visit to Spanish America. He was the discoverer and gave his name to the long and narrow lake between the states of New York and Vermont.

W. L. Grant, ed., *Voyages of Samuel de Champlain, 1604-18* (1952).

CHANCELLOR, RICHARD (?-1556) English navigator. In 1553, while voyaging in search of a *northeast passage to Asia, C. reached the Russian port of Archangel. From there he proceeded over land to Moscow, where he was given permission by *Ivan IV to trade with his country. On his return to England he established the *Muscovy Company (1554). He died on a second voyage to Russia two years later, but the commercial relations between England and Russia, which he had nurtured, continued.

CHAPMAN, GEORGE (c. 1559-1634) English poet, playwright and translator. C. first earned notice with his book of poetry *The Shadow of Night*, published in 1594. A year later this was followed by *Ovid's Banquet of Sense*. He also wrote a number of comedies and two tragedies based on episodes in French history. In 1598 he published a very successful continuation of *Marlowe's unfinished lyric work, *Hero and Leander*. His most famous work, however, was the translation of Homer into English; the complete *Iliad* appeared in 1611, and the *Odyssey* in 1615. Enjoying patronage at the court and fame among fellow authors, he gradually devoted himself more to translating than to writing.

E. Rhys, *Tragedies of George Chapman: Studies of Renaissance Ethics in Action* (1954).

CHARLES D'ORLEANS (1394-1465) French poet. The son of Duke Louis d'Orléans and grandson of King Charles V of France, he had the misfortune of being prisoner at *Agincourt (1415), remaining in captivity in England for twenty-five years. Afterwards he lived at his small court in Blois. His poetry, which included many ballads, was not published until the 18th century, and seems to have been relatively unaffected by his long imprisonment. C. was the father of King *Louis XII.

CHARLES THE BOLD (1433-77) Duke of *Burgundy from 1467. Son of *Philip the Good, he was known from his youth for his combative character, and spent much of his reign in military campaigns. C. assumed the government in 1465, two years before his father's death. His possessions included the duchy and county of Burgundy, as well as *Flanders, Artois, Brabant, Luxemburg, *Holland, Zeeland, Friesland and Hainault. To these territories he aimed to add Alsace and Lorraine, so as to form a middle kingdom – corresponding to the 9th-century Lotharingia – between France and the German Empire. At first he succeeded in forming a powerful alliance against his suzerain, *Louis XI of France, which defeated the latter at the Battle of Montlhery (July 1465). But there were very few tangible gains in this victory. In 1468 C. strengthened his position by marrying Margaret of York, sister of *Edward IV of England and, in October of that year, at a conference at Peronne, he did not hesitate to put Louis XI under arrest, as he suspected him of fomenting a revolt in *Ghent. Nevertheless, by 1471 the French king was able to bring the Swiss to his side and to seize the towns of the Somme.

C.'s great political failure came in September 1473. Emperor *Frederick III, who had agreed to crown him king of Burgundy, deseted him at the last moment. In 1474 Louis XI reversed the alliance against him, bringing to his side Duke René of Lorraine, the free towns of Alsace and the Swiss. Edward IV, his brother-in-law, who invaded France in the summer of 1475, agreed to halt his invasion, signing with Louis XI the Treaty of Picquigny and, during 1476, C. was twice defeated by the Swiss – at Granson and Morat. In January 1477 he again confronted the coalition of the Swiss forces and those of Lorraine near Nancy, and was killed in battle. His mutilated body was later found on the field. His death brought an end to the Burgundian menace to the French monarchy. His defeats by the Swiss were among the first instances when infantry carrying pikes overcame a feudal cavalry.

A. C. P. Haggard, *Louis XI and Charles the Bold* (1913); P. Frédérix, *La mort de Charles le Téméraire* (1966); R. Vaughan, *Charles the Bold; the Last Valois Duke of Burgundy* (1973).

CHARLES V (1500-58) *Holy Roman emperor (1519-56); king of Spain (1516-1556), and Naples; ruler of the Netherlands and Milan; the key figure of European politics in the first half of the 16th century. Born in *Ghent to *Philip the Handsome and *Joanna the Mad, he inherited from his grandparents rights to Spain, *Burgundy, the Netherlands and *Austria. After the death of his father and the derangement of his mother (1506), C. was raised by his aunt *Margaret of Austria, regent of the Netherlands. His religious education was entrusted to Adrian of Utrecht, the future *Adrian VI. He grew up to believe in the ideals of *chivalry and in the mediaeval concept of a universal empire.

Assuming the rule of the Netherlands at 15, C. was proclaimed, in March 1516, the actual ruler of Spain, his mother being unfit to govern. He went to Spain in September 1517 with a retinue of Burgundian advisers, and although he quickly learned the language, he antagonized the country at first by placing the government in the hands of foreign aids. Less than two years later his parental grandfather, *Maximilian I, died, and C. hastened to Germany to secure the imperial crown for himself. He won over his closest rival, *Francis I of France, by buying the votes of the electors with money supplied by the *Fuggers. His election took place on 28 June 1519, and on 23 October 1520, he was

Charles V *by Titian*

crowned King of the Romans at Aachen. However, C.'s accession to the imperial dignity immediately involved him with two of the three great issues which were to mark his political career. The first was a protracted conflict with France; the second, of an accidental nature from the Emperor's view point, was concerned with the rise of *Protestantism in Germany. C.'s early response to this issue, at the Diet of *Worms (1521), was an outright rejection, but in time he had to take account of the changing realities. The third great issue, the defence of Europe from the *Ottoman Turks, began to preoccupy him only some years later.

The revolt of the **comuneros* (1520-21) made C. return to Spain in 1522, remaining there for the next seven years. By giving his personal consideration to this kingdom, he was able to win the loyalty of the nobility and the people, who henceforth supplied most of the officers and soldiers of his armies. Since 1521 war with France over the control of *Milan shifted his attention to Italy. He scored a political victory by having his former teacher, Adrian of Utrecht, elected pope in 1522, and in February 1525 received the news about the capture of Francis I at the Battle of Pavia. C. brought his captive to Madrid and forced him to sign a treaty (14 January 1526) making important concessions, letting him go only after he secured his sons as hostages. Francis, however, soon renounced the agreement that had been extracted under duress. That year, the League of *Cognac, a coalition which included the new pope, *Clement VII, formed against the Emperor. But the Sack of *Rome (1527) shattered the military power of the papacy and, in 1529, the Peace of *Cambrai brought a temporary settlement with France. On 24 February 1530, C. was crowned Holy Roman emperor in Bologna, the last to be consecrated by a pope.

C.'s participation in the Diet of *Augsburg (1530) did not ease the problems of Germany. The Emperor rejected the famous Protestant Confession and, in 1531, the Protestant princes reacted by creating the *Schmalkaldic League. C., nevertheless, went in 1532 to rescue Vienna from the threat of *Suleiman I. He thus relieved the pressure on *Austria, where his brother *Ferdinand had been reigning since 1522. But the Emperor soon carried his campaign against the Turks to another area. In 1535 he personally led an expedition to Tunis, whose hard-won victory gained only minor results. Upon his return to Italy, C. urged Pope *Paul III to convene a general council to consider reform and religious reunion. A war with France followed (1536-38), with military engagements taking place mainly in northern Italy and southern France. In 1540 C. suppressed a revolt in his native city of Ghent. The following year the Emperor led another expedition across the Mediterranean against *Algiers, suffering defeat both at sea and on land.

A new phase of the war with France opened in 1542, with French claims to Milan serving again as the official pretext. While Francis strenghtened his alliance with the Ottoman Turks, who bombarded Nice from the sea and attacked the eastern borders of Hungary and Austria, C. crushed another French ally, the duke of Cleves, and penetrated deep into the north of France (September 1544). At that point, negotiations replaced hostilities, and the two exhausted rivals signed the Treaty of Crépy, whose provisions with regard to Milan were never implemented.

C. now felt ready to tackle the political and religious problems of the empire. He brought over to his side some Protestant princes, among them *Maurice of Saxony and, in 1546, overran southern Germany. On 24 April 1547 he defeated the leaders of the Schmalkaldic League at Mühlberg, taking prisoners *John Frederick of Saxony and *Philip of Hesse. The *Augsburg Interim (June 1548) was then formulated and proposed by the Emperor to Germany as a basis of religious settlement. However, resistance to the imposed settlement, especially in the cities, and the opposition of the princes to his assertion of imperial rule, meant that a forced solution was no longer possible, in spite of the presence of the Emperor and his Spanish troops. In the spring of 1552 a coalition of rebellious princes led by Maurice of Saxony surprised C. near Innsbruck and nearly took him prisoner. The shaken and humiliated Emperor had to agree to the Convention of Passau, which renewed the religious freedom of the Protestants until the next diet (August 1552). About that time C. began an unsuccessful campaign against *Henry II of France so as to regain Metz. But his mind was gradually turning away from political matters. Unwilling to make concessions on religious issues, he designated his brother Ferdinand as his representative at the important Diet of Augsburg (September 1555). On 25 October 1555, at Brussels, C. announced his abdication from the rule of the Netherlands and Naples and, on 15 January 1556, abdicated from the throne of Spain and the Empire. He then retired to a monastery at Yuste, Spain, where he lived in seclusion until his death.

In pursuing the goal of a unified empire in the face of great divisive forces, C. was attempting to accomplish the impossible. Overextended in his commitments and frequently without financial resources, he merely responded to immediate problems, without being able to create lasting new structures. However, the persistent efforts of this earnest and dedicated personage to settle the affairs of *Europe had the effect of turning Spain into a potential master of the Continent. It was this task, the retention of Spanish hegemony, which he bequeathed to his son and successor *Philip II.

K. Brandi, *The Emperor Charles V* (1939);
M. François, *Charles Quint et son temps* (1959);
P. Rossow, *Karl V; Der Kaiser und seine Zeit* (1960).

CHARLES VII (1403-61) King of France. Usually described as a person of weak character, he had a long eventful reign. He became regent of France in 1418, his father Charles VI being insane. His position was very precarious: the English army was in possession of a large territory in northern France, and the French nobility was divided into two great factions, the Burgundians versus the *Armagnacs. In 1419, at a conference in Montereau, the Armagnacs murdered John the Fearless, duke of *Burgundy, in the presence of C., thus forcing the Burgundians into the arms of the English. C.'s insane father, who came under the influence of the Burgundians, then accepted the Treaty of Troyes (1420), which declared his son illegitimate and designated *Henry V of England regent and future heir. Yet after his father's death (1422), C. was nevertheless recognized as king in southern France. But he was almost powerless and under the domination of his Armagnac councillors. That he eventually recovered the occupied parts of the country was due to the popular nationalist movement on his behalf, led by a young woman known as *Joan of Arc. In 1429 she led the French troops against the English who were besieging the city of Orléans, and relieved it. This opened the way to Rheims, where, in the ancient ceremony, C. was crowned on 17 July 1429. However, the King and his advisers declined to do anything to rescue Joan of Arc when she was caught and delivered to the English in May 1430.

In 1435 C. concluded with *Philip the Good of Burgundy the Peace of Arras. The reconciliation strenghtened him vis-à-vis the English, and in 1436 he was able to take Paris. This was followed by a period of military standstill in which unruly bands, dubbed *écorcheurs*, roamed and terrorized the countryside. In the course of these years the King introduced many reforms in the tax system and in the army and, in 1438, issued the Pragmatic Sanction of Bourges, an assertion of the *conciliar idea and of the rights of the crown over the French church. During this part of his reign C. was served by a group of loyal advisers, among them the merchant Jacques *Coeur. His mistress, Agnes *Sorel, was influential in court life and also involved herself in political matters. The fact that his advisers were of relatively low social standing caused resentment among the great nobles, who were joined by the dauphin, the future *Louis XI. Their revolt, known as the *Praguerie* (1440), was suppressed, but the dauphin rebelled again in 1446, and in 1447 took refuge in Burgundy. In spite of these difficulties, C. renewed the war against the English, and in 1450 reconquered Normandy. At the time of his death only Calais remained in English hands.

M. G. A. Vale, *Charles VII* (1974).

CHARLES VIII (1470-98) King of France. The only son of *Louis XI, he succeeded his father in 1483 at the age of 13. However, until 1492 the government was in the hands of his older sister, *Anne of France, and her husband Pierre de Beaujeu. C.'s most important decision was to involve France in an invasion of Italy, where he claimed inheritance rights on the kingdom of *Naples. This expedition was conceived by the ambitious young king as a first step towards a great *crusade to reconquer the Holy Land from the Turks. In order to free his hands in Italy, C. concluded the Treaty of Senlis (1493) with Emperor *Maximilian I and made similar concessions to England and Spain. His march into Italy in 1494 was a triumph. But before long a coalition was formed including the Emperor and King *Ferdinand of Aragon, and, following the Battle of Fornovo (July 1495), forced C. to leave Italy. C. was contemplating a return expedition, when he accidentaly struck his head on a door, while playing games at his beloved chateau of Amboise. He died a few days later.

CHARLES VIII (Karl Knutsson; 1409-70) King of Sweden. Born to a family of the highest Swedish nobility, he took part in an uprising against King Eric in 1436, and, through skilful reversion of his allegiance, was elected regent of Sweden in 1438. In 1448 he was elected king, but was never in full control of the government and had to struggle with *Christian I of Denmark, who claimed the Swedish throne. In 1457 the Swedish nobility actually shifted to the side of Christian I and C. had to leave the government. He was recalled in 1464 and resumed the throne in 1467, but the real power remained in the hands of the nobility.

CHARLES IX (1550-74) King of France. The third son of *Henry II and *Catherine de Médicis, he became king in 1560 at the age of ten, following the death of his brother *Francis II. C. was entirely under the influence of his mother and was unable to prevent the bloodshed caused by the religious wars; the Massacre of *St. Bartholomew (August 1572) occurred in his reign. He seems to have had a genuine love for literature and supported *Ronsard and other members of the *Pléiade.

CHARLES IX (1550-1611) King of Sweden. The third son of *Gustavus Vasa, he and his brother John in 1568 deposed their half-brother, the insane *Eric XIV. Under *John III, C. spent most of his time attempting to preserve the autonomy of his duchy. However, when his brother died in 1592, he stepped forward as the defender of Swedish Protestantism against the pretensions of John III's son, *Sigismund, who was already king of Poland and an orthodox Roman Catholic. In 1595 C. became regent, and undertook a punitive military expedition against Finland. In the civil war which ensued he enjoyed the support of the lower gentry and, in 1598, defeated an attempt by Sigismund to land in Sweden and take over its government. In 1599 Sigismund was deposed by the Swedish representative assembly and, in 1604, C. formally assumed the title of king. However, his reign like his regency, was a time of intermittent wars. Besides Poland, where

Sigismund still nourished hopes of retrieving his lost crown, C. fought against Russia and, in the last year of his reign, started a war with Denmark. He was quite unsuccessful in his military engagements; in 1605 he was decisively defeated by the Polish general Chodkiewicz near Kirkholm. The fact that his defeats did not lose Sweden much territory was only due to the unsettled political conditions in Poland and Russia. The son of a great king, C. was also the father of one, Gustavus Adolphus (1611-32).

CHARONTON, ENGUERRAND (c. 1410-61) French painter. Born in *Lyons, he was particularly active in Avignon, where, after 1447, he painted in a number of churches. His main work, the large *Coronations of the Virgin*, completed in 1454, has stylistic affinities with the works of Jean *Fouquet and Jan van *Eyck.

CHARRON, PIERRE (1541-1603) French preacher and essayist. The son of a Parisian bookseller, he studied law at Orleans and Bourges, but was later ordained priest and acquired a reputation as a preacher. In 1576 he became a canon at Bordeaux, where he met and befriended *Montaigne (1589). *Les Trois Verités*, his defence of Roman Catholicism, was published in 1594 and went through numerous editions. Of his other works the most important was *De la sagesse* (1601). It deals with the conditions of human wisdom: man's knowledge of himself, the manner in which he may free himself from prejudice and the four virtues – prudence, righteousness, strength and moderation – that he must rely on. The essay which, following Montaigne, was marked by an attitude of secular skepticism, is considered a contribution to the development of French free thought.

J. B. Sabrie, *De l'humanisme au rationalisme: Pierre Charron* (1913; rep. 1970).

CHARTIER, ALAIN (c. 1390-c. 1440) French author. As secretary of the dauphin, afterwards King *Charles VII, he was well established at the French court, besides having a brother who served as bishop of Paris. C. impressed his contemporaries with his patriotic zeal. He composed a long poem, *Le livre de quatre dames*, representing the lamentations of four ladies over the misfortunes that had befallen their men at the Battle of *Agincourt. He also wrote a famous letter to Emperor *Sigismund, which contained a eulogy of *Joan of Arc. But his own generation admired C. also for his vivid satire of life at the court, *Le curial*. He was called the father of French literature and enjoyed a great reputation throughout the 15th and 16th centuries. Other works of C.'s in prose include the patriotic *Quadriloge invectif* (1422) and *Le livre de l'espérance* (1429).

CHASTELLAIN, GEORGES (c. 1415-1475) Flemish-Burgundian chronicler and poet. Born in Aalst, *Flanders, he was a soldier in the army of *Philip the Good, then spent several years in France. In 1446 he entered the service of the dukes of Burgundy, serving as secretary, diplomat and, after 1455, official chronicler. His main work was the *Chronique des ducs de Bourgogne*, extending from 1419 to 1474, and containing much information, as well as sound evaluation of some of the main figures. He also wrote poetry, treatises on current political issues, and allegorical plays.

K. Urwin, *Georges Chastellain; la vie, les oeuvres* (1937).

CHATEAUBRIANT, EDICT OF A royal decree signed by *Henry II on 27 June 1551, in an attempt to check the rising tide of Protestantism in France. The Edict extended the force and codified all previous restrictions against the spreading of Protestant ideas. It especially emphasized dispositions against the publishing and sale of reformist literature.

Charles IX *by François Clouet*

CHATILLON, ODET DE (1517-71) French renegade cardinal and *Huguenot leader. The older brother of Admiral *Coligny, he was the last of the Coligny brothers who moved to the side of Protestantism (1561), and as a result lost his Roman Catholic ecclesiastical dignities. Taking a leading part in the early phases of the *Religious Wars, he was forced to escape to England in 1569, and died there, probably a victim of poisoning by one of his aides.

CHAUCER, GEOFFREY (c. 1340-1400) Mediaeval English poet, a key figure in the evolution of English language and literature. Born in London to a wine merchant, he was raised as a page at the court. In 1359 he fell prisoner in France and was ransomed one year later. He then entered the service of Edward III, and was employed by the king on various diplomatic missions abroad. He was sent to France (1369), Flanders (1377), and twice to Italy (1372-73; 1378). Through his wife Philippa, C. was associated with John of Gaunt (1340-99), whose patronage he enjoyed. Under Richard II he was justice of the peace, member of Parliament, clerk of the King's Works and forester for the Crown.

C.'s earliest literary work was deeply influenced by French sources. It followed the traditions of the romances of *chivalry and courtly love, and included a translation of the *Roman de la Rose* and a long elegy on the death of the wife of John of Gaunt, *The Book of the Dutchess* (*c.* 1369). His visits to Italy, however, had a significant effect on his literary vistas. Although it is not clear whether he ever met *Petrarch or *Boccaccio, his later work showed a close affinity to theirs. His *Troilus and Creseyde* (*c.* 1385) was an adaptation of Boccaccio's *Il filostrato*, which exceeded the original in length. *House of France*, a poem which borrowed from *Dante and left unfinished, was followed by *The Legend of Good Women*, stories in verse about famous ladies of the past. In this C. was inspired by a similar work by Boccaccio, while the Italian master's *Decameron* became the immediate model for his greatest and ever-popular, *The Canterbury Tales* (1386-90). A collection of stories told by a group of pilgrims on their way to the shrine at Canterbury, it is full of humour and shows a penetrating observation of human behaviour. It was first published by *Caxton (1477), and was already recognized in the 16th century as the first masterpiece of English letters. C. also wrote two works in prose: a translation of Boethius and an unfinished *Treatise on the *Astrolabe*.

H. S. Bennett, *Chaucer and the 15th Century* (1947).

CHEKE, SIR JOHN (1514-57) English classical scholar. He was born in Cambridge, where he became a fellow of St. John's College in 1529. In 1540 he became regius professor of *Greek, and, in 1544, was appointed tutor to Prince *Edward, whose education he continued to supervise after he became king. A confirmed Protestant, he served in parliament and, in 1553, was made secretary of state and member of the privy council. *Mary Tudor had him arrested for his support of Lady Jane *Grey. Released in 1554, he went into exile, but two years later was seized by emissaries of *Philip II and sent to England where he was induced to make a public recantation and espouse Roman Catholicism. Beside several works on Greek authors and translations, he wrote on theology and on *Kett's Rebellion.

CHELCICKY, PETER (c. 1390-c. 1460) Czech religious leader and author. A peasant who never learned to read Latin, he became one of the principal spiritual leaders of the *Unity of the Brothers. He put an extreme interpretation on the teachings of *Wycliffe and *Hus, rejecting the position of the dominant Hussite church of *Bohemia, and advocating strict adherence to the New Testament. In the social and political sphere, C. opposed commerce in the name of the ideal of self-sustaining peasant life, and rejected government authority. He believed in a sort of rural anarchism, which he identified with the return to primitive Christianity. His *Siet' viery*, written about 1440 and published in 1520, exercised influence on the development of Czech literature.

P. Brock, *The Political and Social Doctrines of the Unity of Czech Brethren* (1957).

CHEMISTRY Strictly speaking, the science of C. is a post-Renaissance development. The 16th century was the great age of *alchemy, which was dominated by the belief in the transmutation of substances, and made no attempt at a systematic study of the relations between them. The iatrochemical ideas of *Paracelsus had a strong affinity with alchemy, and although signalling a potentially new orientation, they were significant at the time chiefly for their attack on the ancient authorities. This tendency was also followed by Jean Baptiste van *Helmont. Actual knowledge of C. during the Renaissance was limited to the practical one which had been acquired in certain industries, such as *metallurgy, ceramics, dyeing and colouring, distillation, and glass and *gunpowder production. The advances made in these fields were summed up by several authors, such as *Agricola's *De re metallica* (1556), which gave a complete account of the mining and metal-working industry.

J. R. Partington, *A Short History of Chemistry*, 3rd ed. (1957).

CHEMNITZ, MARTIN (1522-86) Second-generation German Protestant theologian. He lectured on Lutheran theology at *Wittenberg, but in 1554 became a pastor at Brunswick, where he spent the rest of his life. In his main work, *Repetitio sanae doctrinae de vera praesentia* (1561), he elaborated on *Luther's doctrine of Christ's real presence in the Eucharist. C. also wrote a critical study against the Council of *Trent (1573), but generally followed the moderate position of *Melanchthon.

CHIABRERA, GABRIELLO (1552-1638) Italian poet. Born in Savona, he was raised by an uncle in *Rome and had a stormy adventurous youth, in the course of which he stayed and was involved in quarrels at several Italian courts. In 1581 he returned to Savona where he spent most of the rest of his life. The author of many works of poetry, he is remembered mainly for his *conzonette* and *scherzi*, which had rhythm and were graceful and unpretentious. C. avoided the flamboyance which characterized Italian verse in his time, favouring the manner of the French *Ronsard and *Belleau. However, his long works on religious or moral themes lack an authentic creative merit.

F. Neri, *Il Chiabrera e la Pleiade francese* (1920).

CHIGI, AGOSTINO (c. 1465-1520) Italian banker and patron of the arts. Member of a family of Sienese origins, he began his banking operations in Rome around 1502 and became the chief creditor of *Julius II and *Leo X. Earlier, he loaned money to Cesare *Borgia and to the exiled *Medici and established commercial relations throughout Europe. C. patronized such authors as *Bembo and *Aretino, but is best known for his support of *Raphael, who decorated his palace, later known as the Farnesina.

CHINA Relations of the West with C. during the middle ages were sporadic as for example, Marco Polo's famous visit (1275-91), the mission of John of Monte Corvino (1294) and the later Franciscan missions (1325-28; 1342-48). Regular contacts began in 1514, when the Portuguese entered into commercial relations with Canton. After some years of friction, the Chinese authorities set aside the peninsula of Macao, near Canton, as a permanent Portuguese trading post (1554). But China remained closed to Christian missionaries, a situation which changed only in 1582, when the *Jesuit Michele Ruggieri was permitted to settle in Chao-ching. He was soon joined by Matteo *Ricci, and both began a leisurely exchange with Chinese officials and literati which by 1601 bore fruit, when Ricci was allowed to go north and settle in Peking. When he died, in 1610, China had a small Catholic community of about 2,000 converts. The liberal policy of the early Jesuit missionaries, who mixed Roman Catholicism with traditional Chinese customs, facilitated their penetration, but later became a cause of prolonged controversies.

K. S. Latourette, *A History of Christian Missions to China* (1929).

CHIVALRY Having represented an authentic European ethos in the time of the *Crusades, C. was already in decline when Ramon Lull (*c.* 1235-*c.* 1315) wrote his celebrated *Le libre del orde de cauayleria*. By the early 15th century, it was obvious that what had been a mediaeval code of behaviour was becoming a ceremonial system of courtly etiquette. The new knightly orders, such as that of the *Golden Fleece in *Burgundy, were artificial perpetuations of a decaying tradition. Courtly love (*amour courtois*), the idea that a nobleman could not be a perfect knight unless he loved a lady, was in the early Renaissance a subject of discussion in formal meetings of courtiers. The artificiality of the ideals of C. was nowhere better displayed than in the works of the literary practitioners who actually meant to extol them, the **rhétoriqueurs* of France.

The literary cult of C. continued throughout the Renaissance. Books on the adventurous world of knights and Lull's above-mentioned work, were among the most successful publications of the first English printer, *Caxton. **Amadis de Gaula* was very popular in the early 16th century, and *Ariosto's *Orlando furioso* was a best-seller immediately upon the appearance of its final version (1532). However, the attitude began to change, as romanticism and the enthusiam for the heroic image gave way to satire and parody. This was already detectable in Ariosto, and became fully conscious in *Cervantes' *Don Quixote*. But the ideals of C., as treated by Cervantes, were anything but the object of mere ridicule. Rather, C. was transformed and given an ambivalent meaning. It became a deceptive and universally-valid ideal at one and the same time.

J. Huizinga, *The Waning of the Middle Ages* (1924); R. L. Kilgour, *The Decline of Chivalry as Shown in the French Literature of the Late Middle Ages* (1937).

CHRISTIAN I (1426-81) King of Denmark, Norway and Sweden. C. came to the throne in 1448, when his uncle, who was next in succession, relinquished it in his favour. His accession produced a rift with Sweden, which was not patched up until 1457, and his attempts actually to rule Sweden ended in defeat in 1471. C.'s long reign was interspersed with sporadic conflicts with the Swedish and Danish nobility. In his domestic policy he encouraged trade, awarding commercial privileges to the *Hanseatic League. In 1474 he visited Rome and, after his return, founded a university in Copenhagen and introduced elements of Renaissance culture to his court.

CHRISTIAN II (1481-1559) King of Denmark, Norway and Sweden. Acceding to the Danish throne in 1513, after six years of successful service as viceroy of Norway, C.'s first years as sovereign were marked by a curious relation with his Dutch mistress Dyveke Villemssoon, whose mother, Sigbrit, became his counsellor. He maintained this liaison even after his marriage in 1515 to Isabella, sister of *Charles V, and it was the death of his mistress in 1517, under suspicious circumstances suggesting possible poisoning, that occasioned his first major conflict with the Danish nobility. In 1518 C. began a campaign against Sweden, where the regent Sten *Sture headed the anti-unionist faction. Although he was defeated at first, he later rallied the support of the Unionist Party and vanquished Sture. However, his coronation as king of Sweden in November 1520 occasioned the 'Stockholm bloodbath', in which over 80 dignitaries were beheaded on the flimsy charge of heresy. This caused a renewed revolt led by *Gustavus Vasa, which resulted in a final separation of Sweden in 1523. Earlier that year, C.'s relations with the Danish nobility had also reached a breaking point, as a result of the sweeping legal reforms which he had passed in 1522 in favour of the burghers and the peasantry. In April 1523, when it appeared that his own uncle, Duke Frederick, was in command of the rebellious nobles, C. fled to the Netherlands. In 1531 his brother-in-law, Charles V, helped him to muster an expedition to Norway, but this effort failed. In spite of assurances of safe conduct which had been given to him, he was arrested and kept imprisoned near Copenhagen for the rest of his life.

CHRISTIAN III (1503-59) King of *Denmark and Norway. C. had been influenced in his youth by the teachings of *Luther, whom he heard at the Diet of *Worms (1521). When his father, *Frederick I, died in 1533, his election was postponed for one year, and his proclamation as king in 1534 started an inevitable civil war. Supported by Lutheran nobles and burghers, C. was able to capture Copenhagen in 1536, after besieging it for over a year. He immediately reorganized the Danish church on a Lutheran basis; episcopal property was seized by the crown and the King designated head of the church. In his foreign policy he also adopted a pro-Protestant posture. In 1542 Denmark declared war on *Charles V and closed the passages of the Baltic Sea to shipping. The damage to the commerce of the Netherlands was so great that in 1544 the Emperor made peace with Denmark and relinquished his plan to claim the Danish throne for his niece, the daughter of the imprisoned *Christian II. The rest of C.'s reign was largely peaceful. He left Denmark prosperous and more conscious of its national identity.

CHRISTINE DE PISAN (1365-1431) French poetess and historian. The daughter of an Italian astrologer who served the king of France, she was born in Bologna and brought up at the French court. C. married and had children, but losing her husband at 25, she supported herself as a sort of a court poetess. Her short verses occasionally display an assertive feminist sentiment; her *Poème de la Pucelle* was about *Joan of Arc. Her most important work, however, was *Le livre des faits et bonnes meurs du roi Charles V*, a vivid description of the reign of that monarch.

R. Rigaud, *Les idées féministes de Christine de Pisan* (1911; rep. 1973).

CHRISTUS, PETRUS (?-1473) Flemish painter. C. was the most important painter of *Bruges after the death of Jan van *Eyck. The first record of his presence there is from 1444, three years after the great master's death, but he is generally considered his pupil, and was certainly his follower. One of his most successful paintings, *St. Eligius and the Lovers* (1449), emulates van Eyck's thematic vocabulary and his portrayal of facial expression. Though a very able portraitist, his style is formal and fails to arouse true emotion in his religious scenes.

CHRYSOLORAS, MANUEL (c. 1350-1415) Greek scholar; one of the first to introduce *Greek studies into

Western Europe. Belonging to a distinguished Byzantine family, he was sent to Italy in 1393 by Emperor Manuel Palaeologous to ask for help against the advancing Turks. This visit resulted in his being invited to Florence as a lecturer on the Greek language. He taught there from 1395 to 1397, and among his students was Leonardo *Bruni. Later, C. undertook further diplomatic missions for the Byzantine Emperor, visiting Paris and London. He died while on a mission to Germany, where he was charged with preparing a general council, in which he was to represent the Eastern Church. A relative of his of the following generation, John Chrysoloras, also went to Italy and taught Greek literature.

CHURCH OF ENGLAND (Anglican Church; Episcopal Church) The official, or established, ecclesiastical entity which emerged from the vicissitudes of the *Reformation in England. Created by royal fiat in the Act of *Supremacy (1534), it retained under *Henry VIII most of the doctrinal tenets of Roman Catholicism, and began to absorb Continental *Protestant influences only during the reign of *Edward VI. The first (1549) and second (1552) Books of *Common Prayer, coupled with the permission to the clergy to marry, and the removal of the altars, constituted the real break with the religious traditions of the past. The accession of *Mary (1553) threatened to restore papal domination, and necessitated the reaffirmation of the independence of the English Church early in the reign of *Elizabeth I (1559), and the adoption of the 'Thirty-Nine Articles' (1563), the final doctrinal formula. But the Church of England did not entirely succeed in outgrowing the imprint of its royal sponsorship. On the one hand it drew the criticism of the *Puritans, who objected to episcopal hierarchy and regarded the liturgical changes as half-way measures; on the other, it faced the stubborn resistance of an enclave of Roman Catholic recusants. The result was the continued dependence of the Church on the Crown.

E. T. Davies, *Episcopacy and Royal Supremacy in the Church of England in the 16th Century* (1950);
J. R. H. Moorman, *A History of the Church of England* (1953).

CHURCHYARD, THOMAS (c. 1520-1604) English author. Born in Shrewsbury, he entered the service of Henry Howard, Earl of *Surrey, and was later a soldier-of-fortune fighting in Scotland, Ireland, France and the Netherlands on both the Protestant and Roman Catholic sides. About 1574 he returned to England and was employed by *Elizabeth I as master of pageants, but in 1579 had to flee to Scotland when a passage in one of his works offended the Queen. He was nevertheless able to return to the court in 1584, and later was given a small pension. A prolific writer, C. wrote poetry, tracts describing the wars he had fought, antiquarian and historical works. He enjoyed fame and literary acclaim during his lifetime, but was soon forgotten by the public.

CICERONIANISM A term denoting the tendency of 15th-century humanists writers to immitate the Latin style of the ancient Roman orator, Marcus Tulius Cicero. C. predates the High Renaissance. As a literary trend it began probably with *Petrarch, but reached its peak in the middle of the 15th century. By the end of the century, however, the Ciceronian model was increasingly attacked, and became the subject of fierce literary polemics. The advent of vernacular literature, which gradually took the place of Latin, eventually caused the decline of C. The publication of Erasmus' lively satire *Ciceronianus* in 1528, signalled its end as a respected literary form.

Detail from St. Francis of Assisi *by Cimabue*

CIECO, FRANCESCO (?-1505) Italian poet. Born probably in Ferrara, his name was Francesco Bello, which was changed to Cieco on account of his blindness. He was in the service of several Italian rulers, and wrote *Il Mambriano*, a romance on Carolingian themes which followed *Boiardo's *Orlando innamorato*.

E. Carrara, *Da Orlando a Morgante* (1932).

CIEZA DE LEON, PEDRO (c. 1518-60) Spanish historian. He took part in the final phases of the conquest of Peru, and later supported Pedro de la *Gasca, the governor who suppressed the revolt of Gonzalo *Pizarro (1548-49). He then wrote the *Crónica del Perú*, of which the first part, containing a geographical description of the country, was published in 1553. The other parts of the work on the Inca civilization, the Spanish conquest and the civil wars, were published only in the 19th and 20th centuries.

CIMABUE (c. 1240-c. 1300) An almost legendary figure, considered the first Italian painter to introduce a

more naturalistic quality to the severe Byzantine style of his time. C.'s name is mentioned by *Dante, and there are a few badly-preserved works, mainly in Assisi, which are attributed to him. Otherwise the existence of this teacher of *Giotto's rests almost entirely on hearsay.
A. Nicholson, *Cimabue; A Critical Study* (1932; rep. 1972).

CIMA DA CONEGLIANO, GIOVANNI BATTISTA (1460-1518) Italian painter. Born near Friuli, he was apparently a student of *Vivarini's, but his works bear the marked influence of Giovanni *Bellini. C. executed several altarpieces for churches in and around *Venice. One of his best works, *The Incredulity of St. Thomas* (1501-04), has more than one version, and there is a good number of Madonnas.

CIMINELLI, SERAFINO DE' (1466-1500) Italian poet. A native of Aquila, he was a page at Naples and later moved to Rome, where he won a resounding success as a court poet. He was subsequently patronized by the rulers of *Milan, *Urbino and *Mantua, and was also known as an accomplished musician. Although acclaimed by his own age, his flowery poetry often descends to the level of tasteless extravaganza.

CIRIACO DE' PIZZICOLI (1391-1452) Italian humanist, antiquary and epigraphist. A native of Ancona, he was a self-taught man who devoted himself to collecting ancient Roman and Greek inscriptions, while travelling through Italy and the East as a commercial agent. In 1425 he learned Greek in *Constantinople, where he also acquired a number of important manuscripts. Later he became intimate with some Florentine humanists. From 1435 to 1447 he again travelled in Greece and collected many inscriptions, most of which, however, have not been preserved.
C. C. van Essen, *Ciriaque d'Ancone en Egypte* (1958).

CIVITALI, MATTEO (1436-1501) Italian sculptor. Born in Lucca, he was the pupil, then assistant of Antonio *Rosselino in Florence. He introduced the Florentine style into Lucca, his first great work being the tomb of Piero da Noceto at the cathedral, completed in 1472. C. is also credited with introducing *printing into his native city. For a long time he enjoyed the patronage of Domenico Bertini, for whom he executed many works. He also worked in Genoa. Possessing a sense of harmony and admirable technical skill, C. was perhaps the most renowned non-Florentine sculptor of his time.

CLAVIUS, CHRISTOPH (1537-1612) German mathematician and astronomer. Born in Bamberg, he joined the *Jesuits in 1555, studied at Coimbra and taught at the Order's college in Rome, where he died. Highly regarded by Popes *Gregorius XIII and *Sixtus V, he collaborated in the reform of the calendar, and corresponded with Tycho *Brahe and *Galileo. He published an annotated Latin edition of Euclid's *Elements*, and wrote several works on mathematics.

CLEMENT VII (1478-1534) Pope from 1523. Born as Giulio de' *Medici, he was the son of Giuliano, brother of Lorenzo the Magnificent, who was murdered the year that he was born. He was promoted by his cousin, *Leo X, and made archbishop of Florence (1513) and then cardinal. C. made a bid for the papal throne in the conclave which followed his cousin's death, but had to wait another two years, and was elected in 1523, after *Adrian VI. His policies, which aimed at reducing the imperial power in Italy, led to the Sack of *Rome in 1527. Thereafter he took care to avoid conflict with *Charles V and was, therefore, unresponsive to the request of *Henry VIII to approve his divorce from *Catherine of Aragon, who was the Emperor's aunt. C. showed no understanding of the rising Protestant movement in Germany and declined to adopt measures of reform within the Catholic Church. However, like a true Medici, he was a great patron of arts and letters.
H. M. Vaughan, *The Medici Popes* (1908; rep. 1971).

CLEMENT VIII (1536-1605) Pope from 1592. Born as Ippolito Aldobrandini, C. had advanced slowly in the papal court prior to his election as successor to *Innocent IX. A stern believer in the Catholic doctrines as defined during the *Counter Reformation, he issued a new edition of the **Index* and was responsible for the 1600 execution of Giordano *Bruno. In return for his acceptance of the Edict of *Nante (1598) of *Henry IV of France, he won the implementation of the Tridentine reforms in France. He had previously used his close relations with France to get Spain's agreement to the inclusion of the duchy of *Ferrara in the Papal States. St. Philip *Neri was one of his close advisors.

CLESIO, BERNARDO (1485-1539) Italian cardinal. Born in the castle of Cles in the Trentino, he studied in Bologna, becoming bishop of Trent in 1514. C., who was also the secular authority in Trent, ruled his bishopric-principality in a magnificent manner. In 1530 *Clement VII made him cardinal, and in the course of the next few years he extended his jurisdiction over other ecclesiastical sees. A confirmed opponent of reform, C. was a loyal supporter of the *Habsburgs and served for several years as the trusted councillor of *Ferdinand of Austria. Yet he was a patron of humanists, among them *Erasmus, *Bembo and *Aretino. He also encouraged the introduction of Renaissance art, particularly in architecture, to the Trentino.

CLOUET, FRANÇOIS (c. 1510-72) French painter. The son of Jean *Clouet, he succeeded his father as court painter to *Francis I in 1541. C. excelled in the painting of portraits, and his subjects include many French court personalities of his time, including *Catherine de Médicis, *Mary Queen of Scots and *Henry II. His works, many of which are extremely accurate miniatures, display meticulous attention to detail. C. was greatly esteemed by his contemporaries.

CLOUET, JEAN (?-1541) French painter, probably of Flemish descent, known also as Janet. He first worked in Burgundy, but later became court painter to *Francis I of France. C. did drawings and oil portraits of important people at court. One group of drawings attributed to him has notes in the King's handwriting.

CLOVIO, GIULIO (1498-1578) Italian-Croatian illuminator and painter. Born in Grizane, south of Fiume, he went to Venice in 1516, and became known as Il Macedone. He spent some time in Hungary and Rome, then entered a monastery in Mantua. *Paul III invited him to the papal court, and among his other patrons were Grand Duke *Cosimo I and Pope *Julius III. His illuminated works included many missals and *Books of Hours. Practicing a dying art, he postponed its final demise.
J. W. Bradley, *The Life and Works of Giorgio Clovio* (1891).

COCHLAEUS, JOHANNES (1479-1552) German anti-*Protestant polemicist. Of peasant origin, he acquainted himself with humanist learning in *Cologne, and won fame after 1521 for his bitter attacks on *Luther. In 1526 he entered the service of *Albert of Mainz, and later lived in Meissen (1534) and Breslau (1539). While able to reach the common man, C. lacked high intellectual qualities, and aroused Luther's cold contempt. He participated in several theological conferences, produced a vast number of written works, and took his final revenge in the defamatory commentary on the writings of Luther published in 1549.

CODUCCI, MAURO (c. 1440-1504) Italian architect. Born near Bergamo, he subsequently moved to *Venice, where, together with his contemporary and competitor Pietro *Lombardo, he was responsible for introducing Renaissance architecture. The major works attributed to him are the churches of S. Michele in Isola (1469), S. Zacaria (1480-1500), and S. Giovanni Crisostomo (1497-1504). He also designed a few palaces and the clock-tower at Piazza S. Marco. Plainly influenced by *Alberti, his work still retained much of the former Venetian oriental style.

COELHO, DUARTE (c. 1485-1554) Portuguese colonizer. Following a long career in the service of the Portuguese crown in Africa, India and China, he was given a grant of 60 leagues on the coast of northeast Brazil, corresponding to present Pernambuco and Alagoas (1534). In 1537 he founded Olinda, which became the capital of the colony, built sugar mills and imported slaves from Africa. Later he attempted to oppose the royally-appointed governor-general in Salvador, Bahia, but was not very successful. He was the founder of the Brazilian sugar industry and export.

COEUR, JACQUES (1395-1456) French merchant and banker. The son of a rich merchant from Bourges, he began, in the 1430s, to trade with the Levant, importing to France, via Narbonne and Montpellier, a variety of products, including carpets, silks and brocades. In 1436 *Charles VII made him master of the royal mint and for the next years employed him as a banker, diplomat and administrator of the royal finances. C. loaned the crown money for the war against the English in Normandy, negotiated a commercial treaty with the Sultan of Egypt and, in 1448, represented France at the papal court. In the meantime, his own fortune grew; his beautiful house in Bourges remains as a testimony to its owner's affluence. His manifold concerns and great wealth finally provoked important members of the royal court to turn against him. In 1451 he was accused of poisoning Agnes *Sorel, the King's mistress, who had died more than a year earlier. Charles VII then ordered his arrest and confiscated his property. But in 1455 C. escaped from prison and eventually reached Rome, where *Nicholas V offered him a post as commander of an expedition to aid Rhodes. C. died in Chios during the campaign.

A. B. Kerr, *Jacques Coeur, Merchant Prince of the Middle Ages* (1927).

COGNAC, LEAGUE OF (1526) An alliance between France, *Venice, *Florence and Pope *Clement VII, later joined by *Henry VIII of England, against Emperor *Charles V. The aim of the allies was to form a counterbalance to the growing power of the Emperor, and to keep Italy from falling under Spanish domination. But the imperial attack against Clement VII, which resulted in the Sack of *Rome (1527), hit the League at its weakest point.

The house of Jacques Coeur in Bourges

COKE, SIR EDWARD (1552-1634) Chief Justice of England, legal authority and politician. Educated at Cambridge and Lincoln's Inn, C. quickly became the foremost English lawyer of his time. In 1592 he was made Solicitor General and Recorder of London; in 1593 he served as Speaker of the House of Commons and was appointed by *Elizabeth I Attorney-General of the realm. It was this appointment which originated the long and bitter rivalry between C. and Francis *Bacon, the losing candidate for the office. C.'s most famous prosecution, early in the reign of *James I, was that of Walter *Raleigh, whom he succeeded in having convicted more by arrogant invective and malicious insinuations than by real evidence. In 1605 C. prosecuted the conspirators of the *Gunpowder Plot. The following year he was made Chief Justice of the common pleas. In this position he behaved with characteristic independence and, asserting his own interpretations of the English common law, challenged the royal prerogatives. In 1613 he was promoted to be Chief Justice of the King's Bench – a position of higher dignity but less salary. He was made a privy councillor and was the first to be titled Lord Chief Justice of England. His confrontations with James I led to his dismissal, but in 1621 C. again came out as a champion of constitutionalism when he led the members of *Parliament in a petition asserting their right to freedom of speach. For this he was arrested for several months; nevetheless in 1628 he authored the famous *Petition of Right*. Of his legal writings the most important were the *Reports* (1600-1615); *Institutes* (1628); and *The Complete Copyholder* (1630).

COLET, JOHN (c. 1467-1519) English humanist and reformer of education. The son of a wealthy merchant who was also Lord Mayor of London, C. was educated at Oxford and, in 1493, went to study in Italy. During this three-year period of study abroad, he became a friend of his contemporaries *Budé and *Erasmus and developed a great interest in the new humanist learning. In 1496 he took holy orders and began his famous series of lectures on *St. Paul's Epistles to the Romans* at Oxford; C. discarded the traditional scholastic interpretation of this text in favour of one which emphasized man's sinful nature and his individual search for God's grace. In 1505 he became the dean of St. Paul's Cathedral. In 1509, having inherited his father's fortune, he re-founded St. Paul's school, which was modeled on Italian humanist schools and was the first English educational institution not sponsored directly by the church. The school's first headmaster was the grammarian William *Lilly and the London mercers' guild was made its board of trustees. An older friend of Thomas *More, respected by the young *Henry VIII, C. was an outspoken man who preached boldly against abuses in the Church, and even attacked England's involvement in wars on the Continent. His published writings included commentaries on the Scriptures and letters to Erasmus.

E. Hunt, *Dean Colet and His Theology* (1956);
J. Sears, *John Colet and Marsilio Ficino* (1963).

COLIGNY, GASPARD DE (1519-72) French leader of the *Huguenots. Born to a noble and influential family – his father had the title of Marshal of France – C. entered a military career and distinguished himself in the campaign of 1542-44 against Spain. In 1547 he was entrusted with a high command in the infantry and in 1552 was given the title of Admiral of France. In 1557 he fought bravely but was taken prisoner at St. Quentin, where the Duke of *Alba defeated the French; but was soon freed on payment of a ransom. C. had earlier become a follower of *Calvin, or a Huguenot. In 1555 he had helped Durand de *Villegaignon to establish a Huguenot colony in the harbour of Rio de Janeiro in Brazil. He became known as a foremost spokesman for the Huguenots after the death of *Henry II (1559) when, with Louis, Prince of *Condé, he demanded religious toleration for the French Calvinists. He and Condé were supreme commanders of the Huguenot forces during the *Religious Wars in 1562, and after the death of Condé in 1569, C. became their sole leader. In 1570 he was successful in obtaining the Edict of St. Germain, which reaffirmed the freedom of worship for the Huguenots. Returning to the royal court, he proposed an invasion of the Spanish Netherlands, an idea that favourably impressed the young king, *Charles IX. The queen-mother, *Catherine de Médicis, then concocted a plot to assassinate him and, on 22 August 1572, he was shot and wounded in Paris. Two days later, servants of the *Guises, heads of the Catholic faction and his old enemies, burst into his house and killed him. His murder signalled the beginning of the Massacre of *St. Bartholomew.

J. Shimizo, *Conflict and Loyalties; Politics and Religion in the Career of Gaspard de Coligny* (1970).

COLLEGE DE FRANCE The origins of the C.d.F. go back to 1530, when *Francis I established, upon the request of Guillaume *Budé, lectureships in Greek and in Hebrew, the nucleus of a royal *academy. In 1534 a third lectureship, in Latin, was added, and gave the institution its early name, *Collegium Trilingue*. In spite of the efforts of the University of Paris to block its development, the number of lectureships was increased in 1545 to seven. From then on and until the French Revolution the institution was known as the *Collège Royal*.

COLLENUCCIO, PANDOLFO (1444-1504) Italian diplomat and humanist. Born in Pesaro, he entered the service of the *Sforzas. His many diplomatic missions made him known as a skilful negotiator. Later, however, he was dismissed by Giovanni Sforza (1466-1510), ruler of Pesaro, and was welcomed as a councillor, first by Lorenzo de' *Medici, and later by Ercole I d'*Este of Ferrara. When Cesare *Borgia conquered Romagna, including Pesaro, C. supported him. After Borgia's fall and the recovery of Pesaro by Giovanni Sforza, he was arrested by the latter and executed. C. wrote a history of Naples as well as poetry, and translated Plautus' comedy, *Anfitrione*.

COLLEONI, BARTOLOMMEO (1400-75) Italian *condottiere*. Born in Bergamo to a noble family, he became a mercenary, entering the service of several Italian cities. The Republic of *Venice especially contracted his services, but periodic disagreement with the Venetians made him, between 1443 and 1448, support Venice's rival, *Milan. A contemporary of other great *condottieri*, such as *Gattamelata and Francesco *Sforza, whom he both served and fought, C. was known for the discipline of his troops and for his innovative tactics with *artillery. In 1455 the Venetians appointed him captain-general of their armies for life. Four years after his death, the Republic commissioned the sculptor Andrea *Verocchio to make an equestrian statue of C. It was completed in 1496 and is one of the most magnificent works of Renaissance sculpture.

COLOGNE A centre of commercial, industrial and cultural activity, this German town on the left bank of the Rhine enjoyed, from the 14th century on, *de facto* status of a free imperial city, officially recognized in 1475. While the archbishop of C. retained the imperial electoral right, he did not reside in the city, which, after 1396, was governed by a council elected by representatives of the *guilds. An important member of the *Hanseatic League, C. produced textiles, leather and metal works and, after 1464, was the major centre of printing in northwest Germany. However, the *university was known as a conservative upholder of scholasticism, and a focus of opposition to *humanism. The Reformation did not at first make inroads in C., and attempts by Archbishop Hermann von *Wied to introduce reform from above (1536-40) aroused opposition. A similar situation arose in 1582, when Archbishop Gebhardt Truchsess von Waldburg converted to Protestantism. This

Cologne, *an early 16th-century print*

time, however, the outcome was not only the deposition of the Archbishop by the Chapter and the Pope, but also a war between Protestant and Roman Catholic princes, following which C. came under the influence of the *Bavarian *Wittelsbach family. But, in the meantime, the city's economic status was reduced, and a long stagnation followed.

A. Stelzmann, *Illustrierte Geschichte der Stadt Köln* (1962);

H. Stehkaemper, *Köln, das Reich und Europa* (1971).

COLON, DIEGO (1478-1526) Second Viceroy and Admiral of the Indies. The oldest son of *Columbus, he was educated at the Spanish court, and inherited his father's property and claims on the newly discovered territories. In 1509 he sailed to Hispaniola, accompanied by his wife and relatives, and took charge of its government. In 1515 he had to return to Spain to defend himself against the charge that he had exceeded his powers. He then followed the royal council throughout Spain and, in 1520, received a provisional recognition of his rights as governor over the West Indies islands. Returning to Hispaniola, he was summoned again to Spain in 1523 to answer new charges and died there while awaiting the council's decision. The case of his heirs' rights over the American territories dragged on until 1536, when it was agreed that Luís Colón, C.'s son, would retain the title of Admiral but renounce all other rights in return for an annuity and huge estates in Jamaica and Panama.

T. S. Floyd, *The Columbus Dynasty in the Caribbean, 1492-1526* (1973).

COLONNA A Roman family. The great rivals of the *Orsini, they wielded great power from the 13th century on. In 1417 Oddone C. was elected pope as *Martin V. Fabrizio C. (*c.* 1460-1520) was one of the most famous Italian soldiers of his age, and Marcantonio C. (1535-84) was for many years the commander of the papal troops and played a decisive role in the great naval victory over the *Ottoman Turks at *Lepanto (1571). Highly independent, the C. frequently changed sides in the 15th century, but gradually became a sedate princely family of the *Papal States.

COLONNA, FRANCESCO (1433-1527) Italian author. A Dominican friar, his reputation rests on the *Hypnerotomachia Poliphili*, the story of the love of the charming Poliphil, in which the author put forward a wide range of ideas concerning the arts and moral issues. Combining mediaeval and Renaissance-humanist notions, the work is written in Italian blended with Latin and Greek terms. The work is also significant because of its Venetian edition of 1499, issued by *Manutius, and illustrated with exquisite woodcuts.

E. Kretzulesco-Quaranta, *Les jardins du songe* (1976).

COLONNA, POMPEO (1479-1532) Italian cardinal. A scion of the mighty Roman family, he was naturally inclined to pursue a military career, but was nevertheless

Poliphil asleep under a tree *and* The dream of Polia, *woodcuts from* Hypnerotomachia Poliphili *(1499)*

Vittoria Colonna

made bishop of Rieti in 1507. Following his attempt to lead a rebellion against *Julius II, he was deprived of his ecclesiastical dignities, but *Leo X restored him to favour and even made him cardinal (1517). Quarrelling with *Clement VII, C. took an active part in the Sack of *Rome (1527), on the side of the imperial troops. Afterwards he negotiated between *Charles V and the Pope and served as governor of Naples.

COLONNA, VITTORIA (1490-1547) Italian literary personality and marchioness of Pescara. Belonging to the famous C. family of Rome, at 19 she was married to Fernando de *Avalos the son of the marquis of Pescara. After her husband, who was a military man, died in 1525, she settled in a convent near Rome and became a friend of important reform-minded members of the Catholic Church, such as Cardinals *Contarini and Reginald *Pole. She also became closely associated with the unorthodox current of reformers, represented by Juan de *Valdes, Pietro *Carnesecchi and Bernardino *Ochino, but it is not certain that she herself espoused their Protestant ideas. C. also had many literary friends, among them *Bembo and *Castiglione. But she is best remembered for her friendship with *Michelangelo, who wrote sonnets to her and drew her portrait. Her own book of poems, *Rime spirituali*, was published four times between 1538 and 1544.

A. A. Bernardy, *La vita e l'opera di Vittoria Colonna* (1927).

COLUMBUS, CHRISTOPHER (It. Cristoforo Colombo; Sp. Cristóbal Colón; 1451-1506) The discoverer of *America. Born in *Genoa to a wool weaver, he took to the sea in his youth, as either a sailor or commercial agent. In 1476 he joined an expedition to England, but the ships were plundered by a French corsair off Cape St. Vincent. C., who barely escaped with his life, found shelter at Lisbon, where his younger brother Bartolomé was a chart-maker. In 1477 he completed his voyage to England, and a year later married a Portuguese noblewoman, who bore his first son, Diego (*Colón). It was during the next few years, while he was living in Lisbon and in Madeira, that C. developed his plan for a westward voyage to *India. He may have been encouraged in this idea by *Toscanelli's map and letter, but, considering the atmosphere of the time with respect to geographic knowledge and the interest in *exploration, the concept simply begged to be tested. Failing to convince *John II of Portugal (1483), C. went to Spain and, in 1486, met Queen *Isabella, who appointed a commission to examine the project. Although the commission decided against it (1491), C., who was about to leave Spain, made a last desperate effort and succeeded in persuading the Queen. He was given the title of admiral and perpetual rights as royal administrator for himself and his heirs over the territories that would be discovered.

On 3 August 1492, C. sailed from Palos in the *Santa Maria*, accompanied by two other ships, the *Pinta* and the *Niña*, under the command of the *Pinzon brothers, carrying altogether some 120 men. Passing through the Canary Islands he headed west and, on October 12, sighted land, reaching San Salvador (Watling Island) in

Christopher Columbus

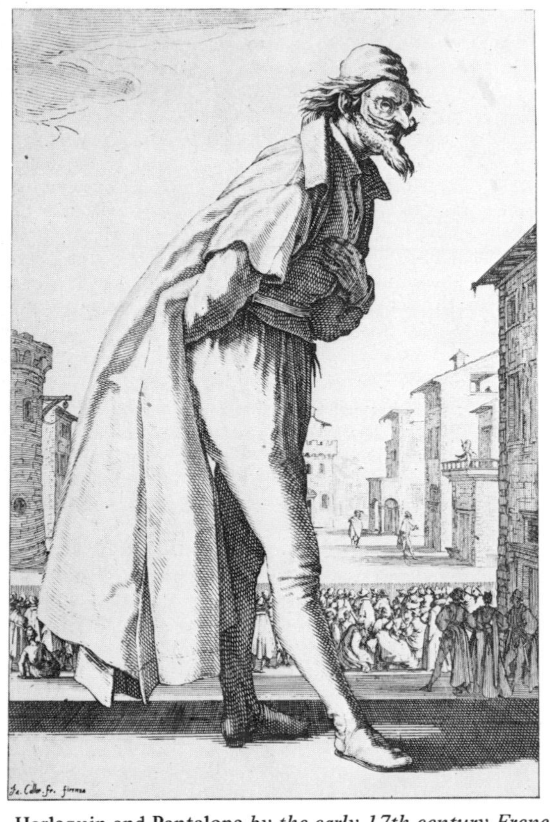

Harlequin and Pantalone *by the early 17th-century French artist Jacques Callot*

the Bahamas. He then sailed along the coasts of Cuba and Hispaniola (Haiti-San Domingo), and took possession of them in the name of Spain. He returned home to report his success, convinced that he had reached the continent of Asia. After an enthusiastic reception in Spain, which included royal honours and the title Admiral of the Ocean Sea and Viceroy of the Indies, C. went on his second voyage (25 September 1493), this time with 17 ships and some 1,500 men. He established a new settlement in Hispaniola in place of the one founded on the first voyage, which had been destroyed. Otherwise he accomplished little beyond exploring the Caribbean Sea and discovering Puerto Rico and Jamaica before returning to Spain early in 1496. On his third voyage, C. landed in Trinidad (August 1498). The sight of the mouth of the Orinoco proved to him the existence of a mainland, and reconfirmed his belief that he had reached the coast of Asia. Relinquishing any further exploration of the coast, he sailed to Hispaniola and took over its government but, in August 1500, following complaints against his administration, he was replaced by *Bobadilla, who sent C. and his brothers to Spain in chains. This outrageous treatment of the discoverer was meliorated in Spain and, on 9 May 1502, C. sailed for the fourth time, and visited the coasts of Honduras and Panama. Failing to find a passage to the West, he became even more convinced that he had reached Asia. He returned to Spain ill in November 1504, and died rather neglected 17 months later.

S. Morison, *Admiral of the Ocean Sea*, 2 vols. (1942); *The Journal of Christopher Columbus*, trans. by C. Jane (1960).

COMMEDIA DELL'ARTE A dramatic genre of popular origins which began in Italy during the second quarter of the 16th century and spread later to other European countries. The C.d'A. was played by professional actors who improvised their texts, following a more-or-less defined and preconceived plot. Each actor interpreted a fixed role of a certain social type, which was recognized by the audience by its characteristic manner of speech, costumes and a mask. The play usually centered on a love affair of two young persons, complicated by the attitude of their elders and the scheming of servants. Among the better known characters of the C.d'A. were: Pantalone, the older person; Harlequin, the clever servant; and Pulcinella the ingenue. The companies, usually comprising nine men and four women, travelled from town to town, performing to popular audiences. The most famous companies, such as *I Gelosi* (1568-1604), were sometimes backed by aristocratic patrons, nevertheless the players were occasionally harrassed by the ecclesiastical authorities. The influence of the C.d'A.

is to be found in the contemporary comedies of *Shakespeare, as well as in the plays of the 18th-century Italian authors, Carlo Goldoni and Carlo Gozzi.
K. M. Lea, *The Italian Popular Comedy*, 2 vols. (1934).

COMMINES, PHILIPPE DE (1445-1509) French historian, considered one of the precursors of modern historiography. Born in *Flanders, he came as a youth to the Burgundian court, entering the service of *Charles the Bold. He is said to have saved the life of *Louis XI at Peronne in 1468, when the King was a prisoner of the Duke's, by interceding on his behalf. In 1472 he went over to the French king, who made him his counsellor, gave him an estate and arranged his marriage into the higher nobility. However, after the death of his protector, C. lost some of his estates and plotted against the regent, *Anne of France. He was arrested for a while and returned to the court only in 1492, when *Charles VIII began his preparations for the invasion of Italy. After Charles' death (1498), C. ceased to be active in French politics.

The *Mémoires*, on which C.'s reputation as an historian is founded, describe the reigns of Louis XI and Charles VIII, covering the years 1464-83 and 1488-95. They are characterized by a flowing narrative, the ability to discern the trend of events and a keen understanding of men's inner motives. C., moreover, emphasized the objective lessons of history and regarded customs and manners as a conditioning factor. The *Mémoires* were first published in 1524.
J. Dufournet, *Etudes sur Philippe de Commynes* (1975);
J. Demers, *Commynes mémorialiste* (1975).

COMMON PRAYER, THE BOOK OF The official liturgy of the *Church of England. The B.o.C.P. was the work of *Cranmer, who meant to produce a revised and simplified English version of the former separate Latin texts. Following the revision of parts of the service under *Henry VIII, the First Prayer Book of *Edward VI was ordered by Parliament into general use in England in the Act of *Uniformity (January 1549). Dissatisfaction among those who wanted more substantial reforms led to the printing of the Second Prayer Book of Edward VI (1552), again the work of Cranmer, who consulted with *Bucer. Its major revisions were in the service of communion, besides omitting prayers for the dead and ordering the officiating clergy to use the surplice instead of vestments. Repealed by *Mary (1553), the B.o.C.P. was restored by *Elizabeth I (1559) with only few changes. Objections by the *Puritans brought some additional minor modifications after the *Hampton Court Conference (1604).

COMPASS An instrument for determining sailing directions by means of a magnetic needle turning freely on a pivot and pointing to the magnetic North. Originally discovered in China, it was brought to the West by the Arabs, and carried by European ships at least since the 13th century. By the 15th century it was fitted with a circular card on which were marked the 32 points of the wind rose. About the end of the century gimbals were introduced, and the existence of variation became known, which helped the navigator to adjust his course in steering the ship.

COMUNEROS, REVOLT OF THE (May 1520-April 1521) A protest movement of the Castilian towns asserting their traditional rights against the rising power of the royal administration. The most extreme demand

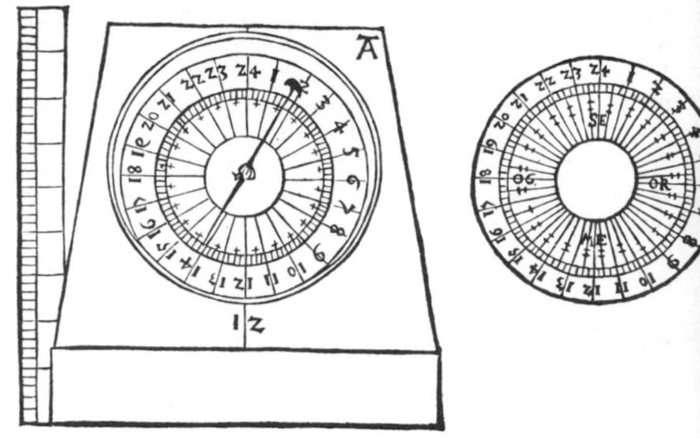

Late 16th-century compass

of the rebels was to assemble the Cortes every three years. The ferocity of the revolt was caused by a distrust of *Charles V's Flemish advisers, which created a general feeling of grievance. The rebels, led by Juan de Padilla of Toledo, won some victories during the summer of 1520. But on 23 April 1521 they were completely defeated, their leaders captured and immediately executed. The Spanish nobility, seemed at first undecided in its response to the movement. But when the revolt took an anti-aristocracy turn, the nobility sided firmly with the monarchy.
H. L. Seaver, *The Great Revolt of Castile* (1928);
J. A. Maravall, *Las comunidades de Castilla* (1963).

CONCILIAR MOVEMENT A movement within the Roman Catholic Church which asserted that the general council was superior to the pope. The movement, which was originated by mediaeval theorists like Marsiglio of Padua (*c.* 1275-1348), found its later ideologists in Pierre D'Ailly (1350-1420) and Jean Gerson (1363-1429), who dominated the Councils of *Pisa and *Constance. The conciliar spirit triumphed at the Council of *Basle (1431-49), but the movement declined during the second half of the 15th century. However, the uneasiness with which the papacy contemplated the prospects of a general council was one of the reasons for the delay in convening the Council of *Trent.
B. Tierney, *Foundations of the Conciliar Theory* (1955);
F. Oakley, *The Political Thought of Pierre D'Ailly* (1964);
E. F. Jacob, *Essays in the Conciliar Epoch* (1963).

CONDE A family of the French aristocracy related to the *Bourbons. Louis (1530-69), the first to be acclaimed Prince of C., had in his youth been exposed to Protestant influence at the court of Navarre. Although a hunchback, he distinguished himself as a military commander in the wars against Spain (1551-57). His services for the crown were not rewarded by *Henry II, and, with the accession of *Francis II (1559), who was under the influence of the *Guises, C. openly assumed the military leadership of the *Huguenots. It was at this point that the title of prince was conferred upon him by his followers. C. supported the Amboise conspiracy (1560) against the King, but delivered himself to the King several months after its failure. The King's death saved him from execution, and, since the Regent *Catherine de Médicis wished to counterbalance the power of the Guises, C. was allowed to resume his role with the Huguenots. He was at their head in December 1562, when they advanced on Paris, but was defeated by François de Guise. This led to the Peace of Amboise and to a four-year interval in the confrontation. However, in 1567 C. broke again from the court. He was defeated a second time near Paris, yet continued his campaigns during the following two years. He was killed in battle at Jarnac, where he was trying to come to the aid of *Coligny.

Upon his father's death, Henry (1552-88), the second Prince of C., became, together with his cousin Henry of Navarre (the future *Henry IV), the recognized leaders of the Huguenots. Both cousins were arrested in the Massacre of *St. Bartholomew (1572) and forced to convert to Roman Catholicism, but both returned to lead the Huguenots, C. becoming one of the principal commanders in the army of Henry of Navarre. In this role he was not noted for either prudence or ability. He died under somewhat mysterious circumstances while recuperating from a wound incurred in battle.

CONDOTTIERI Commanders of mercenary troops who sold their services to the Italian states in the numerous wars during the 14th and the 15th centuries. The first C. were foreigners, but by the end of the 14th century Italian soldiers began to raise mercenary armies and to conquer principalities for themselves. The most famous of the C. was Francesco *Sforza, who became duke of Milan in 1447. The C. and the mercenary bands disappeared as the foreign powers began their invasions of Italy at the end of the 15th century.

CONQUISTADORES A term applied to those Spaniards who conquered the American territories for the Spanish crown. While the upper Spanish nobility led its armies in Europe, it failed to evince much interest in the conquest of America. Many of the C. were adventurers belonging to the minor aristocracy, or to a lower social strata, sometimes even illiterate men of peasant origins, who organized their expeditions with their own resources. They were greedy for riches and fame, fired with a conqueror's missionary zeal and incredible audacity. Penetrating the vast Indian empires with forces numbering a few hundred men, they took possession in the name of their king, more by cunning, clever manipulation of local rivalries or cruel acts of intimidation than by actual military victories. As a reward for the conquest, the leaders of the expeditions received titles of nobility and their men **encomiendas*. The period of intensive conquest of the American mainland lasted from 1519 to 1540. The two most famous C. were *Cortés and *Pizarro.

F. A. Kirkpatrick, *The Spanish Conquistadores* (1934).

CONSEJO DE INDIAS (Council of the Indies) The institutional framework created by *Charles V in 1524 to govern the newly-acquired Spanish dominions in America. Composed of six, later ten, members, the C.d.I. prepared legislation, supervised the administration and also served as the highest court of the American territories. The Council grew slowly during the 16th century, adding new functions and personnel. In 1571 a post was created for an official historian and cosmographer of the Indies.

E. Schäfer, *El consejo real y supremo de las Indias*, 2 vols. (1935-47).

CONSTANCE, COUNCIL OF (1414-17) A general council of the Church convoked in 1413 by *John XXIII to bring an end to the *Great Schism and deal with heresies, especially the teachings of John *Wycliffe and Jan *Hus. Dominated by *conciliar theorists, it promulgated in March 1415 a series of declarations, defining its authority as emanating from God and binding the pope himself. John XXIII, who fled from Constance following the victory of the conciliarists, was charged with simony and promptly deposed by the Council. *Gregory XII resigned (1415), as he had promised to do for the sake of reunifiying the Church, and Benedict XIII, the Avignonese pope, who refused to abdicate, was isolated and finally deposed in 1417. The Council then elected as pope Cardinal Oddo *Colonna, who became *Martin V, thus marking the end of the schism. Before this, the Council had condemned Hus as a heretic and had him burnt at the stake (1415). His companion, Jerome of Prague, received the same treatment (1416). The Council also ordered the body of Wycliffe to be removed from its grave, because of his heretical ideas. Though it was one of the most important church assemblies, it failed to deal with issues of reform.

CONSTANTINOPLE, FALL OF (29 May 1453) By the time *Mehemmed II resolved to bring an end to the Byzantine Empire, C. was a mere shade of its former glory. Emperor Constantine XI had only about 10,000 soldiers to defend the city, against more than ten times that number of besieging troops. Using numerous pieces of *artillery, the Sultan's army pounded the walls of the city for over three months until it forced its way in. The Emperor was killed, the city was given to pillage, and its principal churches converted to mosques. However, when the Sultan implemented his programme of making C. the new capital of his empire, he allowed the residence of Greeks and Armenians in the city and vested their patriarchs with considerable religious authority. In the West, the fall of C. gave rise to a wave of religious indignation and to calls for a *crusade. Yet contemporaries saw in it an event of moral significance, rather than a decisive development of immediate implications.

CONSULADO The Spanish *guild of merchants. It originated in Barcelona which had set up its *Consolat de la mar* in 1347, but was introduced to Castile by *Ferdinand and *Isabella, starting with the C. of Burgos (1494). The C. regulated trade and had its mercantile court. In fact, it was supposed to monopolize wholesale trade on land and sea. The most important C. was the **Casa de Contratación* of *Seville.

CONTARINI, AMBROGIO (?-1499) Italian traveller. A scion of a patrician family of Venice, he was sent in 1474 on a mission to arrange an alliance against the Ottoman Turks with the king of Persia. Travelling through Austria, Poland, the Ukraine and the Crimea, he reached the Caucasus and, in 1475, arrived at Isfahan, where he met Giosafat *Barbaro, who had been sent out the year before. In 1476 he was asked to leave, and on his way back passed through Tiflis, Astrakhan and southern Russia, returning to Venice in 1477. He left a detailed account of his voyage, first printed in 1486.

CONTARINI, GASPARO (1483-1542) Italian cardinal. Belonging to an aristocratic Venetian family, C. pursued a diplomatic career, but at the same time became known for his learning. In 1521 he attended the Diet of *Worms, in his capacity as Venetian ambassador to the

Nicolaus Copernicus

court of *Charles V, and afterwards wrote a book against the teachings of *Luther. Although he was a layman, his reputation as a theologian led *Paul III to make him a cardinal, and to put him on a commission charged with preparing a project for church reform. The *Consilium de emendanda ecclesia* (1537), written largely by C., proposed many radical changes, which were later debated at the Council of *Trent. C. supported the approval of the *Jesuit order. In 1541, at the Conference of Regensburg, he attempted a reconciliation with the Lutherans, and wrote a confession of faith which brought him under suspicion in militant Catholic circles. He died in Bologna the following year.

P. Matheson, *Cardinal Contarini at Regensburg* (1972).

CONTI, NICCOLO DE' (c. 1395-1469) Italian traveller. Born to a well-known Venetian family, he spent the years 1414 to 1439 travelling in the East. He first visited Damascus, where he learned Arabic, then went on to Bagdad and later to India. Eventually he reached Ceylon, Sumatra and Java, passing through Burma and returning via Calicut, Aden and Cairo. His knowledge of the East helped him make a fortune in commercial enterprises after his return to Venice. He gave an account of his travels to *Poggio Bracciolini, who included it in his *De varietate fortunae*; but it was published only in 1723.

COORNHERT, DIRCK VOLCKERTSZOON (1522-90) Dutch humanist, poet, engraver, theologian and politician. The son of a cloth merchant of *Amsterdam, he was educated in Spain and Portugal, and settled in Haarlem (1542), where he worked as an engraver. His translations of *Boccaccio's *Decameron* and *Odyssey* into Dutch had a great impact on the development of prose in the vernacular of the Netherlands. C. took an active part in political life, aligning himself with *William of Orange whose manifestoes he wrote. He was persecuted by the Spanish government and found shelter in Clèves (1568-72), where he taught etching to *Goltzius. His translations from Cicero, Seneca and Boethius were highly praised, but his most important work was on ethics; his *Zedekunst dat is Wellevenkunste* (Morality, or the Art of Good Living) was published in 1586. Advocating religious tolerance it revealed the influence of stoicism. Although he never broke with Roman Catholicism, C. did not care for the sacraments. On the other hand, he attacked the Calvinist doctrines which were then current in the Netherlands and, while emphasizing the need for interior piety, defended liberalism.

COPERNICUS, NICOLAUS (1473-1543) Polish astronomer; father of the heliocentric theory of *astronomy which fundamentally changed man's conception of the universe. Born to a merchant family in Thorn, in Prussian Poland, C. was helped in his education by his maternal uncle, who was a bishop and a learned man. He studied mathematics at the University of Cracow (1491-94), and then went to Italy where he attended schools in Bologna, Ferrara and Padua, taking degrees in canon law and medicine. He left Italy in 1505 and, until 1512, served as his uncle's physician. After the latter's death he moved to Frauenburg in Ermeland, where he held the position of canon at the cathedral. He spent most of the rest of his life there, perfoming his capitular functions as well as those of physician.

C.'s astronomical ideas began to take shape during his student days in Bologna, where he heard the astronomical lectures of Domenico Maria Novara. As a result, he began to question the accuracy of the Ptolemaic system. He hypothesized that if the stars and the earth were assumed to revolve around the sun, the calculation of their movements would be greatly simplified. His ideas were based on theoretical consideration in the manner of geometrical astronomy, with only scanty observed data to support them. However, it eliminated the need for the universe to rotate once a day, as implied in the old notion that the earth was the fixed centre of the universe. C. first made his ideas known in the *Commentariolus*, a brief manuscript which he circulated among his friends. The full exposition of his views, a treatise entitled *De revolutionibus orbium coelestium*, was completed by 1530, but printed only in 1543, shortly before his death. Although he was a Catholic, C.'s theory was at first supported by a number of Protestant personalities. Georg Rheticus, a mathematician from Wittenberg, came to Frauenburg to discuss the theory and received the author's permission to publish his work. Andreas *Osiander wrote a preface to the book. However, the acceptance of the theory came very slowly. Only at the very end of the 16th century, with *Galileo and *Kepler, did the heliocentric system gain a fundamental position in astronomy.

A. Armitage, *Copernicus; the Founder of Modern Astronomy* (1957);
F. Hoyle, *Nicolaus Copernicus* (1973);
H. Kasten, *Copernicus and His World* (1946);
D. Stimson, *The Gradual Acceptance of the Copernican Theory of the Universe* (1972).

COPLAND, ROBERT (?-1547) English printer and author. He may have been an assistant of *Caxton's, and was certainly at the shop of Wynkyn de *Worde. He published few books, but his style was vigorous, and he translated several romances of *chivalry from the French. His best-known work, *Hye Way to the Spyttal House* (1536), is full of curious information about beggars and vagabonds.

F. C. Francis, *Robert Copland* (1961).

CORIO, BERNARDINO (1459-c. 1512) Italian historian. A native of Milan, he served the *Sforza's for a long time, and was commissioned by *Ludovico il Moro to write the history of the city. It was completed after his patron's fall, and first published in 1503 as *Patria historia*. Written in Italian, it covered the history of Milan from its beginnings to 1499. Although it is full of errors and is biased in favour of the *Visconti and Sforzas, the work includes many otherwise unknown sources and valuable descriptions of manners and customs. C. also wrote lives of the Roman and Mediaeval emperors and lesser works.

COPPENHOLE, JAN VAN (?-1492) Leader of the rebellion of *Ghent against *Maximilian of Austria, the future emperor. C. first played a decisive role in the affairs of Ghent in 1484 when he advocated intransigence against Maximilian's claims to the regency during the minority of his son *Philip the Handsome. Forced to flee in 1485, he went to France but returned in 1487 and took advantage of the agitated mood of the population to lead the city against the Regent once more. C. dominated the political life of Ghent until his murder in June 1492. He aimed at conserving and even broadening the city's political autonomy, and exploited the French hostility towards Maximilian. After his death the city surrendered and remained subjugated for a long period.

CORDOBA, GONZALO DE (1453-1515) Spanish military commander, known as *el Gran Capitán*. Born to a noble family, he was orphaned in boyhood and entered the service of the Crown of Castile. He served in the wars against the Portuguese and the Moors, displaying great courage, and was among the officers who received the surrender of *Granada (1492). The opportunity to demonstrate his military talent came in 1495, when he was given command of the Spanish force sent to *Naples to help King *Ferrante against the French invaders. During the next three years he introduced many tactical reforms with regard to the development of infantry, adopting the use of long pikes in the central body, which was flanked by units carrying *arquebuses. He returned to Spain in 1498, following the expulsion of the French, but went back to Italy in 1501, in the capacity of general and viceroy of Naples. He stayed there until 1507, when he was recalled by *Ferdinand the Catholic, who resented his success. C.'s greatest victory was at the Battle of Cerignola (1503), which led to the second expulsion of the French from Naples. The formation he adopted for the infantry units was essentially the one which served the Spaniards in their great victorious combats for the rest of the 16th century.

G. de Gaury, *The Grand Captain* (1955).

CORNARO, LUIGI (1475-1566) Italian student of dietetics. Born in Venice to a distinguished family, he suffered many years from ill health, and claimed to have recovered at the age of forty, when he began to practice dietary regulations and daily exercises. In 1558, aged 83, he published the first of his four treatises, entitled *Della vita sobria*. The treatises came out in several editions and translations, and remained popular for a long time. They celebrated the joy of happy old age, unmarred by physical or mental impairment.

CORNAZZANO, ANTONIO (1429-84) Italian author. Born in Piacenza, he spent many years in the service of the *Sforzas, and the final ones with the house of *Este at Ferrara. He wrote many poems, including the *Sforzeide*, a eulogy of his Milanese masters modelled on Virgil. Of his other writings the most important are a treatise on *dance, a work on military science, *Opera belissima de l'arte militare*, published in 1493, and a collection of licentious tales, *I proverbi*, published in 1525.

CORNEILLE DE LYON (?-1574) French painter. A native of The Hague, he settled in *Lyons, and enjoyed a great reputation for his miniature portraits. Although the correct identification of his works is not without problems, he is known to have painted the portraits of *Francis I, *Henry II and *Catherine de Médicis. His colours are often pale, with plain green ground.

CORONADO, FRANCISCO VASQUEZ DE (c. 1510-54) Spanish explorer. Born in Salamanca, he went to Mexico in 1535, becoming the governor of the northwestern region, known as New Galicia, in 1538. The following year he undertook an expedition to the legendary rich kingdom of Cíbola. Reaching present-day New Mexico, he subjugated the Zuñi Indians, but finding no gold, decided to continue east in search of another legendary country named Quivira. He seems to have crossed parts of Texas and Kansas and, in 1542, returned to Mexico. In 1544 he lost the governorship and died in Mexico City.

F. W. Hodge, ed., *Spanish Explorers in the Southern United States, 1528-1543* (1946).

CORREGGIO (Antonio Allegri; 1494-1534) Italian painter. Confining his activity mainly to the city of Parma in northern Italy, C. worked in relative solitude. He probably never saw the great masterpieces of his contemporaries, *Leonardo and *Raphael, but he must have seen works by their students. C. executed a number of famous *frescoes, the most important of which was in the cupola of the cathedral in Parma. It depicts the Assumption of Mary surrounded by saints and angels, with an illusionist effect on the viewer below, creating the impression that he is looking at a three-dimensional scene. In his oil paintings C. developed compositions of shades, lights and forms which anticipated the *Baroque and which particularly influenced Annibale *Carracci.

S. Brinton, *Correggio* (1907);

E. Panofsky, *The Iconography of Correggio's Camera di San Paolo* (1961);

A. E. Popham, *Correggio's Drawings* (1957).

CORREIA, GASPAR (c. 1495-c. 1565) Portuguese historian. Leaving Portugal for *India in 1512, he became the secretary of Afonso de *Albuquerque and remained in the Far East for the rest of his life. His *Lendas da India*, a description of events which he had witnessed, contained an account of daily life in India, as well as much harsh criticism of the vices of colonial society. C. is believed to have been murdered in *Malacca. His work remained unpublished until the 19th century.

Venus with sleeping cupid *by Correggio*

CORRER, GREGORIO (1411-64) Italian humanist. Born to a distinguished Venetian family, he was taken to Rome by his uncle, a cardinal, who started him on an ecclesiastical career. In 1433 he took part in the Council of *Basle, where he pronounced against papal supremacy. Later, he spent time in Florence (1443), where the papal court was then residing, and felt the vindictiveness of his adversaries inside the Church. Although elected in 1464 Patriarch of Venice, he was not confirmed by Pope *Paul II and died before taking possession. A pupil of *Vittorino da Feltre and a lifelong pursuer of humanist studies, C. wrote on education, composed a Latin drama, adapted Aesop's *Fables* into Latin, and produced a highly interesting autobiography.

C. A. Riccio, *Gregorio Correr* (1900).

CORTE REAL A Portuguese family, several of whose members took part in the late 15th-century *exploration of the North Atlantic. The father, João Vaz Corte Real, is believed to have sailed about 1472 to *Newfoundland. His sons, Gaspar and Miguel, disappeared one after another on expeditions which left from Lisbon in 1500, 1501 and 1502. Miguel is believed to have reached present-day Massachussettes, where he died years later as an Indian chief.

CORTES, HERNAN (1485-1547) Conqueror of Mexico. Born to an impoverished noble family of Castile, he went to Hispaniola when he was 19 and took part in the conquest of Cuba (1511). In February 1519 he sailed to the mainland, leading a small army of 600 men, including 13 musketeers seven small canons and 16 horses. He first defeated an army of Mayans near Tabasco. There he was joined by Jeronimo de Aguilar, a survivor of a shipwreck who had learned the Mayan language, and by a young Aztec woman who was held captive by the Mayans, named Marina, who became his mistress and interpreter. Sailing northwest along the coast, C. landed and founded Veracruz, where he received presents from the Aztec ruler Moctezuma and won the cooperation of local tribes. Before continuing his journey to the interior, he had all his ships destroyed (August 1519). En route to the Aztec capital, Tenochtitlan, he defeated the independent Indians of Tlaxcala, who then became his trusted allies. On 8 November 1519, he entered Tenochtitlan and soon after took Moctezuma hostage. In May 1520 he had to leave the city to confront Pánfilo Narvaez, who had been sent from Cuba to replace him. He succeeded in capturing Narvaez and won his soldiers to his side, but, upon his return, discovered that the Aztecs had risen in rebellion. C. then evacuated the city during the "Sorrowful Night" of 30 June 1520, losing many of his men, horses and guns. He quickly reorganized his diminished forces in Tlaxcala, and, in December 1520, set out with his Indian allies and began a systematic encirclement against the Aztec capital. By May he was able to cut the fresh water supply to the city, which was set in the middle of a lake, and in August 1521 Tenochtitlan fell.

As first governor of Mexico, C. erected the foundations for a new capital city, pacified the surrounding Indian tribes and sent expeditions to Central America. In 1524 he went on an unsuccessful expedition to Honduras and, on returning to Mexico in 1526, found his position weakened. He resumed his work until 1529, when he went to Spain. There *Charles V gave him the title of Marqués del Valle de Oaxaca and a huge **encomienda*. C. returned to Mexico in 1530 as captain-general, not as governor, and continued to organize expeditions along the Pacific coast; in 1536 he visited lower California. In 1540 he returned to Spain, where he died at the age of 63. He was the greatest Spanish **conquistador*, a natural Machiavellian and a great leader of men.

W. H. Prescott, *History of the Conquest of Mexico* (1943);

B. Diaz del Castillo, *The True History of the Conquest of Mexico* (1963);

S. de Madariaga, *Hernán Cortés* (1942).

CORTES, MARTIN (c. 1510-82) Spanish geographer. C. is known primarily for his work on navigation, *El arte de navegar*, which he dedicated to *Charles V. It was published in Cádiz in 1551, had a subsequent edition in *Seville and, in 1561, was translated into English. C. was the first to point out the variability of magnetic declination in the *compass in different areas of the globe.

CORVINUS, JANOS (1473-1504) Duke of Slavonia. An illegitimate son of *Matthias Corvinus, king of Hungary, he was intended by his father to succeed him, but when the latter died suddenly in 1490 C. did not get the support of the nobles. Between 1499 and 1502 he successfully defended Bosnia from the invading Ottoman Turks.

CORYATE, THOMAS (c. 1577-1617) English traveller. The son of a rector of Odcombe, Somerset, he was educated at Oxford. He was court jester of *James I. In 1608 he began a walking tour of France, Italy, Switzerland, Germany and the Netherlands, a lively description of which he published in 1611 as *Coryate's Crudities*. In 1612 he set out on a journey to Greece, the Holy Land, Persia and India. He sent home accounts of his adventures, which were published in 1616, but he never returned, meeting his death at Surat, India. His writings described local mores and he is credited with introducing the use of the fork from Italy into England.

M. Strachan, *The Life and Adventures of Thomas Coryate* (1962).

COSA, JUAN DE LA (?-1510) Spanish explorer and cartographer. A native of Santander, he was the proprietor of the *Santa Maria*, and probably took part in *Columbus' first voyage, and was the cartographer of the second. In 1499 he accompanied Alonso de *Ojeda on the exploration of the coasts of Guayana and Venezuela, a voyage in which Amerigo *Vespucci also took part. His famous map of the world, the first to delineate the American continent, incorporating all the geographic knowledge available then, was published in 1500. Shortly afterwards C. went on another voyage, this time to the coast of Panama and, in 1504, undertook yet another exploration of the north Caribbean coast. The recipient of royal honours and gifts, he served as chief commander of the Spanish coasts (1507). Following an uneventful journey to America in 1508, he went on his seventh voyage with Ojeda. Sailing from Hispaniola in November 1509, they landed near Cartagena, where C. lost his life in combat with the Indians.

Grand Duke Cosimo I de' Medici *by Cellini*

Autumm *by Francesco del Cossa*

COSIMO I (1519-74) Grand-duke of Tuscany. Son of Giovanni dalle Bande Nere de' Medici. He became duke of Florence in 1537 at the age of 18 in the wake of a political crisis which arose when Duke Alessandro de' Medici was murdered. Despite his youth and limited means, he firmly suppressed an attempt by the oligarchy to resume power. In 1539 he married Eleonora de *Toledo, daughter of the Spanish viceroy of Naples, and, with Spanish support conquered *Siena (1555). This and other small territorial conquests later formed the grand-duchy of Tuscany; the title of grand-duke was conferred upon him by *Pius V in 1569. His rule was characterized by intermittent acts of cruelty. Although he managed to retain his independence vis-à-vis Spain, he was less successful in his internal policies. During his long government Florence gradually lost its preeminence as centre of cultural and economic activity.

G. Spini, *Cosimo I de' Medici e la indipendenza del principato mediceo* (1945);

H. M. M. Acton, *The Last Medici* (1958).

COSSA, FRANCESCO DEL (1436-78) Italian painter. C. is mainly known by his decorative works for the

The Duchess of Urbino *by Lorenzo Costa*

*Estes in *Ferrara. In these he followed his senior Cosimo *Tura, but both painters were clearly influenced by *Mantegna. C.'s series of frescoes at the Palazzo Schifanoia at Ferrara depict scenes of hunting and courtly romance according to the months of the year. After their completion (1470), he left Ferrara for Bologna, where he painted religious subjects.

COSTA, LORENZO (c. 1460-1535) Italian painter. Trained in *Ferrara, probably under Ercole de' *Roberti, he moved to Bologna in about 1483. There he executed works for the local rulers, the *Bentivoglios, in partnership with Francesco *Francia. In 1506 he succeeded *Mantegna as court painter at *Mantua. Though weak in his treatment of the human figure, C. was nevertheless able to paint impressive landscapes. His *Isabella d'Este in the Garden of the Muses*, now at the Louvre, is particularly well known.

COTTON, SIR ROBERT (1571-1631) English antiquary. Born to a rich family of Huntingdonshire, he was educated at Westminster School under William *Camden, with whom he maintained a close friendship. During the reign of *James I, C. was received at court and was knighted, but was disgraced in 1615, having been implicated in an attempt to tamper with judicial evidence. He later supported the emerging parliamentary opposition. His collection of manuscripts, books, coins and medals, which he had begun in his youth, became the biggest of its kind in England, and included many old Saxon charters and ancient chronicles. In 1706 it became a national possession.

F. Smith Fussner, *The Historical Revolution* (1962).

COUNTER REFORMATION The broad movement of internal change and religious renewal which characterized the Roman Catholic Church during the 16th and early 17th centuries. The term C.R. was originally employed in reference to the militant reaction of Roman Catholicism to the religious upheaval of the *Reformation. While the term in this sense is valid, it should not be overlooked that the internal reform movement inside the Catholic Church had begun about the same time that *Luther launched his protest against the sale of *indulgences. Thus, like Protestantism, the C.R. was directed, though internally, against such abuses as nepotism, simony, pluralism and absenteeism, and the immorality of the clergy. Unlike Protestantism, it left unchallenged the fundamental doctrines and traditional Catholic beliefs, though it endeavoured to give them authoritative definitions. One of the earliest signs of the C.R. was the advent of new orders, such as the *Capuchins (*c.* 1520). The trend culminated in the founding of the *Jesuit order, which became the militant spearhead of resurgent Roman Catholicism. In Rome, *Adrian VI was the first pope to display reformist zeal, but the movement caught on only with *Paul III (1534-49), whose most important decision, the summoning of the Council of *Trent, had a lasting influence on Catholic doctrine. To the propagandist effort of the C.R. were added repressive measures, exemplified by the **Index Librorum Prohibitorum* and the establishment of the *Inquisition in Italy. On the other hand, the Catholic reformers undoubtedly enjoyed popular support, and the growth of a characteristic 16th-century Catholic mysticism is yet another affirmation of the authenticity of the C.R. In the drive to arrest the territorial expansion of Protestantism, the main achievements of the C.R. were the elimination of the unorthodox undercurrent in Italy and the consolidation of Roman Catholicism in Poland and parts of Germany. The C.R. may be said to have spent its forces at about the opening of the Thirty Years War (1618). It left the Catholic Church devoid of the urbane spirit of the *Renaissance, more disciplined and with the papacy more powerful than before.

E. M. Burns, *The Counter Reformation* (1964);
H. Daniels-Ropes, *The Catholic Reformation* (1962);
A. G. Dickens, *The Counter Reformation* (1969);
B. J. Kidd, *The Counter Reformation, 1550-1600* (1933);
J. C. Olin, ed., *The Catholic Reformation; Savonarola to Ignatius Loyola* (1969).

COUSIN, JEAN (c. 1490-1561) French painter. Born near Sens, he became successful at first as a designer of stained glass and may have executed some of the windows of the Sens cathedral. About 1538 he settled in Paris, where he seems to have worked as a painter, goldsmith and designer of tapestries. Most works are ascribed to C. only by attribution. He was not associated with the contemporary School of *Fontainebleau, and developed the principles and style elements of Renaissance painting on his own. In 1560 he published the *Livre de perspective*, and in 1571 appeared his *Livre de pourtraicture*, two works which enjoyed considerable success. His son, Jean (1522-94), was also a painter as well as engraver, book-illustrator and author.

COUTO, DIOGO DO (c. 1543-1616) Portuguese historian. Born in Lisbon and educated at the royal court, he went in 1559 as a soldier to *India, where he befriended the poet *Camões. He returned to Portugal in 1569, but two years later again sailed East and subsequently settled in Goa where he died. While serving as keeper of the Portuguese archives at Goa (from 1595), C. composed the *Décadas*, a continuation of the work of João de *Barros. An earlier work, *Diálogo do soldado prático*, was very critical of the Portuguese colonial administration. It was published only two hundred years later, but its circulation in manuscript gave the author a reputation as a trouble-maker.

A. F. G. Bell, *Diogo do Couto* (1924).

COVARRUBIAS, ALONSO DE (1488-1570) Spanish architect and decorative sculptor, one of the foremost exponents of the *Plateresque. Born near Burgos, his early work was done in Salamanca and other towns of Old Castile. But his most accomplished works were executed in Toledo. These included a chapel in the cathedral (1531-34), of which he was the master mason, and extensive works at the local Alcázar. C. also worked on the archbishop's palace at Alcalá de Henares. In 1537 he was made royal architect by *Charles V, a post he retained under *Philip II. His opinion was highly respected. In 1542 he was consulted about some works at the cathedral of *Seville.

COVERDALE, MILES (1488-1568) Translator of the first complete English *Bible. A sympathizer of the reformist ideas during his studies in Cambridge, C. had to leave England and spent many years abroad. His translation was first published in *Zurich in 1535 and, two years later, in England. In 1539 he issued the Great Bible, an edition ordered by Thomas *Cromwell. C. then returned to England and, in 1551, was made bishop of Exeter, but had to leave the country again when *Mary acceded to the throne. He returned in 1559 and, in his last years, supported the emerging *Puritan movement.

COVILHA, PERO DE (?-1525) Portuguese explorer. In 1487 C. was sent by the Portuguese crown, together with Afonso de Paiva, to find an overland route to the country of the legendary *Prester John. He went via Naples to Alexandria and Cairo, posing as a merchant, and then continued by way of the Red Sea to Aden, where he parted from his friend Paiva, the latter going on to Ethiopia. C. proceeded to India, visiting Calicut, Cannanore and Goa. On his way back to Egypt he reached the coast of East Africa. A Portuguese Jew, whom he met in Cairo, carried back to Portugal an account of his voyage to India. C. then continued his travels in the Arabian Peninsula, eventually reaching Ethiopia, where his friend Paiva had perished. Here he remained for many years and in 1520, was met by a Portuguese expedition led by Rodrigo de Lima. He died in Ethiopia.

COX, RICHARD (1500-81) English bishop of Ely. Educated at Eton and Cambridge, he pursued an ecclesiastical career and reached a position of influence when he was appointed, with the Greek scholar John Cheke (1554-57), to tutor the future *Edward VI. In 1547 he became chancellor of Oxford University, where he quickly introduced many pro-Protestant reforms. Ousted from his posts at *Mary's accession (1553), he went into exile in *Frankfurt, where he debated John *Knox. He returned in the reign of *Elizabeth I, who in 1559 made him bishop of Ely. C. is described as an honest bur narrow-minded person.

CRANACH, LUCAS (1472-1553) German painter and engraver; known as 'the Elder', to distinguish him from his son of the same name. Having won early fame as a portrait painter, C. settled in *Wittenberg in 1504 and became a court painter to the electors of Saxony. There he met *Luther, whose first engraved portrait by C. dates from 1520, and turned into a partisan of the *Reformation. In later years C.'s prolific production of etchings and woodcuts lowered the quality of his paintings, particularly the colouring. Probably his best painting is his earliest dated work, *Rest on the Flight to Egypt* (1504), which has the Holy Family surrounded by angels in the midst of a Danubian mountain landscape. He continued to paint portraits as well as religious scenes all his life, but at the same time worked on mythological subjects and highly erotic female nudes. His pictures are signed with the initials of his name or with the symbol of a winged snake.

E. Ruhmer, *Cranach* (1963);

M. J. Friedländer and J. Rosenberg, *Die Gemälde von Lucas Cranach* (1932).

CRANMER, THOMAS (1489-1556) English archbishop of Canterbury. Born to a family of Nottinghamshire gentry, C. entered Cambridge University at 14. He remained there as a lecturer and was ordained in 1523. In 1528 he became involved in the theological issues related to *Henry VIII's divorce from *Catherine of Aragon. C.'s position, that the marriage was void from the start, brought him to the attention of the King who appointed him his legal adviser and representative. In 1532, while in Germany on a mission to *Charles V, C. secretly married the niece of the Protestant reformer Andreas *Osiander. Upon his return to England he was made archbishop of Canterbury, and in February 1533 annulled Henry's marriage to Catherine; a few weeks earlier he had secretly celebrated the King's union with *Anne Boleyn. In 1536 C. dutifully pronounced Henry's second divorce. In 1539 he had to send his own wife back to Germany to comply with the *Six Articles, which he opposed. In 1540 he again married the King, to *Anne of Cleve, and soon after divorced them. In all these acts C. was plainly being subservient to the King, having no other choice. However, he took a more independent position under *Edward VI. He welcomed Martin *Bucer to England, issued the Book of *Common Prayer (1549; 1552), and published the 42 *Articles of Religion (1553), which went so far as to deny the doctrine of transubstantiation. When *Mary assumed the crown, C. was accused of heresy and high treason, the result of his reluctant support of Lady Jane *Grey as Edward VI's successor. He was imprisoned for more than two years, recanted his reformist doctrines and reaffirmed papal supremacy. However, before he was burnt at the stake in Oxford (21 March 1556), he publicly reasserted his own true Protestant beliefs, dying a martyr.

F. E. Hutchinson, *Cranmer and the English Reformation* (1951);

Th. Maynard, *The Life of Thomas Cranmer* (1956);

J. Ridley, *Thomas Cranmer* (1962).

Adam and Eve *by Lucas Cranach the Elder*

CRESPIN, JEAN (c. 1520-72) French Protestant reformer, publisher and author. Born at Arras, he first studied law and became an advocate at the courts of Paris. In 1545 he went to *Strassburg and in 1548 to *Geneva. There he founded a printing press, designed to promote Protestantism in France. His own work which dealt with the Catholic persecution of Protestant reformers, appeared in 1554.

CRÉTIN, GUILLAUME (c. 1460-1525) French poet. One of the best-known **rhétoriqueurs*, he enjoyed a considerable reputation during his lifetime. His numerous works included the *Déplorations*, on the death of the musician *Ockeghem, and the first five books of the long *Chronique française*, which contained allegories on patriotic themes. In fact, C. was a transitional figure, whose work was influenced by the Italianate style of poetry. He was respected by *Marot and portrayed, under the name Raminagrobis, by *Rabelais.

CRIVELLI, CARLO (c. 1440-95) Italian painter. Trained in *Venice, probably by *Vivarini, he settled in the nearby provincial Marches; the earliest evidence of his work dates from 1457. C.'s paintings are marked by an intense mood, bordering on fantasy. The ornamentation is exceedingly elaborate, and his use of fruits and vegetables has an annoying effect. The general impression is reminiscent of late Gothic restlessness rather than Renaissance calm and serenity.

CROMWELL, THOMAS (c. 1485-1540) English statesman; the executor of the English *Reformation. The son of a blacksmith, C. is believed to have led an adventurous life in his youth, serving as a soldier in Italy and as a commercial clerk in the Netherlands. Returning to England, he went into trade and money-lending and acquired reputation as a skilful business administrator. Cardinal *Wolsey took notice of him, and in 1524 charged him with the task of suppressing a number of small monasteries. When Wolsey fell in 1529, as a result of his failure to satisfy Henry VIII's demand for a divorce, C. managed to win the King's favour by suggesting to him that he declare himself head of the Church, and prosecute the case in the English ecclesiastical courts. Becoming a member of the Privy Council, C. dedicated his efforts in a characteristically unscrupulous manner to the cause of royal absolutism. After the Act of *Supremacy made Henry the head of the English Church, the King appointed him Vicar General, or his deputy in ecclesiastical matters (1535). At that time C. was also chancellor, and thus in charge of secular affairs too. Between 1536 and 1539 C. supervised the *dissolution of the monasteries. He established a system of espionage among the clergy, suppressed the recalcitrants and dictated church policy. His actions gave rise to much opposition, but it was an issue related to foreign policy which actually led to his downfall. Attempting to align England with the Protestant princes of Germany, C. arranged for the marriage of Henry with *Anne of Cleve. The marriage was a complete disaster, and the King, furious with C. for this fiasco, ordered his arrest on a charge of high treason. He was not even permitted to speak in his own defence, and was beheaded on 28 July 1540.

R. B. Merriman, *Life and Letters of Thomas Cromwell* (1902);
G. R. Elton, *Policy and Police: The Enforcement of the Reformation in the Time of Thomas Cromwell* (1972).

Madonna and Child *by Carlo Crivelli*

CRONACA, IL (1457-1508) The name by which the Italian architect and sculptor Simone del Pollaiolo was known. Born in Florence, he trained there and in Rome, where he studied classical remains. In 1491 he was charged with continuing the work on the Strozzi Palace, Florence, and designed its elegant courtyard. Later, he worked on the cathedral and the Palazzo Vecchio (1495-97), and built the Church of S. Salvatore al Monte, a spacious structure of simple lines in the style of *Brunelleschi.

CROTUS RUBIANUS (c. 1480-c. 1539) Latin name of the German humanist Johannes Jäger. Born in Dornheim, he was educated at Erfurt with Ulrich von *Hutten, with whom he collaborated, in 1515, on the famous collection of satirical letters, the **Epistolae obscurorum virorum*. From 1517 to 1520 he studied in Rome and Bologna and, upon his return, became rector of the University of Erfurt. There, in 1521, he welcomed *Luther on his way to the Diet of *Worms. Later he served *Albert of Prussia at Königsberg but, about 1530, decided to return to Roman Catholicism. He became a canon of Halle at the prompting of *Albert of Mainz. His *Apologia*, which appeared in Leipzig in 1531, aroused the anger of Luther and was answered harshly by the Protestant side. He was the author of several other tracts, the best of which, like the *Epistolae*, is of a powerful satirical bent.

P. Kalkhoff, *Humanismus und Reformation in Erfurt* (1926).

CRUCIGER, CASPAR (1504-48) *Luther's assistant. Coming to *Wittenberg in 1521 from his native Leipzig,

C. studied theology and became a pastor of Magdeburg. In 1528 he returned to Wittenberg and, besides fulfilling his duties as minister, assisted Luther in his work. He participated in the translation of the *Bible and in theological debates and wrote down for posterity many of Luther's sermons. In 1539 he went back to Leipzig for a short time and supervised the implementation of the Reformation in that city. His son, Caspar Cruciger (1525-97), was the successor of *Melanchthon at Wittenberg.

CRUSADE, THE ISSUE OF The history of the great mediaeval crusades came to an end in 1291, when Acre, the last Christian stronghold in the Holy Land, fell to the Moslems. In spite of a religious and ideological climate which favoured the launching of further crusades, the unsettled conditions in Western Europe during the 14th century posed numerous obstacles. But the crusading idea gained force again in the 15th century, in response to the advances of the *Ottoman Turks, who were increasing their pressure on the remains of the Byzantine Empire. In 1396 a crusade, led by Sigismund of Hungary and John the Fearless of Burgundy, and including English, French and German knights, advanced along the Danube to the rescue of the Christian East, but was badly defeated by *Bayezid I at Nicopolis. In 1438, when the Ottoman menace was renewed, the Byzantine emperor, *John VIII, came West, imploring military aid. The result was an unruly crusade with participants of different nationalities, led by Cardinal Giuliano *Cesarini. The crusaders scored a victory against *Murad II at Nish (1443), and forced him to sign a ten-year truce. But later, when they broke the truce and attempted to reach Constantinople, they were defeated by the Sultan near the Black Sea port of Varna (1444).

The fall of *Constantinople (1453) again raised the issue. The hastily assembled army of Janos *Hunyadi, urged by the preacher Giovanni di *Capistrano, compelled *Mehemmed II in 1456 to raise the siege of Belgrade, but otherwise there was little inclination for a united Christian effort. In Burgundy, for example, *Philip the Good held, in 1454, a famous splendid banquet in which his knights ceremoniously vowed to go on a crusade, and then returned to their homes. *Pius II, who made the crusade against the Turks a central issue of his pontificate, came, in 1464, to Ancona only to see the very few thousands who had rallied to his call and then died. After his failure there were no real attempts to organize a united European crusade. But the idea was not abandoned. In Spain, when the **reconquista* reached its final stage in 1492, it was conceived as a crusade. So were later Spanish and Portuguese invasions of North Africa, *Charles V's expedition to Tunis (1535), and, on the other side of the continent, the military struggle against the Turks in the Danube valley, carried on mainly by the Hungarians. The idea also became for a while a conventional argument in internal European politics. In 1494 *Charles VIII justified his invasion of Italy by claiming that it was a preliminary step to a crusade to the Holy Land. Thereafter the argument that a particular political move was undertaken for the sake of a crusade was introduced as a clause to many European treaties. But the open alliance of 1536 between *Francis I and *Suleiman I plainly challenged the assumption that there could be no reconciliation between Christendom and the Islamic world. The contact with newly-discovered non-Christian civilizations in America and elsewhere was also relevant; indeed, while the **conquistadores* carried a sword in one hand and the cross in the other, the *missionaries who followed them renounced the use of violence in favour of a crusade by the power of the Word. Paradoxically, the hardest blow to the sacred value of war against infidels was dealt in Europe: the divisions and animosity which resulted from the *Reformation were so intense, that by mid-16th century Protestant and Catholic parts of Europe considered one another objects for crusades.

A. S. Atiya, *The Crusade in the Later Middle Ages*, 2nd ed. (1965);
A. S. Atiya, *The Crusade of Nicopolis* (1934);
K. M. Setton, *The Papacy and the Levant, 1204-1571* (1976).

CUEVA, JUAN DE LA (c. 1545-1610) Spanish poet and playwright. A native of *Seville, where he spent most of his life, he visited Mexico (1574-77) and, until his return from America, wrote mainly poetry, most of it unpublished. Based on allegorical, didactic and mythological themes, his poems reflected the Italianate tradition. The first of his 14 plays was staged in Seville in 1579. A landmark in the development of Spanish drama, these plays introduced the subject of Spanish history to the stage. The *Muerte del rey don Sancho* and *La libertad de España* are understood to have a political meaning, an admonition to *Philip II to desist from his expansionist designs on Portugal. C.'s treatise in verse, the *Ejemplar poetico* (1609), contained original ideas on the theatre, and explained his approach to the historical drama.

A. I. Watson, *The Political Implications of the Drama of Juan de la Cueva* (1965).

CUJAS, JACQUES (1522-90) French jurist. The son of a fuller of Toulouse, he had exceptional intellectual talents and became well known as one of the leading interpreters of Roman law. In 1554 he left his native town where he had taught, and for some years lectured at Cahors, Valence and Turin, finally settling in Bourges. C. was a follower of *Alciati in attempting to study the development of Roman law in different historical periods. His writings, besides offering a fresh interpretation of the old legal texts, show a clarity of style and profound erudition.

CUNHA, TRISTAO DA (c. 1460-1540) Portuguese navigator. In 1506 he commanded a fleet which sailed East; one of the participants was Afonso de *Albuquerque. On this voyage he discovered the three small volcanic islands in the Atlantic, 2,000 miles west of the Cape of Good Hope, which were named after him. He captured from the Arabs trading posts in East Africa, and helped *Almeida to extend Portuguese influence in India. He returned to Portugal in 1508. In 1513 he led a sumptuous Portuguese embassy to Pope *Leo X. Later, he served on the royal council.

CUSPINIANUS, JOHANNES (1473-1529) German humanist. C. received his early education in Leipzig, but his career as a humanist scholar is associated with the University of Vienna, which he attended at the young age of 17 and where he remained until his death. In 1493 *Maximilian I crowned him poet laureate and, in 1500, made him rector of the University. The Emperor also sent him on various diplomatic missions, and employed him as his counselor. C. promoted humanist studies in Vienna, inviting there the famous Conrad *Celtis. He was the editor of a number of classical authors and mediaeval chroniclers. His own writings included Latin poetry and a work on medicine; of greater value, however, are his historical works, including a treatise on the Turks and their religion, and a book about the history of Austria.

Tower of the Crusader southern wall in Caesarea

The Four Horsemen of the Apocalypse *by Albrecht Dürer*

D

DADDI, BERNARDO (c. 1290-1348) Italian painter. A younger contemporary of *Giotto's in Florence, he may have been the latter's pupil. His painting, however, followed the archaic style of *Siena, distinguished by the employment of gold background. He produced many paintings on small wood panels, and several polyptych altarpieces, some with smiling *Madonnas, which became very popular. Two frescoes in the church of S. Croce, Florence, are also attributed to him.

D'AILLY PIERRE (1350-1420) French cardinal and theologian. A graduate of the University of Paris, he advanced to the chancellorship of that school in 1389 and was close to King Charles VI, who endowed him with several ecclesiastical benefices. In 1397 he was made archbishop of Cambrai. D. played an active role in the developments leading to the conclusion of the Great Schism. Having been created cardinal by *John XXIII in 1412, he took part in the Council of Constance (1414-17), where he defended the *conciliar position. His *Tractatus super reformatione ecclesiae* (1416), is said to have influenced later Roman Catholic reforms, especially those of the Council of *Trent. Essentially a mediaeval philosopher, who often followed the teachings of William of Occam (*c.* 1300-*c.* 1350), D. also wrote the *Imago Mundi* (1410), a widely-read work on geography, known to *Columbus, which contained travellers' tales and quotations from various sources. In this book he suggested that *India might be reached through the West.

DALMAU, LUIS (?-1460) Spanish painter. A native of Valencia, he became a court painter to *Alfonso V of Aragon. In 1431 he went to *Bruges to study the art of oil-painting as practiced by the Flemish school, returning to Valencia in 1437. His only documented work, the *Virgin of the Councillors* (1443-45), reveals the influence of Jan van *Eyck.

DANCE Mediaeval civilization, dominated as it was by religion, viewed dancing as a necessary evil. Although the component of dance undoubtedly always existed, especially in the seasonal festivals of the peasantry, there is very little information on the subject. By the early 15th century there was a marked change, with social dancing of mixed pairs developing into an institutionalized mode of leisure in most European courts. There is no better proof that dance became part of the aristocratic way of life, than the appearance of court dancing-masters and the first dancing manuals. Antonio Cornazzano (1429-84), the court poet of Francesco *Sforza and a prolific writer on various subjects, is also remembered for his *Libro dell'arte del danzare* (*c.* 1460). The *danse basse*, which lasted through the Renaissance, was in essence a processional dance consisting of dignified ceremonial gestures; its movements suited the ladies, who were restricted by their cumbersome clothes. One of the most popular individual dances of this kind was the stately *pavane*. But the gaiety and the general tendency to liberal morals peculiar to the early 16th century led to the introduction of the *danse haute*, which required quicker movements, leaps and a display of physical agility. The earliest of these was the *galliard* of Italian origin, often performed without holding hands, and involving different kinds of thrusting steps and jumps. It was usually danced after a *pavane*. Another popular *danse haute* was the *lavolta*, in which the man turned his partner and lifted her on his knee. Still other dances of this kind were the *courante*, the *allemande*, and the very popular 17th-century *gavotte*.

As always, the lively boisterous dances which reached the social life of the upper class in the 16th century, were stylized adaptations of the dances of the lower strata. In the latter half of the century there was a tendency towards greater uniformity on the one hand, and spectacularity on the other. Dancing schools in and around the main European courts instructed the nobility, which facilitated the transmission of popular dances from one nation to another. In addition, talented impresarios created elaborate spectacles in which singing, dancing, speech and pantomime were performed amid gorgeously decorated settings. These were the Italian *balli*, the French *ballets de cour* and the English **masques*, often planned and enacted with the close cooperation of the royal family itself. Thoinot Arbeau's *Orchesographie* (1588) is considered the best contemporary source on the social dances of the late Renaissance.

C. Sachs, *World History of the Dance* (1937, rep. 1963);

Danse haute *at the French court in the second half of the 16th century*

W. Sorell, *The Dance Through the Ages* (1967);
M. Dolmetsch, *Dances of England and France from 1450 to 1600* (1949);
M. Dolmetsch, *Dances of Spain and Italy from 1400 to 1600* (1959).

DANCE OF DEATH, THE (French, danse macabre; German, Totentanz) An allegorical dance, in which a skeleton representing death leads different types of people to their graves. The theme reflected late-mediaeval fascination with the weird and the gruesome, which was also expressed in European prints of the late 15th and early 16th centuries. The best example is *Holbein the Younger's series of engravings.

J. M. Clark, *The Dance of Death in the Middle Ages and the Renaissance* (1950).

DANIEL, SAMUEL (c. 1562-1619) English poet. Born in Somerset, he was educated at Oxford. His first patron was Sir Edward Dymoke, but in 1592 he joined the circle of the countess of Pembroke, and later had other patrons, until, in 1604, he became a favourite at court. The author of **masques*, pastoral plays and tragedies, D. excelled as a poet. His sonnet sequence, *Delia*, is one of the finest Elizabethan examples of this genre. It was several times revised and republished (1592-1601). His *Musophilus* (1599) was a poetic apologia of literature as a necessary element of life, while his *The Civile Wares* (1595; 1609) was a long poetic chronicle of the Wars of the *Roses. In his *Defense of Rhyme* (1602), he answered the attacks against him made by Thomas *Campion.

C. Schaar, *An Elizabethan Sonnet Problem* (1960).

DANIELE DA VOLTERRA (c. 1509-66) Italian painter. A pupil of *Sodoma, he went to Rome where he decorated the *Farnese palace and several important chapels. At the order of Pope *Paul IV he painted draperies on the nude figures of *Michelangelo's *Last Judgment*. He lived in Rome until he died, doing mostly wall decorations at the Vatican.

DANTE (Dante Alighieri; 1265-1321) Italian poet. Born to a noble Florentine family of modest means, he studied under Brunetto Latini, the compiler of a well-known encyclopaedia. The best-known fact about his early adulthood is his love for Beatrice, who appears in his later writings as both the object of his love and an allegorical symbol of beauty and grace. He wrote his first work, *La vita nuova* (1294), not long after her death. He then married, became a member of the *guild of pharmacists, and between 1295 and 1301 took part in the stormy political life of *Florence. But the victory of the pro-papal faction led to his banishment, and for the rest of his life he wandered from one Italian city to another. When Emperor Henry VII came to Italy (1310), D. supported him, hoping that the renewed imperial authority would result in his return to Florence. However, the Emperor died shortly after (1313), and in 1315 Florence reimposed D.'s sentence. He spent the last four years of his life in Ravenna, where he is buried.

The greatest Italian poet, and one of the most powerful literary giants of all ages, D. is, nevertheless, best understood in the context of mediaeval culture and values. This is amply demonstrated in his treatise on political theory, *De monarchia* (1313), in which he idealized the concept of a universal Christian empire. His *Convivio* (*c.* 1300), a treatise on philosophy, had much in common with mediaeval scholasticism. *De vulgari eloquentia*, traced the origins of languages and defended the literary validity of the vernacular. His grand poetical work *La divina commedia*, describing his visionary journey through Hell, Purgatory and Paradise, links D. with the emerging culture of the Renaissance. Although in this, too, the structure reflected mediaeval theology, morality and politics, it had such a tremendous impact on the humanists of the 14th century that *Boccaccio saw fit to write D.'s life and originated the public readings of the work in Florence. Indeed, it was in the 16th century that the adjective 'divine' was applied to the work. At the same time there were those who dared to criticize D.'s lack of 'purity', and compared him unfavourably to *Petrarch.

T. Chubb, *Dante and His World* (1967);
A. Gilbert, *Dante and His Comedy* (1963);
M. Barbi, *Life of Dante* (1954).

DANTI, EGNAZIO (1536-86) Italian mathematician, cosmographer and architect. Born in Perugia, he was the son of the goldsmith Giulio Danti (1500-75) and younger brother of Vincenzo. In 1555 he joined the Dominican order and, from 1562 to 1574, was at the service of *Cosimo I in Florence, where he also taught mathematics. He translated Proclus and Euclid and, in 1577, published in Bologna a work on mathematics, *Scienze matematiche ridotte in tavole*, which was well received. The author of other scientific works and several maps, he was named papal cosmographer by *Gregory XIII, and took part in the reform of the calendar. In 1583 he became bishop of Altari.

DANTI, GIOVANNI (1478-1517) Italian inventor. Born in Perugia, he became a military engineer and also taught mathematics at Venice, where he died. In 1503 he made a first attempt to fly near Lake Trasimene, launching himself with the aid of two large artificial wings.

DANTI, VINCENZO (1530-76) Italian goldsmith and sculptor. The son of a family of goldsmiths from Perugia, he left his native town in 1557 and settled at the court of *Cosimo I in *Florence. His first important work, a bronze statue of the seated *Julius III, was completed in 1556. His Florentine works show a marked influence of the style of *Michelangelo. They include the *Beheading*

"Death and the Bishop", from Holbein's Dance of Death

Dante *by Luca Signorelli*

Baptism of Christ *by Gerard David*

of St. John the Baptist (1569-71), a bronze group at the Baptistery, and another bronze statue, *Venus Anadyomene* (*c.* 1570). He also executed works in marble and, in 1567, published a theoretical work on the perfect proportions, *Primo libro del trattato delle perfette proporzioni.*

DA PORTO, LUIGI (1485-1529) Italian author. A native of Vicenza, he was wounded while fighting with the Venetian army against the League of *Cambrai in 1511. His *Lettere storiche* related the history of *Venice from 1509 to 1513. In 1524 he wrote the famous tale of the love of *Giulietta e Romeo*, which later was retold by *Bandello and dramatized by *Shakespeare.

DARET, JACQUES (c. 1404-c. 1468) Flemish painter. Born in Tournai, he became an apprentice of Robert *Campin's (1427), together with Roger van der *Weyden. He is known to have worked later in Arras (1433-35), Lille (1453) and *Bruges (1468), but only fragments of larger works have survived. The resemblance between his style and that of the anonymous Master of Flemalle, supports the identification of the latter with his teacher Campin.

DARNLEY, HENRY STUART (1545-67) English noble; second husband of *Mary Queen of Scots and father of *James I. The son of a niece of *Henry VIII, D. first met Mary in France, shortly after the death of her husband *Francis II of France. She fell in love and decided to marry him during his visit to Scotland in 1565, and the marriage was celebrated at the end of July of that year, despite the opposition of Queen *Elizabeth I and the Scot regent, Murray. Soon, however, the marriage fell apart, and D., out of jealousy, cooperated in the gruesome murder of David *Rizzio, his wife's Italian secretary (1566). Later some attempts were made by both wife and husband to mend their relations, but they failed and, in December 1566, D. refused to attend the baptism of his son. By then Mary was already intimately involved with *Bothwell. Early in 1567 she visited her ailing husband and convinced him to go with her to Edinburgh. There, on the night of 10 February, the small house in which he was staying was blown up by gunpowder. D., however, did not die as a result of the explosion, but was strangled to death. The responsibility for the crime was attributed to Bothwell and the Queen.

R. H. Mahon, *The Tragedy of Kirk O'Field* (1930).

DATINI, FRANCESCO (c. 1335-1410) Italian merchant and banker. Born in Prato, he was orphaned and went to work as a boy in Florence. In 1350 he went to Avignon, where he accumulated enormous wealth as a supplier to the papal court. In 1383 he returned to Prato and shortly after to Florence. His business continued to grow and his commercial and financial contacts covered most of Europe and the Levant. The D. commercial records, including letters of instruction, bills-of-exchange and account books, were preserved in his palace at Prato, and are an invaluable source for the economic history of the early Renaissance. D. left most of his wealth to charity.

I. Origo, *The Merchant of Prato* (1957);
C. Ciano, ed., *La 'pratica di mercatura' datiniana* (1964);
C. Villain-Gandossi, ed., *Comptes du sel (Libro di ragione e conto di salle) de Francesco di Marco Datini* (1969).

D'AUBIGNÉ, THEODORE-AGRIPPA (1552-1630) French poet and historian. The son of a *Huguenot noble, he joined the army of the future *Henry IV, whom he also served for many years as councillor. However, after the King's conversion to Roman Catholicism, he retired to his estates and devoted himself to writing. A courageous man endowed with a powerful constitution and personality, he maintained his intransigence to the Edict of *Nantes throughout his life. In 1620 he had to leave France, and spent the rest of his life in *Geneva. His first poetical work, *Le Printemps*, was written in 1570 but published only in 1630; it was dedicated to his youthful love Diane Salviati, a niece of *Ronsard's Cassandre. His greatest poem, *Les Tragiques*, written between 1576 and 1600 and published in 1616, dealt with the time of the *Religious Wars. It is a long political-religious invective, employing morbid symbolism and a prophetic biblical tone, reminiscent of *Dante or Milton. His chief work in prose, the *Histoire universelle* (1616-20), covered the second half of the 16th century. Although somewhat disorganized, it contains a first-hand account of many events of the civil wars. Another of his other works was the autobiography, *Sa vie à ses enfants*.

I. Buffum, *Agrippa d'Aubigné's "Les Tragiques": A Study of the Baroque Style in Poetry* (1951).

DAVANZATI, BERNARDO (1529-1606) Italian author and translator. Born in Florence, he first tried his hand at commerce in *Lyons, but later returned to Florence and devoted himself to literary pursuits. D. translated Tacitus' *Annals* to Italian, and wrote on various subjects including theology, agriculture and economics. His summary of a work by the English Jesuit, Nicholas *Sanders, *Scisma d'Inghilterra* was published in 1602. He was known for his brief concise style.

DAVID, GERARD (c. 1460-1523) Flemish painter. Born in Oudewater in the northern Netherlands, he joined the painters' guild at *Bruges in 1484, and became the last great master of that school. Only three of his paintings are documented, but several more are attributed on good evidence. His religious pictures display a feeling of intimacy and devotion. Basically a follower of the old style, D. deliberately shunned the new Italian influence in favour of a mood of religious fervour typical of northern humanism.

M. J. Friedländer, *Memling and Gerard David* (1970).

DAVIS, JOHN (1550-1605) English navigator. Born near Dartmouth and brought up as a sailor from early youth, D. undertook, between 1585 and 1587, three voyages of exploration in search of a northwest passage to the Pacific. In 1588 he participated in the operations against the Spanish *Armada and, in 1591, accompanied *Cavendish on his second voyage. After Cavendish's death D. continued on his own, discovering the Falkland Islands. In later years he sailed under the command of others and, in 1601, entered the services of the *East India Company. He was killed by Japanese pirates off Sumatra. D. invented a quadrant which carried his name and wrote *The Seaman's Secrets* (1594).

DECEMBRIO Italian humanist family of father and two sons. Uberto (*c.* 1350-1427) was a secretary to the rulers of *Milan and left a number of works on moral and civic issues as well as letters. His elder son Pier Candido (1392-1477), continued his father's career at the Milanese court, but from 1466 to 1474 served Borso *d'Este at *Ferrara. He translated from the Greek Appian, Plutarch and part of the *Iliad*, and wrote biographies of Italian statesmen. His younger brother, Angelo, (*c.* 1415-*c.* 1466), studied under *Gasparino da Barzizza and *Guarino da Verona, and served in Ferrara, *Naples and Spain. An indefatigable collector of manuscripts, he wrote the *Politia litteraria*, a description of the educational circle of Guarino at Ferrara.

DECHAMPS, EUSTACHE (1345-1405) French poet. Born in Vertus, Champagne, he occupied different posts in the royal administration of France and travelled to Bohemia and Hungary. Much of his work described episodes in the *Hundred Years' War, and has been described as historiography in verse. His most famous poem is the ballad *Sur le trépas de Bertrand du Guesclin*, about the great 14th century French soldier. He also composed satirical poems and wrote on moral themes, and a work on the art of poetry, *L'art de dictier et de fere chançons, balades, virelais et rondeaux*.

DECIUS, PHILIPPUS (1454-1535) Italian jurist and political theorist. Born in Milan, he studied law at Pavia and Pisa, where in the course of a long career he lectured on civil law, as well as in Siena and Padua. He frequently got involved in fierce controversies, one of which led to his excommunication and a period of exile in France (1512-15). Most of his works were commentaries on the Roman law. As a political theorist he went against the dominant ideas of his time when he asserted that the ruler is bound by a contract with his people.

DEDEKIND, FRIEDRICH (c. 1525-98) German satirical poet. Born in Neustadt an der Leine, he studied at *Wittenberg, where he wrote his satirical poem in Latin, *Grobianus* (1549). It took its title from a passage in *Brant's *Narrenschiff*, and was an attack on gluttony and drunkenness. It became popular throughout Europe, but his later Latin verse and two plays in German were greatly inferior to it.

E. Rühl, *Grobianus in England* (1904).

DEE, DR. JOHN (1527-1608) English *mathematician, *astrologer and *alchemist. Educated at Cambridge, where he took his Master's degree in 1548, he went to the Netherlands and later to Paris, winning fame for his lectures on Euclid. He returned to England in 1551, becoming an astrologer to Queen *Mary, but was soon imprisoned on a charge of attempting to kill the Queen by magic. Released, he became the favourite astrologer of *Elizabeth I, who frequently consulted him, and also gave instruction to contemporary English navigators. Between 1583 and 1589 he travelled to Bohemia and Poland, where he attempted to win patronship for his experiments in alchemy and communication with the spirits. He then returned to England, becoming, in 1595, Warden of Manchester College. Reputed to be a great sorcerer, D. was also a prolific writer, but died poor.

C. F. Smith, *John Dee* (1909).

DEFENESTRATION OF PRAGUE (23 May 1618) The incident which sparked off the *Thirty Years' War. A delegation of *Bohemian Protestants, led by Count Thurn and followed by a great crowd, broke into the royal castle of Hradschin to protest the infringement of their religious freedoms. The crowd seized Wilhelm von Slawata and Jaroslav von Martinitz, two of the five deputy-governors and their secretary, and threw them out of the window. The three survived the fall of about 70 feet, and only Slawata was injured.

DEI, BENEDETTO (1418-92) Italian traveller and historian. Born in Florence, he fled the city after an abortive conspiracy in which he took part, and spent many years travelling in Africa and Asia. In Constantinople, where he remained for some time, he had access to the Ottoman court. In 1486 he returned to Florence and spent the rest of his life in the service of the *Medici. He wrote *Le memorie storiche*, full of interesting information on geography, economics and the politics of Ottoman Turkey, and another work describing his own time, the *Cronaca*.

M. Pisani, *Un aventuriero del Quattrocento: La vita e le opere de Benedetto Dei* (1923).

DEKKER, THOMAS (c. 1572-1632) English playwright and pamphleteer. He was probably born in London, and it is known that in 1597 he worked for Philip *Henslowe. Between 1598 and 1602 he wrote 44 plays for him, most of which are lost. As pamphleteer D. published, after 1603, a great number of journalistic descriptions of contemporary events, containing satire, social criticism and moral advice. His pamphlets and plays excelled in the portrayal of city life, describing rogues, harlots and simple shopkeepers. His most famous play, *The Shoemaker's Holiday* (1599), was a very popular comedy which exuded humour and realism. On some of his plays he collaborated with others, mainly Thomas Middleton and John *Webster. D. was ridiculed by the reigning literary authority of his day, Ben *Johnson, and responded in kind.

M. T. Jones-Davies, *Un peintre de la vie londonienne: Thomas Dekker* (1958).

DEL CHIERICO, FRANCESCO D'ANTONIO Italian manuscript illuminator active in Florence in the second half of the 15th century. He may have been a pupil of Fra *Angelico, whose style he imitated; his illuminations were more in the nature of small paintings than merely decorative elements. Between 1463 and 1471 he illuminated large liturgical books for the cathedral. The *Medici were his patrons, and some of his work is in the *Laurentian Library. He is also believed to have made illuminations for the rulers of Naples and Urbino, and for *Matthias Corvinus of Hungary.

Entrance to the Castle of Anet by Delorme

DELLA CASA, GIOVANNI (1503-56) Italian author. After a dissipated youth, he was ordained and, in 1544, became archbishop of Benevento. In 1554 he completed *Galateo, ovvero dei costumi,* a work on etiquette, courtly manners and proper social conduct, which was widely popular. He also wrote lyric poetry, distinguished by originality of language and style. He served as papal nunzio to Venice and, shortly before his death, at the court in Rome.

G. Della Casa, *Galateo*, trans. by R. S. Pine-Coffin (1958).

DELLA FONTE, BARTOLOMEO (1445-1513) Italian humanist. Born in Florence, he was a student of *Landino and *Argyropoulos. He lived for a while in *Ferrara (1468-72), later in Rome and, in 1489, went to Hungary at the invitation of King *Matthias Corvinus, but returned shortly to Florence. D. published the first edition of *Artes*, an encyclopaedia by the ancient Roman author Aulus Cornelius Celsus, highly esteemed during the Renaissance. He also wrote commentaries and made translations of the classics, and a highly regarded collection of letters.

DELLA GATTA, BARTOLOMEO (1448-c. 1503) Italian painter. Born in Florence, he became a Camaldolese monk, and spent some years in Rome assisting *Signorelli and *Perugino in their *frescoes at the *Sistine Chapel. Later he became an abbot at Arezzo. Beside painting religious scenes in a dignified style, he illuminated manuscripts and dabbled in music and architectural design.

DELLA ROVERE Italian family which exerted influence on ecclesiastical and political affairs. Originally from Savona, the family rose to prominence when Francesco D. became pope as *Sixtus IV (1471). He furthered the careers of his nephews, especially Giuliano, who later became pope as *Julius II, and Giovanni, who married the daughter of *Federico da Montefeltro. Francesco Maria (1490-1538), the issue of that marriage, succeeded in 1508 to the duchy of *Urbino, and the family continued to rule the duchy through the 16th century. The last of the line was Francesco Maria III (1548-1631), duke from 1574, who towards the end of his life transferred the duchy to the papacy.

DELLA VIOLA, ALFONSO (c. 1508-c. 70) Italian musician. Born in *Ferrara, he entered the service of the house of *Este, writing many *madrigals and *motets. In 1541 he wrote music for *Orbecche*, a tragedy by *Giraldi Cinthio and afterwards composed music for *pastorals. These experiments in combining music and *drama make him a precursor of the late 16th-century Florentine composers who developed the *opera.

DELORME, PHILIBERT (c. 1510-70) French architect. The son of a master mason from Lyons, he visited Italy in his youth and was impressed by the High Renaissance *architecture of Rome. Most of the buildings he designed have perished, with the exception of the tomb of *Francis I (1547) and t':e Anet, a house he built for *Diane de Poitiers (1548-54). His influence on French architecture derived also from his books, *Nouvelles inventions* (1561) and *L'Architecture* (1567). D. was employed on several works for the royal court. In his last years he began to build the palace of the Tuileries for *Catherine de Médicis, but only a small section was actually done by him.

A. Blunt, *Philibert de L'Orme* (1958).

DE' MARCHI, FRANCESCO (1504-76) Italian military engineer. Born in Bologna, he became a professional soldier, acquiring experience in *artillery and fortifications. During many years he served Pope *Paul III and the house of *Farnese, working on the defences of Rome and Parma. He also spent some years in Flanders at the service of *Margaret of Parma. His treatise on fortifications, *Della architectura militare*, won wide acclaim.

DENCK, HANS (c. 1495-1527) German *Anabaptist leader. Born near Munich, he studied at Ingolstadt and then went to *Basle, where he was helped by *Oecolampadius. In 1525 he was forced to leave *Nuremberg by *Osiander on a charge of heresy. He then moved from city to city in southern Germany, and became known as an Anabaptist preacher. Late in 1527 he returned to Basle to seek shelter and died there of the plague.

A. Coutts, *Hans Denck, Humanist and Heretic* (1927);
G. Godbach, *Hans Denck und Thomas Müntzer* (1969).

DENMARK The political history of Denmark in the 15th century is dominated by the issue of maintaining the union with the two other Scandinavian nations. It had been achieved in 1397 by the Union of Kalmar, which gave D., the more populous and wealthiest of the three, an ascendancy over Norway and *Sweden. But whereas the Norwegians reluctantly accepted Danish suzerainty for the next 400 years, the Swedish nobility never ceased to oppose it. The *Hanseatic League further complicated matters by obstinately insisting on its freedom of navigation in the Baltic Straits and, between 1410 and 1435, aided the duchy of Holstein in its long war against King *Eric. The reigns of *Christian I (1448-81) and *John (1481-1513) saw intermittent civil war, particularly in Sweden, and more clashes with the Hanse towns. The final crisis came under *Christian II. He first provoked a Swedish revolt (1520), which irrevocably dissolved the union; at the same time he managed to arouse the Danish nobility and higher clergy who, in 1523, revolted and drove him out the country, placing his uncle *Frederick I (1523-33) on the throne.

Thereafter, the great issues of Danish politics were in the religious sphere. *Frederick I sympathized with the Reformation, but had to be cautious because of his precarious position. For his son, *Christian II, a devout Protestant, the issue affected his right to the crown, which was only acknowledged by the opposition in 1534, after his victory in a civil war. D. then secularized church property and adopted a Lutheran type of national church, with the king as its formal head. The resulting enormous increase in the power of the monarchy was keenly felt during the long reign of *Frederick II, who carried on a savage, seven-year long war with Sweden over Estonia (1563-70). The enmity with Sweden was to result in yet another war, between 1611 and 1613, and a Danish defeat in a third conflict during the latter phases of the *Thirty Years' War.

V. Starcke, *Denmark in World History* (1963).

DESIDERIO DA SETTIGNANO (1430-64) Italian sculptor. The son of a master mason, he settled in

Part of the façade of the Castle of Anet by Delorme

The Tomb of Carlo Marsuppini by Desiderio da Settignano

The Virgin and Child, *bas-relief in marble by Desiderio da Settignano*

*Florence where he produced works in a style influenced by both *Ghiberti and *Donatello. His major accomplishment which he began about 1453, was the tomb of Carlo Marsuppini at the church of S. Croce. Several busts attributed to him show refinement and sensitivity. He is considered one of the major Florentine sculptors of the mid-15th century.

I. Cardellini, *Desiderio da Settignano* (1962).

DES MASURES, LOUIS (c. 1515-c. 1574) French poet and playwright. Born in Tournai, he became a Protestant while on a visit to *Geneva about 1550. In 1563 he published a trilogy of religious plays: *David combattant, David triomphant, David fugitif*. Influenced by similar work of *Beza's, they were intended to raise the spirit of the *Huguenots. In terms of the development of the drama, they marked a transition from the old *Mysteries to later forms of tragedy.

DES PERIERS, BONAVENTURE (c. 1510-44) French humanist writer. He collaborated with *Olivetan on the translation of the Bible (1533-34), was a friend of *Marot and served briefly as secretary to *Marguerite d'Angoulême. In 1537 his *Cymbalum mundi*, a satire on the Christian religion, aroused a public furor, and was burnt by the public executioner. Persecuted as an atheist, D. had to escape and is said to have committed suicide. His collection of licentious short stories, *Nouvelles recréations et joyeux devis*, was published posthumously in 1558.

L. Febure, *Origène et Des Periers ou l'enigme du Cymbalum Mundi* (1942);

J. W. Hassell, *Sources and Analogues of the Nouvelles recréations of Bonaventure des Periers* (1957).

DESPORTES, PHILIPPE (1546-1606) French poet. The son of a wealthy citizen of Chartres, he received a humanist education, then became a priest and visited Italy in company of his bishop. Upon his return to France (1567), he entered the service of the duke of Anjou, the future *Henry III, whose close aide he remained throughout his career. He was given a number of benefices, including the Abbeys of Tiron and Josaphat and, after the King's assassination, joined the *League. A clever opportunist, he later transferred his allegiance to *Henry IV. D.'s early verse was Italianate love poems in a highly technical manner. Of these the *Imitations d'Arioste* (1572) and the *Amours* (1573) became for a time very popular, eclipsing the fame of *Ronsard. Later he turned to religious themes and, in 1591, published a verse translation of the Psalms, a Catholic counterpart to *Marot's. He was the object of criticism by *Malherbe.

M. T. Marchand-Roques, *La vie de Philippe Desportes* (1949).

DEVOTIO MODERNA Latin for 'modern devotion'; the late 14th-century movement of piety, which sprang up in the Netherlands and upper Rhineland. The spread of the movement was linked to the appearance of the *Brethren of the Common Life. *Thomas à Kempis' *The Imitation of Christ* was the foremost example of its devotional literature. The movement attracted men and women of the middle strata, rather than a popular following, and demanded from its adherents spiritual discipline and contemplative efforts.

A. Hyma, *The Christian Renaissance* (rev. ed. 1965).

R. R. Post, *The Modern Devotion* (1968).

DIANE DE POITIERS (1499-1566) Duchess of Valentinois. Mistress of *Henry II of France. Born to a noble family of the Dauphiné and widowed at 33, she became the mistress of Prince Henry 12 years before he came to the throne in 1547. During his reign her position as the first woman in the life of the king almost totally eclipsed the queen, *Catherine de Médicis. This was no mean accomplishment, as D. was 20 years older than her royal lover. After the King's death in 1559 she was forced to leave the court, and retired to her château at Anet. A famous beauty, she was the subject of several works of art.

F. Bardon, *Diane de Poitiers et le mythe de Diane* (1963);

P. Erlanger, *Diane de Poitiers* (1955).

DIAS, BARTOLOMEU (?-1500) Portuguese navigator; first to reach the Cape of Good Hope. There is little information about his life. His voyage to the southern tip of *Africa took place during the years 1487-88, and he is supposed to have died when his ship, which made up part of *Cabral's fleet, was lost in a storm. His discovery made possible the opening of a maritime route to *India.

E. Axelson, *South East Africa, 1488-1530* (1940).

DIAZ DEL CASTILLO, BERNAL (1492-1584) Spanish **conquistador* and author. D. participated in the conquest of Mexico under *Cortés. He later settled in Guatemala, and might not have written his *Historia verdadera de la conquista de Nueva España*, had he not seen the work of Francisco *Gomara on the same subject. Deciding to give a 'true account' of the events, D. told the story of the conquest in the simple language of a soldier. However, it is precisely because of the lack of superfluous stylistic embellishments that his work has remained popular until today. It was first printed in 1632.

B. Diaz del Castillo, *The Conquest of New Spain* (1963).

DIPLOMACY The modern technique of conducting international relations began to take shape during the Renaissance. Although legations from one ruler to another were an accepted procedure before, only in the 15th century did they become permanent. It was appropriate that Italy, with its several city-states, should lead the way and define the early norms of diplomacy. The instructions given by the republic of *Venice to its ambassadors concerning their duties on missions, actually antedate the 15th century. But for Italy as a whole, permanent missions became the rule during the 40 years of relative peace which preceded the French invasion of 1494. Other European nations followed suit and the greater powers relied increasingly on the regular contact with other governments through their embassies, and upon the information supplied by their representatives. *Ferdinand of Spain was the first ruler of a nation-state who sent out resident ambassadors. During the 1490s he set up five permanent legations in Rome, Venice, London, Brussels and at the emperor's court as part of his attempt to encircle France. In 1519 *Henry VIII set up a resident embassy in France, headed by Thomas Boleyn, father of the future queen. The 1520 treaty between Henry VIII and *Charles V included the

Diane de Poitiers

appointment of resident ambassadors. By 1534, when France sent its first resident ambassador to the court of the sultan in Constantinople, the system was well established.

The diplomatic rules of etiquette, hierarchy and immunities were soon defined, but it was some time before they were rigorously complied with. By the mid-16th century two classes of diplomatic envoys were recognized: 'ambassadors' and the less important, but more numerous 'agents'. The person of the diplomatic envoy was considered inviolable, and although the principle of extraterritoriality did not yet apply to the embassies, it was a common practice to abstain from interference in affairs of foreign legations. On the other hand, the foreign diplomat was generally regarded as a potential spy, and subjects of the host country were frequently forbidden to have contacts with him. The Ottoman Turks were notorious for their bad treatment of foreign ambassadors, but the principle of safe-conduct was respected. For example, when in 1584, the Spanish ambassador Bernardino de *Mendoza was suspected of conspiring against *Elizabeth I, he was merely expelled from England.

G. Mattingly, *Renaissance Diplomacy* (1955);
C. Petry, *Earlier Diplomatic History, 1492-1713* (1949).

DJEM (1459-95) Turkish prince, son of *Mehemmed II. After his father's death in 1481, D. went to war with his elder brother, *Bayezid II, for the Turkish throne. Defeated, he fled to Egypt and later found shelter with the Knights of *St. John at Rhodes. In September 1482 the Knights sent D. to France. At the same time they promised Bayezid II to keep his brother in confinement and, in return, received a considerable annual payment from the Sultan. This arrangement meant that D. was a valuable piece of property. In 1489 he was placed in the hands of *Innocent VIII, who immediately began to collect from Bayezid the amounts formerly paid to the Knights of Rhodes. *Alexander VI, who inherited D. from his predecessor, treated him with respect, but conducted negotiations with Bayezid about the price for killing D. When *Charles VIII reached Rome in his invasion of Italy he made the Pope deliver D. to him (January 1495). But the Turkish prince died a few weeks later.

L. Thuasne, *Djem Sultan, fils de Mohammed II* (1892).

DMITRY, FALSE Three pretenders to the Russian throne, who each claimed to be D., the son of *Ivan IV the Terrible. The appearance of the pretenders was occasioned by the extinction, in 1598, of the old Moscovite dynasty, when Boris *Godunov, a man of low origins, succeeded to the throne by election. The first and most important pretender was a boy who had probably been trained for the role by nobles opposed to the new czar. He is usually identified as one Gregory Otrepiev, a former novice in a Moscow monastery. Appearing in Poland in 1603, he received the support of King *Sigismund III and the *Jesuits, and raised an army of volunteers who followed him to Moscow. Although he was defeated, he kept recruiting new followers and, after the sudden death of the czar (April 1605), he entered Moscow (June 1605). However, his Polish orientation and Roman Catholic inclinations irritated the nobility and, in May 1606, he was murdered by Vasily Shuysky. The second pretender was also supported by a large number of Cossacks and Poles. He was active from 1607 and until his murder in 1610, but never reached Moscow, although he was a serious threat to the government. A third pretender appeared in 1611, and was subsequently delivered to the government and executed.

DOLET, ETIENNE (1508-46) French humanist and printer of books. Born in Orléans, D. as a youth went to Italy, where he studied and served as secretary to the French ambassador to Venice. He returned to France a firm believer in secular values and a lover of the classical languages, and gained fame with his *Commentariorum linguae Latinae* (1536) which impressed *Francis I. With the King's permission, D. established a printing press at *Lyons, where he published the works of his friend François *Rabelais, as well as ancient authors in Latin and translations of the Psalms into French. In 1542 D. published a satire by the Calvinist Clement *Marot and some tracts of his own which were declared heretical. He was imprisoned for over a year, released, but later returned to custody on the charge of relapsing into heresy. His case was judged by the theologians of the Sorbonne and, in 1546, he was burned at the stake in Paris.

M. Chassaigne, *Etienne Dolet; portraits et documents inédits* (1930).

DOMENICHINO (1581-1641) Italian painter. Born in Bologna, he was a pupil of Ludovico *Carracci and, in 1602, went to Rome, where he assisted Annibale *Carracci in the decoration of the Farnese palace. After Carracci's death he became one of the most esteemed painters in Rome, and was awarded important commissions and appointed papal architect. Between 1624 and 1628 he executed decorations for S. Andrea della Valle, but quarrelled with *Lanfranco, who was painting the dome of the church. In 1631 he moved to Naples, his main project being the decoration of the chapel of S. Gennaro in the cathedral. One of the earliest masters of the *Baroque, he displayed a particular interest in landscape.

DOMENICO DI BARTOLO (c. 1400-47) Italian painter. He probably studied under *Sassetta at Siena, where he became a member of the painters' guild in 1428. His major work was a series of frescoes in the Ospedale della Scala, Siena (1440-43), on themes of charity and the caring for the sick. He also painted several *Madonnas and polyptych altarpieces. His pictures reflect contemporary *dress and customs.

DOMENICO VENEZIANO (c. 1400-61) Italian painter. Born, as indicated by his name, in Venice, he was working in Perugia in 1438, when he applied to the *Medici for a job. Settling in *Florence, he worked on *frescoes in the choir of S. Egidio (1439-45), which are now lost. His principal documented work is the *Madonna* from the altarpiece of S. Lucia de' Magnoli, now at the Uffizi, Florence. Other works are believed his on the basis of attribution. D.'s influence on mid-15th century Florentine painting is variously evaluated. He is believed to have promoted the growing interest in colour and light. *Piero della Francesca is recorded in 1439 as his assistant.

M. Salmi, *Paolo Uccello, Andrea del Castagno, Domenico Veneziano* (1939).

DOMINICI, DOMENICO (1416-78) Italian theologian. Born in Venice, he studied in Pauda and was warmly received in Rome by *Eugenius IV and *Nicholas V. In

Portrait of a Young Woman *by Domenico Veneziano*

1448 the latter made him bishop of Torcello. D. later became a staunch advocate of Church reform, a subject he elaborated on in his *Tractatus de reformatione romanae curiae*. He continued to wield influence under *Pius II and *Paul II, but failed to convince his fellow prelates of the pressing need for change.

DOMINIS, MARCO ANTONIO DE (1566-1624) Italian polemical author. A former *Jesuit and professor of rhetoric at Brescia, he became in 1602 the archbishop of Spalatto. Accused of Protestant tendencies, he went in 1616 to England, where he was cordially received. There he published *De republica ecclesiastica*, an attack on papal supremacy and the Roman Catholic doctrine of the Eucharist. However, in 1622 he left England in rancour, and went to *Rome, where at first he was welcomed as a sincere repentant. But in 1624 he was arrested by the *Inquisition on a charge of heresy, and died soon afterwards.

DONATÁRIOS A Portuguese term referring to the administrative and economic system which Portugal implemented in its overseas territories during the early phases of colonization. The system was first employed in the Madeira and Azores Islands in the 15th century,

The head of Donatello, from a fresco by Vasari

then in Brazil and Angola. In order to expedite settlement, the crown gave certain individuals the right to colonize and govern designated areas. The D. could distribute land among the settlers and administer justice. Although most grants were hereditary, the crown later succeeded in regaining effective control of the territories.

DONATELLO (1386-1466) Italian sculptor. Born in Florence, he was for a short time an apprentice of *Ghiberti, and may have worked on the doors of the baptistery which his master was commisioned to do. However, of greater importance to his artistic development was the journey to Rome which he undertook about 1402 in the company of *Brunelleschi. In Rome began his interest in the classical form of the human body. He was back in Florence in 1406 and for the next 25 years worked mainly on statues for the cathedral. His works of this period reveal a gradual change from Gothic stiffness to dramatic pose and expression, as displayed in his *St. Mark* and *St. George* (1420). About 1425, D. began a partnership with the younger sculptor and architect *Michelozzo. They produced a number of works in bronze and the relief *Herod's Feast* in the baptistery of *Siena. To this period also belong the tomb of the anti-pope *John XXIII in Florence and the tomb of Cardinal Brancacci, executed in Pisa, but now in Naples.

D. visited Rome again in 1431-33. He did little work there, but may have spent his time examining classical remains. In any event, his work following this journey is

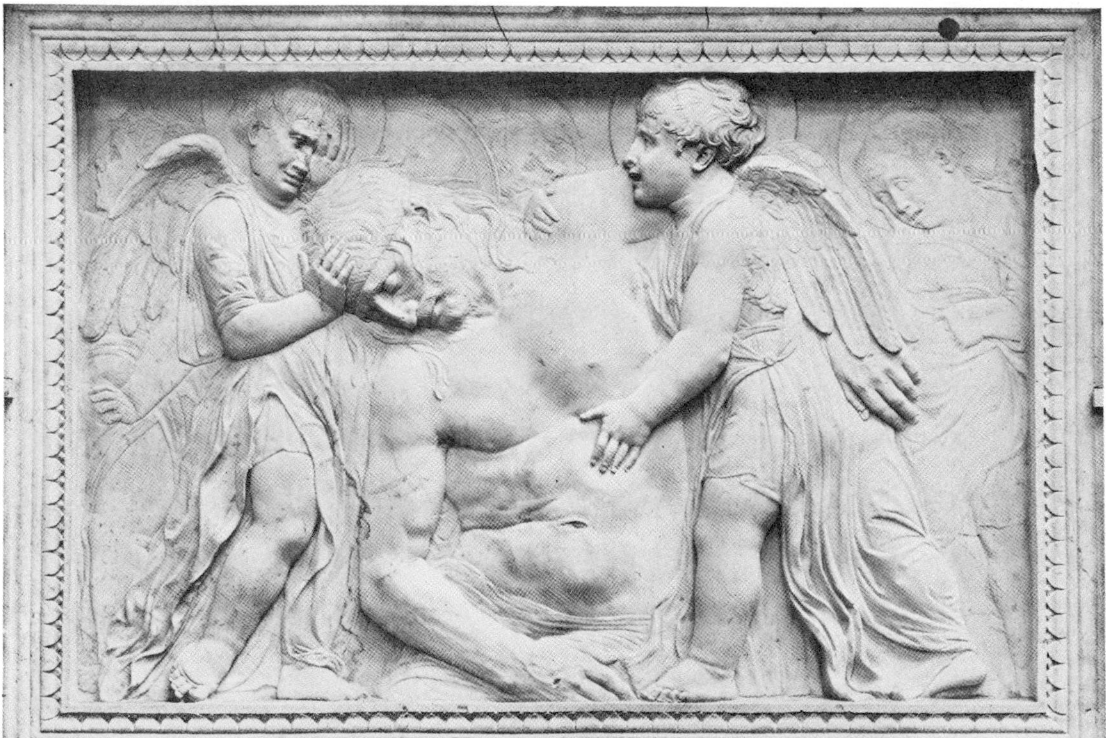

The Mourned Christ *bas-relief in marble by Donatello*

The statue of Gattamelata in Padua by Donatello

inspired by ancient pagan features, as freedom of movement and nudity. His greatest and most famous work of this period is the bronze statue *David* in Florence, the first nude statue of the Renaissance (*c.* 1434). It is graceful and harmoniously balanced, yet very simple in outline. In 1443 D. went to Padua where, in the course of the next ten years, he produced several works, none of which, however, as well known as his equestrian statue of the **condottiere *Gattamelata*. Here too the inspiration of ancient examples such as the *Marcus Aurelius* of Rome is clearly discerned. D. spent the last years of his life in Florence. His orientation was shifting again, and is revealed in the religious feeling of his *Mary Magdalen* in the Baptistery, and the bronze reliefs of the pulpits of San Lorenzo, completed after his death. D. was the greatest sculptor of the early Renaissance, and influenced later Italian sculptors as well as northern Italian painting. Since the end of the last century much of his work has been collected at the Bargello in Florence.

H. W. Janson, *The Sculpture of Donatello*, 2 vols. (1957);
Instituto Nazionale di Studi sul Rinascimento, *Donatello e il suo tempo* (1968).

DONI, ANTON FRANCESCO (1513-74) Italian author. Born in *Florence, he became a friar and then a priest. He travelled from place to place in northern Italy, trying his hand, with little success, at various ventures. A prolific writer of poetry and prose, D. is best known for his *I marmi* (1552), a collection of idle conversations by

Florentines, wherein the author expresses his ideas about different subjects, generally in opposition to the conventions of his time. His *I mondi* (1553) contains a utopian description of a socialist regime.
P. F. Grendler, *Critics of the Italian World, 1530-1560* (1969).

DONNE, JOHN (c. 1572-1631) English poet. Born to a Roman Catholic family, D. was on his mother's side a descendant of John *Heywood and of a sister of Thomas *More's. He studied at Oxford (1584-87) and, in 1592, entered Lincoln's Inn. In early adulthood he seemed more interested in adventures than in studies. From convenience he converted to the *Church of England and, in 1596-97, went with *Essex and *Raleigh on the expeditions to Cadiz and the Azores. Upon his return, he became a secretary to the queen's lord keeper of the Great Seal, whose niece, Ann More, he secretly married in 1601. However, the discovery of the marriage led to his dismissal and, for the next 14 years, he was dependent on patrons, living in poverty with his growing family. In 1615 he took a decisive step and was ordained priest and appointed royal chaplain. Thereafter his promotion was fast. In 1616 he became a reader in divinity at Lincoln's Inn and, in 1621, dean of St. Paul. In his late years he was one of the greatest preachers of the day, and his sermons attracted huge crowds.

D.'s "metaphysical" poetry is one of the outstanding examples of *Baroque literature. It combines intellectual brilliance with intense passion and employs an unusual imagery, deriving from religion, philosophy, science and even ordinary everyday things. Only four of his poems were published during his lifetime, the entire collection appearing only in 1633. His style is uneven, often rugged, but at times pure and beautiful and frequently impressive. His sermons possess the same intensity which marks his verse. He also wrote a polemical tract against Roman Catholicism, a satire on the *Jesuits, and a treatise on suicide. Highly popular in the first half of the 17th century, he was later almost forgotten and was "rediscovered" in the 20th century, chiefly through the efforts of T. S. Eliot.
R. C. Bald, *John Donne: A Life* (1970);
G. H. Carruthers, *Donne at Sermons* (1972);
A. J. Smith, ed., *John Donne: Essays in Celebration* (1972).

John Donne, *an engraving from a book of his poems*

DORAT, JEAN (1508-88) French poet and scholar. Born in Limoges, he became a teacher of classical letters in Paris, and a tutor at the court of *Francis I. Director of the Collège de Coqueret, he inspired *Ronsard and other young members of the *Pléiade, and was recognized as a spiritual father of their group. In 1560 he was appointed head of the department of Greek at the *Collège de France, and later titled 'royal poet' by *Charles IX. D. distinguished himself particularly in his edition of the plays of Aeschylus, to which he introduced many textual emendations.
C. Marty-Laveaux, *Oeuvres poétiques de Jean Dorat* (1875; rep. 1965).

DORIA, ANDREA (1466-1560) Ruler of *Genoa and military naval commander. Born to an old Genoese noble family, D. became a professional soldier, serving, among others, *Innocent VIII, *Ferrante I and his son *Alfonso II. In 1507 he was charged by Genoa with the suppression of a revolt in Corsica, and from then on became a prime mover in the political life of the Republic. At first he opposed the French who attempted to dominate Genoa but, in 1515, went over to their side and fought in their army. In 1525, when the French king fell captive, he entered the services of *Clement VIII for a short time, with the intention of opposing the Spanish forces. However, realizing that ultimately the French were going to be driven out of Italy, and taking advantage of an offer made to him by *Charles V, he changed sides in 1528. D. now became not only the imperial admiral in the Mediterranean but the true head of government in Genoa. Although he refused the title of 'doge', he commanded real power after he reformed the constitution, excluding the non-aristocratic elements and strengthening the rule of an extremely narrow oligarchy. In 1535 he commanded the imperial navy on an expedition to Tunis and, in 1541, accompanied *Charles V to *Algiers, where he helped to save the Emperor from a complete disaster. In fact, Charles V came to trust him so much that he also gave him the command of his forces on the Continent. In 1547 and 1548 D. suppressed two conspiracies against him in Genoa, in the first of which his own nephew and heir was murdered. Between 1553 and 1555, when he was approaching his 90th year, D. still commanded the Genoese forces against the French in Corsica. Shortly before he died he made his great nephew, Gian Andrea

Andrea Doria *by Sebastiano del Piombo*

Doria, his heir. The latter was, in 1571, among the principal Christian commanders at the battle of *Lepanto.

I. Luzzatti, *Andrea Doria* (1943).

DORT, SYNOD OF (November 1618-May 1619) A convention of the Dutch Calvinist church, which dealt with the issue of *Arminianism. In its ranks were several representatives from England, Germany and elsewhere. The assembly was hostile to the Arminians from the start, and produced a highly conservative Calvinist doctrinal statement. Politically, the proceedings were designed to support *Maurice of Nassau in his conflict with Jan van *Oldenbarneveldt. The latter was beheaded right after the conclusion of the synod.

DOSIO, GIOVANNI ANTONIO (1535-1609) Italian architect and sculptor. Born in Florence, he worked for a long time in Rome where, in 1569, he published an illustrated work, *Urbis Romae*, on the city's ancient remains. Later he assisted *Ammanati in architectural work. From 1576 to 1590 he was mainly in Florence, working as an independent architect. He ended his career in Naples.

DOSSI, DOSSO (c. 1490-1542) Italian painter. Born and lived all his life in *Ferrara. D. is considered the last of the masters of that city's school, but in fact his work has little in common with the hard visions of *Tura and del *Cossa. His works reflected the influence of *Giorgione and *Titian, on the one hand, and of *Raphael, on the other. D. excelled in atmospheric landscapes which were part of his allegorical and mythological scenes. An accomplished colourist, his paintings evoke magic and fantasy. His younger brother, Battista, who died in 1548, collaborated with him.

F. Gibbons, *Dosso and Battista Dossi, Court Painters of Ferrara* (1968).

DOUAI A city in *Flanders which, during the reign of *Elizabeth I, became the centre of English Roman Catholicism abroad. This was largely a result of the efforts of William *Allen, who founded the first college in D. in 1568. Subsequently, Catholic missionaries were trained there, who returned to England in secret; they also produced the Catholic English version of the *Bible. English educational institutions at D. were influenced by the *Jesuits.

DOZSA, GEORGE (?-1514) Leader of the great Hungarian peasant uprising. D. was a professional soldier and, in 1514, was chosen by Thomas Bakocz, the Cardinal Primate, to lead a *crusade against the Turks. The thousands who flocked to D.'s gathering armies consisted mainly of landless peasants, and before long the movement assumed the character of social rebellion. After the peasants ignored a royal order to disperse, an army was sent against them, which included hastily-recruited foreign mercenaries. Defeated and captured near Temesvar, D. was burned to death with red-hot irons.

DRAKE, SIR FRANCIS (1545-96) English navigator, military commander and *privateer. Born to a seafaring family in Devonshire, D. accompanied his relative John *Hawkins to the Gulf of Mexico in 1568, and proved his ability as a combatant when they were trapped by the Spaniards in the harbour of San Juan de Ulloa. In 1570 he undertook a privateering expedition on his own and, in 1572, returned again to the Caribbean, plundering Nombre de Dios in the Isthmus of Panama. Late in 1577 he sailed, with the approval of *Elizabeth I, on his famous voyage around the globe, being the first Englishman and the second of any nation to perform this feat. Crossing the Straits of *Magellan in October 1578, he

Sir Francis Drake

The Synod of Dort

raided Spanish ships and towns along the coasts of Chile and Peru. He then proceeded to the northern coasts of the American continent in search of an alternative passage to the Atlantic. Failing to find it, he sailed across the Pacific, reaching the Moluccas in November 1579, Java in March 1580 and the Cape of Good Hope in June. After his return to England, in September 1580, he was knighted by the Queen. In 1585 he again sailed to the Caribbean, attacking Santo Domingo and Cartagena. In 1587, while the Spaniard were fitting the *Armada, D. led a daring expedition into the port of Cádiz, inflicting tremendous damage. He was vice-admiral of the English fleet which defeated the Armada in 1588, and a year later commanded an unsuccessful expedition to Portugal, intending to help *António de Crato regain his throne. D. died in the Caribbean, off Puerto Belo, on board ship, during a final expedition which he had undertaken together with Hawkins.

J. Williamson, *The Age of Drake* (1946);
G. M. Thomson, *Sir Francis Drake* (1972);
H. P. Kraus, *Sir Francis Drake, a Pictorial Biography* (1970).

DRAMA AND THE THEATRE In the ancient world theatre was an integral part of the public life, and performers attained the highest levels of dramatic accomplishment in the approach to fundamental problems of human existence. The Renaissance, in which the forms of classical drama were frequently emulated, returned to this approach after a long period of stagnation. But Renaissance drama developed into something entirely different from the ancient. Not only did it make the theatre a familiar social institution, it also established modern ways of entertainment and, perhaps to a greater extent than any other artistic medium, gave birth to the modern volatile milieu of bohemian society.

Mediaeval drama, originally a mere adjunct of liturgical ceremonies and religious festivals, had developed by the 15th century three distinct features. The oldest consisted of performances based on the *Bible or the lives of the saints, and known as **mysteries* and *miracle plays*. In Italy these were called **sacre rappresentazioni* and in Spain *autos sacramentales*. The next to appear were the **moralities*, allegorical presentations depicting the conquest of the forces of evil. The third type was the *farce*, originally a short interlude in the vernacular, frequently interspersed with dance, song or pantomime. Of these, the mysteries gradually declined in popularity, whereas moralities continued to be performed throughout the 16th century. The farce, on the other hand, assumed, in due course, a more complex form, evolving into the late 15th-century French **soties* and the 16th-century Italian **Commedia dell'Arte*.

The continued exploitation of the farcial element was indeed the main thread around which Renaissance drama evolved. It was the possibility of indulging in hearty social satire that attracted to the dramatic medium some of the leading 15th-century Italian humanists, such as *Vergerio, *Alberti, and *Bruni, and the future *Pius

Commedia dell'Arte; I Gelosi playing before Henry IV of France

II who composed a racy comedy, all these works being in *Latin. Later in the century other humanist authors began to write similar works in the vernacular – for example, in Italy Lorenzo de' *Medici, in Spain Juan de *Encina. In Germany Hans *Sachs cultivated the style of the popular mediaeval farce well into the 16th century. Two other names associated with the growth of the popular theatrical satire in the vernacular were Pierre *Gringore in France and *Ruzzante in Italy.

Popular comedy in its different national genres was to remain a central feature of Renaissance theatre, but it paved the way for the revival of the refined comedy. This was a deliberate creation which turned back to classical times, especially to the works of the Roman playwrights Terence and Plautus, for models and sources of inspiration. Its development began concurrently in the early 16th century in several Italian cultural centres, notably *Rome, *Florence and *Ferrara. It was encouraged by princely patrons and the courtly audiences seeking entertainment. The comedies of *Ariosto, staged by the author himself, revealed his indebtedness to the ancient Roman authors. So, to a lesser degree, did the five comedies of *Aretino. One of the most admired learned comedies of the time was *Calandria* by *Bibbiena; but the work that remains familiar to this day is Machiavelli's *Mandragola*, in which a young man plots the seduction of a married woman. The Italian learned comedy (*commedia erudita*) found imitators in France and England, although in Italy the genre soon became interrelated with that of the emerging *Commedia dell'Arte*.

Even more than the comedy, Renaissance tragedy took shape under the direct influence of classical drama. The first modern tragedy, *La Sofonisba* (1515) by *Trissino, consciously imitated Sophocles and Euripides. But *Giraldi Cinthio, the literary theorist who wrote *Orbecche* (1541) and other tragedies, preferred to follow the exaggerated and unnatural style of Seneca, with its horrifying and bloody scenes. Indeed, the Senecan model exercised a paramount influence on Renaissance tragedy, until the ideas expounded in Aristotle's *Poetics* gained more influence around the turn of the century. Italian tragedy soon became known in France where, in 1552, *Jodelle staged his *Cleopâtre captive*, initiating a new epoch in the French theatre, with the enthusiastic backing of members of the *Pléiade*. In England *Gorboduc* (1562) by Thomas *Norton and Thomas *Sackville marked the appearance of modern tragedy.

The emergence of the tragedy in the middle of the 16th century responded to the particular historical circumstances born of the effects of the *Reformation. With the European cultures charged with emotional tension, there arose a tendency to give the dramatic work a propagandistic content. In England, for example, several plays written around 1538 by John *Bale and structured on the mediaeval moralities pleaded the cause of reform. In France Louis *Des Masures composed his trilogy, *David combattant, David fugitif* and *David triomphant*, which supported the Protestant cause. Similarly, in Germany the medium of the mediaeval drama was used early by Lutherans and Roman Catholic alike to exchange vicious attacks, leading to the anti-papist Latin plays of Thomas *Naogeorg. In the second half of the century, the *Jesuits, who made drama compulsory in the curriculum of their expanding seminaries, staged plays on religious subjects, first in Latin and later in the vernacular.

Late 16th-century sketch of the Swan Theatre, London

By the end of the 16th century European drama had outgrown much of its mediaeval simplicity. Plots and characters were becoming more complex, and authors became skilful in portraying the relative aspects of human existence. With audiences becoming appreciatively more sophisticated, the stage was set for some of the greatest dramas of Western culture. It should be noted, however, that literary greatness here paralleled national cohesion: the "golden age" did not arise in dismembered Italy, divided Germany or France torn apart by civil strife. It arose in Elizabethan England and in Spain of *Philip II and *Philip III.

Spanish drama was marked by its strong native roots, its obvious reliance on the local tradition of the *autos*, comic sketches (*pasos*), and short farcial plays (*entremeses*). The first to popularize this type of drama was the professional actor Lope de *Rueda in the middle of the 16th century. After him Juan de la *Cueva introduced themes from Spanish history. The dramatic works of *Cervantes need not concern us here, as he was essentially a novelist rather than playwright. It was Felix *Lope de Vega who made the Spanish theatre a popular national institution. This took place during the last decade of the 16th century; the fact that before he died in 1635 Lope de Vega had completed about 1500 plays, which were eagerly bought and staged by theatrical impresarios, speaks for itself. Other great contemporary Spanish playwrights were Guillén de *Castro, whose *Mocedades del Cid* (1618) influenced the 17th-century French theatre; Juan *Ruiz de Alarcón, a master of the cleverly structured play; and the creator of the character of Don Juan, *Tirso de Molina.

Elizabethan drama also followed national themes and traditions, as for instance in the *chronicle play*, which dramatized English historical episodes. But in England the influence of Italian literary styles was more noticeable and the reliance on the Senecan model of tragedy endured longer. The great age of the English theatre began in the 1580s, and is associated with names of John *Lyly, Thomas *Kyd, George *Peele and Robert *Greene. The most influential playwright of this early group was probably Christopher *Marlowe, the creator of the tragic hero of demonic dimensions. Ben *Jonson, on the other hand, excelled in the careful architecture of his plays, especially his comedies which abounded with wit and imagination. By the time *James I came to the throne, English drama was in close rapport with a very wide public, and had developed certain professional norms, but also a tendency to cater to the commonest taste. These features of the Jacobean drama are revealed in the works of George *Chapman, Francis *Beaumont and John Fletcher, Thomas *Dekker, John *Marston and several others. It was the peculiar genius of William *Shakespeare, whose career embraces the Elizabethan and part of the Jacobean period, to master all the dramatic techniques of his time and utilize them to achieve his own artistic ends. His dramas reveal careful construction, a discriminating diction, and an unusual attention to the psychological makeup of his characters.

The physical structure of the theatre and methods of staging also underwent considerable changes during the Renaissance. Mediaeval plays were commonly performed out-of-doors on a makeshift stage, a tradition that was retained by the *Commedia dell'Arte*. In the 15th century amateur casts, sponsored by certain *guilds, became quite common. The *Confrèrie de la Passion* of Paris, made up of tradesmen-actors, performed mysteries annually from 1402 until its partial suppression by the French courts in 1548. Another French company, the *Basoche*, was made up of law students, and yet another student society, the *Enfants sans Souci*, became very popular when it began to stage *Maître Pierre Pathelin* (*c.* 1464), the best-known 15th-century secular farce. In time the mediaeval popular theatre added splendid costumes, music, singing and elaborate settings. In Germany the Shrovetide plays of *Nuremberg regularly acted by members of the guilds kept this tradition alive through the 16th century.

After 1500 the popular theatre staffed by amateurs began to be displaced by the professional. The process was slowed by the spread of the refined Italian drama: designed to please a select literate audience, mid-16th century comedies and tragedies were often acted by their author and groups of friends, or by students of the best schools. This type of drama was also meant to revive the physical structure of the ancient theatre: the best-known example is the theatre of the Olympian Academy of Vicenza, designed by *Palladio in 1580 and completed by *Scamozzi in 1585. It was a diminutive indoor Roman theatre with a permanent stage, which extended the full width of the hall and was profusely decorated in the classical style. The Italian influence on staging and costumes was also felt in court spectacles, e.g. the English *masques. In contrast, the Spanish and English theatre buildings of the late 16th century were round timber structures resembling an enclosed yard. The famous Globe Theatre of London was only partly roofed, but had three tiers of galleries. These rudimentary play-houses were built by clever impresarios, who also commissioned authors to write plays, organized acting companies and were, as *Henslowe was called, "bankers" of the theatre. Under their management Renaissance drama reached its ultimate development.

E. K. Chambers, *The Elizabethan Stage*, 4 vols. (1924);
N. D. Shergold, *A History of the Spanish Stage* (1967);
K. Mantzius, *A History of Theatrical Art*, 6 vols. (1937);
B. Gascoigne, *World Theater: An Illustrated History* (1968);
H. Kindermann, *Theatergeschichte Europas*, 9 vols. (1957-70);
S. d'Amico, *Storia del teatro drammatico*, 4 vols. (1953).

DRAYTON, MICHAEL (1563-1631) English poet and dramatist. A page in the household of Sir Henry Goodere, he fell in love with his master's younger daughter, a passion he expressed in his pastoral sonnets *Ideas Mirror* (1594). Because of this love, he is said to have remained unmarried. After his patron's death, he was supported in succession by a number of other prominent persons but, in spite of all his efforts, failed to find favour with King *James I. D. wrote pastoral and historical poems as well as plays, though of the latter only one remains. The work most admired by contemporaries, *England's Heroical Epistles* (1597), was a series of love-letters exchanged by famous English lovers. The most ambitious of his other works was *Polyolbion*, of which the first part appeared in 1612. It was a patriotic epic poem about ancient England, based on *Camden's *Britannia*. D.'s style was accomplished and professional, making up for an essential feebleness.

B. H. Newdigate, *Michael Drayton and His Circle* (1941).

DRESS AND FASHION The deliberate shaping of clothes to the body, the legitimation of the purpose of attracting attention by means of costume – indeed, the modern concept of fashion – may be traced back to the *Renaissance. European mediaeval society chose to hide the contours of the body under shapeless cloaks and conceal women's hair with veils. Only in the 13th century, after the *Crusades had discovered the luxurious fabrics of the East, did garments become more colourful, showing a growing concern for beauty. However, the appearance of 'fashion', that is, a trend which determines the general style of costume, became noticeable only in the second half of the 14th century. Garments and women's head-dresses of the period displayed a flair for the bizarre. Men's hose, for example, were often of a different colour for each leg; their shoes, very long and pointed, were known as *crackowes*, after the Polish city of Cracow. The *houppelande*, an open gown of Flemish origin, became the characteristic formal dress. It was worn short by men and very long, with a train and funnel-shaped sleeves, by women. An innovation of the first half of the 15th century was the *doublet* for men, a short padded garment with sleeves, which covered the body from the neck to a little below the

High Renaissance fashion in Germany, in a painting by Lucas Cranach

Fashions in the second half of the 16th century, in a painting by Frans Pourbus the Elder

Fifteenth-Century Fashions, in a painting by Dieric Bouts

waist. Italian fashions of the 15th century were much freer than those in the rest of Europe, especially in the artful dressing of women's hair, which was often bleached. Italians were also the first to use opulent materials such as silk damasks, velvets and brocades.

In the early 16th century there were many changes in the fashions, tending to create an imposing, even overbearing, image of the individual. Men wore their hair longer and grew their beards. They used heavy, fur-trimmed sleeveless coats and wore gold chains and *medals. Their doublets had longer and wider skirts, with puffed sleeves which were often slashed to show the inner fabric, and they wore small flat hats and very wide shoes. Women wore full skirts with high waists, and their sleeves widening to a bell or puffed shape at the wrists. The bodice was tight-fitting and necklines were low. They also wore chains around their waists, from which they sometimes hung purses and other objects. These styles of the High Renaissance clearly illustrate the ideas of that age: a man's costume enlarged his frame, suggesting power and authority. Women's costumes accentuated femininity, combining an element of natural grace with a hint of sexual allure.

In the second half of the 16th century a definite tendency to stylized rigidity, contrasts with the earlier fashion. The typical courtier in the courts of *Philip II, *Catherine de Médicis or *Elizabeth I wore shor puffed trunk-hose stuffed with horse-hair or wool, which gave his hips the shape of a pumpkin and accentuated the length of his tightly-clad legs. His *doublet* was adorned with much jewelry, and he frequently sported a pointed beard and wore a short cloak. Women wore elaborately decorated and embroidered dresses. Their skirts were exceedingly wide with a very low waistline, resulting in an elongated narrow torso. The stiffness characterizing the fashions of both men and women was further emphasized by the universal wheel-shaped ruff, a frill of several folds of linen, starched and worn around the neck. High fashion at the end of the 16th century projected an air of haughty opulence, but to achieve this effect it distorted the natural lines of the human body.

J. Asser, *Historic Hairdressing* (1966);
M. von Boehm, *Modes and Manners* (1932);
F. Boucher, *A History of Costume in the West* (1967);
M. H. Hill and P. A. Bucknell, *The Evolution of Fashion* (1967);
B. Payne, *History of Costume* (1965).

DROGHEDA, STATUTE OF A measure (also called Poyning's Law, after the governor of *Ireland) which was enacted in December 1494, with the aim of enforcing English royal sovereignty. It established that no Irish parliament could meet without the king's consent and his prior approval of the bills proposed. In addition, laws made by the English parliaments were to apply to Ireland.

DUARTE (1391-1438) King of Portugal from 1433, and author. The son of *John I, he began to take part in the affairs of the kingdom shortly before his father's death. His short reign was dominated by two goals: the military expansion to North Africa, and the further exploration of the African coast. Although significant advances were made with respect to the second goal, the King met with disaster on his expedition to Morocco. In October 1437 the Portuguese attack on Tangiers was

High Renaissance men's fashions in The Ambassadors *by Holbein the Younger*

Madonna and Child *by Duccio*

repelled and one of the King's two brothers who commanded the force, Fernando, was taken prisoner by the Moors. The other brother was *Henry the Navigator. The King, who had had doubts about the wisdom of the expedition, died less than a year later. An educated man given to intellectual pursuits, he wrote the *Leal conselheiro*, a work on the moral guidelines of a king, which also contained original reflections on many other subjects. Another work, *Livro da ensinança de bem cavalgar toda sela*, dealt with horsemanship. A collector of manuscripts, he patronized the chronicler Fernão *Lopes.

A Soares Amora, *El-rei D. Duarte e o "Leal conselheiro"* (1948).

DU BARTAS, GUILLAUME DE SALLUSTE (1544-90) French poet. The son of a wealthy landowner, he studied law at Toulouse (1564-67) and joined the *Huguenots, becoming a close confidant of the future *Henry IV. In 1587 he went on a diplomatic mission to England and Scotland, where he found many admirers of his poetry, including King *James VI. Religiously inspired, though free from extreme partisanship, D. wrote long poems which attracted alike Protestant and Roman Catholic readers. His early works, *Judith*, *Le triomphe de la foi* and *L'Uranie*, were based on biblical themes and had plain didactic qualities. But it was his uncompleted masterpiece. *La semaine ou la création du monde* (1578-84), which achieved enormous success. Describing the seven days of Creation, the fall of Adam and episodes from the Old Testament, the poem was widely translated and influenced similar works outside France, notably John Milton's *Paradise Lost*.

M. Braspart, *Du Bartas; poete chrétien* (1947).

DU BELLAY, JEAN (1492-1560) French churchman and diplomat. He was first bishop of Bayonne, then of Paris, and became a close adviser to *Francis I. He organized the defences of Paris during the invasion of the imperial forces in 1544. D. supported humanist scholars and prompted his king to establish the Collegium Trilingue, later the Collège de France. After the death of Francis I he retired to Rome, where, as cardinal, he held much authority at the papal court.

DU BELLAY, JOACHIM (1525-60) French poet; one of the leading members of a group known as the *Pléiade. Born near Angers, he came to Paris at the suggestion of *Ronsard, who was his friend and poetic rival. D. composed the work which defended the literary ideas of the Pléiade, entitled *Défense et illustration de la langue française* (1549). In 1552 he went to Rome, where he stayed as secretary with Cardinal Jean *Du Bellay, a member of his family, but returned to France in 1555. His poems are lyrical and display refined personal qualities. Among his principal works are *Olive* (1550) and *Divers jeux rustiques*. Afflicted from his youth with hearing problems he eventually became completely deaf and died at the age of 35.

V. L. Saulnier, *Du Bellay*, 3rd ed. (1963);
A. W. Satterthwaite, *Spencer, Ronsard and Du Bellay; a Renaissance Comparison* (1960).

DUCAS, MICHAEL 15th century Byzantine historian. Born into the highest aristocracy, he spent almost all his life in the service of the Genoese ruler of Lesbos. He wrote a history of the Byzantine Empire from 1341 to 1462, to the latter part of which he was an eyewitness. Writing in a plain style, his account was comparatively objective, and he tended to view the Ottoman conquest with a sense of fatalism. His work has been preserved both in the original Greek and in an early Italian translation.

DUCCIO DI BUONINSEGNA (c. 1260-c. 1320) Italian painter. A contemporary of *Giotto, D. worked mainly in *Siena where, between 1308 and 1311, he completed a famous series of paintings, depicting scenes from the life of Christ, for the local cathedral. His work, nevertheless, had only a tenuous impact on the evolving style of art of the Renaissance. In contrast to the naturalism of Giotto, D. retained and, indeed, carried to its conclusion the formal Byzantine style of the previous century. His work is distinguished by superb craftsmanship and profuse gilding.

C. Brandi, *Carmine o della pittura; con due saggi su Duccio e Picasso* (1947).

DUCERCEAU, JACQUES ANDROUET (c. 1510-c. 1584) French engraver and architect. Born at Orléans, he spent three years in Rome and travelled for many years through France. In that period he etched nearly 180 plans and general views of French palaces and chateaux, which served as the basis for his well-known *Les plus excellents bastiments de France* (1576-79). Before that, D. published his *Livre d'architecture* (1559), in which he revealed his admiration for Italian ornamentation. Although not a great practicing architect, he was the founder of a dynasty of builders. This included his two sons, and his grandson Jean Ducerceau, who was active during the reign of Louis XIII. Another grandson was Salomon de *Brosse.

DUFAY, GUILLAUME (c. 1400-74) Flemish composer. A native of Hainault, he began his musical education as a choirboy at Cambrai. At about the age of 20, he went to Italy. He first worked at Rimini, then served in the court of Pope *Eugenius IV, with whom he went to Florence (1428-37). After some years in Savoy he returned to Cambrai (1445), where he was a canon, and he also became canon of *Bruges and Mons. Considered the greatest composer in his time, he wrote many works for *Philip the Good of Burgundy, including the music played at the famous 'Banquet of the Pheasant' in 1454. D. excelled also in the writing of masses, *motets and secular *chansons*. In his masses he was the first to use old secular plainsongs as *cantus firmi*, i.e., single melodies taken as a basis of a composition. He died at Cambrai.

J. F. R. and C. Stainer, *Dufay and His Contemporaries* (1898);
C. van den Borren, *Guillaume Dufay; son importance dan l'évolution de la musique an XVe siècle* (1925);
R. Bockholdt, *Die frühen Messenkompositionen von Guillaume Dufay* (1960).

DUMOULIN, CHARLES (1500-66) French jurist and political theorist. Becoming an advocate at the *parlement* of Paris, D. made a name for himself by his treatises on feudal law, *De feudis* and *Commentarii in consuetudines Parisienses*, both published in 1539. In these works he championed the cause of royal authority, claiming that feudal jurisdiction was but a delegation of the power of the king. Later D. became influenced by Protestant ideas and spent some time teaching law at *Strassburg. After he returned to France in 1557 he was arrested and released only in 1564. During the last years of his life he wrote on religious issues as well.

DUMOULIN, PIERRE (1568-1658) French Protestant leader and theologian. As a small child he was rescued from death in the *St. Bartholomew massacre. He was educated at Sedan, spent three years as a tutor in England (1589-92), and taught Greek and ancient philosophy at Leiden (1592-99). For 20 years he served as pastor of the reformed church of Paris, winning a reputation as an eloquent preacher and an opponent of the *Jesuits. In 1620 he left for Sedan, where he lived for the rest of his life. D. was a prolific writer and corresponded with many English churchmen.

DUNOIS, JEAN (c. 1403-68) French soldier, known as the 'Bastard of Orléans'. The natural son of Duke Louis of Orléans, he was born in Paris and, in 1421, attached himself to the Dauphin, the future *Charles VII. He was defending Orléans in 1429 when *Joan of Arc came to relieve the siege. Later he led the French army in the victories over the English, which made possible the recovery of Paris (1436). In 1439 he was made Count of Dunois. For a time D. cooperated in the movement against Charles VII known at the *Praguerie, but soon resumed command of the royal army. He expelled the English from Normandy and Guienne (1444-50), for which he was entitled Count Longueville. In the early years of the reign of *Louis XI D. joined the League of the *Public Weal, but was later reconciled with the King.

Madonna di Crevole, *Siena, by Duccio*

DUNSTABLE, JOHN (c. 1385-1453) English composer. Probably a native of Dunstable, there is scant information about his life. In 1419 he was made canon of Hereford cathedral, and between 1423 and 1435 appears to have been mostly in France with his patron the Duke of *Bedford. He died in London. His reputation owes not so much to his extant musical works, as to the general acclaim which he was given by his contemporaries who cited his name in one breath with that of *Dufay. Only some of his *motets and masses survive, revealing sensitive, gently flowing harmonies and rhythms.

F. L. Harrison, *Music in Medieval Britain* (1958).

DUPERRON, JACQUES DAVY (1556-1618) French cardinal. The son of a *Huguenot refugee in Bern, he converted to Roman Catholicism shortly after entering the service of *Henry III (1576). After the King's death, he sided with *Henry IV, to whom he gave spiritual guidance. Nominated bishop of Evreux in 1591, he went to *Rome in 1594 to obtain absolution for the King. D. was a strong polemicist who defended papal supremacy. He became cardinal in 1604 and archbishop of Sens in 1606. He wrote on religious and

Adam and Eve *by A. Dürer*

secular subjects. In 1611-12 he conducted correspondence with *James I of England on the question of the true faith.

DUPLESSIS-MORNAY, PHILIPPE (1549-1623) French *Huguenot leader; known as "le Pape des Huguenots". Born to a Protestant family of Normandy, he studied in Paris, fought under *Condé and *Coligny, and almost lost his life in the *St. Bartholomew massacre. Following a sojourn in England, where he had found shelter, he joined the future *Henry IV (1576), whom he accompanied as adviser, diplomatic envoy and military commander, throughout the *Religious Wars. In 1589 he was made governor of Saumur, where he later created the first French Protestant academy (1599). His relations with the King became strained when the latter converted to Roman Catholicism (1593), a rift that was not completely healed even by the Edict of *Nantes. An outspoken polemicist, he debated *Duperron in 1600 at Fontainebleau and, in 1607, made his reconciliation with the King. After Henry's assassination (1610), he counseled moderation. D. composed a number of theological tracts and, in 1611, published *Mysterium iniquitatis sive historia Papatus*, an attack on the Roman Catholic interpretation of the history of the papacy. According to his wife, he was the anonymous author of the **Vindiciae Contra Tyrannos*, but the claim is not universally accepted.

A Huguenot Family in the XVI Century: The Memoirs of Philippe de Mornay, Written by His Wife, trans. by Lucy Crump (1926).

DUPRAT, ANTOINE (1463-1535) French statesman and cardinal. D. was a legal expert who attained considerable standing in 1507 as president of the *parlement* in Paris. He was also close to *Louise de Savoy, mother of Francis d'Angoulême, and when the latter ascended the throne (1515)' D. became Chancellor of France and one of the king's chief policy-makers. Although he was blamed for the king's falling to captivity at the battle of Pavia (1525), he retained his high position in the government. He was created cardinal in 1527 by *Clement VII.

DUPRE, JEAN An influential early French publisher, active in Paris and *Lyons from 1481. Aiming at large-scale distribution, he took account of the public taste and chose his titles accordingly. In 1488 he printed the *Roman des chevaliers de la table ronde*, and a year later published the *Legenda aurea*, the popular collection of over 200 lives of saints, by the 13th-century author Jacobus de Voragine. D. specialized in illustrated quality editions, similar to the German *Koberger.

DÜRER, ALBRECHT (1471-1528) German painter and engraver. The son of a *Nuremberg goldsmith, he first learned his father's trade but, in 1486, was apprenticed to the engraver *Wolgemut, in whose workshop he spent three years. In 1490 he undertook an extended journey throughout Germany, visiting Colmar, where he had meant to meet *Schongauer, who died the previous year, and then Basle and Strassburg. Returning to Nuremberg in the spring of 1494, D. stayed just long enough to get married, and in the autumn went on his first tour of northern Italy. Of this first trip there is only scant testimony, and it appears that for the next ten years he lived and worked in Nuremberg. He returned to Italy for a longer period in 1505, at which time he met in Venice Giovanni *Bellini, was influenced by seeing the works of *Mantegna and probably also of *Leonardo. This second Italian trip, which lasted until 1507, also completed the change in D.'s self-conception as an artist. He began to mingle with some of the most famous German humanists; *Pirckheimer, who lived in Nuremberg, had been his friend even before his second trip to Italy. He had by this time established his reputation as a great master, sought after by German princes and, in 1512, was made court painter of *Maximilian I. For the Emperor D. executed a number of woodcuts for a grand project depicting Maximilian's triumphal arch and a triumphal procession, but the work was not completed. In 1520 he went to the Netherlands, to have his position as court painter confirmed by *Charles V. During this journey, which he recorded in his diary, he met *Erasmus, and was honoured everywhere. Although he remained a Roman Catholic, D. felt sympathy with the Reformation. After his death *Luther wrote in his praise.

D.'s paintings are not numerous. The outstanding ones include the *Adoration of the Magi* (1504), the *Four Apostles* (1526) which he presented to the city of Nuremberg before his death, and the famous *Self-portrait* of his youth, in which he displays himself with an air of bohemian arrogance. But his main achievement was in his vast graphic work, both woodcuts and copper prints. His series *Apocalypse* (1498) was the first book of illustrations in which the text was clearly of secondary importance. Other important series are the *Great Passion* (1510), and *Little Passion* (1511). Of his individual engravings *Adam and Eve* (1504), *The Knight, Death and the Devil* (1513) and *St. Jerome in his Study* (1514), are outstanding. D. also wrote on artistic theory: *Unterweisung der Messung* (*Instruction in Measurement*) printed in 1525 and *Vier Bücher von menschlicher Proportion* (*Four Books on Human Proportions*) published in 1528. The greatest German artist of any time, he transmitted the art of the Italian Renaissance to northern Europe and changed the status of the artistic profession in his own country by adding an intellectual dimension to it.

E. Panofsky, *Albrecht Dürer*, 2 vols. (1943);
M. Brion, *Albrecht Dürer: His Life and Work* (1960);
W. Waetzoldt, *Dürer and His Times* (1955).

D'URFE, HONORE (1568-1625) French author. Of aristocratic background, he became a staunch supporter of the *League, and was twice captured and imprisoned. Even after the last diehard *ligueurs* had made their peace with *Henry IV, D. remained obdurate and, in 1598, withdrew to *Savoy, where he composed pastoral and autobiographical poems. When, in 1600, he returned to France he was reconciled with the King, and married Diane de Chateaumorand, the former wife of his brother, the poet Anne D'Urfé. D.'s famous masterpiece, *L'Astrée*, was written between 1584 and 1589, but published in three parts only between 1607 and 1609. It describes the love of the shepherd Céladon and Astrée, and their eventual marriage after many adventures. A literary expression of D.'s illicit love for his brother's wife, the novel was much admired in the 17th and 18th centuries.

The Seven Candles *by Jean Duvet*

A. Dürer, Self-Portrait

DU VAIR, GUILLAUME (1556-1621) French essayist and statesman. Born in Paris, he became a councillor of the *parlement* (1584) and influenced the political manoeuvers during the latter phase of the civil wars. In 1593 he promoted the acceptance of *Henry IV as king, on condition that he converted to Roman Catholicism. Later he undertook a diplomatic mission to England, served as governor of Provence and, in 1619, was made bishop of Lisieux. D. wrote several essays which aimed at reconciling Christianity with the morality of the ancient Stoic philosophers. His work, which is distinguished by its clear style, influenced the great 17th-century French philosophers Descartes and Pascal. He also wrote a dialogue on the theme of faith in adversity, *De la constance et consolation es calamités publiques* (1593), and a treatise on the French language. He was a friend of *Malherbe.

R. Radouant, *Guillaume du Vair, l'homme et l'orateur* (1908; rep. 1970).

DUVET, JEAN (1485-c. 1562) French engraver. Born in Langres, where apparently he worked most of his life, he may have visited Italy and absorbed the influence of Italian painters and engravers, chiefly that of *Mantegna. His best-known works were 23 etchings which illustrate the Apocalypse (1546-56). He is also known to have produced works for *Francis I and *Henry II. Unaffected by the serene *Mannerism of the contemporary school of *Fontainebleau, his works evoked a dramatic force. He is considered to be the first major French engraver.

Knight, Death and the Devil, *engraving by A. Dürer*

EAST INDIA COMPANY Until the end of the 16th century the European nations made no systematic attempts to take over Portugal's commerce with Asia. When it became clear that there were no northern maritime passages, other nations chartered companies whose purpose was to conduct trade via the Cape route. Of these companies, the English and Dutch were the most important. The English was chartered by *Elizabeth I in 1600 as sharcholders' company. It immediately sent its ships as far as Japan and, by 1611, established a permanent base in India. The Dutch company was organized in 1602, but it included on its board of directors some merchants who had previously traded with India individually with the permission of Portugal. Its progress during the 17th century was even more remarkable than that of the English company.

EBERLIN, JOHANN (c. 1465-1533) German author of popular *Reformation literature. Born in Günzburg near *Augsburg, he joined the Franciscan order and, *c.* 1520, became acquainted with the ideas of *Luther, to whom he gave his utmost support. In 1521 hc published in *Basle a work entitled *Fünfzehn Bundesgenossen*. Through the mouths of 15 protagonists it demanded radical reform in everyday language and with reference to the oppressive social condition of the lower classes. He later spent some time with Luther in *Wittenberg, where his radicalism soften somewhat, and ended his life as a preacher in Erfurt and elsewhere.

EBOLI, ANA DE MENDOZA, PRINCESS OF (1540-92) The beautiful daughter of a Spanish viceroy of Peru, she married, in 1559, the prince of *Eboli, who was much older than she. After his death (1573) it was rumoured that she was the mistress of *Philip II and Antonio *Pérez, and she led the 'Eboli faction' at court. When Pérez was arrested (1579), she was banished from the court. She died in seclusion at Pastrana.

EBOLI, RUY GOMEZ DE SILVA, Prince of (1516-73) Spanish statesman. The son of a noble Portuguese family, he was brought over to Spain as a royal page, becoming a close confident of the future *Philip II. On the latter's accession (1556) he was made Councillor of State and acquired much influence at the court. Subsequently E. came to lead a faction which advocated leniency towards the rebels in the Netherlands, and was opposed to the policies pursued by the Duke of *Alba. After his death, the leadership of the Eboli faction was taken by Antonio *Perez, who had a close relationship with E.'s widow.

ECK, JOHANN (1486-1543) German Catholic theologian; *Luther's most persistent opponent. The gifted son of poor peasants, E. became, in 1510, a professor of theology at Ingolstadt University. His commentaries on Aristotle, which were published as textbooks, reflect his attachment to humanist learning, and he acquired fame and support for his public defence of the lawfulness of charging interest on capital, an issue which he disputed in Augsburg, Bologna and Vienna (1514-16). However, when Luther began the controversy over the *indulgences, E. came out against him and, in June 1519, opened a public disputation with *Carlstadt in Leipzig. Luther, who substituted Carlstadt in July, could hardly match E.'s argumentative thrust on the subject of papal supremacy. Not content with his performance as a debator, E. went to Rome in 1520 and returned as a papal legate, armed with the bull *Exsurge Domine* which excommunicated Luther. From there on he dedicated his efforts to arrest the rising tide of the *Reformation. In 1520 he published *De primatu Petri* which defended Rome; in 1526 he debated the doctrine of transubstantiation with *Oecolampadius; in 1530 he was charged by *Charles V with the task of writing a refutation of the *Augsburg Confession. His collected writings against Luther, *Opera contra Ludderum*, were printed in the years 1530-35.

ECORCHEURS Armed bands of adventurers which plundered parts of *Flanders and northern France between 1435 and 1444. They were led by some minor nobles, and derived their name from their custom of taking all the possessions of their victims. For some time they undermined the security and order in the regions which they ravaged, but when the war against the English resumed, many E. were induced to join the army.

EDUCATION The educational ideals of the late Middle Ages were to produce a professional person in possession of tightly-prescribed knowledge, mostly in theology, *medicine and law. The critical faculties of the student were deliberately restrained, and there also existed a wide gap between the Church-inspired type of E., which dominated grammar schools and *universities, and the instruction given to the children of the feudal nobility. In contrast, the educational aims of the *Renaissance were deeply connected with the new learning of the classics and the humanist ideal of an integrated personality: a many-sided rather than a specialized personality, an orientation towards the accomplishment of civic rather than theoretical goals. The Renaissance saw the beginning of modern liberal E., with its emphasis on literature, history and ethics. The concurrent development of the student's mental and physical abilities was advocated, since the early 15th century, by such humanist as Pietro Paolo *Vergerio and *Pius II. The first educators to test these ideas in practice were *Vittorino da Feltre and *Guarino da Verona. The first-named, especially at his famous school in *Mantua, which was sponsored by the *Gonzagas, included the study of pagan as well as Christian authors, and combined games and *music with the teaching of more conventional subjects. In northern Europe, where the ideas of the Renaissance began to be felt about half a century later, the best educational institution was probably the school of the *Brethren of the Common Life at Deventer, where the new learning was introduced by Alexander *Hegius. There, however, more than in Italy, humanism was given a pietistic bent, producing such personalities as *Erasmus and *Adrian VI. To a certain degree, the example of Deventer inspired the English educators, particularly Erasmus' friends *Linacre and *Colet who, in 1508, founded St. Paul's School. Among English humanists the study of *Greek and classical *Latin authors was considered a proper medium for the upbringing of a Christian individual. Later English educators, such as Roger *Ascham and Thomas *Elyot, continued this trend with somewhat less stress on Christian morality. Juan Luis *Vives, the great Spanish humanist who taught in Flanders, wrote the most mature outline of a humanist approach to E. Rejecting the old scholastic methods, he emphasized the importance of practical knowledge, urged the educator to be aware of his students' psychological makeup, and stressed the need to educate women.

Edward VI *by Holbein the Younger*

Humanist E. in the first half of the 16th century set new universal norms, applicable to the sons of the rising merchant class as much as to the young nobility. It had a cosmopolitan air, and the most famous humanist schools recruited students from all over Europe. The advent of the *Reformation and *Counter Reformation gradually changed this, introducing a spirit of sectarianism and discouraging study abroad. However, the preoccupation with the religious issues during the latter part of the 16th century had its positive results, too: there were widespread efforts to broaden the educational cadres and to provide schooling for a greater segment of the population. The most innovative institution on the Protestant side was the *gymnasium*, a secondary-school combining studies in arts and letters with religious instruction. The best-known school of this kind was founded in *Strassburg in 1538 and headed by Johannes *Sturm; another was the *Oberschule* of *Nuremberg, established through the efforts of *Melanchthon. On the Roman Catholic side the parallel development was the seminary, a diocesan school ordered by the Council of *Trent, of which the *Jesuits were the early promoters. Both the Protestant *gymnasium* and the Jesuit curriculum (*ratio studiorum*), emphasized Greek and Latin grammar, and attempted to inculcate morality and manners by a rhetorical and linguistic training. Originally flexible and aware of the psychological needs of the pupil, but increasingly inclined to regimentation, these institutions set the pattern for the classical school for the next 300 years.

W. H. Woodward, *Studies in Education During the Age of the Renaissance* (2nd ed., 1965);
E. Garin, *L'educazione in Europa, 1400-1600* (1957).

EDWARD IV (1442-83) King of England. The son of *Richard, duke of York, E. ascended the throne amid the unusual circumstances of the Wars of the *Roses. Continuing the fight against the Lancastrians after his father's death in the Battle of Wakefield (December 1460), he was crowned in London on 29 June 1461. Parliament confirmed his coronation shortly thereafter and declared the deposition of *Henry VI. In the first years of his reign his older cousin, Richard Neville, earl of *Warwick, held great influence over the government. His power reached its zenith in 1465, after he had defeated the Lancastrians in the north and captured the fugitive Henry VI. However, the relations between the two deteriorated in 1467, when E., acting against Warwick's counsel, preferred an alliance with Burgundy to a possible accomodation with France. Warwick, aided by E.'s brother, the duke of Clarence, rebelled in 1469. Forced to go into exile in France, he came to terms with Queen Margaret of Anjou, the indomitable wife of the imprisoned Henry VI. In September 1470, Warwick, Clarence and the Lancastrians invaded England and E., finding himself almost deserted, fled in his turn to take shelter in Burgundy with his brother-in-law, *Charles the Bold. With the latter's assistance, he was able to return in March 1471, and crushed the Lancastrians in two successive battles; at Barnet (14 April 1471), where Warwick was slain, and at Tewkesbury (4 May 1471) where Prince Edward, the son of Henry VI, died. E. now treated his enemies in a ruthless manner. On the day he returned to London (21 May) the still imprisoned and insane Henry VI was pronounced dead – probably murdered – in the Tower. The rest of E.'s reign saw renewed English conflict with France, which ended with the Peace of Picquigny, E. accepting a truce of seven years in return for a large sum paid by *Louis XI. In 1478 E. executed his own brother, the duke of Clarence, for his plotting with Warwick back in 1470. He continued to rule autocratically, displaying many traits of a Renaissance despot. He supported the new humanist learning, favoured the printer *Caxton and encouraged the London merchant class.

M. Clive, *This Son of York: A Biography of Edward IV* (1974);

A. R. Myers, ed., *The Household of Edward IV: The Black Book and the Ordinance of 1478* (1959).

EDWARD V (1470-83) King of England. Eldest son of Edward IV, he was seized upon his father's death by his paternal uncle, *Richard, duke of Gloucester, and lodged with his brother in the Tower of London (May 1483). On 6 July, Richard arranged his own coronation, E. and his brother having been declared illegitimate on the grounds that the marriage of their mother, Elizabeth Woodville, to Edward IV had been invalid. Shortly afterwards, probably in August 1483, the two young princes were secretly strangled to death on the orders of Richard III.

EDWARD VI (1537-53) King of England; the only son of *Henry VIII by his third wife *Jane Seymour. A frail child, he was crowned in 1547 at the age of nine, but the actual government was obviously not in his hands. It was first discharged by his uncle, the duke of Somerset and, after his downfall (1550), by the duke of Northumberland. E. is described as an excellent student of classical languages, and may have taken a personal interest in the advances made by the English Reformation during his reign. But he was not by nature a kind person, and although merely a boy, had a haughty conception of his royal power. Shortly before he died he was enticed by Northumberland to exclude his sisters *Mary and *Elizabeth from the succession bequeathing the crown to Lady Jane *Grey; but the plan later failed.

H. Chapman, *The Last Tudor King: A Study of Edward VI* (1959);

W. K. Jordan, *Edward VI: The Young King* (1968).

EGAS, ENRIQUE DE (c. 1455-1534) Spanish architect. Born in Toledo, he was a descendant of master masons from the Netherlands. His first great work was the construction of the Hospital Real in Santiago de Compostela (1501-11). But his most famous edifice was the Hospital de S. Cruz in Toledo (1504-15), with its innovative open-well staircase. E. also designed the burial chapel of *Ferdinand and *Isabella in *Granada. He was considered the foremost exponent of the late-Gothic style of architecture in Spain, and was several times consulted on problems involving the greatest Gothic structure in Spain, the *Seville cathedral.

EGIDIO DA VITERBO (1465-1532) Italian cardinal. In 1488 he joined the Augustinian order and eventually became its Prior General. Later he entered the service of the Vatican, and was employed as a diplomat by *Julius II and *Leo X. The latter made him cardinal in 1517 and sent him to solicit *Charles V's aid for a crusade against the Turks. E. wrote essays and poetry in Italian, as well as theological works. He was known as one of the most erudite humanists of his age.

EGMONT, LAMORAL, COUNT OF (1522-68) Military commander and leader of the resistance to Spanish rule in the Netherlands. Born to a noble family of Hainault, he was a favourite soldier of *Charles V, who showed his appreciation by awarding him the title of prince of Gaveren (1553). He played a leading part in the Spanish victory over the French at St. Quentin (1557) and Gravelines (1558), and in 1559 was nominated governor of Flanders and Artois and member of the council which assisted *Margaret of Parma with the government of the Netherlands. Together with *William of Orange and the count of Horn, E. opposed Philip II's intention of making the Netherlands a complete Spanish dependency and, in 1564, brought about the downfall of the powerful Cardinal *Granvelle. E. now went to Spain and tried to persuade Philip to give the Netherlands more autonomy, but it was in vain. This failure led to expressions of protest by the lesser nobility (1566), bordering on open rebellion. E. tried to disassociate himself from this movement, and even took half-hearted measures against the Flemish Protestants, but he did not disassociate himself entirely from the protesters. In September 1567 the new Spanish commander, the duke of *Alba seized E. and the count of Horn and imprisoned them in Ghent. The move was meant to serve as a warning to the rebels, but it achieved the opposite result. Yet Alba was not about to change course, and on 4 June 1568, E., Horn and other nobles were charged with treason and condemned to death by the infamous "Council of Blood". The next day they were beheaded in Brussels, E.'s personality served as a subject for a drama by Goethe and a musical composition by Beethoven.

B. de Troeyer, *Lamoraal van Egmont; een critische studie over zijn rol in de Jaren 1559-1564* (1961).

EL DORADO (The gilded one) A legendary kingdom of abundant riches. It became the object of searches by Spanish **conquistadores*. The legend began about 1536 with a story reported by *Belalcázar, who had been told by the Indians of Bogotá about a kingdom whose kings, covered with gold dust, would sacrifice themselves before their people by plunging into a lake. In 1541 Gonzalo *Pizarro led an expedition to the Amazon to search for this legendary kingdom. Later a number of other adventurers, throughout the 16th century, tried their luck in vain. Sir Walter *Raleigh's expedition to Guiana in 1617 was the most famous attempt by a non-Spaniard to find El Dorado, but this too was a failure.

W. Raleigh, *Discovery of Guiana*, ed. by V. T. Harlow (1928).

ELEANOR OF TOLEDO (1522-62) Duchess of Florence. The daughter of the Spanish viceroy of Naples, Pedro de *Toledo, she was betrothed in 1539 to *Cosimo I, duke of Florence. The marriage, which amounted to an alliance between Spain and Florence, strenghtened the Spanish influence throughout Italy. As duchess, she was patroness of *Bronzino and other artists and architects.

Eleanor of Toledo *by Bronzino*

ELIZABETH I (1533-1603) Queen of England from 1558. The daughter of *Henry VIII and *Anne Boleyn, E.'s personality was formed by the memory of the terrible fate of her mother, who was executed on a charge of adultery. Danger to her own life during the reigns of her brother *Edward VI, and her sister *Mary Tudor, further added to her natural caution. She saw Thomas Seymour, the widowed husband of her stepmother *Catherine Parr, executed in 1549, having been accused of conspiring to marry her and overthrow the government, and she herself was briefly imprisoned in 1554, at the time of the *Wyatt Rebellion. At her accession, at the age of 25, she was highly qualified to handle the affairs of state. She had been taught classical languages by *Ascham, knew French and Italian, had her way with people, and possessed a high sense of her own authority. She also knew how to take advantage of her peculiar circumstance as a single woman surrounded by men. Her assumption of the crown, following the death of her Roman Catholic sister, was welcomed with enthusiasm and hailed as a victory for Protestantism.

E.'s first decisions bore on the religious issues. She turned the situation back to the state of things during the last years of Edward VI, allowing the repatriation of the Protestant leaders who had been driven out under Mary. She did not, however, encourage further changes, and essentially supported the established *Church of England with its own hierarchy and liturgy; in the later years of her reign extreme *Puritans as well as Roman Catholic missionaries were persecuted by the government. In foreign affairs she at first continued the friendship with Spain and participated in the general settlement of *Cateau-Cambrésis. At the same time she pressed Scotland to break its long-standing alliance with France, and scored a victory in the Treaty of Edinburgh (1560), achieved by her chief adviser, William *Cecil. Encouraged by this success she invaded France in 1562, hoping to recover Calais, but the *Huguenots rallied to the side of the French Roman Catholics to defeat the invaders. This failure in France made E. extremely cautious with regard to foreign wars and cooperation with Protestants on the Continent.

But the most important issue of her first years of government was the one she consistently evaded, namely, her marriage. Although at first public opinion disliked the image of the "Virgin Queen" and clamoured for an heir to the throne, E. postponed her decision, turning the matter into a diplomatic game. She first declined the hand of *Philip II of Spain, the husband of her late sister, and after him a number of other suitable candidates, the last being Francis duke of *Anjou, who visited London in 1579 and 1581. Her personal choice would have been the earl of *Leicester, with whom she developed a romantic liaison early in her reign. After him she had other favourites, the last being the young and impetuous earl of *Essex. But she was always concerned that having an English husband might be more restrictive of her royal authority than a foreigner.

The first, relatively calm, phase of the reign ended with the turmoil of the *Northern Rebellion of 1569. This revolt of Roman Catholic diehards was connected with the fact that a year earlier *Mary Queen of Scots had sought refuge in England. She was kept by the suspicious E. in custody, but her presence encouraged a variety of political schemes and conspiracies. In 1572 the duke of *Norfolk, who had broken his pledge of desisting from such schemes, was accused of taking part in the *Ridolfi conspiracy and executed. But in the meantime E. had been excommunicated by the pope (1570), who declared her deposition, and her relations with Spain deteriorated. The next phase of her reign was, inescapably, one of interminable conflicts.

The conflict with Spain began with a clash of interests outside the boundaries of Europe. It was born of the renewed English attempts at geographic *exploration, which had started before E.'s accession, and the agressive trade voyages of *Hawkins and *Drake to the Caribbean in the 1560s, which eventually developed into simple *privateering. The Queen encouraged these projects, though at first unofficially, and even invested money in some of them. Later she approved *Raleigh's attempts to settle *Virginia. Indeed, her commitment to maritime expansion endured throughout her reign, and was given a final proof in 1600 with the chartering of the English *East India Company. Her active support of the maritime movement naturally enhanced her popularity, and when the conflict with Spain reached its climax her rough sea captains proved the mightiest weapon of of the English arsenal.

E.'s involvement in the Netherlands was for several years confined to the level of indirect aid to the rebels.

Queen Elizabeth I of England *by an unknown contemporary artist*

However, she openly encouraged their separation from Spain, so that in 1583 Philip II was convinced that only a move against England would secure the Netherlands for him. The sending of English troops to the Netherlands under Leicester (1585), the discovery of a series of plots against the Queen, resulting in the banishment of the Spanish ambassador Bernardino de *Mendoza (1586), and the trial and execution of Mary Queen of Scots (1587), led to the launching of the *Armada (1588). The defeat of the Spanish fleet in the English Channel and final destruction in the North Sea encouraged E. to take the offensive. An attempt to put *Antonio de Crato on the throne of Portugal (1589), which ended in a fiasco, was followed in 1596 by the spectacular capture of Cádiz by Essex. The Spaniards on their part supported the long rebellion of Hugh *O'Neill in *Ireland.

Although she emerged triumphant from her long conflict with Spain, E.'s last years were unhappy. During the 1590s the generation of men who had been the maintstay of her regime, including *Cecil and *Walsingham, was disappearing, and the ageing Queen seemed to lose her grip on the political milieu. The situation was dramatized in the fate of Essex, her youthful favourite, who was executed in 1601 following a reckless attempt to organize an uprising. E. cannot be credited directly with the great cultural flowering in the latter part of her reign, especially in the fields of *literature, *drama and the theatre; but she was a great political figure who cleverly manipulated her society and retained power despite numerous obstacles within and without, and some fundamental personal weaknesses to begin with. As such she deserves credit for the great achievements made during her reign.

J. E. Neale, *Queen Elizabeth I* (1934; rep. 1952);
E. Jenkins, *Elizabeth the Great: A Biography* (1959);
N. Williams, *Elizabeth the First, Queen of England* (1968).

ELIZABETH WOODVILLE (c. 1437-92) Queen of England. The beautiful daughter of an English baron and a French woman, she was widowed in 1461. In 1464 she was married secretly to *Edward IV. The marriage was later made public, and E. bore her husband several daughters and two sons, *Edward V and Richard, Duke of York. She also had two sons from her first husband. When *Richard III seized the throne in 1483, and sent her sons to the Tower, she temporarily sought asylum in the sanctuary of Westminster. Upon his fall (1485) she married her daughter Elizabeth to *Henry VII.

ELSHEIMER, ADAM (1578-1610) German painter and engraver. *Frankfurt-born, he travelled south, eventually reaching *Venice (*c.* 1598), where he became acquainted with the work of *Tintoretto. In 1600 he settled in *Rome, becoming a friend of *Rubens and Paul *Bril. His small landscapes, many of them executed on copper, are known for their experimentation in the treatment of glowing sources of light. In this he continued the ideas of *Caravaggio and influenced 17th-century painters, including Rembrandt. His chiaroscuro etchings also made a notable impact. He died in Rome.

W. von Bode, *Adam Elsheimer, der römische Maler deutscher Nation* (1920).

Tobias and the Angel *by Elsheimer*

ELYOT, SIR THOMAS (c. 1490-1546) English humanist writer. The son of a famous jurist, he was a pupil of *Linacre and *More, became an aide of *Wolsey's, and was sent on a diplomatic mission to Spain (1531-32). His manual on the education of the sons of the political elite, *The Boke Named the Governor*, was published in 1531 and frequently reprinted. E. also wrote a manual on health, a series of moral dialogues, and a Latin-English dictionary (1538). This, together with his translations of Isocrates, Plutarch and Plato, influenced the rising status of English as a language of learning.
J. M. Major, *Sir Thomas Elyot and Renaissance Humanism* (1964).

ELZEVIR A firm of Dutch printers and publishers. It was founded by Louis E. (died in 1617), a native of Louvain who had worked at *Plantin's shop in *Antwerp before settling in Leiden (1580). He began to publish in 1593, concentrating on classical authors, and catering especially to the student community of the local university. His son, Bonaventura (1583-1652), and his grandsons, Abraham (1592-1652) and Izaak (1596-1651), printed cheaper editions in large numbers, and spread the firm's name all over Europe.
D. W. Davies, *The Work of the Elzeviers, 1580-1712* (1954).

M. D. LXXXII.

Colophon of the publishing house of Elzevir

ENCINA, JUAN DE (1468-1529) Spanish poet, composer and dramatist. The son of a shoemaker from Salamanca, he enjoyed the patronage of the duke of Alba and, in 1496, published his first work, a collection of poems and eight plays, entitled *Cancionero*. E. visited Italy and spent several years at the courts of *Julius II and *Leo X. Borrowing from the Italian theatre, he introduced to Spain artistic forms of drama and music. He is frequently referred to as the founder of the Spanish theatre.

ENCISO, MARTIN FERNANDEZ DE Spanish explorer and geographer. Having made a fortune in Hispaniola, he financed and accompanied in1510 Alonso de *Ojeda on an expedition to Central America. Later E. quarelled with *Balboa over the command of the expedition, and when he returned to Spain (1513) was instrumental in having Pedro *Arias de Avila sent to replace Balboa. His *Suma de geografía* appeared in Seville in 1519. It was the first work in Spanish to describe the New World.

ENCLOSURES During the 16th century, the practice of enclosing common lands by the local squires and barons caused repeated agrarian unrest in England. The landlords enclosed open fields, in disregard of the ancient commoners' rights to the use of the land, seeking to profit from the rising price of agricultural produce. Where arable land was converted into pasture the discontent was especially bitter. E. were one of the factors that contributed to the *Pilgrimage of Grace, and even more to the 1549 uprising in the eastern counties, known as Kett's rebellion.

ENCOMIENDA The reward which the **conquistadores* received from the Spanish crown; a right to collect tribute and demand services from a designated number of Indian villages. In return for this, the *encomendero* was supposed to care for the Christian education of the Indians. The possession of an E. did not give its holder a title to the Indians land, but the *encomenderos* soon began to act as proprietors and demanded that the institution be given a hereditary character. This led to a conflict with the crown, which in 1542 enacted the "New Laws", designed to restrict the *encomenderos* and bring about the gradual elimination of the system. But a violent reaction to the laws, especially in Peru, resulted in postponements. The E. continued to exist but during the following century lost much of the social and economic importance that it had had in the early phases of colonization.
L. B. Simpson, *The Encomienda in New Spain* (1950).

ENGLAND Of the great European nations E. is the one which least led any of the great movements of the *Renaissance. She was late to absorb the Italian culture of *humanism and she did not distinguish herself, like *Portugal, in the early phases of *exploration. She did not play a decisive part, like *Spain and *France, in the great military conflicts of the early 16th century, nor did she influence, like *Germany, the changing religious life of Europe. And yet, in the final account, this comparatively small nation shared intensely in all these developments. E.'s Thomas *More was probably as great a humanist as any of his generation; although the English *Reformation began as a consequence of a King's uncontrollable obsession, it ended by becoming a symbol of Protestant resistence to the domination of Rome; at the second half of the 16th century, E. suddenly became a nation of great explorers and sea-warriors; and, finally, she contributed extraordinary masterpieces to Renaissance culture in the field of *drama and poetry.

English political history of the first half of the 15th century was shaped by the great victory over the French at *Agincourt (1415). Though the event was of spurious significance, it raised expectations about a permanent reconquest of Normandy and much more. But the English victories had been facilitated by the quarrel between *Armagnacs and Burgundians which debilitated the French; also, the premature death of *Henry V (1422) left the English government increasingly unstable. During the minority of *Henry VI the nobility split into factions around a number of powerful personages who fought amongst themselves fiercely. At the same time the conquests in France began to melt away. In 1450 *Cade's Rebellion expressed the exasperation of the English small landowners with the unending financial demands and the encroachments of the nobility. By then Charles VII of France had completed the reconquest of Normandy, and of the former English possessions in France only Calais remained (until 1558). The stage was thus set for the long and bloody internal conflict which marred the next thirty years, known as the Wars of the *Roses (1455-85).

In terms of the royal succession this period of civil strife saw the House of *Lancaster supplanted by that of *York, represented on the throne by *Edward IV and his cunning brother *Richard III. But the wars had also other effects: they decimated the old nobility, enabling the subsequent rise of new families who favoured a more assertive form of monarchy; secondly, the wars hardly impeded English commercial activities, and the export of wool to the *Netherlands, for example, continued to increase; thirdly, it was at this very time that E. became familiar with certain aspects of Renaissance culture. Humanism entered the schools and *printing, introduced into London by *Caxton, had a beginning.

*Henry VII's victory over Richard III at the Battle of Bosworth Field (1485) opened the way to the century of authoritarian monarchy, as practiced by the House of *Tudor. Under the founder of the dynasty the stress was on the subjection of the unruly nobility. This he accomplished through the suppression of revolts, such as the one connected with the impostor Perkin *Warbeck, and by means of effective judicial institutions, such as the *Star Chamber court. In addition, he improved the royal tax collection, concluded an advantagious commercial treaty with the Netherlands and improved England's international position by allying himself to Spain. The early reign of *Henry VIII saw the continuation of these policies in the able hands of Thomas *Wolsey. But when the King began his conflict with Rome, the tremendous coercive potential of the Tudor system of government suddenly came into the open, including its tendency to destroy its most dedicated servants. The Act of *Supremacy (1534) and the executions of Thomas More, *Anne Boleyn and Thomas *Cromwell were among the main political highlights of the reign, each a testimony to the almost unlimited extent of royal power. Although neither *Edward VI nor *Mary Tudor aspired to be absolute rulers like their father, they certainly benefited from the authoritarian tradition which he had established. *Elizabeth I usually succeeded in tempering this tradition with a measure of discretion. The acquiescence of the nobility and urban middle classes with this type of government explains the relative calm with which the English people accepted the swift and arbitrary shifts in religious matters. A number of rebellions broke out, indeed, but these were generally conspiracies undertaken by small groups, rather than mass resistance. The role played by parliament, a cooperative and frequently subservient institution under the Tudors, also illustrates the nature of the regime.

English foreign policy under the Tudors was preoccupied with the Franco-Scottish alliance. Henry VII accomplished the objective of rendering Scotland harmless by marrying his daughter Margaret to *James IV (1502), but Henry VIII fought Scotland and France together, defeating the French at the Battle of the *Spurs, while the rest of his army crushed the Scots at Flodden Field (9 September 1513). He again defeated the Scots at Solway Moss (25 November 1542), but was somewhat less fortunate in his costly struggle with France (1544-46). Mary Tudor again involved England in a war with France (1557), seemingly for the sole reason of supporting her husband, *Philip II of Spain. However, she lost Calais, and then the Treaty of *Cateau-Cambrésis settled the issues between the two nations. The 1560 Treaty of Edinburgh was a great triumph for Elizabeth I, as it practically terminated French influence in Scotland.

In the years that followed there was a complete reversal of E.'s international alignment. With France prostrate by the *Religious Wars, E. became the only European monarchy that could oppose Spanish domination. To some extent, the change reflected ideological factors: although the Elizabethan religious settlement was of a conservative nature, the nation had acquired a clearly Protestant mentality. There was public sympathy for the rebellion in the Netherlands; there was also enthusiasm for ventures of exploration and overseas expansion, exemplified by *Drake's daring attacks on the Spanish colonies in the Caribbean (1586). The destruction of the *Armada (1588) delivered England from the danger of invasion, but the war with Spain continued for many more years, in fact, until the death of the two protagonists, Philip II (1598) and Elizabeth I (1603). Hatred for Spain came to characterize the English, and *James I, who attempted to renew the Spanish alliance, was espousing an unpopular cause.

For all his personal deficiencies, the first *Stuart king ushered in a new era for E. She was now united with Scotland, her economic interests in *India were becoming established, and in North America the first permanent English colonies were growing. Internally, the cultural processes of the Elizabethan period reached an apogee with *Shakespeare, Ben *Jonson, Francis *Bacon and Inigo *Jones. At the same time the rift between the *Puritans and the *Church of England was steadily widening, and parliamentary opposition to arbitrary royal rule became a dominant feature of national politics. E. was heading for a political revolution.

E. F. Jacob, *The 15th Century, 1399-1485* (1961);
A. R. Myers, *England in the Late Middle Ages, 1307-1536* (1952);
S. T. Bindoff, *Tudor England* (1950);
G. E. Elton, *England Under the Tudors, 1485-1603* (1955);
L. Cahen and M. Braure, *L'évolution politique de l'Angleterre moderne, 1485-1660* (1960);
R. Lockyer, *Tudor and Stuart Britain, 1471-1714* (1964).

ENGRAVING The art of printing pictures on *paper from wooden blocks was essentially a 15th-century phenomenon, which spread through Europe a few decades before the invention of the movable type by *Gutenberg. Woodcuts, probably introduced from *China, were made by incising the surface of a block of wood, leaving lines that were inked and transferred to paper. The medium lent itself to the production of books and, indeed, at the very end of the 14th century "block books", produced by engraving both text and pictures on a single block of wood, were printed in the Netherlands and Germany. After the invention of movable type only the illustrations were made by woodcuts, but as the number of books published continued to increase, E. became a burgeoning industry. Soon the master engraver needed only to draw the lines of the desired picture, and the cutting of the wood was left to his assistants. Outstanding examples of woodcut-decorated **incunabula* were the *Nuremberg Chronicle* of 1493, illustrated by *Wolgemut and published by *Koberger, and the 1499 edition of the *Hypnerotomachia Poliphili* of Francesco *Colonna, issued by *Manu-

The Nativity, *an engraving by Martin Schongauer*

tius in Venice with some 200 exquisite woodcuts. Another fine illustrated book of that period was Erhard *Reuwich's *Peregrinationes in Terram Sanctam* (1486). It is estimated that about one third of all books printed before 1500 were illustrated.

Early in the 16th century wood E. came into its own, becoming an independent artistic medium in its own right. This development is associated with the name of Albrecht *Dürer, probably the greates engraver of all times, who in 1498 issued the first book of woodcuts, in which the text was of secondary value. Thereafter all the major German artists began to make single-sheet woodcuts or series of these prints. They included *Burgkmair at Augsburg, *Altdorfer at Regensburg, *Cranach at Wittenberg, *Baldung at Strassburg and *Holbein the Younger, who in about 1524 completed in *Basle his famous **Dance of Death*. An important innovation was the development of the chiaroscuro technique by the Italian Ugo da Carpi (*c*. 1455-1523). Using successive printings from several blocks, it was possible to get a picture with different shades of colour. Of the wood engravers of the latter part of the 16th century, one may single out Jost *Amman; Hendrick *Goltzius further experimented with the chiaroscuro woodcut early in the 17th century. But by 1550 the great age of wood E. had passed. Not until the present century when it was freshly taken by the German Expressionists, would woodcuts regain the artistic stature they enjoyed in the early 16th century.

What supplanted woodcuts as the principal method of printing pictures were the intaglio techniques using metal plates, usually copper. The artist cut lines into the plate by means of a graver or a sharp iron needle, which served him as a "pencil". The plate was then inked and wiped clean, leaving the ink only in the engraved furrows, and a sheet of paper was pressed upon it. The earliest prints made by this method appeared anonymously about the middle of the 15th century. The first virtuoso engraver of copperplates Martin *Schongauer was, perhaps not accidentally, the son of an Augsburg silversmith. Dürer, who shortly after Schongauer's death in 1491 went to Colmar to see him, also excelled in this medium. Even some of the great Italian artists, who usually confined themselves to painting, did not consider the hard work of copperplate E. beneath their dignity. *Mantegna, who left some 35 engravings in the style of his drawings and paintings, gave his prints a definite sculptural quality. In the early 16th century *Marcantonio Raimondi made copperplate E. a huge business, inundating Europe with thousands of his reproductions of the great works of the Italian masters.

Copper- and iron-plate E. underwent a great change during the 1510s with the invention of etching. In this new technique the artist first drew the desired picture with a needle on a waxed plate, which was then put in an acid solution that eroded the exposed parts, producing printable furrows, like those made by the graver; the

Woman Seated on the Ground, *etching by Parmigianino*

The Judgement of Paris, *engraving by Marcantonio Raimondi, after Raphael*

word etching comes from the Dutch *etsen*, to eat. The new process shortened considerably the time needed for the preparation of the plate. Urs *Graf in *Basle was the first to employ this technique (1513), and Dürer experimented with etching on iron between 1515 and 1518. About 1520 *Lucas van Leyden began to use copper instead of iron, and was followed by most of those who worked in the medium. Among the Italians, *Parmigianino was an enthusiastic practitioner of the etching technique, and the first to surmount the problem of put in shadows. Etching was to come to its full potential in the 17th century in the works of Rembrandt.
D. P. Bliss, *A History of Wood Engraving* (1928);
H. Hyatt Mayor, *Prints and People: A Social History of Printed Pictures* (1971).

ENSINGEN A family of German master masons and architects in the late Gothic style. Ulrich von E., who died in 1419, was for many years in charge of the construction of the great cathedral of Ulm. He designed the original plan of the exceedingly tall single tower. In 1394 he was asked to advise on the cathedral of *Milan, and later on that of *Strassburg. At the same time he also headed the construction of the Frauenkirche of Esslingen. His sons, Kaspar, Mathäus and Mathias, were also well-known architects in the same style.
H. Flesche, *Fünf deutsche Baumeister* (1947).

EPISTOLAE OBSCURORUM VIRORUM (Letters of Obscure Men) While the controversy between *Reuchlin and *Pfefferkorn over the Talmud was going on, two of Reuchlin's supporters, Crotus Rubianus (1486-1539) and Ulrich von *Hutten, published satires which parodied mediaeval Latin and scholastic reasoning. It appeared in two parts, in 1515 and 1517, and became very popular in the humanist camp all over Europe. Making fun of worn-out doctrine and practices, the satires helped to discredit the church on the eve of the Reformation.
H. Holborn, ed., *On the Eve of the Reformation: 'Letters of Obscure Men'* (1964).

EQUICOLA, MARIO (c. 1470-1525) Italian courtier and author. Having been a student of *Ficino's in Florence, he spent most of his life in the service of the house of *Este in Ferrara. He also spent a few years in *Mantua at the court of Isabella d'*Este. His most important work was *Libro de natura de amore* (1525) an encyclopaedic treatise reflecting his *Neoplatonist ideas.
N. Robb, *Neoplatonism in the Italian Renaissance* (1934).

ERASMUS, DESIDERIUS (1466-1536) Dutch humanist; the most outstanding European intellectual of the High Renaissance. He was born in Rotterdam, the illegitimate son of a priest and, in 1475, was sent to

Deventer, where he was educated for eight years by the *Brethren of the Common Life. In 1487 he reluctantly entered the Augustinian order and, in 1492, was ordained priest. Two years later he received permission to reside outside the monastery and, in 1495, arrived in Paris, intending to study philosophy and theology. Here, through his acquaintance with Italian exiles, he was exposed to the secular values of humanist culture. In 1499 he went to England as the tutor of William Blount, Baron Mountjoy. On this first visit E. met John *Colet, who encouraged him to study *Greek as a key to the New Testament and early Christian Fathers. By 1500 he was back on the Continent, where his growing reputation brought him offers of university professorships, which he declined. In 1506, after a second visit to England, he went to Italy, staying in Bologna and Venice, where he worked with the Venetian publisher Aldus *Manutius. On his third and longest visit to England (1509-14) E. stayed for a time at the house of his good friend Thomas *More. There he wrote the *Encomium moriae* (*In Praise of Folly*), a biting satire on the lax morals in the Church, which appeared in 1511. He then became Lady Margaret Professor of Greek and Divinity at Cambridge, where he prepared his Greek edition of the New Testament. From Cambridge he left for *Basle and, in 1516, after his epoch-making critical edition was published, went to Brussels and spent some time in Louvain. He returned to Basle in 1521, remaining for over seven years at the house of the printer *Froben. But, in 1529, with the advent of the Reformation, he left for Freiburg in Germany, where he lived in relative seclusion until 1535. He died in Basle, while supervising the printing of his edition of Origen.

E.'s scholarly and literary output was vast and varied. He first made his name known with the *Adagia* (1500), a collection of 800 ancient Latin proverbs, to which he added his own frequently pungent commentaries. His *Enchiridion militis christiani* (1504), a sort of a handbook of Christianity, emphasized piety, learning and love in preference to the outer forms of religiosity. His famous *Colloquies*, first published in 1516 and frequently reprinted, consisted of dialogues between different characters. These works were full of witty social commentary and, like *In Praise of Folly*, poked fun at the higher clergy, and criticized many aspects of monasticism and superstitious veneration of relics and saints. Of E.'s works on the classical languages the most widely acclaimed was *Ciceronianus* (1528), in which he attacked the slavish imitation of the ancients' style as practiced by the *Ciceronians. Of his treatises on *education the best was probably *De pueris statim ac liberaliter erudiendis* (1529). E. edited many of the ancient classical authors, including Seneca, Suetonius, Cicero, Terence, Livy, Aristotle and Ptolemy. His editions of early Christian authors include St. Jerome, St. Ambrose, St. Augustine and St. Chrysostom, all of which were published by Froben.

Although his writings paved the way for the Reformation, E., who abhorred violence, did not approve of the movement. However, he kept silent for a number of years, and came out against *Luther only in 1524, with his *Diatribe de libero arbitrio* (On Free Will), which was followed by a further exchange between the two. In fact, his position gradually made him an outsider to both the Protestant and the Roman Catholic camps, and

Erasmus *by A. Dürer*

after his death some of his works were put on the *Index. Like other great intellectuals whose ideas effected changes, E. was taken aback by the way in which society reacted to the issues he raised.

J. Huizinga, *Erasmus* (1924);
P. Smith, *Erasmus* (1923);
M. M. Phillips, *Erasmus and the Northern Renaissance* (1950);
R. Bainton, *Erasmus of Christendom* (1969).

ERASTUS, THOMAS (1524-83) German theologian; a Protestant advocate of the supremacy of the state in secular as well as ecclesiastical matters. Born at Baden, he was appointed to the chair of medicine at the university of Heidelberg in 1558. His *Explicatio gravissimae quaestionis* was published in London six years after his death. It argued that civil government should exercise power in the religious affairs as well, including the right to excommunication. The term Erastianism was used in England to describe those who urged the direct interference of the king in the affairs of the church.

ERCILLA, ALONSO DE (1533-94) Spanish poet. Born in Madrid, he was educated at the court, serving as a page to the future *Philip II, with whom he travelled in Europe. In 1555 he went on an expedition to Chile, where he fought the Araucanian Indians, returning to Spain *c.* 1563. His epic poem, *La Araucana*, published in three parts (1569, 1578 and 1589), was based on his experiences in Chile. It described the heroic Indian insurrection and the energetic Spanish response to its challenge. Though widely admired, and held to be the best Spanish epic poem of the Renaissance, it suffers from faults of style and construction.

F. Pierce, *The Heroic Poem of the Spanish Golden Age* (1947).

The Escorial

ERIC (c. 1381-1459) King of *Denmark, Norway and *Sweden. The son of the duke of Pomerania, he was adopted by Margaret, queen of the three Scandinavian countries. Although he was crowned at Kalmar in 1397, he took effective control of the government only after the death of Margaret (1412). Highly ambitious, E. spent much of his reign warring with Holstein and the *Hanseatic League. The costs of his military campaigns made him increasingly unpopular, first in Sweden and then in Denmark; in 1439 he was deposed. After long futile attempts to recover his throne, he retired to Pomerania, where he died.

ERIC XIV (1533-77) King of *Sweden from 1561 to 1569. The only son of *Gustavus Vasa by his first wife, E., who was emotionally unstable, quarrelled with his half-brother John and imprisoned him in 1562. Not long afterwards, he found himself at war with *Denmark and *Poland, a conflict which dragged for the rest of his entire reign. His highhanded methods against the nobility, and his massacre of the aristocratic Sture family (1567), aroused much opposition. Early in 1569 his brother John deposed him, and kept him in jail until he died.

ERSKINE, JOHN (1509-91) Scottish reformer, 5th Laird of Dun. Educated at Aberdeen, he went in 1530 to study in France, and brought back with him to Scotland the first teacher of Greek. He became a supporter of the Reformation, a friend to George *Wishart and John *Knox, whose return from Geneva in 1557 he facilitated. Although a layman, he was appointed in 1560 superintendent for Angus and Mearns. He was four times moderator of the general assembly of the Scottish Reformed Church. In 1572 he agreed at the Leith convention to the introduction of a modified episcopacy. In 1578 he took part in the compilation of the *Second Book of Discipline* and, from 1579, was a member of the King's council.

V. Jacob, *The Lairds of Dun* (1931).

ESCORIAL A palace and monastery northwest of Madrid, built by *Philip II between 1563 and 1584. The E. was intended to serve as residence and court of the kings of Spain and was one of the most ambitious architectural projects of the Renaissance. Although the actual execution of the work was entrusted to Spanish architects, the King consulted Italian experts, including *Palladio and *Vignola. Reflecting Philip's tastes, it included a large church, a seminary and a monastery. Its architecture is characterized by severe rectangular lines and simple décor.

ESPINEL, VICENTE (1550-1624) Spanish writer. Born near Málaga, he spent his youth wandering, studying at Salamanca and Alcalá with brief periods in other places, including Valladolid and Seville. On his way to Italy he was taken captive by Moorish pirates and, after his release, became a soldier in the army of Alexander *Farnese. He was subsequently ordained priest and,

although he never cared much about his religious duties, became the chaplain of one of the richest churches in Madrid (1599). Talented and versatile, he was an innovative poet and musician, and is credited with adding the fifth string to the guitar. His chief work was the *picaresque novel *La vida del escudero Marcos de Obregón* (1618), less cruel and more sensitively humorous than other works of this genre. It later influenced Le Sage's *Gil Blas*.
G. Haley, *Vicente Espinel and Marcos de Obregón* (1959).

ESPINOSA, DIEGO DE (1502-72) Spanish cardinal and statesman. The son of a poor but noble family, he studied civil law at Salamanca, where he later taught. As crown judge in Seville he acquired a great reputation, which prompted *Philip II in 1565 to appoint him president of the Council of Castile and *inquisitor general (1566). He was also made bishop of Sigüenza and cardinal (1568), and during some 5 years enjoyed the complete confidence of the King. E. aroused the enmity of many by his arrogant behaviour. He was criticized for his hard policies as inquisitor and may have been responsible for the regulations which caused the revolt of the *Moriscos. He died suddenly, a day after the King reproved his informal manner with a sharp remark.

ESPINOSA, GASPAR DE (?-1537) Spanish *conquistador*. Born in Medina del Campo, he probably received a legal education, as he was known by the title *el licenciado Espinosa*. He assisted *Arias de Avila with the execution of *Balboa (1519), and founded the city of Panamá. He then undertook an expedition to the region of present-day Costa Rica. Following a period in Spain he returned to America as a royal administrator. He died in Peru, where he had attempted without success to reconcile *Pizarro and *Almagro.

ESQUIVEL, JUAN DE Spanish explorer. He went with *Columbus on the second voyage (1494), and distinguished himself under *Ovando in the conquest of Hispaniola. *Las Casas described E.'s brutal treatment of the Indians. In 1509 he took part in the conquest of Jamaica.

ESSEX, ROBERT DEVEREUX, EARL OF (1567-1601) Appearing at the court of the ageing *Elizabeth I, E. became the Queen's darling at the age of 18. He distinguished himself as a soldier, fighting in the Netherlands in 1585 and commanding forces in Normandy in 1591. In 1596 he inflicted a great humiliation on Spain by capturing the port of Cadiz, and evacuated it only in return for a huge ransom. In 1599 he was made governor of Ireland and charged with the suppression of the O'Neil rebellion. His leniency towarrds the rebels gave his enemies at court the opportunity to manoeuvre for his dismissal. He then began to prepare a palace revolution, but was apprehended, tried on a charge of high treason and executed.

ESTE An Italian noble family which, from the 13th century, dominated the city of Ferrara. In 1452 Borso d'Este (1413-71) was given the title of duke of Modena and Reggio by *Frederick III and, in 1471, Paul II made him duke of Ferrara. The relative independence of the E.s in Ferrara was sharply curtailed by Clement VIII in the late 16th century.

ESTE, ALFONSO D' (1476-1534) Duke of Ferrara. For political reasons, he was married by his father, Duke Ercole I, to Anna Sforza of Milan. After her death in

Robert Devereux, Earl of Essex

1499 he married the daughter of *Alexander VI, Lucrezia *Borgia (1501). Succeeding to the title in 1505, E. first had to suppress a conspiracy against him led by his own brothers, Ferrante and Giulio. In 1508, as a participant of the League of *Cambrai, he destroyed the Venetian fleet in the Po River. On this occasion, as in the Battle of Ravenna (1512), where he fought beside the French, he made excellent use of his artillery, considered at the time the most advanced in Europe. E.'s relations with *Julius II were strained and he carried on a long and bitter feud with *Leo X, who enticed *Charles V to conquer Ferrara. Only Leo's death in 1521 saved the Duke from defeat. Later, he exploited the war between the Emperor and Clement VII in order to recover lost territories.

ESTE, ALFONSO II D' (1533-97) Duke of *Ferrara. The son of Ercole II and *Renée of France, he went at the age of 18 to the court of *Henry II and served in the French army. He returned upon the death of his father in 1559, to begin a long, and peaceful rule. In 1565 he took as his second wife the daughter of Emperor *Ferdinand I, thereby strengthening his ties with the *Habsburgs. Being childless, he conducted fruitless negotiations with the papacy to have his cousin Cesare succeed him, but when he died the duchy went to the Church, and Cesare received only Modena and Reggio. A patron of artists and poets, E. welcomed *Tasso to his court, but in 1579 confined him to a mental hospital. His death brought to an end the splendid rule of the *Este dynasty.

A. Solerti, *Ferrara e la corte estense nella seconda meta del secolo XVI* (1900).

ESTE, BEATRICE D' (1475-97) Duchess of Milan. Born in *Ferrara, she was the daughter of Duke Ercole I d'*Este and a sister of Isabella and Duke Alfonso I. In 1490, aged 15, she married the 38 year-old *Ludovico il Moro Sforza of Milan. She quickly made her presence felt in the Milanese ducal court, encouraging her husband to bring to Milan some of the great artists of the age, including *Leonardo. She also represented her husband on diplomatic missions. She died in childbirth at the age of 22.

ESTE, ERCOLE I D' (1431-1505) Duke of *Ferrara. A son of Niccolò III d'Este (1383-1441), he spent his youth in Naples, returning to Ferrara in 1463 when recalled by his half-brother, Duke Borso d'Este. He succeeded the latter in 1471, and to strengthen his position married the daughter of *Ferrante I of Naples. Although he generally attempted to keep his duchy out of wars, E. joined Lorenzo de' *Medici in the war against *Sixtus IV and, in 1484, had to agree to the loss of some territory to Venice. When the French invaded Italy (1494-95) he did not oppose them, and held on to this policy also when the invasion resumed under *Louis XII (1499). In 1500 he was pressured by *Alexander VI to marry his son Alfonso to the pontiff's daughter Lucrezia *Borgia, and consented after driving a hard bargain. A patron of humanist scholars and artists, he employed the poet *Boiardo and especially encouraged the performance of *drama.

ESTE, ERCOLE II D' (1508-59) Duke of *Ferrara. The son of Duke Alfonso I and Lucrezia *Borgia, he married *Renée of France in 1528 and, in 1534, succeeded his father. His wife's open support of the Reformation complicated for some years his relations with the papacy, and in his last years he confined her to her quarters in the palace. Allied to Spain and the Empire, he changed sides in 1551, joining *Henry II of France and Pope *Paul IV against *Charles V. When he was defeated, he accepted peace in 1558 under terms which allowed him to keep most of his territory.

ESTE, IPPOLITO D' (1479-1520) Italian cardinal; brother of Alfonso d'Este. Destined by his family for an ecclesiastical career, he was made an abbot at the age of five and archbishop at seven. In 1496 he became archbishop of Milan. E. was actually more of a secular prince than a clergyman. He fought with *Ludovico Moro against the French, defended Ferrara against the Venetians and against *Julius II, and supported the arts and letters. *Ariosto, who was his secretary, dedicated his *Orlando furioso* to him.

ESTE, IPPOLITO D' (1509-72) Italian cardinal. Son of Lucrezia *Borgia and Alfonso d'*Este, he was made archbishop of Milan at the age of ten. He served for many years as papal legate to France and was known as a representative of French interests in Rome. A patron of the arts, he built the famous Villa d'Este in Tivoli near Rome, where he assembled great collections of paintings and sculptures.

ESTE, ISABELLA D' (1474-1539) Italian patroness of art and literature. The daughter of Ercole I, duke of *Ferrara, she received a broad humanist education at her father's court and, in 1490, was married to Francesco *Gonzaga of Mantua. She took an active part in the government of Mantua, often substituting for her unfaithful husband, for whom she bore six children. It was due to her impressive presence in Bologna in 1529, prior to the imperial coronation, that the following year *Charles V made her son Federigo a duke. Among the men of letters associated with her court were *Giovio, *Bandello and *Castiglione. *Leonardo drew her portrait and *Mantegna, *Francia, *Costa and others were given commissions by her. Probably the most famous Italian woman of the High Renaissance, E. set examples of manners, tastes and fashions.

J. Cartwright, *Isabella d'Este* (1911);
M. Bellonci, *Segreti dei Gonzaga*, 3rd ed. (1974).

ESTIENNE, CHARLES (c. 1504-64) French physician, author and printer. The third son of Henry Estienne, he studied medicine at Paris and, in 1545, published an anatomical work, *De dissectione partium corporis humani*. His *Epistre* (1542) dealt with ancient *drama, and *Dictionarium historicum ac poëticum* (1553) became a frequently-reprinted encyclopaedia. E. also wrote a guidebook to travel in France and published a volume on agriculture. In 1551, after his brother Robert left Paris, he took charge of the family printing establishment, but after a few years it proved a failure and he went into bankruptcy.

H. W. Lawton, *Charles Estienne et le théâtre* (1928).

ESTIENNE, HENRI (1528-59) Son of Robert Estienne who continued the achievements of his French family of scholars-printers. His printing press in Geneva issued *editiones principes* of Anacreon, Plutarch and Athenagoras, and other classical authors and early fathers of the church. His most famous work was the *Thesaurus linguae graecae* (1572), a comprehensive Greek dictionary in five volumes, which complemented his father's similar work in Latin.

ESTIENNE, HENRY (c. 1460-1520) French printer. Born in Paris, he began printing about 1504, in a shop located near the University. Like his contemporary *Manutius, he concentrated on the classics, as well as theological and scientific works. The founder of the Estienne printers' dynasty, when he died his three sons were still too young to continue the business on their own. It was provisionally headed by their father's foreman, Simon de Colines, who in 1521 married their widowed mother.

ESTIENNE, ROBERT (1503-59) French printer and scholar. Born to a father who had also been a famous printer of scholarly books, E. continued the tradition. He introduced to France the handy size and the founts characteristic of the *Aldine press, and being both a classical scholar and a devout Christian, produced editions of the Bible in Latin (1528; 1532; 1540), the Old Testament in Hebrew (1539-41; 1544-46), and the New Testament in Greek (1550-51). His greatest scholarly achievement was the *Thesaurus linguae latinae* first published in 1531. He also published *editiones principes* of the early Christian fathers, among them Eusebius. E. enjoyed the support of *Francis I, but his annotations of the Bible brought him into conflict with conservative circles. After Francis' death he moved to Geneva where,

in 1551, he reopened his printing press, and subsequently published many of Calvin's works.
E. Armstrong, *Robert Estienne, Royal Printer* (1954).

EUGENIUS IV (1383-1447) Pope from 1431. Born Gabriele Condulmaro, he was the nephew of *Gregory XII, who in 1408 made him cardinal. Upon his election to the papacy he ordered the dissolution of the Council of *Basle, which had been summoned by his predecessor *Martin V. The Council's refusal to obey his order led to a conflict which was suspended temporarily in 1433, with the pope's recognition of the Council's legitimacy. A revolt in 1434 forced E. to leave Rome for Florence and, in 1438, he summoned the Council of *Ferrara, which a year later, in Florence, concluded the union of the Eastern and Western Churches. Although this achievement greatly enhanced his prestige, it also intensified the opposition of the delegates in Basle who, in 1440, elected Amadeus VIII, duke of Savoy, as antipope under the name of *Felix V. But E. was able to retain his control of most of the Church. In 1443 he returned to Rome and, in 1444, organized a *crusade against the Turks. Aenea Silvio Piccolomini (*Pius II), a former adversary, helped him to secure the support of the Church and of the princes of Germany.
J. Gill, *Eugenius IV: Pope of Christian Union* (1961).

EUROPE The term, which had been used by the Greeks and Romans to a more-or-less defined geographic area, almost disappeared from the vocabulary during the Middle Ages. Until well into the 15th century the term 'Christendom' expressed the notion of a continental cultural, political and religious unity. The semantic change was due to begin with the general Renaissance tendency of employing classical terminology, but it was reinforced by the internal religious conflicts in Europe and by the new geographic awareness resulting from the opening up of ways to Africa and Asia, and the discovery of America.
D. de Rougemont, *The Idea of Europe* (1966).

EUSTACHIO, BARTOLOMEO (c. 1510-74) Italian anatomist. Born in San Severino at the Marches, he studied at Rome and, in 1539, was admitted to the court of the Duke of Urbino. In 1549 he went to Rome with Cardinal Giulio *della Rovere, the Duke's brother. Later he was appointed professor of anatomy at the university (1555) and papal physician. In his *Opuscula anatomica* (1564) he described the cardiovascular system, and pioneered the study of the kidneys, the auditory organs and the teeth. The eustachian tube and valve are named after him. E. was a great opponent of *Vesalius, whose anti-Galenic views he never failed to decry. His anatomical drawings, engraved on copper, were discovered and published in 1714.
C. J. Imperatori, *Bartholomaeus Eustachius; His Contribution to the Anatomy of the Ear, Larynx and Bronchi* (1943).

EVERYMAN A famous English *morality play, adapted about 1500 from a contemporary Dutch source. The play's theme is man's moral existence and his accountability before God. Confronted by Death, who had been sent to summon him, E., the protagonist, is forsaken by all his friends, except Good Deeds who stands by him. Before the *Reformation the play enjoyed great popularity, and appeared in several editions.
A. C. Cawley, ed., *Everyman and Medieval Miracle Plays* (1956).

EWORTH, HANS (?-1574) English painter of Flemish descent. Born in *Antwerp, he went to England about 1545 and, after 1554, enjoyed the patronage of the court. Chiefly a portraitist, his style followed that of *Holbein, his predecessor as court painter, to which he added his own *Mannerist imagery. This is best exemplified by the allegorical portrait, *Sir John Luttrell* (1550), whose subject is depicted standing naked to his waist in a stormy sea, his clenched fist raised. He executed several portraits of **Mary Tudor*. His *Queen *Elizabeth Confounding Juno, Minerva and Venus* (1569), was an allegorical scene highly flattering to his patroness.

EXPLORATION It is doubtful whether it is possible to speak of geographic reconaissance prior to the 15th century. Certainly the memorable travels of Marco Polo (1271-95) and John of Monte Corvino (1294) to *China were not part of a coordinated movement of E. If one disregards the stories about the first visit to the Canary Islands (*c.* 1340) and the half legendary 14th-century voyages to the Madeiras and the Azores, the beginning of Renaissance E. can be set at 1415, when *Henry the Navigator began to explore southward along the coast of *Africa. Although the expeditions were still dominated by religious concerns, and although missionary and commercial goals remained essential ingredients of the E. movement for the next 200 years, these voyages were already undertaken with the aim of moving beyond the geographic horizons of the known world.

The Madeiras were discovered, or possibly rediscovered, by the Portuguese in 1418; the Azores reached and colonized between 1439 and 1451. In the meantime, progress continued along the coast of Africa and, in 1456, *Cadamosto discovered Cape Verde Islands. Portuguese E., which slackened after the death of Henry the Navigator, gathered momentum again under *John II. In 1488 Bartolomeu *Dias brought this early phase to conclusion when he rounded the Cape of Good Hope at the southern tip of Africa, demonstrating the feasibility of reaching *India and Far East *Asia by sea.

This was a turning point in Renaissance E. No other nation was about to take from Portugal what was duly hers. Indeed, Vasco da *Gama's 1497 voyage to India and further expeditions by *Cabral (1500), Francisco de *Almeida (1505) and Afonso de *Albuquerque gave the Portuguese an exclusive foothold in the Far East. But by the 1480s sailors of other nations had already begun to consider alternative sea routes to Asia. Italian and German navigators had been in the service of the Portuguese for some time, and it was Christopher *Columbus, a Genoese seaman-merchant resident in Portugal, who proposed the epoch-making voyage across the Atlantic which led to the discovery of *America. That he finally sailed under the Spanish flag only demonstrates to what extent E. had become a goal in which European monarchs were willing to invest. In 1497, as Columbus was preparing for his third voyage, another Genoa-born sailor, John *Cabot, led the first expedition to North America in the service of England. In 1498 the Portuguese sent Duarte Pacheco *Pereira in the direction of South America, and in 1500 the Portuguese brothers Gaspar and Miguel Corte Real sailed from the Azores and visited Labrador and Newfoundland.

During the early 16th century E. retained a certain cosmopolitan character. Thus, for instance, the Floren-

Queen Elizabeth Confounding Juno, Minerva and Venus *by Hans Eworth*

tine Amerigo *Vespucci sailed in the service of both Portugal and Spain; Sebastian *Cabot, an Englishman by adoption, sailed for many years under the Spanish flag, as did the Portuguese *Magellan, while another Florentine navigator, Giovanni *Verrazano, was employed by France. However, the main effort for each country was made by its nationals. As might be expected from the circumstances of the discovery and settlement of the New World, the contribution of Spanish explorers overshadowed the activities of all others. Their main achievement was to chart the Atlantic coasts of North and South America. This post-Columbian phase of discovery opened in 1499 with Alonso de *Ojeda's exploration of the coasts of Guiana and Venezuela. A year later Vicente Yañez *Pinzón reached the mouth of the Amazon, and at about the same time Diego de Lepe explored the coast of the Brazilian hump, the point on the South American continent closest to Africa. Although the Portuguese Cabral, who in 1500 landed near the present city of Salvador on his way to India, is usually credited with the discovery of Brazil, the exploration of its southern coast continued to be of interest to Spain, and in 1516 Juan de *Solis sailed into the estuary of Rio de la Plata. Meanwhile, the Caribbean shores were explored by Columbus on his fourth voyage (1502) and by Pinzón. By 1511 the biggest islands, Hispaniola, Cuba, Jamaica and Puerto Rico were being colonized. In 1512 *Ponce de León discovered Florida and, in 1513, *Balboa crossed the Isthmus of Panama to the Pacific. The discovery of Yucatán was made by Hernández de Córdoba (1517), and was followed by the first proper exploration of the Mexican coast by *Grijalva (1518). In 1519 Alvárez Pineda completed the survey of the Gulf of Mexico, and in the course of the next decade other Spanish navigators investigated the North American coast between the Carolinas and Nova Scotia. Spain crowned her achievements of the first two decades of post-Columbian exploration with Magellan's great voyage which resulted in the first circumnavigation of the globe (1519-1522).

Overland E. of the Americas was an entirely different matter. No one would credit the **conquistadores* with being interested in geographic discoveries per se. But although they were mainly concerned with the quick acquisition of riches, both *Cortés and *Pizarro should be remembered no less as the first Europeans to penetrate the high plateaus of Mexico and Peru. Similarly, Gonzalo *Jiménez de Quesada was the first to sail up the Magdalena River, reaching the highlands of the Colombian Andes near Bogotá, and Pedro de *Valdivia was the first European to reach the fertile valleys of southern Chile. In a number of cases misdirected military efforts, or expeditions which lost their way, turned into almost unbelievable feats of exploration. Thus in 1542 Francisco de *Orellana became the first man to sail the Amazon. Between 1540 and 1542 Francisco Vásquez de Coronado traversed modern Texas, Oklahoma and Kansas in search of the legendary seven cities of Cibola, and in the same years Hernando de *Soto explored the lower Mississipi, where he met his death.

Compared with these mighty achievements of Spain, the accomplishments of other European nations were minor. Portugal was mainly interested in developing its commerce with the Far East, so much so that she even neglected the colonization of Brazil. France followed Verrazano's visits to the bay of New York and the coast of Maine in 1524 with three voyages by Jacques *Cartier to the bay of St. Lawrence and Quebec (1534-41). But the French claim on Canada was not followed up until the early 17th century, when Samuel de *Champlain began to develop the Canadian fur-trade. The case of England was different. Although after the two voyages of John Cabot (1497-98) England seemed to lose interest in further exploration of the North Atlantic, she re-entered the field in the 1550s, when the Spanish activity was declining. This new English interest in exploration was closely connected with the desire of the London merchants to find a *North-East or North-West passage to Asia. It was only fitting that among the leading sponsors of the new movement would be the old Sebastian Cabot, son of John; above all, it received the support of Queen *Elizabeth I.

In terms of tangible results, the first English achievement was *Chancellor's arrival at the northern Russian port of Archangel (1553), which made direct communication with Russia via the White Sea possible. However, the commercial opportunities of this route were necessarily limited, and during the 1560s *Hawkins began to deal in the contraband slave trade between Sierra Leone in Africa and the Spanish settlements in the Caribbean. After the Spaniards attacked Hawkins at the harbour of Vera Cruz, English sailors turned to *privateering. *Drake's raids on the unprotected Spanish settlements on the Pacific coast led to his great voyage which resulted in the second circumnavigation of the globe (1577-80), and a few years later Thomas *Cavendish repeated the feat (1586-88).

In the meantime, attempts to find the northern passages had been resumed. In 1576 *Frobisher made the first of three voyages to Labrador and the Hudson Strait. After him, John *Davis explored the strait which bears his name on the west coast of Greenland (1585-87). Other attempts in the north were made by the Dutch Willem Barents who, between 1594 and 1597, explored the sea that carries his name between Spitsbergen and Novaya Zemlya. In 1607 Henry *Hudson returned to the area and, in 1610, discovered the huge Hudson Bay of Canada. The last great contemporary attempt was made by William *Baffin who, in 1516, explored the area beyond Davis Strait. While northern passages to Asia were not found, the searches resulted in the establishment of the northern English and Dutch fisheries of whales and seals, and the development of the fur trade. Indirectly, they contributed to the settlement of North America.

J. N. L. Baker, *A History of Geographical Discovery and Exploration* (1931);
B. Penrose, *Travel and Discovery in the Renaissance* (1955); J. H. Parry, *The Age of Reconaissance* (1963).

EYB, ALBRECHT VON (1420-75) German humanist. A native of Franconia, he studied in Bologna and Pavia, and later served as canon of the cathedrals of Bamberg and Eichstätt, where he died. In his works, he tried to introduce the culture of humanism into Germany. His *Ehebuch* (1472) discussed conjugal life, and his *Margarita poetica* (1472) was an anthology of ancient Roman writers. The posthumously published *Spiegel der Sitten* (1511), was a kind of an ethical guide, which also contained two comedies by Plautus in a free German translation.

M. Hermann, *Albrecht von Eyb und die Frühzeit des deutschen Humanismus* (1893).

EYCK, JAN VAN (c. 1390-1441) Flemish painter; popularly believed to have invented oil painting, though he actually perfected the technique; the greatest artist of northern Europe in the early *Renaissance. Born near Limbourg, he was employed by John of Bavaria, count of *Holland, at The Hague (1422-24). In 1425 he became court painter to Duke *Philip the Good of *Burgundy at Lille. This patron also entrusted him with diplomatic missions, sending him to Spain (1426) and Portugal (1428). In 1430 he settled in *Bruges, where he married (1434) and established a well-known workshop, thereby starting the famous local school of painting.

E.'s greatest work, the polyptych altarpiece *The Adoration of the Lamb*, at the cathedral of S. Bavon in *Ghent, was completed in 1432. Based on the Apocalypse, the work consists of 12 panels, eight of which are painted inside and out. The inscription on the frame names Hubert van Eyck as the one who had begun the work, indicating the existence of an older brother. However, the work's striking realism and vivid colours clearly point to Jan alone, and today there is a tendency to doubt the contribution of the older brother, about whom, moreover, there is no certain knowledge. Of E.'s other works, the *Madonna of Chancellor Rolin* depicts the earnest-looking Chancellor kneeling in front of a Madonna and Child, creating an irresistible feeling of depth by its masterfully-executed country scenery in the background. The *Arnolfini Marriage* (1434), shows E. at his most sophisticated in the unusually allusive treatment of subject matter. Showing an Italian merchant and his bride in their bedroom, standing hand in hand, the painting emanates a thoroughly secular mood, at the same time conveying a restrained sense of humour. All the other works – about 12 – signed by or attributed to the painter, are either on religious subjects or realistic portraits of individuals in a brilliant technique. E.'s use of oil in his paints and his improved varnish gave his pictures remarkable colouring, which has survived the passage of time. The impression he made on his contemporaries is illustrated by the fact that, a few years after his death, his name was known as far as Germany, Italy and Spain.

L. B. Philip, *The Ghent Altarpiece and the Art of Jan van Eyck* (1971);
L. Baldass, *Jan van Eyck* (1952);
E. Dhanens, *Van Eyck: The Ghent Altarpiece* (1973).

The emblem of the Silk Manufacturers' Guild in the walls of the Artisans' Church at Florence

F

FABER, JOHANN (1478-1541) German Roman Catholic theologian. A native of Württemberg, F. received a humanist education, becoming a friend of *Erasmus and a supporter of the reformist current inside the church. In 1523, he was in Zurich, as the representative of the bishop of Constance, when *Zwingli publicly debated his 67 articles of reform. This led to a rift between the former friends. F. went on to become one of the fiercest enemies of the *Reformation. In 1524 he published the first of many pamphlets against *Luther and, in 1530, was made bishop of Vienna.

FABER, PETER (1506-46) French *Jesuit; the first companion of Ignatius *Loyola. In 1534 F. met Loyola in Paris, where the two of them and Francis *Xavier lived together as students. F. became one of the founders of the *Jesuit order. Attending the Diets of Worms and Regensburg (1540-41), he came to the conclusion that there could be no theological compromise with the *Reformation, and began to work for Catholic reform in Germany, establishing the first Jesuit institutions in the Rhineland. F. was also active in other countries, and his advice was sought several times by *Paul III.

FABRICIUS, GEORG (1516-71) German classical scholar and poet. Born in Chemnitz, he taught at Leipzig and Strassburg and, after 1546, headed a school in Meissen, Saxony. He published editions of Virgil (1551), Horace (1555), and other classical writers and wrote poems in Latin. In 1609 appeared a work of his dealing with the history of Saxony.

FABRIZI, CINZIO ALOISE Italian poet. In 1526 he published in Venice the *Libro della origine delli volgari proverbi*, a work inspired by *Cornazzano's *I proverbi* and dedicated to Pope *Clement VII. It became enormously popular, but its crude obscenity aroused the ire of the Venetian clergy, and led to the institution of censorship by the Republic in 1527.

FACINO CANE (1360-1412) Italian **condottiere*. Of aristocratic origins, he fought for the queen of Naples, Joanna I, and afterwards served Gian Galeazzo *Visconti. After the latter's death (1402), he became the most important person in the political affairs of *Milan as the right-hand man of Giovanni Maria *Visconti; in 1410 he established his own, short-lived government in Pavia.

FACIO, BARTOLOMEO (c. 1400-57) Italian humanist. A pupil of *Guarino da Verona, he worked as a tutor in Venice, Florence and Genoa. In 1444 he was sent by Genoa on an embassy to Naples and became secretary and *astrologer to King *Alfonso of Aragon. His history of the reign of Alfonso is a major source for the study of the Neapolitan cultural milieu in the 15th century. In his *De viris illustribus*, he included biographies of contemporary personalities. F. carried on a long and bitter controversy with Lorenzo *Valla, whose history of Ferdinand of Aragon he had criticized.

FALLOPIO, GABRIELE (c. 1523-1562) Italian anatomist and physician. Born in Modena, he joined the service of the church, but soon turned to medicine, completing his studies in *Ferrara. He then taught in that city and in Pisa. His rising reputation led Grand Duke *Cosimo I to invite him to teach at Padua (1551), where he held the chair formerly occupied by *Vesalius, and was also in charge of the new botanical garden. In his *Observationes anatomicae* (1561) F. made several contributions, especially with regard to the composition and function of muscles. His main achievement, however, was the description of the female sexual organs, including the uterine tubes (fallopian tubes), and the naming of the clitoris, vagina and placenta. He was accused of practicing human vivisection, and may have experimented on condemned criminals.

FAREL, GUILLAUME (1489-1565) French Protestant reformer. A student of *Lefèvre d'Étaples, he collaborated with his teacher in the reform movement which was launched by Bishop *Briçonnet at the diocese of Meaux; but, in 1524, when his activities aroused bitter criticism, he fled to *Basle. Here his attacks on the city's most prominent citizen, *Erasmus, led to his expulsion. F. then moved to Neuchâtel (1530) and from there to *Geneva (1535). Aided by a young assistant, Pierre *Viret, he recruited in 1536 a far more famous personage, John *Calvin, whom he persuaded to stay in Geneva and preach. Although 20 years older than Calvin, F. recognized his leadership. When they both had to leave Geneva in 1538, F. returned to Neuchâtel, but continued to support Calvin, whom he outlived by a year.

FARNESE A noble Italian family which became powerful in Rome during the 15th century. Giulia F., one of the mistresses of *Alexander VI, advanced the career of her brother Alessandro, who, in 1534, was elected to the papacy as *Paul III. In 1545 he made his own son Pier Luigi duke of Parma, and the family continued to rule the duchy until the 18th century. The F.s were great patrons of the arts, and assembled a collection of important manuscripts and early printed books. Cardinal Alessandro F. (1520-89) completed the magnificent Casa Farnesina in Rome, the accumulative creation of Antonio da *Sangallo the Younger, *Michelangelo and Giacomo della *Porta.

FARNESE, ALESSANDRO (1520-89) Italian cardinal, the greatest patron of the arts in his day. The elder son of Duke Pier Luigi Farnese (1503-47), he became bishop of Parma, and at the age of 14 was made cardinal by his grandfather Pope *Paul III. Among the authors he supported were *Bembo, *Caro and *Della Casa, and he encouraged *Vasari to write his *Lives*. He commissioned *Vignola to build the Farnese Villa at Caprarola and was also instrumental in having that architect build the church of Il Gesù. He took part in preparations of the Council of *Trent.

FARNESE, ALESSANDRO (1545-92) Duke of Parma; Italian-Spanish military commander and statesman. The son of Duke Ottavio Farnese, he was educated at the court of his uncle *Philip II. He showed a talent for military affairs, participated under Don *Juan in the Battle of *Lepanto (1571), and, in 1577, was assigned to command the Spanish army in the Netherlands, where Don Juan was regent. When the latter died in 1578, F. succeeded him in the regency. He scored quick victories over the rebels in the south and, in the Treaty of Arras (1579), compelled them to recognize the rule of Spain. However, he still had to deal with some of the important cities, among which were *Bruges and *Ghent and, in 1585, completed the pacification of the south following a year-long siege of *Antwerp. F. was not permitted to carry the war into the northern Netherlands. Instead, he was supposed to cooperate with the *Armada in the invasion of England. After the failure of the Armada (1598), F. intervened in the civil war in France (1589-91), with the aim of preventing Henry of Navarre from ascending the throne. Governor of the Spanish Netherlands for 15 years of continued military action, F. was rated the greatest commander of his time.

FAUCHET, CLAUDE (1530-1602) French historian. Born at Paris, where he lived for most of his life, he wrote *Les antiquitez gauloises et françoises* (1579), a distinguished work on French political and social history of the Middle Ages. His *Recueil de l'origine de la langue et poésie françoise* (1581), was one of the first French literary histories, pioneering the study of the mediaeval *trouvères*.

J. G. Espiner-Scott, *Claude Fauchet* (1938).

FAUST, DR. JOHANN (1480-1538) A German quack, believed to have been also an astrologer and magician, and the subject of the 16th century legend of the ageing scholar who made a pact with the devil. The original Dr. F. was denounced by *Melanchthon, when he attracted multitudes believing in his supernatural therapeutic powers. In 1587 appeared in *Frankfurt the *Historia von D. Johann Fausten dem weitbeschreyten Zauberer und Schwarzkünstler*, a collection of legends compiled by Johann Spies. Promptly translated into English, it inspired *Marlowe's play, the first of many works by some of the greatest masters of world literature on the Faust theme.

G. Bianquis, *Faust à travers quatre siècles* (1955);
E. M. Butler, *The Fortunes of Faust* (1952).

FAWKES, GUY (1570-1606) English Roman Catholic conspirator. Born in Yorkshire, he was raised as a Protestant but converted and, in 1593, served with the Spanish forces in the Netherlands. After returning to England he participated in the *Gunpowder Plot (1604), and was responsible for placing the explosives. He was arrested while keeping watch in the cellar where the gunpowder was stored, and under torture revealed the names of his fellow conspirators. Executed on 31 January 1606, he is still remembered as the famous member of the conspiracy.

FEDERICO DA MONTEFELTRO (1422-82) Duke of Urbino. An illegitimate son of Count Guidantonio of Montefeltro, he was educated at the famous school of *Vittorino da Feltre at *Mantua. From 1444 on he served the *Sforzas and then Florence as **condottiere* and, in 1451, joined the forces of the king of Naples. In 1469, at the head of a joint force of Naples, Milan and Florence, he defeated the papal army and, in 1474, received from *Sixtus IV the title of duke, with a recog-

Federico da Montefeltro *by Piero della Francesca*

nition of his rigths over the territories that he had conquered in Romagna. In 1479 he fought Florence, this time on the side of the papacy. One of the foremost Italian political personalities and military men of his time, F. was a patron of humanist culture and Renaissance art. There is a famous portrait of him by *Piero della Francesca.

FEDERIGO (1451-1504) King of *Naples. The second son of King *Ferrante I, he spent several years at the court of *Louis XI of France before returning to Naples in 1482. In spite of his French sympathies, he fought against *Charles VIII and, in 1496, when his nephew *Ferrante II died, assumed the crown. However, the combined pressure of Spain and France became overwhelming and, in 1501, he abdicated in favour of *Louis XII of France, who compensated him with the county of Maine. He died in Tours, France. His abdication brought to an end the independent kingdom of Naples, which later passed from France to Spain.

FEDERMANN, NIKOLAUS (1501-42) German explorer. An agent for the banking house of *Welser, he went in 1530 to Venezuela as governor, the bankers' rights over this area having been confirmed by *Charles V. In 1531 he organized an expedition from Coro to Lake Maracaibo. Returning to Spain, he was again assigned to Venezuela by the Welsers and, between 1536 and 1539, explored the plains of the Orinoco Basin, crossed the Andes mountains and reached Bogotá, where he met the conqueror of the Chibcha empire, *Jiménez de Quesada. When he returned to Germany, F. was accused by the Welsers of betraying them and arrested. In 1557 his work describing the expedition was published under the title *Indianische Historia*.

FEITORIA (Factory) A trading-post established by the Portuguese in a newly discovered area. In the early days of colonization F.s were maintained along the coast of Africa, in India and Brazil. They usually consisted of a small military garrison rather than a permanent settlement. The F.s around the Senegal and Gambia Rivers in Africa were especially important as centres of the slave trade. Eventually the English, Dutch and French also established 'factories' on the West African coast.

FELIX V (1391-1451) Antipope from 1440 to 1449. Amadeus VIII, duke of Savoy and father of several children, retired in 1434, following the death of his wife, to lead a secluded life near Lake Geneva, at the head of a knightly order which he had created. The delegates of the Council of *Basle, who had broken with *Eugenius IV, chose him as pope in 1440, chiefly because he could maintain himself by his own means. In 1442 he settled in Lausanne, where the Council later joined him in 1448. By then, however, both F. and the Council had been deserted by all and, in April 1449, he resigned. Through French mediation, *Nicholas V pardoned him and gave him the title of cardinal.

FENTON, SIR GEOFFREY (c. 1539-1608) English translator. The son of a noble family, he travelled in his youth in France, Spain and Italy, in the entourage of an embassy. In 1580 he became secretary to the governor of *Ireland, a post he held until his death. In 1567 F. translated from the French *Bandello's *Novelle*, entitled *Tragicall Discourses*, and it became extremely popular in Elizabethan England. He also translated *Guevara and *Guicciardini's *History of Italy*. However, his *A Forme of Christian Pollicie* (1574) contained a harsh endictment of the theatre, based on narrow religious arguments.

Ferdinand I

FERDINAND I (1503-64) *Holy Roman emperor from 1558. The second son of *Philip the Handsome and *Joanna the Mad, and younger brother of *Charles V, he was born and educated in Spain. F. was the favourite of his grandfather *Ferdinand the Catholic, but at his death the crown of Spain went to his older brother. In 1521 Charles compensated him by entrusting him with the government of the *Habsburg possessions in the east, which included *Austria, the duchy of Württemberg and Breisgau. In addition, F., who about that time married Anne, sister of *Louis II of *Bohemia and *Hungary, acquired the rights of succession to the thrones of these two kingdoms, and also served as his brother's substitute in the affairs of the empire. In 1526 Louis died at the Battle of *Mohacs and F. took possession of Bohemia. He was not as successful in Hungary, where the majority of the nobles, headed by John *Zápolya, opposed him, and where much territory was already in the hands of the *Ottoman Turks. Indeed, the Turkish menace grew more serious and, in 1529, they besieged *Vienna and nearly took it. Helped by Charles, F. succeeded in repelling two other invasions, in 1532 and 1541, but for the rest of his life he had to pay tribute to the sultan for the small portion of Hungary which he held.

Elected in 1531 king of the Romans, or heir presumptive to the imperial throne, F. suffered a setback in 1534 when a coalition of princes, led by *Philip of Hesse, restored Duke *Ulrich to the government of Württemberg. In 1546 he aided his brother in the preparations which led to the victory over the *Schmalkaldic League, but shortly afterwards relations between the two became strained, and F. stood by while *Maurice of Saxony defeated the Emperor in 1552. He then negotiated the Treaty of Passau, which established a religious truce and, in 1555, sponsored the settlement known as the Peace of *Augsburg. By then he was already in actual possession of the imperial authority, although he was not crowned until 1558, after Charles V's abdication. In his Austrian possessions F. allowed some Protestant activity, but he defended the Roman Catholic integrity of his own family. He persuaded the estates of Bohemia and Hungary to make the monarchy hereditary instead of elective, thus ensuring the continued domination of the Habsburgs.

A. Lhotsky, *Das Zeitalter des Hauses Österreich; die ersten Jahre der Regierung Ferdinands I in Österreich, 1520-27* (1971).

FERDINAND THE CATHOLIC (1452-1516) King of *Spain; known also as Ferdinand II of *Aragon or Ferdinand V of Castile. The son of *John II of Aragon, he married in 1469 *Isabella of Castile, against the objection of her brother, King Henry IV. The latter's death in 1474 and the death of F.'s father in 1479 gave the young royal couple the combined rule of Castile and Aragon. F., however, was not recognized as king of Castile, although he was allowed to add his signature to his wife's on Castilian decrees; together they came to be known as *los reyes católicos* (the Catholic monarchs). Their reign, which gave Spain a sense of national unity, was marked by four momentous events: the introduction of the *Inquisition (1479), the expulsion of the *Jews (1492), *Columbus' voyage of discovery (1492), and the conquest of *Granada (1492).

A shrewed man, described by contemporaries as an habitual liar, F. was the true architect of Spain's rising power in Europe. Although he also supported the military exploits of Cardinal *Jiménez de Cisneros in North Africa, his main interest was in Italy; there he sent, in 1495, an army commanded by Gonzalo de *Córdoba, which in 1503 gave him the mastery over *Naples. His adversary in Italy was France, which F. successfully encircled by clever *diplomacy. He allied himself with England by marrying his daughter *Catherine to the son of *Henry VII, and with the Empire by giving *Joanna the Mad to the son of *Maximilian I, Philip the Handsome. In 1512 he conquered the part of Navarre which lies south of the Pyrenees. F.'s rule in Spain underwent a crisis following his wife's death in 1504. Claiming the regency of Castile on behalf of his daughter Joanna, the King aroused the opposition of a good part of the Castilian nobility, which backed his son-in-law Philip. But the latter died in 1506, and F. remained in control of the unified kingdom. When the son of his second marriage – to the niece of *Louis XII of France – died, F. favoured the succession of his grandson *Ferdinand. But after his death the older grandson, the future emperor *Charles V, came from the Netherlands and ascended the throne.

J. H. Mariejol, *The Spain of Ferdinand and Isabella* (1961);

J. Vicens Vives, *Historia crítica de la vida y reinado de Fernando II de Aragón* (1962);

W. H. Prescott, *History of the Reign of Ferdinand and Isabella*, 3 vols. (1846).

FERNANDEZ (Hernandez), GREGORIO (c. 1576-1636) Spanish sculptor. A native of Galicia, he was trained at Valladolid, where he established his own workshop about 1605. F. became famous for his altarpieces, which were all carved in wood and painted. He abandoned the use of brilliant colours and gold in favour of a more simple polychromatic arrangement, so as to achieve a naturalist expression. His statues of Christ have a dramatic intensity and their religious fervour makes them outstanding examples of Spanish *Baroque. Most of his works are in Valladolid, but there are some in Madrid and in other towns of northern Spain.

M. E. Gómez Moreno, *Gregorio Fernández* (1953).

FERRANTE I (1431-94) King of Naples. Although he was an illegitimate son of *Alfonso V of Aragon, he was designated by his father as heir to the newly-conquered kingdom of Naples. He ascended the throne in 1458 and withstood many threats, including the long baronial revolt of 1460-65. He took care to make the kingdom of Naples a presence in the Italian political arena of shifting alliances. His greatest rival was Venice which, in 1480, encouraged the Turks to capture Otranto. A second baronial revolt in 1486 was sternly repressed by his son *Alfonso. Shortly before his death, the marriage of his granddaughter Isabella to Gian Galleazzo *Sforza roused the belated reaction of *Ludovico il Moro, uncle of the groom and the real master of Milan. Fearing a Neapolitan attempt to dislodge him from his position in Milan, Ludovico encouraged the French invasion of Naples. F. died while *Charles VIII was preparing the expedition against his kingdom.

FERRANTE II (1467-96) King of Naples; known as Ferrantino. Son of *Alfonso II, he succeeded his father in January 1495, when the latter abdicated the throne, following defeats at the hands of the French and in view of his lacking domestic support. F. continued the struggle under adverse conditions, and mobilized an Italian league, led by Venice, against the French. Moreover, he aligned himself with Spain, which sent an army, under the command of Gonzalo de *Córdoba, to assist him. By the summer of 1496 the French were withdrawing from his kingdom, but F. died before the year was out.

FERRARA Italian duchy and the capital of a rich agricultural region on the river Po, F. was represented in the political rivalries of the Renaissance by its ruling house of *Este. In 1391 preparations were made for the founding of a university, and during the latter half of the 15th century, under Borso d'Este (1450-71) and Ercole I d'Este (1471-1505), the city became one of the main cultural centres in northern Italy. A process of urban beautification endowed her with many palaces. Alfonso I d'Este (1505-34) worked hard to maintain the independence of F. vis-à-vis Venice and the machinations of *Julius II, but after him F. began to decline. In 1598, when the line of Este came to an end, the city was brought under direct papal rule.

W. L. Gundersheimer, *Ferrara: the Style of Renaissance Despotism* (1973).

FERRARA-FLORENCE, COUNCIL OF (1438-45) A general council of the Church, convoked by *Eugenius IV to achieve the union with the Eastern Church and to organize help for *Constantinople against the *Ottoman Turks. Its convening at Ferrara led to a break

between the Pope and the Council of *Basle. The Byzantine emperor *John VIII Palaeologus and Archbishop *Bessarion were the chief representatives of the Eastern Church and accepted a formula of union highly favourable to Rome, but the union was later rejected by a synod of the Eastern Church. In 1439 the council was transferred from Ferrara to Florence, where it transacted most of its important business. In 1442 it was moved to Rome to deal with some minor issues.
J. Gill, *The Council of Florence* (1959).

FERRARI. GAUDENZIO (c. 1475-1546) Italian painter. Born in Piedmont, he worked in his native region and in Lombardy, ending his life in *Milan. His main works were done in the churches of Varallo, where he executed numerous *frescoes treating the life of Chirst. Other works were done in Como, Vercelli, Novarra and Saronno. F.'s painting reflect influences of *Perugino and *Correggio. Rich in colour, they possess an element of dramatic tension.

FERRARI, LUDOVICO (1522-65) Italian mathematician. A temperamental young servant in the house of Girolamo *Cardano, he was taught by his master and became his assistant. In 1540 he succeeded him as public lecturer in Milan. F. defended his teacher in the famous quarrel with Niccolò *Tartaglia. He discovered a solution to the biquadratic equation which was published by Cardano in 1545. This brought him wide acclaim and many offers from powerful patrons. He later taught at Mantua where he became wealthy, ending his life as a famous professor of mathematics in Bologna.

FERREIRA, ANTONIO (1528-69) Portuguese poet and playwright. A graduate of the University of Coimbra, he spent his life as a magistrate in Lisbon, where he died of the plague. A humanist by education and personal inclination, he followed the Italianate style of *Sá de Miranda and advocated the emulation of classical authors. His poetry, published only after his death, appeals to the mind as well as the emotions. His great masterpiece was *A Castro*, a tragedy about the love of Prince Pedro and Ines de Castro and the murder of the latter (1355) by order of the Prince's father, King Afonso IV. Based on a Greek model, the work successfully conveyed psychological tension. F. also wrote two comedies in prose.

FERRUCCI, FRANCESCO (1489-1530) Florentine military commander. Born in Florence, he held several administrative posts, before becoming an officer of the Bande Nere, the mercenary force formerly under the command of Giovanni de' *Medici (1527). In 1529 Florence employed him as military governor of Empoli, where F. distinguished himself by recapturing Volterra, which had declared for the emperor. Advancing by way of Pisa to relieve the siege of Florence, he was intercepted by the Imperial army at Gavinana near Pistoia, and defeated (3 August 1530). Captured, he was brutally put to death. He was remembered as a heroe of Florentine republican freedom.
G. Romagnoli, *Brevi cenni storici sulla vita di Francesco Ferruccio* (1897).

FEUARDENT, FRANÇOIS (1539-1610) French Roman Catholic preacher and author. A member of the Franciscan order, he was ordained in 1561, and undertook a preaching campaign against the *Huguenots. Later he was known as one of the chief spokesmen of the *League. A prolific author of anti-Calvinist literature, he also edited the works of several early Christian fathers.

FEUDALISM A political system founded upon a complicated hierarchy of suzerains and vassals, involving mutual rights and obligations, F. reached its apogee some time in the 13th century. At this time the institutions governing the conduct of the feudal nobility had been defined, establishing norms of mandatory military service, court attendance, and customary payments, or relief, due to the lord. Also by this time *chivalry and knighthood had made their impression on the social life of the feudal class, while the traditional seignorial structure, regulating the relations between the lord and the peasants on his lands, still prevailed. However, changes began to occur even before the onset of the demographic catastrophe and economic depression of the mid-14th century. Already in the 13th century the trend began of commuting the services of the villagers into monetary payments, and lords often agreed to free their peasants from the onerous conditions of serfdom against the payment of a fixed sum. Since the original obligations of the vassal to his lord remained largely unchanged, there was often a considerable gap between the real power at the disposal of each side and the meaning of the legal constraints which tied them together. On the other hand, in the principal feudal monarchies of Europe the royal administration was beginning to lay the foundations for the future central government. Clearly, feudalism was facing manifold disruptive pressures, and the social and economic upheavals of the 14th century only accelerated the process.

In the 15th century new factors hastened the ruin of the old system. First, the rise of international commerce, *mining and industry, and the increasing number of powerful self-governing towns, further reduced the relative importance of most feudal lords. Second, the revolution in the art of warfare, namely the employment of *artillery with its deadly effectiveness against the feudal castle, tipped the balance of power conclusively to the side of the monarchy. Not surprisingly, the 15th century saw the last decisive confrontations between kings and their great feudal barons out of which the centralized monarchy emerged more powerful. In France this happened in the reign of *Louis XI, in England as a result of the Wars of the *Roses, in Spain following the accession of *Ferdinand and *Isabella. By the time the *Italian Wars reached their final stage, the former feudal lords seemed ready for the new status which they were going to have for the next 300 years; that of nobility dedicated to the military, diplomatic and administrative service of a king at the head of a sovereign state.
M. Bloch, *Feudal Society*, trans. by L. A. Manyon (1962);
F. L. Ganshof, *Feudalism*, trans. by P. Grierson (1952).

FEYERABEND, SIGMUND (1528-1590) German printer and publisher. Born in Heidelberg, he was, after 1560, the most important publisher in *Frankfurt. His editions were decorated with woodcuts executed by various artists, among them the prolific Jost *Amman (1539-91). He issued a very successful edition of *Luther's *Bible and scholarly works in Latin. Other members of his family were well-known engravers.

FICHET, GUILLAUME (1433-80) French humanist. Becoming the rector of the Sorbonne at a relatively

Milan's Ospedale Maggiore *by Filarete*

early age, he made energetic efforts to develop the nascent art of printing in France, inviting a number of German typographers from Mainz. His own *Lettres* were published by the university press in 1470. A year later, F. accompanied Cardinal *Bessarion to Rome and became an important official at the papal court.

FICINO, MARSILIO (1433-99) Italian philosopher. Born near *Florence, he studied medicine, philosophy and theology, and in 1456 devoted himself to learning Greek. In 1462 Cosimo de' *Medici put his Greek manuscripts at F.'s disposal, and lent him his villa at Careggi, where F. established the so called *Platonic Academy. Here he wrote his main work, *Theologia platonica* (1469-74; printed 1482), and engaged in teaching and other scholarly pursuits. Gradually his reputation spread throughout Italy and beyond. Ordained priest in 1473, he received an ecclesiastical benefice. He kept up his association with the Medici, with a particularly close connection with Lorenzo. In 1494 when the Medici were expelled from Florence he too had to retire. Of his other philosophical works, *De amore* (1469; printed 1484), was a commentary on Plato's *Symposium*, and *De christiana religione* (printed 1476), dealt with theological questions. He wrote also on astrology and medicine and translated the complete works of Plato (printed in 1484) and Plotinus (printed 1492).

F.'s main contribution to Renaissance philosophy was the revival of classical Platonism. Having studied Plato through the works of St. Augustine, he believed in the compatibility of the Platonic system and Christian theology. Although he retained much of the mediaeval philosophical outlook about God and the universe, he assigned to man a central position in the universal hierarchy, thus giving his philosophy a humanist dimension. His most fruitful concept was the notion of "Platonic love", the ideal of spiritual love and intimate friendship, in contrast with vulgar love. He believed that, in its highest degree, friendship between human beings meant the contemplation and the enjoyment of God, which was the aim of man's existence. His ideas bore a considerable influence on 16th-century philosophy and literature.

P. O. Kristeller, *The Philosophy of Marsilio Ficino* (1943);
R. Marcel, *Marsile Ficin* (1958);
A. B. Collins, *The Secular Is Sacred: Platonism and Thomism in Marsilio Ficino's Platonic Theology* (1974).

FIELD OF CLOTH OF GOLD The name given to the interview between *Henry VIII and *Francis I in June 1520. The meeting held at the Plain of Ardre, France, was conducted in a magnificent manner, accompanied by festivities and games. The French king wanted to draw England over to his side in his conflict with the Empire, but Henry, following *Wolsey's advice, continued to support Emperor *Charles V.

FIESCHI CONSPIRACY (1547) The Fieschi were one of the most powerful families in *Genoa. During the

*Italian Wars they usually supported the French, and when Andrea *Doria, who was allied to *Charles V, came to dominate the city, they attempted to capture the government by a coup d'état. On the night of 2 January 1547, the conspirators murdered Doria's nephew and heir, Giannetino, but dispersed following the accidental drowning of their leader, Gian Luigi Fieschi. Doria then launched a ruthless campaign of retribution against the Fieschi and their party.

FILARETE (Antonio Averlino; c. 1400-69) Italian sculptor and architect. Born in Florence, he studied under *Ghiberti but, in 1433, went to Rome, where he executed two famous doors at St. Peter's (1443), in imitation of the works of Ghiberti and *Donatello. In 1451 he went to work as an architect for Francesco *Sforza of Milan, where he designed the Ospedale Maggiore, the first building of unmistakable Renaissance style in that city. F. wrote an important *Trattato d'architettura* (1464) which described an imaginary model city.

Filarete's Treatise on Architecture, trans. by J. R. Spencer (1965).

FILELFO, FRANCESCO (1398-1481) Italian humanist. Born at Tolentino, he studied under *Gaspanino da Barzizza and, in 1420, went to Constantinople, where he spent seven years mastering the *Greek language. From 1429 to 1434 he taught at Florence, where he quarelled with *Poggio Bracciolini. Later he moved from one city to another, staying for a rather long period in *Milan, where Filippo Maria *Visconti and Francesco *Sforza supported him. Although he wrote extensively, F. is not considered an author of great merit; his collected letters are probably the most interesting part of his work. His significance lies in the type of humanist scholar which he represents. Quarrelsome, extremely proud and quick to offend others, he did not mind putting his pen at the service of many Italian rulers, writing eulogies and ceremonial addresses upon demand. His denunciation of the enemies of Lorenzo de' Medici was rewarded by the latter with an invitation to F. to return to Florence as a professor of Greek, but he died shortly after his arrival.

G. Saitta, *L'educazione del umanesimo in Italia* (1928).

FINIGUERRA, MASO (1426-64) Italian goldsmith. Born in Florence, he learned his craft from his father, becoming the most famous niellist of his time. *Vasari credited him with the invention of copper engraving. Although this is not true, he was certainly among the first Italians to work in this medium.

FIORAVANTI, ARISTOTELE (c. 1415-c. 1485) Italian architect. A descendent of a Bolognese family of architects and engineers, he worked in Rome, Milan and Mantua as well as in Bologna. In 1467 he spent some months working in Hungary and, in 1475, went to Moscow at the invitation of *Ivan III. There he remained until his death, his major project being the building of the church of the Assumption (Uspenskil Sobor) in the Kremlin. F. adapted himself so well to the style of Russian architecture, that only a few details hint that this was the work of a Western architect.

FIORAVANTI, LEONARDO (1518-88) Italian physician. Born in Bologna, he practiced at first in Spain and in Spanish-ruled Sicily and Naples. Later he lived in Rome and Venice, ending his career in Bologna. A prolific author, he published works on the control of plagues (1565), on the connection between medicine and alchemy (1571), and on surgery (1582). F. is credited with the first splenectomy and with the composition of a potion against arsenic poisoning.

D. Giordano, *Leonardo Fioravanti* (1919).

FIORENZO DI LORENZO (c. 1440-c. 1522) Italian painter. Born in Perugia, he is believed to have spent most of his life there, although only two pictures signed by him in that city, exist. His mature style has much in common with that of *Pollaiuolo, and several of the pictures ascribed to him are on the subject of St. Sebastian. His chief work is an altarpiece, *Madonna and Child with St.s Peter and Paul* (1487). In this picture, and in his later works, there is a noticeable influence of *Perugino.

FIRENZUOLA, AGNOLO (1493-1543) Italian author. A Vallombrosan monk who represented his order in Rome, he followed the secular spirit of his age and, in 1526, was dispensed of his vows. In 1534 he settled in Prato where he died. F. wrote poetry, plays and essays, all of vivacious and easy style. His *Asino d'oro* (Golden Ass) was a free adaptation of Apuleius. His *Ragionamenti de amore* (Reasons of Love) contained licentious novels, and his *Dialogo delle bellezze delle donne* (Dialogue on the Charms of Women) is still entertaining. *La prima veste dei discorsi degli animali*, based on Indian didactic fables (taken from a Spanish source) described contemporary human vices. All his chief works were published after his death (1548-50).

M. Oliveri, *Agnolo Firenzuola* (1935).

FISCHART, JOHANN (1547-90) German satirist, called Mentzer because his father had come from Mainz. Born in *Strassburg, he received a humanist education, travelled in Italy, France and England and, in 1574, began a legal career in his native town. His main literary work, the *Geschichtklitterung* (1575), was a translation and free adaptation of *Rabelais' *Gargantua*, narrated in a witty grotesque style. A *Protestant, he wrote against Roman Catholicism and, in his *Jesuiterhütlein* (1580), bitterly attacked the *Jesuits. His *Flöhhaz* (1573) was a lively satire on women, but in *Ehezuchtbüchlein* (1578) he showed greater understanding and enlightened views on marriage. Although not a very original author, his satires exposed the conventional hypocrisies of his time, in defence of true religion and a simple domestic life.

H. Sommerhalder, *Johann Fischart's werk* (1960)

FISH, SIMON (?-1531) English reformer. In 1529 he published a violent attack on the clergy, entitled *Supplication of Beggars*. Addressed to *Henry VIII, it demanded, among other things, the suppression of the monasteries. The work had a wide circulation and merited a written refutation by Thomas *More. F. thus earned the distinction of being one of the earliest English Protestants.

FISHER, JOHN (1469-1535) English bishop of Rochester and martyr of *Henry VIII's Reformation. In his early career he was closely associated with the University of Cambridge, where he helped to introduce the new humanist learning and classical studies. His work there was greatly enhanced by his intimacy with Lady *Margaret Beaufort, the mother of *Henry VII. In 1503 he became the first Lady Margaret professor of divinity, and a year later was made bishop. A man of strong convictions, F. opposed the Lutheran tendencies

Bishop John Fisher *by Holbein the Younger*

which penetrated England from the Continent and, in 1527, wrote in defence of the doctrine of the real presence of Christ in the Eucharist. Moreover, when Henry VIII's intention to divorce *Catherine of Aragon became known, he opposed the King. In 1534, when he refused to swear the oath required by the Act of *Supremacy, he was arrested and after a year's imprisonment, was condemned to death. The fact that *Paul III made him cardinal while he was in jail, angered the King and hastened his death. He was beheaded on 22 June 1535, two weeks before Thomas *More. He was canonized in 1936.

E. E. Reynolds, *St. John Fisher* (1955).

FLACIUS (Matthias Vlacich; 1520-75) Protestant theologian; known also as Illyricus after his native region. He was sent by his uncle to study in Germany and, in 1541, went to Wittenberg where *Luther appointed him, in 1544, to the chair of Hebrew. After Luther's death F. became a leading conservative apologist of his doctrines, and disputed with *Melanchthon on the issues of the *Augsburg Interim and *adiaphora. Forced to leave Wittenberg, he went to Magdeburg, Jena and Regensburg, but, because of the rigidity of his ideas, failed to establish himself in one place. In addition to several theological works, F. was the leading spirit behind the **Magdeburg Centuries*, and, in 1557, published the *Missa Illyrica*, an 11th-century liturgical manuscript, which F. identified as a much earlier document and claimed to be free from the ritual corruptions of the Middle Ages.

L. Haikola, *Gesetz und Evangelium bei Matthias Flacius Illyricus* (1952).

FLAMINIO, MARCANTONIO (1498-1550) Italian poet. A precocious child, he was welcomed by Pope *Leo X to his court in 1514, and the following year he

A woodcut illustration to one of Fischart's anti-Roman Catholic tracts, published in Strassburg

A view of Florence; a late 15th-century woodcut

published his first volume of poems in Latin. He became a friend of famous men of letters throughout Italy, but later attached himself to some of the leading Catholic reformers, associating with Juan de *Valdés in Naples and serving briefly as secretary to Cardinal *Pole. Beginning as an elegant poet on amorous themes, he turned in his last years to religious verse producing a Latin paraphrase of 30 psalms (1546), and hymns of lofty spirituality.

FLANDERS A county in the southern *Netherlands, situated roughly between the river Scheldt and the North Sea. F. played a significant political and economic role in the affairs of western Europe throughout the Middle Ages. However, its most prosperous period began early in the 14th century, when the principal towns of the region, *Bruges, *Ghent, and Ypres, won their freedom from the ruling counts. Under the dukes of *Burgundy in the 15th century, the tendency towards complete urban independence came to a halt. Nevertheless, the Flemish cities enjoyed their golden age as centres of the commerce in cloth, as well as in their cultural activities, which set trends in *painting and *architecture. The gradual economic decline of F. in the latter half of the 15th century, paralleled the rise of neighbouring *Antwerp. It continued in the 16th century, a consequence of the political tensions of the *Reformation and the unsuccessful revolt of the southern Netherlands against Spain. The adjective "Flemish" is frequently applied to an area much larger than F. itself, to include the adjacent counties of Brabant and Hainault, an area that corresponds to present-day Belgium.

J. Lestocquoy, *Histoire de Flandre et de l'Artois* (1949).

FLORENCE The cultural centre of the early Renaissance and an important Italian political entity. In spite of a turbulent history in the late Middle Ages, F. continually expanded, ahead of her Tuscan neighbours the republics of *Siena, Pisa and Lucca. The disaster of the Black Death of 1348 ushered in new internal conflicts in F., in which the greater *guilds, known as the *popolo grasso*, attempted to dominate the government of the republic over the lesser guilds. The outcome was the revolt of the *ciompi*, the lower strata of labourers, who, in 1378, captured the palace of the *Signoria* and proclaimed their leader Michele di Landa as *gonfaloniere*, or head of the civil government. The inevitable suppression of this social revolution was facilitated by defections from the *ciompi*'s ranks, and prepared the ground for a political arrangement which reflected the distribution of economic power. The rich merchant and banking families became the real supports of growing oligarchical structure, and, in 1387, Maso degli *Albizzi, representing the powerful wool guild (*arte della lana*), became the real force in the government. During the 30 years in which he dominated the city, F. engaged in repeated military conflicts with Gian Galeazzo *Visconti of Milan (1390-1402), whose death made possible the conquest of Pisa (1406). The purchase of Leghorn from Genoa (1421), gave F. free passage to the sea and an access to the eastern Mediterranean trade. F. had, by this time, added the silk trade to her thriving economy; banking operations were expanding, and the cultural life was enlivened with names such as *Bruni, *Donatello, *Masaccio and *Brunelleschi.

From here on the history of F. is associated with the name of the *Medici, the descendants of Giovanni Bicci de' Medici, a rich banker who, in 1421, was proclaimed *gonfaloniere*, following a power struggle with the son of Maso, Rinaldo degli Albizzi. Cosimo de' Medici, who was banished from the republic in 1432, returned with popular support two years later and practically ruled F. until his death in 1464. His son, Piero "the Gouty" (1416-69) and Piero's son, Lorenzo the Magnificent (1449-92), continued the Medici dominance, although the latter was several times on the brink of losing his hold over the city and, in 1478, saw his brother Giuliano killed by the *Pazzi conspirators. The early Medici ruled F. cleverly; usually avoiding formal office but influencing the government by means of their financial power. They also avoided unnecessary wars, shifting their alliances to meet the situation, with the aim of maintaining an Italian balance of power. Lorenzo, the

The Town Hall of Antwerp by Floris

most famous Florentine patron of arts, presided over the city's cultural apogee, the age of *Botticelli, *Leonardo, *Ficino and *Politian.

*Charles VIII's invasion of Italy (1494) had a decisive effect on F. The Medici having been forced to leave, a government dominated by the Dominican friar *Savonarola ruled the city in a brief experiment in theocracy, which ended in 1498 with the friar's burning at the stake. The Medici were allowed to return to F. in 1512, and during the time that members of the family, *Leo X and *Clement VII, were popes, their ascendency in F. was maintained by the influence of Rome. But in 1527, the year of the sacking of Rome by the imperial forces, the Florentines again chased out the Medici. This time, however, it was *Charles V himself who forced their restoration (1531) as part of his agreement with Clement VII. From this time on F. and the Medici served Spain's interests in the settlement which she gradually fostered in Italy. This became evident during the long rule of *Cosimo I de' Medici (1536-74), who made F. the capital of his grand duchy of Tuscany, and it continued under his successors. F. still enjoyed her status as an Italian cultural centre, but it was more apparent than real. The end of the 16th century signalled the decline of F.'s economic importance and of her cultural preeminence.

F. Schevill, *History of Florence* (1961);
A. Panella, *Storia di Firenze* (1949);
E. W. Cochrane, *Florence in the Forgotten Centuries* (1973);
J. Lucas-Dubreton, *Daily Life in Florence in the Time of the Medici* (1960);
R. A. Goldthwaite, *Private Wealth in Renaissance Florence* (1968).

FLORIS, FRANS (1516-70) Flemish painter. Born in *Antwerp, he became a master at the painters' guild in 1540 and, between 1541 and 1547, made a journey to Italy, where he absorbed the influences of *Michelangelo and *Raphael. Returning to Antwerp, F. became the foremost exponent of the *Italianate style, producing many paintings on religious and mythological subjects. Much of his work, however, was designed to cater to the changing taste of the Flemish merchant class, and belongs to the contemporary trend of elegant *Mannerism. His older brother, Cornelis (1514-75), was an engraver, sculptor and architect, known for his Antwerp Town Hall (1561-65), the first significant Flemish building in a definite Renaissance style. The two brothers cooperated on the design of Frans' residential palace, built by Cornelis and decorated with external frescoes by the younger brother.

D. Zanta, *Frans Floris* (1929).

FLOTA (The Fleet System) In order to protect their treasure-carrying vessels on their return voyage from America, the Spanish adopted a system of convoys. The system was established in its final form about 1564, and remained in force for the next two centuries. Accordingly, two fleets were dispatched each year: one to Mexico, the other to ports in the Caribbean and the Isthmus of Panama. After unloading their cargo and loading the precious metals of the American mines, the two fleets joined together in Havana, Cuba, for the return voyage to the port of Cádiz in Spain. In spite of these precautions, the Spanish treasure fleet was occasionally harrassed by foreign privateers. On one occasion in 1628 the entire cargo was captured by the Dutch.

C. H. Haring, *Trade and Navigation Between Spain and the Indies in the Time of the Hapsburgs* (1918).

FOGLIETTA, UBERTO (1518-81) Italian historian. The son of a Genoese family, he went in about 1538 to Rome, and was employed at the papal court. In 1559 he published *Delle cose della repubblica di Genova*, a denunciation of the old Genoese oligarchy, which caused his official condemnation at home. His account of the *Fieschi conspiracy, a fragment of an incomplete general history of his times, was published in Naples in 1571. F. served several patrons, including Cardinal Ippolito d'*Este; the beauties of his villa at Tivoli were described in his *Tyburtium* (1569). In 1576 it was possible for him to return to Genoa, whose official historiographer he became, and wrote a history up to the year 1527.

FOIX, GASTON DE (1489-1512) Duke of Nemours; French hero of the *Italian Wars. At the age of 22 this nephew of *Louis XII was given command over the French army in Italy against the forces of the *Holy League headed by *Julius II. Following two victories over the Spanish in Bologna and over the Venetians at Brescia, F. confronted the Spanish army again at the Battle of Ravenna. Although the victory went to the French, he himself died on the battlefield.

FOLENGO, TEOFILO (1491-1544) Italian poet. Born in Mantua, he joined the Benedictines in 1508. In 1524 he left the order by papal permission, but rejoined it in 1530. F. wrote several poems in Latin and Italian, but is chiefly remembered for his *Baldus*, first published in 1518 as part of the collection *Maccheronee*. A clever parody in hexameter, it mixes classical Latin with Italian dialects to create a macaronic burlesque of courtly poetry.

E. Bonara, *Le Maccheronee di Teofilo Folengo* (1956).

FOLZ, HANS German *Meistersinger, active in Worms and *Nuremberg from about 1480 to 1515. He was the founder of the best-known 16th-century centre of Meistersang, and possessed a crude, aggressive style enlivened by coarse humour. By trade a surgeon and barber, F. was a prolific writer, producing also many *Schwänke*, or popular anecdotes, and carnival farces.

R. Henss, *Studien zu Hans Folz* (1934).

FONSECA, PEDRO DA (1528-99) Portuguese philosopher. Having joined the *Jesuit order in 1548, he became famous as a teacher of philosophy at the University of Coimbra (1555-61). He was later set to work on the Jesuit code of education, and performed other functions for his order. His most important work was a four-volume commentary on Aristotle's *Metaphysics* (1577-89). The work essentially follows the scholastic tradition, but F. employed the new tools of Renaissance classical philosophy in his analysis of the text.

FONTAINEBLEAU, SCHOOL OF *Francis I, who failed to persuade any of the great Italian masters with the exception of *Leonardo to come over to France, invited, in 1530, the Florentine painter-designer *Rosso (1495-1540) and, in 1532, the Bolognese painter-sculptor-architect *Primaticcio (1505-70). They took charge of the decoration of Fointainebleau and other royal palaces, and with Niccolo dell'*Abbate, who joined at a later date, were the propagators of an imitative *mannerist style which was elegantly fashionable yet somewhat artificial. They had a great influence on French painting and sculpture in the 16th century.

L. Dimier, *Fontainebleau* (rev. ed., 1967).

FONTANA, DOMENICO (1543-1607) Italian architect and engineer. Born near Lake Lugano, he moved to *Rome where, in 1574, he began to work for Cardinal Montalto. Upon the election of his patron to the papacy as *Sixtus V (1585), F. became his chief architect, and was put in charge of replanning the city of Rome. In 1586 he accomplished his most famous feat, that of moving the old Egyptian obelisk and replacing it in front of *St. Peter's. With Giącomo della *Porta he completed the huge dome of St. Peter's (1586-90) but, in 1592, was accused of mismanaging funds and dismissed by *Clement VIII. His buildings in the Vatican and his Lateran Palace were designed in a style anticipating the *Baroque. After his dismissal, F. went to work on the Royal Palace in Naples, where he died.

The Francis I gallery at Fontainebleau decorated by Rosso Fiorentino

FONTANA, LAVINIA (1552-1614) Italian painter. The daughter of Prospero Fontana, she was instructed by her father, and became famous for her painting of historical scenes and, especially, portraits. One of her best works is a portrait of her patron Pope *Gregory XIII.

Gaston de Foix

Interior of the Vatican Library by Domenico Fontana

Very successful, she was considered one of the ablest painters of her time.

FONTANA, PROSPERO (1512-97) Italian painter. Born in Bologna, he worked in several Italian cities on decorative projects, assisting *Vasari and *Zuccaro, among others. He visited France, working for a short time in *Fontainebleau (1560), then settled in his native city, where he was the first master of Ludovico *Carracci. His later style showed the influence of *Michelangelo and belong to the *Mannerist school. F. also excelled as a painter of portraits.

FOPPA, VICENZO (c. 1427-1516) Italian painter. Born near Brescia, he was trained in Padua and, between 1456 and 1490, resided mainly in Pavia, though occasionally he worked in *Milan, *Genoa and Savona. His early work showed the influence of Jacopo *Bellini, but later he came closer to his contemporary *Mantegna, and absorbed some of the stylistic elements of mainstream Italian painting. Having executed many works for the dukes of Milan, F. became known as the founder of the Milanese school, a style of painting distinguished by its feeling for colour and its restraint, which characterized the north Italian art until it was modified by the example of *Leonardo.

FORD, JOHN (1586-1638) English playwright. His first work, *Fames Memorial* (1606), an elegy on the earl of Devonshire, displayed his romantic quality and a gift for strong portrayal of sorrow and despair. He is known mainly for the series of dramas he wrote in the 1620's and 1630's, starting with *The Witch of Edmonton* (1621), written together with *Dekker. One of his best-known plays, *'Tis Pity She's a Whore* (1633), dealt with an incestuous relationship between a brother and sister.

C. Leech, *John Ford and the Drama of his Time* (1957); M. L. Stavig, *John Ford and the Traditional Moral Order* (1968).

FORMULA OF CONCORD (1577) A doctrinal statement, which became the definitive confession of the great majority of the German Lutheran state-churches. It was the product of efforts by moderate theologians to unify the Lutheran camp. This was followed in 1580 with the *Konkordienbuch* (Book of Concord), which included the Formula, together with early Lutheran confessions. Because of opposition to it outside Germany, the Formula never attained the status of general adherence enjoyed by the Confession of *Augsburg.

FORTEGUERRI A family from Pistoia in Tuscany, which produced several well-known men of letters and ecclesiastical figures. Niccolò F. (1419-73) was made bishop and cardinal by *Pius II, and distinguished himself as a Church diplomat. Scipione F. (1466-1515), a humanist, was an indefatigable promotor of the study of Greek, and assisted *Manutius in Venice. Giovanni F. (1508-82) served Grand-duke *Cosimo I as governor of Pistoia, and wrote a collection of eleven amusing tales.

FORTESCUE, SIR JOHN (1394-c. 1476) English constitutional writer. The son of a noble family of Devonshire, he became, in 1442, chief justice of the King's Bench. Upon the accession of *Edward IV (1461), he took refuge in Scotland and later in France, but subsequently (1473) made his peace with the king. Of his several constitutional treatises, the most famous is *De laudibus legum Angliae* (In Praise of the Laws of England), written for Prince Edward, son of *Henry VI. It contrasts the limited monarchy in England with the absolute monarchy in France, and champions the idea that the English king has no more power than that which the law has delegated to him.

V. Litzen, *A War of Roses and Lilies: The Theme of Succession in Sir John Fortescue's Works* (1971).

FOSCARI, FRANCESCO (1373-1457) Doge of *Venice from 1423. F. came to head the Venetian government after a long career in the service of the republic. His rule was marked by territorial expansion towards Lombardy, though there Venice found herself opposed by Milan. The acquisitions made in his time which included Bergamo and Brescia were confirmed in the Peace of *Lodi (1454). Shortly before his death F. abdicated because of the misconduct of his son.

FOUQUET, JEAN (c. 1420-c. 1480) French painter and *illuminator of manuscripts. Visiting Italy in the 1440s, he adopted many of the techniques of contemporary Florentine painters, which he introduced into his portraits as well as his miniatures, for which he became famous. Favoured by the French court, he painted *Charles VII, his mistress Agnes *Sorel and other personages. In 1474 *Louis XI appointed him royal painter. F.'s most famous work is the *Book of Hours* executed for the royal treasurer Etienne Chevalier, and which included many full-page miniatures. His work lends itself to a comparison with that of Jan van *Eyck, especially in its care for detail and advanced technique. His links with contemporary Italian painting give his art a particular significance.

P. Wescher, *Jean Fouquet and his Times* (1949).

FOURQUEVAUX, RAIMOND DE (1509-74) French soldier, diplomat and author. Born to a noble family of Toulouse, he fought in Italy under *Francis I. In 1557 *Henry II made him governor of Narbonne and, in 1563, he represented his country in Spain. Later he took part in the *Religious Wars. In 1553 he published *Instruction sur le fait de la guerre*, an important source for the study of 16th-century military techniques.

Jean Fouquet, Self-Portrait

FOXE, JOHN (1516-87) English author of a work on Protestant martyrology. A graduate of Oxford, he fled after the accession of *Mary Tudor to the Continent, where he met with the most important reformers and became an ardent follower of *Calvin. When *Elizabeth became queen, he returned to England and was made canon of Salisbury and bishop of London (1560). The English edition of his work, *Acts and Monuments*, better known as Foxe's Book of Martyrs, came out in 1563. It lauded the heroism of the Protestant victims of the reign of Mary, and won immense popularity. As a historical guide it is blemished by exaggerations, but it was successful in heightening Protestant consciousness.
J. F. Mozley, *John Foxe and his Book* (1940).
FOXE, RICHARD (c. 1448-1528) English ecclesiastic, promoter of humanist learning and an important state official under *Henry VII and the early reign of *Henry VIII. He was made in succession bishop of Exeter (1487), Durham (1494) and Winchester (1501), but devoted most of his attention to his duties as minister and diplomat. Having been eclipsed by *Wolsey, F. became more interested in spiritual matters. In 1515 he founded Corpus Christi College at Oxford.
P. S. and H. M. Allen, eds., *Letters of Richard Fox, 1486-1527* (1929).
FRACASTORO, GIROLAMO (1478-1553) Italian physician and poet. Born in Verona, he studied *medicine in Padua and eventually returned to his native city, where he became very successful. In 1530 he published his best-known work, a poem called *Syphilis sive de morbo gallico*, from which originated the medical name of the disease. Dedicated to *Bembo, the poem tells the story of a shepherd who is afflicted by the disease, and suggests certain cures. In his *De contagione et contagiosis morbis* (1546) F. ventured the idea that plagues were spread by germs. He also wrote on astronomy, philosophy and aesthetics, and left an interesting collection of letters to *Ramusio, which were published in 1564.
E. Di Leo, *Scienza e umanesimo in Girolamo Fracastoro* (1937).
FRANCE The political history of Renaissance France is perhaps best understood as a tale of misdirected ambitions. Recovering from the conflict with England, which had been dragging on for over a hundred years, F. actually emerged with its monarchy more powerful than ever and its government increasingly centralized. But with the invasion of Italy in 1494 F. adopted a foreign policy guided by outmoded principles and flimsy goals, and which became increasingly untenable in view of the rising power of the *Habsburgs. By the time this policy was finally abandoned (1559) the nation had lost its internal cohesion and become embroiled in a ferocious conflict over religious issues. But, this fertile land with its population of some 16 million, was obviously capable of renewed vigour. *Henry IV, who slowly secured his hold over a nation weary of the long fratricidal struggle, could later in his reign lay the foundations for French predominance in the politics of 17th-century Europe.

The French defeat by *Henry V of England at *Agincourt (1415) was a catastrophe which the French had brought upon themselves with their quarrels between *Armagnacs and Burgundians. The last-named shortly concluded an alliance with the English (1419), and the Treaty of Troyes (1420) repudiated the Dauphin, the future *Charles VII (1422-61), as heir to the French throne in favour of the king of England and his as yet unborn son *Henry VI. Driven south of the Loire to Bourges, Charles VII suffered a series of defeats at the hands of the Anglo-Burgundian forces, until the appearance of the unlikely saviour, the young prophetess of national redemption, *Joan of Arc. Although she was captured in 1430, her brief leadership had made possible Charles VII's coronation at Rheims and signalled a turn in the French fortunes. The peace of Arras (1435) marked the reconciliation with *Burgundy, followed by the recovery of Paris (1436). A long pause in the fighting – until 1449 – allowed the French to reorganize the army; when the war was resumed they won one victory after another. The last battle of the *Hundred Years' War took place in 1453.

Under *Louis XI (1461-83), F. continued to consolidate. More a political manipulator than a warrior, this monarch displayed the true Renaissance qualities of shrewdness and opportunism in his long struggle against *Charles the Bold of Burgundy. The country moved steadily towards royal absolutism. Escheats and conquest increased the lands under direct royal administration, and the crown officials stamped out banditry and improved the revenue system. At the same time F. was developing economically. Printing was introduced in 1470, and French culture, though not yet fully aware of Italian arts and letters, was enlivened by the paintings of *Fouquet, the poetry of François *Villon and the historical works of Philippe de *Commines. Louis XI's successful policies were continued by his daughter *Anne of France, whose nine-year regency was concluded with the marriage of her young brother *Charles VIII (1483-98) and *Anne of Brittany, thereby effecting a tie between the crown and the most important independent French duchy.

The dashing march of Charles VIII on *Naples (1494-95) is said to have revolutionized the European arts of war and *diplomacy. But to F. the *Italian Wars brought only ephemeral glory. Great French soldiers, such as Gaston de *Foix, *Bayard and the Constable of *Bourbon, distinguished themselves on the battlefields, and great French victories were scored in Agnadello (1509), Ravenna (1512) and *Marignano (1515). Yet Naples, twice conquered, had to be evacuated, and so was *Milan; by the end of the reign of *Louis XII (1498-1515), the French gains had come to nothing. Francis I (1515-47), who carried on the wars in spite of past experience, paid for his folly with the defeat at *Pavia (1525) and his imprisonment in Madrid. In his rage against his captor Emperor *Charles V, he made the first alliance between a European Christian power and the *Ottoman Turks. His son, *Henry II (1547-59), twice renewed the hostilities before bringing the long war to its conclusion in the Peace of *Cateau-Cambrésis (1559). It was during this last phase of the *Habsburg-*Valois conflict that the leaders of the next generation matured, among them *Coligny, *Condé, *Montmorency and the *Guises.

Preoccupied with its military exploits, F. did not significantly participate in early 16th-century movement of *exploration. *Verrazano's voyage (1523) was followed by *Cartier's visits to Canada (1534-41), but the attempts of *Villegaignon and *Ribaut to establish colonies in Brazil and Florida both failed. Meanwhile,

French arts and letters flourished. Although it still relied on Italians like *Rosso and *Primaticcio to come and train her painters and architects, by mid-16th century F. could boast a brilliant group of poets and essayists, led first by *Rabelais and *Marot and later by *Montaigne and *Ronsard.

It was in the gay atmosphere of the reign of Francis I that the problems that were to tear F. apart during the second half of the century began to surface. The first sympathizers with the *Reformation, humanists like *Lefèvre d'Étaples, were easily suppressed, but the next generation of French reformers was more persistent and, after 1541, found a firm foreign base in *Calvin's *Geneva. Persecution only made the number of French Protestants increase, and the Reformation won the hearts and minds of many nobles, including some of the highest rank. Under Henry II the number of heretics sentenced to be burned at the stake became so great, that the special court charged with this task was nicknamed the *chambre ardente*. The outbreak of the *Religious Wars (1562-98), however, was due to a crisis of political legitimacy, during the short reign of the young *Francis II (1559-60) and the minority of his brother and successor *Charles IX (1560-74). Though initially she tried to manoeuvre between the Roman Catholic party and the leaders of the *Huguenots, the queen mother and regent *Catherine de Medicis finally lent her hand to the murder of Coligny and the Massacre of *St. Bartholomew (1572). This atrocity damaged irreparably the position of the **politiques*, the middle party, and ensured the prolongation of the conflict.

F. hit the nadir of anarchy under *Henry III (1574-89). Fearing the *League, which openly invited Spanish aid, the King first acquiesced to the extreme demands of the Roman Catholics but later changed his mind, believing it was in his interest to keep the Huguenots alive. His relations with the League grew still worse and, in 1588, a Parisian popular uprising revealed that he had lost his authority. The subsequent murder of the Guise brothers by order of the King had the result of forcing him to seek shelter in the Huguenot camp of Henry of Navarre who was, since 1584, the first in the line of succession. In 1589 the murder of the King by a monk put a Protestant on the throne of F.

Before *Henry IV could secure the government he had to fight both the French Roman Catholic diehards and Spanish troops under Alessandro *Farnese. But when he converted to the religion of the majority (1593) and was given the papal blessing (1595), the nation swung to his side. The Peace of *Vervins (1598) with *Philip II of Spain, and the Edict of *Nantes (1598), which assured protective rights to the Huguenots, concluded the wars. With the aid of dedicated ministers, especially the Duke of *Sully, Henry IV now began to rehabilitate the French economy and government. Extensive canal digging promoted agricultural development, and the textile industry was encouraged. At the same time, F. renewed its commercial ties with the Ottoman Empire and, with *Champlain, began to develop the fur trade of Canada. This successful *mercantilist policy was accompanied by an effort to restore the authority of the crown. The size of the standing army (formerly some 15,000) was tripled, and extensive building of royal palaces was begun, giving impetus to French decorative arts and architecture. By 1609, when the *Jülich-Cleves contest of succession threatened to disturb the peace of the Empire and Europe, F. was ready to step in.

J. S. C. Bridge, *A History of France from the Death of Louis XI*, 5 vols. (1921-36);
E. Lavisse, *Histoire de France, depuis les origines jusqu'à la revolution*, 9 vols. (1900-11);
R. Mandrous, *Introduction à la France moderne, 1500-1640* (1961).

FRANCESCO DI GIORGIO (1439-1502) Italian painter, sculptor and architect. Born in *Siena, he began his artistic career as a painter. The panels and two altarpieces he produced in Siena are characterized by an air of tenderness. In 1477 he became a military architect to Duke *Federico da Montefeltro at Urbino, for whom he executed bronze sculptures as well as fortresses. F. was extremely versatile and, like *Leonardo, whom he met in 1490, was interested in technology and engineering; he is said to have exploded the first landmine. Although several structures are attributed to him, the only one which is certainly his is S. Maria del Calcinaio at Cortona (1484). His book on civil and military architecture, written towards the end of his life, has a discussion on city planning; but it was published only in the 17th century.

A. S. Weller, *Francesco di Giorgio* (1943).

FRANCIA, FRANCESCO (c. 1450-1518) Italian painter. A native of Bologna, he is thought to have taken up painting in maturity, having previously been a goldsmith. He worked for many years in partnership with Lorenzo *Costa, executing works commissioned by Giovanni *Bentivoglio and by Bolognese churches. His soft style and portrayal of human kindness made his work very popular in his day.

FRANCIABIGIO (1482-1525) The name given to the Italian painter Francesco di Cristofano Bigi. Born at Florence, he studied under *Piero di Cosimo. F. was influenced by *Raphael and by his friend *Andrea del Sarto, whose series of frescoes at the cloister of the Scalzo, Florence he completed. Essentially a painter of the second rank who assimilated the style of the great masters, F. was considered during his lifetime one of the major Florentine artists and received many commissions. As well as frescoes, he did a considerable number of portraits.

S. R. McKillop, *Franciabigio* (1974).

FRANCIS I (1494-1547) King of France from 1515. The son of Charles of Orléans, count of Angoulême, and *Louise of Savoy, F.'s claim to the throne was recognized in his infancy when his cousin *Louis XII became king. His position as heir presumptive was further strengthened in 1514, when he married Claude of France, daughter of Louis and *Anne of Brittany, a union that ensured the eventual incorporation of the duchy of Brittany into the domain of the crown. A skilled athlete and warrior, F. received an irregular education, including some classical studies and much courtly etiquette and *chivalry. Women figured prominently in his life, firstly his mother Louise, whom he revered and who had brought him up after his father's premature death. Secondly, his learned sister *Marguerite d'Angoulême, with whom he spent his childhood. Finally, a succession of mistresses, who confirmed his image as a great lover.

F.'s long reign was marked by his interminable

conflict with *Charles V. Assuming the crown at the age of 20 amid popular acclaim, he immediately set out to accomplish his predecessors' unfulfilled ambitions in Italy. The resounding victory of *Marignano (1515) put him in possession of *Milan and led to the advantageous Concordat of *Bologna (1516) with *Leo X. But in 1519 he lost his bold attempt to gain election as *Holy Roman emperor to Charles V. His sumptuous and friendly meeting with *Henry VIII, known as the *Field of Cloth of Gold (1520), did not result in an English alliance. The war with the Emperor commenced in 1521, adversely for France. In 1523 F.'s erstwhile general, Charles of *Bourbon, defected after a quarrel with the King, and joined the Emperor. The following year Bourbon drove the French out of Italy and invaded Provence and, in 1525, brought upon F. his greatest humiliation, when he defeated and captured him in the Battle of *Pavia. F. was imprisoned for ten months in Spain, steadfastly refusing to accept terms injurious to France. But in the end he signed the Treaty of Madrid (1526), and delivered his two eldest sons as hostages to ensure its fulfilment.

He was no sooner released than he declared the treaty void. He now laid claim to Burgundy and supported the Emperor's enemies in Italy. The war dragged on until concluded with the Peace of *Cambrai (1529), signed by F.'s mother and Charles' aunt, Margaret of Austria. F. left Italy and married the Emperor's sister Eleanor (1530), but he was given back his sons and retained Burgundy. Hostilities were resumed in 1536. Encircled by the *Habsburgs, who now dominated Spain, the Netherlands, Germany and Italy, F. did not hesitate to call upon the *Ottoman Turks for aid and

Francis I *by Jean Clouet*

The staircase at the Château de Blois, built in the reign of Francis I

to support the Protestant *Schmalkaldic League. The pressure of the Turks in *Hungary forced Charles to make an accommodation (1538), but conflict broke out again in 1542, to be settled by another treaty in 1544. While the borders of France underwent further adjustments, F. was barred from realizing any of his ambitions in Italy.

Domestically, F. was more successful in spite of his habitual carelessness with regard to expenditure and administration. A buoyant French economy made possible his costly foreign policies, and for his part the King organized the collection of imposts, which in 1523 and again in 1542 were put under a more centralized system. The machinery of government, especially the Council (*conseil du roi*), was similarly reshaped in an attempt to make the secretaries responsible directly to the King, and the French language became mandatory in all legal matters. During the latter part of his reign the *Reformation began to have its effects in France. Caught between his Roman Catholic ministers and the numerous Protestant sympathizers in his entourage, the King hesitated a while. But after the Affair of the *Placards (1534), he began to move against the reformers. In his last years he issued a number of repressive edicts which led to the execution of several prominent individuals and, in 1545, authorized a wave of persecution and massacres against the old sect of the *Waldensians in southern France.

However, F. is remembered chiefly as a great patron of arts and letters and a consistent supporter of *Renaissance culture. He built numerous chateaux, notably Chambord, Blois and *Fontainebleau, which signalled a new age in French *architecture. At Fontainebleau he established the school of decorative art headed by the Italians *Rosso and *Primaticcio; among other Italian artists whom he invited to France were *Leonardo and Benvenuto *Cellini. The printer Robert *Estienne, the poet *Marot, and the author *Rabelais were all the recipients of his royal favours. In 1530, at the request of Guillaume *Budé, F. founded the *Collège de France as an institution of humanist learning, to counterbalance the conservative University of Paris.

Continually travelling about his kingdom, being in direct contact with people everywhere, F. was forgiven his wasteful foreign adventures and remembered affectionately as *le grand roi*. Succeeding generations were impressed by the fact that, at any rate, he ruled over a unified nation, presenting a much brighter image than the France torn by civil strife of the latter half of the 16th century.

F. Hackett, *Francis I* (1934);
C. Terasse, *François Ier*, 3 vols. (1949-70);
M. Andrieux, *François Ier* (1967);
J. Giono, *Le désastre de Pavie, 24 Février 1525* (1963).

FRANCIS II (1544-60) King of France from 1559. The eldest son of *Henry II and *Catherine de Médicis, he was married in 1558 to *Mary, Queen of Scots, who was two years his senior. Acceeding to the throne at the age of 15, after the accidental death of his father, F., a sickly boy, was greatly influenced by the *Guises, his wife's uncles. This led the prince of *Condé to plan the Conspiracy of Amboise (1560), in which the *Huguenots were meant to take possession of the person of the King. The failure of the conspiracy was followed by F.'s death a few months later.

L. Romier, *La conjuration d'Amboise* (1923).

FRANCK, SEBASTIAN (1499-1543) German humanist author and Protestant reformer. Educated at the universities of Ingolstadt and Heidelberg, he first dedicated himself to the Church, but about 1525 joined the sizeable group of Protestant exiles who had found shelter in *Strassburg. Hence he published his best known work, *Chronica, Zeytbuch und Geschychtbibel* (3 vols., 1531), a historical compilation, which is characterized by broadmindedness, independence of thought and religious tolerance. F. also wrote theological works, and translated Erasmus' *Praise of Folly* into German. He spent his last years in *Basle. Because of his liberality in matters of religion he incurred in his last years the enmity of Protestants and Roman Catholics alike.

W. E. Penckert, *Sebastian Franck* (1943);
S. Wollgast, ed., *Zur Friedensidee in der Reformationzeit* (1968).

FRANCKE, MASTER German painter, active in Hamburg in the first quarter of the 15th century. There are no definite biographical data about him, and only a few works which are attributed to him. However, it is known that in 1424 he began to work on the *Thomas à Becket* altarpiece, which was commissioned by merchants who traded with England. The extant fragments of the work reveal a unique style, influenced by contemporary Flemish art, of which there is no parallel in other German *Hanseatic towns.

FRANCO, NICCOLO (1515-70) Italian poet. Born into a poor family, he became secretary to Pietro *Aretino in Venice, but later quarrelled with him and attacked him in verse. His scurrilous *Priapea*, which enjoyed wide circulation, led to his excommunication. He was arrested in Rome (1558-60), but continued to write, denouncing the late Pope Paul IV. Convicted by the *Inquisition, he was hanged in Rome.

FRANCO, VERONICA (1546-91) Italian poetess. Born in Venice, she left her husband, who was a physician, becoming the best-known Venetian courtesan of her time. She had friends among the artists and writers, and had her portrait painted by *Tintoretto. Her *Terze rime* (1575) were a collection of love poems not entirely lacking in originality.

FRANKFURT AM MAIN A well-established centre of commerce near the confluence of the Rhine and the Main, this German city – to be distinguished from Frankfurt an der Oder in *Brandenburg – was practically independent from the early 14th century and, in 1372, became a free imperial city. For the next two hundred years F. played a certain political role in the affairs of Germany. It was there that the imperial elections were held after the Golden Bull of 1356 and, in the first quarter of the 16th century, the city housed the **Reichskammergericht*, or imperial court chamber. However, the real importance of F. was in its two annual fairs, held in April and September, which attracted merchants from all over Europe. They made F. the capital of the publishing industry. In addition, it had an important banking establishment and a small Jewish community which dealt in money. In 1533 F. joined the

Ecce Homo *by Master Francke*

Reformation, but when *Charles V undertook his campaign against the *Schmalkaldic League, the city surrendered (1546) and, for the next few years, was occupied by imperial troops and had to pay an indemnity. A *modus vivendi* between the Protestant majority and the Roman Catholic minority made F., after 1554, a safe haven for many refugees from England and the Netherlands. Between 1612 and 1616 the city knew great political turmoil, when the middle classes, led by Vicenz Fettmilch, attempted to curtail the power of the small patriciate. Imperial intervention came to the aid of the oligarchy, not only in suppressing the movement, but also in excluding popular participation in government.

F. Bothe, *Geschichte der Stadt Frankfurt am Main* (1966).

FRANKFURT RECESS A document (endorsed 18 March 1558) designed to bridge the gap between the two main Lutheran factions in Germany, the orthodoxes led by *Flacius, and the followers of *Melanchthon. The agreement came about only after the leading Protestant princes took personal interest in the settlement of the disputes, in an effort to consolidate a common front against Roman Catholic critics. Though it was approved by Melanchthon, it was, however, rejected by *Amsdorf and Flacius, and did not achieve its purpose.

FREDERICK I (1471-1533) King of *Denmark from 1523. The younger son of *Christian I, he led in 1522 a revolt of discontented nobles against his nephew *Christian II, forcing him out of the country. His rule was characterized by concessions to the nobility and the estates, and modesty in the conduct of the affairs of the state. After his daughter married *Albert of Prussia (1526), he showed sympathy towards the Reformation. In 1531 F. captured and imprisoned Christian II when the latter attempted to raise a rebellion in Norway, and skilfully parried the threats of Emperor *Charles V, who supported his nephew.

FREDERICK II (1534-88) King of *Denmark from 1559. The son of *Christian III, he began in 1563 the so called Seven Year's War of the North, in which his adversary was his cousin *Eric XIV of Sweden. The war, which was largely a result of F.'s own warlike attitude, became quite unpopular in Denmark, and aroused the enmity of all who suffered from the ruin of the Baltic trade. The peace of 1570 did not result in significant changes in favour of either side. Cured of his aggressive tendency, F. spent the rest of his reign at peace, ensuring Danish dominance of the North Sea and encouraging the expansion of agriculture.

FREDERICK II (1482-1556) Elector Palatine of the Rhine. The fourth son of the Elector Philip, he began his career as a soldier in the service of the *Habsburgs, and became known for his adventurous exploits. In 1521 *Charles V made him one of the chief commanders of the imperial army. The death of his older brother Ludwig in 1544, made him the Elector Palatine, and in this capacity, despite his long association with the Emperor, he allowed the Protestants considerable freedom in his territories. He joined the *Schmalkaldic League, but later surrendered to the Emperor and implemented the *Augsburg Interim (1548). F. then tried to mediate between Charles V and the Protestant princes, thus contributing to the Peace of Passau (1552), granting religious freedom to all who adhered to the Confession of *Augsburg.

FREDERICK III THE PIOUS (1515-76) Elector Palatine of the Rhine. Brought up as a Roman Catholic, he was influenced by his wife, Maria of Brandenburg-Culmbach, whom he married in 1537, to favour the Reformation. He succeeded to the electorate in 1559, and soon began to introduce Calvinist measures in his territories, over the resistance of many Lutheran nobles, including his own son. F. was also involved in religious controversies elsewhere, and sent troops to aid the *Huguenots in France and the rebels in the Netherlands.

FREDERICK III (1415-93) *Holy Roman emperor from 1452. Born in Innsbruck to Ernest, duke of Austria, he inherited in 1424 the family possessions of Styria, Carinthia, Carniola and Gorizia. In the next 15 years he established himself as the most important member of the house of *Habsburg; during this time he went on a pilgrimage to the Holy Land. After the death of his cousin Emperor *Albert II (1438-39), F. became the guardian of his son *Ladislas Posthumus, which gave him the opportunity to make his bid for the imperial throne. In 1440 he was elected king of Germany, and began a long and largely unsuccessful campaign against the *Bohemian nobility, in an attempt to assert the claims which he made on behalf of his ward. His neutrality with regard to the breach between *Eugenius V and the Council of *Basle, and his subsequent support of the Pope, earned him the goodwill of the papacy and, in 1452, he was crowned emperor in Rome by *Nicholas V, at the same time marrying Eleanor of Portugal.

F.'s imperial coronation, the last performed by a pope in Rome, proved to be his last personal triumph. In the same year he was compelled to relinquish his guardianship of Ladislas. He soon lost his influence over German politics, and in his own family was opposed by his brother Albert of Austria, and later by his cousin Sigmund. After the death of Ladislas (1457), F. claimed the thrones of Bohemia and Hungary, only to see the two countries prefer native rulers, *George of Podebrady and *Matthias Corvinus, respectively. Unable to organize the defence of Europe against the advancing *Ottoman Turks, in effective control of a mere fraction of the ancestral Habsburg possessions, the Emperor suffered his greatest humiliation in 1485, when Matthias Corvinus conquered Vienna.

The only political success that F. could claim in the latter part of his reign, the marriage of his son *Maximilian and Mary of Burgundy, daughter of *Charles the Bold, resulted largely from the Duke's desire to be given a royal dignity by the Emperor. F.'s last years were indeed marked by the rising star of this son who, in 1486, was elected king of Germany. It was he who undertook the reconquest of Austria, while his father ended his life in retirement in Linz, occupying himself with *astrology, *alchemy and precious stones.

FREDERICK III "THE WISE" (1463-1525) Elector of *Saxony from 1486 and *Luther's protector. A deeply religious man, he undertook, in 1493, a pilgrimage to the Holy Land and was known for his collection of relics. Interested in the new learning and religious reform, he founded, in 1502, the university of *Wittenberg and invited *Luther to teach there. When the latter was excommunicated (1520), F. protected him, and

Sir Martin Frobisher, *detail from a painting by Cornelius Ketal*

continued to give him shelter even after he had incurred the imperial ban (1521). Although in 1523 he ended the veneration of relics, he may have had second thoughts about the growing radicalism of the reformers. His secretary *Spalatin was the chief link between him and Luther.

FREGOSO A Genoese family which played a prominent part in the political and military life of the republic, it also produced a number of prelates and writers. Originally successful merchants, the F.s gave *Genoa doges, diplomats and admirals. Their ascendancy lasted through the 15th century, when they had the upper hand over the rival family of Adorno. In the 16th century they lost power to Andrea *Doria.

FREMINET, MARTIN (1567-1619) French painter and etcher. Born in Paris, he went in 1592 to Italy, where he was influenced by *Cavaliere d'Arpino. He returned to France in 1602, where he was patronized by *Henry IV who, in 1603, commissioned him to decorate the chapel of the Trinité at *Fontainebleau. This is one of the few works by F. that have survived.

FRESCO Italian for fresh; the favourite Renaissance technique of mural painting. In essence, the idea of the F. was to have the colours integrated into the surface of the wall, so as to achieve an almost permanent union, secure from peeling and damages caused by climatic changes. After the wall had been covered with a special coat on which a rough design of the entire composition was drawn, the artist applied a final layer of plaster and painted it while it was still damp. The great Italian masters excelled in executing F.s with no need for retouching. The art gradually disappeared after the 16th century.

E. Olof, *Fresco Painting* (1947);
The Metropolitan Museum of Art, *The Great Age of Fresco: Giotto to Pontormo* (1968).

FRISCHLIN, NICODEMUS (1547-90) German playwright. A young and brilliant professor at Tübingen, he made many enemies by his criticism of his colleagues and of the vagaries of German politics. Considered one of the last representatives of humanist culture, F. wrote Latin dramas on historical subjects and satires in the style of Aristophanes. His vitriolic writings brought upon him persecution and imprisonment. He died while trying to escape from the fortress of Hohenurach.

D. van Abbe, *Drama in Renaissance Germany and Switzerland* (1964).

FRITH, JOHN (c. 1503-33) Early English *Protestant. Educated at Eton and Cambridge, he became a canon at Oxford, where he soon came under suspicion of favouring reform. In 1528 he fled to the Continent, joined *Tyndale and assisted him in the translation of the *Bible. Returning to England in 1532, he was arrested, charged with the heresy of denying the doctrine of purgatory, and burnt at the stake.

FRITZ, JOSS (c. 1470-1525) German leader of peasants' revolts. A peasant who was born in serfdom, he organized a series of uprisings in the Rhine Valley (1502, 1513 and 1517), which adopted the sign of the *Bundschuh* for their banner. F. was a clever propagandist and was famous for his skill in avoiding capture.

FROBEN, JOHANN (1460-1527) German-Swiss printer. Born in Germany, F. studied the art of printing in *Basle under *Amerbach, with whom he worked in partnership from 1491 until the latter's death in 1513. A scholar himself, he carried on the tradition of accurate printing of biblical and patristic works. F. was an intimate friend of *Erasmus, who lived in his house and for whom he published, in 1516, the first *Greek New Testament. He also published several editions of *Luther's early tracts (1518-20), but when Erasmus and Luther disagreed over the issue of free will, he supported the first. With *Manutius, he was probably the most important European humanist publisher of his time.

FROBISHER, SIR MARTIN (1535-94) English navigator. Between 1576 and 1578 he went on three voyages to find a northwest passage from the Atlantic to the Pacific. Enjoying the support of the London merchants and Queen *Elizabeth I herself, he had to be satisfied with geographical discoveries only. He explored Labrador and crossed the Hudson Strait on his third voyage. In 1585 he accompanied *Drake on his raids on Santo Domingo and Cartagena and, in 1588, fought against the *Armada. He died on the French coast while conducting an expedition intended to aid the future *Henry IV of France.

W. McFee, *Sir Martin Frobisher* (1928).

FROMENT, NICOLAS French painter, active in Avignon from about 1450 to 1490. In spite of his geographic proximity to Italy, his style was closer to the Flemish, tending to crude realism. His most important work was the triptych *The Burning Bush* (1475-76), at the cathedral of Aix-en-Provence. Another well known work is a triptych with portraits of the donors on the outside, *The Ressurrection of Lazarus*, at the Uffizi in *Florence.

FROSCHAUER, CHRISTOPH (?-1564) Swiss printer. In the 1520s, F.'s printing shop in *Zurich made him the most successful publisher in the Swiss Protestant cantons. He was an early follower of *Zwingli and published his complete works, as well as two monumental annotaded editions of the *Bible in German and Latin, and many other religious works. The total output of the firm, until the death of F.'s nephew and heir in 1590, is estimated at some 900 titles.

FRUNDSBERG, GEORG VON (1473-1528) German military commander. He began his career under *Maximilian I, whom he assisted in organizing the **Landsknechte*. Between 1509 and 1514 he commanded the imperial forces against the Venetians and the French in Italy. But his greatest victories were achieved for *Charles V, when, in 1522, he invaded Picardy and then continued to Italy, conquering most of Lombardy. In 1527 F. and his army joined the Constable of *Bourbon in Italy, but his troops mutinied near Bologna, and their commander, finding himself unable to pay them, suffered a mental breakdown. He returned to Germany to die.

FUCHS, LEONHARD (1501-66) German botanist. He studied at the University of Ingolstadt, which was under the influence of the *Reformation, and where he became, in 1526, a professor of *medicine. In 1535 he moved on to Tübingen, where he taught medicine until the end of his life. His main contribution to Renaissance science was the publication, in 1542, of a botanical work describing the foxglove. The fuchsia, a garden plant of red and purple shades, which was brought over to Europe from South America, is named after him.

E. Stübler, *Leonhart Fuchs* (1928).

FUGGER A family of German bankers. The F.s centered their operations in *Augsburg where they settled during the latter half of the 14th century. Their wealth was originally acquired in the textile trade, but during the 15th century they became renowned money-lenders in Germany and elsewhere. They attained their real influence with Jakob (1459-1525), the youngest of seven brothers, who had joined the family business at the age of 19, soon becoming the head of the firm. Under his guidance the F.s acquired copper and silver mines and began their long association with the *Habsburgs – first with *Maximilian I, then with *Charles V, whose election to the imperial office in 1519 was financed mainly by them. The family business continued to thrive under Anton (1493-1560), a personal friend of Charles V, who expanded the commercial and mining concerns of the Fuggers to Asia and America. With their growing importance as bankers they were granted patents of nobility and became patrons of the arts. The decline of the F.s during the latter half of the 16th century was partly due to the political and religious divisions caused by the *Reformation. Devout Catholics, they kept their ties with the Habsburgs and Spain, thus losing opportunities in other parts of Europe. The increasing independence of their agents abroad may have been yet another factor.

Jacob Fugger *by Burgkmair*

R. Ehrenberg, *Capital and Finance in the Age of the Renaissance; A Study of the Fuggers* (1963);

V. Klarwill, ed., *The Fugger News-Letters* (1924).

FUST, JOHANN (c. 1400-66) German printer. A lawyer in Mainz, F. was, with *Gutenberg and with his own son-in-law, Peter Schöffer (1425-1502), a pioneer of *printing. In 1450 he loaned Gutenberg the money which made possible the publication of the *Bible (1452-55) and thus became his partner. In 1455, however, he took over the press from the insolvent Gutenberg and, together with Schöffer, published, on 14 August 1457, a beautiful edition of the *Psalms*, the first printed book which has the exact date of completion and the name of the firm on its title page. F. died while on a business trip to Paris. Schöffer continued to print for many more years.

R. Blum, *Der Prozess Fust gegen Gutenberg* (1954).

G

GABRIELI, ANDREA (c. 1510-86) Italian composer. Born in Venice, he was the pupil of *Willaert, whom he succeeded as *maestro da capella* of St. Mark's, Venice. He was first known as organist, but later became a noted composer. A master of the technique of counterpoint, he wrote many *madrigals and *motets.

GABRIELI, GIOVANNI (1557-1612) Italian composer. A nephew of Andrea Gabrieli (1510-86) a famous organist-composer, he was born in Venice and after being taught by his uncle studied under Orlando di *Lasso in Munich. From 1585 he served as an organist at St. Mark's in Venice. G. wrote choral and instrumental works, and although few in number, they greatly influenced the music of the *Baroque, most especially the evolution of the cantata. His innovations inclued the alternation of vocal and instrumental music, employing vocal solos, duets and choirs, and using the instrument as an integrative element rather than mere accompaniment. His most important compositions are the *Symphoniae sacrae*, choral works which influenced the German composers of the 17th century.

E. Kenton, *Life and Works of Giovanni Gabrieli* (1967); A. Denis, *Giovanni Garbrieli* (1974).

GADDI, TADDEO (c. 1300-66) Italian painter. The son of the Florentine painter Gaddo Gaddi (*c.* 1260-*c.* 1330), he studied under *Giotto, with whom he is believed to have worked for 24 years. Between 1332 and 1338 he completed the fresco cycle of the *Life of the Virgin* in the Baroncelli chapel of S. Croce, Florence; it is considered his best work. Later he worked in Pisa and Pistoia, but spent the last years of his life in Florence, where he was a member of the commission in charge of works on the cathedral. Considered the most important Florentine painter of the 14th century, G. followed the style of his master, though lacking his vigour. His son, Agnolo Gaddi (*c.* 1333-96), was also a successful painter who produced *frescoes in Florence and Prato.

GAETANO DA THIENE (1480-1547) Italian Roman Catholic reformer also known as St. Cajetan. Born in Vicenza, he graduated from the university of Padua (1504) and spent a number of years in the service of Pope *Julius II. In 1516 he was ordained priest in Rome, and about that time founded the *Oratory of Divine Love. In 1524 he and Cardinal *Caraffa (the future *Paul IV) founded a new congregation, which later became known as the *Theatine order. He was canonized in 1671.

P. Chiminelli, *San Gaetano Thiene* (1948).

GAGUIN, ROBERT (c. 1433-1501) French humanist author. Born in Flanders, he entered in his youth the white-robed Trinitarian order, becoming its General in 1473. Although he taught at the Faculty of Canon Law of the Univesity of Paris, G. was mainly interested in the revival of classical Latin and counted *Erasmus and *Reuchlin among his students. Later, he served *Louis XI and *Charles VIII on diplomatic assignments, visiting Italy, England (1489-90) and Germany. His main work, *De origine et gestis Francorum compendio* (1495), dealt with the history of France and served as a model for other historians. He also wrote theological works and translated classical Latin works. One of the most important promoters of humanist culture in France, his letters which were published in 1498 aroused a lively interest.

GAISMAIR, MICHAEL (c. 1490-1530) German rebel. He first appeared in 1525 at the head of the rebellious peasants in Tyrol, and soon fled to Switzerland. Early in 1526 he returned at the head of another peasant force and for several months laid siege to the city of Radstadt, until forced to disperse by the *Swabian League and Archduke *Ferdinand. He found shelter in Italy, where he was murdered by soldiers for the sake of the price set on his head. G., who was influenced by *Zwingli, supported the *Reformation. He went beyond a mere protest of peasant grievances, but fought for a republic dominated by the peasantry, free from domination by nobles, clergy and merchants.

GALILEO (Galileo Galilei; 1564-1642) Italian philosopher, astronomer, physicist and mathematician, the greatest scientist of the late Renaissance and a pioneer of the 17th-century *Scientific Revolution. Born in Pisa to an impoverished Florentine noble who was a musician, he was educated by the Vallombrosan monks and, in 1581, entered the Universtiy of Pisa, which he left after four years without graduating. He continued to study privately mathematics and physics and, in

The Doors of Paradise *at the Baptistery of Florence, by Ghiberti*

Galileo Galilei *by Sustermans*

1586, published his *La bilancetta*, on hydrostatic balance. In 1589, with the help of an influential patron, the Marquis Guidobaldo del Monte, he was appointed lecturer of mathematics at Pisa. Here he upset the faculty by disputing the fundamental assumptions of Aristotelian physics, maintaining that bodies composed of the same material fall at the same speed regardless of their weight. Although the story that he performed an experiment of dropping unequal weights from the Leaning Tower of Pisa, to demonstrate that they fall at the same speed, is a legend, it illustrates the kind of reputation he had. In 1592 he was dismissed and moved to the more liberal University of Padua.

In Padua, where he spent 18 years, G. taught geometry and *astronomy, a subject he had not worked in before. At first he accepted the Ptolemaic premise of the centrality of the earth. In 1597 he changed his mind, after reading *Copernicus, and wrote about it to *Kepler, but thought it prudent not to publish his ideas. For the next few years he concentrated on improving his proportional *compass, and took an interest in heat measurement and in the ideas of the English scientist, William *Gilbert, on magnetism. He never married, but his mistress, Marina Gamba, and he had two daughters and a son.

In 1609 G. heard of the recent invention of the *telescope by a Dutchman, and immediately constructed his own, which he proudly presented to the Venetian Senate. His third telescope, which made things appear 30 times closer, showed the mountains and valleys of the moon, many new stars and Jupiter's satellites. In 1610 he published these discoveries in his *Sidereus nuncius* (*Starry Messenger*), causing a great sensation. With his newly-won European fame, he left that year for Florence, where he became the Grand Duke's mathematician and philosopher. His astronomical observations convinced G. entirely of the validity of the Copernican theory and, in 1613, in a book on sunspots, *Historia e dimostrazioni intorno alle macchie solari*, he forcefully defended the heliocentric theory. This immediately brought him under fire from religious circles in Florence. G. defended himself in a letter addressed to the Grand Duchess Christina, wherein he argued the right of scientific inquiry free from Church intervention. But, in 1616, he was admonished by a papal commission headed by Cardinal *Bellarmine, which found the Copernican ideas heretical ("until corrected"), and threatened him with imprisonment if he taught them again.

Silenced, G. undertook, about 1624, the writing of the *Dialogo dei due massimi sistemi del mondo*, a comparison of the old and new astronomy. Here the Ptolemaic system was subjected to a sharp attack together with old notions of physics and well established philosophical ideas. The book was published in 1632, with the permission of the ecclesiastical authorities, but shortly afterwards G. was ordered to Rome to appear before the *Inquisition. At his trial, early in 1633, he was forced to confess that he had erred in some arguments regarding the motion of the earth. Legend has it that after his recantation he muttered, *Eppur si muove* ("And yet it does move"). He was sentenced to life imprisonment, and the *Dialogo* was ordered burned; but his sentence was soon changed to house arrest and he was allowed to reside at his villa outside Florence. A man of tremendous resilience, G. overcame encroaching blindness to write his last work, *Discorsi e dimonstrazioni matematiche intorno a due nuove scienze* (*Discourses Concerning Two New Sciences*), which was smuggled out of Italy and printed by *Elzevir in Leiden in 1638. A great discoverer, who observed the moon's libration shortly before he lost his eyesight, G.'s contribution to 17th-century science consisted primarily in his methodology and his championship of independent research. His resistence to the *Counter Reformation's intellectual oppression acquired a new significance in the 20th century, in view of the totalitarian systems of our own age.

M. Clavelin, *The Natural Philosophy of Galileo* (1974);

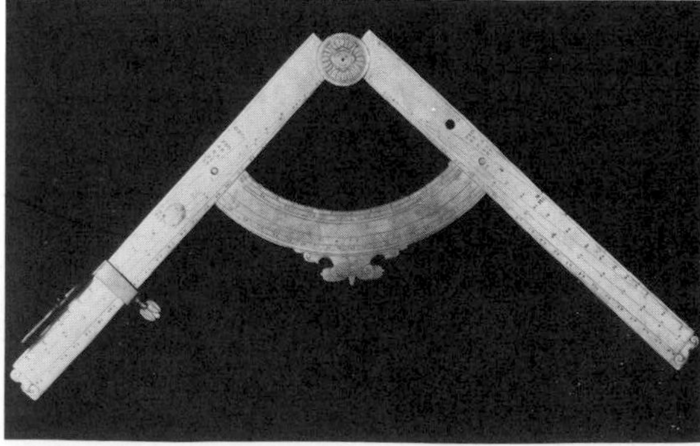

Galileo's geometrical compass

S. Drake, *Galileo Studies* (1970);
L. Fermi, *Galileo and the Scientific Revolution* (1961);
C. A. Roman, *Galileo* (1974).

GALLEON A large sailing vessel, fully rigged and employed either as a warship or in commerce. Although its name is derived from the *galley, the G. was actually a further development of the principles of the *caravel, using square rigs on the main masts and lateen sails on the after masts. It had guns on the broadsides, on one, two or even three decks, and became the 16th-century version of a floating fortress. Originally developed by the Spanish and Portuguese, it was adopted by other nations and maintained with only minor changes until the end of the 18th century.

GALLEY A war vessel, usually of a single deck and propelled by a combination of oars and sails. Employed in the Mediterranean since classical times, the G. was still in use in the navies of the 16th century, despite the development of the *caravel, which used only sails. Most of the ships at *Lepanto (1571) were of this kind. Oarsmen for the G.s were convicted criminals and no better than slaves. The G. disappeared during the 17th century.

GALLICANISM A term denoting the freedom of the French Catholic church from papal ecclesiastical authority. The first instances in which such freedom was demanded occurred before the 15th century. It was declared unilaterally in the *Pragmatic Sanction of Bourges (1438), but conceded by *Leo X to *Francis I in 1516. The Concordat of that year gave the French king the right to nominate bishops and to sanction the validity of papal bulls in his kingdom. Later in the 16th century this privilege served as the basis for the French refusal to implement the decisions of the Council of *Trent.

V. Martin, *Les origines du gallicanisme*, 2 vols. (1939).

GAMA, VASCO DA (c. 1468-1524) Portuguese navigator; the first to reach India by sea. Born to a father who had been employed in the service of the crown, G. was appointed by *Manoel I to lead a voyage of discovery to India. He left Portugal on 8 July 1497, with three vessels, reached the Cape of Good Hope on 18 November, and on 2 March 1498, arrived at the East African sultanate of Mozambique. In Melindi he took aboard a local pilot who directed him across the ocean to the Indian principality of Calicut, which he reached on 20 May 1498. Having exchanged the merchandise which he had brough with him for pepper and cinnamon, he set sail for the turbulent return voyage, which lasted almost 11 months (October 1498-August 1499). G. was received in Lisbon with the greatest honours; he was given the title Admiral of the Indian Ocean. In 1502 he sailed again to India to punish Calicut for the destruction of the Portuguese trading post. During this second voyage he signed treatises with the Indian rulers of Cochin and Cananor, returning to Portugal in 1504. On his third voyage to India in 1524 he went as viceroy, charged with the task of improving the administration of the Portuguese settlements. But he died shortly after his arrival.

E. Sanceau, *Good Hope: The Voyage of Vasco da Gama* (1967);
H. H. Hart, *Sea Road to the Indies* (1952).

GAMBARA, VERONICA (1485-1550) Italian poet. Born into a noble family near Brescia, she married the

A galleon and a galley, engraving after Breughel

lord of Correggio, and after his death (1518) administered the small estate. She wrote about 50 sonnets, mostly in a style imitative of Petrarch, and the best of which touched upon the death of her husband and the devastation of Italy by war. A friend of *Bembo and Vittoria *Colonna, she wrote letters to *Aretino and enjoyed a wide reputation during her life time.

C. de Courten, *Veronica Gambara* (1935).

GANTE, PEDRO DE (1486-1572) Franciscan missionary to Mexico. Born in Flanders and educated by the *Brethren of the Common Life, he arrived in Mexico in 1523 with the first group of missionary Franciscan friars. After learning the Nahuatl language, he launched a massive campaign to convert the Indians, with the aid of his Indian students. He is credited with the founding of numerous churches, schools and hospitals about Mexico City, where he died.

GARAMOND, CLAUDE (1480-1561) Parisian designer of type. Basing his designs on characters developed by other typefounders, such as Geoffroy *Tory, and working for several French printers, G. is credited with substituting the old Gothic lettering with his own graceful roman type, known as *typi regii*. In 1544 he designed the Greek characters of Robert *Estienne's edition of Eusebius, a work commissioned by King *Francis I, and which prompted the naming of this type as *grecs du roi*. G. was the first typefounder who dedicated himself exclusively to the design and cutting of characters. His creations influenced French printing for several hundred years.

GARAY, JUAN DE (1528-83) Spanish colonizer of Argentina. Taken to Peru as a boy, he took part in various expeditions against the Indians of southern Peru, rising in the ranks of the colonial administration. In 1568 he was commissioned to establish settlements in the region of the Rio de la Plata. Sailing south from Asunción de Paraguay, he founded in 1573 the town of Santa Fé on the Rivers Salado and Paraná and, in 1580, Buenos Aires, a site originally settled in 1536 by Pedro de *Mendoza, but later abandoned.

GARCILASO DE LA VEGA (1501-36) Spanish poet and soldier. Born in Toledo to a noble family, he joined the entourage of *Charles V and fought in Italy and in the expedition to Tunis (1535). His work, consisting of some three scores of sonnets, eclogues and odes, shows the influence of Italian literature. Although describing an Arcadian setting in a delicate language and a polished style, his verse has undercurrents of anguish and melancholy. His work was published in 1543, after he had been killed in Provence during military operations. It was received enthusiastically, securing his name as one of the master of Spanish literature.

Garcilaso de la Vega, *Obras* (1966);
Garcilaso de la Vega, *Works*, ed. by H. Keniston (1925).

GARCILASO DE LA VEGA (1539-1616) Spanish historian. Known also as "El Inca", he was born in Cuzco, Peru, the child of an Inca princess and a Spanish **conquistador*. In 1560 he went to Spain, and remained there for the rest of his life. He participated in the suppression of the *Moriscos (1570). Later, he took minor orders and lived in Córdoba where he died. His best known work is the *Comentarios reales* (1609), which describe the history and customs of the Incas. Written as it was many years after he had left Peru, his idealized portrayal of Inca civilization may be questioned. Nevertheless, the work is one of the major sources on the subject. G. also wrote an account of Hernando de *Soto's expedition, entitled *La Florida del Inca* (1605) which has the merit of a literary composition.

Garcilaso de la Vega, *Royal Commentaries of the Incas and General History of Peru*, trans. by H. V. Livermore (1966);
J. Fitzmaurice-Kelly, *El Inca Garcilaso de la Vega* (1921).

GARDINER, STEPHEN (c. 1485-1555) Bishop of Winchester, England. Educated at Trinity Hall, Cambridge, he became master of his college in 1525 and later also chancellor of the university. Employed by *Wolsey in connection with the divorce of *Henry VIII and *Catherine of Aragon, he won the King's favour. When Wolsey was dismissed in 1529, G. stayed on as secretary of state and, in 1531, was made bishop of Winchester. In 1535 he defended royal supremacy over the Church in his *De vera obedientia*, but nevertheless until the end of the reign of Henry VIII, was one of conservative members of the Council, opposing a further drift towards Protestantism. Shortly after the accession of *Edward VI he was imprisoned in the Tower (1548) and remained there throughout the reign. Queen *Mary released him in 1533, restoring his ecclesiastical dignities and nominating him lord chancellor, chief minister and royal advisor. G. was instrumental in the suppression of the *Wyatt rebellion (1554) and was responsible for the execution of those leading reformers who chose to remain in England rather than go into exile. Opinions differ sharply concerning his pendulum-like career.

S. Gardiner, *A Machiavellian Treatise*, ed. and trans. by P. S. Donaldson (1975);
J. A. Muller, *Stephen Gardiner and Tudor Reaction* (1926).

GARETH, BENEDETTO (c. 1450-1514) Italian poet, also known as Il Cariteo. Born in Barcelona, he went to Naples about 1467 and held various offices at the court. An associate of *Pontano and *Sannazzaro, he wrote *Endimione*, a collection of elegant court poems. He went into exile when the French conquered Naples (1495), but returned after it passed to the rule of *Ferdinand of Aragon.

GARNIER, ROBERT (c. 1545-90) French poet and dramatist. A native of Maine, he studied law at Toulouse and published his first love poems in 1565. In Paris he became a friend of *Ronsard and other members of the *Pléiade, but soon moved to Le Mans, where he began a long career as royal advocate and judge. G. was the author of eight plays on classical, contemporary and religious themes. His work signalled a further development of the French tragedy, having some dramatic tension, although not without much rhetoric. His tragicomedy *Brodamante*, drawn from *Ariosto, was reprinted 15 times before the end of the century, pioneering a new dramatic genre. G. was named by *Henry III in 1586 to the Grand Council, and belonged to the *League.

A. M. Witherspoon, *The Influence of Robert Garnier on Elizabethan Drama* (1924).

GAROFALO (1481-1559) The name given to the Italian painter Benvenuto Tisi. Born near *Ferrara, he worked under *Boccacino at Cremona (1508), and visited Venice, Mantua and Rome (1516), where he was influenced by *Raphael. Later he settled in Ferrara, producing many works in an imitative but competent style, working frequently in cooperation with Dosso *Dossi. He was highly admired for his blond Raphaelesque *madonnas. In 1550 he went blind.

GASCA, PEDRO DE LA (1485-1567) Spanish prelate and colonial governor. A graduate of the universities of Alcalá and Salamanca, he rose in the ranks of the Spanish church, serving as member of the Council of the *Inquisition. Later he was also employed by the crown in administrative posts, establishing a reputation as a hard-working and loyal official. In 1546 *Charles V sent him to Peru to preside over the governing council, his task being to put down the revolt of Gonzalo *Pizarro. G. succeeded in bringing over to his side, one by one, the most important of Pizarro's supporters and, in 1548, defeated the rebel in battle. Following the execution of Pizarro he pacified Peru and expanded the Spanish possession to the south. He returned to Spain in 1550 and was made bishop of Palencia and later of Siguenza.

GASCOIGNE, GEORGE (1539-77) English author. The temperamental son of a noble family from Bedfordshire, he left Cambridge before graduating, became a member of Gray's Inn and served as member of Parliament (1557-59). His reputation for wildness prevented his being seated when he was elected again (1572). He then joined the army of the Dutch rebels in the *Netherlands, from which he returned in poor health (1574). G.

produced the first English prose comedy, *The Supposes* (1566), an adaptation of a work by *Ariosto, and also wrote a tragedy, *Jocasta*, based on the *Phoenissae* of Euripides. The revised edition of his collected poems (1575) included his "Notes of Instruction", the first English critical essay on poetry. An innovator of certain literary genres, he produced a 16th-century version of war correspondence in his accounts of military service in Holland. Also important are the *Glasse of Government* (1575), a drama, and his satire in verse, *The Steele Glas* (1576).

C. T. Prouty, *George Cascoigne, Elizabethan Courtier, Soldier and Poet* (1942).

GASPARINO DA BARZIZZA (c. 1360-1431) Italian humanist. He studied grammar and rhetorics in Pavia, where he later taught. In 1407 he moved to Padua, where he established a humanist centre for the study of ancient Latin writings. In 1417 he went to the Council of *Constance as a papal representative. During the last ten years of his life he taught in Milan. G.'s contribution to the growing humanist trend was mainly in the grammatical restoration of Latin to its ancient classical form. He wrote commentaries on the letters of Seneca and on *De officiis* of Cicero, and cleared the texts of other works of Cicero of their mediaeval distortions. In addition, he wrote a treatise on rhetorics and produced models for letter writing.

GATTAMELATA, ERASMO (c. 1370-1443) Italian **condottiere*. In 1437 he was made commander-in-chief of the forces of *Venice, conducting the long campaigns against *Milan, which were concluded only after his death. His main accomplishment was the reconquest of Verona. Shortly after his death the city of Padua commissioned *Donatello to erect the famous equestrian statue of him, which was completed in 1453.

G. von Graevenitz, *Gattamelata und Colleoni und ihre Beziehungen zur Kunst* (1906).

GATTINARA, MERCURINO DI (1465-1530) Italian minister of *Charles V. A successful young lawyer, he entered the service of *Margaret of Austria in 1501. When she undertook the government of the duchy of *Burgundy, G. was assigned important diplomatic tasks, and in 1513 was made a count by *Maximilian I. He continued his role as chief counsellor under Margaret's nephew, *Charles V, whose election as king of the Romans he engineered in 1519. G. pursued a rigid anti-French policy and at one point, after the Battle of Pavia (1525), was ready to tender his resignation because of easy terms accorded the captured *Francis I. In 1529 he was made cardinal.

GEERTGEN VAN HAARLEM (c. 1460-c. 1490) Dutch painter, also called Geertgen Tot Sint Jans (Little Gerard of the Brethren of St. John). Born in Leiden, he worked in Haarlem, where he produced the two panels, originally part of a large altarpiece, *Lamentation of Christ* and the *Legend of the Bones of St. John the Baptist*, now in Vienna. These are superb examples of the late 15th century North European mastery of colour and landscape backgrounds, as yet unaffected by Italian influences. Some 15 smaller works are also ascribed to him.

M. L. Friedländer; *Geertgen van Haarlem und Hieronymus Bosch* (1927).

GEILER VON KEISERSBERG, JOHANN (1445-1510) German religious preacher. Born in the Rhine Valley, he studied at Freiburg and pursued a successful academic career which, in 1476, culminated in the rectorship of the university. In 1478 he became a preacher at the Cathedral of *Strassburg, where he remained for the rest of his life, and was on friendly terms with the local humanists. G. vigorously attacked abuses such as usury and monopolies, and called for ecclesiastical reform. Enjoying a wide popularity among his parishioners, he was compared to *Savonarola, but he did not enter into a direct confrontation with church authorities as did his famous Florentine contemporary. Many of his sermons were published. Jakob *Wimpfeling and Beatus Renanus wrote his biography.

E. J. Dempsey-Douglass, *Justification in Late Medieval Preaching: a Study of Geiler of Keisersberg* (1966).

GELLI, GIAMBATTISTA (1498-1563) Italian author. Born in Florence, he was a shoemaker by trade, and began to study Latin and philosophy at the age of 25. In later years, encouraged by *Cosimo I, he helped to found the Florentine Academy, became the official commentator on *Dante (1553), and championed literature in the vernacular; he himself wrote in colloquial Italian. His best known works are *I capricci di Giusto bottaio* (1546), ten moral essays, presenting the views of a cooper, and *La Circe* (1549), a conversation between Ulysses and 11 persons whom Circe had transformed into various animals. Only the elephant consents to return to his former human state.

A. L. Gaetano, *Giambattista Gelli and the Florentine Academy: The Rebellion Against Latin* (1976).

GEMISTOS PLETHON, GEORGIOS (c. 1355-1450) Greek philosopher. Born in *Constantinople, he spent his youth near the site of ancient Sparta and developed a life-long admiration for Plato; from here the addition "Plethon" to his original name. He came to Italy in 1438, at the age of 83, to attend the Council of *Ferrara-Florence, and impressed the Florentine humanists with lectures on the philosophy of Plato. Cosimo de' *Medici admired him, and is said to have been urged by him to found an academy of *Greek letters. His visit signalled a diminution in the authority of Aristotelian philosophy.

F. Masai, *Pléthon et le platonisme de Mistra* (1956).

GEMMA FRISIUS, REYNERI (1508-55) Flemish geographer and astronomer. Born in Friesland, he studied at the University of Louvain where, in 1541, he was appointed professor of medicine. G. published many scientific works which established his name as one of the leading geographers and *cartographers of his time. Among these were *De principiis astronomiae et cosmographiae* (1530); *Charta sive mappa mundi* (1540), and *De astrolabio* (1556). He was also a well-known mathematician, his *Arithmeticae practicae methodus facilis* was published more than 20 times between 1540 and 1652. *Charles V consulted him on various matters.

G. Kish, *Medecina, Mensura, Mathematica: The Life and Work of Gemma Frisius* (1967).

GENEVA From the beginning of the 15th century this site of the cloth fair on Lake Geneva in the upper Rhone Valley was dominated by the dukes of Savoy. Conscious of the rising power and prestige of their Swiss neighbours, the Genevans sought to win their own independence and, in 1530, won it with the help of the Swiss cantons of Bern and Fribourg. Soon afterwards Guillaume *Farel introduced the Reformation to the city and, in 1535, it decided to become Protestant. An attempt by Savoy to reconquer G. was defeated in 1536 with the aid of Bern, and resulted in the expansion of the territory of the G. canton. In the same year *Calvin first came to G. and, in 1541, returned and made it his permanent home and the capital of French Protestantism. Under his guidance, G. became a refuge for persecuted French, Italian and English Protestants, and the Academy, founded in 1559 and directed by *Beza, added weight to the town's position as a theological centre. After *Calvin's death, G. took part in the *Religious Wars of France. In 1602 the duke of Savoy made a final attempt to take the city by surprise. But his failure confirmed her independence.

J. F. Bergier, *Genève et l'économie européenne de la Renaissance* (1963);
W. F. Graham, *Calvin and his City* (1970).

GENGENBACH, PAMPHILUS (c. 1480-c. 1525) Swiss poet, playwright and printer. Born at Basle, he wrote moralizing Shrovetide plays which were very popular, and poems in the fashion of the **Meistersinger*. Before his death he became a supporter of the Reformation as he made quite clear in his *Die Totenfresser* (1521).

R. Raillard, *Pamphilus Gengenbach und die Reformation* (1936).

GENNADIUS (c. 1400-c. 1468) The name given to the Greek cleric and scholar Georgius Scholarius. He took part in the Council of *Ferrara-Florence, but opposed the union of the Greek Church with Rome. In 1454 the *Ottoman Turks recognized him as the patriarch of *Constantinople. In his last years he wrote a great deal in defence of the Greek Church, for which purpose he interested himself in Western scholasticism.

GENOA The commercial republic of G., which reached in the 13th century the summit of her economic prosperity and political might, lost some of its cohesion in the next hundred years. After 1339 the office of *doge* was held in perpetuity and the republic frequently found itself in the midst of violent factional strifes. From 1421 to 1436 G. was occupied by Filippo Maria *Visconti, duke of Milan and, after the fall of *Constantinople, she lost her interests and colonies in the East. From then on her commercial activities converged on the North African coasts and the western Mediterranean, and she hardly benefited from the opening of the new maritime routes to Asia and America.

Politically, the influence exercised by *Milan was followed, in the 1490s, with a dependency upon France. This led to the sack of G. in 1522 by imperial troops and, finally, to Andrea *Doria's coup d'état. In 1528 Doria made the republic a satellite of *Charles V in return for imperial recognition of its nominal autonomy. After Doria's death, his heirs ruled the republic as a *de facto* dependency of Spain, a relationship which afforded the Genoese banks opportunities for advantageous financing of the Spanish wars on the Continent. By the end of the 16th century, G. no longer counted as a political entity; her possession of the island of Corsica was one of the few reminders of her past colonial greatness.

M. Buongiorno, *Il bilancio di uno stato medievale, Genoa, 1340-1529* (1973).

GEORGE OF PODEBRADY (1420-71) King of *Bohemia from 1458. The son of a noble family, he became the leader of the *Utraquist party and, in 1448, took possession of Prague. He ruled as captain-general and regent until 1453, when he had to relinquish the government in favour of *Ladislas Posthumus. However, in 1457 the sudden death of the young king resulted in the election of G. to the Bohemian throne. Still championing the religious rights of the Utraquists, G. provoked the enmity of Rome, which declared a crusade against him and had him excommunicated (1466). He was forced to fight against an alliance headed by Emperor *Frederick III and his son-in-law *Matthias Corvinus of Hungary, and the latter succeeded in gaining the support of the Bohemian Catholic nobles for his claim to the throne (1469). In order to strengthen his position, G. recognized *Ladislas, son of King Casimir IV of Poland, as his successor. A Bohemian nationalist who defended the independence of his country, he nevertheless, opened the way to a long domination of the Czech people by foreign dynasties after his death.

GEORGE OF TREBIZOND (1396-1484) Greek scholar. A native of Crete, he came to Venice in his youth, studied at the University of Padua (1416) and under *Guarino da Verona and *Vittorino da Feltre. He served as an interpreter at the Council of *Ferrara-Florence, and became secretary to Pope *Eugenius IV. Under *Nicholas V he translated several of the Greek classics, which incurred the criticism of *Poggio Bracciolini. In 1459 he had to leave Rome, returning in 1466. During his long career he was frequently involved in bitter controversies with other scholars. His contribution to Greek studies is matched by his successful manual on Latin style and composition.

GEORGE THE BEARDED (Georg der Bärtige; 1471-1539) Duke of *Saxony. Succeeding his father Albert the Brave in 1500, he began his rule as a supporter of humanist culture and ecclesiastical reforms. But after the Disputation of *Leipzig (1519), in which he personally debated with *Luther, he turned into a irreconcilable foe of the *Reformation. In 1525 he crushed the *Peasants' War at the battle of Frankenhausen, a revolt he viewed as an outcome of the Reformation. Enjoying considerable income from the thriving Saxon mining industry, G. was able to reduce the power of the nobles and strengthen the ducal government. He remained a staunch supporter of the *Habsburgs and Roman Catholicism throughout his long reign. But after his death his successor introduced Protestantism.

GENTILE DA FABRIANO (c. 1370-1427) Italian painter. A native of Lombardy, he probably worked in northern Italy before arriving in Venice (1408), where he began to make his reputation. The fresco which he painted in the Doge's Palace in 1409 was completed by *Pisanello, but destroyed in 1577. In 1412 he left Venice, working in Brescia (1414), Rome (1420) and Siena and, in 1422, went to Florence, where he executed his finest work, an altarpiece on panel depicting *The Adoration of the Magi*, now at the Uffizi. This highly decorative crowded picture, considered the greatest example of the *International Gothic in 15th-century Italy, was created at the time when *Masaccio and *Donatello were about to introduce the new art of humanist realism. Before leaving Florence in 1425, G. completed the *Quaratesi Altarpiece*. For the next two years he worked in Siena and Orvieto, and died in Rome while painting frescoes at the Church of S. Giovanni di

Laterano. Considered one of the major Italian painters of his age, he left traces of his elegant style in each of the artistic centres with which he was associated.
E. Micheletti, ed., *L'opera completa di Gentile da Fabriano* (1976).

GENTILI, ALBERICO (1552-1608) Italian jurist. Born at San Ginesio, he completed his studies of civil law at Perugia. In 1579 he left Italy, having fallen under suspicion of harbouring Protestant beliefs. In 1580 he went to England, where he was given a professorship of Roman law at Oxford. He was consulted by *Elizabeth I in 1584, before her ousting of the Spanish ambassador Bernardino de *Mendoza. He remained in England for the rest of his life, and his opinion was often sought on a variety of legal matters. His principal writings were concerned with problems of international law, especially *De legationibus* (On Embassies) (1585) and *De jure belli* (On the Law of War) (1598). These were the first and imperfect attempts to establish a real legal framework for the relations between states, and had a significant influence on *Grotius.
G. Molen, *Alberico Gentili and the Development of International Law* (1937).

GERHAERT VAN LEYDEN The name by which the sculptor Nicolaus Lerch is known. Originally from the Netherlands, he is first heard of in Strassburg, where he became a citizen in 1464. Later he worked at Trier, Constance and Baden. He died probably in 1487 in Vienna where he had been commissioned to do the tomb of *Frederick III at St. Stephen's. Following a style still influenced by the Gothic, his figures exude sympathy and humour.
O. Wertheimer, *Nicolaus Gerhaert* (1929);
E. D. Schmid, *Der Nördlinger Hochaltar und sein Bildhauerwerk* (1971).

GERMANY The history of G. in the 15th and 16th centuries does not quite parallel that of the loose institutional framework known as the *Holy Roman Empire. In the Golden Bull of 1356 the Empire had confirmed the political division of G. into autonomous principalities presided over by a titular head; nevertheless, economic, social and cultural processes encouraged the development of an identity, which reached a high point on the eve of the *Reformation. However, the existence in G. of over 350 separate authorities, divided among secular and ecclesiastical princes, counts and prelates and imperial towns, did not make for national consolidation. When the Reformation superimposed a religious division on top of the political one, the fate of G. was sealed: not for 300 years would it regain the intense feeling of nationhood.

The long reigns of Emperors *Sigismund (1410-37) and *Frederick III (1440-93) saw an entrenchment of political particularism. Although internal strife may have diminished, compared with the disastrous second half of the 14th century, there was a new pretext for war in the *Hussite movement of *Bohemia. The early 15th century saw changes with relation to the larger German political components: the *Teutonic Knights were beginning to lose to *Poland their preeminence in the Baltic region; the houses of *Hohenzollern and *Wettin assumed the rule over *Brandenburg and *Saxony respectively, and the *Habsburgs retained the imperial crown from the brief reign of *Albert II (1437-39) on. These years saw the *Hanseatic League flourishing, *mining and metallurgy expanding, and many German towns were building impressive cathedrals in the late Gothic style. Perhaps the best sign of the improved conditions was the rapid development of *printing in the second half of the 15th century, a process invented and disseminated through Europe mostly by Germans. Chronologically it corresponded to the founding of new German *universities. Even the peasant revolts, mostly of local character, could not darken the general picture of material prosperity.

The reign of *Maximilian I (1493-1519) promised to be an era of fulfillment. *Humanism had promoted in G. a climate of patriotism, in which German folk legends and old imperial traditions proliferated. Painters and engravers, such as *Dürer, *Cranach and *Altdorfer, presided over an unusually creative generation, marking a zenith of German art. German *banking houses were taking over from the Italians the control of international commerce and industry; indeed, the liveliness of German public life suggested envy of Italy and resentment towards Rome. The constitutional reforms of the Empire, agreed from 1495 on, seemed to be coping with the task of political unification, producing new juridical institutions (**Reichskammergericht*). But before long the Emperor himself gave up the challenge of reform in favour of external wars and the building of Habsburg might outside G. His grandson, *Charles V (1519-56), who was anything but a German, was forced from the start to leave things as they were.

Paradoxically, the spontaneous expressions of unity reached a high point when *Luther began his opposition to Rome, launching the *Reformation (1517). But the ensuing clamour for change was soon translated into social protest and revolt. The *Knights' War (1522-23) and the *Peasants' War (1524-25), though prompted by different, even opposing social classes, represented elements that unlike the urban merchants and artisans had suffered during the preceding years. By the mid-1520s the *Protestants gained control of some of the most important principalities and, after 1531, they were organized in the *Schmalkaldic League, a political division bent on military resistance.

Imperial involvement in Italy, wars with France, and especially the presence of the *Ottoman Turks on the borders of *Austria, delayed the decisive conflict inside G. But at last Charles V, temporarily free of foreign conflicts, gathered the necessary means to settle accounts with the Protestant princes. His victory in the Battle of *Mühlberg (1547) resulted in the captivity of the two major leaders of the Protestants, *Philip of Hesse and *John Frederick I of *Saxony. Seemingly master of the stiuation, the Emperor issued the *Augsburg Interim (1548), and made the imperial towns which had joined the Schmalkaldic League suffer the consequence of defeat. It was now the turn of that unlikely champion of Protestantism, *Maurice of Saxony, to undo the imperial gains. In 1552, taking Charles V by surprise, he defeated him and forced upon him the Convention of Passau. The final settlement of the struggle between German Roman Catholics and Protestants was the work of Archduke *Ferdinand, soon to assume the imperial crown. The Religious Peace of *Augsburg (1555) established the principle that each subject should follow the religion of his ruler and gave official recognition to the Lutherans, but not to the Calvinists.

Conrad Gesner, from title page of his book

German politics of the second half of the 16th century showed the weariness from past convulsions. Lutheranism made some gains, and achieved a definite doctrinal basis in the *Formula of Concord (1577). At the same time Calvinism was planted in the *Palatinate under *Frederick III, the Pious (1559-76). But religious changes on the Protestant side were generally insignificant, the really meaningful development being the recuperation of German Roman Catholicism, which became noticeable during the last quarter of the century. Under *Maximilian II (1564-76), imperial attention was drawn mainly to *Hungary. His son *Rudolf II (1576-1612) was an eccentric person absorbed in *astrology, who was progressively pushed out of the political scene by his brother and successor *Matthias (1612-19). The reemergence of the old spirit of religious intransigence in politics was signalled by the creation of the *Protestant Union (1608), and its counterpart the Catholic League (1609). The conflict over the *Jülich-Cleves succession followed, which was a local rehearsal of the outbreak of the *Thirty Years' War.

H. Holborn, *A History of Modern Germany: The Reformation* (1959);
K. Brandi, *Deutsche Geschichte im Zeitalter der Reformation und Gegenreformation* (1941);
F. Hartung, *Deutsche Geschichte im Zeitalter der Reformation, der Gegenreformation und des 30jährigen Krieges* (1963);
J. Lortz, *The Reformation in Germany*, 2 vols. (1969).

GERSON, JEAN LE CHARLIER DE (1363-1429) French theologian. A student of Pierre *D'Ailly, with whom he remained a lifelong friend, he succeeded his teacher-friend in 1395 as chancellor of the University of Paris. In 1397 he moved to *Bruges, where he devoted three years to writing. He returned to his post in Paris and began to take part in the general affairs of the Church, aiming at bringing an end to the *Great Schism. Together with D'Ailly he attended the Council of *Constance, where he defended the *conciliar idea and *Gallicanism, and joined in the condemnation of Jan *Hus. From 1419 to the end of his life he lived in seclusion at *Lyons. A prolific writer, G. is especially noted for his spiritual guides, inspired by mystical feelings and advocating a direct, personal approach to God. *Thomas à Kempis' *Imitation of Christ* was long believed to be his.

J. L. Connolly, *John Gerson, Reformer and Mystic* (1928).

GESNER, CONRAD (1516-65) Swiss zoologist. Born in Zurich, he studied medicine in Basle and then returned to his native town, where he practiced and worked on his zoological and botanical researches. His first work of merit, however, was the *Bibliotheca universalis* (1545), an ambitious catalogue of all past writers and their works. The *Historia animalium*, his great work on zoology, was published in four volumes between 1551 and 1558. It included his survey of mammals, birds and fishes; a fifth volume dealing with snakes was published posthumously. G. also wrote on linguistics and about his mountain excursions.

H. Fischer, *Conrad Gesner, 1516-1565; Universal gelehrter, Naturfoscher, Arzt* (1967).

GESSO A substance used during the Renaissance as a coating on wood panels or canvas, to serve as the ground for the painting. It was made of plaster mixed with glue and was applied in several layers. Its use enhanced the brilliance of colours and gilding, and it could also be shaped by relief impression. One of the earliest descriptions of the use of G. is in Cennini's *Libro dell' arte*.

GESUALDO, CARLO (c. 1560-1615) Italian composer. Prince of Venosa. Born at Naples into a noble family, he became one of the most skilled lute players of his time. In 1590 he is said to have instigated the murder of his wife, whom he suspected of having a love affair with another Neapolitan noble. G. spent the best years of his life at the court of the house of *Este in *Ferrara (*c.* 1592-97). During these years he published his first four books of *madrigals. He ended his life in Naples, where the fifth and sixth books were published (1611), containing bold complex compositions of extremely modern spirit, quite different from the contemporary modes of expression. G.'s technical innovations were designed to relate his music artistically to the meaning of the words.

G. E. Watkins, *Gesualdo; the Man and His Music* (1976).

GHENT A great Flemish centre of the commerce in cloth during the late Middle Ages, G. tried to maintain its political autonomy and republican government in the 15th century, in the face of the rising power of the dukes of *Burgundy. It fought both *Philip the Good and *Maximilian but, in 1539, failed in its last revolt against *Charles V, who then put an end to its autonomy. In the second half of the 16th century the city was for a while a centre of Calvinism (1578-84), but was forced back into Roman Catholicism by *Farnese. Its

ld man with his grandson *by Domenico Ghirlandaio*

The Adoration of the Kings *by Gentile da Fabriano*

Cloth manufactories, late 15th century. Canterbury, England

commerce, which had been in continuous decline, suffered further from its separation from the northern Netherlands and *Philip II's hostile relations with England.

H. van Werveke, *Gand, esquisse d'histoire sociale* (1946).

GHENT, PACIFICATION OF (November 1576) A treaty, concluded by all the provinces of the Netherlands, for a common policy against Spain. Committing the members to a united effort to expell the Spanish troops, it stipulated that religious questions would be resolved by a representative assembly of all 17 provinces. The treaty was adopted at a time of disorder and pillage by Spanish soldiers, following the death of the governor Luís de *Requesens. The new governor, Don *Juan of Austria, at first confirmed the measures of the P. of G., but the war soon began again.

GHETTO A term which came to signify a compulsory urban residential quarter for *Jews. Although during the Middle Ages Jews tended to live together in their own quarters, it was only in the 16th century that they were compelled to live in a walled section, and having only a few gates which were closed at night. It is believed that the term originated in Venice, where in 1516 the Jews were permitted to settle on condition that they would be confined in a quarter near a foundry; the Italian word for that being *getto* or *ghetto*. The militant religious climate of the *Counter Reformation contributed to the spread of this restrictive measure to other Italian cities, especially during the second half of the 16th century.

S. Waagenaar, *The Pope's Jews* (1974).

GHEYN, JACOB DE (1565-1629) Dutch engraver. Born (probably) in Antwerp, to a father who was a glass painter and miniaturist, he learned engraving under *Goltzius (1585-90). Later he worked for the court of Orange at The Hague, designing gardens for *Maurice of Nassau. His numerous engravings reflected the bold free style of his master and were widely appreciated. His son, by the same name, was also an engraver.

GHIBERTI, LORENZO (1378-1455) Florentine sculptor. He began his working career as a goldsmith and painter, but in 1402 won the competition for the commission to execute a pair of doors for the baptistry, which was sponsored by the important guild of wool merchants (*arte della lana*). Among the seven artists who participated were *Brunelleschi and Jacopo della *Quercia, but G.'s elegant model finally won over Brunelleschi's. The work on the doors lasted from 1403 to 1424; among his assistants during this time were *Donatello and Paolo *Uccello. After he completed this work, which showed 28 scenes from the New Testament, he was commissioned to do another pair of doors (1425-52). These so-called "gates of paradise", a term coined by *Michelangelo, are G.'s masterpiece. They contain ten gilded reliefs showing scenes from the Old Testament, on themes suggested by Leonardo *Bruni. In contrast with the first pair of doors, the second was done in a realistic style which used to great effect the principles of perspective. G. also made a number of statues, and relief works for the baptistry of *Siena, and may have tried his hand at architectural designs. Although a great master, he was not a bold innovator, and his second famous pair of doors actually adopted principles which had been developed by his former student *Donatello. G. left a written work, his three

Landscape with Farm, *an etching by de Gheyn*

Commentaries, which include his views of the artists of the 14th century and his own autobiography. He was the first Renaissance artist to write about himself.

J. von Schlosser, *Leben und Meinungen des florentinischen Bildners, Lorenzo Ghiberti* (1941);
L. Goldscheider, *Ghiberti* (1949);
R. Krautheimer, *Ghiberti's Bronze Doors* (1971).

GHIRLANDAIO, DOMENICO (1449-94) Florentine painter. A contemporary of *Botticelli and the first teacher of *Michelangelo, he headed a very active workshop and was one of the most popular painters of his time. Most of his important work was done in *fresco, of which he was considered a great master. He was supported by Lorenzo de' *Medici and, in 1481,

A detail of Ghiberti's doors of the Baptistery, Florence

The Rape of the Sabines *by Giambologna*

was invited by *Sixtus IV to work on the decoration of the *Sistine Chapel. G. is best described as a sober realist, whose art continued the traditions established by *Giotto and *Masaccio, rather than an innovator. Some of his paintings, such as the famous *Old Man and Boy*, have a tendency towards naturalist accuracy. His work consciously reflected contemporary figures, customs and ideas and lent itself to analysis as a social document.

G. S. Davies, *Ghirlandaio* (1908).

GIAMBOLOGNA (Giovanni da Bologna or Jean de Boulogne; 1529-1608) Born at Douai, Flanders, he studied in Italy, remaining there throughout his long career, becoming the greatest sculptor of the second half of the 16th century. Most of his works were done in Florence where he settled about 1556, but his first major project, the *Fountain of Neptune*, was executed in Bologna (1563-67). G.'s most famous work is the *Rape of the Sabines* (1579-83) at Florence's Loggia della Signoria. A complex sculpture of three figures, it was carved from a single piece of marble. He was also renowned for his small bronze statues, such as the *Medici Mercury* (1564), which seem to be floating in the air. A continuator of the style of *Michelangelo and essentially a *Mannerist, G.'s work exudes harmony and elegance. It had many imitators throughout Europe.

GIANNOTTI, DONATO (1492-1573) Italian political writer. Born in Florence, he studied and taught law at Pisa. In 1530 he was banished by the returning *Medici on account of his support for the republic (1527-30). Later he entered the service of several prelates, and finally as the secretary of Pope *Pius V. Influenced by the republican thought of *Machiavelli, he wrote on the forms of government of Florence and of Venice. The oligarchical nature of the latter he frankly admired. His last work, *Discorso delle cose d'Italia*, suggested an alliance with France against the *Habsburgs.

GIBERTI, GIAN MATTEO (1495-1543) Bishop of Verona and Catholic reformer. The son of a Genoese sailor, he became the secretary and close friend of Cardinal Giulio de' *Medici, and was made bishop in 1524, shortly after the latter ascended the papal throne as *Clement VII. G. was also close to *Paul III and, in 1536, was appointed by him to the Commission of Nine, which included *Contarini, *Sadoleto and *Pole, and which produced a plan of church reform preparing the way to the convening of the Council of *Trent. He was a student of patristic literature and issued editions of some Greek Church Fathers.

GIL DE HONTAÑON Two Spanish architects, Juan (*c*. 1480-1526) and Rodrigo (*c*. 1505-1577), father and son, who produced some of the finest examples of the Late Gothic style. Juan G. was in 1513 put in charge of the construction of the Cathedral of Salamanca and, in 1525, began work on the Cathedral of Segovia. Earlier, he had built the new lantern for the Cathedral of *Seville (1513) and a cloister at Palencia. Rodrigo, who had been trained by his father, continued the work in Segovia, and also built parts of the Cathedrals of Astroga, Salamanca and Palencia. While following a basically late-mediaeval structural design, he decorated the outer walls in a **Plateresque* manner. His best known structure is the impressive façade of the University of Alcalá (1537-53).

GILBERT, SIR HUMPHREY (1539-83) English explorer. An older half-brother of Walter *Raleigh, G. was educated at Eton and Oxford, earned some distinction as a soldier and subsequently found his way to the court of Queen *Elizabeth I. He became interested in finding a northwestern route to China and, in 1576, published his *Discourse of a Discovery for a New Passage to Cataia*. The book aroused the interest of the merchants of London, who had outfitted the three unsuccessful voyages of *Frobisher. In 1578 G. sailed to the North Atlantic, empowered with a patent given him by Elizabeth, and accompanied by Raleigh, but returned without having discovered anything. He sailed again in 1583 and took possession of Newfoundland in the name of his Queen, leaving behind him a small settlement, the first English colony on the new continent. He and his crew lost their lives on the return voyage.

GILBERT, WILLIAM (1544-1603) English scientist. Born in Colchester to a distinguished family, he was educated at Cambridge and, in 1569, completed his medical studies. In 1576 he became a member of the College of Physicians and, in 1601, was appointed physician to *Elizabeth I, a position he retained for a few months under her successor *James I. G.'s main work was *De magnete* (1600), an account of his many years of experimentation. His experiments had led him to conceive of the earth as a great magnet, thereby explaining the behaviour of the magnetized needle. G. was the first to distinguish between force of magnetism and electricity. He also wrote on astronomy.

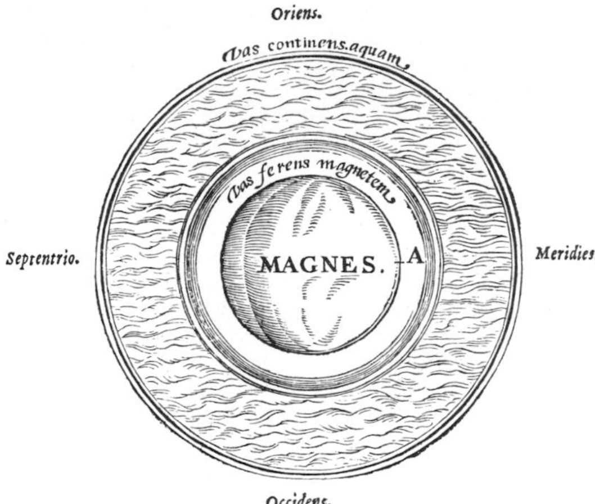

Gilbert's Philosophia Nova

R. Harré, *The Method of Science* (1970);
D. H. D. Roller, *The De Magnate of William Gilbert* (1959).

GILIO DA FABRIANO, ANDREA Italian art theorist. In 1564 he published the *Dialogo degli errori della pittura*, dedicated to Cardinal *Farnese, a great patron of the arts. Embodying the attitude of the Council of *Trent with regard to art, G. criticized the display of nudity in pictures and demanded from the artist a strict adherence to biblical sources and Roman Catholic doctrines. His was the most important officially inspired reaction against what was considered as the profane qualities of *Mannerism.
F. Zeri, *Pittura e contrariforma* (1957);
A. Blant, *Artistic Theory in Italy 1450-1600* (1940), 103-136.

GIOCONDO, FRA GIOVANNI DEL (c. 1433-1515) Italian humanist and architect. Born in Verona, he became a Dominican friar and subsequently made his reputation both as an architect and a collector and publisher of manuscripts. He built the Palazzo del Consiglio in Verona, begun in 1476. About 1500 he discovered in Paris the correspondence of Trajan and Pliny the Younger and, in 1511, published in Rome the first illustrated edition of Vitruvius. G. also assembled ancient Roman inscriptions, published posthumously. In 1514 he was summoned to Rome to collaborate with *Raphael and Giuliano da *Sangallo on plans for *St. Peter's.

GIOLITO, GABRIELE (c. 1510-78) Italian printer. Born into a Venetian family of printers, he joined the business in 1536 and later opened printing shops in other cities, including Bologna and Naples. G. was famous for his friendship with leading Italian authors, and favoured the publication of vernacular literature, issuing many editions of the popular works of *Petrarch, *Boccaccio and *Ariosto. Late in his career the restrictive climate of the *Counter-Reformation caused him to change his orientation and he began to put out works on theology, too. His firm 'La Fenice' remained active until 1606.

GIORGIONE (Giorgio Barbarelli; 1477-1510) Venetian painter. G.'s reputation as a major artist contrasts with the dearth of information about his life and work. A student of Giovanni *Bellini, he left less than half a score of works, some of which were probably completed by *Titian. His great achievement was the creation of the atmospheric picture, a style of painting in which landscape, light, human figures and nature are blended together to evoke in the viewer a certain mood. His three great masterpieces are: *The Tempest, Fête Champêtre* and the *Sleeping Venus*. All three are superb examples of High Renaissance art in as much as they accomplish the secularization of feeling.
T. Pignatti, *Giorgione* (1971);
L. Baldass, *Giorgione* (1965);
M. Conway, *Giorgione: A New Study of His Art as a Landscape Painter* (1929).

GIOTTO (1266-1337) Italian artist; considered the father of Renaissance painting. G. was born in Florence where he is believed to have studied under *Cimabue. He was recognized as a great revolutionary of art by his contemporaries, and was mentioned with admiration by *Dante and *Boccaccio. In 1334 he was commissioned by Florence to erect the bell tower of the Cathedral, a

COMINCIA LA
DECIMA ET VLTIMA
GIORNATA DEL DECA
merone: nellaquale Sotto il regi
mento di Pamphilo si ra-
giona di chi
LIBERALMENTE O MAGNI-
ficamente operasse alcuna cosa.

GIORNATA DECIMA.

NCHORA *eran uermigli certi Nuolletti nell'occidente; essendo gia quegli dell'oriente nelle loro estremità simili ad oro lucentissimi diuenuti per gli solari raggi, che molto loro auicinandosi gli ferieno: quando Pamphilo leuatosi; le donne e' suoi compagni fece*
K K

A page from Boccaccio's Decameron, *published by Giolito in 1550*

project completed long after his death. G.'s major works are the fresco cycles in Assisi and in the Arena chapel in Padua; the first depicts scenes from the life of St. Francis, the second the life and Passion of Christ. G. broke away from the flat Byzantine style of his times. He introduced foreshortening and elements of *perspective, which lent his paintings a sense of spaciousness. Moreover, the human figures in his works radiated feeling and are related to each other in a dramatic context. His three-dimensioanl naturalism was achieved with the simplest means and economy of detail. Although he was highly praised, his genius was beyond the comprehension of his immediate followers. Not until *Masaccio, about a 100 years later, did Florentine painting return to the path first opened by G.

M. Baxandall, *Giotto and the Orators; Humanist Observers of Painting in Italy and the Discovery of Pictorial Composition, 1350-1450* (1971);
B. Cole, *Giotto and Florentine Painting, 1280-1375* (1976).

GIOVANNI DALMATA (c. 1440-c. 1509) The name given in Italy to the Dalmatian sculptor and architect Ivan Duknovic. He went to Italy in his youth and trained in several places, especially in Rome with *Bregno. Later he worked with *Mino da Fiesole on the tomb of *Paul II (1474), and executed the tomb of Cardinal Rovenella at the church of S. Clemente, Rome (1476-77). G. also designed parts of the Palazzo Venezia, Rome. From 1481 to 1490 he was in Hungary, working for King *Matthias Corvinus.

GIOVANNI DI PAOLO (1403-82) Italian painter. Born in *Siena, he spent his entire career in his native city, though he may have visited *Florence. Beside *Sassetta he is considered the leading Sienese 15th-century painter. His works display a feeling for fantasy, gracefulness and decoration, which represents a sharp contrast to his realistic Florentine contemporaries. Between 1450 and 1460 he painted a series of panels illustrating scenes from the life of John the Baptist, which are among his best surviving works. His style reflects a strong influence of the *International Gothic.

C. Brandi, *Giovanni di Paolo* (1947).

GIOVIO, PAOLO (1483-1552) Italian historian and collector. Born in Como, he studied medicine at Pavia and Padua, becoming the physician and the friend of many European statesmen and rulers. Both *Leo X and *Clement VIII were his patrons and the latter made him, in 1528, bishop of Nocera. In 1536 he left Rome and returned to Como, where he built a museum of artistic objects, antiques and rarities. His main work, *Historiarum sui temporis libri* (1550-52), dealt with the history of Italy after the French invasion of 1494. Before that he had published a historical treatise which dealt with the Ottoman Turks. He also wrote biographies. Though lacking in depth, his works contain much information on non-political themes.

GIRALDI CINTHIO, GIAMBATTISTA (1504-73) Italian author. Born in *Ferrara, he became, in 1525, professor of philosophy at the local university and, in 1537, was given the chair of literature. From 1542 to 1560 he served as secretary to the dukes of the ruling house of *Este, but fell out of favour and left his native city. He ended his career as a teacher of rhetoric in Pavia. G. wrote an important tragedy, *Orbecche* (1541), and eight other plays. He is, however, especially remembered as the author of two theoretical works on the moral intent of literature: *Intorno al comporre delle commedie e delle tragedie* (On the Composition of Comedies and Tragedies) (1543) and *Intorno al comporre dei romanzi* (On the Composition of Novels) (1548). G. recommeded staging horrible events, to evoke, in a Senecan manner, the innermost emotions of the spectator. His collection of 113 tales, entitled *Hecatommithi*, was first published in 1565, and enjoyed an ephemeral popularity.

P. R. Horne, *The Tragedies of Giraldi Cinthio* (1962).

GIROLAMO DA CARPI (1501-56) Italian painter and architect. A native of *Ferrara, his career was linked with the ruling house of *Este, for which he designed and decorated several villas and palaces. An eclectic *Mannerist though not without ability, his paintings show the influence of *Correggio and *Parmigianino. G. was also known as a portraitist. His architectural work is influenced by *Bramante and *Giulio Romano.

GIULIANO DA MAIANO (1432-90) Italian sculptor and architect. The older brother of *Benedetto da Maiano, he worked mainly in Tuscany, but ended his life in Naples (1484-90), where he served as architect to King Ferrante I. A follower of the style of *Brunelleschi, his best structures are the cathedral at Faenza, begun in 1474, and the Spannochi Palace at Siena. Much of his work was done in cooperation with his brother.

GIULIO ROMANO (1499-1546) Italian architect and painter. Born in Rome, he became the trusted pupil of *Raphael, whom he assisted in several works, mainly in the *Sala del Incendio* in the Vatican. After his master's death (1520), G. completed some of his works, and decorated with *frescoes the Villa Madama, a work commissioned by the future *Clement VII. In 1524 he had to leave Rome, having designed indecent prints, and went to *Mantua. Here he executed for Federigo *Gonazaga his most important work, combining architecture, painting and decoration, the Palazzo del Tè. This and other buildings of his in Mantua demonstrate his penchant for illusive effects, and overwhelm the viewer by their irregular proportions. His break with the harmonious vision of the High Renaissance makes him one of the first promoters of *Mannerism in *architecture. Also, his paintings show inventiveness and exuberance, as, for example, the *Sala dei Giganti* at the Palazzo del Tè and the scenes of the Trojan War at the ducal palace.

F. Hartt, *Giulio Romano*, 2 vols. (1958).

GIUSTINIANI An important Venetian family, to which belonged a number of statesmen, prelates, military commanders and authors. Lorenzo (1380-1456) was the first Patriarch of *Venice and wrote mystical tracts. His brother, Leonardo (1388-1446), wrote popular poems set to music and known as *Giustiniane*; Leonardo's son Bernardo (1408-89), wrote a Latin history of Venice. A Genoese family of the same name, but probably not related, became known at the end of the 16th century through its son Pompeo (1569-1616), a general who served in the Spanish army in the Netherlands, and later in Crete against the *Ottoman Turks.

GLAREANUS, HEINRICH (1488-1563) Swiss humanist and a theorist of *music. A native of the canton of Glarus, hence his name, he studied in Bern and *Cologne and, in 1512, was crowned poet-laureate by *Maxi-

The Fall of the Giants, *a fresco by Giulio Romano in Mantuas' Palazzo del Tè*

milian I. Following a short stay in France (1521), he founded a school in *Basle but, in 1529, left with *Erasmus for Freiburg, where he taught history, classical literature and music. For a time G. sympathized with the Reformation, but never broke with the Catholic Church. He was the author of a treatise on geography and a panegyric to Switzerland in verse, and edited the works of Livius, Boethius and others, adding his own commentaries. His most important work was the *Dodecachordon*, first published in Basle in 1547. This is a systematic exposition of his theory on the musical modes, which he expanded from 8 to 12. It enjoyed a great success and established the nomenclature in the subject.

H. Glareanus, *Dodecachordon*, translated by C. A. Miller, 2 vols. (1965).

GLOUCESTER, HUMPHREY, DUKE OF (1391-1447) English statesman. The fourth son of Henry IV (1399-1413), he was appointed by the dying *Henry V, his brother, regent during the minority of the infant *Henry VI (1422), but subsequently shared power with a council. Although generally popular, he made rash decisions with regard to foreign affairs and soon entered into a bitter quarrel with his uncle, Cardinal Henry *Beaufort. In 1426 this necessitated the intervention of his brother, the duke of *Bedford. After the latter's death (1435), G. was next in line of succession, but his warlike policies gave rise to a growing opposition. In 1441 he suffered a great humiliation when his second wife, Eleanor Cobham, was convicted of seeking to cause the death of the young king by *witchcraft. At Henry VI's coming of age (1442), G. lost all influence in the government. In 1447 he was accused of treason and arrested, but died before he could stand trial. G. was a great patron of learning. He collected classical manuscripts, which he bequeathed to Oxford, and encouraged contacts between English and Italian scholars.

K. H. Vickers, *Humphrey, Duke of Gloucester* (1907).

GODUNOV, BORIS (1551-1605) Tsar of Russia from 1598. The son of a family of Tartar origins, he entered the service of *Ivan the Terrible, and reached the highest rank of the nobility when his sister was chosen to wed the *tsarevich* Fyodor (1580). Upon the death of Ivan, G. was appointed one of the guardians to the young tsar (1584). Within a year he was the all-powerful regent of the kingdom, and crushed all the attempts of the great nobles to destroy him. As the real ruler of Russia for some two decades, he expanded the colonization of the south Volga region, building many fortresses to hold back the Tartars. He encouraged contacts with the West, allowing English merchants to come and trade, and permitted some activity of Protestant preachers. In 1595 he gained back from Sweden the areas that had been lost during the previous reign. When Fyodor died leaving no heirs, G. was elected tsar by an assembly of the nobility (21 February 1598). His reign was marred by his obsessive suspicions of possible attempts against

The Adoration, *from the Portinari Altarpiece by Hugo van der Goes*

his life, which led him to employ spies and to suppress potential rivals, especially the Romanovs, with whom he carried a long-standing feud. He died when the so called False *Dmitry was advancing into Russia from Poland.

S. F. Platonov, *Boris Godounov, tsar de Russie* (1929).

GOES, HUGO VAN DER (c. 1440-82) Flemish painter. Little is known of his early life. He became a member of the painters' guild of *Ghent in 1467. His major work is the *Portinari Altarpiece*, a painting showing the adoration of the newborn Christ by angels and peasants. It was commissioned by an agent of the *Medici bank, who sent it in 1475 to Florence, where it influenced such painters as *Ghirlandaio; the painting is now at the Uffizi in Florence. G. did decorative works for the wedding of *Charles the Bold and Margaret of York (1468), and for the funeral of *Philip the Good (1473). Then he entered a monastery as a lay brother, and continued to paint. A year before his death he suffered a mental collapse. His melancholy and religious intensity are clearly projected in the works attributed to him. He was considered the greatest Flemish painter of his time.

E. Panofsky, *Early Netherlandish Painting* (1953);
F. Winkler, *Das Werk von Hugo van der Goes* (1964).

GOÍS, DAMIÃO DE (1502-74) Portuguese humanist and historian. Educated at the court of *Manoel I, he was sent in 1523 as a Portuguese commercial representative to *Antwerp, and was later assigned to diplomatic posts at various European courts. G. became acquainted with some of the principal spiritual figures of the time, including Cardinal *Sadoleto, *Luther and *Erasmus, whom he visited in Freiburg in 1533-34. Of cosmopolitan nature and outlook, his first important work, *Fides, religio, moresque Aethiopum* (1540), dealt with Christianity in Ethiopia, on the basis of reports by Portuguese travellers; another work was devoted to the Portuguese in *India. In 1546 *John III appointed him royal archivist, and he began to work on his greatest book, *Cronica do felicíssimo rei dom Manoel*, which was published in four volumes (1566-67). A year later he published the shorter *Cronica do príncipe dom João*. These works dealt with the eventful period of Portuguese history at the turn of the 15th century, and displayed an objective and critical approach. During the last years of his life G. was harassed by the *Inquisition because of his friendship with Protestant leaders. He was arrested in 1571, but was released shortly before his death.

E. Hirsch, *Damião de Gois; The Life and Thought of a Portuguese Humanist* (1967).

GOLDEN FLEECE, ORDER OF THE An exclusive brotherhood of nobles created in 1430 by *Philip the Good, duke of Burgundy. Limited at first to 24 and then to 30 members, the order was an expression of the affection for chivalric tradition which characterized social life at the Burgundian court. Although preceded by the English Order of the Garter (founded in 1348), it was the Burgundian model which inspired similar versions in France, Denmark, Hungary and elsewhere. Dissolved by the death of *Charles the Bold, the order was restored in 1478 by *Maximilian of Austria, its members assuming for a time the role of mediators between the Archduke and his unruly subjects. In 1516 *Charles V extended the membership to Spanish nobles. After his death, both the Spanish and Austrian *Habsburgs claimed the right to award membership in the order.

GOLTZIUS, HENDRICK (1558-1617) Dutch engraver. Born in Utrecht, he lost the power of his right hand while still a baby, and learned to draw with the muscles of his arm and shoulder. G. was trained as an engraver by *Coornhert in Cleves. At Haarlem, where he did most of his work, he developed a style of line-engraving which to the modern eye appears like crude newspaper photographs. He was one of the last great masters of engraving who devised models for others to copy. Besides metalplate line-engravings he produced colour and chiaroscuro woodcuts.

O. Hirschmann, *Verzeichnis des graphischen Werks von Hendrick Goltzius*, 2nd ed. (1976).

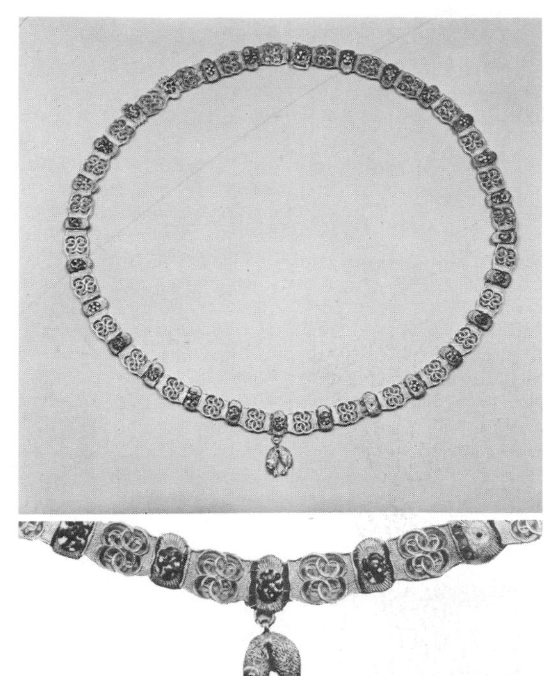

Chain of the Order of the Golden Fleece

Coloured woodcut by Goltzius

Hercules killing Cacus *by Goltzius*

GOMARA, FRANCISCO LOPEZ DE (c. 1511-65) Spanish humanist historian. He studied in Alcalá and Rome and in 1541, while on the expedition of *Charles V to *Algiers, met Hernán *Cortés, whose secretary and chaplain he became and remained until the latter's death in 1547. Between 1552 and 1554 he published the *Historia de las Indias*, a history of the Spanish conquest of America, in two parts, the second of which treated Cortés' campaign in Mexico. Despite the fact that G. never visited the New World his work became very popular, but the unreserved eulogies which he heaped on Cortés gave rise to criticism among veterans of the conquest and prompted Bernal *Díaz del Castillo to compose his *True History of the Conquest of Mexico*. G. also wrote a history of the reign of Charles V.

F. López de Gomara, *Cortés: The Life of the Conqueror of Mexico by his Secretary*, trans. by L. B. Simpson (1964).

GOMARISTS Followers of the Dutch Calvinist Francis Gomar, a professor of theology at the University of Leiden between 1594 and 1611, who held rigidly intolerant principles, in opposition to the more liberal ideas of *Arminius. The Synod of *Dort (1618-19) which condemned the Arminians, was a sort of victory for the G. However, in spite of Gomar's presence the synod did not affirm some of his more extreme views with regard to *predestination. Later he held a professorship at Groningen. His followers were also known as Contra-*Remonstrants.

GONÇALVES, NUNO Portuguese painter; active in the third quarter of the 15th century. His main work, the six-panelled St. Vincent altarpiece, shows identifiable Portuguese historical figures and reveals a strong influence of the Flemish school, especially that of *Bouts. Another altarpiece was destroyed by earthquake in 1755.

GONGORA Y ARGOTE, LUIS DE (1561-1627) Spanish poet. Born in Córdoba, he studied in Salamanca, then took minor orders and was made a prebendary of the cathedral of his native town. He first went to Madrid in 1609, and returned in 1617 as royal chaplain to *Philip III. He went back to Córdoba a year before his death. His early *romances*, or ballads, were in the Italianate style and his *letrillas*, or songs, displayed wit and humour. In the fifth decade of his life he began to cultivate the style that came to bear his name (*gongorismo*), and which influenced Spanish verse for the rest of the 17th century. This was a deliberately artistic poetry, addressing itself to a narrow intellectual audience, with a classical Latin vocabulary and mythological imagery. His best known works in this grand manner are: *Fábula de Polifemo y Galatea* (1612-13) and the *Soledades* (1612-17).

P. Darmangeat, *Gongora* (1964);

F. Lázaro Carreter, *Estilo barroco y personalidad creadora* (1966).

GONZAGA An Italian political family which, from the beginning of the 14th century, was identified with the

Ludovico Gonzaga and His Family, *a fresco by Mantegna*

town of *Mantua. The early G.'s were satisfied with the military title of *capitano generarle* but Francesco G., who allied Mantua with *Venice against *Milan, obtained from the Emperor in 1408 the title of marquis. The G.'s consolidated their rule in the 15th century, by means of astute politcal moves and matrimonial alliances. Federico G., who ruled between 1519 and 1540, was in 1530 given the title of duke by *Charles V. In the latter part of the 16th century the G. pursued a pro-Spanish policy.
M. Bellonci, *Segreti dei Gonzaga* (1971);
S. Brinton, *The Gonzaga* (1927).

GONZAGA, ERCOLE (1505-63) Italian cadinal. The second son of Francesco *Gonzaga and Isabella d'*Este, he was made bishop at 16, and studied at Bologna (1521-25) before being created cardinal in 1527. From 1540 on he acted as regent of *Mantua, governing it on behalf of his young nephews, Francesco (1540-50) and – later – Guglielmo (1550-87). An able administrator he contributed to Mantua's economic prosperity. In 1561 he presided over the Council of *Trent.

GONZAGA, FEDERICO II (1500-40) Ruler of *Mantua. The son of Francesco Gonzaga and Isabella d'*Este, he succeeded his father in 1519. He served at the beginning as commander of the papal armies, but soon adopted a policy in support of *Charles V. As a result, he was able to extend his territories and, in 1530, was given the title of duke. A great patron of the arts, G. is remembered as the builder of the Palazzo del Tè, designed by *Giulio Romano.

GONZAGA, FRANCESCO (1466-1519) Ruler of *Mantua. The son of Federico I Gonzaga (1442-84), he succeeded his father at 18 and in 1490 married Isabella d'*Este. In 1495 he commanded the Italian army which fought the French at Fornovo, but later allied himself with *Louis XII of France and took part in the Battle of Agnadello against *Venice (1509). Shortly afterwards, he was taken prisoner by the Venetians; after his release went into semi-retirement, leaving his wife in position of influence in the government of Mantua.

GONZAGA, GIANFRANCESCO (1395-1444) Ruler of *Mantua. The son of Francesco Gonzaga, the first marquis, he succeeded to the title in 1407 and, in 1413, assumed control of the government. G. was the rival, first of *Venice, then of Filippo Maria *Visconti of Milan. He later allied himself with Venice, commanding the Repuplic's army, but in his last years fought against her again. In 1433 he had his title of marquis confirmed by Emperor *Sigismund. G. brought to his court the educator *Vittorino da Feltre (1423) and supported his famous school.

GONZAGA, GIULIA (1513-66) Italian noblewoman, a patroness of unorthodox Italian reformers. Famous for her beauty and intelligence, she was widowed in 1528, after one year of marriage, remaining in possession of the small principality of Fondi. Many Italian literati and artists visited the place, making her the subject of their works. The legends surrounding her personality moved the Turkish admiral, Khair-ed-Din *Barbarossa, to attempt her kidnapping in 1534, so as to send her to *Suleiman I. In 1533 she retired to a convent near Naples. She had previously been associated with persons such as Vittoria *Colonna, *Valdes and *Carnesecchi, and in Naples became deeply involved in the crypto-movement of Catholic reform. Suspected of heresy by the *Inquisition, she refused to go into hiding, but died in her convent before she was apprehended.

GONZAGA, LUDOVICO (1414-78) Ruler of *Mantua. The son of Gianfrancesco Gonzaga, he was educated by *Vittorino da Feltre and in 1443 married Barbara of Brandenburg, the niece of Emperor *Sigismund. Succeeding his father in 1444, he spent the first ten years of his government chiefly in fighting against Venice, but after the Peace of *Lodi (1454) settled to a long and comparatively peaceful rule. G. was a great patron of the arts, who engaged *Mantegna to work for him, and erected churches designed by *Alberti. Among the humanists who filled his court were *Filelfo and *Platina.

GOTHA, LEAGUE OF The first coalition of German Protestant princes, formed in February 1526, known also as the League of Torgau after the town where the alliance was concluded. The moving spirit of this coalition was the young *Philip of Hesse, and it included electoral *Saxony, Magdeburg and Prussia. In view of *Charles V's recent victories in Italy, and the fact that the overwhelming majority of the German princes were still Roman Catholic, the G. was a bold step.

GOUDIMEL, CLAUDE (1505-72) French *Huguenot musician. He studied music in Rome, where for a time he sang in the papal chapel. His religious views changed later, and, in 1564, he arranged melodies for the French psalter of *Marot and *Beza. G.'s influence on the development of Protestant music went beyond the boundaries of France. He was killed at Lyons during the *St. Bartholomew massacre.

GOUJON, JEAN (c. 1510-1564) French sculptor. Born in Normandy, he executed some works in Rouen (1540-

Diana *by Goujon*

42), before going to Paris and joining the architect *Lescot. Among the works on which they collaborated were the Hôtel Carnavalet, where G. created four allegorical figures representing the *Seasons* (1547), and the *Fountain of the Innocents*, commissioned by Lescot in 1549, with its graceful undulating bodies of the *Nymphs*. About that time, G. also began to execute bas-reliefs and other works at the Louvre, where he produced the *Caryatids* (1550-51), a group of statues representing young girls in Grecian style. He left Paris and disappeared in 1562 at the outbreak of the *Religious Wars. G. is considered the major Renaissance sculptor in France. In 1547 he engraved the plates for the first French translation of Vitruvius.

P. du Colombier, *Jean Goujon* (1949).

GOWER, GEORGE (c. 1540-1596) English painter. The son of an old family of Yorkshire, he was appointed painter to Queen *Elizabeth I (1581), with the exclusive right of painting her portraits. He also worked on the decorations of the royal palaces, but only one of his works survives, a self-portrait dated 1579; other paintings are ascribed to him on grounds of stylistic affinity.

GOWER, JOHN (c. 1330-1408) English poet. Born into a Kentish family, he was a landowner in Suffolk and Norfolk and lived for some time in London. G. was acquainted with *Chaucer, who mentioned him in his *Troilus and Criseyde*. In 1398 he married Agnes Groundolf, though probably it was not his first marriage. G.'s work consist of an English poem, *In Praise of Peace*; a long poem in French, *Mirour de l'Omme*; the Latin *Vox clamantis*, a social satire dealing with the peasants' revolt of 1381; and his major poem in English, *Confessio amantis*. This is a collection of stories from different sources, told as the confessions of a lover. Though lacking Chaucer's genius, G.'s work was long considered a classic. It is indeed the product of a gifted mind, but suffers from unnecessary digressions.

J. H. Fisher, *John Gower; Moral Philosopher and Friend of Chaucer* (1965).

GOZZOLI, BENOZZO (1420-98) Italian painter. Born in Florence, he is first mentioned in 1444 as an assistant of *Ghiberti. In 1447 he went to work for Fra *Angelico but, in 1449, began to paint for himself, though still under the influence of Fra Angelico. His best *fresco was executed in 1459, at the chapel of the Medici-Ricardi Palace in Florence. Entitled *The Journey of the Magi*, it has a completely secular outlook and depicts members of the *Medici family. Basically a late follower of the *International Gothic style, G.'s frescoes exude charm and grace. He later worked in San Gemignano and Pisa.

A. Padoa Rizzo, *Benozzo Gozzoli, pittore fiorentino* (1972).

GRAF, URS (c. 1485-1527) Swiss goldsmith, engraver and mercenary soldier. A native of *Basle, where much of his artistic career was made, G. repeatedly enlisted as a soldier; he took part in the Battle of *Marignano (1515). He worked for the printers *Amerbach and *Froben, producing hundreds of book illustrations. His best known are white-line woodcuts containing powerful, aggrandized images of **Landsknechte*.

W. Lüthi, *Urs Graf und die Kunst der alten Schweitzer* (1928).

GRAFTON, RICHARD (?-1572) English printer. A London merchant who became an ardent Protestant, he joined in 1536 with Edward Whitechurch (died 1562) to print at *Antwerp *Coverdale's translation of the *Bible. This led to a permission by Thomas *Cromwell to print the Great Bible, a venture that he began in Paris but had to complete in London (1539). In 1542 he was given the right to print the prayer books of the *Church of England and, in 1549 and 1552, published the first and second *Books of *Common Prayer*. In 1553, having published a proclamation on behalf of Lady Jane *Grey, he lost his position as royal printer.

J. A. Kingdon, *Richard Grafton* (1901).

GRANADA, CONQUEST OF THE KINGDOM OF (2 January 1492) The Spanish **reconquista*, which had

The Mourned Christ, *relief in marble by Jean Goujon*

come to a halt in the early part of the 15th century, resumed its crusading character after the fall of *Constantinople in 1453. However, it was only under *Ferdinand and *Isabella that the victory over the last Moorish kingdom was accomplished. The campaign, conducted as a series of siege operations, began in 1482, and the Spanish took advantage of internal feuds in the Moorish camp to seize one strategic stronghold after another in that mountainous region. The terms of surrender gave the Moors the right to retain their property and religion and a measure of autonomy, but after 1499 the Spanish crown decided on a policy of forcible conversion, which led to Moorish resistance. In 1502 all the unconverted Moors were expelled from Spain by royal decree, thus giving rise to the problem of the *Moriscos.

GRANADA, LUIS DE See LUIS DE GRANADA.

GRANJON, ROBERT French printer and designer of type. Born in Paris, he was first active there but, in 1556, moved to *Lyons where he designed characters for the printing of *music. He then spent some time in Rome, experimenting with the type of oriental letters, and later worked on Greek typeface in Paris. G. also tried to create a new type, called Civilité, to be used by all French printers, but it won a limited acceptance. Essentially a follower of *Garamond, whose typeface he perfected, G.'s work was widely admired by his contemporaries, especially his type ornaments.

GRANNACCI, FRANCESCO (1477-1543) Italian painter. Born in Florence, he studied together with *Michelangelo at the studio of Domenico *Ghirlandaio. His works, which are mainly in Florence, reflect the styles of the great masters of the High Renaissance. He is remembered chiefly for his friendship with Michelangelo.

GRANVELLE, ANTOINE PERRENOT DE (1517-86) Statesman and administrator in the service of *Philip II. His father, who was of Flemish descent, served *Charles V in responsible government posts. He prepared his son for the same tasks, but also took care to endow him with ecclesiastical benefices. In 1560 he was assigned to his most important position as counsellor to *Margaret of Parma, regent of the Netherlands and, in 1561, was created a cardinal. However, he soon found that his notions of royal absolutism were not acceptable to the nobles of the Netherlands and, in 1564, he had to leave. He continued nevertheless to serve Philip as viceroy of Naples (1571-75), and after 1579 as a royal counsellor in Spain. G. advocated a hard policy towards the rebels in the Netherlands and was detested in the Protestant countries.

M. van Durme, *Antoon Perrenot van Granvelle* (1953).

GRASSER, ERASMUS (c. 1450-1518) German sculptor. A native of Bavaria, where he spent most of his life, he is known primarily for his *Moorish Dancers*, a group of small grotesque individual figures carved in wood. They were made for Munich's Town Hall and reflect a style which follows the Gothic tradition, though with some Italian influence.

P. M. Halm, *Erasmus Grasser* (1928).

GRAZZINI, ANTON FRANCESCO (1503-84) Italian playwright and poet also known as Il Lasca. Born in Florence, he was an apothecary, and also took part in city's literary life. He was among the founders of the *Accademia della Crusca*. His best work is *Le Cene* (1558), a collection of short stories told in a vivid language. He wrote several comedies which are characterized by his delight in intrigue, and composed poems ranging from the lyrical to the burlesque.

The Flag Carrier *by Urs Graf*

G. D. Bonino, ed., *Opere di Anton Francesco Grazzini* (1974).

GREAT SCHISM (1378-1417) A period of almost four decades in which the papacy and the entire Western Church were divided between a Roman line and an Avignonese line of popes. The schism followed seventy years of papal residence in Avignon (the so called Babylonian captivity), and also reflected European political antagonisms. Only at the Council of *Constance and the unanimous election of *Martin V (1417), was unity restored.

J. B. Morrall, *Gerson and the Great Schism* (1960);
W. Ullmann, *The Origins of the Great Schism* (1948).

GREBEL, CONRAD (c. 1498-1526) Swiss *Anabaptist leader. The son of a patrician family in *Zurich, he was given a humanist education in Vienna and Paris. When he returned to Zurich in 1520, he was caught by the religious excitement and became a follower of *Zwingli. By 1523 G. had rebelled against both his family and his religious mentor. He married a woman of humble origins and led a small group of followers who argued against infant baptism, favouring the biblical manner of adult, or believer's baptism. On 21 January 1525, he performed the first ceremony of rebaptism in Zurich, administered to *Blaurock at the home of *Manz. Banished with his friends from Zurich, he died of the plague the following year.

H. S. Bender, *Conrad Grebel* (1950).

El Greco's self-portrait as John the Evangelist

GRECO, EL (Domenikos Theotokopoulos; 1541-1614) Spanish painter. Born in the Venetian colony of Crete and probably trained in Byzantine icon painting, he eventually reached Venice, where he met the aged *Titian. In 1570 he went to Rome where he executed works for Cardinal *Farnese. Nevertheless, in 1577, concluding that his foreign origins barred him from being properly appreciated in Italy, G. decided to go to Spain. He settled permanently in Toledo, the city with which he became identified, and was soon given a number of important commissions. Between 1577 and 1579 he painted three altars in the church of San Domingo el Antiguo, *El Espolio* (*Disrobing of Christ*) in the Toledo cathedral and a work for the chapter house of the *Escorial. These led to a commission for a large painting for *Philip II. But the resulting *Martyrdom of S. Maurice and the Theban Legion* (1582) was disliked by the King for its distortive *Mannerism and eerie colour, and the painter never succeeded in making his work acceptable to the royal court. He had, however, other admirers and, in 1588, completed what is probably his best known picture, the *Burial of Count Orgaz*, at the church of San Tomé, Toledo. G. also painted many portraits, as well as secular subjects and landscapes such as his famous *View of Toledo* (1610). But the religious feeling, intense emotionalism and a visionary mood pervade almost all his works. His elongated human figures, which suggest devotion and self-mortification, and his heightened scale of contrasting colours combine to produce an air of mystical intent. Standing at the threshold of the *Baroque, this naturalized Greek was the first great Spanish painter.

L. Goldscheider, *El Greco*, 2nd ed. (1949);
P. Keleman, *El Greco revisited; Candia, Venice, Toledo* (1961);
H. E. Wethey, *El Greco and His School*, 2 vols. (1962).

GREEK, THE STUDY OF Although knowledge of the classical *Greek authors never quite died out in the Middle Ages, it was sustained almost entirely by translations, as for example Aristotle, the principal ancient source of mediaeval scholasticism. The revival of the learning of Greek began in Italy in the second half of the 14th century. *Petrarch, who was the first to show interest in it, probably never fulfilled his ambition to read Homer and Plato in the original, but *Boccaccio made better progress and even established a lectureship in Greek in Florence for his friend Leontius Pilatus (1360-63). That city, where a number of famous Byzantine scholars who had come West taught, remained a centre during the 15th century. The study of Greek authors was flourishing long before the fall of *Constantinople, which brought reinforcements of eastern scholars to the West. By the time the Byzantine empire fell, *Filelfo and Leonardo *Bruni had already completed their translations of Plato, and *Nicholas V, a Florentine and founder of the papal manuscript collection, had entrusted a number of eastern and Italian scholars with the translation of other Greek authors. *Vittorino da Feltre (1378-1446), who for the last 20 years of his life directed a school for the *Gonzaga children in *Mantua, taught Homer, Herodotus, Xenophon and others there.

The introduction of printing to Italy made possible the publication of the most important Greek texts, starting with an edition of Homer in Florence in 1488, edited by Demetrius *Chalcondylas. But it was Aldus *Manutius who became the foremost printer of Greek authors. Between 1494 and 1515 he published about 30 *editiones principes* of such authors as Aristophanes, Thucydides, Sophocles, Theophrastus and Euripides. Robert *Estienne was another outstanding printer of Greek writings and, between 1544 and 1550, published Eusebius, as well as several editions of the Greek New Testament. His son, Henri *Estienne, compiled the important *Thesaurus linguae Graecae*.

In the late 15th century the study of Greek spread outside Italy. *Linacre and *Grocyn introduced it to England, *Budé, who was a student of *Lascaris, promoted it in France, and Rudolf *Agricola carried it from Italy to Germany. *Erasmus, the greatest humanist of the age, particularly encouraged the study of Greek and, in 1516, brought out the first edition of the Greek New Testament ever published. A tradition of Greek erudition was thus formed. During the latter part of the 16th century it was carried on by many European universities, of which Leiden, where *Scaliger was active (1593-1609), is an outstanding example. By that time G. had become part of the curriculum for European youth of both the Roman Catholic and the Protestant countries of the Continent. In English grammar schools, the German gymnasium or *Jesuit educational establishments, the student was expected to learn Greek, although less intensively than *Latin. The educational status and mandatory character which the study of Greek attained in the 16th century continued for about 300 years.

J. E. Sandys, *A History of Classical Scholarship*, vol. 2 (1908);

H. T. Peck, *A History of Classical Philology* (1911);
R. Pfeiffer, *History of Classical Scholarship* (1976).

GREENE, ROBERT (1558-92) English poet, dramatist and prose writer. Educated at both Oxford and Cambridge, he travelled – according to his own somewhat inconsistent account – in France and Italy, and about 1585 settled in London to a life of frivolous pleasures. His output during the brief period before his premature death was impressive, including almost 40 published works. Most of them did not endure past his own age. Of his prose romances, *Pandosto, the Triumph of Time* (1588), provided *Shakespeare with the story on which he based *The Winter's Tale*; G., moreover, was the first to refer to Shakespeare explicitly; he called him "an upstart crow, beautified with our feathers". Of his plays, *Alphonsus, King of Aragon* (1588) and *Friar Bacon and Friar Bungay* (1591), were inspired by *Marlowe. Of greater interest are his prose repentence pamphlets, wich contain many autobiographical details and references to the social milieu in which he lived. The best known of these is *A Groatsworth of Wit Bought with a Million of Repentance* (1592).

E. J. Castle, *Shakespeare, Bacon, Jonson and Greene; A Study* (1897, rep. 1970).

GREENWOOD, JOHN (c. 1562-93) English *Puritan leader. A graduate of Corpus Christi College, Cambridge (1581), he became clergyman of the *Church of England, but in 1586 was arrested for organizing a separatist community in London. Released after four years, he was apprehended again in 1592 and condemned to death with his friend Henry *Barrow for publishing seditious literature. The two were hanged together.

GREGORY XII (c. 1325-1417) Pope from 1406 to 1415. Born Angelo Correr in Venice, he became bishop of Castello in 1380 and, ten years later, was named Latin patriarch of Constantinople. Elected pope in 1406, he promised to resign if the schismatic antipope of Avignon would do so too, thus clearing the way for the election of a single pope by both Roman and Avignon cardinals. His final resignation, however, did not come until 1415, following many fluctuations which saw him deposed by the Council of Pisa (1409) and reinstated by the Council of *Constance. His resignation made possible the election of *Martin V, and brought an end to the *Great Schism.

GREGORY XIII (1502-85) Pope from 1572. Born Ugo Buoncompagni in Bologna, he studied and taught law at the famous university of his native city. In 1539 he went to Rome entering the service of *Paul III as a legal expert. He was ordained priest and attached himself to the *Carafa family, but escaped the consequences of their downfall following the death of *Paul IV. After the Council of *Trent in which he had taken part, *Pius IV made him cardinal (1563). In 1572 he was elected to succeed *Pius V, his candidacy being favoured by *Philip II. During his pontificate efforts were made to win back areas which had been lost to Protestantism, but with little result. His moves against *Elizabeth I and his attempts to renew the fight against the Turks were also largely unsuccessful. However, he fared better with regard to internal reforms in the Church, founding many religious schools, which were entrusted to his favoured order, the *Jesuits, and encouraging missionary work, particularly in Asia. His name is linked with the calendar reform, which took place in 1582: a commission of scientists, appointed by him, corrected the error of ten days, which had accumulated on the Julian calendar, and introduced a system to prevent the recurrence of new errors. The Gregorian calendar was immediately adopted in Catholic countries and gradually gained a universal status. G. also issued an amended edition of the Canon law, and spent vast sums on architecture and on the beautification of Rome. His heavy taxation and pressure on the lesser nobility of the *Papal States led to the spreading of banditry, which was suppressed only after his death.

GREGORY XIV (1535-91) Pope from December 1590. Born Nicolo Sfondrati, to a noble family from Cremona, his brief pontificacy was characterized by his support of *Philip II which had contributed to his election, and by his backing of the *Guises against *Henry IV in France.

GRENVILLE, RICHARD (1542-91) English privateer; one of the outstanding sailors of the age of *Drake and *Hawkins. In 1585 he went to the West Indies to harrass Spanish shipping, also taking with him 100 colonists, whom he landed, according to the instruction of Walter *Raleigh, in Roanoke Island near the coast of present-day North Carolina. In 1588 he was among the English commanders who defeated the *Armada and, in 1591, sailed as second-in-command on an expedition to the Azores, where his squadron waited for the returning Spanish treasure fleet (*flota*). Having been warned that the Spaniards were accompanied by a greatly superior force, the commander-in-chief, Lord Thomas Howard, got away with most of the English fleet, but G. was surrounded and killed after a fierce battle.

A. L. Rowse, *Sir Richard Grenville of the Revenge* (1940).

GRESHAM, SIR THOMAS (1518-79) English financier, merchant and royal supplier. The son of a lord mayor of London, his association with the court began in 1551, when he negotiated loans for *Edward VI. *Mary Tudor and *Elizabeth I continued to employ him, mainly as financial agent in *Antwerp. G. paid and renewed the loans of the English crown with such skill that his credit was better than that of *Philip II, the ruler of the Netherlands. In 1566 he founded the Royal Exchange, which was opened by the Queen herself in 1571, as the official location of financial transactions. His name is associated with the "Gresham's Law", the assumption that bad money drives good money out of circulation; this phenomenon, however, was also commented on by others at the time. But G. had bold ideas regarding the possible manipulation of the rate of exchange, which were in advance of his age. A prominent member of the *Merchant Adventurers Company, he was one of the wealthiest persons in England and contributed funds for education.

R. A. de Roover, *Gresham on Foreign Exchange* (1949);
F. R. Salter, *Sir Thomas Gresham* (1925).

GREVIN, JACQUES (1538-70) French dramatist and poet. In the years 1560-61 this young author wrote two comedies, a collection of love poems, entitled *L'Olympe*, and a tragedy, *César*, which he claimed to be the first in the French language, dismissing *Jodelle's *Cléopâtre* which had not yet been published. Over this he quarelled with *Ronsard. At about the same time he became a *Protestant, and subsequently went into exile in Turin, where he died.

E. S. Ginsberg, ed., *César* (1971).

GREY, LADY JANE (1537-54) Queen of England for nine days. A great niece of *Henry VIII, she was educated by Roger *Ascham and was reputed to be fluent in Hebrew, Greek and Latin. When the health of *Edward VI began to fail, the duke of *Northumberland resolved to have her succeed as queen, as a way of retaining his control of the government. He, therefore, married her to his son and persuaded the dying king to name her as his heir, disregarding his older pro-Catholic sister *Mary. Proclaimed queen by the duke in July 1553, she was arrested shortly afterwards, when Mary captured the government with overwhelming popular support. Committed to the Tower of London, she and her husband were executed in the following year.

GREY, WILLIAM (?-1478) English prelate. Born into a noble family, he was educated at Oxford, and then went to *Cologne to study theology. About 1442 he went to Italy, visiting several cities and attending the classes of *Guarino da Verona, at Ferrara. He remained in Italy for over 12 years returning after his nomination as bishop of Ely by Pope *Nicholas V in 1454. Thoroughly familiar with Italian humanism, G. brought with him to England a valuable collection of books. Many of these he gave to Balliol College, Oxford, where they formed the nucleus of a library. He took part in politics, trying to moderate between the various *Yorkist factions during the War of the *Roses. In 1469 he became high treasurer, a post he held for one year.

GRIFFO, FRANCESCO Italian designer of type. Born in Bologna, G. made his reputation during the last decade of the 15th century as the chief typefounder of Aldus *Manutius. He produced excellent models of roman founts, such as those designed for Francesco *Colonna's *Hypnerotomachia Poliphili* (1499). But his main achievement was the invention of italics, the type based on the cursive of the papal chancery, which Manutius used for his cheap and compact editions of classical authors.

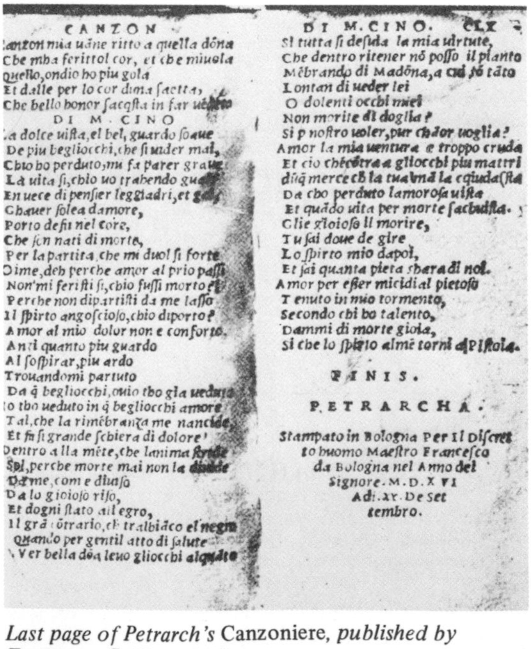

CANZON
Canzon mia uāne ritto a quella dōna
Che mha ferittol cor, et che miuola
Quello, ondio ho piu gola
Et dalle per lo cor dma saetta,
Che bello honor sacqsta in far uēdetta
DI M. CINO
La dolce uista, el bel, guardo soaue
De piu begliocchi, che si uider mai,
Chio ho perduto, mi fa parer graue
La uita si, chio uo trahendo guai
En uece di pensier leggiadri, et gai
Ghauer solea damore,
Porto desii nel core,
Che son nati di morte,
Per la partita, che mi duol si forte
Oime, deh perche amor al prio passo
Non mi feristi si, chio fussi morto
Perche non dipartisti da me lasso
Il spirto angoscioso, chio diporto?
Amor al mio dolor non e conforto.
Anzi quanto piu guardo
Al sospirar, piu ardo
Trouandomi partuto
Da q̄ begliocchi, ouio tho gia ueduto
Io tho ueduto in q̄ begliocchi amore
Tal, che la rimēbranza me nancide,
Et fu si grande schiera di dolore
Dentro alla mēte, che lanima sentie
Sol, perche morte mai non la diuide
Da me, com e diuiso
Da lo gioioso riso,
Et dogni stato allegro,
Il grā cōtrario, ch tral biāco el negro
Quando per gentil atto di salute
Ver bella dōa leuo gliocchi alquāto

DI M. CINO. CLX
Si tutta si desuia la mia uirtute,
Che dentro ritener nō posso il pianto
Mēbrando di Madōna, a cui sō tāto
Lontan di ueder lei
O dolenti occhi miei
Non morite di doglia?
Si p nostro uoler, pur chador uoglia?
Amor la mia uentura e troppo cruda
Et cio chēcōtra a gliocchi piu mattri
dūq mercē ch la tua lmā la cōiudastra
Da cho perduto lamorosa uista
Et quādo uita per morte sacquista.
Glie gioioso il morire,
Tu sai doue de gire
Lo spirto mio dapoi,
Et sai quanta pieta shara di noi.
Amor per esser micidial pietoso
Tenuto in mio tormento,
Secondo chi ho talento,
Dammi di morte gioia,
Si che lo spirto almē torni a Pistoia.

FINIS.

PETRARCHA.

Stampato in Bologna Per Il Discret
to huomo Maestro Francesco
da Bologna nel Anno del
Signore. M. D. X VI
Adi. xx. De Set
tembro.

Last page of Petrarch's Canzoniere, *published by Francesco Griffo (1516)*

GRIJALVA, JUAN DE (c. 1480-1527) Spanish explorer. Born in Cuellar near Segovia, G. participated in 1511 in the conquest of Cuba under Diego *Velázquez. In 1518 he took charge of an expedition to Yucatán, exploring also the coasts of Mexico, and established the first contact with the Aztec empire. However, his excessive cautiousness led Velázquez to replace him and to put *Cortés at the head of a second expedition to Mexico (1519). He was killed in Nicaragua by rebelling Indians.

GRIMALDI A noble Genoese family which furnished that city with many political and military personalities. The rise of the family began during the 12th century. It first accumulated wealth through trade, then went into banking. During the 15th century one branch of the family took power in the principality of Monaco, where its descendants still govern. The G.s also distinguished themselves as benefactors of their city.

GRINDAL, EDMUND (1519-83) Archbishop of Canterbury. Educated at Cambridge, he became a chaplain to *Edward VI, but after the king's death fled to the Continent, returning only with the accession of *Elizabeth I. Although his views were far more radical than those of the Anglican hierarchy, he was made bishop of London and, in 1570, archbishop of York. In 1575 he succeeded *Parker as archbishop of Canterbury. However, his time in office was marred by a suspension of his jurisdiction for five years (1577-82), as a result of his leniency towards the *Puritans and his strained relations with the Queen.

GRINGORE, PIERRE (c. 1475-c. 1539) French actor, poet and satirist. Famous during his life, his wanderings left some uncertainties about his biography. As a poet he belonged to the school of the **rhétoriqueurs*, but he was more popular as an actor and playwright, and was considered the best author of the **soties*, the French topical farces. G. managed the theatre society of the *Enfants Sans Souci* and acted in the political satire which he wrote himself, *Jeu du Prince des Sots* (1511), a scathing attack on Pope *Julius II. A protegé of Louis XII, he left Paris after the accession of King *Francis I.

R. L. Frautschi, ed., *Pierre Gringore's 'Les fantasies de Mère Sote'* (1962).

GROCYN, WILLIAM (c. 1446-1519) English humanist scholar. Educated at New College, Oxford, of which he became a fellow in 1467, he continued to teach at Oxford until he was over 40 years old. He then went to Italy and studied Greek under *Politian and *Chalcondylas (1488-90). After his return to Oxford he became known as the foremost English classical scholar, and counted *Colet, *Erasmus and *More among his students. In 1496 he left Oxford for London. G. was a lifelong friend of *Linacre.

R. Weiss, *Humanism in England during the Fifteenth Century* (1957).

GROLIER DE SERVIERES, JEAN (1479-1565) French statesman and bibliophile. Born at *Lyons into a family of Italian origin, he entered the service of the King, becoming under *Francis I treasurer general of France (1537). Previously, during his service in Italy, G. had begun to collect books with exquisite bindings, many of which were made under his own direction. He became

the best-known bibliophile of his day. Some 400 of his richly-ornamented volumes have survived.
British Museum, London, *Bookbindings from the Library of Jean Grolier* (1965).

GROOTE, GEERT DE (1340-84) Dutch mystic and religious leader. Born in Deventer, he studied in Paris and later taught at the University of Cologne. In 1374 he underwent a spiritual crisis and retired for three years of ascetic life in a monastery. In 1379 he began to preach, gathering around him a number of followers with whom he established in Deventer the first community of the *Brethren of the Common Life. His work was carried on by his pupil, Florentius *Radewyns.
T. P. Van Zijl, *Gerard Groote; Ascetic and Reformer* (1963).

GROPPER, JOHANN (1503-59) German Roman Catholic theologian. As an assistant to the archbishop of *Cologne, Hermann von *Wied, G. became known first for his efforts to reach a theological understanding with the Protestant reformers, and later for his uncompromising opposition to them. In 1538, he published the *Enchiridion*, which contained an exposition of fundamental Catholic doctrines, and on this basis negotiated with *Bucer. Active in almost all the religious controversies which took place in Germany under *Charles V, he refused to follow his archbishop's inclination towards Protestant views and, in 1546, contributed to his deposition. In 1555 *Paul IV offered to make him cardinal, but he declined.

GROTIUS, HUGO (Huig van Groot; 1583-1645) Dutch statesman, jurist and theologian. The son of a prominent family of Delft, he was educated at the university of Leiden under *Scaliger, and at a very early age joined the staff of *Oldenbarneveldt, the person in charge of the foreign policy of the *United Provinces. Appointed Advocate-General of *Holland and Zeeland (1607), he was sent as envoy to England in 1613 and, upon his return, was made Pensionary of Rotterdam. In the meantime, G. had published theological tracts in support of the *Arminians. This and his continued association with Oldenbarneveldt led to his arrest in 1618, when the Arminian party was crushed by *Maurice of Nassau and the Synod of *Dort. Sentenced to life imprisonment, he made his escape in 1620 with the aid of his wife, and settled in Paris. In 1622 he wrote his chief theological work, *De veritate religionis Christianae*, in which he attempted to demonstrate that the natural order of man's life conformed to the teachings of Christ. His great work on international law, *De jure belli ac pacis*, was first published in Paris in 1625. Although resting in some respects on traditional grounds, it ushered in the concept of the Law of Nature, an idea which, as defined by G., became a fundamental proposition of the social and political thought of the 17th century.

In 1631 G. returned to Holland, but was soon banished and moved to Germany. In 1635 he became the envoy of Queen Christina of Sweden to the French court. During the next ten years he was mainly concerned with the problems of achieving Christian reunion. G. also wrote biblical exegesis, edited and translated classical texts, wrote poetry and two Latin tragedies. One of the few great intellectuals of the transition from the Renaissance to the Enlightenment, he contributed to both and belonged to either. He died in Rostock, on his way from Sweden to France.
H. Vreeland, *Hugo Grotius* (1917);
W. S. M. Knight, *The Life and Works of Hugo Grotius* (1925).

GRÜNEWALD, MATHIAS (c. 1475-1528) German painter. There are scant biographical data about G., and few of his paintings survived. From 1508 on he was working for Archbishop Albert of Mainz. Later he lived in Frankfurt and in Halle, where he died. His best known painting is the Altarpiece of Isenheim, now at the nearby Colmar museum. It covers 11 panels and portrays the Crucifixion in a manner that makes the viewer shudder in awe. The most moving detail in G.'s tormented figure on the cross are Christ's upturned fingers; St. John is standing on the right, pointing to the cross. G.'s other paintings are also distinguished by their intensity and violence, occasionally bordering on the macabre. But although his tortured world appears very different from the serenity and harmony of most High Renaissance painters, G. has more in common with the technique and outlook of his age than may be surmised at first glance.
E. Ruhmer, *Grünewald: Drawings* (1970);
L. Nochlin, *Mathis at Colmar: A Visual Confrontation* (1973);
G. Scheja, *The Isenheim Altarpiece* (1969).

GRUTER, JANUS (1560-1627) English classical scholar. The son of an English mother and a Flemish father, he received his education at Cambridge and Leiden, but most of his teaching career was at Heidelberg. G. supervised numerous editions of classical Latin authors, including Tacitus, Cicero and Livy. His most important work was a collection of ancient inscriptions.

GUARDATI, TOMMASO (c. 1420-c. 1480) Italian author, known also as Masuccio Salernitano. Born at Salerno, he spent many years at the court of Naples, where he wrote *Il Novellino* (1476), a collection of 50 short stories. Some of these are licentious and satirical in the manner of *Boccaccio's *Decameron*. His tale of Mariotto and Gianozza is similar to *Bandello's Romeo and Juliet.
G. Petrocchi, *Masuccio Guardati e la narrativa napoletana del quattrocento* (1953).

GUARINI, GIAMBATTISTA (1538-1612) Italian poet and playwright. He was born in *Ferrara to a family of old humanist traditions, which descended from *Gharino da Verona. In 1567 he entered the service of the duke of Ferrara and was sent as ambassador on many diplomatic missions; later he also served the rulers of *Florence and *Urbino. A friend and imitator of *Tasso, G. wrote a famous pastoral drama, *Il pastor fido*, first published in 1590. Although quite long, the play was full of grace and refinement, and became popular throughout Europe, and was translated into several languages. Other works of G. were much less successful than "The Faithful Shepherd".
N. J. Perella, *The Critical Fortune of Battista Guarini's "Il pastor fido"* (1973).

GUARINO DA VERONA (1374-1460) Italian humanist and educator. The orphan of a simple artisan, he studied in Padua and Venice and, in 1403, went to Constantinople, where he mastered the Greek language under *Chrysoloras. In 1408 he became a teacher of classical letters at Florence, but later moved to Venice and, in 1418, returned to Verona. In 1436 he was invited to *Ferrara by its ruler and undertook the instruction of the latter's son with other young persons, and also taught at the university. G. translated Herodotus, Plutarch and Strabo, and wrote a highly-regarded book of grammar, *Regulae grammaticales*, published in 1470. As an educator, he favoured a programme combining pagan and Christian writings, and emphasized gymnastics, *dance, swimming and hunting, to balance the theoretical studies. He was also known for his correspondence with his former students, in which he encouraged and advised them.

W. H. Woodward, *Vittorino da Feltre and Other Humanist Educators* (1921).

GUAS, JUAN (c. 1435-1496) Spanish sculptor and architect. The son of a French sculptor, he settled in Spain with his father. His first works were done in Toledo. He soon became known as one of the chief exponents of the ornamental *Plateresque style. He headed the works on the cathedrals of Segovia (1473-91) and Toledo (1483-95); was appointed by Queen *Isabella royal architect, and assigned to build the monastery of S. Juan de los Reyes (1489-90). Of his other works the best known is the façade of the Infantado Palace at Guadalajara (1480-83).

GUEVARA, ANTONIO DE (c. 1480-1545) Spanish author. Born in the village of Treceno near Santander, he was educated at the court of Queen *Isabella and, in 1504, joined the Franciscan order. *Charles V made him preacher of the royal chapel (1521), member of the Council of the *Inquisition (1523), bishop of Guadix (1528), and of Mondonedo (1537). In 1535 he accompanied the Emperor on the expedition to Tunis. G. wrote a series of works on moral and political themes, which were translated and widely read throughout Europe. His most important work, the *Reloj de príncipes y libro aureo de Marco Aurelio* (1529), was both a biography of the ancient Roman emperor and a treatise on the ideal Christian ruler. *Menosprecio de corte y alabanza de aldea* (1539) dealt with vice, wich G. associated with urban life, as against moral purity which he ascribed to rustic existence. Also popular were his guides to religious life, *Oratorio de religiosos* (1542) and *Monte Calvario* (1548), and the collection of his letters. His writings abound with witty anecdotes and much inaccurate information, combining to produce a charming and fashionable moralizing literature.

J. Gibbs, *La vida de fray Antonio de Guevara* (1961).

GUEUX The name, meaning 'beggars', given to the Calvinist rebels in the Netherlands. Meant as a term of contempt, the rebels themselves adopted the name with pride. The invasions of the G. from the sea in 1572 signalled a new uprising in the Netherlands which eventually resulted in the independence of the northern provinces.

GUICCIARDINI, FRANCESCO (1483-1540) Italian historian, diplomat and statesman. Born to a respected Florentine family, he studied law at Ferrara and Padua and, in 1512, was sent as ambassador to the court of *Ferdinand of Aragon. G. was for many years the faithful servant of the *Medici and served in various important administrative, military and governmental posts for the two pontiffs of that family, *Leo X and *Clement VII. When the Medici returned to rule *Florence in 1530, he acted as an adviser to Alessandro Medici. When the latter was murdered (1537), G. retired to his villa and devoted himself to writing. His many works included commentaries on the Florentine government, political discourses, a treatise on the *Discorsi* of *Machiavelli, memoirs and letters. His outstanding work is the *Storie fiorentine dal 1378 al 1509*, written when the author was in his twenties, and the *Storia d'Italia*, which describe the period of the Italian Wars until 1534. G.'s historical writing is marked by objectivity and the minute descriptions of political events.

R. Ridolfi, *The Life of Francesco Guicciardini* (1968);
V. Luciani, *Francesco Guicciardini and His European Reputation* (1936);
F. Gilbert, *Machiavelli and Guicciardini: Politics and History in Sixteenth-Century Florence* (1964).

GUIDI, GUIDO (c. 1500-59) Italian physician. Born in Florence, he became known as one of the best-known medical men of his age. In 1542 he went to France to serve as physician to *Francis I. There he also lectured at the *Collège de France and befriended *Cellini. In 1547 he returned, at the invitation of Grand Duke *Cosimo I, and became professor at the university of Pisa. He wrote several works on medicine, and a study of *anatomy, *De anatomia corporis humani*, published in 1611. The Vidian nerve and canal are called after him.

GUIDOBALDO DA MONTEFELTRO (1472-1508) Duke of Urbino. The son of *Federico da Montefeltro, he succeeded his father in 1482. He fought against the French (1494-95) but, in 1497, was taken prisoner in a war against the *Orsini and released only after payment of heavy ransom. In 1502 he fled from Urbino when attacked unexpectedly by Cesare *Borgia. He recovered the duchy the following year after the death of *Alexander VI. In 1504 he adopted as his successor Francesco Maria *della Rovere, a nephew of Pope *Julius II, who had appointed G. captain general of the papal army. An undistinguished military man, he was known for his learning, sound administration and refined court, which included the author *Castiglione.

R. de La Sizeranne, *César Borgia et le duc d'Urbino 1502-03* (1924).

GUILDS The system of self-governing associations of artisans or merchants for the promotion of their members' economic and social interests, became a permanent feature of European life from the early 12th century. The Renaissance inherited the system and in some respect entrenched it even further. For example, in order to reap the benefits of trade and industry, European monarchs of the 16th century gave certain G. monopolies over particular aspects of the national economy, and tried to regulate membership and technological procedures. With some modifications, therefore, the mediaeval guild system easily lent itself to the practical requirements of *Mercantilism. At the same time, however, many other dynamic factors tended to make the guild system obsolete. Primarily, the interventionist policies of the state gradually killed the autonomous and voluntary spirit which had characterized the G. in their heydey. Secondly, new industries, especially those requiring large-scale entrepreneurial methods, such as *mining, could only with difficulty be brought under the old system. Thirdly, the great change of values, the new emphasis on the worth of the individual which reduced religious restraints on economic activities, especially in Protestant countries, also had an adverse effect on the status of the G. New forms of economic cooperation, such as joint-stock companies for *exploration and trade, were linked to guild tradi-

Francis Preaching to the Birds *by Giotto, from the fresco series on the life of St. Francis in Assisi*

Above: Angels Playing Music *and* Madonna with Child: *two panels of the Isenheim Altarpiece by Grünewald*

Left: The Disrobing of Christ *by El Greco*

The Fall of Jericho, *a miniature by Jean Fouquet in an illuminated manuscript of Josephus "Antiquities of the Jews"*

tion but, in reality, pointed to the ineffectiveness of the old system in the face of new conditions.

S. L. Thrupp, "The Guilds", *The Cambridge Economic History of Europe*, III, 230-80;
P. Boissonnade, *Life and Work in Mediaeval Europe* (1927).

GUISE An aristocratic family, a branch of the house of Lorraine, which played a decisive role in the political life of France during the time of the *Religious Wars, as leaders of the extreme Roman Catholic party. Claude, the first duke of Guise, became a prominent military commander under *Francis I. He fathered 12 children, among whom were Francis, second duke of Guise, Charles, cardinal of Lorraine, and Mary (1515-60), wife of *James V of Scotland and mother of *Mary Queen of Scots. Henry, third duke of Guise, was the leader of the *League. But his brother Charles, duke of Mayenne, finally submitted to *Henry IV in 1596.

H. D. Sedgwick, *The House of Guise* (1938).

GUISE, CHARLES DE (1525-74) Also known as Cardinal de Lorraine. The brother of Francis, second duke of *Guise, he was destined for the Church, becoming archbishop of Rheims at 13 and a cardinal at 22. He showed extreme intolerance towards the growth of Calvinism in France, and his intransigence contributed to the outbreak of the *Religious Wars and to the *St. Bartholomew massacre (1572). G. also took part in the general affairs of the Church, participating in the Council of *Trent, corresponding and preaching, always with the intention of fighting the spread of Protestantism. A patron of men of letters, he was the founder of the University of Rheims.

GUISE, FRANCIS DE (1519-63) Second duke of *Guise. Winning fame in his youth as an energetic military commander, he distinguished himself in numerous battles and, in 1558, scored his most remarkable victory in the capture of Calais from England. During the brief reign of *Francis II, whose young wife *Mary Stuart was the Duke's niece, he dominated the government. But when *Catherine de Médicis became regent for *Charles IX, the duke of Guise allied himself with *Montmorency, and put himself at the head of the extreme Catholic party. The massacre of *Huguenots by his troops at Vassy (March 1562), sparked off the *Religious Wars. G. scored several partial victories over the Huguenots before he was shot to death by an enemy.

GUISE, HENRY OF (1550-88) Third duke of *Guise. The son of Duke Francis of Guise, he emulated his father as a military commander, and already in his youth took part in the *Religious Wars. In the St. *Bartholomew Massacre in 1572, he was responsible for the assassination of *Coligny and other *Huguenot leaders. When the *League was organized (1576), G. became its chief commander, reaching the summit of his power in May 1588, when he entered Paris at the head of some 30,000 men. He cherished hopes of succeeding *Henry III and dominated the estates of Blois, in which the King was pressured to suppress the *Huguenots entirely and, in addition, to relinquish some of the royal prerogatives. On 23 December 1588, he was assassinated by order of the King.

A. Bailly, *Henri le Balafré, duc de Guise* (1953).

GUNPOWDER An explosive mixture of saltpetre, charcoal and sulphur, which made possible the Renaissance revolution in warfare. G. reached the West probably from China or India, by the intermediary of the Arabs. The first to mention the manufacture of G. in Europe was the mid-13th century English scientist-monk Roger Bacon, but it was applied to *artillery only in the first half of the 14th century. In the early 15th century its value was so recognized, that rulers took measures to supervise its manufacture, and established monopolies over the sources of saltpetre. At first, G. was used in firearms in a loose mixture known as serpentine, but in the 15th century, a process was devised by which the mixture was moistened, made into cakes and granulated. The "grains", of irregular shape, controlled the burning and were better suited to the firing of guns.

H. W. L. Hime, *Gunpowder and Ammunition* (1904);
A. Marshall, *Explosives*, 3 vols. (1917-32);
J. R. Partington, *A History of Greek Fire and Gunpowder* (1960).

GUNPOWDER PLOT (1604-05) A conspiracy in England that aimed at blowing up the Houses of Parliament, while the king was there. The explosion was meant to signal a Roman Catholic uprising. However, the conspirators, a small group led by a fanatic named Robert Catesby, and a soldier of fortune named Guy *Fawkes, were betrayed by one of their number and apprehended in time (November 1605). They were executed early in 1606.

H. R. Williamson, *The Gunpowder Plot* (1941).

GUSTAVUS VASA (1496-1560) King of Sweden from 1523 and founder of the *Vasa dynasty. A scion of one of the most powerful families of the Swedish aristocracy, he took part in the struggle against *Christian II of Denmark and, in 1518, was one of the hostages taken by that king. Escaping from his captors, G. returned to Sweden in 1520. After the "Stockholm Bloodbath" of November of that year, in which many of the nobles who were opposed to Christian were killed, he began to reorganize the opposition. With some foreign help, mainly from German merchants of Lübeck, as well as popular support, he was able to chase out the Danes. Dissolving the union, he was elected king of independent Sweden on 6 June 1523.

On the internal scene, the most decisive acts of his reign was the forced introduction of the *Reformation. In this he was aided by the fact that several important members of the clergy had been exiled as supporters of Christian. In 1527 the Diet of Västeras gave G. complete power over the property of the church, thereby strengthening the monarchy and providing him with the means to appease the restless nobles with ecclesiastical estates. However, the rupture with Rome was a gradual process, responding to political expediencies, and it was not until 1550 that a Lutheran type of church became established.

In 1544 G. accomplished his design of consolidating the royal power by getting the Swedish *Riksdag* to declare the monarchy hereditary rather than elective. A strong personality, who was capable of ruthlessness in dealing with his opponents, he managed to crush a series of revolts during the first 20 years of his reign, and left the nation united and stable at the time of his death. G. also intervened occasionally in the affairs of Denmark and of Germany. In 1537, following a war with Lübeck which had played part in his accession to the throne, he ended the commercial monopoly of the *Hanseatic

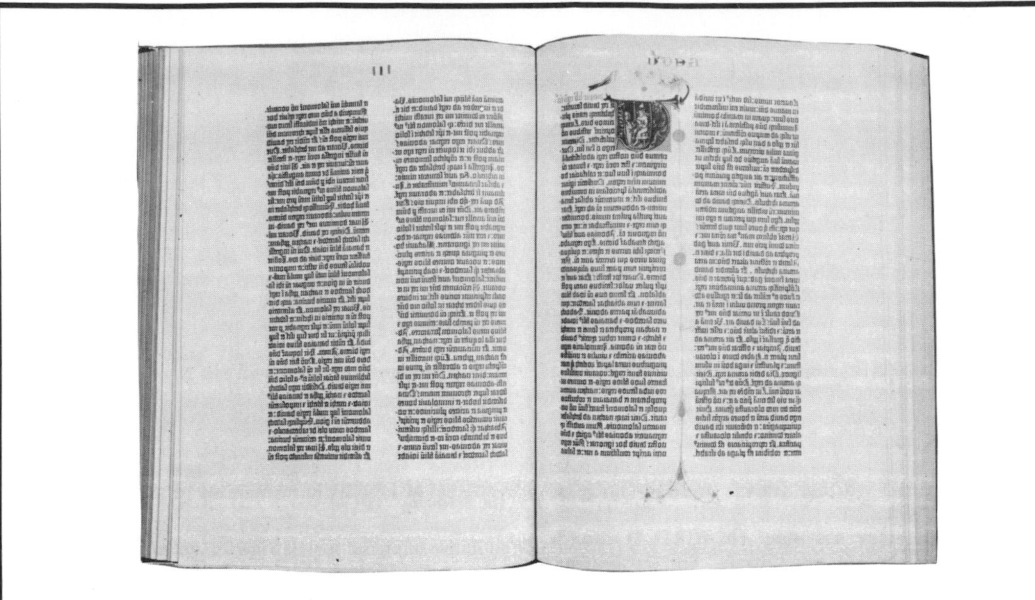

Gutenberg's Bible

League in the Baltic Sea and, between 1555 and 1557, fought *Ivan IV of Russia.

S. Wikberg, *Gustav Vasa*, 2 vols. (1945).

GUTENBERG, JOHANN (c. 1399-1468) German inventor of *printing. Of a distinguished family of Mainz, he became a goldsmith and settled in Strassburg (1430-44) where he began to conduct the experiments which eventually led to his invention. Around 1448 he returned to Mainz and, in 1450, borrowed from Johann *Fust 800 guilders, a sum later doubled when Fust became his partner in their joint printing venture. The partnership came to an end in 1455, Fust foreclosing on the loan and assuming sole ownership of the printing equipment. G. remained in Mainz and, in 1465, received a pension from Archbishop Adolf. There is no evidence that he was involved in printing after 1460.

G.'s invention was the development of the technique of cutting punches, stamping matrices and casting type. It is impossible to state with confidence which of the earliest printed books in Mainz were entirely his own creation, or what was the contribution of Fust and his son-in-law Peter *Schöffer's. G. is usually credited with the production of the 42-line Bible, printed between 1452 and 1456, and with another early printed Bible which had 36 lines to a page. In 1460, after his separation from Fust and Schöffer, he is believed to have produced the *Catholicon*, a popular dictionary printed in comparatively small type.

A. Ruppel, *Johann Gutenberg, sein Leben und Werk*, 2nd ed. (1947);
E. Beck, *Johannes Gutenberg; from Lead Letter to the Computer* (1968);
H. Lülfing, *Johannes Gutenberg und das Buchwesen des 14. und 15. Jahrhunderts* (1969).

HABSBURG, HOUSE OF The most important European dynasty of the 16th century; famous for their ability to enlarge their possessions by intermarriage. Based in the valley of the Danube, the H. first won European prominence when Rudolph I was elected to the throne of the *Holy Roman empire in 1273. Having lost the empire in 1308, they regained it in 1438 with the election of *Albert II and, with one minor exception, supplied all its rulers until its dissolution by Napoleon (1806). The efforts of the H. to expand their domain beyond the boundaries of Germany came to fruition in 1477, when *Maximilian, son of *Frederick III, married Mary, heiress of *Charles the Bold, duke of Burgundy. Subsequently, the marriage of their son, *Philip the Handsome, with *Joanna the Mad of Spain resulted in a further tremendous expansion of their possessions under *Charles V: besides *Austria, *Bohemia and the *Netherlands, these now included *Spain and her overseas empire and the kingdom of *Naples. The problems of ruling over this 'universal monarchy', led Charles V to divide his lands between his brother *Ferdinand, who retained the family estates in Austria, and his son *Philip II, who in 1556 acceeded to the throne of Spain, the Netherlands and Naples. Although Ferdinand was given the imperial title, it was the H. Spain of Philip which played the role of a European superpower during the second half of the 16th century.

A. Wandruska, *The House of Habsburg* (1964).

HABSBURG-VALOIS STRUGGLE A long and bitter conflict between the ruling family of France, represented by *Louis XII, *Francis I, and *Henry II, and Emperors *Maximilian I and *Charles V. The areas contested between the two dynasties included the duchy of Milan and the kingdom of Naples, the duchy of Burgundy and the provinces of Flanders and Artois in the Netherlands, and territories along the borders of France and Spain. The first military confrontation took place in 1513, and most of the important battles occurred in Italy, mainly between the armies of Charles V and Francis I. *Philip II and *Henry II put an end to the conflict in 1559 by signing the Treaty of *Cateau-Cambrésis.

HAKLUYT, RICHARD (c. 1552-1616) English author on *exploration. The son of a well-to-do family of Herefordshire, he was educated at Westminster School and Oxford and, about 1580, took holy orders. When he was still at Oxford his interest in geography, *cartography and the exploits of English navigators made his name known, and he soon became one of the foremost advocates of further searches for *northeast and northwest passages and of the colonization of North America. His first work, *Divers Voyages Touching the Discoverie of America* (1582), was a compilation of various foreign sources and secured him in 1583 the post of chaplain to the embassy in Paris. In 1584 he wrote a secret report, *The Discourse on the Western Planting*, which was presented to the queen, and in which he recommended *Raleigh's *Virginia project. His major work, *The Principall Navigations, Voyages and Discoveries of the English Nation*, appeared in one volume in 1589, shortly after his return from France. This epic of English sea adventure and exploration, later expanded into three volumes (1598-1600), contained embellished accounts of the maritime expeditions and urged further undertakings. H. assisted in the creation of the *East India Company and continued to back the Virginia ventures for the rest of his life.

J. A. Williams, *Richard Hakluyt and His Successors* (1946).

HALLER, BERCHTOLD (1492-1536) Swiss reformer. A priest who had been educated in conservative *Cologne, he became a follower of *Zwingli and, in 1525, made public his Protestant convictions by ceasing to perform the mass in his community in Bern. In 1528 he composed the "Theses of Bern", a set of ten doctrinal positions meant to answer the arguments of Johann *Eck. By that time H. was recognized the leader of the Reformation in Bern. He was a staunch enemy of the *Anabaptists.

HAMILTON, JOHN (1511-71) Scottish archbishop of St. Andrews. The natural son of the first earl of Arran, he was destined for the Church but, taking advantage of his family's position, went into politics. In 1543 he was appointed keeper of the Privy Seal and, in 1545, bishop of Dunkeld. A close friend of Cardinal *Beaton, he succeeded him to the see of St. Andrews (1546), and became known as a stringent opponent of the Protestants. He later became a close supporter of *Mary,

Queen of Scots, whose son he baptized (1566), and annulled *Bothwell's marriage, enabling him to marry the Queen (1567). Joining her also in the last futile attempt to regain the throne, H. was captured after her flight in Dumbarton Castle and hanged at Stirling.

HAMILTON, PATRICK (1503-28) The first victim of the persecution of Protestantism in Scotland. H., who held a church lay benefice, was drawn to the ideas of *Luther while studying in Paris. In 1526 he visited *Wittenberg where he met Luther and *Melanchthon, and when he returned to Scotland was accused of heresy. Refusing to recant, he was burnt at the stake before the college of St. Andrew's.

HAMPTON COURT CONFERENCE A meeting, presided over by *James I, between a group of bishops representing the *Church of England and *Puritan leaders. The King, following the intransigent example of the bishops, refused to alter the episcopal structure, accepting only a few changes in the Book of *Common Prayer and a new translation of the *Bible (the Authorized Version, 1611). However, the failure to gain concessions strengthened the Puritan opposition which now assumed the form of a movement with distinct political significance.

HANSEATIC LEAGUE An alliance of cities in northern Germany which dominated the Baltic trade. It began as an association of German merchants trading abroad, but after its first plenary diet in 1356 the H. assumed a political as well as economic significance. At the height of its power, in the first quarter of the 15th century, the H.L. included more than 70 regular members and controlled most of the commerce of the area between London in the west and *Novgorod in the east. It waged war successfully against *Denmark to keep open the Baltic straits, and reserved commercial privileges to natives of the member cities. The leading towns were Lübeck, Hamburg and Bremen; other important members were *Cologne, Magdeburg, Breslau, Danzig and Cracow. Cities in which the H.L. had trading privileges were *Bruges, *Antwerp, *Ghent, London, York, Hull, Norwich, and the principal towns of Denmark, Norway and *Sweden. Most German towns on the northeastern shores of the Baltic belonged to the H.L. The consolidation of the power of the Scandinavian monarchies, and the rising commercial influence of the Dutch in the 16th century, signalled the decline of the H.L., which had already been adversely affected by the convulsions of the *Reformation.

P. Dollinger, *La Hanse*(1964).

HARCADELT, JACOB (Arcadelt; c. 1514-c. 1575) Dutch composer. Born in the Netherlands, he went to Italy, where he served as singing master in Florence and at the papal court in Rome (1540-49). Although he composed masses and *motets, H. became known especially for his *madrigals, five books of which were published in Venice between 1539 and 1544. In 1555 he joined the service of the cardinal of Lorraine, duke of Guise and, in 1557, published in Paris 3 books of masses. One of the most prominent northern musicians of his time, he ended his life in France.

HARRISON, WILLIAM (1534-93) English historian. Born in London, he served for most of his life as parish rector in the county of Essex and, in 1586, became canon of Windsor. His *Historicall Description of the Islande of Great Britayne* (1577), was an entertaining and highly informative survey of Elizabethan England. It made part of *Hollinshed's *Chronicles*, and was written in a homely but vivid style, shedding particular light on social customs and institutions.

HAWES, STEPHEN (c. 1474-c. 1523) English poet. Educated at Oxford, he was a member of the court of *Henry VII and wrote a number of allegories, characterized by a moralistic and didactic tone. His most famous work, *The Pastime of Pleasure*, published in 1509, dealt with love and death, but devoted much space to describe the education of its hero.

J. M. Bredan, *Early Tudor Poetry* (1920).

HAWKINS, SIR JOHN (1532-95) English *privateer, slave trader and naval commander. Conducting his commercial maritime activities from the port of Plymouth, H. was the first English sailor to trade in slaves with the Spanish settlements of the Caribbean. In 1562 he bought a cargo of slaves in the African coast of Guinea, and sold them in Hispaniola at a huge profit. The Spanish authorities tried to stop him in 1564, but to no avail. On his third voyage (1567-68) he took with him his young cousin Francis *Drake and came accompanied with battle-ships, but lost most of his fleet in the Mexican harbour of San Juan de Ulloa. H.'s second and third trading expeditions were undertaken with the backing of Queen *Elizabeth I. The destruction of his fleet became one of the reasons of the deterioration of relations between England and Spain. In 1573 H. became treasurer of the English navy and, in 1588, distinguished himself in the battle of the *Armada, commanding a part of the English fleet. He was knighted by the Queen, and, in 1590, undertook another expedition to the Caribbean and yet another one with Drake. He died in mid-voyage.

J. A. Williamson, *Hawkins of Plymouth* (1949).

HAWKWOOD, JOHN (c. 1320-94) English **condottiere*. The son of a noble family, he went to France during the early phase of the *Hundred Years' War, and from there proceeded to Italy at the head of a company of soldiers. H., whom the Italian called Giovanni Acuto, spent 35 years of his life in the service of Pisa, Milan, Padua and Florence. He died in Florence, whose government honoured his memory by commissioning Paolo *Uccello to paint his statuesque image mounted on a horse in a fresco at the cathedral.

HEBREW, THE STUDY OF Whereas the study of Greek had been neglected by mediaeval Christian Europe, Hebrew remained as both the literary and liturgical language of the European Jews; it was, however, shunned by Christian scholars. Indeed, there was a certain fear that H. might lead the student to stray from doctrinal orthodoxy. The new interest in H. after the second half of the 15th century was a by-product of the humanist methods of textual criticism, which led many scholars to the conviction that biblical exegesis ought to be based on the original sources. One of the first to promote H. was Giovanni *Pico della Mirandola; in 1490 he met with and encouraged the greatest pre-Reformation Hebrew scholar, Johann *Reuchlin. Although Reuchlin's *De rudimentis hebraicis* (1506) was not the first Hebrew grammar to be printed, it became the principal source for the study of the language. By the second decade of the 16th century H. had spread throughout the great European centres of learning. Secular heads of states who sponsored humanist learning

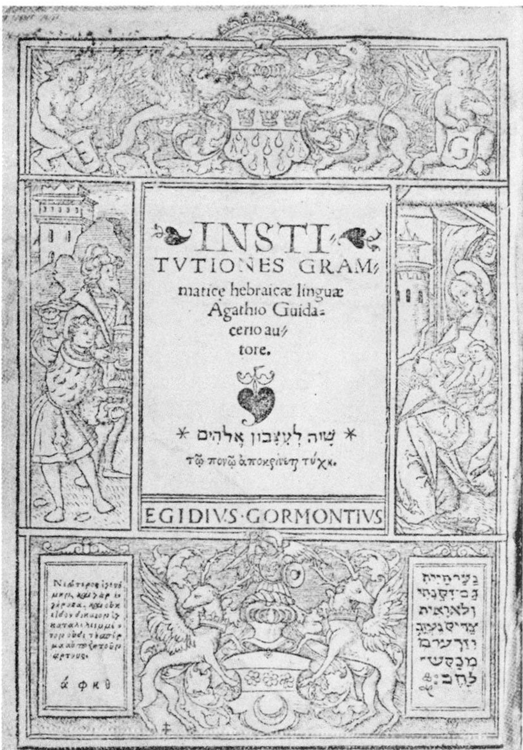
INSTITUTIONES GRAMmatice hebraicæ linguæ Agathio Guidacerio autore.
EGIDIVS·GORMONTIVS

Frontpage of a Hebrew grammar published in Paris c. 1530

recognized this development and established chairs of Hebrew in universities in England, Spain, France and Germany. The long and involved controversy between the Reuchlin and *Pfefferkorn, on the eve of the Reformation, was also an indirect proof of the new significance which Hebrew had won among Christian scholars. For obvious reasons, H. was pursued more freely in Protestant areas. The greatest Hebrew scholar of the mid-16th century, Sebastian Münster, actually converted from Roman Catholicism to Lutheranism. Reuchlin's true post-Reformation heir was Johannes *Buxtorf of Basle. His *Epitome grammaticae hebraeae* became the most popular Hebrew grammar of the 17th century.

W. Schwarz, *Principles and Problems of Biblical Translation: Some Reformation Controversies and Their Background* (1955).

HEDIO, KASPAR (1494-1552) German Protestant reformer. Born in Ettlingen, he was educated in Pforzheim and the universities of Freiburg and *Basle, where he was ordained priest. In 1520 he became a preacher at the court of Archbishop *Albert of Mainz but, in 1523, had to leave because of his sympathy with the Reformation and went to *Strassburg. There he married (1524), and became active with *Bucer in the promotion of educational institutions. H. took part in the Colloquy of *Marburg (1529) and other important Protestant meetings, and influenced the growth of Protestantism in the *Palatinate, Baden and Württemberg. He was also a classical scholar, and translated works of the early Christian Fathers and Josephus Flavius, as well as contemporary Renaissance authors. Of his own works the most important are those on the history of the Church, justifying the *Reformation.

HEEMSKERK, MAERTEN VAN (1498-1574) Dutch painter. Trained first at Heemskerk and Delft, he worked from 1527 to 1529 with Jan van *Scorel in Haarlem and, in 1532, went to Italy. His work showed exaggerated influences of the Italianate style even before this journey; during his four years in Italy he copied the works of *Michelangelo. In 1537 he settled in Haarlem, where he became a leading member of the guild and executed many portraits and Italianate religious paintings. Also important are the drawings of Roman antiquities which he made in Italy.

C. Hülsen and H. Egger, eds., *Die römischen Skizzenbücher von Marten van Heemskerk*, 2nd ed. (1973).

HEGIUS, ALEXANDER (1433-98) German educator. A student of Rudolf *Agricola, he was appointed, in 1465, to head the school of the *Brethren of the Common Life in Deventer. By introducing humanist ideas and methods, H. made the school a centre of new learning north of Italy. *Erasmus and the future *Adrian VI were among his many pupils.

HEIDELBERG CATECHISM A Calvinist confession of faith composed in Heidelberg in 1562 and accepted in the following year as the established doctrine of the

Portrait of a Young Woman Spinning *by Marten van Heemskerk*

Palatinate. Prepared at the bidding of the Elector *Frederick III, it became, thanks to its moderate formulation, the basic doctrinal statement of many Calvinist churches in Germany and the Netherlands.

HEINSIUS, DANIEL (1580-1655) Dutch classical scholar. Born in *Ghent, he was appointed, in 1605, professor and librarian at the University of Leiden. His *De tragoediae constitutione* (1611), which dealt with Aristotle's *Poetics*, had a great influence on the changing conceptions of the *drama. H. also edited several Greek and Latin authors, among them Livy and Virgil, and wrote commentaries on the plays of Seneca and Terence.

HELMONT, JEAN BAPTISTE VAN (1577-1644) Flemish medical chemist. The son of an aristocratic family in Brussels, he devoted himself to the study of medicine, for which he travelled for years in Switzerland, Italy, France and England. After his marriage in 1609 he settled in Vilvorde, near Brussels, where he pursued his scientific experiments. H. was the discoverer of carbon dioxide, which he called *gas sylvestre*, and was the first to realize that there are gases distinct from the atmospheric air. He was inclined to believe that water was the essence of all matter, and identified fermentation with the physiological processes of digestion and nutrition. On the other hand, he was a practicing *alchemist, and like *Paracelsus, ascribed different functions in the human body to supernatural influences. In his choice of drugs he paid attention to their chemical qualities, thus becoming one of the founders of iatrochemistry. An edition of his collected works was published in 1648.

W. Pagel, *The Religious and Philosophical Aspects of van Helmont's Science and Medicine* (1944).

HELVETIC CONFESSION The first Swiss confession; an attempt to formulate a single Protestant religious statement for the whole of Switzerland. It was agreed upon by *Bullinger and *Myconius at *Basle in 1536, and was accepted by most Swiss cantons. In 1566 Bullinger issued a second confession at the request of the German Elector *Frederick III the Pious. This document replaced the *Zwinglian orientation of the first with many Calvinist teachings, and won wide acceptance in Switzerland and parts of Germany.

HENLEIN, PETER (1480-1542) German locksmith and mechanical inventor. About 1510 he invented the mainspring and produced clocks in the shape of small boxes. These were the earliest pocket watches. Modified versions of these appeared in *Nuremberg shortly after his death, and were popularly known as "Nuremberg eggs".

HENRIQUE, CARDINAL (1512-80) King of Portugal from 1578. The third son of *Manoel I, he was destined for the Church, and became archbishop of Braga in 1532. In 1542 he was created cardinal, and in due course became also archbishop of Lisbon and Coimbra. H., who was known for his piety, succeeded to the throne after the death of King *Sebastian, his grand-nephew, in the Battle of Alcacerquivir. He ruled for 17 months only. His refusal to support the claims of his illegitimate nephew, *Antonio de Crato, facilitated the conquest of Portugal by *Philip II of Spain immediately after his death.

HENRY IV (1425-74) King of Castile from 1453. The son of *John II, he is remembered for his notoriously weak character, which gave rise to disorders in Castile. His second wife, Joan of Portugal, bore him a daughter, whom the King at first repudiated, and who was popularly known as *Juana la Beltraneja, after her mother's reputed lover. H. tried to dissuade his half-sister *Isabella from marrying *Ferdinand of Aragon. When she disobeyed him, he excluded her from the succession. But when he died most of the Castilian nobility rallied to Isabella's side.

A marble bust of Henry II of France by Pilon

HENRY II (1519-59) King of France from 1547. The second son of *Francis I, he was married in 1533 to *Catherine de Médicis, but the woman who dominated his life was his mistress *Diane de Poitiers. The death of his older brother opened his way to the throne. In his 12-years' reign France was almost constantly at war with Spain and the Empire. H. fought *Charles V in Italy, and over the bishoprics of Metz, Toul and Verdun (1552-53). He renewed the war in 1557, this time against *Philip II of Spain, leading France to a defeat in St. Quentin, followed by the victory of the capture of Calais from the English (1558). Internally the reign saw the rising influence of the Constable of France, Anne of *Montmorency, and the house of *Guise, which gave H. his most trusted military commanders. Though he concluded an alliance with the German Protestant princes (1552), the King conducted a relentless persecution of the French followers of the Reformation. The special court created by the *parlement* of Paris in 1547 to try heretics sent so many to the stake, that it was named the *chambre ardente*. H. died of injuries received in a tournament during the festivities which followed the signing of the Treaty of *Cateau-Cambrésis.

HENRY III (1551-89) King of France from 1574. The third son of *Henry II and *Catherine de Médicis, he first bore the title of duke of Anjou. Under his brother, *Charles IX, he was given command of the royal army, defeating the *Huguenots at Jarnac and Moncontour (1569). The favourite son of his mother, he cooperated with her in instigating the Massacre of *St. Bartholomew, and in 1573 she helped him to be elected to the vacant throne of *Poland. However, the Polish episode was cut short by the death of his brother in 1574, and H. hastened back to France. His reign saw the prestige of the crown descending to its lowest point. In 1576 he agreed to terms of peace with the Huguenots, which provoked an immediate Catholic reaction and made the King change his mind and resume the war. But the real crisis of his reign began in 1584, when the death of the King's brother, Francis, put the leader of the Huguenots, Henry of Navarre, in immediate succession to the throne. The War of the Three Henrys (1585-87) ended with Henry, duke of *Guise, enjoying immense popularity among the French Catholic majority, and on 12 May 1588 (Day of the Barricades), the King was driven out of Paris by the supporters of the *League. H. then arranged the murder of the two Guise brothers (December 1588), but finding himself without any real power fled to the camp of Henry of Navarre. There, while besieging Paris, he was stabbed to death by a fanatical Dominican friar, Jacques Clement (August 1589). Obviously inclined to homosexuality, H. was given to pleasure and kept a group of young effeminate courtiers, popularly known as *mignons*. With his death the *Valois line expired.

Catherine de Médicis, Henry III and the Duke of Anjou in a 16th-century tapestry

Henry IV of France

P. Erlanger, *Henri III*, 2nd ed. (1971).

HENRY IV (1553-1610) King of France from 1589. The son of *Antoine de Bourbon and *Jeanne d'Albret, queen of Navarre, he was brought up by his mother as a Protestant, and at the age of 16 took part in the *Religious Wars on the *Huguenot side. Becoming king of Navarre when his mother died in June 1572, he married, on August 18, *Marguerite de Valois, the daughter of *Catherine de Médicis and sister of *Charles IX. The arrival of many Huguenots to Paris to celebrate the marriage led to the *St. Bartholomew's massacre (August 23-24), in which H. himself was forced to convert to Roman Catholicism so as to save his life. In 1576, however, he regained his freedom and rejoined the Protestants, establishing himself at their head. In 1584 the death of the duke of Anjou, brother of *Henry III, made H. the heir presumptive to the crown of France, but his claim was rejected by the *League. Although he defeated the royal army at Coutras during the so called War of the Three Henrys (1585-87), his prospects of mounting to the throne were as dim as ever. But, in 1588, Henry III broke with the League, and finding himself without support, fled to H.'s camp. The following year, before he was killed by an assassin, he pronounced H. his legitimate heir. However, the League, aided by *Philip II of Spain, continued to oppose the new king, and it was not until 1593 that H., realizing that he could not remain a Protestant and rule a predominantly Roman Catholic nation, decided to convert, declaring "Paris is well worth a Mass". In 1594 he was crowned at Chartres, and took possession of the capital and, in 1596, the opposition of the League came to an end.

In his domestic policies, H.'s most important measure was the Edict of *Nantes (1598), which settled the status of the Huguenots. During his reign much was done to heal the wounds of the last 50 years. The judicial machinery was brought under control, the financial basis of the monarchy reformed, agriculture and industry were encouraged, the army was reorganized, and French architects began to adorn Paris with splendid palaces. France's system of canals dates from this reign. In his foreign policy, H. terminated, in 1598, the conflict with Spain, and most of the time had friendly relations with England, the Italian states, the *United Provinces and the Ottoman empire. Known for his easygoing manners, his many love affairs and his concern for the poor, he is remembered as the most popular king of France. By his second wife, *Marie de Médicis, whom he married in 1600, he had six children. He was assassinated in Paris by François Ravaillac, a Catholic fanatic, who succeeded thus in undoing the King's plan to mobilize an international military coalition against Spain and the Empire.

H. D. Sedgwick, *Henry of Navarre* (1930);
R. Mousnier, *L'assassinat d'Henri IV* (1964).

HENRY V (1387-1422) King of England from 1413. The eldest son of Henry IV (1399-1413), he displayed a martial talent from an early age and, in 1411, led his first expedition to France. Immediately after succeeding his father, H. took advantage of the French disarray, due to the conflict between the *Armagnacs and the Burgundians, and prepared a larger expedition. Landing in Normandy in 1415, he met, on 25 October, a French force much larger than his own and dealt it a crushing defeat in the Battle of *Agincourt. He returned to France in 1417 and, during the next three years, conquered considerable areas in the north, including Rouen. By the terms of the Peace of Troyes (1420), H. married Catherine of Valois, the daughter of Charles VI of France, and was recognized as heir to the French throne. In 1421 he fought again in France, this time against the armies loyal to the Dauphin, the future *Charles VII; he died suddenly in the following year.

E. F. Ernst, *Henry V and the Invasion of France* (1950).

HENRY VI (1421-71) King of England. Succeeding to the throne in 1422, when he was only nine months old, he was proclaimed king in both London and Paris, which the English dominated at the time. During his long minority the government was in the hands of his two uncles, the duke of *Gloucester, who became Protector of England, and the duke of *Bedford, who acted as regent of France. However, the war in France was becoming a heavy burden, and the loss of the Burgundian alliance in 1436 led to the French capture of Paris in the following year. The King, declared of age in 1437, was a gentle person, and inclined to support the peace party of the *Beauforts. But his inability to take decisive action inevitably encouraged the war party to put obstacles in the way.

In 1444 a truce was finally sought with France, and the following year H. married *Margaret of Anjou. She was a forceful personality and, though only 16 at the time, soon learned to dominate him. But as the French renewed the war in 1449 the marriage and the Queen herself became generally unpopular. In 1450, after the French had taken Normandy, the opposition party, led by Richard, duke of *York, brought about the impeachment of the chief minister, the duke of *Suffolk, who had enjoyed the King's favour. The crisis was patched up by making York governor of Ireland, but he returned the same year and, in a early showdown with the new chief minister, the duke of Somerset, forced his way into the Royal Council. The *Cade's rebellion, an uprising of small landowners in Kent, which also took place in 1450, was suppressed, but dramatized the weakness of H.'s government.

In 1453, another defeat in France combined with the King's manifest insanity, set the stage for the Wars of the *Roses. York, through his power in the Council, became regent but relinquished the post in January 1455, when the King recovered. Forstalling an attempt by the Queen and Somerset to bring about his ruin, York went north and returned in May 1455 to defeat the royal army in the first Battle of St. Albans. The civil war had begun. In the years that followed H. became increasingly a pawn between the warring parties. In July 1460 he was compelled to recognize York as his heir, and when the latter was killed (October 1460), his son Edward captured the throne, forcing H. to flee to exile in Scotland. He was caught and imprisoned in 1465, remaining for five years in the Tower of London. Between October 1470 and March 1471, he was nominally restored, though *Warwick, who had successfully revolted against *Edward IV, controlled the government. But Edward's return sealed H.'s fate, and he was murdered when the latter made his victorious entrance into London (May 1471). His tomb in Surrey later became a place of popular devotion.

M. E. Christie, *Henry VI* (1922);
E. F. Jacob, *The 15th Century* (1961).

HENRY VII (1457-1509) King of England from 1485, and founder of the *Tudor dynasty. The son of a Welsh noble, Edmund Tudor, he inherited a doubtful claim to the English throne from his mother, Lady *Margaret Beaufort. Throughout the reign of *Edward IV, H. was kept by older members of his family in exile in Britanny, France, a living symbol of the claims of the house of *Lancaster. His opportunity came when *Richard III ascended the throne (1483), and provoked much opposition by his ruthlessness. On 22 August 1485, H. defeated Richard in the memorable Battle of Bosworth Field, in which the latter was killed. Proclaim-

Henry VII of England, bust by Torrigiano

ed king he married, in 1486, Elizabeth of *York, daughter of Edward IV, thus uniting the houses of Lancaster and York. However, his control of the country was not secure, a situation which encouraged the appearance of two pretenders to the throne, the second of whom, Perkin *Warbeck, was captured only in 1497.

Although he warred with France (1492) as well as with Scotland, H.'s reign was essentially peaceful, as he preferred to achieve his objectives by diplomatic manoeuvres and marriage alliances. He betrothed one of his daughters to *James IV of Scotland, gave another to *Louis XII of France and, in 1501, cemented an alliance with Spain by marrying his eldest son Arthur to *Catherine of Aragon. His reign saw a tremendous increase in the power of the monarchy, the result of the enforcement of Statute of Liveries (1487), which forbade private armies of the nobility, and the creation of the court of *Star Chamber. H. was extremely thrifty, and squeezed as many taxes as he could out of his subjects, sometimes resorting to outright requisition. He encouraged commerce, gave high positions in government to members of the clergy and the middle class, and sent *Cabot on his voyages in the North Atlantic.

J. D. Mackie, *The Earlier Tudors* (1951);
G. Temperley, *Henry VII* (1914);
E. N. Simons, *Henry VII: The First Tudor King* (1968).

HENRY VIII (1491-1547) King of England from 1509. The second son of *Henry VII, he was given a broad humanist education. In addition to theology, he was taught Latin, French and Spanish, was a skilled musician and a fine horseman. When his older brother, Arthur, died in 1502 H. was betrothed to the latter's widow, *Catherine of Aragon, who was six years older than he. He married her upon his assumption of the crown, having obtained a special dispensation from Pope *Julius II. She bore him six children, but only one, the future Queen *Mary Tudor, survived.

Taking charge of the government of England at the age of 18, H. quickly entered Europe's political and martial arena. In 1511 he joined the *Holy League on the side of Spain and the Empire and, in 1513, scored a victory over the French in the famous Battle of the *Spurs. In the same year his army defeated *James IV of Scotland at Flodden Field, where the Scottish king met his death. The following year H. made peace with both France and Scotland. In 1520 he met with *Francis I of France in the *Field of Cloth of Gold, one of the most sumptuous Renaissance diplomatic events. A consistent opponent of *Luther, he published in 1521 the *Assertio septem sacramentorum* (Assertion of the Seven Sacraments), a work which won him the title "Defender of the Faith" from Pope *Leo X. Although he was never a man who would let other people's ideas, or the weight of circumstances, override his personal whims, he seemed content to leave the affairs of state during the first part of his reign to Cardinal *Wolsey, the son of a butcher and a graduate of Oxford University, who supervized the day-to-day management of England's fortunes.

Although many attempts have been made to adduce more serious causes for the dramatic events of the second part of his reign, it is a fact that they all proceeded from the King's desire to marry his young mistress *Anne Boleyn. Although there was little likelihood

Henry VIII by Hans Holbein

that Rome would consent, and despite the fact that his Spanish wife was quite popular in England, H. began pressing for a divorce in 1527. Wolsey, who was the papal legate, tried to establish a legal basis for it on the grounds of the invalidity of a marriage to a brother's widow. But he consumed two fruitless years heading a commission together with the Italian emissary of the pope, Archbishop Lorenzo *Campeggio. In 1529 the case was returned to Rome. Enraged, H. dismissed Wolsey from the chancellorship and had him prosecuted under the Statute of Praemunire, which forbade appeals to Rome. Following *Cranmer's advice, he consulted theologians at the universities of England and on the Continent, and a number of them, who were outside the sphere of influence of Emperor *Charles V, returned favourable opinions. To further pressure Pope *Clement VII, H. began a campaign of coercion against the English church. In 1530 he extracted from the clergy a huge fine for having acquiesced with Wolsey's alleged offences. In 1532 he compelled the English church to recognize his authority in all ecclesiastical matters, by the act known as the *Submission of the Clergy. Finally, having made Cranmer archbishop of Canterbury, he got him to invalidate the marriage to Catherine of Aragon and to marry him to Anne Boleyn (May 1533). As a result, in July 1533 the Pope excommunicated the King.

The break with Rome was consummated in 1534 in the Act of *Supremacy, by which Parliament made the King and his successors the supreme heads of the *Church of England. Those who refused to take the oath of supremacy, such as Thomas *More and Bishop John *Fisher, were executed. At the same time, H.'s new right hand man, Thomas *Cromwell, proceeded to reform the church, supervizing, between 1536 and

1539, the dissolution of the monasteries, whose enormous wealth was confiscated by the crown. The doctrinal changes which accompanied these reforms were negligible: the *Articles of Religion of 1536 and 1539 were Roman Catholic in essence. Indeed, the Henrican Reformation was mainly a political movement, an experiment in enforcing the royal will upon a subservient clergy and parliament. By 1536 the original cause of all that, Anne Boleyn, was beheaded after being convicted of adultery, and her daughter, *Elizabeth, was deprived of her rights of succession. The only serious attempt of resistance to the changes, the uprising known as the *Pilgrimage of Grace (1536), was put down first by promises of pardon, then by mass executions.

H.'s career as a husband continued to affect his politics. His third wife, *Jane Seymour, whom he married soon after the execution of Anne Boleyn, died in 1537 following the birth of his only son, the future *Edward VI. The King then waited for a while and, in 1540, married *Anne of Cleves to cement an alliance with the Protestant princes of Germany. Displeased with his fourth wife, he divorced her, but revenged himself on Cromwell, who had negotiated the marriage, by having him charged with high treason and beheaded. Immediately after, he married *Catherine Howard (July 1540), thirty years younger than himself, only to become suspicious of her conduct and have her tried and executed in 1542. His sixth and last wife, *Catherine Parr, whom he married in 1543, outlived him, though she was similarly the object of his obsessive suspicions. Each of his marriages to an English woman entailed a choice of new courtiers from among the bride's relations. This intensified the hostility among the factions at the court, and resulted in a climate of insecurity and fear. The last noble to be executed for high treason during the reign of H., was the young earl of *Surrey. His father, the duke of *Norfolk, was also waiting the executioner's axe, and was saved by the King's death.

During his last years H. renewed the wars with Scotland and France. In 1542 his army, commanded by Norfolk, routed the Scots under *James V at Solway Moss and, in 1544, he captured Boulogne from France. The war was terminated two years later in a treaty advantageous for England, but the expenditure had exhausted the English treasury. It was during this war that England first began to build a naval force.

A promoter of improved firearms, an occasional poet, the patron of *Holbein the Younger, H. nevertheless does not entirely fit the image of a Renaissance prince. His love of music recalls the ancient Nero, and he also foreshadows the modern totalitarian ruler of the type of Stalin who, like H., succeeded in terrorizing the entire ruling classes. He might be described as a Machiavellian ruler, but for the fact that he was often driven by reasons other than of state.

A. F. Pollard, *Henry VIII* (1902);
J. J. Scarisbrick, *Henry VIII* (1968);
F. Hackett, *Henry VIII* (1929);
H. M. Smith, *Henry VIII and the Reformation* (1948).

HENRY THE NAVIGATOR (1394-1460) Portuguese prince (*infante*); the architect of his nation's movement of naval exploration. Son of King John I, he participated in the capture of Ceuta (1415) and, about 1420, was made head of the knightly Order of Christ. At this time he organized the first sailing expeditions, whose initial aim was the appropriation of the Canary Islands and the exploration of the coast of *Africa beyond Cape Bojador. The second goal was accomplished by Gil Eanes in 1434, and resulted in Afonso Gonçalves Baldaia's exploration of Rio de Oro and Pedra de Galé in 1436. H., who had in the meantime begun the colonization of the Madeira Islands, settled in 1438 near Sagres in the south of Portugal, where he brought together a group of navigators and cartographers. His efforts were renewed in 1441, when Nuno Tristão reached Cape Blanco and, for the next three years, continued southward along the African coast as far as the Senegal River and Cape Verde. In the 1450's other navigators employed by H., among them the Italian *Cadamosto, reached the coast of Portuguese Guinea and, by the time he died, Pedro de Cintra had advanced as far south as Sierra Leone. Although after his death there was a long hiatus in the Portuguese movement of exploration, which was renewed in the 1480's, H.'s relentless work of some 40 years had set the course of Portuguese and European history to the eventual reconnaissance of the entire globe.

E. Sanceau, *Henry the Navigator* (1946);
J. Cortesão, *Os descobrimentos portugueses* (1959);
B. W. Diffie, *Prelude to Empire* (1967);
E. D. S. Bradford, *Southward the Caravels; The Story of Henry the Navigator* (1961).

HENSLOWE, PHILIP (?-1616) English theatre manager. Born probably in Sussex, he settled near London before 1577 and, having made his money in business, built the Rose Theatre (1587). He later built other theatres, notably the Fortune (1600), in which his partner was his son-in-law the actor Edward Alleyn. H. employed a number of acting companies and some of the best known Elizabethan playwrights, among them *Dekker, *Drayton and *Chapman. A shrewed businessman, he frequently underpaid his employees. His account books, known as "Henslowe's diary", cover the years 1592-1603, and contain much data about plays, authors, and the costs of theatrical production.

E. L. Rhodes, *Henslowe's Rose; the Stage and Staging* (1976).

HERING, LOY (c. 1485-c. 1554) German sculptor. A native of Bavaria, he worked in *Augsburg and several other south German towns, mainly on small religious subjects and tombs. Though showing traces of the Gothic style, H. is considered the first to introduce High Renaissance motifs into German sculpture. Some of his figures were adapted from *Dürer's prints, and display elegance and charm.

HERLIN, FRIEDRICH (c. 1435-1500) German painter. Born at Rothenburg, he divided his career between his native town and Nördlingen, where he died. His works, mostly on religious themes, display a strong influence of Roger van der *Weyden.

HERNANDEZ DE CORDOBA, FRANCISCO (?-1517) Spanish navigator. Having taken part in the conquest of Cuba, he was sent by Governor *Velázquez in 1517 to lead an expedition in search of new lands. At the head of a fleet of three ships he discovered Yucatán and established the first contact with the Mayan civilization. After a skirmish with the Indians in which he lost many of his men, he sailed along the coast of Mexico and then returned to Cuba, where he died. His expedition was shortly followed by those of *Grijalva and *Cortés.

HERNANDEZ DE CORDOBA, FRANCISCO (?-1526) Spanish **conquistador*. In 1523 he was sent by Pedro *Arias de Ávila on an expedition to Nicaragua and present-day Costa Rica. He discovered the river Desaguadero, which connects Lake Nicaragua and the Atlantic Ocean, and founded several settlements, hoping to consolidate his own rule in the area. In 1526 he submitted to "Pedrarias", who came to Nicaragua, but the latter caused him to be executed.

HERRERA, FERNANDO DE (1534-97) Spanish poet. Born in *Seville, he spent most of his life in his native city, where he enjoyed the patronage of the Count of Gelves. Much of his elegant love poetry was addressed to the Countess, and is written in the manner of *Petrarch's sonnets to Laura. His most important poetic works are the two patriotic odes on the victory of *Lepanto (1571) and the death of King *Sebastian of Portugal at the Battle of Alcacerquivir (1578). His poems were first published in 1580, and a fuller edition, but with many alterations, appeared posthumously in 1619. In 1580 he edited the works of *Garcilaso de la Vega, together with comments and an exposition of his own literary theories. This work influenced later Spanish poets. H. also wrote a prose history of the naval wars against the *Ottoman Turks, published in 1572, and a life of Thomas *More (1592). He devised his own system of orthography and punctuation. His rich language and harmonious, classically inspired poetry earned H. the title "El Divino".

O. Macri, *Fernando de Herrera* (1959);
M. G. Randel, *The Historical Prose of Fernando de Herrera* (1971).

HERRERA, FRANCISCO (c. 1576-1656) Spanish painter and engraver. Born in Seville, he divided his career between his native city and Madrid. He was known for his excellent draftsmanship, but also for his bad temper. H. is frequently mentioned with Juan de las *Roelas as the leading Spanish painter during the transition from *Mannerism to the *Baroque. His style reflected the influence of *Caravaggio, and foreshadowed Spanish naturalism of the 17th century. Diego Velásquez (1599-1660) is said to have been his pupil for a short time. H.'s son Francisco Herrera el Mozo (1622-85), who ran away from his father to Italy, later became a famous painter and architect.

HERRERA, JUAN DE (c. 1530-97) Spanish architect. Acquiring his stylistic tastes in Flanders and Italy, where he spent many years with the Spanish army, he was, in 1563, appointed by *Philip II to continue the building of the *Escorial. It is his other works, however, such as the palaces of Aranjuez and Simancas, which reveal his Italianate tendencies. He also built the *Casa de Contratación at *Seville (1582) and designed the architecturally influential, but unfinished cathedral of Valladolid (begun 1585).

HERRERA Y TORDESILLAS, ANTONIO DE (1549-1625) Spanish historian. The son of a noble family from the vicinity of Segovia, he studied in Italy and was made the official historiographer of the *Spanish empire in America by his patron *Philip II. Most of his efforts were devoted to the writing of the *Historia general de los hechos de los Castellanos en las islas y tierra firme del mar oceano*, an account of the Spanish discovery and conquest of America up to 1554. Based on earlier authorities, the work was published in Madrid, in four volumes, between 1601 and 1615. It became the most widely known contemporary history of the subject.

HERVETUS, GENTIAN (1499-1584) French humanist and Roman Catholic leader. Born near Orléans, he became a well-known authority on the *Greek language and, in 1544, translated Aristotle's *De Anima*. He then went to Rome, where he attached himself to Cardinal *Pole and took an active part in the discussions of the Council of *Trent. Translations of the Greek Fathers of the Church further enhanced his name. Ordained in 1556, he became a close aide of Charles de *Guise, cardinal of Lorraine and, in 1561, published *De reparanda ecclesiasticorum disciplina*, a treatise advocating strict supervision of church government as means of Catholic reform. H. was an opponent of the *Huguenots. He published a French translation of the decrees of the Council of Trent (1564), and a translation of St. Augustine's *Civitas Dei*.

HEYWOOD, JOHN (1497-c. 1580) English poet and playwright. Believed to have studied at Oxford, he became about 1519 a singer and musician at the court of *Henry VIII, and married the niece of Thomas *More. He wrote four plays (two others are attributed to him), and several *masques, which were performed in the reign of *Mary, whose favourite he was. To her he dedicated his allegorical poem, *The Spider and the Fly* (1556). A fervent Roman Catholic, he emigrated about 1564 and ended his life at the *Jesuit college in *Antwerp.

R. G. W. Bolwell, *The Life and Works of John Heywood* (1921).

HILLIARD, NICHOLAS (c. 1547-1619) English painter. The son of a goldsmith of Exeter, he began painting miniature portraits at the age of 13. In 1569 he painted his first portrait of *Elizabeth I and in the same year was appointed the Queen's Limner and Goldsmith. He is known to have visited France and, about 1577, was attached to the duke of *Anjou, Elizabeth's young French intended. He also designed the Queen's Great

Hilliard, a miniature portrait of the artist's wife

Seal and wrote a short treatise on miniatures, *The Art of Limning*, published in 1612. Despite his position in court (he was retained as royal portraitist by *James I), his later years were marred by financial problems. H.'s miniatures, oval in shape and designed to be worn, were in the Italian style and showed similarities with the work of *Clouet. He is considered the first important native English painter.

E. Auerbach, *Nicholas Hilliard* (1961).

HIRSCHVOGEL, AUGUSTIN (1503-53) German engraver. Born in *Nuremberg, he was the son of a stained-glass artist, and practiced this art as well as pottery, in addition to engraving. His most remarkable works are landscape etchings, which betray the influence of Wolf *Huber. He also excelled as a cartographer, working for *Ferdinand I in Vienna, where he died.

K. Schwartz, *Augustin Hirschvogel; ein deutscher Meister der Renaissance* (1917).

HISTORIOGRAPHY The writing of history, a sensitive indicator of man's changing view of himself, acquired during the *Renaissance a new purpose and its early modern character. Mediaeval annals and chronicles, even when not entirely credulous, were generally based on an uncritical view of people, events and textual sources. This was true even in the late 14th century, when the French Jean Froissart (*c.* 1333-*c.* 1400) produced his famous *Chronicles* of the *Hundred Years' War; a highly descriptive work, it presented history merely as a sequence of unrelated episodes. Perhaps the main achievement of the Renaissance was the introduction into the writing of history analyses of motives and causes, and the claim that it had a practical use, especially for the statesman. Although during the *Reformation much historical writing was tinted by religious partisanship, it was nevertheless distinguished by a generally higher standard of scholarly objectivity than in the past, and some impressive attempts to collect and study relevant documents. Also, in process of studying the movement of maritime *exploration and discovery, historians now began to pay greater attention to social and cultural matters.

Renaissance historiography evolved as a by-product of *humanism. Out of admiration for classical culture, 15th-century historians began to emulate the style of Livy and Tacitus and dealt with history in terms similar to those used by the ancient Greek and Roman authors. Leonardo *Bruni, frequently called the first modern historian, portrayed the history of Florence as a struggle for civic liberties, regarding his native city as the centre of the world. His contemporary *Poggio Bracciolini even surpassed Bruni in Roman-inspired rhetoric, and so did Bernardo *Giustiniani in his history of Venice. Another early humanist historian of Venice, Marcantonio Coccio (1436-1506), better known as Sabellicus, kept up the equation of a Renaissance city-state with an ancient polis, and in his *Enneades* produced the first humanist world history. These early humanist historical writings were still largely uncritical towards their subject matter. This fault was shared by Lorenzo *Valla in his historical work, but by his demolition of the legendary Donation of Constantine, Valla set historical scholarship an example of textual criticism and new norms of dealing with sources. At the same time Flavio *Biondo made a fundamental contribution to historical retrospection when he coined the term *Medium Aevum for the long period which separated his own age from classical antiquity. As regards political history, Italian humanism achieved its most mature stage with *Machiavelli and *Guicciardini, in the early 16th century. Although still upholding the classics as models, these authors reached a degree of detachment which allowed them to evaluate man's behaviour in secular and rational terms. They tackled such questions as 'what are the teachings of history', and 'to what degree does man control his own destiny'. But whether the sophisticated political H. of the High Renaissance should be viewed as a scholarly accomplishment of the humanist school remains an open question. In his *Memoirs* covering the reign of *Louis XI of France, Philippe de *Commines revealed the same sense of realism in treating political events, though without adhering to the classical models of humanist H.

Throughout Europe, most of the works on history written just before 1500 still retained the mediaeval tradition of starting with the creation of the world and a summary of biblical events. The best example is *Schedel's *Nuremberg Chronicle* of 1493. But the influence of humanist H. now began to be felt outside Italy. *Aventinus in Germany and *Vadianus in Switzerland were among the first notable humanist historians of the north to follow the style of Bruni and Biondo. In England the career of the Italian Polydore *Vergil demonstrated the importance which the new historiography had won; Thomas *More and later Francis *Bacon continued this tradition with their works on the reigns of *Richard III and *Henry VII. In Scotland the master of Latin style, George *Buchanan, wrote a history of his nation in a straightforward narrative, though containing much political bias. The most important Spanish historians to treat national topics were Jeronimo *Zurita who dealt with *Aragon, Diego *Hurtado de Mendoza, who described the rebellion of the *Moriscos of Granada in a style inspired by Tacitus, and Juan de *Mariana, the Jesuit philosopher who produced a vivid history of Spain.

The Reformation, by opening the debate about the true form of Christianity, was responsible for the development of a new type of religious H. One of the earliest statements of the Protestant position was contained in a history of the popes by the English reformer Robert *Barnes. The most elaborate Protestant history of the Church was the **Magdeburg Centuries*, a cooperative effort, edited by Matthias *Flacius, which attempted to disprove Catholic dogma. For the other side, *Baronius responded with his *Annales ecclesiastici*, perhaps even more polemical, but utilizing a considerable number of documents from the Vatican archives. On both sides, however, there were some historians capable of impartiality and even self-criticism. *Sleidanus comes to mind with regard to the Protestant camp, *Sarpi with the Roman Catholic.

Among the typical genres of the Renaissance one finds historical works dealing with the antiquities of Italy or national antiquities elsewhere. Biondo, the most significant early writer in this genre, was later followed by the English William *Camden. The field of historical biographies had its earliest exponents in *Petrarch and *Boccaccio, and late in the 16th century in the work of Brantôme and *Vasari's famous biographies of Italian artists. Contemporary history was first treated by Enea Silvio Piccolomini (*Pius II), followed by a famous work of

Paolo *Giovio, who in turn inspired the French *Thuanus. In his treatise on the study of history Jean *Bodin produced a pioneering work on methodology which particularly stressed the influence of climate and topography.

The discovery and conquest of the New World were immediately recorded by some of the most prominent participants in the events. *Columbus and *Vespucci, wrote long letters about their voyages, and *Cortés described his conquest of Mexico. Of the early historians of the *conquista* who had spent time in America were *Las Casas, *Díaz del Castillo, *Oviedo and *Cieza de Leon. But the history of exploration and discovery seemed to hold a general fascination, and it did not take long for historians who never left the shores of Europe to begin writing about the distant continents. The first was an Italian humanist who had settled in Spain, Pietro Martire d'*Anghiera. He was followed by, among others, Francisco *Gomara and by the most popular author on the Spanish conquest of the New World, Antonio de *Herrera y Tordesillas. Among the Portuguese the work of João de *Barros acquired particular fame. The history of English voyages of exploration by Richard *Hakluyt is in a category by itself, since here the aim of the historian was both to record the past and to convince the reader of the need for further efforts.

H. E. Barnes, *A History of Historical Writing* (1962);
J. W. Thompson, *A History of Historical Writing*, 2 vols. (1942).

HÖCHSTETTER A German family of merchants and bankers from *Augsburg. The H. belonged to the patrician class of their city since the early 15th century. They rose to their highest prominence during the lifetime of Ambrosius H. (1463-1534), and in the first quarter of the 16th century were the third most important Augsburg banking house, after the *Fuggers and *Welsers. However, Ambrosius, who for several years attempted to monopolize the European market of quicksilver, went into bankruptcy in 1529 and ended his life in jail.

R. Ehrenberg, *Capital and Finance in the Age of the Renaissance* (1928).

HOEN, CORNELIUS (?-1524) Dutch Protestant reformer. Born probably in Gouda, he became an advocate at The Hague. About 1521 he wrote a short treatise on the significance of the Eucharist, wherein he rejected the doctrine of transubstantiation in favour of a symbolical interpretation. A friend of his brought the work to *Luther in Wittenberg and to *Zwingli in Zurich, and it influenced the latter's thought. H. was prosecuted by the *Inquisition at The Hague, imprisoned and made to pay a fine. His work was published anonymously in Zurich in 1525.

HOFFMANN, MELCHIOR (c. 1500-43) German *Anabaptist leader. A furrier from Swabia, he became influenced by *Luther's ideas and began preaching about 1523, while on business trips to the north Baltic region. For the next few years he spent most of his time in Sweden and Denmark, preaching, debating and writing eschatological commentaries on the Book of Daniel. In 1529 he joined the Anabaptists in *Strassburg, and from 1530 to 1533 preached successfully amongst the simple working men of East Friesland. Returning to Strassburg, which he regarded as the New Jerusalem awaiting the imminent second coming of Christ, he was arrested and held in jail for almost a decade, until his death. His followers were often referred to as 'melchiorites'.

HOFFMEISTER, JOHANNES (c. 1509-47) German Roman Catholic leader. Having joined the Augustinian order in his youth, he became known as a staunch opponent of the *Reformation. His effectiveness as preacher hastened his promotion in the ranks of his order, and brought him invitations to deliver sermons on important occasions. H. preached at the Diet of Worms of 1545, which preceded *Charles V's offensive against the Protestant princes.

HOFHAIMER, PAUL (1459-1537) German organist and composer. Born in Radstadt, he was considered to be the best organist of his age. From 1480 to 1519 was chiefly in Innsbruck, where he played in the imperial chapel. After the death of *Maximilian I, who had conferred upon him a title of nobility, he settled in Salzburg. His many compositions for the organ are lost. He also set to music 35 odes of Horace. Several simple German songs of his have survived.

H. J. Moser, *Paul Hofhaimer; ein Lied- und Orgelmeister des deutschen Humanismus*, 2nd ed. (1966).

HOHENZOLLERN A German family which gradually gained political importance during the 15th and 16th centuries as the ruling dynasty of *Brandenburg and Prussia. Divided into two branches, the Swabian and the Franconian, the H. began their rise in 1415 when Frederick, Burgrave of *Nuremberg and head of the Franconian line, was made Margrave of Brandenburg by Emperor *Sigismund. Their power did not extend outside the confines of Germany until the 17th century.

H. Eulenberg, *The Hohenzollerns* (1929);
O. Hintze, *Die Hohenzollern und ihr Werk* (1915).

HOLANDA, FRANCISCO DE (1517-84) Portuguese painter and author. Trained as a miniaturist, he visited Italy twice, spending several years there. He was a friend of *Michelangelo, *Serlio and *Clovio. On his return to Portugal he was commissioned to make portraits of the royal family. While working on these he also wrote a treatise entitled *Da pintura antigua* (On Ancient Painting), which dealt with contemporary art theories. It was, however, published only at the end of the 19th century. H. was also architect and made plans for the city of Lisbon. An interesting book of sketches he made on his travels is in the library of the *Escorial.

HOLBEIN THE ELDER, HANS (c. 1465-1524) A painter of the *Augsburg school and the senior member of a family of painters. His paintings of altars in Augsburg and Frankfurt am Main show a compromise between the Late Gothic and the Renaissance styles. He also made designs for glass painting and windows.

HOLBEIN THE YOUNGER, HANS (c. 1497-1543) German painter and designer. Born in Augsburg to a family of important artists (his father, Hans *Holbein the Elder, his uncle Sigmund and his brother Ambrosius), H. began his career in Basle in 1515. He broke completely from the Gothic style, especially after his travels in Italy in 1518, where he probably came into contact with *Leonardo's circle. In Basle he was given a commission to decorate the town hall, and became closely associated with Basle publishers and their humanist friends, designing woodcuts for title pages and book illustrations, including the illustrations for *Erasmus' *Praise of Folly*, the title pages for *More's *Utopia* and for *Luther's German translation of the

Hans Holbein the Younger Self-Portrait

New Testament, as well as the famous 51 plates of the **Dance of Death*. Among his paintings from the Basle period are the portrait of the scholar *Bonifacius Amerbach* (1519), the marvellous portrait of *Erasmus* (1523), and a group portrait of his own wife and children (1526). In 1526 H. left Basle for England, bringing a letter of introduction from Erasmus. It was on this first visit that he painted a portrait of *Thomas More* and a group portrait of *More's family* (of which only a drawing and copies remain). After another sojourn in Basle (1528-32), he settled in England, first working for the German Steelyard Merchants, and from 1536, as court painter for *Henry VIII. About 150 of H.'s portraits of royalty and nobility, are an imperishable record of the Tudor court. The better known are the numerous portraits of *Henry VIII*, **Anne of Cleves* (1539) and *Christina, Duchess of Milan* (1538). His other work for the court included ornamental design, miniatures, fashion design and mural decorations. Prolific and versatile, his drawings are remarkable for their precise naturalism and his portraits for their objective realism, H. was undoubtedly the greatest German painter of his generation.

R. C. Strong, *Holbein and Henry VIII* (1967). (ME)

HOLBEIN RUGS Name used to describe several types of 16th- and 17th-century Anatolian carpets, the patterns of which appear in paintings by Hans *Holbein the Younger.

HOLINSHED, RAPHAEL (?-1580) English historian. His *Chronicles of England, Scotland and Ireland* appeared in 1577, and were reprinted in 1586. This work, with its patriotic strain, was probably the most popular of several works of its kind. It furnished *Shakespeare with much of his sources on English history. Not much is known of H.'s life. He is supposed to have been educated at Cambridge, and later worked as a translator and compiler in London. The *Chronicles* was a work which incorporated uncritically many sources, including parts written by others, such as *Harrison's survey of England.

W. G. Boswell-Stone, *Shakespeare's Holinshed: the Chronicle and the Plays Compared* (1907; rep. 1968).

HOLL, ELIAS (1573-1646) German architect. Born in *Augsburg, he acquired the principles of Renaissance *architecture in Venice (1600-01), and introduced them to his native city. The famous Augsburg Town Hall was built by him between 1615 and 1620. It contained huge rooms and a profusion of gilt decoration, and is considered the most outstanding building of early 17th-century German architecture.

H. Hieber, *Elias Holl; der Meister der deutschen Renaissance* (1923).

HOLLAND The most important province of the northern *Netherlands, situated between Utrecht and the Zuider Zee on the east, and the North Sea on the west. The economic growth of the county of H. coincided with the rule of the dukes of *Burgundy in the 15th century. It was based on maritime trade, on herring fisheries and the cultivation of land reclaimed from the sea. During the revolt of the Netherlands against Spain H. emerged as the centre of the independence movement, and the most powerful of the seven *United Provinces. The term H. was frequently used in reference to the Dutch republic as a whole. *Amsterdam, Haarlem, the Hague, Rotterdam, Leiden, Delft and Dort are all located in this province.

HOLY LEAGUE A political alliance established in October 1511 between Pope *Julius II, *Ferdinand of Spain, *Henry VIII of England and the republic of *Venice, against France and her Italian allies. Following the Battle of Ravenna (April 1512), which was won by the French, Emperor *Maximilian I also joined the H.L. As a result, France had to leave Italy, allowing the return of the *Medici to *Florence and Massimiliano *Sforza to *Milan. The bloodless Battle of the *Spurs was fought by Henry VIII as member of the H.

HOLY ROMAN EMPIRE More than a cohesive political entity it was a lofty and never-fulfilled idea of Christian unity. The H. proclaimed at the coronation of Charlemagne in Rome in 800, was identified by the 13th century with the territories of *Germany and part of *Italy. But the failure of Emperor Frederick II (1212-50), who was king of Sicily, to rule Germany and Italy signalled the decline of the century-long efforts of the Hohenstaufens and, during the 14th century, the H. fell into disarray. Emperors now came from different houses; with the exception of Henry VII (1308-13) and Louis IV of Bavaria (1314-47) none of them attempted the incorporation of Italy; in Germany the real power was in the hands of the territorial princes. An acknowledgement of this state of affairs was made in the important constitutional document of 1356, promulgated by Charles IV of Luxemburg (1347-78) and known as the Golden Bull. Henceforth, the election of the emperor, styled King of the Romans or King of Germany until his coronation by the pope, was entrusted to an electoral college of three ecclesiastical and four secular princes. These were the archbishops of Mainz, Trier and *Cologne, the king of *Bohemia, the count palatine of the Rhine, the duke of *Saxony and the margrave of *Brandenburg. The elected king did not need the approval of the pope to exercise his royal rights immediately. The new arrangement gave supreme rights to the main territorial princes, thus, if not exactly 'legalizing anarchy' in James Bryce's famous dictum, it certainly consolidated an already established German particularist system.

The eventual securing of the imperial crown by the *Habsburgs, who provided all the emperors from 1438 on, did not change things significantly. Under the rather powerless *Frederick III the affinity between the H. and Germany was further emphasized in the title "Holy Roman Empire of the German Nation". His son Maximilian I consented to the introduction of several internal reforms which included the creation of *Reichskammergericht*, or a system of imperial courts, and an improved machinery for tax collection, but these did not detract from the power of the princes and proved relatively ineffective. *Charles V saw his grand ambitions for the H. come to nought in the havoc wrought by the *Reformation. The absence of central authority gave greater influence to the imperial diet (*Reichstag*), in which the electors, the princes and the free imperial cities were all represented. After Charles V, emperors were no longer crowned by the pope, and the Treaty of Westphalia (1648), marking the end of the *Thirty Years' War, confirmed the character of the H. as a loose federation of numerous principalities and towns presided over by the rulers of *Austria.

J. Bryce, *The Holy Roman Empire* (1864; new edition 1925);
G. Barraclough, *The Origins of Modern Germany* (1946).

HOMBERG, SYNOD OF An assembly of Protestant reformers, convoked at Homberg by *Philip of Hesse on 21 October 1526. Intending to establish the religious structure of Hesse, the assembly discussed proposals submitted by François *Lambert, but did not reach any definite results. Later a committee agreed upon far-reaching changes which allowed each community its own self-government. The decisions were not implemented, due to *Luther's objections.

HOOFT, PIETER CORNELISZ (1581-1647) Dutch historian, poet and playwright. Born to a wealthy merchant family in *Amsterdam, he acquired a literary education in France and Italy, where he was influenced by diverse authors, such as *Montaigne, *Tasso and *Guarini (1598-1601). Marked by his humanist learning, the early poems and plays reveal the author's liberal political outlook and his hope of a true Dutch cultural renaissance. In 1609 he was appointed sheriff of Muiden, where he gathered around him a circle of fellow artists which became known as the *Muiderkring*. His plays *Geeraerdt van Velsen* (1613) and *Beato* (1617) dealt with Dutch historical themes and combined a sense of patriotism with ideas about government and society. Of H.'s other plays the most successful was the comedy *Warenaar* (1616), an adaptation of Plautus' *Aulularia* to the Amsterdam scene. His most famous prose work was a chronicle of the Dutch struggle for independence from Spain, a project which he began in 1628. The 27 volumes of his *Nederlandsche Historiën*, covered the years 1555 to 1587. Modelled on Tacitus, this masterpiece influenced Dutch authors until the 19th century.

HOOKER, RICHARD (1554-1600) English political theorist. Educated at Oxford, H. taught for several years at the university before becoming an Anglican clergyman in 1584. His treatise, *The Laws of Ecclesiastical Polity*, in four books, was first published in 1594 (Book V came out in 1597, Books VI-VIII were added only after the author's death). Its principal aim was to defend the established church against *Puritan criticism, but he touched upon numerous other basic issues of political power. His theory of government had a contractual basis, and posited an original agreement between society and its chosen ruler. While certainly not a champion of absolute royal power, he held that, by refusing to conform to the usages of the *Church of England, the Puritans were denying their essential political obligations.

P. Munz, *The Place of Hooker in the History of Thought* (1952);
G. Hillerdal, *Reason and Revelation in Richard Hooker* (1962).

HOOPER, JOHN (1475-1555) English Protestant reformer. Educated at Oxford, H. was for many years a Cistercian monk. After the dissolution of the monasteries he came to London and became known as an advocate of further reforms. From 1547 to 1549 he was in Zurich, where he became close to *Bullinger and, upon his return to England, was made chaplain of *Somerset and bishop of Gloucester. His radical ideas, favouring religious simplicity, were embodied in his *A Godly Confesssion and Protestation of the Christian Faith* (1551), which later influenced the *Puritans. In 1552 H. was made bishop of Worcester, but after the accession of *Mary (1553) was arrested and tried as a heretic. He was burnt at the stake in 1555.

HORN, PHILIP DE MONTMORENCY, COUNT OF (1518-68) Flemish statesman. One of the most trusted Flemish nobles under *Charles V, he served him in administrative and military positions and was awarded the Order of the *Golden Fleece. Nevertheless, under *Philip II he joined *William of Orange and Count *Egmont in protesting the religious repressions of Cardinal *Granvelle. When the duke of *Alba took over the government of the Netherlands (1567), H. decided to remain, despite the warnings of William of Orange. He was arrested with Egmont, tried as a traitor by Alba's "Council of Blood", and executed in Brussels on 5 June 1568.

HOSIUS, STANISLAS (1504-79) Polish Roman Catholic leader. Born in Cracow, he studied in Bologna, where he first came in contact with the movement of Catholic reform. In 1543 he was ordained priest and, in 1551, was made bishop of Ermland. He then began an energetic campaign of preaching against Polish Protestants, and published polemical writings in defence of Roman Catholicism. A friend of *Canisius, he soon earned the respect of the papacy, was created cardinal (1561) and entrusted with the preparation of the last phase of the Council of *Trent. In 1564 he succeeded in having the Polish church approve the decrees of Trent, and in order to facilitate their implementation encouraged the coming of the *Jesuits. He passed his last ten years in Rome.

L. Bernacki, *La doctrine de l'eglise chez le cardinal Hosius* (1936).

HOTMAN, FRANÇOIS (1524-90) French political theorist. Born in Paris, he was a well-known legal

Portrait of the Humanist Jacob Ziegler by Wolf Huber

authority and, in 1567, became a professor of law at Bourges. H. was one of the advisers of the Prince of *Condé, the *Huguenot leader, and barely escaped death during the St. *Bartholomew Massacre. Finding shelter in *Geneva, he composed his *Francogallia*, which was published in 1573. Written in a passionate style, the book treated the history of France in an attempt to prove that the king was always legally subordinate to the national representative body, the *États-Généraux*. While this work contains many inaccuracies, it is distinguished as one of the most interesting 16th-century arguments that sovereignty resides in the people.

B. Reynolds, *Proponents of Limited Monarchy in Sixteenth-Century France; Francis Hotman and Jean Bodin* (1931);
J. Franklin, *Constitutionalism and Resistance in the Sixteenth Century* (1969).

HOUTMAN, CORNELIS DE (c. 1565-99) Pioneer of Dutch penetration of the Far East. In 1592 he visited Lisbon and gathered information about the spice trade. In 1595 he sailed to the East at the head of a small fleet, and although the voyage did not fulfil the commercial expectations around it, H. signed a treaty with the sultan of Bantam, who commanded the Sunda Strait between Java and Sumatra.

HOWARD OF EFFINGHAM, CHARLES, LORD (1536-1624) English naval commander. A grandson of the second Duke of *Norfolk, he participated in 1569 in the suppression of the *Northern Rebellion. In 1585 he was appointed Lord High Admiral and commanded the English navy in 1588 during the attempted invasion of the *Armada. Although not a great naval officer, he acted prudently and knew how to inspire the famous captains under his command with a sense of a unity of purpose. With the Earl of *Essex he commanded, in 1596, the expedition against Cádiz but, in 1601, helped to suppress the revolution which the latter was preparing. He continued to hold high offices also under *James I.

HUBER, WOLF (c. 1490-1553) German painter and engraver. Probably a pupil of *Altdorfer, by whom he was clearly influenced, he settled in 1515 in Passau. H.'s paintings show a remarkable feeling for landscape and so do his drawings and woodcuts. He is considered, after Altdorfer, the outstanding exponent of the so called Danube School.

HÜBMAIER, BALTHASAR (c. 1485-1528) German *Anabaptist leader. Born near Augsburg, he studied under Johann *Eck and in 1516 went to Regensburg where he took part in the expulsion of the Jews. Attracted by the teachings of *Zwingli, he went to Zurich in 1523, but soon joined the radical movement of the Anabaptists. H. then became a preacher among the peasants of Waldshut, Austria, and subsequently settled in Nikolsburg, Moravia (1526), where he presided over a sizeable community. He was arrested and delivered to the Austrian authorities, condemned as a heretic and burned at the stake in Vienna. In his writings he rejected infant baptism as idolatry, advocating adult baptism based on personal faith.

T. Bergsten, *Balthasar Hübmaier; Seine Stellung zur Reformation und Täufertum, 1521-28* (1961);
G. H. Williams, ed., *Spiritual and Anabaptist Writers* (1957).

HUDSON, HENRY (?-1611) English explorer. There is no information about his life before 1607, when he undertook a voyage on behalf of the *Muscovy Company. Seeking to reach *China by a northern route, he sailed to Greenland and then eastward along the ice pack, until he arrived at present-day Spitsbergen. As a result of this voyage English whale fisheries were established in the area. H. again tried to find the *northeast passage in 1608, and sailed between Spitsbergen and Novaya Zemlya, but had to return when his path was blocked by the ice. In 1609 he undertook a third voyage, this time on behalf of the Dutch *East India Company to search further for a northeast passage. He was again stopped by ice around Novaya Zemlya, and quarrels broke out among his mixed English and Dutch crew; he then changed course and sailed west across the Atlantic. Reaching *Virginia, H. followed the coastline northward in the hope of finding the legendary channel that was said to connect the Atlantic and Pacific oceans. With this idea he sailed up the Hudson River, as far as the vicinity of present-day Albany. Upon his return to England (November 1609), he was forbidden to sail under the flag of another nation and, in April 1610, departed on a voyage in search of a northwest passage on behalf of a number of London merchants. In August he reached Hudson Bay, which he explored, and spent the winter at the southwest corner of James Bay. When the expedition continued its way in June 1611, a mutiny broke out among the men, and H., his son and seven others, were put on a small boat and sent to their deaths. Although he was not the first to visit the bay, strait, and river which carry his name, his voyages signalled the beginning of systematic commercial exploitation of these places.

L. Powys, *Henry Hudson* (1928);
P. Vail, *Magnificent Adventures of Henry Hudson* (1965).

HUGUENOTS The name given to the Calvinist Protestant party in France at the outset of the *Religious Wars. It appeared about 1561, probably as a nickname based on the old legend of King Hugo; another possibility is that it is a corruption of the German word *Eidgenossen* (confederates). By the time they became a political entity, the H. had some 2,000 congregations and accounted for as much as 15 per cent of the population. Although among their leaders were some great aristocrats, the vast majority were of the lesser nobility and the urban middle class. The H. withstood over 30 years of civil wars until they won full freedom of worship in the Edict of *Nantes (1598), awarded by their own former leader King *Henry IV.

H. M. Baird, *History of the Rise of the Huguenots*, 2 vols. (1900);
R. Stephan, *L'épopée huguenote* (1945);
A. J. Grant, *The Huguenots* (1934).

HUGUET, JAIME (?-1492) Spanish painter. Born in Tarragona, he was active in Barcelona from 1448. He was a follower of *Martorell and is considered the greatest representative of the 15th century Catalan school. His altarpiece in the church of San Antonio Abad (1455) was destroyed in the early 20th century, but his *Consecration of St. Augustine*, completed in about 1486, is at the Barcelona museum. Like his Catalan predecessors, H. was influenced by the Flemish style, but his works reveal a growing maturity and high quality of technique and composition.

J. Ainaud de Lasarte, *Jaime Huguet* (1955).

HUMANISM The major cultural-intellectual trend of the *Renaissance. The term was coined in the 19th century, and is probably understood by most people today as concerned with human interests and ideals. Originally, however, it referred to an education favouring classical studies and, more specifically, to the teachings and cultural ideas of Renaissance scholars who laid stress on the works of ancient *Greek and Roman authors. Historically, the term goes back to the late 14th century when scholars first began to refer to the *studia humanitatis*, the liberal arts, in which they included grammar, rhetoric, poetry, history and ethics. The adjective "humanist", to designate the person engaged in these studies, came into use around the year 1500. By that time humanist education was contrasted with the mediaeval scholastic curriculum, which emphasized logic, natural philosophy and metaphysics.

As a movement having conscious goals, humanism was pioneered by *Petrarch. It was he who first stressed rhetoric, poetry and language in contrast to contemplative speculations. He began a collection of classical manuscripts and in his writings opened a new historical perspective of the world of antiquity. His younger contemporary, *Boccaccio, extended this interest in classical history and mythology, and originated the study of Greek. The movement might have remained confined to literary and antiquarian scholarship, but for Coluccio *Salutati, a chancellor of the Republic of Florence, who applied the new humanist vocabulary to the language of statecraft and *diplomacy. Salutati's work was followed in the early 15th century by the next Florentine chancellor, Leonardo *Bruni, who is considered the founder of the Florentine tradition of civic H., marked by a special interest in the study of history and politics. Much later this tradition reached its apogee in the works of *Machiavelli and *Guicciardini.

Meanwhile, H. was spreading all over Italy and enveloping an ever wider range of interests. In *Gasparino da Barzizza and his pupil *Filelfo it produced the familiar types of roving scholars, successively patronized by different rulers. Niccolò *Niccoli, *Poggio Bracciolini, *Ciriaco de' Pizzicoli and Giovanni *Aurispa were among the earliest indefatigable collectors of numerous Roman and Greek manuscripts. *Vergerio, *Vittorino da Feltre and *Guarino da Verona were the first great theorists and practitioners of humanist *education. While Enea Silvio Piccolomini, the future *Pius II, raised the humanist art of rhetoric to new heights, Lorenzo *Valla broke new ground in the field of historical textual criticism. Leone Battista *Alberti, on the other hand, extended humanist theory to visual aesthetics, particularly to *architecture. The cumulative contribution of all these intellectual pioneers was to transform the cultural life of Italy during the first half of the 15th century.

Italian H. of the second half of the 15th century shifted its emphasis. If the former generation sought to emulate classical antiquity in a broad and obvious manner, the next was more selective and specialized. With Ermolao *Barbaro and *Politian, the study of the ancient authors became a true scholarly occupation, and humanists began their fruitful cooperation with the *printing industry, turning out carefully-edited texts of the classics. At the same time, certain currents of thought were given particular attention and employed as means of conciliation between humanist culture and Christianity. Marsiglio *Ficino was the foremost promotor of *Neoplatonism. His pupil, Giovanni *Pico della Mirandola, went even further in his search of philosophical truths and made use of Arabic and *Hebrew sources.

By the end of the 15th century H. acquired a permanent foothold throughout Europe. Such persons as Robert *Gaguin and *Lefèvre d'Étaples in France, Rudolph *Agricola, Conrad *Celtis and Johann *Reuchlin in Germany, William *Grocyn, Thomas *Linacre and John *Colet in England, adapted the humanist ideas of Italy to the cultural conditions of their own countries. In northern Europe H. tended to become closely involved with moral and religious issues; in Germany it developed a patriotic tone. This character of Northern H. made it an even more revolutionary factor than its more secular Italian parent, and may have hastened the emergence of the *Reformation. Of the leading second-generation Northern humanists, the French Guillaume *Budé continued to stress classical philology, while the Spanish Juan Luís *Vives represented a current more concerned with social and moral questions. Germany's Ulrich von *Hutten was a notable representative of the more destructive aspect of the movement, whereas in England Thomas *More personified the inner struggle of a humanist who was also a devout Christian. The greatest pre-Reformation humanist, *Erasmus, combined in his career most of these themes. A classical scholar, he also dealt with such topics as education and ethics, became famous for his scathing social satires, but shunned the Reformation.

The decline of H. as a strong Continental intellectual movement began with, and as an outcome of, the Reformation. As broadmindedness gave way to sectarianism, the liberal outlook essential to H. came under heavy pressure. But much of the European culture of the 16th and later centuries remained intimately associated with the achievements of the movement. The Protestant and Roman Catholic systems of education alike continued to emphasize the study of the classics, and European *drama and *literature retained for a long time their affinity to classical models, as was much of the work in *political theory and *historiography. Indeed, the sense of identity of modern man could not have evolved without the contribution of Renaissance humanism.

H. Baron, *The Crisis of the Early Italian Renaissance*, 2 vols. (1955);
W. J. Bouwsma, *The Culture of Renaissance Humanism* (1973);
E. Garin, *Italian Humanism* (1965);
R. Weiss, *The Dawn of Humanism in Italy* (1947).

HUNDRED YEARS' WAR (1338-1453) This long military conflict, begun by Edward III of England when he asserted his claim to the French throne (1340), seemed to be nearing its end with the truce of 1396, after the French victories had recovered much of the earlier English gains. However, internal quarrels between the *Armagnacs and the Burgundians debilitated France, and made possible the renewed English invasion under *Henry V and the great victory at *Agincourt (1415). The Treaty of Troyes (1420), which recognized Henry V as heir to the French throne, could not take effect because of the sudden death of the English king (1422); but until 1428 the English military domination was complete and they controlled Paris and most of the area north of the Loire, except Orléans. The French recovery was inspired by the dramatic appearance of *Joan of Arc (1428-30). After the first French victories there was a reconciliation between *Charles VII and *Burgundy (1435) and, in 1436, Paris was recovered. Although in the next 13 years there were several extended periods of truce, the English position steadily deteriorated. When the war was resumed in 1449 they immediately lost Rouen, after which the French captured the whole of Normandy and Gascony. On 17 July 1453, the Battle of Castillon brought the long conflict to an end. French *artillery completely crushed the army of John Talbot, who was killed. Of all its former possessions in France, England retained only Calais.

E. Perroy, *The Hundred Years' War* (1951).

HUNGARY Situated in the plains of the middle Danube Valley, H. began to take part in the affairs of Europe with its conversion to Christianity in the 11th century. The political history of the Magyar people reached a turning point in 1301 when the last descendant of the ancient Arpád dynasty died childless. In accordance with the old tribal tradition, the monarchy was made elective and, for the next two centuries, a series of foreign kings became or claimed to be the rulers of H. An arrangement which left considerable freedom to the Hungarian nobility, the system worked well enough under Louis I the Great (1342-82), but *Sigismund (1387-1437), who was also emperor and king of *Bohemia, caused dissatisfaction by his neglect of the kingdom. After the brief reign of Emperor *Albert II (1437-39), H. went to the weak *Vladislav III of Poland (1440-44), who met his death at the Battle of Varna. The next king, *Ladislas Posthumus (1444-57), was only four years old at his accession and was made to leave H. as a result of a feud with the nobles, and died shortly after. Nevertheless, it was during these last two reigns that H. came to play a cardinal role as defender of Christendom from the *Ottoman Turks. The struggle, which was led by Janos *Hunyadi, a powerful frontier governor, climaxed in the heroic defence of Belgrade (1456). Hunyadi died soon after, but his young son *Matthias Corvinus (1458-90) was elected king. During his long reign H. became the strongest military power of Central Europe, developed economically and was exposed to Renaissance art and culture.

After his death, the work of Matthias Corvinus was allowed to decay. Under the next sovereign, *Ladislas II of Bohemia (1490-1516), royal authority collapsed, and the nobility, led by the *Zápolya family of Transylvania, extracted from the crown important privileges. In 1514 a great peasant revolt, led by George *Dozsa, was repressed, resulting in the enforcement of serfdom. *Louis II (1516-26), only ten years old upon his accession to the throne, lost his life when he led the Hungarians to their disastrous defeat at the hands of the Turks in the Battle of *Mohács. Without a king, the nobility became divided between John Zápolya and *Ferdinand of Austria. A long war ensued in which Zápolya did not hesitate to call upon the Turks for help. When he died (1540), Cardinal *Martinuzzi, regent, and guardian of his son, John Sigismund Zápolya (1540-71), recognized the suzerainty of the Turks: in 1541 they took Buda and the entire central part of the country, and remained in control of it for almost a century and a half.

For the rest of the 16th century, H. was thus divided between three governments: the northwestern narrow strip belonged to the *Habsburgs, for which, however, they paid, tribute to the Sultan; the centre was under Turkish military rule, while in the east, Transylvania was a Turkish dependency. Nevertheless, late in the century a succession of Hungarian princes took advantage of the declining power of the Turks to make Transylvania practically independent. What further distinguished this region was the adherence of many Hungarian nobles to Calvanism. The *Counter-Reformation efforts to return Hungary to Catholicism did not begin until early in the 17th century.

O. Zarek, *The History of Hungary* (1939).

HUNYADI, JANOS (c. 1387-1456) Hungarian political and military leader. Born to a noble family of Transylvania, he entered the service of King *Sigismund (about 1410), and took part in the *Hussite Wars (1420). Having distinguished himself as soldier and as councillor, H. became highly influential with *Vladislav III, who rewarded him with governorship of Transylvania and the command of the fortress of Belgrade. From 1441 on H. was responsible for defending the Balkans from the Ottoman Turks. He defeated *Murad II in a series of campaigns in 1443, and forced him to accept a ten-year truce; but then he himself promptly violated the treaty and was defeated at Varna in 1444, a battle in which Vladislav died. In spite of this, H. became in 1446 the regent of Hungary in the absence of the boy-king *Ladislas Posthumus. He retained a prominent position, as captain general of the kingdom, after *Frederick III returned Ladislas to Hungary (1453). IN 1455 he defended Belgrade against the renewed advance of the Turks under *Mehemmed II. Combining astute offensive actions with successful static resistance, he forced the besiegers to withdraw. He died soon afterwards of the plague. His son, *Matthias Corvinus, was later king of Hungary.

HURTADO DE MENDOZA, DIEGO (1503-75) Spanish statesman and historian. Born to a noble family in Granada, he studied at Salamanca and in Italy. *Charles V sent him to *Henry VIII of England, and in 1539 appointed him ambassador to *Venice. There he collected rare manuscripts, including the one that served for the first printing of Josephus Flavius (1544). Employed for many years as a trusted administrator, he was banished from the court in 1568 by *Philip II and retired to his native town, where he dedicated himself to writing. His major work, *History of the War of Granada*, dealt with the *Morisco rebellion of 1568-70. It was intelligently written and contained a good deal of criticism of contemporaries, but was rather slavish in its attempt to imitate Tacitus. He also wrote poetry, and was believed to be the author of **Lazarillo de Tormes*, the famous *picaresque novel.

A. González Palencia and E. Mele, *Vida y obra de Hurtado de Mendoza*, 3 vols. (1941-43).

HUS, JAN (1374-1415) Czech reformer; the most important forerunner of the 16th-century *Reformation in central Europe. Born to a peasant family, he entered the university of Prague about 1390, took his Master's degree in 1396 and, in 1398, began to teach there. Having been ordained, he quickly acquired a reputation as a preacher at the Bethlehem Chapel in Prague (1402). That year he was made rector of the university. At this time H. came under the influence of *Wycliffe, whose ideas were introduced into *Bohemia by *Jerome of Prague, a friend of H. He began to criticize the moral conduct of the clergy and translated Wycliffe's writings into Czech. Popular with his own countrymen, he was increasingly attacked by the non-Czech Faculty and students of the University, who incited Archbishop Zbynek of Prague to take measures against him. But, in 1409, a royal decree of King *Wenceslaus gave the Czech nation control over the university, causing the German students to leave, and making the University a Wycliffe stronghold. Soon the Archbishop forbade H. to preach and, early in 1411, he was excommunicated by Pope *John XXIII, who also put Prague under an interdict.

In 1412 H. denounced the papal legate who came to Prague to promote the sale of *indulgences. The affair caused a public riot, and the King then made H. leave Prague with his followers and take refuge with some Czech nobles. He then wrote his main work, *De Ecclesia* (*On the Church*), wherein, following Wycliffe, he advocated the purification of the Church. Having been given a safe-conduct by Emperor *Sigismund, he left in October 1414 to appear before the Council of *Constance and answer charges brought against him. But when he arrived at Constance he was put under arrest, and at his trial (June 1415) was not allowed to speak in his own defence. Refusing to make a public recantation, he was burnt at the stake on 6 July 1415. In Bohemia his execution gave rise to vehement protests

Hus burning at the stake. Illustration in a contemporary manuscript

against the conduct of the council and the breach of faith by the Emperor. Declared a national hero, his followers began driving out Catholic priests and renounced the authority of Rome. The rebellion, a movement both religious and political, soon led to the *Hussite Wars.

M. Spinka, *John Hus' Concept of Reform* (1966);
J. Herben, *Huss and His Followers* (1926);
J. Macek, *The Hussite Movement in Bohemia* (1958).

HUSSITE WARS (1420-36) A protracted series of military campaigns in which the Czech followers of Jan *Hus, though disunited, successfully resisted outside attempts to destroy their religious and political independence. The wars opened with the proclamation of a crusade against the Hussites by *Martin V, and the invasion of *Bohemia by King *Sigismund. Repelled, Sigismund tried again, but was defeated by Jan *Zizka (1422). In 1427 another crusade, led by the English Cardinal Henry *Beaufort, was crushed at Tachov and, in 1431, a third crusade was routed at Domazlice. The Council of *Basle then opened negotiations with the Hussites, which led to the agreement known as the *Compactata* (1433). The agreement conceded the Czechs' principal demands: communion in both kinds, expropriation of Church property and freedom of preaching. The extreme faction, the *Taborites, who refused to accept the settlement, were defeated by the more moderate *Ultraquists and the imperial forces at the Battle of Lipany in 1434. In 1436 the *Compactata* was officially promulgated and the Czechs acknowledged Sigismund as their king. The wars, which ravaged Bohemia for 15 years, involved forces of several European nations and caused much destruction. They resulted, however, in a Czech national church which remained independent until it was suppressed by the *Counter Reformation, following the defeat of the Bohemian rebels in 1620.

J. Macek, *The Hussite Movement in Bohemia* (1958);
H. Kaminsky, *A History of the Hussite Revolution* (1967).

HUT, HANS (1491-1527) German *Anabaptist preacher. An eloquent and radically-inclined bookbinder from Franconia, he collaborated with Thomas *Münzer in the *Peasants' War and, after its suppression, joined the

Anabaptist leader Hans *Denck in Augsburg. Later he also had some connections with the Anabaptist community of Nikolsburg, Moravia, which was led by *Hübmaier. He was known for the apocalyptic message of his sermons. Apprehended by the authorities on a visit to Augsburg, he is said to have set fire to himself in prison. During his years of wandering and preaching a legend had grown around his personality, ascribing to him an almost magical power to win the hearts of peasants and labourers.

R. M. Jones, *Studies in Mystical Religion* (1923).

HUTTEN, ULRICH VON (1488-1523) German humanist, patriot and an imperial knight. H. personifies some of the major cultural, social and political trends in Germany at the beginning of the 16th century. On his visits to various universities and travels in Italy he befriended many of the leading humanists, including *Erasmus. H. wrote satires and poetry in both Latin and German and in 1517 was crowned poet laureate by Emperor *Maximilian I. It was H. who published in Germany a version of *Lorenzo Valla's *Donation of Constantin* (1517) and was a major contributor to the *Epistolae Obscurum Virorum* (Letters of Obscure Men) (1515-17), a scathing satire on the ignorance and obscurantism of monks. But H. was also a German nationalist and in his Latin dialogue *Arminius* (written in 1520 but published in 1528) the hero is depicted as a symbol of German resistance to Rome throughout the ages. Unlike his friend Erasmus, H. was an ardent supporter of *Luther from the beginning. In Luther's

Ulrich von Hutten

Music and text of a Protestant hymn, published in Prague (1566)

cause he published, in Latin and in German, a series of satiric pamphlets entitled *Gesprächbüchlein* (Little Conversation Book) (1522). Luther, however, did not give his support to the war of the imperial knights against the German princes and prelates, which was led by H. and Franz von *Sickingen in 1522. It was a last attempt of this declining class to assert its power. The revolt ended in total disaster when the knights were defeated by an alliance of princes at the Landstuhl. Franz von Sickingen was killed and H. exiled from the Empire. He fled to Switzerland where, penniless and sick, he was given refuge by *Zwingli and died soon afterwards. H. was romanticized in German literature as a fierce fighter for freedom and as a national hero.

H. Holborn, *Ulrich von Hutten and the German Reformation* (1937). (M.E.)

HUTTER, JAKOB (?-1536) German *Anabaptist leader. Joining the Swiss Anabaptists at an early stage, H. became one of the leaders of the movement in the Tyrol. But, in order to avoid persecution, he took his followers to Moravia and organized them in agricultural settlements embodying the principles of communism and pacifism (1533-35). Shortly afterwards he was seized by the Austrian authorities and burned at the stake in Innsbruck. But the so called Huttertite Brethren continued to exist, moving first to Russia, in the early 17th century, and to the United States in the 19th.

H. Fischer, *Jakob Hutter* (1956);
J. W. Bennett, *Hutterian Brethren* (1967).

HYMNS The *Reformation, which ushered in an age of religious fervour, put an emphasis on congregational singing of prayers or texts in praise of God. *Luther especially recognized the value of hymn singing in the vernacular and himself composed many, the most famous of which is *Ein feste Burg ist unser Gott*. *Calvin, on the other hand, allowed only the singing of biblical texts, a restriction that explains the popularity of the *Marot-*Beza psalter among the *Huguenots. Among the early collaborators of Luther's in the development of Protestant hymns was Michael Weiss. In England Miles *Coverdale was probably the first to introduce Protestant hymnology. Congregational singing has remained, since the 16th century, an identifiable trait of many Protestant churches.

A. L. Jefferson, *Hymns in Christian Worship* (1950).

Holland in winter

מאימתי קורי' את שמע בערבי' משעה שהכהנ' נכנסים לאכול בתרומתן עד סוף הא האשמורת הראשונה דברי ר' אליעזר וחכמי' אום' עד חצות רבן גמליאל אום' עד שיעלה עמוד השחר. מעשה ובאו בניו מבית המשתה אמרו לו לא קרינו את שמע אם' להם אם לא עלה עמוד השחר חייבין אתם לקרות. ולא זו בלבד אמרו אלא כל מה שאמ' חכמי' עד חצות מצותו עד שיעלה עמוד הש השחר. הקטר חלבי' ואברי' מצותן עד שיעלה עמו' השחר וכל הנאכלי' ליום אחד מצותן עד שיעלה עמוד השחר א"כ למה אמרו חכמים עד חצות כדי ל להרחיק אדם מן העבירה.

מאימתי קורין את שמע בערבין. משעה שהכהני' נכנסי' לאכו' בתרומת' כהני' שנטמאו וטבלו והעריב שמשן והגיע עתם לאכול בתרומה: עד סוף האשמורת הראשונה שליש הלילה כדמפרש בגמ' ומשם ואילך עבר זמן דלא מקרי תו זמן שכיבה דלא קרינן ביה בשכבך ומקמי הכי נמי לאו זמן שכיבה הלכך הקורא קודם לכן לא יצא ידי חובתו. אם כן למה קורין אותה בבה"כ כדי לעמוד בתפלה מתוך דברי תורה והכי תני בברייתא בברכות ירושלמי ולפיכך חובה עלינו לקרותה משתחשך ובקריאת פר' ראשונה שאדם קורא על מטתו יצא: עד שיעלה עמוד השחר שכל הלילה קרוי זמן שכיבה:

מאימתי קורין וכו' פי' רש"י ואנן היכי קרינן מבעוד יום ואין אנו ממתינין לצאת הכוכבים כדמפ' בגמ'. על כן פי' רש"י שק"ש שעל המטה עי' עיקר והוא לאחר צאת הכוכבי' והכי איתא בירו' אם קרא קודם לכן לא יצא וא"כ למה אנו מתפ' מתפללין ק"ש בבה"כ כדי לעמוד בתפלה מתוך דברי תורה. תימ' לפי' והלא אין העולם רגילין ל' לקרות סמוך לשכיבה אלא פר' ראשונה וא"כ ג' פרשיות היה לו ל' לקרות. ועוד דצריך לברך בק"ש שתים לפניה ושתי' לאחריה בע' בערבי'. ועוד דאותה ק"ש סמו' למטה אינו אלא בשביל המזיקי' כדאמ' בסמוך ואם ת"ח הוא אי' אינו צריך ועוד ק' דא"כ פסקי' כר' יהושע בן לוי דאמ' תפלות באמצע תקנום פי' באמצע בי' שני ק"ש בין ק"ש של שחרית ובין ק"ש של ערבית ואנו קי"ל כר' יוחנן דאמ' לקמן איזהו בן העה"ב זה הסומך גאולה של ערבי' לתפלה לכן פר"ת דאדרב' ק"ש של בי' הכנס' עיקר ואת היאך אנו קורין כ"כ מבעוד יום וי"ל דקי"ל כר' יהודה דאמ' פ' תפלת השחר דזמן תפלת מנחה עד פלג המנחה דהיינו י"א שעו' פחו' רביע ומיד כשיכלה זמן המנחה מתחיל זמן ערבי' ואת"ה היאך אנו מתפללי' תפלת מנחה סמו' לחשכה ואפי' לאחר פלג המנחה. י"ל דקי"ל כרבנן דאמ' זמן תפלת המנחה עד הערב ואמ' לקמן השת' דלא איתמ' הלכתא לא כמר ולא כמר דעבד כמר עבד ודעבד כמר עבד. מ"מ קשי' דהוי סתרי אהדדי שהרי מאיזה טעם א' אנו מתפללין ערבי' מיד לאחר פלג המנחה משו' דקי"ל דשעת המנחה כלה לדברי ר' יהודה ומיד הוי זמן ערבי' ובזמ' התפל' עצמה לא קי"ל כר' יהודה אלא כרבנן. על כן אומ' ר"י דודאי ק"ש של בית הכנסת עיקר ואנו שמתפללי' ערבי' מבעו' יום ס"ל כהני תנאי דגמ' דאמ' משעה שקדש היו' וגם משעה שבני

הקטר חלבי' ואברי' של קרבנות שנזרק דמן ביום: מצותן להעלות כל הלילה ואינן נפסלין בלינה עד שיעלה עמוד השחר והן למטה מן המזבח דכתי' לא ילין לבקר. חלבים של כל קרבנו' אברי' של עולה: כל הנאכלי' ליום אחד כגון חטאת ואשם וכבשי עצרת ומנחות ותודה: מצותן זמן אכילתן עד שיעלה עמוד השחר והוא מביאן להיות נותר דכתי' בתודה לא יניח ממנו עד בקר וכלם מתודה ילמדו: א"כ למה אמרו חכ' חכמי' עד חצות בק"ש ובאכילת קדשי': כדי להרחיק אדם מן העבירה ואסרום באכילה קודם זמנן כדי שלא יבא לאכלן לאחר עמוד השחר ויתחייב כרת. וכן בק"ש לזרז את האדם שלא יאמר יש לי עוד שהות ובתוך כך יעלה עמוד השחר ועבר לו הזמן. והקטר חלבים דקתני הכא לא אמרו בו חכמי' עד חצות כלל ולא נקט להו הכא אלא להודיע שכל דבר הנוהג בלילה כשר כל הלילה והכי נמי תנן בפ"ב דמגלה כל הלילה כשר לקצירת העומר ולהקטר חלבי' ואברים: גמ' היכא

אדם נכנסין להסב דהיינו סעודת ע"ש והיא היתה מבעוד יום. ומאותה שעה הוי זמן תפלה. וגם ראי' דרב הוה מצלי של שבת בע"ש ומסתמא גם היה קורא ק"ש מכל אות' הראיו' משמע דאותו ק"ש של בה"כ הוא עיקר והא דקאמ' בירושלמי למה היו קורין בבה"כ וכו' אומ' ר"ת שהיו רגילין לקרות ק"ש קודם תפלת' כמו שאנו רגילין לומר אשרי תחלה ואותו ק"ש אינו אלא לעמוד בתפלה מתוך דברי תורה ומכאן נראה מי שקורא ק"ש על מטתו שאין לברך וגם אינו צריך לקרות אלא פרשה ראשונה. גמ'

א ב

Tractate Berakhot, *illuminated manuscript. Soncino Press, London 1484*

I

IACOPINO DEL CONTE (1510-98) Italian painter. The pupil of *Andrea del Sarto in Florence, he was later influenced by *Michelangelo. Essentially a *Mannerist, his best work is in the frescoes illustrating the life of St. John, at S. Giovanni Decollato, Rome. He also excelled as a portraitist.

IACOPO DEL SELLAIO (1442-93) Italian painter. The son of a Florentine saddler, he was a pupil of Fra Filippo *Lippi. His several versions of the *Madonna Adoring the Child*, reflect the influence of *Boticelli. Other pictures of his, on religious subjects, ancient history and mythology, are all in the linear Florentine style of the second half of the 15th century.

IBRAHIM PASHA (c. 1490-1536) Ottoman military leader. A captive of Christian parentage who was brought up at the Sublime Porte, he was in 1523, appointed by *Suleiman I Grand Vizier and governor of several provinces in the Balkans. His first military expedition was against Egypt (1524), but in 1526 he was put in charge of the Danubian army and, in 1529, commanded the siege of *Vienna. I. represented the Sultan in negotiations with *Charles V over *Hungary. In 1534 he led a successful military campaign against Persia and conquered Baghdad. His soaring prestige aroused the suspicion of the Sultan who had him executed.

ILLUMINATED MANUSCRIPTS The art of embellishing handwritten texts with painted pictures, ornamental letters and a variety of other decorations, reached its highest degree of sophistication at precisely the time that *printing was about to appear. This last great phase of the art was distinguished by a series of works in the *International Gothic style, commissioned by the dukes of Berry. Jacquemart de Hesdin, active from about 1380 to 1410, created four famous Books of Hours, the most splendid of which was *Les Petites Heures du Duc de Berry*. He was followed by the *Limbourg brothers, whose *Les Très Riches Heures du Duc de Berry*, begun about 1411, is perhaps the greatest treasure of 15th-century illumination. While most I. of this period were religious texts, there are also examples of beautiful miniature pictures ornamenting secular books. These were made, among other places, in Aix-en-Provence, at the court of René, duke of Anjou, and in Tours, the residence of Jean *Fouquet. The last-named, who also produced a famous Book of Hours for the royal treasurer Etienne Chevalier, illustrated Josephus' *Antiquities of the Jews* with 21 full-page miniatures. These were among the last great I. The advances made by printing and wood *engraving soon undermined the need for and the practice of the old art.

J. A. Herbert, *Illuminated Manuscripts* (1912);
D. Miner, *Illuminated and Illustrated Books* (1949).

INCUNABULA Books made during the earliest period of printing, from *Gutenberg to 1500. In Latin the word I. means swaddling clothes. In the course of the 17th century it came to describe the period 'when the art of typography was in its cradle'. The term became so widespread that eventually the word 'incunabulum' came to designate any single printed item of the 15th century.

INDEPENDENTS Members of an English movement of the Reformation practicing the principle of the autonomy of each local church; also known as Congregationalists. Early in the reign of *Elizabeth I, dissatisfaction with the conservative practices of the *Church of England created the phenomenon of mixed gatherings of men and women who listened to their own preachers and devised their own manner of worship. The most radical group were the *Brownists, who injected into their congregationalism elitist conceptions. Persecuted, most I. went underground, but only to reappear in the reign of Charles I. Others were driven to exile in Holland and subsequently became the founders of the first colonies in New England.

INDEX LIBRORUM PROHIBITORUM (List of Banned Books) The official list of works whose reading was forbidden by the Catholic church. Attempts to censor printed books were made by Rome as early as 1501, but the institution of the I. as it is popularly known, was a response to the menace of Protestantism which became an important instrument of the *Counter Reformation. Cardinal *Caraffa, the future *Paul IV, who headed the Roman *Inquisition, ordered, in 1543, that no book, old or new, be printed without previous inspection by the ecclesiastical authorities. In 1557, as pope, he issued

Vniuersis Cristifidelib; pñtes litteras inspecturis Paulinus Chappe Consiliari⁹ Ambasiator ꝛ pcurator generalis Serenissimi Regis Cypri ĩ hac pte Salutẽ in dño Cũ Sãctissim⁹ ĩ xpo pr ꝛ dñs nr̃ dñs Nicola⁹ diuĩa puidẽtia papa v⁹. Afflictiõi Regni Cypri misericorditer ꝯpatiẽs contra pfidissiõs crucis xpi hostes Theucros ꝛ Saracenos gratis ꝯcesserit omib; xpifidelib; vbilibet ꝯstitutis ipõs p aspsionem sãguis dñi nri ihũ xpi pie exhortãdo qui infra trienniũ a prima die Maii Anni dñi Mccccli incipiendum p defensiõe catholice fidei ꝛ Regni pdicti de facultatib; suis magis vel min⁹ prout ipoꝝ videbit ꝯscientiis procuratorib; vel nũciis Substitutis pie erogauerint vt Confessores ydonei seculares vel regulares p ipsos eligendi ꝯfessionib; eoꝝ auditis p ꝯmissis etiã Sedi aplice reseruatis excessib; crimib; atq; delictis quãtũcũq; grauib; p vna vice tãtũ debitã absolutionẽ impẽdere ꝛ penitẽtiã salutarẽ iniũgere Necnõ si id huiliter petierĩt ipõs a quibuscũq; excõicationũ suspensionũ ꝛ Interdicti Aliisq; sentẽtiis cẽsuris ꝛ penis ecclesiasticis a Iure vel ab hoĩe pmulgatis quib⁹ forsan innodati existũt absoluere. Iniũcta p modo culpe penitẽtia salutari vel aliis que de Iure fuerint iniũgenda ac eis vere penitẽtib; ꝛ confessis. vel si forsan propter amissionem loquele ꝯfiteri non poterint signa ꝯtritionis ostendendo plenissimã oĩm petoꝝ suorũ de quib; ore ꝯfessi ꝛ corde ꝯtriti fuerĩt Indulgẽtiã ac plenariã remissionẽ semel in vita et semel in mortis articulo ipĩs aũcte aplica ꝯcedere valeãt. Satisfactõe p eos fcã si supuixerint aut p eoꝝ heredes si tunc trãsierint Sic tñ q post indultũ ꝯcessum p vnũ ãnũ singulis sextis feriis vel quadã alia die ieiunẽt. legitiio impedimẽto ecclesie pcepto Regulari obseruãtia. pnia iniũcta voto uel alias non obstañ. Et ipĩs impeditis in dicto ãno uel eius parte Anno sequenti uel alias quam primũ poterint ieiunabunt. Et si ĩ aliquo ãnoꝝ vel eoꝝ parte dictũ ieiuniũ cõmode adimplere nequiuerint Confessor ad id electus in alia ꝯmutare poterit caritatis opera que ipĩ facere etiã teneãt Dũmodo tñ ex ꝯfidentia rẽissionis hmõi quod absit peccare non presumant Alioquĩ dicta concessio quo ad plenariã remissionẽ in mortis articulo et remissio quo ad pcã ex ꝯfidentia vt pmittit' ꝯmissa nulli⁹ sint roboris uel momẽti Et quia deuoti in xpo Fridericus Schulem [illegible] Sebaldi Iuxta dictũ indultum de facultatibus suis pie erogauit merito huiusmodi indulgentiis gaudere debet In veritatis testimonium Sigillum ad hoc ordinatum presentib; litteris testimonialib; est appensum Datum Nuremberge Anno dñi Mccccl[illegible] die uero [illegible] Mensis Marcy

Forma plenissime absolutionis et remissionis in vita

Misereatur tui ꝛc Dns nr̃ ihesus xps p suã sctissimã et piissimã mĩa; te absoluat Et aũcte ipi⁹ beatoꝝq; petri et pauli apłoꝝ ei⁹ ac aũcte aplica michi ꝯmissa et tibi ꝯcessa Ego te absoluo ab omib; pctis tuis ꝯtritis ꝯfessis ꝛ oblitis Etiã ab omib; casib⁹ excessib; crimib; atq; delictis quãtũcũq; grauib; Sedi Aplice reseruatis Necnon a quibuscũq; excõicationũ suspensionũ et interdicti Aliisq; sniis cẽsuris ꝛ penis ecclesiasticis a Iure vel ab hoĩe pmulgatis si quas incurristi dando tibi plenissimã oĩm pctoꝝ tuoꝝ indulgentiã ꝛ remissionẽ Inquãtũ claues sancte matris ecctie in hac pte se extendũt. In nomine patris ꝛ filii et spiritus sancti Amen.

Forma plenarie remissionis in mortis articulo

Misereatur tui ꝛc Dñs noster ut supra Ego te absoluo ab omib; pctis tuis ꝯtritis ꝯfessis ꝛ oblitis restituendo te vnitati fideliũ ꝛ sacramentis ecctie Remittendo tibi penas purgatorii quas propter culpas et offensas incurristi dando tibi plenariam oĩm pctorũ tuorũ remissionẽ. Inquãtũ claues sctẽ mris ecctie in hac parte se extendũt. In noĩe pris et filii et spũs sancti Amen.

A 15th-century letter of indulgence

the first Index. It was approved by the Council of *Trent and, in 1571, *Pius V established a special commission to make periodic revisions of the lists. Not only Protestant works were prescribed, but also Catholic authors, early humanists like Boccaccio and some works of Erasmus. The I. remained in existence for several centuries, but gradually lost its effect.

F. S. Betten, *The Roman Index of Forbidden Books* (1935).

INDIA On 17 May 1498, Vasco da *Gama landed near Calicut on the Malabar coast, thus opening naval communication between I. and Europe. In the next ten years the Portuguese established a number of **feitorias*, especially at Cochin and Cananor, and, in 1509, they defeated at Diu a Moslem fleet which sought to prevent their gaining control of the Indian spice trade. The two persons most responsible for consolidating the Portuguese presence in I. were Francisco de *Almeida and Afonso de *Albuquerque. In 1510 the latter acquired Goa for Portugal, and it became the headquarters of the *Estado da India*. The Portuguese were not after extensive territorial conquests and satisfied to gain certain strongholds which gave them commercial advantages. Not being very strong militarily, they contrived to exploit the rivalry among the different Indian rulers. They also promoted Roman Catholicism. In 1542 Francis *Xavier arrived at Goa and, in 1557, this administrative centre was important enough to be made a diocese. In the early 17th century Roberto de *Nobili won more converts to Christianity. However, the Portuguese gradually lost the audacity and determination which characterized their early relations with I. and, by the end of the century, they began to face the challenge of other nations. The first Dutch fleet arrived in 1595, and the first English expedition in 1601. By the second decade of the 17th century these two nations put an end to Portuguese commercial monopoly, although a long time had to pass before any European nation gained decisive influence in I.

R. S. Whiteway, *The Rise of Portuguese Power in India, 1497-1550* (1952).

INDULGENCES The general remission of penalties imposed on repentant sinners was a phenomenon which appeared first in the 12th century, in association with the *Crusades. First promised to those who took up the cross, the Church later broadened the I. to include the remission of temporal punishment to reward monetary contributions. During the latter half of the 15th century the remission was extended to the punishment of the living and the dead in purgatory, and the sale of I. was expanded and became a form of regular fund-raising. It was conducted by professional salesmen, who omitted the requirement of repentance, and offered their merchandize as an unqualified immunity from the consequences of sin. *Julius II and *Leo X both authorized the sale of I. so as to raise funds for the building of St. Peter's. In April 1517, when Johann *Tetzel approached Wittenberg on an I.'s selling campaign, *Luther composed his 95 theses attacking the manner of the sale and the principle behind it. It was the immediate cause of the *Reformation. Although the Council of *Trent did not change the doctrine sanctioning I., their sale was prohibited in 1567 by *Pius V.

INFESSURA, STEFANO (c.1436-c.1500) Italian historian. Born in Rome. he was attached to the powerful house of *Colonna, which he served as administrator. His *Diario della città di Roma*, written partly in Latin, is a lively account of the period from 1303 to 1494. It is generally critical of the popes, especially of *Sixtus IV.

INGEGNERI, MARCANTONIO (c.1545-92) Italian composer. Born at Verona, he became in 1572 choirmaster at Cremona where, between 1580 and 1582, he was the teacher of *Monteverdi. He composed *madrigals for 5 voices, masses and *motets, but is chiefly remembered for the 27 Responsoria for Holy Week (1588). These were for a long time attributed to *Palestrina, before they were recognized as the work of their true author.

INNOCENT VIII (1432-92) Pope from 1484. Born in Genoa as Giambattista Cibo, he studied at Padua before taking holy orders. In 1469 he was made bishop of Savona and in 1472 of Molfetta. His election to the papal throne was strongly supported by Cardinal Giuliano della Rovere, the future *Julius II. Spiritually, his reign was a failure, characterized by the pope's moral laxity and secular concerns. Yet I. was not even an effective ruler of the Papal States, which were overun by the armies of *Naples. His attempt to organize a *crusade against the Ottoman Turks came to nought, but because he held the sultan's brother, *Djem, I. was able to extract from *Bayezid II an annual payment.

INNOCENT IX (1519-91) Pope for two months in 1591. Born Giovanni Antonio Facchinetti in Bologna, he had a long ecclesiastical career, and practically managed the papal affairs under his predecessor *Gregory XIV.

INQUISITION, THE The establishment by the church of Rome of special ecclesiastical courts whose business it was to put down religious heresy, took place in the 13th century. It was then that the use of torture against the accused was first allowed and the practice established of delivering the extreme offenders to the secular government for execution. The *auto da fé* (act of faith), the public ceremonial procession which preceeded the

Manner of burning at the stake those who had been condemned by the Inquisition, a later version of 16th-century auto da fé *at Paris*

St. Dominic at the Tribunal of the Inquisition *by Pedro Berruguete*

sentencing and burning at the stake, was also of mediaeval origin. However, during the Renaissance the institution was revived and adapted to the new conditions. In 1479 *Ferdinand and *Isabella received papal approval for the institution of the I. in Spain. It was given a highly centralized structure and was especially directed against the **marranos*. Later, it also persecuted the **moriscos*, the **alumbrados* and suspected *Protestants. It was this form of I. which appealed to Cardinal *Caraffa (the future *Paul IV) who, in 1542, was authorized by *Paul III to establish the Sacred Roman Congregation of Universal Inquisition, better known as the Holy Office. Consisting at first of six cardinals, and afterwards (1587) of 13, it was given authority as a final court of appeal over the entire Christian world. Designed to fight the spread of the *Reformation, especially in those areas which had a Roman Catholic majority, the employment of the I. was nevertheless dependent on the cooperation of secular rulers. The political might of Spain aided its spread to the Italian states. In France it was employed especially in the reign of *Henry II, but in the *Netherlands its practices hastened the revolt against Spain. The continued existence of the I. in Italy, Spain and Portugal contributed to the process of intellectual decay.

H. C. Lea, *History of the Inquisition in Spain*, 4 vols. (1922);
C. Roth, *The Spanish Inquisition* (1938);
A. L. Maycock, *The Inquisition* (1926).

INTERCURSUS MAGNUS A commercial agreement which, in 1496, reestablished the prosperous cloth trade between England and the Netherlands. This trade had come to a halt in 1493, when Perkin *Warbeck, the pretender to the English throne, was given shelter and support in the Netherlands. In the I. *Henry VII extracted a promise to expel the pretender. The agreement also established fixed duties on goods exported by one country to the other and expanded the freedom of trade.

INTEREST During the Middle Ages, the charging of interest on loans had been condemned by the Church as usury. However, the concept acquired a partial legitimation in the Renaissance. Although the gulf between moral restriction and economic reality had been evident since the 12th century, it was deepened by the expansion of international *banking in the course of the 15th century. Credit became more readily available and in fact, tended to lower the rate of interest. An early response to this new situation were the *Monti di Pietà. On the eve of the Reformation, an interpretation distinguishing between usury and justified interest was forcefully argued by Johann *Eck, who was backed by the *Fuggers. Yet Eck's great rival, *Luther, repeatedly condemned the charging of interest, and so did *Zwingli. *Calvin, on the other hand, in a famous letter of 1574, denied that accepting payment for the use of money was in itself sinful. He pointed out that the money is used by the borrower to procure revenues for himself, and implied that only the taking of interest from borrowers in distress constituted sinful usury.

Legislation to regulate the rate of interest was first passed in Protestant countries. In 1571 England enacted a law permitting an interest of up to ten per cent, though this law still left creditors liable to prosecution in ecclesiastical courts. Other Protestant nations followed suit in the course of the 17th century. In the Catholic parts of Europe the prohibition against interest-usury was not lifted until much later.

B. N. Nelson, *The Idea of Usury* (1949);
R. H. Tawney, *Religion and the Rise of Capitalism* (1922).

INTERNATIONAL GOTHIC A term commonly applied to a style of painting of the period of transition from the Middle Ages to the Renaissance. The I. is characteristic of works done just before and after 1400 in Burgundy and northern France, from where it spread to Italy, Gemany and other countries. While retaining much of the mediaeval Gothic it introduced elements of realism in the treatment of landscape and costume, adding rudimentary perspective and an ornamental feeling for detail. It was a style that consciously pursued elegance. Its best representative work is the *Très Riches Heures*, an illuminated manuscript made about 1415 by the three *Limbourg brothers for the duke of Berry.

L. Castelfranchi Vegas, *Die internationale Gotik in Italien* (1966).

IRALA, DOMINGO MARTINEZ DE (1487-1557) Spanish **conquistador*. Born in the northern province of Guipuzcoa, he went to Paraguay from Buenos Aires at the head of an expedition of Pedro de *Mendoza's. In

1537 he founded Asunción. In 1542 *Cabeza de Vaca came from Spain to replace him as governor, but I. turned the colonists against him, deposed him and reassumed the governorship (1545), remaining the uncontested strong man of Paraguay until his death. I. is also remembered for the many children he sired on his numerous Indian wives.

IRELAND Conquered in 1171 by Henry II of England, more by a display of arms than a military campaign, I. was always an uneasy English possession. In the course of time, some of the English nobles who had settled there adopted the Gaelic tongue and taken Irish wives; native families, such as the O'Neills and the O'Donnells continued to dominate the north. Attempts to make English institutions work, chiefly by banning intermarriage and enforcing the English language, law and customs, characterized the crown's policy during the 14th century. But early in the 15th century the English lord-lieutenant, Sir John Talbot, engaged in a bitter struggle against local "degenerate English" lords, and the area under his effective command was limited to a short strip between Dublin and Dundalk. Richard, duke of *York, who went to I. in 1449, was acclaimed there heir to the English throne. The next lord deputies in charge were Yorkists, of which Gerald Fitzgerald, earl of Kildare, an Anglo-Irish magnate, became the most powerful. He was confirmed in his office by *Henry VII, in spite of his past political affiliation, and removed only in 1494, after he had welcomed to I. the two pretenders Lambert *Simnel and Perkin *Warbeck. The new English governor, Sir Edward Poynings, arriving at the head of an army, had the Irish parliament pass the Statute of *Drogheda. However, Kildare soon recovered his office and held it until his death in 1513. The same developments took place under *Henry VIII, when an English governor sent by the King quickly left, and was replaced by Kildare's son. But when the Fitzgeralds declined to support the King's break with Rome (1534), they precipitated a conflict which led to their destruction. In 1541 the Irish parliament affirmed Henry VIII as "King of Ireland", and during the next century there was no Irish-born lord lieutenant.

I., nevertheless, resisted the implementation of Protestantism, especially the abolition of the Mass under *Edward VI. There was a respite under *Mary Tudor, but with the religious settlement of *Elizabeth I (1560), resistance flared up again, leading eventually to the three great rebellions of Shane O'Neill (1559), James Fitzmaurice Fitzgerald of Desmond (1568-83), and Hugh *O'Neill (1595-1603). The first of these was essentially a case of insubordination by a chief of a native clan, but the second became a religious movement which received aid from Rome and Spain. The third actually saw Spanish troops joining the rebels, and culminated in a full-scale military campaign, headed on England's side by *Essex and *Mountjoy. It was, in fact, the first time that I. was subdued militarily.

E. Curtis, *A History of Medieval Ireland, 1086-1513* (1938);
R. D. Edwards, *Church and State in Tudor Ireland* (1935);
J. C. Beckett, *A Short History of Ireland*, 5th ed. (1973).

ISAAC, HEINRICH (c.1450-1517) Flemish composer. Having spent his youth in the Netherlands, he went to Italy, where he supervised *musical performance in churches, and later found employment in Florence under Lorenzo de' *Medici. In 1484 he went to Innsbruck and later entered the service of Emperor *Maximilian I, living in Vienna and Constance. Eventually he returned to Italy and died in Florence. The author of sacred and secular compositions, he, like his compatriot *Josquin Després, was one of the best-known composers of his age. He introduced to Germany the rich new style of High Renaissance polyphony, and is especially remembered for the melody *Innsbruck, ich muss dich lassen (Innsbruck, I Must Forsake Thee)*, which much later was harmonized by Bach.

ISABELLA THE CATHOLIC (1451-1504) Queen of Castile from 1474. The daughter of John II of Castile, she altered the face of the Iberian Peninsula when, in 1569, she married *Ferdinand of *Aragon, against the wishes of her brother King *Henry IV. After his death she gained the support of the majority of the Castilian nobles, against the claims of her niece *Juana la Beltraneja and, following the victory at the Battle of Toro (1476), secured the crown for herself. After 1479, when Ferdinand succeeded to the throne of Aragon, I. and he ruled Spain jointly, though without actually uniting their kingdoms.

Imbued with a deep sense of royal authority, I. succeeded in the first years of her reign to strengthen the central government considerably. She curbed the privileges of the great nobles and military *orders and, in 1480, introduced the institution of *corregidor*, who henceforth governed the Castilian town on behalf of the crown. I. and her husband were present at the conquest of *Granada, and supported expeditions against the Moslems in North Africa. A highly religious person, I. backed the *Inquisition, which she had introduced in 1478, and was the real author of the expulsion of the *Jews (1492). But she was also largely responsible for the fact that *Columbus sailed on his voyage of discovery under the flag of Spain. She had one son, who died before she did, and four daughters. Of these, two married *Manoel I of Portugal, and the others were *Joanna the Mad and *Catherine of Aragon.

M. Ballesteros Gaibrois, *La obra de Isabel la Católica* (1953);
C. Silio, *Isabel la Católica* (1967);
W. T. Walsh, *Isabella of Spain* (1931).

ITALIAN LEAGUE (1454) Immediately following the Peace of *Lodi, Francesco *Sforza of *Milan established with *Venice and *Florence a league of alliance for the duration of 25 years. Soon afterwards, the *papacy and *Naples joined the three original members. The aim of the league was to maintain the status quo between the participants, and members promised not to contract separate alliances. It stabilized Italian politics for almost two generations, but the system which it supported ended with the French invasion of 1494.

ITALIAN WARS (1494-1559) The name given to a series of European military conflicts of which *Italy was the main theatre. The wars began with the French invasion of Italy in September 1494, King *Charles VIII leading some 30,000 troops. The French king took *Florence and, in February 1495, entered *Naples, on which he had a rather flimsy claim. His easy victories led to the formation of a league between *Venice, *Milan, the papacy, Spain and the Empire. On his way back north *Charles VIII fought the first great battle of the wars at Fornovo (July 1495), which he won. But soon after his garrison in Naples was decimated by a plague and defeated on the battlefield by Gonzalo de *Córdoba. The kingdom was then delivered to *Ferrante II.

Four years later the wars were renewed by *Louis XII of France, who laid claim to Milan. With the co-operation of Venice he forced *Ludovico Moro to flee to Germany, captured the city (September 1499), and, in 1500, signed with *Ferdinand the Catholic the Treaty of Granada, by which Spain and France were to share Naples between them. In 1501 King *Federico of Naples did indeed abdicate in favour of the French king, but the allies soon fell out, starting a war over the control of Naples (1502-04). The most decisive battle was held at Cerignola (April 1503), and was won by Córdoba, thereby securing complete Spanish domination over the southern half of the Italian Peninsula.

The wars were renewed following the establishment of the League of *Cambrai (1508). Still the master of Milan, Louis XII defeated the Venetians at Agnadello (May 1509). He captured Cremona and Bergamo, handed over Verona, Vicenza and Padua to *Maximilian I, enabling *Julius II to conquer Ravenna and Rimini. But Venice having been humiliated, France's former allies turned against her, the Pope taking the lead in organizing the *Holy League with Spain, Venice and England to drive the French out of Italy. Although the French defeated the Spaniards at Ravenna (April 1512), they were driven out of Milan, and crushed by the Swiss at Novara (June 1513). Two months later *Henry VIII defeated them in the Battle of the *Spurs.

Upon his accession, *Francis I of France renewed the wars with the aim of recovering Milan. Allied with Venice he won a great victory over the Swiss at *Marignano (September 1515), which gave him not only the mastery over Milan but led to the Concordat of *Bologna with *Leo X (1516). The peace that followed lasted six years. In 1522 *Charles V, supported by the Pope and by England, took Milan from the French. The war was now waged also in the Netherlands and on the Spanish-French border, culminating in the Battle of *Pavia (February 1525), where Francis was taken prisoner by the Spanish. After he signed the Treaty of Madrid (January 1526) and was liberated, the French king hastened to conclude the League of *Cognac (May 1526) with Venice, Florence and Pope *Clement VII. As a result, the Sack of *Rome by the Imperial army followed (May 1527). Florence revolted against the *Medici (1527-30); Andrea *Doria changed sides from the French to the Empire, making *Genoa the ally of the Emperor (1528). The Peace of *Cambrai (August 1529) brought a temporary settlement.

When hostilities reopened in 1536 it became even more than before a *Habsburg-Valois struggle. Again the main bone of contention was Milan, which Charles V, after the death of Massimiliano *Sforza (1535), claimed as its imperial suzerain. The Truce of Nice (June 1538) established peace, Spain retaining Milan but conceding the French acquisitions in Piedmont. In the renewed fighting in 1542 the action was mainly outside Italy, and ended with the Treaty of Crespy (September 1544). Although the provisions of this agreement were not implemented, war was avoided until 1552, when *Henry II of France, allied with the German Protestant princes, seized Metz, Toul and Verdun. The Truce of Vaucelles (February 1556) left France in possession of these cities. But Charles V having abdicated, the French allied around Pope *Paul IV and renewed the fighting in Italy against *Philip II of Spain. The latter's wife, *Mary Tudor, then brought England into the conflict. The defeat of France at St. Quentin (August 1557) led to the recall of the French troops from Italy. They managed to capture Calais (January 1558), before the Treaty of *Cateau-Cambrésis brought the long wars to a conclusion (April 1559).

The I. W. had an enormous influence on European military tactics and the development of arms, especially *artillery. In addition, they intensified the contacts between the different parts of the Continent, bringing first Frenchmen, then Spaniards and Germans, into direct contact with Renaissance-Italy arts and fashions. During this long conflict international politics began to assume a more secular nature, sometimes bordering on opportunism, and the concept of a European balance of power began to emerge. Ironically France, the initiator of the wars, gained nothing of significance, but Italy was the chief loser: with Spain firmly established in Naples and Milan, the political dismemberment of the country and its domination by foreigners was accomplished.

E. Fueter, *Geschichte des europäischen Staatensystems von 1492 bis 1559* (1919);
F. L. Taylor, *The Art of War in Italy, 1494-1529* (1921);
F. Ercole, *Da Carlo VIII a Carlo V: la crisi della liberta italiana* (1932);
E. Cavaignac, *Politique mondiale, 1492-1757* (1934).

ITALIANATE STYLE By the end of the first quarter of the 16th century, the style of the High Renaissance in Italy, as practiced by its great masters, had reached northern Europe. The fusion of native tradition and Italian influences differed, of course, from one place to another. It first reached Germany, where *Dürer set the example, and a few years later the Netherlands, where Jan Gossaert, called *Mabuse (who died about 1533), and Bernard van Orley (1493-1542) paved the way. In France the I. was promoted by the king, *Francis I, who invited *Leonardo and *Andrea del Sarto and imported the painters who are known collectively as the School of *Fontainebleau.

ITALY It does not happen often in history, that a nation assumes an overwhelming cultural preponderance in a defined civilization, though it does not lead in the arena of international politics. During the 15th and 16th centuries Italians revolutionized European arts, letters and fashions. What they accomplished in *painting, *sculpture and *architecture became the foundation upon which the modern world has built. If their contributions to *drama and *literature, *music, *historiography and *political theory were less outstanding, still they initiated trends and frequently provided the most decisive examples; they were second to no other nation in the sciences, and excelled in most fields which required practical knowledge. At the same time I. was the battlefield for other nations, and its internal division was deepened by foreign domination. Not until the 19th century were the Italians able to achieve political unity, and not until far into the 20th did they realize that the lack of military might was not perhaps a national failure after all.

During the later Middle Ages Italy was bitterly divided between supporters of the papacy and the Empire. The conflict which gave rise to prolonged internal feuds in many Italian cities, lessened in intensity after the unsuccessful expedition of Emperor Henry VII (1310-13), and while the papacy continued its exile in Avignon (1305-78). Left to themselves by absentee emperors and popes, the Italian city-states continued to fight each other, and a new phenomenon, the company of mercenary troops led by a **condottiere*, made its appearance. This development was paralleled by significant changes in government, the decline of the communal system and the rise of tyrannical dynasties. During the 14th century the *Gonzagas established themselves in *Manuta, the *Este at *Ferrara, *Bentivoglio at Bologna, *Malatesta at Rimini. These and other families in similar positions were subsequently ennobled and converted their possessions into duchies and marquisates. The consolidation of these small states under despotic rulers was accompanied by the eclipse of some of the old commercial republics, such as *Genoa, *Siena and Pisa. Thus, at the beginning of the 15th century, despite the formal division into numerous small states, there were in I. five major powers: the prosperous republic of *Venice, the strong duchy of *Milan under the *Visconti, the republic of *Florence, soon to be secured by the *Medici, the *papacy and the kingdom of *Naples.

In the period which ended with the Peace of Lodi (1454) there were some outbreaks of internal fighting. This was the time when Naples passed to the Aragonese dynasty, Venice expanded west and the papacy began to emerge as a secular power. For the next forty years a delicate balance of power was maintained by the *Italian League. Though the stability of some of the states was occasionally threatened by conspiracies against the ruling family, I. as a whole enjoyed a climate of peace and cultural splendour, marred only by brief outbreaks such as the war of *Sixtus IV and *Ferrante I against Lorenzo de' *Medici (1479-80).

The French invasion of 1494, which marked the opening of the prolonged *Italian Wars, destroyed the internal political fabric which had been so carefully woven. The ruling houses of some of the leading city-states were overthrown and Italians were defeated successively by the French, Spaniards, Swiss and Germans. Though they did score a few victories, they hastened their own destruction by their lack of unity and their willingness to cooperate with foreign powers. The political division of I. was settled by *Charles V at *Bologna in 1530: Venice's hold over her Lombard possessions was confirmed, and the families of Este and Gonzaga were secured in their respective duchies; the Medici were allowed to return to Florence and the last *Sforza permitted to remain until his death in Milan. But after 1535, with Spanish viceroys in Naples and Milan, the entire system depended on the Emperor and later on his son *Philip II.

Perhaps the only factor to gain from the past convulsions was the papacy. It now ruled over a considerable part of central I. – the so-called *Papal States – extending from the Adriatic to the Tyrrhenian Sea. Pope *Paul IV even dared to challenge the Spanish power by joining *Henry II of France in a war against Philip II. But the Treaty of *Cateau-Cambrésis (1559) reconfirmed the Spanish-dominated system, and the papacy had to be content with small territorial gains, such as the inclusion of *Ferrara into its rule in 1598, with the extinction of the line of Este. The most obvious illustration of Italian acquiescence with the leadership of Spain was the Battle of *Lepanto where the day was won for the Christian side, by Spain's Italian satellites (1571). Thereafter, however, Venice began to decline, and with the death of Philip II, so did Spain herself. The last decades of the 16th century saw the consolidation of *Savoy in the northwest reaches of Italy, but it was still a long time before it would play a primary role in national politics. By the 17th century I. became a rather somnolent country, its intellectual and artistic decline reflecting its political impotence.

L. Salvatorelli, *A Concise History of Italy* (1940);
N. Valeri, *L'Italia nell' eta dei principati dal 1343 al 1516* (1950);
P. Laven, *Renaissance Italy, 1464-1534* (1965);
L. Simeoni, *Storia politica d'Italia* (1950);
H. B. Cotterill, *Italy from Dante to Tasso, 1300-1600* (1919).

IVAN III (1440-1505) The first Russian prince to establish contact with the West. He became grand duke of Moscow in 1463 and enlarged his territory by incorporating neighbouring principalities, including the Republic of Novgorod. In 1480 he stopped paying tribute to the khan of Kazan, bringing to an end the suzerainty of the Mongols over Russia. Married in 1473 to Sophia, a Byzantine princess, I. declared himself successor to the Byzantine emperors and adopted their symbols of authority. He invited to his court men of different nationalities, including Greeks and Italians.

IVAN IV "THE TERRIBLE" (1530-84) Becoming grand duke of Moscow at the age of three, I. was the first Russian ruler to be crowned tsar in 1546. He set

Ivan IV The Terrible

out to enlarge his territory eastwards, conquering the Tartar Khanates of Kazan (1552) and Astrakhan (1556). The conquest of Siberia began in 1581. He was less successful in the west, his two wars with Poland (1563-70, 1578-82) ending in defeat. In 1571 the Crimean Tartars invaded Russia and held Moscow for a time. The first phase of I.'s reign, until 1560, was marked by cooperation with the *boyars*, the higher barons. Later he launched a bloody campaign against them and other, real or imagined, subversive elements. In 1570 he committed a massacre in the town of Novgorod, whose inhabitants he suspected of treason, and in 1581 he slew his own heir in a fit of rage. After the arrival in Moscow of Captain Richard Chancellor in 1553, I. established commercial relations with England. In 1568 he offered England a treaty, giving its merchants exclusive rights in return for England's political support against Poland. However, he rejected the Elisabethan type of government which did not correspond with his concepts of royal absolutism. Traditionally thought of as a deranged tyrant, he has been described otherwise in Soviet historiography.

*An illustrated manuscript from Italy (*c. *1400)*

J

JAGIELLO The dynasty which ruled *Poland during most of the 15th and 16th centuries. In 1386 Jagiello, Grand Duke of Lithuania, married Queen Jadwiga. Converting to Christianity and promising to unite his duchy to Poland, he took the name of *Vladislav II. After his death (1434) his second son, *Casimir IV, actually accomplished the union. During his long reign he curtailed the power of the *Teutonic order and secured *Bohemia and *Hungary for his son *Ladislas. In the last quarter of the 15th century the house of J., reached the height of its power and might have gained a permanent hold on Eastern Europe. But wasteful wars and the growing independence of the Polish nobility debilitated the J. The dynasty came to an end in 1572, with the death of *Sigismund II.

JAMES I (1566-1625) King of England from 1603; formerly, James VI of Scotland. The only child of *Mary, Queen of Scots, by her second husband Henry *Darnley, he was proclaimed King of Scotland upon his mother's forced abdication in 1567. Educated in his youth by the aged George *Buchanan, he mastered Latin and French and was given instruction in theology. He grew a physically weak person, with definite literary tastes of his own. Although he was declared in possession of royal power in 1578, until 1585 he was quite helpless in his relations with the unruly and divided Scottish nobility; in 1581, for instance, he was seized by one faction at the castle of Ruthven, and broke away from his captors only in 1583. In 1586 J. became the ally of *Elizabeth I, who supported him with a pension. He expressed little objection to the execution of his mother (1587), and when the Spanish *Armada sailed, showed readiness to cooperate with England (1588). In 1589 he married Anne, daughter of *Frederick II of Denmark. In the following years he succeeded in some measure in enforcing his royal authority upon the Scots, although as late as 1600 he was the target of a conspiracy against his life. For most of this time he had the support of the *Presbyterian party, but lost it when he favoured a system of episcopacy. In dire need of funds, which reduced his army to little more than a body-guard, J. waited for the death of Elizabeth I, whom he was to succeed by right of his mother's descent from *Henry VII. He travelled to London immediately after hearing of her death, and after his coronation (July 1603) assumed the title King of Great Britain.

Inevitably, he was treated as a foreigner by some of his English subjects, but that he alienated so many of them was his own doing. Initially susceptible to the *Millenary Petition, he rejected the *Puritan demands at the *Hampton Court Conference (1604), although he did authorize a new translation of the *Bible, which was completed in 1611. At the same time, and in spite of his peace treaty with Spain (1604), J. aroused the anger of the English Roman Catholics, who had expected greater leniency. In 1605 a small group of Catholics organized the abortive *Gunpowder Plot, which was followed by stringent measures against the *Recusants. Afterwards J. also had disagreements with the *Church of England, stemming from his concept of the divine right of kingship.

J.'s differences with his subjects on the religious plane were translated to politics. He was repeatedly refused money by his parliaments, where a Puritan trend was beginning to assert itself. The trend was kept under control as long as the affairs of state were managed by Sir Robert *Cecil (1563-1612), son of the chief minister of Elizabeth I, who continued the policies of the previous reign. But when the young George Villiers (1592-1628), later Duke of Buckingham, became the most influential person in the government (1615), parliamentary opposition became more pronounced, especially with regard to the attempted rapprochement with Spain. Francis *Bacon, who was impeached in 1521, was a victim of this opposition. In spite of the fact that in 1624 J. reversed his policy and declared war on Spain, he did not succeed in restoring parliamentary confidence.

J. was peculiarly fond of handsome young male companions and *masques were his favourite court entertainment. He was also an author, his published works including poetry, translations and several treatises in prose. Of these, *Daemonology* (1597) urged the suppression of *witchcraft. *Basilikon Doron* (1599) and *The True Law of Free Monarchies* (1598) expressed his intrasigent ideas on the divine right of kings, describing them as "breathing images of God upon earth". His

James I

Counter Blast to Tobacco (1604) makes J. a precursor of 20th-century drive against smoking.
C. and H. Steeholm, *James I of England* (1938);
S. J. Houston, *James I* (1975);
C. Williams, *James I* (1934, reprinted 1951).

JAMES I (1394-1437) King of Scotland from 1406. The son of King Robert III (1390-1406), he was captured in 1406, while on his way to France, and held in England for 18 years. He was knighted by *Henry V in 1421, and fought with the English army in France. In 1424, after the death of his uncle the Duke of Albany, who had ruled Scotland as regent, he returned and assumed power. He energetically suppressed the nobility, and tried to improve the judicial and administrative machinery, acting also against Rome's arbitrary manipulation of Scottish ecclesiastical benefices. He was assassinated by a group of conspiring nobles. J. was interested in music and the arts and wrote a poem, *The Kingis Quair*.
E. W. M. Balfour-Melville, *James I* (1936);
J. Norton-Smith, ed., *'The Kingis Quair' by James I of Scotland* (1971).

JAMES II (1430-60) King of Scotland from 1437. The surviving son of *James I, he succeded to the throne after his father's assassination. During his minority the country was dominated by the unruly barons, but after he came of age, J. reasserted the royal power. He conducted a long and bloody struggle against the mighty Douglas clan (1452-55), and continued the traditional Scottish alliance with France. He met his death in battle while raiding the northern borders of England.

JAMES III (1451-88) King of Scotland from 1460. Succeeding to the throne when he was only eight years old, J. took charge of the government in 1469, beginning a feud-ridden reign. In 1479 he arrested his two brothers, one of whom mysteriously died and the other fled to England. His country was attacked by *Edward IV of England (1482), and, by 1488, he had lost the support of his subjects and faced a general revolt, the rebels declaring for his young son, the future *James IV. Defeated, he was stabbed to death by a soldier. J.'s fondness for music and architecture and his dislike of martial activities were said by contemporaries to have cost him the loyalty of his nobles.

JAMES IV (1473-1513) King of Scotland from 1488. The son of *James III, who had lost his life in a revolt of the nobles, he began his reign by pursuing a policy of hostility to England; between 1495 and 1497 he sheltered at his court Perkin *Warbeck, the pretender to the English throne. However, in 1502, he made peace with *Henry VII, married his daughter Margaret and joined with England and Spain in an alliance. The King's European prestige increased so long as the alliance continued, and he was also able to introduce some changes in the administration of his country and improve the quality of the Scottish navy. But, in 1512, he began to quarrel with his brother-in-law *Henry VIII and concluded a treaty of friendship with *Louis XII of France. In 1513 he declared war on England and invaded it; on 9 September he was defeated and killed at Flodden Field. His reign signalled Scotland's entrance into the European political system.
R. L. Mackie, *King James IV of Scotland* (1958).

JAMES V (1512-42) King of Scotland. Upon the death of his father at Flodden in 1513, this 17-month-old baby was declared king, the actual administration of the kingdom being entrusted to his cousin, the duke of Albany. The regency, a turbulent period, ended in 1524 with Albany's leaving the country for France, but J. did not assume the actual government of Scotland until 1528, when he managed to break away from the control of his stepfather, the earl of Angus. His uncle *Henry VIII of England suggested that he marry *Mary Tudor, but he preferred to marry the daughter of *Francis I (1536), and when she died soon after coming to Scotland, he took another French bride, Mary of Guise (1538). J.'s friendship with France and his adherence to Rome eventually caused a breach with his uncle. Though lacking the wholehearted support of the nobility, J. attempted to take the offensive in his conflict with England. But his army was defeated at the Battle of Solway Moss (25 November 1542), and the King died less than a month later. A popular monarch, who used to mingle with his people, he was the father of *Mary, Queen of Scots, who was born shortly before he died.
D. Hay, ed., *The Letters of James V* (1955).

JANE SEYMOUR (?-1537) Queen of England; third wife of *Henry VIII. J. married the King in 1536, shortly after the execution of *Anne Boleyn. She died one year later, having borne the King a male child, the future *Edward VI.

JANISSARIES Elite military units of the *Ottoman Turks. The J. were created to meet the need of the sultans for a loyal imperial guard. They began in the 14th century, when the Ottomans raised levies of young Christian boys from the Balkans for this purpose. They

Jane Seymour *by Hans Holbein the Younger*

were separated from their families, forced to accept the Moslem faith and given rigid military training. Supplemented by periodic forced recruitment, the number of J. reached about 15,000 in the reign of *Suleiman I. At this time there were signs of restlessness in their ranks, and the Sultan decided to mitigate their severe Spartan existence. They were allowed to marry and, subsequently, to have their sons admitted to the corps, which thus took on a hereditary character. By the early 17th century, J. were permitted to engage in trade, to substitute in one way or another for their own military service and the recruitment of Christians was discontinued. In effect, this military body became a privileged and powerful caste.

N. Weissmann, *Les Janissaires; étude de l'organisation militaire des Ottomans* (1964).

JANSSENS, ABRAHAM (1575-1632) Flemish painter. Born in *Antwerp, he visited Rome between 1598 and 1601. There he acquired some stylistic elements from *Caravaggio, and the classical inspiration for his later work. In 1606 he became dean of the Antwerp painters' guild. His best works deal with historical scenes, although he also executed portraits and beautiful religious pictures. His ability as a painter declined his later years, and his reputation was eclipsed by a fellow citizen of Antwerp, Peter Paul *Rubens.

JAPAN In the 16th century J.'s relations with the West were marked by a relative tolerance, which gradually hardened into rejection. In 1549, six years after the Portuguese had begun to trade with J., St. Francis *Xavier arrived in Kyushu with his *Jesuit companions. During his two-year stay, the foundations of Christianity in J. were laid. The number of converts increased. The progress of Roman Catholicism in J. was impressive enough for *Sixtus V to create, in 1588, the first Japanese diocese. However, the previous year a nationalist reaction had set in, led by Toyotomi Hideyoshi. His decree of 1587, which proscribed missionary activity, was not strictly enforced, but, in 1597, it was followed by a wave of persecution in which about 40 Christians, missionaries and converts, were killed. A second wave of persecution came in 1614 and continued until 1639, when the Tokugawa government put an end to J.'s commercial relations with Portugal. In 1640, when a Portuguese ship arrived in Nagasaki from Macao, most of its passengers were put to death, to dramatize J.'s determination to exclude all foreigners. The severance of relations with the West occurred precisely because Christianity was all too successful, claiming, when the missionary effort was at its peak, between 1587 and 1596, up to 250,000 converts in all social strata.

R. H. Drummond, *A History of Christianity in Japan* (1971).

JEAN DE BRUGES Flemish painter, also known as Jean de Bondol, who worked at the royal court of France (1368-81) as a miniaturist and designer of tapestries. His style, uniting care for detail and elegance with a realistic depiction of landscape and the human figure, makes him a significant early practitioner of the *International Gothic.

JEANNE D'ALBRET (1528-72) Queen of Navarre. The daughter of King Henry d'Albret and of *Marguerite d'Angoulême, sister of *Francis I, she was married

Janissaries

to *Antoine de Bourbon, becoming queen in 1550. J. was famous for her high sense of duty and cleverness, and for her public declarations in support of Protestantism. After the death of her husband (1562), she skilfully guarded the independence of Navarre. In 1572, just before her own death, she arranged the marriage of her only son, the future *Henry IV of France, to Marguerite, daughter of *Catherine de Médicis.

JENSON, NICOLAS (c. 1420-80) French type-designer and publisher. Born near Troyes, he was a die-cutter and learned *printing in Germany where, according to one version, he was sent by *Charles VII. However, he did not return to France but went to Venice where, in the last decade of his life, he published about 150 titles, including Virgil, Caesar, Suetonius, Pliny the Elder, Cicero, Eusebius and St. Augustine. J. was the originator of the "roman" typeface, though he printed also in "gothic" type as, for example, in his Latin *Bible of 1476. His clear roman face was much admired, and won him a title of nobility conferred by *Sixtus IV.

JEROME OF PRAGUE (c. 1370-1416) Bohemian follower of Jan *Hus. After having established a close relationship with Hus, he went to England (1398) to study *Wycliffe's doctrines. He then visited a number of European theological centres, returning to *Bohemia in 1407. J. dedicated himself to propagating church reform, bringing upon himself charges of heresy. In 1415 he went with Hus to *Constance. Perceiving the danger to his life he tried to escape, but was subsequently arrested and condemned to be burnt at the stake.

JESUITS (Society of Jesus) The most important Roman Catholic monastic order to be established in the 16th century, and a decisive instrument of the *Counter Reformation. Created by Ignatius *Loyola and six companions in Paris in 1534, it was approved by *Paul III in 1540. The J. were conceived by their founder as an elite corps, obedient soldiers of the Church in the fight against heresy at home, and zealous missionaries spreading the faith among the heathens. Their regulations, besides the usual vows of poverty and chastity, included a special pledge of obedience to the pope, undertaken by the novice after a long probation period. The J. did not confine themselves to monasteries, but lived in missions, novitiates and colleges, and dedicated much of their efforts to teaching. The constitution of the order was autocratic and followed a military model. Each district, or "province", was governed by a provincial, assisted by a number of advisors. At the head of the order stood the general, elected for life, who resided in *Rome.

At the time of Loyola's death (1556), the order counted only about 1,000 members; but these were already heading over a hundred colleges. The number of J. heading schools increased greatly in the following century, and they became the most important *educational cadre in the Roman Catholic countries. The order drew many talented persons to its ranks. After its founder's death it was led by Diego *Lainez and St. Francis *Borgia, and it reached a stage of exceptional expansion and influence under the fifth general, Claudius *Acquaviva. The J. were in the forefront of the effort to regain *Austria, *Bavaria and the Rhine Valley back to Roman Catholicism; after 1578 they were also active in England. St. Francis *Xavier was the first and most important of many J. missionaries who worked in *India, *Japan and *China. America was reached by the J. after the Dominicans and Franciscans had already converted the main nuclei of the Indian population; they, therefore, dedicated their efforts to the frontier areas and, in 1610, founded the first of their famous missions to the Guarani Indians of Paraguay. Some of the most influential Catholic theologians and *political theorists of the latter part of the 16th century came from the ranks of the order, including Juan de *Mariana, Roberto *Bellarmine and Francisco *Suarez.

T. J. Campbell, *The Jesuits, 1534-1921* (1921);
J. Brodrick, *The Origins of the Jesuits* (1940);
R. Fülöp-Miller, *The Power and Secret of the Jesuits* (1930).

JEWEL, JOHN (1522-71) English bishop of Salisbury and an apologist for the *Church of England. Educated at Oxford, he took a leading part in the reforming activities in the reign of *Edward VI, but had to leave England when *Mary became queen. His years of exile on the Continent cured him of his zeal, and when he returned, upon the accession of *Elizabeth I, he became a strong defender of the established church. In 1560, he was made bishop of Salisbury and, in 1562, published *The Apology of the English Church*, in which he upheld the doctrine of the divine right of kings, and, although he did not recognize the authority of the Council of *Trent, demanded that Protestants be admitted to this body. His book was appreciated by Elizabeth, and was accepted as an official statement of the Anglican position.

W. M. Southgate, *John Jewel and the Problem of Doctrinal Authority* (1962).

JEWS In the last centuries of the Middle Ages European J. became increasingly subject to waves of persecution, economic restrictions and policies of religious intolerance. They were expelled from England in 1290 and from France in 1306 and 1394. In Germany the Black Death (1348-49) occasioned popular riots against

A 15th-century woodcut depicting Jews performing a ritual murder of a Christian boy

the J., who were accused of causing the plague, and they were expelled from many places. During the 15th century J. were banished from *Saxony (1432), *Augsburg (1439), *Bavaria (1450), Mainz (1483), Magdeburg (1493), *Nuremberg and Ulm (1499), and other cities. By the end of the 15th century much of western Europe was practically *Judenrein* (free of J.). The Renaissance with its spirit of openness and secularism might have benefitted the J., but nevertheless they remained largely on the margin of European history, and this state of affairs lasted throughout the periods of the *Reformation and *Counter-Reformation. It was only in the 17th century, with the establishment of a prosperous Jewish community in the *United Provinces, their return to England (1655), as well as the massacre of thousands of J. in the Ukraine by Bogdan Chmelnycky's Cossacks (1648-49), that they actually entered the modern history of Europe.

The major event, which dominated European Jewish history in the 15th and 16th centuries, was the expulsion from Spain (1492). The Spanish Jewish community had long been a part of the general life of the country, Jewish bankers financed the last phases of the **reconquista*, and men of Jewish descent were involved in preparation of *Columbus' voyage of discovery. But from 1391 on Spanish J. were divided into those who practiced their religion openly, and the **marranos*, i.e., J. who had been forced to convert. The decision of *Ferdinand and *Isabella to expel the J. was made in the hope that it would bring about the complete assimilation of those who remained. Approximately half the exiles went first to Portugal, from which they were in turn expelled in 1496. The suffering and death of countless refugees, the loss of prosperity and the humiliation, the complete annihilation of Jewish culture in the Iberian Peninsula, left psychological scars on the entire European diaspora.

The Spanish exiles eventually settled in North Africa, Southern France and Italy, and in the *Ottoman empire. New Jewish centres sprang up in Constantinople, Adrianople and Salonika, and some J. rose to prominence in the Ottoman government. The most outstanding example was the Mendes family, headed by Don Joseph *Nasi, Portuguese *marranos* who had moved east via *Antwerp and *Venice. But although they made great efforts to recover their social and economic status elsewhere, Spanish J., the *sepharadim*, tended to religious introspection and were susceptible to Messianic expectations. The writings of Don Isaac *Abrabanel contained visions of the coming redemption of the Jewish people, and there were similar works by other Spanish exiles. The enthusiasm that accompanied the appearances of Shlomo *Molkho and David Ha-*Reuveni testified to the eschatological mood of J. during the first half of the 16th century. Later in the century this mood inspired the leaders of the *Kabbalistic centre of Safed in the Holy Land, where also the first great code of modern Jewish religious law was written, the *Shulhan Arukh ("Prepared Table")* by Joseph Caro (1488-1575).

In Christian Europe the J. were probably best off in Italy. Although banished from *Naples (1541), they had prosperous communities in the north, especially in *Mantua and in *Venice, which became a centre of *Hebrew printing. But in the course of the 16th century their circumstances became much more restricted. The Counter-Reformation prompted the authorities to

Von den Jüden vnd jren Lügen.
D. M. Luth.
Gedrückt zu Wittemberg / Durch Hans Lufft.
M. D. XLIII.

Titlepage of Luther's tract on the Jews (1543)

enforce the **ghetto* system, which separated J. from Christians.

The situation in *Poland was different – there J. had settled as a result of intermittent persecutions in Germany, and in the 16th century they prospered as merchants and agents of the Polish nobles, and were permitted extensive autonomous institutions. While this

German peasant and Jewish moneylender, *an illustration from a book printed in Augsburg (1531)*

prosperity was to account for the future numerical preponderance of East European Jewry, it could not but arouse the resentment of the local peasantry, who saw the J. always as middlemen between themselves and their landlords.

Late in the 16th century Spanish and Portuguese *marranos* took advantage of the newly won Dutch independence and established the community of *Amsterdam. This became a model of Jewish settlements in western Europe in the 17th century, and the springboard of their return to England and their first settlements in the New World.

Individual J. made a number of contributions to Renaissance culture. Jewish *cartographers in Majorca designed the famous Catalan map of 1375. Later, Abraham *Zacuto became the outstanding authority on *navigation in Spain and Portugal. J. were often the physicians of Renaissance rulers, and served in some Italian courts as musicians and *dance instructors. But although a number of Jewish poets and dramatists produced works in Hebrew in emulation of Renaissance literary innovations, most of these were clearly derivative. A major contribution by a Jewish author to Renaissance thought were the *Dialogues on Love* of Judah *Abrabanel. The interest shown by humanist scholars in the *Hebrew language and the *Kabbalah, could be translated into a more liberal attitude toward the J., as evidenced by *Pico de la Mirandola and, especially, Reuchlin. But *Luther's anti-Semitic outbursts encouraged a hostile attitude among Protestants and, in 1555, Pope *Paul IV issued restrictive orders concerning the J. which ended the former openness on the Roman Catholic side. Only at the end of the 16th century, with scholars such as Johannes *Buxtorf, a liberal approach toward Judaism was manifested again.

S. W. Baron, *A Social and Religious History of the Jews*, 3 vols. (1965);
Y. F. Baer, *A History of the Jews in Christian Spain*, 2 vols. (1961);
G. Scholem, *Major Trends in Jewish Mysticism* (1941);
M. L. Margolis and A. Marx, *A History of the Jewish People* (1965);
C. Roth, *The Jewish People* (1966).

JIMENEZ DE CISNEROS, FRANCISCO (1436-1517) Spanish churchman and statesman. After studying at Salamanca, he had a taste of Italian *humanism in *Rome and, in 1465, returned to Castile to begin a long ecclesiastical career. He spent some years with the Observantine branch of the Franciscans, leading the life of a hermit. In 1492 he was appointed confessor to Queen *Isabella and soon became influential in the affairs of state. In 1494 he became the head of the Franciscans in Castile and, in 1495, was elevated to the highest ecclesiastical office in Spain, the archbishopric of Toledo. After the death of Queen Isabella (1504), J. smoothed the disagreement between *Ferdinand and his son-in-law, *Philip the Handsome, and following the latter's sudden death briefly held the regency of Castile. Created cardinal (1507), he organized and led a military *crusade against the Moslems in North Africa, taking Oran and Tripoli (1509-11). He reached the highest point of his political career in 1516, when he succeeded Ferdinand as regent of Spain. He then suppressed the opposition of certain nobles, and prepared the country for the arrival of *Charles V. He did not, however, live to see the young monarch, but died on his way to meet him.

J. introduced many religious reforms and advanced the new learning in Spain. In 1500 he founded the University of Alcalá, whither he invited foreign scholars and, in 1502, ordered the work on the *Complutensian Polyglot*, a *Bible combining the *Hebrew, *Greek and *Latin version. It was completed only five years after his death.

J. Garcia Oro, *Cisneros y la reforma del clero español* (1971);
J. P. R. Lyell, *Cardinal Ximenes* (1917).

JIMENEZ DE QUESADA, GONZALO (c. 1500-79) Spanish **conquistador*. Born probably in Córdoba and by profession a lawyer, he went to America in 1535 as a magistrate of Santa Marta, a settlement on the Caribbean coast of present-day Colombia. In April 1536 he led an expedition of 900 men to the land of the Chibcha Indians, and using methods not unlike those employed by *Cortés in Mexico and *Pizarro in Peru, succeeded in gaining control of the country. In 1538 he founded Santa Fé de Bogotá and there, in 1539, welcomed the expeditions of *Federmann and *Belalcázar. Together with these two he went to Spain, where the Crown awarded him only the office of *regidor*, or town councillor, for life, and an **encomienda*. He settled in Bogotá, dedicating his last years to the search for *El Dorado.

R. B. Cunninghame Graham, *The Conquest of New Granada* (1922).

JOACHIM I (1484-1535) Elector of Brandenburg from 1499. J. was first involved in the politics of Germany in 1519, when his vote was eagerly solicited during the imperial election. Supporting *Charles V, he later espoused the cause of the Emperor's enemies, but the Reformation drove him back to the imperial camp. A devout Catholic, he became one of the chief German princes who sought to suppress the reform movement. Nevertheless, certain members of his family were influenced by *Luther's doctrines, including his wife, who left him in 1528 for this reason.

JOACHIM II (1505-71) Elector of Brandenburg from 1535. Raised at the court of *Charles V, he took part in the imperial campaigns against the Turks. After his succession to the electorate he abandoned his father's religious policy, and allowed Lutheran preaching (1539). In 1543 he changed the ecclesiastical organization of Brandenburg and, although at the beginning he retained many of the old customs, his territories gradually joined the side of the Reformation. In internal German affairs J. attempted to mediate between the Emperor and the *Protestant princes. He did not join the *Schmalkaldic League and, after the Battle of Mühlberg (1547), persuaded *Philip of Hesse to surrender to the Emperor. He supported the *Augsburg Interim (1548), backed the peace of Passau (1552) and took part in making the religious peace of *Augsburg (1555).

JOAN OF ARC (Jeanne d'Arc; 1412-31) French national heroine of the latter phase of the Hundred Years' War, known also as the Maid of Orléans and *La Pucelle*. The daughter of a peasant family of the village of Domremy in Champagne, she was a taciturn religious person, who could neither read nor write. From about the age of 13 she had visionary experiences, in which voices, which she identified as belonging to certain

Joachim II *by Lucas Cranach the Younger*

A 15th-century small statue of Joan of Arc

saints and angels, urged her to assume the task of saving France from the English conquest. In 1428 she tried and failed to convince the commander of the French troops at Vaucouleurs of the genuineness of her mission. But, in 1429, when some of her prophecies had been fulfilled, she was allowed to come before the Dauphin at Chinon, and recognized him immediately in spite of his disguise. A commission of theologians having found her views untouched by heresy, she was sent at the head of an expedition to relieve the siege of Orléans (April-May 1429). Wearing white armour and carrying a banner, she succeeded in inspiring the French troops. On 17 July 1429, she was present at the coronation of the Dauphin as *Charles VII at Rheims, an event made possible by the relief of Orléans. In September she was wounded during an attempt to recapture Paris. She rejoined the French army in the spring of 1430 but, on 24 May, was taken prisoner near Compiègne and, on 21 November, was sold to the English by the duke of Burgundy. Charles VII did nothing to rescue her. Imprisoned in an iron cage at Rouen, she was tried for heresy and witchcraft on 21 February 1431, by a court presided by the bishop of Beauvais. On 30 May she was burnt at the stake in Rouen, declaring as the flames engulfed her that the voices she had heard were true. Her sentence was revoked by *Calixtus III in 1456. J.'s status of national heroine is a comparatively modern phenomenon, stimulated by French Catholic patriotism of the late 19th century. She has been the subject of a number of literary works, notably by Voltaire, Schiller, Mark Twain and George Bernard Shaw.

A. Buchan, *Joan of Arc and the Recovery of France* (1948);
J. Cordier, *Jeanne d'Arc; sa personnalité, son rôle* (1948);
R. Pernoud, *Joan of Arc by Herself* (1966).
H. Guillemin, *The True History of Joan of Arc* (1972).

JOANNA II (1371-1435) Queen of Naples. Succeeding to the throne in 1414, upon the death of her brother, this middle-aged widow soon became notorious for her young lovers, a reputation equalled only by her capacity for political blunders. In over two decades of her reign the kingdom was in continuous turmoil. In 1422 she called to her aid the young *Alfonso V of Aragon, whom she promised to make her heir instead of Louis III of Anjou. But after Alfonso captured Naples, J. broke with him and adopted Louis as her son. In 1432 her lover-counsellor Giovanni Caracciolo was murdered, and the Queen again faced a rebellion by her barons. Louis having died fighting the rebels (1434), she named his brother René heir to the throne, but the internal dissensions in the kingdom made it possible for Alfonso to conquer Naples in 1442.

JOANNA THE MAD See JUANA LA LOCA.

JODELLE, ETIENNE (1532-73) French poet and playwright. Born of a noble family in Paris, he is known as the author of the first French tragedy, *Cléopâtre captive*. It was presented before the court of King *Henry II in Rheims in 1553, with the author in the role of Cleopatra and Remy *Belleau and others in the cast. After the performance, J. was honoured by his friends of the *Pléiade with a procession led by a goat adorned with flowers, a celebration which caused *Beza to accuse *Ronsard of renewing the pagan worship of Bacchus. J. wrote two other plays and verses. He was patronized by *Catherine de Médicis, but subsequently lost favour at the court and died in poverty.

JOEST, JAN (c.1450-1519) Dutch painter. Born at Calcar, he probably worked in his native city until about

1510, when he settled in Haarlem. In 1515 he worked in Cologne, and he may have also visited Italy. J.'s style reflects the influence of *Mostaert. His best work is *Scenes from the Life of Christ* (1505-08) painted for the church of St. Nicholas at Calcar.

JOHAN, PEDRO (1398-c.1458) Spanish sculptor. A native of Catalonia, he first worked in Barcelona on decorations of the façade of the Town Hall. In 1425 he began the altarpiece for the cathedral of Tarragona, carved in alabaster, and later executed a similar work in Saragossa. It seems that he went in 1447 to Naples, at the invitation of *Alfonso of Aragon.

JOHN II (1397-1479) King of Aragon from 1458; brother of *Alfonso V the Magnanimous and father of *Ferdinand II. During his brother's reign he often served as regent of Aragon, while the King spent many years in Italy. His reign was marked by constant conflicts, first with his own son Charles, prince of Viana, who died in 1461, then with his Catalan subjects and with *Louis XI of France. J.'s great achievement was the marriage of his younger son with princess *Isabella of Castile in 1469, thus preparing the union of the two most important kingdoms of the Iberian peninsula.

JOHN II (1405-54) King of Castile from 1406. Succeeding to the throne when he was less than two years old, he had a long reign, almost half a century long, much of it characterized by feudal anarchy. The strong man of the reign, Alvaro de Luna, was the real ruler of the country until he was dismissed by the king. By his second marriage to Isabella of Portugal J. was the father of *Isabella the Catholic. His immediate successor was his son from his first marriage, *Henry IV.

JOHN (Hans; 1455-1513) King of *Denmark and Norway from 1483, and of *Sweden from 1497. The son of *Christian I, he had to overcome a conflict with the Danish diet over the extent of royal power before being allowed to succeed his father in 1483. He was recognized in Sweden only after Sten *Sture had been forced to resign the regency but, in 1501, the Swedish nobility again rose in rebellion and he lost control over that kingdom. J., supported by his brother, the future *Frederick I, was also confronted by a peasant revolt in Denmark and by insubordination on the part of the nobility, which he gradually quelled. Shortly before his death he conducted a war against Sweden and *Lübeck (1510-12), as a result of which the power of the *Hanseatic League in the Baltic Sea was reduced.

JOHN I (João I; 1357-1433) King of Portugal from 1385. Establishing his rule by defeating the Castilians in the Battle of Aljubarrota (14 August 1385), his long reign saw the beginning of Portuguese overseas expansion. In 1415 he captured Ceuta, thus gaining a foothold for Portugal on the North African coast. By marrying Philippa, daughter of John of Gaunt, he allied his country to England. She bore him five sons, of whom the most outstanding was *Henry the Navigator.

JOHN II (João II; 1455-95) King of Portugal from 1481. J. inherited a weakened monarchy, the result of shaky internal conditions during the reign of his father *Afonso V, he soon had to crush an aristocratic revolt, led by the duke of Braganza and supported by Spain. This was accomplished by 1483. Leading Portugal in her continued efforts of maritime exploration, the greatest achievement of his reign was the rounding of the Cape of Good Hope by *Dias in 1488. The year before the King had sent Pero de *Covilha to search for an overland passage to India. J. meant to follow up Dias' discovery with a sea voyage to India, but postponed its departure until he solved his disputes with Spain by the treaty of *Tordesillas (1494). But he died the following year, leaving the task to his brother *Manoel I.

JOHN III (João III; 1502-57) King of Portugal from 1521. The son of *Manoel I, he succeeded to the throne when his nation was at its historical zenith. This fact was demonstrated in 1524, when he took to wife the sister of *Charles V, and the latter married J.'s sister. A religious man, he permitted, in 1536, the establishment of the *Inquisition and encouraged the *Jesuits in Portugal and her overseas possessions. During his reign Martin Afonso de Sousa began the Portuguese settlement of Brazil, to which, in 1549, the King added the first trappings of royal government. He was less successful in his attempts to consolidate the Portuguese holdings in India and East Asia.

JOHN III (1537-92) King of Sweden from 1569. The son of *Gustavus *Vasa, he became governor of Finland in 1556. But when his half-brother *Eric XIV mounted the throne (1560), J.'s authority was restricted and, in 1562, he was imprisoned. Freed in 1567, he joined his younger brother, the future *Charles IX, in a rebellion (1568) which deposed Eric. He was crowned in the following year, and immediately began peace negotiations with *Denmark, ending the seven-year war with that nation (1570). He conflicted with Muscovite *Russia over Estonia. In 1577 he appears to have arranged the murder of the deposed and imprisoned Eric. Interested in matters of theology, J. tried to find an accomodation with Roman Catholicism by restoring old rituals and liturgy. He raised his son *Sigismund as a Catholic, and arranged his election to the throne of *Poland in 1587. His religious policies however, met with many objections especially from his brother Charles, and late in his reign he abandoned his projects.

JOHN ALBERT (Jan Olbracht; 1459-1501) King of Poland from 1492. The second son of *Casimir IV, he distinguished himself as a soldier from an early age, but as a monarch indulged in wasteful military projects. In 1497 he led a vast army to Moldavia in what was intended as a great campaign against the *Ottoman Turks. Instead, he was attacked by the voivode of Moldavia, who was in alliance with the Turks, and was forced to withdraw after many losses. Although he succeeded in curtailing the independence of the *Teutonic Order, he conferred on the Polish gentry many privileges, thus weakening the power of the monarchy.

JOHN CASIMIR (1543-92) Count Palatine of the Rhine. The fourth child of the Elector of the *Palatinate *Frederick III, he was brought up by his father a Calvinist and, between 1567 and 1575, participated in the *Religious Wars of France on the side of the *Huguenots. In 1583 he became the regent during the minority of his nephew Frederick IV, and restored Calvinism in the Palatinate. Earlier, he intervened in the rebellion of the *Netherlands against Spain, coming to the aid of *Ghent at the head of troops subsidized by *Elizabeth I (1578-79). His attempts to rally the Protestant princes of Germany did not produce tangible results.

JOHN, ELECTOR OF SAXONY (1468-1532) The younger brother of *Frederick III the Wise, he succeeded him as elector in 1525 and like him also supported *Luther. In 1526 he joined *Philip of Hesse in the league of Gotha, and in the same year began to implement the *Reformation in Saxony. J. was one of the original *"Protestants" at the Second Diet of Speier (1529); he objected to the election of *Ferdinand of Austria as king of the Romans, and became one of the leaders of the *Schmalkaldic League (1531). He consented to the religious Peace of Nuremberg, which permitted the Protestants to practice their religion until the meeting of a new diet, but died in the same year.

JOHN THE FEARLESS (1371-1419) Duke of *Burgundy from 1404. Son of Duke Philip the Bold, he participated in 1396 in the *Crusade of Nicopolis where he was taken prisoner by the *Ottoman Turks, and was released only after ransom was paid. He then assumed the government of Burgundy, and entered into a bitter feud with Louis of Orleáns, brother of the king of France, over the leading influence at the court. In 1407 he arranged the murder of his rival, and by this act provoked a civil war between his own supporters and the *Armagnacs (1411). J. took no part in the Battle of *Agincourt (1415), where the French were crushed by *Henry V of England. In 1418 he entered Paris with his troops, massacred the Armagnacs and took charge of King Charles VI. The English seizure of Rouen induced the warring French parties to seek reconciliation. J. therefore met the Dauphin, the future *Charles VII. In their second meeting on the bridge of Montereau (September 1419) the Duke was assassinated by one of the latter's attendants. He was succeeded by his son *Philip the Good.

R. Vaughan, *John the Fearless* (1966).

JOHN FREDERICK I (1503-54) Elector of Saxony. The son of the Elector *John, he was brought up as a confirmed supporter of the *Reformation, and was deeply devoted to *Luther. Succeeding his father in 1532, he became with *Philip of Hesse the leader of the *Schmalkaldic League, which he had helped to create back in 1530; however, he did not always agree with Philip's precipitated methods. In 1541 he quarelled with *Maurice, the new ruler of ducal Saxony, and a military confrontation between them was averted only by Philip's mediation. But when, in 1546, *Charles V renewed the war against the Schmalkaldic League, he took advantage of that old quarrel and made a compact with Maurice, promising him the electoral dignity. Although he succeeded in repelling Maurice from his territories (November 1546), J. was defeated and taken prisoner by the Emperor at Mühlberg (24 April 1547). Having been condemned to death, he saved himself by signing the so-called Wittenberg Capitulation, which transferred much of his territory and the electoral rights to Maurice. He retained only the regions around Weimar, Gotha, Eisenach and Coburg, as well as the title of duke, and was held in captivity until 1552; he refused, however, to make any relgious concession. In 1554 he concluded a treaty with Maurice's successor, and acquiesced with the loss of the electoral rights.

JOHN FREDERICK II (1529-95) Duke of Saxony. Eldest son of *John Frederick I, he administered his territories during the latter's captivity, and succeeded him after his death in 1554. Determined to regain the electoral dignity of which his father had been forcibly deprived, he took as his counsellor Wilhelm von Grumbach, a former aid of *Albert Alcibiades. His protection of Grumbach despite repeated exhortations caused *Maximilian II to put him under the imperial ban and, in 1567, he was deposed by Augustus I elector of Saxony. He was then delivered to the Emperor, and held in captivity in Vienna until his death. His wife Elizabeth joined him in his prison. His brother John William took possession of his territories.

JOHN VIII PALAEOLOGUS (1390-1448) Emperor of Byzantium. He succeeded to the throne in 1425 and, in 1438, came to the West in an effort to bridge over the religious differences and rally support against the *Ottoman Turks. The union of the Eastern and Western churches, which he concluded at the councils of Ferrara (1438) and Florence (1439), was later rejected in Constantinople, while the *Crusade which came to his aid was defeated by *Murad II at Varna (1444). By the time J. died, the Turks had already reduced the territory under his government to the capital and its vicinity alone.

JOHN XXIII (?-1419) Antipope from 1410 to 1415. Born Baldassare Cossa, the son of an impoverished noble Neapolitan family, he was involved in his youth in naval warfare and piracy, but later studied law and entered the service of the Church. Created cardinal by Boniface IX (1402), and papal legate of Bologna (1409), he was elected pope in 1410 by a group of supporters who defected from *Gregory XII and Benedict XIII of Avignon. His declared intention was to end the *Great Schism, for which he convened the Council of *Constance (1414). But his insincerity became apparent when he fled from the council in disguise (March 1415), in an attempt to undermine its authority. Imprisoned and delivered back to the council by Duke Friedrich of Austria, he was deposed on 29 May 1415, and held in custody in Germany for the next three years. In 1419 he was set free and went back to Italy, where the legitimate pope, *Martin V, made him cardinal-bishop of Tusculum. He died soon afterwards.

JONAS, JUSTUS (1493-1555) German reformer; one of Luther's closest aids. Educated at the universities of Erfurt and Wittenberg, he returned to Erfurt in 1518 as professor of law. In 1521, when Luther passed through Erfurt on his way to the Diet of *Worms, J. joined him and from then on remained with him. He accompanied him and *Melanchthon to the conference with the Swiss reformers at Marburg (1529), translated his writings and preached in his funeral (1546). Shortly afterwards he had to leave Wittenberg because of the *Schmalkaldic War.

JONES, INIGO (1573-1652) English architect and designer of *masques. The talented son of a London clothworker, he was helped by a wealthy patron to go on a study trip to Italy(1603). Soon after he returned to England he became popular at the court as a designer of costumes and architectural decorations for masques. In 1612 he again went to Italy together with the earl of Arundel, returning a year and a half later, thoroughly acquainted with the architectural principles of *Palladio. From 1615 he was the royal architect, a position he held until the outbreak of the Civil War (1642). The downfall of Charles I was a grave setback for J., who was forced to pay a heavy fine, but in the last years of his life he apparently regained his status as the leading English architect. J. was a true practitioner

Queen's House, Greenwich, by Inigo Jones

of the Renaissance architectural values of classical proportions. These are best exemplified in his Queen's House, Greenwich, begun in 1616, and in his Banqueting House, Whitehall, London (1619-22). Although some of his structures were destroyed, enough remained to inspire the Palladian revival in English architecture of the 18th century.

J. Summerson, *Inigo Jones* (1966);
M. T. Jones-Davies, *Inigo Jones, Ben Jonson et le masque* (1967).

JONSON, BEN (1572-1637) English poet and dramatist. Born in London a month after his father, a minister, died; his mother later married a master bricklayer. He attended Westminster School, where he was taught by William *Camden, and after a brief attempt at following his stepfather's occupation (1589), went as a soldier to the Netherlands (*c.* 1591). There he killed an enemy in single combat in front of the two armies, stripping his opponent of his weapons. Returning to England he married (1594), and had three children; but he never settled to the role of family man. He may have worked as a wandering actor; his literary career began in 1597, when he completed a satiric comedy of Thomas *Nashe, *The Isle of Dogs*. This landed him in prison when the theatres were suppressed on account of the play, but he was soon released and, in September 1598, won fame with another comedy, *Every Man in His Humour*. A quarrel with the actor Gabriel Spencer in the same month ended in the latter's death. Jailed, J. converted to Roman Catholicism and escaped hanging only by pleading benefit of the clergy. He was released after being branded on the thumb as a felon. He then wrote for different theatrical companies and, in 1601, conducted with *Marston and *Dekker the "war of the theatres", satirizing the other two and being satirized by them.

By this time J. was attracting literary friends and some wealthy patrons, and with *Sejanus* (1603) he ventured into the field of tragedy. The play failed, but in that year he was introduced to the court of *James I and, in 1604, wrote his first **masque* on which he collaborated with Inigo *Jones. In 1605 he voluntarily joined the imprisoned Marston and *Chapman, who had got in trouble for their satirical comments on the Scots in the comedy *Eastward Ho*, in which J. had collaborated. The next ten years were his best. He wrote his four great comedies: *Volpone* (1606), a satire on human cupidity, *Epicoene or the Silent Woman* (1609), *The Alchemist* (1610) on the ingenuous who are duped by tricksters, and *Bartholomew Fair* (1614). Although his second tragedy on a Roman theme, *Catiline* (1611), also failed, he achieved celebrity with his numerous masques. Visiting France (1613) as the tutor of Walter *Raleigh's son, he was awarded a pension by its king. In 1616 he published the first folio of his *Works*. In 1618-19 he walked to Scotland, where he was warmly acclaimed, and upon his return was made an honorary graduate of both Cambridge and Oxford. But his creative powers, were beginning to fail. His last comedies were not as successful as the first and, in 1631, he quarrelled with Inigo Jones, whose decorations for the masques eclipsed J.'s text. He later satirized Jones in *The Tale of a Tub* (1634). Stricken with paralysis in 1628, he was confined to his home in Westminster for most of his last years.

J. was the towering English literary figure of his age. In the 17th century his plays were considered greater than *Shakespeare's. In the Devil Tavern, surrounded by fellow authors and admirers, he expounded his theory of humour and passed judgment on classical works and of his contemporaries. Much of his poetry, written in a plain style, has not survived the test of time, and today his masques are of interest only to literary scholars. Much the same may be said of his criticism, letters and epigrams. But his great comedies were brilliantly planned and exploited the humour in the situation while presenting the characters as universal human types. They rank with the finest English dramas.

L. C. Knights, *Drama and Society in the Age of Jonson* (1937);
M. G. Chute, *Ben Jonson of Westminster* (1953);
G. B. Jackson, *Vision and Judgment in Ben Jonson's Drama* (1968).

JOOS VAN CLEVE (c. 1490-1540) The name by which the Flemish painter Joos van der Beke is known. A native of Cleves, he became a master of the *Antwerp guild of painters in 1511. It is believed that he made several working trips to the courts of France and England, and to Italy. He executed many triptych altarpieces and *Madonnas in a rich decorative manner which derived from the 15th century Flemish school. His religious works are generally marked by a peaceful air, free from tension and tragedy. In his last years *Italianate elements became noticeable, particularly the influence of *Leonardo. J. also excelled as a portraitist; pictures of *Maximilian I, *Henry VIII and *Francis I are attributed to him.

JORIS, DAVID (1501-56) Dutch *Anabaptist leader and visionary. The son of a shopkeeper who settled in Delft, he first worked as a glass painter, but, imbued with the ideas of the *Reformation, he began about 1524 to attack Roman Catholic doctrines. In 1528 he was subjected to public disgrace and banished from Delft, in consequence of his violation of the sacramental host. J. then chose the life of a wandering preacher. In 1533 he joined the Anabaptists, being particularly influenced by Melchior *Hofman and, in 1544, settled with

April, *from "Les très riches heures" of the Duc de Berry, a 15th-century illuminated manuscript*

The Virgin of the Rocks *by Leonardo da Vinci*

David Joris *by Jan van Scorel*

a few followers in Basle. There he lived, unknown to the local authorities until his death, corresponding with his many supporters in Holland. In his treatises, written in Dutch, J. told of the second coming of Jesus Christ, styling himself Christus David, that is, the prophet who heralds the second coming. Much of his writing consisted of eschatological monologues. Three years after his death his son-in-law denounced him to the Basle authorities, who had his body exhumed and burnt.

D. Joris, *Concerning Heretics*, ed., by R. Bainton (1965).

JOSQUIN DESPRÉS (c. 1440-1521) Flemish composer. A native of Hainault, he was the pupil of *Okeghem. In early adulthood he spent a few years in Italy. In 1486 he became a musician at the papal court, remaining there until 1499. Afterwards he went to France and later to Germany. A clergyman, he eventually returned to Hainault, where he died as Canon of Condé. A master of the technique of counterpoint, J. wrote many masses, *motets and secular songs, and acquired a reputation throughout Europe. He is considered as one of the most important Flemish precursors of the great Renaissance Italian choral school of *Palestrina.

A. Schering, *Die niederländische Orgelmesse im Zeitalter des Josquin* (1912; reprinted 1971).

JUAN OF AUSTRIA, DON (1545-78) Spanish military commander. An illegitimate son of *Charles V, whose mother belonged to a wealthy family of Regensburg, he was raised by foster parents who did not reveal to him his father's identity. In his will, however, the Emperor enjoined his son and heir *Philip II to care for his natural brother and, in 1559, J. was recognized as a member of the royal family. Demonstrating an inclination towards military life, he led, in 1568, an expedition against Algiers and, in 1569, was sent to quell the revolt of the *Moriscos. His greatest achievement came in October 1571, when at the age of 26 he commanded the Chirstian forces which crushed the Turkish navy at the Battle of *Lepanto. In 1573 he captured Tunis, but it was lost in the following year. In 1576 he was appointed governor of the *Netherlands, where the recent Pacification of *Ghent had united all the provinces in opposition to Philip II. At first he made some concessions to the rebels, but later changed his policy and in January 1578 defeated them at Gemblours, a battle in which Alexander *Farnese greatly distinguished himself. He died of a fever eight months later.

JUAN DE AVILA (1500-69) Spanish preacher and mystic. Born to a wealthy family near Toledo, he studied at Salamanca and later under Domingo *Soto at Alcalá. He was ordained in 1525 and, in 1528, decided to devote himself to preaching to the people of Andalusia. Greatly successful in *Seville, *Granada and Córdoba, J. was at one point accused before the *Inquisition of spreading seditious ideas, but was cleared of all blame. He was a close adviser of *Teresa de Avila and gave his support to the first Spanish *Jesuits. Of his writings the most widely read was *Audi filia* a work on religious devotion. His collection of letters on spiritual guidance, *Cartas espirituales*, was also influential.

JUAN DE DIOS, ST. (1495-1550) Spanish founder of the Brothers Hospitallers. Born in Evora, Portugal, he was for many years a soldier but, in 1539, in Granada he turned to a life of religious devotion after hearing the preacher *Juan de Avila. At first his public penitence caused him to be considered a madman but, in 1540, he followed his mentor's suggestion to look after the sick, and founded the first of many hospitals later associated with his name. Caring especially for the mentally afflicted, he succeeded in enlisting the aid of the Church hierarchy and wealthy people, and was supported by the early *Jesuits. The rapid expansion of his hospitals actually took place after his death and, in 1572, the order of the Brothers Hospitallers was approved by *Pius V. By the mid-17th century the order was maintaining 80 hospitals in Spain alone.

A. Alarcon Capilla, *La Granada de oro; San Juan de Dios* (1950);

G. Russotto, *L'ordine ospedaliero di S. Giovanni di Dio* (1950).

JUAN DE FLANDES (?-1519) Flemish painter at the court of *Isabella of Castile. He came to Spain about 1496 and is believed to have painted for the Queen many small religious pictures, 15 of which are extant. His chief work was the altarpiece of the cathedral of Palencia, begun in 1506.

E. Bermejo, *Juan de Flandes* (1962).

JUAN DE JUANES (c. 1523-79) The name given to the Spanish painter Juan Vicente Macip, active in Valencia. He was the son of the painter Vicente Macip (*c.* 1490-1550), whose religious works in Valencia and the cathedral of Segorbe (1535) showed old Flemish influences. J.'s work is marked by his complete adoption of the *Italianate style. His Raphaelesque *madonnas were particularly admired, one of them becoming the object of popular devotion.

JUAN DE JUNI (c. 1507-77) The Spanish version of the name of the Burgundian sculptor, Jean de Joigny.

Pope Julius II *by Raphael*

He came to Spain about 1533, and worked in several places before settling in Valladolid (1540). His numerous sculptures on religious subjects are dramatically expressive, making him one of the forerunners of the *Baroque in Spain.

JUAN DE LA CRUZ, ST. (1542-91) Spanish mystic. He entered the Carmelite order in 1564 and was ordained priest in 1567. Attempting to implement the ascetic norms advocated by *Teresa de Avila, J. encountered strong opposition within his order. Imprisoned several times, he finally left for a remote monastery in Andalusia where he died. J. wrote works of poetry and prose of meditative and mystical character; they were published after his death. He was canonized in 1726.

JUANA LA BELTRANEJA (1462-1530) Spanish princess; pretender to the throne of Castile. Daughter of Henry IV of Castile, J.'s royal paternity was in doubt and was ascribed to her mother's lover Beltrán de la Cueva. In 1468 her vacillating father was forced to declare his sister *Isabella as successor to the throne but, when he died, a faction of Castilian nobles rallied to the side of J. (May 1475), who also received aid from her uncle, *Afonso V of Portugal. However, her cause and the plan for a marriage with her uncle came to nought when her supporters were defeated at the Battle of Toro (1476). In 1479 she retired to a convent.

JUANA LA LOCA ("The Mad"; 1479-1555) Queen of Castile and mother of *Charles V. The daughter of *Ferdinand and *Isabella, she was married in 1496 to the son of *Maximilian I, Archduke Philip the Handsome, to whom she bore two sons and four daughters. In 1502 the **cortés* of Castile recognized her right to the throne, and she became queen upon the death of her mother in 1504. However, her mental condition, aggravated by her husband's infidelities, was so unstable that she could not rule, and the actual business of government was conducted by her father and, for a short time, her husband. J. withdrew completely from reality when her husband died in 1506. In the next five decades until her death she was confined to a palace near Valladolid, her father and later her son ruling in her name.

JUD, LEO (1482-1542) Swiss reformer. Educated in Basle, he became one of the closest supporters of Zwingli, and settled in Zurich in 1522. Besides his crucial support of Zwingli, J. pursued an extensive career as a translator of the Old and New Testaments.

JÜLICH-CLEVES SUCCESSION (1609-14) An international conflict between Catholic and Protestant powers, which may be described as a general rehearsal for the *Thirty Years' War. The territories of Jülich, Cleves, Berg, Mark and Ravensberg, in the lower Rhineland, were claimed in 1609 by two principal would-be *Protestant heirs, John Sigismund of *Brandenburg and Wolfgang William of Neuburg. Although the two reached an agreement to hold the territories jointly until a final settlement could be made, Emperor *Rudolf II intervened, sending his own representative, Archduke Leopold, to take possession. The confrontation led to a mobilization of forces by other princes of the rival denominations and, in 1610, Dutch and English troops under *Maurice of Nassau joined the conflict. At a later stage Spanish troops also entered the scene but, in late 1614, the Treaty of Xanten brought an end to the conflict, the territories having been divided between the two original claimants.

JULIUS II (Giuliano della Rovere, 1443-1513) Pope from 1503. Born in Savona to an impoverished noble family, his education had been supervised by his uncle, who in 1471 became Pope *Sixtus IV. Having been brought up by the Franciscans, he was showered by his uncle with ecclesiastical benefices and dignities, including several bishoprics and a cardinalate. In 1480 he went as papal legate to France to settle the Burgundian question, and under Pope *Innocent VIII, played a leading role in the papal court. The election of *Alexander VI (1492), a personal enemy, forced him to take shelter in France, where he encouraged *Charles VIII to undertake an expedition against *Naples. He returned to Italy with the French and tried unsuccessfully to depose the pope, but having failed concluded with him a formal reconciliation (1498), though he continued to avoid the papal court. He returned to Rome immediately upon hearing of the death of Alexander VI (1503). Following the brief pontificacy of *Pius III, he was himself elected pope.

Driven by an ambition to renew the secular strength of the *papacy, J. scored his first important victory when he forced Cesare *Borgia to leave Italy. He united behind him the leading Roman families, including the *Orsini and *Colonna, and opened negotiations with the

Federico da Montefeltro *by Justus of Ghent*

French and the Empire with a view to procuring allies for his plan to drive *Venice from Romagna. In 1506 he secured Perugia and *Bologna for the papacy, following a military campaign and, in 1508, pitted against Venice the League of *Cambrai. However, following the defeat of the Venetian army at Agnadello (1509) by *Louis XII of France, J. turned against the latter and, in 1511, joined the *Holy League against France.

The French king then convened a council in *Pisa (1511) to depose the Pope, a move that J. countered by summoning the Council of *Lateran. This body actually met in 1512, although by then the French were already leaving Italy, after Emperor *Maximilian I had joined their opponents. Victorious, the Pope died early in the following year.

Although early in his pontificacy J. issued a bull which condemned simony in the papal elections, J. was not interested in the spiritual affairs of the Church. His calls for a *crusade against the Turks and his proclamations about needed reforms were lip-service paid to enhance his political designs, and he especially took recourse to the selling of *indulgences. But he was a great statesman and military leader and one of the outstanding Renaissance patrons of art. He employed *Bramante, who began the building of *St. Peter's (1506), commissioned the Vatican *frescoes of *Raphael and the painting of the Sistine Chapel by *Michelangelo.

J. Klaczko, *Rome and the Renaissance; the Pontificate of Julius II* (1903);

E. Rodocanachi, *Le pontificat de Jules II* (1928).

JULIUS III (1487-1555) Pope from 1550. Born Gianmaria del Monte, he was of humble background, but rose quickly in the hierarchy, becoming archbishop of Siponto in 1511. Paul III made him cardinal, and appointed him papal legate to the Council of *Trent, of which he was the first president (1545). Elected pope in 1550, his first act was to reconvene the Council (1551), but, faced with the strong opposition of the Spanish delegates, he suspended it the following year. He supported the *Jesuits, whose college at Rome was confirmed in 1553, and never entirely relinquished the issue of reform. However, there were no real changes during his pontificate.

JUSTE Surname of three Italian brothers, sculptors from San Martino near Florence, who settled in Tours, France, in the early 16th century. The most important of the brothers, is Jean J. (1485-1549), who in 1513 was appointed royal sculptor. Their chief work was the tomb of *Louis XII and *Anne of Brittany, executed in Tours (1517-18) and placed in the abbey of Saint-Denis (1531). A superb example of the Italianate style, it portrays the kneeling king and queen surrounded by the 12 apostles and 4 allegorical figures.

JUSTIFICATION BY FAITH A fundamental concept of Protestantism regarding man's salvation. Quoting passages in St. Paul's *Ephesians* (2:8-9) and *Romans* (3:28), *Luther held that man becomes the recipient of God's mercy through faith alone (*sola fide*). Salvation does not depend on merit and good works, faith itself being a gift of grace by which God mysteriously elects to save a man. Man justifies himself by his supreme trust and passive expectation of God's forgiving mercy.

G. W. H. Lampe, ed., *The Doctrine of Justification by Faith* (1954).

JUSTUS OF GHENT (Joos van Gent) Flemish painter. The dates of the birth and death of this artist are not known. There is only one authenticated work of his, the *Communion of the Apostles*, in Urbino (1473-74); he is usually identified as Joos van Wassenhove, a friend of Hugo van der *Goes at *Ghent, who went to Italy, where he executed several works at the court of *Federigo da Montefeltro. His most important achievement in Urbino was a series of 28 portraits of *Famous Men*. J. is not heard of after 1475.

Musée de Beaux-Arts, Ghent, *Juste de Gand, Berruguette et la cour d'Urbino* (1957).

The Adoration of the Kings *by Kulmbach*

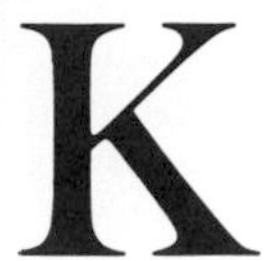

KABBALAH (Heb.: Received knowledge) Term denoting sum of Jewish esoteric and mystical works. The K. was given its textual consolidation in Spain in the early 14th century with the final composition of the *Zohar* (Book of Splendour). It was widespread among the exiled Spanish Jews who, in the 16th century, founded Kabbalistic centres in North Africa, the Ottoman Empire and, especially, in Safed in the Upper Galilee, where it was taught by Moses Cordovero, Isaac Luria and Joseph Caro. Earlier, in the 15th century, the K. had been studied by some Christian humanists, who believed that it represented a lost tradition of the earliest state of mankind. The most famous Christian student and promoter of the K. was *Pico della Mirandola, who was followed by *Reuchlin. Other students included Cornelius *Agrippa and *Paracelsus. By the early 16th century the study of the K. had become a humanist vogue, a subject which interested many, but was properly grasped by very few.
G. Scholem, *Major Trends in Jewish Mysticism* (1941);
J. L. Blau, *The Christian Interpretation of the Cabala in the Renaissance* (1944).

KEMPE, JOHN (c.1380-1454) English statesman, Archbishop of Canterbury. Educated at Oxford, he became an ecclesiastical lawyer and later entered the royal service and was made chancellor of Normandy. In 1419 he became bishop of Rochester which he soon exchanged for the bishopric of London. A protegé of Cardinal Henry *Braufort, he succeeded him in 1426 as chancellor of England, and was also that same year made archbishop of York. Although he had to resign the chancellorship in 1432, he continued to take part in political affairs siding with those who favoured peace with France. He regained the chancellorship in 1450, becoming cardinal and Archbishop of Canterbury two years before his death.

KEPLER, JOHANN (1571-1630) German astronomer. Born near Württemberg, his father was a soldier of fortune. After a sickly childhood, he entered the University of Tübingen in 1589. In the five years which he spent there he pursued mainly classical studies, but came to espouse the theories of *Copernicus and, in 1594, was appointed professor of mathematics at Gratz. There K. dealt with *astrology as well as *astronomy, and married a wealthy heiress (1597). In 1600 he was invited by Tycho *Brahe to be his assistant at Prague. Brahe's sudden death in 1601 left him in possession of the latter's instruments and accumulated data, and brought him the appointment of Court Mathematician and Astronomer to *Rudolf II. K.'s first task was to edit Brahe's catalogue of 777 stars (1602-03). Nevertheless, his own first publication in Prague was again a work on astrology, written to satisfy the inclinations of his imperial patron.

K. continued to elaborate Brahe's data for over 20 years and, in 1627, published the *Rudolphine Tables*,

Johann Kepler

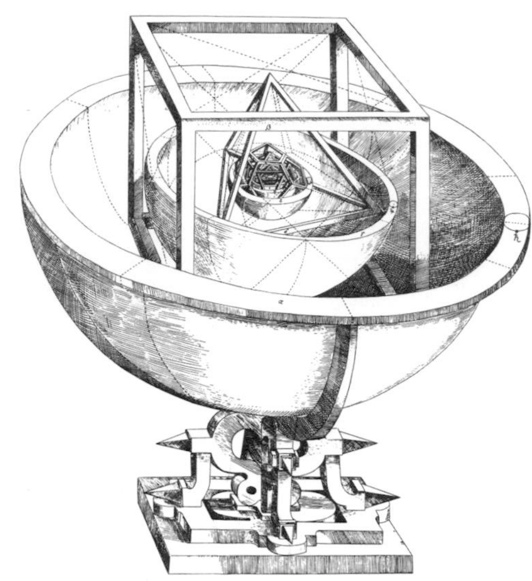

Kepler's Planetary Model based on perfect geometrical forms

giving the exact positions of 1005 stars, which remained in standard use for over a century. Meanwhile, he had published a number of treatises which boldly introduced new astronomical concepts. His *De stella nova in pede Serpentarii* (1606), which dealt with a new star that had appeared in 1604, was followed in 1609 with his innovative *Astronomia nova, seu physica coelestis tradita commentariis de motibus stellae Martis* (*New Astronomy, or Celestial Physics Delivered in Commentaries on the Motions of Mars*). Attempting to reconcile the observed astronomical data with the Copernican system, it proposed that planets revolved around the sun in elliptical paths, the sun being one of its two foci; next, that the radius vector of each planet sweeps over equal areas of the ellipse in equal times. The work also included a theory of celestial forces, and was, in fact, an attempt to explain the physical mechanism accounting for the motion of the planets. K. extended this theory in his *De harmonice mundi* (1619), in which he proposed a third law relating the periods of revolution of the planets with their mean distances from the sun. In his *De cometis*, published in the same year, he suggested that comets are made of "ether" and move in straight lines, being driven away by the sun. He also wrote on the principles of the *telescope and on logarithms, *Chilias logarithmorum* (1624), besides many other works of lesser importance.

Although his patron Emperor Rudolf was dethroned in 1611, K. was kept on by his successor *Matthias. In 1613 he remarried, his first wife having died, and the latter part of his life was passed at Linz, where he taught mathematics. He died in Regensburg. K. is recognized with his contemporary *Galileo as the real founders of modern astronomy.

A. Koestler, *The Watershed; a Biography of Johannes Kepler* (1961);
A. Beer, ed., *Kepler – Four Hundred Years* (1975).
M. Caspar, *Kepler* (1959).

KERLE, JACOB VAN (c.1531-91) Flemish composer. Born at Ypres, he went to Italy in his youth. From 1562 to 1575 he was at the service of Cardinal Otto von Truchsess, Archbishop of Augsburg who directed him to write music for special prayers on behalf of the Council of *Trent. Later he was at the court of Emperor *Rudolf II in Prague, where he died. The author of masses and *motets, K. was not a great innovator, though considered one of the chief composers of religious music of his time.

KETEL, CORNELIS (1548-1616) Dutch painter. Born at Gouda, he was trained in Holland, and spent 2 years working in France, at *Fontainebleau and Paris (1566-68). In 1573 he went to England, where he became a celebrated portrait painter. His portrait of Queen *Elizabet, is lost, but the one of the sailor Martin *Frobisher, survives. From 1581 on he resided mainly in *Amsterdam.

KETT'S REBELLION An agrarian uprising in England during the summer of 1549, led by the tanner Robert Kett. The rebellion was fanned by grievances stemming from landlords' appropriation of common lands by *enclosures. The rebels, numbering some 16,000, camped near Norwich where Kett held court, assuming the title of King of Norfolk and Suffolk. On 27 August 1549, he was defeated and taken prisoner by the earl of Warwick; he was executed at the end of that year.

KEY, LIEVEN DE (1560-1627) Dutch architect. Born in *Ghent, he spent many years in London (1580-91), but eventually reached Harlem, where, in 1593, he became a municipal architect. His works include churches and public buildings in Haarlem and Leiden, which parallel the style of Hendrik de *Keyser in *Amsterdam.

KEYSER, HENDRIK DE (1565-1621) Dutch sculptor and architect. Born in Utrecht, he eventually reached

Amsterdam's Westerkerk by Hendrick de Keyser

*Amsterdam, where he became a master stonemason (1591) and municipal architect (1612). K. combined the Renaissance style with Dutch architectural traditions, as shown in his several churches in Amsterdam. He also built the tomb of *William of Orange at Delft (1614-21), which is his chief sculptural work. Other important buildings which he designed were the house of the *East India Company (1605), and the Amsterdam Stock Exchange (1608).
E. Neurdenburg, *Hendrik de Keyser* (1931).

KLESL, MELCHIOR (1552-1630) Austrian ecclesiastic and statesman. The son of a Protestant baker, he converted to Roman Catholicism, became the chancellor of the university of Vienna and, in 1598, bishop of that city. About that time he threw his lot in with Archduke *Matthias, and helped his political manoeuvres to wrest control of the *Habsburg empire from his brother *Rudolf II. When Matthias became emperor (1512), K. became his right-hand man. Formerly a rigid opponent of Protestantism, he gradually became more cautious in his attitude to the religious question, aware of the dangers it held for the stability of the imperial government in Austria, Bohemia and Hungary. Shortly after the outbreak of the *Bohemian rebellion (1618) he was arrested by the supporters of Duke Ferdinand, Matthias' heir presumptive and an extreme Roman Catholic militant, and the Emperor was unable to come to his aid. K. was released in 1622. After spending several years in Rome, he was allowed to return to his diocese in 1627.

KNIGHTS' WAR, THE (1522-23) A political-military movement among the imperial knights of Swabia and Franconia which sought to play an independent part in the political life of Germany. It was led by Franz von *Sickingen, whom Ulrich von *Hutten served as propagandist and ideologist. The movement meant both to assert the independence of the knights as a class, in opposition to the powerful territorial princes, and to further the cause of the Lutheran resistance. Its principal goal was the secularization of the ecclesiastical domains and, in order to accomplish this, Sickingen besieged the archbishop of Trier in his city (August 1522). But he had to lift the siege and, having been condemned by the imperial council, was in turn attacked by the electors of the Palatinate and Trier and the landgrave of Hesse. The movement was finally crushed in the summer of 1523, Sickingen being killed and Ulrich von Hutton taking refuge in Switzerland. The castles of more than a score of Franconian Knights were destroyed.
W. R. Hitchcock, *The Background of the Knights' Revolt, 1522-1523* (1958).

Brent Knipperdollinck *engraving by Aldegraver (1536)*

KNIPPERDOLLINCK, BRENT (c. 1490-1536) German Anabaptist leader. A wealthy cloth merchant of *Münster, he had been introduced to Anabaptism during a business journey to Sweden together with Melchior *Hoffmann. Attaching himself from there on to the radical group in Münster, K. came, in 1534, under the influence of Jan *Bockelson. When the latter became the virtual dictator of Münster (April 1534), K. served as his righthand man and, after August 1534, as his 'prime minister', Bockelson having been proclaimed himself king. Arrested during the fall of the city (June 1535), he was tortured and put to death on 22 January 1536.

KNOLLYS, SIR FRANCIS (1514-96) English minister of Elizabeth I. A scion of a family whose members had served the first *Tudors, he began his career at court under *Henry VIII, but was raised to a distinguished position by Elizabeth, whose cousin he was by marriage. K. was entrusted by the Queen with receiving the fugitive *Mary Stuart (1568). He was appointed to the Privy Council and served also as treasurer of the royal household. A *Puritan who was sometimes critical of the Queen's policies, he remained one of her closest advisers until his death.

KNOPKEN, ANDREAS (c. 1493-1539) German reformer. Born near Küstrin, he studied at Frankfurt-on-the-Oder, and later under *Bugenhagen at Treptow (1514-17). Having been ordained, he became a chaplain in Riga (1517-19). After a visit to Treptow and other places, he returned to Riga in 1521 and began to expound the ideas of the *Reformation. Following a disputation in June 1522, of which he was declared the victor, the city adopted the new religious doctrines, and K. was elected archdeacon of the principal church. A close follower of *Luther and *Melanchthon, he stressed the Lutheran concept of *justification by faith. His early victory in Riga had been made possible by the assistance of the *Livonian order.

KNOX, JOHN (c. 1513-72) Scottish Protestant reformer. Born to a well-off peasant family in Haddington, he was educated at Glasgow. He may have taken minor orders in 1530 but, on returning to his native town he became a notary. In 1546 he espoused the Reformation under the influence of *Wishart and, in the following year, became a preacher of the Protestant garrison of St. Andrews. In June 1547 he was taken prisoner by the French, who captured St. Andrews

Operis tanti pars non vilis Homines quatimur fortune salo. Rapidos rector
comprime fluctus. Et quo celum regis immensum Firma stabiles federe terras.
Prosa quinta libri pmi.
Hec vbi continuato dolore delatraui. illa vultu placido. nihilq meis questibus
mota. P. Cū te inquit mestū lacmantēq vidissem illico miser exulēq cognoui.
Sedq̄ id longinquū esset exiliū. nisi tua pdidisset oro nesciebā. Sz tu q̄ procul

Gothic type used by Koberger in his edition of Boethius' De consolatione *(1476)*

Castle, was shipped to France and sent to the *galleys. Released in 1549, he went to England. In 1551 he became chaplain to *Edward VI. He assisted in the revision of the Book of *Common Prayer (1552) and championed reforms in the performance of the Mass. On the accession of *Mary Tudor, he fled to France, then went to *Geneva, where he first met *Calvin, thence to *Frankfurt (1554), where he was for a short time a minister of the English exiles and, finally, to Scotland (1555). But the continued persecution of the Protestants under Mary of *Guise forced him to return to Geneva (1556). His famous antifeminine diatribe, *The First Blast of the Trumpet Against the Monstruous Regiment of Women*, was published in 1558. Directed against Mary of Guise, it also angered *Elizabeth I, who refused him passage through England.

K. returned to Scotland in 1559. His position became secure after the death of Mary of Guise and the conclusion of the Treaty of Edinburgh with England (1560), which ended the alliance with France and assured the triumph of Protestantism. He now published what became the basic works of Scottish *Presbyterianism: the *Confession of Faith* and the *First Book of Discipline* appeared in 1560; in the same year his theological work, the *Treatise on Predestination*, was published in Geneva. The Scottish book of religious service, the *Book of Common Order*, was based on the one K. had written for his Geneva congregation in 1556.

When the young *Mary Stuart came to Scotland (1561), K. at once clashed with her over her attachment to Roman Catholicism. He was visiting in England when *Darnley was murdered, but was back in time to celebrate her abdication and preach at the coronation of her infant son. He became a close confident of the regent *Murray but, when the latter was murdered, had to leave Edinburgh and go to St. Andrews (1570).

A forceful preacher, K. crucially influenced the rising Scottish Presbyterian movement. Though the final consolidation of Presbyterianism took place only after his death, he certainly laid its foundations. A narrow-minded man, he was courageous and bold in his dealings with the nobility and royalty. His *History of the Reformation in Scotland* was published posthumously, and remains one of the chief sources on the subject.

J. G. Ridley, *John Knox* (1968);
L. E. Percy, *John Knox* (1937).

KOBERGER, ANTON (c. 1440-1513) German publisher. The most successful large-scale printer of the early period, he issued in his native *Nuremberg over 200 **incunabula*. K. catered to the public taste, accompanying his folios with woodcut illustrations, which were often coloured by hand. He was the publisher of *Schedel's *Liber chronicarum* (1493), better known as the *Nuremberg Chronicle*, for which he employed the engraver Michael *Wolgemut. At one point his workshop

Crucifixion, *attributed to Konrad von Soest*

employed 24 presses and over 100 men in different phases of production, and his books sold throughout Europe. He was ennobled and admitted to the town council, but his heirs, who lacked his entrepreneurial spirit, had to liquidate the business in 1526.

KOCHANOWSKI, JAN (1530-84) Polish poet and humanist. Of noble family, he attended the universities of Cracow and Königsberg and then visited and studied in Italy and France. Returning to Poland in 1559, K. entered the service of the crown, remaining in it until 1570. He was the first Polish poet who wrote in the vernacular, employing Renaissance stylistic elements. His works had both religious and secular themes and evoked patriotic feelings.

KOECK, PIETER (1502-50) Flemish painter, architect, designer of tapestries and writer. Born in Aalst, he was a pupil of van *Orlay at Brussels, and in 1527 became a member of the painters' guild at Antwerp. Previously he had visited Italy, and in 1533 went to Constantinople, with the aim of making designs of tapestries for the sultan, or perhaps learning the secrets of oriental rug-making. A book he wrote on the Ottoman way of life, together with his drawings, was later published by his widow. Attached to the court of *Charles V, he went in 1535 with the imperial fleet to Tunis. In 1549 he helped with the decorations for the triumphal entry of Charles and his son *Philip into Antwerp. K. translated *Serlio's work to Flemish (1539). Pieter *Breughel was his son-in-law.

G. Marlier, *La Renaissance flammande: Pierre Coeck d'Alost* (1966).

KOELHOFF, JOHANN (?-1493) German printer. Having learned his craft in Venice under the brothers *Speier, he went to *Cologne in 1472 and helped to make it a leading centre of printing in western Germany.

His son of the same name (died 1502) issued in 1499 the *Chronicle of Cologne*, a profusely illustrated book, which includes the first comments about the origin of printing.

KONRAD VON SOEST (c. 1378-?) German painter. Born in Dortmund, he seems to have been trained in *Cologne; his main work, the altarpiece of Nieder-Wildungen was done in 1404 or 1414. His technique reveals an understanding of *perspective, but his style is largely archaic, though with a link to the Burgundian school. Other works attributed to him are in the churches of Dortmund and Soest.

KOSTER, LAURENS (1405-84) Dutch printer of block-books. A native of Haarlem, K. was for a long time credited by his countrymen with the invention of movable type *printing. In fact, his contribution was limited to the art of xylography, and he is recorded as the holder of important posts in the government of his native town. The legend which had him a predecessor of *Gutenberg, has been proven to be just that.

KRAFT, ADAM (c. 1455-1508) German sculptor and architect. A native of *Nuremberg, he worked mainly in this city, and his earliest work, a statue, is in the church of St. Sebald. His masterpiece, the canopy over the altar in the church of St. Lorenz (1493-96), is carved in a florid Gothic style and is over 60 feet high. Richly decorated, it has numerous human figures and animals. His other works also display the elaborate manner of Late Gothic stone carving.

W. Schwemmer, *Adam Kraft* (1958).

The Nativity *by Konrad von Soest*

Kraft's sculptured self-portrait

KRANTZ, ALBERT (1450-1517) German historian. Born in Hamburg, he studied at Rostock and *Cologne. Later he taught at Rostock, where he became rector of the university. In 1493 returned to Hamburg, where he took part in the civil and religious affairs of the city as dean of the cathedral chapter. K. wrote several historical works, the principal one being *Vandalia, sive historia de Vandalorum vera origine*, an account of the primitive peoples of Germany. Inspired by the writings of *Pius II, it is considered one of the earliest works of humanist *historiography in Germany.

V. A. Nordman, *Die Wandalia des Albert Krantz; eine Untersuchung* (1934).

KULMBACH, HANS SÜSS VON (c. 1480-c. 1522) German painter and engraver. Born in Kulmbach, Franconia, he studied under Jacopo de' *Barbari and later became an assistant of *Dürer at *Nuremberg, with whom he was on very close terms. In 1514 he was in Cracow, Poland, where he executed *Scenes from the Life of the Virgin*, which show an unmistakable influence of the great German master.

KYD, THOMAS (1558-94) English dramatist. Born in London, he was educated at the Merchant Tailors' school, and seems later to have been in the service of an aristocratic person. About 1591 he was sharing lodgings with Christopher *Marlowe. In 1593 he was imprisoned on suspicion of treasonable activity and tortured, but was soon released. K. was the author of *The Spanish Tragedy* (1592), the first Elizabethan revenge play, which anticipated the structure of many subsequent works including *Hamlet*. It was one of the most popular plays in the last years of the reign of Elizabeth I, and was several times reprinted. The only other play which is ascribed to him with certainty is *Cornelia* (1594), an adaptation of a work by the French writer Robert *Garnier, which was not intended to be performed on the stage.

A. Freeman, *Thomas Kyd: Facts and Problems* (1967).

L

LABÉ, LOUISE (1524-66) French poetess. Born in *Lyons to a prosperous merchant, she became known for her charm and wit and had many admirers, including Maurice *Scève. She married a wealthy, elderly man who died after several years, leaving her a considerable fortune. In 1555 she published a volume of love sonnets, together with a short discourse on the nature of love. Her style is simple, but her poetry is intensely emotional.
D. O'Connor, *Louise Labé* (1926).

LA BOÉTIE, ÉTIENNE DE (1530-63) French author. Born in Sarlat, he received a legal education and was appointed a councillor of the *Parlement* of Bordeaux, where he met and befriended *Montaigne. His writings included sonnets, a translation of Xenophon and a commentary on the religious edict of 1562. His most important work, *Discours de la servitude volontaire*, published in 1576, dealt with politics and attacked royal absolutism in the name of popular sovereignty.
P. Bonnefon, *Estienne de la Boétie; sa vie, ses ouvrages et ses relations avec Montaigne* (1888; reprinted 1970).

LADISLAS POSTHUMUS (1440-57) King of *Hungary and *Bohemia. The only son of Emperor Albert II and the daughter of Emperor *Sigismund, he was born four months after his father's death and given to the guardianship of his cousin, Emperor *Frederick III. The child, whose election to the Hungarian throne was confirmed in 1444, was released by his guardian only in 1452 and, in 1453, was also crowned king of Bohemia. Under the influence of his uncle Ulrich, Count of Cilli, he entered into a bitter feud with Janos *Hunyadi, the regent of Hungary. This conflict climaxed in March 1457, when L., violating earlier assurances, put to death a son of Hunyadi who had been accused of the murder of Ulrich. Forced to leave Hungary, he returned to Prague, where he died suddenly of the plague.

LADISLAS II (1456-1516) King of *Bohemia and of *Hungary. The son of Casimir IV of Poland, he was elected in 1471 through the influence of his father to the throne of Bohemia, following the death of *George of Podebrady. His election was contested by *Matthias Corvinus, who was supported by a minority of the Bohemian nobility. But L. eventually reached an agreement with his rival, and following his death (1490), was also elected king of Hungary. He was a much less energetic monarch than his predecessors either in Hungary or Bohemia.

LAETUS, JULIUS POMPONIUS (1425-98) Italian humanist. Born in Salerno, he studied at Rome, where he succeeded Lorenzo *Valla as a professor of Latin. L. was the founder of the *Roman Academy, whose members met to discuss questions about classical antiquity. In 1468 *Paul II suppressed the academy for its alleged paganism. L., who was imprisoned and tortured, was able to re-establish the academy under *Sixtus IV. He had a great reputation as a teacher and philologist. He wrote commentaries on Virgil, edited Pliny and Sallust and wrote on later Roman history. The Roman Academy flourished under *Julius II and *Leo X, but disbanded in 1527.

LAFRERI, ANTONIO (?-1577) Roman book-illustrator, of French origin. A native of Burgundy, he settled in Rome, where many of the copperplates of *Marcantonio Raimondi came into his possession. During the 1540s he began to issue individual prints illustrating views of modern and ancient Rome, and after 1548 offered more than 130 such engravings under the title *Speculum romanae magnificentiae (Mirror of Rome's Magnificance)*. This work, in great demand by tourists, made L. the first great publisher of prints.

LAINEZ, DIEGO (1512-65) Spanish *Jesuit; *Loyola's successor as general of the order. After studying philosophy at Alcalá, he went to Paris in 1533, and joined the small group around Loyola. Most of his later years were spent in Italy, teaching, preaching and laying the foundation of the *Jesuit order. As papal theologian he took part in the debates of the Council of *Trent, and influenced the decrees on the issues of justification and grace. He became the Italian provincial of the Jesuits in 1552, vicar in 1556 and general in 1558.

LA MARCHE, OLIVIER DE (c. 1425-1502) *Burgundian ducal councillor and historian. The descendant of a noble family long in the service of the dukes of Burgundy, he became a page at the court of *Philip the Good and faithfully served *Charles the Bold as secretary and ambassador. After the latter's death at Nancy (1477), where L. himself was taken prisoner, he served his

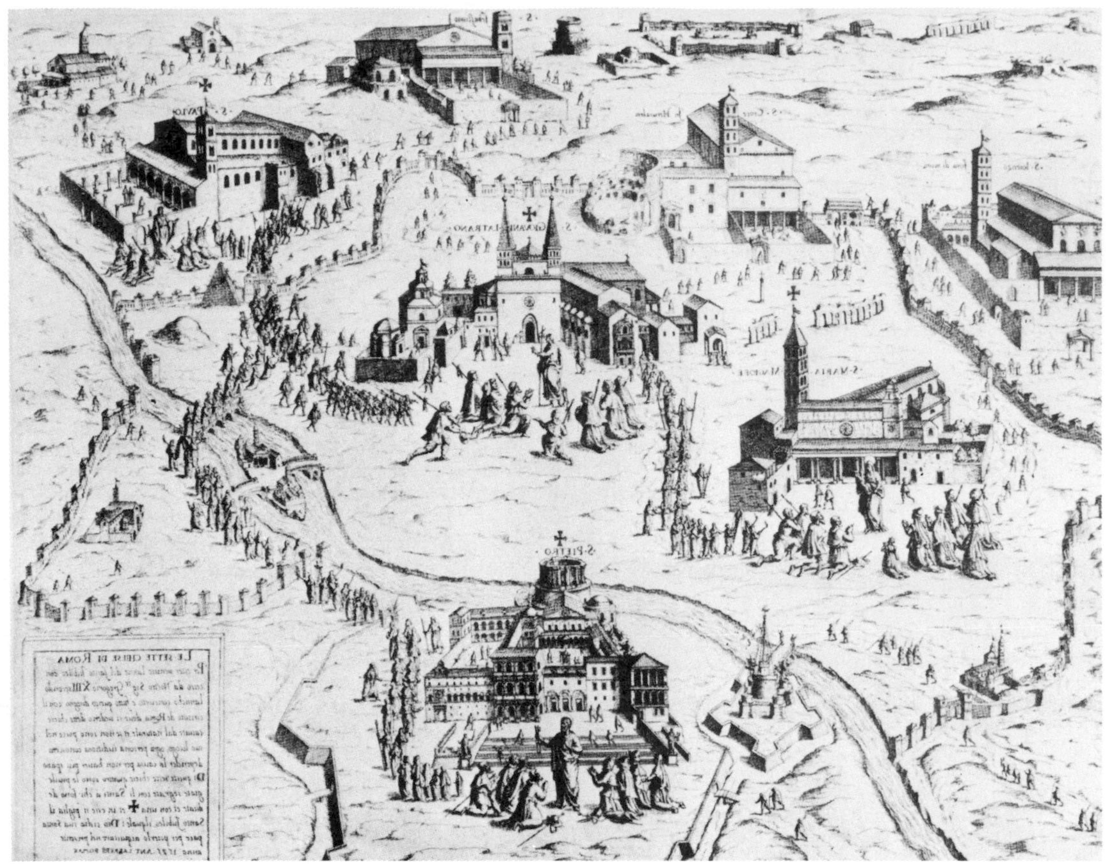

The Seven Churches of Rome *by Lafreri*

daughter *Mary and her husband Archduke *Maximilian and, in 1480, was put in charge of the education of their son *Philip the Handsome. L.'s works included poetry in praise of his patrons, an account of their rule, and a description of the Order of the *Golden Fleece. His most important work was the *Mémoires*, covering the years 1435 to 1488. An essential source on the history of Burgundy, it fails to rise to the critical level of his contemporary Philippe de *Commines.

LAMBETH ARTICLES (1595) A body of theological statements expressing the position of the Church of England, especially on the question of predestination. Espousing an extreme Calvinist position, the L. maintained that God decreed the election or non-election of the individual from eternity, and that those who were saved were so by God's pleasure only and not by their own works. Supported by Archbishop *Whitgift, the L. provoked the anger of Queen *Elizabeth I.

LAMBERT, FRANCIS (1486-1530) French Protestant reformer. Having joined the Franciscans at Avignon in 1501, he became a well-known preacher but, in 1522, left the order, establishing contact with *Zwingli in Zurich and then with *Luther at Wittenberg (1523). In 1526 he went to Hesse at the invitation of the Landgrave *Philip, and presented to the *Homberg Synod a plan of reform distinguished for the democratic and liberal character of its projected church organization. *Luther objected to the plan, but the proposal to establish a university was carried out, and L. was, in 1527, appointed professor of exegesis at Marburg, the first Protestant university. He was the author of several tracts against *Erasmus.

LAMBERTI The family name of two Florentine sculptors, father and son, who had a share in introducing the early Renaissance style into Venice. Niccolò L. (died 1451), a slightly-older contemporary of *Ghiberti and *Donatello, worked on doors for the cathedral of Florence. In 1416 he was invited to Venice, where he executed sculptural decorations for S. Marco with the assistance of his son Piero (1393-1435), and Paolo *Uccello. The son, who died before his father, is credited with some sculptures in the Florentine church of Orsanmichele and with the tomb of Onofri Strozzi in the church of S. Trinità (1420). From 1424 on he was in charge of building a new wing of the Ducal Palace in Venice, where he also executed many sculptures. One of his chief works was the monument of Doge Tommaso Mocenigo in the church S. Giovanni and S. Paolo. He died in Padua.

LAMBIN, DENYS (1520-72) French classical scholar. A native of Picardy, he studied in Italy and, in 1560, became a professor of Latin at the *Collège de France. A year later he was appointed to the chair of Greek. L.

won wide repute for his editions of classical Latin authors, especially Horace (1561), Lucretius (1564) and all of Cicero (1566). His commentaries on the plays of Plautus were also admired.

LANCASTER, HOUSE OF The English royal family to which belonged Henry IV (1399-1413), his son *Henry V and his grandson *Henry VI. John of Gaunt (1340-99), the fourth son of Edward III (1327-77), who became duke of Lancaster by marriage, was the father of Henry IV. During the Wars of the *Roses the Lancastrian faction was decimated by the House of *York, and lost their control of the government. Prince Edward, the son of Henry VI and the last direct heir to the house of Lancaster, was killed in 1471 at Tewkesbury. *Henry VII, who ascended the throne in 1485 after his victory over *Richard III, claimed to unite the houses of Lancaster and York when he married Elizabeth, daughter of *Edward IV.

LANDINO, CRISTOFORO (1424-1504) Italian humanist. A member of *Ficino's *Platonic Academy of *Florence, he excelled as poet and philologist. He wrote commentaries on Horace and Virgil and translated Pliny the Elder. His *Quaestiones camaldulenses* was a dialogue written in the style of Cicero.

LANDO, ORTENSIO (c. 1512-c. 53) Italian humanist. Born in Milan, he made an extensive study of the classical writers and travelled in the service of various patrons in Italy, Germany and France. He was the author of many works. *Cicero relegatus et Cicero revocatus* (1534) attacked Cicero and then defended him. *Forcianae quaestiones* (1536) dealt with contemporary mores. The *Paradossi* (1543) and the *Confutazione* (1543) were of a satirical nature. He also wrote stories and translated Thomas *More's *Utopia* into Italian.

P. F. Grendler, *Critics of the Italian World, 1530-60* (1969).

LANDSKNECHTE German mercenary infantry of the 16th century. The term, meaning 'men of the plain', distinguished them from the Swiss mercenary 'men of the mountain', whom they emulated. The L. were created by *Maximilian I. Armed with long lances, they were organized in regimental units which were subdivided into companies. Recruited by officers of the Emperor, they established a reputation for loyalty and discipline, though were prone to mutiny when they were not paid. After the Battle of Ravenna, the L. were considered the best European infantry. Under such commanders as Georg von *Frundsberg, they performed tactical movements which made possible their deployment in conjunction with cavalry and *artillery.

LANFRANCO, GIOVANNI (1582-1647) Italian painter. Born in Parma, he was a pupil of Agostino *Carracci. He went to Rome, where his first important commission was the decoration of the ceiling of the Casino Borghese. He soon became known for his skills at achieving illusionist effects. L.'s growing fame incensed *Domenichino, who had also been a pupil of the Carracci and with whom he shared the important commission of S. Andrea della Valle in Rome. Later L. painted the dome of the chapel of S. Gennaro in the cathedral of Naples (1640), the walls of which had also been decorated by Domenichino. He died in Rome.

LANG, MATTHÄUS (1468-1540) German cardinal and statesman. Born in *Augsburg, he was educated at Ingolstadt, Tübingen and Vienna, and in 1494 became

Landsknechte, *a drawing by Urs Graf*

the secretary of *Maximilian I. He soon became the Emperor's trusted councillor, was given several ecclesiastical benefices, including, later, the archbishopric of Salzburg; after 1508 he was the imperial chancellor. In 1512 *Julius II created him cardinal, but he was not a consecrated priest until 1519. Following Maximilian's death, L. played a leading part in arranging the election of *Charles V, and influenced the young Emperor to act against Luther.

LANGEN, RUDOLF VON (1438-1519) German humanist. Educated by the *Brethren of the Common Life, he became the leading spirit of the cathedral-school at *Münster. He emphasized the study of the classics, and generally displayed a more liberal approach to education than was common in northern Europe at his time.

LA NOUE, FRANÇOIS DE (1531-91) French *Huguenot soldier and author; known also as Bras-de-Fer (Ironarm). Of a noble parentage, he became renowned for his bravery in the first two *Religious Wars. In 1570 he lost his left arm, which was replaced with an iron limb ending with a hook. After the St. Bartholomew massacre he commanded the Huguenot stronghold of La Rochelle (1574-78) and, in 1580, was taken prisoner by the Spaniards while fighting with the Calvinists in the Netherlands. During his five years' imprisonment he wrote the *Discours politiques et militaires*, an account of the French civil wars which was first published in 1587. This work, combining memoirs with moral and political thought, enjoyed further editions as well as translations. He fought at the side of *Henry IV in the Battle of Ivry

(14 March 1590), and died of wounds received in siege operations a later later.

H. Hauser, *François de la Noue* (1892; reprinted 1970).

LARIVEY, PIERRE (c. 1540-1611) French playwright. Born in Troyes to Italian parents, he was the most important author of French comedies in the 16th century. His comedies were published in two instalments, in 1579 and 1611. Although they were adaptations from Italian authors, they had a lively spirit of their own. A comic scene from his most famous comedy, *Les Esprits*, was later used by Molière.

LA SALE, ANTOINE DE (c. 1386-c. 1460) French writer. A page and then a soldier in the service of the dukes of Anjou, he was in 1429 made governor of Arles. In 1435 became tutor to the son of *René of Anjou. In 1448 he joined the household of the counts of Luxemburg, and there wrote most of his works. His literary masterpiece is the romance *Le Petit Jehan de Saintré*, describing the relations between an adolescent and his patroness. He also wrote the satirical *Le quinze joies du mariage*, and some didactic works. The famous 15th-century farce *Pathelin* is believed to be his, and he is also sometimes credited with *Cent nouvelles nouvelles*, a collection of licentuous stories, reminiscent of *Boccaccio's *Decameron*.

F. Desonay, *Antoine de la Sale, aventureux et pédagogue* (1940).

LASCARIS, CONSTANTINE (1434-1501) Byzantine scholar who exerted a great influence on the development of Greek studies in Italy. Born to a noble family in *Constantinople, he fled the city after its capture by the Turks in 1453, and went to Milan, where he was employed as tutor by Francesco *Sforza. His *Erotemata*, a grammatical compendium, was the first book ever printed in Greek (1476). A friend of *Bessarion, he was a great collector of manuscripts and had numerous students, among them *Bembo. He taught at Rome and Naples, but the last thirty years of his life were passed in Messina, Sicily.

LASCARIS, JOHANNES (1445-1534) Greek scholar. Possibly a younger brother of Constantine, he went to Italy at an early age and taught Greek in Florence. He collected valuable Greek manuscripts for Lorenzo de' *Medici. In 1495 he went to France and taught Greek in Paris. Under *Louis XII he was sent as ambassador to Venice (1503-05). The editor of several classical works, he ended his life at Rome.

LAS CASAS, BARTOLOMÉ DE (1484-1566) Spanish Dominican missionary, bishop of the region of Chiapas in Central America (1544-47), historian and champion of the rights of the American Indians. Born in *Seville, he came in 1502 to Hispaniola, where he participated in the conquest and was awarded an **encomienda*. In 1512, being already a priest, he took part in the conquest of Cuba. Two years later, however, he decided to dedicate his life to the cause of the Indians. Returning to Spain, he was given the title Protector of the Indians by the crown and went back to America, authorized to seek a solution to the problem of ending the system of *encomiendas*. He was opposed by the Spanish settlers, who were responsible for the failure of his model Indian village on the coast of Venezuela (1521); but he was supported by *Charles V, who, in 1542, issued the "New Laws" which restrained the practice of *encomiendas*. In 1550 L., in a debate before the *Consejo de Indias, defended the principle that the Indians were not to be conquered by the sword and enslaved, but rather brought to the Christian faith through preaching in a peaceful manner. In 1552 he published the *Brief Account of the Destruction of the Indies*, which criticized harshly the attitude of the Spaniards to the Indian. Translated by the enemies of Spain into other European languages, it supplied the foundation for the growth of the *Black Legend. His great work, *Historia de las Indias*, which he completed in 1561, dealt with the history of America from the discovery to 1520. He took great care to present the Indians as human beings, endowed with reason, feelings and emotions. As a militant radical who had fought for a human cause, social justice and racial equality, L.'s personality is of great relevance in the present age.

L. Hanke, *Bartolomé de las Casas* (1951);
J. Friede and B. Keen, eds., *Bartolomé de las Casas in History* (1971).

LASKI, JAN (1499-1560) Polish Protestant reformer. A nephew of Archbishop Jan Laski (1456-1531), an important Polish statesman and an extreme opponent of the Reformation, L. first encountered *Zwingli, Guillaume *Farel and *Erasmus while studying in Germany and Italy. After his return to Poland, he was made bishop of Vesprim in 1529, and archdeacon of Warsaw in 1538. That same year, however, he became an avowed follower of *Calvin and left Poland. In 1542 he was chosen to conduct the religious affairs of Emden in Friesland, and from there influenced the growth of Calvinism in Holland. He went to England in 1550, at the invitation of *Cranmer, to act as minister of the community of foreign Protestants, and remained there, until the accession of *Mary Tudor, taking part in the deliberations that led to the publication of the *Book of *Common Prayer* in 1552. In 1556 L. was permitted to go back to Poland, where he attempted to unite all the Protestant currents. But his authority was recognized by the Polish Calvinists alone.

G. Dawid, *Le protestantisme en Pologne jusqu'en 1570* (1927).

LASSO, ORLANDO DI (1532-94) Flemish composer. L.'s nationality is problematic: born in Mons, Flanders, he was in his youth taken to Sicily, where he sang as a choirboy at the court of the Spanish viceroy; he always preferred the Italianized form of his name. In 1553 he became a choirmaster in Rome, but left this post after a year. Following a visit to his native Flanders, he went to Munich in 1556, at the invitation of *Albert V, duke of Bavaria. Here he lived until his death, writing and performing music and educating students, among them Giovanni *Gabrieli. A prolific composer, he left over a thousand works, mainly *motets and other liturgical compositions. His *Primo libro dei motetti* was published in Antwerp as early as 1555, establishing his reputation as a master polyphonist. In contrast with his contemporary *Palestrina, L.'s music is harmonically oriented, intended more to impress than to arouse devotion.

W. Boetticher, *Orlando di Lasso und seine Zeit* (1958).

LASTMAN, PIETER (1583-1633) Dutch painter. Born in Amsterdam, he went in 1604 to Italy, where he befriended *Elsheimer and was influenced by *Caravaggio. He returned in 1607 and settled in his native city, where he enjoyed a considerable reputation. His mature style combined exotic themes and animated gestures. One of his pupils was Rembrandt (1606-69), who for several years copied L.'s works.

K. Freise, *Pieter Lastman; sein Leben und seine Kunst* (1911).

LA TAILLE, JEAN DE (c. 1535-1608) French poet and dramatist. Educated in Paris, he studied law at Orleans, and subsequently served in the royal army and possibly also with the forces of the *Huguenots. His natural bent, however, was literary. In 1572 and 1573 he published *Saul* and *La famine*, two of the best early French tragedies. He also published two tragedies by his decreased brother Jacques (1542-62), and a treatise *L'art de la tragédie*. The last-named work summarized contemporary views on the art of the tragedian, emphasizing the need to arouse the viewers' emotions and to follow certain formal rules. L. also wrote a number of political tracts.

T. A. Daley, *Jean de la Taille* (1934).

LATERAN, FIFTH COUNCIL OF (1512-17) The last great council of the Church prior to the *Reformation, convoked by *Julius II and continued by *Leo X. The Council was summoned in response to the Council of Pisa (1511), a body composed of prelates opposed to Julius and sponsored by *Louis XII of France. A product of political expediency, the Council was not interested in the reform of the Church and devoted most of its attention to minor theological issues. It proclaimed papal superiority over councils and decreed a three-year tax on Church property to raise funds for a crusade against the Turks.

LATIMER, HUGH (c. 1485-1555) English reformer; bishop of Worcester. The son of a prosperous Leicestershire farmer, he received a humanist education in Cambridge and, in 1522, was ordained priest. L. then earned a reputation as a powerful preacher, and although he was suspected by the ecclesiastical authorities because of his outspoken criticism of abuses, he had friends in the court who interceded on his behalf. *Henry VIII's break with Rome strengthened his position. He was made the king's chaplain and, in 1535, appointed bishop of Worcester. In this capacity he continued to support reforming measures. But in 1539, when the Act of *Six Articles was passed, he resigned his sec, was imprisoned for some time and then remained in obscurity until 1546, when he was imprisoned again. The accession of *Edward VI brought his release, and by 1548 he had regained his reputation as a popular itinerant preacher, aiding the spread of Protestant ideas. In the reign of Queen *Mary L. was again imprisoned (1553). In 1554 he was compelled to dispute the doctrine of transubstantiation with Catholic theologians at Oxford. Refusing to recant, he was burnt at the stake with *Ridley in Oxford on 16 October 1555.

H. S. Darby, *Hugh Latimer* (1953).

LATIN LANGUAGE AND LITERATURE In contrast with *Greek which was all but forgotten, Latin continued to serve as a literary medium and remained a living language used by the Church and the *universities throughout the Middle Ages. As a result of its special status it evolved steadily until it differed from the language of the ancient Romans by the addition of words from the vernacular and the adoption of a simplified coarser syntax. One of the principal aims of the early humanists, beginning with *Petrarch and *Boccaccio, was to lift Latin from the barbarous state to which it had sunk and restore its pristine purity. This concern was intimately connected with the growing interest in retrieving and editing the works of classical Latin authors, activities pursued in the first half of the 15th century by humanists such as *Salutati, *Poggio Bracciolini and *Niccoli. The fact that some of these persons served as secretaries of the republic of Florence and the papal court helped to spread the neo-Latin style. Lorenzo *Valla's *Elegancies of the Latin Language* (1435-44), a call for a rigorous restoration of Latin as it had been in antiquity, became widely diffused. It was printed in 1471 and saw more than fifty editions in the next sixty years. Niccolo *Perotti's *Rudimenta grammatices* (1468) was the first new Latin grammar, printed as early as 1473. Soon the new Latin penetrated other countries. In Spain the main innovations in teaching the subject were introduced by Antonio de *Nebrija, whose *Introductiones latinae* supplanted old Latin grammar. In England the new grammatical handbooks from Italy were adopted in the last quarter of the 15th century but, in 1510, when *Colet founded St. Paul's School he asked *Linacre to prepare a special Latin grammar for the school.

The transformation of Latin in the 15th century had repercussions in the realms of the literary dialogue, the stylized letter, *drama, poetry and *historiography. But by the early 16th century excessive emphasis on style, known as *Ciceronianism, produced an inevitable reaction. What was more, in *literature Latin was losing ground to the vernacular languages. It remained the language of law and science, reigned supreme in the academic milieu and in theology, and was one of the principle subjects required in elementary and, especially, secondary *education. Not until the present century could a person boast of a proper Western education without being able to cite from memory a few lines of Cato, Cicero, Ovid or Virgil.

P. van Tieghem, *La littérature Latine de la Renaissance* (1966).

LAUBER, DIEBOLD A German scribe and dealer in manuscripts, active in Hagenau, Alsace, from about 1425 to 1467. Some 50 illuminated manuscripts in German and Latin are known to have been produced in his workshop. He may be compared with the Florentine bookseller Vespasiano da *Bisticci, and like him seems to have suffered from the advent of *printing.

LAUDONNIERE, RENE GOULAINE DE (?-c. 1582) French colonizer and writer. Born in Poitou, he became a *Huguenot and, in 1562, accompanied Jean *Ribaut on the first French expedition to Florida. He returned to it in 1564, in command of a second expedition, and established Fort Caroline on the south bank of St. Johns River. The settlement was attacked by Indians and the colonists were on the verge of mutinying, when Sir John *Hawkins visited the place and sold L. food and one of his ships (August 1565). Soon after also Ribaut arrived, with orders for L. to return to France to answer charges laid against him. But before he could do so, the settlement was attacked and destroyed by the Spaniards under Menéndez de Aviles. L., one of the few to escape the massacre, arrived in France in 1566. His account of the affair, *Histoire notable de la Floride*, was published in 1586.

C. E. Bennett, *Laudonnière and Fort Caroline; History and Documents* (1964).

LAURANA, FRANCESCO (c. 1430-1502) Italian sculptor and architect. Born in Dalmatia, a Venetian territory, he first appeared in Naples about 1455 as a sculptor working on the *triumphal arch of *Alfonso V. He later worked in Provence and, from 1467 to 1472, in Sicily. He was again in Naples in 1472-75 but spent his last years mostly in southern France, building the chapel of St. Lazare in Marseilles and doing sculptural work in Avignon. L. was a pioneer of Renaissance sculpture in Naples and France, he is best remembered for his series of busts of women.
R. W. Kennedy, *Four Portrait Busts by Francesco Laurana* (1962).

LAURANA, LUCIANO (c. 1420-79) Italian architect. A native of Dalmatia who settled in Italy, he first lived in Venice, but is especially remembered for the palace at *Urbino he built for Duke *Federico da Montefeltro. Combining elements of a residential house and a fortress, the palace has a beautiful inner courtyard surrounded by an arcade of Corinthian columns. L. may have been inspired by the Duke's painter *Piero della Francesca. His work was completed by *Francesco di Giorgio.

LAURENTIAN LIBRARY A collection of some 10,000 manuscripts and early books gathered by Cosimo de' *Medici, his son Piero the Gouty, and his grandson Lorenzo the Magnificent. Containing some of the oldest versions of the classical and early Christian authors as well as texts of the *Bible, the library building was designed by *Michelangelo and completed by *Ammanati and *Vasari. It was opened by Grand Duke *Cosimo I in 1571.

LA VALETTE, JEAN PARISOT DE (1494-1568) Grand Master of the order of *St. John. A descendant of a noble family of Toulouse, he became the head of the Malta-based order in 1557. He distinguished himself by his defence of the island, which in 1565 withstood a four-months siege of 40,000 Ottoman troops with some 200 vessels. Immediately afterwards he began the building of the new capital of the island, Valetta, which is named after him.

LAZARILLO DE TORMES A short novel published in 1554 as *La vida de Lazarillo de Tormes y de sus fortunas y adversidades*. It is the story of a young man who is first the servant of different masters and later his own master. It is a scathing satire on Spanish society, and includes bitter comments on the idleness of the aristocracy and the immorality of the clergy. The work combines humour and realism and is considered the first **picaresque* novel. The author is unknown, and for a long period it was ascribed to *Hurtado de Mendoza.
The Life of Lazarillo de Tormes. His Fortunes and Adversities, trans. by W. S. Merwin (1962).

LEAGUE, THE (1576-95) A political-military organization of the Roman Catholic party in France, formed with the intention of combating the *Huguenots. The L. represented an aristocratic and Catholic disapproval of the manner in which the monarchy compromised with Protestantism. Although *Henry III himself joined it in 1577, the actual leadership was in the hands of Henry, duke of *Guise, while *Philip II and Rome supplied inspiration and support. The cohesion and influence of the organization increased after 1585, when it was joined by treaty to Spain. In 1588 it dominated Paris, in spite of the King's objections and when its head, the duke of Guise, was murdered by order of Henry III, the duke's brother led the L. in an open revolt against the King. When Henry III was stabbed to death (31 July 1589), the L. refused to recognize *Henry IV, declaring the old cardinal of Bourbon king, under the name of Charles X. But the victories of Henry IV in the next few years, together with his ability to win the support of moderate Catholics, undermined the L.'s strength. When he returned to Roman Catholicism in 1594 and entered Paris, the L. simply melted away.
M. Wilkinson, *A History of the League or Sainte Union, 1576-1595* (1929).

LE BÉ, GUILLAUME (1525-98) French type designer. Born in Troyes, he was an apprentice of the printer Robert *Estienne, but in 1545 left for Venice, where he worked for different printers. L. designed Greek and Roman type, but is best known for his Hebrew founts, in which he produced exquisite letters in a manuscript style. He passed most of his latter years working in France.

LE CLERC, FRANÇOIS (?-1563) French *privateer. Having lost a leg in a sea battle he was known also as *Jambe de Bois* ("Wooden Leg"). *Henry II of France employed him to attack the Spanish merchant marine and American settlements. In 1553 he raided the island of Hispaniola, and a year later attacked Havana. In 1555 he harassed Spanish shipping to the Canary Islands. A *Huguenot, he took part in the first phase of the *Religious Wars, but died during a sea voyage not long afterwards.

LEFÈVRE D'ÉTAPLES, JACQUES (1455-1536) French humanist and precursor of the Reformation. L. received his doctorate in Paris and, having been ordained priest, he went, in 1492, to study in Italy. Influenced by *Barbaro, he devoted himself to the texts of Aristotle, but was also interested in *Neoplatonism and in the mediaeval mystics. At a later stage of his intellectual development, L. became interested in ancient Christian literature and biblical philology. In 1512 he published a commentary of St. Paul's Epistles, which influenced the evolution of *Luther's thought on the subjects of grace and faith. This was followed by a commentary on the Gospels (1522), a translation into French of the New Testament (1523) and the Psalms (1525).

From 1507 L. was supported by a former student of his, Guillaume *Briçonnet, who made him librarian of the monastery of St. Germain-des-Prés, and afterwards, the vicar-general of the diocese of Meaux. However, the reforming activities of L. and a circle of younger followers at Meaux resulted in their condemnation by the University of Paris and, in 1525, the aged humanist-reformer had to seek shelter in *Strassburg. During the last years of his life he enjoyed the protection of the King's sister, *Marguerite d'Angoulême. Although substantially in agreement with the ideas of the Reformation, L. did not openly break with the Catholic Church.
A. Renaudet, *Prereforme et l'humanisme à Paris pendant les premieres guerres d'Italie* (1953);
W. L. Gundersheimer, ed., *French Humanism, 1470-1600* (1969).

LEICESTER, ROBERT DUDLEY, EARL OF (1532-88) Lover of *Elizabeth I. The son of the duke of *Northumberland, L. was not welcome at the court during the reign of *Mary Tudor. But things changed when Elizabeth I ascended the throne. Conveniently losing his first

A scene from the Histories of St. Thomas *by Filippino Lippi at the Caraffa chapel in S. Maria Sopra Minerva, Rome*

Portrait of the Collector Andrea Oddoni *by Lorenzo Lotto*

Robert Dudley, Earl of Leicester

wife in 1560, L. became the Queen's favourite, indeed the only person whom she ever seriously entertained marrying. In 1564 she made him earl of Leicester and, although the idea of marriage was discarded, she remained partial to him and allowed him to retain a strong influence in the government. L. conducted a long but indecisive campaign against William Cecil, the Queen's chief adviser. Described as an arrogant and unreliable person, he nevertheless became a supporter of the *Puritans, and defended their interests at the court. In 1585 he commanded an English expeditionary force in the Netherlands and, in 1588, when the *Armada was about to invade England, was entrusted with the command of the English army. He died of a sudden illness in that year.

M. Waldman, *Elizabeth and Leicester* (1945).

LEIPZIG, DISPUTATION OF A debate held at Leipzig, beginning 27 June 1519, between Johann *Eck and Andreas *Carlstadt, who was joined on 4 July by *Luther. In the course of the debate Luther asserted that general councils of the Church may err and had erred in the past, especially with regard to the works of John *Hus. While the disputation furnished Eck with evidence for papal excommunication of Luther, it helped to crystallize the latter's doctrinal opposition to Rome. The event is recognized as an important landmark in the development of the *Reformation.

LEIPZIG INTERIM A religious settlement adopted by *Saxony in December 1548. It was drafted by *Melanchthon, who felt that some concessions to the *Augsburg Interim, imposed by the victorious *Charles V, were unavoidable. The L. reaffirmed *justification by faith, but allowed some Roman Catholic sacraments, including the mass, as *adiaphora. Many Lutheran leaders disagreed with Melanchthon.

LE JEUNE, CLAUDE (c. 1527-1600) French composer. Born in Valenciennes, he became choirmaster to Francis of *Anjou and afterwards entered the service of *Henry IV. Earlier, L. was associated with members of the *Pléiade*, and wrote music to their verses. He eventually became a *Huguenot, and composed music to a famous series of metrical psalms, which were published after his death in 1606. He also wrote many *madrigals and *motets.

LELAND, JOHN (c. 1506-52) English antiquary. Born in London, he was educated at St. Paul's School and later attended Cambridge and Oxford. Taking holy orders, he became chaplain to *Henry VIII and, in 1533, was appointed King's Antiquary. About 1536 L. undertook a survey of England, which resulted in a detailed antiquarian and topographical records. The bulk of his work remained in manuscript for a long time, but a summary was published in 1549 as *The Laboryouse Journey and Serche of Johan Leylande for Englandes Antiquities.*

T. D. Kendrick, *British Antiquity* (1950).

LEMAIRE DE BELGES, JEAN (1473-c. 1525) French poet and prose writer. Born in Bavay in Hainault, he was taught the art of poetry at Valenciennes by his uncle Jean Molinet a librarian to the dukes of Burgundy. He later studied at Paris and Lyons and, in 1503, entered the service of *Margaret of Austria, regent of the Netherlands, to whom he dedicated the *Épîtres de l'amant vert*. Supposedly composed by the princess' green parrot, the poems described the bird's distress at the absence of his beloved mistress, and eventual suicide. In this, as well as in other works, L. freed himself from many of the shortcomings of the **rhetoriqueurs*. He absorbed Italian influences and employed constructions of language and imagery which make him the precursor of the *Pléiade*. His major work, the *Illustrations de Gaule et singularitez de Troye* (1510-13), was written in prose while he was at the court of *Anne of Brittany. It was an adaptation of a mediaeval legend about the founding of the kingdom of France by the son of Hector the Trojan hero.

LEO X (Giovanni de' Medici: 1475-1521) Pope from 1513. The second son of Lorenzo de' *Medici, he was destined for the Church, and through the influence of his father was created cardinal at the age of 13. He was given a secular humanist education, but before going to Rome in 1492, he spent two years in Pisa studying theology and canon law. After the election of *Alexander VI he stayed away from Rome, and after the fall of his brother Piero from power (1494), he had to leave Florence too, and went to Germany, Holland and France. He returned to Rome in 1500, being welcomed by Alexander VI and, in 1503, supported the election of *Julius II. In 1511 the latter appointed L. papal legate of *Bologna and Romagna, and shortly afterwards commissioned him to lead the papal army against Florence. He was instrumental in effecting the return of the Medici to Florence (1512), being recognized at that time as head of the family, after the death of his elder brother some years before. At the age of 38 he succeeded Julius II, following a long and stormy conclave.

L. inherited from his predecessor the fifth *Lateran Council (1512-17) which he continued and brought to a

Pope Leo X *by Raphael*

conclusion, without dealing with any of the real abuses of the Church. He took interest in the controversy between *Pfefferkorn and *Reuchlin, enjoining the latter to silence in 1520. But he completely misunderstood the nature of the revolt of *Luther, whom he excommunicated in the same year, and shortly before his death awarded *Henry VIII of England the title Defender of the Faith for his work against Luther. Yet, he encouraged in his court a group known as the *Oratory of Divine Love, and thus linked his name with the origins of the Roman Catholic internal movement of reform.

More concerned with politics than religion, L. cooperated early in his pontificacy with Spain, England and the Empire against *Venice and *Louis XII of France. But following *Francis I's victory at *Marignano (1515), he had to sign the Concordat of *Bologna, in which, however, he gained the abolition of the *Pragmatic Sanction of Bourges. He then went to war with the duchy of *Urbino (1517), where he placed his young nephew Lorenzo de' *Medici and, in 1519, made an attempt to sieze *Ferrara. His costly policies left the papal treasury empty and in his last years L. abandoned his support of France and allied himself with Emperor *Charles V.

Liberal and pleasure-loving, L. was a great patron of artists and men of letters. He delighted in public celebrations and spectacles in which the Church and the clergy were occasionally subject to ridicule, and enjoyed the company of Pietro *Bembo and Jacopo *Sadoleto, whom he made his secretaries. *Raphael was his favorite painter and architect, but he also employed *Sansovino and *Michelangelo. He welcomed to his court the poets *Vida and *Trissino and the writer *Bandello, and made efforts to raise the level of the University of Rome by bringing over many teachers from outside. His liberal attitude was extended also to the *Jews.

E. Rodocanachi, *Le ponteficat de Leon X* (1931);
G. Truc, *Leon X et son siècle* (1941);
H. M. Vaughan, *The Medici Popes* (1908).

LEO AFRICANUS, JOHANNES (c. 1495- c. 1550) The name given upon his conversion to Christianity to the Moslem scholar Al-Hasan Ibn Muhammed Al-Wazzan Al-Zaiyati. Born in Granada, he was raised in Morocco and, in 1516, went on a diplomatic mission to Mecca and Constantinople. In 1520 he was captured by Christian corsairs and brought to Rome, where he was baptized by Pope *Leo X. He wrote an Arabic-Hebrew-Latin dictionary (1524), a geographical description of Africa in Italian (1526), and a collection of biographies of eminent Arabs (1527). Later on he left for Tunis, where he reverted to Islam.

LEON, LUIS DE (1527-91) Spanish religious author and poet. At 17 he joined the Augustinian order, and later studied and taught theology at Salamanca. Imprisoned by the *Inquisition in 1572 because of his translation of the 'Song of Songs' into Spanish, he was released in 1576 after a long trial, in which his Jewish descent did nothing to help his case. It is told that he resumed his lectures at Salamanca with the words: 'Hesterno die dicebamus' ('as we were saying the other day') . . . Of his moral and religious works in prose, *De los nombres de Cristo* and *La perfecta casada* (1583) dealt, the first with the diverse appellations of Christ in the Bible, the second with the moral norms of marriage. In his poetry, however, he showed, an inclination towards non-Christian classical authors, and translated Horace, Virgil, Homer and the Italians *Bembo and *Petrarch. His lasting fame as a poet rests on about 20 lyrical poems which celebrate the mysteries of the universe in a serene contemplative manner. These were published only after his death in 1631.

A. F. G. Bell, *Luís de León* (1925).

LEONARDO (Leonardo da Vinci; 1452-1519) Italian painter, sculptor, scientist, military engineer and inventor; the foremost embodiment of the ideal of universal genius bequeathed by the Renaissance to the modern world. Born at Vinci, a small town west of Florence, he was the illegitimate child of a wealthy Florentine notary and a peasant girl, and passed his childhood at the home of his paternal grandparents. Displaying at an early age a talent for drawing, his father apprenticed him at the age of 13 to the Florentine sculptor Andrea *Verrocchio, who trained him both in sculpture and painting. Although he became a free master in the city's painters'

The Mona Lisa *by Leonardo da Vinci*

The Musician *by Leonardo, at the Ambrosiana, Milan*

guild in 1472, he remained with Verrocchio until 1478. His earliest authenticated work is an angel with some of the landscape background on the left side of Verrocchio's *Baptism of Christ*. Another early work is the unfinished *Adoration of the Magi* of 1481. That year L. left Florence for Milan, entering the service of *Ludovico il Moro *Sforza, to whom he had recommended himself primarily as a military engineer. He lived in Milan for 17 years, working in several different capacities, among which was designing the sets and costumes for court spectacles. His most important works of this period included the *Virgin of the Rocks* of which there are two versions, several court portraits, and the *Last Supper* (1496-97), a large *fresco, which began to deteriorate almost immediately, in the convent S. Maria delle Grazie. It is characteristic that the great equestrian statue of the duke, which preoccupied him for many years was never finished. Its full-size clay model was destroyed by French soldiers, who used it as a target for archery practice.

The fall of his patron in 1499 as a result of the renewed French invasion of *Italy, forced L. to leave Milan. By 1500 he was back in Florence, advising the local government on architectural matters. His large drawing and painting, *Virgin and Child With St. Anne* (1501) aroused excitement; at the same time he pursued his scientific and anatomical research. In 1502 he entered the service of Cesare *Borgia as a military engineer, and for ten months travelled in central Italy, making sketches of city plans and topographical maps. He returned to Florence in 1503 and was commissioned to paint a large mural at the Palazzo Vecchio on the *Battle of Anghiari*. He never completed the project, but the preparatory cartoons aroused admiration. Much of his lasting fame, however, derived from a small portrait which he executed that year, the *Mona Lisa*, depicting the calm but somewhat enigmatic face of the wife of a Florentine merchant, against the background of an atmospheric landscape. The picture was later bought by Francis I and brought over to France.

With the permission of the Florentine government, L. went back to Milan in 1506, and remained there for another seven years as the honoured artistic adviser to the French governor. He returned to Florence only for brief periods, mainly in connection with an inheritance lawsuit between himself and his legitimate half-brothers following the death of their father. One of his main projects in Milan was the erection of another equestrian monument, this time of the native pro-French general *Trivulzio, but like the earlier monument it was never finished. This did not lessen the admiration and respect shown him by King *Louis XII; but in 1512 the French were forced out of Milan, and the representative of the house of Sforza, who returned, could hardly overlook the fact that L. had not remained loyal to the old ducal family. The aging artist left for Rome where he arrived late in 1513. He was lodged in the Vatican by Giuliano de' Medici, brother of the newly elected *Leo X, and occupied most of his time in scientific research and mechanical studies. The Pope himself was captivated by the geniuses of *Raphael and *Michelangelo, both younger than L. and at the height of their artistic powers. After his patron died in 1516, L. turned to the new French king, *Francis I, then in Italy following his victory at *Marignano. He accepted the invitation of the young monarch and in 1517 went to France, where he became First Royal Painter, Architect and Engineer and was given a residence at Cloux, near Amboise, where he died. Several works are ascribed to these last two years of his life, including the design of the famous spiral staircase of the Château of Chambord, but it seems that mainly he continued his work on the diverse subjects that had always preoccupied him before, while serving as a sort of general adviser to the admiring French court.

L.'s paintings are few in number. In addition to those already mentioned, there are the early and masterly *Ginevra de' Benci*, portraying the determined face of a young woman; *Cecilia Gallerani* (*c.* 1483), showing the mistress of Ludovico il Moro holding an ermine, and lastly, *St. John* (*c.* 1515), a rather unsuccessful attempt to combine pose and mystery. Yet with his stress on psychological characterization, his use of **sfumato* and his conception of atmospheric and dramatic unity, L. was undoubtedly the master who pioneered the new human awareness which marked the painting of the High Renaissance. His sculptural monuments were never executed. He was particularly interested in the technical problems of bronze casting, but all that remains of his activity as a sculptor are a few debatable minor works. The part of his extant work which best demonstrates the genius of his art and craftsmanship are the drawings. His papers were first bequeathed to his young friend Francesco Melzi, and during the 17th century they dispersed, the bulk going to the *Ambrosiana Library in Milan and the royal collection of England. These include notebooks in his left-handed "mirror script", and contain

Madonna of the Rocks *by Leonardo da Vinci*

Five Grotesque Heads *by Leonardo da Vinci*

some 3500 pages and thousands of drawings in ink and chalk. They cover an astonishingly wide range of subjects – studies of human beings and animals, plants and natural forces such as wind and water-currents, fantastic creatures, anatomical studies, architectural and mechanical sketches, maps and emblems. Many of the drawings are preparatory studies, but some, like the caricatures, are independent series. It is here that L.'s awareness of the human capacity for violence is revealed, as well as his preoccupation with the instability of man's existence,

Self-Portrait *by Leonardo da Vinci*

reflected in his juxtapositions of beauty and ugliness.

As a scientist L. is perhaps best known for his anatomical researches. He claimed to have dissected over 30 bodies, and was the first to draw correctly the position of a foetus in the womb. He devoted years of study to the movement of water, and wrote on this as well as on the flight of birds, mathematics, geology and other scientific subjects. His manuscripts contain schemes for flying machines, fortifications, new types of arms, including a military chariot which resembles a tank, and a bathyscape. Although he explored most aspects of the physical world, he never attempted to systematize his observations. Most of what he wrote is in the form of disconnected notes, and the only one of his treatises which exerted real influence is the *Trattato della pittura* (On Painting), an orderly compilation from his notes made by Melzi after L.'s death. A short version of this was published in France in 1651.

The final evaluation of L.'s work and personality is something which each one has to make for himself. To some his towering intellectual and artistic talents are the most significant fact about the man. Others are disturbed by his latent sense of impotence, i.e., his inability to carry out many of his main artistic and almost all of his scientific ideas. Whatever the case, no-one can question his stature as one of the giants of modern civilization.

K. Clark, *Leonardo da Vinci* (1939);
R. L. Douglass, *Leonardo da Vinci: His Life and His Pictures* (1944);
I. B. Hart, *The World of Leonardo da Vinci* (1961);
J. P. Richter, *Literary Works of Leonardo da Vinci* (1970);
V. P. Zubov, *Leonardo da Vinci* (1968).

LEONE DA MODENA (1571-1648) Jewish author. Born in Venice, he displayed already in his childhood unusual intellectual gifts, and received a broad education in Jewish and general subjects. A prolific writer and a famous preacher, he became known for his learning among Christians. His essay on Jewish customs, *Riti ebraici* (1637), was later translated into English and aroused interest when a new attitude of tolerance towards *Jews was emerging. L. led an unsettled life. He took up one profession after another, and became a habitual gambler. Among his works was an attack on the *Kabbalah, wherein he disproved the antiquity of the Zohar.

C. Roth, *Leone da Modena and the Christian Hebraists of his Age* (1927);
E. Rivkin, *Leon da Modena* (1952).

LEONI, LEONE (1509-90) Italian sculptor. Born in Arezzo, he had an eventful career working in several Italian cities, and later as a sculptor for *Charles V in Germany and the Netherlands. He finally settled in Milan, where he also designed coins, and *medals of Cardinal *Granvelle and *Michelangelo. His son Pompeo, also a sculptor, went to Spain where he completed the bronze statues which his father had cast for the main chapel of the *Escorial. Pompeo then executed on his own several monuments in Spain. He is also remembered as the possessor of *Leonardo's papers and notebooks, which he rearranged. He died in 1610.

F. Plon, *Les maîtres italiens au service de la maison d'Autriche; Leone Leoni et Pompeo Leoni* (1887).

LEOPARDI, ALESSANDRO (c. 1466-c. 1523) Italian sculptor, goldsmith and architect. Born in Venice, he worked at the mint, and later took up bronze casting. In 1492 he completed the casting of the monumental equestrian statue of *Colleoni by *Verrocchio. Later, he worked with Antonio *Lombardo on the tomb of Cardinal Zeno at S. Marco (1503-04), and made the richly-ornamented bronze bases for standards at the Piazza S. Marco. His main building is the church of S. Giustina in Padua, completed after his death.

A group of sculptures by Leoni in Milan

A contemporary print describing the Battle of Lepanto

LEPANTO, BATTLE OF (7 October 1571) A great naval battle in the Ionian Sea, near the entrance to the Gulf of Patras, in which the Turkish fleet was destroyed by a combined Christian force under Don *Juan of Austria. The battle followed a long period of rivalry between Spain and the Ottoman Empire for the domination of the Mediterranean, but was an immediate result of the renewed Turkish pressure on the possessions of Venice. In 1570, when the Turks demanded the cession of Cyprus, the Venetian government appealed to *Pius V who summoned a Holy League of Christian princes. It included ships from Spain, Venice, Genoa, the Grand Duchy of Tuscany and lesser Italian city states. Don Juan, who commanded a slightly smaller fleet, sank and captured more than three-quarters of the Turkish fleet of 250 galleys, and freed about 12,000 Christian galley slaves. The victory won a tremendous acclaim in Europe, but the Turks quickly built a new fleet, retaining command of the sea. In May 1573 Venice made peace with the Ottoman Empire, in which it not only gave up Cyprus, but paid a war indemnity of 300,000 ducats and, in 1574, the Turks were able to retake Tunis, which had fallen to the Spaniards after Lepanto. Nevertheless, coming as it did after a series of military victories under *Suleiman I, Lepanto was the first great Turkish defeat and was, therefore, seen as the beginning of the Ottoman decline.

M. Lesure, *Lepante; la crise de l'Empire Ottoman* (1972).

LERMA, FRANCISCO DE SANDOVAL Y ROJAS, DUKE OF (1552-1625) Spanish statesman. Of ancient noble parentage, he was attached to the court of *Philip II, but was not given a position of responsibility until 1598, when the young *Philip III succeeded his father. A favourite of the new king, he was given the title of duke (1599), and during the next two decades virtually took charge of the government of Spain. As prime-minister, however, L. proved disastrous. Amassing an enormous fortune for himself and his relatives, he pursued a costly intransigent foreign policy and neglected the army and navy. In 1609 he had to agree to a 12-year truce with the Dutch, unable to continue the war as a result of the bankruptcy of the treasury. That year he also caused the expulsion of the *Moriscos from Spain, a total of approximately 300,000. L. fell from power in 1618, the victim of a palace intrigue in which his own son played a prominent part. Under Philip IV some of his properties were taken from him. He was the first in a series of royal favourites (*privados*), a permanent feature of Spanish government in the 17th century.

LESCOT, PIERRE (c. 1500-78) French architect. The son of a well-to-do family, he studied architecture and was fortunate in having the sculptor *Goujon for a collaborator. Their most important joint endeavour was the square court of the Louvre, with its high French roofs and exquisite sculptural wall decorations (1546-51). They also collaborated on the Hotel Carnavalet and the Fountain of the Innocents (1547-49).

LESLIE, JOHN (1527-96) Scottish clergyman, bishop of Ross. Educated, like many of his countrymen, in France, he attached himself to *Mary, Queen of Scots, and in 1566 was consecrated bishop. After Mary's flight to England he became her liaison with *Elizabeth I, and in 1571 was arrested for his part in the project regarding Mary's marriage to the duke of *Norfolk. He then left England for Rome where, in 1578, he published a history of Scotland. He spent most of the rest of his life in France. Much of what he wrote was in defence of his Queen.

LESSIUS, LEONHARD (1554-1623) Flemish theologian. Born in Brecht, he was educated at Louvain and, in 1572, joined the *Jesuits. He became a teacher at the Jesuit College of *Douai (1574-81) then went to Rome, where he was influenced by *Suarez. Later he taught at Louvain (1585-1600). Enjoying a great reputation for learning among contemporaries, he was consulted by many about religious questions, and published several widely debated theological works. His most important work, *De justitia et jure* (1605), was frequently reprinted in the 17th century. It dealt at some length with the ethics of commerce and the charging of *interest. He also wrote on asceticism and on questions of personal morality.

K. van Sull, *Léonard Lessius* (1930).

L'ESTOILE, PIERRE DE (1546-1611) French chronicler. Born in Paris, where he spent most of his life, he studied law at Bourges and served as a royal official. In 1601 he retired and began to write his *Memoires-Journaux*, a description of the events of his own time, (first published in 1621). Dealing with the years 1574 to 1611, it contains vivid descriptions of everyday life, and is critical of the extremist Roman Catholic party. It is one of the foremost sources of French history of that period.

The Paris of Henry of Navarre as Seen by Pierre de L'Estoile (1958).

LE TAVERNIER, JEAN The name of two Flemish illustrators of the 15th century. The first, based at Oudenaarde, executed works for the dukes of *Burgundy (1440-61), in a style reminiscent of van Eyck's. His chief work is the *Chroniques et Conquêtes de Charlemagne*. The second, if indeed he had a separate existence, resided in Bruges (*c.* 1450-70).

LEU, HANS (c. 1490-1531) Swiss painter. The son of a German religious painter who had settled in Zurich, he travelled in Germany, where he became an admirer of *Dürer and *Altdorfer. From 1513 he worked in Zurich, where he painted many small altarpieces. At the beginning of the Reformation he became a soldier, and led an unsettled life. He painted several pictures on themes of

Façade of the square court of the Louvre by Lescot and Goujon, with the Pavillon de l'horloge *by Lemercier*

The Library at Fontainebleau

violence and death. He was killed in the battle of Kappel, in which *Zwingli lost his life.

H. Debrunner, *Der Zürcher Maler Hans Leu im Spiegel von Bild und Schrift* (1941).

L'HOPITAL, MICHEL DE (1503-73) French political leader and author. The son of an exiled physician, he studied law in Italy and served Emperor *Charles V and the papal court before returning to France in 1534. He then managed to procure a post at the **Parlement* of Paris, and in time became the confidant of certain members of the royal family. When, in 1560, *Francis II made him chancellor of France, one of his first acts was the registration of an edict barring the introduction of the *Inquisition. Pursuing a moderate course between the two warring religious parties, L. sponsored the Colloquy of *Poissy (September 1561), and initiated the Decree of January 1562, which granted the *Huguenots measures of toleration. He also contributed much to the reform of the royal administration. Nevertheless, his policy of defending the interests of the state over those of any religious party made him the foe of the Catholic party and, in 1568, after the renewal of the civil war, he resigned. He spent the rest of his life in retirement at Vignay, where he devoted himself to writing. A loyal supporter of *Catherine de Médicis, he was the first to articulate the position of the **politiques*.

C. T. Atkinson, *Michel de l'Hôpital* (1900).

LIBAVIUS, ANDREAS (1550-1616) German *alchemist. Born in Halle, Saxony, he was a follower of *Paracelsus. In his chief work, *Alchymia* (1597), and in another work published in 1604, he defended the alchemist's endeavour to achieve the transmutation of metals. He described the laboratory methods of his day, but criticized Paracelsus for relying on magic and *astrology, and tried to eliminate many superstitious practices. Representative of the transition in the history of science, L. is frequently cited as the one who foreshadowed the development of experimental *chemistry.

LIBERALE DA VERONA (c. 1445-c. 1529) Italian painter and miniaturist. Trained at Verona, he was influenced by *Mantegna while on a visit to Padua and, between 1467 and 1474, was mostly in Siena, where he illuminated books for the cathedral library. He returned to Verona in about 1488 and established a successful workshop. His later style is distinguished by rythmic lines and live colours, in contrast to Mantegna's classicism.

LIBRARIES In the Middle Ages L. were mainly monastic. By the 14th century some *universities and particular monarchs also owned collections of books, but none of these held more than a few hundred. The gathering of works by classical authors was a 15th-century innovation, introduced by some of the leading Italian humanists and their princely patrons. *Niccoli, *Poggio Bracciolini and Lorenzo *Valla were some of the notable discoverers of old manuscripts in monasteries, who helped to put together more complete collections of the ancient *Latin authors. Cardinal *Bessarion, and after him *Lascaris, performed the same task with regard to Greek authors.

By the mid-15th century this trend was so well established that Pope *Nicholas V launched an ambitious project to acquire all the ancient classics. It is believed that he assembled some 5,000 volumes, and although many were later lost, his collection constituted the nucleus of the Vatican Library. Other great Italian collectors were *Federico da Montefeltro, a dedicated procurer of classical manuscripts, and Cosimo de' *Medici. In 1433, while exiled in Venice, he began the famous *Laurentian Library, named after his grandson Lorenzo, who further expanded it. The greatest book collector of the 15th century, however, was *Matthias Corvinus, the cultured humanist-monarch of Hungary. The number of volumes in his great library in Buda was estimated in tens of thousands.

The advent of printing further stimulated the formation of libraries. The significant reduction in the cost of books permitted many well-off persons to amass impressive libraries. Among these were Hartmann *Schedel and Willibald *Pirckheimer in Germany at the turn of the 15th century, and the English Sir Robert *Cotton one hundred years later, whose collection was the nucleus of the British Museum Library. Sir Thomas *Bodley, a contemporary of Cotton, pioneered the large public, or institutional library, a development which made itself felt throughout Europe during the 17th century. The first library open to the public was the *Ambrosiana of Milan in 1609.

A. Hessel, *A History of Libraries* (1950);

The Month of January *by the Limbourg brothers*

The Avenue of the Hundred Fountains by Pirro Ligorio

F. Wormald and C. E. Wright, eds., *The English Library Before 1700* (1958);
C. F. Buhler, *The Fifteenth-Century Book* (1960).

LIEDET, LOISET Flemish illuminator, active in Bruges between 1445-75. He executed several works for the dukes of *Burgundy. One of his illuminations for the *Histoire de Charles Martel et de ses successeurs* (1469-75), now in the royal library at Brussels, is signed. Another famous manuscript which he illuminated is the *Chronicles* of Froissart, at the French national library.

LIGORIO, PIRRO (c. 1510-83) Italian architect. Born in Naples, he was also a painter and an archaeologist; early in his career he excavated the site of Hadrian's villa outside Rome. His main creation was the Villa d'Este in Tivoli, commissioned by Cardinal Ippolito d'*Este in 1550. It is especially remarkable for its descending gardens and fountains. He then built the elegant Casino of *Pius IV in the Vatican gardens (1558-62). After 1568 he was active in *Ferrara.

LILIO, LUIGI (c. 1510-76) Italian physician. At his death he left in manuscript a work entitled *Compendium novae rationis restituendi kalendarium*, which proposed a reform of the calendar. Presented by his brother to Pope *Gregory XIII, it was approved in 1582, replacing the Julian calendar.

LILLY, WILLIAM (1468-1522) English humanist and educator. A graduate of Oxford, L. learned Greek while on an extended voyage to the East. Following a pilgrimage to the Holy Land, he spent some time with the Knights of *St. John at Rhodes, and then studied at Rome and Venice. The first teacher of Greek in London, he was invited by *Colet in 1510 to be the first headmaster of the school of St. Paul's. He was the principal author of a *Latin grammar which remained in use until the 19th century.

LIMBOURG BROTHERS The family name of three brothers, Pol, Hennequin and Herman, creators of the

most famous *illuminated manuscript of the 15th century, a *Book of Hours*, completed in about 1416 for the duke of Berry. Broadly following the style of *International Gothic, their paintings combined gorgeous colour with realism and a highly decorative effect.
M. Meiss, *French Painting in the Time of Jean de Berry; the Limbourgs and Their Contemporaries*, 2 vols. (1974).

LINACRE, THOMAS (c. 1460-1524) English humanist scholar and physician. He was educated at Canterbury by his uncle, the Benedictine prior William of Selling, the first Englishman who had studied Greek in Italy (1464-67). In 1480 he went to Oxford, where, in 1484, he was elected Fellow of All Souls. The following year he went to Italy with his uncle, who introduced him to *Politian. L. remained in Italy for ten years, studying Latin, Greek and *medicine. Upon his return to England he was recognized not only as an authority on the classics but as a great physician as well. In 1509 he was appointed physician to *Henry VIII, and later tutored Princess *Mary. In 1518 he founded the Royal College of Physicians with the aim of improving the standards of

Detail from the Adoration *by Fra Filippo Lippi*

Filippo Lippi, Madonna Adoring Her Child

the profession. L. translated into Latin three treatises on medicine by Galen, which were published in Paris and Cambridge between 1517 and 1521. In addition, he wrote two works on Latin grammar and composition. A friend of *Colet, *Erasmus and *More, he was, with *Grocyn, a leading promoter of humanist learning in England.
C. D. O'Malley, *English Medical Humanists: Thomas Linacre and John Cains* (1965).

LINCK, WENCESLAUS (1483-1547) German Protestant reformer. A graduate of the university of Leipzig, he joined the Augustianians and became prior of the Order's cloister at *Wittenberg, where *Luther was subprior. In 1520 he succeeded *Staupitz as vicar-general of the Order in Germany. He soon joined Luther's movement and, in 1523, resigned his office and became a preacher in Altenburg. After 1525 he was active in *Nuremberg.

LINSCHOTEN, JAN HUYGHEN VAN (1563-1611) Dutch explorer. Born in Haarlem, he went to Lisbon on business and, in 1583, sailed to *India, where he spent six years. After his return to Holland L. wrote two books, published in 1595-96, which stimulated the first Dutch expedition to the East under *Houtman. In 1594 he accompanied William *Barents on his *exploration of the Arctic region and, in 1595, went again with Barents, reaching Novaya Zemlya and Kara Sea. A description of these voyages, which sought to find a northern route to India, was published in 1601.
C. M. Parr, *Jan van Linschoten: The Dutch Marco Polo* (1964).

LIPPI, FRA FILIPPO (c. 1406-69) Italian painter. The son of a Florentine butcher who died when he was a child, he was placed by his mother in a Carmelite monastery, where he learned his craft. His first *frescoes were plainly influenced by *Masaccio, but after he returned from a period of work in Padua (1434-37), he began to make his own contribution to Renaissance painting, the depiction of the human figure in a religious context but in a gently realistic manner. This is exemplified in his graceful madonnas, such as the famous *Virgin Adoring the Child*, now at the Uffizi, with its boy-angel who faces the viewer with a playful smile. A protegé of the *Medici, L. later added the influence of Fra *Angelico, and in 1452 undertook the decoration of the cathedral of Prato, which he adorned with scenes from the lives of St. Stephen and St. John the Baptist. He died at Spoleto. His son Filippino Lippi (1457-1504), born of his union with the nun Lucrezia Buti, which was given a retroactive papal dispensation, was a pupil of *Botticelli and himself a well-known painter under Lorenzo de' *Medici. His principal works included the completion of Masaccio's frescoes at the Brancacci Chapel, frescoes in the chapel of Filippo Strozzi at S. Maria Novella, Florence, and religious scenes in the Caraffa chapel in S. Maria sopra Minerva in Rome (1488-93).

R. Oertel, *Fra Filippo Lippi* (1942);
K. Neilson, *Filippino Lippi* (1938).

LIPSIUS, JUSTUS (1547-1606) Flemish classical scholar and philosopher. Born near Brussels and raised as a Catholic, he turned to Lutheranism during his stay at the University of Jena (1572-75), and embraced Calvinism when he taught at the University of Leiden (1579-91). In 1592 he joined the University of Louvain, returning at the same time to Catholicism. He remained at Louvain for the rest of his life. His shifting from one religious doctrine to another represented an aloofness from dogmatism, and a belief in the need for religious unity, which was expressed in his *Politicorum libri sex* (1589). Most of his works, however, dealt with classical philosophy and Roman antiquity, and included editions of Tacitus and Seneca.

J. L. Saunders, *Justus Lipsius: The Philosophy of Renaissance Stoicism* (1955).

LISMANINI, FRANCESCO (?-1566) Italian Protestant reformer in Poland. Born in Corfu, he joined the Franciscan order and went to Poland about 1546 as court preacher to its queen Bona Sforza. Encouraged by her son King *Sigismund II Augustus, he went in 1553 to Switzerland, returning a confirmed Calvinist. He then cooperated with Jan *Laski in his attempts to unite the various currents of Polish Protestants, ending his life in Königsberg.

LITERATURE, THE RISE OF VERNACULAR The Renaissance did not create the national literatures of Europe; already in the 13th century there were literary works in the vernacular, such as verses of the French *troubadours*, the German *Minnesinger*, or the practitioners of the *dolce stil nuovo* in Italy, and lyric poetry was increasingly cast in local idioms. The same is true of the older French epic poems, the *chansons de geste*, which furnished the basis for the development of the romances of chivalry, tales of heroic adventures, frequently combining prose and verse. At the same time, the *Roman de la rose* was the best example of the long allegorical poem. In a sense, therefore, European vernacular literature may be said to have been born in the fully matured *feudal society. Nevertheless, the Renaissance was a time of crucial importance to the development of vernacular literature as well as the *drama. Some of the major modern literary forms were created by the literary giants of the age. The languages themselves underwent a process of consolidation, and literature became the outstanding cultural pastime which it has remained until our own day.

Any survey of Renaissance literature must begin with the names of three great Italians: *Dante, *Petrarch and *Boccaccio. The first, a fervent advocate of the vernacular, supplied in his *Divine Comedy* an eternal model of a poem of overpowering passion and force. The second was the earliest celebrated master of the sonnet. The third, with his *Decameron*, began the modern form of prose narrative which culminated in the novel. Two other outstanding authors of this period of transition from Middle Ages to Renaissance were *Chaucer in England and *Villon in France. However, in the 15th century the paths opened by these great masters had not yet been made into highways. In Italy vernacular literature actually suffered a setback in the competition against *Latin. In France the flourishing school of the **rhétoriqueurs* was chiefly preoccupied with formal, complicated problems of rhyme schemes and metaphors. In Germany the **Meistersinger* presented a similar phenomenon. Indeed, in its subject matter as in its sensibilities, most of the literary creation of the late 15th century still showed a mediaeval spirit. But this spirit, which on the one hand strove to maintain the artificial ideals of *chivalry, expressed itself also in short farcical stories, often combinig satire and obscenity. These were known in France as *fabliaux*, and were represented in Germany by the **Schwänke*.

The advent of *printing in the second half of the 15th century brought vernacular literature to a much wider public. This was almost immediately reflected in the success of works as *Malory's *Morte d'Arthur* and **Amadis de Gaula*. The time-tested combination of the themes of love and war thus quickly reasserted itself, its most notable expressions being the four great Italian epic romances in verse: *Morgante Maggiore* by *Pulci, *Orlando innamorato* by *Boiardo, *Orlando furioso* by *Ariosto and *Gerusalemme liberata* by *Tasso. The fact that approximately one hundred years passed between the publication of the first work and the last, testifies to the enduring popularity of this literary genre. It had many imitations outside Italy, such as *The Faerie Queene* by the English *Spenser. Another popular genre of an epic work was the *pastoral romance. Here too the pattern was set in the late 15th century by an Italian author, *Sannazaro, whose *Arcadia* inspired a prose work having the same title by Sir Philip *Sidney, which was published as late as 1590. Both in verse and prose, the romances of the High Renaissance showed an increasing tendency to use classical mythological themes and images. Epic poetry attempted to follow the style of the ancients, especially Virgil, and even the setting was sometimes ancient Greece. In the second part of the 16th century, however, a certain realism in the characterization of heroes and analysis of their motives began to be manifested.

Dependence on classical models was even closer in the field of refined lyric poetry. The Renaissance revived the ode, the eclogue and the elegy in imitation of the great Roman and Greek lyricists, Horace, Catullus, Ovid and Pindar. But Renaissance lyricism is especially remembered for the tremendous proliferation of the sonnet. A poem of 14 lines, it was generally addressed to an unreachable or unresponsive lady and dealt with themes of exalted passion and love. Following Petrarch, the most prominent Italian sonneteer of the 15th century was *Politian, followed by his patron, Lorenzo de' *Medici. In the next generation *Bembo's sonnets stand out, as well as those of *Michelangelo and his friend Vittoria *Colonna. By this time the form had struck root in other European countries: *Boscán and *Garcilaso de la Vega introduced the Petrarchan sonnets to Spain; *Marot, the first to write them in French, was soon followed by a group of poets from *Lyons, including Maurice *Scève and Louise *Labé. In England the first sonnet sequences were by Thomas *Wyatt and the Earl of *Surrey, and the form became widespread during the reign of *Elizabeth I. The last and best-known English sonneteer of the age was, of course, *Shakespeare, whose name is linked with the sonnet in which the fourteen lines are divided into three quatrains followed by a rhymed couplet.

In prose the short entertaining narrative, introduced by Boccaccio, was already in the late 14th century followed by *Sacchetti. Other Italian story-tellers made their contributions in the course of the next one hundred years, but it was not until the mid-16th century, when *Bandello published his *Novelliere* in France, that this genre reached its greatest popularity. The Italian novel had several imitators in Elizabethan England, notably *Fenton and *Painter. Other nations were more inclined to adhere to local traditions. In Germany the most popular collection of rude satiric tales, **Till Eulenspiegel* (1515), was soon followed by *Pauli's *Schimpf und Ernst* (1522) and, by the mid-century, an entertaining collection of tales by *Wickram. In France it was the grotesquely satirical *Rabelais who won the widest popularity as a prose writer. In Spain in the early 16th century a work usually described as a novel in a dramatic form, *La Celestina* by Fernando de *Rojas, established a tradition of realistic prose. Later, the publication of **Lazarillo de Tormes* (1554) introduced the Spanish *picaresque novel, and further displayed the preoccupation of local authors with social reality, a counterbalance to the romances of chivalry which were still in vogue. It was out of the contrast between these two literary traditions that *Cervantes' *Don Quixote* (1605) emerged, a masterful combination of the imaginary quality of the romance and the earthly flavour of the picaresque.

Although must of what was written during the Renaissance has little appeal for the 20th-century reader, it is nonetheless an essentially modern literature. Moreover, by the second half of the 16th century European writers displayed many of the characteristics of their modern counterparts, including a true bohemian spirit and avant-gardistic tensions. In France the immediate example of this are the **Pléiades*, in Spain the careers of Cervantes and *Lope de Vega, in England the *University Wits, the lackadaisical practitioners of rogue literature. Writers everywhere developed a real concern for intellectual values and theories of esthetics, and became painfully aware of the importance of originality.

W. Sypher, *Four Stages of Renaissance Style: Transformation in Art and Literature, 1400-1700* (1955);
D. Bush, *Prefaces to Renaissance Literature* (1965);
C. S. Baldwin, *Renaissance Literary Theory and Practice* (1939).

LITHUANIA Emerging from a tribal state of organization only in the 13th century, the Lithuanian people were nevertheless able to ward off the threat of the Prussian-Livonian military orders, and at the same time expand southward to the plains between the Dniester and Dnieper rivers. In the late 14th century they controlled vast stretches of land between *Poland and *Russia. Having until then preserved their national religion, the Lithuanians converted to Christianity when Grand Duke *Jagiello married the Polish heiress Jadwiga and became king of Poland as *Vladislav II (1386). Henceforward Lithuania was linked by a dynastic union to Poland, although there were some attempts of resistence to the ties. In 1501, when Alexander, Grand Duke of Lithuania and brother of the deceased *John Albert, was elected king of Poland (1501-06), the two offices of grand duke and king were combined in one person. Finally, in 1569 *Sigismund II (1548-72) effected the Union of *Lublin.

The Cambridge History of Poland, 2 vols. (1941).

LITTLE MASTERS (German: Kleinmeister) A group of German engravers, active in the first three decades of the 16th century, who executed very small prints of biblical and mythological scenes. The most important representatives of this art were *Dürer's followers at Nuremberg, the *Beham brothers and Georg *Pencz. *Altdorfer and *Aldegrever also excelled in producing very small copper plates.

LIVONIAN ORDER A German military order of knights that established itself during the 13th century in the Baltic region north of *Lithuania. In 1237 it became amalgamated with the *Teutonic Knights, and in its heyday in the 14th century controlled Livonia itself as well as Estonia and Courland, including the cities of Riga, Dorpat and Reval. Though not as powerful as its Prussian counterpart, the order nevertheless succeeded in defending itself against its rising neighbours, *Lithuania and *Russia. Following the lead of *Albert of Prussia it allowed the introduction of the Reformation. Its rule ended as a result of the *Livonian War.

LIVONIAN WAR (1558-82) A series of military clashes for the Baltic province of Livonia, principally between Poland and Sweden, on the one side, and *Ivan IV of Russia, on the other. The Tsar began the conflict in 1558, when he seized the Baltic ports of Narva and Dorpat from their former rulers, the *Livonian Order, a decaying branch of the *Teutonic Knights. This provoked a Swedish invasion of Estonia (1561), and the capture of the southern part of Livonia by Poland in the same year. Other events in the conflict were the defeat of the Russians by the Swedes at Wenden in 1578, and the victorious invasion of Russia by *Stephen Bathory in 1581. The peace of 1582 gave most of Livonia to Poland.

LOBO, FRANCISCO RODRIGUES (1580-1622) Portuguese author. Born to a noble family of Leira, he studied at Coimbra but returned to his native region where he passed most of his life. L. wrote a number of *pastorals in prose and verse, the most successful of which was the *Primavera* (1601), frequently reissued and considered a model of inspired scenery description in Portuguese

Madonna *by Stephen Lochner*

literature. Writing at a time when Portugal was under Spanish rule, he composed an historical epic poem with a certain patriotic import. He was much admired for his stylistic elegance.

LOCHNER, STEPHAN (c. 1410-51) One of the most important German painters of the first half of the 15th century. He was active mainly in *Cologne. The only undoubtedly authentic work of his is the *Altar of the Patron Saints* (1442-47) in the cathedral of Cologne. It depicts the adoration of a fragile-looking Christ, and is related in imagery and technique to the *International Gothic. Other works are ascribed to L. on the basis of stylistic affinity.

LODI, PEACE OF (9 April 1454) A treaty signed between *Milan, *Genoa and *Mantua, on the one side, and *Venice and the *papacy, on the other, fixing the northern boundaries of Italy. Partly a response to the fall of *Constantinople, the treaty ended a long period of constant wars between the Italian city-states and established a measure of equilibrium and coexistence. *Florence, an ally of Milan, and *Naples also supported the settlement.

LOLLARDS The name given to the followers of John *Wycliffe and to English religious dissenters of the 15th century. The L. were opposed to Church hierarchy and emphasized redemption through faith. They rejected a number of Catholic doctrines, including Transubstantiation, favouring the preaching and reading of the *Bible. Persecuted under the statute *De haeretico comburendo* (1401), many L. were made to recant, but others continued as an underground movement, persisting in small enclaves throughout the 15th century. The adherents were mainly among town labourers and artisans, and the movement probably contributed to the acceptance of the Reformation in England, although it was certainly not a decisive factor.

A. G. Dickens, *Lollards and Protestants in the Diocese of York, 1509-1558* (1959);
J. A. F. Thomson, *The Later Lollards, 1414-1520* (1965);
K. B. McFarlane, *Lancastarian Kings and Lollard Knights* (1972).

LOMAZZO, GIOVANNI PAOLO (1538-1600) Italian art theorist. Born in Milan, he studies painting under Gaudenzio *Ferrari, and entered the service of Grand Duke *Cosimo I in Florence. At the age of 33 blindness forced him to stop painting. He then wrote the *Trattato dell'arte della pittura, scultura ed architettura* (1584), one of the best-known treatises on art of the late 16th century. A champion of the *Mannerist 'serpentine line', L. connected artistic qualities with certain stars, mixing *astrology and aesthetics. His treatise was translated into English and French. His autobiography, together with a number of poems, appeared in 1587.

Scritti sulle arti di Gian Paolo Lomazzo, 2 vols. (1973-75).

LOMBARD, LAMBERT (1506-66) Flemish painter and engraver. Born in Liège, he was probably a pupil of *Mabuse's, but studied Italian painting during a visit to Rome (1537-39). After his return, he headed a school of painting in Liège, and had many pupils, among them Frans *Floris. Most of L.'s paintings have been lost, but there are copies, as well as drawings and engravings. He enjoyed a considerable reputation in his lifetime, and was praised by *Vasari, with whom he corresponded.

Musés de l'Art Wallon, Liège, *Lambert Lombard et son temps* (1966).

LOMBARDO, PIETRO (c 1435-1515) Italian sculptor and architect. Born near Lake Lugano he may have visited Florence, but his career is associated with the republic of Venice. He first worked mostly as a sculptor, completing, among other works, the tomb of Doge Pietro *Mocenigo (1485), with sculptures showing some influence of *Donatello. His best-known building is the small church, S. Maria dei Miracoli (1480-89), a well-proportioned two-story structure, surrounded by pillars and topped by a half-barrel roof. In his later works he was assisted by his sons, Antonio (1485-1516) and Tullio

The Palazzo Vendarmin Calergi by Pietro Lombardo, Venice

(*c.* 1455-1532). A number of Venetian palaces are ascribed to them.

LOPE DE VEGA, FELIX (1562-1635) Spanish playwright and poet. Born to a poor family in Madrid, he attended, between 1577 and 1582, the universities of Alcalá and Salamanca, but left without a degree and subsequently led the life of an actor and a soldier. In 1588 he was banished from Madrid for mistreating his mistress, an actress, and joined the *Armada in Lisbon. Afterwards L. served a number of dignitaries, among them the duke of Alba and the count of Lemos. From 1605 until his death he enjoyed the patronage of the young duke of Sessa. He was twice married, and had many mistresses. After the death of his second wife (1613) he was ordained priest, but soon returned to his illicit amorous relationships, and was involved in many literary quarrels in which aspects of his private life gave his enemies plenty of ammunition. L. was not welcomed at the court but, in 1627, was given the title of doctor of theology by Urban VIII. By the time he died his name was famous throughout Spain, and his death was mourned by the whole nation.

L.'s literary production is staggering, his non-dramatic works alone filling more than 20 volumes. He wrote pastoral romances, ballads, elegies and over 1500 sonnets, in the styles of *Sanazzaro, *Ariosto, *Tasso and a host of others. But it was his dramas which enshrined his name in world literature. It is estimated that he wrote about 1500, of which 468 have survived. Written with great facility, they range from farces to melodramas and religious plays (*autos*), and employ mythological and historical themes, foreign as well as Spanish; a great number deal with the author's contemporary society. Revealing his tremendous imagination, the works are also filled with trivialities, and the structure of the plays is sometimes careless. L. was faithful to his own declared goals: in his verse treatise on drama, *Arte nuevo de hacer comedias en este tiempo* (1609), he held that the playwright's foremost duty was to satisfy the public demand. In this he was supreme, beyond any shadow of doubt.

R. Schevill, *The Dramatic Art of Lope de Vega* (1918);
H. Rennert, *The Life of Lope de Vega* (1937);
J. H. Parker and A. M. Fox, eds., *Lope de Vega Studies (1964).*

Madonna and child *by Pietro Lorenzetti*

LOPES, FERNÃO (c. 1380-1460) Portuguese historian. He is first heard of in 1418, when he managed the royal archives. In 1434 King *Duarte commissioned him to write the chronicles of previous reigns, of which those dealing with the years 1357 to 1411 are extant. His masterpiece, *Crônica de D. João I*, utilizes much documentary evidence and material taken from other contemporary chronicles. Critical, straightforward and an able reporter of crucial historical events, L. is considered an outstanding exponent of 15th-century Portuguese prose.

A. de Magalhães Basto, *Fernão Lopes e a Crônica de 1419* (1959).

LOPES, GREGORIO (c. 1490-c. 1550) Portuguese painter. Born in Lisbon, he was court painter to *Manoel I and *John III. His best works are a series of pictures of religious subjects which he painted for the convent of Christ at Tomar (1536-38). He also left portraits of persons associated with the royal court. He was the foremost painter of Portugal's golden age.

LOPEZ, RODRIGO (?-1594) The physician of *Elizabeth I. The son of a **marrano* Portuguese family, he went to England in 1559 and became known as a medical expert. He treated *Leicester and *Walsingham and, in 1586, was appointed the Queen's physician-in-chief. His success and his Jewish ancestry made him many enemies and, in 1594, he was charged by the Earl of *Essex with taking part in a plot to murder *Antonio de Crato and the Queen. Essex himself presided over the special court which condemned L. to death. He was hanged a few months later, after the Queen approved the sentence. L. is commonly regarded as the historical figure which inspired *Shakespeare's Shylock.

L. Wolf, *Jews in Elizabethan England* (1927).

LORENZETTI, PIETRO AND AMBROGIO Italian painters, brothers, who were active in *Siena between 1320 and 1347. A follower of the style of *Duccio, Pietro is particularly remembered for his work at Assisi, where there is a tragic-looking *Madonna and Child* of his, and his *Carmine Altar* (1329) and the *Birth of the Virgin* (1342), both in Siena. In contrast with Pietro's rather

Detail from the Carmine Altarpiece *by Pietro Lorenzetti*

staid and hieratic style, Ambrogio displayed a more secular orientation. He apparently spent some years in Florence, and reveals a distinctly un-Sienese affinity with *Giotto. His best-known works are the *frescoes of *Good and Bad Government* in Siena's Town Hall (1337-39). These include allegorical representations of political values in the form of massive women, and panoramas of Siena, showing a surprising mastery of the elements of *perspective.
G. Rowley, *Ambrogio Lorenzetti*, 2 vols. (1958).

LORENZO DI CREDI (c. 1456-1537) Italian painter. The son of a Florentine goldsmith, he studied with *Leonardo under *Verrocchio, becoming the latter's righthand man. It is almost impossible to distinguish between L.'s work and Verrocchio's in the period 1478 to 1488. Later, he executed a number of altarpieces in Florence. He is believed to have destroyed all his secular works under the influence of *Savonarola (1497). A competent artist, he was overshadowed by the great innovators of his age.

LORENZO MONACO (c. 1370-1425) Italian painter. Born in Siena, whose school of painting influenced his work, he went to Florence and lived as a monk in the monastery of S. Maria degli Angeli. His *Adoration of the Magi*, was probably his last work (now at the Uffizi), and shows an unmistakable affinity with the *International Gothic. However, in that style he was soon outdone by *Gentile da Fabriano.

LOTTO, LORENZO (c. 1480-1556) Italian painter. Born in Venice, he was probably a pupil of *Vivarini, and was strongly influenced by Giovanni *Bellini. He left Venice too early to have been influenced by *Titian, and worked in Treviso and Bergamo; about 1510 he visited Rome. Upon his return to Venice, about 1526, he began to emulate Titian's colour scheme, but his work is clearly marked by his own restless personality. Continually changing styles and residences, L. ended his life at a monastery in Loreto, which he entered in 1552. He left an interesting document, his account book from 1538 on.
B. Berenson, *Lorenzo Lotto* (1901).

LOTZER, SEBASTIAN (1490-c. 1525) German rebel. Born near the imperial city of Memmingen in *Bavaria, he joined the Reformation early and, in 1523-24, published five pamphlets advocating broad religious reforms. In 1525 he joined the rebellious peasants in Swabia and composed the "Twelve Articles", their most significant revolutionary programme. Following the suppression of the *Peasants' War he disappeared.

LOUIS OF ANJOU (1403-34) Duke of Anjou. The son of Louis II (1377-1417), duke of Anjou and titular king of *Naples, he succeeded his father and, in 1420, sailed to Naples to claim his kingdom, having been promised the support of Pope *Martin V. Queen *Joanna II of Naples then adopted as her heir *Alfonso of Aragon, provoking a war between the Angevins and the Aragonese. In 1423 the Queen reversed her position, declaring L. her adopted son and heir, and he was sent to govern the duchy of Calabria. In 1433 he was repudiated by the Queen in favour of Alfonso, but quickly reinstated. He was killed while conducting a war against the prince of Taranto, an ally of Alfonso's. His claim to Naples was taken up by his brother, *René of Anjou.
E. G. Léonard, *Les Angevins de Naples* (1954).

LOUIS II (1506-26) King of *Hungary and *Bohemia.

Portrait of a Young Girl *by Lorenzo di Credi*

A prematurely-born son of *Ladislas II, he succeeded to the throne at the age of ten. He was given to pleasure and seemed to be growing old in his youth. For most of his reign the government was run by regents, who were harassed by the proud Hungarian aristocracy. L.'s name is especially remembered in connection with the resistance against the offensive of the *Ottoman Turks under *Suleiman I. L. assembled and led the great Hungarian army which met the Turks at *Mohacs, but was completely defeated and died while in flight from the battlefield.

LOUIS XI (1423-83) King of France from 1461. The son of *Charles VII, he had an austere upbringing and was married in 1436 against his wishes to Margaret of Scotland. In 1440 he joined the Praguerie, a movement of the nobility directed against the king and, in 1446, was exiled by his father to the Dauphiné; he never saw him again. There L. strengthened his position as a semi-independent ruler. After his first wife died, he married (1452) Charlotte of Savoy, who bore him five daughters and a son. In 1456, when his father approached the Dauphiné with his army, L. took shelter at the court of

Madonna with Child and St. Peter Martyr *by Lorenzo Lotto*

*Philip the Good of *Burgundy, with whom he remained until he succeeded his father in 1461.

As king, L. pursued from the start a policy designed to strengthen the monarchy in alliance with the urban middle classes. Of his father's councillors he retained those of lowly origins and who were known for their anti-feudal attitudes reinforcing them later with the famous historian Philippe de *Commines. His policies estranged him from his former protector Philip the Good, and soon the great nobility confronted him with the League of the *Public Weal, which defeated him at the Battle of Montlhéry (16 July 1465) and compelled him to sign the Treaty of Conflans. But it was with the accession of *Charles the Bold to the duchy of Burgundy that L. encountered his real enemy. Charles' alliance with England made the conflict unavoidable, but L. scored the first victories. Then, in a meeting between the two in Peronne (October 1468), the Duke, accusing L. of encouraging sedition among his subjects in *Flanders, arrested him and released him only when he had signed a humiliating treaty. L. responded by intensifying his repressive measures against the high nobility and by aiding the *Lancastrians against *Edward IV, Charles' brother-in-law (1470). Not until 1472, when his own brother's death weakened the internal coalition against him, was L. able to make real progress. He then forced the Duke of Brittany to make peace and, in 1473, crushed the powerful house of *Armagnac. In the meantime he continued successfully to wage war in the south, as a result of which the Pyrenees became France's southern boundary.

The struggle against Charles the Bold took longer, and necessitated cooperation with foreign allies. In 1474 L. formed the Union of Constance against Burgundy, with the Swiss and Sigismund of Austria. On his side, Charles called for help on Edward IV, who invaded France; but L. met the king of England at Picquigny (1475) and bought him off with a substantial sum of money and the promise of an annual pension. L. then continued his successful repression of the recalcitrant French nobles, while the Swiss defeated the Duke of Burgundy at Granson and Morat, and finally at Nancy (1477) where he met his death. L. immediately seized Burgundy, but failed in his attempt to conquer *Flanders. Subsequently he concluded with *Maximilian, husband of Charles' heiress, *Mary of Burgundy, the Treaty of Arras (1482) by which he retained most of his conquests, including the long-contested Somme towns in Picardy and Artois. The extinction of the line of Anjou (1480) had earlier given L. control of the duchies of Anjou and Bar and, in 1481, Maine and Provence also went to the crown. With this the whole of the eastern French border, except Lorraine, was unified under the monarchy.

L. was the true designer of the centralized French monarchy of modern times. He made the *taille*, a property-tax paid by all except the nobles and the clergy, the main source of government revenue, to which were added the *gabelle*, the salt-tax, and the *aides*, which were other, indirect taxes. The estates-general were called only once during his reign (1469), and after hearing that the king could collect the revenue without them, declared Normandy inalienable from the crown and bid him to rule by royal decree in the future. He expanded the economy by introducing the silk industry to *Lyons (1466), and

A medal depicting Louis XI

encouraged the production of textiles in the north of France. Travelling constantly about his kingdom, he ran the government while being in direct contact with his people. He was, however, impatient of any restraint upon his personal authority, and was continually at odds with the **Parlement* of Paris. A brilliant diplomat, a compulsive talker and totally unscrupulous, L.'s brand of Machiavellism was tempered only by outward signs of religious piety. He built shrines, endowed many churches and prayed often and went on pilgrimages. Yet this behaviour may have been designed to keep the support of the Church. L. is described as a physically feeble and ugly person, with a long hooked nose. For most of his life he dressed simply and was recognized by his old felt hat. Yet 'the Spider', as he was nicknamed, was the greatest European monarch of his time.

P. Champion, *Louis XI* (1927);
R. Gandilhon, *Politique économique de Louis XI* (1941);
C. Hare, *The Life of Louis XI* (1907).

LOUIS XII (1462-1515) King of France from 1498. The son of *Charles, duke of Orleans, he married in 1476 his cousin Jeanne of France, daughter of *Louis XI. In 1488 he led a revolt against the regent *Anne of France, for which he was imprisoned. Later he took part in *Charles VIII's invasion of Italy, distinguishing himself in battle near Milan (1495). L. became king in 1498, following the death of his childless predecessor. He immediately obtained from *Alexander VI a divorce from his wife, and married *Anne of Brittany, the widow of Charles VIII. In 1499 he renewed the war in Italy, conquering *Milan, to which he had a flimsy claim. He then continued south towards *Naples, which he took in 1501, following an agreement with *Ferdinand of Aragon. But in 1502 the allies became estranged and over the next few years, they intermittently waged war and negotiated their differences, Naples being eventually secured by Spain. Late in 1508, L. joined the League of *Cambrai, also adhered to by *Maximilian and *Julius II, and aiming at the despoilment of *Venice. This led to L.'s great victory over the Venetians at Agnadello (May 1509), but before long he had to contend with his former allies who, in 1511, joined Venice in a 'Holy League' against France. Although L. triumphed at Ravenna (1512), he lost at Novara (1513) and also at the Battle of the *Spurs the same year. When he died there was little to show for his ambitious Italian campaigns, and the French royal treasury was empty. L. fostered the introduction of Italian Renaissance culture to France. In 1511 he sponsored the schismatic Council of *Pisa, which he hoped to use as an instrument against Julius II.

J. A. Néret, *Louis XII* (1948).

LOUIS OF NASSAU (1538-74) Dutch leader of the rebellion against Spain. The younger brother of *William of Orange, he was one of the nobles who presented the petition of grievances of 1566 to *Margaret of Parma. Upon the arrival of the duke of *Alba (1567), he left with his brother but, in 1568, invaded Friesland at the head of rebel forces. Defeated by Alba, he joined the *Huguenots under *Coligny at Jarnac and, in 1572, invaded the southern Netherlands from France. He was defeated again at Mons, and had to withdraw. On his third attempt, in 1574, L. penetrated the Netherlands from Germany at the head of a mixed army, seeking to relieve the siege of Leiden. But he lost his life at the Battle of Mookerheide together with a younger brother, Henry.

LOUISE OF SAVOY (1476-1531) Mother of *Francis I of France. The daughter of the duke of Savoy, she was married in 1488 to Charles of Valois, great-grandson of

Louise of Savoy

Charles V of France, to whom she bore *Marguerite d'Angoulême (1492) and Francis (1494). After her husband's death (1496), she lived at court with her children for several years, awaiting the death of the childless *Louis XII, whom her son would succeed. With the accession of Francis (1515), she began to take part in the government. She and the royal adviser *Duprat were blamed for the King being taken captive at the Battle of Pavia (1525). In 1529 L. with *Margaret of Austria, initiated the negotiations which led to the Peace of *Cambrai.

LOYOLA, ST. IGNATIUS (1491-1556) Spanish founder of the Society of Jesus, (see *Jesuits). Born to a noble family in the Basque region, he served as a page in the court of *Ferdinand the Catholic, and afterwards did military service in the army of the overlord of his family, the duke of Najera. In 1521, while taking part in the defense of Pampeluna in *Navarre against the French, he was wounded by a canon ball which shattered his leg. Lamed for life, he was released by the French and sent in a litter to his family castle where he silently endured an operation in which his leg was broken and reset. While recuperating, he began reading about the life of Christ and the saints, and transposing his love of *chivalry to religion, resolved to become a 'knight for Christ'. He made a pilgrimage to the abbey of Montserrat, near Barcelona, where he hung up his sword at the altar and exchanged clothes with a beggar. He then spent a year in seclusion in nearby Manresa (1522-23), experiencing a prolonged spiritual crisis, from which resulted his *Spiritual Exercises*, written there but revised and expanded in later years. It suggested methods to conquer the passions and dedicate oneself single-mindedly to the service of God. From Manresa L. set out on a pilgrimage to Jerusalem, stopping in Rome and Venice on his way. He returned from the Holy Land in 1524, and in his thirty-third year devoted himself to studies of Latin and theology, first in Barcelona then at Alcalá. There he gathered around him a group of fellow-students, and was arrested briefly by the *Inquisition on suspicion of a link with the **Alumbrados*.

In 1528 L. went to Paris, where he attended for two years the Collège Montaigu and later the Collège Sainte-Barbe. It was there that the original group of Jesuits was formed. It included six members, among them Diego *Lainez, Alfonso *Salmeron, Francis *Xavier and Peter *Faber. In 1534 they vowed to dedicate themselves to a life of poverty, to make a pilgrimage to the Holy Land or, if this was not possible, to go to Rome and place themselves at the service of the pope. Although the vows were made individually, the scene in the church of Montmartre amounted to the founding of a new order. Late in 1535 L. went to Spain and thence to Italy, where his companions joined him in 1537. They were given the blessing of *Paul III for the pilgrimage to the Holy Land, and L. and several others were ordained priests. The pilgrimage, however, was not undertaken. Instead, they began to preach at Rome and, in 1540, Paul III sanctioned the Society of Jesus, of which L. was elected the first general (1541). His remaining years were spent in untiring work on behalf of the order. His *Spiritual Exercises* were published in Spanish and in a Latin translation approved by Rome, and he composed the *Constitutions* (1447-50), the rule of the order which established its quasi-military hierarchy, and its emphasis on obedience.

Ignatius of Loyola

By the time he died the Jesuits numbered about a thousand, with members in all Roman Catholic Europe, as well as in *India and the New World, including many talented men of upper-class background. Having been a young officer given to mundane concerns, L. overcame his wounds and disability, and combined tenacity of purpose with spiritual vision to become perhaps the most original Roman Catholic figure of the 16th century. Intuitively reacting to the climate of his day, he contributed to the resurgence of Roman Catholic missionary zeal, education and reform at a moment when it seemed to be losing the moral war to the *Reformation.

P. van Dyke, *Ignatius Loyola, The Founder of the Jesuits* (1926);
J. Broderick, *St. Ignatius Loyola* (1956);
H. Rahner, *Ignatius von Loyola* (1956).

LÜBECK Baltic port city. The most important member of the *Hanseatic League, L. dominated the Baltic herring trade since its foundation in the 12th century. It reached the zenith of its commercial prosperity two centuries later and, in 1370, was the leading member of the coalition which forced the Peace of Stralsund upon *Denmark. A rift between the *guilds and the merchants caused numerous conflicts at the end of the 14th century, and between 1408 and 1416 the merchants were temporarily excluded from the government. At that time L. counted some 20,000 people, and its population continued to grow. But the commercial development of southern Germany and *Flanders affected L. adversely. With its northern orientation, it found itself in the 16th century fighting a losing battle against the rising Scandinavian monarchies. Between 1501 and 1512 it clashed with Denmark, and shortly afterwards helped *Gustavus Vasa to win independence for *Sweden (1520-23). But this did not prevent L. from engaging in a long naval war with Sweden later in the 16th century. L. joined the Reformation in 1530. Between 1534 and 1536 burgomaster Jürgen Wullenweber led an anti-aristocratic government, but the patrician classes were soon back in power. Later, the city suffered great hardships during the *Thirty Years' War.

A. Bralwn, *Der Lübecker Salzhandel bis zum Ausgang des 17. Jahrhunderts* (1923);
W. Ebel, *Lübisches Kaufmannsrecht* (1952).

LUBLIN, UNION OF (1 July 1569) The formal act of unification of Poland and the Grand Duchy of *Lithuania, effected despite opposition by the Lithuanian nobility. The two nations were to have one king and a common representative assembly, but Lithuania was assured of a separate administration.

LUCAS VAN LEYDEN (1494-1533) Dutch painter and engraver. The precocious son of a painter from Leiden, he attracted attention as a boy and at the age of 15 was already known as a painter. In 1521 he met *Dürer in Antwerp and exchanged prints with him. In 1527 he travelled in the Netherlands and entertained fellow painters in a number of towns. Afterwards his health failed; he died at Leiden after a long illness. His extant paintings, of delicate style and great sensitivity, deal mostly with biblical themes. A notable exception is his intense self-portrait, a wood panel completed *c.* 1520. But his contemporary fame, reaching as far as Italy, was based on his numerous copper *engravings. The earliest of these include the *Ecce Homo*, the *Expulsion of Adam and Eve*, and the *Milkmaid*, all done in 1510, in a masterful technique which assured L. a place of honour at the side of Dürer and *Marcantonio Raimondi. In his last years he experimented with the new technique of etching.

J. Lavalleye, *Pieter Breugel and Lucas van Leyden* (1967).

LUDER, PETER (c. 1415-74) German humanist. He was born near Heidelberg and studied there (1430). Later he went to Italy where he became acquainted with humanist thought. L. taught at Heidelberg, Erfurt and Leipzig. He was the first to introduce humanist subjects into German *universities.

The Milkmaid, *engraving by Lucas van Leyden*

The Pilgrims, *engraving by Lucas van Leyden*

LUDOVICO 'IL MORO' SFORZA (1452-1508) Duke of Milan. Son of Francesco *Sforza and Bianca Maria Visconti, he became the guardian of Gian Galeazzo, son of his brother, Galeazzo Maria, who was assassinated in 1476. He gradually established himself as the real master of Milan. At first he allied himself with Naples and had young Gian Galeazzo marry Isabella, granddaughter of King *Ferrante I. Later he became fearful of Neapolitan designs against him and supported *Charles VIII's invasion of Italy. In 1495 he changed again and joined Rome and Florence against France, thus contributing to its withdrawal from Italy. The death of Gian Galeazzo, who was probably murdered, left him duke of Milan. But in 1499 *Louis XII of France invaded again, with Milan his first target. L. had to leave the city and returned a few months later, accompanied by a contingent of German and Swiss soldiers. His own soldiers delivered him to the French (1500), and he was held prisoner in France until his death eight years later. L. was famous for his patronage of artists, especially *Leonardo. His young wife, Beatrice d'Este, who died in 1497, was also a patron of the arts.

LUINI, BERNARDINO (c. 1481-1532) Italian painter. Born at a village on Lake Maggiore, he went to Milan where he was influenced by a number of artists, but eventually became the best-known practitioner of the style of *Leonardo. A prolific artist, most of his works are kept in or around Milan. They include *frescoes and oils, and are distinguished by their rich colouring and fair charming women. A painter of considerable skill, he lacked true intellectual powers.

LUIS DE GRANADA (1505-88) Spanish mystic. The son of a poor family, he became a Dominican friar at

Granada in 1524. After 1544 he spent ten years preaching in Córdoba. In 1557 he was made head of the Dominican order in Portugal, and became the spiritual councillor of the queen. The author of a number of works on asceticism and meditation, his most important books were *De la oración* (1533) and *Guía de pecadores* (1555). This popular 'guide to sinners' was investigated by the *Inquisition, but the charge that the author's ideas resembled those of the *Alumbrados was later dropped. L. exercised considerable influence on late 16th-century Roman Catholic devotional authors.
E. A. Peers, *Studies in the Spanish Mystics* (1927);
R. L. Oecholin, *Louis de Grenade, ou rencontre avec Dieu* (1954).

LUKAS OF PRAGUE (c. 1460-1528) Czech leader of the Hussite *Unity of the Brethren. Brought up as an *Utraquist, he studied at the University of Prague and some time in the 1480's joined the Brethren, among whom he quickly achieved a position of prominence. In 1500 he was chosen their bishop, and in this capacity established contact with *Luther, although no agreement was ever concluded between them. L. wrote theological and liturgical works.
P. Brock, *The Political and Social Doctrines of the Unity of Czech Brethren* (1957).

LUNA, ALVARO DE (1388-1453) Spanish statesman. The natural son of an Aragonese nobleman, at the age of 20 he entered the service of *John II of Castile, who after a short time made him very powerful. In 1423 he

Ludovico il Moro Sforza

Drawing of a Woman *by Bernardino Luini*

was made constable of Castile, and attempted to impose the royal authority over the great nobility. In 1427 *Alfonso of Aragon caused L.'s banishment from the court by accusing him of the destruction of the Aragonese faction in Castile. He returned, however, in 1429, and retained his influence until 1439, when he was exiled for the second time. Regaining his position at the court once again, he fought and defeated the Moors of Granada (1441-45), but fell finally from power, when Queen Isabella of Portugal joined his enemies. Accused of treason, he fled, but was arrested and decapitated at Valladolid. L. was the author of the *Libro de las virtuosas e claras mujeres*, a work which reflected his high moral principles and political ideas.
L. Suárez Fernández, *Nobleza y monarquía* (1959).

LUNGHI, MARTINO (c. 1530-91) Italian architect. Born near Milan, he eventually reached Rome, where in 1575, he was appointed papal architect. Influenced by *Vignola, he completed some of the buildings of the Capitol, and built the churches of S. Girolamo degli Schiavoni (1588-90) and the Chiesa Nuova. Among his other works, the courtyard of the Borghese Palace is a good example of his Mannerist style. His son Onorio (1569-1619) was also a noted Roman architect, and was followed by his own son, Martino the Younger (1602-57). The last two collaborated on the church of S. Carlo al Corso, Rome (1612-27), in a distinctive *Baroque style.

LUTHER, MARTIN (1483-1546) German religious leader, founder of the *Reformation. Born in Eisleben,

Martin Luther *by Cranach*

*Saxony, he was the second son of a successful miner from Thuringia. At 13 his father sent him to school at Magdeburg for a year, then to Eisenbach for three years (1498-1501). L. then entered the University of Erfurt, where he studied philosophy and received a master's degree in January 1505. Revealing marked intellectual ability, he was intended by his father to become a lawyer, but L. abruptly gave up the legal studies and entered the monastery of the Observantine Augustinians at Erfurt (July 1505). Ordained priest in 1507, he was shortly afterwards recommended as an instructor to the newly-founded University of *Wittenberg. He arrived there in 1508, and lectured on ethics while continuing his studies of divinity. In 1509 he returned to Erfurt and, in 1510, was sent by his order to Rome, where he spent the winter months without betraying any concern about the secular court of Pope *Julius II. He returned to Wittenberg in 1511 and, in 1512, received a doctorate in theology and became a professor of biblical studies at the university, a post he held continuously until his death. His exegetical lectures of 1515-16 on Paul's Epistle to the Romans, and those of 1516-17 on the Galatians, were beginning to attract the attention of students and fellow lecturers. At the same time he acquired experience as a preacher and, from 1515, served as vicar of his order, a post that entailed the supervision of eleven monasteries.

L.'s religious crisis probably stemmed from his anxiety for his own salvation, and consequently his tendency to approach theological problems directly, rather than from a speculative approach, in the current scholastic fashion. He surmounted personal doubts by forming his own interpretation of crucial passages in the New Testament, and devised the concept of *Justification by Faith which became a cornerstone of his theology. Yet it is doubtful whether L.'s inner crises would have had such resounding effect, had he not also intuitively known that the time was ripe for a new spiritual message. The appearance of the seller of *indulgences, Johann *Tetzel, in the vicinity of Wittenberg supplied the necessary stimulus for action and prompted him to draw up his famous 95 Theses, which he pinned to the doors of Wittenberg's Castle Church on 1 November 1517. Here he challenged not only the sale of indulgences, but also the actual authority of the Church to remit sins; guilt, repentance and pardon being entirely dependent upon the sinner's change of heart and God's forgiveness. Although the theses were presented as a challenge to a disputation, which did not take place, they immediately aroused tremendous interest, and quickly spread throughout Germany, making the name of L., a household word, while the sale of indulgences suffered a sharp decline.

Denounced to Rome as a heretic, L. entered into a controversy with several conservative opponents, among them Johann *Eck and the Italian Dominican Silvestre *Mazzolini. He was summoned to Rome, but the summons was changed to an appearance before the papal legate *Cajetan at *Augsburg. This meeting, in October 1518, changed nothing and L., who enjoyed the protection of *Frederick the Wise of Saxony, returned to Wittenberg. In December Karl von *Miltitz, a personal emissary of *Leo X, likewise failed to persuade L. to issue a retraction. Meanwhile public opinion in Germany and elsewhere was becoming increasingly favourable toward L., who was revealed as a competent and incredibly prolific publicist. In July 1519 he took part in a crucial disputation with Eck at *Leipzig, where for the first time he publicly announced that popes and general councils were not infallible.

L.'s break with Roman Catholicism culminated in 1520 when he published his three famous treatises. The first, *An den christichen Adel deutscher Nation* (To the Christian Nobility of the German Nation), called upon the German princes to reform the Church by their own initiative. It attacked the celibacy of the clergy, pilgrimages, the veneration of saints, religious orders and the authority of the pope. The second, *Von der babylonischen Gefangenschaft der Kirche* (On the Babylonian Captivity of the Church), rejected the old sacramental system, allowing only baptism and the Eucharist. The third, *Von der Freiheit eines Christenmenschen* (On the Liberty of the Christian Man), had a more devotional tone, and elaborated on the liberation of the Christian man by inner faith, contrasting this with the obligation to perform good works. The treatises, especially the first two, were written in vehement style and language which themselves barred any attempt at reconciliation. On 15 June 1520, Leo X published the bull *Exsurge domine* which cited L.'s heretical ideas and gave him 60 days to recant. L. responded by burning it and, on 3 January 1521, the Pope issued another bull, *Decet romanum pontificem*, which excommunicated him.

Summoned to appear before the Diet of *Worms, (17-18 April, 1521), L. lived up to the great test by remaining faithful to his beliefs before Emperor *Charles V. As a declared heretic he would have been placed under the imperial ban and liable to be put to death. But the Elector of Saxony arranged to have him seized and taken to a place of hiding, Wartburg Castle near Eisenbach, and there he spent the next ten months (May 1521-February 1522). His sudden disappearance gave rise to all kinds of rumours and caused widespread indignation at his possible assassination by the emissaries of Rome. While L. was in hiding, his followers, especially in Wittenberg, began openly to abandon the old religious ways. Priestly celibacy was discarded, monks and nuns left their convents, and churches were cleansed of pictures and images. L., who was in communication with the outside, encouraged these changes in his letters and pamphlets. In Wartburg he also began his translation of the *Bible into German, first rendering the New Testament from the Greek. The whole work, including the Old Testament translated from the Hebrew, was published in 1534, and exercised a profound influence on the formation of the German language.

L. returned to Wittenberg in March 1522 in order to put a stop to the accelerating pace of religious reforms, which were becoming a threat to the civil order. He abolished the private mass, confession and fasts, but made the changes gradual, slowly introducing liturgical innovations. He did not involve himself in the *Knights' War (1522-23), but condemned the popular rebellion against constituted authority in the *Peasants' War (1524-25). When he failed to mediate between the peasants and the Elector of Saxony, he composed the harsh pamphlet of May 1525, *Wider die mördischen und räubischen Rotten der Bauern* (Against the Murderous and Thieving Peasant Bands). Written under the impression of reports about the brutalities of the rebels, it called for their merciless extermination by any horrible means. Immediately after the suppression of the rebellion, he married a 26-year old former Cistercian nun, Katherine von Bora. Eventually he settled into a comfortable life as the head of a large family, which included five children and several destitute relatives, though this did not lessen his tremendous activity. He appreciated his wife and consulted her frequently.

The Diet of *Speyer (1526) resulted in the first conditional recognition of the Reformation. From here on the struggle for the survival of Protestantism in Germany was carried mainly by the subscribing secular rulers. L. on his part became more concerned with the unity of the movement, which by then had split into several major factions. His meeting with *Zwingli and others at the Colloquy of *Marburg (1929) only sharpened their differences. In 1530, unable to attend the Diet as he was still formally under the imperial ban, he let *Melanchthon take his place, approving the latter's *Augsburg Confession, which became the most important exposition of Lutheran principles. His own *Schmalkaldic Articles (1537) reiterated the differences with Roman Catholicism. Remaining always in close rapport with the Protestant princes, he gave his consent in 1539 to the bigamous marriage of *Philip of Hesse, signing a document to that effect, together with Melanchthon and *Bucer. L.'s last years were passed in ill health and incessant work. He became more flexible on theological matters, and continued to labour for unity in the midst of growing dissention among his followers. He died in Eisleben during a journey in mid-winter to arbitrate an inheritance dispute between the counts of Mansfeld.

L. was the author of a massive body of works, mostly small treatises and pamphlets. Of special interest are his replies to *Erasmus and *Henry VIII of England, his *hymns, and his *Tischreden*, conversations at table which his students recorded. As a preacher, he possessed a great command of language and ready metaphors which aroused the enthusiasm of his listeners. But he could be harshly abusive towards his opponents, and became gradually more intolerant of such groups as *Anabaptists and *Jews. Indeed, his vulgar outburst against the Jews, uttered in his later years, is frequently cited as the precursor of modern German anti-Semitism. But, although he remained to the end of his life bound by the narrow cultural horizons of his early youth, his personality is still eminently relevant to the present age. Few troubled souls in the entire history of mankind found courage such as L. showed to confront their society with moral means alone, and to effect such decisive changes.

R. H. Bainton, *"Here I Stand!" A Life of Martin Luther* (1950);
E. H. Erikson, *Young Man Luther* (1958);
G. Ritter, *Martin Luther: His Life and Work* (1963);
J. M. Todd, *Martin Luther: A Biographical Study* (1964);
A. G. Dickens, *The German Nation and Martin Luther* (1974).

LYDGATE, JOHN (c. 1370-c. 1450) English poet. A Benedictine monk at the abbey of Bury St. Edmunds, he probably spent some years in London and in France, and wrote for the royal court. Between 1421 and 1432 he was a prior at Essex. L. was an enthusiastic follower of *Chaucer, but his huge output of verse, much admired at the time, is now considered rather prolix. As well as long moralistic and devotional works, he wrote about historical events in classical antiquity. Many of these were popular with the first English publishers.

W. F. Schirmer, *John Lydgate* (1961).

LYLY, JOHN (c. 1554-1606) English author and playwright. The son of a clergyman, he was educated at Oxford, graduating in 1575. He then went to London and, in 1578, published *Eupheus: or The Anatomy of Wit*, a romance in prose which was very successful. Here L. employed a witty style embellished with contrasting descriptive phrases, which became known as 'euphuisms', and which influenced several contemporary English authors. In 1580 he produced a patriotic sequel, *Eupheus and His England*, and in the next few years wrote eight comedies based on classical themes and mythology. As a playwright too, L. was a skilful manipulator of language, and excelled in constructing plots of love and intrigue, highly popular with his public. But, although L. undoubtedly raised the dramatic standards of his day, he was soon surpassed by others. After 1590 the favour previously shown him at the court turned into neglect, and in his last years he implored *Elizabeth I to renew her kindness, but to no avail.

G. K. Hunter, *John Lyly; The Humanist as Courtier* (1962).

LYNDSAY, SIR DAVID (c. 1490-c. 1554) Scottish poet. Born to a noble family, he served for many years in the courts of *James IV and *James V and, after 1531, was also employed on several important ambassadorial missions. L.'s literary works, written at the court, were verses on historical, moral or political themes, marked by a lively spirit of satire. He is especially remembered for his long *morality play, *Ane Satyre of the Thrie Estaits*, the only surviving example of this genre in Scotland. The play mirrors contemporary social and religious issues.

W. Murison, *Sir David Lyndsay* (1938).

LYONS Situated at the confluence of the Rhone and the Saône, this ancient Roman town grew during the Renaissance into a major centre of French commerce and industry, second only to Paris. The *Hundred Years' War, which disrupted the commercial routes in the north of France, served to make L. the site of celebrated annual fairs and a home for numerous Italian banking firms. To this was added, in the mid-15th century, a thriving silk industry, which remained the basis of the city's prosperity for several hundred years. The industry was especially favoured by *Louis XI who, in 1466, settled Italian silk workers in L. In 1473 the city's first printing press was opened; by the end of the 15th century there were forty presses, many of which were operated by German immigrants. More receptive than Paris to the manifold secular aspects of humanist culture, L. became the home of a famous school of poetry, led by Maurice *Scève, and of a number of important painters and architects. During the protracted *Religious Wars the city often sided with the *League, but it supported King *Henry IV once he was welcomed by Paris.

M. Bresard, *Les foires de Lyon aux XVe et XVIe siècles* (1914).

M

MABUSE (Jan Gossaert; c. 1478-1533) A Flemish painter of the Italianate school named after his native city. About 1508 he went to Italy, where he became skilled at portraying muscular nudes and architectural settings. M. is usually cited as an example of the ill-assimilated Italian influence, the stylistic concepts of which combined with the old Flemish models of painting to introduce an element of disharmony into his works. In his workshop at *Antwerp he also executed many individual portraits in a style inspired by *Leonardo.

MACHIAVELLI, NICCOLO (1469-1527) Italian statesman, playwright, historian and political theorist; his name is commonly associated with the modern concept of political power as an end that justifies the means. Born in Florence to a noble family of modest means, his education included a good knowledge of Latin, but not of Greek, and he received his first public appointment in 1494, becoming a clerk in the second chancery of the republic. This was when the *Medici fell from power, and M.'s service in the government of Florence was to last until their return. In 1498 he was elevated to the rank of second chancellor and secretary of the *dieci*, the council of ten in charge of foreign affairs. This opened before him the world of *diplomacy. In 1500 he went to France to negotiate the question of Pisa with *Louis XII. From October 1502 to January 1503 he stayed at the camp of Cesare *Borgia, where he witnessed the execution of Vitellozzo *Vitelli. Later he was sent as envoy to the camp of Pope *Julius II. At this point in his career M. was closely associated with the powerful *gonfaloniere* of Florence, Piero *Soderini who, during 1506 and 1507, employed him in the organization of a standing militia of infantry in the Florentine countryside. M. conceived of the militia as possessing the qualities of the citizen-army of the ancient Roman republic, but it proved to be no match to professional soldiers. In December 1507 he was sent to the court of *Maximilian I, which gave him an opportunity to see Switzerland and the Tyrol and, in 1510, he again went to France. Although Pisa, whose surrender M. had long been trying to achieve, fell in 1509, the scheme of alliances which he had hoped to maintain soon collapsed. In 1512 the Medici returned to power in Florence, aided by Spanish troops. M. immediately lost his position and, in 1513, was even imprisoned for about a month and tortured. Retiring to his small estate near San Casciano, he spent the rest of his life as a private citizen, frequently mingling with the simple villagers. He continued to correspond with intellectual friends, and repeatedly made attempts to gain the favour of the Medici, but with little success. It was during his retirement that he wrote all his works.

Il principe (The Prince), M.'s most famous work, was written quickly in 1513, but not published until 1532. Purporting to instruct a ruler on how to gain power and keep it, the author counselled the use of any act, even vicious ones, such as lies, deception and murder, that would further self-preservation and perpetuation in power, which becomes an end in itself. While the precepts in this work have found followers among heads of

Machiavelli

states until our own times, many pages of *The Prince* read like a manual of instructions for a rising Mafia boss. The fate of Cesare Borgia, who served as his model, might have warned M. that he may have over-rationalized the case. If he really believed that only by means of unscrupulous audacity and terror could the liberation of Italy from foreign invaders be accomplished, he certainly deceived himself.

M. presents a more balanced political theory in the *Discorsi sopra la Prima Deca di Tito Livio* (*Discourses on the First Ten Books of Livy*), begun in the same year as *The Prince*, but completed much later and published in 1531. The reflections on the history of ancient Rome afforded him an opportunity to consider many aspects of the nature of the state, and to display his republican sympathies. The *Libro della arte della guerra*, written in 1519 and published in 1521, was a treatise on military matters in which he championed the use of infantry and belittled the significance of *artillery. The *Istorie fiorentine*, commissioned by the future *Clement VII in 1520 and published in 1532, was a vividly-written history of Florence, which also attempted to analyze and reason every major change in the life of the republic. Of his other works the comedy *Mandragola*, published in 1524, is a cynical tale of a cunning adventurer and his hypocritical companion who take advantage of the stupidity and weakness of a husband, his wife and her mother. Abounding with wit and lust, the play was an astounding success. The 'Machiavellian' image of M. was established during the 16th century, largely by non-Italians who knew only *The Prince*. The French *Huguenot writer, Gentillet, in his *Antimachiavel* (1576), was probably the principal source of this image.

F. Chabod, *Machiavelli and the Renaissance* (1958);
R. Ridolfi, *The Life of Niccolo Machiavelli* (1963);
J. H. Whitefield, *Machiavelli* (1947).

MACHAUT, GUILLAUME DE (c. 1300-77) French *musician and poet. Born near Rheims, he took holy orders and in 1323, became secretary to the king of Bohemia, John of Luxemburg. In 1337 he was appointed canon of Rheims, and after the death of his first patron (1346) served the king of Navarre. M. was a great representative of the musical school known as *Ars Nova*. He wrote a mass for four voices, 23 *motets and music for his numerous *ballads* and songs. Most of his works have a poliphonic setting, and he was the first French musician to use the binary rhythm. He was also an important poet, his most original work being the *Livre du Voir Dit* (*c.* 1364). His poems dealt with themes of courtly love and didactic allegories, where he introduced a more realistic style, which influenced 15th century French poets as well as *Chaucer.

A. Machabey, *Guillaume de Machaut, la vie et l'oeuvre musicale*, 2 vols. (1955);
S. Lavarie, *Guillaume de Machaut* (1969);
G. Reaney, *Guillaume de Machaut* (1971).

MACHUCA, PEDRO (?-1550) Spanish painter and architect. Following a period of study in Florence, where he learned the principles of Renaissance architecture from Giuliano da *Sangallo, he returned to Granada (1520). At first he worked mainly as a painter but, in 1527, was nominated by *Charles V chief architect of the Alhambra and undertook the building of a palace. This Palace of Charles V, so different from the adjacent mediaeval Moorish architecture, is an almost classic example of the High Renaissance style as practiced by *Bramante and *Raphael. It was completed by his son.

MADERNO, CARLO (1556-1629) Italian architect. Born near Lake Lugano, he began his career as a sculptor and, in 1588, joined his uncle Domenico *Fontana in Rome. After the latter lost his position and was forced to go to Naples (1592), M. completed some of his buildings. He is chiefly remembered for completing the building of *St. Peter's (1607-26), where he added the long nave and designed the façade. But his two masterpieces are the church of S. Susanna, whose dynamic style seems to point to the *Baroque, and S. Andrea della Valle, a Roman basilica with a dome second only to St. Peter's. M. also built residential palaces in Rome and supervized works of decoration at St. Peter's.

U. Donati, *Carlo Maderno, architetto ticinese a Roma* (1957).

MADERNO, STEFANO (1576-1636) Italian sculptor. Born in Bissone in the north of Italy, he went to Rome, where he specialized in the reproduction of classical sculptures. Of his own works, the best is *Santa Cecilia* (1599) in the church of that name in Trastevere, Rome. The saint is shown in the recumbent position in which she had been found shortly before. Later, M. executed a statue of St. Charles *Borromeo at the church of S. Lorenzo in Damaso, Rome, and assisted in sculptural works at the church of S. Maria Maggiore. He exchanged sculpture for an administrative post during the last years of his life.

MADONNA (Italian: My Lady) The representation of the Virgin Mary holding the infant Christ. An artistic theme, which reached its highest expression during the High Renaissance, it first appeared in the 2nd century, but it was not until the late Middle Ages that it became popular in western Europe. The increasing appeal of the image of the Virgin to painters had to do with her growing importance in Christian theology, the debates concerning the concept of Immaculate Conception, and particularly, the profuse popular literature about her life. The first Italian Renaissance painters who depicted the Virgin, *Cimabue, *Giotto and *Duccio, portrayed her seated in majesty, surrounded by angels. During the 15th century the image softened, the M. beginning to resemble a beautiful young matron. The trend is eminently noticeable in the works of Fra Filippo *Lippi, and culminated in the engaging M.s of Giovanni *Bellini and *Raphael.

J. Guitton, *The Madonna* (1963).

MADRIGAL During the 14th century this term was applied in Italy to vocal compositions for two or three voices, often on secular amorous themes. It reappeared in the 16th century when Flemish composers active in Italy and their Italian followers began to write vocal pieces for up to six singers. These were secular unaccompanied choral works, whose themes were nature and love, and almost all the great composers of the period wrote them. England, which discovered the M. around the last quarter of the 16th century, developed its own native school.

A. Einstein, *The Italian Madrigal*, 3 vols. (1949).

MADRUZZO, CRISTOFORO (1512-78) Italian cardinal. A scion of an important old political family of Trento (Trent), he rose rapidly in the hierarchy of the Church, becoming prince-bishop of Trento in 1539, and cardinal

Interior of St. Peter's, Rome, by Carlo Maderno

in 1543. His most important achievement as bishop was the opening of the Council of *Trent (1545). Essentially a politician, M. was a faithful supporter of the *Habsburgs and, in 1556, was nominated by *Philip II as governor of *Milan. In 1567 he left the post and resigned his see in favour of his nephew Ludovico Madruzzo (1532-1600). He ended his life in Rome.

MAGDEBURG CENTURIES The popular name for the *Ecclesiastica historia secundum singulas centurias*, first published in Basle, in 13 volumes, between 1559 and 1574. The collective work of a group of Lutheran scholars, headed by Matthias *Flacius, it depicted the history of Christianity as a process of degeneration since the Apostolic age, making necessary and culminating in *Luther's revolt. Although they were extremely partisan in their use of sources and their anti-papal attitude, these volumes, each covering a century, were nevertheless the first attempt at a comprehensive church history. The response from the Catholic side was *Baronius' *Annales Ecclesiastici*.

MAGELLAN, FERDINAND (Fernão de Magalhães; 1480-1521) Portuguese sailor; the first to circumnavigate the globe. Born to a family of the minor nobility, he was educated at the court and, in 1505, sailed to *India with its first Portuguese viceroy, Francisco de *Almeida. Spending the next seven years in the East, M. fought at Cannanore, participated in the voyage of Diogo Lopes de Sequeira to *Malacca and explored the route to the Spice Islands (*Moluccas). In recognition of his distinguished service in the East, he was given a higher title of nobility upon his return to Portugal (1512). In 1513 he was wounded and lamed for life in the conquest of Azannor in Morocco. Shortly afterwards he was accused of improper behaviour, and was given to understand that he was no longer welcome at the Portuguese court. M. decided to try his luck elsewhere. In 1517 he renounced his nationality, a formal act which included a farewell interview with the king, and went to Spain. There he outlined his plan of sailing to the Spice Islands of the East by a westward route via the long-sought straits at the extreme southern end of the Americas. The plan was approved by Juan *Rodríguez de Fonseca and confirmed by *Charles V (1518). On 10 August 1519 M. set sail from *Seville, commanding a fleet of five ships. Of his 270 men 37 were Portuguese, 30 Italians and 19 Frenchmen, as well as a few Germans, Flemings, Greeks, Africans and one Englishman; nearly two-thirds of the crew were Spaniards.

The small fleet reached the Brazilian coast in late November 1519, and, in March 1520, arrived at the port of St. Julian in the land which M. named Patagonia. While wintering there, he had to crush a mutiny. On October 21 he reached the strait that bears his name, a 300-mile long, narrow tortuous labyrinth, in which many

Ferdinand Magellan

ships have foundered since then. M. somehow managed to make the crossing in five weeks, only one ship deserting and returning to Spain. The passage of the Pacific, so named by M., took 98 days and cost many lives, the result of scurvy, thirst and starvation. Finally, on 6 March 1521, the fleet reached the Ladrones Islands where fresh food was available. On 16 March it reached Samar Island in the *Philippines and, on 7 April arrived at Cebu. Received warmly by the local ruler, who declared his intention to convert to Christianity, M. offered to aid him in the conquest of the island of Moctan. He lost his life in the battle (27 April 1521). His men quickly realized that their supposed ally was only waiting for an opportunity to betray them, and sailed out of the Philippines with the two remaining vessels. They stopped at Borneo, reaching the Moluccas on 6 November. Only one ship, the *Victoria*, laden with spices and commanded by Sebastian del Cano, was able to make the return trip (21 December 1521). It doubled the Cape of Good Hope in mid-April 1522, and reached the Cape Verde Islands in July. In September, three years after it had set out, it arrived at Seville with 31 men on board. As for M., although he did not live to complete the great voyage, he died knowing that he had proved the feasibility of his grand designs.

E. Roditi, *Magellan of the Pacific* (1972);
F. H. H. Guillemard, *The Life of Ferdinand Magellan* (1890).

MAINARDI, BASTIANO DI BARTOLO (c. 1460-1513) Italian painter. Born in San Gemignano, he was trained in Florence by his brother-in-law Domenico *Ghirlandaio, whose collaborator he became. He made numerous pictures for churches in Florence and San Gemignano, which show the influence of Ghirlandaio as well as of *Verrocchio.

MAITLAND, SIR RICHARD (1496-1586) Scottish Lord of Lethigton, statesman, historian and poet. The son of Sir William Maitland, who died with *James IV in the Battle of Flodden (1513), he was educated at St. Andrews and Paris, and served *James V. About 1561 he went blind but continued to serve *Mary Stuart as keeper of the Great Seal (1562-67), and remained active until two years before his death. M. wrote satirical and patriotic verse which described the troubled conditions in Scotland. He is chiefly remembered, however, for his collection of early Scottish poetry known as the *Maitland Folio Manuscript*. To this his daughter later added another anthology called the *Maitland Quarto Manuscript*.

MAITRE DE MOULINS The name given to the unknown painter of the altarpiece in the Cathedral of Moulins, who is identified as the creator of several other works. He was active during the last two decades of the 15th century, but his style is still relatively free from Italian influences. He has been frequently identified with Jean *Perréal.

MAJESTÄTSBRIEF (Letter of Majesty) A royal charter awarded on 9 July 1609, to the estates of *Bohemia by *Rudolf II, permitting the free exercise of religion. Since the majority of the Czech people were either *Utraquists or belonged to the *Unity of the Brothers, the M. was understood as a measure of protection against enforced Roman Catholicism. However, *Matthias, who assumed the crown of Bohemia in 1611, soon began to infringe upon the provisions of the charter, and the ensuing tension eventually lead to the outbreak of the *Thirty Years War.

Portrait of Cardinal Charles of Bourbon *by the Maître de Moulins*

Bust of Sigismondo Malatesta

MAJOR, JOHN (1470-1550) Scottish Catholic theologian. Leaving his native country to study abroad, he entered in 1493 the University of Paris, remaining there afterwards as a teacher of philosophy. In 1518 he returned to Scotland to lecture first at the University of Glasgow and later at St. Andrews, where he taught for the last two decades of his life. A prolific writer, he wrote several theological treatises as well as commentaries to Aristotle and some mediaeval philosophers. M. was known for his support of the conciliar position, which was that the General Council should take the lead in the reform of the Church. But his best-known work is the *History of Great Britain*, first published in Latin in 1521. Famous in his lifetime as an author and teacher, his lectures were attended by the young John *Knox and George *Buchanan.

MALACCA A strategically-located town in Malaysia, which lends its name to the straits that separate the Malayan peninsula from Sumatra. It was attacked in 1509 by the Portuguese commander Diogo Lopes de Siqueira and conquered in 1511 by Alfonso de *Albuquerque. The Portuguese then made M. the centre of their Far-Eastern spice trade, enjoying a monopoly for a considerable length of time. When the Lisbon market was closed to Dutch and English traders (1594), these nations began to attack M., with the aim of winning a direct access to the trade. The Dutch finally succeeded conquering the place in 1641.

MALATESTA, SIGISMONDO (1417-68) Italian ruler of Rimini; the most important representative of the family which dominated that city and other parts of the Romagna from 1324 to 1500. The natural son of Pandolfo Malatesta (1370-1427), he became one of the most notorious **condottieri* of his age. From 1433 to 1464 he fought in almost all the internal wars of Italy,

The Tempio Malatestiano, Rimini, designed by Alberti for Sigismondo Malatesta

changing sides often and perfidiously. In 1447, after he had broken his pact with *Alfonso V of Aragon, he had to fight against an alliance which included *Federico da Montefeltro, and finally accepted an unfavourable settlement (1459). He turned next against *Pius II, who had mediated between him and his enemies, and as a result was excommunicated (1460). In 1462, in a unique and peculiar ceremony, M. was consigned to hell by the Church and burned in effigy in Rome. Shortly afterwards he was defeated in battle and had to accept harsh conditions of peace, including the reversion of all of his lands to the papacy after his death. In 1464 he went to fight the Ottoman Turks in the Morea on behalf of *Venice, but he was unsuccessful and returned to Rimini after a year.

M. was a great patron of the arts, and wrote some poetry himself. He commissioned the architect *Alberti to design the Tempio Malatestiano in Rimini, which was decorated by *Piero della Francesca and *Agostino di Duccio with *frescoes and reliefs. He also supported humanist scholars. His contemporaries accused him of cruelty and immorality. The charges, though exaggerated were probably not entirely groundless.

C. Tonini, *Campendio della storia di Rimini* (1926).

MALDONADO, JUAN (1533-83) Spanish biblical exegete. Educated at the university of Salamanca, he entered the *Jesuit Order and, in 1564, became a professor at the College de Clermont in Paris. His lectures attracted many students, and he was later accused of teaching unsound doctrines; in 1576 he left Paris. His *Comentarios a los Evangelios*, published posthumously, remained popular for a very long time.

MALESPINI, CELIO (1531-c. 1609) Italian adventurer and man of letters. Born in Venice, he served as a soldier in the Spanish army in the Netherlands, and later moved from place to place in Italy, engaging in different and not always honest occupations. He translated Brunetto Latini's *Tresor* to Spanish and Antonio Torquemada's *Jardín de flores curiosas*. In 1609 he published in Venice a collection of 202 stories under the title *Duecento novelle*. Though mostly based on themes of *Boccaccio's and others, about 80 of the stories are original, and reflect the authors turbulent biography.

MALHERBE, FRANÇOIS DE (1555-1628) French poet. Born in Caen, the son of a Protestant lawyer, he studied in Basle and Heidelberg before entering the service of Henri, Duke of Angoulême, in Aix-en-Provence. Between 1586 and 1596 he lived in his native town, and later in Aix where he met *Du Vair. M., who for many years searched for a powerful patron, found one in 1605, when *Henry IV, on the recommendation of Cardinal *Duperron, made him the official court poet. He became the exacting mentor of young authors and retained the royal patronage also under *Marie de Médicis.

M.'s early poems were written under the influence of the *Pléiade. Among these was the intense *Les larmes de Saint Pierre* (1587). But gradually he became concerned with linguistic and stylistic purity, criticized *Ronsard, and devised poetic rules which emphasized logic and clarity. This made for rigorous stiff verses, best exemplified in his *Consolation á Du Périer* (1599) and in his rendering of the psalms, *Paraphrase du psaume CXLV* (1628). M.'s collected poems were published in 1630 and exercised a great influence during the 17th century. Nicolas Boileau (1636-1711), with his exaggerated declaration, *'Enfin, Malherbe vint!'* hailed him as the true founder of French poetry.

R. Fromilhague, *La vie de Malherbe* (1954);
R. Winegarten, *French Lyric Poetry in the Age of Malherbe* (1954).

MALORY, SIR THOMAS (1408-71) English author, whose identity is uncertain. He is now commonly believed to have been a knight from the estate of Newbold Revell of Warwickshire, who, in 1436, served under the Earl of Warwick in the siege of Calais; later he was involved in several violent incidents, including robbery, spending most of his last 20 years in prison. M.'s famous collection of legends, *Morte d'Arthur*, was completed in jail in 1470. It consisted of eight tales adapted from French sources, dealing with the exploits of King Arthur, Merlin the Magician, Tristan, Lancelot and Guinevere. Written in a simple, straightforward and powerful prose style, the work was first published by *Caxton in 1485. It was frequently reprinted, and was the most widely-read English literary work in the 16th century.

E. Vinaver, *Malory* (1929).

MALOUEL, JEAN (c. 1360-1419) Flemish painter who worked in France. A native of Guelder, he settled about 1380 in Dijon. In 1396 he worked for a year in Paris for Isabel of Bavaria, but from 1397 to 1415 was again mainly in Dijon, as court painter to the dukes of *Burgundy. Several paintings are attributed to him, the best known of which is the *Martyrdom of St. Denis*, now in the Louvre. He was uncle of the *Limbourg brothers, and his work was one of the earliest influences of Flemish style of realism on French painting.

MANDER, KAREL VAN (1548-1606) Flemish painter and author. Born to a noble family of Meulebeke, he studied at *Ghent, where for several years he devoted himself to the writing of religious plays. Between 1574 and 1577 he visited Rome. He then worked with other artists on a *triumphal arch for *Rudolf II in Vienna. Subsequently he settled in Haarlem, where he wrote a famous book on the lives of the painters of Northern Europe, *Het Schilderboek*, published in 1605. He died in *Amsterdam. An undistinguished Mannerist painter, M. is remembered principally for his book, which was an imitation of *Vasari's.

MANETTI, GIANOZZO (1396-1459) Italian humanist. Born in Florence to a wealthy family of merchant bankers, he took an active part in the political life of the republic and was entrusted with many high offices and diplomatic assignments. In 1453 he chose to go into exile and entered the service of Pope *Nicholas V, for whom he prepared a new Latin translation of the New Testament from the Greek. He ended his life at the court of *Alfonso V in *Naples. A master of the three classical languages, M. wrote histories of Greece and Pistoia, biographies of classical writers and of the leading early humanists. His *De dignitate et excellentia hominis*, which was published in *Basle in 1532, contained a summary of his humanist views. Although he had been a deeply devoted Catholic, the work was placed on the *Index in the late 16th century.

MANFREDI Italian political family which ruled several towns in Romagna, especially Faenza. The M. emerged as a politically important family during the 13th century. In 1379 Astorre I was declared *signore* (lord) of Faenza. The family reached its apogee during the reign of Galeotto M. (1477-88). He encouraged the production

A 16th-century clock, showing the hours and the date

Christ in Gethsemane *by Andrea Mantegna*

of majolica, for which Faenza became famous, was patron of humanists and artists and collected a well known library. After his death by assassination the family was unable to recover its power. Its rule over Faenza was ended in 1501 by Cesare *Borgia.

MANFREDI, BARTOLOMMEO (1580-1621) Italian painter. Born near *Mantua, he was trained in Rome where he became known as a disciple of *Caravaggio. It was through him that the latter's light-and-shadow innovations were transmitted to northern Europe. More concerned with norms of taste and dignified postures than his mentor, M. was fond of painting card-players, bandits and soldiers. He became quite popular in Rome and elsewhere in Italy, and enjoyed the support of important patrons.

MANNERISM A term used by modern scholars to denote Italian art between the zenith of the High Renaissance (*c.* 1520) and the emergence of the *Baroque (*c.* 1600), but also with regard to the art of the rest of Europe, particularly France and Spain. The term derives from the Italian word *maniera*, meaning personal style, employed by *Vasari when in reference to the young artists who produced works 'in the manner' of the late *Michelangelo. M. was a deliberate departure from the classically-inspired harmony of *Raphael and *Bramante, and the subjection of the established norms of colour and form to the artist's personal expression, inventive vision or even his mere whim. Much of the work that comes under this classification has a quality of affectation, as if the artist were straining to impress the viewer. The painters *Parmigianino, *Pontormo, *Bronzino and Il *Rosso were among the leading Italian Mannerists, the last-named being reponsible for the transmission of the style to the French school of *Fontainebleau. In Spain M. is exemplified in the eminently religious vision of El *Greco. Michelangelo is considered to be the first mannerist architect, especially with regard to his *Laurentian Library in Florence. *Giulio Romano's Palazzo del Tè in *Mantua is another early example.

W. F. Friedlaender, *Mannerism and Anti-Mannerism in Italian Painting* (1957);
L. Murray, *Mannerism* (1969).

MANOEL I (1469-1521) King of Portugal from 1495. The grandson of *John I, he succeeded his cousin *John II. His reign corresponds to the grand age in Portuguese history, i.e. the opening of direct sea trade with *India by Vasco da *Gama, the discovery of Brazil by *Cabral and the consolidation of the Portuguese presence in the East, through the efforts of Francisco de *Almeida and Afonso de *Albuquerque. In addition to his constant support for these ventures, M. devoted time and effort to religious activities. He built many monasteries, attempted to organize a *crusade against the *Ottoman Turks and expelled from his dominions the *Jews (1496) and the Moors. M. was an ally of his great neighbour Spain, marrying in succession the daughters of *Ferdinand and *Isabella, Isabella and Maria, and after the latter's death, Leonora, sister of Emperor *Charles V.

MANSFELD The name of a county near *Saxony, and of one of the oldest ruling families of Germany. Count

The cathedral of St. Basil in the Kremlin, Moscow, built during the reign of Ivan IV

The Feast of the Sea Gods *by Giulio Romano and Primaticcio, at the Palazzo del Tè, Mantua*

Albrecht III von M. (1480-1560) was the territorial lord of *Luther's family and among the first princes to back the *Reformation. He lost his possessions after the Battle of *Mühlberg, but recovered them in the Peace of Passau (1552). Count Peter Ernst I von M. (1517-1604) was an important military commander in the service of the *Habsburgs, and in 1592 succeeded Alessandro *Farnese as governor general of the Spanish *Netherlands. His son Count Peter Ernst II von M. (1580-1626) was also a famous soldier. Though a Roman Catholic, he joined the *Protestant Union in 1610. Later, he distinguished himself on the Protestant side during the early phases of the *Thirty Years' War.

MANSUETI, GIOVANNI DI NICCOLO (c. 1465-c. 1527) Italian painter. Born probably in Venice, there are few certain facts about his life. He described himself as a pupil of Gentile *Bellini and was influenced by *Carpaccio. His chief work is *Miracle of St. Mark and of the True Cross* (1494), in the Academy of Fine Arts, Venice. This and other large paintings of his reflect contemporary architecture and costume, giving a true picture of Venice of his time.

MANTEGNA, ANDREA (1431-1506) Italian painter. Born to a poor family in Vicenza, M. was adopted by the painter and antique-collector Francesco Squarcione, who made him his favourite pupil. In his youth he mastered the art of the *fresco, and at the age of 17 began to execute works in this medium at Padua, where he soon established a reputation as the best painter in the city. M. was certainly inspired by the old *Giotto frescoes in Padua, and even more by *Donatello's masterpiece, the equestrian statue **Gattamelata*, which had been completed in 1453. He was also influenced, and established close contacts with the Venetian painter Jacopo *Bellini, whose daughter Nicolosia he married in 1454. Around 1460 M. left Padua and entered the service of Ludovico *Gonzaga, the ruler of *Mantua. After a short period in Rome (1488-90), he returned to Mantua. M.'s frescoes reflect his interest in classical antiquity and are often adorned with archaeological remains. Of the paintings he did in Mantua the famous *Parnassus*, now at the Louvre, was commissioned by Isabella d'*Este. Also well-known are the frescoes in the so-called *Camera degli Sposi* of the Castello, which include portraits of the Gonzaga family. His technical virtuosity was dramatically displayed in one of his last pictures, the *Dead Christ*, in which an extreme foreshortening of the body was accomplished with accuracy. M. was equally the master of prints, many of them modelled after his paintings. He influenced many of his immediate followers, including *Raphael.

W. G. Constable, *Mantegna and Humanism in Fifteenth-Century Italy* (1937);
K. A. Haenlein, *Studien zur Kunst Andrea Mantegnas* (1969).

MANTOVANO, BATTISTA (1448-1516) Italian poet and humanist. Born Giovanni Battista Spagnoli, he entered the Order of the Discalced Carmelites, of which he eventually became the general (1513). He composed religious poems in Latin, imitating the style of Virgil. He wrote ten eclogues, an epic poem dedicated to *Alfonso of Aragon, and the *De calamitatibus nostrorum temporum*, in which he criticized aspects of humanist culture. The author of many other works, M. became known also outside the confines of Italy.

V. Zabughin, *Un beato poeta* (1917).

MANTUA A town in the north of Italy, the capital of the political entity ruled by the *Gonzaga family. Under their leadership, M. became an important political and cultural centre. In the 15th century it boasted the first humanist school of *Vittorino da Feltre, founded in 1423, churches designed by *Alberti and the works of *Mantegna During the high Renaissance, M. opened its gates to many of the most famous artists, including *Leonardo, *Raphael and *Titian. A famous project undertaken then, the Palazzo del Tè, was built and decorated by *Giulio Romano and *Primaticcio. The cultural apogee of M. was during the rule of Francesco II *Gonzaga, whose wife Isabella d'*Este (1474-1539) invited to the court such men as *Boiardo, *Bembo, *Castiglione, *Pomponazzi and *Ariosto. This golden age continued through the 16th century, coming to an end in the devastating War of the Mantuan Succession (1628-31).

MANUEL II PALAEOLOGUS (1350-1425) Emperor of the Byzantine empire from 1391. The second son of Emperor John V, he was made co-emperor in 1373, but, in 1376, was imprisoned with his father by his elder brother. After his father regained the throne (1376), he reigned as co-emperor in Thessalonica. Upon his father's death he escaped from the court of *Bayezid I, where he was held in custody, and was crowned at *Constantinople. This resulted in the siege of the city by the *Ottoman Turks, who compelled the Emperor to pay them annual tributes. The *crusade organized on his behalf was crushed by the Turks at Nicopolis (1396). In 1399 M. went to Italy, England and France to seek help. Returning in 1402 he found that the Ottomans had been weakened by dynastic troubles. He was thus allowed almost 20 years of relative peace, until in 1422 *Murad II again laid siege to Constantinople. In 1424 M. agreed for the second time to pay tributes. He died as a monk in the following year.

J. W. Barker, *Manuel II Palaeologus; a Study in Late Byzantine Statesmanship* (1969).

MANUTIUS, ALDUS (1450-1515) Italian printer and humanist. Born in Bassiano in the *Papal States, he was educated under *Guarino da Verona in *Ferrara and became an intimate friend of *Pico della Mirandola. Two nephews of Pico's, the princes of Carpi, whose tutor he had been, gave M. the funds to establish his famous printing shop in *Venice in 1490. His main aim was to publish the classic *Greek authors, which he did with the help of a team of Greek scholars. He issued the works of Aristotle (1495-98), Aristophanes (1498), Thucydides, Sophocles and Herodotus (1502), Europides and Xenophon (1503), Plutarch (1509) and Plato (1513), as well as many lesser Greek authors. A scholar himself, he was both editor and publisher of many of these *editiones principes*. M. also published some ancient *Latin authors and several contemporary humanists, such as *Bembo, *Sannazzaro and *Politian. His contributions to printing include an elegant cursive type design, later known as

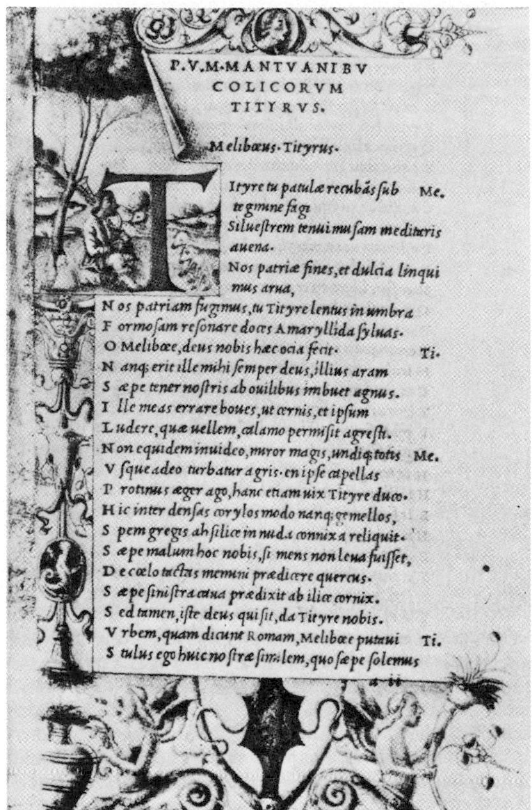
P.V.M.MANTVANI BV
COLICORVM
TITYRVS.

Melibœus. Tityrus.

Tityre tu patulæ recubās sub tegmine fagi Me.
Siluestrem tenui musam mediteris auena.
Nos patriæ fines, et dulcia linquimus arua,
Nos patriam fugimus, tu Tityre lentus in umbra
Formosam resonare doces Amaryllida syluas.
O Melibœe, deus nobis hæc ocia fecit. Ti.
Nanq; erit ille mihi semper deus, illius aram
Sæpe tener nostris ab ouilibus imbuet agnus.
Ille meas errare boues, ut cernis, et ipsum
Ludere, quæ uellem, calamo permisit agresti.
Non equidem inuideo, miror magis, undiq; totis Me.
Vsque adeo turbatur agris. en ipse capellas
Protinus æger ago, hanc etiam uix Tityre duco.
Hic inter densas corylos modo nanq; gemellos,
Spem gregis ah silice in nuda connixa reliquit.
Sæpe malum hoc nobis, si mens non leua fuisset,
De cœlo tactas memini prædicere quercus.
Sæpe sinistra caua prædixit ab ilice cornix.
Sed tamen, iste deus qui sit, da Tityre nobis.
Vrbem, quam dicunt Romam, Melibœe putaui Ti.
Stultus ego huic nostræ similem, quo sæpe solemus

A page in italic type printed by Manutius

'italic', but more important were his innovations as publisher. He printed large editions of cheap, compact and yet meticulously scholarly books, which sold so well that soon other European printers began to imitate him. His son Paulus (1512-74) continued the firm after his death, concentrating on the edition of Latin classics. A grandson, Aldus the younger (1547-97), was a renowned scholar and published a collection of Italian works.

A. Firmin-Didot, *Alde Manuce et l'hellenisme a Venise* (1966);
M. Ferrigni, *Aldo Manuzio* (1925).

MANZ, FELIX Swiss *Anabaptist. A former priest who supported *Zwingli from 1519, M. joined Conrad *Grebel and a few other radicals in 1523 in the demand to do away with infant baptism. In January 1525, at a meeting at his home in Zurich, the first ritual of adult baptism took place. Imprisoned and subsequently banished, M. worked for about a year among the peasants, was recaptured and, in January 1527, was tied to a hurdle and executed by drowning.

MARBURG, COLLOQUY OF (1-3 October 1529) A conference convoked by landgrave *Philip of Hesse with the view to achieving unity among the several Protestant reformers of Switzerland and Germany. The chief speakers were *Luther, who was accompanied by *Melanchthon, *Jonas, *Brenz, *Cruciger and *Osiander, and *Zwingli, accompanied by *Oecolampadius; *Bucer and Jacob *Sturm of *Strassburg were also present. The dis-

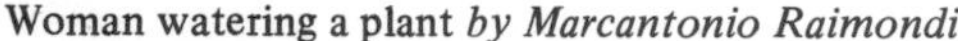

Woman watering a plant *by Marcantonio Raimondi*

The Bathers, *engraving by Marcantonio Raimondi*

cussion was held in the presence of the landgrave, Duke *Ulrich of Württemberg and about 50 others. Agreement was quickly reached on 14 of the 15 articles which Luther had drawn up, including issues such as baptism and *justification by faith, but there was a sharp dissension over the question of the real presence of Christ in the Eucharist. Immediately afterwards Luther revised the articles in a manner that made it possible for all parties to subscribe in spite of differences, and in the following year these served as a point of departure for the drawing of the Confession of *Augsburg.

W. Köhler, *Das Marburger Religionsgespräch* (1929).

MARCANTONIO (Marcantonio Raimondi, c. 1480-c. 1534) Italian engraver; a master at reproducing works of his great contemporaries. He passed his youth in Bologna and his earliest prints date from 1505. According to *Vasari, he aroused the anger of *Dürer by copying the German master's woodcuts on copper-plates. In 1510, in Florence, he engraved scenes from a large cartoon by *Michelangelo, entitled The Battle of Pisa. That year he went to Rome and concentrated on reproducing the drawings of *Raphael. This developed into a sizeable and successful operation, M. heading a workshop which employed a number of other engravers. In 1527, during the Sack of *Rome, he was caught by the rioting Spanish soldiers and had to pay a heavy ransom, leaving the city in consequence. He died in Bologna.

MARCELUS II (1501-55) Pope for one month. Born Marcello Cervini, he had a long career prior to his election. He was created cardinal by *Paul III and, in 1545, presided over the opening of the Council of *Trent. Under *Julius III he organized the Vatican library.

MARCOLINI, FRANCESCO (c. 1500-59) Italian printer and type designer. Born in Forli, M. worked in Venice where he began printing in 1535. He became a friend of *Titian and *Aretino, whose *La cortigiana* was the first book he published. Although he also experimented with the printing of musical notes, he concentrated on the works of contemporary Italian authors, among whom were *Doni, and the theoretician of architecture *Serlio.

MARENZIO, LUCA (c. 1553-99) Italian composer. Born at Coccaglio near Brescia, he served as a choirboy in the latter city, and about 1578 entered the service of Cardinal Luigi d'Este in Rome. His first book of *madrigals, for which he is mostly remembered, was published in Venice in 1580. In 1588 he visited Florence, and after another period at Rome went to Poland, where he became the highly esteemed director of music at the court of *Sigismund III (1591-93). The last years of his life were spent mainly in Rome, in close association

with the papal court. Besides 9 books of madrigals, he wrote *motets and a few masses. In 1588 his madrigals were introduced into England in a collection entitled *Musica transalpina*, which had a strong influence on English composers.
H. Engel, *Luca Marenzio* (1956);
D. Arnold, *Marenzio* (1965).

MARGARET BEAUFORT, LADY (c. 1441-1509) Mother of *Henry VII. A great-granddaughter of John of Gaunt, she married in 1455 Edmund Tudor, a son of the widow of Henry V by a Welsh man. Her husband died before she gave birth to their son, Henry (1456), and, in 1459, she married again. During the Wars of the *Roses her son – who, after 1471, was the Lancastrian claimant to the throne – was sent to safety in Brittany. M. married for the third time in 1482. After Henry's victory in the battle of Bosworth (1485), she arranged his marriage with Elizabeth of *York, so as to reconcile the two rival houses. She took an active part in furthering the cause of humanist and religious studies. She established the Lady Margaret chairs at the universities of Oxford and Cambridge, and founded Christ College at Cambridge. John *Fisher was her protégé and religious counselor. Lady M. was the reputed author of a devotional treatise, and translated from the French extracts of Thomas à Kempis' *The Imitation of Christ*, which were published in 1503.

MARGARET OF ANJOU (1429-82) Queen of England. The daughter of *René of Anjou, titular king of Naples, Sicily and Jerusalem, she was chosen in 1445 to be the wife of *Henry VI of England, because of her family relationship with the king of France. By 1453, when she gave birth to a son, Edward, M. was already deeply involved in English politics. She aspired to the regency during her husband's first attack of insanity, but the office was assumed by Richard, Duke of *York. After the defeat and death of the Duke of Somerset (May 1455), whom she had ardently supported, she led the opposition to York. A strong and willful woman, she did not give up the struggle when her husband was taken captive at Northampton (July 1460). A new army, which she raised in the north of England, defeated and Killed York at Wakefield (December 1460).

M.'s partisans, however, were soon beaten at Towton (March 1461), and the Queen had to find shelter in Scotland. After two years of futile attempts and adventures, she went to France where she stayed with her son until 1470. When the Earl of Warwick chased *Edward IV and nominally restored her husband to the throne, M. went back to England, only to lose her son at the battle of Tewkesbury (May 1471) and be taken prisoner. In 1475, when *Louis XI and Edward IV concluded the treaty of Picquigny she was ransomed by the French king. Early in 1476 she returned to France, where she spent the remainder of her life in poverty.
J. J. Bagley, *Margaret of Anjou, Queen of England* (1948).

MARGARET OF AUSTRIA (1480-1530) Duchess of Savoy and regent of the Netherlands. The daughter of *Maximilian I, she had been meant to be the wife of *Charles VIII of France, but after the latter took *Anne of Brittany she married the heir of the Spanish crown (1497) and, after his death, the Duke of Savoy (1501). In 1504 her second husband died, and in 1507, following the death of her brother *Philip, her father made her regent of the Netherlands. M. brought up her nephew, Philip's son, the future Emperor *Charles V, who let her remain regent until her death.

Marguerite de Valois *by François Clouet*

MARGARET OF PARMA (1522-86) Regent of the Netherlands from 1559 to 1567. The daughter of *Charles V by a Flemish woman, she was married in 1533 to Duke Alessandro de' *Medici, and after his assassination, to Ottavio *Farnese, Duke of Parma (1542). In 1559 her half-brother *Philip II made her regent of the Netherlands, where she had to face the rising tide of protest against the religious conformity enforced by Spain. By following the advice of Bishop *Granvelle she lost the support of the higher nobility and, in 1567, retired, leaving her post to the Duke of *Alba. Her son, Alessandro *Farnese, later returned to the scene as Spanish military commander and governor.

MARGUERITE D'ANGOULÊME (1492-1549) French writer, patroness of art and literature and Queen of *Navarre. The older sister of *Francis I, she was famed for her intellect and personal charm. In 1509 she married Duke Charles of Alençon, and after his death in 1525 became the wife of Henry d'Albret, King of Navarre, to whom she bore *Jeanne d'Albret, mother of *Henry IV. After her brother's accession to the throne (1515), M. used her influence with the King to support humanist cultural activities. She was the patroness of Clement *Marot and *Rabelais, and interceded on behalf of the reformist group of Meaux, led by Bishop *Briçonnet and *Lefèvre d'Étaples; although she did not save the printer *Dolet from being burnt at the stake. M. was probably inclined herself towards the Reformation and wrote poetry of deep religious devotion, but she died a Roman Catholic. Her principal work was the *Heptameron*, first published in 1558 under the titlename, *Histoire des amants fortunés*. It was a collection of 70 stories arranged in the manner of *Boccaccio's *Deca-*

meron. Although the work followed an established model, it possessed many original qualities and was enveloped in a poetical spirit. Some of the tales, however, have erotic themes, which are quite surprising considering the status of the author.

P. Jourda, *Une princesse de la Renaissance* (1932; reprinted 1973);
S. Putnam, *Marguerite of Navarre* (1936);
N. Tetel, *Marguerite de Navarre's Heptameron* (1973).

MARGUERITE DE VALOIS (1553-1615) Daughter of *Henry II of France and *Catherine de Médicis, and the object of contemporary gossip; known as *"La reine Margot"*. In 1572 her mother married her to Henry of Navarre, the future *Henry IV, a union that was supposed to stabilize the internal political conditions in France, but which instead precipitated the *St. Bartholomew massacre. Rightly or wrongly, she had a reputation as an extravagant personality, inclined towards amorous adventures. In 1598 Henry was granted papal permission to divorce her, but later seemed to be on good terms with his ex-wife. She was the author of well-written memoirs.

C. Haldane, *Queen of Hearts; Marguerite of Valois* (1968).

MARIANA, JUAN DE (1536-1624) Spanish historian and political philosopher. Born at Talavera, he studied at the prestigious university of Alcalá and at 17 joined the *Jesuit Order. In 1561 he went to teach theology at Rome, where *Bellarmine attended his lectures, and from 1564 to 1569 lived in Sicily. Thereafter, for five years he lectured before large audiences in Paris, but in 1574 returned to Spain and settled in Toledo, devoting himself to writing. His *History of Spain* in Latin came out in 1592. This national history celebrating the greatness of Spain was so successful that M. later proceeded to cover the reigns of *Charles V, *Philip II and *Philip III, and translated the work into Spanish. His name is perhaps better known for his *De rege et regis institutione* (1598), a treatise on the origin and nature of the state, in which he argued the right of rebels to depose a tyrannical prince. The *Gunpowder Plot in England and the murder of *Henry IV of France were later viewed as acts inspired by the teachings of the Jesuits, of whom M. was held to be an authoritative spokesman. However, the general of the Order, *Acquaviva, condemned M.'s ideas, and the author's last years were marred by the examination of his works by the *Inquisition.

G. Lewy, *Constitutionalism and Statecraft during the Golden Age of Spain; A Study of the Political Philosophy of Juan de Mariana* (1960).

MARIE DE MEDICIS (1573-1642) Queen-regent of France. The daughter of Francesco de' *Medici, Grand Duke of Tuscany, she was married in 1600 to *Henry IV of France, mainly because of his financial obligations to her family. She bore her husband two sons and three daughters, and, when he died in 1610, became regent. The period of her regency was marked by unrest in the French nobility, directed mainly against her favourite, Concini, the husband of her childhood friend Leonora Galigai. In 1617 Concini was murdered, and his wife burnt at the stake as a witch; the Queen-regent was banished from the court to Blois. In 1621 she briefly recovered her position at the court through her new favourite, Richelieu, but the latter soon amassed enough power to become master of the situation. M. made yet another attempt to control the government during the Day of Dupes (12 November 1630). But Richelieu was too strong to topple and M. escaped France and took shelter in Brussels. She died in Cologne five months before her great rival.

MARIGNANO, BATTLE OF (13-14 September 1515) One of the decisive battles of the Italian Wars, in which the French, under the young *Francis I, defeated near Milan a force of 25,000 Swiss infantrymen. To a large extent this was a victory of *artillery and *arquebus over pikes, and it undermined the reputation for invincibility which the Swiss had enjoyed.

MARINO, GIAMBATTISTA (1569-1625) Italian poet. A lawyer's son, he was born in Naples, where he studied law, but gave it up in 1590, becoming the protégé of a succession of patrons. In 1598 he was arrested in connection with the death of his young mistress, and was again imprisoned in 1600 for falsifying documents to help a friend. M. then fled to Rome, where he was protected by Cardinal Pietro Aldobrandini, whom he accompanied on travels through Italy. Subsequently he settled in Turin (1608-15), and there entered into a literary feud with the poet Gaspare Murtola, which ended in a duel and M.'s imprisonment. He then moved to Paris, where he sought the protection of *Marie de Medicis and Louis XIII and, in 1523, returned to Italy, ending his life in his native city of Naples.

A master of superb technical skills, a virtuoso in the use of words and the modulation of language, M. was considered the greatest Italian poet of his age. Nevertheless, he had many difficulties in getting his works published on account of their content, which offended established morality. He first won fame with the *Canzone de' baci* (1592). His chief work, the mythological poem

Marie de Médicis *by Pourbus the Younger*

Adone (1623), on the love of Venus and Adonis, made use of classical sources; the posthumously published *La strage degli innocenti* (1632), was shortly translated into English. M.'s poetical sensuality exercised a great influence on the poetry of the *Baroque in Italy and elsewhere and his followers were often referred to as 'Marinisti.'

J. V. Mirollo, *The Poet of the Marvelous* (1963);
C. Colombo, *Cultura e tradizione nell' 'Adone' di Marino* (1967).

MARINUS VAN REYMERSWAELE (c. 1497-c. 1567) Flemish painter. The son of a member of the painters' guild of *Antwerp, where he was evidently influenced by Quentin *Massys, he spent much of his career elsewhere. After leaving Reymerswaele he went to Middelburg where, in 1567, he was punished and later banished for taking part in the pillage of the church of West Minster. M. is known for his pictures of St. Jerome and his depictions of bankers, usurers and tax-gatherers, dressed in fancy costumes, and painted in a carefully detailed manner. These personifications of avarice were very popular and made the painter's name known as far as Italy and Spain.

MARLOWE, CHRISTOPHER (1564-93) English playwright and poet. The son of a shoemaker from Canterbury, he obtained his Bachelor's degree from Corpus Christi College, Cambridge, in 1584 and, in spite of irregular attendance, was awarded the Master's degree in 1587. By that time M. spent most of his time in London leading a dissolute life. He was arrested at least once, was engaged from time to time in spying for the government, and acquired a reputation as an atheist for his blasphemous talk. His relationship with the authorities was rather ambiguous when he was killed in a tavern quarrel.

Considered the most important predecessor of *Shakespeare, M. is the certain author of six plays. The widely-acclaimed two-part *Tamburlaine the Great*, staged in 1587-88 and printed 1590, chronicled the life of the 14th-century Mongol conqueror; it was the first great English tragedy. *Dr. Faustus*, staged in about 1589 but printed only in 1604, developed the themes of the 'Faust-book', a popular work about an early 16th-century alchemist-astrologer, which had been first published in German in 1587. *The Jew of Malta*, performed about 1589, dealt with the avaricious Barabas, a rich Jew whose greed is in sharp contrast with the virtues of his daughter Abigail. The play became very popular, but was printed only in 1633, in a version which is not necessarily similar to M.'s original text. His other plays were: *Edward II* (staged 1591); *The Massacre of Paris* (1593); and *The Tragedy of Dido*, which was later completed by *Nashe. His *Hero and Leander*, a poem derived from the ancient Musaeus, was also left unfinished and was completed by *Chapman.

M.'s great innovation in *drama was the introduction of the heroic struggle of an individual driven by overpowering ambition, but doomed to failure. His protagonists, impelled towards their fate by brutal acts and passionate discourses, became the models for Shakespeare, who, however, surpassed M. in characterization and psychological penetration.

J. Bakeless, *The Tragical History of Christopher Marlowe*, 2 vols. (1942);
J. B. Steane, *Marlowe: A Critical Study* (1964).

MARMION, SIMON (c. 1425-89) Flemish-French painter and illuminator. He is known to have worked in Amiens (1449-58), where he executed a work in the town hall, and afterwards in Valenciennes. Although he enjoyed a considerable reputation in his lifetime, only one work, a series of subjects from the life of St. Bertin, is believed to have survived. As an illuminator he decorated manuscripts for *Philip the Good and *Charles the Bold of *Burgundy, which were distinguished by their bright colours.

MARNIX VAN ST. ALDEGONDE, PHILIPS VAN (1540-98) Dutch poet and theologian. Born in Brussels to a noble family, he studied in France, in Italy and in *Geneva (1560-61). Becoming a firm Calvinist, M. attached himself to *William of Orange, whom he served in different capacities. He was imprisoned by the Spanish (1573) and later held office as burgomaster of *Antwerp until his retirement from political life in 1585. Of his early works the best known is the satirical attack on Roman Catholicism, *Biencorf der H. Roomsche Kercke* (1569), which was translated into German and English, and later rendered into French as *Tableau des differandes de la religion* (1598). He also translated the Psalms, and is popularly believed to be the author of the Wilhelmus, the Flemish national song.

I. van Kalken and T. Jonckheere, *Marnix van St. Aldegonde* (1952).

MAROT, CLEMENT (1497-1544) French poet. Born in Cahors to a father who was himself a poet and the secretary of *Anne of Britany, he was educated at the University of Paris, but soon gave up his legal studies to become a page in the royal court. His first poems were dedicated to the young *Francis I, and in 1518 he became a personal attendant of the King's sister, *Marguerite d'Angoulême. M. accompanied the royal court to the meeting at the *Field of Cloth of Gold (1520), which he celebrated in verse and, in 1525, was wounded and taken prisoner at *Pavia. He was released, but early in 1526 was arrested at the Châtelet on charges of heresy. He regained his freedom through the intervention of a friendly ecclesiastical dignitary. That year he inherited his father's post as the King's *valet de chambre*. In 1527 he attempted to rescue a friend from prison but was caught and was set free by the King. In 1532 appeared his first book of poetry, *Adolescence Clementine*, which was a resounding success. In 1535 M. was implicated in the Affair of the *Placards and fled from the court. He first sought shelter with Marguerite d'Angoulême at Béarn, but subsequently went to Italy and entered the service of *Renée, Duchess of Ferrara. In 1537, he took advantage of the opportunity offered to the French Protestants to return on condition that they recant. On his way back to Paris he stopped at *Lyons, where he met Maurice *Scève. In 1539, having regained his standing at the court, he presented the King with his translation of 30 psalms in verse. These became popular at once, and were adopted by the French Protestants. In 1543 M. found it prudent to leave France again. He went to *Geneva, where he published an edition of 50 psalms; in 1562 Theodore *Beza brought up the number to 150, and issued the entire French psalter. But M. did not feel comfortable in *Calvin's puritan city, and before long he left for Piedmont. He died in Turin.

M. is considered the first great French poet of the Renaissance. With him ends the influence of the **Rhé-*

toriqueurs, and he was the first to introduce the sonnet. His best known works were the *Temple de Cupidon* (1515), an allegory with persons from the *Roman de la Rose*, and *L'Enfer*, written in 1526 but published only in 1542, which dealt with his imprisonment at the Châtelet.
P. Jourda, *Marot* (1956);
C. A. Mayer, *Clement Marot* (1972).

MARPRELATE TRACTS (1588-89) A series of sharp satirical pamphlets, printed and distributed clandestinely in London, attacking the episcopal hierarchy of the *Church of England. Signed 'Martin Marprelate' (mar a prelate), their scurrilous language aroused a fierce reaction against the *Puritans. The bishops then employed a number of hack writers, including Thomas *Nashe, to return the attack, and caused foreign Calvinists to be expelled.
W. Pierce, *An Historical Introduction to the Marprelate Tracts* (1908).

MARRANOS A pejorative designation – meaning pigs – to the crypto-*Jews of Spain and Portugal, i.e., those who adhered to their faith in secret after they had been forced to undergo baptism. The M. became an acute problem in Spain in 1391, when thousands of Jews simulated conversion to Christianity in the face of widespread riots against them. Over 100,000 then became *Nuevos Cristianos* or *conversos*, and their number swelled afterwards with additional forced recruits. Obliged to lead a double life, outwardly Christians, inwardly observing Jewish laws, the M. were accused of religious insincerity and at the same time often envied for their economic success and ability to advance socially. Following another wave of massacres of Jews (1473-74), the *Inquisition was established to deal with the problem of false converts. The concept of *limpieza de sangre* (purity of blood) was used to separate people of Jewish and Moorish descent from other Spaniards. Under Tomás de *Torquemada, the first Grand Inquisitor, more than 2,000 M. were burned at the stake. After the expulsion of the Jews from Spain (1492), Portugal had its own community of M., when many of the Spanish exiles who settled there were driven to simulate conversion (1497). While most Spanish and Portuguese M. continued to live as suspected Christians, many escaped the tight supervision to which they were subjected and sought religious freedom in America, North Africa, the *Ottoman Empire, or under Protestant governments. The most famous community of former M. was the Jewish congregation founded in *Amsterdam in 1597.
C. Roth, *A History of the Marranos* (1941).

MARSTON, JOHN (1576-1634) English playwright. An attorney's son, he graduated from Oxford in 1594, but rejected his father's profession in favour of literature. His first works, an erotic poem and a volume of satires, both published in 1598, were condemned by the religious authorities, but also attracted attention. He then began writing for the theatre and, between 1599 and 1608, produced a number of satirical comedies and melodramas, which were quite popular. M. had a feud with Ben *Jonson, who ridiculed him in his *The Poetaster* (1601). He was twice jailed for the politically-offensive elements in his plays. In 1609 he entered the Church and was ordained, ending his life as the pious rector of Christchurch, Hampshire.
A. Caputi, *John Marston, Satirist* (1961).

MARSUPPINI, CARLO (1398-1453) Italian humanist. Born in *Genoa, he grew up in *Florence, where he became close to the *Medici family and, in 1444, succeeded Leonardo *Bruni as chancellor of the republic. A man of vast culture, he was the author of letters and some poetry. In 1452 *Nicholas II asked him to translate the *Iliad* into Italian, but he died before he had accomplished much.

MARTIN V (1368-1431) Pope from 1417. Born Oddo *Colonna, he was the scion of one of the great Roman families. As bishop and cardinal, from 1408 on, he took part in the movement for the reunification of the Church. Elected unanimously by the Council of *Constance, he was able to enter Rome in 1420 and began to restore its ruins and to reconstitute Church rule over the *Papal States. M. called and dissolved the Council of Siena (1424) and appointed Cardinal Giuliano *Cesarini to precide over the Council of *Basle (1431). He died just as the council was about to begin and his pontificate marked the end of the *Great Schism.
P. Partner, *The Papal State Under Martin V* (1958).

MARTINEZ DE TOLEDO, ALFONSO (1398-1470) Spanish author. Having been a prebendary at Toledo and archpriest of Talavera, he became chaplain to *John II of Castile. His prose works include the lives of St. Isidoro and St. Ildefonso, but his main work is *Corbacho o reprobación del amor mundano*, first published in 1495. Borrowed from Italian sources it is an attack on worldly love, combining popular speech with a satirical observation of the contemporary mores. Enormously successful in its time, the work is one of the earliest masterpieces of Spanish literature.
C. J. Whitbourn, *The Arcipreste de Talavera and the Literature of Love* (1970).

MARTINI, SIMONE (c. 1284-1344) Italian painter. A Sienese disciple of *Duccio, he first won acclaim in 1315, when he executed a large fresco of an enthroned madonna in the Palazzo Pubblico of his native city. Invited to Naples by King Robert of Anjou, he painted the latter's coronation by his brother Louis, bishop of Toulouse (1317). M. later executed altar-pictures in Pisa and Orvieto and a series of frescoes in Assisi. In 1340 he went to the papal court at Avignon where he met *Petrarch, for whom he illuminated a manuscript of a commentary on Virgil, now in the *Ambrosiana of Milan. Most of his work, however, was done in Siena, where he enjoyed the highest esteem. His *Guidoriccio da Folignano*, done in 1328, is the first equestrian portrait of the Renaissance.
G. Contini and M. C. Gozzoli, eds., *L'opera completa di Simone Martini* (1970).

MARTINUZZI, GEORGE (1482-1551) Hungarian statesman and cardinal. A Croatian by birth, the son of a Venetian mother, from whom he took his Italian name, he was the trusted adviser of John *Zapolya, and at his death (1540), assumed the role of regent for the infant John Sigismund Zapolya (1540-71). To strengthen his position against the claims of Archduke *Ferdinand of Habsburg, M. accepted the suzerainty of the *Ottoman Turks, and succeeded in keeping Transylvania practically independent. In 1545 he changed his policy, and tried to form a united front with Ferdinand against the Turks; the treaty confirmed at the diet of Kolozsvar (1551), accepted the reunification of Hungary under the Habsburgs. However, being concerned that *Suleiman I might counteract the move by a massive military attack, he sought to appease the Turks. Ferdinand's officers then denounced him to the Archduke as a traitor, and arranged his murder.

MARTORELL, BERNARDO (?-c. 1453) Spanish painter and illuminator. Active in Barcelona, he is recorded as working there and in other Catalan cities from about 1433. His earliest important work was the altarpiece for the church of Pubol, Gerona (1437). His pictures betray a Flemish influence and meticulous care for detail; they are embellished with many flowers and animals.

J. M. Gudiol Ricart, *Bernardo Martorell* (1959).

MARY I (Mary Tudor; 1516-58) Queen of England from 1553. The daughter of *Catherine of Aragon and *Henry VIII, she adhered to her Roman Catholic faith, in spite of the extremely harsh treatment by her father and the seclusion imposed on her during the reign of her half-brother *Edward VI. M. mounted the throne supported by popular acclaim, which made it easy for her to crush the attempt of the Duke of *Northumberland to crown his daughter-in-law, Lady Jane *Grey. She began moderately, content to repeal the ecclesiastical legislation of Edward VI and some of the anti-papal acts of Henry VIII. But the announcement of her betrothal to *Philip of Spain ignited the *Wyatt Rebellion, and following its suppression, M. took stern measures, having Lady Jane Grey and her husband executed and committing her sister *Elizabeth to the Tower for some time. After her marriage (July 1554), she welcomed Cardinal *Pole back to England and, in 1555, embarked upon a policy of complete restoration of Roman Catholicism. The right of the ecclesiastical courts to try heretics was restored and in the next three years some 300 Protestants were burned at the stake, including *Cranmer. These persecutions, which won the Queen her derisive nickname, 'Bloody Mary', ended her popularity. The failure of her marriage to a man ten years younger than herself further reduced her support and increased her bitterness. In 1557, under the influence of her husband, now king of Spain, she joined her country to his in a war against France. But this only led to the French conquest of Calais in 1558. She died late that year, a forlorn and unhappy woman.

D. M. Henderson, *The Crimson Queen, Mary Tudor* (1933);
B. White, *Mary Tudor* (1935);
H. F. M. Prescott, *A Spanish Tudor; The Life of Bloody Mary* (1940).

MARY OF BURGUNDY (1457-82) Duchess of *Burgundy. The only daughter of *Charles the Bold, she inherited all his possessions when he was killed at Nancy in 1477. *Louis XI of France, who seized Burgundy, wanted her to marry his young son *Charles. But M. preferred Archduke *Maximilian of Austria, and retained the loyalty of the *Netherlands by granting the estates-general certain rights over the government. She had three children, the oldest being *Philip the Handsome, father of Emperor *Charles V.

MARY OF LORRAINE (Mary of *Guise; 1515-60) Queen-regent of Scotland. The daughter of Claude, first Duke of Guise, she was married to Louis of Orléans, to whom she bore a son (1535), but her husband died and, in 1538, she married *James V of Scotland. The only child who survived of this union was *Mary, Queen of Scots, born in 1542, shortly before her father's death. M. then claimed the Scottish regency, meaning to oust

Mary Tudor *by Anthonis Mor*

the regent and heir-presumptive James, Earl of Arran. She was actively helped by Cardinal *Beaton and, in 1543, became the most powerful member of the council, but did not assume the regency until 1554, when Arran resigned. Ruling while her daughter was in France, she naturally meant to expand the French influence in Scotland, but failed to win support for her proposal that Scotland join France in the war against England (1557). In 1558 she began to act against the Scottish Protestants, provoking a rebellion and, subsequently, English intervention, which had national overtones, due to her deployment of a French garrison. She was driven out of Edingburgh, but recaptured it (1560). Shortly before her death she called on the nobles of both parties to swear allegiance to her daughter, then Queen of France.

E. M. H. M'Kerlie, *Mary of Guise-Lorraine, Queen of Scotland* (1931).

MARY, QUEEN OF SCOTS (Mary Stuart; (1542-87) Queen of Scotland. The only lawful child of *James V and *Mary of Lorraine, she was the granddaughter of Margaret *Tudor, daughter of *Henry VII, and thus could lay claim to the thrones of both Scotland and England. M. was proclaimed queen upon the death of her father, which occurred when she was only a week old. In 1548 she was sent to France in fulfilment of a treaty with Scotland and, in 1558, married the dauphin. The following year her husband acceeded to the throne

Mary Queen of Scots *by François Clouet*

as *Francis II, but after his death in 1560 the beautiful and intelligent young widow decided to return to Scotland, where her mother, the regent, had just died. M. assumed royal power in 1561, and immediately clashed with John *Knox, the narrow-minded leader of the *Presbyterians, who attacked her as a Roman Catholic. In other ways she seemed well on the way to establish her authority over her wayward subjects. In 1565, following several unsuccessful marriage negotiations, she fell in love with and married Lord *Darnley, a handsome English kinsman of hers and in 1566, gave birth to his son *James, the future king of Scotland and England.

M.'s problems began before the birth. Her marriage was a failure and her jealous husband plotted the murder of her Italian secretary and confidant, David *Rizzio. The Queen, who had also antagonized some of the nobles, linked her fate with a new man, the Earl of *Bothwell. Early in 1567 Bothwell arranged the murder of Darnley and, on 15 May, married the Queen in a Protestant ceremony. Whether M. was privy to the conspiracy to kill Darnley is still debated. Her guilt was supposed to have been proved at the time by the 'Casket Letters', poems and letters written by her to Bothwell, which were produced in evidence by the regent *Murray in 1568. Though today the letters are considered highly dubious, this does not clear the Queen of possible complicity. On the other hand, the whole question of authorship of the letters is trivial when considered from the point of view of today's marital standard of ethics. Following Bothwell's defeat and exile from Scotland in the summer of 1567, M. was forced by the nobles to abdicate in favour of her infant son. Imprisoned on the island of Lochleven, she escaped on 2 May 1568, but was defeated by Murray ten days later and fled to England.

*Elizabeth I, who had ample reason to fear that M. might become a centre of intrigue against her own government, placed her in custody. In the last 18 years of her life she was transferred from castle to castle and was very closely watched. English Roman Catholics and Elizebeth's political opponents conspired to free her, with the aim of either returning her to Scotland or having her replace Elizabeth on the throne of England. Although M. was not party to the early conspiracies, she did know and consented to the later ones, after years of imprisonment made her despair. Finally, in October 1586, she was tried and found guilty in connection with the conspiracy of Anthony Babington. She faced her executioner with calm pride, while her son James, now king of Scotland, made no effort to save her.

A tragic and romantic figure, M. has been the subject of many literary works, beginning with authors of her own time. She had been the queen of two countries and could claim the throne of a third. But she had no deep roots in any nation, a disadvantage which even her acknowledged royal rights could not make up for.

A. Fraser, *Mary Queen of Scots* (1969);
N. Morrison, *Mary Queen of Scots* (1961);
J. Phillips, *Images of a Queen* (1964).

MARZIO, GALEOTTO (1427-c. 97) Italian humanist, physician and astronomer. Born at Narni, he studied medicine at Padua, and during his long career travelled widely in Italy and abroad. He stayed at various times at the court of *Matthias Corvinus of Hungary, who in 1478 intervened in his behalf with the Republic of Venice, were M. had been arrested by the *Inquisition for his work *De incognitis vulgo*. M. exchanged invectives with *Filelfo and *Merula. His writings contained new ideas, especially on *astronomy, in which field he is sometimes described as a forerunner of *Copernicus.

MASACCIO (1401-28) A nickname, meaning 'the clumsy one', by which the Italian painter Tommaso Guidi is known. The son of a notary, he is first heard of in 1422 as a member of the Florentine painter's guild. His earliest extant work is the polyptich painted for the Carmelite church at Pisa in 1426. The central panel, a *Madonna and Child* (now in London), demonstrates that M. discarded the *International Gothic style then current in Florence for one of human realism and drama in the tradition of *Giotto. Immediately afterwards he began the famous *frescoes in the Brancacci Chapel of Sta. Maria del Carmine in Florence. Although there is no certainty as to which of the scenes that have survived were painted by M., and which by *Masolino and Filippino *Lippi, it is beyond doubt that his share undoubtedly includes the *Tribute Money*, with the firm faces of Christ and his disciples, and the anguished and naked Adam and Eve in the *Expulsion from Paradise*, and perhaps five other scenes. Here M. did for Florentine *painting what his contemporary *Donatello did for *sculpture; he introduced elements of *perspective to create an overall harmony, but at the same time gave the human image an intense monumental quality. These frescoes were for a long time admired as models of the genre. M.

did not live to earn the rewards. He died in Rome, where it seems he went to evade his creditors.
K. Steinbart, *Masaccio* (1948);
U. Procacci, *All the Paintings of Masaccio* (1962).

MASO DI BANCO A mid-14th-century Italian painter, follower of *Giotto, believed to have painted several *frescoes, notably those illustrating the legend of St. Sylvester in the Bardi Chapel of S. Croce, Florence. He had Giotto's sense of mass, space and harmony, but his contribution to the development of the Florentine realism did not immediately attract followers, until the revival of Giottesque tradition in the 15th century.

MASOLINO (1383-c. 1447) The name given to the Italian painter Tommaso da Panicale. Born near Florence, he became a member of its painters' guild in 1423; shortly afterwards he went to Hungary, and returned in 1427. M. executed a number of frescoes at the famous Brancacci Chapel of the Church of the Carmine in Florence. His style is so influenced by *Masaccio's that it is difficult to distinguish between them. However, his work tends to accentuate detail of costume in a manner reminiscent of *International Gothic. Later he worked for Cardinal Branda Castiglione in Rome and in the north of Italy.
E. Micheletti, *Masolino da Panicale* (1959).

MASQUES English term for the court spectacles in which song, *dance, and drama were combined in a performance marked by lavish costumes and stage sets. The M. were meant to entertain, and usually presented an allegory. The actors were nobles and members of the royal entourage, and some of the best known authors and artists of the day cooperated in their creation. Ben *Johnson was the greatest of all M. writers of the age, and Inigo *Jones the outstanding designer of sets and costumes. Although they were performed intermittently throughout the 16th century, the M. became the foremost form of court entertainment during the reign of *James I.
E. Welsford, *The Court Masque* (1927);
M. T. Jones-Davies, *Inigo Jones, Ben Jonson et le masque* (1967).

MASSYS, QUENTIN (1464-1530) Flemish painter. The son of a clockmaker of Louvain, he settled in 1491 in *Antwerp, where he became the first painter of note of

The Banker and His Wife *by Quentin Massys*

the expanding metropolis. It is not known who had taught him, but his early style followed those of *Bouts and *Memling. Later his work clearly showed the influence of *Dürer, who came to visit him in 1520, of *Holbein, and of the great Italian masters. M. executed religious scenes, distinguished by the great care given to decorative details and the tendency to express facial tenderness. He also did excellent individual portraits and a number of pictures of male and female moneylenders, in which there is a caricature-like display of covetousness and avarice.

MASTER OF. . . A term used to describe authors of important anonymous works of art. Employed by art historians in the last 200 years, it has been applied principally to works of the early *Renaissance, especially certain prolific Flemish painters. The 'M.' is usually named after the place from which the work derives, or where it is presently installed, or after the main subject of the work. In many instances a famous work, or group of works ascribed to an anonymous master were later satisfactorily shown to have been created by a known historical figure. An outstanding case is that of the Master of Flemalle, later identified as Robert *Campin. In other cases, such as the *Maître de Moulins (*c.* 1480-1500), creator of the tryptich at the cathedral of that town, attempts to identify him are still going on. The term is also used in reference to anonymous early *engravers. Among these are the prolific mid-15th-century German Master E. S., so-called after his signature and distinguished by his devotional subjects, and his contemporary, the Master of the Playing Cards, whose human figures, flowers and animals are both realistic and elegant. The late 15th-century German engraver, the Master of the Housebook, influenced Dürer with his subjects taken from everyday life. The device of referring to the 'Master of. . . ' has facilitated the comparative study of early Renaissance art, but has also occasioned wild speculation and much partisan scholarship.

Philadelphia Museum of Art, *Master E. S.* (1967);
M. Huillet d'Istria, *La peinture française de la fin du Moyen Age; Jean Perreal et le Maître des Moulins*(1961);
H. Lehmann-Haupt, *Gutenberg and the Master of the Playing Cards* (1966);
A. Stange, *Der Hausbuchmeister* (1958).

Early 16th-century print showing computation with abacus and Arabic numerals

MATARAZZO, FRANCESCO (c. 1443-1518) Italian humanist also known as Maturanzio. Born near Perugia, he learned *Greek during a year that he spent in Rhodes (1472-73), and afterwards held offices in Perugia, as protegé of the *Baglioni family. His best work is a history of Perugia covering the years 1492 to 1503.

MATHEMATICS During the Renaissance, the science of M., as that of *astronomy, grew on the foundations of ancient Greek and Hindu knowledge, transmitted to Europe in the Middle Ages by the Arabs. *Regiomontanus in the mid-15th century is generally considered the first important Renaissance mathematician, and in his *De triangulis* originated the separate study of trigonometry. By the end of the century expressions like *million*, *billion* and *zero*, were introduced, as well as the symbols for addition and subtraction, expanding the accepted mathematical terminology. Further progress was made with the publication of the works of ancient Greek mathematicians, chiefly Archimedes. By early 16th century European M., especially the field of algebra, had advanced beyond the level achieved at any time in the past. A highly significant achievement was related to the solution to cubic equations. The credit was claimed by Niccolo *Tartaglia, but it was first published by Girolamo *Cardano in his *Ars magnae* (1545), giving rise to a famous feud between the two. Cardano also published calculations on probabilities in games of chance. Of the non-Italian mathematicians Simon *Stevin introduced the use of decimal fractions and François *Viète inaugurated the accepted letter symbols in algebra. In the early 17th century, John *Napier invented logarithms as well as the decimal point. However, Renaissance M. still lacked uniformity and was scarcely related to the other sciences. The application of M. to physics and mechanics was mainly a 17th-century accomplishment.

J. F. Scott, *A History of Mathematics from Antiquity to the Beginning of the 19th Century* (1958).

MATTEO DI BASCIO (c. 1495-1552) Italian religious reformer. Born in Bascio, he joined the Observantine branch of the Franciscans. In 1525 he went to Rome and received from Pope *Clement VII as a personal privilege, the right to wear a garment with a pointed hood (*cappuccio*), and to preach, while practicing rigorous rules of poverty in emulation of St. Francis. With his small group of followers he founded the *Capuchin order whose vicar general he became in 1529. However, realizing it had not been his intention to create a new order, he resumed his itinerant preaching, returning later to the ranks of the Franciscans. In 1547 he accompanied the imperial troops to the Battle of *Mühlberg. He died in Venice.

MATTEO DI GIOVANNI (c. 1435-95) Italian painter. The son of a tinker of Borgo San Sepolcro, he settled in *Siena, and became its most famous painter of his day. The creator of elegant *Madonnas, he skilfully introduced into his work a sense of drama and realism, as may be clearly observed in his several versions of the *Massacre of the Innocents*.

MATTHIAS (1557-1619) German emperor from 1612. The third son of *Maximilian II, he opened his career with a rash step, accepting the invitation of the rebels in the *Netherlands to assume the governorship, although it meant a conflict with his great-cousin *Philip II of Spain. His three years in Brussels (1578-81), however, turned out to be only an episode. Returning to *Austria, M. was appointed its governor in 1593 by his brother *Rudolf II, in time to suppress the peasant uprising of 1595. By this time he was the next in the line of succession to his mentally-unbalanced brother; in 1605, with the consent of other members of the *Habsburg family, he persuaded the Emperor to give him the government of *Hungary. No longer troubling to disguise his intention of supplanting his brother on the throne, M. won over to his side the estates of Austria, Moravia and Hungary, mainly by means of concessions on the religious issue. In June 1608 he forced his brother under a threat of war to recognize his right to these lands. A reconciliation between them was effected in 1610, Rudolf retaining the imperial title and the control of *Bohemia. But in 1611 the dissatisfied Bohemians invited M. to come and assume the government, which he did, thereby dispossessing Rudolf of his last kingdom.

Rudolf died soon after (January 1612), and in June M. was crowned Emperor. Heeding the advice of his councillor Melchior *Klesl, he pursued a moderate policy with regard to the sensitive religious problems. In 1617 he gave in to the demand of his young cousin Ferdinand, Duke of Styria and Carinthia, to have him elected and crowned king of Bohemia and Hungary, as a preliminary step to securing his succession to the imperial throne. Ferdinand's known Roman Catholic intransigence ignited a revolt in Prague (23 May 1618), the first incident of the *Thirty Years' War. This immediately produced a reaction in Vienna, where Klesl was demoted and arrested by Ferdinand's supporters. M., now old, ill and childless, could only helplessly watch the situation, dying early in the following year.

MATTHIAS CORVINUS (MATYAS HUNYADI; 1440-90) King of *Hungary from 1458. The second son of Janos *Hunyadi, he was given early military training and was knighted at 14, during the siege of Belgrade. When his father died (1456), M. was seized by enemies of his family and almost lost his life. Having been spared on account of his youth, he found shelter with *George of Podebrady, whose daughter he married and, in 1458, was elected king by a majority of the Hungarian magnates. His long reign saw numerous successful campaigns. He first fought the *Ottoman Turks, asserting his rights over Bosnia, but soon became embroiled in a long struggle with Emperor *Frederick III, who had the support of a minority of the Hungarian nobility. When the conflict with the Emperor was temporarily settled in 1462, to M.'s advantage, he again turned to fight the Turks. In 1469 he turned against his father-in-law George of Podebrady, having been elected king of *Bohemia by the Czech Catholic party. This long struggle, in which Poland opposed him, was concluded only in 1478, M. obtaining Moravia and Silesia but relinquishing the throne of Bohemia to *Ladislas II. M. now renewed the war against his old rival the Emperor (1481). In 1485 he conquered Vienna, which he made his capital, and quickly annexed much of the rest of Austria. He thus became the greatest monarch of Central Europe, and contemplated securing for himself the title of emperor, so as to lead a great *crusade against the Turks. He died suddenly in Vienna, leaving no legitimate heir, but only his young natural son by a German woman, Janos *Corvinus, whose succession was fiercely opposed by M.'s third wife, Beatrice of Naples.

Matthias Corvinus in a 16th-century manuscript

A brilliant military leader, M. was also a learned man who embodied the ideals of a Renaissance prince. His court at Buda attracted many humanist scholars, poets and artists. His main achievement as a patron of culture was the Bibliotheca Corvina, a collection of some 50,000 manuscripts and printed books, which was the largest of its kind at the time. But the collection was dispersed soon after his death.

J. Balogh, *Die Anfänge der Renaissance in Ungarn; Matthias Corvinus und die Kunst* (1975);
C. Csapoki, *The Corvinian Library* (1973).

MATTIOLI, PIERANDREA (1500-77) Italian *botanist. Born in Siena, he became a physician, practising in Siena, Rome, Trento and Gorizia and at the courts of

Emperors *Ferdinand and *Maximilian II. He later spent much time in botanical studies. The first edition of his great work, known as *Comentarii a Dioscoride*, was published in Venice in 1544. It had numerous editions and was translated into Italian, French, German and Czech. It contained almost all that was known about plants and their medical properties, since classical times. It was frequently reissued with rich illustrations. Later editions included the descriptions of newly discovered plants of Asia and America.

MAURICE OF NASSAU (1567-1625) The second son of *William of Orange, and grandson on his mother's side of *Maurice of Saxony, he succeeded his father after the latter's assassination in 1584, his elder brother Philip having been rejected because of his Spanish affiliation. M. devoted himself to a thorough study of the art of war and, in 1588, became the commander in chief of the armed forces of the *United Provinces. During the next three decades he supervized the military affairs, leaving Johan van *Oldenbarneveldt, a close friend of his father's, in charge of the civil and political matters. He won his first victories in 1591 when, taking advantage of Alessandro *Farnese's involvement in France, he conquered the province of Gelderland. He was opposed to the 1609 Twelve Years' Truce with Spain, although it was supported by Oldenbarneveldt, which caused strained relations between the two. In 1618 during the bitter national-religious controversy between the *Arminians and *Gomarists, M. supported the latter group and had Oldenbarneveldt arrested and condemned to death on a charge of treason; he was beheaded on 13 May 1619. Henceforward, M. was for all practical purposes the sole ruler of the United Provinces, but his performance as a commander diminished and, when the war with Spain resumed in 1621, he suffered some reverses. He died childless and was succeeded by his younger brother.

MAURICE OF SAXONY (1521-53) Elector of *Saxony. The elder son of Henry, Duke of Saxony, he married in 1541 the daughter of *Philip of Hesse and in the same year succeeded his father as duke. Shortly afterwards, he quarrelled with his cousin *John Frederick I, elector of Saxony, and only the intervention of Philip of Hesse and *Luther averted war between them. M., however, was determined to acquire the electoral dignity and, in 1546, when *Charles V was reopening hostilities with the *Protestant princes, he left their ranks and made a secret treaty with the Emperor. In November he invaded the territories of John Frederick, from which, however, he was soon compelled to withdraw. But on 24 April 1547, Charles V defeated and captured John Frederick in the battle of *Mühlberg, and by the so-called Wittenberg capitulation the elector was coerced to surrender his rights and much of his territory in favour of M.

Invested with the electoral dignity at the diet of Augsburg in February 1548, M. soon changed sides again. Entrusted by the Emperor in 1550 with the suppression of Magdeburg, he granted the city easy terms of surrender and, on January 1552, signed a treaty with *Henry II of France. In March he surrounded the imperial troops, taking them by surprise, captured Augsburg and almost seized the Emperor himself, who fled from Innsbruck to safety through the Brenner Pass. The treaty of Passau, which the Emperor was forced to sign (August 1552), stipulated that M.'s father-in-law, Philip of Hesse be released from his four year long captivity and that liberty of religion be granted to the Protestants until the next diet. M. then undertook to fight the Turks in Hungary, but instead returned in the summer of 1553 to lead the armies of several princes against the ravaging troops of *Albert Alcibiades, with whom he had cooperated in 1546. In the fierce battle of Sievershausen M. was clearly the victor, but he was wounded by a stray bullet and died two days later. More soldier than prince, he was, in spite of himself, a great champion of the cause of Protestantism.

MAXIMILIAN I (1459-1519) *Holy Roman Emperor from 1493, known as 'the Last of the Knights'. The eldest son of Emperor *Frederick III, he was born near Vienna. M. first assumed the responsibilities of government in 1477 when he married the heiress of the Netherlands, Mary, daughter of *Charles the Bold. He successfully withstood the attacks of *Louis XI of France, defeating the French at Guingate in 1479, but his position was weakened by the death of his wife in 1482. Seeking to continue his rule of the Netherlands as regent on behalf of his son *Philip the Handsome, he provoked an uprising of some of the principal cities of *Flanders, led by *Ghent. In 1488 he suffered his greatest humiliation when he was detained for three months by the citizens of *Bruges. Although later he was able to revenge himself on his captors, M. soon underwent another humiliation. In 1490 he married, by proxy, *Anne of Brittany, but late in 1491 she became the wife of *Charles VIII of France, who at the same time renounced his previous betrothal to M.'s daughter Margaret.

By then M. was looking eastwards. In 1490 he secured the Tyrol, where he made his residence; in 1491 he drove the Hungarians out of Austria, and, in 1492, drove the Turks from Carinthia. He became Emperor in 1493. The following year he married Maria Bianca Sforza, daughter of a duke of *Milan, as a result of which he became interested in Italy. In 1494 he fought against rebels in the Netherlands and, in 1496, married his son Philip to *Joanna, daughter of *Ferdinand and *Isabella, thus paving the way for the mightiness of the house of *Habsburg in the 16th century. In the imperial Diet of Worms of 1495 M. launched a series of measures designed to reorganize the structure of the Empire. These innovations, which included the creation of the **Reichskammergericht*, were continued at the subsequent Diets, but the changes agreed on turned out to be more apparent than real, and the Emperor, encountering much opposition, preferred to rule through his own commissions. In 1499 M. lost the war against the Swiss and recognized their independence. His long conflict with *Louis XII over Milan did not bring military success either, and in the Treaty of Blois (1504) he relinquished the duchy to the French king.

After the death of his son Philip in 1506, M. established his daughter *Margaret as regent of the Netherlands and guardian of his grandson *Charles, the future emperor. In the following years he was particularly active in Italy. In 1509 he joined the League of *Cambrai against *Venice, and after *Julius II made a separate peace with Venice (1510), he cooperated with Louis XII against the Pope in summoning a general council of the Church. Then, in 1513, he joined the *Holy League against France, and in the same year was present at the English camp during the Battle of the *Spurs. In 1516

M. actually seized Milan, but his troops mutinied and he was forced to leave Italy, ceding the duchy to *Francis I. All these wars and skirmishes reflected the Emperor's adventurous spirit rather than a clear political design. In fact, M. achieved more by clever matrimonial schemes than on the battlefield. In 1515 he arranged a double marriage between two of his grandchildren and *Louis of Hungary and his sister, which union eventually led to the annexation of *Bohemia and *Hungary by the Habsburgs.

A dreamer who hoped to revive the mediaeval empire, and who pretended to lead Europe in a *crusade against the Turks, M. was unable even to secure the election of his grandson Charles as king of Germany in the Diet of Augsburg of 1518. But although he was politically ineffectual, the Emperor's public image was magnificent, worthy of his grand tomb at Innsbruck. Himself a military man, he was the patron of humanist scholars and artists, notably *Dürer and *Burgkmair. He was also a writer, the author of two poetical allegories: *Weisskunig*, an unfiinished autobiography, and *Teuerdank*, describing his adventures while journeying to meet his first wife, published in 1517. His minor writings included a treatise on hunting, *Geheimes Jagdbuch*.

R. W. Seton-Watson, *Maximilian I* (1902);
C. Hare, *Maximilian the Dreamer* (1913);
G. E. Waas, *The Legendary Character of Kaiser Maximilian* (1971);
H. Wiesflecker, *Maximilian I, Österreich, das Reich und Europa an der Wende zur Neuzeit* (1971).

MAXIMILIAN II (1527-76) *Holy Roman Emperor from 1564. The son of *Ferdinand I and Anne, daughter of the king of *Hungary and *Bohemia, he was educated in *Spain. In 1548 he married his cousin Maria, daughter of *Charles V. From 1552 on, M. was in Vienna where he took part in the administration of the lands of the Austrian *Habsburgs and in their defence against the *Ottoman Turks. Although formally he remained a Roman Catholic, he was influenced by Lutheran ideas, a fact which aroused concern in one religious camp and hopes in the other. When he succeeded his father as emperor and king of Bohemia and Hungary, M. allowed considerable freedom to the *Protestants in *Austria. Most of his reign was consumed in efforts, largely unsuccessful, to overcome the Turkish threat. But although he remained on close terms with his cousin *Philip II, he did not join the Spanish monarch either before or after the Battle of *Lepanto (1571).

V. Bibl, *Maximilian II, der rätselhafte Kaiser* (1929).

MAYENNE, CHARLES, DUKE OF (1554-1611) French leader of the *League. The son of Francis, second duke of *Guise, he was an aide to his brother Henry, third duke of *Guise. When the latter was murdered at Blois (1588) by order of King *Henry III, M. marched to Paris, which was faithful to the League, and was declared before the **parlement* 'lieutenant-general of France'. After Henry III was assassinated (1589), M. proclaimed the old Cardinal of Bourbon King of France as Charles X. He conducted a series of battles against *Henry IV, in which he was helped by Spanish troops sent by *Philip II. But gradually he turned away from the intransigence of the extreme *liguers* and, in 1595, made peace with Henry IV.

MAZZOLINI, SILVESTRE (1456-1523) Italian Dominican friar, also known as Prierias. A native of Piedmont

Maximilian I *by Dürer*

who had taught at Bologna, he was appointed in 1514 by *Leo X to a chair of theology in Rome and, in 1515, published a work on church doctrines and ethics which was very popular. In 1518 he was one of the first to attack Martin *Luther with his *Dialogus de potestate papae*, which expounded the Roman Catholic views on *indulgences. Luther replied to him sarcastically.

MECHANICS It might have been thought that during the Renaissance man's quickly-developing inventiveness would have harnessed the natural forces, such as wind and water, to move machines. But this was not the case. Indeed, most of the European mechanical inventory of the 16th century had been developed during the Middle Ages. However, the Renaissance did see improvements added, and old machines given wider applications. The water-wheel, usually driven from underneath, was the most widely used power generator. Constructed of wood and metal, it was an assembly of wheels, cogs and pulleys and was used in mills to grind corn, crush olives, saw wood and many other tasks. The windmill, on the other hand, was more typical of northern Europe. It reached its highest degree of perfection in the 16th century in the Netherlands, where two major types were developed: a post-supported rotating mill and the tower mill, of which only the cap, carrying the wind-shaft, had to be rotated. Dutch engineers led all others in mill construction, and also excelled in building wind-powered pumps, employed in reclaiming land from the sea. Many other kinds of pumps were employed by the *mining industry, as well as for supplying potable water to cities. A large array of these mills and pumps was described by Agostino Ramelli in his *Le diverse et artificiose machine* (1588). It is true that some Renaissance authors, notably *Leonardo, suggested the idea of steam-powered machine, but it seems that no experiments were made at the time.

The Renaissance, however, saw impressive advances in the area of time-measuring devices. The first all-mechanical clocks were made around 1300. These were large iron structures driven by weights which sounded the hours, and were placed high in the bell-towers of the main cathedrals. By the early 15th century the crafts had developed to the stage that scaled-down clocks for homes could be made. In the 16th century springs were introduced, instead of weights for the clock's driving power, though this involved a difficulty, inasmuch as it was necessary to equalize the force of the uncoiling spring. The problem was solved differently in various places, the German device of a friction brake being the most successful. Early spring-driven clocks took the shape of small metal drums with dials on the top, but in the second half of the 16th century they were mostly designed as profusely-decorated small towers. Their accuracy was within a quarter of an hour per day, and usually a single hand was employed. In his last years *Galileo experimented with the pendulum, which he perceived as an accurate time regulator. But the first pendulum clock was constructed only in 1656 by the Dutch Christian Huygens.

The Card Players *by Israel Meckenem*

Late 16th-century watches from Augsburg

Mid-16th century table clock

The watch, which appeared in the 16th century, was a further example of Renaissance technical proficiency and craftsmanship. Basically it was a reduced version of the domestic clock, small enough to be carried on the person. Peter *Henlein of *Nuremberg, the inventor of the mainspring, is usually cited as the first maker of watches. But Henlein's metal drum was actually a table clock, and it was not until about 1550 that the first oval-shaped watches appeared in Nuremberg, becoming quickly known as 'Nuremberg eggs'. While based on much the same mechanical principles, these were highly decorative objects, and sometimes encased in porcelain. But in the third quarter of the century watchmaking spread from Nuremberg to England, France and other countries, and finally established a new centre in *Geneva. Here a group of French and Italian watchmaker-goldsmiths, mostly religious refugees, founded a guild, based on a rigid system of apprenticeship and closely-kept trade secrets. This was the beginning of the famous Swiss watch industry.

C. Singer et al., eds., *A History of Technology*, vols. 2-4 (1956-58);

The Last Judgement *by Michelangelo, in the Sistine Chapel*

F. Klemm, *History of Western Technology* (1958);
F. A. B. Ward, *Time Measurement: A Historical Review* (1961);
E. Bruton, *Clocks and Watches, 1400-1900* (1967).

MECKENEM, ISRAEL VAN (1450-1503) German engraver. Born in Bamberg, he was probably the son of an engraver, and became the most prolific master of his age, ranking as highly in technique as his contemporary *Schongauer. Many of his 600 or so copperplates were based on the works of others, including some anonymous German masters who had also influenced Schongauer.

MEDALS One of the most original creations of Renaissance art, the medal appears in the early 15th century, as what might be termed a display coin. Representing humanist admiration of the style of classical antiquity, the early M. were modelled on old Roman coins. *Pisanello, who cast his M. from moulds, was their true originator. It was he who established their form: a profile portrait on one side, and an inscription combined with an emblem on the other. By the late 15th century, M. were made in France and other countries, and their wearing as decorative pieces became fairly widespread. The first known Jewish medal, for example, dating from 1503, is an indirect evidence of the proliferation of the art. Famous M. were struck for *Elizabeth I, following the English victory over the *Armada (1588). This may have been one of the first instances when M. were awarded as a sign of reward for distinguished military service.

A. Armand, *Les medailleurs italiens des quinzieme et seizieme siecles*, 3 vols. (1966);
D. M. Friedenberg, *Jewish Medals: From the Renaissance to the Fall of Napoleon, 1503-1815* (1970).

MEDICI A family which became dominant in the political life of Florence in the early 15th century. The M.'s political power was founded on *banking; already Giovanni Bicci de' M. (1360-1429) was believed to be the wealthiest person in Italy. His son, Cosimo the Elder, was involved in a struggle with other families of the Florentine oligarchy, which he won in 1434. Thereafter the M.s remodelled the city government to suit their own purpose, and continued to dominate the republic until 1494 when Piero, son of Lorenzo, was deposed during the French invation. The M.s returned to Florence in 1512 with the aid of Spain. By now, however, their power extended to Rome, and two members of the family reached the papal throne – *Leo X (1513-21) and *Clement VII (1523-34). The M.s again lost their hold on Florence between 1527 and 1530, but were reestablished a second time with the help of Spain, Alessandro receiving from *Charles V the title of Duke. After the murder of Alessandro in 1537 – by Lorenzino, a distant relative – the government passed to the other branch of the M.s, represented by *Cosimo I. This M. obtained for himself and his heirs the title of grand duke and established the M.s as one of the ruling houses among European princes. The M. dynasty of Florence expired in the 19th century.

F. Schevill, *The Medici* (1949);
R. A. De Roover, *The Medici Bank* (1948);
H. M. M. Acton, *The Last Medici* (1959).

MEDICI, ALESSANDRO DE' (c. 1510-37) First *Medici duke of Florence. An illegitimate son of Lorenzo de' Medici (1492-1519), Duke of Urbino, he was ap-

Young Man with a Medal *by Botticelli*

pointed by his uncle Pope *Clement VII co-ruler of Florence, together with his brother Ippolito (1523). Both were expelled in 1527, but in 1530 Alessandro returned, aided by Emperor *Charles V whose natural daughter, *Margaret of Parma, he married. In 1532 he was given the title of duke. His rule was characterized by cruelty and his own licentious behaviour. He was murdered by a relative, Lorenzino de' Medici.

MEDICI, COSIMO DE' (1389-1464) Florentine statesman, called 'Cosimo the Elder'. Son of the rich Giovanni Bicci, he spent his first 40 years mainly in commerce and banking, entering the stormy political life of Florence only after his father's death. In 1433 he was banished to Padua, but in the following year returned and established himself as the most influential citizen of the Republic. By instituting changes in the councils of government and raising the level of taxation, he succeeded in forcing some hostile members of the oligarchy to emigrate, thus strengthening his position. While the banking operations of the Medicis grew tremendously

Margaret of Austria, kneeling, and her mother, Mary of Burgundy, in an early 16th-century stained-glass

during the period that he was in power, the Republic also benefited. He encouraged commerce and agriculture, erected many public buildings and was popular with the lower classes. He especially stimulated the arts and the new humanist scholarship, helping *Ficino to set up the *Platonic Academy and commissioning works from *Brunelleschi, *Donatello and *Ghiberti. He also started the great Medici collection of manuscripts which is part of the *Laurentian Library.

K. S. Gutkind, *Cosimo de' Medici* (1938).

MEDICI, GIOVANNI DE' (1498-1526) Italian military commander, called Giovanni delle Bande Nere, because, upon the death of *Leo X and later, when he himself died, his soldiers changed their banners from white to black. He belonged to the junior branch of the Medici family and was orphaned at a very young age. Raised at the house of Jacopo Salviati, he married his daughter Maria, by whom he had a son, the future *Cosimo I. Giovanni dedicated himself to the military profession, becoming at an early age one of the best Italian soldiers of his time. He fought for Leo X, then for the French, and lost his life while fighting in the armies of the *League of Cognac.

MEDICI, GIULIANO DE' (1478-1516) Duke of Nemours. The third son of Lorenzo the Magnificent, he had to leave *Florence upon the fall of his brother Piero (1494), and found shelter at the court of *Guidobaldo da Montefeltro. He returned to Florence in 1512, with the aid of his other brother Cardinal Giovanni de' Medici. When the latter became Pope *Leo X, he named M. supreme commander of the papal armies, and arranged his marriage to Filiberta of Savoy, niece of *Francis I of France, who awarded him the title of duke (1515). Dying soon afterwards, M. is chiefly remembered on account of his monument, the work of *Michelangelo, in the church of S. Lorenzo, Florence.

MEDICI, LORENZO DE' (1449-92) Florentine statesman known as Lorenzo the Magnificent (grandson of Cosimo the Elder and son of Piero the Gouty). He was educated by the finest teachers and entered political life at the age of 17. Upon the death of his father (1469) he vigorously took over the leadership of Florence, but soon involved the Republic in a war against Volterra (1472). An opposition to him arose, which culminated in an attempt on his life in the church of Santa Maria del Fiora on 26 April 1478. His younger brother Giuliano was stabbed to death by the conspirators, but Lorenzo escaped and then suppressed his enemies by the harshest measures. Since *Sixtus IV supported the conspirators, he excommunicated Lorenzo, imposed an interdict on Florence, and joined King *Ferrante of Naples in an alliance against the Republic. In 1480 this alliance scored a victory over the Florentines, threatening Lorenzo's rule. In consequence, Lorenzo personally undertook a diplomatic mission to Naples and succeeded in persuading Ferrante to restore the peace. The fortunate outcome of his gamble brought him out of the crisis stronger than ever. Lorenzo's fame, however, rests principally on his association with contemporary artists, philosophers and poets. He was not merely their patron, but sought their company and believed himself to be one of them. He wrote poetry, a play and a book on falconry. His secular concerns and tastes brought upon him the criticism of *Sovonarola during the last years of his life.

E. Bizzari, *Il Magnifico Lorenzo* (1950);
E. L. S. Horsburgh, *Lorenzo de Magnificent and Florence in Her Golden Age* (1908);
C. M. Ady, *Lorenzo de' Medici and Renaissance Italy* (1955);
E. Armstrong, *Lorenzo the Magnificent and Florence in Her Golden Age* (1896).

MEDICI, PIERO DE' (1416-69) Florentine statesman and banker, known as Piero the Gouty. The son of Cosimo the Elder, he succeeded his father in 1464 as head of the banking family and the unofficial ruler of Florence. His frequent illnesses, the effects of gout, made him vulnerable, and his enemies thought that they could destroy him. But he energetically foiled their attempts (1465), and sent many to exile. A great patron of artists and humanists, he was the father of Lorenzo the Magnificent.

MEDICI, PIERO DE' (1472-1503) Italian ruler of *Florence. The eldest son of Lorenzo the Magnificent, he succeeded him in 1492 as head of the Medici family. When the French armies passed through Tuscany on their way to Naples, M. reversed his former position and went to the camp of *Charles VIII offering his cooperation. This caused a revolt in the city (9 November, 1494), in which the Medici lost power and were banished. M. made unsuccessful attempts to return, being favoured by Pope *Alexander VI. He died in battle at the crossing of the Garigliano River, where he fought on the side of the French.

MEDICINE The changes in medical science during the Renaissance did not amount to a revolution. The fact

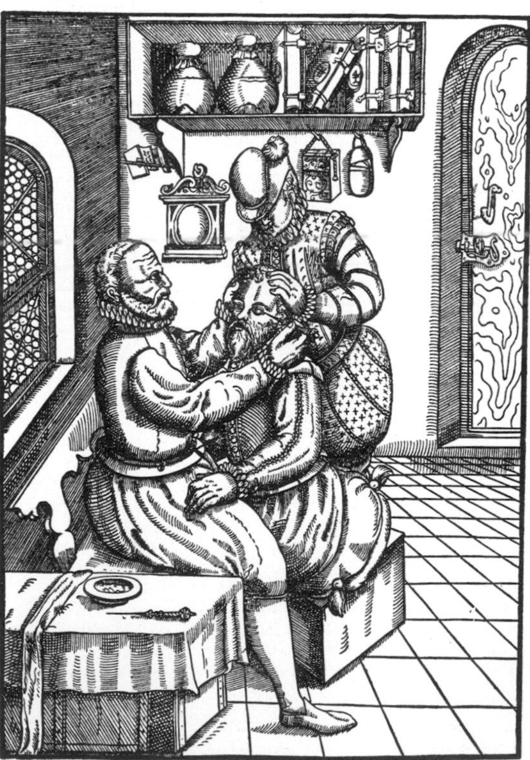

The Eye Doctor and his Patient *from* Ophthalmoduleia *by Bartisch (1583)*

Blood letting – standard medical treatment, in a miniature from a 15th-century illuminated manuscript

that William Harvey's discovery of the circulation of blood encountered so much opposition when it was published in 1628, says much about the conservative orientation of the contemporary medical profession. Nevertheless, considering that well into the 15th century European medicine depended almost entirely on ancient Greek and Roman sources transmitted by the Arabs, the advances made in the next 200 years were impressive. The most significant achievements of the Renaissance were scored not in medicine proper, but in the related field of *anatomy. Naturally, the better understanding of the human body made for many improvements in the treatment of wounds. Diseases were better understood and identified, and the training of physicians incorporated some clinical methods. Of greater significance was the fact that the medical world was awakened from its millennial stupor by innovative theories, such as those expounded by *Paracelsus, which, if they did not contain scientific truths, at least exposed the deficiencies of the knowledge inherited from the ancients.

Mediaeval medicine had reached an apogee of sorts in the 13th century. Schools such as those of Salerno and Montpellier had absorbed the works of the great ancient authorities Hippocrates and Gelen, as well as those of the great Moslem physician Avicenna (980-1037) and the Jew Maimonides (1135-1204). The resulting science relied heavily on *astrology and *alchemy. Blood-letting was used as means of 'cleansing' the body of its ailments, and drugs were frequently prescribed on the basis of belief in their inherent powers, ratner than any demonstrated effects. The medical practice of the Renaissance continued the mediaeval separation between the university-trained 'Doctor', who wore a long robe and spoke in Latin, and the homely barber-surgeon, who performed blood-letting and treated wounds in addition to cutting hair. The latter category was organized in

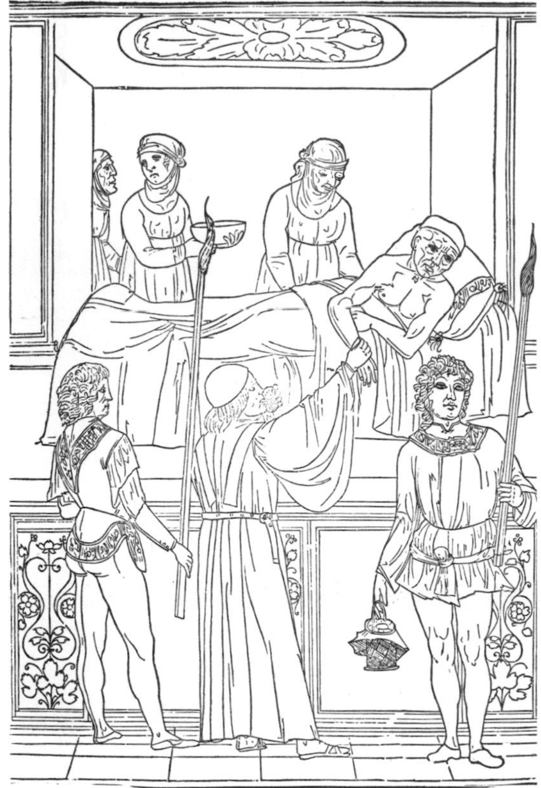

Physician visiting a plague victim, 15th-century woodcut

*guilds, and its status was slowly rising. In 1540 *Henry VIII granted the English barber-surgeons the right to be addressed as 'Masters'. Earlier the same King had chartered the first College of Physicians, founded by *Linacre, which was granted control of the practice of medicine in London. With regard to the leading schools of medicine, Italy retained its long-time European pre-eminence, which became even greater in the 16th century thanks to the great school of Padua. But as the age drew to a close, the University of Leiden was beginning to lead in the field of medical instruction, and with it began the dominance of the medical institutions of northern Europe in the 17th century.

European hospitals, run by religious orders, grew in number during the Renaissance. But crowding and bad sanitation were generally the rule, and the hospital was viewed as the place where the poor sick went to die. There also existed a number of asylums for the mentally ill, of which England's Bedlam was the oldest. Periodic regional epidemics continued to take their heavy toll and, after 1495, a new disease became widespread, *syphilis. Girolamo Fracastoro (1478-1553), who gave the new disease its name, published in 1546 a work called *De contagione*, wherein he advanced ideas about ways to contain infection and control epidemics. But the views of this Veronese poet-physician were too advanced for his time. It is characteristic that the great Renaissance medical reformer, who was a pioneer in the better treatment of wounds and amputations, was not a university-trained physician but a former apprentice of a Parisian barber-surgeon. Ambroise *Paré substituted soothing dressing for searing oil in treating gunshot wounds, and taught the use of arterial ligatures instead of cautery in amputations. With regard to the treatment of diseases and internal disorders, the leading theory still maintained that they resulted from a change in the proper balance of four elements: heat, cold, wetness and dryness. This so-called 'humoral pathology', was a mediaeval heritage, and it actually gained authority in the 16th century, thanks to the publication of the works of Galen, and survived the Renaissance. The most celebrated attempt to displace Galen was made by members of the iatro-chemical school, chiefly Paracelsus and van *Helmont. While not in agreement among themselves, both opted for drugs made of chemical substances, mainly metallic preparations. They also devised theories which ascribed to supernatural forces control over the human body. In the final account, Paracelsus merely exchanged one grand theory for another, the difference being that his own, of a *Neoplatonist orientation, was more in line with the philosophical temper of his times. The medical man of the Renaissance, on the whole, did not possess the means to explain the causation of disease.

R. H. Major, *A History of Medicine*, 2 vols. (1954);
M. Foster, *Lectures on the History of Physiology During the 16th, 17th and 18th Centuries* (1901);
A. Castiglioni, *A History of Medicine* (1958);
C. Singer and E. A. Underwood, *A Short History of Medicine* (1962);
E. Long, *A History of Pathology* (1965).

MEDINA SIDONIA, DON ALONSO PEREZ DE GUZMAN, DUKE OF (1550-1615) Spanish commander of the *Armada. Born to one of the noblest and wealthiest families of Spain, he was put in charge of the planned invasion of England (1588), in spite of the fact that he had never shown any special military talents. In justice, it should be noted that he tried to avoid the assignment, complaining to the king that he always felt sick at sea. Returning to Spain after his humiliating defeat, he still retained the confidence of *Philip II, who kept him in his post as admiral.

MEDIUM AEVUM (Middle Ages) A term first employed by the Italian humanist and historian Flavio *Biondo (1392-1463), to signify the long interval between the ancient Roman world and the rebirth of classical learning in the 15th century. Renaissance humanists saw the M.A. as a thousand years of decline and degeneration, and their own time as a new golden age. Thus, the term M.A. testified to the emergence of a new historical consciousness and the consolidation of what became the accepted periodization of the history of Western civilization: the Ancient World, the Middle Ages and the Modern Period.

MEHEMMED I (1387-1421) Sultan of the *Ottoman Turks from 1413. The youngest son of *Bayazid I, he secured the sole government of the Ottoman empire after a long struggle against his older brothers (1402-13). Though his reign was short, he had to face the threat of a pretender who claimed to be a missing brother, and a religious revolt. This explains his friendly attitude towards the Byzantine Empire.

MEHEMMED II (1432-81) Sultan of the *Ottoman Turks from 1451. The son of *Murad II, he first as-

Mehemmed II *by Gentile Bellini*

sumed power in 1444, replacing his father at the head of the government for two years. He again took over when his father died, and immediately began preparations for the most resounding military victory of the Turks, the conquest of *Constantinople. The old Byzantine metropolis fell in 1453, and the sultan made it the capital of his empire. In 1458 he completed the conquest of Serbia, where two years earlier he had failed to take Belgrade; in 1463 he seized Bosnia. M. smashed the Venetian and Genoese empires in the Aegean and Black Sea, seizing Negroponte, Scutari and Kaffa. But he was unable to wrest the island of Rhodes from the Knights of *St. John (1480). In the last year of his life his forces attacked the kingdom of *Naples, taking Ontranto. A superb military organizer, M. certainly earned his title: 'The Conqueror'.
F. C. Babinger, *Mehmed der Eroberer und seine Zeit* (1953).

MEHEMMED III (1566-1603) Sultan of the *Ottoman Turks from 1595. The son of *Murad III, he secured the throne for himself by executing nineteen of his brothers. A war with *Austria was waged throughout his reign. After early losses he conquered Erlau in Hungary in 1596, and defeated the *Habsburgs at Mezö-Keresztes. He scored other victories in the war of sieges that ensued. However, a revolt in Asia Minor and a new war with Abbas I of Persia augmented the serious difficulties which he was unable to solve before his death.

MEISTERSINGER German versifiers, first on religious-moral themes, later on secular subjects, who were organized in *guilds which flourished in the 15th and 16th centuries. Continuing earlier, mediaeval traditions, the M. claimed to possess the skills and knowledge of the craft of peotry, justifying their self-proclaimed 'mastership'. The elaborated a highly formal manner of *Meistersang*, a poetic composition sung to the tune of a traditional melody. Hans *Folz, in the early 16th century, introduced more freedom into the art by adopting new melodies. Hans *Sachs, who followed him in *Nuremberg, brought the reputation of the M. to its height.
B. Nagel, *Der deutsche Meistersang* (1967);
A. Taylor, *The Literary History of Meistergesang* (1937).

MEIT, CONRAD (1485-1544) German sculptor. Born at Worms, he worked in different places. In 1511 he was at *Wittenberg, in the service of *Frederick the Wise of Saxony. Later he moved to the Netherlands where, between 1526 and 1532, he executed his masterpiece, the tombs for *Margaret of Austria and her family at Notre-Dame-de-Brou, Bourg. M., who excelled also as wood-carver, adopted the Italianate style, but without surrendering his own artistic character. About 1536 he settled at *Antwerp, where he spent the last years of his life.

MELANCHTHON, PHILIP (1497-1560) German Protestant reformer. Born into a well-off family of Bretten in Baden, he was *Reuchlin's great-nephew. In 1509 he began his studies at Heidelberg, and three years later moved to Tübingen, where he received his M.A. degree. In 1518, on the recommendation of Reuchlin, M. was appointed a professor of *Greek at the university of Wittenberg. There, while quickly acquiring a reputation

Melanchthon *by Lucas Cranach*

Platina appointed Librarian of the Vatican by Sixtus IV *by Melozzo da Forli*

as a brilliant teacher, he met and was influenced by *Luther and, in 1519, took part in the Disputation of *Leipzig. In 1521, when Luther was confined in the Wartburg, M. substituted for him as the leader of the Reformation in Wittenberg. During this time he tended to follow the radical approach of *Carlstadt and wavered in his attitude towards the *Zwickau Prophets. At the same time he published the *Loci communes*, the first comprehensive doctrinal statement of the Reformation. After Luther's return (1522), M. helped him with the translation of the *Bible, and was also with him in the Colloquy of *Marburg (1529). In 1530 M. was the leading Protestant representative at the Diet of *Augsburg. There he prepared the important *Augsburg Confession, which reflected his conciliatory spirit towards Roman Catholicism.

From here on and despite the rejection of the Confession by the Emperor, M. was viewed as the Protestant leader most likely to achieve a possible compromise and reunion with Rome, which caused him to be criticized by the more radical followers of Luther. In 1537 he appended to the *Schmalkaldic Articles a clause explaining the conditions under which he would recognize the authority of the pope. Ten years later, when the Protestant princes were defeated by *Charles V in the Battle of *Mühlberg, M. gave a partial approval to the *Augsburg Interim (1548). As a result he found himself involved in a bitter controversy with regard to the concept of **adiaphora*, which split the Protestant camp. From Wittenberg M. continued to lead the Protestant community of Saxony, a task that devolved upon him when Luther died (1546). But he was never able to heal the internal rifts which had opened in the German Reformation. Although somewhat weak as a leader, M. was a superb theologian who provided the Reformation with doctrinal statements at different stages of its development. He also left his mark on Protestant *education, organizing schools, writing textbooks and promoting the study of the classics and humanist values.

F. Hildebrandt, *Melanchthon: Alien or Ally?* (1946).

MELOZZO DA FORLI (1438-94) Italian painter. The son of an established family of Forli, he was probably a pupil of *Piero della Francesca. The affinity between the two may be perceived in M.'s best known picture, **Platina Appointed Librarian of the Vatican by *Sixtus IV* (1477). Most of the other works ascribed to him have survived only as fragments. M. was famous as one of the inventors of the technique of extreme foreshortening, a feat in which he can be compared with his contemporary *Mantegna. This was especially displayed in his *Ascension of Christ*, painted in Rome in 1472.

A. Schmarsow, *Joost van Gent und Melozzo da Forli* (1912).

MELVILLE, ANDREW (1545-1622) Scottish religious leader. After studying in France and teaching at the *Geneva Academy, he returned to Scotland to become the principal of Glasgow University (1574), and principal of St. Mary's College, St. Andrew's (1580). As Moderator of the General Assembly, he clashed with *James VI and had to leave Scotland (1584). Returning in 1585 he regained his post, becoming rector of St. Andrew's in 1590 but, in 1606, he was summoned to London to a discussion on the Scottish Church, and was arrested and held in the Tower for four years for his contemptuous attack on the *Church of England. The author of many reforms which consolidated Scottish *Presbyterianism, he ended his life in France as professor of divinity at Sedan.

MEMLING, HANS (c. 1430-94) Flemish painter. Born near Mainz, he is believed to have been a pupil of Roger van der *Weyden. About 1465 he settled in *Bruges, where he established a very successful workshop. The city *guilds were among his best customers, but he was also patronized by the *Burgundian court and had an international clientele. At the end of his life he was one of the most prosperous citizens and left a considerable property. M. painted in a style which recalled both van der Weyden and van *Eyck, but characterized by softness and an almost delicate transparency of colours. His human figures have warmth and sweetness, and there is careful attention to detail. He executed several works for the St. John's Hospital at Bruges; the shrine of St. Ursula is one of the masterpieces of his maturity. Several of his pictures were subsequently taken to Germany, Italy, France and elsewhere.

M. J. Friedländer, *Memling and Gerard David* (1970).

MEMMI, LIPPO Italian painter of the Sienese school. He was a brother-in-law of Simone *Martini, whose style he emulated, and with whom he sometimes collaborated. His first documented work is *The Virgin in Majesty* (1317) in the Twon Hall of S. Gemignano. The

Annunciation at the Uffizi, Florence, completed 1333, is signed jointly with Martini, but is entirely dominated by the latter. M. may have visited and worked at the papal court at Avignon. Of his other works the *Madonna del popolo* (1320), at the church of the Servites in Siena, is distinguished by its delicate taste. Not a great master, M. is considered the most perfect example of mid-14th century Sienese modelling and refinement. He is not heard of after 1347.

MENA, JUAN DE (1411-56) Spanish poet. Born in Córdoba, he studied at Salamanca, and later went to Italy, where he became interested in ancient Latin writings. Back in Spain, he became secretary to king *John II of Castile and a friend of the marquis of Santillana, for whom he wrote the allegorical poem *La coronación* (1438). M. also translated into Spanish a mediaeval Latin rendering of the *Iliad* and, towards the end of his life, began a poem on classical themes which remained uncompleted. His major work, *El laberinto de fortuna* (1444), dealt with contemporary political events and remained very popular until the 17th century.

M. R. Lida de Malkiel, *Juan de Mena, poeta del prerrenacimiento español* (1950).

MENDIETA, GERONIMO DE (1525-1604) Spanish missionary and historian. Born at Vitoria in northern Spain, he joined the Franciscans and in 1554, arrived in New Spain (Mexico), where he quickly distinguished himself as an indefatigable worker among the Indians. From 1569 to 1573 he was in Spain, making known his opinions about the need of improving the conditions of the Indians. After his return he filled several ecclesiastical posts in the vicinity of Mexico City, where he died. His *Historia eclesiastica indiana* was completed in 1596, but remained in manuscript until 1870. It describes the christianization of the Caribbean and New Spain from the arrival of *Columbus, and is marked by its open criticism of Spanish colonization.

J. L. Phelan, *The Millenial Kingdom of the Franciscans in the New World*, 2nd ed. (1970).

MENDOZA, ANTONIO DE (1490-1552) First Spanish Viceroy of New Spain. Born to a noble family in Granada, he was employed by *Charles V as an ambassador before being sent to Mexico in 1535. M. was the real founder of the administrative machinery which maintained Spanish colonial rule in America for another three centuries. He organized the collection of tribute from the Indians, regulated the mining industry, established the first mint, a foundry, schools for the sons of the Indian nobility, and backed the **encomienda* system. In 1551 he was sent to perform a similar task in Peru, but died a year after his arrival.

A. S. Aiton, *Antonio de Mendoza, First Viceroy of New Spain* (1927).

MENDOZA, BERNARDINO DE (1540-1604) Spanish diplomat and author. Of aristocratic family, he completed his studies at Alcalá (1557) and joined the army, participating in campaigns in the Mediterranean. The Duke of *Alba was the first to employ him on diplomatic missions in Italy (1567), and also entrusted him with important military commands in the *Netherlands (1572-74). M. first visited England in 1574. He returned as resident ambassador of *Philip II in 1578, and for the next six years involved himself in the internal affairs of the country, aiding *Jesuit infiltrators, scheming with the supporters of *Mary Queen of Scots and maintaining contacts with plotters against *Elizabeth I. In 1584 he was ordered to leave, his expulsion being taken by Philip II as a personal insult. He was then posted to France (1584-91), where he became an ardent supporter of the *League. Returning to Spain after the victory of *Henry IV, he lost his eyesight and spent his last years in a monastery, writing and translating. His main work, a book on military matters, *Teorica y practica de la guerra* (1595) was frequently republished.

D. Jensen, *Diplomacy and Dogmatism: Bernardino de Mendoza and the French Catholic League* (1964).

MENDOZA, PEDRO DE (1487-1537) Spanish conquistador. The son of a wealthy family of Almeria, he fought in Italy, and joined the household of *Charles V. In 1535 he headed a well-equipped expedition of 11 ships to South America, and after a pause at the harbour of Rio de Janeiro, reached the Rio de la Plata, where he founded the colony of Buenos Aires. Members of this colony subsequently sailed up the Paraná and Paraguay rivers, and established a settlement at Asunción. M. himself, hard pressed by constant Indian attacks, decided to abandon the site (Buenos Aires) and go back to Spain, but died on his return voyage.

P. Groussac, *Mendoza y Garay; las dos fundaciones de Buenos Aires* (1916).

MENDOZA, PEDRO GONZALEZ DE (1428-95) Spanish cardinal and archbishop of Toledo. The talented son of the Marquis of Santillana, he completed his studies at the university of Salamanca in 1452, and a year later was made bishop of Calahorra. Becoming cardinal and chancellor of Castile (1473) under *Henry IV, M. lent his support to *Ferdinand and *Isabella, who were already married. In 1474 he championed Isabella's right to succeed her brother and, in 1476, joined the King and Queen at the Battle of Toro, defeating the supporters of *Juana la Beltraneja. Keeping his post as chancellor, M. remained the chief advisor to the royal couple until his death. In addition to his political concerns, he promoted the development of a humanist culture in Spain, translated classical authors into Spanish and patronized Pietro Martire di *Anghiera. In 1482 he became archbishop of Toledo, the highest position in the Spanish ecclesiastical hierarchy, which he left to his protegé *Jiménez de Cisneros.

A. Merino Alvárez, *El cardenal Mendoza* (1942).

MENENDEZ DE AVILES, PEDRO (1519-74) Spanish naval commander of noble family, he distinguished himself under *Charles V while fighting the corsairs of the Atlantic. In 1554 he accompanied the future *Philip II to England. When the latter became king (1556), M. was made commander of the American **flota*. In 1557 he carried on his ships the troops that scored the Spanish victory at St. Quentin. Out of favour for a period, M. was later made governor of Florida (1565) and ordered to destroy the *Huguenot colony of Jean *Ribaut. He accomplished his mission in a thorough and brutal fashion, slaughtering all the Frenchmen suspected of Protestantism, and founded St. Augustin, the first European settlement in the present territory of the United States. As governor of Cuba he organized the Spanish defenses. Shortly before he died, he was called to Spain to assume command of the **Armada*.

MENTELIN, JOHANN (?-1478) German printer. Born in Schlettstadt, he became the first printer in *Strassburg, where he was active from 1458 on. In 1460 he issued a

49-line *Bible, which held the complete text in 850 pages, compared with *Gutenberg's 1,286, and in 1466 printed the first Bible in German. M. catered to the general public and published popular romances of *chivalry. Aided by his son-in-law Adolf Rusch, M trained many of the early printers of Strassburg.

MERBECKE, JOHN English theologian and musician, active in the reigns of *Henry VIII and *Edward VI. In 1544 he was sentenced to be burned at the stake for having compiled the first English concordance to the *Bible. Pardoned through the intercession of Bishop *Gardner, he printed the work in 1550. In the same year he published the Book of *Common Prayer together with musical notations. M. was for many years an organist at Windsor, and died about 1585.

MERCANTILISM A term, first employed by Adam Smith in his *The Wealth of Nations* (1776), in reference to the system in which the acquisition of precious metals was the chief interest of national economy. The development of the mercantilistic system runs parallel to the political history of the *Renaissance, the growth of the European nation-states, and the age of geographical exploration and discoveries. In order to promote their exports so as to achieve a favourable balance of trade, governments attempted to exclude foreign merchants from trading with their colonies, placed high tariffs on foreign wares, and encouraged exportable domestic industries. During the 16th century Spain was especially well placed to practice a mercantilistic policy with regard to her new American colonies. That it nevertheless declined economically in the 17th century, despite her continuous importation of precious metals from Mexico and Peru, underscored the weakness of the system.

E. F. Heckscher, *Mercantilism* (1931);
D. C. Coleman, ed., *Revisions in Mercantilism* (1969);
W. E. Minchinton, ed., *Mercantilism: System of Expediency* (1969).

MERCATOR, GERARDUS (Gerhard Kremer, 1512-94) The foremost cartographer of the 16th century. Born at Rupelmonde, Flanders, he studied at Louvain, where, in 1537, he published his first map of Flanders and, in 1538, his first map of the world. For the next 50 years he continued to produce maps, terrestrial globes and wrote treatises on cartography, geography and the principles of measurement, gradually outgrowing the influence of the ancient geographer Ptolemy. His most important innovation was a map for use in navigation, which he published in 1568. It introduced 'Mercator's projection', a system in which the meridians are represented by straight parallel lines at equal intervals, and the latitudes by straight parallel lines, at right angle to the meridians, at increasing intervals. M. was patronized and honoured by *Charles V. But, being harassed by the authorities of Louvain on account of his Protestant sympathies, he emigrated in 1552 to Duisburg in Germany, where he became the cosmographer of the Duke of Cleves. M.'s maps and terrestrial globes were distinguished by a care for detail and accuracy.

A. S. Osley, *Mercator; A Monograph on the Lettering of Maps in the 16th Century Netherlands* (1969).

MERCHANT ADVENTURERS So called because its members 'adventured' abroad. An English trading *guild, formed in London in the early 15th century. By mid-century it dealt largely in the export of cloth to the Netherlands, its Continental centre being first *Bruges, and after 1446, *Antwerp. The *Intercursus Magnus of 1496 had the effect of promoting the commerce of the M.A., whose extensive activities in the Netherlands continued until the 1560s, when the tension caused by the religious strife and the repressive rule of the Duke of *Alba drove it to Hamburg. Although it later regained a mart-town in Holland, the end of the 16th century saw a decline in the company's commercial supremacy.

MERCURIALE, GIROLAMO (1530-1603) Italian physician. Born in Forli, he studied at Bologna and Pavia, and practised in Rome. In 1569 he became professor of *medicine at Padua, and later was at the service of Emperor *Maximilian II, ending his career as a lecturer at the universities of Bologna and Pisa (1587-93). The author of works on diverse medical subjects, he is mainly remembered for *De arte gymnastica*, first published in Venice in 1573. It described and recommended gymnastic exercises for all conditions of age and health.

MERICI, ST. ANGELA (1474-1540) Italian founder of the *Ursulines. She entered a branch of the Franciscan Order, devoting herself to the aid of young girls and the care of sick women. In 1524 she went on a pilgrimage to the Holy Land. After her return she founded a school for girls in her own home, and in 1535 was joined by 12 other women in founding a religious congregation named after her patron St. Ursula. She was canonized in 1807.

MERULA, GIORGIO (c. 1430-94) Italian humanist. Born in Alessandria, he studied in Milan under *Filelfo, and afterwards worked as a private tutor in *Milan, and taught Greek and rhetorics in *Mantua and *Venice (1465-82). In 1483 *Ludovico il Moro invited him back to Milan where he began to write a history of the *Sforzas, while searching for historical documents. This led, in 1493, to the discovery by M.'s secretary of important Greek and Latin classical manuscripts in the monastery of Bobbio. M. published editions of Cicero, Cato and Plautus with commentaries.

MESTA A Spanish corporation which included all the great sheep-raisers of Castile. Originally established by Alfonso X in 1273, the M. attained a powerful position early in the 15th century, when it dominated Spain's thriving export of wool. Possessing its own court, finance and officials, it regulated the migration of the flocks between the plains of Estramadura and the Castilian highlands in search for pasture. The Crown favoured the organization because it was the backbone of an industry which supplied much of the royal revenues. With the decline of the commerce in wool in the reign of *Philip II, elements opposed to the corporation, such as the towns and the Church, won the upper hand and pressured the king to restrict its privileges. The decline of the M. during the 17th century reflected the general stagnation of the Spanish economy.

J. Klein, *The Mesta: A Study in Spanish Economic History* (1920).

MICHELANGELO (Michelangelo Buonarroti; 1475-1564) Italian sculptor, painter, architect and poet; the most influential personality of *Renaissance art. Born in Caprese, Tuscany, where his father was a magistrate, he belonged to a minor Florentine noble family. In 1488 he was apprenticed to Domenico *Ghirlandaio who taught him the elements of the *fresco, but he soon transferred to the school in the garden of San Marco

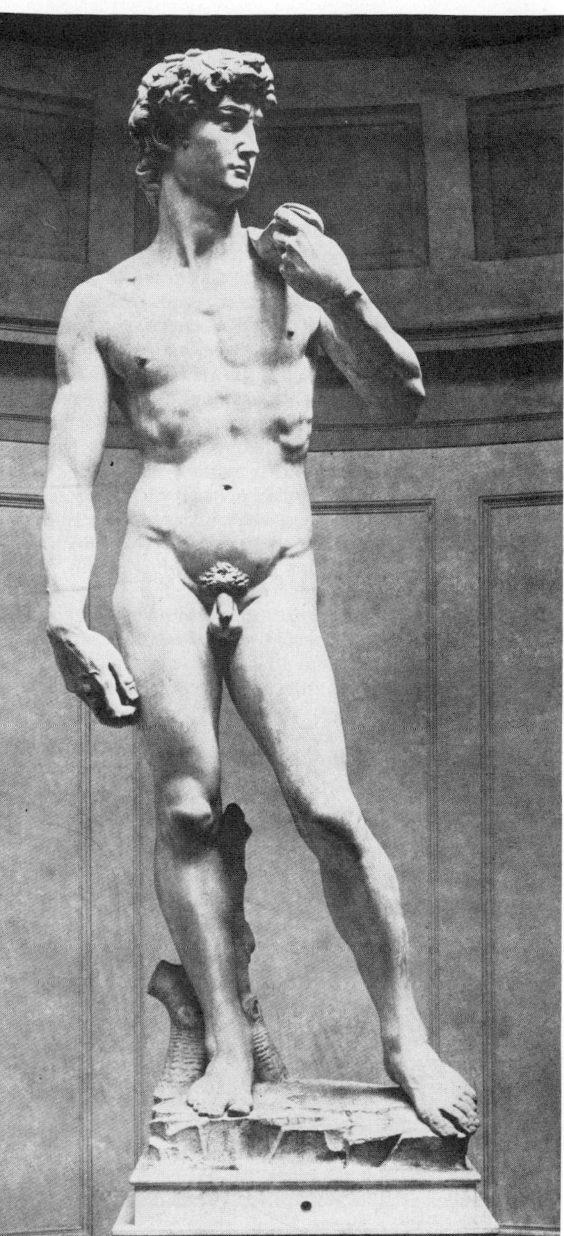

David *by Michelangelo*

which had been set up by Lorenzo de' *Medici where he became a pupil of the sculptor *Bertoldo di Giovanni, himself a former assistant of *Donatello. Showing exceptional talents, he was introduced to Lorenzo, for whom he probably did his earliest work, the relief of the *Battle of the Centaurs*, left unfinished at Lorenzo's death in 1492. In 1494, when the Medici fell from power, M. left Florence for Bologna where he worked on the tomb of St. Dominic and, for his living, taught the writings of *Dante and *Petrarch. In 1496 he was in Rome, where he produced the two marble statues which established his reputation: the first was the *Bacchus*, now at the Bargello, Florence, the second the *Pietà* (1497-1500), showing the grieving Mary with the body of Christ in her lap. One of the greatest works of art at *St. Peter's, the combination of a young, beautiful mother nursing the body of a full-grown dead man is nevertheless harmonious, and emanate a sense of sublime tragedy.

M. returned to Florence in 1501. For the next three years he worked on what has become the best-known Florentine work of art, the colossal *David*. Carved from a huge block of marble that 40 years earlier defied the chisel of *Agostino di Duccio, this confident-looking nude youth is almost 18 feet high and reveals the master's thorough knowledge of the human body. Though it is inspired by a classical sense of beauty it is full of modern virile energy. Evoking boundless admiration, the statue was immediately placed before the palace of the *Signoria* (1504); but in 1882 it was moved, for safety's sake, to Florence's Academy. While working on the *David*, M. produced other sculptures and painted the well-known *Holy Family*, now at the Uffizi. He then received a commission to paint a monumental fresco at the Palazzo Vecchio, which should have faced *Leonardo's *Battle of Anghiari*. He chose for his subject the battle of Cascina of 1364, but produced only the cartoon of the *Bathers*, showing nude figures in violent action. He left the project unfinished and, in the spring of 1505, went to Rome at the invitation of *Julius II to work on the Pope's monumental tomb.

M.'s first plan for this work was a huge free-standing structure with numerous sculptured figures. He spent the winter of 1506 cutting marble at the quarries of Carrara, but upon his return to Rome quarrelled with Julius and fled to his family in Florence, while the Pope besieged the republic with demands to send him back. He soon made up the quarrel and during 1507 was primarily busy with Julius' great bronze statue which commemorated the Pope's victory over Bologna; it was destroyed by the Bolognese in 1511. In 1508, back in Rome, he began the celebrated frescoes on the ceiling of the *Sistine Chapel. Portraying the Creation of the World and other scenes from the Book of Genesis, together with the prophets of the Old Testament and the pagan Sybils, the grandiose scheme was accomplished in four years, the painter having worked for most of the time lying on his back atop a high scaffold, assisted only by paint mixers. Its completion in 1512 confirmed M.'s name as the greatest living artist of his age, and originated the legend about the superhuman nature of his artistic drive. He immediately returned to work on Julius' tomb, but the Pope died in 1513, and the new contract which M. signed with the heirs reduced the original project, though it was still of majestic proportions. Of the second project M. completed during the next three years *Moses* and the two *Slaves*, which are in the Louvre. The work was then practically abandoned, although a third contract in 1516 was followed by another in 1532, and a final one in 1542. The old master's assistants then completed the small monument in S. Pietro in Vincoli, Rome, of which the fierce-looking seated Moses, holding the Tables of the Law, is the principle figure.

M.'s abandonment of Julius' tomb was a result of his employment by the new pope, *Leo X, a son of Lorenzo de' Medici. In 1516 he commissioned M. to do the façade of the church of S. Lorenzo in Florence. This was the

Moses *by Michelangelo, in S. Pietro in Vincoli, Rome*

artist's first great venture into *architecture, a field in which he was to exercise a tremendous influence, but the magnificent scheme came to nought after four years and much wasted effort. In 1524, after a period spent in lesser works, M. returned to the Medici sepulchral chapel, and also undertook the building of the *Laurentian Library, both attached to S. Lorenzo and commissioned by the new Medici pope, *Clement VII. The chapel, of a revolutionary design, was never properly completed, but it houses his famous tombs of Lorenzo, Duke of Urbino, and Giuliano, Duke of Nemours, both portrayed in sculpture, seated and in a contemplative mood, above two pairs of reclining allegorical figures. The work on the library and the chapel was interrupted in 1527 with the expulsion of the Medici from Florence. M., an ardent republican, threw himself into the politics of his city, going on diplomatic missions to Venice and taking charge of the construction of Florence's fortifications. In 1529 he fled the besieged city and at some point even considered going to France, but he returned to Florence in time to take part in her submission to the Medici in 1530. While most of the rebel leaders were punished, he was pardoned and allowed to continue his work on the Medici Chapel and the library. Finally, in 1534, he left Florence for Rome, where he was to live and work for the last 30 years of his life.

His first commission there was the painting of the *Last Judgment* on the wall behind the altar of the Sistine Chapel (1536-41). When shown to the public, the work created a sensation: Its style and mood were markedly different from the frescoes on the ceiling, serenity and harmony having been replaced with an intense brooding atmosphere of a crowded, fear-driven humanity. The success brought M. another commission from *Paul III to paint two more frescoes in the Vatican's new Pauline Chapel (1542-50), but these were less impressive. During these years the aging master was more active as an architect: in 1536 he had begun the reconstruction of a group of buildings on the Capitol, where he introduced big, two-story columns. In 1546 he was commissioned by Paul III to complete the *Farnese Palace, and redesigned Antonio da *Sangallo's façade and courtyard. In the same year he was also given his most important commission as an architect, namely the works on *St. Peter's. Although he here succeeded two great masters, *Bramante and Sangallo, M. did not hesitate to alter the plan, reverting to a centralized concept for the building. By the time of his death the supports and the lower portion of the dome had been built. The dome itself, the work of Giacomo della *Porta, differed substantially from M.'s idea, as were most of his other designs for St. Peter's. Nevertheless, the entire present structure reflects his conception more than that of any other architect. Additional architectural designs of M.'s were executed in S. Maria Maggiore (1560), in the reconstruction of Porta Pia (1561-64), and in the portion of the Baths of Diocletian which was converted into the church of S. Maria degli Angeli (1561), all in Rome.

Pietà *by Michelangelo, in the cathedral of Florence*

Michelangelo *by an anonymous artist*

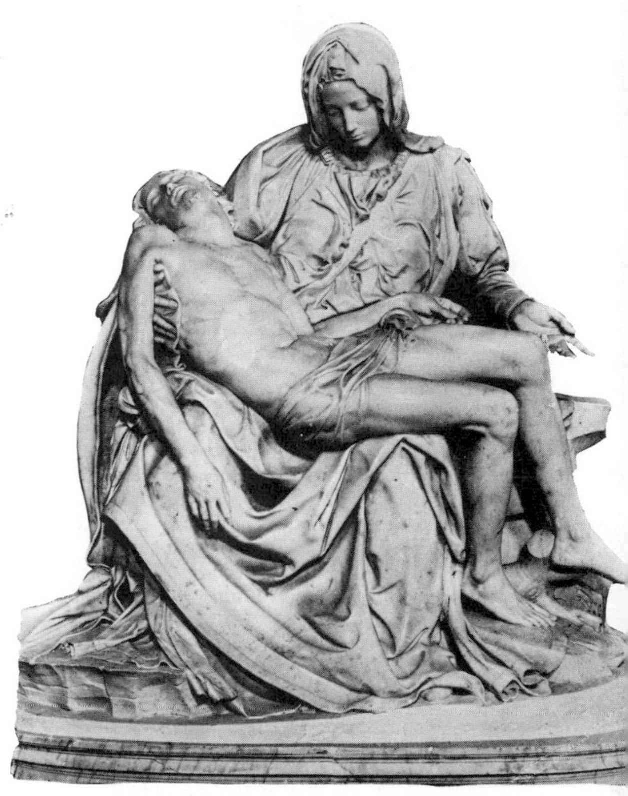

Pietà *by Michelangelo, in St. Peter's, Rome*

In his later years M. wrote poetry. He addressed sonnets to the youthful Tommaso Cavalieri and, from about 1537 until her death in 1547, was a close friend and literary companion of the poetess Vittoria *Colonna. Although often fragmentary in expression, his literary style had something of the force of his sculpture. At the same time he also produced numerous drawings, many of them in highly-finished red or black chalk, on classical themes and Christian subjects, especially the Crucifixion and Resurrection. On the verge of his 90th year he was still working in marble. His last sculptures were intensely religious works, of an entirely unclassical style, on the subject of *Pietà*.

M. is described as a man of medium height, his bearded face marred by a broken nose, the result of a blow he received in his youth from the sculptor *Torrigiano. He was given to frequent changes of mood, was known for his explosive temperament and an emotional intensity, which his contemporaries referred to in terms as *furia* and *terribilità*. He was incontestably the greatest sculptor who ever lived, and the person who established modern civilization's image of the artist. He was also a great genius in the arts of painting, drawing and architecture; the last-named he provided with a new vocabulary of ornaments and a novel treatment of mass and space, later adopted by the *Mannerists and the *Baroque. A *Neoplatonist, M. believed that the sculptural form was latent in the stone, the artist's mission being to 'liberate' it. His conception of man as a creature combining physical beauty, energy and intelligence endeared him to his contemporaries and posterity. Even today he is the single Renaissance genius most persistent in the awareness of modern man.

C. de Tolnay, *Michelangelo*, 5 vols. (1943-50);
R. J. Clements, *Michelangelo's Theory of Art* (1962);
M. Salinger, *Michelangelo: The Last Judgment* (1963);
R. W. Carden, ed., *Michelangelo: A Record of His Life as Told in His Own Letters and Papers* (1913);
M. Salmi, ed., *The Complete Work of Michelangelo* (1966);
R. Schott, *Mechelangelo* (1968).

MICHELOZZI, MICHELOZZO (1396-1472) Italian architect and sculptor. The son of an immigrant who came to Florence from Burgundy, he first worked as an assistant of *Ghiberti, and, from 1425 to 1438, in partnership with *Donatello. He then abandoned sculpture in favour of architecture. His patron Cosimo de' *Medici, commissioned him in 1444 to build the Medici palace, and, between 1458 and 1461, he constructed the Villa Medici in Fiesole near Florence. M. also introduced the Renaissance style outside Florence. In 1462 he worked in Milan and soon afterwards designed a palace in Dubrovnik. His style was strongly influenced by *Brunelleschi, whom he succeeded for a while as the architect in charge of the cathedral of Florence. He was responsible for numerous other buildings in and around that city.

L. Gori Montanelli, *Brunelleschi e Michelozzo* (1957).

The Palazzo Medici-Ricardi, Florence, by Michelozzo Michelozzi

MIEREVELT, MICHIEL VAN (1567-1641) Dutch painter. Born in Delft, he studied under Blocklandt at Utrecht (1579-83). He quickly established himself as a successful protraitist and headed a large studio. He became court painter to the princes of Orange, and was employed also by Archduke *Albert, in spite of his *Anabaptist affiliations. The creator of historical and mythological scenes in an elegant *Mannerist style, M. is estimated to have produced about 10,000 portraits.

MILAN Mistress of the rich plains of Lombardy in northern Italy, M. was ruled from 1262 by the *Visconti family. In 1395 Gian Galeazzo *Visconti was given the title of duke of M. by Emperor *Wenceslas. He began the building of the famous cathedral and of the Certosa in narby Pavia. His son Filippo Maria *Visconti died in 1447, leaving no heir, which prompted the inhabitants to renew the communal system of government. But this so-called Ambrosian Republic lasted only three years and, in 1450, Francesco *Sforza captured the government by force. The uninterrupted reign of the Sforzas ended in 1500, when *Ludovico Moro was ousted by the French invaders. Thereafter the city was headed by Massimiliano Sforze (1512-15), who was protected by *Maximilian I, but it was no longer an independent polity and, from 1515 to 1535, changed hands between the *Habsburgs and the *Valois. Thereafter, and until 1714, M. was a Spanish possession. M. was rather late in acquiring the cultural expressions of the Renaissance, though under Ludovico Moro it enjoyed artistic glory when both *Leonardo and *Bramante worked there. After it lost its political independence the city also declined as an economic force.

C. M. Ady, *A History of Milan Under the Sforzas* (1907); D. Muir, *A History of Milan Under the Visconti* (1924).

MILLENARY PETITION An appeal signed by some one thousand *Puritan clergymen to *James I on his arrival in England (1603), asking for changes in the established liturgy and rituals. Among the more significant demands were objections to the use of the sign of the cross in baptism, the ring in marriage and the mandatory surplicc in rituals. James' answer to the petition was to convene the *Hampton Court Conference.

MILTITZ, KARL VON (c. 1480-1529) German papal chamberlain and emissary. The scion of a noble Saxon family, he established himself at the papal court. In 1518 he was sent by *Leo X to present *Frederick the Wise with the Golden Rose, a greatly prized honour. The main aim of his mission was to convince the Elector of Saxony to abandon Martin *Luther. M. had three conferences with Luther, and even went so far as to attack the seller of *indulgences, Johann *Tetzel, but nothing came out of his efforts.

P. Kalkoff, *Die Miltitziade; eine kritische Nachlese zur Geschichte des Ablaßstreites* (1911).

MINIMS An order of friars founded in 1435 by St. Francis de Paola (1416-1507), with the aim of living a life of humility and abstention. Its rule, confirmed by Pope *Alexander VI in 1501, included clauses forbidding the consumption of meat, milk and eggs. The order spread quickly, attaining the height of its influence about the time of the beginning of the *Reformation, when its black-clad members possessed over 400 houses throughout Europe.

MINING AND METALLURGY The 15th century saw a great expansion in the production of metals, especially iron, necessitating extensive changes in the operation of mines. The most important European ore beds of iron, copper, silver and gold were located in *Bohemia, *Hungary, *Saxony, Silesia and Tyrol. Significant deposits were also exploited in *Sweden and *Spain. In the late Middle Ages all these were worked by small miners' companies but, in the 15th century, as they grew in importance, they began to employ thousands of workers each, and the possession of mines became a matter of great economic and political advantage. The Italian alum deposits of Volterra, for instance, containing a sulfate used in dyeing by the textile industry, were the object of a war in 1472, in which *Florence appropriated the mines. The papacy, on the other hand, made of its own alum mines at Tolfa, discovered in 1461, an important source of revenue with which it financed, among other things, preparations for war against the *Ottoman Turks. By the early 16th century some of the rising German

Blast furnaces, from Agricola's De re metallica

Recovering gold from amalgam, an illustration from a book on metallurgy (1580)

*banking families entered the European mining world. Taking advantage of the precarious finances of the *Habsburgs, they sought to win control of the rich mines, accepting rights of operation as securities for loans. The *Fuggers thus acquired the leases of mines in the Tyrol and Hungary, and later the right to operate the Spanish mercury mines of Almadén. Mercury being an essential component in a new technique of separating silver from copper, this gave the Fuggers a strong position in the European metal market.

The working of mines continued to be largely manual and performed under dangerous conditions, with primitive drainage and ventilation. But techniques of metallurgy of the 15th century showed marked improvement. Blast furnaces were developed to a degree of efficiency that permitted the casting of iron cannons. Most of the advances originated in Germany, where in the early 16th century some 100,000 people were employed in mining and the related industries. They operated large reverberatory furnaces for bronze smelting, made widespread use of water power for the working of metals, and through the *Stückofen*, a large brick furnace, could produce up to 50 tons of iron a year. The importance of the industries was reflected in the growing literature on the subject. At first anonymous booklets were published, such as the *Probierbüchlein* (1510), describing the methods of smelting, refining and assaying. *Biringuccio's *De la pirotechnia* (1540) was the first systematic account, followed by the classic work of Georg *Agricola *De re metallica* (1556). Here almost everything concerned with mining processes was painstakingly described, including working conditions, tools and hauling machines, methods of driving shafts and tunnels and the construction of timber supports. Not until the 18th century, when they underwent a revolution with the introduction of new industrial methods, did M. and M. see so much progress.

Besides iron, which was in relatively good supply, silver was available in the 16th century in unprecedentedly large quantities. About 1450 the *saiger* process was devised in Saxony, in which silver was extracted by alloying crude copper containing silver with lead, and then melting off the lead and recovering the silver. This process was employed in 1516, when silver was struck in Joachimsthal, Bohemia; the coins first known as *Joachmisthalers* were later named *thalers* and then *dollars*. The *saiger* process was also used in the Mexican and Peruvian mines of the *Spanish empire in America. But in 1557 the Spaniards discovered the *patio* process, in which mercury was used to form amalgams in order to refine both gold and silver from their ores. This process gave Europe the huge quantities of silver which caused the *price revolution in the second half of the 16th century. The principal Spanish silver mine in

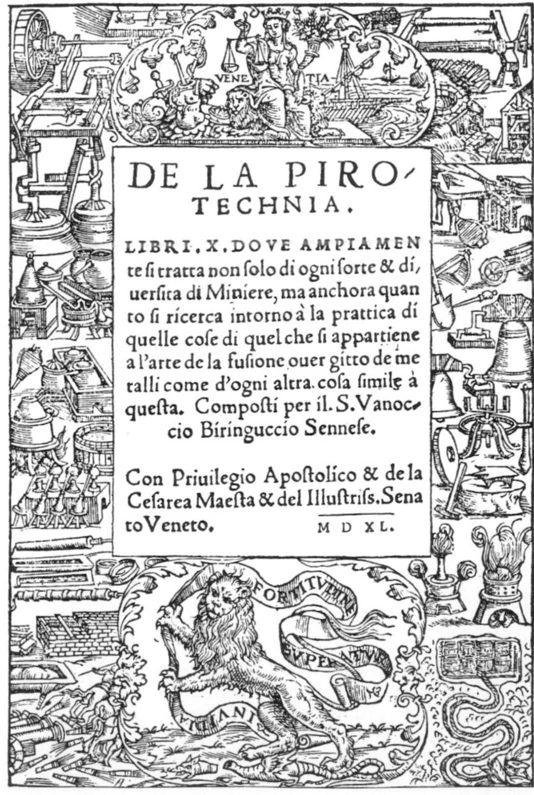
DE LA PIRO-
TECHNIA.

LIBRI.X.DOVE AMPIAMEN
te ſi tratta non ſolo di ogni ſorte & di,
uerſita di Miniere, ma anchora quan
to ſi ricerca intorno à la prattica di
quelle coſe di quel che ſi appartiene
a l'arte de la fuſione ouer gitto de me
talli come d'ogni altra coſa ſimile à
queſta. Compoſti per il. S. Vanoc-
cio Biringuccio Senneſe.

Con Priuilegio Apoſtolico & de la
Ceſarea Maeſta & del Illuſtriſ. Sena
to Veneto. M D XL.

Title page of Biringuccio's De la pirotechnia

America was the immensely rich mountain of Potosí, in the Andean region of what is now Bolivia. Its operation was facilitated by the existence of an independent source of mercury in Peru in the famous mine of Huancavelica.

T. A. Rickard, *Man and Metals*, 2 vols. (1932);
G. Schreiber, *Der Bergbau in Geschichte, Ethos und Sacralkultur* (1962);
J. Schreiber, *Le fer à travers les âges* (1956);
M. Bargallo, *La minería y la metalurgia en la América española durante la época colonial* (1955);
A. P. Whitaker, *The Huancavelica Mercury Mine* (1941).

MINO DA FIESOLE (c. 1430-84) Italian sculptor. Born in Poppi, he was the pupil of *Desiderio da Settignano, and worked both in Florence and Rome. He was most successful in his male busts, which are inspired by classical Roman sculpture. He also built sculptured tombs, such as that of Francesco Tornabuoni in S. Maria Sopra Minerva, Rome (1480), and Count Ugo in the Badia, Florence (1482).

MINTURNO, ANTONIO (?-1579) Italian cleric and literary theorist of the *Counter-Reformation. Born in Traetto, he went to Rome in 1521. His early literary works were in a secular vein, but later he began to advocate a Roman Catholic orientation in literature. He was made bishop of Uggento in 1559, and died as bishop of Crotone. His most important works were the two essays on poetry, the first *De poeta* (1559) in Latin, the second *L'arte poetica* (1594) in Italian.

MISSIONS In the Middle Ages attempts to propagate Christianity among the Moslems, associated with the names of St. Francis of Assisi and Ramón Lull, became most intense in the 13th century in consequence of the *crusades. This relationship between the processes of territorial expansion and missionary activity reappeared in a modified form during the Renaissance. Not surprisingly, it was Spain and Portugal, representing Roman Catholic Europe, which led the overseas missionary movement. The most active early missionaries in America came from the ranks of the Dominican, Franciscan and Augustinian friars, and included the towering figure of Bartolomé de *las Casas. The coming of the *Counter-Reformation brought about a change in the missionary cadres. New orders, such as the *Capuchins and especially the *Jesuits, entered the field. Jesuit missionaries registered their greatest successes in the possessions of Portugal – in Brazil, where Fathers *Anchieta and *Nobrega were active, and in *India, *Japan and *China, the arena of the greatest 16th-century missionary St. Francis *Xavier. Late in the century Matteo *Ricci and Roberto de *Nobili introduced new methods to the Eastern mission. The papacy increasingly concerned itself with directing the overseas missionary activities and, in 1622, the Sacred Congregation of the Propagation of the Faith was created by Gregory XV in Rome to supervise the works.

K. S. Latourette, *History of the Expansion of Christianity*, 7 vols. (1937-45);
S. C. Neill, *Christian Missions* (1964);
S. Delacroix, ed., *Histoire universelle des missions catholiques*, 4 vols. (1956-59).

MOCENIGO An aristocratic family which gave the Republic of *Venice several *dogi*, prelates, statesmen and military commanders. Tommaso M. (1343-1423) was *doge* from 1414, and made an agreement with the *Ottoman Turks. Pietro M. (1406-76) was *doge* during the last two years of his life only, but gave his name to a Venetian monetary unit which was in use throughout northern Italy. Alvise M. (1507-77), *doge* from 1570, headed the Republic at the victory of *Lepanto and the loss of Cyprus.

MOHACS, BATTLE OF (29 August 1526) A battle near the Hungarian town of M., where the *Ottoman Turks under *Suleiman I defeated the Hungarian nobility led by King Louis II. The king himself died in his flight from the battlefield, and Suleiman advanced and briefly occupied the Hungerian capital Buda. The battle marked a high point in the Ottoman penetration of Europe; in 1529 Suleiman failed in his attempt to capture *Vienna.

MOLCHO, SOLOMON (c. 1500-32) Would-be Messiah of the *Jews. The son of Portuguese **marranos*, he met David *Reuveni in Lisbon in 1525, and as a result returned to Judaism and left Portugal for Turkey. There he studied *Kabbalah and, in 1529, published in Salonica a work in Hebrew, in which he interpreted the Sack of *Rome as a sign of the coming redemption of the Jews. Appearing in Italy, he began to preach in the Jewish community of Ancona, but was denounced to the ecclesiastical authorities. He then went to Rome (1530) and Venice (1531). Upon his return to Rome he was condemned to death, but released by personal intervention of *Clement VII. In 1532 M. met again with Reuveni in the north of Italy. They decided to seek the aid of *Charles V, and to propose that the Emperor issue a Cyrus-like declaration, designed to enlist the Jewish people in the struggle against the *Ottoman Empire. Instead they were arrested at Regensburg by order of the Emperor. M. was brought to Mantua where he was tried and burnt at the stake. M.'s influence reached as far as Poland, many Jews believing him to be a true messiah. M. himself seems to have been strongly motivated by an urge to atone for his non-Jewish youth. He vehemently critized Christianity and openly sought martyrdom.

MOLINA, LUIS DE (1535-1600) Spanish theologian. A member of the *Jesuit Order, who taught at Coimbra and Evora, he published in 1588 a controversial work on the questions of free will and divine grace, *Concordia liberi arbitrii cum gratiae donis*. His ideas, emphasizing the divine prescience of free human action, and termed 'Molinism', were espoused by the Jesuits who defended them in bitter controversies with conservative Dominican theologians.

A. Bacilieri, *Luis de Molina* (1921);
F. Stegmüller, *Geschichte des Molinismus* (1935).

MOLUCCAS Also known as the Spice Islands. A group of islands situated in the South Pacific, between Celebes and New Guinea, they were a main source of cloves, nutmeg and other sought-after spices. The Portuguese established themselves there in 1514, but the Spaniards also claimed the islands, and sent out the expedition of *Magellan, which reached them by a westwardly route (1521). However, in 1529 the Portuguese claim to the M. was recognized. They rules the islands from their capital at Ternate, until supplanted by the Dutch in the first half of the 17th century.

MOLZA, FRANCESCO MARIA (1489-1544) Italian poet. Born in Modena, where he also died, M. had a reputation for scandalous living as much as for his Latin and Italian verses. He wrote en elegy on *Catherine of Aragon's separation from *Henry VIII, five short stories which were published in 1549 and his best-known work, a pastoral, *La ninfa tiberina* (1538).

MONASTERIES, DISSOLUTION OF THE The origins of the movement to suppress monasticism in England preceded the beginnings of the Henrician Reformation itself. As early as 1523, *Wolsey was granted a papal permission to close down forty small M., to raise money to establish Christ Church College at Oxford. Once the Act of *Supremacy (1534) was passed, the M. were marked as a prime target for reform. In February 1536, Parliament, acting upon reports of inspection conducted by *Cromwell, authorized the dissolution of all M. whose yearly income was less than £200. This led to increased criticism of monastic life and to government pressure which caused many of the great religious houses to declare their own dissolution. Then, in 1539, Parliament authorized a total suppression, which meant the end of about 500 M. A special court was set up to deal with the properties. Besides the fundamental effect on the structure of the church, the dissolution increased the income of the crown and created a secular majority in the Upper House of Parliament. The English gentry took much of the land which was put up for sale, and many peasants were driven out of their homes as a result of the change in ownership.

G. Baskerville, *English Monks and the Suppression of the Monasteries* (1937).

MONE, JEHAN (c. 1500-c. 48) Franco-Flemish sculptor. Born in Metz, he spent most of his career in the Netherlands, working in Brussels, *Antwerp and Malines, and becoming court sculptor to *Charles V. One of his first works for the Emperor was the high altar at Hal, near Brussels (1533). Another important project was the majestic tomb of Guillaume de Croy at Anghien. Excelling in the use of marble, M. was the first *Italianate sculptor of the Netherlands; he broke completely with the Gothic tradition.

MONTAGNA, BARTOLOMEO (c. 1450-1523) Italian painter. Born at Orzinuovi near Brescia, he was probably a pupil of *Mantegna and was influenced by Giovanni *Bellini at Venice. In 1483 he completed in the Scuola di San Marco, Venice, large works on biblical themes. Afterwards he resided mainly in Vicenza, where he enjoyed a great notoriety, but worked also in Verona and Padua. His religious paintings are characterized by the stately dignity of the figures, his *madonnas personifying the qualities of quiet, solemn nobility. His style was imitated by his son Benedetto M. (1481-1558), and other painters of Vicenza.

T. Borenius, *The Painters of Vicenza* (1909).

MONTAIGNE, MICHEL DE (1533-92) French essayist. Born to a wealthy family of Bordeaux, of old noble lineage on his father's side, he was a descendant of Spanish Jews on his mother's side. To ensure his mastering Latin, he was given a German tutor who could not speak French, and at the age of six was sent to the College de Guienne at Bordeaux, where he studied under *Buchanan and *Muret. At 13 he began to study law, probably at Toulouse. In 1554 he became a counsellor of the **parlement* of Bordeaux. For the next 17 years M. led the life of a well-placed official, occasionally taking part in military affairs and making a number of appearances at the court. He married in 1565 and, after the death of his father, succeeded to the title and the possessions of his family (1568). In 1571 he sold his magistracy and retired

Montaigne

to the Château de Montaigne, to devote himself to study and writing. The first two books of his *Essais* were published in 1580. In the same year M. set out on a journey to Switzerland, Bavaria, Venice and Rome, where he had an audience with the pope and stayed for five months. This journey was recorded in a *Journal de voyage*, a not particularly inspired work, which was discovered and published only in the 18th century. His sojourn at Lucca, where he was taking the baths for his health, was cut short by the announcement that he had been elected mayor of Bordeaux (1581). Returning immediately to France, he filled the post until 1585, when he resumed the life of contemplation in his rural retreat. In 1588 he published a new revised edition of the *Essais*, to which was added the Third Book. For this he visited Paris, where he met a young feminine admirer, Marie de Gournay (1565-1645). Some years later, after his death, she brought out a third edition of his work, based upon the second one and on the author's handwritten notes. M.'s acquaintance with the future *Henry IV, then the leader of the *Huguenots, caused him to be imprisoned by the *League when he visited Paris. He was soon released and returned to his château, where he remained until his death from complications of quinsy.

The *Essais* are collections of M.'s personal experiences and his reflections on the human condition. Among the themes discussed are sadness, fear, friendship, education, the force of habit, the value of classical literature, the art of conversation, prayer, death and cannibalism. An admirer of Plutarch and a master of the racy phrase and of a style marked by flexible construction, M. is the creator of the modern essay. But it is not just for his formal literary accomplishments that he became justly

St. Peter Distributing Alms, *a fresco by Masaccio in the Brancacci Chapel of Florence's S. Maria del Carmine*

A scene from the life of St. Catherine by Masolino, at the Basilica of S. Clemente, Rome

famous. Writing in an era of extreme intolerance he was highly rational in his views and arguments, and possessed a great critical sense, treating skeptically any preconceived idea. His writing is a true continuation of the humanist tradition. Emphasizing love of nature and commenting with appreciation on the practical wisdom of simple folk, he was always aware of the essential limitations of man. His essays, which were greatly influential in 17th-century France, were translated into English in 1603, inspiring such authors as *Bacon.

D. M. Frame, *Montaigne's Discovery of Man* (1955);
A. Cresson, *Montaigne, sa vie, son oeuvre* (1947);
A. M. Boase, *The Fortunes of Montaigne* (1935).

MONTANES, JUAN MARTINEZ (c. 1580-1649) Spanish sculptor. Born and raised in Andalusia, he worked for most of his life in *Seville, working chiefly in wood, which he then coloured. Between 1607 and 1620 he produced a number of impressive altars for the cathedral of Seville and neighbouring churches. He excelled in realistic depictions of the figure of Christ.

MONTANO, BENITO ARIAS (1527-98) Spanish theologian and orientalist. In 1562 he earned distinction as a theological adviser to the Council of *Trent. In 1568 *Philip II put him in charge of the publication of the polyglot *Bible, which came out of the press of *Plantin in *Antwerp (1571) in eight volumes. He was later suspected of having tampered with the authorized text of the Vulgate, but, with the support of his king, he was cleared and put in charge of the *Escorial library. M. was an authority on oriental languages and his Bible had a Syriac text in addition to the Hebrew. In 1575 he edited a Latin translation of the writings of the 12th-century Jewish traveller Benjamin of Tudela. He also published biblical commentaries.

MONTCHRESTIEN, ANTOINE DE (c. 1575-1621) French dramatist and economist. Educated in Caen, he published his first tragedy at the age of 21, and produced five more plays in the next seven years. In 1605 he killed a man in a duel and fled to England, where he got interested in economic questions. Upon his return to France he published the *Traité de l'économie politique* (1615), in which he suggested extensive social reforms. A man of action, M. settled in Orléans, where he sought to test his ideas by establishing a steel foundry. He was killed while fighting on the Protestant side during the *Huguenot uprising of 1621. His tragedies employed themes from Greek mythology, Roman history and the Bible, except for *L'Ecossaise*, which was about the life and death of *Mary Queen of Scots.

R. Lebegue, *La tragedie française de la Renaissance* (1943).

MONTEFELTRO An italian family which – except for short intervals – ruled *Urbino from 1234 to 1508. Champions of the interests of the Ghibeline party in central Italy, the family helped Emperor Henry VII in his offensive in Italy (1310-13), and continued a long struggle against the supporters of the *papacy. However, the enmity with Rome was ended during the rule of Antonio who, in 1377, recovered Urbino, adding later Gubbio (1388). His son Guidantonio married a relative of Pope *Martin V, who favoured the family in its feud against the *Malatestas of Rimini. Oddantonio M. was created duke in 1443. After his death in a conspiracy, his half-brother *Federico brought the family to the height of its power (1444-82). His own son *Guidobaldo was dispossessed in 1502 by Cesare *Borgia, but recovered the duchy a year later. With his death the line became extinct and was replaced by the *Della Rovere.

G. Franceschini, *Saggi di storia montefeltresca e urbinate* (1957).

MONTEMAYOR, JORGE DE (c. 1520-61) Spanish author. Of Portuguese and Jewish parentage, he was born in Coimbra and went to Spain in 1548, where he served as a musician to members of the royal family. He returned to Portugal in 1551, but soon went back to Spain. Later he fought with the Spanish army in the Netherlands, but found his death in a fight over a woman in Italy. M. was the author of a famous *pastoral novel, *La Diana* (1559), which was translated into French, English and German, going through almost 40 editions in the next 100 years. The story of elegant shepherd lovers in an idealized nature setting, the book influenced works in this genre by *Sidney and *D'Urfé. M. also wrote poems and plays.

J. B. Avalle-Arce, *La novela pastoril española* (1959).

MONTESINOS, ANTONIO DE (c. 1486-c. 1530) Early Spanish defender of the American Indians. A member of the Dominican Order, which he had joined in 1502, he went to Hispaniola in 1510. There he preached, in the following year, a sermon against the enslaving of the Indians. This aroused the anger of the Spanish colonists, and he had to return to Spain. There he apparently influenced the enactment of the Laws of Burgos (1512), the first attempt to regulate the relations between Spaniards and Indians, which inaugurated the **encomienda* system. M. returned to America where he remained for much of the rest of his life. The author of a tract on the legal rights of the Indians, he was soon followed by a man of greater stature, Bartolomé de *las Casas.

MONTEVERDI, CLAUDIO (1567-1643) Italian musician; the first great composer of *operas. Born in Cremona, he studied composition in *Mantua and, in 1602, succeeded his teacher Ingegneri as chief musician for the dukes of *Gonzaga. His first opera, *Ariana*, was composed in 1607 to celebrate the marriage of his patron, his second, *Orfeo* (1608), scored an immediate success and had a decisive influence on the evolution of modern opera. In 1613 M. became *maestro di cappella* of St. Mark's in Venice. Here he composed many liturgical works which were distinguished by their ornamental characteristics. Ten years before his death he became a priest.

A. Arnold, *Claudio Monteverdi* (1963);
L. Schrade, *Monteverdi* (1950).

MONTI DI PIETA Charitable lending institutions which loaned small sums of money on the security of pawned items. The M. di P. were established as a morally-sanctioned answer to the growing practice of high-interest lending in the latter part of the Middle Ages. They were set up by the Franciscans, the first institution being established in Perugia in 1461. The M. di P. spread quickly in Italy. By the 16th century they had acquired a mixed character of pawn shops and savings banks. Low interest rates were charged on loans secured against pawned objects; also, deposits were accepted from small investors and interest paid to them. The introduction of the M. di P. involved their promoters in a controversy: their opponents argued that their institution was an attempt to legalize usury. The debate was finally decided in favour of M. di P. during the pontificacy of *Leo X.

Rather than having an economic impact *per se,* the M. di P. signalled a general change of attitude with regard to the problems of lending, financing and interest.
B. N. Nelson, *The Idea of Usury* (1949);
J. T. Noonan, *The Scholastic Analysis of Usury* (1957).

MONTLUC, BLAISE DE (1502-77) French military commander and historian. The eldest son of a noble family from Gascony, he served under *Bayard in Italy and won fame in the eight months defence of Siena (1555). He also participated in the French *Religious Wars and, in 1574, was made marshal of France by *Henry III. His posthumous reputation, however, rests on the *Commentaires*, his memoirs which give an admirable description of contemporary military tactics. The work is written in a conversational manner and is considered a literary gem.

MONTMORENCY, ANNE DE (1493-1567) Duke and Constable of France. Named after his godmother, *Anne of Brittany, he was brought up with the future *Francis I, and became one of the king's trusted military commanders. He distinguished himself in the battle of *Marignano (1515), defended Mézières (1521) and was taken prisoner with the king at *Pavia (1525). In 1538 Francis made him constable, the highest military office, but in 1541 he left the court, returning only in the reign of *Henry II, who made him a duke (1551). M. was again taken prisoner at St. Quentin (1557), regaining his freedom only with the signing of the Treaty of *Cateau-Cambrésis (1559). By this time, however, the *Guises had become the main influence at the court, and M., who joined them, generally followed their lead. He won the first battle of the *Religious Wars at Dreux (1562), but was himself taken prisoner for the third time. Released by the Peace of Amboise (1563), he died fighting the *Huguenots in the battle of St. Denis (1567).

MOR, ANTHONIS (c. 1517-77) Dutch painter. Born in Utrecht, he was a pupil of Jan van *Scorel, and became a court painter of the Spanish rulers of the Netherlands, where he was patronized by *Granvelle, the future cardinal. In the 1550s he visited Italy and worked in Spain. His painting of *Mary Tudor suggests that he may have also visited England. M. was the master of the full-length courtly portrait in realistic style, and exercised considerable influence in northern Europe.

MORAIS, FRANCISCO DE (c. 1500-72) Portuguese novelist. A treasurer of the household of King *John III, he came in 1540 to Paris as secretary to the Portuguese ambassador. There he began to write *Palmeirim de Inglaterra*, a romance of chivalry, which became immensely popular, and is considered, after **Amadis de Gaula*, the second great work in this genre. Completed about 1544, it was first published in Spanish translation (1547), the first Portuguese edition coming out in 1567. Written in a clear style, the romance was praised even by *Cervantes. M. also wrote three moral dialogues. He was assassinated in Evora.
H. Thomas, *Spanish and Portuguese Romances of Chivalry* (1920).

MORALES, CRISTOBAL DE (1500-53) Spanish composer. Born in *Seville, he was trained there and in 1526 became choirmaster at Avila. He later went to Rome, where he joined the papal choir (1535-45). During this period he wrote most of his 25 masses, many *motets and other liturgical works, which brought him wide acclaim. After his return to Spain, M. was choirmaster at Toledo (1545-47), then entered the service of the duke of Arcos. After 1551 he lived in Málaga, where he died. A prolific author, he ranks with *Palestrina and *Victoria as one of the most powerful masters of 16th century religious *music.

MORALES, LUIS DE (c. 1509-86) Spanish painter. Born in Badajoz, he is sometime considered the first Spanish painter of the Renaissance whose work displays a distinctive national character. M. painted only religious subjects, which expressed intense devotional feelings and brought him the popular nickname El Divino. But *Philip II, who invited him to participate in the decoration of the *Escorial, disliked his *Christ Carrying the Cross* and discharged him. His style, inspired by the Italian masters, especially *Leonardo, is essentially *Mannerist. His chief work are 20 panels on the life of Christ, painted between 1563 and 1568 for the church of Arroyo del Puerco.
J. A. Gaya-Nuño, *Luís de Morales* (1961);
E. du Gué Trapier, *Luís de Morales and Leonardesque Influences in Spain* (1953).

MORALITIES (or Morality Plays) A form of early Renaissance drama which came to be so designated because of their didactic nature. Purporting to convey an essential moral truth, their protagonists personified abstract qualities, namely, basic types of virtue or vice. The M. were a 15th-century development of the *Mysteries and Miracle plays, and reached the height of their popularity on the eve of the Reformation. The famous English Morality Play, *Everyman*, was adapted from the Dutch

Title page of an English morality play

Sir Thomas More *by Holbein the Younger*

version about 1500. The M. signified the transition from religious to a secular form of *drama. As time went on they tended to become less allegorical and more realistic.
H. Craig, *English Religious Drama of the Middle Ages* (1955).

MORE, SIR THOMAS (1477-1535) English humanist and statesman. His father was a barrister and then a judge at the King's Bench. M. received his education at St. Anthony's school in London; in the household of John Morton (archbishop of Canterbury and chancellor); at Oxford (1492-94), and later prepared for the bar at New Inn and at Lincoln's Inn. While studying Common Law, M. resided in the Carthusian Monastery and even contemplated becoming a priest.

At Oxford M. made the acquaintance of the English humanists – *Grocyn, *Colet, *Linacre – who had lately returned from Italy imbued with the new learning. From Linacre M. received his first instruction in Greek and was later to become an ardent defender of Greek studies in Oxford and of *Erasmus' version of the Greek New Testament. Erasmus and M. first met in 1497 and developed a life-long intimate friendship. Erasmus described M.'s household as a new Platonic academy, since M. devoted much of his time to the education of his family, including his wife and daughters. The attractive atmosphere of that household was immortalized in the drawing by *Hans Holbein the Younger, who also painted a portrait of M. Together they translated some of Lucian's dialogues into Latin and when, in 1509, Erasmus wrote his famous *Praise of Folly* (*Moriae Encomium*), he dedicated it to M.

Another important influence on M. was the Italian humanist of the preceding generation, *Pico della Mirandola. In 1510 M. published a life of Pico together with translations from his works and letters. Between 1513 and 1518 the Latin and English versions of M.'s *Life of Richard III* came out – the first masterpiece of English historiography. This work inspired *Shakespeare and suceeding historians, and is at least partly responsible for the popular but inaccurate portrayal of Richard III as a tyrant and murderer.

M. is best remembered, however, for his *Utopia*, which was published in Louvain in 1516. The word was coined by him from the Greek *ou-topos* (no-place) and *eu-topos* (good-place). *Book I* is an acute analysis of the social, economic and political evils of contemporary Europe, and England in particular. *Book II* depicts an ideal imaginary society in the New World, where all evils were abolished through communism, the absence of money and rigid supervision. The ambiguity and ironic tone of the work left it open to many interpretations and various ideological camps were later to claim it for their own.

In the happy island of Utopia religious tolerance allowed the worship of different gods, and only a few basic tenets were compulsory. But in reality M. was not a tolerant man. Like his humanist friends, he realized the need to correct certain abuses in the Catholic Church, yet he strongly opposed the Lutheran Reformation which endangered the hegemony of the papacy. He wrote many anti-heretical works, especially in controversy with the English Protestants (*The Confutation of Tyndale's Answer*, 1532-33). In his official capacity he severely persecuted heretics and even described himself as *hereticis molestus*.

M.'s political career began in 1504, when he became a member of parliament. Later he became one of the two under-sheriffs of London (1510-18). In 1518 he was appointed the king's Master of Requests. On various occasions he was the king's emissary in diplomatic negotiations on the Continent. In 1521 M. was knighted and appointed sub-treasurer to the king. In 1523 he was elected speaker of the House of Commons. After the fall from power of *Cardinal Wolsey, in 1529, M. was made Lord Chancellor – the first layman to hold this office. But his opposition to *Henry VIII on the issue of the divorce from *Catherine of Aragon soon made his position intolerable and he resigned from office in May 1532. But, the king would not allow him to spend the rest of his life in quiet retirement: in April 1534 M. was committed to the Tower for refusing to swear the oath to the Act of Supremacy, which made the king supreme head of the Church of England. During his imprisonment he wrote *A Dialogue of Comfort Against Tribulation*. On 1 July 1535, M. was indicted for high treason and was put to death five days later. *John Fisher, bishop of Rochester, and the Carthusian monks shared his fate; they were the first martyrs of the English Reformation. M. was canonized by Pope Pius XI in 1935.
R. W. Gibson and J. M. Patrick, *St. Thomas More: A Preliminary Bibliography of His Works and of Moreana to the Year 1750* (1961);
E. E. Reynolds, *The Field is Won: The Life and Death of Saint Thomas More* (1968). (ME)

MOREELSE, PAULUS (1571-1638) Dutch painter and architect. Born in Utrecht, he was a pupil of *Mierevelt

Portrait of a Young Man *by Moretto*

of Delft. In 1596 he was established as a master in his native town, and not long afterwards visited Italy. In 1611 he helped to found the Utrecht painters' *guild, of which he was the first head. Like his teacher, he excelled in portraits, which were very popular and brought him substantial income.

MOREL, JACQUES (c. 1395-1459) French sculptor. Born in *Lyon, he belonged to a family of sculptors, both his father and grandfather having been employed at Avignon. In 1418 he was put in charge of the works at Lyon's cathedral, completing the tomb of cardinal de Saluces, which was destroyed in 1562. Later, he executed the tombs of the duke of Bourbon and his wife at Souvigny (1448-53), and the tomb of *René of Anjou at Angers, which was left incomplete at the time of his death. A follower of the art of *Sluter, his style is less powerful, but reveals considerable technical skill.

MORETTO (1498-1554) The nickname, meaning 'the dark one', bestowed on the Italian painter, Alessandro Bonvicino. Born near Brescia, he studied and worked mainly in that city, but he was also a student of *Titian's and was influenced by him and other Venetian painters. M. excelled in full-length portraits in decorative settings with deep perspective. His works in oil are more important than his frescoes; his art is characterized by an air of peacefulness. He was the teacher of *Moroni.

MORISCOS REBELLION, THE (1568-70) Forcibly converted from Islam to Christianity after the conquest of *Granada (1492), the M. accumulated many grievances over their treatment by the Old Christians of Andalusia, and clung to their old customs and to the Arabic language. The rebellion, a reaction to a royal decree of 1567 which had prohibited the old customs, dress and language, was extremely difficult to suppress and lasted over two years. *Philip II then ordered the dispersion of the M. throughout Spain and brought thousands of families from the northern regions into Andalusia.

MORONE, DOMENICO (c. 1442-c. 1517) Italian painter. A Veronese, he headed a school of painting influenced by *Mantegna. His earliest fresco in Verona dates from 1471. In 1494 he painted for Francesco *Gonzaga *The Expulsion of the Bonaclosi*, a large battle scene, at the ducal palace in Mantua. His later work was done in collaboration with his son and pupil Francesco (*c.* 1471-1529), who continued to work in the classically inspired manner.

MORONE, GIOVANNI (1509-80) Italian cardinal. Born to a wealthy Milanese family, he was made Bishop of Modena in 1529 and, in 1536, was sent as papal legate to Germany. M. then identified himself with a small but prominent minority of Catholic reformers, who were willing to address the issues raised by the Protestants. He was created cardinal in 1542 and participated in the preparations for the Council of *Trent, but in 1557 was imprisoned on the orders of *Paul IV and charged with heresy. Cleared of these charges under Paul IV's successor, *Pius IV, he presided over the final sessions of the Council of Trent (1563) and served as a papal diplomatic emissary. In his later years his orientation changed to one of stringent orthodoxy.

MORONI, GIAMBATTISTA (c. 1525-78) Italian painter. The pupil of *Moretto at Brescia, his first independent works date from about the time of his master's death (1554). M. further developed the Lombard full-length portrait in a style of straightforward, quiet realism. Praised for his portraits by the old *Titian himself, he was less original in his religious works.

MORTON, JOHN (c. 1420-1500) English cardinal and statesman. Educated at Oxford, where he studied law, he was for a long time identified with the Lancasterian

The Young Tailor *by Moroni*

Charles Bount, Baron of Mountjoy

party but, about 1473, made his peace with *Edward IV, who employed him on diplomatic missions. Made bishop of Ely (1479), he was arrested by *Richard III (1483), but soon joined the future *Henry VII on the Continent. After the latter's accession to the throne, M. became his adviser. In 1486, M. was made Archbishop of Canterbury, and he was created cardinal in 1493. A patron of learning, M. was frequently blamed for the harsh methods which the royal administrators used to raise money. The taxes and forced loans raised during this period were known as 'Morton's fork', and there were frequent demands for his removal from office.

MOSER, LUCAS German painter of the St. Mary Magdalen altar in the church of Tiefenbronn near Pforzheim (1431). Plainly influenced by Flemish masters like *Campin and van *Eyck, this is the only extant work by this artist and is equally famous for the inscription that the artist added: 'Cry, Art, and mourn loudly, no one now desires you!'

MOSTAERT, JAN (c. 1475-1555) Dutch painter. Born in Haarlem, he was trained in his native town, but by 1504 was already sufficiently renowned to become court painter of *Margaret of Austria, regent of the Netherlands. Accompanying his patroness on her travels, M. visited Italy and assimilated some Italianate motifs. Essentially, however, he retained the older style of the Netherlands, as may be seen in his best-known work, the *Deposition* tryptich in Brussels. He painted many portraits and imaginary scenes of the New World. He died in Haarlem, where many of his works were destroyed by fire in 1576.
S. Pierron, *Les Mostaert* (1912).

MOTET A musical term referring to vocal works, with or without accompanyment, intended for liturgical use. Originating in France in the 13th century, where it was particularly favoured by Philippe de Vitry (1291-1361), the M. became popular in other European countries during the 15th century. Rich M.s, employing choral polyphony, were composed by *Ockeghem and *Obrecht, and in the 16th century, when it reached its height, many M.s were written by *Lasso, *Palestrina and *Byrd. The M. retained its popularity in the early 17th century, but subsequently lost favour to the *cantata*.
H. Leichtentritt, *Geschichte der Motette* (1908);
M. Bukofzer, *Studies in Medieval and Renaissance Music* (1950).

MOUNTJOY, CHARLES BLOUNT, BARON OF (1563-1606) English lord-lieutenant of *Ireland. One of the rising English military commanders in the latter part of the reign of *Elizabeth I, he was at first *Essex' rival for the favours of the Queen, but later became his friend and, in 1597, went with him on the ill-fated expedition to the Azores. In 1600 he succeeded Essex as governor of Ireland and, by 1602, completely crushed the Spanish-supported rebellion of Hugh *O'Neill. He continued in office under *James I, who made him Earl of Devonshire.

Portrait of a Young Man *by Jan Mostaert*

MÜHLBERG, BATTLE OF (24 April 1547) The decisive battle in the *Schmalkaldic War between *Charles V and the German Protestant princes. Having subjugated south Germany, the Emperor appeared with his Spanish army in *Saxony. Crossing the Elbe River at M., he defeated the Elector *John Frederick I and took him prisoner. As a result of the defeat, Protestant resistance collapsed and in the next diet the Emperor was able to dictate the *Augsburg Interim (1548).

MULTSCHER, HANS (c. 1400-67) German painter. Born in Reichenhofen, he went about 1427 to Ulm, where he worked for much of the rest of his life. His best work is the Wurzbach altarpiece (1437) of eight panels, now in Berlin, but to him is also attributed the high altar of the cathedral of Sterzing in Tyrol, dated 1457. His figures, probably in imitation of contemporary Flemish painting, are gross and have an air of caricature about them. M. also sculpted in wood.

N. Rasmo, *Der Multscher-Altar in Sterzing* (1963).

MÜNSTER, ANABAPTIST KINGDOM OF (1534-35) The capital of Westphalia in northwest Germany, M. had been, since the late 15th century, a centre of *humanism. During the 1520s the town espoused the Lutheran Reformation and, in 1532, rose against its bishop-prince,

Adoration of the Kings *by Hans Multscher, a panel from the Wurzbach altarpiece*

Thomas Münzer in the Battle of Mülhausen

led by the preacher Bernt *Rothmann, and a rich cloth merchant Bernt *Knipperdollinck. In 1533 many Dutch *Anabaptists arrived in the city and converted Rothmann to their beliefs. The stage was thus set for the appearance of Jan Matthys, a baker from Haarlem and a passionate follower of Melchior *Hofmann, who was preceded by his young emissary, Jan *Bockelson. In February 1534 an internal revolution took place. The Anabaptist proletariat seized the government from the Lutheran middle classes and drove them out of the city. Swept with chiliastic expectations, the town was declared a 'New Jerusalem', whose people would be spared the wrath of God on the coming day of judgment. Matthys, assuming dictatorial powers, confiscated the property of the rich and began to destroy all the books except the Bible. Meanwhile the bishop-prince had begun to lay siege to M., and early in April Matthys was killed while leading a sortie against the besiegers. The government of the town was promptly taken over by Bockelson, a charismatic figure who instituted polygamy and in August proclaimed himself king. Initially successful in defending the town against the bishop's mercenary troops, he resorted increasingly to terror as conditions grew worse. On 24 June 1535, having been brought to the brink of starvation, the town was taken; Bockelson was captured alive, while most of his followers perished in a massacre. The episode, which was used to discredit the entire Anabaptist movement, had actually occurred in response to an unusual set of conditions, an overpowering moral and religious climate and the influence of strange personalities. It remains the most famous example of mass ecstatic antinomianism in modern history.

N. Cohn, *The Pursuit of the Millennium* (1957), pp. 272-306.

MÜNSTER, SEBASTIAN (1488-1552) German geographer, cosmographer and Hebrew scholar. Entering the Franciscan Order at seventeen, he was taught by Konrad *Pellikan, who, in 1504, published the first Hebrew grammar. The latter came to favour the Reformation, and so did M. from about 1524. From 1529 until his death he taught at Basle, where he published the first German translation of the Bible from the Hebrew. His best-known work is the *Cosmographia univesalis* (1544), a geographical description of the world, which was written in German and later translated into several languages. M. also wrote Hebrew and Chaldee grammars.

MÜNZER, THOMAS (c. 1490-1525) German religious leader and revolutionary. A priest who had studied at Leipzig and Frankfurt, he joined the Reformation very early, and in 1520 became a preacher at Zwickau. There he enunciated radical religious and social ideas, which led to his expulsion after a brief and stormy ministry. M. then tried to settle in Bohemia and, when he failed, went to the small town of Alstedt (1523), where his bold liturgical innovations attracted large audiences. By this time he had become a fierce opponent of *Luther, whom he accused of moral opportunism, and it was at the latter's instigation that he had to leave (July 1524). Finding shelter at Mühlhausen, M. reached the climax of his career when he led the rebellious peasants in Thuringia. Preaching the imminent coming of the Kingdom of God and the destruction of all earthly rulers, he also spoke of equality and a kind of communist social order. On 15 May 1525, he and his peasant followers were defeated and dispersed in a battle near Frankenhausen. Captured in his hiding place, he was tortured and executed.

A. Meusel, *Thomas Müntzer und seine Zeit* (1952);
E. Sommer, *Die Sendung Thomas Münzers* (1948);
N. Cohn, *The Pursuit of the Millennium* (1957), pp. 251-71.

MURAD I (1326-89) Sultan of the *Ottoman Turks. Succeeding his father Orkhan about 1360, he began the conquest of the Balkan peninsula, and made Adrianople his capital. M. then defeated an expedition of forces from the West and, in 1371, crushed the Bulgarians at the battle of Samokovo. In 1382 he conquered Sophia and Nish. Although he was killed at the battle of Kossovo, by this time the Ottomans were in control of most of the Balkans and had reduced the Byzantine empire to a state of vassalage.

I. Beldiceanu-Steinherr, *Recherches ser les actes des regnes des sultans Osman, Orkhan et Murad I* (1967).

MURAD II (1404-51) Sultan of the *Ottoman Turks from 1421. Succeeding his ineffectual father Mehemmed I (1413-21), he first had to suppress a rebellion in Asia Minor, before continuing the Turkish advance in the Balkan peninsula. In 1430 he conquered Salonika but, in 1443, was defeated at Nish by a *crusade of Christian forces, composed chiefly of Hungarians, Poles and Germans and led by Janos *Hunyadi. The following year M. dealt the crusaders a crushing blow at the battle of Varna. Then for two years he retired from the government, which was taken over by his son, but upon his return conquered the Morea (1446) and later defeated the Hungarians again at the second battle of Kossovo (1448).

MURAD III (1546-95) Sultan of the *Ottoman Turks from 1574. The son and successor of *Selim II, M. was mostly concerned with the eastern borders of his empire, engaging in a long military conflict with Persia, from whom by 1590 he had wrested Tabriz and Hamadan, and conquered Tiflis and vast territories around the Caspian Sea. In 1593 he began to war with *Austria, and the conflict continued after his death until 1606. However, his reign actually witnessed the decline of Ottoman power, as a result of administrative fragmentation, exhaustion from constant wars, financial difficulties and the moral deterioration of the elite military corps, the *Janissaries.

MURET, MARC-ANTOINE (1526-85) French humanist scholar. A young teacher at the Collège de Guienne in Bordeaux, where he taught *Montaigne and wrote a Latin tragedy (1546), he lectured in succession in Poitiers, Paris and Toulouse and, from 1555 to 1558, taught in Venice. In 1563 he went to Rome, where he passed the rest of his career. M. published numerous editions of classical Latin authors, including Catullus, Horace, Terence and Cicero. His commentaries on Plato, Aristotle and Tacitus were likewise admired. Though a Frenchman, he was one of the last great classical scholars of the Renaissance in Italy.

C. Dejob, *Marc-Antoine Muret; un professeur français en Italie* (1881; reprinted 1970).

MURMELIUS, JOHANNES (1480-1517) German humanist educator. A native of the duchy of Guelder, he was a pupil of *Hegius at Deventer. Later he taught at the cathedral school of Münster, at Alkmar (1513) and finally in Deventer. His most influential work was *Pappa puerorum*, a Latin grammar.

MURNER, THOMAS (1475-1537) German satirist. Born in Alsace, he joined the Franciscan Order in his youth, but from 1495 devoted several years to travel and study in Freiburg, Paris and Cracow. Settling in *Strassburg (1502), he published several satirical works in a popular style, full of bitter criticism of the lax morality in the Church. His growing fame brought him the title of imperial poet laureate, bestowed by *Maximilian I (1506). Although he championed the cause of reform in his writings, M. opposed *Luther. He spent a few years at Lucerne, where he organized opposition to *Zwingli. In 1529 he had to leave, and ended his life in his native town in Alsace. Of his works, the *Narrenbeschwörung* (1512) is probably the best known.

MURRAY, JAMES STEWART, EARL OF (c. 1531-70) Regent of Scotland. The natural son of *James V of Scotland by Lady Margaret Erskine, he was the older half-brother of *Mary Queen of Scots. He attended the University of St. Andrew's and, in 1548, accompanied Mary to France. Afterwards M. took an active part in Scottish politics. In 1560 he supported the English efforts to put an end to the French influence in Scotland, though he favoured the return of Mary from France (1561), and served as her home secretary. But after her marriage to *Darnley, he became estranged from the Queen, and following her abdication at Lochleven, took on the regency (1567). When Mary escaped to England, M. produced the so-called Casket Letters, which purported to prove her complicity in the murder of Darnley (1568). He was assassinated by a political opponent, James Hamilton.

MUSCOVY COMPANY An English commercial company, incorporated in 1555, following *Chancellor's voyage to Russia. The volume of trade conducted by the M.C. between England and Russia was limited, but it made continuous efforts to search for a north-east passage to Asia.

MUSIC Refined music in Mediaeval Europe consisted of religious *hymns. At first represented by the purely vocal and monophonic Gregorian chant, it was later accompanied by the primitive organ and developed the florid polyphonies which gave birth to the *Motet. In the 12th century appeared the first performers of secular songs in the vernacular such as the French *troubadours*, and later the German *Minnesinger*. By the 14th century secular music became popular in the courts of kings and princes, where, according to contemporary depictions, a variety of musical instruments was in use, including several types of fiddles, trumpets and drums and an early

Signa
Repetitionis.
Comunientiæ.
Concordantiæ.
Finalis.

PARADIGMATA
graduum.
DISCANTVS.
Prolatio maior.

A page out of Listenius' Musica *published in Leipzig*

version of the clavichord. The growing complexity of the art gave rise to the school known as *ars nova*, from the title of a work by its main founder, Philippe de Vitry (1291-1361). Employing in a more liberal way religious and secular musical elements, it enriched the rhythmic and melodic expression. The best-known composers of the 14th century were the Frênch Guillaume de Machaut (*c.* 1300-77), an author of many secular songs and the creator of the first Mass, and Francesco Landino (1325-97), a blind Italian who wrote secular music of genuine feeling and subtlety. The complexity of 14th-century secular music is exemplified by the *caccia*, a piece written for two voices, which dealt with such subject matter as hunting scenes – hence the origin of the term – in strict canonic imitation.

In the 15th century the centre of musical creativity moved north, while reacting to the varied complexity of the recent past by returning to the tradition of harmonic suavity. English composers like John Dunstable (*c.* 1385-1453) became famous at that time, but the leading role was played by Franco-Flemish composers at the ducal court of *Burgundy, notably the great Guillaume *Dufay (*c.* 1400-74). Of the other outstanding representatives of the Flemish School, Jean *Okeghem and Jacob *Obrecht contributed to harmonic unity and extended the range of voices, while *Josquin Després and Heinrich *Isaak developed the balanced, soaring polyphony, which reflected the artistic temper of the High Renaissance. This brought to perfection the technique of counterpoint, as recognized by the foremost contemporary musical theorist, Johannes *Tinctoris. At the same time, modern musical notation began to emerge from a series of simplifications of complex older systems. The process of the development and diffusion of musical composition was in turn accelerated by the new *printing industry. Most music, however, was still written for vocal performance. Instrumental music was just making its appearance, though it progressed rapidly during the next hundred years. By far the most popular instrument was the lute, followed by the major instrument of liturgical music, the organ. By the end of the 15th century there were also several types of keyboard instruments, but ensembles were not standardized and reflected the number and type of players available.

In the 16th century the centre changed again, with Italy gaining in importance. The *frottola*, a simple song that could be performed by one voice, or by a group with instrumental accompaniment, became the prevailing form of refined secular music. Its diffusion throughout Europe was aided by the activity of a Venetian musical publisher, Ottaviano de' Petrucci (1466-1539), who issued eleven collections of *frattole*. About 1530 it gave birth to the *Madrigal, which remained the most important form of vocal chamber music until the end of the century. Although Italy remained predominant in the field, Flemish composers also made their mark, such as Adrian *Willaert and Cipriano de *Rore. Most of these worked in Italy, and Orlando di *Lasso, the brilliant Flemish-Italian composer, in his long career spent time also in England, France and Germany. The presence of Italian influence in England is noted in the work of William *Byrd and other composers of madrigals.

The *Reformation and *Counter-Reformation had a direct influence on music. *Luther, himself a talented musician and composer of *hymns, never tired of praising music as the noblest of arts. Congregational singing rather than the chanting of the choir became an integral part of the service in the Lutheran churches, and was adopted also by the followers of *Zwingli. *Calvin, who favoured the singing of psalms, inspired the musical arrangements of the *Huguenot composer Claude *Goudimel. The Protestant endeavour was eventually to make Germany the capital of European music, a process in which Heinrich *Schütz is the most important link leading up to Johann Sebastian Bach (1685-1750). But the immediate great accomplishments in liturgical music belonged to the Roman Catholic side, where two composers especially distinguished themselves. The first was Giovanni da *Palestrina, perhaps the greatest composer of the Renaissance and an author of masses of lofty religious feelings. The second was the Spaniard Tomás Luís de Vitoria, whose music has a mystical quality. Both emphasized the subordination of the musical forms to the meaning of the texts, a view which won the approval of the Council of *Trent.

The Organ Player and His Wife *by Israel van Meckenem*

In the second half of the 16th century Venice was an important musical centre. Here Giovanni *Gabrieli introduced daring experiments in the alternation of vocal and instrumental music and was succeeded as the principal composer of sacred music in 1613 by Claudio *Monteverdi. The latter, however, is better remembered as the first great composer of **operas*, a new form

Young Woman playing the Lute *by an anonymous artist*

which combined secular music with *drama to produce a highly entertaining new form. Although a late 16th-century creation of highly intellectual young Florentines led by Jacopo *Peri, the *opera* was really developed in the following century through efforts of Venetian and Neapolitan composers. A parallel development in sacred music was the *oratorio*, which originated in the circles around St. Philip *Neri, and employed a soloist and narrator, as well as chorus and orchestra. However, both the opera and oratorio, as well as the tender cantata, properly belong to the music of the *Baroque.
G. Reese, *Music in the Renaissance* (1959);
M. Bukofzer, *Music in the Baroque Era* (1947);
N. D. Ferguson, *A History of Musical Thought* (1959);
H. D. McKinney and W. R. Anderson, *Music in History* (1966);
A. Einstein *A Short History of Music* (1947).

MUSKET A type of infantry gun which replaced the *arquebus in the second half of the 16th century. The M. was not really a further development of the arquebus. At first it looked like a small piece of artillery and had to be rested on an iron fork to be fired. Much heavier than the arquebus, the M. was more powerful and had almost twice its range. It was first introduced in the Spanish army by the Duke of *Alba, and by the 17th century was in general use throughout Europe. By then it was improved so that it could be fired without a support.

MUSURUS, MARCUS (c. 1470-1517) Greek scholar in Italy. Born in Candia, Crete, he came to Florence to study under *Lascaris and then went to Venice, where he became the chief Greek editor for Aldus *Manutius. In 1499 his work on Greek etymology appeared, and he also prepared a grammar of that languages. A teacher of Greek at Padua and Venice, his reputation prompted *Leo X to invite him to Rome and appoint him archbishop of a Greek archdiocese. He died a year after his arrival in Rome.
D. J. Geanakoplos, *Greek Scholars in Venice* (1962).

MUZIANO, GIROLAMO (1528-92) Italian painter. Born near Brescia, he studied there and in Venice, where he was influenced by *Titian. About 1548 he visited Rome, and with the support of *Michelangelo, was awarded several important commissions. He reached the zenith of his career during the pontificacy of *Gregory XIII, who appointed him superintendant of art works at the Vatican. His masterpiece is *The Ressurrection of St. Lazarus*, originally painted for the church of S. Maria Maggiore, Rome. M. combined a talent for drawing figures with a feeling for landscapes, wherein he made use of his native Brescian scenery. He was a founder of the Academy of St. Luke.
U. da Como, *Girolamo Muziano* (1930).

MUZIO, GIROLAMO (1496-1576) Italian writer. Born in Padua, he spent much of his life as a courtier at various Italian courts, dying at La Paneretta, near Siena. He wrote several books of poetry, and treatises on various subjects, including the *Battaglie per la difesa dell'italica lingua*, defending the Italian language. Also important are his treatises against the Reformation. In one of his last works, published the year he died, he proposed the union of Italy.

A Musketeer *from an engraving published in 1587*

V. Di Tocco, *Ideali d'indipendenza in Italia durante la preponderanza spagnuola* (1926).

MYCONIUS (Oswald Geisshäusler; 1488-1552) Swiss Protestant reformer. Born in Lucerne, he received a humanist education in *Basle. There he was influenced by *Erasmus (1510-14), from whom he also received his name. In 1516 he became a teacher at the *Zurich cathedral and, in 1518, helped his friend *Zwingli to get elected as people's priest. M. openly joined the Reformation in Lucerne in 1522, and the following year returned to Zurich to assist Zwingli. In 1532 he succeeded *Oecolampadius as chief pastor in Basle, where he composed the First Basle Confession (1534). A biblical scholar, M. also wrote a short biography of Zwingli (1532).

MYCONIUS, FRIEDRICH (1490-1546) German Protestant reformer. Born in Lichtenfels am Main, he joined the Franciscans in 1510 and was ordained in 1516. While training for the priesthood he met and was offended by Johann *Tetzel. In 1524 he openly joined *Luther and became the leading reformer of Gotha. Later he was active in Thuringia and, in 1529, was with Luther in the Colloquy of *Marburg. He remained an active leader of the Lutheran camp throughout his life. In 1538 he undertook a brief trip to England, in an attempt to gain the support of *Henry VIII. M. wrote a history of the Reformation.

H. U. Delius, ed., *Der Briefwechsel des Friedrich Myconius, 1526-46* (1960).

MYSTERIES AND MIRACLE PLAYS The name given to two related forms of late mediaeval religious drama. The Mysteries dramatized a biblical episode, such as the Fall of Adam or the story of Cain and Abel; the Miracles treated non-biblical subjects, such as the lives of the saints and salvation through the intercession of divine powers. Performed in the open, especially during Holy Week and Easter, they attained the height of their popularity in the 14th and 15th centuries, later falling into decay with the advent of more secular forms of *drama. The oldest Mystery, incompletely preserved, is *Adam*, which dates from the 12th century. The English Chester Plays and York Cycle belong to the 14th century, the latter group containing almost 50 plays.

H. Craig, *English Religious Drama in the Middle Ages* (1955);
G. Frank, *The Medieval French Drama* (1954).

MYSTICISM Extreme forms of religious devotion, designed to achieve direct knowledge of God by insight or intuition, have existed side by side with official Christianity throughout the Middle Ages. But, it was in the 14th century, probably in consequence of the Black Death, that mystical tendencies seemed to proliferate. One of the most influential of the late mediaeval mystics was the Flemish Jan van Ruysbroeck (1293-1381), whose numerous writings in the vernacular had a direct effect on the *Devotio Moderna. Among others were St. Catherine of Siena (1347-80) and St. Bridget of Sweden (1303-73), both of whom tried to heal the Great Schism; the number of women mystics was significantly high.

M. was not a noticeable feature of the progressively secular 15th century, although such developments as the movement led by *Savonarola in Florence hinted at a possible reaction. But with the upheaval of the 16th century mystical forms of religiosity had a great resurgence. In the Roman Catholic world probably no other period produced as much inspirational mystical literature as that of the *Counter-Reformation. The mystical vocation was central to the enterprises developed by the great leaders of the Catholic reformation, St. Ignatius *Loyola and, somewhat later, St. Philip *Neri. M. in southern Spain produced such lasting examples of spiritual devotion and ecstasy as the lives of *Juan de la Cruz or *Luís de Granada. The greatest feminine voice of 16th-century mysticism, St. *Teresa of Avila, also came from Spain. Among other famous women mystics of the age were the Italian St. *Catherine of Genoa and St. *Catherine de' Ricci. In Spain, however, M. was for a long time held in suspicion, and most of the Spanish spiritual leaders were examined at one time or another by the *Inquisition. In Protestant Europe the original enthusiasm, liturgical simplicity and spontaneous devotional spirit seemed at first to eliminate the need for individualistic religiosity, but at the turn of the 16th century the increasing rigidity of Protestant theology prompted the mystical works of Johann *Arndt and Jacob *Boehme.

W. R. Inge, *Christian Mysticism* (1899);
H. C. Graef, *Histoire de la mystique* (1972);
R. M. Jones, *Spiritual Reformers in the 16th and 17th Centuries* (1959);
T. Katsaros, *The Western Mystical Tradition* (1969).

Nuremberg, *a woodcut in Schedel's* Nuremberg Chronicle *(1493)*

St. Luke *by Nanni di Banco*

NANNI DI BANCO (c. 1384-1421) Florentine sculptor. A somewhat older contemporary of *Donatello, his early death cut short a promising career. In 1407 and 1408 he worked with Donatello in the Cathedral, where he made the sculpture of *Isaiah.* His best work was done in the church of Orsanmichele, Florence. Here, among other works, he was responsible for the Tabernacle of the Shoemakers and the Tabernacle of Constructors and Sculptors (1408-15). His work shows similarities of style with that of Donatello.

NANTES, EDICT OF A decree signed by *Henry IV at Nantes on 13 April 1598 awarding the *Hugenots religious freedom with certain limitations. According to the edict they could hold services in every district except Paris and a few other cities, enjoy the same political rights as Catholics and serve in the royal administration. In addition, they were allowed to maintain garrisons in about 200 towns at the state's expense. In spite of some Catholic opposition, the E. of N. laid the foundation for religious coexistence in France.

NAOGEORGUS, THOMAS (1511-63) Latinized name of the German dramatist Thomas Kirchmeyer. A follower of *Luther, he defended Protestantism in two Latin dramas: *Pammachius* (1538) was a violent attack on the papacy as a diabolical institution; *Mercator* (1540), a *morality play, had some comic situations, but also included a great deal of anti-Roman Catholic invective. He also attacked the papacy in his epic *Regnum papisticum* (1555).

F. Wiener, *Naogerogus im England der Reformationszeit* (1907).

NAPIER, JOHN (1550-1617) Scottish mathematician. Born into an aristocratic family, he was educated at St. Andrews and in his youth travelled on the continent. In 1593 he published a work on the Revelation of St. John, a sharp refutation of Roman Catholicism. N. experimented with mechanical inventions, and also took an interest in the use of manure in agriculture. His main achievement, however, was a new method of calculation by 'artificial numbers', which he called logarithms. His work, containing the explanation of the method and a table of logarithms, came out in 1614, and was adopted at once, facilitating and shortening the time needed for

Four Saints *by Nanni di Banco, Florence*

computation. He also wrote a work which introduced the present form of decimal factions, and, in 1615, published a method for mechanized use of logarithms by little rods (called Napier's bones). N.'s tables of logarithms were improved by Henry Briggs (1556-1631), his calculating rods by William Oughtred (1574-1660).
E. W. Hobson, *John Napier and the Invention of Logarithms* (1914).

NAPLES, KINGDOM OF N., being the largest part on the Italian mainland, belonged to the Norman kingdom of Sicily between the 11th and the 13th centuries. Following the Sicilian insurrection against Charles of Anjou – an event known as the Sicilian Vespers – in 1282, the island passed to the crown of *Aragon, whereas N. led an uneasy existence under the frequently divided Angevins. During the reign of *Joanna II (1414-35), the last ruler of the dynasty, N. reached a state of near-total anarchy. Then *Alfonso V of Aragon, who conquered N. in 1443, reunified it with Sicily and inaugurated a period of cultural splendour at his court, patronizing humanist scholars, painters and architects. After his death, N. was once again separated from Sicily, which remained attached to the crown of Aragon, and went to Alfonso's illegitimate son *Ferrante ((1458-94). During the first years of his reign the kingdom played a successful role in the Italian political arena but, in 1485, fell prey to a long and bloody baronial revolt. This became a prelude to the event that altered the fate of N., and much else – the invasion of Italy by *Charles VIII of France (1494).

The French conquest of N. opened an international conflict with the participation of the Empire and Spain. In 1503, after three descendants of Ferrante I had either abdicated or died, *Ferdinand the Catholic captured the kingdom, thanks to the victories of his general Gonzalo de *Córdoba, and organized it under Spanish rule. Although both Sicily and N. were now Spanish possessions, they were governed separately, N. being administered by a viceroy and lacking the representative institutions which modified the power of the Spanish government in Sicily. The most important of the 16th-century Spanish Neapolitan Viceroys was Pedro de *Toledo. His authoritarian methods provoked protests, and some rebellions erupted in the late 16th century, leading to the great popular revolt led by the fishmonger Masaniello in 1647. But N. remained under Spanish rule until the 18th century, when it was once again joined together with Sicily into an independant kingdom under Charles of Bourbon (1738).
A. F. C. Ryder, *The Kingdom of Naples Under Alfonso the Magnanimous* (1976);
A. Ghirelli, *Storia di Napoli* (1974).

NARDI, JACOPO (1476-1563) Italian historian. Born in Florence, he was in his youth a supporter of *Savonarola, and remained an ardent republican. He took part in the republican regime of Florence between 1527 and 1530, and in 1533 was banished by Alessandro de' *Medici to Livorno (Leghorn). In 1535 he protested against the latter before *Charles V. Afterwards he resided mainly in Venice. He wrote two comedies, a free translation of Livy and two political treatises. His main

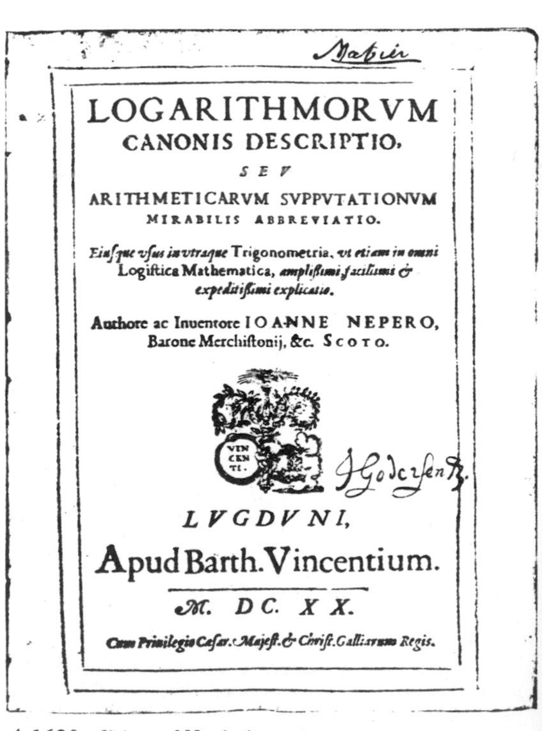

Napier

LOGARITHMORVM
CANONIS DESCRIPTIO,
SEV
ARITHMETICARVM SVPPVTATIONVM
MIRABILIS ABBREVIATIO.
Eiusque usus in utraque Trigonometria, ut etiam in omni Logistica Mathematica, amplissimi, facillimi & expeditissimi explicatio.
Authore ac Inuentore IOANNE NEPERO,
Barone Merchistonij, &c. SCOTO.

LVGDVNI,
Apud Barth. Vincentium.
M. DC. XX.
Cum Priuilegio Cæsar. Majest. & Christ. Galliarum Regis.

A 1620 edition of Napier's work on logarithms

work is the *Istorie della città di Firenze*, a republican-oriented history of Florence from 1494 to 1532, published posthumously in 1582.

A. Pieralli, *La vita e le opere di Jacopo Nardi* (1901).

NARVAEZ, PANFILO DE (1478-1529) Spanish **conquistador.* Born in Valladolid, he went to America as a young man and, in 1511, joined Diego *Velásquez in the conquest of Cuba. In 1520 the latter sent him with some 800 men to Mexico to intercept *Cortés. Instead, his camp was attacked by Cortés, and N., who lost an eye in the scuffle, was held prisoner for two years. In 1528 N. led 400 men to Florida, an expedition from which only four survivors returned.

NASHE, THOMAS (1567-1601) English author. After studying at Cambridge, he joined Robert *Greene in London, where he led a turbulent life and frequently engaged in bitter controversies, while working as a literary hack. His *Anatomie of Absurdities* was printed in 1589, and his powerful social satire, *Pierce Pennilesse, His Supplication to the Divell,* in 1592. N. wrote the first English **picaresque* novel, *The Unfortunate Traveller, or the Life of Jack Wilton* (1594), and a *masque, *Summers Last Will and Testament,* published in 1600. He also wrote plays, pamphlets and poems. His work is of uneven quality. His prose abounds with linguistic inventions and colloquialisms, but he was frequently carried away by his own fluency.

G. R. Hibbard, *Thomas Nash* (1962).

NASI, DON JOSEPH (c. 1520-79) Jewish banker and statesman. Born to a **marrano* family in Portugal, he was taken in 1536 to *Antwerp by his aunt, Dona Gracia Nasí (1510-69). There he became a banker to *Charles V. Suspected by the *Inquisition, N. left for Italy in 1547 and, in 1554, joined his aunt in Constantinople, married his cousin, and openly returned to Judaism. He soon became a confidant of *Suleiman I, and when *Selim II gained the sultanate (1565), was given the title of Duke of Naxos, together with many commercial privileges. N. advised the Sultan to support the Protestant states, and persuaded him to undertake the conquest of Cyprus (1571), which was a Venetian posession. After the death of Selim II his influence gradually declined. A great benefactor of his co-religionists, N. cooperated with his aunt in settling Jews in Tiberias which, with seven neighbouring villages, had been granted him in 1561. A famous early attempt to restore the Jews to their ancient land, it achieved but modest results.

C. Roth, *The House of Nasí, the Duke of Naxos* (1948); P. Grunebaum-Ballin, *Joseph Nasí, Duc de Naxos* (1968).

NAVAGERO, ANDREA (1483-1529) Italian poet. The son of a noble Venetian family, he received a broad humanist education and was employed as editor of classical texts by Aldus *Manutius. Later, he was made director of the Library of S. Marco, and undertook diplomatic missions on behalf of Venice. While in Spain in 1526 he befriended Juan *Boscan, who consequently introduced the Italianate style into Spanish literature. N.'s own poetry in Latin is superior to the Italian. He also wrote letters and notes about his diplomatic voyages, and was famous for his cultivated gardens at Treviso and Murano.

NAVARRE A small kingdom in the southern slopes of the western Pyrenees, it expanded after the 10th century to include territories on the northern, or French, side of the mountains. By the 13th century it began to feel the increasingly determined pressure of its great neighbour Castile, but its independence was respected as long as the **reconquista* movement was unfinished. But, in 1484, N. passed by marriage to the French house of Albret and, in 1516, *Ferdinand the Catholic conquered the Spanish part of the kingdom, which left the king of N. merely a French magnate. This was, essentially, the position of Queen *Jeanne d'Albret of N., from whose union with *Antoine de Bourbon came the future *Henry IV of France. Upon his accession N. was united to France.

NAVARRETE, JUAN FERNANDEZ DE (c. 1526-79) Spanish painter, surnamed "El Mudo", because he was a deaf-mute. Born at Logroño, he went in his youth to Italy and worked under *Titian in Venice. Many years later *Philip II called him back to work on the decorations of the *Escorial, and from 1568 he served as court painter. Of the 32 altarpieces that he was commissioned to paint for the chapels of the Escorial, only 8 were completed. N. was the originator of *tenebrismo*, the use of chiaroscuro to achieve dramatic effects. *Abraham and the Three Angels* (1576) and the *Burial of St. Lawrence* (1579) are among the most famous of his works.

NAVARRO, PEDRO (c. 1460-1528) Spanish military commander and engineer. Beginning his career as a mercenary soldier, he saw action in Italy and North Africa, and joined the expedition of Gonzalo de *Córdoba to Italy. There he began to display his skill at breaching fortified walls with explosives. His most successful operation was in 1503, when he mined the French garrison of *Naples. By that time he had also earned a reputation as a commanding officer and, in 1509-10, fought in Oran and Tripoli. In 1512 he was taken prisoner at the Battle of Ravenna, and after three years of captivity entered the service of the new French king, *Francis I. In 1525 he was taken prisoner at *Pavia by his own countrymen, but was released after the Treaty of Madrid (1526). In the service of France he took charge of the *artillery.

NAVIGATION So long as European seafaring was confined to the Mediterranean, the Baltic and coastal shipping, moving a vessel from one point to another remained a simple procedure. A ship rarely lost sight of land for more than 24 hours, when sailors depended on dead reckoning to be verified by natural landmarks. Crossing the Atlantic Ocean, and eventually all the navigable seas of the globe, necessitated many changes. *Ships were designed differently, *cartography made great strides forward, and navigation became for the first time dependent on instruments. The crucial instrument had, in fact, been developed before the 15th century. This was the *compass, in use since the 13th century, which gave the navigator his steering course. To this he could add in the early 16th century the log for measuring the ship's speed. It consisted of a block (log chip) fastened to a long line knotted at regular intervals. When the log was streamed the speed at which the knots ran out over the stern was timed.

For finding his latitude, 15th century navigator came to rely on celestial observations, a practice that was related to advances in *astronomy. Celestial measurment proceeded from the principle that the height of a star, that is the angle between a star and the observer's horizon, made possible the determination of the observer's latitude. In the northern hemisphere, the Pole Star lent itself easily to such measurment. But in the southern hemisphere other stars or the sun had to be used, which necessitated almanacs containing tables of declination of the heavenly bodies. Two 15th-century scientists in particular contributed to the calculations involved in celestial navigation: *Regiomontanus and *Zacuto of Salamanca. The actual measurement by seamen was taken with the aid of an *astrolabe, an old instrument which was adopted by Portuguese explorers in the second half of the century. About 1496 the first manual of navigation, *O regimento do astrolabio,* was published in Portugal, containing tables of declination and general instructions of measurement and calculation. At that time a handier instrument was developed, the *quadrant, which simplified the taking of measurements at sea. The cross-staff and back staff were further developments of the 16th century.

The new requirements of steering ships made it mandatory for the navigator to have some theoretical knowledge. In Spain the **Casa de Contratación* added, in 1508, the office of chief pilot (*piloto mayor*), who headed the first European school of navigation, validated nautical charts and instruments and examined pilots for the Atlantic traffic. The first to hold this position was the famous Amerigo *Vespucci; another prominent *piloto mayor* was Sebastian *Cabot. However, in spite of the general admiration for the Spanish method, other nations were not quick to emulate them. Indeed, N. during the 16th century and after remained an art which combined skill, experience and first-hand knowledge of sea currents, weather conditions and prevailing winds.

E. G. R. Tailor, *The Heaven-finding Art: A History of Navigation from Odysseus to Captain Cook* (1956);
C. Singleton, ed., *Art, Science and History in the Renaissance* (1967), pp. 189-237.

NEBRIJA, ANTONIO DE (c. 1444-1522) Spanish humanist. Born at Lebrija in Andalusia, he assumed for his name a modified pronounciation of his native place. He studied at Salamanca and then went to Italy, and spent 10 years studying *Hebrew and *Greek in Bologna. After his return, N. served for many years as professor of grammar and rhetoric at Salamanca but, in 1513, moved to the new university of Alcalá, where he headed the project of the Complutensian Polyglot *Bible. The most important of his works was the *Arte de la lengua castellana* (1492), the first grammar of a modern European language. He had previously published a Latin grammar (1481) and, between 1492 and 1495, edited a Latin-Spanish, Spanish-Latin dictionary.

NEOPLATONISM The philosophy of Plato, which influenced such philosophers as Plotinus, in the 3rd century, and Proclus in the 5th, and even St. Augustine's *The City of God*, became in the 15th century a major force in the resurgence of philosophical studies. Probably the first major Renaissance Neoplatonist was *Nicholas of Cusa. His concept of God as a transcendental infinite unity wherein all contradictions are resolved (*coincidentia oppositorum*), was plainly based on the Platonic tradition. But the introduction of Plato into the culture of the age is usually ascribed to the Greek scholar *Gemistos Plethon, whose admiration for the ancient Greek philosopher prompted *Cosimo de' *Medici to found Florence's *Platonic Academy (1459). The head of this school, Marsiglio *Ficino, was responsible for completing the translation of Plato, and also translated Plotinus and Proclus. In his *Platonic Theology* of 1482 all three authors were treated as sources of divine revelation quite in harmony with Christianity. Ficino's younger friend, Giovanni *Pico della Mirandola, was also influenced by Neoplatonism, but claimed to harmonize in his thought the philosophies of Plato and Aristotle. In the early 16th century Neoplatonism spread outwards from Florence and influenced the thought of such humanists as *Erasmus, Thomas *More, and much later, Giordano *Bruno and Johan *Kepler.

Neoplatonism emphasized a hierarchical conception of the universe and the knowledge of God as the ultimate end of human existence. Stressing idea over matter, believing that the human soul is endowed with certain virtues and is capable of an inner ascent to God, it reflected an approach quite in tune with an age in which man's creative powers seemed supreme.

N. A. Robb, *The Neoplatonism of the Italian Renaissance* (1935);
P. O. Kristeller, *Renaissance Thought* (1961);
R. Klibansky, *The Continuity of the Platonic Tradition* (1950).

NERI, ST. PHILIP (1515-95) Italian Catholic reformer. The son of a Florentine family, he went to Rome in 1533 and studied theology. In 1538 he abandoned his studies and began a life of religious devotion as a layman. In 1548 he, with other laymen, organized a fraternity for the assistance of pilgrims and the poor, and founded the hospital of Sta. Trinità dei Pellegrini. Ordained finally in 1551, he began to gather around him young priests with whom he would enter into informal discussions, which included prayers and the singing of hymns. Although he was censured for his activity by *Paul IV (1559), he was later allowed to continue the work. In 1564 he established the first Oratory, a community of followers who devoted their afternoons to religious talks, preaching and prayer in the vernacular. The historian *Baronius was one of the members, and *Palestrina contributed music to the hymns. The Oratory was criticized in the reign of *Pius V but, in 1575, *Gregory XIII recognized it as a congregation of 'secular priests', and gave them a small dilapidated church in Rome, which they rebuilt. The Oratories later spread through Italy, Spain and Portugal, and in the early 17th century were introduced into France. N., who was formally elected provost of the congregation in 1577, acquired a reputation as the 'Apostle of Rome'. He was succeeded by Baronius and canonized in 1622.

L. Ponelle and L. Bordet, *St. Philip Neri and the Roman Society of His Times* (1933);
L. Bouyer, *The Roman Socrates* (1958);
R. Addington, *The Idea of the Oratory* (1966).

NEROCCIO DEI LANDI (1447-1500) Italian painter and sculptor. Born in Siena, he studied under *Vecchietta. Between 1467 and 1475 he worked in partnership with *Francesco di Giorgio. Possessing a delicate and charming style, he painted, in addition to religious subjects, on mythological and classical themes. His sculptures, on the other hand, project natural harmony and force. Some of the best examples are at Siena's cathedral.

G. M. Coor, *Neroccio dei Landi* (1961).

NETHERLANDS, THE (The Low Countries) During the Middle Ages these rich provinces on the flat, alluval plains by the North Sea reflected the disintegration of

Lorenzo de' Medici by Giorgio Vasari

Madonna and Child *by Hans Memling*

the Carolingian empire and the politics of *feudal particularism. In the late 14th century the Dukes of *Burgundy began the task of moulding the many duchies, marquisates and counties into a unified political body. Despite linguistic and ethnic distinction, by the 15th century a considerable degree of central administrative authority had been achieved. Under the imperial dynasty, the *Habsburgs, the N. seemed to be progressing towards political consolidation but, after nearly a century of increasingly rigid Habsburg rule, a reaction set in and the issue of religious tolerance finally exploded in a revolt against Philip II. By 1579, although many battles were yet to be fought, the political division of the N. was determined: while the south continued under Spanish government, the seven northern provinces formed an independent republic.

The importance of the N. lay in their commerce, industry and agriculture, the outcome of natural conditions and a favourable location combined with considerable human effort and ingenuity. In the south, *Flanders whith its cities of *Bruges, *Ghent and Ypres remained dominant for most of the 15th century, but *Antwerp in nearby Brabant quickly forged ahead, followed by Mechlin and Brussels, the last-named being the seat of the government under the Habsburgs. North of the estuaries of the Meuse and the Rhine, *Holland and Zeeland with their systems of dykes and drained land became famous for their *agricultural methods and cattle breeding. by the mid-16th century the Dutch had taken over much of the maritime carrying trade between western Europe and the Baltic.

The death of *Charles the Bold at Nancy (1477) resulted in a constitutional crisis in the N. In order to get the recognition of her subjects, *Mary of Burgundy had to grant them the *Grand Privilège*. It gave the estates-general the right to assemble on their own initiative and to decide important issues, such as war and peace. But Mary's death (1482) reopened the crisis. During the minority of her son *Philip the Handsome, the towns, especially Flanders, rose against the regent, *Maximilian of Austria, precipitating a decade of instability. Philip's formal accession in 1493 ushered in peace and prosperity. But after his marriage to the heiress of Spain, *Joanna the Mad, the Archduke's interests ranged wider than the N., and his early death, in 1506, cut short the process of centralization. Although *Margaret of Austria proved a much more successful regent than her father Maximilian had been, she was restricted by an aristocratic *Grand Conseil* and during the latter part of her long regency (1507-30), merely substituted for her nephew Emperor *Charles V. The latter, in his turn, not only extracted from the N. considerable sums to finance his wars, but also excluded the *guilds from town government to the benefit of the patrician classes. This attitude towards the N. culminated in 1548 when, at the Diet of *Augsburg, the Emperor attached the 17 provinces to the Empire. These now included: Brabant, Limburg, Luxemburg, Gelderland, Flanders, Artois, Hainault, Holland, Zeeland, Namur, Tournai, East and West Friesland, Mechlin, Utrecht, Overyssel and Groningen.

Nevertheless, Charles V remained popular to the end. His son, Philip II, who took over when his father abdicated in 1555, faced a delicate situation. For several decades the *Reformation had been making inroads into the N., and by the middle of the century Calvinism had particularly gained hold in the northern Dutch provinces. Philip's half sister, *Margaret of Parma, who served as regent (1559-67), first followed the advice of Cardinal *Granvelle in enforcing Roman Catholicism. This provoked the resistance of the nobles on both constitutional and religious grounds, and led to Granvelle's recall (1564). The lesser nobility then petitioned the regent to abolish the *Inquisition (1566), but was rebuffed in an incident from which originated the name **Gueux* for the extreme insurrectionary party, That summer the populace of several cities rose in a series of iconoclastic riots that prompted the leaders of the higher nobility, *William of Orange and the Counts of *Egmont and *Horn, to come to the aid of the government. But the nobles were unable to control the movement, and Philip's announcement that he was sending the Duke of *Alba from Spain with an army of 20,000 men reopened the crisis. Shortly after Alba's arrival Margaret of Parma resigned. William of Orange, who had foreseen the consequences, went into exile, and Egmont and Horn were arrested. Their execution in 1568, after a mock trial, signalled the opening of the revolt. Alba did his best to inflame the popular animosity towards Spain by his ruthless suppression of any opposition, confiscations and the imposition of heavy taxes.

The first attempts of William of Orange and his brother *Louis of Nassau to invade the N. were unsuccessful. But, in 1572, the Sea Beggars (Gueux) captured Brill. This victory was followed by uprisings in Holland, Zeeland and Utrecht, and the installation of William of Orange as *stadtholder*. Moreover, by now the conflict had assumed international proportions: *Elizabeth I. was helping the rebels, and so were some German Protestant princes, while the French monarchy was not about to miss an opportunity to aggravate Spain's difficulties. Alba, recalled in 1573, was succeeded by *Requesens. The latter defeated the rebels at Mookerheide (1574), but was unable to subdue the liberated provinces. At the time of his sudden death, two years later, the Spanish troops were demoralized and on the verge of mutiny. In November 1576 the unpaid soldiers unleashed in the so-called Spanish Fury, a riot of pillage and massacre in Antwerp which lasted 11 days. The horrified southern provinces joined the north in what proved a temporary anti-Spanish alliance, known as the Pacification of *Ghent.

The position of the new Spanish governor, Don *Juan of Austria, was so weak that he began by making concessions. Then, in January 1578, he took advantage of the strength of Roman Catholicism in the south and the hostility of the Walloon nobility to William of Orange, to gain a victory at Gemblours. Eight months later he died of typhus, and the command passed to Alessandro *Farnese, a brilliant soldier who was also a shrewd statesman. His first political achievement was the Union of *Arras (January 1579), linking a group of the southern provinces. The seven northern provinces immediately formed the *Union of Utrecht, which was followed in 1581 by a formal declaration of independence.

The conflict in the N. continued for another 30 years. Indeed, it was not until 1648 that the independence of the *United Provinces was formally recognized by Spain. But its hopes of regaining the entire N. came to an end during the 1580s. Farnese saw the discredited Francis of *Anjou leaving in 1583, and benefitted from the murder of William of Orange in 1584. In 1585 he completed the pacification of the south by capturing Antwerp and, in 1585-87, made the English troops under *Leicester taste the bitterness of defeat. But the destruction of the *Armada in 1588 meant the collapse of Philip II's plans for both England and the N., and Farnese's involvement in the *Religious Wars of France relieved the pressure on the Dutch. After Farnese died in 1592, Philip II had difficulties in finding a successor, finally appointing to the task *Albert of Habsburg. In accordance with the terms of the peace of *Vervins (1598), Albert married the Infanta and became the ruler of the southern N., which were to be governed apart from the Spanish crown. The war between Albert and *Maurice of Nassau continued intermittently until the 12 years' truce of 1609.

P. Geyl, *The Revolt of the Netherlands* (1932);
H. Pirenne, *Early Democracies in the Low Countries* (1915; rep. 1963);
P. J. Blok, *A History of the People of the Netherlands*, 5 vols. (1898-1912).

NEUDORFER, JOHANN (1497-1563) German type designer and art historian. Born in *Nuremberg, he became one of the most famous masters of calligraphy of his time, and influenced the conclusive form of the Fraktur, or German Gothic lettering. In 1547 he published a collection of biographical notes on contemporary German artists, which remains an important source.

NEUMEISTER, JOHANN (?-1522) German printer, who may have been a pupil of *Gutenberg's. From 1470 to 1474 he worked in Foligno, where he published the first edition of Dante's *Divine Comedy*, then in Mainz (1479) and in Albi (1480). In 1483 he settled in *Lyons, which he helped to make into an important centre of printing. N. excelled in the publication of liturgical books, and also produced famous illustrated editions of *Torquemada's *Meditationes* (1479, 1481), with metal cuts after paintings by Fra *Angelico.

NEVILLE, GEORGE (c. 1433-76) English archbishop of York. The son of the Earl of Salisbury and younger brother of the Earl of *Warwick, he became the bishop of Exeter in 1456. Following the victories of the House

A 15th-century monument to Pope Nicholas V at the Vatican

Nicholas of Cusa

of *York he was made chancellor in 1460, and archbishop in 1465. From there on his fortune followed that of his brother's, and after the latter's death (1471) he was imprisoned for three years. N. was one of the first leading English clergymen to promote the study of *Greek.

NEWFOUNDLAND The first English possession in the New World. The aboundance of cod fish and the favourable geographic location made this island a natural target of English overseas *exploration, and it seems it was visited by fishermen even before John *Cabot discovered it in 1497. The Portuguese brothers *Corte-Real, also came to N. and early in the 16th century it became the fishing grounds for English, French, Portuguese and Spanish vessels. In 1583 Sir Humphrey *Gilbert formally annexed N. to England, founding the first settlement. Though it failed, repeated attempts of colonization finally secured the island for England in the 17th century.

NICCOLI, NICCOLÓ (1364-1437) Italian humanist. Born in Florence, where he spent most of his life as a merchant, he became an admirer of the 'new learning' and an indefatigable collector and copyist of ancient manuscripts. A friend of *Poggio, *Bruni and *Valla, N. did not leave any writings of his own. At his death his collection of some 800 manuscripts was redeemed from his creditors by Cosimo de' *Medici, and placed at the convent of S. Marco, becoming the first public library.

NICHOLAS V (Tommaso Parentucelli; 1397-1455) Pope from 1447. The son of a physician, he studied at Bologna and was introduced to the culture of humanism while spending a few years in Florence as tutor in a wealthy family. He then served for many years in the household of the bishop of Bologna (1423-43), whom he was appointed to succeed by *Eugenius IV. Employed by the latter on a mission to Germany, he was elevated to the cardinalate in 1446, and was elected pope a year later. Pursuing a policy of reconciliation, he was able to achieve the abdication of *Felix V and the dispersion of the Council of *Basle. In 1452 he crowned Frederick III, the last German Emperor to have his imperial coronation at Rome and, in 1453, withstood a political crisis, including a Roman conspiracy against his life. The fall of *Constantinople, which happened that year, helped N. to convince the other Italian states to join the discussions which led to the peace of Lodi (1454). N. was the first Renaissance pope: he collected a great number of manuscripts of classical works, encouraged the humanists, invited to Rome a number of Byzantine scholars, and founded the Vatican library. He devoted large sums to the rebuilding and beautification of Rome, and commissioned painters and architects to prepare the city for the jubilee year of 1450, which celebrated the reunification of the Church.

K. Pleyer, *Die Politik Nikolaus V.* (1927).

NICHOLAS OF CUSA (Nicolaus Cusanus; 1401-64) Cardinal, statesman and philosopher. A son of a fisherman from Kues of Cusa on the river Moselle, from which he derived his name, he was educated at the school of the *Brothers of the Common Life in Deventer, and later studied Greek and Hebrew in Padua. He entered the service of the Church and rose quickly in its ranks. At the Council of Basle during the schism with the papacy he strongly defended the conciliar idea in a work entitled *De concordancia Catholica.* However, in 1437 he went over to the Roman side, and travelled to Constantinople on a mission to bring unity between the Eastern and Western churches. From 1440 to 1447 he was the papal legate in Germany and, in 1448, was created cardinal. Two years later he became Bishop of Brixen, a position that brought him into conflict with the Archduke of Austria. A longtime friend of Pius II, he supported his call for a crusade against the Turks and, in 1459, served as governor of Rome in the Pope's absence. The last four years of his life were dedicated mainly to writing.

In addition to his tracts on ecclesiastical political issues, C. wrote a number of philosophical treatises, as well as on physical science and the reform of the calendar. His main philosophical work, *De docta ignorantia* (1440), maintained that since human knowledge is mere conjecture, the true grasp of God is a matter of

Roberto de Nobili in sannyasi *dress*

insight, untuition and mystical speculation. While still related to the main currents of mediaeval philosophy, his thought included many innovative ideas. In the late 16th century, Giordano *Bruno acknowledged his influence.

P. E. Sigmund, *Nicholas of Cusa and Mediaeval Political Thought* (1963).

NICHOLAS OF FLUE, ST. (Brother Klaus; 1417-87) Swiss hermit. A well-to-do member of his community, he obtained his wife's consent in 1467, to retire to a life of devotional solitude. His growing reputation for holiness caused people to seek his blessing and spiritual advice. In 1481 he arbitrated the differences between the Swiss cantons, thus averting a possible civil war.

NICCOLO DALL'ARCA (c. 1435-94) Italian sculptor. Born in Bari, he was given his surname after the canopy he made for the tomb of St. Dominic at Bologna, together with several small figures of angels and saints (1469-94). His earlier *Pietà*, at the church of S. Maria della Vita, Bologna, is much more dramatic and emotional. A sensitive artist who responded to various influences, his work lacks stylistic unity.

NICLAES, HENDRIK (c. 1502-80) German-Dutch *Anabaptist leader. The son of merchants of *Münster, he sought shelter in *Amsterdam after being charged with heresy and, in 1540, founded a small sect called the Family of Love. It had strong antinomian and mystical tendencies, and subsequently gained adherents among the English *Puritans. N. spent many years in Emden, writing and organizing his followers. But in his last years he was persecuted and had to change his residence several times. His sect lasted as late as the 17th century.

NIFO, AGOSTINO (c. 1469-c. 1546) Italian philosopher. A native of Calabria, he studied at the university of Padua, and later taught there as well as in Naples, Pisa and Salerno, where he died. N. wrote on various subjects and was not scrupulously consistent. In his *De intellectu et daemonibus* (1492) he championed Averroism, but in *De immortalitate animae* (1518), dedicated to Pope *Leo X, he reverted to Thomism and attacked the ideas of *Pomponazzi. His *De regnandi peritia* (1523) dedicated to *Charles V, borrowed much from *The Prince* by *Machiavelli. He also wrote on economics, and commentaries on the works of Aristotle.

NIÑO, PEDRO ALONSO (1468-c. 1505) Spanish navigator. Born near Huelva, he was known as El Negro. He gained experience by joining several Portuguese expeditions to *Africa, and in 1498 accompanied *Columbus on his third voyage. In 1499 he undertook with Cristóbal Guerra the exploration of the coast of Venezuela, returning to Spain with pearls and dye-wood. He was accused of theft and died in prison.

NIZOLIO, MARIO (1498-1576) Italian philosopher. Born in Brescello, he taught at the University of Parma and died in Sabbioneta. He won his reputation with the *Thesaurus Ciceronianus*, a widely-read defence of the *Ciceronian style, first published in 1536. A second work of his, on the true principle of philosophy, distinguished between the language of the ancient philosophers and the philosophical content of their works. It was first published in 1553, and was reissued twice during the 17th century by Leibnitz, who was a great admirer of N., under the title *Antibarbarus philosophicus.*

NOBILI, ROBERTO DE (1577-1656) Italian *Jesuit missionary. Of noble family, he joined the Jesuits in 1597 and, in 1606, arrived at Madure, *India. He quickly learned the local languages, and not only preached in the native tongue but adopted the way of life of the local ascetics and accomodated himself to the Hindu caste system. In this way he succeeded in converting to Christianity many members of the higher castes. N. translated the catechism, hymns and other religious literature into Sanskrit and Tamil. In 1610 he wrote the *Apologia*, a defence of his missionary methods, in which he replied to those who accused him of tolerating idolatry. Approved by Rome (1623), he continued his missionary activity until 1643.

V. Cronin, *A pearl to India: The Life of Roberto de Nobili* (1959).

NOBREGA, MANOEL DE (1517-70) Portuguese *Jesuit missionary. He went to Brazil in 1549 with the first Jesuit missionaries to go to America. He opposed the enslavement of the Indians by the European colonists and pleaded for their Christianization by peaceful means. His letters are an important source for the early history of Brazil.

NOGAROLA, ISOTTA (1418-66) Italian humanist. Born at Verona, she studied there under Martino Rizzoni, a pupil of *Guarino da Verona, together with her sister Ginevra. After 1441 she pursued the study of theology. She wrote a Latin dialogue and letters, and is considered the first Renaissance woman who made a contribution to humanist culture.

NONCONFORMISTS A term applied in England to those who, while not necessarily disagreeing with the fundamental doctrines of the established church, refused to conform to its discipline, particularly with regard to matters of ritual and ceremony. The earliest Nonconformists, or Dissenters, were *Puritans and such independent groups as the *Brownists and *Barrowists.

NOORT, ADAM VAN (1562-1641) Flemish painter. Born in *Antwerp, he probably visited Italy in his youth. He lived in his native city, where he painted mainly portraits and historical scenes. A relatively small number of his works has survived. He is chiefly remembered as a teacher, counting among his pupils *Rubens, and his son-in-law Jacob Jordaens (1593-1678).

NOOT, JONKER VAN DER (1539-95) Dutch poet. Born in Brecht, he fled in 1567 from Antwerp to England, and lived there for a few years, presenting himself as a persecuted Calvinist. He then went to Germany and France and, in 1578, returned to Antwerp a pro-Spanish Roman Catholic. N. was the first Renaissance poet of the Netherlands. His *Het Bosken,* published in London in 1570, followed *Ronsard. Other works of his were promptly translated into German and French. He spent his last years in Antwerp as a hack poet. Between 1580 and 1595 there were several editions of his *Poëtische Werken.*

L. Forster, *Die Niederlande und die Anfänge der Barocklyrik in Deutschland* (1967).

NORFOLK, THOMAS HOWARD, 3RD DUKE OF (1473-1554) English statesman and military commander. The son of the 2nd Duke of Norfolk, who had held prominent positions and military posts under *Henry VII and the early years of the reign of *Henry VIII, he succeeded to the title in 1524, becoming an influencial member of the King's Council. His power grew after the fall of *Wolsey (1530) and, in 1536, he handled with tact and firmness the rebellious movement known as the *Pilgrimage of Grace. His influence grew even more after the fall of *Cromwell (1540), and his religious views had a bearing on the conservative trend which characterized Henry VIII's last years. However, late in 1546 he was arrested on the charge of treason, and witnessed the execution of his son, the Earl of *Surrey. He himself was rescued from a similar fate by the death of the King (1547). Remaining in custody during the reign of *Edward VI, he was released and restored to a position of influence with the accession of *Mary (1553). N.'s most important acts in the last year of his life were to condemn *Northumberland to death and help suppress the *Wyatt Rebellion.

NORFOLK, THOMAS HOWARD, 4TH DUKE OF (1536-72) Leader of the English aristocracy under *Elizabeth I. The grandson of the Duke of Norfolk, he aroused the suspicion of the Queen when he gave his consent to a proposed marriage with *Mary Stuart (1569). Arrested, he was released the following year, but soon became involved in the *Ridolfi Conspiracy and imprisoned by *Cecil in the Tower of London (1571).

Thomas Howard, Duke of Norfolk *by Holbein the Younger*

Although he denied the charges, he was convicted of high treason and executed.

NORTH, SIR THOMAS (1523-1601) English translator. Born in London to a middle class family, he became known for his popular translations. *The Diall of Princes* (1557) was a translation of a work by the Spanish Antonio de *Guevara. He then translated the *Moral Philosophy* of the Italian *Doni (1570), and a book of oriental fables *Kalilah and Dimnah*. In 1579 appeared his translation of Plutarch, *Lives of the Noble Grecians and Romans*, from the French version of Jacques *Amyot. It later supplied *Shakespeare with material for his classical history plays.

NORTHEAST AND NORTHWEST PASSAGES The idea that there may be northern sea passages to *Asia, similar to those at the southern tips of *Africa and South America, was first tested by John *Cabot in his voyage of 1498. A more determined search by English navigators was made only half a century later. The northeast voyage of 1553 resulted in *Chancellor's reaching Archangel and opening commercial relations with Moscovite Russia. In 1576 *Frobisher renewed the search for a northwest passage. He was followed by *Davis (1585-87), and by *Hudson (1607), among other. The expeditions undertaken in the second half of the 16th century had the backing of Queen *Elizabeth and the London merchant class.

NORTHERN REBELLION (1569) A rebellion in northern England against *Elizabeth I, approximately in the same place where the *Pilgrimage of Grace had taken place 23 years before, and where there was widespread feeling against the governing Council of the North, an organ of the monarchy. The rebels, led by the Earls of Northumberland and Westmorland, were also inspired by Catholic sympathies. They believed in rumours of Spanish aid from the Netherlands, where the Duke of *Alba was in command. Nothing came out of these hopes, and the plan to release *Mary Queen of Scots likewise failed. By December 20th the leaders were in flight to Scotland. But the rank and file suffered severe punishment, and some 600 people were hanged.

NORTHUMBERLAND, JOHN DUDLEY, DUKE OF (1502-53) English Lord Protector in the reign of *Edward VI. The son of an unpopular minister of *Henry VII's, he earned a reputation as a military commander in the last years of the reign of *Henry VIII. He was nominated to the council that was to rule during the minority of Edward VI, and was also given the title of Earl of Warwick. In September 1547 he distinguished himself under the Protector *Somerset at the battle of Pinkie against Scotland and, in August 1549, suppressed the *Kett's Rebellion. Shortly afterwards (October 1549) he took advantage of his influence in the council to topple Somerset and assume the office of Protector. As head of the government he encouraged further moves towards Protestantism. He became Duke of Northumberland in 1551 and, in 1552, had Somerset executed for treason. Trying to prevent *Mary, the leader of the Catholic party, from inheriting the throne after the death of her sickly brother, N. persuaded Edward VI to name as his heir Lady Jane *Grey, who he married to his own son. As soon as the King died (July 1553) N. proclaimed his daughter-in-law queen. But his supporters were few and his failure was complete. Arrested, he was executed on 22 August.

NORTON, RICHARD (1498-1588) English Roman Catholic rebel. The sheriff of Yorkshire, he took part in the *Pilgrimage of Grace in 1536, and rose again in 1569 to join the Earls of Northumberland and Westmoreland in the *Northern Rebellion. Seven of his eleven sons were at his side in the abortive attempt to free *Mary, Queen of Scots, who was being held in Tutbury. He escaped to Scotland and thence to Flanders, where he was given a pension by *Philip II. He died in exile.

NORTON, THOMAS (1532-84) English poet and playwright. Born in London, he was educated at Cambridge and, in 1555, admitted to the inner Temple. In 1562 he became a member of Parliament. He took part in numerous political religious controversies, writing against Roman Catholicism, and serving as an official prosecutor of Roman Catholics. N. is remembered chiefly as the co-author of *Gordobuc,* the first English tragedy based on a classical model, which he wrote with Thomas *Sackville in 1560. It was first performed in 1562 and printed in 1565. His poetry appeared in Tottel's *Miscellany* (1557), and he also translated Calvin's *Institutes* (1561).

F. P. Wilson, *The English Drama, 1485-1585* (1969).

NOSTRADAMUS (1503-66) The Latinized form of the name of the French astrologer and physician Michel de Nostradame. Born at Saint-Rémy, of Jewish descent, he studied at Avignon and Montpellier. He first practised medicine at Agen, but in 1544 settled at Salon, near Aix, where he was reputed to have effected remarkable cures during an outbreak of the plague. He began to make prophecies about 1547 and in 1555 published a book of rhymed prophecies under the title *Centuries*. Obscure and symbolic, some of the predictions appeared to have been fulfilled, bringing the author enormous fame, and invitations to the court of *Catherine de Médicis and *Charles IX. The work has continued to attract interest and a great deal of controversy. It remains a classic of its kind.

E. Cheetham, ed., *Prophecies on World Events by Nostradamus* (1974);
J. Laver, *Nostradamus, or the Future Foretold* (1952).

NOVGOROD, REPUBLIC OF Situated on the Volkhov river about 120 miles south of present-day Leningrad, the city enjoyed self-rule since the 12th century, and was the hub of a commercial empire which stretched as far as the Urals. In the early 15th century N. had a population of about 400,000 and maintained its traditional trading relations with the *Hanseatic League. At this time it became a bone of contention between *Lithuania and the grand princes of Moscow. After its defeat by the Muscovites in 1456, N. lost its sovereignty by degrees, and was forced deeper into Moscow's sphere of influence. In 1570 *Ivan IV 'the Terrible', suspecting a revolt, massacred thousands of its inhabitants and deported many others. The city retained an important position as *Russia's main link with the Baltic, but it came to an end with the founding of St. Petersburg by Peter the Great in 1703.

NUNES, PEDRO (1492-1577) Portuguese geographer and mathematician. Born in Alcacer do Sal, he was a professor of mathematics in Coimbra and, in 1529, was made royal cosmographer. N. demonstrated that the Spice Islands (*Moluccas) were situated in the part of the globe which by the Treaty of *Tordesillas belonged to Portugal. He published a translation of Ptolemy with comments (1537), and wrote a treatise on the art of *navigation, *De arte atque ratione navigandi* (1546), which is the finest contemporary exposition of the Portuguese technique of exploration. He was also active in Spain, where he resided from 1538 to 1544, but later returned to Coimbra, where he died.

NUREMBERG Founded in the 11th century, this Bavarian town developed rapidly as a centre of trade and industry. In 1219 Emperor Friedrich II conferred upon it the status of a free Imperial town. In 1356 it was the site of the diet which promulgated the Imperial constitution known as the Golden Bull. Ruled by a council of 42, which was dominated by the powerful merchant families, N. achieved unprecedented prosperity by the year 1500, when together with *Augsburg it became the main commercial link between Italy and northern Europe. In addition, it excelled in most kinds of metal and mechanical works. The finest suits of *armour, guns, terrestrial and celestial globes, and the finest pocket watches, known as 'Nuremberg eggs', were made there. The city also had a thriving printing industry and was, unquestionably, the foremost artistic centre of Germany. The artist Albrecht *Dürer and the engraver Michael *Wolgemut lived in N., as did some of the most important German sculptors: Adam *Kraft, Veit *Stoss and Peter *Vischer. Among its celebrated humanists were Martin *Behaim, *Regiomontanus and Willibald *Pirckheimer, and the city was also famous for its school of **Meistersinger*, the most important exponent of which was Hans *Sachs.

In 1525 N. became the first Imperial city to adopt the Reformation and, in 1526, the famous *gymnasium,* planned by *Melanchton, was opened. The subsequent political and religious strife in Germany eroded the city's economic position. It was compelled by *Charles V to pay fines, and began to decline in the second part of the 16th century. It was severely hurt by the *Thirty Years' War, when it was subjected to a long siege. N. retained its formal autonomy for two centuries longer.

E. Kusch, *Nürnberg: Lebensbild einer Stadt* (1950).

NUREMBERG, CATHOLIC LEAGUE OF (1538) A political union of the Roman Catholic princes of Germany, designed as a counter-force to the Protestant *Schmalkaldic League. But, although it was sponsored by Archduke *Ferdinand of Austria, the Emperor's brother, it failed to gather enough power. As a result, and because of the imminent danger of a Turkish attack on Austria, a military conflict between the two Leagues was averted, and another temporary agreement, the Frankfurter Respite, was concluded in 1539.

NUREMBERG, RELIGIOUS PEACE OF (1532) A temporary settlement of the religious conflicts in Germany, agreed in Nuremberg between Emperor Charles V and representatives of the Protestant princes. It postponed the resolution of the conflict until the meeting of a general council, or the next German diet. Although meant as a temporary measure, the agreement was an indirect recognition of Protestantism and welcomed by *Luther as such. It lasted several years and actually gave the German reformers valuable time for further expansion.

Florence's Loggia dei Lanzi designed by Orcagna, with statues by Cellini and Giambologna

O

OBRECHT, JACOB (1453-1505) Dutch composer. The son of a trumpeter in the service of the Duke of Cleves, he was choirmaster at the cathedral of Cambrai in 1484. He then went to *Bruges and, in 1487, visited Italy, where the ruler of *Ferrara wanted him to remain when O. impressed him with his music. O. was later active in Bruges and *Antwerp but, in 1504, returned to Ferrara, where he died of the plague. Much of his music, on liturgical themes and secular songs, has survived, and is considered of great significance.

OCHINO, BERNARDINO (1487-1564) Italian leader. born in Siena, he joined the Observantine Franciscans and became their general, but in 1534 joined the new and more austere order of the *Capuchins. A preacher of great eloquence, O. soon rose to become vicar-general of his new order (1538). Then he fell under suspicion of adopting a Lutheran position on the *justification by faith and, in 1541, fled to *Geneva to avoid the *Inquisition. In 1545 he became the pastor of the Italian congregation in *Augsburg but, in 1547, had to leave and went to England where he was given a royal pension. Here he wrote a dialogue attacking papal authority, and a critique of some aspects of *Calvin's doctrine. At the accession of *Mary he went to Zürich (1555). In 1563 he had to move again because of his tolerant views on polygamy and other controversial doctrines. He died in Moravia.

OCKEGHEM, JEAN OF (c. 1430-95) Flemish composer. Having trained as a choirboy at the cathedral of *Antwerp, he went to France, and by 1454 was already known as a composer and chaplain for *Charles VII. Later he settled in Tours, in the Abbey of St. Martin, where he died. O. was an important developer of polyphony, and the author of many masses and motets. His chansons, too, earned him great popularity. He was also a favourite composer of *Louis XI and *Charles VIII.

OECOLAMPADIUS, JOHANN (1482-1531) German Protestant reformer. Born in the Palatinate, he was educated at Bologna, Heidelberg and Tübingen, and became an established authority on the three classical languages. In 1515 he was appointed preacher at the cathedral of Basle, but he also worked for the publisher *Froben, and helped in the preparation of *Erasmus' Greek edition of the New Testament. He was an early supporter of Luther, but between 1520 and 1522 seemed to have been troubled by doubts and gone into a monastry in Bavaria. In 1523 he became a pastor and professor at the University of Basle, and from there on dedicated himself to the cause of the Reformation. Although he did not do too well in his disputation with *Eck in Baden (1526), O. influenced the decision of the city of Bern to join the reformers, following a disputation which was held there in 1528. In 1529 he took part with his close friend *Zwingli in the Colloquy of Marburg. After his death, his position as leader of the Reformation in Basle was filled by Oswald *Myconius.
G. Rupp, *Patterns in Reformation* (1969)

OJEDA, ALONSO DE (1466-1510) Spanish explorer. Born in Cuenca, he joined *Columbus on his second voyage, and played an important part in the conquest of Hispaniola (1493-95). In 1499-1500 he commanded a famous voyage of discovery, in which he was accompanied by Juan de la *Cosa and Amerigo *Vespucci. They explored the coasts of Guiana and Venezuela ('Little Venice'), which O. named thus when he saw Indian huts standing on stilts near Lake Maracaibo. Later he was appointed governor of the Caribbean coast of present-day Colombia. In 1509 he tried to establish a settlement at the site where later the city of Cartagena was founded. There was an attack by local Indians, and O.'s companion, Juan de la Cosa, was killed. O. himself was wounded by a poison dart during a second landing. He died not long after his return to Hispaniola.

OLDENBARNEVELT, JOHAN VAN (1547-1619) Dutch statesman. Of middle-class background, he studied law in Louvain, Bourges and Heidelberg, before settling in The Hague, where he became a devoted follower of *William of Orange. He took part in the revolt against Spain and, in 1576, obtained the post of Pensionary in Rotterdam, which made him a member of Estates of *Holland. O. encouraged the Union of *Utrecht (1579), and had a hand in the decision of Holland and Zeeland to offer William the title of Count (1584). When the latter was assassinated, O. promptly persuaded the Estates to make young *Maurice of Nassau *stadtholder*

The execution of Oldenbarnevelt

and captain-general (1585). In 1586 he was appointed Land's Advocate of Holland, an office which his energy and skill made into the leading political post in the *United Provinces. During his 32 years in the office, O. practically held the union together, resisting separatist tendencies and supplying the needed leadership in times of crises. He was particularly successful in his foreign policy, concluding an alliance with France and England (1596) which was the first significant international recognition of Dutch independence.

O.'s political standing was for many years strengthened by the support he received from Maurice of Nassau, who generally confined himself to the military sphere. But gradually the relationship between them deteriorated. The 12-years truce with Spain, which O. concluded in 1609, meant a recognition of Dutch independence by the former ruler of the northern Netherlands, yet it was signed in spite of Maurice's misgivings, and the reluctance of the orthodox Calvinist clergy and *Amsterdam merchants. Soon the fierce debate between *Gomarists and Arminians divided the Dutch even more profoundly, O. being with the latter. The final crisis came in 1617, when Maurice came out openly in favour of the Gomarists, rallying around him O.'s opponents. In August 1618 Maurice, having been given supreme powers by the Estates-General, arrested O. and his supporters. The aging statesman was charged with treason, a totally baseless accusation – he may have been guilty of a haughty attitude towards his opponents. Condemned by a packed court, he was beheaded at The Hague.

J. L. Motley, *Life and Death of John of Barneveld,* 2 vols. (1874);
J. den Tex, *Oldenbarnevelt,* 2 vols (1973).

OLIVER, ISAAC (c. 1560-1617) English painter. Born into a French *Huguenot family, he was taken to England as a child, and there became an assistant of the miniaturist Nicholas *Hilliard. In the 1590s he was Hilliard's leading rival, and began to introduce changes into the art of miniature painting, doing both portraits and historical scenes.

OLIVETAN (c. 1506-38) French Protestant translator of the *Bible. Born Pierre Robert, he was a cousin of *Calvin, and earned his name by his habit of burning the midnight oil. O. exercised some influence on young Calvin's decision to espouse the Reformation. He became a *Greek and *Hebrew scholar, and while preaching the new doctrines in Piedmont began his translation, doing the Old Testament directly from the Hebrew. The complete work was published in Neuchâtel (1535). In his last years he was with Calvin in *Geneva.

O'NEILL, HUGH, EARL OF TYRONE (c. 1540-1616) Irish rebel. A child of one of the noble clans of Ulster, he seemed at first to depart from the rebellious tradition of his family, and actually helped the English troops suppress the Desmond rebellion (1579-83). In 1595, however, he joined the uprising that had begun two years earlier and, placing himself at its head, appealed for aid to *Philip II of Spain. But the mighty Spanish armada which sailed in 1596 was dispersed by gales and, in 1599, *Elizabeth I sent *Essex to *Ireland at the head of some 22,000 men. A truce was arranged, as Essex was inclined to accept O.'s demands, which included complete religious freedom. But the next commander of the English forces renewed the fighting, and even the Spanish expedition which landed in 1601 could not save O. and the Irish from the relentless punitive expeditions. In 1602 O. surrendered, but in the reign of *James I he rose again. In 1607 he fled to Rome and there he died.

OPERA A drama presented by means of music and singing, which made its first appearance in 1600, when Jacopo *Peri's *Euridice* was produced in Florence. Three years earlier Peri had composed music for a work called *Dafne*, now lost. Also in 1600 Giulio Caccini (*c*. 1550-1610), another Florentine, composed his own musical set to *Euridice;* the libretti of these three pioneer O.s were all written by Ottavio *Rinuccini. Growing out of the late Renaissance attempts at musical dramatization, and experiments with the *madrigal, the first O.s were largely musical court spectacles. Claudio *Monteverdi, whose *Orfeo* (1607) is the first great O., was responsible for its further musical development, and for its early acceptance as a popular public entertainment. His other great work, *L'incoronazione di Poppea,* was performed in Venice in 1642.

D. J. Grout, *A Short History of the Opera* (1947);
A. Loewenberg, *Annals of Opera* (1955).

OPITZ, MARTIN (1597-1639) German poet. Educated at Heidelberg, where he gathered around him a circle of young poets, he went in 1620 to Holland, and there met and was influenced by the Dutch poet-philologist Daniel Heinisius (1581-1655). In 1627 Emperor Ferdinand II ennobled O., who was then serving as secretary to Count Donha, the man who made Silesia Roman Catholic. After 1635 O. was a historiographer to Ladislas IV of Poland, and resided at Danzig.

Known as the father of German poetry, O. won a reputation with his first works. *Aristarchus,* written when he was 21 and published in 1624, and *Buch von der deutschen Poeterey,* published in the same year, set the style, language and meter that governed German poetry of the 17th century. His German adaptation of *Rinuccini's *Dafne,* to which *Schütz wrote music, is considered the first German **opera.* Other works of O.'s testify to his versatility and fine technique. While not a great innovator, he was a talented practitioner of the literary genres fashionable in his time.

K. Garber, *Martin Opitz, Der Vater der deutschen Dichtung* (1976).

A miniature of the Countess of Bedford by Isaac Oliver

OPORINUS, JOHANNES (1507-68) Swiss printer, publisher and scholar. Born in *Basle, he studied in *Strassburg and then returned to his native town, where he taught Greek and for some time worked for *Froben as an editor (1530-33). Later he opened his own publishing house, issuing scientific texts with his own comments, and translations of the classics. The best-known work printed by him was *Vesalius' *De humani corporis fabrica* (1543) illustrated with numerous woodcuts. In 1542 he published a Latin translation of the Koran with introductions by *Luther and *Melanchthon.

M. Steinmann, *Johannes Oporinus: Ein Basler Buchdrucker um die Mitte des 16. Jahrhunderts* (1966).

ORATORY OF DIVINE LOVE A Catholic reform movement led by devout churchmen of the court of *Leo X. It began in 1517, and counted among its members Gaetano da Thiene, Giampietro *Carafa and *Sadoleto. Their aim was to bring about a moral regeneration from within the Church. A few years later some of the participants founded the *Theatine Order.

ORCAGNA (c. 1308-68) The name by which the Italian painter, sculptor and architect Andrea di Cione is known. A native of *Florence, he joined the painter's guild in about 1343. He executed his best-known painting, an altarpiece for the Strozzi chapel in S. Maria Novella, between 1354 and 1357. His principal sculptural work, the great tabernacle in the church of Orsanmichele, Florence, was executed with the help of several assistants and is dated 1359. That same year he also supervised the work on the duomo at Orvieto. Returning to Florence in about 1362, he took part in redesigning the plan of the cathedral. The famous Loggia dei Lanzi at the Piazza della Signoria is commonly ascribed to O., as well as some lesser works. His three brothers, Jacopo, Matteo and Nardo, assisted him, and were well-known artists in their own right. Essentially a follower of *Giotto, O.'s style lacks depth, and also shows some hieratic Byzantine influences similar to the Sienese paintings. He is, nevertheless, considered the greatest Florentine artist of the mid-14th century.

K. Steinweg, *Andrea Orcagna* (1929).

ORDERS, MILITARY The European military orders of the 15th century were old and staid institutions dating from the time of the early *crusades. They included the *Teutonic Knights of Prussia, the Knights of the Order of St. *John, fought against the *Ottoman Turks in the Aegean sea, the three Spanish military orders (Santiago de Compostella, Alcántara and Calatrava), and the Portuguese Order of Christ. Having always enjoyed considerable autonomy and immense wealth, the three Spanish orders were brought by *Ferdinand and *Isabella under the direct authority of the monarchy, the King himself assuming their grand-mastership (1487-94). In 1523 Pope *Adrian VI incorporated all three orders into the crown of Castile. The German order was practically abolished in 1525. The Knights of St. John were, from 1530, for almost three centuries the rulers of the stagnant island of Malta. By the 16th century autonomous military orders had become obsolete, the Malta one being an exception to the rule.

E. Gallego Blanco, ed., *The Rule of the Spanish Military Order of St.James, 1170-1493* (1971).

ORDERS OF CHIVALRY The orders of *chivalry of the 14th and 15th centuries were a phenomenon quite different from the military *orders. The latter originally embodied monastic and feudal ideas, and eventually became organizations of great economic and political power. By contrast, the O. of the late Middle Ages and early Renaissance were exclusive aristocratic clubs, ideally dedicated to the pursuit of moral good, but often preoccupied with the details of impressive ceremonies and complicated court rituals. The first was the English Order of the Garter, decreed by Edward III in 1348, with membership limited to the king and 25 knights. The Burgundian Order of the *Golden Fleece, which followed it in 1430, was to begin with similarly limited. It became the model of many other orders which were founded by kings and great nobles. Chief among these were the Order of St. Michel, founded by *Louis XI of France in 1469; the Order of the Elephant, founded by *Christian I of Denmark in 1462. (The Order of the Annunziata was founded in *Savoy as early as 1362.) These O. continued to flourish during the 16th century, their constitutions being periodically amended and their membership enlarged according to circumstances. Surviving as decorative aristocratic associations, they remained in vogue until the end of the 19th century.

R. W. Barber, *The Knight and Chivalry* (1974);
L. Gautier, *Chivalry* (1965).

ORDERS, RELIGIOUS The final great phase of mediaeval monasticism was at the end of the 12th and the beginning of the 13th century. Several influential new orders, such as the Carmelites, Dominicans, Franciscans, Mercedarians and Augustinians, were established, introducing into European society the mendicant friars who, unlike the monks of the older orders, lived in the towns, preaching, working or begging for their keep. In the next two centuries these orders, scrupulously poor to begin with, relaxed their rules considerably, and by the 15th century were subjected to criticism from within and without. The conservative Dominicans, for instance, as upholders of mediaeval scholasticism, drew sharp attacks from the humanists. By the time of the Reformation the monastic ideal seemed to have lost its appeal to the educated, and monks were often the object of ridicule and contempt. Nevertheless, the mendicant orders retained much of their vitality, and the Spanish ones, in particular, were zealous missionaries among the New World natives in the early 16th century.

In northern Europe the *Reformation dealt a final blow to monasticism. In England, where at first Protestantism did not seem entirely victorious, the Dissolution of the Monasteries (1536-39) signalled the first obvious break with the old religion. Nevertheless, the 16th century was one of the great ages of Roman Catholic religious orders. The search for new religious forms that would reflect the changing social conditions had begun in the 15th century, in such movements as the *Brethren of the Common Life, and the changes in the old orders, producing, for example, the austere Observants branch of the Franciscans. The first important new order in the 16th century, the *Capuchins, arose in this context. They were followed first by a small group, the *Barnabites, and shortly afterwards by the immensely influential *Jesuits. One of the most significant orders to appear later in the century was that of the Oratorians of St. Philip *Neri. Even more than the 13th-century orders, the *Counter-Reformation emphasized work among the secular society, and supplied new leadership in missionary work and *education.

M. Heimbucher, *Die Orden und Kongregationen der katholischen Kirche*, 2 vols. (1933-34).

ORDOÑEZ, BARTOLOMÉ (?-1520) Spanish sculptor. There is not much information about the early part of his career. He probably came from Burgos, and is known to have collaborated in 1517 with Diego de *Siloe on the church of San Giovanni a Carbonara, Naples. That year he was commissioned to decorate with carvings the choir of the cathedral of Barcelona. O. then executed the tombs of some Spanish dignitaries and, about 1519, began to work on his masterpiece, the monument of *Philip the Handsome and Joanna the Mad at the royal chapel at Granada. It is a remarkable work in a harmonious High Renaissance style clearly influenced by *Michelangelo. He died at Carrara, Italy, where he was working with some Italian assistants.

M. Gómez-Moreno, *Las águilas del renacimiento español* (1941).

ORELLANA, FRANCISCO DE (c. 1500-49) Spanish **conquistador* and explorer. A participant in the conquest of Peru, he was in 1537 charged with the task of re-establishing the Spanish colony at Guayaquil. He then joined Gonzalo *Pizarro's expedition to the eastern slopes of the Andes in search of gold (1540), but, in December 1541, left the main party at the head of a group of 57 men. Entering the Amazon, they followed the great river to the Atlantic, which O. reached in August 1542 with a dozen survivors. In 1543 he returned to Spain, and was appointed governor of the lands he discovered. He then sailed back (1546), intending to establish a settlement at the mouth of the Amazon, but lost many men to the plague at the Cape Verde Islands, and died shortly after his arrival.

ORESME, NICOLE (c. 1320-82) French philosopher and economist. Born near Caen, Normandy, he studied theology and, from 1356 to 1361, was master of the Collège de Navarre, Paris. In 1362 he became canon and, in 1364, dean of the chapter of the cathedral of Rouen. He served as chaplain and advisor to King Charles V, a position which led to his election in 1377 as bishop of Lisieux, where he died. O. left works in different fields, including *mathematics and *astronomy. At the bidding of Charles V he translated from the Latin Aristotles' *Ethics* and *Politics*. His chief work is *De moneta*, a comprehensive treatise on money. Although he relied heavily on Aristotle, and took no account of the actual commercial and *banking practices of his time, it did contain new ideas, particularly about monetary circulation. It was first published in 1484 and was frequently reprinted.

C. Johnson, ed., *The De Moneta of Nicholas Oresme* (1956);
G. W. Coopland, *Nicole Oresme and the Astrologers* (1952).

ORIGINAL SIN, DOCTRINE OF THE The belief that all human beings are born sinful, a basic tenet of Christianity, was given an extreme interpretation by *Luther and *Calvin. According to them, Adam's Fall resulted in a hereditary sin imputed to all men from birth – thereby destroying freedom of choice. This view differed from the Roman Catholic doctrine, according to which infants were cleansed of their original sin by baptism. Although both Roman Catholics and Protestants agreed upon man's essential sinfulness, the emphasis laid by the the latter on the hereditary nature of original sin, led to excessive pessimism.

N. P. Williams, *Ideas of the Fall and of the Original Sin* (1927).

ORLEY, BERNARD VAN (c. 1490-1541) Flemish painter. Visiting Italy twice, he was influenced by the works of Raphael and Michelangelo and became one of the principal practitioners of the Italianate style in the Netherlands. Based in Brussels, he was a court painter during the regency of *Margaret of Austria. Although he also produced stained glass and tapestries, he is especially remembered for his sweet Raphaelesque madonnas.

ORSI, LELIO (1511-87) Italian painter. Born in Reggio, his work shows the influences of *Correggio – whose pupil he may have been – and of *Michelangelo. He was also an architect. In 1546 he was banished from Reggio and, after visits to Venice and Rome, settled at Novellara, where he died. Most of his *frescoes at Reggio and Novellara have perished. His extant works reveal an elegant *Mannerist style, which is sometimes oriented towards drama.

Portrait of a Man *by Bernard van Orley*

ORSINI An important Roman family, the great rivals of the *Colonnas. After the popes returned to *Rome in the 15th century, the O. were often their close supporters. Niccoló O. (1442-1510) was an able **con-dottiere* who commanded for a time the papal troops, and the family distinguished itself in 1527, in the vain attempt to defend Rome against the imperial troops. The O. held titles of nobility and provided the Church with prelates.

ORTA, GRACIA DE (c. 1500-68) Portuguese botanist. Born in Spain into a **marrano* family, he studied medicine in Salamanca and Alcalá before moving to Portugal in 1526. There he held a chair at the University of Lisbon. In 1534 he went with Martim Afonso de *Sousa to *India, and settled in Goa. There he served as physician to the Portuguese viceroys and neighbouring local dignitaries. Though outwardly Christian, he secretly practiced Judaism, and after his death he was condemned by the *Inquisition. O.'s reputation rests on his *Coloquios dos simples e drogas e cousas medicinais da India,* the first treatise on tropical medicine and pharmacology. It was published in Goa in 1563, together with an ode by Luis de *Camoes. The most original work published by the Portuguese in the East, the work also contains material on Indian history, fauna and flora.

C. R. Boxer, *Two Pioneers of Tropical Medicine* (1963).

ORTELIUS, ABRAHAM (1527-98) Flemish cartographer. Born in *Antwerp, he was trained in the various processes of map *engraving, and in about 1554 established his own shop, which also dealt in coins, *medals and antiques. O. was not a great authority on the mathematical aspect of carthography, and is believed to have taken up map designing under the influence of his friend *Mercator. At any rate, he always acknowledged his debt to the cartographers whose maps he reworked. His great *Theatrum orbis terrarum* was first published in 1570, and was later frequently reissued with further corrections and additions. The original edition included 70 maps covering the whole world, and was the first modern atlas. He also wrote works on geography and numismatics. In 1575 he was honoured by *Philip II, who appointed him royal geographer.

OSIANDER, ANDREAS (1498-1552) German Protestant reformer. Two years after he was ordained priest in 1520, he joined *Luther, and became the foremost leader of the Reformation in *Nuremberg. In 1529 he participated with Luther in the Colloquy of Marburg, and during the next year attended the Diet of *Augsburg. When the Imperial armies became the masters of Germany, O. left Nuremberg for the duchy of Prussia and, in 1549, was appointed to the chair of theology at the University of Königsberg. His *De justificatione* (1550) started a fierce debate with the followers of *Melanchthon, concerning the presence of Christ among the faithful. O. maintained that *justification by faith entailed the transfer of divine righteousness to the believer. He also wrote several other scholarly and theological works.

M. Stupperich, *Osiander in Preussen, 1549-52* (1973).

OSONA, RODRIGO DE The name of two Spanish painters, father and son, active in Valencia at the end of the 15th and early 16th century. Rodrigo the Elder's work still reveals marked Flemish influences, but his son's is much more inclined to the *Italianate style. Excelling in the execution of altarpieces depicting traditional religious scenes, some of the best works of Rodrigo the Younger are at the Prado, Madrid.

OSTENDORFER, MICHAEL (c. 1490-1559) German painter and engraver. A pupil of *Altdorfer, he imitated his master's style, and resided throughout his career in Regensburg. He excelled in woodcuts, producing many works on religious subjects. One of his best-known engravings is a genealogy of the *Ottoman sultans with their portraits.

OTTOMAN TURKS, THE A Moslem tribe which settled in north-western Asia Minor in the late 13th century, it became within one hundred years, under the dynasty of Osman I (1290-1326), a prime factor in European history. By the end of the 15th century they had destroyed the remnants of the old Byzantine empire, established their own, conquered the Balkan peninsula and seemed intent on advancing into the heart of Europe. Although they failed to take Vienna in 1529, the Turks conquered *Hungary (1541), and remained there until the end of the 17th century. Their presence and continued menace to *Habsburg territories helped the cause of Protestantism by keeping the German emperors occupied with the external danger. Though they were to begin with an occasional target of Christian crusading spirit, the O. gradually became major partners of the Renaissance European state system.

The first victories of the Turks over the Byzantines were won in the reign of Orkhan I (1326-60). In 1345, at the invitation of a Byzantine emperor, they crossed into Europe and, by 1354, had established their first settlement in Thrace. *Murad I (1360-89) moved the capital to Adrianople, and signed advantageous treaties with *Genoa and *Venice. Penetrating deep into the Balkans, he established Turkish suzerainty over the Bulgarians, Macedonians and Serbs. Their threat to the Byzantine empire, which they had meanwhile reduced to the paying of tribute, prompted the *crusade of Nicopolis (1396), an expedition of knights of assorted western nationalities that ended in disaster. During the early years of the 15th century there was a pause in Turkish expansion, caused by Tamerlane's attack on the Asian part of the O. empire (1402), as well as by internal dissensions. But under *Murad II (1421-51) the Turks occupied parts of Greece and, following a defeat by Janos *Hunyadi at Nish in 1443, crushed the Hungarians and their crusader allies at Varna (1444), and once again in the second battle of Kossovo (1448).

Under *Mehemmed II 'The Conqueror' (1451-81), the Empire became consolidated, and organized its administrative framework, which was to last a long time. His reign opened with the conquest of *Constantinople, which became the new Turkish capital. Although the Sultan failed to take Belgrade (1456), he practically reduced to complete obedience the entire area from the Wallachia, on the other side of the Danube, to Bosnia on the Adriatic Sea, and as far as the Aegean Sea. One after another, the last pockets of resistance failed, and by the end of the reign the only unconquered enclaves in the Empire were the island of Rhodes, ruled by the Knights of St. *John, and Cyprus and Crete, which were ruled by Venice. Adopting a policy of flexible tyranny, the Turks took advantage of the ethnic differences among their subjects, and contented themselves to be the military and administrative echelons. They succeeded in converting some of the upper classes in the subject nations to Islam, but generally tolerated the different religions in their realms. The *Janissaries were their elite warriors, inculcated with boundless loyalty to the sultan. Although this arrangement was to be the cause of the eventual decline of the O., it made for a satisfactory association of the heterogenous elements of the Empire for several generations.

*Bayezid II (1481-1512) relaxed the pressure on the West. He launched the three-year war against Venice (1499-1503) only after the death of his brother *Djem, who had been kept hostage in Italy. *Selim I (1512-20), who had forced his father to abdicate, turned his energies to other directions, undertaking military expeditions to Persia (1514), Syria (1516) and Egypt (1517). By the end of his reign the Ottomans controlled the Arabian peninsula, and the sultan became the protector of the holy places of Islam and a caliph, its spiritual head. The Empire now included the entire eastern part of the Mediterranean.

The O. reached their zenith under the next sultan, *Suleiman I (1520-66). He immediately renewed the pressure on the West, capturing Belgrade (1521) and Rhodes (1522) and, in 1526, dealt King *Louis of Hungary a crushing defeat at *Mohacs. Three years later he made an almost successful attempt to conquer *Vienna (1529). Soon the Ottoman-Habsburg struggle extended to the western Mediterranean, where a talented Turkish admiral, Khair-ed-Din *Barbarossa, established two powerful bases in *Algiers and Tunis. Since about 1525 Ottoman military ventures had been undertaken in agreement with *Francis I, the Habsburgs' leading Christian rival. This alliance was given formal recognition in 1535, when France was awarded the first *Capitulations. The war at sea and on land continued, with temporary truces, throughout Suleiman's reign. After 1541 the Turks held Buda, the Hungarian capital.

Under the pleasure-loving *Selim II (1566-74) the Empire seemed as strong as before. Although its forces lost the great naval battle of *Lepanto (1571), it was able to achieve its strategic aims: the cession of Cyprus by Venice (1573), and the recapture of Tunis from Spain (1574). But with *Murad III (1574-95) the decline of the O. became noticeable. The earliest symptoms were diminished administrative cohesion and moral decay. However, when the war with the Habsburgs in Hungary was renewed in 1593, after a truce of almost a quarter of a century, the O. were no longer able to control their vassal principalities of Transylvania and Moravia, or to repeat the military successes of their heyday. By the peace signed at Sitvatorok in 1606, the sultan renounced his suzerainty over Transylvania. But the O. withdrawal from the Balkan did not begin until the long war, which ended with the treaty of Karlowitz (1699).

D. M. Vaughan, *Europe and the Turk* (1967),

P. Coles *The Ottoman Impact on Europe* (1968).

OUWATER, ALBERT VAN Dutch painter, active from about 1440 until 1470. A citizen of Haarlem, he was famous for his landscape backgrounds, but the only authenticated work of his which survives, *The Ressurection of Lazarus* (Berlin), has for a background a romanesque church. His figures reveal a clear influence of Jan van Eyck's realistic style. O. was the master of *Geertgen van Haarlem. He is sometimes described as the father of "Dutch painting".

OVANDO, NICOLAS DE (1460-1511) Spanish governor of Hispaniola. An official of the military order of Alcántara, he was in 1502 appointed by the crown to replace the highhanded Francisco *Bobadilla. In his seven years of office he completed the conquest of the island, divided the Indian population among the Spaniards in **encomiendas*, organized the work in the mines and plantations, and began the importation of slaves from Africa. In 1509 he returned to Spain.

OVIEDO, GONZALO FERNANDES DE (1478-1557) Spanish historian. A scribe in the court of *Ferdinand and *Isabella, he sailed to America six times on official missions and ended his life in Santo Domingo. He wrote several books, including a novel, but his great work was the *Historia general y natural de las Indias*, first published in *Seville in 1535. Based on first-hand information, it is an extensive account of the Spanish discovery and conquest of the Indies, celebrating Spain's achievements during her most glorious years. From 1532 until his death O. held the office of royal chronicler of the Indies.

OXENHAM, JOHN (?-1575) English *privateer. In 1572 he joined *Drake's expedition which captured Nombre de Dios in the Isthmus of Panama. On their march across the Isthmus both Drake and O. announced their intention to attack the Spaniards in the Pacific coast, where they least expected foreign privateers. In 1574 O. returned to Panama, and penetrated inland on foot. He was discovered, however and pursued by the Spanish authorities and finally captured. Most of his men were executed immediately, and O. was sent to Lima and hanged there.

P

PACHECO, FRANCISCO (1564-1654) Spanish painter and author. Born in Sanlucer de Barrameda, he settled in *Seville, where he established a successful workshop and later a painting academy (1611). One of his pupils was Diego Velásquez (1599-1660), who married his daughter. P. served as a painting censor for the *Inquisition in Seville. He was one of the founders of the Spanish naturalist style, and an important figure during the transition from *Mannerism to *Baroque. Between 1623 and 1625 he worked in Madrid, but after his return to Seville he dedicated himself to writing. His *Arte de la pintura, su antiguedad y grandeza* was published in 1649.

PACHER, MICHAEL (c. 1437-98) German painter. P. worked in the churches of small towns in the Tyrol; his style reveals the influences of his Italian contemporaries, especially of *Mantegna. His best work was the great altarpiece of 1481 in the parish church of St. Wolfgang, in Austria. The polychromed sculptural figures in his paintings suggest that he also practised woodcarving.

PACINI, PIERO (c. 1440-c. 1513) Italian printer. Born at Pescia, he was possibly the best-known Florentine publisher of the late 15th century. He specialized in Italian works with woodcut illustration, among which were Aesop's *Fables* (1496) and *Petrarch's *Trionfi* (1499). In 1505 he printed the *Lettera delle isole nuovamente ritrovate* of Amerigo *Vespucci.

PACIOLI, LUCA (1445-c. 1510) Italian mathematician. Born in Borgo San Sepolcro, he went in his youth to Venice, where in about 1465 he became a tutor in the household of a merchant. He became an expert in commercial bookkeeping and, after he joined the Franciscan order (1470), devoted himself to teaching and lecturing on mathematics in Perugia, Rome, Naples, Milan, and other places. His *Summa de arithmetica, geometria, proportioni et proportionalità* (1494) was the first textbook of mathematics ever published, although it was mostly derivative. P. also wrote on mathematical games. In 1503 he published in Venice *De divina proportione*, where he deduced principles of proportion in *architecture, and in the structure of the human body, reflecting the author's association with artists such as *Piero della Francesca and *Leonardo.

S. Morison, *Fra Luca Pacioli of Borgo S. Sepolcro* (1933);
J. B. Geijsbeek-Molenaar, ed., *Ancient Double-Entry Bookkeeping; Lucas Pacioli's Treatise* (1974).

PADILLA, JUAN DE (1468-c. 1522) Spanish poet. Born in Seville, he became a Carthusian monk and is therefore also known as "El Cartujano". The author of several romances, he is especially remembered for his two long religious poems, *Retablo de la vida de Jesús Cristo* (1513) and *Los doce triunfos de los doce apostolos* (1521). He imitated the style of the 15th-century poet Juan de *Mena, and made use of allegory.

PADILLA, JUAN DE (1484-1521) Leader of the unsuccessful *Comuneros revolt in 1520-21 against *Charles V. Born in Toledo to a noble family, he was unsuccessful in gaining royal favour and, out of a sense

The Betrothal of the Virgin *by Michael Pacher*

High Renaissance painting: Madonna and Child *by Boltraffio*

The Mathematician Luca Pacioli *by Jacopo de' Barbari*

of bitterness, became the captain of the rebel forces. The insurrectionists first thought of forming a national government headed by Queen *Joanna the Mad, and captured the castle of Tordesillas where she was kept. Popular demands for democratization of the movement then alienated the nobles. After being replaced, P. was recalled when the new captain was defeated. After some military success, his forces were defeated at Villalar on 23 April 1521. He was captured and executed the next day.

PAGNINI, SANTI (?-1541) Italian biblical scholar. A native of Lucca, he entered the Dominican order, acquiring such a reputation for his knowledge of oriental languages that Pope *Leo X invited him to teach in Rome. In about 1518 he completed a Latin translation of the *Bible directly from *Hebrew and *Greek. Published in *Lyons (1527) and later in *Cologne (1541), this was the first translation to divide the Bible into separate verses. P. also compiled a Hebrew grammar and dictionary which went through numerous editions.

PAINTER, WILLIAM (1540-94) English writer. In 1561 he became a clerk of the ordnance in the Tower of London. Charged with embezzling government property, he was not prosecuted. P.'s fame rests mainly on his work, *The Palace of Pleasure* (1566-67), a collection of classical and contemporary Italian and French amorous tales, translated into English which served as a source for Elizabethan dramatists including *Shakespeare.

PAINTING An artistic medium which reached its historical zenith during the 15th and 16th centuries, Renaissance P. has remained the aesthetic complex upon which the modern world largely relies for its norms of beauty and grace. Its influence over painters of later generations was overwhelming, perhaps even debilitating, and even today the average man tends to appreciate paintings according to recognizable Renaissance criteria. The principal techniques, as well as the conventional range of subjects and the manner of representing them, were developed and matured during that period.

Renaissance P. began in Italy at the end of the 13th century in the work of several precursors of exceptional talent. Following the half-legendary Florentine *Cimabue, his fellow-citizen *Giotto introduced revolutionary elements of three-dimensional reality and a heroic human expression, breaking away from the hieratic symbolism of the Middle Ages. He also revived the art of the *fresco, which replaced the mosaic and became the favourite Renaissance medium of monumental painting.

Flemish School of the 15th century: Madonna and Child *by Dieric Bouts*

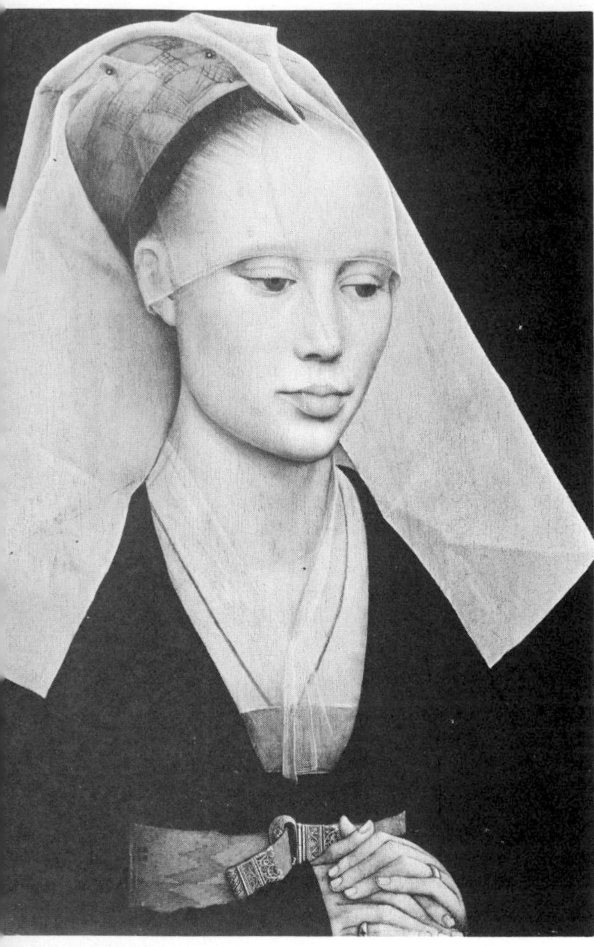

Portrait of a Lady *by Roger van der Weyden*

His contemporary *Duccio in Siena still clung to Byzantine stylistic elements, and so, to a large extent, did Simone *Martini. The latter, however, was the first to paint a non-religious picture, depicting a mounted **condottiere*. The younger Sienese, Ambrogio *Lorenzetti, painted allegories on civic life, and adopted the realistic style.

Giotto's manner of painting was continued in the 14th century by his Florentine followers, including Taddeo *Gaddi, Bernardo *Daddi and *Maso, often referred to collectively as the "Giottesques". But *Orcagna, in the third quarter of the century, reverted to the rigid Byzantine style. The transition was not restricted to Italy. The stylized elegance of the *International Gothic, at once aristocratic and bizarre, was then spreading through western Europe, having a particular effect on the art of *illuminated manuscripts. In Italy its outstanding follower was *Gentile da Fabriano, followed by less influential figures, such as *Stefano da Verona, and their joint disciple, *Pisanello. It is not a chronological coincidence that the realist reaction to International Gothic began about 1425 in both Italy and *Flanders. In *Bruges Jan van *Eyck, one of the most original artists of all ages, combined a new technique of oil painting with elements of *perspective, and a penetrating eye for the human expression, to launch an immensely influential school. His best successor was Roger van der *Weyden, and among other gifted representatives were Dieric *Bouts, Hugo van der *Goes and Hans *Memling. New norms of painting established by these masters were assimilated as far as Spain and Portugal, and had a fruitful influence even on the Italians. In Germany the effect was noticeable in the work of 15th-century painters, such as Konrad *Witz, Lucas *Moser, and Hans *Multscher. In France, on the other hand, the situation was more complicated, there being a strong tendency to continue the traditions of International Gothic, as well as to absorb outside influences The more conservative tendency is most noticeable in the illuminated manuscripts of the *Limbourg brothers and, later, *Bourdichon. The famous *Pietà*, painted by an unknown artist of the Avignon school *c.* 1450, is a masterpiece combining sensitivity with realism, while the works of *Fouquet and *Charonton reveal familiarity with Flanders and Italy.

For all that, the future of European P. was forged in Italy. In Florence *Masaccio revived Giotto's realist style in his frescoes at the Brancacci Chapel (1425-27). From *Brunelleschi he learned the principles of scientific perspective, and from *Donatello the interest in classical forms and the nude; the modulation of light and shade, however, which gave his paintings a new three-dimensional plasticity, was entirely his own. His contribution was felt only partially in the elegant religious works of Fra *Angelico, but it fascinated Paolo *Uccello and was emulated by Andrea del *Castagno. Outside Florence, *Piero della Francesca and *Mantegna were the two most influential masters of this kind of P., the first with his clarity and order, the second with the statuesque qualities and classical reconstructions. Mantegna was also a chief contributor to the rise of the Venetian school, though here the influence of *Antonello da Messina was equally decisive. In the second part of the 15th century Florentine painters, stressing fine draftsmanship and linearity, were still leading Italy in the quality of their work. They developed an interest in mythological subjects, exemplified first on a monumental scale by *Botticelli, and acquired a better knowledge of human *anatomy, as may be seen in the works of *Pollaiuolo and *Signorelli. Their *Madonnas, in the manner of Fra Filippo *Lippi, represented femininity and motherhood. Portraits, an increasingly popular genre, were strickingly naturalistic, as in the works of *Ghirlandaio, and revealed early attempts at psychological characterization.

Italian P. of the High Renaissance was a relatively short but abundantly fruitful age, corresponding with the first quarter of the 16th century. The combined achievement of *Leonardo, *Michelangelo, and *Raphael was a style embodying classical beauty, harmony and grace, which came to be viewed as the ultimate fulfilment of universal artistic ideals. Technically, they surpassed all their predecessors, a fact that may be verified by an examination of their drawings in particular. In addition, each made a distinct personal contribution: Leonardo with his innovative modelling, Michelangelo with his heroic sculptural figures, Raphael

Adoration of the Kings *by Mabuse*

with his serene balanced compositions. Lesser geniuses abounded, such as *Andrea del Sarto of Florence, the master of gentle postures, and *Corregio of Parma, whose ecstatic religious works and illusionist fresco domes inspired the painters of the late 16th century.

The true heirs of the balanced style of the High Renaissance were the Venetians. In the late 15th century Giovanni *Bellini founded a school of painting which emphasized landscape, light and colour. He was followed by *Giorgione, the master of atmospheric pastoral scenes, and by *Titian, whose work brought Venetian P. to a level of perfection that won the admiration of all of Europe. *Tintoretto's agitated nature made his work somewhat exceptional among his great contemporaries. But it was *Veronese who brought the Venetian tradition of serene decorative splendour to its high point.

At the same time, the generation that came after the High Renaissance masters in Florence and Rome developed individualistic tendencies, and was later described by the general term *Mannerism. The departure from the ideal of natural harmony in the work of *Pontormo, *Rosso, *Giulio Romano and *Parmigianino, was partly a response to a changing cultural climate, partly the product of artistic preoccupations, such as the pursuit of original aesthetic effects. *Bronzino, the master of detached analytical portraiture, and the painter-art historian *Vasari, were among the leading exponents of late Italian Mannerism.

The Italianate style began to influence the painters of northern Europe as early as the first years of the 16th century. The process was particularly noticeable in Germany, where *Dürer, an enthusiastic champion of the Italians, dominated a great artistic generation. Whereas *Cranach's acceptance of the new trend was largely superficial, it was plainly evident in the portraits of *Burgkmair, and is discernible in the landscapes painted by *Altdorfer and his followers, the so-called Danube School. *Holbein the Younger, whose superb portraits display High Renaissance dignity and poise, introduced this P. to England. At the same time Flemish and Dutch painters, led by *Mabuse, Quentin *Massys and Jan van *Scorel, began to emulate Michelangelo and Leonardo with various degrees of success. Nevertheless some of the best northern painters resisted the Italian influences, remaining faithful to the expressive Gothic tradition, or to their own personal visions. This was, notably, the case with *Bosch and *Breugel in the Netherlands, and *Grünewald in Germany.

By the middle of the 16th century, painters outside Italy came under the influence of Mannerism. *Primaticcio and Rosso, who headed the *Fontainebleau

Mannerist landscape painting: Fantastic Landscape *by Niccolò dell'Abate*

Diana of Poitiers Emerging from her Bath *by Clouet*

School in France, helped to develop a style designed to please rather than impress, and this was complemented by the courtly portraits of Jean and François *Clouet. The Mannerist style was introduced into England by Hans *Eworth, and was continued in the exquisite miniatures of Nicholas *Hilliard. In the Netherlands, Frans *Floris and Maerten van *Heemskerk were its leading practitioners. Towards the end of the century, the break with the High Renaissance concepts of serene harmony produced occasional extremist creations on eerie and fantastic subjects. The tendency is best exemplified in the works of *Arcimboldi and *Spranger at the *Habsburg court in Prague. But it is also found in the work of El *Greco in Toledo, Spain, whose pictures with their disproportionate figures and greenish tones created a feeling of intense, anguished religiosity.

By the end of the 16th-century European painting was due for a major revision. The new style, later named

*Baroque, orchestrated colour and form into a grand whole, designed to evoke an emotional response in the viewer. It began in Rome, where *Caravaggio was active in the 1590s, and where in 1604 Annibale *Carracci completed the fresco decorations of the Palazzo Farnese. Among the most important early followers of the two were *Lanfranco and *Domenichino. But the outstanding figure of the early Baroque was undoubtedly *Rubens, who mastered the new style while working in Italy. With his return to Antwerp in 1508, the centre of European P. may be said to have moved west, anticipating the emergence of the great 17th-century schools of the Netherlands, Spain and France.

J. Lassaigne, *The Fifteenth Century: From Van Eyck to Botticelli* (1955);
L. Venturi, *The Sixteenth Century: From Leonardo to El Greco* (1956);
C. Gilbert, *History of Renaissance Art* (1973);
P. and L. Murray, *The Art of the Renaissance* (1963).

PALATINATE (German: Pfalz) Extending to the left and right of the middle Rhine, this large principality played a distinctive role in German politics of the *Reformation. Its name dates back to the 12th century, when Frederick Barbarossa gave the office of count palatine to his half brother, who linked the dignity with family possessions of the Hohenstaufens. Heidelberg on the Neckar, where, in 1386, the famous university was founded, became the capital. The *Wittelsbachs, who ruled the P. throughout the 13th and 14th centuries, made it known as the Rhenish or, later, as the Electoral Palatinate, so as to distinguish it from the Upper Palatinate (Oberpfalz) in *Bavaria. The count palatine held the first place among the secular electors of the Empire. When Count Rupert, who had also been king of Germany, died in 1410, the principality underwent successive changes. Later, Frederick I the Victorious (1449-76), extended his lands in Alsace and north along the Rhine.

In 1556 elector Otto Henry made Lutheranism a state religion. He died without sons in 1559 and was succeeded by *Frederick III, the count palatine of the branch of Simmern. In 1561 the new elector embraced Calvinism and became an active supporter of the French *Huguenots and the Dutch rebels. His son Louis VI reverted to Lutheranism, but following his death (1583), *John Casimir took over the government, ruling on behalf of his young nephew, Frederick IV, from 1583 to 1592, and again aiding the Calvinists. Frederick IV was one of the main architects of the *Protestant Union (1608). In 1619, his son Frederick V contributed to the outbreak of the *Thirty Years' War by accepting the throne of *Bohemia offered him by the Czech rebels. During the course of this long conflict, the P. suffered disastrously and the ruling dynasty was suspended. It was restored again, however, as a result of the Peace of Westphalia (1648).

PALEARIO, AONIO (c. 1500-70) Italian humanist and religious martyr. Born at Veroli, he studied in Rome, which he left in 1527 to go to Siena. In 1536 his religious poem, *De immortalitate animorum*, was published in Lyons. In 1542 he was accused of writing a heretical tract known as *Libellus de morte Christi*, but the charge did not prevent his appointment to a chair of rhetoric at Lucca (1546-55). It was probably there that he wrote his caustic attack on the papacy, *Actio in pontifices romanos et eorum asseclas*, first published in Amsterdam in 1696. Forced to move to Milan, he was there denounced to the *Inquisition (1559), but was again acquitted. However, in 1567 the charges against him were renewed, and the following year he was sent to Rome, where he was imprisoned for two years before being hanged and burned as an unrepentant heretic.

G. Morpurgo, *Un umanista martire: Aonio Paleario* (1912).

PALESTRINA, GIOVANNI PIERLUIGI DA (c. 1524-94) Italian composer. Born at Palestrina, near Rome. As a boy he went to Rome and in 1537 joined the choir of Sta. Maria Maggiore. In 1544 he became an organist and a singer in the Cathedral of Palestrina. In 1551, soon after the bishop of his town became Pope *Julius III, P. was invited to Rome and served as a choirmaster at the Capella Giulia. Three years later he published his first book of masses which he dedicated to Julius III. In return, despite the fact that P. was married, the pope made him a member of the pontifical choir. In 1555 the pope died and was succeeded by *Marcellus II who retained the position for less than a month. Marcellus claimed that it was important to understand the words of the service, and that the music should clarify them rather than become in itself an essential part of the liturgy. With this idea in mind, P., after the death of the pope, wrote the *Missa Papae Marcelli*. During the same year he also published a collection of secular compositions, his *First Book of Madrigals*. The next pope, *Paul IV, decreed that only unmarried men could serve in the pontifical choir. P., who had been married since 1547, had therefore to leave, then becoming the director of the choir of St. John Lateran, for which he composed his *Lamentations*. In 1561 he became choirmaster at Sta. Maria Maggiore, and also entered the service of Cardinal Ippolito d'*Este in Tivoli. From 1571 until his death he was again choirmaster of the Capella Giulia, and during these years composed hymns for St. Philip *Neri's Oratory, many *Motets to words taken from the "Songs of Songs" and the mass *Assumpta est Maria*, first performed in 1585. Between 1581 and 1594 he published 17 volumes containing various types of composition.

Perhaps the most famous composer of the 16th century, in order to be in line with the concern expressed by the Council of *Trent that music should not obscure the text, P. wished to show that words could be clearly audible even in contrapuntal music. His music, a true expression of the ideals of the *Counter Reformation, is highly systematized and well regulated, both ecclesiastical and secular compositions containing a great variety of rhythms.

H. Coates, *Palestrina* (1938);
K. Jeppesen, *The Style of Palestrina and the Dissonance* (1946). (ND)

PALISSY, BERNARD (1510-89) French potter and author. Born in Agen, he learned glass painting and eventually settled in Saintes, near La Rochelle. For 16 years (1538-54) he conducted experiments in an attempt to produce a pure white enamel to be used for decorative purposes. According to the account he gives, he sacrificed almost everything toward this end, at times burning his furniture in order to keep alight the fire in his oven. His enameled pottery and clay sculpture brought him the patronage of *Montmorency, who rescued him from

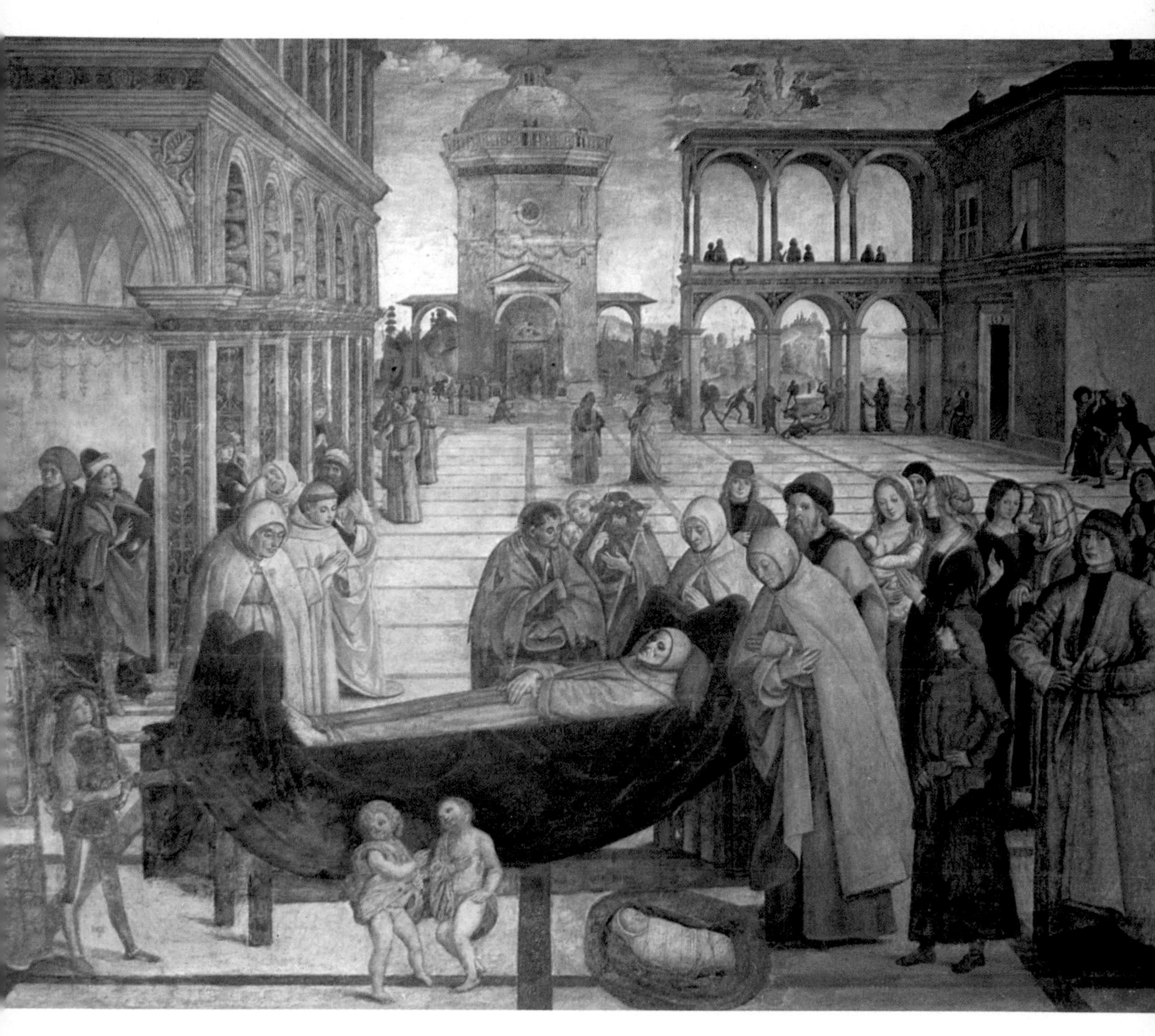

ıe Burial of St. Bernardino *at S. Maria Aracoeli, Rome*

The Punishment of Korah, Dathan and Abiram, *a fresco by Botticelli in the Sistine Chapel*

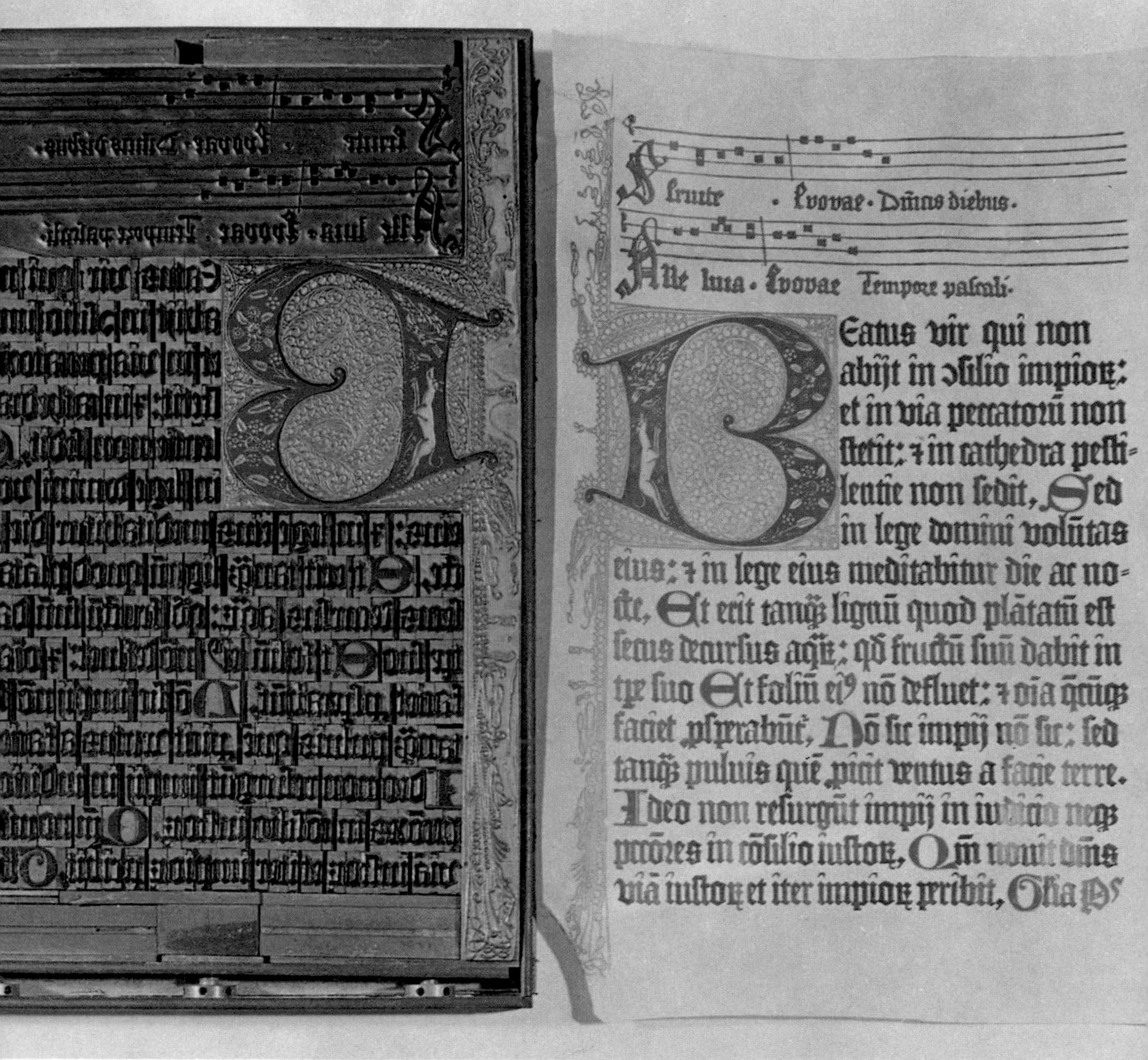

Seruite · Euouae · Dñis diebus ·
Alle luia · Euouae Tempore pascali·

Beatus vir qui non
abijt in ɔsilio impiorꝫ:
et in via peccatorũ non
stetit: ⁊ in cathedra pesti-
lentie non sedit, Sed
in lege domini volũtas
eius: ⁊ in lege eius meditabitur die ac no-
cte, Et erit tanꝙ lignũ quod plãtatũ est
secus decursus aq̃rꝫ: qđ fructũ suũ dabit in
tp̃e suo Et foliũ ei⁹ nõ defluet: ⁊ oĩa q̃cũqꝫ
faciet ꝓsperabũt, Nõ sic impij nõ sic: sed
tanꝙ puluis quẽ ꝓicit ventus a facie terre.
Ideo non resurgũt impij in iudicio neqꝫ
pctõres in cõsilio iustorꝫ, Qm̃ nouit dñs
viã iustorꝫ et iter impiorꝫ peribit, Gl̃ia Ps

The first book printed in colours; a page from the psalter of Fust and Schöffer prison in Bordeaux where he was put on the charge of being a *Huguenot preacher (1562). When he came to Paris, he was supported by *Catherine de Médicis, for whom he made many works of art including a pottery grotto. There, from 1575, in addition to his artistic output, he lectured on scientific subjects, publishing a popular pamphlet on natural history, *Discours admirables* (1580). In another work, *De l'art de la terre*, he described his working methods as a potter. Sentenced again to imprisonment for his religious beliefs in 1588, he died in the Bastille the following year.

The Admirable Discourse of Bernard Palissy, trans. by Aurele La Rocque (1957);

E. Dupuy, *Bernard Palissy: l'homme, l'artiste, le savant, l'écrivain* (1902; rep. 1970).

PALLADIO, ANDREA (1518-80) Italian architect. Born in Padua, he ran away to Vicenza at the age of 16 and went to work as a stonecutter. The poet *Trissino, whose protegé he became, provided him with the essentials of a humanist education and also named him after the ancient Greek goddess Pallas Athena. P. formed his style during three visits to Rome (1541, 1547 and 1549). He received his first important commission in 1546, when he won the competition to rebuild the Palazzo della Ragione in Vicenza. Most of his later works were also executed in his adopted town, although in the last 20 years of his life he frequently worked in Venice, where he built several beautiful churches. P. excelled in the building of harmonic, classically-inspired residential palaces and country villas. He favoured the use of impressive columns to support the entire structure, one on top of the other, as in his Palazzo Chiericati in Venice. His best-known residential house is the Villa Rotunda (1550-51) near Vicenza, a square building of four identical façades with a large round dome over its central hall. P. employed sculptors and painters, including *Veronese, to decorate his buildings. He wrote several books, the most important being the *Quattro libri dell'architettura* (1570), and, already in his lifetime, attained a reputation as the foremost theoretician and practitioner of the Graeco-Roman form. Famous throughout Europe, he influenced many architects, among them the English Inigo *Jones, and left a lasting impression on Italian architecture.

J. Ackermann, *Palladio* (1967);

R. Wittkower, *Palladio and Palladianism* (1974).

PALLADIUS, PEDER (1503-60) Danish theologian. When he was rector of Odense, he decided to join the *Reformation. In 1531 he came to study at *Wittenberg, spending six years there. In 1537 he returned with *Bugenhagen to Denmark where he was consecrated bishop of Zeeland, the most important Danish ecclesiastical office. An effective preacher and spiritual administrator, he wrote the *Visitatsbog* (Visitation Book), a seminal work in the annals of Danish Lutheranism.

PALMA GIOVANE, JACOPO NEGRETTI (1544-1628) Italian painter. Born in Venice, he was the great-nephew of *Palma Vecchio. P. completed one of *Titian's *Pietà* after the latter's death. Undoubtedly influenced by this master, he eventually developed his own *Mannerist style. P. lived mainly in Venice, where he was regarded as second only to *Tintoretto and *Veronese. When they died he remained the unrivalled master in Venice, a position he held throughout the first quarter of the 17th century.

PALMA VECCHIO, JACOMO NEGRETTI (1480-1528) Italian painter. A native of Lombardy, he settled in Venice where he earned fame for his lush, very appealing portraits as well as for his depiction of biblical themes. P. painted popular female half-figures, and religious scenes with heavy-set, female saints, typically Venetian in quality. First influenced by Giovanni *Bellini, his later work shows clear traces of *Giorgione and *Titian.

G. Gombosi, *Palma Vecchio* (1937).

PALMEZZANO, MARCO (1456-1539) Italian painter. Born at Forli, he adopted the style of his master *Melozzo da Forli, and completed some of his frescos. Later he became subject to several influences, including that of *Mantegna. He left a great number of pictures, mostly on religious subjects and a few portraits.

PALMIERI, MATTEO (1406-75) Italian humanist. A native of Florence, he studied under famous humanists, served in the government of the republic and wrote both in Latin and Italian. His *De temporibus*, covered the years 449-1449, and is one of the first attempts to write a history of the Middle Ages. P. wrote a history of Florence and the history of the war with Pisa. In the *Della vita civile*, which he wrote in Italian, he discusses the qualities needed for managing a family, guiding a state and being a good citizen. *La città di vita* is a long poem imitative of *Dante. By P.'s request, it was published only after his death.

PALSGRAVE, JOHN (c. 1480-1554) English scholar. Born in London, he studied at Cambridge and Paris, where he acquired a thorough knowledge of French. He became a tutor to Princess Mary, sister of *Henry VIII, whom in 1514 he accompanied to France. Later he taught the duke of Richmond, the King's natural son, becoming rector of St. Dunstan-in-the-East, London (1533). In 1545 he was appointed rector of Wadenhoe, Northamptonshire, where he died. He is known for *Lesclaircissement de la Langue Françoyse*, published in 1530, designed as a French grammar and dictionary, which has indirectly become a valuable source of information on early 16th century English.

PANNARTZ, ARNOLD AND SWEYNHEYM, KONRAD German printers; active from about 1465 to 1477. Learning their craft in *Gutenberg's Mainz, in 1463 they went to Italy and set up the first press outside Germany in the Benedictine abbey of Subiaco near Rome. There, in 1465, they printed Cicero's *De oratore* in round character, thus innovating the earliest form of roman type. In 1468, with the aid of Cardinal Juan de *Torquemada, they moved to Rome where, during the next four years, they printed 46 volumes in editions of 275 copies each, among which were important classical and Christian patristic texts. Before his death, Sweynheym prepared the 27 copper plates for the maps of Ptolemy's *Cosmographia*, which was published in Rome in 1478. Prefaces to the classical texts of Pannartz and Sweynheym were written by Giovanni Andrea *Bussi.

PANNONIUS, JANOS (1434-72) Hungarian humanist. Born to one of the noblest Magyar families, he was sent to *Ferrara in 1447, and educated by *Guarino da Verona. From 1454 to 1458 he studied canon law in Padua; upon his return to Hungary he was made bishop of Pécs (1459), serving in the court of King *Matthias Corvinus. He again visited Italy on a diplomatic mission in 1465. Later, because of his part in a conspiracy

Villa Capra near Vicenza by Palladio

against the king he had to flee Hungary and died in exile. P. wrote Latin poetry which brought him recognition already in his youth. One of his best-known elegies was addressed to *Mantegna, who had painted his portrait. He also translated from Plutarch, Homer and other classical authors.

PANORMITA (1394-1471) The name given to the Italian humanist Antonio Beccadelli. Born in Palermo, he studied in Sienna, and in 1425 published in Bologna a Latin collection of obscene and satirical epigrams entitled *Hermaphroditus*. In 1429 he became court poet of Filippo Maria *Visconti, but in 1434 exchanged patrons, going to the court of *Alfonso V of Aragon, whose secretary and trusted adviser he became. P. was instrumental in encouraging the growth of humanist studies in Naples. He wrote a biography of Alfonso, as well as poems and letters in a graceful Latin style.

L. Barozzi, *Studi sul Panormita e sul Valla* (1891).

PANORMITANUS (1386-1445) Italian archbishop of Palermo, hence his name, also known as *Abbas Modernus*. A native of Sicily, he was born as Nicolo de' Tudeschi, became a Benedictine monk and later studied and taught canon law at *Bologna. In 1425 he became an abbot of a monastery near Messina, and in 1435 was made archbishop. P. was the author of several commentaries on canon law, but he is also remembered for his role at the Council of *Basle where he defended *conciliarism against the notion of papal supremacy, and supported antipope *Felix V.

PAPACY During the Renaissance the P. ceased to be the universal centre of Christianity. Although the various popes were deeply involved in the political and cultural events of the period, their influence in religious matters was declining, a process which not even the *Counter Reformation could arrest. The end of the *Great Schism in 1417 marked a new period in the history of the institution. Again there was only one Papal centre, and the popes seemed to regain much of the power and prestige which had been lost during the years of the Avignonese papacy and the Schism. But, in the 15th century, the P. had to confront the rising power of monarchs who wanted to establish state churches. There was an acknowledged need for reform within the Church, but nothing was done about it until the second half of the 16th century. In the meantime, the popes directed their attention to the worldly interests of the *Papal States, handling political affairs just like secular rulers.

What was more, from *Nicholas V (1447-55) until about the mid-16th century, the P. became a leading centre of culture. *Rome rivalled Florence as a magnet for Italian and European humanists and artists who received patronage from the various popes.

The decadency of the P., its secularization and the need for reform were the conditions that gave rise to the challenge of Martin *Luther in 1517. *Leo X (1513-21) and *Clement VII (1523-34) did not understand the implications of what was happening and that the unity of the Church was being rapidly eroded. Only belatedly did the *Reformation make the popes aware of the necessity for reform of the Church from within. Pope Paul III (1534-49), began the enterprise, of which the most significant accomplishment was the Council of *Trent. Efforts to reform the Church and strengthen the P. were continued by Paul's successors. However, the P. could never regain its mediaeval function as a central force of Western civilization.

M. Creighton, *A History of the Papacy during the period of the Reformation*, 6 vols. (1887-94);
F. X. Seppelt, *Das Papsttum im Spätmittelalter und in der Zeit der Renaissance* (1941). (ND)

PAPAL STATES When the papacy was translated to Avignon (1309-77), it completely lost control over the territories in central Italy which formerly had come under its temporal jurisdiction. Romagna, the Marches and Umbria became the property of single families, ruling independent baronies and cities; these, while claiming to exercise power granted them by the Church, actually governed in their own right. The first significant attempts to restore papal jurisdiction were made by *Martin V (1417-31). But during most of the rest of the 15th century papal government in much of these areas existed in name only. A determined effort to recover effective control was then undertaken by *Alexander VI through his son Cesare *Borgia, with the intention of giving him the opportunity of seizing power himself. Frequently cited as the real founder of the P., *Julius II renewed the attempt, regaining Romagna and bringing *Bologna under his jurisdiction. After him *Leo X continued consolidating his authority over the area till the Sack of *Rome (1527), which occurred during the pontificacy of *Clement VII, left the papal government in shambles. It was the same pope, however, who, by crowning *Charles V emperor at Bologna in 1530 prepared the way for a long alliance between Rome and the Spanish monarchy, thus enabling later popes to recover full dominion and even to enlarge the area under their rule. During the governments of *Paul III and later under *Sixtus V and *Clement VIII, the nobility was reduced to obedience and the *Inquisition gained power. Modena was recovered from the *Este family, and, in 1598 *Ferrara itself was taken. By that time the P. stretched from coast to coast, including the March of Ancona, the duchies of Parma and Piacenza held by the house of *Farnese, and, in addition Romagna, Spoleto, Bologna, Perugia and Orvieto.

P. Partner, *The Papal State Under Martin V* (1958);
J. Guiraud, *L'état pontifical après le grand schisme* (1896).

PAPER Mediaeval manuscripts were usually copied on parchment, but the great increase in the number of books arising from the introduction of *printing necessitated the use of a cheaper, more easily produced material. First made by the Chinese, paper was brought to Europe by the Arabs in the 12th century and, by the late 14th century, was a commonly known commodity. The European paper industry of the 15th and 16th centuries used old rags as the chief raw material. These were shredded in a mill driven by waterpower, the small pieces that resulted being soaked in water to create a liquid pulp. With the aid of a large flat wire sieve the papermaker then formed thin sheets of evenly distributed pulp, which he put on alternate layers of felt, squeezed in a press and dried. At the time printing made its appearance paper was selling for less than a fifth of the price of parchment; consequently, the latter material, as well as calfskin-made-vellum, was employed only in luxury printing. Paper continued to be made of rags in Europe until the mid-19th century when the method of producing it from wood-pulp was developed.

PARABOSCO, GIROLAMO (c. 1524-57) Italian writer and musician. Born in Piacenza, he wrote 8 comedies, a tragedy, a mythological poem, entitled *Adonis*, and a poem in praise of the women of Venice. His best-known work is *I Diporti* (1550), a collection of 17 stories, which, though not entirely original, abound with comic situations. From 1551 he served as organist at St. Mark's, Venice, where he also composed *motets.

PARACELSUS (Philippus Aureolus Theophrastus Bombastus von Hohenheim; 1493-1541) Swiss physician and *alchemist who introduced the use of *chemistry into *medicine. He adopted the name Paracelsus (above Celsus), to show that he considered himself greater than Celsus, the 1st century Roman physician. Born to a poor German physician in a village near Einsiedeln, now in Switzerland, he first began to study metals and chemistry when he moved to Villach in Southern Austria. In 1507 he went to the university of *Basle and later attended several other European universities though, it seems, without obtaining a degree. Very critical of his professors, he claimed that knowledge should be gained through experience, and spent ten years wandering and trying to learn about medicine, alchemy and the treatment of diseases which other physicians considered incurable. On his return to Villach in 1524 he had already become famous, and he was appointed town physician and lec-

Paracelsus

turer at the university of Basle in 1526. His lectures, which were given in German rather than in Latin as was customary at the time, drew students from all over Europe. In them P. discarded the accepted Greek and Arab medical authorities and publicly burned the works of Galen and Avicenna. He attacked remedies common in his time and claimed that nature is the best healing power. His intolerance made him many enemies, and in 1529 he had to leave Basle, and begin to wander once more. A prolific writer on medicine, philosophy and alchemy, he published the *Die große Wundartzney* (The Great Book of Surgery) in 1536. He died in Salzburg under mysterious circumstances.

Paracelsus' theories involved many magical elements and were based on a visionary belief in the constant influence of the universe on man's life. He found new remedies for medical treatment, however, and unlike the prevalent concept, which regarded disease as a bodily imbalance, stated that each disease has its own cause which requires treatment. He was the first to claim that a disease can be cured by its antidote (i.e., by what has caused it, if given in small doses). He replaced vegetable remedies by the introduction of chemical drugs such as mercury, sulphur, iron and copper sulfate. Holding views, which were at once lofty and bizarre, he has long been regarded as one of the most fascinating personalities of Renaissance science and philosophy.

B. de Telepnef, *Paracelsus: A Genius Amidst a Troubled World* (1945); W. Pagal, *Paracelsus* (1958); H. M. Pachter, *Magic Into Science; the Story of Paracelsus* (1951). (ND)

PARE, AMBROISE (1510-90) French surgeon, regarded as the greatest surgical reformer of the 16th century. After studying in Paris, he became an army surgeon in 1537. His aptitude gained him promotion to becoming a royal surgeon in 1552. He introduced significant improvements in the treatment of gunshot wounds, and in 1545 published an account of the new method in his *La methode de traicter les playes faicted par harcquebutes*. Another contribution he made was to reintroduce the practice of tying together large arteries that had become divided so that they could knit together again. He also introduced the use of artificial limbs made of gold or silver, and invented many surgical instruments. His innovations were, however, not immediately accepted. Unlike most surgeons of his time, he tried to avoid operating if it was not absolutely necessary.

S. Paget, *Ambroise Paré and his Times* (1897).

PARKER, MATTHEW (1504-75) Archbishop of Canterbury during the first part of *Elizabeth I's reign. Born in Norwich, he went to Corpus Christi College, Cambridge. Ordained in 1527, he was associated with the Cambridge reformers, a group which had Lutheran sympathies. He was chaplain to *Anne Boleyn and later to *Henry VIII. In 1544 he became master of Corpus Christi College and, a year later, Vice Chancellor of Cambridge. When *Mary Tudor became queen in 1553, he was deprived of his office because of his Protestant sympathies. Until the accession of Elizabeth I he had to go into hiding. In 1559 P. was elected Archbishop of Canterbury, in this capacity helping Elizabeth to establish the Anglican Church. He was a moderate reformer and tried to find a compromise between Catholics and Protestants. In 1566, however, he published the Book of *Advertisements and in 1568 issued a new authorized translation of the *Bible. Preferring scholarship to controversy, he also published several mediaeval chronicles and assembled a collection of many manuscripts.

V. J. K. Brook, *A Life of Archbishop Parker* (1962).

PARLEMENT The French superior court of justice in Paris, which also held important administrative duties and legislative powers. The product of the long evolution of the mediaeval *curia regis* or king's court, the P. was given its definitive structure of separate *chambres* in the course of the 15th century, during which time several provincial P.s were also created. Since it was charged with the registration of royal decrees, the P. claimed the right to withhold the promulgation of new measures, subjecting new laws to close scrutiny and frequently using its right to remonstrate with the king. In the 16th century the P. became involved particularly with religious issues. While defending the principles of *Gallicanism, it usually assumed an extremist attitude towards suspected Protestants.

E. Maugis, *Histoire du parlement de Paris de l'avénement des rois Valois jusqu'à la mort d'Henri IV*, 3 vols. (1913).

PARLER German family of master masons responsible for important works in the late Gothic style during the second half of the 14th century. Johannes Parler, the founder of the dynasty, first worked at Cologne, but it was his son Peter Parler (*c.* 1330-99) who became famous for his work on the cathedral of Prague. He was the first artist who left posterity a bust of himself.

PARMIGIANINO, FRANCESCO MAZZOLA (1503-40) Italian painter, one of the early leading *Mannerists. Born in Parma, he was a pupil of *Corregio whose influence can be seen in P.'s first important work, *Mystic Marriage of St. Catherine*. In 1522 he was commissioned to paint two series of frescoes in Parma. Two years later he went to Rome where he began to paint in the style of *Raphael and *Michelangelo. His most important work done in Rome is his *Vision of St. Jerome*, but his work was interrupted by the Sack of *Rome (1527). He went to Bologna where he painted one of his masterpieces, *Madonna with St. Margaret and Other Saints*. He also made a portrait of *Charles V who came to Bologna in 1530. In 1531 P. returned to Parma and signed a contract to decorate S. Maria della Steccata. He managed to paint the frescoes in the church, but was delayed in the execution of the rest of the work and apparently was arrested for this by his patrons in 1539. Released shortly afterwards, he went to Casalmaggiore where he died. P.'s works show the Mannerist ambiguity of space composition and the distortion of human figures expressed in the long necks and small heads of his Madonnas. The figures in his paintings are elegant and graceful. He was probably the first Italian artist to make etchings, as well as chiaroscuro woodcuts, out of his designs.

S. J. Freedberg, *Parmigianino: His Works in Painting* (1950). (ND)

PARRASIO, AULO GIANO (1470-1522) Italian humanist. Born in Cosenza, as Giovanni Paolo Parisio, he later refashioned his name to have a "classical" sound. He studied Greek in Corfu and became a member of *Pontano's academy in Naples and of the Roman Academy of Pomponius *Laetus. From 1499 to 1506 he taught in Milan, and from 1514 to 1517 lectured again in Rome, where he was invited by Pope *Leo X. P. wrote commentaries on works by classical authors and published an edition of Cornelius Nepos (1500). He also retrieved a number of Roman texts, and enjoyed a reputation as one of the most learned humanist scholars of his time.

PARSONS, ROBERT (1546-1610) English Roman Catholic leader. Educated at Oxford, he became a fellow of Balliol College. Forced to leave England in 1574, he went to Rome, becoming a *Jesuit in 1575. In 1580 he infiltrated England in the company of *Campion, a mission which ended in the latter's arrest and execution. Again compelled to leave, during his subsequent sojourn in Scotland, and later in France and Spain, P. engaged in plots against *Elizabeth I. In 1594 he published *The Conference About the Next Succession to the Crown of England* under the name of Doleman. Here he argued the claims of the Spanish Infanta to the English crown, on the grounds that subjects are obliged to put religion before anything else and are therefore permitted to choose a sovereign who is of their religion.

PARUTA, PAOLO (1540-98) Italian historian and political theorist. Born in Venice, he belonged to a distinguished family and passed most of his life in the service of the Republic, and was entrusted with diplomatic missions. His dialogue *Della perfezione della vita politica* (1579) defended political activity as a noble pursuit, affirming – in contrats to *Machiavelli – that a statesman must comply with certain moral principles. Commissioned by Venice to complete the history of the Republic begun by Pietro *Bembo, he wrote the *Istoria veniziana*, which was published posthumously in 1605. He also wrote the *Storia della guerra di Cipro*, which dealt with the surrender of the island of Cyprus to the *Ottoman Turks. Of his other works, the *Discorsi politici*, published in 1599, was noted especially for its detailed discussion of the government of Venice.

F. Zanoni, *Paolo Paruta nella vita e nelle opere* (1904).

PASQUIER, ESTIENNE (1529-1615) French lawyer and historian. Born in Paris, he studied at Toulouse and Bologna, making his name in 1565, when he successfully handled a legal case attempting to ban *Jesuits from teaching at the university of Paris. P. defended many prominent people, and later occupied positions at the courts of Poitiers (1579). Tours (1583) and Paris (1585). Possessing a clear style, he composed poetry as well as writing on jurisprudence, but his main contribution, the encyclopaedic *Recherches de la France*, published in ten volumes between 1561 and 1621, was in the field of history. Although lacking a systematic plan, the *Recherches* contained a great deal of information on the development of French institutions, customs and language.

PASSAROTTI, BARTOLOMEO (1529-92) Italian painter. Born in Bologna, he went in 1551 to Rome, where he worked under *Vignola and Taddeo *Zuccari. He returned to Bologna in about 1565, opened a large studio and became a partisan of the Venetian school which emphasized colour, in opposition to Florentine *mannerism. A teacher of Agostino *Carracci, he excelled as a portraitist and painted peasant types, with fruits, flowers and still-life. His religious painting in the leading churches of Bologna show the influences of *Correggio and *Parmigianino, and point towards the *Baroque.

PASSE, CRISPIN (1564-1637) Dutch engraver and painter. A native of Zeeland, he became in 1585 member of the guild of *Antwerp, then settled at Cologne (*c.* 1594-*c.* 1613), but ended his life in Utrecht. Together with his three sons and one daughter, he produced a large number of portraits. Several of the works were printed in London, Paris and Frankfurt, spreading the reputation of the father and sons as outstanding engravers of portraits.

PASSION PLAY A dramatic presentation of biblical episodes concluding with the birth, life and death of Christ, it was a 15th-century development of the mediaeval *Mysteries. The best-known performances of the P. during the Renaissance were given by the *Confrérie de la Passion*, a Parisian group which, in 1402, secured a royal patent to stage the plays and performed them until they were banned by a decree of the **parlement* in 1548. The performances were continued, however, in the French provinces and elsewhere. In 1633 the peasants of the village Oberammergau in Bavaria vowed to stage the P. at ten-year intervals, as an expression of gratitude for their deliverance from a ravaging plague. With some interruptions, the play has been staged by hundreds of residents of the village since then.

PASTI, MATTEO DE' (?-1468) Italian architect and sculptor. Born in Verona, he is chiefly remembered as the architect who carried out *Alberti's plans for the *Tempio Malatestiano* of Rimini. He is credited with several reliefs, which compare well with those executed there by *Agostino di Duccio. He also struck *medals.

PASTON LETTERS One of the major sources on the social history of England during the 15th century. Covering the years 1422-1509, this collection consists of letters exchanged by members of the Paston family of Norfolk and a considerable number of public documents. Many of the letters are from and to prominent contemporary personalities, but their great value lies in the light they shed on the life of a middle-class family.

H. S. Bennett, *The Pastons and their England* (1922).

PASTOR, ADAM (?-c. 1560) The name adopted by the German *Anabaptist leader, Rudolf Martens. Probably born in Münster, he was particularly active in Clèves. In 1547 he worked together with Menno *Simons, but shortly afterwards entered a dispute with him over questions related to the Trinity. Later, he seems to have wandered about from place to place in the lower valley of the Rhine, dying in Emden.

PASTORAL The artistic treatment of bucolic life, usually dealing with shepherds, their songs, loves and sorrows. The P. tradition originated in classical antiquity; one of the foremost examples of this way of presenting nature as an imaginary golden world of youth and beauty was given in Virgil's *Eclogues*. The tradition was revived during the Renaissance, finding expression in *literature, *drama, *painting and *music. *Boccaccio already resorted to it in his novel *Ameto*, but the true harbinger of the fashion was *Sannazaro's *Arcadia* (1504), followed by *Sydney's work with the same title, *Montemayor's *Diana* (1559), Tasso's *Aminta* (1581) and Guarini's *Il pastor fido* (1583). In painting *Giorgione's *Fête champêtre* comes to mind, together with other 16th-century north-Italian descriptions of idyllic scenery. In music, the P. theme was particularly influential in the development of *opera. Creating a deliberately artificial world of poetic glamour, the P. persisted until the 18th century as a recurrent artistic phenomena.

W. W. Greg, *Pastoral Poetry and Pastoral Drama* (1906); H. Genouy, *L'Arcadia de Sidney dans ses rapports avec*

Madonna and Child *in a fantastic landscape by Patinier*

l'Arcadia de Sannazaro et la Diana de Montemayor (1928).

PATENIER, JOACHIM (1485-1524) Flemish painter. Probably born in *Antwerp, he became a member of the painter's guild there in 1515. In 1521 he acted as Dürer's host during the latter's voyage through the Netherlands and the German master used him as a model for one of his drawings. P. was a friend of Quentin *Massys, who took care of his children after his death. Although many pictures are attributed to him, only a few have been verified as his according to documentary evidence. P. was one of the first painters to emphasize landscape at the expense of human figure, which he usually made small and impotent in contrast to the power of nature.

PATRIZZI, FRANCESCO (1413-92) Italian humanist. Born in Siena, he was a protegé of Pope *Pius II, who in 1461 made him bishop of Gaeta. There he devoted himself to humanistic studies, and wrote two widely-known treatises. *De institutione reipublicae* defended the republican form of government; *De regno et regum institutione* discussed the nature of monarchy. Both works were published posthumously and translated into several languages.

PATRIZZI, FRANCESCO (1529-97) Italian philosopher. Educated in Padua, he was appointed to the chair of philosophy in *Ferrara in 1578. In 1592 he was invited by the pope to teach in Rome. Philosophically he was a supporter of Plato, and had controversies with the Aristotelians. He published works on science, history and rhetoric. In his major work, *Nova de universis philosophia* he claims that Light, which emanated from God, is the first element.

PAUL II (1417-71) Pope from 1464. Born in Venice as Pietro Barbo, he was educated in Florence, becoming bishop of Cervia and Vicenza before he was made cardinal by his uncle Pope *Eugenius IV. Upon his election to the papacy he refused to conform with the demands made of him by the cardinals who wanted to strengthen their influence. Trying to centralize all powers in his hands, he opposed the tendency on the part of secular rulers to consolidate their hold over state churches. He intervened in the religious struggles in *Bohemia, excommunicating *George of Podebrady in 1466. His efforts to form a Christian alliance against the Turks ended in failure. In 1468 P. dissolved the humanist Roman Academy of Pomponius *Laetus, and charged its members with opposing Christian ideals. He built the luxurious palace of St. Mark (today Palazzo Venezia), where he resided from 1466.

R. Weiss, *Un umanista Veneziano; Papa Paolo II* (1958).

PAUL III (1468-1549) Pope from 1534. Born Alessandro Farnese, to a distinguished Italian family, he was educated in Rome and in the house of the Medici in Florence. In 1493 he was made a cardinal; in this office he served under four different popes, and then was himself unanimously elected Pontiff. Though addicted to worldly pleasures and prone to nepotism, P. has gone down in history as a reformer. In 1536 he appointed a comission to examine the conditions prevalent in the Church and to suggest reforms. In 1540 he gave his blessing to the newly-formed *Jesuit Order, and, in 1542, approved the establishment of the *Inquisition at Rome. His most noteworthy act in the area of reform was the fact that, in 1545, he consented to open the Council of *Trent which aimed at the comprehensive reorganization of the Roman Catholic Church.

In 1538 P. had placed England under a ban and excommunicated *Henry VIII. All P.'s efforts to combat the spread of Protestantism were unsuccessful, however. He was also a great patron of the arts. In this capacity, he comissioned Michelangelo to continue construction of *St. Peter's.

W. Friedensberg, *Kaiser Karl V und Papst Paul III* (1932); L. Dorez, *La cour du pape Paul III*, 2 vols. (1932).

PAUL IV (1476-1559) Pope from 1555. Born as Giampietro *Carafa to a noble family of Neapolitan origin. Educated in Rome, mainly by his uncle, Cardinal Oliviero Carafa, who also introduced him to the papal court. As bishop of Chieti (1504-29), he played a prominent part in founding the *Theatine order. In 1536 he became a cardinal and a member of the reform comission. He was responsible for the reorganization of the Roman *Inquisition in 1542. When he was elected to the papacy he increased the Inquisition's role in bringing about Church reform and extirpating heresy. He did not reconvene the Council of *Trent, but continued to reform the Church from within. He fought against simony and the corruption of the clergy, introducing firmer disciplinary measures. P. had a very repressive attitude also toward the Jews. In 1555 he established the *ghetto in Rome, and enforced rules which excluded them from public life.

In foreign policy P. was an opponent of the *Habsburgs, but failed in his effort to drive the Spaniards out of Naples. Defeated by the duke of *Alba, P. had to make peace with him in 1557. Where the Protestants were concerned, however, he rejected any efforts to reach an agreement and denounced the Peace of *Augsburg. During his last years P. became extremely unpopular because of his highhanded policies and his nepotism.

G. M. Monti, *Ricerche su Paolo IV Carafa* (1925).

Pope Paul III *by Titian*

PAUL V (1552-1621) Pope from 1605. Born in Rome as Camillo Borghese. P. became a cardinal in 1596 and vicar of Rome in 1603. As a pope he had to face several problems arising out of the general confrontation of papal authority with the power of the state. In 1606 he placed Venice under a ban because of her refusal any longer to accept papal jurisdiction and eccelesiastical immunity. P. forbade English Roman Catholics to take the new oath of allegiance introduced by *James I. Otherwise, he tried to remain neutral where politics was concerned. When the *Thirty Years' War broke out, for instance, he did not, as one might have expected, publicly announce his support for the Catholic nations. P. promoted missionary activity in Asia, Africa and America. It was during his administration that *Galileo was condemned as a heretic. (ND)

PAULI, JOHANNES (c. 1453-1530) German author. A Franciscan friar, in 1519 he published a collection of anecdotes, entitled *Schimpf und Ernst*, which included moralizing tales in a coarse humouristic bent. These enjoyed an enormous vogue, going through 30 editions. Other works of his were not so successful.

PAVIA, BATTLE OF (24 February 1525) A decisive battle in the *Italian Wars between France and Spain. Wishing to establish their hegemony over Lombardy, the French were besieging the city of Pavia, 20 miles south of *Milan, when an attack by the Spanish army led to their defeat. *Francis I who was commanding the French army, was captured and sent to Madrid, where he was forced to conclude a treaty that was afterwards repudiated.

PAZZI CONSPIRACY (April 1478) A plot against the *Medici in Florence. Organized by persons related to Pope *Sixtus IV and most probably with the knowledge of the pope himself, the conspiracy was carried out by a group led by Jacopo Pazzi, head of a notable Florentine family. The conspirators struck while the two brothers, Lorenzo and Giuliano, were attending mass at the cathedral; They killed Giuliano but only wounded Lorenzo. The latter then suppressed his enemies, emerging from the affair stronger than before. Because he ordered the execution of Archbishop Salviati, who was a member of the conspirators, the pope excommunicated Lorenzo, joining Naples in a war against Florence (1478-80).

N. Rubinstein, *The Government of Florence Under the Medici, 1434-94* (1966).

PEASANTS' WAR, THE (1524-25) A series of risings in southwest and central Germany, inspired by the religious zeal and defiance of authority of the leaders of the Reformation, and aimed at restoring the traditional rights of the peasants and ameliorating their lot. The revolt broke out at Stühlingen in the Black Forest in June 1524, and quickly spread into the Rhineland, Swabia, Franconia and Thuringia. The demands of the peasants, best expressed in the Twelve Articles of Memmingen, were concerned with forest, grazing and fishing rights, with tithes and feudal exactions, and the lay election of the clergy. These were all presented as customary rights that had been abused and abrogated by the nobility. In certain areas the peasants received support from the towns and from the lesser nobility. In Franconia they were inflamed by the ideas of Andreas *Carlstadt, in Thuringia by the preaching of *Thomas Müntzer. Bands of peasants pillaged the countryside and destroyed abbeys and manor houses. The revolt failed for lack of united leadership; in the battle of Frankenhausen, on 15 May 1525, the peasants suffered a decisive defeat at the hands of the forces of the Protestant Philip of Hesse and the Catholic Duke George of Saxony. Thomas Müntzer was executed and the rebels crushed. Thereafter the peasantry of Southern Germany ceased to have a political significance.

*Luther's reaction to the revolt received a great deal of attention from contemporaries and historians. The peasants cited Luther's plea for the liberty of Christian men, and his enemies laid the blame for all religious and civil disobedience at his door. But Luther disassociated himself from the rebels. In May 1525 he wrote *Admonition to Peace*, which was a mild tract, recognizing the justice of some of the peasants' claims. But, the threat to order and the excesses of the peasants alarmed him, and he published the violently-phrased leaflet *Against the murdering, thieving hordes of peasants* – calling on the princes to punish the rebels with all severity. This tract alienated many of Luther's radical followers and placed him definitely on the side of established authority.

Abraham and Hagar, *engraving by Georg Pencz*

E. B. Bax, *The Peasants' War in Germany* (1903); (ME) G. Frantz, *Der deutsche Bauernkrieg*, 7th ed. (1965).

PECOCK, REGINALD (c. 1393-1461) English churchman. Born in Wales, he was educated at Oxford, becoming a fellow of Oriel College in 1417. In 1431 he was appointed Master of Whittington College, London, and in 1444 Bishop of St. Asaph, becoming Bishop of Chichester in 1450. He then wrote his best-known work *The Repressor of Overmuch Blaming of the Clergy* directed against the *Lollards. Although he upheld the traditional practice of the Church, his writings were examined in 1457 and he was accused of heresy. Convicted, he made a public recantation, but was deprived of his bishopric and spent the rest of his life in seclusion in the Abbey of Thorney. P.'s writings are written in English and display an impressive argumentative ability.

V. H. H. Green, *Bishop Reginald Pecock* (1941).

PEDERSEN, CHRISTIAN (c. 1480-1554) Danish humanist and *Bible translator. In 1529 he published at *Antwerp his first Danish translation, based on the Vulgate and on *Erasmus' Greek edition of the New Testament. A second version, undertaken after the victory of the *Reformation in Denmark, appeared in 1550, and is known as the *"Christian III Bible". P. also published a Latin-Danish dictionary, a translation of the 13th-century *Gesta Danorum* of Saxo Grammaticus, and other mediaeval chronicles.

PEDRO DE ALCANTARA (1499-1562) Spanish Franciscan friar. Born in Alcantara, he studied at Salamanca and in 1515 joined the Observantine branch of the Franciscans. He rose in the hierarchy of his order but, not being satisfied with the strictness of the rule, in 1540 he retired to a hermitage in Portugal where he was joined by other friars, thus giving rise to the reformed movement of the Descalced Franciscans, also known as the "Alcantarines". Later their centre moved to the convent of Pedroso, Spain, where P. settled in about 1556. A close supporter of *Teresa of Avila, he was the author of a popular work on ascetism and meditation, *Tratado de la oración y meditación* (1556). P. was canonized in 1669.

PEELE, GEORGE (1556-96) English dramatist and poet. Born in London and educated at Oxford, where he probably wrote his first surviving work, an abridgement of the *Iliad* entitled the *Tale of Troys*. In 1581 he moved back to London where he wrote his first play, *The Arraignment of Paris* (1584), which combined mythological and pastoral elements. His later works were playhouse dramas, such as *The Battle of Alcazar* (1594), *The Old Wives Tale* (1595) and *Edward I* (1593). P. also wrote poems about significant events of his day.

PELLIKAN, KONRAD (1478-1556) German scholar. A native of Alsace, he entered the Franciscan order, becoming well-versed in oriental languages. He published the first comprehensive introduction to the study of *Hebrew, *De modo legendi et intelligendi hebraeum*, in *Strassburg in 1504. Joining the *Reformation, he became a professor of theology at *Basle in 1523, moving to *Zurich in 1526 to be a theology professor there. P.'s important commentaries on the *Bible came out in seven volumes between 1532 and 1539.

PENCZ, GEORG (c. 1500-50) German painter and engraver. Born in *Nuremberg, he probably studied under *Dürer. A close friend of the brothers *Beham, he was accused of heresy together with them in 1524, but was allowed to remain in Nuremberg. P. produced exquisite engravings of small size. He twice visited Italy, where he familiarized himself with the work of *Marcantonio Raimondi. Like the Behams he is grouped among the "Little Masters".

PENNI, GIANFRANCESCO (c. 1488-1528) Italian painter, known as *il Fattore*. Born at Florence, he worked as an assistant of *Raphael, whom he accompanied to Rome. He was employed by the master in some of his major *frescoes and the tapestry cartoons. After Raphael's death he worked briefly with *Giulio Romano.

PENRY, JOHN (1559-93) English *Puritan. A native of Wales, he was educated at Cambridge and Oxford, and soon became a follower of Robert *Browne. In 1587 he published an attack on episcopacy which provoked action by Archbishop *Whitgift; although this could not be proved, in 1588 many believed him to be the real author of the *Marprelate Tracts. P. then fled to Scotland, but on his return in 1592 he was arrested and charged with having slandered the queen. Found guilty, he was hanged in the following year.

PEREIRA, DUARTE PACHECO Portuguese explorer and navigator. In 1498 he sailed along the south-western coast of *Africa, and in 1500 joined *Cabral on the voyage of the discovery of Brazil. P. later served in *India as commander of the Portuguese force at the trading station of Cochin. When the station was attacked by the ruler of Calicut, P. managed to defeat him with a small force, following which he became known as the "Portuguese Achilles". From 1520-22 he was governor of Portuguese East Africa. P. wrote a very useful manual on navigation called *Esmeraldo de Situ Orbis*.

PEREZ, ANTONIO (1539-1611) Spanish statesman. The illegitimate son of the secretary of state of *Charles V and *Philip II, he was educated in Alcalá and Salamanca and sent to Italy for further study. On his return to Spain, P. became the confident of the Prince of Eboli who, in 1567, convinced Philip II to make P. his secretary of state for Italy. During the ten years that he filled positions at court, P. amassed a great deal of power. In 1578, however, he was accused of the murder of Juan de Escobedo, a confidant of Don *Juan of Austria, and in 1579 arrested together with his mistress, the princess of Eboli. His trial lasted for many years, but in 1590 he succeeded in escaping from prison, finding shelter in discontented *Aragon. There P. producing documentary evidence to the effect that Philip II had been an accomplice in the murder of Escobedo, incited the population to revolt. In 1591 he fled the advancing royal troops and found shelter in France.

His memoirs describe the corruption at the Spanish court.

G. Marañon, *Antonio Pérez* (1958).

PERI, JACOPO (1561-1633) Italian composer. Born in Rome, he spent most of his creative years in Florence where he held the position of musical director to the ruling grand-ducal family, the *Medici. Interested in the revival of the ancient Greek drama, a subject which was discussed in Florentine literary and artistic circles, in 1594 P. composed music to *Dafne*, a libretto by *Rinuccini. This *opera, now lost, was performed in 1597. Also with a libretto by Rinuccini, his second opera, *Euridice*, which has survived, was staged in 1600, with P. himself taking the role of Orpheus. P.'s long recitatives were meant to reproduce ancient Greek declamations.

PERKINS, WILLIAM (1558-1602) English theologian. Educated at Cambridge, where he became a fellow (1584-94), he acquired a reputation for his preaching at the university and for the *Puritan orientation of his writings. His treatise on *predestination in 1598 resulted in a reply by *Arminius. P. assumed an extreme Calvinist position.

PEROTTI, NICCOLO (1429-80) Italian humanist. A student both of *Vittorino da Feltre at *Mantua (1445-46) and of *Guarino da Verona, he entered the service of Cardinal *Bessarion in 1447. In 1455 he became a papal secretary, and in 1458 was appointed archbishop of Siponto. P. translated classical Greek authors and wrote a Latin grammar and a guide to the writing of letters. His most important work was the *Cornucopia*, a large commentary on the 1st century Roman author Martial, published posthumously by his nephew in 1489. P.'s *Rudimenta grammatices*, the first modern Latin grammar, was printed in 1473 and enjoyed a wide acclaim.

PERRÉAL, JEAN (c. 1460-1530) French painter, sculptor and architect, known also as Jehan de Paris. The son of a poet-painter associated with the court, he became the most famous French artist of his time, working in the service of *Charles VIII, *Louis XII and *Francis I. He accompanied the French army to Italy three times, was an expert arranger of public festivities and received special patronage from Queen *Anne of Brittany. P. painted a number of portraits of royal French personages, struck *medals and designed churches and sculptured tombs. Only partially influenced by the Italian style, however, he is frequently identified with the anonymous *Maître de Moulins.

M. H. Goldblatt, *Deux Grand Maîtres français: le Maître de Moulins identifié, Jean Perréal* (1961);
M. Huillet d'Istria, *La peinture française de la fin du Moyen Age; Jean Perréal et le Maître de Moulins* (1961).

PERSPECTIVE The technique employed by Renaissance artists to create a pictorial representation of physical reality. The geometric principles of the system, said to have been formulated by *Brunelleschi, were adapted by *Masaccio and *Donatello. The first written description of the technique appeared in *Alberti's *De pictura* (1435). It was based on the assumption that, although they might appear to, parallel lines never meet. All parallel lines receding into the picture were made to converge at a single "vanishing point" at about the centre of the viewer's horizon. The picture plane was thus given scales of proportion conducive to the production of an illusion of tri-dimensional depth. The final result was higly aesthetic, although sometimes it carried an air of artificiality. Some 15th-century artists, such as *Uccello followed by *Mantegna and *Piero della Francesca, delighted in foreshortening or in applying the rules of perspective to a single object, such as a pointed arm or a body lying perpendicular to the viewer, producing some highly impressive results.

PERUGINO, PIETRO VANNUCCI (c. 1450-1523) Italian painter of the Umbrian school. Born near Perugia, he went to Florence in about 1470 and was the pupil of Andrea del *Verrochio together with *Leonardo. The first work undisputedly by P. is *St. Sebastian* (Cerqueto, near Perugia) dated 1478. In 1481 he was one of the artists who were invited by Pope *Sixtus IV to decorate the Sistine Chapel with frescoes from the lives of Moses

Madonna and Child with Two Women *by Perugino*

Portrait of a Young Man *by Perugino*

The Handing of the Keys to St. Peter *a fresco by Perugino in the Sistine Chapel*

and Christ. There he painted one of his masterpieces, *Christ Giving the Keys to St. Peter*, in which his concept of atmospheric space as well as his simple and clearly organized style are revealed. P.'s other frescoes at the Sistine Chapel were taken down for *Michelangelo's *Last Judgement*. When he returned to Florence, he worked in the Palazzo della Signoria. Later, he traveled to Perugia and Rome and received a great number of commissions. Some of his most notable works of the period are *Virgin Appearing to St. Bernard* (1489), *Nativity*, which he painted for Pope *Julius II in 1491, and *Pietà* (1495).

During the years 1500-04 Perugino was the master of *Raphael. From about 1505 he began to repeat and rearrange his earlier figures, meeting with the criticism of the Florentines. He left Florence for Perugia revisiting Rome only once in 1508 to paint the *Stanze* for Pope *Julius II. He died of the plague at Fontignano, near Perugia.

E. Camesasca, *Tutta la pittura del Perugino* (1959).(ND)

PERUZZI, BALDASSARE (1481-1536) Italian architect. Born in Siena, he studied painting under *Pinturicchio, and in 1503 became an assistant of *Bramante's in Rome, helping him with the designs for St. Peter's. His first important work was the Farnesina in Rome (1509), often cited as one of the finest examples of High Renaissance residential architecture. After the death of *Raphael, P. succeeded him in some of his architectural works. He fled Rome for Siena in 1527, but returned soon afterwards and cooperated with Antonio da *Sangallo on the Villa Farnese (1530). His last work in Rome, the Palazzo Massimo alle Colonne (1532), deviated from the balanced harmony of the High Renaissance in its use of contrasting and curving forms. P.'s drawings and sketches were used by his student *Serlio in his famous book on architecture. Generally a practitioner of the classically delicate and proportional High Renaissance structure, P. is considered one of the most significant architects of his age.

Petrarch *by Andrea del Castagno*

Interior of the Palazzo Massimo alle Colonne by Peruzzi

PETRARCH (Francesco Petrarca; 1304-74) Italian poet, regarded as the father of *Renaissance humanism. P. was born in Arezzo, the son of an exiled Florentine notary, but was brought up in Avignon, where his father moved in order to be close to the papal court. He spent nine years studying civil law at the universities of Montpellier and Bologna, and it was during this time, much to his father's disapproval, that he began to show an interest in vernacular poetry and in the study of classical Latin literature. After his father's death in 1326, P. returned to Avignon, but abandoned the practice of law for a life of literary pursuits. Although he took holy orders and was supported by an income from ecclesiatical sources, he actually lived as a layman. Shortly after his return, P. fell in love with Laura, a mysterious married woman who was the symbol of beauty and the sublime in his numerous Italian sonnets. He continued to write about her even after her death in 1348, later assembling these poems in *Il Canzoniere*. P. was recognized as an outstanding poet and was crowned poet laureate in Rome in 1341. His visit to Rome led, in

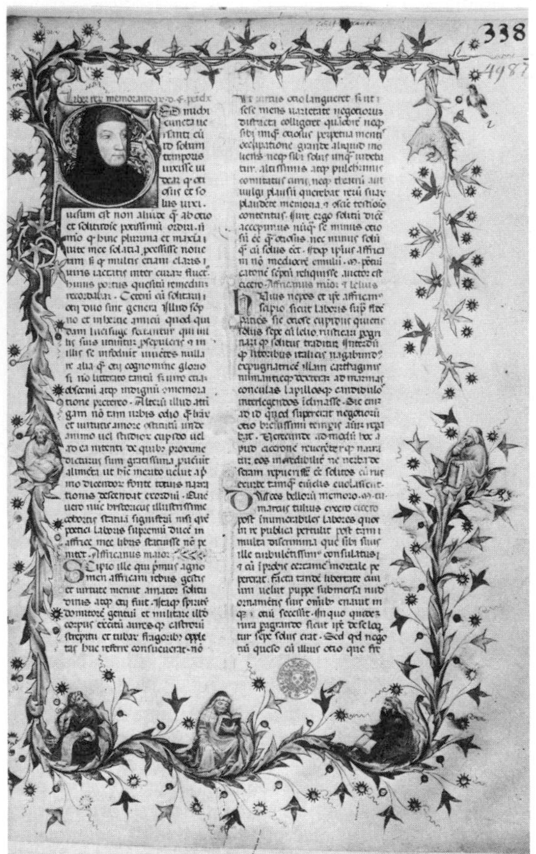

Petrarch's portrait in a 15th-century manuscript

1343, to his appointment as emissary to Naples by Clement VI. Later P. lived either in Vaucluse in southern France, or in northern Italy, in Parma, Milan, Padua and Venice. He died at Arqua near Padua.

P.'s Italian poetry was not the part of his work which most influenced the thought and letters of the Renaissance; rather it was his espousal of the classics. He discarded the mediaeval scholastic tradition in favour of Cicero, Vergil, Horace and St. Augustine. He tried to make his Latin style conform with that of the classical authors, and wrote about ancient Rome, e.g., *Africa*, a poem on the campaigns of Scipio Africanus, which he began in 1338 and *De viris illustribus*, a collection of biographies of Roman personalities. However, he soon moved away from a mainly scholarly interest in the classics, and tried to find in them the inspiration of both a stylistic model and moral wisdom. His attempt to reconcile the study of antiquity with Christian ethics is demonstrated in the *Familiares*, an anthology of 350 letters, to which he later appended another collection of 125 letters, the *Seniles*. P. also wrote a number of religious, contemplative or ethical works, on the subject of spiritual inner peace. The most important was the *Secretum meum* (1343), a sincere confession of his moral failings, consisting of three dialogues between the author and St. Augustine.

The influence of P. on the development of humanism should also be seen in light of his personal example as a new type of scholar. Throughout his life he corresponded with numerous other scholars; particularly famous was his friendship with *Boccaccio which began in 1350. To this may be added his travels in France, Germany and elsewhere, in order to copy classical manuscripts. Finally, in anticipation of the High Renaissance type of humanist and, indeed, of the modern intellectual, he was continually responsive to the problems of his time; for example, in 1347 he declared his support for the Roman revolution of Cola di Rienzo, believing that this movement was about to revive ancient republicanism.

J. W. Shitefield, *Petrarch and the Renaissance* (1943);
E. H. Wilkins, *Life of Petrarch* (1961);
M. Bishop, *Petrach and His World* (1963).

PETRI, OLAUS (Olaf Petersson; 1493-1552) Swedish leader of the *Reformation. P. was about to enter on an ecclesiastical career when he became a follower of *Luther and *Melanchthon in Wittenberg. Ordained after his return to *Sweden in 1519, he soon began to expound the new doctrines. Becoming a friend of Laurentius *Andreae, the king's secretary, he had an influence upon the conversion of Gustavus *Vasa to Lutheranism. Moving to Stockholm, P. became very much involved with preaching during 1526. Together with Andreae and with his brother Laurentius Petri (1499-1553), he translated the New Testament into Swedish. His work bore fruit in 1527, when the Diet of Västeras decided to break with Rome and confiscate Church property. After the establishment of the Swedish Reformed Church (1529), P. wrote a number of liturgical works and his brother, Laurentius, was appointed Archbishop of Uppsala. Falling into royal disfavour, in 1539, the brothers were arrested and even condemned to death, only to be later released and returned to their posts. After P.'s death, Laurentius carried on as the leader of Swedish Lutheranism, and was responsible for consolidating the Church's independence from the Crown.

C. J. I. Bergendoff, *Olavus Petri and the Ecclesiastical Transformation in Sweden, 1521-1552* (1928).

PETRUCCI, PANDOLFO (1452-1512) Ruler of Siena. The scion of a distinguished Sienese family, he became involved in the troubled political life of the city. In 1487 he returned from exile and formed a government which enjoyed popular support. Aided by his brother Giacopo, he gradually became the sole ruler of the city. In 1502 he was compelled by Cesare *Borgia to leave Siena, but returned after a few months, with the support of *Louis XII of France. This did not hinder him from siding with *Julius II against the French in 1511. His son Borghese succeeded him as ruler of Siena, until he was exiled in 1515. Another son, Alfonso, was created cardinal by Julius II, but later conspired against Pope Leo X and was murdered in prison in Rome (1517).

PETTIE, GEORGE (1548-89) English writer. Educated at Christ Church, Oxford, he later went through military service. His most important work is *A Petite Pallace of Pettie His Pleasure* (1576), a collection of 12 romantic tales. One story is based on a mediaeval legend and the rest on classical themes, mainly from Ovid and Livy, all, however, were written in a contemporary style. Revealing the influence of William *Painter's *Palace of Pleasures* (1567), P.'s work was very popular, going into six editions, and in turn, influencing the style of John

*Lyly in *Euphues* (1578). P. also published *The Civil Conversation* (1581), a translation of dialogues on polite conversation by Stefano Guazzo.

PEUERBACH, GEORG (1423-61) German humanist. A native of *Austria, he went to Italy to study *mathematics and there became friendly with *Nicholas of Cusa In 1454 he was made a royal astronomer to King Ladislas of Hungary, shortly afterwards becoming a teacher of *astronomy at the University of Vienna. His greatest achievements were in trigonometry. P. was the teacher of *Regiomontanus.

PEUTINGER, CONRAD (1465-1547) German humanist-antiquarian and political figure. Born in *Augsburg, he studied law in Italy and, in 1490, began to take part in the local government of his native town, subsequently serving for many years as secretary of the council (1497-1534). *Maximilian I made him member of the imperial council, where he championed the interests of the great commercial houses, having himself married into the *Welser family. Owing to his opposition to the Reformation which was continually growing in influence, he had to resign from his post on the city council in 1534. P. collected many antiquities, salvaging a number of important mediaeval chronicles which he edited. He also published Roman inscriptions and promoted the study of German antiquity. His name, however, is mainly remembered because of the Peutinger Table, a 13th-century copy of an ancient Roman road map of the world, which was given to him in 1494 by his friend, Conrad *Celtis. Composed of 11 sheets and almost seven meters long, this is the main specimen of ancient cartography that has survived.

PFEFFERKORN, JOHANN (1469-1522) A converted Jew, notorious for his diatribes against Judaism and the liberal aspects of *humanism. Having converted to Christianity in about 1504, and patronized by the Dominicans of Cologne, P. published several tracts in which he attacked the Talmud and urged that Jews be compelled to attend Christian sermons. In 1509 he was empowered by *Maximilian I to confiscate Jewish literature "hostile to Christianity". Pursuing his task in a highhanded manner, which included the extortion of bribes from Jewish communities, P.'s methods aroused protests and culminated in an inquiry by the archbishop of Mainz, who referred to the opinion of *Reuchlin. When he learned that Reuchlin was about to deliver a largely favourable opinion on the Talmud, P. attacked him violently in his *Handspiegel wider und gegen die Juden* (1511). Reuchlin responded with his *Augenspiegel*, and the resulting controversy became a debate over the significance of the Hebrew language, scholastic learning and the values of humanism. At a certain point, the Emperor intervened, binding both sides to desist from further attacks. But, between 1515 and 1517, two of Reuchlin's supporters published **Epistolae Obscurorum Virorum*, a mimicking satire, supposedly written on behalf of P., which discredited the Church.

PFISTER, ALBRECHT (?-c. 1466) German printer. For a long time secretary to the bishop of Bamberg, he began to work as a printer in about 1460. During the next few years he published the first books in the vernacular, including the *Edelstein* (1461), and *Die vier Historien* (1462) both of them moralizing fables. P. first had the idea of using hand-coloured woodcuts as illustration. He also published a *Biblia pauperum* (Bible of the poor), a pictorial account of scenes from the life of Christ.

PHILIP I, THE HANDSOME (1478-1506) King of Castile and founder of the *Habsburg dynasty in *Spain. The son of *Maximilian I and Mary of Burgundy he inherited Burgundy and the Netherlands in 1482. In 1496 he married *Joanna, daughter of *Ferdinand and *Isabella. The couple was recognized by the Spanish nobles as the rightful successors to the Spanish crown, and upon Isabella's death in 1504 they became heirs to Castile, but were opposed by Ferdinand who wanted to retain Castile and Aragon under his rule. In 1506, when P. returned from the Netherlands to realize his claim, he had to confront Ferdinand's opposition. Rivalry between the two was prevented by P.'s sudden death at Burgos. This, coupled with Joanna's insanity, allowed Ferdinand to get his way. P. was the father of emperors *Charles V and *Ferdinand I.

PHILIP II (1527-98) King of Spain from 1556. The sickly child of Emperor *Charles V and Isabella of Portugal, he was born in Valladolid and educated in Spain. In 1543 he married his cousin Maria of Portugal, who gave birth to a son, Don *Carlos, before her death in 1545. In 1548 P. went to Brussels in what was at that time the *Netherlands, to get acquainted with his future subjects. Having already had administrative experience, he was entrusted with full responsibility for the government of Spain on his return to that country in 1551. His father again summoned him to Brussels in 1554 to arrange his marriage with *Mary Tudor, Queen of England, a union intended to bolster P.'s future position against France. P., however, was not popular in England and his second wife, over ten years older than he, was childless. Upon his father's abdication, P. found himself king not only of Spain, but also of *Naples, *Milan, the Netherlands and the empire of Spanish America. At first he continued to live in Brussels, from where he directed the war with France (1556-59). His father and his second wife both died in 1558. This heavy toll within the royal family, however, did not prevent Spain being successful on the battlefield. The war ended with a comprehensive settlement, in Spain's favour, being signed at *Cateau-Cambrésis. Previously, P. had entertained the idea of marrying *Elizabeth I of England, so as to keep his alliance with that country intact. Immediately after signing the treaty with France, however, Elizabeth of Valois, daughter of *Henry II of France became his third wife. In August 1559 he returned to Spain, never again leaving the country.

Although P. detested war, he was nevertheless convinced that it was the mission of Spain to fight infidels and heretics. Against the former he came off quite well; in 1571 the Spanish-led Christian naval forces dealt the *Ottoman Turks their heaviest defeat at the Battle of *Lepanto. The flaw in P.'s foreign policy stemmed from his inability to accommodate the demands of those he viewed as heretics, i.e., his rebellious subjects of the Netherlands. His response to the disturbances of 1567 was to dispatch the duke of *Alba to enforce complete submission. The result was a war which outlasted his long reign, and which gradually crippled Spain, while involving her in the affairs of England and of France.

At first he attempted to deal with the Netherlands as a local problem. The change of policy which took place in the 1580s may have been affected by the fact that, at that time he seized possession of *Portugal. The deaths of King *Sebastian (1578) and Cardinal *Henrique (1580) enabled P. to advance a claim to the Portuguese throne, which he finally took by force of arms, thus uniting the Iberian peninsula under one government. While this expansion of Spanish power raised the alarm of England and France, it raised P.'s hopes in the possibility of crushing the Netherlands by attacking from both sides of the English channel. In 1588, after long preparations, he sent the *Armada to invade England, with the result that he brought upon Spain one of her worst defeats. It was easier to make headway in France, where the *League was in any case committed to Spain, and where P. meant to champion the claims of his daughter by his French wife. In view of *Henry IV's conversion to Roman Catholicism, however, and his growing internal support, he had to give up his aims in this direction also. In 1596 a second attempt to invade England by sea also failed and, in 1598, P. accepted the terms of the Peace of *Vervins, which recognized a government for the southern Netherlands separate from that of Spain.

A devout Roman Catholic, P. was very rigid and and suspicious by nature. Although he may not exactly have been the cruel monster he was made out to be by Protestants, his relationship with some of his most important generals and councillors, including the duke of Alba, his half-brother Don *Juan of Austria, Antonio *Perez and Alessandro *Farnese, nevertheless ended in disaster. His eldest son, Don Carlos, died in jail, arrested for having plotted against his father, and his court, especially during the latter part of his reign, was the scene of factional intrigues. Although in general he received the loyal support of the majority of his Spanish subjects, his reign witnessed two local rebellions, that of the *Moriscos in Granada (1568-70) and also an uprising in *Aragon (1591-92). P.'s painstaking dedication to paper work bordered on obsession. Alone he hovered over an avalanche of reports and memoranda, giving his personal attention to almost every affair of government, petty or great. Yet when it came to decision making he would frequently temporize. More than any other monarch he was responsible for the detailed but inefficient governmental system which accompanied Spain's

Philip II aged 59

Philipp II *by Titian*

decline during the next two centuries. The same is true of his attitude to the empire of Spanish America, where he consolidated a system of administration which culminated in stagnation soon after his death. Silver from Spanish America helped P. maintain the Spanish preponderance in European affairs during most of his reign; in fact, however, this was due at least as much to circumstances beyond his control, particularly to the long civil wars in France.

In 1563 P. began building a new architectural complex, El *Escorial, where he spent much of his last years, finally dying there. P. was a patron of the arts, inviting several Italian painters and sculptors to his court, and buying many works of *Titian, although he had a dislike for the style of El *Greco. His reign ushered in the golden age of Spanish *literature and *drama, and when he died it was not yet clear that most of Spain's power was over. From his fourth marriage with his cousin Anne of Austria, P. had a son who succeeded him as *Philip III of Spain.

W. H. Prescott, *History of the Reign of Philip the Second*, 3 vols. (1855-59);
R. B. Merriman, *The Rise of the Spanish Empire in the Old World and the New*, vol. 3, *Philip the Prudent* (1934);
J. H. Mariejol, *Philip II the First Modern King* (1933);
W. Walsh, *Philip II* (1940).

PHILIP III (1578-1621) King of Spain from 1598. The son of *Philip II, he fulfilled the worst fears of his father and left most of the affairs of state to his favourite, the duke of *Lerma. In this way began the regrettable tendency of delegating the administration of affairs of state to royal favourites which lasted throughout the 17th century. During the early part of P.'s reign there was fighting in the Netherlands and in 1618 the *Thirty Years' War broke out, during which P. supported the emperor and the Roman Catholic German princes. An important event in the domestic affairs of the country during P.'s reign was the expulsion of the *Moriscos from Spain (1608-14), the action of a weak government seeking popularity that resulted in economic problems. Although P. was a religious man and devoted much of his energies to advancing the interests of the Church, he also spent a lot of money on himself.

PHILIP OF HESSE (1504-67) German landgrave; the ablest leader among the Protestant princes. Born in Marburg, he inherited the landgraviate of Hesse from his father, Landgrave William II. P. began his rule in 1518. In 1523 he married Christina of Saxony. He joined Martin *Luther in 1524, already at that time viewing the religious conflict also in political terms. Stressing the importance of unity among all the Protestant princes, he participated in the suppression of the *peasant's revolt in 1525. In 1526, after the Diet of *Speyer, he began to reform the church in his own state. A year later he founded the first Protestant university at Marburg. Wanting to form an all-embracing Protestant alliance, P. tried to moderate between Luther and *Zwingli, but the conference which he organized between the two at *Marburg in 1529, failed. He played an important part in the creation of the *Schmalkaldic League (1530), which was to serve as a defensive alliance of the Protestant princes.

P. lost some of the princes' support owing to his bigamous marriage to Margaret von der Saal in 1540. Though sanctified by Luther, the marriage was not recognized by several princes. His final decline from power came with the successful attack of *Charles V on the inactive Schmalkaldic League in 1546. P. was imprisoned, to be released only in 1552, after the unexpected attack of the Protestant princes on the imperial forces. Nevertheless, P.'s aim, equality between the Catholic and Protestant princes, was achieved in the Peace of *Augsburg of 1555. In his later years Philip devoted most of his time to the internal affairs of his state. He ruled Hesse skillfully, and was called by his contemporaries Philip "the Magnanimous".

A. O. Hancock, "Philip of Hesse's View of the Relationship of Prince and Church", *Church History*, XXXV (1966); H. J. Hillerbrand, *Landgrave Philip of Hesse* (1967). (ND)

PHILIP THE GOOD (1396-1467) Duke of *Burgundy from 1419. He succeeded to the title after the murder of his father, John the Fearless. Having blamed the Dauphin Charles (later *Charles VII of France) for the murder of his father, P. signed the Treaty of Troyes (1420), which adopted King *Henry V of England as successor to the French throne. His collaboration with the English lasted over ten years. He betrayed *Joan of Arc to them in 1430. Later, in the Treaty of Arras (1435), P. recognized Charles as king of France, and in return was given some additional territories.

P., wishing to expand his holdings, seized possession of smaller neighbouring duchies. His greatest acquisition was the duchy of Luxemburg in 1443. He had difficulties in controlling the Low Countries, which rebelled several times, until his victory at the Battle of Gavere (1453), which forced *Ghent to submit. P.'s projected crusade against the Turks, which he tried to initiate in 1453, failed, but not before he gave a famous banquet for the knights, in 1454, at which they all vowed to liberate the East, and then went home. During his reign the duchy of Burgundy prospered, and his court was rich and extravagant. In 1430 he founded the chivalrous Order of the *Golden Fleece. He was a great patron of artists and his court was the centre of the rising Flemish school of painting. Among the famous artists of his court was Jan *van Eyck.

J. Calmette, *The Golden Age of Burgundy* (1962).

PHILIPPINES These islands, between the Pacific and China Sea, were discovered by *Magellan (1521), who met his death there. In 1542 Spain dispatched an expedition to these islands, and named them P. in honour of Philip, the son of *Charles V. In 1564 Miguel López de Legaspi went there from Mexico and established a settlement, which after 1571 was located at the bay of Manila. For the next 200 years Spain conducted its commercial contacts with the P. by dispatching a ship once a year from the harbour of Acapulco in Mexico. Barred from the *Moluccas spice commerce, the Spaniards dealt mainly in silks and cinnamon.

W. L. Schurz, *The Manila Galleon* (1939).

PHILOSOPHY In the 13th century mediaeval scholastic P., a method of speculation aimed at a systematic understanding of revealed truths, reached its hight in the work of St. Thomas Aquinas (1225-74). Aquinas was followed by other great thinkers, including Duns Scotus (1264-1308) and William of Occam (*c* 1300-49), but soon afterwards the whole tradition went into decline, while never completely disappearing, as can be seen from the work of the late 16th-century philosopher Francisco *Suarez. It is generally agreed, however, that the Renaissance constituted a barren period where philosophical work in general is concerned. Indeed, not until the 17th century, with the works of Descartes, Spinoza and Leibnitz, did thinkers resume a systematic investigation of the areas of logic, ethics and metaphysics.

Although Renaissance thought did not necessarily shun abstract speculation, it was generally oriented toward-concrete, man-related issues. This trend was intimately connected with *humanism, the major intellectual movement of the period, leaving a mark in the fields of *historiography and *political theory. The most important philosophical current of the Renaissance was *Neoplatonism, which emerged with *Nicholas of Cusa, *Ficino and *Pico della Mirandola, and continued to affect the thinking of *Bruno and *Campella late in the 16th century. The Aristotelian tradition of stressing logic and method, however, found worthwhile exponents in *Pomponazzi and *Zabarella, although even they were inclined to give their philosophy a humanistic bent. A period of almost constant changes, Renaissance thought and philosophy were dominated by tendencies towards idealization and romanticism. Imagination, intuitive reasoning and mysticism were more typical of the age than analytic speculation.

E. Garin, *La cultura filosofica del Rinascimento italiano* (1961);
P. O. Kristeller, *Eight Philosophers of the Italian Renaissance* (1964);
N. W. Gilbert, *Renaissance Concept of Method* (1960).

PHILPOT, JOHN (1516-56) English Protestant reformer. Educated at Oxford, he became a fellow there in 1534. Later he developed enthusiasm for the teachings of *Calvin and, under *Eduard VI, was made archdeacon of Winchester. His attack on the concept of transubstantiation in an ecclesiastical convocation held during the reign of *Mary Tudor led to his arrest in 1553. Two years later he was convicted of heresy and burnt at the stake.

PHRANTZES, GEORGIUS (1401-?) Byzantine historian. In 1478 he completed in Corfu a history of the Byzantine empire covering the period from 1258. Alongside *Ducas' this is the best contemporary account. It exists in a long and short versions. P.'s writing is characterized by his animosity towards all foreigners, *Ottoman Turks as well as western Europeans.

PICARESQUE A term applied to the Spanish novel whose hero is usually a person at the bottom echelons of society. In Spanish *picaresco* means roguish. Novels of this genre served as a counterpart to the adventurous romances of *chivalry which took the knight errant for their hero. The P. novels frequently emphasized the vulgar aspects of human existence, vice and carnal love. The earliest example was **Lazarillo de Tormes*; a later successful work was *Guzman de Alfarache* by Mateo *Aleman. The Spanish theme of hero-vagabond was soon adopted by authors of other European nations, the best-known example being Le Sage's *Gil Blas* (1715).

PICCININO, NICCOLO (c. 1386-1444) Italian **condottiere*. Born near Perugia, he became a mercenary, a lieutenant of *Braccio da Montone, whom he succeeded in 1424. He served briefly Florence, then became a captain of the army of Filippo Maria *Visconti (1425). He won many victories for the Duke of Milan, and was rarely defeated. In 1441, when the campaign in Lombardy was turning in his favour, Visconti became suspicious of his rising power, suspended the fighting and gave his natural daughter in marriage to Francesco *Sforza, P.'s enemy. From here on he encountered misfortune. He died on his way to Milan, whither he was summoned by Visconti, after hearing of the defeat of his troops in his absence. His son Jacopo (1423-65) was captain of the army of the Ambrosian Republic of *Milan (1447-50), and also served Venice and King *Alfonso V of Aragon. Later, he gave his support alternately to *Ferrante I and the claimant to the kingdom of Naples, Jean of Anjou. Accused by Ferrante of treachery, he was arrested and put to death.

PICCOLOMINI The name of an important Sienese family. Wealthy merchants, they had already asserted themselves as leaders of the Guelph party in the 13th century. The family's heydey was during the pontificacy of *Pius II (1458-64). One of his nephews, Francesco Todeschini, whom he made cardinal, later became pope as *Pius III (1503). Another nephew, Antonio, was given in 1461 by *Ferrante I the title of Duke of Amalfi. Antonio's nephew, Alfonso, was in 1528 appointed by *Charles V to a high military post in Naples, becoming shortly afterwards the overseer (*capitano del popolo*) of Siena. Suspected of dealing with France, he was compelled by the Emperor to relinquish this position (1541). Other members of the family distinguished themselves as military commanders during the second half of the 16th century and the *Thirty Years' War.

PICCOLOMINI, ALESSANDRO (1508-78) Italian humanist. Born in Siena, he had a distinguished career as a lecturer on philosophy at Padua and Rome. Of his literary works the best known are *La Raffaella* (1540), a dialogue on women, two comedies, *Amor costante* and *Alessandro* (1545-49), and a collection of *sonnets, *Cento sonetti* (1549). He wrote on philosophy and science, and translated classical works.

F. V. Cerreta, *Alessandro Piccolomini, letterato e filosofo senese del Cinquecento* (1960).

PICO DELLA MIRANDOLA, GIOVANNI (1463-94) Italian humanist philosopher. The son of the ruling family of the small duchy near Modena, when he was 16 he came to Florence where he first became associated with *Ficino's *Platonic Academy. From 1480 to 1486 he studied in Padua, then he studied again in Florence, and then in Paris. Endowed with a brilliant mind and an unusual capacity to absorb knowledge, he learned not only *Greek, but also *Hebrew and Arabic, and began to delve into the Jewish *Kabbalah. In 1486 he announced that he was about to hold a disputation over 900 theses which embodied his philosophical views, but before he could do so, *Innocent VIII condemned his opinions. In 1489 he again found shelter in Florence where, protected by Lorenzo de' *Medici, he lived until his death at the early age of 31. In 1492 he wrote *De Ente et Uno*, a philosophical treatise dedicated to his friend, Angelo *Poliziano. Shortly before his death his thought and manner of life took a religious turn, and he became an adherent of *Savonarola. His most influential work, however, the *Oratio*, was written in 1486. It presented man as a completely autonomous being, who could reach perfection by his own efforts and through philosophical meditation. P.'s works were published, together with a biography, by his nephew in 1496, and they have been frequently reedited and translated since.

P. Kibre, *The Library of Pico della Mirandola* (1936);
E. Cassirer, ed., *The Renaissance Philosophy of Man* (1948);
A. Dulles, *Princeps Concordiae: Pico della Mirandola and the Scholastic Tradition* (1941).

PIENZA A small town in the vicinity of *Siena whose name was changed in 1462 from Corsignano, in honour of Pope *Pius II who had been born there. Earlier the Pope had commissioned the Florentine architect Roberto *Rosselino to adorn the town with new public buildings in the Renaissance style. By 1462 he had completed the cathedral, the *Piccolomini palace, the bishop's palace and some lesser buildings. It is perhaps the earliest of urban renewal in modern history.

PIERIN DEL VAGA (1501-47) Italian painter. Born in Florence as Pietro Buonaccorsi, he took his nickname from one of his teachers. He became an assistant to *Raphael in Rome. In 1527 he went to Genoa, where he executed frescoes on mythological subjects in the *Doria Palace. From 1534 to 1538 he worked in Pisa. Later, he lived in Rome, where he continued to paint

Resurrection *by Piero della Francesca*

Fire in the Forest *by Piero di Cosimo*

frescoes in a style reminiscent of *Michelangelo. The best of these are in the Palazzo Massimo alle Colonne.
Galleria dagli Uffizi, Florence, *Mostra di disegni di Pierino del Vaga* (1966).

PIERO DELLA FRANCESCA (c. 1420-92) One of the most important Italian painters of the 15th century. Born at Borgo San Sepolcro in Umbria, where he spent most of his life, his paintings show an interest in *perspective and a scientific approach. The earliest record about him shows that in 1439 he worked with *Domenico Veneziano on a series of frescoes for the hospital of S. Maria Nuova in Florence. There he was influenced by the techniques of the early Renaissance art, with their emphasis on colour and light in painting. By 1442, P. was back in Borgo, where he was elected town councillor. In 1445 he was commissioned to do an altarpiece for the company of the Misericordia of Borgo. His work shows his Florentine influence and the importance he placed on geometry.

In 1451 he completed the fresco of *Sigismondo *Malatesta before St. Sigismund* at Rimini. In 1451 he began one of his masterpieces, the *Legend of the True Cross,* in S. Francesco at Arezzo, which remained unknown until late in the 19th century. The work reveals P.'s mature style, emphasizing clarity of structure and use of perspective. Another notable work of that period is the *Madonna in Childbirth,* an unusual topic for that period. In the late 1450s he painted the *Flagellation of Christ* which, as well as being a fine example of the use of architectural space, also arouses controversy because of its focus on three unidentified persons, while Christ remains in the background. The fresco of *The Resurrection* in Borgo, a powerful depiction of the risen Christ, is also of that period.

P. spent 1459 in Rome, painting frescoes for Pope *Pius II in the Vatican. Later he was patronized by Duke *Federico da Montefeltro, whose portrait he painted together with that of the duchess. P. spent the last two decades of his life at Borgo. Notable paintings of that period are the unfinished *Nativity*, and the *Madonna with the Duke of Urbino as Donor.* Later in his life he wrote two treatises: *De perspectiva pingendi* (On Perspective in Painting) and *De quinque corporibus regularibus* (On the Five Regular Bodies). According to 16th-century tradition P. was blind in his last years. He was not very influential at his time, and was more famous for his scientific works than for his paintings. Modern scholarship has, however, come to appreciate his restrained, discriminating style, and at present he is probably considered the greatest Italian master of the mid-15th century.
P. Bianconi, *All the Paintings of Piero della Francesca* (Eng. trans. 1962).
K. Clark, *Piero della Francesca*, 2nd ed. (1969). (ND)

PIERO DI CONSIMO (c. 1462-1521) Italian painter. Born in Florence as Pietro di Lorenzo, he took his name from his teacher Cosimo *Rosselli. His mature work, however, clearly shows the influence of *Signorelli and *Leonardo, and is distinguished by fantastic imagery especially in his mythological subjects. P. was known as a great portrait painter, a reputation which is attested today by his nude bust of a woman with a snake around her neck, *La Bella Simonetta*. P. was also famous as a designer of *triumphal pageants and, in 1511, he arranged a particularly moving spectacle to illustrate the triumph of death. Several of his younger Florentine contemporaries were influenced by him and he was the master of *Andrea del Sarto. During his last years he is supposed to have turned increasingly to religious subjects.

PIETÀ The representation of the dead Christ lying in his mother's arms, sometimes surrounded by other mourning figures. The theme, first expressed in the art of 14th-century northern Europe, developed parallel to that of the *Madonna (the Virgin Mary) holding in her arms the infant Christ. The theme of *pietà*, Italian for pity, was intended to evoke compassion and religious devotion. Probably the most famous example is the marble sculpture by *Michelangelo in *St. Peter's.

PIGAFETTA, ANTONIO (c. 1491-c. 1535) Italian navigator. Born in Vicenza, he spent some years as a seafaring soldier in the Mediterranean. In 1519 he joined *Magellan's expedition in *Seville. During the great voyage, P. became a confident of the Portuguese captain, who entrusted him with delicate assignments. He was at the side of Magellan when the latter was killed in the *Philippines (1521), and was one of the 18 survivors of the first circumnavigation of the globe who returned to Spain in 1522. In 1525 he was asked by Federico II *Gonzaga to write an account of the expedition. Entitled *Primo viaggio intorno al globo terraquio*, this account is the most important document on Magellan's voyage.

PIGHIUS, ALBERT (c. 1490-1542) Dutch theologian. A native of Kampen, in 1523 he came to Rome by invitation of his fellow-countryman, *Adrian VI. The author of a number of treatises concerning current religious issues, in 1538 he published the *Hirarchiae ecclesiasticae assertio*, a defence of the Roman Catholic Church as the upholder of religious truth. P. countered the Protestant stress on predestination by emphasizing man's free will, an issue, on which he conducted an exchange with *Calvin.

PILGRAM, ANTON (c. 1460-c. 1515) German sculptor and architect. Probably born in Brno, where he is recorded to have worked between 1502-1508, he came to Vienna in approximately 1512. There, in addition to other works, he executed two busts of himself in a realistic mode. P. is considered one of the most important German architects in this transitory style which, while conserving much of the Gothic, is marked by an awareness of Italian Renaissance architecture.

PILGRIM FATHERS (1620) Founders of the Plymouth colony, in the present state of Massachusets, which was the first colony in New England. 35 of the 102 pilgrims were *Puritans fleeing persecution. Their pilgrimage aboard the *Mayflower* was financed by a London stock company, and their disembarkation point was at Cape Cod. There they signed the Mayflower Compact, a political agreement among themselves, and chose the Plymouth site for their settlement. The term "Pilgrim Fathers" was given them in 1820 by the orator Daniel Webster.

PILGRIMAGE OF GRACE The name given to a series of uprisings which occurred in northern England between October 1536 and January 1537. Although economic factors were involved, the rebels emphasized the moral and religious nature of their discontent, their demands including the reinstitution of the monasteries. The main uprising in Yorkshire was led by Robert Aske, who was joined by many members of the local gentry and, at one stage, led a force of about 30,000 men. The rebels took York but, trusting the promises made him by the king's emissary, Aske persuaded them to disband. A further outbreak then gave Henry VIII a pretext to suppress the movement completely. Over 200 persons, including Aske and other members of the local gentry, were executed.

PILKINGTON, JAMES (c. 1520-76) English Protestant reformer. Educated at Cambridge, he became a fellow there and later president of St. John's College. An outspoken critic of Roman Catholicism, he fled England after the accession of *Mary Tudor, returning under *Elizabeth I, to be appointed regius professor of divinity at Cambridge. In 1560 he was made bishop of Durham, where his decidedly Protestant views aroused the enmity of many and resulted in an unsuccessful attempt to have him arrested during the *Northern Rebellion of 1569. His writings included commentaries on the Prophets.

PILON, GERMAN (c. 1535-1590) French sculptor whose works were mainly monumental tombs, and show a transition between *Mannerist and Baroque art. Born to a sculptor in Paris, his first known work was the decoration of the tomb of *Francis I. In 1565 he was commissioned by *Catherine de Médicis to decorate the tomb of *Henry II, a work which lasted almost until his death. He sculptured the kneeling bronze figures and the marble, seminude figures of the King

Nymphs *bronze sculpture by Germain Pilon*

The Coronation of Pius II *by Pinturicchio*

and Queen. In 1570 he sculptured the marble *Virgin and Child*, and designed decorations for the wedding of *Charles IX. The King appointed him a royal sculptor, and he began to work on portraits. From 1572 he was controller of the mint and in 1575 he produced a series of bronce medallions. P.'s early works were influenced by the school of *Fontainbleau, but his later ones mark the beginning of a distinctive French style.

PINTO, FERNAO MENDES (c. 1510-83) Portuguese writer. Leading a life of adventure from youth on, in 1537 he went to the Far East, visiting, according to his own account, various places in Ethiopia, India, China and Japan during the next 20 years. After his return to Portugal in 1558, P. began to write his famous *Peregrinacam*, first published in 1614. The work, which abounds with exaggerated descriptions and unlikely episodes, enjoyed success in the Spanish, English, French and German translations, and is regarded one of the foremost examples of Renaissance travelogues.

G. Le Gentil, *Fernão Mendes Pinto: Un précurseur de l'exotisme au XVIe siècle* (1947).

PINTO, HEITOR (1528-84) Portuguese writer. Born in Covilha, he joined the Hieronymite Order in 1543, later studying at Coimbra, where he began to teach theology in 1551. P. was a great biblical scholar, but is remembered less for his erudite commentaries than for his *Imagem da vida cristã*, a work in 11 dialogues which dealt with faith, friendship, philosophy and other moral themes. Published in two parts in 1563 and 1572, it was widely translated, going into numerous editions till the end of the century. In 1583, because of his opposition to the Spanish annexation of Portugal, P. was himself exiled to Spain.

PINTURICCHIO, BERNARDINO (1454-1513) Italian painter. A disciple of *Perugino, whom he assisted in 1481 with the frescoes at the *Sistine Chapel, P. was essentially a decorative painter. His best-known ornamental frescoes were done in the *Borgia apartments in the Vatican (1492-95), at the commission of *Alexander VI. Ten years later he executed another famous series in the Libreria del Duomo at Siena, which treated scenes from the life of *Pius II. He also produced many paintings, his earlier work being distinguished by its elegance and splendid portraiture.

E. M. Phillips, *Pintoricchio* (1901).

PINZON Three Spanish brothers all of whom became navigators. The P.s accompanied *Columbus on his first voyage of discovery. The eldest, Martin Alonso (*c.* 1440-93), was in charge of the Pinta, with his brother Francisco as pilot. Twice during the voyage he found himself cut off from Columbus, but nevertheless arrived back in Palos in the same day. Five days after their return, however, he died. Vicente Yanez (*c.* 1460-1524) was in command of the Niña. In 1500 he led an expedition to the mouth of the Amazon and explored the northern coasts of Brazil.

PIRCKHEIMER, WILLIBALD (1470-1530) German humanist. When he was a very young man, he travelled to Italy to study at Padua and Pavia; in 1497, he became a town-councillor at Nuremberg, where his lifelong

Willibald Pirckheimer *by Dürer*

The Wooers Surprising Penelope *by Pinturicchio*

friendship with *Dürer began, other humanist friends of his being *Reuchlin, *Celtis and Erasmus. P; wrote on history and astronomy and translated Greek authors into Latin. At first a supporter of *Luther, he returned to the Catholic faith in 1521, under the influence of his devout sister Charitas.

PISA, COUNCIL OF (1409) A general council of the Church convoked by a group of cardinals to end the *Great Schism. It was attended by some 500 ecclesiastical delegates and representatives of the European princes. The council announced the deposition of the two rival popes, Benedict XIII and *Gregory XII, and chose Alexander V to succeed them as the single pope of a united Christendom. However, the latter soon died and was replaced in 1410 by Cardinal Baldassare Cossa, who took the name of *John XXIII. Since neither the Avignonese nor the Roman pope had resigned, the immediate result of the council was to aggravate the rift by adding a third claimant to the papal throne. But, by demonstrating that a major portion of the church was determined to put an end to the schism, the council paved the way for the final resolution of the problem at *Constance.

PISA, COUNCIL OF (1511) An ecclesiastical council convened at Pisa through the initiative of *Louis XII of France, with the purpose of deposing Pope *Julius II. Attended also by delegates sent by Emperor *Maximilian I, the latter soon fell out with the French King. Supported by only a minority of the cardinals, the council was declared schismatic by the pope, who countered it by convening the fifth *Lateran Council in 1512. The French withdrawal from Italy that same year ended the Pisan experiment.

PISANELLO, ANTONIO (c. 1395-1455) Italian painter and medalist; a major exponent of the *International Gothic style. Born in Pisa he was trained in Verona and wandered through many Italian courts. Between 1415 and 1422 he worked with *Gentile da Fabriano, by whom he was very much influenced, on frescoes in the Doges' palace in Venice, and after 1427 in St. John Lateran in Rome; all these works, however, were destroyed. His frescoes are detailed and their subject is

The Vision of St. Eustace *by Pisanello*

mainly knights and *chivalry. His most notable paintings are *St. Eustace* and *Madonna with Saints Anthony and George* which he painted early in his life, and *S. George and the Princess of Trebizond* (1432).

P. was the first artist who worked on *medals, which he began at a later phase in his life. Among the portraits on his medals were those of *John VIII Palaeologus, the Byzantine emperor, and *Alfonso of Aragon. In addition, P. worked on painted portraits, mostly in profile. P.'s drawings were kept in the Louvre and they reveal his varied techniques. Many of them are realistic drawings of animals executed in detail and with scientific accuracy. (ND)

PISANO, ANDREA (c. 1290-c. 1348) Italian sculptor and architect. Born at Pontedera, near Pisa, he moved to Florence where he was greatly influenced by *Giotto. In 1330 he was commissioned to make the bronze doors of the Baptistery, a work which he completed in 1336. The panels of the doors represent 20 scenes from the life of St. John the Baptist, and eight figures of the Virtues. When Giotto died in 1337, P. completed his work on the Campanile of the cathedral. Other sculptural works of his are *Christ Blessing* and *St. Reparata*. In his capacity as architect, when Emperor Henry VII presented a threat to Florence, P. raised the fortification walls of the city in 1312. P.'s last undertaking, which he was not able to complete, was as the architect of the cathedral of Orvieto.

PISANO, NICOLA (c. 1220-c. 84) AND GIOVANNI (c. 1250-c. 1317) Italian sculptors, father and son, who created a new sculptural style. Nicola was probably born in Apulia, but he spent most of his life in Pisa. There he produced his first great work, the marble pulpit of the Baptistery. With the help of Giovanni, he completed the pulpit of the Cathedral at Siena in 1268, and later designed the fountain in the *piazza* at Perugia. Nicola introduced the use of classical motives combined with a late Gothic style. His early works still present static, impersonal and idealized figures, but in his later ones there is a transition. The figures are more realistic and they are presented in states of action and emotion. Giovanni's principal works were the planning and decoration of the façade of the Cathedral at Siena (1284-95), the pulpit of St. Andrea at Pistoia (completed 1301), and the pulpit of the Cathedral of Pisa. Giovanni's forms are more dramatic and less detailed than those of his father, but he continued the combination of classical and Gothic motives.

PITHOU, PIERRE (1539-96) French political writer. the son of a distinguished *Huguenot family, he converted to Roman Catholicism in 1573 and became a well-known lawyer. In 1593, together with other moderate Catholic writers, he compiled a famous pamphlet, *La satyre menippée*, which is said to have gained *Henry IV access to Paris. His immensely successful book, *Les libertés de l'eglise gallicane*, published in 1594, declared that the pope could exercise no temporal authority in France and that his spiritual jurisdiction was also subject to limitation, being restricted to those conciliar decrees which the French monarchy recognized as valid. This extreme assertion of *Gallicanism was given royal sanction in the 17th century. P. also edited classical texts, collected manuscripts on early conciliar history, and prepared an edition of canon law. Henry IV appointed him attorney of the **parlement* of Paris.

PITTI, LUCA (1395-?) Florentine merchant and official. Member of an ancient aristocratic family, he served as a Gonfalonier of Justice. In 1454 he tried to take over the power from Cosimo de' *Medici by changing the method of election to the signoria; however, he had to turn to Cosimo for help and the latter's power was restored. In 1466 he plotted against Cosimo's son, Piero. When his conspiracy failed, P. went over to Piero's side. He is remembered particularly for having commissioned the Pitti Palace; begun by *Brunelleschi in 1435, it was only completed by *Ammanati in 1570. The most monumental palace in Florence, it is a treasure of Renaissance art.

PIUS II (Enea Silvio Piccolomini; 1405-64) Humanist writer. Pope from 1458 to 1464. Born near Siena, he showed a talent for literature at an early age and studied in *Florence. He acted as secretary to the Bishop of Ferma, attending the Council of Basle together with him in 1432. During the next few years he filled various posts and carried out diplomatic assignments for the Council. Rising in influence, he took part in the election of Amadeo VIII, Duke of Savoy, as Pope Felix V (1440), and was made his secretary. Felix, however, had been elected in opposition to the reigning pope, Eugenius IV, and had only minority support, and P. soon shifted his ground.

The Sculpture Hall at the Pitti Palace, Florence

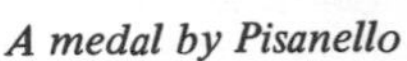

A medal by Pisanello

In 1442 P. went to Germany, where he was given a warm reception and various honours by *Frederick III. It was there that he wrote a very popular novel of love and adventure, *Historia de duobus amantibus*, as well as Latin poetry and a comedy, *Chrisis*. Then, not long after he had become famous as a secular writer, P. underwent a spiritual change which, in 1446, made him enter a religious order. Becoming a supporter of Eugenius IV, he was made Bishop of Trieste in 1447 and Bishop of Siena in 1450, working effectively to lessen friction between Rome and Germany. P. was made a cardinal in 1456 and was elected pope in 1458.

As pope, P. dedicated most of his efforts to organizing a crusade against the Turks, but he received little support from the Congress of Mantua which he convened in 1459. He then tried to achieve his goal by strengthening the spiritual supremacy of the papacy. In 1460 he issued the bull *Execrabilis*, reprobating the notion that the church councils could have more weight than the pope. In 1461 *Louis XI of France was persuaded by P. to renounce the ancient liberties of the French church, only to reassert them again later. In 1462 a bitter conflict broke out between P. and between George of Podebrady, King of Bohemia, and his supporters in Germany, continuing until after P.'s death. In spite of his difficulties with the European princes, P. declared a crusade in 1463 and took up the cross himself, hoping that his personal example would win him volunteers. The only response, however, came from Venice, which offered him a small fleet of twelve ships. While desperately awaiting the crusaders, P. died in Ancona, a disappointed man.

P. also wrote on the history of the Council of Basle, on the reign of Emperor Frederick III and on the kingdom of Bohemia. Of particular interest is his autobiography, which tells the story of his pontificate until 1463.

R. J. Mitchell, *The Laurels and the Tiara: Pope Pius II, 1458-64* (1963);
Pius II, *Memoirs of a Renaissance Pope* (1959).

PIUS III (Francesco Todeschini; 1440-1503) Pope from 22 September to 18 October 1503. Though occupying the papal throne for less than four weeks, P. had, prior to his election, enjoyed a long ecclesiastical career. As nephew of *Pius II he was made Archbishop of Siena when he was only 20 years old. Later serving as papal legate to Germany, P. was also employed by *Sixtus IV, *Innocent VIII and *Alexander VI. His election to the papal throne took place while Cesare *Borgia was threatening the Vatican. P.'s reaction to this threat was not altogether courageous.

PIUS IV (Giovanni Angelo Medici; 1499-1565) Pope (1559-65). Although he bore the name of Medici, P. was not related to the Florentine family. He was born in Milan, studied in Bologna and entered the papal court as a notary and administrator. *Paul III, his patron, made him Archbishop of Ragusa in 1545, and four years later he became a cardinal. The death of his benefactor that same year seems to have affected his position. He was given only modest assignments under *Julius III and, because of his pro-Habsburg sentiments, was at odds with *Paul IV. When the latter died, P. was absent from the papal court in Milan. His election to the papacy was due mainly to the fact that the electoral college was evenly divided, a situation favouring the choice of a moderate candidate. The conclave lasted over three months. Notwithstanding his reputed moderation, P. opened his reign with the arrest of the protegés of his predecessor (June 1560), the brothers Carlo and Giovanni Carafa. Carlo, a cardinal, was executed on a charge of murder and treason. P. soon surrounded himself with protegés of his own family and was aided in particular by his nephew Carlo *Borromeo. His greatest accomplishments was the reconvening, in January 1562, of the Council of *Trent, which had been suspended for about ten years, bringing it to a conclusion in December 1563. On the basis of the Council's decrees, he issued a new catechism and revised the Index of prohibited books. P. also dedicated his efforts to the building of St. *Peter's, and encouraged the execution of other churches and monuments. He extended especial patronage to *Michelangelo.

PIUS V, ST. (1504-72) Pope (1566-72). Born to a poor family near Alessandria, he became a Dominican at the age of 14, changing his name from Antonio Ghislieri to Michele. He worked his way up as an inquisitor in the hierarchy of the Church, at first in Como, near the Swiss border (1550), than as Commissary General of the Roman Inquisition (1551), and, finally, in 1558, he was created Grand Inquisitor for life of the Roman Church. His promotion was due to the support of *Paul IV, an extreme disciplinarian from the doctrinal point of view, who also consecrated him as bishop (1556) and cardinal (1557). Although the Grand Inquisitor was out of favour during the pontificate of *Pius IV, he emerged victorious from the conclave in which he was championed by Cardinal Carlo *Borromeo in January 1566. As pope he introduced a mode of ascetic austerity into the Vatican and implemented the decisions of the Council of *Trent, especially with regard to censorship. He had *Breviarium Romanum* (1568) and the *Missale Romanum* (1570) published, thus establishing liturgical uniformity. In a futile attempt to regain England for Roman Catholicism, P. excommunicated Queen Elizabeth I and gave his support to Catherine de *Médicis in her stand against the *Huguenots. The most successful of P.'s international dealings was against the Turks: he brought together the naval coalition, led by Spain and Venice, which won the Battle of *Lepanto in 1571. His achievements as a great restorer of the church were confirmed by his canonization in 1712.

PIZARRO, FRANCISCO (1470-1541) Conqueror of Peru. An illegitimate child who never learned to read, P. went to America in 1509. In 1519 he settled in Panama and, together with *Almagro, began exploring southwards along the Pacific coast. After reaching as far south as Guayaquil, he went to Spain in 1528, to have *Charles V appoint him governor of Peru the land he was delegated to conquer. P. returned to the New World accompanied by his four half-brothers and other volunteers, and, in late 1530, sailed from Panama. He landed in Guayaquil and marched south into Peru, where he met Atahualpa, the chief ruler of the Inca, at Cajamarca. On 16 November 1532 P. tricked Atahualpa into his own camp and took him captive in a surprise attack. The Indian monarch was promised his freedom in exchange for enough gold objects to fill his prison cell; but P. broke the agreement and had him executed. He then captured Cuzco, the Inca capital (November 1533), and in 1535 founded a new capital, Lima, on the coast. Soon after he had to put down an Indian revolt, and, in

Peasant Wedding *by Pieter Breughel*

Madonna with St. Margaret and Other Saints *by Parmigianino*

1537, lost Cuzco to his former associate Almagro, who had just returned from Chile. Their confrontation ended in the Battle of Las Salinas, which P. won. He then extended Spanish rule to present-day Bolivia and Ecuador, and sent *Valdivia to conquer Chile. He was murdered at his home in Lima by followers of Almagro's son.
W. H. Prescott, *History of the Conquest of Peru* (1847); P. A. Means, *The Fall of the Inca Empire and the Spanish Rule in Peru, 1530-1780* (1932).

PIZARRO, GONZALO (c. 1506-48) Spanish **conquistador*. A younger brother of Francisco *Pizarro, he came to America with his brother in 1529 and joined the expedition to Peru. After the Incas had been conquered and their uprising crushed, P. helped to defeat *Almagro in 1537. In 1539 he became governor of Quito and led an expedition to the jungles of the eastern Andes in search of *El Dorado. A splinter group, headed by *Orellana, separated from P.'s main party undertook to cross the Amazon. In 1542, however, P. returned to Quito empty-handed. Shortly afterwards, when the New Laws were issued limiting the privileges of the holders of Indians in **encomienda*, P. led a revolt against the royal administration. In 1546 he killed the viceroy, Blasco Nuñez Vela, in battle, thus becoming virtual ruler of Peru. The new viceroy, Pedro de la *Gasca, however, succeeded in defeating him and had him executed as a traitor.
R. Arciniega, *Dos rebeldes Españoles en el Peru; Gonzalo Pizarro y Lope de Aguirre* (1946).

PIZARRO, HERNANDO (c. 1490-1578) Spanish **conquistador*. He went to the New World in 1529, with his elder half-brother Francisco *Pizarro, and distinguished himself in the conquest of Peru. In 1534 he was entrusted with the cargo of gold sent to the royal treasury of Spain. Returning to Peru, he was captured in 1537, together with his brother Gonzalo *Pizarro, by *Almagro but was soon released; in the following year he defeated and executed Almagro. In 1540 he was again sent with the treasure to Spain, but arrested upon arrival and held in confinement for some 20 years.
J. Lockhart, *The Men of Cajamarca* (1972).

PLACARDS, AFFAIR OF THE (18 October 1534) A scandal caused by the distribution of Protestant propaganda in Paris, which touched off a wave of persecution. Until this time *Francis I wavered in his attitude towards the French Lutherans. These broadsides, which attacked Roman Catholic doctrines in a very vehement language, aroused his outrage. In the course of the following year, hundreds of Lutherans were imprisoned on charges of heresy, and about two dozen burnt at the stake.

PLANTIN, CHRISTOPHER (1514-89) Printer in *Antwerp. A Frenchman by birth, in 1549 he settled in Antwerp, soon becoming a large-scale publisher whose books acquired a reputation for the accuracy and design with which they were produced. His list included classical authors and works on medicine and science. He was particularly famous, however, for his editions of the Bible, printing the *Biblia Regia*, an eight-volume Polyglot Bible sponsored by *Philip II between 1568 and 1572. After his death, the firm was continued by his son-in-law, Jan Moretus (1543-1610).
C. Clair, *Christopher Plantin* (1960);
L. Voet, *The Golden Compasses*, 2 vols. (1969-72).

Francisco Pizarro, Conqueror of Peru

PLATERESQUE The name given to the decorative style of architecture popular in Spain during the 16th century. The P., corresponding to Spain's period of apogée, consisted in lavish ornamentation derived from either oriental or western sources, added to a building irrespective of its basic structure. The most famous practitioners of the style were Alonso de *Covarrubias and Rodrigo Gil de Hontañon. The word P. means in Spanish "silversmith-like". The *manuelino* is a related style of architecture in Portugal.

PLATINA, BARTOLOMMEO (1421-81) Italian humanist. He first served Francesco *Sforza, then became a tutor for the *Gonzagas at *Mantua. Between 1457 and 1461 he studied Greek under *Argyropoulos at Florence. In 1462 he came to Rome where he joined the circle of Pomponius *Laetus and alienated *Paul II. But *Sixtus IV made him librarian of the Vatican. P. wrote a number of treatises concluding a very famous history of the popes, *Liber de vita Christi ac omnium pontificum* (1474), in which he flattered his patron.

PLATONIC ACADEMY In the second half of the 15th century, a group of scholars in *Florence who considered themselves a revival of the academy formed by Plato in Athens. Led by Marsilio *Ficino and enjoying the patronage of Cosimo and Lorenzo de' *Medici, the P. became a centre of learning and for the diffusion of modernized and Christianized Platonism. Other notable members included *Pico della Mirandola, *Politian, Cristofero Landino and Gentile de' Becchi.

PLATTER, THOMAS (1499-1582) Swiss humanist. Born in Grächen, Wallis, to a poor family, he was a shepherd, soapmaker and wandering teacher, later he became a printer and schoolmaster in *Basle. While he was a young man, he joined the Reformation, becoming a supporter of *Zwingli, and in 1536 published the first edition of Calvin's *Institutes*. At the age of 75 he wrote an autobiography in a popular style which is a valuable source on the period. His son Felix Platter (1536-1614), city physician of Basle, was the author of *Praxis medica* (1602-08); he, like his father, left an interesting autobiography. Felix's son, Thomas Platter the Younger (1574-1628), also a physician, wrote an account of his travels in Europe which included a description of a performance at London's Globe Theatre in 1599.

A. L. Schnidrig, *Thomas Platter* (1955);
H. Hecht, *Thomas Platters des Jüngeren Englandfahrt im Jahre 1599* (1929).

PLEIADE, THE A French school of poetry launched in 1549 by *Ronsard and *Du Bellay with the publication of the latter's *Defense et illustration de la langue française*. In addition to the two main leaders, the founding group included their friends *Baïf, *Jodelle, *Belleau and Ponthus de Thyard, and their teacher at the College de Cocqueret, Jean Dorat. The declared aim of the P. was to make the French language a dignified instrument for poetry. This was to be achieved by writing poems modelled on the great classical or Italian authors, especially Pindar, Anacreon and Horace. The artistic notions of the P. influenced French poetry until the end of the 16th century.

H. Chamard, *Histoire de la Plèiade*, 4 vols. (1939-40);
G. D. Castor, *Plèiade Poetics* (1964).

PLEYDENWURFF, HANS (c. 1420-71) German painter. He was probably born in Bamberg, but was active in Nuremberg from 1457. His mature style is influenced by Flemish realism, although it still retains much of the *International Gothic, and of the primitive local traditions. Known primarily for his large *Crucifixion*, now in Munich, P. was the teacher of *Wolgemut. His son Wilhelm P. (d. 1494) was one of the greatest masters of the woodcut in his time, and collaborated with Wolgemut on the *Nuremberg Chronicle*.

PO, FERNANDO Portuguese explorer. Only a few details about him are recorded. Possibly of German origin, he was employed by Fernão Gomes, who had received from the crown the right to trade with the Guinean coast of Africa. In 1471 P. discovered an island which he named Formosa, but which was later called after him.

POGGIO, BRACCIOLINI, GIOVANNI FRANCESCO (1380-1459) Italian humanist. Born to an impoverished family, P. learned Latin and trained himself as a scribe. In 1404 he entered the service of the papal chancery and, in a layman capacity's he served eight popes in Rome and elsewhere during almost 50 years. In 1453 he became chancellor of *Florence, a post he held until shortly before his death. P. discovered many classical works, including some manuscripts of Cicero, Lucretius, Livy and Quintilian, in monastic libraries throughout Europe. He also wrote witty satires in Latin, filled with irreverence toward religion and the clergy. He collected Roman inscriptions and wrote a work describing Rome's ancient monuments. His intense relations with other humanists of his time frequently brought him into vehement controversies; especially acerbic were his feuds with Lorenzo *Valla and *Filelfo.

POISSY, COLLOQUY OF A conference between French Roman Catholic bishops and Protestant theologians held in Poissy near Paris in September 1561. The dialogue, led by the Jesuit *Lainez and the Protestant theologian *Beza, had been convened by *Catherine de Médicis with the aim of reaching some kind of agreement on fundamentals, but no real meeting-point was achieved. On 17 January 1562, however, the queen regent published the famous edict which for the first time gave a measure of recognition to the *Huguenots.

POLAND The political history of Poland during the 15th and 16th centuries was dominated by the rule of the *Jagiello dynasty and their effort to preserve the union with *Lithuania. This dynastic alliance began in 1386, when Jadwiga, who was elected queen by the Polish aristocracy, married Jagiello, prince of Lithuania. With the help of Lithuania, the Poles hoped to be able to stop the threat posed by Germany, especially that of the *Teutonic Knights. In 1410 Jagiello, who had assumed the title of *Vladislav II, defeated the knights at Tannenberg. His son *Casimir IV completed the subjugation of the order, following a long war which ended with the second peace of *Thorn (1466). The royal union with Lithuania became political only in the Diet of Lublin (1569). In the meantime another important alliance was achieved by Casimir IV (1447-92), when he acquired *Bohemia for his son, *Ladislas II (1471). The result was the creation of a large empire, which, during the end of the 15th century, threatened to become the greatest power in eastern Europe.

That this was not realized is accounted for by the internal political conditions of Poland. Under the Jagiellos the nobility (*szlachta*) became increasingly more powerful. Both the greater and lesser nobility participated in the royal council which was turned into the national Diet (*seim*) after 1493, with an upper and a lower house. In 1505 the constitutional act *Nihil Novi* decreed that no new law could be passed without the Diet's consent. According to the *liberum veto*, any member of the Diet could veto any measure, though in reality the majority could have forced its will. The strengthened power of the aristocracy made for a renewal of the feudal system in Poland, and the serfdom of the peasantry was legalized in the 16th century.

In the 15th and 16th centuries Poland grew wealthy and developed an important foreign trade. The *Reformation, which penetrated the country during the 16th century made inroads, especially among the nobility, which resulted in religious conflicts. These were resolved in the Compact of Warsaw (1573), which introduced constitutional equality to all religions. But after that the Roman Catholics, led by the *Jesuits, became more powerful, and effected the adherence of the *Uniate Church of Rome.

The end of the Jagiello rule marks the beginning of the decline of Poland. After the death of the last Jagiello, *Sigismund II (1548-72), a system of electing foreign kings was introduced. Through this method, sponsored by the powerful magnate Jan *Zamoiski, the Polish aristocracy aimed at safeguarding its privileges, and their agreements with the kings strictly limited the royal power. The first king to be elected in 1573 was Henry of Valois, who returned to France in 1574 and became *Henry III. After him the crown was held by the Hungarian *Stephen Bathory (1575-86). By the time of the outbreak of the *Thirty Years' War P. was ruled by a Swedish prince of the house of *Vasa, Sigismund III (1587-1632). (ND)

POLE, REGINALD (1500-58) English cardinal and archbishop of Canterbury. Related on his mother's side to the royal family, he was educated at Oxford and then in Italy and France where he was able to make the acquaintance of leading humanists of the day. As an emissary of the Church, P. rejected *Henry VIII's attempt to obtain the Pope's approval for his divorce from *Catherine of Aragon. This led to a quarrel between the King and himself, as a result of which P. left England and went to Italy in 1532. There, in 1536, he was made cardinal by Pope *Paul III. Although he helped the Pope in his efforts to form a coalition against England, together with his friend *Contarini, he was one of the Catholic clergymen who sought to reform the Church from within and reconcile it with *Protestantism. As one of the presiding legates at the Council of *Trent, he spoke of the need for such reforms. When *Mary Tudor became queen of England in 1553, P. was appointed papal legate to England. There he was responsible for the reinstitution of Catholicism and the introduction of several Church reforms. In 1556 he was appointed archbishop of Canterbury. A year later, as a result of a conflict between England and Pope *Paul IV over political issues, his appointment was terminated and he was denounced as a heretic. A man of high moral character, he died a few hours after Queen Mary.

W. Schenk, *Reginald Pole, Cardinal of England* (1950).

POLIDORO DA CARAVAGGIO (c. 1500-43) Italian painter. Born at Caravaggio near Bergamo, he came to Rome in his youth, where he was influenced by *Raphael. He acquired a reputation for the mythological and historical scenes with which he decorated the façades of Roman houses, although none of these have survived. His best extant work is *St. Mary Magdalen*, a fresco in the church of S. Silvestro al Quirinale, which is noted for its landscape background. He left Rome in 1527, and later worked in Messina, where he was assassinated.

A. Marabottini, *Polidoro da Caravaggio*, 2 vols. (1969).

POLITIAN (Angelo Poliziano; 1454-94) Italian poet. and humanist. Born at Montepulciano, he left for Florence around the year 1469, after the murder of his father. In Florence he studied Latin, Greek and philosophy and, at the age of 17, composed Latin poems and Greek epigrams praising several Florentine citizens. P. translated four books of the *Iliad* into Latin and dedicated the first two to Lorenzo de' *Medici. Lorenzo became his patron, taking him into his household in 1473, and making him the tutor of his son, Piero. At about that time P. published first editions of a number of Roman poets, and wrote his most important poem in the vernacular, *Stanze per la giostra*. In 1479, owing to a quarrel with Lorenzo's wife, he left the Medici house and went to *Mantua. Patronized by Cardinal Francesco Gonzaga, in 1480 he wrote a dramatic play in the vernacular called *Favola d'Orfeo*. In the same year, however, he was recalled to Florence, and began to lecture on Latin and Greek at the university. His lectures attracted scholars from all over Italy and Europe. In 1489 he published the *Miscellanea*, a learned work on

A illustration from Thomas More's Utopia *(1516)*

classical philology. P.'s works are based on classical motifs, which he used in a new way to suit the atmosphere of the second half of the 15th century. In Latin, as well as in Italian, he was a born poet. (ND)

POLITICAL THEORY Alternating between a tendency to set up ideal models and attempts to describe the actual norms of political behaviour, P. in the Renaissance was never entirely divorced from its past. Though capable of bold innovations, it was still influenced by traditional concepts of authority and the purpose of political organization. What distinguishes Renaissance political thought from its mediaeval predecessors were the issues it discussed, which reflected the changing historical circumstances. P. in the Middle Ages had been concerned with such themes as papal *versus* imperial authority, Roman law and feudal custom, universal monarchy and Christian unity as opposed to particularism. The Renaissance had to deal with the emergence of the modern, centrally-governed state. The view that politics constituted a distinctive area of human behaviour acquired wider currency, and political authority was defined in utilitarian, secular terms – quite unlike the mediaeval tendency to address it in moral concepts. But to stress the secularization of political thought during the Renaissance is to over-emphasize one particular aspect. The prolific political literature of the 16th century also dealt with such issues as religious tolerance and non-resistance to constituted authority, as well as with the right of rebellion and the divine right of kings. A significant feature of Renaissance political thought was the wide range of the subjects it dealt with.

In the first half of the 15th century political writers were still preoccupied with problems of Church authority, rekindled by the *Great Schism (1378-1417). The leading contributors, including Pierre *D'Ailly, Jean *Gerson, Francesco *Zabarella, tended to deny the absolute power of the pope, defending with different degrees of emphasis the rights of the general Church council. This approach was also adopted by *Nicholas of Cusa in his *De concordantia catholica* (1433), although he stressed harmony rather than authority. The defence of the *conciliar idea was significant, as it implied a possible support for constitutionalism against absolutism in the realm of national politics also. The 15th century, when the struggle between *feudalism and the centralized monarchy was not yet over, witnessed the growing power of *representative institutions. Some of the most penetrating contemporary observers of political events, like *Commines in France, upheld the right of subjects, represented by their Estates, to consent to extraordinary taxation. In England, *Fortescue described the government of his own country as *dominium politicum et regale*, whereby the king could not make laws without the consent of Parliament, and the people acknowledged the authority of a strong hereditary monarchy. Later, Claude de *Seyssel expounded similar views in his *Grant monarchie de France* (1518).

European political thought was enriched by the systematic study of and commentary on the Roman law, begun in the 12th century. Among the "civilians", who usually championed the cause of absolute monarchy, there were in the first half of the 16th century such outstanding thinkers as *Decius, *Alciati and *Cujas. *Budé, who turned from legal studies to classical scholarship, exemplified the diminishing influence of Roman law and the effect of humanist culture on political thought. At that time much of the political writing that came from humanist circles consisted of edifying expatiation on the duties of the ruler in a high didactic style. Yet the *Neoplatonist ideas which marked the thought of the High Renaissance produced More's *Utopia* (1516), which describes an ideal community whose static serenity stood in sharp contrast to the moral and cultural upheavals of More's times. Although it was never intended to be an actual political model, More's book inspired other works in the same vein, of which one of the better known is *Campanella's *Civitas solis* (1623).

More's idealism was at one pole of the humanist political theory; the other was expressed in *Machiavelli's realistic analysis in his famous work, *The Prince*. The author's shrewdness, his cold objective attitude and his ability to abstract politics from moral considerations impressed his 16th-century readers. But it is not for these qualities alone that Machiavelli is often described as the pioneer of modern political theory: in his search for the factors which stabilize society, he stressed the functions of religion and patriotism, and what he had to say on these and other matters, particularly on the nature and mechanics of political leadership, to some extent remains valid until our own day. In Italy Machiavelli was followed by *Guicciardini, like him a keen observer who wrote on politics in a detached objective manner. In the late 16th century their line of thought reappeared in the works of Giovanni *Botero.

However, at the very time when Machiavelli's theories were gaining currency, P. became impregnated with theological considerations, as a result of the advent of the *Reformation. Both *Luther and *Calvin taught that resistance to rulers was wicked. They preached submissiveness and encouraged state control of religion and morals, favouring a rigidly intolerant rule. Calvin, especially, decried all acts of rebellion, claiming that an evil ruler is an affliction from heaven and that remedy could come only through prayer and the help of God. It was only later, in the teachings of *Knox and as an outcome of historical circumstances in Scotland, Holland and France, that the Calvinists reversed their position. Curiously enough some of the foremost Roman Catholic political authors of the *Counter-Reformation formulated ideas which paralleled those of the Calvinists. Roberto *Bellarmine, for example, asserted the rights of the popes to depose heretical rulers, though he emphasized the secular nature of monarchies and conceded that the pope had no power in secular matters. Other famous *Jesuit political authors, especially Juan de *Mariana and Francisco *Suarez, dealt with resistance to arbitrary royal power, claiming that government derived its authority from a contract between the ruler and the people, a breach of which permitted the latter to exercise its constitutional rights. On the opposite side of the political spectrum was the English Richard *Hooker, who chided the *Puritans for their opposition to a state-sponsored church. Although this was probably not his intention, Hooker's line of argument ultimately supported the divine right of kings; but the most elaborate statement in support of this position was made by the Scot William *Barclay. Another contributor to this doctrine, who emphasized the hereditary nature of monarchy and its all-encompassing power was King *James I.

France, because of turbulent internal conditions in the latter half of the 16th century, became a breeding ground for conflicting political theories. One of the most influential authors, writing on the threshold of the *Religious Wars, was Charles *Dumoulin. His works, dealing with French customary law, were an apologia for the growing power of the monarchy, a process which had begun under *Louis XI and continued in the reigns of *Louis XII, *Francis I and *Henry II. French champions of a limited monarchy belonged to the beleaguered *Huguenot camp. In his *Francogallia* (1573) François *Hotman tried to substantiate constitutional theories, claiming that the Estates-General had always exercised restrictions on the monarchy. A famous Huguenot political tract, the **Vindiciae Contra Tyrannos* (1579), went even further, and defended active resistance to kings, on the basis of a contractual theory that the ruler is accountable to the people for the justice and legality of his rule. The most valuable French contribution, however, came from the middle party, the **politiques* as, for example, Jean *Bodin, the author of the *Six livres de la Republique* (1576). Here, in the midst of the storm, an attempt was made to establish a set of principles upon which order and unity could be maintained. Bodin's main answer was to propose the concept of *sovereignty, the supreme and perpetual power over the state and its subjects, unrestrained by law. To the sovereign he attributed the right to make peace or war, appoint magistrates and decide all judicial matters. Stating his argument in legal terms, and generally eschewing moral and theological considerations, he certainly did not mean to support the divine right of kings. But the fact that his "well-ordered state" vested sovereignty in a single person, made him the prophet of the absolute monarchies of the 17th and 18th centuries.

J. W. Allen, *A History of Political Thought in the 16th Century* (1928);

R. W. and A. J. Carlyle, *A History of Medieval Political Theory in the West*, vol. VI, *Political Theory From 1300 to 1600* (1936);

G. H. Sabine, *A History of Political Theory* (1937).

POLITIQUES The middle-of-the-road current of opinion in France during the *Religious Wars. Already in the early 1560s the term was employed with reference to the policies of *Catherine de Médicis and her chancellor, Michel de *L'Hôpital. The P. stood for strong monarchical power, but accepted the idea of tolerance towards the *Huguenots, claiming that the function of government was not to suppress heresy but to maintain peace and order. At a later stage many P. made common cause with the Huguenots against the *League.

W. F. Church, *Constitutional Thought in 16th Century France* (1941).

POLLAIUOLO, ANTONIO (c. 1432-98) AND PIERO (1443-96) Florentine painters and sculptors, brothers. Pupils of *Castagno, their interest was in the human body in movement. Antonio, who was also a goldsmith, is famous for bronze works such as *Hercules and Antaeus* which once belonged to the *Medici. As a painter, he worked in collaboration with his brother. Their major work was the *Martyrdom of S. Sebastian* (1475), which reveals interest in topographical landscape. The movement of the figures is tense and violent, as it is in other of their works, such as *Hercules and Nessus*. Piero was mainly a painter. His principal late works are *Coronation of the Virgin, Three Saints* and *Prudence*.

The P. brothers owned a very successful workshop, which created works of art in all the major contemporary techniques. Antonio was evidently also an expert of *engraving. His famous print *The Battle of the Naked Men*, reveals an interest in *anatomical study, and he is said to have been the first artist to dissect human bodies in order to study the shape of muscles and bones. Late in his life Antonio worked in Rome on the bronze papal tombs of *Sixtus IV (1493) and *Innocent VIII (1494-98).

A. Sabatini, *Antonio e Piero Pollaiuolo* (1944).

POMPONAZZI, PIETRO (1462-1525) Italian philosopher who introduced humanistic ideas into mediaeval Aristotelianism. Born in *Mantua, he studied medicine and philosophy at Padua, where he became a professor of philosophy in 1488. In 1509 he went to *Ferrara and from there moved to *Bologna where he did most of his writing. His philosophy is based on the 2nd century Aristotelian commentator, Alexander of Aphrodisias. P.

The Battle of the Naked Men, *engraving by Antonio Pollaiuolo*

Self-Portrait by Pontormo, a detail of the Deposition

had a naturalistic concept of the human soul, and claimed that there was no rational proof for immortality. In his major work, *De immortalitate animae*, published in 1516, he rejects the earlier interpretations of Aristotle and claims that, according to him, the soul is mortal. P. says that reward and punishment are received in this world, and that the idea of the immortality of the soul is based only on faith and not on natural reason. His work was officially condemned and burnt in Venice. He defended himself saying that he was loyal to the Church, but he differentiated between science, which included philosophy, and theology. In his other important work, *De fato, libero arbitrio, et de praedestinatione* (1520), he deals with the problem of predestination and freedom. His conclusion is that the two can not be reconciled. P. believed that human dignity consisted not in theoretical speculations, but in moral virtue. Human beings, accordingly, fulfilled themselves by pursuing achievable goals.

A. H. Douglas, *The Philosophy and Psychology of Pietro Pomponazzi* (1910);
B. Nardi, *Studi su Pietro Pomponazzi* (1965);
E. Cassirer et al., eds., *The Renaissance Philosophy of Man* (1948), 257-381.

PONCE DE LEON, JUAN (c. 1460-1521) Spanish **conquistador*. The son of a noble family, he was raised at the royal court and most probably accompanied *Columbus on his second voyage. In 1502 he participated in the conquest of Hispaniola under *Ovando, and in 1508 himself led an expedition to Puerto Rico. In 1510 P. resisted and suppressed a revolt of the local Indians. Removed from his post as governor (1511), he decided to look for new conquests, and in 1513 sailed north of Cuba in search of the legendary island of Bimini and the miraculous "fountain of youth". On March 27 he landed near St. Augustin, Florida and explored the eastern shores of the peninsula. Returning to Puerto Rico, he spent most of his time there until 1521 when he attempted to establish a permanent settlement on the western coast of Florida. The colony, however, was soon attacked by the Indians, and P. returned to Cuba, where he died.

E. M. King, *The Fountain of Youth and Juan Ponce de Leon* (1963).

PONTANO, GIOVANNI (c. 1422-1503) Italian humanist. Born at Cerreto near Spoleto, in his youth he settled in Naples, and came to be a trusted servant of *Alfonso V and his heirs. In 1471 he became the head of a humanist circle known as the Accademia Pontaniana. From 1486 on he held the most important post in the kingdom as secretary of state, but when the French captured the city of Naples (1496), he refused to join *Ferrante II, who continued the fight, and surrendered to *Charles VIII. P. wrote extensively on history, philosophy, astrology, literature and religion, and is often cited as an example of the wide-ranging humanist scholar. However, much of his writing was of inferior quality, and probably his major achievement was the consistent promotion of humanist culture in southern Italy.

PONTORMO, JACOPO DA (1494-1557) Italian painter, one of the earliest *Mannerists. Born in Pontormo, he went to Florence in 1506, and for a while worked under *Leonardo, and then with *Andrea del Sarto. Already his early paintings, such as *Visitation* (1516) and *Joseph in Egypt*, show that he adopted a new style. In 1518 he finished his altarpiece *Holy Family with S. John the Evangelist*. Its unquiet atmosphere and restlessness mark a complete departure from the style of the High *Renaissance. In addition, his paintings often lack *perspective, a major factor in 15th-century painting. In 1521 he decorated the *Medici Villa at Poggio a Cajano with mythological subjects. P. was strongly influenced by *Dürer, as is reflected in his series of frescoes on the Passion (1522-25), the *Supper at Emmaus* and the *Deposition of Christ*, both painted in 1525. His later works, especially the frescoes in St. Lorenzo of which only drawings remained, show the influence of *Michelangelo. P. also painted several portraits. He worked in solitude and reclusion, but some details of his character are revealed from his diary of the years 1554-57. *Bronzino was his pupil and chief assistant.

E. B. Toesca, *Il Pontormo* (1943). (ND)

PONZIO, FLAMINIO (c. 1560-1613) Italian architect. Born in Milan, he learned his craft in Rome, where he executed most of his projects, finally dying there. P. attached himself to the *Borgheses, and received the patronage of Pope *Paul V, a member of the Borghese family. His major early work was the façade of the Sciarra-Colonna palace, constructed in a traditionally classical style. In 1611 he completed the Pauline Chapel at S. Maria Maggiore, an original creation, that already has much of the *Baroque. Other buildings by P. also show the mark of transition from *Mannerism to Baroque.

POOR LAW English law for the relief of the poor. During the 16th century several laws concerning poor

Lady in Red Dress *by Jacopo Pontormo*

Façade of the Church of Gesù, Rome, by Vignola, modified and completed by Giacomo della Porta

relief were enacted and, in 1601, collected into a comprehensive legal system. Accordingly, each parish had to collect rates for poor relief and work had to be provided for the able-bodied. It also stipulated that able-bodied persons had to work and that begging and vagrancy were prohibited.

PORCARI, STEFANO (?-1453) Italian humanist and rebel. The son of an ancient Roman family, he was noted for his rich classical culture and devotion to republican ideals. In Florence (1427-28) he befriended *Manetti and *Poggio Bracciolini. Later he served *Eugenius IV as governor of Bologna and Orvieto. When the Pope died (1447), P. incited the citizens of Rome to revolt against the "government of the priests". *Nicholas V then exiled him to Bologna. In 1452 he made another attempt, returning in disguise, but was captured and hanged in Rome, in the midst of popular apathy.

PORDENONE, IL (Giovanni Antonio Licino; 1483-1539) Italian painter. Born near the northern Italian town from which he derived his name, he was influenced by the Venetians, especially *Giorgione. P. excelled in the treatment of light and shade and the various colour tones. In Venice, where he mainly lived, he for some time rivalled *Titian himself. The domes he painted in Treviso (1520) and Piacenza (1530) reveal his mastery of the technique of illusionism. He died in *Ferrara, where he had settled by the invitation of the duke.

PORTA, ANTONIO DELLA Italian sculptor. Between 1491 and 1498 he worked on the Certosa di Pavia, and immediately afterwards executed low reliefs and six imperial busts in the city of Pavia itself. In 1501 he established a workshop in Genoa, where he also produced carved doors for several palaces. He was known for his rich decorative style.

PORTA, GIACOMO DELLA (c. 1533-1602) Italian architect. A Lombard who became the assistant of *Vignola, except for the years 1565-70 which he spent in *Genoa, during his whole career he worked in Rome. P. succeeded Vignola as architect of the church of Gesù, for which he designed the façade (1573-84). He also followed in his master's footsteps as chief architect of *St. Peter's, between 1588 and 1590 completing the great dome, originally planned by *Michelangelo. In addition, mostly using a markedly Mannerist style, P. was the architect of many churches, palaces and villas in and around Rome.

PORTA, GIAMBATTISTA DELLA (c. 1535-1615) Italian physician, science writer and playwright. Born in Naples, he became famous at an early age when he published *Magia naturalis* (1558), a treatise on magic and physics, which also dealt with magnetism and contained the first written description of a *camera obscura*. In other works he dealt with optics, astronomy, cryptography, geometry, fortifications and other subjects. His plays, mostly comedies, were adaptations of classical works, but were written in a lively modern language.

PORTA, GIOVANNI GIACOMO DELLA (c. 1485-1555) Italian sculptor. Born near Como, he worked in Milan and Pavia; in 1531 he settled in Genoa where he made several important works, including an altar in the cathedral. His nephew Guglielmo della Porta (1500-77), who worked together with him in Genoa, moved to Rome in 1537, where *Michelangelo became his collaborator. Guglielmo's most important work was the monument for Pope *Paul III at *St. Peter's in the Vatican.

PORTUGAL During the 15th and 16th centuries P. was at the height of its power, influence and prosperity. The country's expansion into *Africa, *Asia and America was not only a major factor in its own history but also in the development of European ties with those areas. During most of the period the country was ruled by the House of Aviz (1385-1580), this dynasty having been founded by *John I (1385-1433), after he defeated the Castilians in the Battle of Aljubarrota. In 1411 peace was concluded with Castile, and the following years were devoted to campaigns in north Africa. The policy of expansion was initiated by the conquest of Ceuta in Morocco (1415), which marked both the renewal of warfare with the Moslems and the beginning of sea exploration along the coast. The movement was given an important impetus by Prince *Henry the Navigator (1394-1460), who was the first to make exploration into a systematic campaign. Expeditions were then turned into a national enterprise to promote the economic and political interests of the country. However, conflicts with Castile were renewed in the reign of *Afonso V (1438-81), owing to the latter's claims to the Castilian throne. Portugal was defeated at the Battle of Toro in 1476. The Azores and the uninhabited Madeira, the first Portuguese colonies, were rapidly exploited for economic purposes, especially exportation of sugar to Europe from about 1445 on. Next came the *feitorias along the African coast. The Portuguese expansion in Asia began in the reign of *John II (1481-95), whose foreign policy deliberately

The Port of Lisbon in the 16th century

encouraged naval exploration. This energetic king also strengthened the royal administration and restricted the power of the nobility. Portuguese hegemony in Africa and Asia was recognized by Spain in the Treaty of *Tordesillas (1494), which limited the latter's claims to lands discovered west of the Atlantic. That treaty, as well as others, prevented an open struggle between the two sea powers. Portuguese ascendancy reached its height with the great discoveries during the reign of *Manoel I (1495-1521): Vasco da *Gama's voyage to *India (1497-98), the discovery of Brazil by Pedro *Cabral (1500) and the securing of an east Asian empire by Francisco de *Almeida and Afonso de *Albuquerque. Commercial relations with China were also established and maintained through the colony of Macao founded in 1557. By then Portuguese possessions stretched across half the globe and its economy was very prosperous. Lisbon had replaced Venice as the main centre for eastern wares. The success and wealth of the country also found expression in the art and literature of the period, in which there was a gradual transition from mediaeval forms to those of the Renaissance.

At the end of the 15th and during the 16th century, there were close ties between the royal families of

P. and Spain, both nations feeling the need to defend their overseas interests. The Spanish influence in P. is demonstrated by the expulsion of the *Jews from the country in 1497, in spite of the fact that they had only been admitted to P. by John II five years earlier and also by the establishment of the Inquisition in P. in 1536. At the end of the 16th century, however, it was becoming obvious that, with the disastrous defeat of the crusade against the Moors in Morocco in the Battle of Alcacerquivir (1578), P. was politically on the decline. In that battle the Portuguese king *Sebastian I was killed and, following the two years' reign of the aging Cardinal Henrique, P. was invaded and captured by *Philip II of Spain. In the Union of 1580 P. in fact lost her independence which was regained through popular revolt only in 1640.

O. Marques, *A Sociedade Medieval Portuguesa* (1964);
H. V. Livermore, *A History of Portugal* (1966, 1969);
D. Peres, *A History of the Portuguese Discoveries* (Engl. trans. 1960). (ND)

POSSEVINO, ANTONIO (c. 1533-1611) Italian *Jesuit missionary. Born in Mantua, he joined the Jesuits in 1559 and was immediately given important assignments in Protestant territories. In 1560 he worked among the *Waldesians in Piedmont. Between 1563 and 1572 he was in France, where he founded several colleges. In 1573 he became secretary of the order, and in 1579 visited *Sweden, where he secretly brought *John III back to Roman Catholicism. His mission to Russia (1580), where he mediated between *Ivan the Terrible and *Stephen Bathory of Poland, did not produce concrete results. Following some years in Poland, he returned to Italy, spending most of the rest of his life at Padua as a teacher at the local Jesuit college. A great missionary and diplomat, P. is an essential figure of the *Counter-Reformation. Of his writings, *Moscovia* (1586) described his embassy to Russia and *Judicium* (1594) attacked *Machiavelli.

P. Pierling, *Un nonce de la Pape en Moscovie* (1884).

POSTEL, GUILLAUME (1510-81) French scholar. A graduate of the university of Paris, where he had learned Hebrew and Arabic, P. was a man of extraordinary opinions. His major work, *De orbis terrae concordia* (1544) was intended to convert Moslems to Christianity. Shortly after its publication he joined the *Jesuit Order, from which he was soon thrown out. Later, he defended *Servetus and tried to appear before the Council of *Trent. Finally he was denounced to the *Inquisition, and ended his life in enforced seclusion.

POURBUS A dynasty of Flemish portrait painters who were active during the entire second half of the 16th century. In 1538 Pieter P. (1510-84), settled in *Bruges, where he married his master's daughter and became a municipal surveyor as well as a member of the painters' guild. He executed many religious scenes, characterized by the detached look on the faces in his portraits. His son, Frans the Elder (1545-81), was actually a pupil and follower of Frans *Floris, whose niece he married in 1569. Frans the Younger (1569-1622) had a truly international career. Becoming court painter to Archduke *Albert in Brussels in 1596, in 1600 he went to *Mantua where he served the *Gonzagas. In 1609 the invitation of *Marie de Médicis brought him to Paris. He remained attached to the French court almost until his death, executing many portraits of the royal family and entourage with much care for the details of rich dress and jewellery.

POYNINGS, SIR EDWARD (1459-1521) English soldier and diplomat. Having fled from England in 1483, after taking part in an unsuccessful uprising against *Richard III, P. attached himself to the future *Henry VII, who later knighted him (1491) and employed him as a trusted aide. In 1494 he was sent as lord deputy to *Ireland, where he defeated Perkin *Warbeck, and passed the Statute of *Drogheda, also known as Poyning's Law. Recalled in 1496, he was given important administrative assignments in England. Under *Henry VIII P. served as member of the Council and was entrusted with diplomatic missions.

PRAGMATIC SANCTION OF BOURGES (1438) A unilateral decision issued by a French assembly of the nobility and higher clergy, presided over by *Charles VII. It enunciated both conciliarist and *Gallicanist principles, declaring the pope was obliged to follow the decisions of the general Church Council, and that the French church had the right to rule itself. Motivated by the crisis that had broken out at the Council of Basle, the P. became the basis of French ecclesiastical independence from Rome.

PRAGUERIE In 1440, a revolutionary movement of the higher French nobility against *Charles VII. The name refers to the capital of *Bohemia, where the *Hussite wars were raging at that time. The movement was a reaction to the French king's anti-feudal measures which forbade the maintenance of troops without his permission. Charles' young son, the future *Louis XI, also joined the rebels, who, in addition, included the dukes of Bourbon and Alençon and the counts of Vendôme, *Armagnac and *Dunois among their number. The urban middle class, however, stood by the monarchy, and the revolt was put down within several months.

PREDESTINATION The doctrine according to which certain persons were predestined for salvation was given its most important early definition by St. Augustine at the turn of the 4th century and was generally incorporated as part of mediaeval theology. It became a matter of fundamental controversy during the *Reformation, however, when *Calvin, claiming that Christ's death benefited the elect alone, and insisting that those to whom salvation was denied were damned from eternity even though it was no fault of them, turned it into a crucial point in his theological system. This complete denial of the efficiency of human will with respect to salvation later led to bitter divisions among the Calvinists themselves, especially in Holland where the Synod of *Dort (1618-19) suppressed the followers of *Arminius and reaffirmed a rigid predestinarian interpretation. Roman Catholic theologians of the *Counter-Reformation were inclined to emphasize man's freedom of choice, though without denying the concept of predestination.

B. Warfield, *Calvin and Augustine* (1956);
F. Wendel, *Calvin: The Origins and Development of His Religious Thought*. (1963).

PREDIS, AMBROGIO DE' (c. 1455-c. 1517) Italian painter and illuminator. Born at Milan, he became in 1482 court painter to *Ludovico il Moro Sforza. In 1483, together with his brother, Evangelista, and *Leonardo, he undertook to paint an altarpiece, the central panel of which is Leonardo's *Virgin of the*

Rocks, whereas the wings are by the Predis brothers. Influenced by Leonardo, P. was a successful portrait painter. He also worked at the court of Emperor *Maximilian I.

PRESBYTERIANISM A form of church government by presbyters or elders, first introduced into *Scotland by John *Knox. Strongly influenced by the doctrines and organizational methods of *Calvin and claiming to follow the ancient models of church rule, the system stressed the self-government of each congregation by its own minister and elders, and set up a hierarchy of courts; large areas were governed by synods and the entire national church controlled by general assemblies consisting of an equal number of ministers and elders. In England the *Puritans were a group most close to P.

J. N. Ogilvie, *The Presbyterian Churches of Christendom* (1925);

G. D. Henderson, *Presbyterianism* (1954).

PRESTER JOHN A mythical Christian ruler of a kingdom in the East; the legend of P. has been known in Europe since the 12th century. Originally identified with certain kings of central Asia, in the 15th century P. was generally held to have been the emperor of Ethiopia. In 1487 the Portuguese Pero de *Covilha was sent to Ethiopia to establish contact with P., however, there were also opinions which located his kingdom in the Congo or in *India.

A. P. Newton, ed., *Travel and Travellers in the Middle Ages* (1926).

PRICE REVOLUTION, THE The term given to the European inflationary current which caused a rise in the price of commodities, especially foodstuffs, during the second half of the 16th century. Although, by comparison with 20th-century rates of inflation, the rise was not exceptional, it created an alarm, as until then prices had tended to remain stable for a long period. The inflation was due to importation of vast quantities of silver from Mexican and Peruvian mines which poured into Spain and the rest of Europe; between 1550 and 1600 the yearly average of silver importation multiplied almost five times. The first to explain the P. by taking into account the influx of precious metals from America, was Martín de Azpilcueta Navarro (1491-1586), a professor at the university of Salamanca. A similar explanation was given by Jean *Bodin. With the decline in the production of American mines after 1600, prices in Europe again began to stabilize.

E. J. Hamilton, *American Treasure and the Price Revolution in Spain* (1934);

M. Grice-Hutchinson, *The School of Salamanca; Readings in Spanish Monetary Theory, 1544-1605* (1952).

PRIEUR, BARTHELEMY (?-1611) French sculptor. A pupil of Germain *Pilon, he continued his classical style. P.'s best-known work is the tomb of the Constable *Montmorency in Paris on which he collaborated with the architect *Bullant.

PRIMATICCIO, FRANCESCO (c. 1504-70) Italian *Mannerist painter, sculptor and architect. Born at Bologna, he went to *Mantua in about 1526, and worked with *Giulio Romano in the decoration of the Palazzo del Tè. In 1532 he was invited to France by *Francis I to help in the decoration of the palace of Fontainebleau. Together with *Rosso he is known as the founder of the School of *Fontainebleau, and had a decisive influence on the development of 16th-century French art. When Rosso died in 1540 P. became the chief artist of the works being carried out at Fontainebleau. A major contribution of his was the *Gallery of Ulysses*, containing 58 episodes from the Odyssey. After 1552 he cooperated with Niccolò dell'*Abbate. His stucco decorations were highly admired. Although he made visits to Italy, P. remained in France until his death.

St. George *by Primaticcio*

PRINTING AND PUBLISHING The mechanical multiplication of texts and *engraved pictures; an enduring contribution of the Renaissance to modern civilization and the earliest form of contemporary mass media. Printing, especially during the first 75 years, presented a veritably revolutionary phenomenon. It substituted for the expensive handwritten mediaeval codices, bringing books within the reach of an ever-increasing number of people. By these means it encouraged the rise of vernacular *literatures and contributed to the spread of *humanist learning. The fervour which marked the European intellectual milieu on the eve of the Reformation was, in fact, a direct result of the acceleration in the communication of ideas made possible by printing. Moreover, the initial success of the Reformation itself owed much to the availability of the printed word.

The art of printing on *paper began in China, first by means of seal-impressions and block-printing, and then, after the 11th century, through use of movable type made out of clay, wood and, later, metal. The development of printing in Europe repeated this process. First to appear were the block-prints of which the earliest extant example dates from 1423. However,

Printing, *a woodcut by Jost Amman*

while a good number of books were printed from wood blocks, only a few survived, and even these date from comparatively late. The introduction of movable type by Johann *Gutenberg of Mainz was, in fact, merely one of a series of his innovations. He not only replaced wood by metal and the block by single letters; he also adapted the wooden screw-and-lever press from the Rhenish winepress and prepared an ink which would adhere to metal types. Technically, however, his most difficult achievement was the invention of matrices, brass moulds from which thousands of replicas of the same lead letter could be reproduced. Actually, the technical stage which he reached in his 42-line Bible (1452-56) was not surpassed for another 300 years.

The printers of Mainz, led by Peter *Schöffer, tried at first to keep the knowledge of the new art a closely guarded secret. But this was possible only for a short time; in the 1460s printing began to spread throughout Germany and Europe, establishing itself in *Strassburg in 1460, in *Cologne in 1464, in *Basle in 1467 and in *Nuremberg in 1470. Earlier, however, two printers, *Pannartz and *Sweynheym, trained at Mainz, had built the first press outside Germany in the monastery of Subiaco near Rome where, in 1464, their first book appeared. Most of the printers who helped spread the technique in Europe were German emigrants. In 1469 the first press was established in Venice, in 1470 presses were set up in Paris and Utrecht; in 1471 in Milan, Naples and Florence; in 1473 in *Lyons; in 1474 in Budapest, Cracow, Valencia, Louvain and Bruges; and in 1476 the first English press was opened by *Caxton in Westminster.

The earliest printed books were initially regarded by many wealthy collectors as inferior versions of the manuscript volumes they were intended to imitate. But printing soon developed its own destinctive look. The title-page was used by Schöffer as early as 1463 and by 1470 he and others were printing book notices. At the same time there were developments in the basic designs of type. While most German printers inclined to use the "Fraktur" or Gothic type, Italian printers promoted the mainstream "roman" variety. This last, first employed by Pannartz and Sweynheym in 1465, was given a clearer oval shape in 1470 by *Jenson, the first non-German printer to work in Venice. These years also saw the earliest printing of Greek and Hebrew script (1465 and 1473). Musical notes were first published in 1473 and mathematical figures in 1482. The first atlas, Ptolemy's *Cosmography,* came out in Bologna in 1477.

Early European printers were also their own publishers. They chose the titles, produced the books and sold their merchandise locally or through the aid of an international network of booksellers. The fact that Latin was an international language helped make a book published in Germany marketable elsewhere. Soon it was discovered, however, that in each of the main European nations there was also a public ready to buy books in the vernacular, especially romances

Varia Sebastiani
Brant Carmina

Quę tibi diua miser christipara/carmina lusi
Cęlicolisq; aliis:suscipe grata velim.
Et mihi pro reliquis erratibus optima virgo
Exores veniam: criminibusq; precor.
Nam pro laude tui nati/superiq; tonantis:
Cuncta hec concinui que liber iste tenet.
1498

Woodcut illustration; titlepage of a book of poems

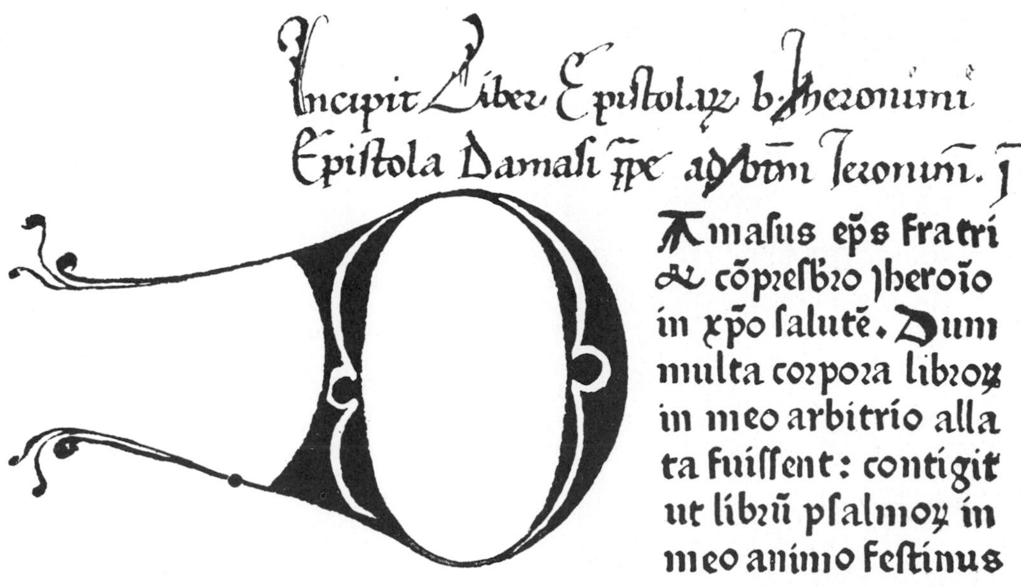

Incipit Liber Epistolaꝝ b. Iheronimi
Epistola Damasi pape ad btm̄ Ieronimi. j.
Damasus eps̄ fratri & cōpresbiro Iheroīo in xp̄o salutē. Dum multa corpora libroꝝ in meo arbitrio allata fuissent: contigit ut librū psalmoꝝ in meo animo festinus

Early 'gothic type'; titlepage of Hieronymus's Epistolae, *published by Mentelin in Strassburg,* c. *1467*

of love and adventure and volumes adorned with woodcut illustrations. Publishing for this kind of clientèle was practiced to a certain extent by Caxton who as well as being a printer, was also the translator of many books that he produced. But it was Anton *Koberger of Nuremberg who became the greatest publisher and businessman of the **incunabula* period. At the height of his carreer in the 1490s he owned some 24 printing shops, each of which employed woodcut illustrators and commercial agents doing business in each of the main European countries.

Early in the 16th century Germany lost its foremost position in printing. In France, Lyons developed into an important centre and a little later printers in Paris established a reputation for producing liturgical works and superbly ornamented *Books of Hours. During the High Renaissance Italian printing held the ascendency, with Venice as the capital, a development closely linked with the name of Aldus *Manutius, the scholar-turned-publisher, who filled Europe with cheap octavo-editions of the classics. From his printing shops also came a new popular design of type, the "italics" which is distinguished by its lightness. Johannes *Froben of Basle was a contemporary of Aldus who also specialized in the publication of scholarly works and used to refer to his intimate friend, *Erasmus, as a literary adviser. A third company to link scholarship with the publishing trade belonged to the French family *Estienne. Although they enjoyed the patronage of *Louis XII and *Francis I, in 1551, fearful of religious persecution, Robert Estienne emigrated to *Geneva, which became a prominent mid-16th century printing centre. Further experimentation proceeded with typography, especially with italics. During the first half of the 16th century the French produced a number of innovative type designers associated with this development, among whom were Geoffroy *Tory, Claude *Garamond and Robert *Granjon.

The French ascendancy over the art of printing lasted approximately until the outbreak of the *Religious Wars. In the 1560s pride of place in this field again moved on, this time to the Netherlands, where the firm of *Plantin in *Antwerp built the biggest press in Europe. In spite of the revolt raging against Spain, Plantin enjoyed a lasting vogue, catering for a

εφιεμαι και λιαν ἐυχομαι ἀισθανεσθαι σε τι/
να ευροντα διδασκαλον περι τα λογικα ἢ δι
αλεκτικην καὶ περὶ την φιλοσοφιαν ὀυπερ γε
νομενου μαντευομαί σε ἕτερον ἰταλίας ανθ/
ος εσεσθαι πείσθου μοι πειθου παῖ φιλτατε.

Hoc græcum ita sonat.
Aueo & uehementer opto audire inuentum
esse tibi præceptorem in logicis seu dialectica
& in philosophia: Quod si feceris vaticinor
te alterum Italiæ florem futurum obtempera
mihi obtempera Fili carissime.

Printing of Greek and Latin characters, Ferrara, 1476

A reconstruction of the Gutenberg press at Mainz

Roman Catholic public. In Calvinist Leiden, also in the Netherlands, a rival firm was opened by Louis *Elzevir in 1587. Again following Aldus' example of linking publishing with the scholarly world, he first based his market on the local student body of Leiden university. Soon, however, his books were selling abroad, his company being able to maintain its international trade throughout the 17th century.

S. H. Steinberg, *Five Hundred Years of Printing* (1955);
T. F. Carter, *The Invention of Printing in China and Its Spread Westward*, 2nd ed. (1955);
H. Barge, *Geschichte der Buchdruckerkunst* (1940);
A. F. Johnson, *Type Designs: Their History and Development* (1959);
W. T. Berry, *Annals of Printing: A Chronological Encyclopaedia from Earliest Times to 1950* (1960);
W. Chappell, *A short History of the Printed Word* (1970)

PRIVATEERS The license for private ships to attack and plunder the fleet of the enemy began before the second half of the 16th century. The political, religious and economic conditions during the reigns of *Elizabeth I and *Philip II, however, particularly encouraged privateering, most of it conducted by English ships against Spain. Although P. belonging to the Dutch and French Huguenots also participated in the naval raids on the Spanish galleons, it was England that produced the most notorious P. of the kind, with *Hawkins and *Drake heading the list.

PROTESTANT A term coined at the diet of Speyer (1529), where a minority of the followers of *Luther "protested" against the resolution of the Roman Catholic majority to put into execution the decrees laid down by the diet of *Worms. With its strong anti-papal connotation the word came to include all those who sympathized with the *Reformation, whether they were the followers of Luther, *Calvin or *Zwingli.

PROTESTANT UNION OF GERMANY (1608) An alliance of the German Protestant princes, led by the elector of the *Palatinate and including *Brandenburg, *Strassburg, *Nuremberg, Württemberg, Baden and Ulm. It was supposed to check the encroachments of Roman Catholic princes, but instead promoted the creation of a Catholic League in 1609. Later abandoned by Brandenburg and never joined by *Saxony, the P. was actually a failure, a point amply proven after the outbreak of the *Thirty Years' War.

PROVOST, JAN (c. 1462-1529) Flemish painter. Born in Mons, he was in 1491 in Valenciennes, where he married the widow of Simon *Marmion. In 1493 he became a member of the painter's guild of *Antwerp, but the following year settled in *Bruges. where he remained for the rest of his life. His only signed work is the *Last Judgement*, which is in Bruges. Other works are ascribed to him with some degree of certainty, which reveal traces of the *Italianate style. In 1521 *Dürer stayed at his house while on a visit to the Netherlands, and is known to have painted his portrait.

PUBLIC WEAL, LEAGUE OF THE (Ligue du Bien Public) A movement among the higher feudal French nobility opposing *Louis XI of France. Formed in 1465 and, supported mainly by Burgundian forces, it overcame the royal troops at Montlhéry and besieged Paris. The king, who relied on the lesser nobility and the townsfolk, had to make concessions to the rebels, but in 1466 he regained much of his losses. Then, however, he found himself confronting the powerful alliance of England and *Charles the Bold of Burgundy.

PUCELLE, JEHAN (c. 1300-c. 55) French illuminator. Working in Paris, he was the first illuminator to sign and date his work. P. is one of the early major protagonists of the style known as *International Gothic. His works reveal knowledge of the elements of *perspective, and familiarity with Italian painting. Some 15 manuscripts of his thriving workshop have survived, the most famous of which are the *Belleville Breviary* (1323-26), and the **Book of Hours of Queen Jeanne d'Evreux* (1325-28).

K. Morand, *Jean Pucelle* (1962).

PULCI, LUIGI (1432-84) Italian poet. Born in Florence to a noble family, he was closely associated with the *Medici, especially with Lorenzo the Magnificent who introduced him to the contemporary circle of poets, artists and philosophers by whom he was surrounded. P.'s works are full of humour, mockery and criticism. His minor works include letters and satirical sonnets. His masterpiece, the epic poem *Morgante Maggiore*, is taken from the themes of Carolingian chivalry, which P. turned into parody. He was the first Italian poet to revive the chivalrous epic, but in a comic and popular way.

PURITANS A term that came into use in the 1560s to describe the people who called for a simpler form of ritual in the *Church of England. The P., however, soon went beyond criticism of the standard forms of religious worship per se and attacked the very principle of episcopacy, i.e., Church government by bishops, while laying stress on the individual's sense of duty and moral conduct. By the end of the reign of *Elizabeth I, there were P. both inside and outside the official Church of England. The former were represented by leaders such as *Cartwright, who advocated *Presbyterianism, and, belonging to the latter category of those who had split off from the main body of the Church, there were the Nonconformists, Separatists, or Independents earlier examples of which were the *Brownists and the *Barrowists.

PURVEY, JOHN (c. 1353-1428) English follower of *Wycliffe. Educated at Oxford, where he met Wycliffe, he completed a revision of his English *Bible after the old man's death. Resigning his ecclesiastical benefice at Kent, he became a *Lollard preacher.

PUTTENHAM (George or Richard) English literary critic. He is credited with the authorship of *The Arte of English Poesie*, published anonymously in 1589. Written several decades earlier, the work is the most systematic contemporary treatise on the subject. It contains a discussion of poetry, mainly the ancient, a section on the rules of versification and the author's observations on good manners. The two brothers P., one of whom is believed to have been the author, were nephews of Sir Thomas *Elyot.

PYNAS, JAN (c. 1583-1631) Dutch painter. Born in Haarlem, he went to Italy in 1605, together with *Lastman. Later he worked in *Amsterdam, where he also produced etchings. His brother, Jacob P. (*c.* 1585-1648) was also a painter. Both are said to have taught Rembrandt, if briefly.

PYNSON, RICHARD (?-1530) English printer. A native of Normandy who emigrated to England, he became an assistant to *Caxton, establishing himself as an independent printer in London in approximately 1490. Among his first published books were a Latin grammar and an illustrated edition of *Chaucer's *Canterbury Tales*. P. was a business rival of Wynkyn de Worde. He issued less books than the latter, but of higher quality. As royal printer to *Henry VIII he had the honour of publishing the king's answer to *Luther in defence of the sacramental system.

The main door of the Basilica of San Petronio by Jacopo della Quercia, Bologna

with a Veil *by Raphael*

Madonna del Granduca *by Raphael*

Madonna of the Roses *a glazed terra-cotta sculpture by Luca della Robbia*

QUADRANT A simplified version of the *astrolabe for measuring the altitude of the stars. The instrument consisted of a graduated 90 degree arc with a movable radius on which a sight was mounted. It was developed late in the 15th century and was used by *Columbus to sight the Polar star on his first voyage. In addition to being lighter and simpler, the Q. greatly improved the precision of the astrolabe.

QUENTELL, HEINRICH (? -1501) German printer. Born in *Strassburg, he was active at *Cologne, and is believed to have published the illustrated editions of the *Bible in Low German dialects (1479). The business was continued by his son and grandson until well into the 16th century. The Q. press specialized in Latin philosophical and theological texts for the local university students, and also published *Tyndale's Bible.

S. Corsten, *Die Anfänge des Kölner Buchdrucks* (1955).

QUERCIA, JACOPO DELLA (1374-1438) Italian sculptor. Born in Siena, he was a contemporary of *Ghiberti, to whom he lost, in 1402, the competition for designing the doors of the Florence baptistery. Most of his works were done in Siena, but his relief works and his *Virgin with Child* at the basilica of St. Petronio in Bologna were later much admired by *Michelangelo. Other works of his were done in Lucca and Ferrara.

A. C. Hanson, *Jacopo della Quercia's Fonte Gaia* (1965);
O. Morisani, *Tutta la Scultura di Jacopo della Quercia* (1962).

QUEVEDO Y VILLEGAS, FRANCISCO GÓMEZ DE (1580-1645) Spanish poet, novelist and satirist. Born in Madrid, he attended the universities of Alcalá and Valladolid between 1596 and 1606, studying art and theology. Later he had to leave Spain, probably in consequence of a fight, and went to Italy. In 1613 he became a counselor to the duke of Osuna, who was then viceroy of Sicily and later of Naples. When the duke fell from power Q. was imprisoned (1620), and a year later was exiled. He returned to Spain and served in the court of Philip IV. In 1639 he was arrested because of an anti-government poem, which was attributed to him. Released in 1643, he spent the rest of his life in retirement.

Q.'s poetry is of diverse topics and styles. He wrote love sonnets, poems on time and death, as well as satirical verses. His prose satires were aimed at the social and political life and the popular beliefs of the time. Most notable are the *picaresque novel *La historia de la vida del Buscón* (1626), the burlesque *Sueños* (1627), and the political satire *La hora de todos* (1635-36). Q. also wrote non-satirical works on moral and political subjects, such as *Marco Bruto* (1644), a defence of monarchy versus democracy.

L. A. Martin, *La vida turbulenta de Quevedo*, 2nd ed. (1945);
D. W. Bleznick, *Quevedo* (1972). (ND)

QUIÑONES, FRANCISCO DE (1480-1540) Spanish cardinal. Joining the Franciscans in about 1498, he became minister general of the Observants' branch of the order in 1523. That year he sent the famed missionary group of Franciscans, the so-called Twelve Apostles, to Mexico. He remained minister general until 1528, and during that time was employed by *Clement VII in the negotiations with Emperor *Charles V. He was created cardinal immediately after the Sack of *Rome (1527) and, in 1529, he was involved in the divorce case of *Henry VIII and *Catherine of Aragon. At the pope's order he prepared a new Breviary, which was issued by *Paul III in 1535. It reflected Q.'s awareness of the need for reform, by reducing the number of prayers, especially the readings from the Lives of the Saints, putting greater emphasis on reciting the Psalms and reading the *Bible. It was a great success, and was reissued about 100 times between 1535 and 1558. However, its disregard for tradition was attacked by the Council of *Trent, and led to its suppression by *Paul IV. The English Book of *Common Prayer showed the influence of Q.'s Breviary.

Marquis d'Alcedo, *Le Cardinal Quinones et la sainte-Ligue* (1910).

Du ſolt nit laßen das glid an dir
So yedes Zaichen ſein ader rur

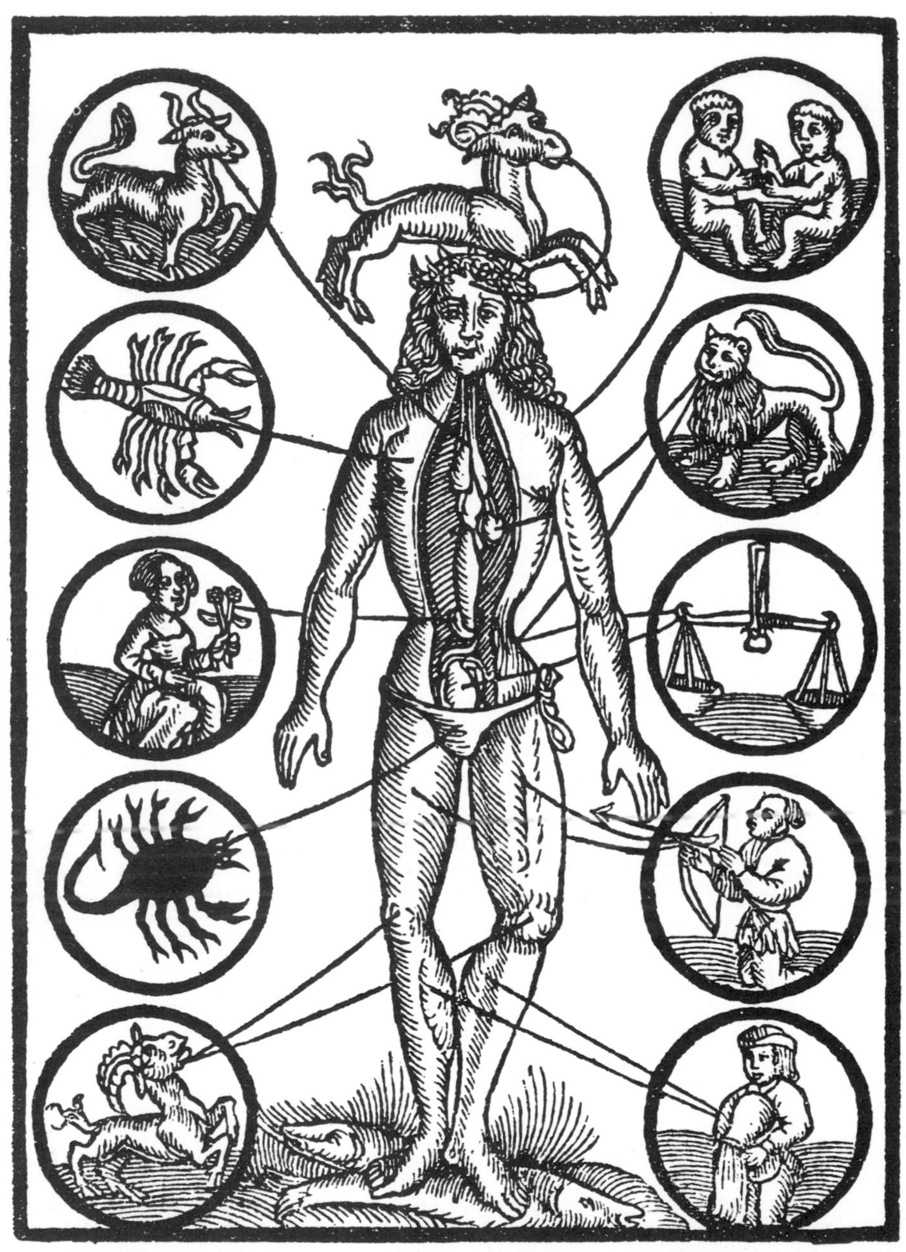

Klarhayt der zeit beſſert alle Laß tag

Woodcut from Regiomontanus' calendar (1512)

R

Les grandes et inestimables Cronicqs: du grant et enorme geant Gargantua: Contenant sa genealogie, La grādeur et force de son corps. Aussi les merueilleux faictz darmes quil fist pour le Roy Artus, cōme verrez cy apres. Imprime nouuellemēt. 1532

Titlepage of the 1532 edition of Gangantua *by Rabelais*

RABELAIS, FRANÇOIS (1483-1553) French humanist writer, author of *Gargantua* and *Pantagruel*. R. was the son of a lawyer, born near Chinon in Touraine. Little is known of his early life. He took holy orders in a Franciscan monastery and, in 1524, obtained permission to remove to a Benedictine house in Maillezais. In 1530 he broke his vows. R. studied medicine in Paris and at Montpellier, and lectured on the works of the ancient Greek physicians. In 1532 he was appointed physician at the hospital of Lyons. It was during this period that he discovered his writing talent. *Pantagruel* was published under a pseudonym, in 1532 or 1533; *Gargantua* in 1534; the *Tiers Livre de Pantagruel* in 1546; part of the *Quart Livre* in 1548, and the entire book in 1552. In 1562 and 1564 appeared the so-called *Cinquiesme et Dernier Livre*, but its authenticity is questionable: some scholars believe that it is based on drafts left by R.

The work, composed in the course of 20 years, does not form a single whole. A fantastic tale about a family of giants, it is full of humour and wisdom, and creates a vivid picture of French society in the early 16th century. It also expresses the enthusiastic humanism of the author, his love of life in all its manifestations, and his dislike of asceticism and religious hypocrisy. The work is outstanding for its rich use of Renaissance French. Although condemned as heretical by the Sorbonne and the Parlement of Paris, this delightful satire entranced the French court and aristocracy, and had a profound influence on many French writers of succeeding generations. (ME)

English translations by Sir Thomas Urquhart and Pierre Matteux (1929);

M. A. Screech, *The Rabelaisian Marriage: Aspects of Rabelais' Religion, Ethics and Comic Philosophy* (1958).

RADEWYNS, FLORENTIUS (1350-1400) Dutch religious reformer. The most important student of Geert de *Groote at Deventer, he succeeded him in 1384 as the leader of the *Brethren of the Common Life. R. realized Groote's plans of expansion, founding new communities of the Brethren, notably those of Zwolle and Windesheim.

RADOM, CONSTITUTION OF (1505) A law enacted by the Polish diet (*seim*) and approved by King

Alexander (1501-06), curtailing the already-limited power of the monarchy. It introduced the principle of *Nihil novi* (no innovations), giving the gentry, as represented in the local diets, the right to approve new laws, taxes and troops. Although it reaffirmed the shaky union with *Lithuania, declaring that the crowns of Poland and the Grand Duchy of Lithuania would always be worn by the same person, the R. was a great political victory for the **szlachta*.

RADZIWILL, MIKOLAJ (1515-65) Polish statesman and soldier. A scion of an old aristocratic family with immense power in *Lithuania, he was titled imperial prince by *Charles V in 1547 and, in 1551, was named palatine of Vilna. *Sigismund II sent him on diplomatic missions to Germany and France, where he espoused the *Reformation, having been influenced by the teachings of *Calvin. He promoted the spread of Protestantism in Lithuania and, in 1563, made possible the publication of the Radziwill Bible, the first Polish translation of the *Bible. Shortly before he died he defeated the Russians who had invaded Livonia. R.'s sons later returned to Roman Catholicism and supported the *Counter-Reformation policies of *Sigismund III.

RAFFAELO DA MONTELUPO (c. 1505-c. 66) Italian sculptor and architect. Trained by his father, Baccio, he worked in Rome (1524-27), which he left after the sack. He worked in Loreto (1530-33), and in Florence, where he executed his masterpiece, the statue of *St. Damian*, at the church of S. Lorenzo, after a design by *Michelangelo (1538). He returned to Rome (1543-52) and was the architect of Castello S. Angelo. Later, at Orvieto, he supervised the works of the cathedral.

Sir Walter Raleigh

RALEIGH, SIR WALTER (1552-1618) English military and naval commander, courtier and explorer. Born in Hayes Barton, Devon, he attended Oriel College, Oxford. In 1569 he fought as a volunteer with the *Huguenots in France. In 1578 he joined his half-brother Sir Humphrey *Gilbert, in an expedition to the West Indies. He drew the attention of Queen *Elizabeth I during his service in Ireland, in which he fought against Irish rebels. Upon his return to England, in 1582, he became the Queen's favourite. He was rewarded with estates in Ireland (on which he later planted potatoes), and was knighted in 1584. In 1587 he was appointed captain of the Queen's guard. His affair, or secret marriage to one of the Queen's maids of honour, Elizabeth Throgmorton, led to a fall from favour. He was imprisoned in the Tower of London in 1592, but was soon released.

R. took part in several expeditions. Between 1584 and 1589 he sent three expeditions to the present-day North Carolina, in order to establish a colony there. But the colony, which was named *Virginia, was not successful. In 1595 he went to Guiana in South America, and described the expedition in his book, *The Discovery of Guiana* (1596). He discovered gold in the area where *Eldorado was believed to be. He was involved in the English attack on Cádiz (1596), and in an expedition to the Azores (1597). In 1600 he was appointed governor of the island of Jersey.

When *James I succeeded to the throne (1603), R. was accused of complicity in a plot in favour of Lady Arabella *Stuart. He was charged with treason, condemned to death, reprieved and imprisoned for 12 years in the Tower of London. He was released in 1616, in order to lead another expedition to Guiana, in search of gold, but warned not to attack the Spaniards, whom the King wished to pacify. The expedition failed, and there was a fight with the Spaniards. When R. returned to England (1618) the King ordered the execution of his death sentence. R. wrote both poetry and prose. His poems were collected and published after 1618. During his imprisonment, he wrote *The History of the World* (1614), from the Creation until the 2nd century B.C. He views history as a record of God's providence.

J. H. Adamson and H. F. Folland, *The Shepherd of the Ocean: An Account of Sir Walter Raleigh and His Times* (1969). (ND)

RAMUS, PETRUS (1515-72) French humanist. Educated in Paris, he made a name for himself, as a fierce opponent of the Aristotelian system, in his public defence of his M.A. thesis in 1536. In 1543 he published his two major works, *Aristotelicae animadversionis*, and *Dialecticae institutiones*, which were condemned by the University of Paris. Although *Francis I confirmed the judgement against him, R. was helped by important patrons who, in 1551, secured for him a lectureship at the Collège Royal. In 1562 he became a Calvinist and went to Germany, but eventually returned to France. He was murdered in the *St. Bartholomew's Night massacre. R. attempted to combine logic and rhetoric in a method of deduction which would lead to finite scientific truths. His ideas exercised considerable influence in European universities.

W. J. Ong, *Ramus: Method and the Decay of Dialogue* (1958).

RAMUSIO, GIAMBATTISTA (1485-1557) Italian compiler and editor of the history of *exploration. Born at

Self-Portrait by Raphael (left) with a portrait of Sodoma; from a fresco at the Stanza della Segnatura

Treviso, he studied at Padua. He served as a diplomat for the republic of *Venice, and later as secretary of its Senate and the Council of Ten. His collection of travellers' reports and accounts of exploration, entitled *Delle navigationi e viaggi*, was published in three volumes between 1550 and 1559. A classic of the literature on geography, soon to be imitated by Richard *Hakluyt and others, it dedicated a volume each to the continents of Africa, Asia and America.

RAPHAEL (Raffaello Sanzio; 1483-1520) Italian painter and architect, the youngest and least problematic of the three great artistic geniuses of the High Renaissance. Born in *Urbino, he was the son of the painter Giovanni Santi (*c.* 1440-94), who was also his first teacher. He was orphaned at the age of 11, and was for some years in the care of a stepmother and an uncle. In about 1499 he joined the workshop of *Perugino in Perugia. Although he immediately showed superb technical skills, R.'s first works owed much to his master. At 19 he began to execute independent works. His first signed and dated picture, *Lo Sposalizio* (1504), depicting the betrothal of the Virgin, is greatly superior to Perugino's work on the same theme, on which it had been modelled. Shortly after he finished this work, R. left Umbria for *Florence, carrying a letter of recommendation to Piero *Soderini from Giovanna, duchess of Sora. He quickly learned the lessons of the great Florentine masters, including *Leonardo's manner of modelling, and *Michelangelo's emphasis on drawing, and began his long-lasting friendship with Fra *Bartolommeo. This first visit to Florence lasted only a few months. In 1505 he was again in Perugia, painting his first fresco, and that year he also visited Siena. A short visit to Urbino in 1506 preceded his return to Florence, where he worked for the next two years, producing some of his best pictures. To this period belong most of his beautiful *Madonnas, generally identified by the names of their early owners. Also outstanding are his portraits of Agnolo and Maddalena Doni.

At the end of 1508 R. went to Rome, where he soon became the favourite artist of Pope *Julius II. In 1509, when Michelangelo was working in the nearby *Sistine Chapel, R. began the decorations of a number of rooms in the Vatican belonging to the papal apartments. The first of these, known as the *Stanza della Segnatura* (papal signature room), was completed between 1509 and 1512. In it are the two frescoes on the themes of theology and philosophy, the *Disputa* and *School of Athens*, sometimes described as the finest examples of classical harmony in High Renaissance mural painting. The other three *Stanze* are stylistically different, with drama and juxtapositions of colour replacing the serenity of the first room. The change is probably due to the influence of Michelangelo, and is also noticeable in the *Triumph of Galatea* (1514), a fresco R. painted in the Villa Farnesina, a palace belonging to Agostino *Chigi. Depicting the nymph Galatea riding on a shell pulled by a pair of dolphins, it is a masterpiece of composition,

The Triumph of Galatea *by Raphael*

the strong movement of all the other figures being balanced by the nymph's beautiful face in the centre.

By this time R. had many assistants, and it is not easy to distinguish his own hand from those of his pupils. However, the portraits of Julius II and *Leo X, and of Baldassare *Castiglione, a friend and admirer, were certainly executed by himself. His workshop continued to produce graceful Madonnas, and in about 1516 he completed one of his most famous pictures, known as the Sistine Madonna, now at Dresden. Made for the monastery of San Sisto in Piacenza, it shows the Virgin appearing through drawn green curtains, standing on a white cloud, while St. Barbara and St. Sixtus are kneeling in adoration. The conception is full of vision and majesty, yet the style is broad and simple. Between 1515 and 1516 R. also designed the famous cartoons for the wall tapestries for the Sistine Chapel. The tapestries were finished in 1519 and are still in the Vatican. Seven of the ten original cartoons later became part of the English royal collection.

In 1514 R. was appointed by Leo X chief architect of *St. Peter's, a post to which he was recommended by *Bramante shortly before he died. R. had already executed an architectural project in 1509, when he designed S. Eligio degli Orefici, a small, domed church near the Tiber. In architecture, as in painting, he was an outstanding exponent of High Renaissance classical harmony. But his buildings are few and he relied closely on the style of Bramante. His Villa Madama in the outskirts of Rome had a circular courtyard and reflected his interest in Roman antiquities. However, the part actually completed was largely the work of *Giulio Romano, who carried out the stucco reliefs. R. last architectural designs were the Chigi Chapel in S. Maria del Popolo, Rome (1519), and the Palazzo Pandolfini, Florence, completed some ten years after his death. R. also modelled a few sculptures, though he did not actually execute them. He designed silverware and pottery, and influenced the art of *engraving through the works executed by *Marcantonio Raimondi from his sketches.

R.'s last major work was *The Transfiguration*, commissioned by Cardinal Giuliano de' Medici, the future *Clement VII, in 1517. It was still unfinished when he died suddenly at 37, following a brief illness, and was completed by Giulio Romano. Often compared to Mozart, whom he resembles in many respects, R., unlike the musical genius, died at the height of his career, was treated with deference by dukes and cardinals and admired by all. His versatility and the apparent ease with which he created, produced his popular image as the greatest painter of all times. Although he lacked Leonardo's intellectual stature and Michelangelo's heroic dimensions, R. is nevertheless a cardinal personality in the history of Western art. Whether by careful planning or a magical touch, he established norms of beauty and grace which were for many generations regarded as artistic ideals, and never cease to impress the beholder.

O. P. Oppe, *Raphael* (1909);
E. Camessasco, ed., *All the Paintings of Raphael*, 4 vols. (1963); O. Fischel, *Raphael* (1964);
J. Pope-Hennessy, *Raphael* (1970);
L. Dussler, *Raphael: A Critical Catalogue of His Pictures, Wall-Paintings and Tapestries* (1971).

RATDOLT, ERHARD (1447-1528) German printer. Born in *Augsburg, he was taken to Mainz as a boy, and there introduced to the new art of printing, probably by *Gutenberg himself. In the 1470s he was in Venice, where he lived for over ten years, rivalling the fame of *Jenson with his inventiveness. R. was the first to design a title-page, the first to advertise a type-face catalogue, the first to print books of geometry with diagrams and pictures in three colours. In 1486 he was invited by the bishop of Augsburg to return to his native city, which he soon helped to make into the centre of colour-printing in Germany. R. also produced the first edition of mathematical and astronomical works, as well as some beautiful prayer books with colourful woodcuts.

RATGEB, JERG (1480-1526) German painter. Born at Herrenberg, he worked in his native town, as well as in Stuttgart and *Frankfurt, and died at Pforzheim. His best work, the *Herrenberg Altarpiece* (1519), now at Stuttgart, is composed of 8 panels describing the Passion of Christ, in a manner both realistic and fantastic. R. took part in the *Peasants' War. He is frequently compared with *Grünewald.

RATISBON, CONFERENCE OF (1541) A conference of Protestant and Roman Catholic theologians held in Ratisbon (Regensburg) during the German Diet. The main Protestant spokesmen were *Melanchthon and *Bucer, the Catholic side being led by *Eck and *Gropper. Significant agreement on doctrinal matters was reached, but the objections of *Luther and the adverse attitude of the Protestant princes prevented further progress.

RECONQUISTA The centuries-long military effort of Christian Spain to reconquer the land from the Moslems. Making great strides in the 13th century, the R. slackened during the second half of the 14th century, but resumed its effort after the union between Castile and *Aragon, which was effected by the marriage of *Ferdinand and *Isabella (1469). These monarchs completed the R. in 1492 with the conquest of *Granada.

RECORDE, ROBERT (c. 1510-58) English mathematician. Of noble Welsh family, he was educated at Oxford and Cambridge, where he was awarded a medical degree in 1545. Later, he taught briefly at Oxford. He was probalby physician to *Edward VI and *Mary Tudor, but died in prison, after having been imprisoned for debts. R.'s extant works are on arithmetic, geometry and astronomy, and on algebra, which he was the first to introduce into England. His *The Grounde of Artes* (1540) saw numerous editions, and remained the standard work on arithmetic well into the 17th century.

RECUSANTS A term employed for those who refused to attend the services of the *Church of England. First it was widely applied, but after about 1570 it came to be used in regard to Roman Catholics especially. R. were liable to pay fines, which in 1581 were raised to 20 pounds per month, an amount that only the very rich could afford. But the penal laws were only infrequently applied. During the 1580's R. were considered a political menace, because of the activities of *Jesuit infiltrators among them.

REDMAN, HENRY (?-1528) English master mason. In 1515 he succeeded his father as builder of Westminster Abbey. He designed Cardinal *Wolsey's palaces at York Place and Hampton Court (1515-16), and Christ Church College at Oxford (1525). Several other buildings are attributed to him, on some of which he collaborated with William *Vertue.

REFORMATION, THE A term designating the long crisis in Western Christianity during the first half of the 16th century, which ended the absolute supremacy of Rome, and saw the consolidation of new creeds and national churches. The need for reform had been felt keenly much earlier. Traditionally, *Wycliffe and his followers, the *Lollards, in England, and *Hus in *Bohemia, are described as important precursors of the movement that was to assault the hierarchical character of the Church over 100 years later. But many of the causes of the R. culminated in the 15th century. There was dissatisfaction with papal pretensions to supreme jurisdiction in ecclesiastical affairs, and dismay at the growing worldliness of Rome. At the same time, the clergy found the lower classes increasingly hostile on account of the heavy burden of ecclesiastical fees, an attitude often expressed in popular satires. Most damaging to the old system was the impact of *humanism: the new scholarship, with its highly developed sense of criticism, and with better knowledge of the biblical and patristic sources, revealed gaps in the traditional dogma. Such fundamental usages of the mediaeval Church as the veneration of saints and relics and the sale of *indulgences, were denounced as imcompatible with the biblical sources as revealed by the new critical approach. The humanists, moreover, exacerbated the declining prestige of the church by direct assaults. Most crucial was the influence of books such as *Erasmus' *Praise of Folly* (1511), and the mocking satires of the **Epistolae obscurorum virorum* (1515).

When *Luther published his 95 theses (1517) he was expressing ideas which were in currency throughout Europe. However, the early successes of the R. depended upon the reaction of one nation. It was the overwhelming response of the German people to Luther's early writings, especially to the three treatises of 1520, which led to the decisive encounter at the Diet of *Worms (1521), and the beginning of political support for the R. The *Peasants' War of 1525 was probably the decisive turning-point in the turbulent course of the next few years. Luther's uncompromising backing of the existing social system gained him the support of important princes, including *Philip of Hesse, *Albert of Prussia and *John of Saxony. From here on, the reform movement could be defended by force of arms, if necessary, a point underscored at the Diet of *Speyer (1529), and by the formation of the *Schmalkaldic League (1531). By now *Denmark and *Sweden, too, had begun to favour the Lutheran camp, which had spread to the German provinces in the Baltic, to *Brandenburg, Württemberg and Brunswick. The victories of *Charles V in the *Schmalkaldic War (1546-47), endangered the gains of the German Lutherans, but they soon recovered, when *Maurice of Saxony launched a surprise attack against the Emperor (1552). In 1555 the Religious Peace of *Augsburg gave formal recognition to the Lutheran position in Germany.

Wherever Lutheranism was implemented monasteries disappeared, clerical celibacy was abolished and the number of sacraments cut from seven to two, namely Baptism and the Eucharist. Various Roman Catholic practices such as fasts and confessions were discontinued, churches stripped of excessive decoration, and the

The Protestant Lord's Supper. *A Reformation print showing Luther and Hus administering Holy Communion to John Frederick I of Saxony*

liturgy recast in the vernacular and simplified. *Justification by faith replaced the doctrine of Transubstantiation as the fundamental concept with regard to salvation, and the reading of the Scriptures and singing of *hymns became its foremost outward expressions. At the same time, control of the churches was left almost entirely in the hands of secular rulers, leading to the gradual decline of Lutheranism, especially in the period following the *Formula of Concord (1577).

Shortly after Luther began his campaign in Germany, another important centre of the R. was founded in *Zurich by *Zwingli. The Swiss movement was far more radical, going even further in search of liturgical simplicity, and denying the presence of Christ in the Eucharist, a rite which, according to the reformers of Zurich, was primarily of memorial significance. After Zwingli's death in battle (1531), the centre of Swiss R. moved to *Geneva, where in 1541 *Calvin founded a theocratic regime. His doctrines gradually gained adherents in *France, the *Netherlands and *Scotland. In the last-named it resulted in a reaction against the traditional French political influence, and the advent of *Presbyterianism, under the leadership of John *Knox. In France the Calvinist *Huguenots became locked in the *Religious Wars, which began in 1562 and ended only in 1598, with the granting of the Edict of *Nantes. In the Netherlands, Calvinism supplied the religious impetus for the great revolt against *Philip II, and later became the creed of the independent *United Provinces.

The Reformed Churches, as the Calvinist bodies were commonly designated, shared with the Lutherans the doctrinal stress on *original sin and justification by faith. They differed, however, in their belief in absolute *predestination. With regard to the sacraments, Calvin tended to follow Zwingli's symbolic views. He also rejected the ceremonial use of crucifixes, a practice which had been retained by the Lutherans. Viewing man as essentially depraved, weak and ignorant, Calvinism was inclined to regulate social life and control manners. In this it responded to the spiritual needs of the nascent north-European commercial classes.

In addition to creeds which can be traced back to one of the three great leaders of the R., there appeared a number of other, often more radical, religious movements. This was inevitable at a time when the old faith had been shaken, while the new was still inchoate. The most important representatives of these movements were the *Anabaptists, who were persecuted by Protestants and Roman Catholics alike. There were other groups, such as the *Unitarians, influenced by the teachings of Faustus *Socinus, and special cases, such as that of *Servetus. It is important to note, however, that there were vast areas where the R. gained adherents, or even became the dominant religion, but later retreated before the Catholic *Counter-Reformation. This was not the case in Italy, where the newly-instituted *Inquisition quickly suppressed the incipient Protestantism of *Ochino, *Vermigli and a few others. But in Poland and *Hungary, there were for a long time many protestants among the nobility, and their number decreased only in the 17th century. There was a similar development in some parts of Germany, particularly *Austria. Perhaps the most dramatic reversal occurred in *Bohemia: here an independent national church and its reformed liturgy had existed since the 15th century, but after the defeat of the Czechs in 1620, the victorious *Habsburgs enforced Roman Catholicism.

The history of the R. in England is unique and distinctive. As had happened in Sweden, Denmark and the main German Protestant principalities, England's break with Rome by the Act of *Supremacy (1534), was a political event. It augmented the power of the monarchy, while the dissolution of the *monasteries (1536-39) filled the royal coffers. But the pretext for these drastic steps, *Henry VIII's determination to dissolve his marriage to *Catherine of Aragon, never measured up to the consequences, and the King, moreover, did not allow changes of doctrine and liturgy. The process of religious reform was begun by Thomas *Cranmer in the reign of *Edward VI (1547-53), and had not taken extensive root by the time of the accession of *Mary Tudor (1553-58), who restored Roman Catholicism. Her successor, *Elizabeth I reestablished the *Church of England (1559). But although England became, during the second half of the 16th century, the bulwark of European Protestantism, the religious climate within the country was anything but conducive to further reform. The *Puritans, an English variety of Calvinism, were persecuted by the authorities, as were the Roman Catholic diehards. Under *James I (1603-25) the issue of religious freedom raised by the Puritans combined with that of political liberty, to confront the monarchy

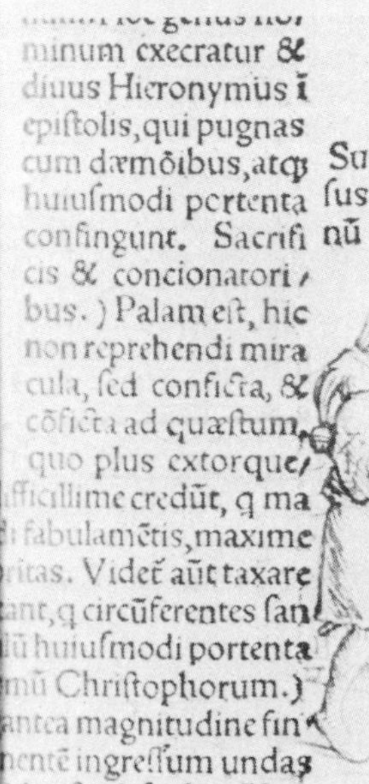

Two illustrations by Holbein to Erasmus' Praise of Folly, *ridiculing the cult of saints*

with an increasingly powerful internal opposition.

P. Smith, *The Age of the Reformation* (1920);
H. Belloc, *Characters of the Reformation* (1936);
R. H. Bainton, *The Reformation of the Sixteenth Century* (1952);
N. Sykes, *The Crisis of the Reformation* (1946);
H. J. Grimm, *The Reformation Era, 1500-1650* (1956);

G. E. Elton, *Reformation Europe, 1517-1559* (1963);
J. Hurstfield, ed., *The Reformation Crisis* (1966);
S. E. Ozment, ed., *The Reformation in Medieval Perspective* (1971);
L. W. Spitz, ed., *The Reformation: Basic Interpretations* (1972).

REGIOMONTANUS (Johann Müller; 1436-76) (The name is a Latin translation of Königsberg, R.'s native city.) German scholar, mathematician and astronomer. At 15 he went to Vienna to study astronomy, and also studied *Greek under *Bessarion. When the latter returned to Italy, R. accompanied him, and until 1468 studied and taught at Padua and Rome. Following a short period as librarian of King *Matthias Corvinus of Hungary, he went to Nuremberg (1471), where a wealthy patron helped him build an observatory. In 1475 he was invited by the pope to return to Rome, to assist in the reform of the calendar, but died shortly after his arrival there. R. wrote several important astronomical works. His mathematical treatise on trigonometry was printed in 1533. The most significant astronomer to precede *Copernicus, he improved by his observations the astronomical tables then in use.

M. C. Zeller, *The Development of Trigonometry from Regiomontanus to Pitiscus* (1946).

REGNIER, MATHURIN (1573-1613) French satirical poet. Born at Chartres, he was the nephew of the poet *Desportes. He went to Rome in 1587 in the service of Cardinal François de Joyeuse. In 1609 he was made canon of Chartres. R. wrote on the daily life and typical characters of his age, although his 16 satires are written in the style of Horace and Juvenal. His language is popular and colourful. His most notable work is the satire *Macette*.

REICHSKAMMERGERICHT (Imperial Cameral Tribunal) A judicial organ, created at the Diet of Worms in 1495, to deal with conflicts among the principalities of Germany. In part an expression of the personal authority of *Maximilian I, the R. also represented the general movement to introduce reforms in the internal structure of the *Holy Roman Empire, led by Berthold of Hennenberg, archbishop of Mainz (1484-1504). Although the Emperor had the right to appoint the chief justice and his deputies, most of the other 22 judges were nominated by the electors and the Imperial Estates. In 1500 and 1512 ten provincial court districts (*Reichskreise*) were created, comprising a number of principalities each; later an attempt was made to establish a general poll-tax (*gemeiner Pfennig*) to finance the court. In the early 16th century the R. was located mostly at *Frankfurt. Although it introduced an element of cohesion into German internal affairs and legal systems, it did not necessarily strengthen the authority of the Emperor.

REINHOLD, ERASMUS (1511-53) German astronomer. He studied at *Wittenberg where, in about 1536, he became professor of mathematics. A friend of *Rheticus, he persuaded *Melanchthon and *Cruciger to support the publication of *Copernicus' book on the heliocentric theory (1543). Later, he published new editions of Ptolemy and *Regiomontanus.

REJ, MIKOLAJ (1505-69) Polish writer. Self-educated, he was a courtier for some years, and later settled down as a prosperous country squire. Often called the father of Polish literature, he endeavoured to raise the status of the vernacular. His work, however, also reflected the older traditions of moralization, and touched upon religious and political questions. He wrote several plays based on the classics, a collection of epigrams, poems and prose, the best of which is a description of the life of the Polish gentry. In 1546 he became a Calvinist and made a prose translation of the Psalms.

RELIGIOUS WARS OF FRANCE (Guerres de Religion; 1562-98) A prolonged political crisis in France, involving a series of civil wars, and later direct and indirect foreign intervention. The origins of the conflict were partly religious, partly political. In spite of relentless persecution under *Henry II, the Reformation gained adherents among the French nobility and the urban middle-class. In the court they were represented by Admiral *Coligny, his two brothers and *Condé, and fiercely opposed by the rising family of *Guise. The death of Henry II (1559) precipitated the crisis, the throne having been inherited by the young and ineffectual *Francis II, who was dominated by the Guises. Following the accession of the ten-year-old *Charles IX (1560), and concurrent with the rise to power of the queen mother, *Catherine de Médicis, there was an unsuccessful attempt at reconciliation at the Colloquy of *Poissy (1561), which produced the first recognition of the *Huguenots. However, the massacre of some 60 Huguenots while at religious services in Vassy (1 March 1562), by troops of Francis, duke of Guise, sparked off the wars.

In the first war the Huguenots, led by Condé, were defeated at the Battle of Dreux (1562). Then, early in the following year, the duke of Guise was murdered, and a truce was signed. In 1567 the Huguenots, in response to rumours about possible Spanish intervention, renewed the conflict with a march on Paris. They were stopped by *Montmorency at St. Denis, and in the ensuing battle the old constable lost his life. Following yet another truce, a third war broke out in 1568, this time provoked by the Catholics, who attempted to seize Condé and Coligny. The former was killed at the Battle of Jarnac (1569), and shortly afterwards the latter was defeated at Moncontour (1569). But the Peace of St. Germain (1570) affirmed the conditional freedom of worship for the Huguenots guaranteed by royal recognition of four Protestant strongholds – or places of refuge –, La Rochelle, Montauban, Cognac and La Charité.

The fourth war (1572-73) broke out immediately after the Massacre of *St. Bartholomew's Night. Having lost some of their best leaders in the massacre, the Huguenots nevertheless resisted effectively, and succeeded in winning a virtual autonomy in certain regions of central and southern France. This war ended in a compromise, confirmed by the Edict of Boulogne (July 1573), when Henry, Charles IX's brother and commander of the besiegers of La Rochelle, was elected king of Poland. He returned to France in 1574, to mount the throne as *Henry III, and was immediately confronted with a powerful movement embracing the entire south of France, when the **politiques* joined forces with the Huguenots. There was no serious fighting in this fifth war, mainly because of the King's financial straits. The Huguenots gained a new leader when Henry of Navarre escaped from the court and returned to Protestantism. At the same time the King's young brother, the duke of

Alençon, joined the *politiques*. Henry III then accepted the Peace of Monsieur (May 1576), which gave the Huguenots their most favourable settlement, allowing them complete freedom of worship throughout France with the exception of Paris.

The Roman Catholic reaction to this development was manifested in the formation of the *League, and in 1577 the sixth war broke out. It lasted a few months, ending with the Edict of Poitiers, which was less favourable to the Huguenots. However, none of the provisions of the previous terms of peace had actually been fulfilled and, in 1580, the seventh war, known as the "Lovers' War", opened with the slaughter of Catholics in Cahors, a town claimed by Henry of Navarre as part of the dowry of his wife, the King's sister. The Peace of Fleix, at the end of the year, left the situation unchanged. The eighth war, known as the "War of the Three Henrys", was a longer and more complicated affair. It began in 1585, with Henry III allied to the League, which was headed by Henry, duke of *Guise. In spite of the victory of Henry of Navarre at Coutras (20 October 1587), the Huguenots were unable to obtain a favourable peace. But on 12 May 1588 the League-dominated Paris humiliated the King, when militant Roman Catholics rose in a popular insurrection (Day of the Barricades). Forced to flee the city, Henry III took his revenge in December, when he ordered the murder of Henry of Guise at the meeting of the Estates-General at Blois. Finding himself completely deserted, the King then fled to the camp of Henry of Navarre, where, in the following year, he was stabbed to death by a fanatic Roman Catholic monk (31 July 1589).

His claim to the throne being rejected by the Roman Catholic party, Henry of Navarre continued the war, aiming above all to conquer Paris. The next important battle was held at Ivry (14 March 1590), where he defeated the duke of *Mayenne. Alessandro *Farnese then marched from the Netherlands to the aid of Paris, at the behest of *Philip II. Forced to raise the siege of the capital, Henry in 1592 invested Rouen, which was also relieved by Farnese. A second siege of Paris, and Henry's conversion to Roman Catholicism (1593), led to his coronation in Chartres (1594) and the surrender of the capital to him. With the capitulation of Mayenne (1595) the wars were over. The settlement between the monarchy and the Huguenots was sealed in 1598 by the Edict of *Nantes.

G. Livet, *Les Guerres de Religion* (1962);
E. Armstrong, *The French Wars of Religion* (1892);
J. W. Thompson, *The Wars of Religion in France* (1909);
J. H. M. Salmon, ed., *The French Wars of Religion: How Important were Religious Factors?* (1967).

REMONSTRANTS The name given the followers of *Arminius in Holland. It originated in an Arminian doctrinal statement of 1610, which rejected several Calvinist notions about predestination and the meaning of Christ's death on the Cross. The *Gomarists, followers of Francis Gomar, who opposed the Arminians, were also known as Contra-Remonstrants.

RENAISSANCE A term of French origin which came to identify the 15th and 16th centuries, as a distinct period in the history of Western civilization, which saw a transition from the tradition-minded mediaeval world to a new, change-oriented society of plural, moral and religious values. Some of the more important historical developments during the R. included: a tremendous activity and interest in the realms of scholarship, literature and the visual arts, which in turn enhanced both the secular and the religious critical spirit and the back-to-the-sources movements, namely, the *Reformation and the *Counter-Reformation, the appearance of the printed book as the first product of mass culture and communication; the advent of firearms, which undermined the previous patterns of feudal military organization and warfare; the movement of *exploration, which brought Europeans into economic and cultural contact with all other parts of the globe. Other developments during the R. which affected the transition may have been less noticeable at the time but historically significant, for instance, the emergence of the national state under centralized royal authority and the formation of economic organizations, anticipating industrial capitalism.

That such diverse developments should be grouped under a term meaning "rebirth" or "renovation", is due to the contemporary feeling that arts and letters were being revived according to the ancient classical models after a long interval, which was referred to as **medium aevum*, or the Middle Ages. *Vasari, in the mid-16th century used the word *rinascità* to describe the Italian cultural movement which began with *Cimabue and *Giotto, in the late 13th century, and culminated in the achievements of his own age. The use of the term R. to describe a distinct period of Western civilization is, however, of relatively recent use. The first to do this was the historian Jules Michelet who, in 1855, thus subtitled his work on the history of France in the 16th century. The term reappeared five years later in the title of *Burkhardt's famous book: *The Civilization of the Renaissance in Italy*. From there on the French term was increasingly employed in other languages, prevailing over other versions, such as *Renascence*, while in Italian the word *Rinascimento* is in use.

The chronological boundaries and subdivisions of the R. have never been rigidly defined. With regard to Italy, it is possible to point out early manifestations in the arts, literature, philosophy and politics throughout the 14th century. But for European civilization as a whole, the year 1415 may be considered a convenient starting point. The date of the last great mediaeval battle fought at *Agincourt, it also corresponds to the beginning of Portuguese exploration of the coast of Africa. In addition, it was about then that a conscious classically-inspired style became manifest in Florentine *sculpture, *painting and *architecture, a development paralleled in northern Europe by the advent of Flemish realism. These were the years in which the movement of Italian *humanism was becoming widespread, and its application to the field of *education. With regard to religion, the *Great Schism came to an end in 1417, but at the same time mediaeval Christian unity was again shaken, this time by the reform movement of Jan *Hus. Finally, significant developments in *shipbuilding and *mining, and experiments with block-*printing, ushered in a period of technological innovation.

The Early R. (*c.* 1415-92/94) was followed by a relatively short period of intense human creativity and adventure, known as the High R., which was brought to an abrupt end in the Sack of *Rome of 1527. Characterized by a kind of general euphoria, this period saw the discovery of the New World and the first circumnavigation of the globe, while in the arts it was dominated by the genius of *Leonardo, *Michelangelo and *Raphael. Politically, the High R. corresponds to the first part of the *Italian Wars, and it includes the early phase of the *Reformation.

The rest of the 16th century is sometimes denied the adjective "R." This period is marked by long religious conflicts, such as the revolt of the *Netherlands and the civil wars in France. On the *Protestant side, followers of *Calvin become more influential than the Lutherans; while Roman Catholicism is affected by the *Counter-Reformation. In the arts, the style known as *Mannerism gives way early in the 17th century to the first phase of the *Baroque. However, certain developments in the second half of the 16th century in France, England and Spain, reflect the continuation of the cultural values which had matured in Italy. This is true especially with regard to *literature and *drama, which with *Cervantes and *Shakespeare, gained great universal masterpieces. But from any point of view, the Renaissance does not extend beyond the outbreak of the *Thirty Years' War (1618).

V. H. H. Green, *Renaissance and Reformation: A Survey of European History Between 1450 and 1660* (1965);
D. Hay, *Europe in the Fourteenth and Fifteenth Century* (1966);
H. S. Lucas, *The Renaissance and Reformation* (1960);
E. Lucki, *History of the Renaissance 1350-1550*, 5 vols. (1963-1965);
E. F. Rice, *The Foundations of Early Modern Europe, 1460-1559* (1970);
K. E. Dannenfeldt, *The Renaissance: Medieval or Modern?* (1959);
T. Helton, *The Renaissance: A Consideration of the Theories and the Interpretation of the Age* (1961);
L. W. Spitz, *The Renaissance and Reformation Movements*, 2 vols. (1972);
W. H. Werkmeister, ed., *Facets of the Renaissance* (1959).

A portrait of S. Carlo *by Guido Reni, at the Church of S. Carlo ai Catinari, Rome*

RENÉ OF ANJOU (1409-80) Duke of Anjou, Lorraine and Bar, count of Provence and titular king of *Naples. Born in Angers, he was the second son of Louis II, duke of Anjou and, in 1419, his maternal great-uncle named him heir to the duchy of Bar. He claimed Lorraine in 1431, when its ruler, who was his father-in-law, died, but was defeated in battle, taken captive and turned over to *Philip the Good of Burgundy. He was released conditionally when he pledged his sons as hostages (1432). In 1434 he inherited Anjou and Provence from his deceased brother, Louis III. Shortly afterwards he was required by Philip to return to captivity, and obtained his freedom in 1437 only upon the payment of a heavy ransom. He now set about taking possession of the kingdom of *Naples, after the death of its queen, *Joanna II, who had adopted him as her son and heir. His wife, Isabella, was already there, defending her husband's claim against that of *Alfonso of Aragon. Arriving in 1438, R. held out for four years. In 1442 he left the besieged Naples and returned to France.

R. now set out to support his brother-in-law, King *Charles VII of France, in his conflict with England. He contributed to the peace treaty of 1444 by marrying his younger daughter, *Margaret of Anjou, to King *Henry VI of England; but the war was resumed a few years later, R. fighting on the French side. For the last 25 years of his life he concentrated on the government of Anjou and Provence, where he encouraged the arts and literature. He is believed to have dabbled in painting, and several works, in a marked Flemish style, have been attributed to him. He wrote – or at least dictated – poetry, an allegorical romance, a treatise on tournaments, and other works. Although not a successful military leader, he was one of the greatest European princes of his time.

A. Lecoy de la Marche, *Le roi René; sa vie, son administration, ses travaux artistique et litteraire*, 2 vols. (1875; rep. 1969);
J. Levron, *La vie et les moeurs du bon roi René* (1953).

RENEE OF FRANCE (1510-74) Duchess of Ferrara. The daughter of *Louis XII and *Anne of Brittany, she married (1528) Ercole d'*Este, who became duke of Ferrara in 1534. In Ferrara R. patronized humanists and sheltered French religious refugees. In 1536 *Calvin visited her, and asked her for material support. Under his influence, and that of the French poet Clement *Marot, she became a Protestant. Her husband, who disapproved of her views, took away her children and she was imprisoned in 1554. She recanted soon after and was released, but later returned to the Protestant faith. In 1560, after the duke's death, she returned to France and lived in Montargis. Her château became the centre of Protestant propaganda and a refuge for *Huguenots. During the *Religious Wars her château was attacked by Catholic troops, and besieged by her son-in-law, the duke of *Guise (1563).

RENI, GUIDO (1575-1642) Italian painter. Born in Calvenzano, he studied in Bologna under *Calvaert, but was also influenced by Ludovico *Carracci. In 1600 he went to Rome, where he painted in an idealized Raphaelesque style, quite different from that of the greatest masters of the day, *Caravaggio and Annibale Carracci. He continued to work mainly in Rome until 1614, when he returned to Bologna, which he subsequently left only twice – in 1622 and 1625 – to work in Naples and Rome. R. executed many frescoes, of which the *Aurora* (1613), on the ceiling of the Casino Ludovisi, Rome, is probably the best. In his last years his religious works tended towards superficiality and sentimentality.

C. Gnudi, *Guido Reni* (1955).

REPARTIMIENTO (Spanish: distribution) A term used by the Spanish conquerors of America for the allotment of Indian labour. During the early period the term was employed interchangeably with **encomienda*. After 1550 it came to mean a system of forced labour, in which Indians had to take turns working on farms, in the textile workshops and, especially, in the mines. By the late 16th century the sytem had become grossly oppressive, but remained in force for another 200 years.

REPRESENTATIVE INSTITUTIONS In the later Middle Ages the periodic assembly of estates, or representative bodies of organized social classes, became a widespread phenomenon throughout Europe. From a constitutional view point, these assemblies were extensions of the royal council (*curia regis*), itself a primary institution under the feudal monarchies. There were the estates of the higher clergy, the nobility, and the "third estate", generally knights and prosperous burghers. The representation of the bourgeoisie was an inevitable outcome of the growing economic power and semi-independence of many cities. Alongside the clergy and nobility, it had become an important source of extraordinary revenue to the royal treasury. In addition, the monarchs learned to manipulate the representatives of the cities against the other two estates, although in time the bourgeoisie learned to assert its own particular interests. Convening the estates generally remained the prerogative of the ruler, who also determined the subjects of their deliberations. The vote was often taken by the estates as a whole, requiring unanimous decisions. Moreover, the sovereign need not consider the resolutions as binding. The power of the assembly over the monarch corresponded to the latter's financial needs of the moment. It is questionable whether these assemblies were genuine forerunners of today's national legislative bodies. In England, and to a lesser extent Sweden and Denmark, a process of gradual evolution may be discerned. In other European countries the Estates General – also called diets – virtually disappeared in the 17th century, with the rise of the absolute monarchies. Historically, these institutions were part of European political life for about three centuries – from the beginning of the 14th to the end of the 16th. In their heyday they constituted the periodic solemn reunion between the ruler and his people, and were thus considered by many to be the source of absolute authority.

In France the estates (*Etats-Généraux*) came into being in 1302, when King Philip IV summoned to Paris representatives of the clergy, nobles and towns, in order to get their support in his conflict with Pope Boniface VIII. The next meeting, six years later, approved the King's suppression of the Knights Templars. Later developments established a division between the estates of northern France (*Langue d'Oil*) and those of the south (*Langue d'Oc*). The former made an attempt, between 1355 and 1357, to control the government when King John II was held captive by the English. It resulted in a brisk constitutional movement, led by the mayor of Paris Étienne Marcel, which, however, collapsed after his assassination (1358). Later the French kings were careful not to let the estates have a say in the actual conduct of government. *Louis XI, the architect of the centralized French monarchy, called the estates only once, to Tours (1468), an assembly which he dominated completely. At another meeting in Tours (1484), during a regency, an attempt was made by the representatives to ensure regular assemblies every two years, but it was not done and under *Louis XII, *Francis I and *Henry II the estates met only once. The period of the *Religious Wars saw a revival: assemblies were held at Orleans (1560-61), Pontoise (1561), Blois (1576), again at Blois (1588-89) and Paris (1593). Beside granting subsidies, they approved regencies, discussed issues of religious toleration, and were even asked to support a change in the laws of succession to the throne. The last assembly of the French estates took place in Paris during the regency of *Marie de Médicis (1614). The estates were not recalled until May 1789, a few weeks before the outbreak of the French Revolution. France also had provincial estates, more easily controlled by the Crown, which convened regularly to vote financial subsidies.

In the *Netherlands, the estates reflected the economic importance of the great marts of *Flanders. In the 15th century they were convened periodically by the dukes of *Burgundy, and became even more powerful during the political crisis which followed the death of *Charles the Bold (1477). *Charles V tried to govern without them, but the fact that they were regularly called upon to furnish the ruler with taxes and war subsidies, made them an important institution. They were instrumental in coordinating the revolt of the different provinces against Spain and consequently, in 1585, *Philip II sharply curtailed the powers of the estates-general in the southern Netherlands.

In *Spain, the representative tradition was perhaps the oldest in Europe, the estates-general (*Cortes*) of Castile, *Aragon, Valencia and Catalonia having been in existence and holding regular meetings since the 13th century. There were, however, important differences between the estates of Castile and the three Aragonese assemblies. The last were held regularly (in Catalonia, at intervals of three years), whereas the Castilian assembly was summoned only at the king's discretion, and was barred from legislating, being allowed to petition only. Under *Ferdinand and *Isabella the Castilian Cortes were called frequently, but attendance was sometimes limited to representatives of the towns, without the clergy and nobility. These weak and numerically-small assemblies could not counter royal power. Some of the demands of the towns during the revolt of the **Comuneros* (1520-21) related to the regular convening of the Cortes. Afterwards the Castilian institution became entirely dominated by the monarchy. The Cortes of

Aragon retained most of its privileges, even after the revolt of 1591-92, but under *Philip II very long periods were allowed to lapse between one assembly and the next. The decline of the Spanish assemblies also affected the *parlamenti* of *Naples and *Sicily, which were ruled by Spain. The Neapolitan assembly met for the last time in 1642. Elsewhere in Italy representation by estates was never a significant institution, except in Piedmont under the dukes of *Savoy.

In *Germany the diet (*Reichstag*) of the *Holy Roman Empire was the equivalent of a national estates-general. It was given its definitive form in the Golden Bull of 1356, and played an important role in German politics throughout the *Reformation. But, in contrast with other European estates, this was a meeting of rulers in their own right, rather than a representative assembly of a king's subjects. Estates (*Landtag*), however, existed in the main German principalities, the most important being those of *Austria, *Saxony, *Bavaria and *Brandenburg. These developed in the 15th century when during a period of continuous unrest, they compelled the princes to make important political concessions. But they lost much power in the second half of the 16th century, and after the *Thirty Years' War, offered little resistance to the rising tide of absolutism.

In *Bohemia the estates consisted of representatives of the nobles, burghers and peasants, but the last two categories could only advise, the nobles only having the right to vote. Here the existence of the estates was inevitably embroiled with the issues of religious toleration and foreign rule. The estates, which led the rebellion against the *Habsburgs in 1618, fell victim to the victorious royal absolutism, following the defeat of the Czechs at the Battle of the White Mountain (1620). In *Poland and *Hungary, too, the representative assemblies were above all concerned with defending the exclusive interests of the nobility. In the 16th century the Polish *sejm* actually acquired such powers, that it could easily obstruct any royal initiative. However, far from promoting constitutionalism, it helped to perpetuate a semi-feudal regime and political impotence.

The English Parliament was marked by many of the disabilities of the European representative assemblies, but by the end of the 16th century, it had acquired sufficient prestige for *Hooker to declare it "that whereupon the very essence of all government within this realm doth depend". Like the Spanish Cortes, Parliament was a creation of the 13th century. Already the "Model Parliament" of 1295 included over 100 members of the highest nobles and clergy, and in addition, two knights from each shire and two representatives from each borough. During the 14th century the knights and burgesses, known as the "commons", were regularly present. Parliament acquired important judicial functions, and in the reign of Edward III (1327-77), royal officials were impeached by it for the first time, the Lords acting as jury and the Commons as prosecutor. Thus, by the beginning of the 15th century, Parliament had grown beyond its original functions of taxation and council to the king. Petitions, which previously were often altered by the crown before being enacted into law, were now taking the form of bills and statutes, establishing the right of the Commons to initiate legislation. Parliament was summoned less frequently by the kings of the house of *York, and under the *Tudors, especially in the reign of *Henry VIII, it became an instrument of royal absolutism. But the mere fact that it had to be employed so as to approve by law the drastic changes effected by the English Reformation, tended to confirm its constitutional role. *Elizabeth I also viewed Parliament as a powerful instrument in the hands of the monarchy. But while she refused to let it share in the government, her parliaments increased in membership and developed closely-guarded procedures. In the last parliaments of her reign, the often-repeated claim of the Commons to the right of free speech became prelude to the attacks on the royal prerogatives during the reign of *James I.

E. Picot, *Histoire des états-généraux de 1355 a 1614*, 2nd ed., 5 vols. (1888; rep. 1969);
F. L. Carsten, *Princes and Parliaments in Germany From the 15th to the 18th Centuries* (1959);
A. Marongiu, *Il parlamento in Italia nel medio evo e nell'età moderna* (1962);
H. G. Koenigsberger, *Estates and Revolutions* (1971);
J. Russell Major, *Representative Institutions in Renaissance France* (1960);
F. M. Stenton, *The History of Parliament* (1955).

REQUESENS, LUIS DE ZÚÑIGA Y (1528-76) Spanish governor of the Netherlands from 1573. At the time of his appointment to the Netherland R. was governor of *Milan. He was chosen by *Philip II as successor to the duke of *Alba, and instructed to carry out a policy of reconciliation. R. tried at first to compromise with the rebels, but his efforts were unsuccessful and he renewed the war. In 1574 he gained a victory over *Louis of Nassau at Mookerheide. In 1575 he began the siege of Zuriczee, but was recalled to Brussels in March 1576, because of insubordination in the Spanish cavalry. On his way there he contracted the fever which led to his death. The Spanish army, which remained unpaid and without a supreme commander, subsequently ran wild. In November it sacked the city of *Antwerp in what is known as the "Spanish Fury".

RESENDE, GARCIA DE (c. 1470-1536) Portuguese chronicler and poet. Born in Évora, he served in the royal court, first as a chronicler and, from 1491, as private secretary of King *John II. He remained a courtier in the reigns of *Manoel I and *John III and, in 1513, accompanied the Portuguese ambassador, Tristão da *Cunha, on a visit to Pope *Leo X. R.'s *Chronica de D. João II* (1545) is based on an earlier one by Rui de Rina, but it contains personal anecdotes and some descriptions of the atmosphere of the age. His *Miscelanea* surveys social life and major events of his lifetime. The *Cancioneiro geral* (1516) is a collection of poems of the period including some of his own.

RETZ (RAIS), GILLES DE LAVAL, SEIGNEUR DE (c. 1404-40) French soldier, notorious sadist. Having fought with distinction at the side of *Joan of Arc in the Battle of Orleans, he was made marshal of France, but soon retired to his castle in Brittany. He turned to alchemy, and rumours spread about his secret magical experiments and rituals, involving atrocities perpetrated on human beings. Tried by an ecclesiastical court, he confessed to the murder of over 100 boys, and was executed at Nantes. His history is believed to have supplied Charles Perrault (1628-1703) with material for the story of Bluebeard.

J. Benedetti, *Gilles de Rais* (1971).

REUCHLIN, JOHANN (1455-1522) German humanist. Born in Pforzheim, he studied classical languages at Freiburg, Paris and Basle, and at the age of 20 compiled a Latin dictionary which was very successful. Between 1477 and 1481 he studied law in Orleans and Poitiers, and then entered the service of the duke of Württemberg, with whom he went on his first trip to Italy (1482). His second visit (1490), on which he met *Pico della Mirandola, was also undertaken at the service of the duke. In 1496, however, he had to move to Heidelberg, because of the hostility of the duke's successor. While there, he wrote two Latin comedies *Henno* and *Sergius*. After a third visit to Italy in 1498, R. was able to return to Württemberg, and from 1502 to 1513 served as judge of the Swabian League. Later, he was a lawyer at Stuttgart, and taught at the universities of Ingolstadt and Tübingen.

R. was the foremost Hebrew scholar of his time, having begun to study that languague about 1485, with the aid of learned Jews. He also studied the *Kabbalah, about which he wrote two works, *De verbo mirifico* (1494) and *De arte cabbalistica* (1517), which were meant to demonstrate the truth of Christianity, and contained numerous speculations. His most important work, however, was *De rudimentis hebraicis* (1506), a Hebrew grammar and dictionary, which greatly advanced the study of the language among Christian scholars. In the last 12 years of his life R. became involved in a famous controversy with *Pfefferkorn over the confiscation and burning of Jewish literature. In his opinion to *Maximilian I (1510), he opposed the act on grounds of humanist principles and the interests of scholarship, and was attacked by Pfefferkorn and his supporters, the Dominican friars of Cologne. R. responded with his satirical *Augenspiegel* (1511), and the controversy became a war of pamphlets, culminating in the celebrated **Epistolae Obscurorum Virorum* (1515-17). *Leo X finally decided the case against R. (1520), and condemned his *Augenspiegel*. Although by that time R.'s name was linked with *Luther's, and in spite of the fact that many of the reformers supported him, he remained loyal to Rome, and sought to discourage his great nephew *Melanchthon from joining the *Reformation.

M. Krebs, ed., *Johannes Reuchlin, 1455-1522* (1955);
L. W. Spitz, *The Religious Renaissance of the German Humanists* (1963).

Woodcut illustration in Breydenbach's Peregrinationes in Terram Sanctam *by Erhard Reuwich*

REUVENI, DAVID (c. 1485-c. 1538) Jewish messianic leader. His origins are shrouded in mystery. He claimed to be an emissary of the lost tribes of Reuben, Gad and Manasseh, and he certainly spent some years in Alexandria and Jerusalem, before appearing in Venice in 1523. Aided by the local Jews, he went to Rome, where he was given an audience with Pope *Clement VII, to whom he proposed an alliance with his brother Joseph, sovereign of the legendary Jewish kingdom in the East, against the *Ottoman Turks (1524). Armed with a letter of recommendation from the Pope, R. went to Portugal (1525), and there spent two years, enjoying ambassadorial status. Having kindled the national pride of the **marranos*, he encouraged Shlomo *Molcho to return openly to Judaism; he also aroused great expectations in the Jewish communities of North Africa. Ordered to leave, he was imprisoned in Provence, ransomed by local Jews and, in 1530, reappeared in Venice. At this point, although still considered an authentic leader by many Jews, he was denounced by some as an impostor, and the accusations were transmitted by the duke of Mantua to Clement VII and *Charles V. In 1532 he went with Molcho to meet the Emperor at Regensburg, but was imprisoned and subsequently sent to Spain, where he died. R. was careful to present himself as an ambassador and military commander, rather than a divinely-inspired prophet of redemption. Nevertheless, his widely reported plans of conquering the Holy Land at the head of a Jewish army, could not but encourage deep messianic stirrings.

E. N. Adler, ed., *Jewish Travellers*, 2nd ed. (1966);
A. S. Aescoli, *Sippur David Ha-Reuveni* (1940).

REUWICH, ERHARD Dutch engraver. Born in Utrecht, active from about 1475 to 1500; believed to be the first artist to illustrate books and be named in them. In 1483 he accompanied the canon Bernhard von Breydenbach on his pilgrimage to the Holy Land. His sketches, which included a map of *Venice and panoramas of Corfu and Rhodes, were later cut in wood and incorporated in Breydenbach's *Peregrinationes in Terram Sanctam*, published in Mainz by *Schöffer in 1486. The book had an immense success and was translated into other languages.

RHENANUS, BEATUS (1485-1547) German humanist scholar. Born in Schlettstadt, he studied at the University of Paris, graduating in 1505. He then worked as editor for the French printer Henry *Estienne. In 1511 he went to Basle and joined the printer Johannes *Froben, and for the next 16 years collaborated with him on a series of classical works, including Pliny, Tacitus, Livy and Velleius Paterculus. R. also associated with *Erasmus, Froben's intimate friend, and collected his letters for publication. In 1527, after the printer's death, R. returned to his native city. Like Erasmus, he supported *Luther at first, but later reversed his position.

RHETICUS, GEORG (1514-76) German astronomer and mathematician. Born in the Tyrol as George Joachim von Lanchen, he Latinized his name after the Roman name of his native land, Rhaetia. He espoused the astronomical theories of *Copernicus, with whom he stayed for a time in 1539. In 1541, while teaching at *Wittenberg, he published a summary of the heliocentric theory entitled *Narratio de libris revolutionum Copernici*. This was the prelude to the publication of Copernicus' own work two years later. R. wrote other astronomical works and important tables of trigonometry, published posthumously by his disciples. He died in Hungary.

E. Rosen, ed., *Three Copernican Treatises: The "Comentariolus" of Copernicus, the "Letter Against Werner", the "Narratio prima" of Rheticus*, 3rd ed. (1971).

RHETORIQUEURS A French school of formal poetry which flourished during the 15th century. The term, of a pejorative connotation, was coined by the poet Guillaume Coquillart (*c.* 1420-1510), who referred to his contemporaries such as George Chastellain (*c.* 1410-75), as "les grands rhétoriqueurs". The R. emphasized technique and style over content to a degree that they seemed to be seeking the most complicated way of saying nothing; mediaeval themes of courtly love and chivalry still supplied much of their subject matter.

RIAÑO, DIEGO DE (?-1533) Spanish architect. Active in *Seville, he became the best known exponent of the *Plateresque style in Andalusia. From 1523 he was in charge of works at Seville's cathedral, where he designed the great sacristy and the chapter hall. His best known building is the profusely ornamented Seville Town-Hall, which was built after his death in accordance with his plans.

RIARIO An Italian family of modest origins, which became highly influential during the pontificate of *Sixtus IV (1471-84). The Pope, whose sister, Bianca della Rovere had married Paolo R., showered favours on his nephews. Pietro, the eldest was made cardinal, archbishop of Florence and papal legate for Itlay. When he died (1474), the Pope created the youngest brother, Raffaele (1460-1521), cardinal. In 1478, probably without his uncle's knowledge, the young man took part in the *Pazzi Conspiracy. Another nephew, Girolamo, was in 1473 given the town of Imola, which the Pope had acquired from Galeazzo Maria *Sforza, and in 1480 he was also made lord of Forli. He married Caterina, Sforza's natural daughter, and served as commander of the papal army. He was murdered in 1488, by political enemies supported by Lorenzo de' *Medici, who repaid the family for its part in the Pazzi Conspiracy.

RIBALTA, FRANCISCO (c. 1555-1628) Spanish painter. His master was probably Juan Fernández de Navarrete (1526-79), known as El Mudo. R. was familiar with Italian art, but was one of the first Spanish painters who broke with the *Italianate style. Only one painting, *The Nailing to the Cross* (1582), survives from his early period. In 1598 R. moved to Valencia where he opened a studio, and was patronized by the archbishop Juan de Ribera. His greatest works belong to this period, and they are distinguished for their realism of form and light, and a simplicity of composition. Among the works painted after 1612 are, *The Singer, Christ Embracing St. Bernard* and *Portacoeli Retable*. R. was one of the pioneers of the new trend in Spanish painting, projecting native qualities of simplicity, dramatic content and religious ardour.

RIBAUT, JEAN (1520-65) French navigator and colonizer. A native of Dieppe, he was sent by *Coligny in 1562 to establish a *Huguenot colony in North America. He sailed to the region then known as Florida, and founded a settlement in present-day Port Royal, South Carolina, but it was later abandoned. In 1565 he was sent to aid Fort Caroline, another French settlement, which was threatened by the Spaniards under *Menéndez de Aviles. Thinking to surprise the Spaniards at nearby St. Augustine, R. left Fort Caroline, which was promptly captured by Menéndez. R.'s ships were then wrecked by storms, and he too was caught by Menéndez and executed.

RIBEIRO, BERNARDIM (c. 1482-1552) Portuguese poet and novelist. Born in Torrão he studied law at the university of Lisbon between 1507 and 1512. He went to Italy probably in 1521 and, in 1524, became secretary of *John III. In later years he suffered from a mental illness, and he died in Lisbon. It was probably during his sojourn in Italy that R. wrote the chivalric and pastoral novel, *O Livro da Menina e Moça*, first published in 1554 in Ferrara, in which it is thought he may have related his own story. In it love is presented as a force of fate which directs the actions of lovers. It was, perhaps, the most sensitive treatment of the theme of love between a man and a woman in 16th-century literature, but the text as it is today, appears to include many passages written by another hand. R. also wrote several eclogues.

RICCI, MATTEO (1552-1610) *Jesuit missionary. Born in Italy, R. went to Goa, *India, in 1578. In 1582 he went to Macao where he began a systematic study of Chinese languages and customs. He dressed in the local costume and impressed the Chinese with his mathematical and astronomical knowledge, gradually attracting men of the social elite to the Roman Catholic faith. In 1599 he was given permission to settle in Nanking and, in 1601, arrived at Peking, where he remained until his death. By making allowances for local customs and beliefs, R. facilitated conversion and founded in *China a Christian community, estimated at over 10,000. He wrote a catechism in Chinese, made translations of the Bible, and left journals of his missionary work.

V. Cronin, *The Wise Man from the West* (1955).

RICH, BARNABE (c. 1540-1617) English writer. He was for many years a professional soldier (1562-74) and took up writing while still serving the Crown as an informer in Ireland, where he died. R. wrote romances imitating the euphuistic prose-style of John *Lyly. His best-known work is *Rich: His Farewell to Militarie Profession* (1581), a collection of eight tales, one of which served *Shakespeare as a source of *Twelfth*

Richard III of England

Night. He also wrote reports on Ireland, commentary on manners, pamphlets and translations.
T. Cranfill and D. Bruce, *Barnaby Rich* (1953).

RICHARD III (1452-85) King of England from 1483; last of the house of York. Born at Fotheringhay Castle, Northamptonshire, he was the youngest son of Richard, duke of York. When his eldest brother drove out the Lancastrian king *Henry VI and became King *Edward IV (1461), R. was made duke of Gloucester. Afterwards, he proved to be an able and loyal administrator in the north. It was, however, said that he had a hand in the murder of Henry VI at the Tower of London (1471), since he was there on the night it happened. Upon Edward's death (April 1483), R. became the protector, ruling on behalf of his brother's twelve-year-old son, *Edward V. He clashed sharply with the queen mother, *Elizabeth Woodville and, charging her supporters with treason, he arrested and executed some of them without trial. Edward IV's marriage to her was then pronounced invalid and their children illegitimate, and R. was proclaimed the rightful heir to the throne. He was crowned on 25 June 1483. R. placed Edward V and his brother in the Tower. The two children were probably murdered in August 1483 and it was rumoured that R. was responsible. It is not clear if this was true, or a fabricated charge designed to discredit him, but the children were never seen again and the king's popularity was hurt. A rebellion against him, led by the duke of Buckingham (October 1483) failed. In 1485 Henry Tudor, earl of Richmond, the Lancastrian claimant to the throne, landed with his army in Wales. In the battle of Bosworth Field R.'s force was defeated and he himself was killed. Henry became the first ruler of the house of *Tudor as *Henry VII. R.'s personality is controversial. He was often illustrated, especially by 16th-century writers, as a villain, a tyrant and a hunchback (*Shakespeare, *Richard III*). Some modern historians describe him as a potentially able monarch, but their arguments are not more convincing than those of his old detractors.
P. M. Kendall, *Richard III* (1955). (ND)

RICHARD, DUKE OF YORK (c. 1410-60) English claimant to the throne and instigator of the Wars of the *Roses. Although his father was executed in 1415 on charges of conspiracy, R. was allowed to succeed him to the titles of his family. He distinguished himself in France, where as regent he scored several military successes (1436-37; 1440-45). To stop his meddling in the government, his enemies, the *Beauforts, had him nominated as governor of Ireland (1449) but, in 1450, he returned, and by a show of force was admitted to the royal council. His object was to dominate the government, which he accomplished in 1453 when he became Protector during Henry VI's first attack of insanity. In 1455, when the king recovered, R. had to relinquish the post. Unwilling to see his enemy, the Duke of Somerset, return to power, he staged an uprising and defeated the royal army at St. Albans (May 1455). He was made Protector again (1455-56), and three years of relative peace ensued, until, in 1459, the Yorkist rebellion was renewed with much greater intensity. In the Battle of Northampton (10 July 1460), R. managed to capture the king and extract from him an acknowledgement of his claim to the throne. But Queen Margaret, who continued the fight, defeated R. in the Battle of Wakefield (30 December 1460), where he died. However, his sons reigned as Edward IV (1461-83) and Richard III (1483-85).

RICHIER, LIGIER (c. 1500-67) French sculptor. A native of Lorraine, he was born into a family of sculptors and possibly visited Rome in his youth. His work combines Italian influences with older, naturalist traditions as, for example, in the group he carved for the church of S. Etienne of S. Mihiel (1553). Other works are marked by a religious intensity bordering on the macabre. A *Huguenot, he had to leave France in 1564, and died in Geneva.

RICHINI, FRANCESCO MARIA (1584-1658) Italian architect. Born in Milan to a father who was an established military engineer, he was sent to Rome by Cardinal Federico *Borromeo, to complete his education. Upon his return to Milan (1603), he was at once hired to work on the *duomo* and, in 1607, began the building of the church of S. Giuseppe. Completed in 1630, it is one of the earliest structures in the *Baroque style. R. supervised the construction of several other churches and was employed continuously by Milan's Spanish government. Most of his churches have not survived. Of his other buildings, the best are the Brera Palace, begun in 1615, and the Ospedale Maggiore, both in Milan, distinguished for their elegant collonaded courts.

RIDLEY, NICHOLAS (1500-55) English reformer; Bishop of London. Educated at Cambridge, Paris and Louvain, he became a fellow of Pembroke Hall, Cambridge, advancing eventually to the mastership of the college (1540). A few years earlier he had become an

A Man and a Woman *by Peter Paul Rubens*

St. Francis Denying His Earthly Father *by Sassetta*

intimate of *Cranmer, who made him a royal chaplain and procured for him the see of Rochester (1547). In 1550, when *Bonner was deprived of his post, R. succeeded him as Bishop of London. Until the end of the reign of *Edward VI, he was a consistent champion of Protestantism, to the extent of supporting the claim of Lady Jane *Grey (July 1553). As soon as *Mary assumed the throne he was imprisoned in the Tower. Compelled to dispute the doctrine of transubstantiation at Oxford (1554), he was tried for heresy and, on 16 October 1555, was burnt at the stake together with *Latimer.

RIDOLFI CONSPIRACY, THE (1571) Roberto Ridolfi was a Florentine banker, resident in England, who acted as an emissary between the bishop of Ross, *Philip II, *Pius V, *Mary Stuart and the Duke of Norfolk, when they planned a Catholic rebellion in England. According to the plan, the uprising was to be supported by troops sent by the Duke of *Alba, the governor of the Netherlands, and Mary – wedded to Norfolk – was to supplant *Elizabeth on the throne. The plot was discovered in September 1571. Ridolfi, who was out of England, got away, but Norfolk was executed and other leading plotters were imprisoned.

RIEMENSCHNEIDER, TILMAN (c.1460-1531) German late-Gothic sculptor, whose career reflected the rising social status of artists during his time. Born either in Heiligenstadt or Osterode, he was the son of the master of the mint in Würzburg, where he opened a workshop, which became very successful. He served as a councilman of the city (1504-20) and as burgomaster (1520-25). During the *Peasants' War he was imprisoned. His work, in wood and stone, is marked by religious feeling. His earliest known works are the altarpiece of St. Mary Magdalene (1490-92) and the limestone statues of *Adam* and *Eve* (1491-93). Among his other works are the *Altar of the Holy Blood* (1501-05) and *The Virgin and Child* (1520). R.'s works are harmonious and balanced.

K. Gerstenberg, *Tilman Riemenschneider* (1943).

RINUCCINI A distinguished Florentine family, whose members filled important offices of the Republic, while others were military commanders, churchmen and humanists. Alamanno (1419-99) was the author of an anti-*Medici dialogue, *De libertate* (*on Liberty*). Alessandro (1555-1622) composed *Diva Catharina martyr*, a Latin poem on a religious theme.

RINUCCINI, OTTAVIO (1562-1621) Italian poet. Born into an old Florentine family, he was closely associated with the ruling house of the *Medici. R. wrote a number of poetical works on secular and religious themes, but is known chiefly for his three melodramas, *Dafne* (1594), *Euridice* (1600) and *Arianna* (1607), the first operatic libretti. These charming works were set to music by *Peri, Giuglio Caccini and *Monteverdi. In 1600 R. accompanied *Marie de Medicis to France, where he remained for three years.

A. Civita, *Ottavio Rinuccini e il sorgere del melodrama in Italia* (1900).

RIVAUDEAU, ANDRÉ DE (c. 1540-80) French Protestant poet and dramatist. He was born in Poitou, where his biblical tragedy *Aman* (1566) was performed. The tragedy follows classical rules though it ends happily. Its style is rhetorical and there is little action. R. also wrote poems, some on biblical subjects, and a translation of Epictetus.

RIZZIO, DAVID (1533-66) The Italian-born secretary and confidant of *Mary Queen of Scots. The son of a musician of Turin, he went to Scotland in 1561 and was retained by the Queen. At first she employed him as a musician but in 1564 made him her secretary. During the following year his influence grew, and the Queen's reliance on his advice became even greater after her estrangement from her second husband *Darnley. Whether he was her lover or not remains an open question, but his conduct certainly encouraged such rumours and turned the Scottish nobles against him. On the evening of 9 March 1566 he was dragged from the Queen's presence by a group of conspirators, acting together with Darnley, and murdered.

ROBBIA, LUCA DELLA (c. 1399-1482) Florentine sculptor. His first and most important work was the *Cantoria* (*Singing Gallery*) in the cathedral at Florence (1431-38), where it hangs opposite a similar work by *Donatello. The *Cantoria* consists of ten reliefs, showing children singing, dancing and playing musical instruments. The architectural design shows an influence of *Brunelleschi and the work is clearly inspired by classical models. Between 1437-39 R. worked on five reliefs on themes of human labour for the *campanile* of the cathedral. In 1439 he was commissioned to work on marble altars for two chapels in the cathedral, and produced *St. Peter Delivered from Prison* and *The Martyrdom of St. Peter*. His other works in the cathedral include bronze doors for the sacristy.

R. was the first artist who used glazed terra-cotta for monumental sculpture, which he substituted for marble in some cases. One of his notable works in terra-cotta is the *Resurrection* (1442), over the north door of the sacristy in the cathedral. His flourishing workshop in Florence was continued by his nephew Andrea della Robbia (1435-1525), and by the latter's sons Giovanni (1469-*c.* 1529) and Girolamo (1488-1566). (ND)

ROBERTI, ERCOLE DE' (c. 1448-96) Italian painter. The ablest follower of *Tura and *Cossa in *Ferrara, he may have been the latter's assistant. In 1486 he succeeded to Tura's position as court painter to the *Estes. His austere style, marked by hard outlines and monochromatic treatment of colour, projected intense fervour. The style is well demonstrated in his small but well-known *Pietá*.

B. Nicholson, *The Painters of Ferrara* (1950).

ROBIN OF REDESDALE (1469) The assumed name of the leader of an uprising against King *Edward IV of England. The insurrection began among the peasants of Yorkshire, whose discontent was exploited by Sir William Conyers. The rebels were encouraged by the Earl of *Warwick, who joined them. They defeated the royal army and forced the King to issue a general pardon. But Edward IV soon extricated himself and Warwick fled to France.

ROBINSON, JOHN (c. 1575-1625) English *Puritan leader. He probably studied at Cambridge, and was ordained in the *Church of England. Later he became a Puritan pastor in Nottinghamshire. In 1608 he left with his followers for Leiden, Holland, where he joined the university as a student in theology. He helped to organize the sailing of the *Pilgrim Fathers (1620), but did not go with them. R. wrote several theological treatises of marked Calvinist orientation, including a defence of the Synod of *Dort.

ROBORTELLI, FRANCESCO (1516-67) Italian classical scholar. Born in Udine, he studied in Bologna, and taught at Lucca, Pisa, Venice and Padua. He edited the works of classical authors, both Roman and Greek, the most important of which was an annotated Latin edition of Aristotle's *Poetics*, published in Florence in 1548. He died in Padua.

RODRIGUEZ DE FONSECA, JUAN (1451-1524) Spanish bishop and statesman. Of a family of which several members had served in the ecclesiastical hierarchy, he was chaplain to Queen *Isabella and, in 1494, was made bishop of Badajoz. Later he was given the dioceses of Córdoba (1499) and Palencia (1505). In 1514 he was transferred to the prestigious see of Burgos, where he died. R., however, devoted most of his attention to the affairs of the state. He went on important diplomatic missions for *Ferdinand and Isabella, and from 1493 until shortly before his death, supervised all matters concerning the *exploration, conquest and settlement of America. He organized the **Consejo de Indias* and the **Casa de Contratación,* and communicated directly with most of the Spanish navigators and **conquistadores* of the early 16th century.

ROELLAS, JUAN DE LAS (c. 1558-1625) Spanish painter. Born in Seville, he studied in Venice and excelled as a draughtsman. Until 1624 he lived and worked in Madrid and Seville. He then moved to Olivárez, where he spent the rest of his life as a prebendary of the chapel. Some of his main works are: *Death of St. Isidore, Martyrdom of St. Andrew, Conception* and *Moses Striking the Rock.* His style was greatly influenced by Italian *Mannerism.

ROGERS, JOHN (c. 1500-55) English reformer and *Bible editor. Educated at Cambridge, he became, in 1534, a chaplain to the English merchants at *Antwerp. There he befriended *Tyndale, and after the latter's death (1536), published from his notes a complete English translation of the Bible (1537). The edition is known as Matthew's Bible, from the name assumed by its editor. About that time R. became a Protestant, and got married. He returned to England in 1548, and was a lecturer in divinity at St. Paul's Cathedral, but was arrested early in *Mary's reign and charged with heresy. Following a year's imprisonment, he was convicted and burnt at the stake.

ROGERS, WILLIAM (c. 1545-c. 1605) English engraver. The first Englishman to make a significant contribution to the art of *engraving, he probably learned his craft in the Netherlands. He was well-known for his protraits and title-pages. He engraved the images of many of the political figures of the time, including Queen *Elizabeth, the earl of *Essex and *Henry IV of France.

ROJAS, FERNANDO DE (c. 1465-1541) Spanish author. Spending most of his life in the town of Talavera, of which he became mayor, R. was author of *La Celestina,* one of the most influential works of Spanish literature. Known also as *Comedia y tragicomedia de Calisto a Melibea,* it was first published in Burgos in 1499, and reissued in many editions throughout the 16th century. The novel described the tragic love of Calisto and Melibea and the murder of Celestina, the bawd who was their go-between. For the first time in Spanish literature, a moral work portrayed human emotions in a realistic manner. The author's Jewish origins have caused some scholars to view the tragic elements of the work as an expression of his own insecurity amid the surrounding society.

La Celestina, a Novel in Dialogue, trans. by L. B. Simpson (1955).

ROLLENHAGEN, GEORG (1542-1609) German dramatist. Born near Berlin, he studied theology at *Wittenberg. He served as a Protestant pastor and schoolmaster, and wrote pedagogical and astrological works, as well as dramas. His three biblical dramas, *Abraham* (1569), *Tobias* (1576) and *Lazarus* were written to be performed by his pupils. They have elements of moral satires. His most famous and popular work was the animal epic drama, *Froschmeuseler* (1595), which described a war between frogs and mice. A moral, religious and social satire, it is directed, in part, at the implications of the *Reformation.

ROMAN ACADEMY An organization of humanists in Rome, founded by Pomponius *Laetus, which attempted to revive ancient Roman past by means of literary discussions, performance of classical plays and the celebration of the old festivals. It was suppressed by *Paul II in 1468, but revived by his successor *Sixtus IV. It attained its greatest reputation as a literary society during the pontificates of *Julius II and *Leo X.

ROMANOV, HOUSE OF The dynasty which ruled Russia from 1613 until the February Revolution of 1917. They were descendants of the 14th-century Muscovite boyar Andrey Ivanovich Kobyla, who was of Prussian or Lithuanian descent. They took their name from Roman Yuriyev (d. 1543), whose daughter, Anastasia Romanovna, married Tsar *Ivan IV, the Terrible. Her brother, Nikita, was president of the regency council under Tsar Fyodor I. His grandson, Michael Romanov, was elected Tsar ending a decade of anarchy (*Times of Trouble 1604-1613).

R. N. Bain, *The First Romanovs* (1905).

ROME During the Renaissnace R. may have ceased to be the religious capital of the Christian world, but she enjoyed a splendid period as a great centre of artistic and intellectual life. As governors of the city, the popes took care of its municipal needs, restoring old churches and public buildings, and erecting new ones. They patronized the great artists and scholars who flocked to Rome and employed them in grand projects. It is estimated that from the late 14th century to about 1600 the population of R. grew from a few thousands to about 130,000.

The rule of the papacy over Rome and its inhabitants was resumed with the election of Pope *Martin V (1417-1431), which ended the *Great Schism. The son of an important Roman family, he began the work of reconstruction of churches. However, the major innovations began during the pontificates of *Nicholas V (1447-55) and *Sixtus IV (1471-84). It was then that the streets of Rome were widened and paved, and new buildings rose. These popes also encouraged artists and scholars. Nicholas was the founder of the Vatican Library, while Sixtus erected the Sistine Chapel. Their policy was continued by their successors, and by the end of the century R. was beginning to rival Florence as the cultural centre of the Renaissance. The city also flourished during that period. The popes were financed by the great Italian banking families, who stimulated a flow of capital into the city. Local industry and commerce did not develop on a large scale, but the city was in a position to consume important luxuries. The golden age of R. corresponds with the High Renaissance, especially the pontificates of *Julius II and *Leo X. The greatest painters, sculptors and architects – *Michelangelo, *Raphael, *Bramante and, for a short time *Leonardo – worked in the city, as did poets and humanist scholars such as *Bembo, *Trissino and *Bandello. Many architectural and decorative projects were undertaken of which the most important was the beginning of the building of *St. Peter's. And yet in the popular imagination, particularly outside Italy, life in R. was described as corrupt and debauched, and the city was blamed for the assorted moral ills which afflicted Christianity as a whole. In spite of its reconstructed fortifications R. could not withstand the forces of *Charles V. The Sack of *R. (1527) caused the death of thousands of Roman citizens and the destruction of churches, houses and palaces. Nevertheless, within a few decades, R. recovered from these events. Under Pope *Sixtus V (1585-90) new projects were carried out, new streets were built and the city was supplied with drinking water, piped in by an aquaduct from about 20 miles away. In addition, the Lateran Palace and Vatican Library were built, and the dome of St. Peter's completed. R. was then one of the best planned cities in Europe.

P. Paschini, *Roma nell Rinascimento* (1940);
J Klaczko, *Rome and the Renaissance* (1903);
F. Gregorovius, *History of Rome in the Middle Ages*, 13 vols. (1894-1900). (ND)

ROME, SACK OF (6 May 1527) The conquest of the city of Rome by German and Spanish mercenaries. The act was a violation of the 1526 peace treaty between Pope *Clement VII and *Charles V, who, however, disclaimed responsibility for the attack. The pillage lasted for eight days. Some 30,000 citizens were killed, and churches and palaces destroyed. The Pope himself was captured. The R. drove away many of the artists and writers who had been working in Rome, and is described as the historical end of that period of intense creativity known as the High Renaissance. (ND)

RONCALLI, CHRISTOFORO (1552-1626) Italian painter, named after his birthplace near Voltera, *il cavaliere da Pomerancio*. He went to Rome in his youth and later became a protegé of Pope *Paul V, for whom he painted many frescoes in the Vatican and Quirinal palaces, and in several important churches. He also worked in Naples. He painted in the style known as *Mannerism, and is especially noted for the landscape backgrounds of his works.

RONSARD, PIERRE DE (1524-85) French poet. Born to a noble family at Château de la Possonnière near Vendôme, he was at first educated at the Collège de Navarre in Paris, but later transferred to the court, where he was a page of the Dauphin's. In 1537 he accompanied the French wife of *James V to Scotland, and spent three years in that country. Returning to France (1540), he entered the service of the future *Henry II, and went on embassies to the Netherlands, to Scotland, Germany and Italy. His budding diplomatic career was brought to an end at the age of eighteen by an attack of deafness. Dedicating himself to the study of classical literature, he enrolled at the College de Coqueret, where he was taught by Jean

Ronsard

*Dorat. His friend, *Baïf, accompanied him there, sharing his room; also present were *Jodelle, *Belleau and Ponthus de Tyard. In 1548 they were joined by *Du Bellay, the seventh member of the group that became known in 1549 as the *Pléiade. Although Du Bellay wrote the manifesto which expressed the literary views of the group, R. was its true leader, and the first to publish poetry which demonstrated the new style. These were the first four books of the *Odes* (1550), graceful amorous verses, influenced by Horace, Pindar and *Petrarch. They created a scandal by their implied repuditation of the poetry of *Marot, but won R.'s admiration of the court. His victory was ensured in 1552 with the publication of *Amours de Cassandre,* 225 sonnets celebrating his love for a young woman of Italian origin, whom he apparently met at a ball in Blois and continued to adore after her marriage.

Acclaimed "prince of poets", R. wrote a fifth book of *Odes* (1552) and two continuations of the *Amours* (1555-56), and his first *Hymns* (1555-56), poetry of an heroic and epic character addressed to friends and patrons. He was showered with favours by *Henry II and supported by the King's sister, Marguerite de Valois, and is also said to have been encouraged by the young *Mary Stuart. He was even more fortunate in the reign of *Charles IX (1560-74), who titled him royal poet, gave him a residence at the court and bestowed on him several abbacies and priories. In this new role, responding to the issues of the *Religious Wars, R.'s poetry assumed a partisan tone: his *Discours des misères de ce temps* (1562) defended Roman Catholicism and treated Protestantism satirically. His *Elégies, mascarades et bergerie* (1565) were mainly intended for the entertainment of the court. *La Françiade* (1572),

The Nativity *by Antonio Rosselino*

a mythological epic poem on the French monarchy, had little success and was never completed. In the preface to it, however, R. expounded his aesthetic theories, developed from the earlier *Abrégé de l'art poétique* (1565). In his last years R. turned away from the court, living in his priories, where he spent his time gardening and revising his poems. Among his best late works are the sonnets and elegies, *Sur la mort de Marie* and the *Sonnets pour Hélène* (1578).

R.'s biography by his friend Claude Binet (1553-1600) presented him as the greatest French poet of his time, a view with which modern criticism concurs. But for more than two centuries after his death R. suffered from his condemnation by *Malherbe and was disregarded. His fresh love poems, technical virtuosity, gorgeous imagery and brilliant descriptive powers are again appreciated, in spite of his frequent lack of restraint and excessive dependence on Greek mythology.

P. Laumonier, *Ronsard, poète lyrique* (1906);
M. Raymond, *L'influence de Ronsard* (1927);
R. Lebegue, *Ronsard; l'homme et l'oeuvre* (1966);
M. Bishop, *Ronsard, Prince of Poets* (1940).

RORE, CIPRIANO DE (1516-65) Flemish composer. Born probably in Antwerp, he studied in Italy and, in about 1546, became musical headmaster at *Ferrara. In 1561 he moved to Parma, where he remained until his death. R. excelled in the composition of madrigals. He was influenced stylistically by *Willaert, and inspired later composers such as *Lasso and *Palestrina.

RORITZER A family of German architects who worked in the late-Gothic style, active in the 15th and early 16th centuries. Based in Regensburg, where they were in charge of building the cathedral, they also worked on Munich's *Frauenkirche,* Nuremberg's St. Lorenz and Vienna's St. Stefan. Matthäus, representing the third generation of the family, published in 1486 a valuable little book, *Von der Fialen Gerechtigkeit.* It described how to set out Gothic finials.

ROSES, WARS OF THE (1455-85) The rivalry of the royal houses of Lancaster and York for the throne of England and the intermittent wars in which they fought for three decades in the 15th century. The name is of a later origin and derives from the fact that the *Tudors, who represent both houses, adopted as their emblem the red and white roses. The causes of the wars were not necessarily the hereditary claims to the crown professed by representatives of the two houses. *Richard, duke of York was only a distant descendant of Edward III (1327-77), and his claim to be the heir of *Henry VI could not be pressed after the king sired a son, Edward, in 1453. The true reasons, therefore, should be sought in the endemic feuds of the nobility, its frustration following a series of defeats in France, and the feeble leadership of Henry VI. The first battle at St. Albans (22 May 1455) between the duke of York and the royal army did not immediately lead to the victor's claim on the throne, but only to a temporary assumption by the Yorkists of the principal offices of government. But, in 1459, when the conflict was renewed, the parties had grown more intransigent and, in 1460, following his victory at Northampton, York asserted his claim, and the captured Henry VI had no choice but to acknowledge it.

The conflict is considered to have ended with the Battle of Bosworth (22 August 1485) in which *Richard III was killed, but the fighting had not continued uninterruptedly. Under *Edward IV there were extended lulls; in fact, most of the major battles took place between 1459 to 1461, and 1469 to 1471. In a sense, the Yorkists had defeated the Lancastrians, and it was only the dissention in their own camp which ignited the latter phase of the wars. Moreover, the final Tudor-Lancastrian victory of *Henry VII might not have been possible without *Richard III's first damaging, by his own behaviour, the cause of York.

The economic and social development of England was not much affected by the wars. Indeed, at the same time there was an upsurge in commerce and a distinct rise in the status of the merchant class, which was felt in the lower House of Parliament. On the political side, however, the wars had yet another result: by destroying some of the old nobility, they paved the way for the rise of the strong Tudor government.

E. F. Jacob, *The Fifteenth Century, 1399-1485* (1961);
A. B. Chrimes, *Lancastrians, Yorkists and Henry VII* (1964);
R. B. Mowat, *The Wars of the Roses* (1914).

ROSICRUCIANS A secret society, which took its name from the emblems of the Rose and the Cross. It was founded in about 1614, when two anonymous pamphlets, generally attributed to Johann Valentin Andreae (1586-1654), were published in Germany. One of these, *Chymische Hochzeit Christiani Rosenkreutz,* described the fictitious founding of the society in 1484 by one Christian Rosenkreutz, who had learned the "secrets of nature" in the East. Subsequently, a number of associations were organized which took this name. Their principal interest was in *alchemy, and

they aroused much interest in the mid-17th century.
A. E. Waite, *The Brotherhood of the Rosy Cross* (1924).

ROSSELLI, COSIMO (1439-1507) Italian painter. A native of Florence, he was the pupil of Benozzo *Gozzoli. His most distinguished commission came in 1481, when he was invited to paint frescoes for the *Sistine Chapel in Rome. A solid but uninspired painter, he was the teacher of Fra *Bartolommeo and *Piero di Cosimo.

ROSSELLINO, ANTONIO (1427-79) Italian sculptor. Born at Settignano near Florence, he was trained by his elder brother Bernardo. His first signed and dated work is the bust of *Giovanni Chellini.* A later bust is that of *Matteo *Palmieri*. His most important work is in the chapel of the Cardinal of Portugal, in S. Miniato al Monte outside Florence: the pavement, the episcopal throne and the cardinal's tomb (1461-66). A later work of similar style is the tomb of Mary of Aragon in the Piccolomini chapel in Naples. In that chapel is also his last and finest relief, *Nativity* (1470s). Of his sculptures, *St. Sebastian* (1466) and the *Young St. John* (1477) are well known. R.'s works have a classical elegance and are noted for their dynamism.

ROSSELLINO, BERNARDO (1409-60) Italian sculptor and architect. The elder brother of Antonio R., he was active in Florence, where he also did architectural design and decorative work. His main sculptural creation is the tomb of Leonardo *Bruni at the church of S. Croce (1444-50), which became a model for tombs in niches for a number of other humanists. As an architect he first carried on *Alberti's designs for the Rucellai Palace (1446-51), the courtyard of which he designed. In 1451 Pope *Nicholas V appointed him papal architect. He built the palace and cathedral of Pienza for *Pius II, and the Palazzo Venezia in Rome (1455) is also attributed to him.

ROSSI, ROBERTO DE' (1355-1417) Italian humanist. Member of an ancient family of Florence, he held various offices in the Republic until 1393. An educated man, he was one of the first Florentines to read classical *Greek, which he taught privately, as well as Latin. Among his pupils was Cosimo de' *Medici.

ROSSO, IL (Giovanni Battista Guasparre; 1494-1540) Italian painter. Born in *Florence, he began painting in his native city, but about 1523 began to travel extensively through Italy. In 1530 *Francis I invited him to France, where he executed his most important work, a series of frescoes on allegorical subjects in the palace of *Fontainebleau. R. is considered one of the earliest *Mannerists, and is distinguished by the intensely emotional quality of his works. His influence was particularly strong in France, where his frescoes were copied in engravings and in tapestries.
K. Kusenberg, *Le Rosso* (1931).

ROTA, BERNARDINO (1508-75) Italian poet. Born in Naples, where he was a well-known figure in literary circles, he was the author of 26 sonnets lamenting the death of his wife (1559). These and others of his poems are marked by a restrained and somewhat artifical style. He also wrote poetry in Latin, and two comedies, *Scilinguato* and *Strabalzi*.

ROTHMANN, BERNT (c. 1495-1535) German *Anabaptist leader. The son of a blacksmith, he acquired a university education, and became a chaplain at *Münster; in 1531 he openly espoused the Lutheran reforms. Together with *Knipperdollinck he led the rising of the guilds against the prince-bishop of *Münster (1532), but soon afterwards abandoned Lutheranism, affiliating himself with the Anabaptists (1533). R. supported the dictatorship of Jan Matthys and the subsequent rule of Jan *Bockelson, whose court preacher he became. His pamphlets, *Restitution rechter und gesunder christliche Lehre* and *Von der Rache*, published respectively in October and December 1534, expressed the moral orientation of the millennial regime, justifying polygamy and inciting extreme hate towards "non-believers". R. was killed when Münster fell to the besiegers.

ROTTENHAMMER, JOHANN (1564-1625) German painter. Born in Munich, he spent some years as a young man in Rome, and later in Venice, where he was particularly influenced by the elegant style of *Veronese. After working in several Italian cities, he returned to Germany and settled in *Augsburg. R. excelled in small paintings of mythological subjects with carefully executed landscape backgrounds. He was patronized by Emperor *Rudolph II.

ROUSSEL, GERARD (c. 1500-50) French humanist and religious reformer. Born near Amiens, he was a devoted pupil of *Lefèvre d'Etaples', and, in 1521-22, edited two works of Boethius and Aristotle. He followed his teacher to Meaux, where he became canon of the cathedral and preached in favour of reform. In 1524 he was suspended by Bishop *Briçonnet, for fear of the conservatives' reaction, and left France, spending several years in *Strassburg. He returned in 1535 at the invitation of *Francis I and, in 1536, became bishop of Oloron, where he was protected by *Marguerite d'Angoulême. As bishop he preached a great deal, emphasizing the study of the *Bible and the administration of the Eucharist in both kinds, for which he was condemned by the University of Paris. He died in Mauleon from injuries received when a Roman Catholic fanatic attacked with an ax the pulpit from which he was preaching.
C. G. A. Schmidt, *Gerard Roussel, predicateur de la reine Marguerite de Navarre* (1845; reprinted in 1970).

ROXELANA (c.1505-61) Favourite wife of *Suleiman II, also known as Khurrem (The Cheerful One). A former Russian slave, she found the way to the Sultan's harem, although she was not beautiful and rather fat. She gave the Sultan three sons and a daughter, and in the latter part of the reign became his closest adviser. With her talent for intrigue, she succeeded, in 1553, in getting rid of Mustafa, the Sultan's older son by another woman, whom she accused of treason, and so ensured the succession of her own son, the future *Selim II.

RUBENS, PETER PAUL (1577-1640) Flemish painter. The son of a former town-councillor of *Antwerp, he was born in Siegen, Westphalia, where his family was living in exile because of the father's conversion to Calvinism. In 1587, the father having died, the family returned to Antwerp. There R. studied at the *Jesuit College, and later became a page to the countess of Lalaing. He received his artistic training first with Tobias Verhaecht and later with Adam van *Noort and Otto van *Veen. In 1600 he went to Italy, where he became court painter to the duke of Mantua, Vincenzo *Gonzaga. The duke sent him to Rome (1601-02),

St. Catherine, *an etching by Peter Paul Rubens*

where he was influenced by the works of the masters of the High Renaissance and by *Caravaggio. In Mantua he painted a triple altar for the duke's chapel (finished 1605). He also visited the court of *Philip III in Spain (1603) and worked in Milan and Genoa, where he painted the *Circumcision* for the altar of the Jesuit church. After two more years in Rome he returned to Antwerp (1608), and remained there for the rest of his life. In 1609 he married Isabella Brant, a handsome woman who appears in many of his works. R.'s love for Italian art was expressed not only in his paintings. His book, *Palazzi di Genova* (1622), illustrated the great Renaissance palaces of Genoa. Elements of Italian architecture are also found in the Church of St. Charles *Borromeo, which he designed at Antwerp. He was a religious painter, too, as well as a court portraitist. His first important works after his return from Italy, *The Raising of the Cross* (1610) and *The Descent from the Cross* (1611-14) at the cathedral of Antwerp, and *The Miracle* at the cathedral of St. Bavon, made him the leading painter in Flanders and throughout Europe. R. was a great artistic entrepreneur. In his busy workshop he employed many assistants, produced a large number of works, and frequently had them engraved and printed, thereby enhancing his international reputation. His fame brought him commissions from European monarchs, and he decorated the palaces of *Marie de Médicis and Philip IV of Spain.

R. was also employed in diplomatic missions. In 1628 he was sent by the regent of *Netherlands to Madrid to negotiate a peace treaty between Spain and England, to end the war which was disastrous for *Flanders. After nine months, during which time he also painted the portraits of the royal family, R. was sent by Philip IV on a peace mission to England. His efforts were successful, and a peace settlement was concluded between the two countries in 1630, though it did not last long. R. was knighted by King Charles I, and commissioned to decorate the ceiling of the royal banqueting house in the Whitehall Palace. The panels, which Rubens finished in Antwerp in 1634, represent the reign of King *James I. In England he also painted *The Blessings of Peace* and *Peace and War.*

Back in Antwerp R., now 53, remarried (1630), four years after the death of his first wife. His second wife was 16-year-old Hélène Fourment. She was the model of many of his late mythological works and portraits. He now began to concentrate on landscape painting, and also did pictures of his young children. His most notable works of that period are the *Landscape with a Rainbow* (*c.* 1636), and *Château de Steen* (*c.* 1635-37). Another important work of his late years is *Horrors of War* (1637-38), an allegory on the suffering of Europe. R. was also a great art collector as well as a designer of tapestries, book illustrations and *triumphal processions. He was the first complete *Baroque painter, a virtuoso of visual effects and an artist of inexhaustible vitality.

P. Cabanne, *Rubens* (1967);
C. V. Wedgwood, *The World of Rubens 1577-1640* (1967);
A. M. Jaffé, *Rubens and Italy* (1977). (ND)

RUCELLAI An old Florentine family of wool merchants and bankers, which played a prominent part in the political life of the republic. Giovanni R. (1403-81) supported Cosimo and Lorenzo de' *Medici. He commissioned the architect *Alberti to design the famous R. palace, as well as other buildings. His son Bernardo (1448-1514), who married Lorenzo's sister, patronized Florentine humanists, and was himself the author of two historical works. Another son, Pandolfo (1436-97), was an ardent supporter of *Savonarola.

F. W. Kent, *Household and Lineage in Renaissance Florence; the Family Life of the Capponi, Ginori and Rucellai* (1977).

RUCELLAI, GIOVANNI (1475-1525) Italian humanist and dramatist. Born in Florence, his mother was the sister of Lorenzo de' *Medici. He studied the classics and entered the ecclesiastical service. His classical tragedy, *Rosmunda,* is based on Sophocles' *Antigone*. Other works of his are *Oreste*, which is based on Euripides' *Iphigenia in Tauris,* and the poem on bees, *Api.*

RUDOLPH II (1552-1612) Holy Roman emperor from 1576. Son of Emperor *Maximilian II and Maria, daughter of *Charles V, he was born in Vienna and educated in Spain. Before succeeding his father as emperor, he was crowned king of *Hungary (1572) and king of *Bohemia (1575). During the first 20 years of his rule, R. was actively involved in the affairs of the Netherlands and in the defence of the Empire against the *Ottoman Turks. Domestically, he reversed the tolerant policy of his father in religious matters. One of his first acts was to limit the freedom of worship of the Austrian Protestants, which had been granted by Maximilian II, and to curtail their political privileges. As a result Catholic princes were encouraged to impose their religion by force. R.'s measures caused discontent and unrest in the Empire, and led to uprisings of the Austrian peasants (1594-97) and of the Hungarians in 1604.

R. was subject to fits of severe depression, which grew worse after 1598. His weakness and incompetence finally caused the Habsburg archdukes to declare him incapable, and to recognize his younger brother, *Matthias, as their head (1606). In 1608 R. had to cede Hungary, *Austria and Moravia to Matthias, who granted religious freedom to his subjects. Pressed by the Czechs, R. then issued the *Majestätsbrief* (1609), which granted them similar concessions. When further disorders broke out in Bohemia, it was invaded by Rudolph's cousin, Leopold, and the inhabitants called on Matthias for help. In 1611 R. was forced to cede Bohemia to his brother, who also succeeded him as Emperor after his death.

R. was greatly interested in the arts and sciences. He was the patron of Tycho *Brahe and *Kepler and the astronomical tables produced by them are known as the "Rudolphine Tables". He was also a great art collector, but his intolerance and insanity made him unpopular.

R. Evans, *Rudolph II and his world; a study in intellectual history 1576-1612* (1973). (ND)

Emperor Rudolf II

RUEDA, LOPE DE (c.1510-65) Spanish dramatist and actor. Born in *Seville, he first worked as a goldbeater. Later, he became an actor, and between 1558 and 1561 was a manager of a theatrical company. His most important achievement was the creation of the *paso*, a one act prose interlude based on everyday life and written in popular style. The *paso* contributed to the popularization of the theatre. R.'s other plays, comedies and dramatic dialogues were based on Italian models. He was praised by *Cervantes as a talented actor, an excellent writer and a major figure in early Spanish *drama.

RUGGERI, UGO (c.1450-c.1508) Italian printer. Born in Reggio Emilia, he studied law at Bologna. In about 1473 he became interested in the new art of *printing and henceforth devoted himself to it. Active chiefly in Bologna, he printed many books on law, and popular editions in Italian. His books were carefully designed and accompanied with prefaces written by him. He also cast cannons for Giovanni *Bentivoglio.

RUÍZ, JUAN (c.1280-c.1353) Spanish poet, known also as the Archpriest of Hita. Almost nothing is known of his life, except the details contained in his great poetic work, *Libro de buen amor*. Written about 1330 and revised in 1343, it includes, among others: tales of several love-affairs, told in the first person, allegories, hymns to the Virgin, anti-clerical satires, fables and anecdotes told by their characters. The language is rich and inventive, and the whole work is full of irony, ambiguity and parody, with a sensuous, life-loving strain, despite its declared didactic and moralistic aims. Considered the most remarkable Spanish poetic work of the late Middle Ages, it had a great influence on Spanish literature during the 15th century.

C. Gariano, *El mundo poético de Juan Ruíz* (1968);
M. R. Lida de Malkiel, *Two Spanish Masterpieces: the 'Book of Good Love' and The Celestina* (1961);
G. B. Gybbon-Monypenny, ed., *'Libro de buen amor' Studies* (1970).

RUIZ DE ALARCÓN, JUAN (c.1581-1639) One of the principal dramatists of 17th-century Spain. Born in Mexico, he emigrated to Spain in 1613 and there began to write. He published only 24 plays, less than the usual playwright's output in those days. His comedies concentrate on the topic of moral choice and the superiority of ethics. Himself a hunchback, he often referred to the misfortune of having a physical defect, in a manner which suggests a portrayal of his own problems. This is especially noticable in the character of Don Juan in *Las Paredes Oyen*. His most important satirical comedy is *La verdad sospechosa* (*c*. 1619), about an inveterate liar. The theme was taken up by Corneille in *Le menteur* (1643). Other important plays of his are *Los pechos privilegiados,* on loyalty to the monarch, and *El tejedor de Segovia,* a romantic historical play. Not much is known about R.'s life and the dates of the composition or first performance of his plays. They were published in two instalments in Madrid (1628) and Barcelona (1634). A careful writer, who gave much thought to the structures and plots of his plays, he abandoned the theatre in 1626 for a position in the *Consejo de Indias.

M. V. Melvin, *Juan Ruíz de Alarcón* (1942).

RUPERT (1352-1410) German king from 1400. The son of the elector palatine Rupert II and Beatrice, daughter of the king of Sicily, he succeeded his father in 1398 as a ruler of the *Palatinate. When, together with other electors, he deposed Emperor *Wenceslas in 1400, he was at once chosen king of Germany. In 1401 he led an expedition to Italy, hoping to get himself crowned emperor, but his troops dispersed near Brescia and he had to return. His resources were obviously inadequate for the effective leadership of the *Holy Roman empire, and his authority was challenged by many German princes until he died.

RUPPEL, BERTHOLD (?-1495) German printer. Having been taught the art of printing by *Gutenberg himself in Mainz, he introduced it to *Basle. His first book appeared there in 1464 and, in 1467, he published a popular commentary on the Book of Job by the 4th-century St. Gregory of Nyssa. R. was also one of the first printers to advertise his wares.

RUSSIA In the 15th century R. was still divided into several states, but the strategically-located principality of Muscovy (Moscow) became increasingly preeminent. Having shaken off the nominal suzerainty of the Tatars, the Muscovite princes sought to annex the other principalities, including Tver and Ryazan, and especially the *Novgorod republic. This policy, which was systematically followed by *Ivan III (1462-1505), led to conflicts with *Poland and *Lithuania, the powerful neighbours in the west. At the same time, there was a tendency to establish closer ties with western Europe, which R. needed for its technical development. Ivan III, who took for his second wife Sophia, a niece of the last Byzantine emperor, employed the famous *Fioravanti, and other Italian architects in building the Kremlin. He was the first to use the title *Tsar* (Russian-Caesar), i.e. Emperor.

*Vasily III (1505-33) took Pskov (1510), Smolensk (1514) and Ryazan (1517). He was succeeded by his son *Ivan IV, the Terrible (1533-84), in whose long and eventful reign the territorial expansion continued, particularly to the east and southeast. Ivan IV bought arms from Germany, and permitted a community of foreign skilled workers and merchants to settle in Moscow. In 1553 he welcomed the English navigator Richard *Chancellor, and in 1555 established diplomatic and trade relations with England. He waged an intermittent war with Poland and *Sweden over *Livonia (1558-82), but gained little tangible result.

Ivan IV's weak son Fyodor I (1584-98) was followed by the gifted "upstart" Boris *Godunov (1598-1605). But the opposition of the great nobles, the *boyars*, to his rule encouraged a series of pretenders, known as the False *Dmitrys, and led to a prolonged period of anarchy, called the *Time of Troubles (1604-13), which invited the intervention of both Poland and Sweden. In 1609 *Sigismund III of Poland invaded and besieged Smolensk, hoping to win the Russian crown. A popular nationalist movement then organized an army, aided by Sweden, and drove the Poles out. In 1613 Michael *Romanov was elected Tsar by the *zemsky sobor* (National Assembly), ending the prolonged turmoil and beginning the rule of the last Russian royal family.

G. Vernadsky, *Russia at the Dawn of the Modern Age* (1959);

A. E. Prasniakov, *The Formation of the Great Russian State* (1970). (ND)

RUSTICI, GIOVAN FRANCESCO (1474-1554) Italian sculptor. Born into a wealthy family of Florence, he studied under *Verrocchio. His sculpture shows strong classical inspiration, as well as the influence of *Leonardo and *Michelangelo. His best work, the bronze *John the Baptist Preaching*, composed of three carefully modelled figures, is above an entrance of Florence's Baptistery. In 1528 he went to France at the invitation of *Francis I, and died in Tours. But none of his French works have survived.

RUYSBROECK, JAN VAN (1293-1381) Flemish *mystic. Brought up by an uncle, canon of St. Gudule's at Brussels, he was ordained priest in 1317. He continued to live with his uncle and another canon, and in 1343 the three retired to a hermitage at Gronoendael, where they were joined by disciples. In 1350 the group adapted the rule of the Augustinian canons, R. assuming the position of prior. His mystical writings, in Flemish, had a direct influence on the movement known as *Devotio Moderna, and on the later *Brethren of the Common Life. In his *Spiritual Marriage* he elaborated a gradual system of moving from the stage of active life, through the inward to the contemplative life, by which the individual rises to Christian perfection.

A. Wautier d'Aygalliers, *Ruysbroeck the Admirable* (1925; reprinted 1969);

M. d'Asbeck, *La mystique de Ruysbroeck l'Admirable* (1928).

RUZZANTE (c. 1502-42) The name by which the Italian playwright and actor Angelo Beolco was known, who was the most famous comedian of his time. A native of Padua, he came of a prominent family of merchants, but chose the career of an actor, excelling in the portrayal of uneducated simple folk, whose coarse language and lack of sophistication aroused laughter. Beside a number of comedies, he wrote also poetry. His works were first published in 1548.

A. Mortier, *Un dramaturge populaire de la Renaissance italienne: Ruzzante,* 2 vols. (1926);

M. Prosperi, *Angelo Beolco nominato Ruzzante* (1970).

S

SA, MANOEL DE (c. 1530-96) Portuguese *Jesuit scholar. Educated at Coimbra, he taught at the university of Alcalá in Spain (1551-57), and then went to Rome, where he became a professor of theology at the Jesuit College. His dictionary of moral theology, *Aphorismi confessariorum* (1595), became widely known.

SA, MEM DE (c. 1500-72) Portuguese governor of Brazil. The illegitimate son of a prelate, he was the younger brother of *Sá de Miranda. In 1557 he was sent to Brazil, where his main accomplishment was the destruction of the French colony at Fort Coligny, a task that necessitated two expeditions, in 1560 and 1567. Not far from this site S. founded Rio de Janeiro. From his seat at Bahia, he supervised the development of Portuguese settlements and supported the missionary activity of the *Jesuits.

L. Norton, *A dinastia dos Sás no Brasil* (1965).

SABELLICUS (1436-1506) The name given to the Italian humanist and historian Marcantonio Coccio. Born at Vicovaro, he was a member of the *Roman Academy and later taught at *Venice, where he was associated with Aldus *Manutius. His *Rerum venetarum ab urbe condita* (1486) was a history of Venice from its foundation. In 1504 he completed the *Enneades sive rapsodiae historiarum*, a history of the world in 92 books, the first humanist work of its kind. Although using relatively few sources, it treated the history of antiquity with a sense of perspective. S. was skeptical of biblical miracles, which he viewed as similar to classical fables.

SABINUS, GEORG (1508-60) German neo-Latin poet. Born in Brandenburg, he was a student of *Melanchthon's at *Wittenberg, and married his daughter in 1536. While on a visit to Italy, he befriended *Bembo. From 1538 on he lived mostly in Frankfurt-on-the-Oder, where he was a professor of eloquence. Besides writing fine, moving Latin poems, he edited Cicero and wrote on Ovid. His best work are the *Elegies* (1550).

SACCHETTI, FRANCO (c. 1330-c. 1400) Italian prose writer and poet. Born probably in Ragusa, he was a scion to a noble Florentine family. He travelled extensively and, about 1362, settled in Florence, where he served in several official posts. Some of his writings dealt with religious, moral and political matters, while his poetry was cast in the traditional, contemporary forms. But his best known work was a book of amusing short novels, *Trecentonovelle*, first printed in 1724. The stories, reduced from the original 300 to just over 200, consist mainly of anecdotes and jokes. Some were derived from traditional tales, and others were based on S.'s observation of everyday life and common people.

L. Caretti, *Saggio sul Sacchetti* (1951).

SACHS, HANS (1494-1576) German poet and dramatist. Born in *Nuremberg, he became a shoemaker in 1509. He wandered around Germany, studying the art of the **Meistersinger*, and later returned to Nuremberg, where

Hans Sachs *by Jost Amman*

he became the most significant 16th-century representative of the school. He supported *Luther, and praised him in his poem *Die wittenbergisch Nachtigall* (The Nightingale of Wittenberg), 1523. He wrote other works which supported the *Reformation, but in 1527 the city council forbade their publication. S. wrote over 6,000 works, in many different genres: meistersongs, *dramas, narratives, fables and others. He drew on biblical, classical, Germanic and mediaeval legends, and on Renaissance themes. His language was live and free, and he often described everyday life and his fellow citizens. His best poems are humorous, short and of popular style. Among these are *Sankt Peter mit der Geiss* (1555), and *Der Müller mit dem Studenten* (1559). Equally successful were his short anecdotal Shrovetide plays, which were full of humorous situations. Richard Wagner commemorated S. in his comic opera, *Die Meistersinger von Nürnberg* (1868).

H. von Wendler, *Hans Sachs* (1953);
E. Geiger, *Der Meistergesang des Hans Sachs* (1956);
H. Cattanés, *Les "Fastnachtsspiele" de Hans Sachs* (1923).

SACKVILLE, THOMAS (1536-1608) English statesman, dramatist and poet. Born in Sussex, he was a cousin of *Anne Boleyn's. In 1553 he settled in London, and two years later he was elected to the Parliament. Among the offices he held was that of commissioner at state trials, and it was he who announced the sentence of death to *Mary Queen of Scots. In 1599 he became the Lord High Treasurer. His most notable works were written during the 1550s. The most remarkable are the collection *A Mirror for Magistrates* and the tragedy *Gorboduc*. This, the earliest English *drama in blank verse, was written with Thomas *Norton and performed before *Elizabeth I in 1562.

SACRA CONVERSAZIONE (Italian: holy conversation) The depiction of the Virgin and Child with saints. This development in the portrayal of the theme of the *Madonna belongs to the 15th century. Its composition became increasingly articulate, and it may be viewed as a stage preceeding the secular presentation of the Madonna during the High Renaissance.

Sacra Conversazione *by Domenico Veneziano*

SACRAMENTARIAN CONTROVERSY The debate within the Protestant camp about the presence of Christ in the Eucharist. It was disputed in the Colloquy of *Marburg (1529), where *Zwingli and *Oecolampadius argued that the bread and wine of the Eucharist were the body and blood of Christ only in a "sacramental", or metaphorical sense. The word "sacramentarians" thus came to be used for all who denied the actual presence of Christ's body and blood.

SACRA RAPPRESENTAZIONE Italian religious *drama during the Renaissance. These were dramatic performances which corresponded to the *mysteries and *moralities of northern Europe. Their subjects were taken from biblical tales, legends of the lives of saints and stories of moral significance. They were very popular until the middle of the 16th century.

SA DE MIRANDA, FRANCISCO DE (1485-1558) Portuguese poet. Born into a noble family in Coimbra, he studied at the university of Lisbon, where he took a law degree in 1516, and spent time at the royal court. In 1521 he went to Italy, where he became acquainted with Renaissance poetic forms through direct contact with the foremost Italian literary personalities of the age. Returning to Lisbon in 1526, he introduced the sonnet, eclogue and Italian manner of versification. His comedy, *Os Estrangeiros* (1527), was the first Portuguese play written in classical manner. There are also new verse forms in his *Fabula do Mondego* and in his eclogue, *Aleixo*. In 1530 he married, left Lisbon and settled at his estate at Alto Minho. His poetry was thereafter filled with criticism of the Portuguese society. His most notable eclogue, *Basto* (1532) is a long debate between two shepherds. The poetic *Cartas* and other satires are directed against social corruption and growing materialism. In 1538 he wrote a second classical comedy in prose, *Vilhalpandos*, which was performed at the court. Afterwards his creative powers dwindled, though he continued to write short poems and maintained extensive literary contacts. Although his works were first published in 1595, his influence on Portuguese poetry was already felt in his own lifetime.

SADOLETO, JACOPO (1477-1547) Italian cardinal, humanist scholar and Catholic reformer. Having acquired a reputation as a student of classical languages, he was appointed secretary to *Leo X and, in 1517, made bishop of Carpentras. In 1536, when *Paul III bestowed the cardinalate on a number of reform-minded ecclesiastics, S. was included among them, and, in 1537, was appointed by the pope to the Commission of Nine under *Contarini, which was charged with preparing the agenda for the Council of *Trent. S. made several attempts to win Protestants back to Roman Catholicism. In May 1539 he addressed a letter to the people of Geneva, which was rejected by *Calvin. In 1542, as papal legate, he attempted a reconciliation between *Charles V and *Francis I, to open the way for the convening of the general Church council, but was unsuccessful.

SAGREDO, DIEGO DE Spanish theorist of *architecture. A chaplain of Queen *Juana the Mad, he was the author of the first Spanish work on Renaissance architecture. Entitled *Medidas del Romano*, it was published in Toledo in 1526, and saw several editions and translations. Following the ancient Vitruvius, the author advocated a combination of the old Roman style with the Spanish **plateresque*.

SAHAGUN, BERNARDINO DE (c. 1500-90) Spanish ethnographer. A native of Leon, he joined the Franciscan order (1524) and, in 1529, went to Mexico as a missionary. Later he taught at the College of Santiago Tlaltelolco, where sons of the Indian nobility were instructed. There he began to gather material for his *Historia general de las cosas de Nueva España*, written in Spanish and Nahuatl, with many illustrations, about the Aztec civilization. S.'s methods were quite modern, including questioning elderly Indians, who supplied him with information on conditions before the Spanish conquest. Completed in 1577, after almost 30 years, the work was not allowed to be printed and remained in several manuscript versions, the fullest being that of the Florentine Codex. It was first published in 1830.

M. S. Edmonson, ed., *Sixteenth-Century Mexico: The Work of Sahagún* (1974).

SAINT-ANDRÉ, JACQUES D'ALBON (c. 1505-62) French soldier. Having distinguished himself in the wars against Spain, he was made marshal of France and governor of Lyonnais by *Henry II. In 1557 he was taken captive at St. Quentin, but released in time to participate in the negotiations leading to the peace of *Cateau-Cambrésis (1559). In April 1561 he formed a triumvirate with *Montmorency and Francis, duke of *Guise, against the *Huguenots and the queen-regent, *Catherine de Médicis, thereby precipitating the outbreak of the *Religious Wars. He was killed at the Battle of Dreux.

SAINT-GELAIS, MELLIN DE (1487-1558) French poet. Born in Angoulême, where his father later became bishop, he studied in Italy and acquired a reputation as a physician, *astrologer, musician and poet. About 1515 he became court poet to King *Francis I, contributing semi-dramatic texts to the court festivities. A follower of *Marot, he is credited with popularizing the *sonnet in France. Under *Henry II, S. was ridiculed by the young members of the *Pléiade, and lost the favour of the court to *Ronsard. In 1554 his translation of *Trissino's *Sofonisba* was staged before *Catherine de Médicis.

H. J. Molinier, *Mellin de Saint-Gelays* (1910; rep. 1968).

SALES, ST. FRANCIS DE (1567-1622) Prominent French Catholic and devotional author. Born to a noble family in Savoy, he became a priest in 1593, somewhat against the wishes of his father, and undertook missionary work in Chablais, where there was a strong Calvinist strain. In 1602 he was made bishop of Geneva. Shortly thereafter he met the widow Jeanne Frances de Chantal with whom he founded, in 1610, a religious order of women dedicated to charity, the Visitation of the Holy Mary. In his missionary work he emphasized conversion by persuasion and personal example. His collected sermons and writings fill more than 20 volumes, of which *The Introduction to the Devout Life* (1608), is a classic of Catholic spiritual literature. He was canonized in 1665. The Salesian order founded in 1841 is named after him.

R. Kleinman, *Saint François de Sales and the Protestants* (1962).

SALMASIUS, CLAUDIUS (Claude Saumaise; 1588-1653) French classical scholar. A native of Saumur, he was educated at Paris, where he was befriended by *Casaubon, who convinced him to convert to Calvinism. He established his name as a scholar at the age of 19, when he discovered a celebrated ancient manuscript at Heidelberg. In 1608 he edited two 14th-century manuscripts which attacked papal supremacy, and later published various classical works, and his immense *Plinianae exercitationes*, which dealt with Pliny's geography. In 1632 he became professor of Greek at Leiden, and published two treatises on the legitimacy of usury (1638-39). In 1649 he wrote a defence of the exiled king of England, Charles II, which provoked a reply from Milton. His wide reputation for learning brought him an invitation from Queen Christina, but after a short stay in Sweden, he returned to Holland where he remained until his death.

SALMERON, ALFONSO (1515-85) Jesuit preacher and theologian. Born in Toledo, he studied at the university of Alcalá and, from 1533, in Paris. He was a member of the first *Jesuit group established by Ignatius *Loyola, and contributed to the formation of the order. As a theologian, he participated in the Council of *Trent. S.'s major work was a 16-volume commentary on the New Testament, based on his lectures.

SALUTATI, COLUCCIO DI PIERO (1331-1406) Italian humanist, chancellor of Florence. Born in Stignano in Valdinievole, he studied law in Bologna and became a notary and a public official. He served as chancellor of Todi (1367) and of Lucca (1371), and then was elected chancellor of Florence (1375), a post which he held to the end of his life. He was the first humanist chancellor of the Republic, and his reputation made the position suitable for learned men. S. admired Latin language and literature and used them skilfully in his correspondence. By his use of the classical language he tried to make the classics relevant to worldly affairs. His official letters were highly praised and served as models for diplomatic correspondence. During the 1390s, when Florence was threatened by Gian Galeazzo *Visconti of Milan, S.'s writings appealed to the Florentine's love for liberty and civic pride. In his philosophical writings S. stresses the power of free will over that of fortune. These ideas are presented in his *De fato et fortuna* (On Fate and Fortune) (*c.* 1396). Among his other writings are *De Tyranno* (On the Tyrant) (1400), a discussion on monarchy, *De seculo et religione* (On the World and Religion) (1381), in which he compares secular and monastic life, and *De Laboribus Herculis* (On the Labours of Hercules) (*c.* 1391), an allegory which interprets the labours of Hercules as symbols of active civic life. An influential person and a respected statesman, as well as a notable humanist, S. successfully combined active life with scholarship.

B. L. Ullman, *The Humanism of Coluccio Salutati* (1963);
A. Petrucci, *Coluccio Salutati* (1972). (ND)

SALVIATI A distinguished old Florentine family many of whose members were public officials, churchmen and humanists. The S. usually followed the lead of the *Medici, although Francesco S., whose appointment as archbishop of Pisa was blocked by Lorenzo the Magnificent, took a prominent part in the *Pazzi Conspiracy (1478). Jacopo S. (d. 1533) married Lorenzo's daughter Lucrezia; he was the father of two cardinals and grandfather of Grand Duke *Cosimo I. Leonardo S. (1540-

89) was a well-known poet and dramatist who wrote an essay on the language of *Boccaccio's *Decameron*.

SALVIATI (1510-63) Italian painter, whose real name was Francesco di Rossi. Born in Florence, he was a pupil of *Andrea del Sarto. In about 1530 he entered the service of Cardinal Salviati in Rome, hence his name, and achieved fame with his *frescoes on religious themes, some executed together with his friend *Vasari. In 1539 he went to Venice, where he was likewise successful. In 1544 he undertook the decoration of Florence's Palazzo Vecchio at the invitation of *Cosimo I. In 1554 he went to France, and worked for the cardinal of Lorraine, but returned to Rome late in the following year. *Paul IV then commissioned him to decorate the *Farnese Palace, his last great work. A restless *Mannerist, S. was particularly adept at painting frescoes characterized by rich pictorial content and inventiveness. He also designed tapestries and was famous for his portraits.

SAMBIN, HUGUES (c. 1520-c. 1601) French architect and sculptor. Born at Gray, he worked in *Burgundy and died in Dijon. His most important building was the Palais de Justice at Besançon (1581). A work on architectural terms published in 1572 contained his beautiful engravings of sculptural forms.

SAMBUCUS, JOHANNES (1531-84) Hungarian physician and humanist. He studied in *Wittenberg, Ingolstadt, *Strassburg and Paris, and received his medical training in Padua between 1553 and 1557. After teaching for some time at Bologna, he became physician and librarian at the *Habsburg court in Vienna. He wrote a commentary on Dioscorides (1549), published a Latin translation of an Arabic work on the interpretation of dreams (1577), an edition of the laws of *Hungary, and other works.

H. Gerstinger, ed., *Die Briefe des Johannes Sambucus* (1968).

SAMPIERO DA BASTELICA (Sampiero Corso; 1498-1567) Corsican military leader and patriot. Trained as a soldier in the mercenary army of Giovanni de' *Medici, he later joined the French forces and, in 1545, returned to his native Corsica, then largely under *Genoese rule. After a period in prison he went to France and persuaded *Henry II to conquer the island, an operation which was carried out with the cooperation of the Turkish fleet (1553). This caused Emperor *Charles V to intervene, and by the Treaty of *Cateau-Cambrésis (1559), Corsica was returned to Genoa. But S. continued his resistence to the Genoese, and even visited *Constantinople to seek the aid of the *Ottoman Turks. Although he failed to obtain outside assistance, he landed on the island in 1564 with 50 men and soon mustered an army of several thousands. War was waged for over two years, until S. was murdered by political enemies.

SANCHEZ COELLO, ALONSO (c. 1531-88) Spanish painter. Of Portuguese parentage, he was born near Valencia, and studied at Brussels, where he met and was influenced by Anthonis *Mor. In 1571 he succeeded him as court painter to *Philip II. S. was particularly known for his formal courtly portraits, in which he continued Mor's style.

SANCHEZ COTAN, JUAN (1561-1627) Spanish painter. Born at Orgaz, near Toledo, he excelled in painting still-life. In 1604 he became a Carthusian monk, and thereafter executed works on religious themes, too. His best-known picture is *Still Life with Cabbage*, now in San Diego, California. From 1615 to 1617 he painted in the cloister of the Carthusian monastery of Granada, illustrating the life of St. Bruno and other saints of his order.

SANCHEZ, TOMAS (1550-1610) Spanish theologian. In 1567 he joined the *Jesuits and became master of novices at Granada. His most famous work was *Tratado sobre el matrimonio*, a comprehensive work on the religious and moral aspects of matrimony. It was widely read during the 17th century.

SANDERS, NICHOLAS (c. 1530-81) English Roman Catholic polemicist. Educated at Oxford, he taught canon law there in the reign of *Mary Tudor. In 1559 he fled to Italy, where he became a priest. For some time he attached himself to Cardinal *Hosius, but in 1565 he was appointed professor of theology at Louvain. There he published several treatises in defence of strict papal authority over the Church. In 1572 he went to Rome and consulted *Gregory XIII on the situation of Roman Catholicism in England. In 1577 he went to Spain to urge *Philip II to declare war on England. That

Courtly Portrait of a Lady *by Sanchez Coello*

The Church of S. Biagio near Montepulciano by Antonio da Sangallo

year appeared in Latin his *Origin and Progress of the English Schism*, a pro-Catholic history of the Reformation in England. In 1579 he went as papal legate to join the Desmond insurrection in *Ireland. He died there after being pursued for two years by government forces.
T. M. Veech, *Dr. Nicholas Sanders and the English Reformation* (1935).

SANDYS, EDWIN (1519-88) English archbishop of York. A graduate of Cambridge, he held a number of ecclesiastical posts before becoming vice-chancellor of the university in the reign of *Edward VI. He was imprisoned for his support of Lady Jane *Grey (1553), but presently left England, returning only upon the accession of *Elizabeth I. He became in turn bishop of Worcester (1559), London (1570) and archbishop of York (1575). Although a fervent Protestant, he was frequently at odds with the *Nonconformists.

SANGALLO, ANTONIO DA (1455-1534) Italian architect, known as S. the Elder, to distinguish him from his nephew. A brother and pupil of Giuliano, he began his career as a military engineer. His architectural masterpiece is the Church of S. Biagio at Montepulciano (1518-29), a centrally-planned structure, modelled on Giuliano's S. Maria in Carceri at Prato, but profoundly influenced by the massive style of *Bramante. Several palaces in Montepulciano and Rome are also attributed to him.

SANGALLO, ANTONIO DA (1484-1546) Italian architect; nephew of Giuliano. Born in Florence, he was the first architect to be educated as such. Establishing a name quite early as a technical expert in his field, he worked for some time with *Bramante and, in 1520, succeeded *Raphael as the chief architect of *St. Peter's, a post he was to hold for 20 years. His most important individual work was the elegant and monumental *Farnese palace in Rome, which *Michelangelo completed after his death. Like his uncles, S. was employed as a military engineer in fortifications around Rome. Considered at the time the leading Roman architect, his works followed the Renaissance classical style.
G. Giovannoni, *Antonio da Sangallo, il Giovane*, 2 vols. (1952).

SANGALLO, GIULIANO DA (1445-1516) Italian architect. Born in Florence, he visited Rome in his youth, where he studied ancient remains, but it was probably his Florentine predecessors, such as *Brunelleschi, who had the greatest influence on his development. S.'s style was distinguished by a deliberate pursuit of an organic Graeco-Roman model. This may be seen in his S. Maria delle Carceri in Prato (1485), and in his most famous building, the Villa *Medici at Poggio a Cajano, which was completed in 1491. In his later years he erected military fortifications in Rome, including the Castello S. Angelo, and worked with *Raphael on *St. Peter's (1514-15). His brother Antonio (1455-1534) was also one of the prominent architects of the age.
G. Marchini, *Giuliano da Sangallo* (1942).

SANMICHELI, MICHELE (1484-1559) Italian architect. Born in Verona, he studied under his father, who was also an architect. In 1527, following a period of

The Logetta by Jacopo Sansovino at the piazetta of San Marco, Venice

work in and around Rome, he returned to the north of Italy, working mostly in Verona and *Venice. S. became a very famous military engineer-architect, and was placed by the Republic of Venice in charge of its fortifications, including those in Corfu and Crete. His buildings, including a few churches, were sometimes reminiscent of fortresses, and generally of a massive appearance. In his residential palaces in Verona he began with a High Renaissance style which he had brought from Rome, but later developed his own architectural Mannerism.

SANNAZARO, JACOPO (1455-1530) Italian poet and humanist. Born in Naples, he lived for many years at the court of the local ruling family and, in 1501, accompanied King *Federigo to exile, returning to Naples only after the king's death. S. was one of the leaders of *Pontano's circle. His most important work, the *Arcadia*, was an autobiographical allegory about unrequited love, written in Italian, in poetry and prose together. Published in 1501, it had a strong influence on the development of Italian vernacular literature; it was also translated into other languages. Another renowned work was the long Latin poem, *De partu Virginis* (1513), which took as its theme the birth of Christ and won the praise of *Leo X.

L. Monga, *Le genre pastoral au XVIe siècle: Sannazar et Belleau* (1974).

SANO DI PIETRO (1406-81) Italian painter. Born in *Siena, he was a pupil of *Sassetta, and headed the largest Sienese workshop. He produced numerous rather cold-seeming works on religious themes in the style of his master.

SAN PEDRO, DIEGO DE Spanish author of romances and poet, active in the later 15th century. He was possibly of Jewish descent, but very little is known about his life. His two romances in prose, *Arnalte y Lucenda* (1491) and *La cárcel de amor* (1492), were influenced by similar works of Italian authors, chiefly *Boccaccio's *Fiammetta*. They developed the theme of the faithful lover, and were widely popular, and were translated into Italian, French and English. S. also wrote poetry, including a popular narrative of Christ's death.

SANSEVERINO The leading noble house of the kingdom of *Naples. Conspicuous since the 11th century, the S. succeeded in acquiring a great many fiefs, and during the 14th and 15th centuries gave their allegiance to various foreign claimants to the throne. Ultimately they supported *Alfonso V of Aragon and his heirs, who rewarded them with high public offices. Ferrante S., prince of Salerno, was a famous military commander in the army of *Charles V, and a patron of Bernardo *Tasso. He had to flee to France in 1552 after he protested against the creation of the Neapolitan *Inquisition.

SANSOVINO, ANDREA (1467-1529) Italian sculptor. Born Andrea Contucci, he was renamed after his birthplace when he settled in *Florence where he studied under *Pollaiuolo. Most of his works were executed in S. Maria del Popolo, *Rome (1505-09). Between 1513 and 1527 he was often in Loreto, where he made some series of reliefs. His style displays grace and sensitivity.
G. H. Huntley, *Andrea Sansovino* (1935).

SANSOVINO, FRANCESCO (1521-86) Italian scholar. Born in Rome, he was the son of Jacopo *Sansovino, and spent most of his life in Venice. He was a prolific writer of poetry, history and philosophy. Among his works are *Del governo dei regni e delle repubbliche* (1561), on the forms of government in Italy, and *Origini e fatti delle famiglie illustri d'Italia*, descriptions of the principal Italian cities and their noble families. His 14 volume *Venetia* (1581), was the first attempt to survey the city's art and architecture, including the works of his father.

Admiral Alvaro de Santa Cruz

SANSOVINO, JACOPO (1486-1570) Italian sculptor and architect. Born in *Florence as Jacopo Tatti, he adopted the name of his master, the sculptor Andrea *Sansovino (1467-1529). In 1505 he went to Rome, where he was active mainly as a sculptor, but where he also made a thorough study of the architectural work of *Bramante. The Sack of *Rome (1527) drove him to *Venice, where he settled permanently, and where he soon became the leading architect. His best-known building, the Old Library at the Piazzetta S. Marco, was begun in 1536. The two superimposed rows of arcades are supported by Doric columns below and Ionic above, and accompanied by superb sculptural ornamentation. The building, intended to house manuscripts bequeathed to the Republic by *Bessarion, however, was not completed until 1588. Other outstanding structures by S. were the Ca' Grande, designed in 1532, a palace with an impressive façade, and the Mint (*La Zecca*), completed in 1545. Of his many sculptures the most famous are the *Mars* and *Neptune* in the Doge's Palace (1554). A major practitioner of the splendid style of the High Renaissance, S., a friend of *Titian and *Aretino, left an unmistaken imprint on Venetian architecture.
G. Mariacher, *Il Sansovino* (1962).

SANTA CRUZ, ALVARO DE BAZAN, MARQUIS OF (1526-88) Spanish admiral. Born in Granada, he was the son of a Spanish naval commander. He joined the navy in his youth, and participated in battles against the French, the *Ottoman Turks and the Moorish kingdoms of North Africa. In 1569 he was created marquis. He then commanded the Spanish ships in several successful naval battles, including the Battle of Lepanto against the Turks (1571), and the capture of Tunis (1573). In 1580 his fleet aided in the conquest of Portugal, and in 1583 won the battle for the Azores against a superior combined French and English fleet. As a reward, S. was titled "captain general of the ocean". He now approached King *Philip II with the proposal to conquer England. His plan was accepted and he was appointed naval commander of the mission. S. had organized most of the *Armada before he died on February 1588. A few months later the Armada sailed to its disaster under the command of the duke of *Medina-Sidonia. S. was the most successful naval commander in the heyday of Spanish power.
G. Mattingly, *The Defeat of the Spanish Armada* (1959).

SANTA HERMANDAD A centralized militia, created in 1476 by *Ferdinand and *Isabella to combat brigandage. Based on the mediaeval popular bands of the Castilian towns, the S. was also meant to aid in the last efforts of the **reconquista* and to strengthen the crown's stand against the powerful magnates. It had its own courts and was controlled by a council responsible to the crown. By 1498, however, the institution had accomplished much of its aims, and the crown agreed to suppress the council; the organization continued to exist as a sort of rural police.

SANTI, GIOVANNI (c. 1440-94) Italian painter and writer. Born in *Urbino, he became court painter of *Guidobaldo da Montefetro. More important than his paintings, however, is his chronicle in verse of the dukes of Urbino, where contemporary artists are mentioned and evaluated. He was *Raphael's father and first teacher.

SANTILLANA, IÑIGO LOPEZ DE MENDOZA, MARQUIS OF (1398-1458) Spanish statesman and poet. Of noble descent, he served the court of *John II of Castile, and distinguished himself in military service. He took a prominent part in bringing about the downfall of Alvaro de *Luna (1453), and was later created marquis (1455). In his last years he devoted himself to writing, composing a collection of didactic sayings, *Proverbios de gloriosa doctrina*, and a dialogue in a similar vein *Diálogo de bias contra fortuna*. His *Comedieta de Ponza*, influenced by *Dante, described the battle in which *Alfonso V of Aragon fell in Genoese captivity (1435). Other works of his also betrayed the influece of Italian models.

M. Pérez y Curis, *El marqués de Santillana* (1916);
R. Lapesa, *La obra literaria del marqués de Santillana* (1957).

SANUDO, MARINO (1466-1533) Italian historian; known as "the younger", to distinguish him from the early 14th-century traveller and writer by the same name, who had attempted to revive the idea of the *Crusades. Like his namesake, S. was a native of *Venice, and received an excellent classical education. He held public office in Verona and in the Great Council of Venice. His outspokenness caused him to be denied the post of official historian of the Republic, and it was only in 1531 that his merits were recognized by the Senate, which granted him an annual pension. S. wrote an account of a journey in 1483 through Venetian-owned territories, and a description of the war with *Ferrara. His *Le vite dei dogi* gave the lives of the Venetian chiefs of state until 1494. Most important were his *Diarii* in 58 volumes, covering the years 1496 to 1533. These diaries include daily comments on the government of Venice, together with many documents, and reports on events in Italy and other countries. It is an essential source of information on the period.

SARACENI, CARLO (c. 1580-1620) Italian painter. Born in Venice, he went to Rome in about 1600, and remained there for most of his life. He may have been a pupil of *Elsheimer's, but he was also strongly influenced by *Caravaggio. Of his small landscapes on copper the best are those on mythological themes. In 1616 he worked with *Lanfranco on *frescoes in the Sala Regia of the Quirinal Palace. Later he made altarpieces for Roman churches. He died in Venice, where he had been commissioned to decorate the hall of the Great Council.

SARMIENTO DE GAMBOA, PEDRO (1532-92) Spanish navigator and historian. Born in Alcalá, he became a soldier and, in 1555, a seaman, whose services were much sought after because of his knowledge of astronomy and navigation. He took part in the reconaissance of the Pacific (1567-69), and accompanied viceroy Francisco de *Toledo on his inspection of Peru (1570-72). S. then wrote his *Historia Indica*, an important account of the Inca empire, which emphasized the cruelty and the illegal nature of the government of the pre-conquest rulers of Peru. Diametrically opposed to the better-known view of the Incas of *Garcilaso de la Vega, it was published only in 1906. After *Drake's passage through the Strait of Magellan, S. was sent there from Peru to fortify the place (1579). He proceeded to Spain and, in 1580, *Philip II made him governor of the Strait. He sailed there at the head of 16 ships (1581), and for the next five years made repeated attempts to establish settlements near today's Punta Arenas, on the western side of the Strait, but was forced to give up because of the cold. On his return to Spain (1586) he was captured by English ships, but released after an audience with *Elizabeth I. However, before he reached Spain he was again captured, this time by French *Huguenots, and only set free upon the payment of a ransom in 1590.

S. Clissold, *Conquistador; The Life of Don Pedro Sarmiento de Gamboa* (1954).

SARPI, PAOLO (1552-1623) Italian historian. Born in Venice, he was still in his youth when he joined the Servite order, of which he eventually became Procurator-General (1585-88). When *Paul V put Venice under an interdict because it had enacted laws which restricted the right of the Church to own property, S. supported his native city. In 1606 he was appointed theological consultor of the Republic, and took such a strong anti-papal stand that in 1607 he was attacked by rowdies and left for dead. His chief work, *Istoria del concilio tridentino* (1619) expressed his criticism of Rome, and explained the *Reformation as a reaction to abuses in the Catholic Church. The major part of the work attacked papal and *Jesuit manipulations at the Council of *Trent. He also wrote on the government of Venice.

P. Sarpi, *History of Benefices and Selections from History of the Council of Trent*, trans. and edited by P. Burke (1967).

SASSETTA (Stefano di Giovanni; 1392-1450) Italian painter. A native of Siena, he is first heard of in connection with an altarpiece executed in 1423-26. His best-known work is a series on the *Life of St. Francis*, painted between 1437 and 1444 for the church of S. Francesco, Sansepolcro, and now dispersed. Plainly aware of contemporary Florentine realism, and displaying some stylistic affinities with *International Gothic, S. is basically a continuator of the linear tradition of representation of the 14th century. Together with *Giovanni di Paolo he was the greatest Sienese painter of his time.

SATTLER, MICHAEL (c. 1490-1527) German *Anabaptist leader. Born near Freiburg, he became a Benedictine monk and prior of the monastery of St. Peter. In 1523 he left, married and went to *Zurich, where he joined the first group of the Swiss Anabaptists. In 1525 he was expelled by the *Zwingli-dominated town council and, in 1526, spent some time in *Strassburg where he had friendly discussions with *Capito and *Bucer. In that year he attracted many followers around Horb. In February 1527 he presided over a meeting of Swiss and German Anabaptists which adopted the *Schleitheim Confession. Shortly afterward he and his wife were seized in Horb, and taken to Rottenburg. Condemned as heretics, S. was burned at the stake and his wife executed by drowning.

SAVERY, ROELAND (1576-1639) Flemish artist. Born in Courtrai, he was trained in *Amsterdam by his elder brother Jacques (died 1602). Later he worked for

Diana and Her Nymphs Surprised by Acteon *by Titian*

S. Maria della Consolazione, Todi, built in 1508 on a circular plan, after a design by Bramante

St. Francis Marrying Poverty *by Sassetta*

*Henry IV in France and for Emperor *Rudolf II in Prague (1604-12). During these years he painted mythological scenes with a variety of animals, and a series of atmospheric landscapes of the Tyrol. Later, he was again in Amsterdam and worked briefly for Emperor *Matthias. In 1619 S. settled in Utrecht, where he enjoyed a considerable reputation. Of his later works, the best are the flower paintings.

SAVILE, SIR HENRY (1549-1622) English scholar and educator. A graduate of the university of Oxford, he acquired a wide reputation for his Greek scholarship and knowledge of mathematics and, in 1578, was appointed Greek tutor to *Queen Elizabeth I. From 1585 he served as warden of Merton College and, in 1596, became provost of Eton, too. The most important of his editions of classical writings was a sumptuous eight-volume folio of St. Chrysostom (1610-13). He founded professorships of geometry and astronomy at Oxford, translated Tacitus, and published a collection of old English chronicles. Himself a collector of manuscripts, he helped found the *Bodleian Library.

SAVOLDO, GIOVANNI GIROLAMO (c.1480-c.1548) Italian painter. He was born in Brescia, but little is known about his life, except that he worked mainly in Venice, where he was influenced by Giovanni *Bellini and *Giorgione. One of his best-known works, *The Transfiguration* in Florence's *Uffici, has a lyrical, sentimental quality. Other works also show an interest in the effects of luminosity and attention to details of materials.

A. Boschetto, *Giovan Gerolamo Savoldo* (1963).

SAVONAROLA, GIROLAMO (1452-98) Dominican friar and reformer, who dominated the political scene in Florence between 1494-98. Born in Ferrara, he entered the Dominican order of Bologna in 1475. In 1482 he was sent to Florence as a preacher in the convent of San Marco. There he began his prophetic sermons, talking about the necessary reforms in the Church. He left Florence in 1487 but was recalled in 1490, at the request of Lorenzo de' *Medici, and became the prior of San Marco (1491). In his fiery sermons, which drew large crowds, he attacked corruption and criticized the Medici government. He predicted the invasion of Italy by *Charles VIII of France, and called for repentance for the sake of a better future. When Piero de' Medici was driven out of Florence (1494), S. became the virtual leader of the city. He supervised the establishment of a popular theocratic government, based on a great council consisting of 3,200 citizens, and carried out social and moral reforms which were widely popular. He objected to the alliance of the Italian cities against France, which Florence therefore did not join.

Savonarola *by Fra Bartolommeo*

However, his rigorous campaign against immorality made him many enemies. Opposition formed in the city, and was supported from the outside by the Medici, who sought to return to power. S. was also opposed by Pope *Alexander VI, who wanted Florence to join the Italian alliance, and who saw him as a threat to his own authority. In a series of measures the Pope tried to eliminate the friar's power. First he invited him to Rome to explain his revelations, but S. rejected the invitation. He then ordered him to abstain from preaching. S. stopped preaching for a while, but in 1496 launched a new series of sermons directed against the corruption of Rome herself. In 1497 he was excommunicated by the Pope and, when he continued his sermons, Florence was threatened with an interdict. Famine, war, plague and the fear of excommunication reduced S.'s popularity and the tide turned against him. The *signoria* asked him to stop preaching and encouraged riots against him. S. was challenged to an ordeal by fire by Franciscan friars, an event which ended in turmoil and confusion. The next day a mob attacked San Marco and S. was arrested. He was tortured and sentenced to death as a heretic. He was hanged on 23 May 1498 with two of his disciples and their bodies were burned.

D. Weinstein, *Savonarola and Florence: Prophecy and Patriotism in the Renaissance* (1970);
R. Ridolfi, *The Life of Girolamo Savonarola* (1959);
G. Soranzo, *Il tempo di Alessandro VI e di Fra Girolamo Savonarola* (1960) (ND)

SAVOY An independent duchy in northwest Italy, it was ruled for a long time by the house of S., whose territories included Piedmont and Vaud. Commanding the most important passes of the western Alps, S. was French-oriented, and took little interest in the political affairs of Italy. Amadeus VIII, who received the ducal title from Emperor *Sigismund in 1416, acquired the county of *Geneva and some territories in Italy. In 1434 he withdrew to a life of seclusion in Ripaille, from which he emerged in 1440 when the Council of *Basle elected him pope, taking the name Felix V. After his death (1451) S. entered a period of decline, characterized by French interference, internal conflicts in the ruling house, and haphazard attempts of the Estates-General to fill the void.

During the *Italian Wars S. was the battleground between France and the *Habsburgs. Duke Charles III (1504-53), who tended to support Emperor *Charles V, lost Geneva, which joined the *Swiss Confederation, and was deprived of most of his lands by Francis I. Emmanuel Philibert (1553-80), continued to support Spain in its war with France. He commanded the Spanish forces at the Battle of St. Quentin (1557), where he gained complete victory over the French, and S. was restored to him in the Treaty of *Cateau-Cambrésis (1559). He reorganized his estates, but failed in his attempt to convert the *Waldenses by force (1560-61). In 1563 he transferred the capital from Chambéry in S. to Turin in Piedmont. In subsequent years, S. kept manoeuvering between France and the Habsburgs. When Charles Emmanuel I (1580-1630) sided with Spain, *Henry IV of France occupied the duchy. The territories were regained by Victor Amadeus I (1630-37), who married Christina, a daughter of the French king, and sealed an alliance with France. After his death, Christina served as regent for her son, until 1663. A prolonged conflict between the French and Spanish factions weakened the duchy, until its re-emergence as a strong military state in the 18th century.

C. Dufayard, *Histoire de Savoie* (1930);
H. Ménabréa, *Histoire de la Savoie* (1958);
P. Guichonnet, ed., *Histoire de la Savoie* (1973). (ND)

SAXONY An electoral duchy in east Germany which played an important role during the 15th-16th centuries. The rank of elector of S. was bestowed in 1423 on Frederick I, margrave of Meissen and member of the House of *Wettin. The name S. was then applied to all the Meissen lands, including Osterland and large parts of Lusatia and Thuringia. The territories were divided by Frederick's grandsons, Ernest and Albert, in the Treaty of Leipzig (1485). Ernest obtained most of Thuringia, Saxe-*Wittenberg and the electoral rank. Albert received Meissen and northern Thuringia. In 1486 Ernest was succeeded by his son, *Frederick III the Wise, under whom the duchy prospered and became the most influential state in Germany. In 1502 he founded the university of Wittenberg and appointed Martin *Luther as lecturer. His support and protection of Luther made S. the centre of the *Reformation. *John Frederick I the Magnanimous, who became elector in 1532, led the *Schmalkaldic League together with *Philip of Hesse. When the League was defeated in the *Schmalkaldic War (1546-47), John Frederick was captured by *Charles V. It was a turning point in the history of S. The electoral title and most of its territories were transferred to the Albertine line, then headed by *Maurice of S., who supported the Emperor. The Ernestine line was left with Thuringia, which was divided into several duchies. In a short time Maurice changed sides, and S. joined the *Protestant princes again. Maurice organized the war of 1552, in which Charles was defeated, and signed the Treaty of Passau.

Maurice was succeeded by his brother *Augustus I (1553-86), who made a significant contribution to the internal development of the duchy. Its economy developed, mainly thanks to its mines. Augustus also made some significant administrative changes, and he made the capital, Leipzig, a centre of arts. In the early stages of the *Thirty Years' War (1618-48), George I (1611-56) led the German Protestant princes and fought with Sweden against the Emperor. But in 1635 S. concluded the Peace of Prague with the Emperor. As a result, the electorate suffered greatly from the Protestant armies, and its population was reduced from three to one and a half millions. At the end of the war S.'s influence and leadership in Germany was in decline. It finally lost its central position among the German Protestant states to *Brandenburg-Prussia.

R. Kötzschke und H. Krezschmar, *Sächsische Geschichte*, 2 vols. (1935). (ND)

SCALIGER, JOSEPH JUSTUS (1540-1609) French scholar. Born in Agen, he was taught by his father, before going to Paris, where he studied Greek and oriental languages. In 1562 he converted to Calvinism and, in 1565, undertook a long excursion to Italy in company of a nobleman of Poitou, who became his patron. Between 1567 and 1570 he fought on the side of the *Huguenots, and for two years taught at *Geneva (1572-74). Thereafter he dedicated himself to his studies, moving from one castle of his patron's family to another, according to the vicissitudes of the *Religious Wars. In 1593 he accepted the offer of the university of Leiden to succeed *Lipsius. Although he hardly lectured, he helped make Leiden the greatest European centre of classical studies of the time. Combining wide learning with a sharp critical faculty, S. published editions of classical Roman writers, including Festus (1575), Catullus, Tibullus and Propertius (1577), Apuleius (1600) and Caesar (1606). His edition of Manilius (1579) showed his interest in ancient astronomy, and was followed by a study of the chronology of antiquity, *De emendatione temporum* (1583). These, together with the *Thesaurus temporum* (1606), make him the father of modern methods of chronology, in addition to his being the greatest figure in the history of French classical studies.

G. W. Robinson, ed., *Autobiography of Joseph Scaliger* (1927);
C. Nisard, *Le triumvirat litteraire au XVIe siecle; Juste Lipse, Joseph Scaliger et Isaac Casaubon* (1852; rep. 1970).

SCALIGER, JULIUS CAESAR (1484-1558) French classical scholar. Born and educated in Italy, he went to France at the age of 42, and became the physician of the bishop of Agen. An ardent *Ciceronian, he published in 1531 a small tract against *Erasmus, and repeated the attack in 1536. His *De causis latinae linguae* (1544) was a detailed exposition of the principles of Latin, but his major contribution was the *Poëtice* (1561), one of the earliest systematic treatises of the art of poetry, which contained the first definition of the classical rules of tragedy. He was the father of Joseph Justus *Scaliger.

V. Hall, *Life of Julius Caesar Scaliger* (1950).

SCAMOZZI, VINCENZO (1552-1616) Italian architect. The son of a carpenter-mason of Vicenza, he was the pupil of *Palladio's, whom he succeeded as the outstanding architect of northern Italy. His dependence on his master can be seen in his early work, the Villa Rocca Pisana at Lonigo, a residential house on top of a hill commanding a spectacular scenery. After Palladio's death (1580) S. completed some of his structures in Venice and, in 1585, added the permanent stage to the master's theatre of the Olympian Academy at Vicenza; later he designed another classically-inspired theatre at Sabbioneta (1588). In 1599 he travelled in Germany and France and, in 1604, visited Austria. Like his master, S. also wrote on the subject of architecture. His *Discorsi sopra le antichita di Roma* (1582), dealt with the remains of ancient Rome; his *L'idea dell' architectura universale* (1615) is considered the final statement on the principles of architecture by a major Renaissance builder.

SCARSELLA, IPPOLITO (1551-1620) Italian painter, etcher and miniaturist. Born in *Ferrara, he was trained in *Venice, and was active in several places in northern Italy, but mainly in his native town. His extensive output is of unequal quality, the religious paintings being rather better than the mythological scenes.

SCEVE, MAURICE (1501-64) French poet. A native of Lyons, he is credited with having found the grave of Petrarch's Laura in Avignon, a discovery which may have been of largely imaginary significance. S. was originally influenced by the poetry of *Marot, but his great work, *Délie, object de plus haulte vertu*, published in 1544, is recognized as one of the finest poetic creations of the *Renaissance. Dealing with the vicissitudes of love, it displays the poet's psychological insight and gift for symbolic images. His vocabulary, which contains many mythological and biblical terms, endows his poetry with a metaphysical air.

P. Quignard, *La-parole de la Délie; essai sur Maurice Scève* (1974).

SCHAFFNER, MARTIN (1478-c. 1546) German painter. Born in Ulm, where he spent most of his life, he was a successful artist and his altarpieces were much in demand. In his last years, however, he turned increasingly to portrait painting. His style shows the influence of *Burgkmair and *Schäuffelin, combining German traditions with the new Italian trends. S. left a considerable number of signed and dated works.

SCHÄUFFELIN, HANS LEONHARD (c. 1480-1538) German painter and wood engraver. Born in *Nuremberg, he worked under *Dürer, whose style he assimilated, though he had an independent and rich imagination of his own. In 1505 he left and for a while worked in Augsburg, later becoming a burgher of the town of Nördlingen (1515). S. illustrated Emperor *Maximilian I's *Theuerdank*. He enjoyed a wide reputation and almost never did his own carving. His son Hans the Younger (*c.* 1515-82) was also a well-known engraver.

F. Winkler, *Die Zeichnungen Hans Süss von Kulmbachs und Hans Leonhard Schäuffelins* (1942).

SCHEDEL, HARTMAN (1440-1514) German humanist. Born in *Nuremberg, he studied at the university of Leipzig (1456-60) and, in 1463, went to Italy, where he studied medicine. Having become a practicing physician, he eventually returned to his native city (1480), where he remained for the rest of his life. Intimately connected with artists, printers and fellow humanists, S.'s major contribution was the *Liber chronicarum,* a compilation of earlier chronicles, which was intended as a kind of world history. Known also as the Nuremberg Chronicle, it was published in 1493 by *Koberger and illustrated with 1809 woodcuts by Michael *Wolgemut and others. S. was a great collector of printed books and manuscripts.

SCHEDONI, BARTOLOMEO (1578-1615) Italian painter. Born in Modena, he was mainly active in Parma, in the service of the house of *Farnese. His early works reflect the influence of *Corneggio and are among the best examples of Italian *Mannerism. Later he assimilated the style of *Caravaggio, handling light effects with great charm. Regarding his early death, it was said to have been an outcome of his uncontrollable passion for gambling.

SCHEIDT, KASPAR (c. 1520-65) German satirist. He is known primarily for *Grobianus; von groben sitten und unhöfflichen geberden* (1551), a German adaptation of the work of *Dedekind. His work, however, is much more extensive. It contains open and detailed descriptions of vulgar behaviour and rude customs. Immensely popular in Germany, it was also adapted and translated into other European languages.

SCHIAVONE (1522-63) The popular nickname of the Italian painter Andrea Meldolla. Born in Zara, he was active in Venice. He was obviously influenced by both *Titan and *Parmigianino; the latter he also imitated in his etchings. He painted *frescoes on the façades of Venetian palaces, but none of these have survived. His best extant work uses mythological subjects in a romantic and dramatic vein.

SCHIAVONE, GIORGIO (c. 1436-1504) Italian painter of Slavonic origin, hence his nickname. Born in Dalmatia, he went to Padua in 1456 and signed a contract with *Squarcione, agreeing to work for him in return for artistic instruction. He left in 1461 and returned to Dalmatia. Later he worked in Zara and Skradin. His few extant paintings combine classical architectural motifs and a stress on decorative features, such as fruits, with a rather awkward treatment of the human figure.

SCHINNER, MATTHIAS (1456-1522) Swiss cardinal. Born in Mühlebach, he was educated in *Zurich. In 1500 he was made bishop of Sitten. In 1509 Pope *Julius II made him legate to Switzerland, his task being to win the Swiss over to the papal side. He was created cardinal in 1511. In 1513 he organized Swiss troops to help the *Sforzas, defeating the French at Novara. In 1515 he personally led the Swiss to their defeat by *Francis I at *Marignano. More a ststesman and soldier than a religious person, S. reacted favourably to the early manifestations of the *Reformation.

A. Büchi, *Kardinal Mattäus Schiner als Staatsmann und Kirchenfürst* (1937).

SCHLEITHEIM CONFESSION A doctrinal statement adopted on 24 February 1527 by a gathering of *Anabaptists at Schlatt near Schaffhausen. Drafted probably by Michael *Sattler, it consisted of the seven following articles: (1) Baptism was to be given to those who have repented and mended their ways; (2) An Anabaptist who sinned was to receive two private admonitions and a third, public one, before being excommunicated; (3) The Lord's Supper (a rite of memorial character), was to be shared only by the baptised; (4) Anabaptists were to separate themselves from worldly enjoyments, such as visiting drinking-houses; (5) Pastors were to be chosen for their integrity; (6) Anabaptists were not to bear arms, nor undertake magisterial duties; (7) Anabaptists were forbidden to take oaths. The confession was widely circulated and is the most representative of the various Anabaptist teachings. It was immediately attacked by *Zwingli and, in 1544, was also censured by *Calvin.

SCHMALKALDIC ARTICLES Confession of faith written by Martin *Luther in 1536. The articles were prepared for presentation before a general council convoked by Pope *Paul III, and they served to define which issues could be negotiated with the Catholics and which not. At a meeting between the members of the *Schmalkaldic League and several theologians at Schmalkalden (1537), the articles were not officially accepted. Still, they were signed by 44 theologians, published in 1538, and were included in the Book of Concord (1580). The S. are in three sections: the first discusses the unity of God, the Trinity, the incarnation and Christ; the second deals with Christ and *justification by faith; the third lists the 15 articles which could be discussed by Catholics and Protestants, such as sin, the law, repentance, the sacraments and a definition of the church.

SCHMALKALDIC LEAGUE A defensive alliance of the Protestant German states and imperial towns against

Preclarū hoc opus prime ſecūde ſancti tho
me de aquino. Alma in vrbe moguntina. in-
clite nationis germanice. quā dei clementia
tam alti ingenij lumine. dono q3 gratuito. cete
ris terrarū nacōib3 pferre illuſtrareq3 digna-
ta ē. Artificioſa quadā adinuencōe imprimē-
di ſeu caracterizandi abſq3 vlla calami exara
tione ſic effigiatū. et ad euſebiā dei induſtrie
eſt conſummatū. p petrū ſchoiffer de gernß-
hem. Anno dñi milleſimoquadringenteſimo
ſeptuageſimo pmo. Octaua die nouembris.
Sit laus deo.

Titlepage of Thomas Aquinas' Summa Theologica, *published by Peter Schöffer in 1471*

Emperor *Charles V. Formed on 27 February 1531, at Schmalkalden, it was led by *Philip of Hesse and *John Frederick I of *Saxony. In 1532, when Charles was threatened by the Turks, he signed a truce with the S. known as the Peace of *Nuremberg. But after the Emperor made peace with France (1544), and since the Protestants refused to attend the Council of *Trent, he decided to open war. By then the S., which had been inactive all this time, had become relatively weak.

SCHMALKALDIC WAR (1546-47) A series of campaigns in Germany, in which Emperor *Charles V defeated the *Schmalkaldic League of Protestant princes and cities. The Emperor gained an important ally by concluding a secret agreement with Duke *Maurice of Saxony, which facilitated the imperial conquest of southern Germany. He then advanced north and scored a decisive victory at the Battle of *Mühlberg (24 April 1547).

SCHÖFFER, PETER (c. 1425-1503) German printer. Born in Gernsheim in the Rhine valley, he worked for a time as a book copyist in Paris. Later he became an assistant of Johann *Fust of Mainz, whose daughter he married. With *Gutenberg and Fust S. was a pioneer of the art of *printing, and is traditionally credited with perfecting the method of stamping matrices. In 1457 he issued with Fust the superbly-designed great psalter. They were the first to print in colours and, in 1465, were the first to use Greek type. Upon Fust's death (1466), S. inherited the business. He continued to introduce innovations, using book advertisements and titlepages, although he did not fully grasp the importance of the latter. His son Johann continued the firm until his death in 1531, publishing a complete edition of Livy in Latin (1518-19) and in German translation, and works on classical scholarship.

SCHONGAUER, MARTIN (c. 1430-91) German painter and engraver. A descendant of a prominent *Augsburg family, he was raised in Colmar, Alsace, where his father, a goldsmith, had settled in about 1440. In 1465 he was registered for one semester at the university of Leipzig, but in 1469 was already back in Colmar, where he lived until shortly before his death. S. was obviously influenced by the painting of Roger van der *Weyden, although his style was softer than the Flemish master's. It is known that his work was much in demand, but only a few paintings remain, the most famous being the *Madonna of the Rose Garden* (1473) in the church of St. Martin, Colmar. He is, however, best remembered for his numerous copperplate engravings, which were among the first to give an artistic expression to popular imagery. Over one hundred of these have survived, mostly on religious themes. His reputation attracted the young *Dürer to Colmar, but he arrived in 1492, after S.'s death.

E. Flechsig, *Martin Schongauer* (1951).

SCHÖNSPERGER, JOHANN (1481-1523) German printer. Based in *Augsburg, he was, with *Ratdolt, the most important printer in that city. He is known especially for the books he printed for Emperor *Maximilian I, who named him imperial court printer. In 1513 he completed a sumptuous prayer-book for the Emperor in an edition of ten copies on vellum, using magnificently-designed Gothic type. In 1517 he published Maximilian's own *Theuerdank*.

Madonna With a Rose *a drawing by Martin Schongauer*

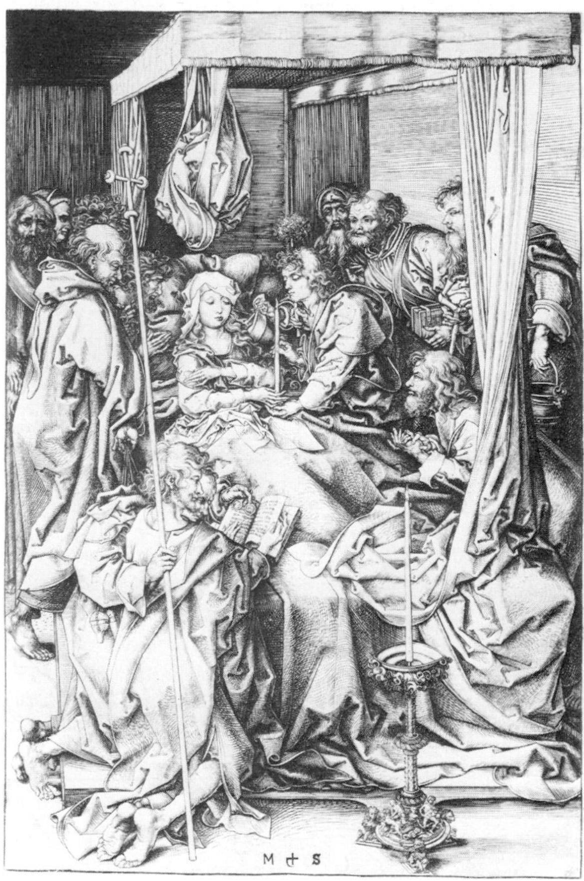

Death of the Virgin *engraving by Martin Schongauer*

SCHÜTZ, HEINRICH (1585-1672) German composer. He completed his musical education in Venice (1609-12), where he was influenced by Giovanni *Gabrieli. In 1612 he became court organist at Cassel, and after 1617 served as musical arranger and conductor at the Saxon court in Dresden. One of the foremost exponents of the *Baroque in music, S. especially developed the Passion, a musical setting for the narrative of the redemptive sufferings of Christ, which he divided among several vocal soloists, each portraying a different character. Considered an essential link between Renaissance and the "classical" music of the 18th century, his work exercised a particular influence on Johann Sebastian Bach (1685-1750).

SCHWANK German word, meaning a hoax or a comic tale, denoting a popular form in German Renaissance literature. A continuation of a mediaeval tradition, the *Schwänke* were collections of comic anecdotes that frequently included crude and obscene elements. A number of these would be told in connection with a certain personality, the most famous being the legendary Till Eulenspiegel, identified with a peasant adventurer

Portrait of a Woman *by Jan van Scorel*

who probably lived in the 14th century. Other famous *Schwänke* were created by *Pauli and *Wickram. Hans *Sachs versified his *Schwänke* and charged them with moral meaning.

H. Fischer, ed., *Schwankerzählungen des deutschen Mittelalters* (1967).

SCHWENKFELD, CASPAR (1489-1561) German radical reformer and mystic. A native of Silesia, he was of a noble family. He was impressed, early in the Reformation, by the ideas of *Luther, to which he gave a highly spiritual interpretation. In 1522 he visited *Wittenberg, but he soon came to oppose Luther's views on the Eucharist, and the concept of *justification by faith, stressing the inward baptism of the spirit. In 1529, forced to leave his estate in Silesia, he became a travelling preacher, going to *Strassburg and other cities of southern Germany. His major work, *Konfession und Erklärung*, was published in 1540. It upheld a mystical doctrine of the deification of Christ's humanity. Persecuted by Protestants and Roman Catholics alike, S. died in Ulm, but his small group of followers survived as a religious sect in Silesia, and in the 18th century established a community in North America.

P. L. Maier, *Caspar Schwenkfeld on the Person and Work of Christ* (1959).

SCIENTIFIC REVOLUTION, THE A term commonly employed to describe the changes in scientific theory and methodology in the 16th and 17th centuries. Broadly viewed, it resulted from the repudiation of the concept of science as a finite body of knowledge derived from classical antiquity and treated as an extension of philosophy. Its pioneers were the bold 16th-century innovators who broke new ground in several scientific branches. *Copernicus, who introduced the heliocentric theory, *Paracelsus, who rejected the old medical theories, and *Vesalius, who systematized the study of *anatomy, made possible the emergence of science as a vocation. In the second half of the 16th century, Tycho *Brahe, Simon *Stevin, Johann *Kepler and *Galileo Galilei further contributed to the new scientific studies of *astronomy and mechanics by direct observation. Advances in *mathematics and the use of many new instruments, especially the *telescope, enabled these scientists to pursue their researches employing measurable and demonstrable methods. Philosophically, the new scientific methodology was expressed by Francis *Bacon, who urged that science be based on experience and that the experimental method become the key to increased knowledge. Early in the 17th century the S. gathered momentum with Harvey's discovery of the circulation of the blood (1628), and further progress in physiology became possible presently through the use of the microscope. In the 17th century important contributions to science and scientific methodology were made by René Descartes (1596-1650), Blaise Pascal (1623-62), Robert Boyle (1627-91), Gottfried Wilhelm Leibniz (1661-1729) and Isaac Newton (1642-1727).

H. F. Kearney, *Origins of the Scientific Revolution* (1964);

M. Boas, *The Scientific Renaissance, 1450-1630* (1962).

SCOREL, JAN VAN (1495-1562) Dutch painter, architect and humanist. Born in Schoorl, Holland, he was the son of a priest. He studied painting from the early age, first at Alkmaar and then in Amsterdam and Utrecht. In 1518 he began a period of wandering, during which he studied briefly with Albrecht *Dürer. His first patron was Count Cristoforo Frangipani, for whom he painted an altarpiece (1520). In the fall of 1520 he went to Jerusalem, with a group of Dutch pilgrims, and remained there for several months. The following year he went to Rome (1521), where he was patronized by Pope *Adrian VI, whose portrait he painted. In Rome he studied the works of *Raphael and *Michelangelo, and the influence affected his style for the rest of his life. Back in the Netherlands, he was appointed a canon in Utrecht. He devoted his time to painting and was quite successful. His paintings include many landscapes. In addition, he worked on the restoration of the church of St. Mary's in Utrecht, and on cleaning the Van *Eyck altarpiece in Ghent. S.'s works mark the transition in Dutch painting from 15th-century realism to the new form of the northern style of High Renaissance.

G. J. Hoogewerf, *Jan van Scorel* (1923). (ND)

SCOT, REGINALD (1538-99) English writer. Born into a noble family of Kent, he studied at Oxford but spent his life as a gentleman in his native county. His *Perfect Platform of a Hop-garden* (1574) was the first practical English treatise on hop cultivation. More important was *The Discoverie of Witchcraft* (1584), an exhaustive survey and criticism of contemporary superstitions and persecutions of witches. S. stressed the imaginary nature of suspicions of *witchcraft, and the fact that the majority of the accused were simple, poor and aged persons. His work was answered by, among others, the future *James I who, after he ascended the throne of England, ordered S.'s work burned.

SCOTLAND Scottish history in the 15th and 16th centuries is marked by prolonged internal disorders,

David *by Donatello*

intermittent struggles with England, and the continuation, during most of the period, of the traditional alliance with France. The Stuart line, which had ruled since 1371, tried to strengthen the central authority against the barons. It conducted a long feud with the earls of Douglas, who were subdued in 1452. But the weakness of the monarchy continued. It was partly due to frequent regencies. Every king, until the accession of Charles I (1625), inherited the crown as a minor. Under *James IV a semblance of order was established, and in 1502 he concluded a "treaty of perpetual peace" with England. But when England threatened France, Scotland reverted to its traditional alliance. In 1513 James IV invaded England, only to be defeated and killed at the Battle of Flodden Field. Another disastrous invasion of England took place late in the reign of *James V, who refused to join his uncle *Henry VIII against Rome and remained an ally of France. Again the Scots were defeated, this time at Solway Moss (1542). During the regency of *Mary of Lorraine (1554-60) S. suffered from the intervention of both France and England. French influence over the country aroused resentment, and combined with the decline of the Scottish Roman Catholic Church to promote the cause of Protestant preachers such as John *Knox. The long political crisis thus facilitated the Scottish Reformation. In August 1560 parliament abolished papal authority and adopted a reformed confession of faith. The previous month France and England both withdrew their troops and Scotland was neutralized. When *Mary Queen of Scots came over from France and began her short reign, she was a Catholic sovereign in a Protestant state. But, in 1567 she was forced to abdicate and escaped to England.

The crowns of England and Scotland were united after the death of Elizabeth I (1603), when James VI of S. became also *James I of England. It was a personal union, but subsequently proved to be a turning point in Scottish history.

W. C. Dickinson, *Scotland from the Earliest Times to 1603* (1965);
R. Mitchison, *A History of Scotland* (1970). (ND)

SCRIPTORIS, PAUL (c. 1450-1505) German theologian. Born in Weil, he joined the Observantine branch of the Franciscan order and was educated in Paris. Later he was the guardian of the Franciscan monastery in Tübingen, where he lectured on the theology of Duns Scotus (1265-1308), counting *Wyttenbach and *Staupitz among his listeners. S. studied Greek and was active as a preacher. Although not a humanist, he is sometimes described as an early precursor of the type of German theologian that emerged on the eve of the *Reformation.

SCROTES, GUILLIM (?-1553) Flemish painter. In 1537 he was appointed painter to the regent of the Netherlands, Mary of Hungary. He is known to have painted the portraits of *Charles V and his family and, in 1546, was in the service of *Henry VIII of England. Several portraits of English nobles are ascribed to him, all in a courtly *Italianate style.

SCULPTURE Of all the visual arts in the Renaissance, S. mostly followed the classical models of ancient times. In contrast with *painting, and to an extent also *architecture, there survived a good number of examples, especially of the Roman period. The discovery of

The Presentation to the Temple *by Giovanni Pisano*

great ancient works, such as the Laocoön group and Apollo del Belvedere, helped to maintain the inspiration. In addition, most of the basic techniques, including bronze casting and stone- and wood-carving, had been in existence, although the Renaissance artists improved these and revived distinctive mediums, such as terracotta. But this did not make Renaissance S. any a less innovative – indeed, it was the work of its great masters, like *Donatello and *Michelangelo, rather than the classical remains, that later generations of sculptors came to imitate.

The beginnings of Renaissance S. are usually traced back to late 13th-century Italy, where Nicola *Pisano and his son Giovanni employed classical forms taken from ancient Roman sarcophagi. The classical motif, however, was also used by their contemporary Gothic sculptors in northern Europe, whereas in Italy the work of the Pisani had no real following during the 14th century. While Andrea *Pisano's bronze doors of Florence's Baptistery show the unmistaken influence of *Giotto, *Orcagna, who in 1359 completed the Tabernacle of Orsanmichele, Florence, worked in a flowery Gothic style. The decisive change came in the early 15th century, and is linked to a concrete event, the competition won by *Ghiberti for the second set of bronze doors for the Florence Baptistery (1402). Jacopo della *Quercia, one of the losers in the competition, the only non-Florentine among these pioneers, produced the reliefs in a dramatic classical style in S. Petronio, Bologna. But monumentality, which became the most recognizable quality of the new style, was a contribution of the genius of Donatello. Two works of his in particular influenced the evolution of Renaissance S.: *David* (c. 1434), the first modern free-standing bronze nude, and **Gattamelata* (1443-53), inspired by an ancient Roman monument and the first grandiose bronze outdoor equestrian statue.

A host of 15th-century Florentine sculptors followed Donatello, obviously influenced by him. Yet they all made a distinctive individual contribution: Luca della *Robbia became famous for his glazed terracotta *Madonnas; the *Rosselino brothers and *Desiderio da Settignano executed elegant tombs of humanist figures, a genre further developed by Antonio *Pollaiuolo in his bronze papal tombs at *St. Peter's – the latter was also the first to take an interest in *anatomy and the movement of the human body; while *Verrocchio, creator of the equesterian statue of *Colleoni in Venice, contributed the Renaissance image of energy; *Bertoldo di Giovanni, head of the school in S. Marco's garden, Florence, became the link between the heritage of Donatello and Michelangelo. Among the non-Florentine sculptors of this period, *Bregno in Rome and Francesco *Laurana in Naples, were two of the most outstanding.

Michelangelo dominated the S. of the High Renaissance. He conceived it as chiselling at the block of stone until the statue hidden in it is revealed. Although interested almost exclusively in the human male body, he succeeded in expressing the widest range of emotion; heroism and virility in his early work, restraint and resignation in his later years. Before his absolute command of the medium, would-be rivals, such as Baccio

The Shouting Knight *by Briosco*

*Bandinelli, never posed a real challenge. In fact, a talented admirer like *Cellini realized the futility of emulation, and took up an elegant style, emphasizing technical skill, as exemplified in his bronze *Perseus* in Florence's Loggia dei Lanzi. Another contemporary, who excelled in the casting of bronze, was Andrea *Briosco of Padua. Andrea *Sansovino and his pupil, the sculptor-architect Jacopo *Sansovino represent yet another High Renaissance current of classical monumentality. Yet by mid-16th century, *Mannerism became manifested in S. In Florence it was represented by *Ammanati, and more convincingly, in the virtuoso works of *Giambologna and in Vincenzo *Danti's bronze statues. The *Leoni of Milan, father and son, and Alessandro *Vittoria of Venice, belong to the same period and style.

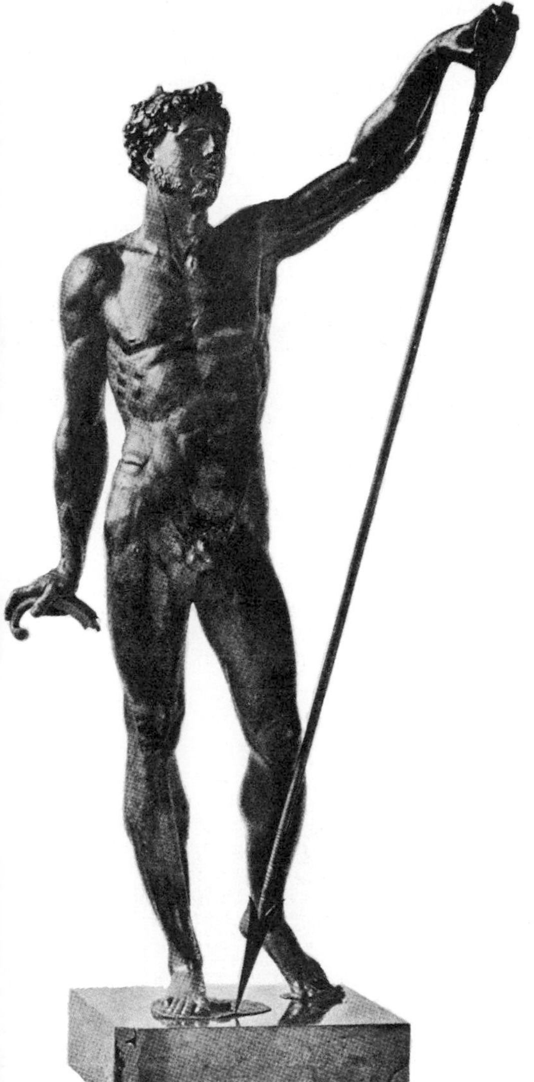

Meleager *by Jacopo Sansovino, a High Renaissance statuette in bronze*

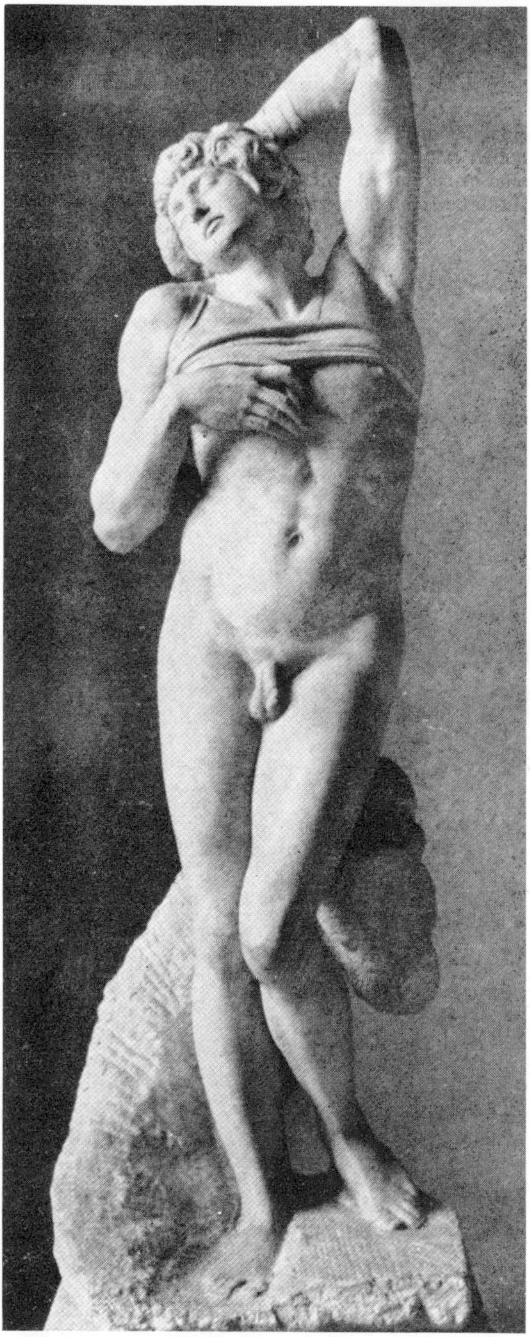

Dying Slave *by Michelangelo*

In northern Europe S. followed a different course. First to break away from mediaeval Gothic and introduce an overpowering realist dimension was the Dutch Claus *Sluter, in his works for the dukes of *Burgundy in the late 14th century. But Sluter's influence was more immediately felt in Flemish painting than in his own medium. North European 15th-century depictions of the **Pietà* and carved tombs actually continued the Gothic tradition, although at times it was highly charged with emotional content; the best example is the sepulchre of Solesme by the French Michel Colombe (1435-95). In Germany a number of great masters enriched the cathedrals of the main towns with elaborate altars, stalls, pulpits and tabernacles, showing a superb skill in wood carving. Among these were Jörg *Syrlin of Ulm and Veit *Stoss, who divided his carreer between Cracow and *Nuremberg. Adam *Kraft and the *Vischer family, also of Nuremberg, produced outstanding works in stone and bronze respectively.

North European sculptors gradually developed a more realistic style of representation, but it was not until the 16th century that they adopted the classically-inspired elegance of the Italians. The change sometimes followed a visit by an Italian master, as in the case of the impact left by Pietro *Torrigiano in England and Spain. Some artists, such as the Spaniard Alonso *Berruguete, acquired the new style in Italy, whereas much later Adriaen de *Vries, a Dutch pupil of Giambologna, propagated Italian Mannerism in several places north of the Alps. The most important sculptor in the High Renaissance style in Germany was Conrad *Meit of Worms, and in the Netherlands, Cornelis *Floris of *Antwerp; but in both cases traces of the late Gothic lingered on. In France, on the other hand, Jean *Goujon and Germain *Pilon achieved a distinctive style that influenced French S. for a long time afterwards. During the *Counter-Reformation, religious inspiration sometimes led to the abandonment of marble and bronze in favour of polychromed wood carving. In Spain this led to the powerful depictions of Christ By Gregorio *Fernández and Juan Martínez *Montañes, as a prelude to the coming *Baroque.

Lead statuette of a seated woman by Adriaen de Vries

C.Gilbert, *History of Renaissance Art* (1973);
G. H. Chase and C. R. Post, *A History of Sculpture* (1924);
H. D. Molesworth, *European Sculpture from Romanesque to Rodin* (1956);
F. Cronheim, *Italian Sculpture, 1250-1700* (1967);
J. Pope-Hennessy, *Italian Renaissance Sculpture,* 2nd ed. (1971);
C. Seymour, *Sculpture in Italy, 1400-1500* (1966).

SEBASTIAN I (1554-78) King of Portugal from 1557. Born in Lisbon after the death of his father, he succeeded his grandfather, *John III, at the age of three. The period of regency ended in 1568, when S. assumed power. Educated by the *Jesuits, and extremely religious, his ambition was to mount a great crusade against the Moslems of North Africa. When a war of succession broke out in Morocco (1578), S. decided to help one of the contenders, hoping thus to lounch his crusade. He organized a force and sailed to Morroco, but at the Battle of Alcacerquivir (4 August 1578) his troops were defeated and he himself was killed. S. left no heirs. After his death his old uncle, Cardinal *Henrique, ruled for a short period and, in 1580, *Philip II invaded Portugal and the country was annexed to Spain. Rumours that S. was still alive led to the formation of a movement called "Sebastianism", which was popular during the years of Spanish domination (1580-1640). Its members held that S. would return and free Portugal from the rule of Spain. There were also several pretenders who claimed to be S. (ND)

SEBASTIANO DE PIOMBO (c.1485-1547) Born Sebastiano Luciani in Venice, he was a pupil and friend of *Giorgione, who influenced his early work. In 1511 he went to Rome and was commissioned by Agostino *Chigi to help in the decoration of the Villa Farnesina, where he painted several *frescoes. He attached himself to Raphael, whose style he imitated in portraits of men and women. Later he came under the influence of *Michelangelo, with whom he corresponded. To this period belongs his powerful *Pietà* (c.1517), with its sculptural figure of the dead Christ. After the Sack of *Rome (1527), he worked in *Mantua and Venice, but in 1531 returned to Rome and was appointed keeper of the papal seal (*il piombo* in Italian, hence his nickname). The best work of his late years are the portraits, executed in a rigorous classical style, yet sensitive and colourful.

L. Dussler, *Sebastiano del Piombo* (1942).

SEGNI, BERNARDO (1504-1558) Italian historian. Born in Florence, he was sent by *Cosimo I as ambassador to the imperial court, and served in various other public offices. He made several translations of classical works, especially of Aristotle and Sophocles, but is chiefly remembered for his two historical works:

St. John Chrysostom Surrounded by Saints
by Sebastiano del Piombo

Istorie fiorentine, being a history of Florence from 1527 to 1555, and *Vita di Niccolò Capponi*. They were first published in 1723.

SEISENEGGER, JACOB (1505-67) German painter. Born in Linz, he became, in 1531, court painter of the *Habsburgs. In the following year he painted a full-length portrait of *Charles V, which was reproduced by *Titian and so admired by the emperor, that he made the latter his official painter. S.'s style was electic, combining Italian and North European influences.

SELIM I (1470-1520) Ottoman Sultan from 1512. Youngest son of *Bayezid II, he revolted against his father and in 1512 dethroned him and vanquished his brothers. He devoted most of his energies to territorial aggrandizement. Being a Sunnite Muslem, he turned against his Shi'ite subjects, slaughtering about 40,000 of them in Anatolia. He then defeated the Shi'ite Persian Shah, Ismail I, at the Battle of Chaldiran in Armenia (23 August 1514). He proceeded against the Mamluk Sultan of Egypt, conquering Syria, Egypt and Palestine. S. almost doubled the area of the Ottoman empire, and he was acknowledged as the protector of the holy cities of Arabia, which made him the leader of the Moslem world. He is described as bloodthirsty and authoritarian, motivated by insatiable military ambitions. He planned to renew the Turkish pressure on Christian Europe, but died while preparing an expedition against Rhodes.

SELIM II (1524-1574) Ottoman sultan from 1566. Son of *Suleiman I and his favourite *Roxelana, he was known as "the Sot". His reign marked the beginning of the downward trend in the power and ability of the Ottoman sultans. Preferring to lead a life of pleasure, he relied on his advisers in affairs of state. Foremost among these was Muhamad *Sökölli, who had been trained by Suleiman and was able to continue his politics and keep the order in the empire. In 1568 a peace treaty was concluded with *Austria, and the Ottomans consolidated their rule in Moldavia and Walachia. In 1570-71 they captured Cyprus from *Venice. This expedition led to a formation of a Christian league which destroyed the Ottoman navy at *Lepanto in October 1571. But the league was unable to defeat the new navy that the Turks quickly put together, and the 1573 peace treaty with Venice recognized the hegemony of the Ottoman empire in the Mediterranean. In 1574 the Ottomans recaptured Tunis, which had been conquered by the Spaniards in 1572. Internally, however, S. could not impose his rule over the *Janissaries. He died when he slipped on the marble floor of his bathroom.

SEPARATISTS A term used in England to denote the groups that separated themselves from the established church. Principally, it referred to the *Independents, a movement which appeared towards the end of the reign of *Elizabeth I, and included the *Brownists and other *Puritan congregations.

SEPULVEDA, JUAN GINES DE (c. 1490-c. 1573) Spanish humanist. Born near Córdoba, he studied there as well as at Alcalá and Bologna. He acquired a wide reputation for his elegant Latin style, and wrote a history of the reign of *Charles V. S. was a follower of Aristotle, whose *Politics* he translated. In his *Democrates alter* he defended the right of Spain to wage war and enslave the American Indians. In 1550 in Valladolid he participated in a debate against *Las Casas, both contestants claiming victory at the end.

A. F. G. Bell, *Juan Ginés de Sepúlveda* (1924);
L. Hanke, *The Spanish Struggle for Justice in the Conquest of America* (1949), 110-132.

SERCAMBI, GIOVANNI (1348-1424) Italian writer and statesman. Born in Lucca, he was a supporter of the ruling family, the Guinigi, and served as soldier and public official. He is known mainly for his *Novelle,* 155 short stories, often witty and licentious, set in a similar framework as *Boccaccio's *Decameron*. He also wrote the *Croniche delle cose di Lucca*, a history of the city from 1164 to 1423, and *Monito*, a tract on government.

G. Beretta, *Contributo all'opera novellistica di Giovanni Sercambi* (1968).

SERDINI, SIMONE (c. 1360-c. 1420) Italian poet. Born in Siena, he spent many unhappy years in the service of princely patrons, and ended by taking his own life in prison. He wrote love poems and moralistic ones, filled with mythological imagery, and bitter songs railing at his ill fortune. His work is highly influenced by *Dante.

SERIPANDO, GIROLAMO (1493-1563) Italian theologian, general of the Augustinian order, cardinal and legate at the Council of *Trent. Born probably in Naples, he entered the Augustinian monastery of San Giovanni a Carbonara in Naples in 1507. He was elected general of the order in 1539. He served as a theological councillor in the early sessions of the Council of Trent, where his contributions were of great value. S. emphasized the superiority of the Scriptures over tradition, and the importance of the study of biblical languages. In 1554 he was elected archbishop

The Castle of Ancy-le-Franc by Serlio

of Salerno. In 1561 he was created cardinal and sent as a legate to the Council of Trent by Pope *Pius IV. In the Council he principally directed the work on the dogmatic decrees. A conflict with the pope, arising from his view that a bishop should live at his diocese, led to his recall, but he died suddenly in Trent. S. left many works, including commentaries on *Paul's Epistle to the Galatians* and *Epistle to the Romans*, and commentaries on the Council of Trent.

SERLIO, SEBASTIANO (1475-1554) Italian architect. Born in Bologna, he went to Rome where he became the student of *Peruzzi. After the Sack of *Rome (1527), he moved to *Venice and, about 1540, accepted an invitation to go to France, where he advised on the building of *Fontainebleau. His historical importance, however, derives from his books – a series, *L'Architettura*, was published in six parts between 1537 and 1551. It was based on material left by his master Peruzzi. Though the books were of a practical nature, consisting of a group of architectural models, they had a considerable influence on the diffusion of the High Renaissance Italian style throughout Europe. His ideas were followed in particular by French architects.

SERVETUS, MICHAEL (1511-53) Spanish physician and martyred theologian. The son of a royal notary, he was born in Tudela. He studied at Toulouse and then travelled to Bologna, *Basle and *Strassburg, where he met *Bucer. In 1531 he published *De trinitatis erroribus libri VII*, in which he challenged the accepted definitions of the Trinity, and which caused him to be described as a heretic. S. then turned to medicine, a field in which he developed many new ideas, especially on the circulation of the blood. Between 1541 and 1553 he was physician to the archbishop of Vienne. In his final year he published a new work, *Christianismi restitutio*, wherein he put forward his ideas denying the divinity of Christ. Arrested by the *Inquisition in Vienne, he escaped, but was condemned in his absence by civil authorities in *Lyon, on evidence partly supplied by *Calvin. It is not clear why he went to *Geneva – perhaps he hoped for support from the opposition to Calvin. However, he was recognized and arrested and, after refusing to recant, was burnt at the stake (27 October 1553).

J. Fulton, *Michael Servetus; Humanist and Martyr* (1953);
R. H. Bainton, *Hunted Heretic: The Life and Death of Servetus* (1953).

SEVILLE The chief city of Andalusia, its location and link with the Atlantic via the Guadalquivir River gave it a natural economic predominance in southern Spain. The city was reconquered by the Christians in 1248 and, by the 15th century, had become a commercial centre for Spain and other Mediterranean lands. The discovery of America made S. into one of the major ports of Europe. it was here that the *Casa de Contratación was located, and all shipping to and from the New World directed. S.'s population, estimated at about 70,000 in 1500, more than doubled during the next hundred years. In that time it also acquired a university and a number of important printing houses. In the early 16th century it displayed its new prosperity by completing the building of the then largest cathedral in Europe. S. also became an important artistic centre of poetry, painting and woodcarving. But while its commercial life reached its zenith in the first years of the 17th century, most of the products which left its port were of foreign manufacture. Spanish industry failed to feed S. with the goods it needed in order to keep up its *mercantilist functions. The city then began a gradual decline.

H. and P. Chaunu, *Seville et l'Atlantique*, 8 vols. (1955).

SEYSSEL, CLAUDE DE (1450-1520) French jurist and political thinker. Born in Aix le Bain in the Savoy, he became a minister of King *Louis XII, chancellor of

Titlepage of Serlio's Architettura *published in Venice*

France and ambassador to England. S. lauded the king in his *Histoire singuliere de Louis XII* (1508), and *Les louanges de Louis XII* (1508). His best-known book is *Le grant monarchie de France* (1518), written during his retirement at the request of Louis' successor, King *Francis I. The book is considered the best example of French political thought in the early 16th century. S.'s position on the French monarchy and constitution was favourable. He viewed the French constitution as containing checks and balances, and maintained that the king's power was circumscribed by religion, existing rules and custom. S.'s ideas were influential during the 16th century, and later French political thinkers commented on them and expanded them.

J. H. Hexter, *The Vision of Politics on the Eve of the Reformation; More, Macchiavelli and Seyssel* (1973).

SFORZA The ducal dynasty which ruled *Milan from 1450 to 1499 and, with interruptions, until 1535, producing also a number of rulers of lesser principalities, as well as prelates and military commanders. The founder of the house was a wealthy peasant from the vicinity of Ravenna, Muzio Attendolo (1369-1424), who became a *condottiere*, and was given the appellation *Sforza*, meaning strength. His natural son Francesco, also a *condottiere*, became in 1450 duke of Milan, and was succeeded by his son Galeazzo Maria in 1466. In the meantime, Francesco's brother Alessandro (1409-73), had in 1445 taken possession of Pesaro in the *Papal States, a territory which was ruled by his descendants until 1512.

The main branch of the Sforzas in Milan had its heyday under *Ludovico il Moro, but after his fall in 1499 the fortunes of the family declined sharply. His two sons, Massimiliano (1493-1530) and Francesco Maria (1495-1535), rulers of Milan in the years 1512-15 and 1522-34 respectively, had to rely on Swiss mercenaries and imperial troops, and were no more than puppets. With the death of Francesco Maria the family's role in Italian politics came to an end.

C. M. Ady, *History of Milan under the Sforza* (1907); G. Franciosi, *Gli Sforza* (1931).

SFORZA, CATERINA (c.1463-1509) Italian countess of Forli, a natural daughter of Galeazzo Maria *Sforza. In 1477 she married Girolamo *Riario, nephew of *Sixtus IV who, in 1480, received from his uncle Forli and Imola. After her husband was murdered (1488), she fiercely defended herself and continued to rule Forli on behalf of her son Ottaviano. She was aided by Jacopo Feo, her lover, and succeeded in crushing another uprising, when the latter was slain (1495). Shortly afterwards she married Giovanni de' *Medici, of the Florentine family, who died, too, but by whom she had a son, the future **condottiere* Giovanni delle Bande Nere. In 1499 she had to leave Forli and take shelter in a nearby fortress, where she was besieged for several months by Cesare *Borgia, before being taken captive. Released in 1501, she subsequently retired to Florence, where she died. Called a virago by contemporaries she was also admired for her beauty and courage.

SFORZA, FRANCESCO (1401-66) Duke of *Milan. The illegitimate son of the **condottiere* Muzio Attendolo, he followed in his father's footsteps and, after serving Queen *Joanna II of Naples, went to fight for Filippo Maria *Visconti of *Milan (1426). During the next 20 years he several times left Visconti and entered the service of his enemies, but each time was recalled. In 1432 Visconti betrothed his only child, the eight-year-old Maria Bianca, to S., but the marriage took place only in 1441. Even then relations between S. and his father-in-law were so stormy that in the last three years of Visconti's life S. fought against him, on the side of *Venice; he was about to change sides again in 1447, when he received news of Visconti's death. S. then became the general of the Ambrosian Republic, which was declared by the inhabitants of Milan. But, in 1450, he seized power in the city and became its sole ruler. After the Peace of *Lodi (1454), he steered Milan through a period of tranquil prosperity, expanding his territories by a clever series of alliances which led, in 1464, to the inclusion of *Genoa. S. employed the humanist *Filelfo and the architect *Filarete, but although he promoted Renaissance culture in his court, he himself always adhered to the dignified frugal mode of his martial years.

SFORZA, GALEAZZO MARIA (1444-76) Duke of *Milan. The son of Francesco *Sforza, he was in France, fighting the League of the *Public Weal at the side of *Louis XI, when his father died. He hastily returned and assumed the government of Milan. An intelligent and cultured person, he promoted the silk industry and the cultivation of rice, and made his court a centre of humanist learning and arts. But he was also capable of cruelties, such as banishing and probably poisoning his mother Maria Bianca *Visconti, and he led an extravagant and dissolute life. His main accomplishment was keeping Milan at peace. He was murdered in church by three conspirators.

SFORZA, GIAN GALEAZZO (1469-94) Duke of *Milan. In 1476, aged seven, he succeeded his father Galeazzo Maria *Sforza, but was actually under the guardianship of his uncle *Ludovico il Moro who, in 1489, arranged his marriage with Isabella, granddaughter of King *Ferrante I of Naples. S. never actually wielded power as duke, and when he died it was rumoured that he had been poisoned by his uncle. His daughter Bona (1493-1557) became the wife of *Sigismund I, king of Poland.

SFUMATO Italian for smoked, a word employed by *Leonardo to describe the manner in which he blended colours by soft stages. so as to make the transition from one to the other almost imperceptible. The softness of contour thus achieved became a characteristic element of High Renaissance *painting, and was adopted by *Raphael and others.

SHAKESPEARE, WILLIAM (1564-1616) English dramatist and poet, who for the last two centuries has been regarded the foremost playwright of Western culture. S. was born in Stratford-on-Avon, Warwickshire, the son of a glove-maker who, in 1568, served as high bailiff of the town, but who later sank into debt. Educated probably at Stratford's grammar school, he married Anne Hathaway in 1582, and less than nine months later the couple's first child, Susanna, was born. In 1585 were born the twins, Hamnet and Judith. Nothing more is known about S. until 1592, when Robert *Greene described him as an "upstart crow, beautified with our feathers", thereby attesting his presence in London as a successful actor and playwright. His first published work, *Venus and Adonis* (1593) was a narrative poem on amatory themes, dedicated to the young Earl of Southampton. It was followed by *The Rape of Lucrece* (1594), dedicated to the same patron; both works were written during the closure of the theatres on account of the plague. Also to this period (about 1594-96) belong most of his 154 **Sonnets*, which seem to have circulated for a long time in manuscript, and published in 1609 without the author's permission. Divided into three quartains and a final couplet, many of these poems are either addressed or refer to a young gentleman, possibly the same Earl of Southampton.

In 1594 S. joined the Lord Chamberlain's Men, one of the two theatrical companies of London – the other was called the Lord Admiral's Men. He wrote and acted, and soon became a leading member of the company and one of its shareholders. In 1599, when the company leased the Globe Theatre, S.'s interest in the property amounted to one tenth. Upon the accession of *James I the company changed its name to The King's Men and, in 1608, took over the Blackfriars' Theatre, where S.'s initial interest was one-seventh. This gave him a comfortable income, at least until 1613, when the Globe was destroyed by fire. He bought a large house in his native town (1597) and made other acquisitions. As an actor he took part in plays by other authors, such as Ben *Johnson's *Every Man in His Humour* (1598) and *Sejanus* (1603). Thereafter he probably devoted himself to writing and, about 1610, retired to Stratford, where he continued to write until 1612. Although he lived on his own in London for a long time, S. seems to have led a quiet life, keeping away from turbulent tavern gatherings. He is mentioned as witness in two law-suits, but otherwise left a sober and stolid image, quite unlike that of Johnson or *Marlowe.

The bulk of S.'s literary output consists in the following 37 plays: *Henry VI Parts 1, 2 and 3* (written about 1590); *Richard III* (1592); *The Comedy of Errors* (1592); *Titus Andronicus* (1593); *The Taming of the Shrew* (1593); *The Two Gentlemen of Verona* (1594); *Love's Labour's Lost* (1594); *Romeo and Juliet* (1594); *Richard II* (1595); *A Midsummer Night's Dream* (1595); *King John* (1596); *The Merchant of Venice* (1596); *Henry IV, Parts 1 and 2* (1597); *Much Ado About Nothing* (1598); *Henry V* (1598); *Julius Caesar* (1599); *As You Like It* (1599); *Twelfth Night* (1599); *Hamlet* (1600); *The Merry Wives of Windsor* (1600); *Troilus and Cressida* (1601); *All's Well That Ends Well* (1602); *Measure for Measure* (1604); *Othello* (1604); *King Lear* (1605); *Macbeth* (1605); *Antony and Cleopatra* (1606); *Coriolanus* (1607); *Timon of Athens* (1607); *Pericles* (1608); *Cymbeline* (1609); *The Winter's Tale* (1610); *The Tempest* (1611); *Henry VIII* (probably with John Fletcher, 1612). Twenty of the plays were first published in cheap quarto editions, some with badly corrupt texts. The first collected edition, known as the First Folio, was published in 1623. The first edition to divide the plays into acts and scenes was that of Nicholas Rowe (1709).

S. used several identifiable sources. For the plays based on English history he relied mainly on *Holinshed's *Chronicles of England, Scotland and Ireland* (1586). For his Roman tragedies he used *North's translation of Plutarch's *Lives*. Some of his themes were based on works by earlier English authors., such as John *Gower, and some borrowed from his English or foreign contemporaries, including the Italians *Ariosto, *Bandello and Giraldi Cinthio, and the Spaniard *Montemayor. His dramatic art is usually divided into four main periods: the plays written before 1594 suggest an experimental stage, the comedies being imitative and excessively farcical, and the tragedies and histories lacking depth and characterization. Between 1594 and 1599 there are English histories and romantic comedies, where the elements of emotion, mood and idyllic atmosphere begin to assert themselves, but are not yet fully integrated. In the following decade S. wrote his most powerful works, including *Hamlet, Othello, King Lear* and *Macbeth*, in which he dealt with universal moral questions in intense and polished dramatic form. The last plays, written between 1608 and 1612, are mainly tragi-comedies, or "romances", in which grace and romantic charm are used to resolve melodramatic plots of tragic potential.

William Shakespeare

S.'s plays are far from flawless: there are gaps in the construction of the plots, and they frequently betray the haste in which they were written. Their greatness is due to the playwright's linguistic virtuosity and his profound understanding of human nature. As his style evolved, the flowery language of the early plays matured into poetic metaphors, without suffering a diminution of range, which still encompassed obscenity and the sublime. While not attempting to impart moral truths, the plays dealt with the most fundamental problems of human behaviour; lust for power, love, friendship, jealousy, and tension between the individual and the surrounding society, are portrayed in a manner which has lost none of its freshness. During the 19th century, the fact, that S.'s formal education ended with grammar school gave rise to speculations, that the real author of the plays was someone of noble descent, or at least a university graduate. The most famous of these theories is the one which ascribed the plays to Francis *Bacon. Contemporary scholarship has rejected these theories, but certain elusive qualities about S., the man and playwright, are bound to remain an added attraction of his work.

E. Chambers, *A Short Life of William Shakespeare* (1935);
H. Craig, *An Interpretation of Shakespeare* (1948);
F. E. Halliday, *Shakespeare in His Age* (1956);
M. R. Martin and R. C. Harrier, *The Concise Encyclopedic Guide to Shakespeare* (1972);
A. L. Rowse, *Shakespeare the Man* (1973);
S. Schoenbaum, *William Shakespeare; A Documentary Life* (1975).

SHAXTON, NICHOLAS (c. 1485-1556) Bishop of Salisbury. Educated at Cambridge, he was a member of the university committee which supported the divorce of *Henry VIII from *Catherine of Aragon (1530). Later he became a protegé of *Cromwell's and supported the Act of *Supremacy. This resulted in his appointment to the see of Salisbury (1535). An ardent Protestant, he resigned his see in 1539 because of his opposition to the *Six Articles. In 1546 he was imprisoned with others on a charge of heresy and, to save himself from the stake, recanted and preached at the burning of several of his companions. In spite of the accession of *Edward VI he did not return to his former views, and under *Mary Tudor was reappointed to an ecclesiastical office and took part in the suppression of Protestants.

SHIPS AND SHIPBUILDING The Renaissance, which saw tremendous advances in the art of *navigation, and great feats of sea *exploration, was also a time of significant developments in the design and building of ships. In about 1400 European ships were still structurally inferior to those used in many parts of the East. Indeed, the innovations which were to establish European supremacy on the seas during the next two centuries, were to a great extent the result of borrowings, adaptions and subsequent improvements of foreign models. The standard Mediterranean vessel of the 15th century was still the *galley, combining oars and sails. At that time the Portuguese, followed by Castilians, were developing the *caravel, a smaller and faster craft, which came to be the preferred vessel for ocean sailing. In the 16th century the lessons learned in the early voyages made possible the construction of a larger ship, known as *galleon, serviceable both in commerce and naval warfare.

The evolution of ship design during this period was strongly affected by the introduction of the lateen rig, resulting in changes in the number of masts and the shape of the hull. Mediaeval ships, already equipped with rudders, had used a single mast and a square sail;

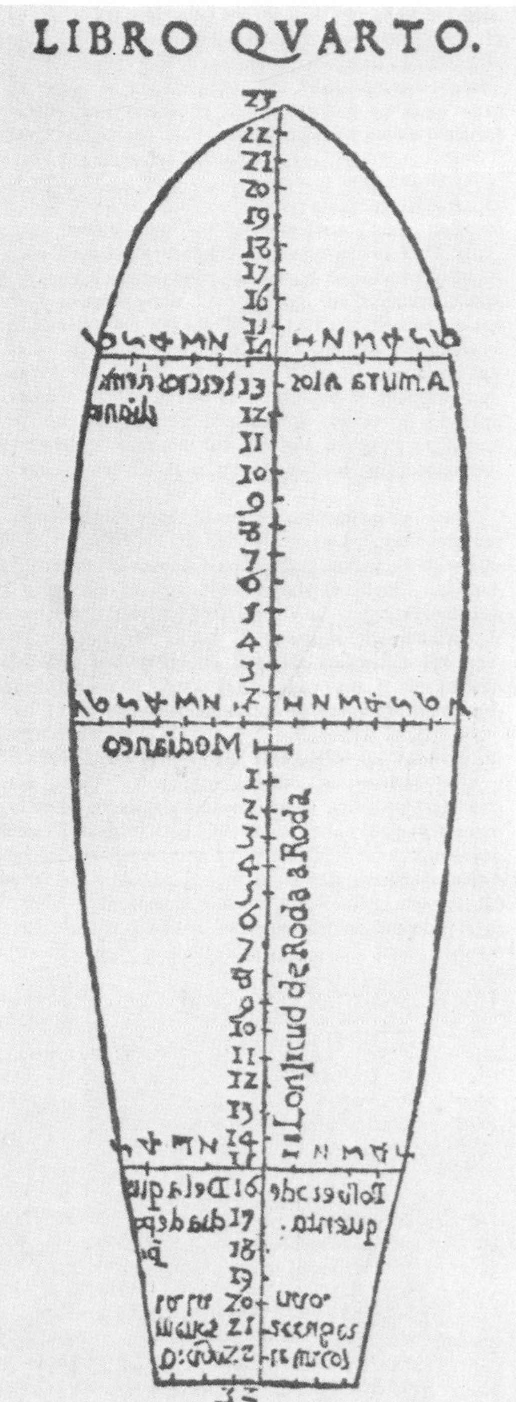

A ship's plan, from a Spanish work published in 1587

they could be quite large, but lacked manoeuvrability. The triangular lateen rig, used by the Arabs and adopted by the Portuguese, could, by simple adjustments, make

The Venetian "Arsenal" shipyard in 1500; detail from a print by Jacopo de' Barbari

a ship sail under almost any wind conditions. Moreover, it permitted the use of more than one mast, and their number was increased first to two, then to three, each carrying a single lateen sail. Towards the end of the 15th century Iberian ship designers began to combine lateen and square rigs. This allowed them to increase the size of their vessels to suit long ocean voyages. Thus, the *caravela redonda*, used by *Columbus and Vasco da *Gama, carried square sails on the foremast. Later, this successful combination of lateen and square rigs was extended to big ships such as the galleon, with four and five masts.

A second innovation which influenced ship design was naval *artillery. Mediaeval battle ships had fore and aft castles designed to facilitate boarding of enemy ships. When guns made their appearance, they were mounted in these castles. But as it was impossible to carry many guns on top without affecting the ship's balance, later designs placed the heavy guns closer to the waterline, firing through portholes in the ship's side. The first to employ this revolutionary arrangement were the French early in the 16th century. It became a standard design, and big ships would carry tiers of guns between several decks. The development of broadside artillery caused in turn a change of construction. In big Spanish ships especially, the waterline width was almost twice as much as that of the upper deck.

Shipbuilding became an important industry. The Venetian Arsenal, for example, was a state-owned shipyard which, in the mid-16th century, covered some sixty acres of buildings, land and docks and employed over 10,000 skilled workers. Hierarchically

A late 16th-century English drawing for the construction of a ship

organized and closely supervised by the Venetian senate, it was Europe's first great industrial establishment. Lisbon, too, had a large shipyard which, as late as the last quarter of the 16th century, built vessels, then believed to be the largest in the world. The English royal dockyard and naval station was established in the early 16th century at Woolwich, near London. It was here that Henry Grace à Dieu was launched (1514, and rebuilt 1536), an enormous vessel reputed to exceed 1,000 tons. It had five masts and two tiers of guns on the broadsides, but was not yet fully shaped as a galleon and is usually called a carrack. The big ships of the English fleet which defeated the Spanish *Armada (1588) were smaller in size, but already surpassed their opponents in manoeuvrability and effective deployment of their guns.

F. C. Lane, *Venetian Ships and Shipbuilders of the Renaissance* (1934);
R. Anderson, *The Sailing Ship; Six Thousand Years of History* (1927);
F. C. Bowen, *From Carrack to Clipper* (1948);
C. E. Gibson, *The Story of Ships* (1949).

SHIRLEY, JOHN (c. 1366-1456) English collector of manuscripts. Believed to have travelled widely in foreign countries, he made translations from Latin into English, and is chiefly known as the transcriber of the works of *Chaucer and *Lydgate.

H. S. Bennett, *Chaucer and the 15th Century* (1947).

SHUTE, JOHN (?-1563) English painter of miniatures and writer on architecture. In 1550 he was sent to Italy by his patron, the duke of *Northumberland, and there collected material for his survey of the art of building, *The First and Chief Groundes of Architecture* (1563). Influenced by the writings of *Serlio, it had four editions during the next 15 years.

SICILY After the Sicilian Vespers, the great revolt of 1282, the island passed into the rule of the kings of *Aragon. According to the settlement reached in 1302 between the Aragonese and the Angevin dynasty of *Naples, the latter retained the title of "Kings of the Island of Sicily", whereas Frederick II (1296-1337), and Frederick III (1355-77) after him, agreed to style themselves "Kings of Trinacria". The second half of the 14th century, however, was marked by dynastic feuds among the Aragonese, until, in 1412, Ferdinand I (1412-16) incorporated Sicily into the crown of Aragon. This was followed by the introduction of the office of viceroy in 1415, ruling on behalf of the king. But the local barons remained powerful and the Sicilian parliaments were regularly summoned.

S. enjoyed a period of economic and cultural activity under *Alfonso V (1416-58), who made it a base for his conquest of Naples, encouraged humanism in Palermo, and founded a school in Catania. After his death the island was again separated from Naples, but they were reunited in 1503 by *Ferdinand the Catholic. Early in his reign, *Charles V faced a revolt (1516), which later assumed a popular dimension, causing the baronial class to align itself on the side of the viceroys. For the rest of the 16th century the population increasingly felt the pressure of the Spanish administration. The *Inquisition was introduced and the *parlamenti* lost some of their autonomy. Resentment against foreign domination finally broke out in a great popular uprising in Palermo in 1647. But Sicily was to remain under the Spanish crown until the Treaty of Utrecht (1713).

G. Ganci Battaglia, *Storia di Sicilia* (1960);
D. MacSmith, *Medieval Sicily, 800-1713* (1968);
H. Koenigsberger, *The Government of Sicily Under Philip II* (1951).

SICKINGEN, FRANZ VON (1481-1523) German leader of the *Knights' War. Born into a noble family in the fortress of Ebernburg near Worms, he became a captain of mercenary troops, whom he sometimes employed to plunder merchants. Before he decided to support the election of *Charles V to the imperial throne in 1519, S. had fought in the service of *Francis I of France and carried on an open war against the towns of Worms and Metz. The Emperor gave him the title of councillor. Shortly afterwards S. was persuaded by Ulrich von *Hutten to back *Reuchlin in his controversy with the conservative Dominicans, and offer his protection to the followers of *Luther. In 1422, with Hutten as his political mentor and Martin *Bucer his chaplain, S. led an army against Richard von Greiffenklau, archbishop of Trier, announcing the complete secularization of all ecclesiastical principalities. But his campaign failed, the union of imperial knights proved ineffective and he was declared an outlaw by the imperial governing council. In May 1523 he died from his wounds at the castle of Landstuhl, which was beleaguered by electors of the Palatinate and Trier and the landgrave of Hesse.

W. R. Hitchcock, *The Background of the Knights' Revolt* (1958).

SIDNEY, SIR PHILIP (1554-86) English writer, soldier and courtier. The son of Sir Henry Sidney, whom *Elizabeth I made governor of *Ireland, and nephew of the earl of *Leicester, he married the daughter of Sir Francis *Walsingham. Young S. travelled in Europe, became a favourite of the Queen and was described as the ideal courtier; cultured, loyal and brave. He wrote *In Defense of Poesie* (1580), a beautiful essay in which he championed poetic imagination, and the *Arcadia*, published posthumously (1590), a *pastoral romance in prose on love and chivalry. His sonnet sequel *Astrophel and Stella* (1591) was also widely admired. In 1585 he went with Leicester to the Netherlands and was mortally wounded at the Battle of *Zutphen. Dying, it is said, he gallantly refused a cup of water, giving it to another wounded soldier.

J. G. Nichols, *The Poetry of Sir Philip Sidney* (1974);
M. W. Wallace, *The Life of Sir Philip Sidney* (1515; rep. 1967).

SIENA During the 13th and part of the 14th century, this city-state in Tuscany was an important commercial centre rivalling its northern neighbour, *Florence. The rivalry was not only economic, but political, since S. was pro-imperial (Ghibelline), and Florence mainly pro-papal (Guelf). In 1260 S. defeated Florence at Montaperti, but turned Guelf in 1268 after its defeat at Tagliacozzo. Through the 14th and 15th centuries, S.'s commerce and banking were in decline. Investments were taken elsewhere and, unlike Florence, S. did not recuperate well from the Black Death which had hit it in 1348, and probably halved its population. In addition, Florence blocked its northern routes to the rest of Europe.

S. was under oligarchic rule for about two centuries, and internal strife among the classes was endemic. Between 1487 and 1512 the city was ruled by Pandolfo *Petrucci, an exiled aristocrat who seized power. He formed alliances with Florence and France, and tried to restore order, but his methods were brutal and despotic. His family continued to rule until 1524, and then the Sienese sought the protection of Emperor *Charles V. Subjection to the Holy Roman Empire led to renewed fights and revolts, and in 1552 the Emperor's forces were driven out. In 1554 Spanish forces besieged the city, which held out for a whole year before succumbing. Philip II then gave S. to *Cosimo I (1557), making it a part of the grand duchy of Tuscany.

S. played an important part in the development of Renaissance art. In the 14th century the Sienese school produced great artists, such as *Duccio di Buoninsegna, Simone *Martini, the *Lorenzetti brothers and Lipo *Memmi. Its art preserved an affinity with the Gothic style until the end of the 15th century, though it also had admirers of the classical style, such as the sculptor Jacopo della *Quercia. The last great painters of Renaissance S. were *Beccafumi and *Sodoma.

F. Schevill, *Siena; the History of a Medieval Commune* (1909; rep. 1964);
T. Burckhardt, *Siena; the City of the Virgin* (1960);
E. G. Gardner, *The Story of Siena and San Gemignano* (1926). (ND)

SIFERWAS, JOHN Flemish illuminator, active in England from about 1380 to 1421. His chief work was the *Louterell Psalter*, today at the British Museum. He is also credited with the decoration of the Missal of the Monastery of Sherborne.

SIGISMUND (1368-1432) Holy Roman emperor from 1410. Born in *Nuremberg, he was a younger son of Emperor Charles IV (1346-78). Upon his father's death he became the margrave of Brandenburg. In 1385 he married Maria, daughter of King Louis I of Hungary and Poland and, in 1387, was crowned king of Hungary, while the Polish crown went to Louis' younger daughter, Jadwiga. In 1396 S. fought against the Turks who attacked Serbia and Bulgaria, but was defeated at Nicopolis. In 1400 his brother, Emperor *Wenceslas, was deposed by the German princes and ten years later his successor Rupert died. S. was then elected king of Germany and crowned in 1414 at Aachen. His greatest achievement was the convening of the Council of *Constance (1414-18) which ended the *Great Schism. S. invited Jan *Hus to defend his views at the council, promising him a safe-conduct, but then accepted the council's verdict that Hus was a heretic and approved his execution. When Wenceslas died (1419), S. inherited the Bohemian crown, but was crowned only in 1436 because of the *Hussite Wars. The King and the German princes were unable to defeat the Hussites, and a compromise was achieved in the *compactata* of Prague (1433). That year he was crowned emperor by Pope *Eugenius IV. The last emperor of the house of Luxemburg, he was succeeded by his son-in-law Albert V of Habsburg, duke of Austria. The imperial throne became then hereditary in the house of *Habsburg. (ND)

SIGISMUND I (1467-1548) King of Poland from 1506. The son of *Casimir IV and Elizabeth of Habsburg, he ruled Glogow, Silesia, from 1499, and became margrave of Lusatia and governor of Silesia in 1504. Two years later he succeeded his brother Alexander as king of Poland and grand duke of Lithuania. He was at war against Muscovy almost throughout his reign. In 1535 the Polish army defeated the invading forces of *Ivan IV, but failed to take Smolensk. Conflicts with the *Teutonic Knights in Prussia ended when, in 1521, Poland subdued the order. In 1525 the order was dissolved, and Polish suzerainty over Prussia was confirmed. Four years later the duchy of Mazovia was annexed to the Polish state. Domestically, S. was at odds with the *Szlachta*, and relied for support on the great nobles. During his reign the peasants lost most of their rights, and ultimately became serfs. S. was tolerant toward non-Catholics and protected the Greek Orthodox subjects and the *Jews. Poland expanded during his reign, both economically and culturally; its connection with Italy and the influence of the Italian Renaissance being enhanced by S.'s marriage to Bona *Sforza, daughter of the duke of Milan. (ND)

SIGISMUND II (1520-72) King of Poland from 1548. In 1530 he was declared co-ruler with his father, *Sigismund I. He ruled Lithuania from 1544 and four years later succeeded to the Polish throne as well. S. had to face the threats of the *Ottoman empire and *Russia. He succeeded in ending the Russian attacks on the lands of the *Livonian order by concluding the Treaty of Vilna (1561), which integrated the Livonia into Lithuania. His great achievement was the transformation of the personal union between Poland and Lithuania into a hereditary one. By the Union of *Lublin (1569), Poland and Lithuania were formally joined. Domestically, S. continued the policy of religious tolerance of his father, in spite of the growing strength of the *Reformation. He married three times but remained childless, and was therefore the last of the *Jagiellonian dynasty. (ND)

SIGISMUND III VASA (1566-1632) King of Poland from 1587 and of Sweden from 1592 to 1599. Son of King *John III Vasa of Sweden and Catherine of Poland, he was given a Roman Catholic education, which facilitated his election by the Polish senate. In 1592 he married Archduchess Anne of Austria and, in that year, succeeded to the Swedish throne, with the permission of his Polish subjects. However, as a Roman Catholic he was not very popular in Sweden. The regent he had left there, his uncle Charles (later *Charles IX of Sweden), rebelled against him in 1598. S. was deposed in 1599, but he did not renounce his claims and launched the Swedish-Polish War which lasted 35 years. During the *Time of Troubles in Russia (1598-1613), S. intervened and claimed the Russian throne for his son. The Polish army occupied Moscow (1610-12) but was driven out, retaining Smolensk until 1654. Between 1617 and 1621 S. fought the Turks in Moldavia. In 1621 the Swedish army, led by King Gustavus II Adolphus, invaded Poland and occupied much of Polish Livonia. The Peace of Altmark with Sweden (1629) put a temporary end to the Polish-Swedish wars. During the *Thirty Years' War S. remained neutral. As a foreigner he was not popular in Poland. Opposition to him erupted in a civil war (1606-08), when he wanted to introduce majority vote in place of unanimity in the Polish diet. In 1596 he transferred the Polish capital from Cracow to Warsaw.

SIGNORELLI, LUCA (c.1445-1523) Italian painter. Born in Cortona, Umbria, he was probably, like *Perugino, a pupil of *Piero della Francesca. The influence of Piero can be discerned in an early fresco of S.'s *Madonna and Child Between SS. Jerome and Paul* (1474). While working in Florence (1475), he was also influenced by the brothers Pollaiuolo. Thereafter, the principal feature of his style was the human body in movement and in his interest in anatomy he is considered a predecessor of *Michelangelo. In 1480 he was invited to help in the decoration of the *Sistine Chapel; the fresco *The Testament of Moses* is attributed to him. In 1497 he painted ten of the frescoes depicting the life of St. Benedict at the monastery of Monte Oliveto Maggiore near *Siena. His most important works were the frescoes *The End of the World* and *The Last Judgement,* with the *Resurrection of the Dead, Heaven* and *Hell* in the Chapel of S. Brizio at Orvieto Cathedral. Begun in 1499, the work includes scenes from Dante, Vergil, Ovid and Horace. There are powerful nude human figures in strained poses and

The Condemned to the Infernal Fire *by Luca Signorelli at the cathedral of Orvieto*

grotesque muscular devils bathed in a doomesday atmosphere. Some of his later works are the *Deposition* (1515/16), the *Assumption* and the *Immaculate Conception* (begun in 1519). He ended his life at Cortona, the owner of a large workshop which produced altarpieces in a pre-High Renaissance style.
M. Salmi, *Luca Signorelli* (1953). (ND)

SIGONIUS (1520-84) The Latinized name of the Italian historian and humanist Carlo Sigonio. Born in Modena, he distinguished himself at an early age by his knowledge of Greek, and had a long carreer as a teacher in Modena, Venice, Padua and Bologna. His major work is a study of Italian history between 570 and 1200, entitled *De regno Italiae* (1574). But he also wrote on ancient Roman and Athenian history. Other works of his were in the field of philology. In his historical writings he shows a special interest in the influence of law on the development of institutions. His edition of Livy earned much acclaim but, in 1583, he published in Venice a volume purporting to contain a work of Cicero, but suspected of being his own.

SILOE, DIEGO DE (c. 1495-1563) Spanish architect and sculptor. He was the son of Gil de Siloe, a sculptor of French origins, who was the last great exponent of the Gothic style in Spain and died in about 1500. S. visited Italy in his youth. In 1523 he completed the *Escalera Dorada* (gilded stairway) in the cathedral of Burgos. The dome and Corinthian columns which he designed for the cathedral of Granada (where he succeeded Enrique de *Egas in 1528), display his familiarity with Renaissance Italian architecture. He also built churches in Ubeda, Málaga and Guadix.
M. Gómez-Moreno, *Las águilas del Renacimiento español* (1941).

SIMNEL, LAMBERT (?-1525) English impostor. The son of an artisan, he was trained by die-hard partisans of the house of *York to impersonate the young Earl of Warwick, as an heir of *Edward IV in the hope of toppling the first Tudor king, Henry VII. During the rebellion S. played an entirely passive role, the actual command being in the hands of another Yorkish claimant, John de la Pole, earl of Lincoln, who met his death at the Battle of Stokes (16 June 1487). Captured, S. was punished with contempt, being made a lowly servant at the king's court, later becoming a falconer.

SIMONS, MENNO (1496-1561) Dutch *Anabaptist leader, founder of the Mennonite communities. A parish priest at Friesland, he began leaning towards Lutheranism, but in 1536 joined the persecuted Dutch Anabaptists. This move was partly a reaction to the recent annihilation of the Anabaptist kingdom of Münster, an experience of which S. strongly disapproved although his own brother had taken part in it. Resolving to show the remnants of the shattered movement the true way to God, he began organizing and preaching, stressing adult baptism, silent prayer and inward state of faith. S. forbade the taking of oaths, thereby excluding his followers from magistracy and military offices. He was active at Amsterdam, Groningen, Emden and in villages between Hamburg and Lübeck. His

Tomb of Bishop Luís de Acuña at Burgos, by Diego de Siloe

The monument of Sixtus IV at St. Peter's by Pollaiuolo

followers, dubbed Mennonites as early as 1545, grew in number in the 17th century. Later they established communities in America.

J. C. Wenger, ed., *The Complete Writings of Menno Simons* (1956).

SINAN MI'MAR (1489-1578) The greatest architect of the *Ottoman empire. Born in Anatolia, the son of a Christian Greek, he was in his youth forcibly enrolled among the *Janissaries. He first distinguished himself as a military engineer, one of his feats being a bridge erected across the Danube, late in the reign of *Selim I. Most of his work was done under *Suleiman I the Magnificent. According to his own account, he built 334 structures, including mosques, schools, hospitals, palaces, bathhouses, bridges and tombs. His best works are in Istanbul (*Constantinople), notably the Suleimaniye (1550-56), a mosque with an immense cupola. However, he himself considered the Selimiye (1570-74) in Adrianople, a square building of enormous proportions, to be his masterpiece.

A. Stratton, *Sinan* (1972);
E. Egli, *Sinan, der Baumeister osmanischer Glanzzeit* (1954).

SINOPIA A red pigment used in *fresco painting. It was originally imported from the Black Sea, and employed by artists from the 14th century on to make a complete preliminary sketch of the work. These sketches came to be known as *sinopie.*

SIRMOND, JACQUES (1559-1651) French Roman Catholic scholar and educator. Entering the *Jesuit order in 1576, he taught at the College de Clermont (1581-90), and then became secretary to the general of the order, *Acquaviva, in Rome (1590-1608). Later, he was rector of the Jesuit college of Paris, and served as confessor to Louis XIII of France. S.'s editions of early and mediaeval Christian fathers – including Paschasius Radbertus (1618) and Eusebius of Caesarea (1643) – are famous. Of his own writings, the *Concilia antiqua Galliae* (1629) dealt with the early history of the Church in France.

SISTINE CHAPEL The principal chapel of the Vatican, used for important ceremonies and for the conclave, the sequestration of the college of cardinals during the election of a new pope. The decorations of the chapel are perhaps the most famous of the Renaissance. Pope *Sixtus IV, who had the chapel built, invited *Perugino, *Ghirlandaio, *Botticelli and *Rosselli to paint frescoes on its walls (1481-82). But the most celebrated decoration of the S. is the ceiling, painted between 1508 and 1512 by *Michelangelo. Three decades later he painted *The Last Judgment* on the altar wall.

SIX ARTICLES, ACT OF THE (June 1539) An English law passed at the demand of *Henry VIII, with the aim of arresting the progress of the *Reformation. It reaffirmed the doctrines of transubstantiation and communion in one kind, enforced the celibacy of the clergy and reconfirmed auricular confession, in addition to other conservative measures. Bishop Hugh *Latimer resigned his see of Worchester in disapproval, but most of the clergy acquiesced, although they tended not to comply with the requirements, which they dubbed "the whip with six strings."

SIXTUS IV (1414-84) Pope from 1471. Born Francesco *della Rovere in Cella Ligure, near Savona, he entered the Franciscan order and studied philosophy

Interior of the Sistine Chapel with Michelangelo's famous ceiling and his Last Judgement *in the background*

and theology at the universities of Padua and Bologna. He won a great reputation while teaching at several universities and, in 1464, was chosen minister general of his order. In 1467 he was created cardinal by Pope *Paul II, whom he succeeded four years later. S. was mainly concerned with strengthening the authority of the *Papacy, and sought to limit the power of the cardinals. He was not greatly concerned with international affairs, except for his abortive crusade against the Turks (1472).

S. elevated members of his family to high positions and through them became involved in the political conflicts of the Italian states. His most famous intrigues was the *Pazzi Conspiracy (1478), which was directed by his nephew, Girolamo Riario. S. excommunicated Lorenzo de' *Medici and entangeled Naples in a two-year war with Florence (1478-80). His coalition with Venice led to her attack on Ferrara in 1482.

S. was not much concerned with abuses in the Church, and his contributions to ecclesiastical affairs were few. In 1478 he annulled the decrees of the Council of *Constance (1414-18). To his credit are some important improvements in *Rome: paving and widening streets, erecting and restoring many churches, and opening a new hospital. He had the *Sistine Chapel built and invited such artists as *Boticelli, *Perugino and *Ghirlandaio to decorate it. He also rearranged and enlarged the Vatican library. (ND)

SIXTUS V (1520-90) Pope from 1585. Born Felice Peretti, he joined the Franciscan order in 1533 and was ordained in 1547. In 1557 he became the head of the *Inquisition in Venice. His severity and zeal led to his recall in 1560. Pope *Pius V made him vicar general of the Franciscans, bishop (1566), and then cardinal (1570). Having spent some years in retirement during the pontificate of *Gregory XIII, he succeeded him as pope. S. was a reformer who effectively enforced the decrees of the Council of *Trent. His measures dealt with discipline of the clergy, finance and reforming the central administration of the Church. On the international level, he was involved in the French *Religious Wars, in connection with which he negotiated with *Philip II of Spain and with Henry of Navarre (later King *Henry IV of France). S. fixed the number of cardinals at 70, suppressed banditry in the *Papal States and endeavoured to beautify the city of *Rome. The dome of *St. Peter's and several other important architectural projects were completed during his energetic pontificate.

R. Canestrari, *Sixto V* (1954).

SKANDERBEG, GEORGE CASTRIOTIS (1405-68) Albanian military leader, Brought up as a Moslem at the court of *Murad II, he served in the Ottoman army and was known as Iskander Bey. In about 1443 he deserted and, converting to Christianity, began a long campaign against the Turks in his native Albania. In his guerilla war S. was aided by *Venice and later also by the papacy. Called "the dragon of Albania" and "the athlete of Christendom", he succeeded in preserving his people's independence until his death. Afterwards, many of his followers went to Italy, but most Albanians acquiesced with Turkish rule.

F. S. Noli, *George Castrioti Scanderbeg* (1947).

SKELTON, JOHN (c. 1460-1529) English poet and satirist. Born probably either in Norfolk or Cumberland, he was educated both at Oxford and Cambridge. In 1498 he took holy orders. About that time he was appointed tutor to Prince Henry (later *Henry VIII), and later wrote his satire *Bowge of Courte*. In about 1502 he became Rector of Diss in Norfolk. He then wrote some of his best poems, such as *Philip Sparrow, Ware the Hawk* and *The Tunning of Eleanor Rumming*, which is a comedy on low life. His poetic style, called "Skeltonics", consists of short lines with irregular but persistent rhyme. S. wrote political ballads against the Scots and some of his satires were directed against the friars. Later, he attacked Cardinal Thomas *Wolsey, about whom he wrote *Colin Clout, Speke Parrot* (1521) and *Why Come Ye Not to Court* (1522). It is likely that because of his attacks on the Cardinal, he had to seek sanctuary at Westminster, where he apparently remained until his death. S.'s reputation was great. *Erasmus referred to him as "the incomparable light and glory of English letters".

S. E. Fish, *John Skelton's Poetry* (1965);
A. R. Heiserman, *Skelton and Satire* (1961);
L. J. Lloyd, *John Skelton; a Sketch of His Life and Writings* (1938). (ND)

SLAVERY An institution which had characterized the economies of the ancient Greek and Roman societies, S. disappeared gradually in Europe during the Middle Ages. In the West it survived on a large scale until about the 10th century, when the rise of *feudalism created milder forms of serfdom. Thereafter S. remained significant in certain regions only. (The term itself, from the mediaeval Latin *sclavus,* derived from the word Slav, the ethnic name of the people from whom most of the slaves came between the 11th and 14th century.) Enslavement of prisoners, however, was common whenever Christians fought Moslems. It persisted on both sides in Spain throughout the **reconquista*, and in the 16th century was practised by the *Ottoman Turks and Moslem kingdoms of North Africa, where Christian captives were sometimes used, after appropriate treatment, to guard harems as eunuchs. On the other hand, captured Orientals and Turks were highly prized in Italy, and were used to perform hard tasks in industry and as house servants. Some religious orders, such as the Trinitarians and Mercederians, devoted themselves to redeeming Christians from servitude at the hand of Moslems. The Church, though critical, did not condemn S., which retained a legal status.

During the Renaissance the institution was intimately connected with the movement of *exploration and the early contacts of Europeans with the black peoples of *Africa. The initiative was taken by the Portuguese: it has been estimated that, between 1444 and 1505, some 140,000 slaves were shipped from their slave trading stations at Rio de Oro, Senegal, Sierra Leone and Guinea. After the discovery of America the enslavement of Africans increased considerably. In the beginning, the European colonists attempted to take slaves from the native Indian population – the practice continued a long time among the Portuguese settlers in Brazil, whereas the Spanish forbade the outright sale of Indians, and regulated the exploitation of the native population through the **repartimiento* and the **encomienda*. Both the Spanish and Portuguese, however, encouraged the importation of black slaves to work in the coastal plantations of South America and the Caribbean. Despite successive condemnations by *Paul III (1537) and *Pius V (1567), the slave trade between Africa and America continued to grow. By the 1560s it had become so lucrative that the English John *Hawkins considered it worthwhile to engage in illegal trade and risk reprisals by the Spanish authorities. In the early 17th century S. was introduced into the young English colonies of North America. By that time ships of all major European countries, including the Dutch and French, were engaged in the cross-Atlantic slave trade, which was not ended until the 19th century.

H. A. Wyndham, *The Atlantic and Slavery* (1935);
C. Verlinden, *L'esclavage dans l'Europe méditerranéenne* (1955):
J. A. Saco, *Historia de la esclavitud de la raza africana en el nuevo mundo,* 2 vols. (1879-83).

SLEIDANUS (Johannes Philippson; 1506-56) German historian; named after his native town Schleiden in the Rhine Valley. He studied at Cologne, Paris and Orleans and, having settled in France, was employed in 1540 by *Francis I as a diplomat. At that time, he was already under Protestant influence and, in 1544, undertook the writing of a history of the *Reformation, a task in which he was supported by *Philip of Hesse and other Protestant princes. In 1554 he was made professor of jurisprudence at Strassburg.

His main work, *Commentaries on the Political and Religious Conditions in the Reign of Emperor Charles V,* originally written in Latin, appeared in Strassburg in 1555, and was translated into English five years later. Backed by a large selection of documents, it is the best contemporary account of the Reformation. A student of *Commines, whom he had translated, S. was broadminded, surprisingly impartial, and interested in the political background of the Reformation, and the constitutional aspects of the positions adopted by the German princes. Probably because of its objectivity, the work did not yet enjoy much popularity at the time of its publication.

SLUTER, CLAUS (c. 1350-1406) Dutch sculptor. Born probably in Haarlem, he joined the stonemasons' guild of Brussels in about 1380. In 1389 he succeeded Jean de Marville as chief sculptor for Philip the Bold, Duke of *Burgundy, and took charge of the two great works then in progress: the portal of the ducal chapel, and the Duke's tomb at the Charterhouse of Champmol, near Dijon. In 1395 he was commissioned to execute a monumental Crucifixion group for the Charterhouse – its base, known as *The Well of Moses*, still survives. In 1404 he retired to a monastery in Dijon. Some of his works were then completed by his nephew Claus de Werve. An artist of intense and individual genius, S. broke with the decorative elegance of *International Gothic and introduced into northern Europe a realist style which influenced painters as well as sculptors. The life-size statues of the portal are interrelated, and the masterful execution of the draperies endows them with an imposing physical presence. The six life-size figures of the prophets which surround the base of the Crucifixion group are unique psychological studies of agony. The influence of S. in northern Europe can be compared with that which *Donatello would exercise 20 years later in Italy.

H. David, *Claus Sluter* (1951);
A. J. Kleinclausz, *Claus Sluter et la sculpture bourguignonne* (1905).

Wollaton Hall by Smythson

SMYTH, JOHN (c. 1554-1612) English founder of the Baptist sect. Educated at Cambridge, he first pursued an ecclesiastical career in the *Church of England, but subsequently became a *Puritan preacher (1603). In 1609 he left with other exiles for *Amsterdam, where he established the first Baptist church. Doctrinally related to the *Anabaptists of the first part of the 16th century, the Baptists practiced adult baptism, and emphasized religious toleration. In 1612, after the death of S., a group of his followers, led by Thomas Helwys (*c.* 1550-1616), returned and founded the first congregation in England. They struck stronger roots later in the 17th century.

SMYTHSON, ROBERT (c. 1536-1614) English architect. Not much is known about his life. He is recorded as chief mason of Longleat, Wiltshire (1567-80), and later lived in Wollaton, Nottinghamshire. S. left many plans and drawings, on the basis of which a number of houses in Nottinghamshire and Yorkshire are attributed to him. His chief creation was Wollaton Hall (1580-88). Following a modified Renaissance style inspired by *Serlio, his designs are noted for their emphasis on many large windows, symmetry and refinement.

SOCINUS, LAELIUS (1525-62) AND FAUSTUS (1539-1604) Italian Protestant reformers, uncle and nephew, who came of a noble Sienese family. Laelius was educated as a jurist and, in 1547, left Italy and travelled to the centres of the Reformation in northern Europe. He was in contact with *Melanchthon, *Bullinger and *Calvin and, although sometimes suspected for his radical theological ideas, was given shelter and died in Zurich. Faustus, who had not known his uncle very well, was for 12 years (1563-75) in the service of Isabella de' Medici, daughter of the grand duke of Tuscany, and then moved to *Basle. He was later active in Transylvania and, in 1579, went to Poland, where he spent the rest of his life. In his writings he championed anti-Trinitarian ideas, denying the divinity of Christ and upholding the uniqueness of God. He also expressed doubts about the natural immorality of man.

D. M. Cory, *Faustus Socinus* (1932);
G. Pioli, *Fausto Socino* (1952).

The Archangel Michael *by Sodoma*

St. Catherine *by Sodoma (detail)*

SODERINI, PIERO (1452-1522) Florentine statesman. He began his political career under Lorenzo de' *Medici and his son Piero. After Piero's expulsion from the city (1494), S. gradually gained influence over the government and, in 1502, he was elected head of the republic, *Gonfaloniere di Giustizia*, for life. A moderate ruler and a good administrator, he made some significant reforms in matters such as public finances and the judiciary. Following the ideas of his protégé *Machiavelli, he introduced a system of national militia, in preference to foreign mercenaries. During his rule Florence captured Pisa (1509), thereby ending the war between them. When the Medici returned (1512), aided by Pope *Julius II, Piero deposed S. and exiled him. He then first went to Siena and later to Ragusa; later Pope *Leo X invited him to Rome, where he died. (ND)

SODOMA (Giovanni Antonio Bazzi; 1477-1549) Italian painter. Born in Vercelli in Piedmont, he was a pupil of Giovanni Spanzotti (1490-97). Later he was deeply influenced by *Leonardo and *Raphael. S.'s works exemplify the transition from the style of the High Renaissance to *Mannerism. In 1501 he was invited to Siena, where he remained for most of his life. Between 1505 and 1508 he worked in the nearby monastery of Monteoliveto Maggiore, where he completed a series of frescoes, begun by *Signorelli, on the life of St. Benedict. In 1508 he was invited to Rome and painted in the Stanza della Segnatura in the Vatican. In 1509 this work was continued by Raphael, but some of S.'s ceiling decoration remains. In Rome he also painted scenes from the life of Alexander the Great in the Villa Farnesina (1513). Other notable works of his are the St. Catherine frescoes in S. Domenico, Siena, the *Christ of the Column*, the *Descent into Limbo* and *St. Sebastian*. (ND)

SÖKÖLLI, MUHAMAD PASA (1505-79) Ottoman grand vizier under *Selim II. Born in Sokal, Bosnia, he was recruited into the Ottoman service and, in 1546, became high admiral of the fleet. Later he was governor general of Roumania. Between 1559 and 1561 he led Selim's forces to victory over his brother in the conflict over the succession, and then married Selim's daughter. From his accession in 1566 Selim relied on him and left most of the affairs of state in his hands. However, he failed to prevent the wars with Venice (1570-71) and with Persia (1578). Under Selim's successor, *Murad III, S. lost much of his power, though he remained grand vizier. He died at the hands of assassins.

SOLARI, GUINIFORTE (1429-81) Italian architect and sculptor. A native of Milan, he succeeded *Filarete as architect of the Ospedale Maggiore. Later he built the nave of S. Maria delle Grazie and supervised the works of Milan's carthedral. He also was for some time architect of the Certosa di Pavia, which had been begun by his father Giovanni (1410-80). Both father and son remained faithful to the vocabulary of Italian Gothic *architecture.

SOLARI, PIETRO ANTONIO (c. 1450-93) Italian architect and sculptor. The son and pupil of Guiniforte *Solari, he worked on the Milan cathedral and, in about 1490, went to Moscow, where he worked with another Italian architect, Marco Ruffo, on the "Faceted Palace" in the Kremlin. Unlike the Moscow work of *Fioravante, this is done in Italian Renaissance style.

SOLARI, SANTINO (1576-1646) Italian architect. Born near Lugano, he did much of his work in Austria, where he helped to introduce the Renaissance style. In 1612 he became architect to the bishop of Salzburg, for whom he built the *Lustschloss* at nearby Hellbrunn (1613-19). His most important work was Salzburg Cathedral (begun 1614), in the Italian manner. In addition to other buildings in Salzburg, he worked in Innsbruck and in Einsiedeln, Switzerland.

SOLARIO, ANDREA (c. 1470-c. 1520) Italian painter. A native of Milan, he was obviously influenced by *Leonardo, who worked there, and later by the Venetian painters. Some works of his also reveal the influence of the Flemish school, perhaps the result of a period of work in France (1507-09). His *Madonna with a Green Cushion*, later acquired by *Marie de Médicis and now at the Louvre, shows his considerable techincal skill. His older brother Cristoforo (*c.* 1460-1527) was a sculptor and architect, who worked in Milan for *Ludovico il Moro and later in *Ferrara.

SOLIS, JUAN DE (1470-1516) Spanish navigator. He acquired much of his seafaring experience while accompanying Vicente Yañez *Pinzon on two voyages of exploration along the Atlantic coast of South America. In 1511 *Ferdinand I appointed him *piloto mayor* (chief pilot), an office in which he succeeded *Vespucci. In

1515 S. commanded a small fleet of three ships sailing down the coast of South America in search of a passage to the Pacific. Entering the estuary of Rio de la Plata, he advanced to the mouth of the Paraná, where he was killed by Indians.

SOLIS, VIRGIL (1514-62) German engraver. A citizen of Nuremberg, he produced over two thousand copper-plate engravings, etchings and woodcuts. He was also famous as a great illustrator of religious works. His engravings were on a broad range of subjects and were very popular in their time.

I. O'Dell-Franke, *Kupferstiche und Radierungen aus der Werkstatt des Virgil Solis* (1977).

SOMATIANS A religious order founded in 1532 by St. Jerome Emiliani (1481-1537), a native of Venice and a former soldier, who became a priest and decided to dedicate his life to working among the poor. The orders' first establishment was in the town of Somasca, between *Milan and Bergamo. Devoting themselves to the care of orphans and the sick, the S. were approved by *Pius V in 1568, and made their presence felt in northern Italy.

P. Paschini, *L'ordine dei Chierici Regolari Somaschi* (1928);
I. Landini, *S. Girolamo Emiliani* (1946).

SOMERSET, EDWARD SEYMOUR, FIRST DUKE OF (c. 1500-52) Protector of England during the first three years of the reign of *Edward VI. His career at the court began in the reign of *Henry VIII, after his sister *Jane Seymour married the King and gave birth to a son. Created earl of Hertford, he commanded the English forces in the invasion of Scotland, in 1544. Two years later he successfully manoeuvered the downfall of the duke of *Norfolk. Thus he paved the way to his election as Lord Protector by the council of regency. Elevated to the rank of duke, S. ruled England from early 1547 until his downfall in October 1549. He promoted religious reforms, but was not entirely successful in the wars against Scotland and France, and seems to have lost his authority when he allowed the execution of his younger brother, Thomas Seymour (*c.* 1508-59), on charges of treason. Ousted by his former supporter, *Northumberland, S. was sent to the Tower, but released after a few months. The two then seemingly made peace, S. marrying his daughter to Northumberland's son. But when political conflict reopened, S. was arrested, condemned of felony and executed.

A. F. Pollard, *England Under Protector Somerset* (1900).

SONCINO A Jewish dynasty of printers, originally from Germany, who had the most important Hebrew printing presses in Italy. Two of its members, Samuel and Simon, settled in Soncino, near Cremona (1454), and there the press was established by Joshua Solomon (d. 1493). The first book he published was the talmudic tractate *Berakhot* (1484); later he issued a complete Hebrew *Bible (1488) and other works. These were the first printed Hebrew editions of the Bible and Talmud. Joshua's nephew, Gershom ben Moses (d. 1534), printed works in Hebrew, Latin, Greek and Italian. He published important manuscripts, and made many innovations in the field of Hebrew typography. He was the first to use woodcut illustrations in Hebrew works and to print secular Hebrew books. Gershom also worked in other cities in Italy, including Brescia, Fano, Pesaro and Rimini, and produced more than 100 volumes in Hebrew and about as many in other languages. Eventually he left Italy and worked first in Salonika (from 1527) and then in Istanbul (from 1530). His work was continued by his son Eliezer (d. 1547). The last of the S. was Eliezer's son, Gershom (d. 1562), who worked in Cairo, Egypt. The Hebrew press in Prague was probably founded by the family in 1512.

M. Marx, *Gershom Soncino's Wanderyears in Italy, 1498-1527* (1936; rep. 1969). (ND)

SONNET A poetic form developed in Italy in the 13th century and employed by *Petrarch, which in the 16th century was introduced into the *literature of France, Spain, England, and other European countries. The Petrarchan sonnet consisted of 14 lines, divided into eight (an octave) and six (a sextet), the first group being rhymed *abba abba*, the second *cdcdcd*. There were, however, several variations. The Shakespearean sonnet, for example, is divided into three groups of four (quartains), followed by a detached rhymed couplet.

SOREL, AGNES (c. 1422-50) French mistress of *Charles VII. Born into a noble family of Touraine, she became the King's mistress in about 1442, and gave him four daughters. In her last years she wielded great influence on the affairs of the state by means of royal councillors, such as Etienne Chevalier and Jacques *Coeur. Her death, soon after the birth of her fourth daughter, was rumoured to have been caused by poisoning. The dauphin, the future *Louis XI, was suspected, and later Jacques Coeur was accused of the deed.

J. d'Orliac, *The Lady of Beauty: Agnes Sorel, First Royal Favourite of France* (1931).

SOTIE A type of French satirical play in the 15th century. Partly a farce, partly a satire on political or moral themes, it was intended above all to provoke laughter and amusement. The actors, *sots* or fools, wore the traditional jester's costume with bells on their legs. The best-known company of *sots* were the *Enfants sans souci*, and the most famous author, Pierre *Gringore. The S. represented a theatrical development in France, similar to the *commedia dell'arte* in Italy.

SOTO, DOMINGO (1494-1560) Spanish theologian. A graduate of the universities of Alcalá and Paris, and a pupil of Francisco de *Vitoria, he entered the Dominican order in 1524. In 1532 he became a professor of theology at the universtiy of Salamanca. In 1545 *Charles V sent him as an imperial theologian to the Council of *Trent, where he distinguished himself by his erudition. Later he served as the emperor's confessor and, in 1552, succeeded Melchor *Cano as the principal theologian at Salamanca. In his several treatises on theology, S. upheld Thomistic doctrines. In his commentaries on Aristotle (1545) he proposed a theory about the trajectory of missiles which anticipated *Galileo's.

B. Hamilton, *Political Thought in the 16th-Century Spain* (1963).

SOTO, HERNANDO DE (c. 1500-42) Spanish explorer. Born in Extremadura, he was educated at the university of Salamanca. In 1519 he went to Panama to join his patron, Pedro *Arias de Avila. In 1523 he participated in the conquest of Nicaragua, where he served as military commander for several years. Between 1531 and 1535 he took part in the conquest of Peru and was the first European to enter Cuzco, the Inca capital. In 1535 he returned to Spain a wealthy man. Hearing tales of great riches in the Mississipi Valley, he obtained the approval of *Charles V of an expedition to North America, and in 1537 was made royal deputy of the Floridas. Two years later he began to explore the area of what was to become the southeastern United States. In 1541 he arrived at the banks of the Mississipi River, and followed it in search of the fabled treasures. He died on this journey and was buried in the river.

SOUSA, MARTIM AFONSO DE (1500-64) Portuguese colonial administrator. Of noble family, he distinguished himself as a soldier and, in 1531, went at the head of a naval expedition to the shores of Brazil, where he discovered the Bay of Guanabara, which he named Rio de Janeiro. He founded Sao Vicente, the first Portuguese permanent settlement, near present-day Sao Paulo. Returning to Portugal, he was appointed governor of *India in 1534. There he intervened in the wars between the rulers of Cochin and Calicut, but returned to Portugal before assuming the post of viceroy. In 1542 he was sent again to India and remained there for three years, heading what was generally described as a corrupt, ineffective administration.

SOUTHWELL, ROBERT (1561-95) English poet and Roman Catholic martyr. Born into a Catholic family in Norfolk, he was educated at *Douai and in 1580 became a member of the *Jesuit order and went to study in Rome. In 1586 he went as a missionary to England and for six years carried out his clandestine work in London and elsewhere, aided by a number of high-ranking Roman Catholic nobles. In 1592 he was betrayed and delivered to the authorities. Tortured and confined for over two years in the Tower, he was subsequently hanged as a traitor. Most of his poems were written in prison and published soon after his death. *Saint Peter's Complaint* (1595) tried to express the eternal through the imagery of the temporal, and *Maeonia* (1595) contained shorter poems of ecstatic religious fervour. S. also wrote some prose treatises to uplift the hearts of the persecuted English Roman Catholics.

SOVEREIGNTY A political term denoting absolute and unlimited authority in the state. The concept was developed by the French political thinker, Jean *Bodin (1530-96), who defined it as "the supreme power of the state over citizens and subjects, unrestrained by law". Bodin's theory came in response to the anarchy in France during the *Religious Wars (1562-98). He presupposed that people wanted to live in a society regulated by law, and maintained that to avoid anarchy there can be only one supreme authority whom the people must obey. The concept of sovereignty was often used by later political thinkers to explain the supreme power of the ruler, the state or the people.

F. H. Hinsley, *Sovereignty* (1966);
B. de Jouvenal, *Sovereignty* (1957). (ND)

SPAIN A partly barren land, separated from the rest of the continent by the chain of the Pyrenees and sparsely populated, S. was ill-suited for the part of a European superpower. Yet early in the 16th century the country suddenly became the hub of a huge empire which stretched on both sides of the Atlantic. Spanish soldiers were fighting in *Italy, *Germany and on the coasts of North Africa, while the **conquistadores* took possession of the gold and silver mines of the New World, which were to finance Spanish supremacy during the rest of the century. Spanish might reached its zenith in 1580, when *Philip II annexed *Portugal. But at about the same time the revolt of the *Netherlands demonstrated the limits of S.'s military force, and the defeat of the *Armada was soon to inflict a painful humiliation. By the early 17th century it was clear that the country's power was declining. While enjoying still a period of artistic creativity, she failed to develop her industries and her influence on European politics steadily lessened.

Conditions in S. at the beginning of the 15th century were hardly propitious for the emergence of a powerful monarchy. Divided between the kingdoms of Castile and *Aragon, S. also still contained small Moslem principalities in the south. In Castile, the largest polity, feudal anarchy during the long reign of *John II (1406-54) obstructed all attempts to strengthen royal power; as the career of Alvaro de *Luna showed. The crown remained weak in the reign of *Henry IV (1454-74). Then, in 1469, the king's half-sister, *Isabella, against his wishes married *Ferdinand, heir to the kingdom of Aragon. She assumed effective control of the government after the defeat of the supporters of *Juana la Beltraneja at the Battle of Toro (1476), and three years later Ferdinand succeeded to the throne of Aragon, and the two kingdoms were unified under the couple's rule.

The rise in royal power was felt immediately. Already in 1476 an effective militia force, known as the *Santa Hermandad, was organized and employed by the crown against the powerful nobles and military *orders. At the same time the monarchy won control of the towns through the introduction of the office of *corregidor* (1480). Another new institution, the *Inquisition (1478), although intended to deal with the problem of the **marranos*, also became a potent royal instrument; here, however, the benefits reaped in the short run later came to be one of the causes of Spanish stagnation. Resuming the **reconquista*, the envigorated monarchy completed the subjugation of *Granada, the last Moslem Iberian state, in 1492. Two other events in that remarkable year were of crucial importance for the future of S.: the expulsion of the *Jews (followed by the Moslems in 1502), and *Columbus' voyage of discovery to the New World. Shortly afterwards Ferdinand began his intervention in the *Italian Wars, and by 1503 was in possession of the kingdom of *Naples. By concluding marriage-alliances with the *Tudors and the *Habsburgs, S. succeeded in isolating France and becoming a first-rate European power. Spanish *armies in Italy under Gonzalo de *Córdoba, and in North Africa under Cardinal *Jiménez de Cisneros, were beginning to demonstrate the qualities which earned them reputation as the best in the 16th century.

The accession of *Charles V (1516), a Flemish prince of the house of Habsburg, soon to be elected emperor, did not pass without opposition. S. now added the *Netherlands and *Germany to her military commitments. The young king's entourage of foreign advisers aroused resentment, the immediate expression of which was the revolt of the **comuneros* (1520-21). Afterwards, however, Charles took care to win the hearts of his Spanish subjects, who rallied to his side and served him faithfully in numerous campaigns in Italy and France, and against the *Ottoman Turks. His son, *Philip II (1556-98), saw S. as the guardian of Europe against the continued Ottoman menace and, in addition, the champion of Roman Catholicism against the rising tide of Protestantism. The treaty of *Cateau-Cambrésis (1559) affirmed Spanish domination in Italy and, in 1571, S. celebrated a tremendous naval victory over the Turks in the Battle of *Lepanto. Credit for these achievements was at least partly due to such great generals as the duke of *Alba, Don *Juan de Austria and, later on, Alessandro *Farnese, and brilliant admirals like *Menendez de Aviles and *Santa Cruz. Nevertheless, Tunis, captured in 1573, was lost in the following year, and the revolt in the Netherlands, which had apparently been suppressed, suddenly assumed alarming dimensions. The Dutch, lead by *William of Orange, liberated their country from Spanish domination and, in 1579, concluded the Union of *Utrecht, declaring their independence two years later. In spite of the increasing supply of precious metals which poured in from its New World colonies, S.'s policies in northern Europe were headed for failure. In the long war with England, which followed the sailing of the Armada (1588), Cádiz was captured by *Essex in 1596, and sporadic hostilities continued until after the death of Philip II. Nor did the Spanish intervention in the last phase of the *Religious Wars of France produce tangible gains when it ended with the conciliatory Peace of *Vervins (1598).

The great century of Spanish might and diplomacy, the 16th was also a golden age of scholarship, arts and letters. *Humanism, introduced from Italy in the late 15th century, centred around the University of Alcalá, its notable figures being *Nebrija and *Vives. The science of *historiography was advanced in the works of *Hurtado de Mendoza, *Zurita y Castro and Juan de *Mariana, among many others. Spanish theologians, like Francisco de *Vitoria, Melchor *Cano and later, Francisco *Suárez, led the revival of Roman Catholic thought; the mystics *Luís de Granada and *Teresa de Avila wrote some of the most inspired pages of Christian devotional literature. The *Jesuits, that indispensable instrument of the *Counter-Reformation, founded by Ignatius *Loyola, were led primarily by Spaniards.

The cultural flowering continued during the first decades of the 17th century. In painting the genius of El *Greco was followed by that of Diego Velasquez (1599-1660). *Cervantes published his immortal *Don Quixote*, and Spanish *drama saw its golden age with the works of *Lope de Vega and *Ruíz de Alarcón, while *Quevedo enriched Spanish poetry with his sonnets and satirical verses. Politically, however, S. was already entering a long period of lethargy. Under the religious and incompetent *Philip III, the duke of *Lerma initiated the pernicious system of rule by royal favourites (*privados*).

R. B. Merriman, *The Rise of the Spanish Empire in the Old World and the New*, 4 vols. (1918-34);
C. E. Chapman, *A History of Spain* (1927);
R. Trevor Davies, *The Golden Century of Spain, 1501-1621* (1937);
R. Altamira y Crevea, *A History of Spain* (1949);
H. Livermore, *A History of Spain* (1958);
J. H. Elliott, *Imperial Spain, 1469-1713* (1963);
J. Lynch, *Spain Under the Hapsburgs*, vol. 1 (1964).

SPALATIN, GEORG (1484-1545) German humanist and reformer. Born near Nuremberg, he studied in Erfurt and after being ordained priest in 1508 was appointed tutor to the children of the Elector of Saxony, *Frederick III the Wise (1509). S. presently became the elector's secretary and confident. Since at the same time

Spain as the head of Europe, engraving from Sebastian Münster's Cosmographia *(1527)*

he befriended *Luther, under whom he studied the Bible, he was able to intercede on his behalf. He accompanied the elector to the Diet of Worms (1521), and, under his successor John Frederick, who had been his pupil, advocated the complete Protestant reform of Saxony. S. translated Luther's writings from the Latin and corresponded with him. His *Annales reformationis* was published in 1718.

J. Höss, *Georg Spalatin* (1956).

SPANISH EMPIRE IN AMERICA First sighted by *Columbus in 1492, the coasts of the New World soon became the object of reconnaissance by Spanish navigators. When this movement of *exploration reached its high point with *Magellan's first circumnavigation of the globe (1519-21), Spain began the conquest of the American mainland. During almost three decades the **conquistadores* criss-crossed Central, South and parts of North America, subjugating native Indian empires and annexing to the Spanish crown territories larger than all of Europe. In the second half of the 16th century the new lands were placed under administrative rule becoming an indispensible factor in Spain's predominance in the Old World, chiefly because of their rich mines of silver. Apart from the Portuguese presence on the coast of Brazil, Spain had the New World to herself during most of the 16th century. She laid the foundation for the first modern interracial society, and implanted her language, culture and institutions from California in the north to Chile and Rio de la Plata in the south.

The first moves in the building of the empire were made in the Caribbean Islands and the Isthmus of Panama, where explorers and settlers like Diego de *Velásquez, *Balboa and Pedro *Arias de Avila were active. Hernán *Cortés' epoch-making expedition to Mexico in 1519 ushered in the heroic phase of the conquest. Within three years the powerful Aztec empire had been subjugated. Between 1523 and 1525 Pedro de *Alvarado conquered Guatemala. The conquest of Yucatán was undertaken in 1527 and, in 1531, after several years of preparation, Francisco *Pizarro began his expedition against the Incas of Peru. Venezuela was conquered from the late 1520s, with the help of the German banking house of *Welser, and in 1538 Gonzalo *Jiménez de Quesada won New Granada (present-day Colombia) from the Chibcha Indians. Chile, first visited by Diego de *Almagro in 1535, was conquered by Pedro de *Valdivia in 1541. Some years earlier Pedro de *Mendoza had attempted to colonize the estuary of the Rio de la Plata, but failed. However, Paraguay was settled in 1537, and Buenos Aires was founded (for the second time) in 1580 by Juan de *Garay.

Spain administered these enormous areas through the *Consejo de Indias*, a supreme council responsible for their government, justice, legislation, taxation and ecclesiastical affairs. Commerce with the colonies was restricted to Spanish merchants and controlled by the **Casa de Contratación* of *Seville. The chief officials representing the crown in America were the two viceroys, residing in Mexico City and Lima. They were assisted by lesser officials (*corregidores, alcaldes mayores*), and their authority was balanced by the **audiencias*, i.e. judicial and administrative courts. Some districts were placed under captain-generals with their own *audiencias*, and ruled directly from Spain. The **flota* system, adopted for reasons of security, completed this essentially centralized framework of government. Inevitably, conditions in the new lands meant that there would be considerable difference between the formal structure and its actual implementation.

Under the first viceroys, men of the stature of Antonio de *Mendoza, Luís de *Velasco and Francisco de *Toledo, the new colonies grew and prospered. Towns were built, *universities established in Mexico City and Lima (1551) and, by the middle of the century, the *mining centres of Guanajuato and Zacatecas in New Spain (Mexico) and Potosí in upper Peru began to produce vast quantities of silver. But this economic growth slackened after a few decades. This was the result of several factors, such as the exhaustion of the mines and the rigid *mercantilist policies of the Spanish government. But perhaps the crucial factor was the condition of the Indian population: the Spaniards exploited the natives through the **encomienda*, and instituted a system of forced labour known as **repartimiento*. The results were seen within a hundred years of the conquest: a demographic catastrophy in which the Indian population declined to about 10 per cent of its original size. This extreme case of depopulation, the result – among other causes – of widespread series of epidemics, sharply reduced the production capacity of the colonies, a situation that even the stepped-up importation of African *slaves could not resolve. Not until the 18th century did Spanish America resume its economic growth.

E. F. Bourne, *Spain in America,1450-1580* (1904; rep. 1962);
W. Diffie, *Latin-American Civilization: Colonial Period* (1945);
C. H. Haring, *The Spanish Empire in America* (1947);
C. Gibson, *Spain in America* (1966);
J. H. Parry, *The Spanish Seaborne Empire* (1966).

SPENGLER, LAZARUS (1479-1534) German Protestant leader. Born in *Nuremberg, he was appointed its first town clerk (1507) and member of the council (1516). He supported *Luther from the beginning and, in 1519, published a popular pamphlet on his behalf. Denounced by Johann *Eck, his name was included in the papal bull of excommunication against Luther. S. then desisted from open advocacy of reform, but began again after 1525, when he published several Protestant tracts. He was influential in aiding the gradual development of the Reformation in Nuremberg, though he advised against joining the Protestant *Schmalkaldic League.

SPENSER, EDMUND (c. 1552-99) English poet. Born probably in London, he attended the Merchant Taylors' School (1561-69). He continued his education at Cambridge where he received his B.A. degree in 1573 and the M.A. in 1576. In 1578 he became secretary to the bishop of Rochester. A year later, he published his first important work, *The Shepeardes Calendar*. It is a series of pastoral poems, one for each month of the year, which deal with some contemporary topics and with time and its effect on man. In 1580 S. became secretary to Lord Grey de Wilton, who had been newly appointed lord deputy of *Ireland. S. became attached to Ireland and eventually settled down as a landlord of Kilcolman Castle in County Cork (1586). He gives an account of the situation in the country in *A View of the Present State of Ireland* (written 1595-97, but published only in 1633). The first three books of his greatest work, *The Faerie Queene*, were published during his visit to London (1589-90) and Books IV-VI appeared in 1596. The theme of this great poem are the moral qualities required by statesmen, each book dealing with a certain virtue. S. employed his own verse form, which has become known as the spenserian stanza. From the first, *The Faerie Queene* was immensely successful, and Queen *Elizabeth I gave the poet a pension. Following this success, other poems of his were published in a volume called *Complaints* (1591). His second marriage is recorded in *Epithalamion*, and in the love sonnets *Amoretti*, both published in 1595. A description of his visit to London was given in his autobiographical poem, *Colin Clouts Come Home Againe* (1595). In 1598 S.'s castle at Kilcolman burnt down and he went to England to report on the incident. He died a year later and was buried in Westminster Abbey. S. was the leading poet of Elizabethan England. His poetry has a misty quality, enhanced by his use of coined words, allegory and subtle sound effects.

L. Bradner, *Edmund Spenser and the Faerie Queene* (1953);

M. Evans, *Spenser's Anatomy of Heroism* (1970);
P. J. Alpers, ed., *Edmund Spenser; a Critical Anthology* (1969);
R. M. Cummings, ed., *Spenser; the Critical Heritage* (1971). (ND)

SPERONI, SPERONE (1500-88) Italian humanist. Born in Padua, he studied there under *Pomponazzi, and spent most of his life there. He worte poetry, critical studies of Virgil, *Dante and *Ariosto, and numerous dialogues on a variety of subjects. The most important of these was *Delle lingue* (1542), a defence of the vernacular, which followed *Bembo's ideas and in its turn influenced *Du Bellay's *Deffense et illustration de la langue française* (1549). His tragedy, *Canace* (1546), followed Aristotle, and was designed to provoke feelings of pity. It involved the author in a long literary controversy.

F. Cammarosano, *La vita e le opere di Sperone Speroni* (1920).

SPEYER, DIETS OF Two important diets of the *Holy Roman Empire, in which the German Protestant princes made the first attempts to unite. The Diet of 1526 was supposed to put into effect the Edict of *Worms, but in view of the emperor's political difficulties, the Roman Catholic majority at the diet gave way to the minority, led by Landgrave *Philip of Hesse. It was determined that, until the convocation of a general ecclesiastical council, each ruler and his subjects "would live, govern, and act in such a way as everyone trusted to justify before God and the Imperial Majesty". This was the earliest official recognition of the followers of *Luther.

In the diet of 1529 the imperially-controlled majority was bent on annulling the earlier resolution. After this was done, a number of Lutheran princes and cities made the famous "protestation", from which the term *Protestant derives.

E. Mayer, *Der Speierer Reichstag 1529* (1929).

SPEYER, JOHANN AND WENDELIN OF German printers. Two brothers, natives of the town of Speyer, they arrived in *Venice in 1467 and, in 1469, opened the first printing establishment, Johann having been granted a five-year monopoly. Their first book, Cicero's *Epistolae ad familiares* (1469), was printed in clear "roman" type in an edition of 300 copies, which was quickly followed by a second of a similar size. After Johann's death in 1470, his brother continued to print until 1477. He produced dozens of titles, especially Latin classics, as well as an Italian translation of the *Bible (1471) and poems by *Petrarch.

SPIEGEL, HENRIC LAURENS (1549-1612) Dutch poet and humanist. Born in Amsterdam, he was brought up a Roman Catholic and, in 1578, objected to the Calvinists' takeover of the city. He was influenced by the Dutch humanist *Coornhert. In his *Nieuwe Jaerslieden* (1578-1601) he attacked tyranny. His major work is *Hertspiegel* ("Heart-Mirror", 1614). In this long poem he reveals his philosophical views and his religious beliefs. Another work of his is the unfinished *Lieden op't Vader Ons*. S. was a member of the movement which promoted the use of the Dutch language, and expressed his opinions on its importance in his "dialogue on Dutch Literature" (1584).

SPIERA, FRANCESCO (1502-48) Italian Protestant. A distinguished lawyer in Cittadella, near Padua, he began to have doubts about the Roman Catholic faith, preached Protestant doctrines and was tried before the *Inquisition in Venice. Having made a public recantation, he was allowed to return to his home. Later he sank into a state of profound depression which ended in his death. His case was frequently cited by 16th-century Protestants as an example of what happened to those who discovered the religious truth and denied it.

SPINELLO, ARETINO (c. 1346-1410) Italian painter. Born in Arezzo, he was probably trained in Florence, where he executed his first works. From 1361 to 1384 he worked chiefly in his native city; in 1387 he completed a fresco cycle on the life of St. Benedict in the sacristy of S. Miniato, Florence. He then painted frescoes in the Campo Santo of Pisa (1391-92) and, in 1400, was back in Florence, painting scenes from the lives of St. Philip and St. James in the church of S. Croce. His last works were executed in Siena's Palazzo Pubblico (1408-10). A fast-working narrative painter, S. borrowed from *Giotto, and increasingly from his contemporary Sienese masters.

SPORTS, THE BOOK OF The name given to the declaration issued by *James I of England in 1618 which defined the recreation permitted on the Sabbath after church. It allowed dancing, archery, maypoles and other physical leisure activities, but outlawed bear-baiting and "interludes", or short farcial plays. The S. was opposed by the *Puritans, who believed in stricter observance of the Sabbath. It was later reinforced by Charles I (1633), but eventually repealed by the Puritan-dominated Long Parliament.

SPOTTISWOODE, JOHN (1565-1639) Scottish archbishop of St. Andrews. Educated at the University of Glasgow, he became one of the leaders of the *Presbyterian movement, but later shifted his allegiance to James VI who, upon becoming *James I of England (1603), made him bishop of Edinburgh. He then espoused *Erastian views and became the chief instrument of the King in modelling the Scottish Kirk according to Anglican principles. He was made archbishop in 1615, continuing his close association with the monarchy under Charles I.

SPRANGER, BARTHOLOMEUS (1546-1611) Flemish painter. The son of a rich merchant of *Antwerp, he was taught by a number of artists, and was particularly influenced by Frans *Floris. From 1565 he travelled widely in France and Italy, worked for *Maximilian II in Vienna (1575) and, in 1581, settled in Prague as court painter of *Rudolf II, who in 1588 awarded him a title of nobility. In Italy he had been impressed by the works of *Correggio and *Parmigianino, and in his *Mannerist paintings exploited the erotic potentials of the nude. His friend, van *Mander, later introduced his style from the imperial court into Holland.

SPURS, BATTLE OF THE An almost bloodless battle fought on 16 August 1513 near Terouenne, France, in which the English under *Henry VIII defeated a French relief force. The English name of the encounter referred to the hasty French retreat from the battlefield. The battle was an outcome of Henry VIII's joining the *Holy League in 1511. In the following year he made peace with *Louis XII.

SQUARCIONE, FRANCESCO (1394-1468) Italian painter and teacher of artists. Born in Padua, he began

The Martyrdom of St. John the Evangelist *by Spranger*

as a tailor, before turning to painting in about 1429. His two extant rather mediocre works do not account for his reputation, so much as the fact that he was the teacher of a number of north-Italian painters, the so-called "Paduan School", including *Mantegna, Giorgio *Schiavone, Marco *Zoppo and Cosimo *Tura. S. had his pupils sign contracts in which they promised to work for him for a certain time; he also adopted some of them as his sons. However, judging from the fact that his best pupils preferred to break the contracts and run away, he must have been a harsh master. No traces of his collection of antique sculpture remain, and the classical orientation of the works of Mantegna and Zoppo is perhaps better attributed to the cultural climate of mid-15th-century Padua, a university-town in which humanist studies were beginning to flourish.

STAMPA, GASPARA (c. 1523-54) Italian poetess. Born in Padua, she was orphaned at an early age and raised in Venice with her sister and brother, all three becoming famous for their musical and literary gifts. Most probably a courtesan, she had several lovers, but fell in love with a Venetian noble, Collaltino di Collalto, who left her after three years. Her *Canzoniere*, first published in the year of her death, traces of the tragedy of her life. It contains love poems which are sensual and

Venus and Adonis *by Spranger*

sincere expressions of the feelings and passion of a tormented soul.

G. A. Cesareo, *Gaspara Stampa, donna e poetessa* (1920); L. Pompilj, *Gasparina* (1936).

STANCARO, FRANCESCO (1501-74) Italian theologian and reformer. Born in Mantua, he entered a religious order and studied theology. He became a Protestant in 1540, was suspected of heresy and left. He first went to Vienna (1544), and later to *Basle, where he published a *Hebrew grammar (1547). A year later, in Cracow, he published his 50 articles, entitled *Canones reformationis* (1548). He was seized as a heretic but escaped to Königsberg (1551), where he taught school. Later, he debated with Andreas *Osiander, and wrote his *Apologia contra Ostiandrum*. He continued to travel during his last years, visiting Poland, Hungary and Transylvania.

STANLEY, THOMAS (c. 1435-1504) English statesman, first earl of Derby. S. was a squire to *Henry VI, when he married Eleanor, daughter of the earl of *Warwick, the Yorkist leader, and his political positions remained ambiguous. He did not participate actively in the Wars of the *Roses, but was often suspected as a traitor. In 1460 he fought at Henry's side in the Battle of Northampton, but the victorious Yorkists appointed him chief justice of Chester and Flint, and he became a counselor of *Edward IV. In 1482 he married *Margaret Beaufort, mother of Henry *Tudor (later *Henry VII). After the latter's landing in England, he remained neutral, while his brother fought with the Tudor forces and, after the Battle of Bosworth (27 Oct. 1485), he placed the crown on Henry's head. He was rewarded with the title Earl of Derby.

STAPLE, COMPANY OF MERCHANTS OF THE Beginning in the early 14th century, the kings of England assigned certain towns on the Continent staples, i.e., exclusive dealers in the main English exports. In 1392 the Continental staple was formally established in English-ruled Calais. The English wool export was handled there by a company of merchants with a monopoly granted by the crown. The arrangement did not help the expansion of English wool export, but the company periodically helped the crown with large loans, and thus retained its privileges; from 1466 on it also administered the port. However, the increasing English export to the Netherlands diminished the importance of Calais, and the company lost its preeminence to the *Merchant Adventurers. Its decline was completed after the conquest of Calais by the French in 1558.

E. E. Power *The Wool Trade in English Medieval History* (1941);
E. M. Carus-Wilson, *Medieval Merchant Venturers,* 2nd ed. (1967).

STAPLETON, THOMAS (1535-98) English Roman Catholic author. Having been a prebendary of Chichester under *Mary Tudor, he left England after the accession of *Elizabeth I and, in 1569, joined William *Allen in *Douai. There S. taught divinity for many years and, in 1590, *Philip II appointed him professor of theology in Louvain. A prolific writer, he defended the authority of the Church, but did not entirely subscribe to the supremacy of the pope. His *Tres Thomae* (1588) dealt with Thomas the Apostle, Thomas à Becket and Thomas More.

STAR CHAMBER, COURT OF An English judicial court, created by *Henry VII in 1487 to deal with criminal charges against persons too powerful for the ordinary slow courts. Composed of a special committee of the Royal Council, it was based on a mediaeval tradition by which the Council was always superior to any other court. There is a theory that it was named after the chamber in which the promissory notes of the 13th-century Jewish moneylenders (*Shetar* in Hebrew), were deposited at the expulsion of the Jews. The S. served the *Tudors effectively in dealing with internal opposition. It had no jury, and could use torture in examining suspects and witnesses. Very popular in the first decades of its existence, it was later criticized for its harsh methods and abolished in 1641.

STARKEY, THOMAS (c. 1490-1538) English political thinker. A graduate of Oxford University, he taught natural philosophy at Magdalen College. In about 1531 he entered the service of Reginald *Pole in Italy and, in 1534, became chaplain to Pole's mother in England. He was made a royal chaplain shortly afterwards. In 1535 he was ordered by *Henry VIII to write Pole to persuade him to return to England, and to seek his opinion on the King's divorce. Though his efforts were fruitless, he was rewarded by the King and made master of Corpus Christi (1536). His best-known works are *Exhortation to Christian Unity* (written about 1534), and the *Dialogue between Cardinal Pole and Thomas Lupset* (written between 1536-38). The *Dialogue* describes the evils of life in England at the time, and discusses the question of public good. The author tries to discover the nature of the true commonweal, and how it can be established in England. Permeated with humanist utilitarianism, it stands beside *More's *Utopia* as the most outstanding English political writing of the age.

STATIONERS' COMPANY Trade association of London's printers and booksellers, established in 1403. In 1557 *Mary Tudor granted the S. monopolistic control of all book publishing. Intended in part as an instrument against the printing of heretical and seditious writings, it gave the company a powerful semi-official standing, which it kept through the 16th and 17th centuries.

STAUPITZ, JOHANN VON (c. 1470-1524) German vicar-general of the Augustinian friars. After studying at the university of Leipzig, he joined the Augustinians (1490), becoming a prior of a monastery at Tübingen (1497) and a doctor of theology (1500). He was invited by *Frederick III the Wise, Elector of Saxony, to help with the organization of the new university of *Wittenberg, becoming the first dean of its faculty of theology (1503-12). In 1503 he became vicar-general of the order in Germany and in this capacity took interest in *Luther, whom he chose to succeed him at Wittenberg. After Luther's attack on the sale of *indulgences, S. refused to take disciplinary measures against him. In 1520 he resigned the vicariate, but three years later Cardinal Matthäus *Lang made him abbot of the wealthy Benedictine abbey of St. Peter at Salzburg. Shortly before his death he began to preach against the *Reformation.

E. Wolf, *Staupitz und Luther* (1927).

ST. BARTHOLOMEW'S NIGHT, MASSACRE OF A massacre of the French Protestants (*Huguenots), in which it is estimated that 10,000 people lost their lives. It began on the night of 23-24 August 1572 in Paris, lasted for two days and then spread to the French provinces. It happened shortly after a great number of Huguenots arrived in Paris to witness the marriage of Henry of Navarre and *Marguerite de Valois on 18 August, and was preceded by an attempt on the life of *Coligny on 22 August. The following night Coligny was murdered in his house by Henry Duke of *Guise, and this, and the ringing of church bells, gave the signal to begin the slaughter. Young Henry of Navarre and the prince of *Condé were spared on condition that they become Catholic. Made possible by the recent joining of forces between *Catherine de Médicis and the extreme Catholic party, the massacre did not destroy the Huguenots, who continued to fight stubbornly for their religious freedom.

S. England, *The Massacre of Saint Bartholomew* (1938);
P. Erlanger, *Le massacre de la Saint-Barthelemy* (1960).

STEENWYCK, HENDRICK VAN (c. 1550-1603) Dutch painter. Born near Overyssel, he was a pupil of Hans

Vredeman de *Vries, and excelled in the painting of small interiors of Gothic churches. He acquired a considerable reputation and, when religious persecution obliged him to leave the Netherlands, he was welcomed to Frankfurt. His son of the same name (c. 1580-1649), continued to work in a similar style, surpassing his father.

STEFANO DA VERONA (1374-c. 1450) Italian painter, also known as Stefano di Giovanni or Stefano da Zevio. A native of Verona, where he spent most of his life, he was one of the foremost practitioners of the *International Gothic in an elegant, decorative and poetic manner. His **Madonna* in an enclosed garden, in Verona, has an unreal atmosphere. His *Adoration of the Magi* (1435), considered his principal work, is in Milan.

STEINHÖWEL, HEINRICH (1412-82) German humanist. Born at Weil, he studied in Vienna and Padua, and later practised *medicine in Esslingen and Ulm. He made free German translations of *Boccaccio's *De claris mulieribus* and *Guiscardo e Sigismunde* (1473), and published a collection of fables in 1477, under the title *Aesop.* these and other translations contributed to the development of German prose *literature in the vernacular. He also wrote *Regimen sanitatis* (1472), a treatise on hygiene.

M. O. Walshe, *Medieval German Literature* (1962).

STEPHEN BATHORY (1533-86) King of Poland from 1575. Scion of an ancient family of the Hungarian aristocracy, he spent his early years at the court of *Ferdinand I, but later became the trusted aid of *John Zapolya. His support of the rights of the latter's son and successor, John Sigismund, caused him to be imprisoned for a period by *Maximilian II. In 1571, after the death of John Sigismund, he was elected prince of Transylvania by the Hungarian estates. The election was followed by a civil war in which S. proved his military skill, and which strengthened his surprising claim to the throne of Poland, recently evacuated by *Henry of Valois. Elected and crowned at Cracow (May 1575), he was at first in extremely difficult situation, but after crushing the internal opposition, led by the city of Danzig (1577), consolidated his government. It is to S.'s credit as a ruler that he was able to persuade the Polish nobility to raise money for a campaign against *Ivan the Terrible of Russia. The war ended in 1582 with the cession of Livonia to Poland. S. encouraged the *Jesuits in Poland, and had plans to unite it with Hungary, but died before his design could be carried out.

J. Dabrowski, *Etienne Bathory, roi de Pologne, prince de Transylvanie* (1935).

Cars propelled by wind, developed by Simon Stevin

STERNHOLD, THOMAS (c. 1500-49) English writer. A native of Gloucestershire, his metrical English rendition of the Psalms, published shortly before his death, became very popular. It influenced the development of *hymns. S. served in the court of *Henry VIII, and was a member of parliament.

STETHAIMER, HANS (c. 1360-1432) German architect and painter. Born probably in Burghausen, he was one of the most important German architects in the late Gothic style, designing "Hall-Churches" with aisles as high as the nave. On his tomb at Landshut, Bavaria, are listed seven churches which he had built. His best works are in Landshut and Salzburg, Austria.

E Hanfstaengl, *Hans Stethaimer* (1911).

STEVIN, SIMON (1548-1620) Dutch mathematician and engineer, Born in *Bruges, he became a bookkeeper in *Antwerp, but later joined the service of *Maurice of Nassau, for whom he improved the defense system of sluices in the dykes. This made possible the flooding of lowlands against Spanish troops. S.'s small work, *De Thiende* (Decimals), published in 1585, introduced the use of decimal fractions. In 1586 he formulated the first basic theories of hydrostatics, related to the pressure of liquids on given surfaces. He also wrote on geography and experimented with falling bodies, his attempts to refute Aristotelian physics coming a few years before *Galileo's.

E. J. Dijksterhuis, *Simon Stevin; Science in the Netherlands Around 1600* (1970).

STIMMER, TOBIAS (1539-84) Swiss painter and book illustrator. Born at Schaffhausen, he came of a well-known family of painters and followed the style of *Holbein. He is especially remembered for his decorative *frescoes in Schaffhausen and Baden-Baden. In 1574 he decorated the astronomical clock of the cathedral in *Strassburg.

ST. JOHN, KNIGHTS OF THE ORDER OF Known also as the "Hospitallers" or "Knights of Rhodes" and, after 1530, "Knights of Malta". A product of the age of the Crusades, this order of warriors bound by religious vows established itself in 1309 on the island of Rhodes. During the second half of the 15th century it was the core of Christian resistance to the *Ottoman Turks in the Aegean Sea but, in 1522, *Suleiman II conquered Rhodes, causing the knights to seek temporary refuge in Crete. In 1530 they received the island of Malta from *Charles V, and it remained their permanent base until it was captured by Napoleon in 1798.

STONE, NICHOLAS (1583-1647) English sculptor. A native of Devonshire, he went to *Amsterdam, where he worked with Hendrik de *Keyser, whose daughter he subsequently married. He returned to England in 1613 and became known at first for his elegant tombs, and later for his impressive sculptural monuments and figures in London's principal churches. After 1619 he worked with the architect Inigo *Jones and, in 1632, oecame master mason to the crown. His later style, tending towards naturalism, showed the influence of Italian and classical art. He employed many assistants, a fact which is betrayed by the uneven quality of his works. An excellent craftsman, he was the most important English sculptor of the first half of the 17th century. He left a record of his activities in his *Note-Book* and *Account Book*.

W. L. Spiers, ed., *The Note-Book and Account Book of Nicholas Stone* (1918).

STORCH, NICHOLAS An illiterate German clothmaker from Zwickau who, in 1521, led a group of followers to Wittenberg, where they became known as the *Zwickau Prophets. He later preached in various places in Germany and Poland, his ideas broadly corresponding to those of the *Anabaptists. He died in Bavaria in 1530.

STOSS, VEIT (c. 1447-1533) German sculptor. Born in Swabia, he was trained in *Nuremberg, where he lived for the better part of his career. But his best-known work was done in Cracow, where he carved the huge altarpiece of the German church of St. Mary (1477-89), in a style which is essentially Gothic, though dramatically powerful and with realist qualities. Also in Cracow is his tomb of King Casimir IV. Upon his return to Nuremberg, S. was accused of forging a document, a charge which marred the rest of his life. Until 1496 he worked in Bohemia and Hungary. Later he produced wood and stone sculptures for the churches of St. Sebald and St. Lorenz, Nuremberg. His last important work was the carved altarpiece for the cathedral of Bamberg (*c.* 1520-23). A painter and engraver too, he was a virtuoso of wood-carving.

E. Lutze, *Veit Stoss* (1938).

STOW, JOHN (c. 1525-1605) English historian and antiquary. Born in London, he was a tailor until the early 1560s, when he began to collect manuscripts and to write chronicles. Despite of his lowly origins, he became a member of the Society of Antiquaries, founded about 1586. He first published an edition of Chaucer (1561) and a *Summary of English Chronicles* (1565). His first original work was *The Annales of England* (1580). S.'s most famous work is *A Survey of London* (1598; revised by him in 1603). It contains information about the history of London, and details of the life, customs, people, government and scenery in London. S. was employed by Archbishop *Parker to edit mediaeval chronicles. It was said that he had spent all his money in the search for records.

F. Smith Fussner, *The Historical Revolution* (1962), 211-30.

ST. PETER'S The great cathedral at the Vatican in *Rome; the largest single building designed and constructed during the Renaissance. Erected on the site where St. Peter is believed to have been crucified, the idea of building it was first promoted by *Nicholas V. However, it was only in 1506, under *Julius II, that work began according to a plan by *Bramante, and it took over a century to complete. In the meantime a series of architects altered the original design. Bramante's successor was *Raphael, followed by *Peruzzi and *Sangallo. *Michelangelo, who was in charge of the works between 1547 and 1564, redesigned it and built the drum beneath the dome, which was completed by Giacomo della *Porta (1590). The building was finished

A group of angels from Christ's Baptism *by Veit Stoss*

in 1614, but during the following years Giovanni Bernini (1598-1680) continued to work on the interior and built the magnificent colonnades surrounding the piazza at the front of the church. It remains one of the greatest examples of monumental architecture.

M. Sharp, *A Guide to the Churches of Rome* (1966).

STRAPAROLA, GIANFRANCESCO (c. 1480-1557) Italian novelist. He was born at Caravaggio, but little is known about his life. His *Sonetti* (1508) were undistinguished, and he is chiefly remembered for *Le piacevoli notti* (The Pleasant Nights), a collection of 75 popular stories, published in Venice in 1550 and 1553. These include tales which combine the ordinary with the supernatural, and animal fables. They were translated into other languages and influenced the growing of fairy tales in the 17th century.

G. Mazzacurati, *Società e strutture narrative dal Trecento al Cinquecento* (1971).

St. Peter's

STRASSBURG An important commercial centre in Alsace, west of the Rhine river, this city became the heart of German humanism in the 15th century. Such scholars as *Wimpfeling and Sebastian Brant resided there, and the city was also an important centre of early *printing. In 1381 S. became member of the league of Swabian towns, and it supported the Swiss cantons during their war against *Charles the Bold (1474-77). Led by Martin *Bucer, the *Reformation was accepted in S. at about 1523. The Mass was suppressed and convents abolished (1529). The city's political activities during that period were directed by Jacob *Sturm. Under his leadership S. was among the "protesters" at the second Diet of *Speyer (1529), and joined the *Schmalkaldic League in 1531. S. participated in the League's war against Charles V and, though forced to submit to the Emperor, it obtained favourable terms (1548). S. did not actively participate in the *Thirty Years' War (1618-48), withdrawing from the *Protestant Union in 1621, and remaining neutral to the end. In the same year the Emperor *Ferdinand II established the university of S., on the basis of its existing academy.
M. U. Chrisman, *Strasbourg and the Reform* (1967).

STRIGEL, BERNHARD (c. 1460-1528) German painter. A pupil of *Zeitblom at Ulm, he settled in nearby Memmingen, and became famous for works he did for *Maximilian I, including the emperor's portraits. His altarpieces combined German traditions with Italian influences.

STRIGEL, VICTORINUS (1524-69) German Protestant theologian. A native of Swabia, he was the student of *Melanchthon at Wittenberg and, in 1548, became professor at Jena. In 1563 he began to teach at Leipzig but, following objections to his teachings, moved to Heidelberg in 1567. S. wrote biblical commentaries as well as on philology and theology. In an age of growing Lutheran rigidity, he continued to represent Melanchthon's liberal outlook on issues such as *original sin, divine grace and free will.
V. A. Nordman, *Victorinus Strigelius als Geschichtslehrer* (1930).

STROZZI A Florentine family of wealthy merchants, which played an important part in the political life of their city. Prominent since the 13th century, the S. went into *banking in the 14th century. During the 15th century they were often the political rivals of the rising *Medici, whom they also tried to outdo as patrons of artists and humanists. Their palace in Florence, designed by *Benedetto da Majano and completed by Il *Cronaca (1489), is one of the best examples of early Renaissance architecture. The family had branches in other Italian cities, of which that of

*Ferrara is especially remembered thanks to the courtiers, the poets Tito Vespasiano S. (1424-1505) and his son, Ercole (*c.* 1473-1508). Later in the 15th century the family made its peace with the Medici. After 1527 it supported the French, which again pitted it against the Medici, who supported Spain. Filippo S. (1489-1538) became an opponent of Duke Alessandro de' Medici and, in 1533, had to leave Florence for Venice. After Alessandro's death he attempted to rally the Florentine exiles against *Cosimo I, but was captured and put to death. Filippo's sons Piero (*c.* 1510-58) and Leone (1515-54), both distinguished themselves later as military commanders in the service of France.

STROZZI, PALLA (c. 1373-1462) Italian merchant and humanist. Belonging to the distinguished Florentine merchant family, he was interested in humanist studies. In 1395 he helped to bring Manuel *Chrysoloras to Florence and studied *Greek under him. A great collector of Greek manuscripts, he made his home in Florence a centre of Greek studies, and founded the city's first public library. When Cosimo de' *Medici returned from exile, S., a supporter of the losing party, was banished (1434). He ended his life in Padua, where he continued to back humanist endeavours.

STUART, ALEXANDER (c. 1493-1513) Scottish humanist. The natural son of *James IV, king of Scotland, he was appointed archbishop of St. Andrews in about 1505. In 1506 he went to the Netherlands and France, and settled in Padua (1508), where he studied rhetoric and logic under *Erasmus. The latter praised his character and eagerness to study. Around 1510 he was appointed lord chancellor of Scotland. He patronized learning and was the founder of the college of St, Leonard's. He joined his king in the attempt to invade England, and was killed in the Battle of Flodden Field (9 September 1513).

STUART, ARABELLA (1575-1615) English figure in succession intrigues against *James I. A first cousin of the King, she was a member of the English branch of the Stuart family, and viewed by some as legitimate successor to Elizabeth I. She continued, however, to reside at court until 1610 when, contrary to the King's wishes, she married Sir William Seymour. Detained by royal orders and confined separately, the lovers escaped, Seymour reaching Ostend. But Arabella was captured at sea, brought back to England and committed to the Tower. Heartbroken and progressively deranged, she died after four years of imprisonment.

P. M. Handover, *Arabella Stuart* (1957).

STUBBS, JOHN (c. 1543-91) English *Puritan pamphleteer. Educated at Cambridge, he was the brother-in-law of Thomas *Cartwright and, in 1579, published an attack on the proposed marriage of *Elizabeth I with Francis, duke of *Anjou. For this S. was sentenced to have his right hand cut off, and while the sentence was carried out, he supposedly waved his hat with the other hand, protesting his loyalty to the Queen. Later, he wrote a response to William *Allen and, in 1589, became a member of parliament.

STUMPF, JOHANNES (1500-78) Swiss historian and theologian. Born in Bruchsal, Germany, he studied in Heidelberg and *Strassburg and, in 1521, entered the order of St. John. In 1522 he was appointed prior and people's priest in Bubikon, *Zurich, where he stayed until 1543. S. was an early supporter of *Zwingli, whose views on the Eucharist he strongly defended. His *Schweizer und Reformationschronik* contains Zwingli's first biography. He wrote several works on geography, history and theology, the most famous of which was a Swiss chronicle, *Gemeiner loblicher Eidgenossenschaft Städten, Landen und Völkern chronikwürdiger Taten Beschreibung* (1546-48).

STURE The name of three Swedish regents, distantly related, who led the resistance to Danish domination at the end of the 15th and early 16th century. Sten S. the Elder (*c.* 1440-1503) became regent upon the death of *Charles VIII and, in 1471, defeated an invading force led by *Christian I of Denmark. He did much to centralize the country's administration. Svante S. (*c.* 1460-1512) succeeded as regent in 1503, but was much less effective. Sten S. the Younger (*c.* 1492-1520), an ambitious manipulator, attempted to reduce further the power of the nobility; he died of wounds received during the invasion of *Christian II.

STURM, JACOB (1489-1553) German politician and Protestant reformer. Born in *Strassburg, he was educated at the universities of Heidelberg and Freiburg. In 1524, after converting to Protestantism, he became a member of the Strassburg municipal government, where he became a leading figure. He represented the city in the German diets which dealt with the *Reformation. S. supported a union among the various Protestant groups, and participated in the debate between *Luther and *Zwingli at *Marburg (1529). Since no compromise was reached, he supported a Zwinglian line in the *Tetrapolitan Confession, which he presented to the Diet of *Augsburg (1530). S. was largely instrumental in the participation of Strassburg in the *Schmalkaldic League. After its defeat by *Charles V in 1547, he was able to obtain favourable terms for his city from the Emperor.

STURM, JOHANNES (1507-89) German Protestant educator. Born in Schleiden, Westphalia, he was educated ad the university of Louvain, and at the *Collège de France in Paris, where he then lectured on medicine and the classics (1530-36). Being a successful teacher, he was invited in 1537 by the magistrates of *Strassburg to open a classical Latin school in the city. S. opened the Strassburg Gymnasium in 1538. Its students were mainly sons of noble and wealthy families. The curriculum emphasized the liberal arts, stressed *Greek and classical *Latin, and included *music, logic, oratory *drama and *mathematics. S. converted to Lutheranism, but criticized the Lutheran church of Strassburg. As a result he was expelled in 1581. Eventually allowed to return, he died in poverty. Among his notable works are: *The Book on the Right Method of Founding Schools for Literary Education* (1537), and *Classical Letters* (1565). S.'s Gymnasium became a model for Protestant schools, and his theories on education had a lasting influence in Europe. (ND)

SUAREZ, FRANCISCO (1548-1617) Spanish philosopher and theologian. Born into a family of jurists in Granada, he went to study law in Salamanca in 1561, and joined the *Jesuits in 1564. From 1571 he taught philosophy and theology in several Spanish universities, and later at the Jesuit college in Rome (1580-85). From 1585-93 he taught at Alcalá. In 1597 he received King *Philip II's appointment to the chair of theology at the university of Coimbra in Portugal, where he remained until a little before his death. S.'s doctrines inspired a school of thought called "Suarism", which was influential in European universities for more than a century. His major work, *Disputationes Metaphysicae* (1597), deals with the problems of human will and the idea of the general versus in particular. He relied on Aristotle and Thomas Aquinas, but also on other scholastic philosophers. At the request of Pope *Paul V he wrote apologetic works, two of which are *De Virtute et Statu Religionis* (1608-09), and *Defensio Fidei Catholicae* (1613). In these works S. opposes the theory of the divine rights of kings, and expresses his political and legal philosophy: the people are the original holders of political authority; the state is founded by a social contract, and the people have the right to life and liberty. This theory led him to criticize the acts of the Spanish colonists in the Indies. In his book, *De Bello et de Indis,* he argues that the Indies are also sovereign states. Possibly the greatest Jesuit theologian, S. is considered one of the founders of international law. According to his theory, all nations are members of one community, and the relations between them are governed by a body of international law.

R. Wilenius, *The Social and Political Theory of Francisco Suárez* (1963).

J. Fichter, *Man of Spain; A Biography of Francis Suárez* (1940). (ND)

SUBMISSION OF THE CLERGY (15 May 1532) The act by which the English clergy surrendered to the demands of King *Henry VIII. In this act the right of final approval of ecclesiastical laws was given to the king of England. The agreement was reached after the House of Commons complained to Henry VIII about the privileges of the Church in matters of legislation, and about abuses in the church. The clergy agreed not to legislate without royal consent, and to submit existing laws to the censorship of a commission of 16 members of parliament and 16 clergy. The submission was enacted by parliament in 1534. The S. also abolished the absolute autonomy of the church courts, and made the king the supreme authority in appeals on ecclesiastical matters.

SUFFOLK, WILLIAM DE LA POLE, DUKE OF (1396-1450) English statesman. Having distinguished himself in negotiating with France, he attached himself to the *Beaufort party, and rose to prominence in the government when *Henry VI was declared of age (1422). In 1445 he arranged the King's marriage to *Margaret of Anjou and, in 1447, caused the arrest of his old rival the duke of *Gloucester, who died in prison shortly afterwards. His pacific policy towards France gave rise to accusations against him in 1449, when the French began their conquest of Normandy, and to these were added charges of greed, accumulation of public offices and misuse of royal funds. Impeached in parliament, he tried to escape to Flanders, but was intercepted by a ship sent after him and beheaded.

SULEIMAN I (1494-1566) Sultan of the *Ottoman empire from 1520, called the Magnificent, and by the Turks Kanuni, the Lawgiver. His rule was the golden heydey of the empire, and he extended its power and influence in Europe and Asia. The only son of Sultan *Selim I, he was made governor of Kefe in 1509 and later was transferred to Manisa in Western Anatolia. When he succeeded to the throne, he began a series

Sultan Suleiman I, *a 16th-century European engraving*

of military ventures and domestic reforms. His first military campaigns were directed against the Christian states in central Europe and the Mediterranean. In 1521 he attacked *Hungary and captured Belgrade, and a year later seized Rhodes from the Knights of *St. John. His next campaign in Hungary ended in a triumph at *Mohács and the death of the Hungarian king, *Louis II (1526). His efforts to prevent an intervention of the *Habsburgs in Hungary culminated in a siege on *Vienna (1529); it failed, but he did incorporate Budapest into his empire. Though he concluded a peace treaty with *Austria in 1533, the conflict over the control of Hungary reopened in 1540. The country was divided, with the Habsburgs ruling in the north and the Ottomans in the centre and in Transylvania. Nevertheless, the war in Hungary was resumed in 1541. The peace that was signed in 1562 did not end the confrontations.

In the east S. fought the Persians and recaptured Tabris, and conquered Baghdad and the area of Lake Van (1534). Ottoman naval domination was established in the Mediterranean by admiral Barbarossa (Khayr-ed-Din) who, in 1538, defeated the fleets of Venice and Spain, off Preveza. Tripoli was taken by the Ottomans in 1551, but an attempt to take Malta in 1565 failed. From 1535 on, S.'s struggle against the Habsburgs was supported by France, with which he had a formal alliance and which he granted the first *Capitulations. S. organized his vast empire well. He established an able administration, and was served by capable viziers, such as Ibrahim Rüstem and Muhamad *Sökölli. He initiated and revised laws, trying to adjust them to the needs of the empire. During his reign the Ottoman empire flourished economically and culturally. The arts, literature and architecture were developed. The cities, especially the capital, Istanbul, gained new public buildings. In his later years S. had to deal with quarrels among his sons. Two of them, Mustafa and Bayezid, were executed, and the Sultan chose *Selim, son of his beloved wife *Roxelana, as his successor. S. died in September 1566, while besieging the fortress of Szigetvar in Hungary.

R. B. Merriman, *Suleiman the Magnificent, 1520-66* (1944);

D. M. Vaughan, *Europe and the Turks* (1954);

A. H. Lybyer, *The Government of the Ottoman Empire in the Time of Suleiman the Magnificent* (1913). (ND)

SULLY, MAXIMILIAN DE BETHUNE, DUKE OF (1560-1641) French statesman in the reign of Henry IV. Born in Rosny, he was brought up as a *Huguenot and was sent as a boy to the court of Henry of Navarre (later King *Henry IV of France). During the *Religious Wars (1562-98), he joined Henry's forces and was wounded at the Battle of Ivry (1590). He helped arrange Henry's marriage with *Marie de Médicis (1600), negotiated the Peace of Savoy (1601), and was ambassador extraordinary to England (1603). He served as a member of the King's financial council in 1596, and became finance minister by 1598. His measures were effective and helped to rehabilitate France's economy after its prolonged internal conflicts. However, his new tax, the Paulette, made French office-holders into a closed caste. In return for an annual tax, offices were made hereditary, and could be passed on at will or sold. For his loyalty to the King, he was granted several titles of nobility and, in 1606, was created duke of Sully and a peer of France. His major role in the government ended after Henry's assassination (1610) and he resigned in 1611. While in retirement, he wrote his *Memoires* (1638).

H. Pourrat, *Sully et sa grande passion* (1942).

SUMMENHART, KONRAD (c. 1450-1502) German theologian. A native of Württemberg, he studied in Paris and, from 1489, lectured on theology and philosophy at Tübingen. Trained in the scholastic tradition, his work showed little trace of the new humanist currents in Germany. But some of his works touched critically upon ecclesiastical matters, especially monastic abuses, which qualifies him as a precursor of the *Reformation.

SUPREMACY, ACT OF An act passed in England in 1534 which declared the king the supreme head of a national church. The act legalized the claims of *Henry VIII in ecclesiastical matters, and marked the establishment of the *Church of England. All office holders had to take an oath of loyalty, swearing to accept the results of the break with Rome and the supremacy of the king, or be charged with treason. The S. was repealed by *Mary Tudor, but renewed by *Elizabeth I, as the first act of her reign. In this and the Uniformity Act of 1559, the Queen was declared supreme governor in all spiritual and ecclesiastical matters.

SURREY, HENRY HOWARD, EARL OF (1516-47) English poet. The son of the third duke of *Norfolk, he became acquainted with the new modes of poetry while on visit to Italy. Later he fought against Scotland and, during his father's ascendancy at the court of Henry VIII, was made governor of Boulogne, France. But in 1546 he and his father were arrested and falsely accused of high treason. On 21 January 1547, he was executed, the last victim of *Henry VIII. His poems were published, together with those of Thomas *Wyatt in 1557, and his translations from Virgil's *Aeneid* appeared about the same time.

F. H. Ridley, ed., *The Aneid of Henry Howard, Earl of Surrey* (1963).

SWABIAN LEAGUE A confederation of south German princes, free cities and knights for the common defence of law and order. It was created in 1488 with the encouragement of Emperor *Frederick III, and was continually backed by the *Habsburgs, who saw in it an effective instrument for the political stability of Germany. In 1519 the S. achieved a major victory when it defeated Duke *Ulrich of Württemberg, in 1523 it crushed the *Knights' War of Franz von *Sickingen and, in 1525, defeated the *Peasants' War. Later, the divisions caused by the *Reformation crippled the S. and, by 1530, it was to all intents and purposes dissolved.

SWABIAN WAR (1499) War between Emperor *Maximilian I and the *Swiss Confederation. When the Emperor made a final attempt to bring the Swiss back under imperial jurisdiction and taxation, resistance led to a war in which the Emperor was defeated twice: at Calven (May 1499), and a Dernach (July 1499). The Peace of Basle, which followed the S., granted the Swiss Confederation virtual independence.

SWART VAN GRONINGEN, JAN (c. 1495-c. 1560) Dutch painter and engraver. Not much is known about his life. In 1522 he worked at Gouda, and later in *Antwerp, where he died. He may have visited *Venice, and his work shows familiarity with the style of the

Henry Howard, Earl of Surrey *by Holbein the Younger*

The representatives of the cantons swearing the oath at the founding of the Swiss Confederation

Italian High Renaissance. He contributed most of the woodcuts in the 1528 Dutch edition of the *Bible, published in *Antwerp.

SWEDEN Becoming a member of the Scandinavian Union, with *Denmark and Norway in 1397, S. consented to be ruled from Copenhagen, where the monarch of the three kingdoms resided. The awkwardness of this arrangement became clear already in the reign of *Eric (1412-39), whose wars and heavy taxation aroused the enmity of the lower classes and hindered S.'s commercial relations with the *Hanseatic League. The king was deposed in an uprising and, in 1448, a Swedish noble, Karl Knutsson, was crowned king as *Charles VIII. Twice exiled, Charles VIII managed to retain the crown until his death in 1470, while obstructing the attempts of *Christian I of Denmark to conquer the country. The rise of the *Sture family began in his reign, and they dominated the next 50 years, as regents nominated by the Swedish royal council. The final confrontation with Denmark, still determined to impose the union, came in 1520, when *Christian II asserted his rights and defeated the Stures in battle. Crowned king, he ordered the massacre of 80 Swedish nobles (the Stockholm Bloodbath) in November 1520. The atrocity stirred a new nationalist revolt, led by *Gustavus Vasa, who was supported by *Lübeck. In 1523 he was elected king at Strängnäs. The tremendous increase of the royal power unter the *Vasas was largely due to the decision of Gustavus I to introduce the *Reformation, a step undertaken chiefly out of political consideration. In 1527, at the Diet of Västeras, the property of the Church was transferred to the monarchy, bishops were made dependent on the crown and the payment of Peter's pence to Rome was discontinued. Two years later changes were introduced into the religious service. The king, who at first encouraged the Lutheran preaching of the *Petri brothers, later curbed their activities and strove to make the process slow and gradual. But S. nevertheless became the first nation of Europe to espouse the Reformation.

In spite of several revolts, which he suppressed, and wars with Lübeck and *Ivan IV of Russia, Gustavus Vasa was able to persuade the Swedish *Riksdag* to make the monarchy hereditary, leaving his son *Eric XIV at the head of a strong government (1560-68). The latter, a headstrong and unstable person, embroiled his country in wars with Denmark and *Poland. His half-brother *John III (1569-92), who deposed him, married Catherine, daughter of *Sigismund I of Poland, and entertained ideas of restoring S. to Roman Catholicism. This would have been done, had his son, *Sigismund III of Poland, ascended the throne. But when John died, his brother Charles, the last surviving son of Gustavus Vasa, came forward as the defender of Swedish Protestantism. Ruling as regent, he defeated an attempt by Sigismund III to enter the country (1598), declared his deposition (1599) and, in 1604, assumed the crown as *Charles IX. He was quite unsuccessful in his wars against Poland, *Russia and Denmark, but under his son Gustavus Adolphus (1611-32), S. entered its greatest period as a European power.

I. Anderson, *A History of Sweden* (1968);
C. J. Hallendorf and A. Schüch, *History of Sweden* (1929; rep. 1970);
V. Moberg, *A History of the Swedish People,* 2 vols. (1972-74).

SWISS CONFEDERATION In 1291 three forest cantons, Schwyz, Uri and Unterwalden, formed an "Everlasting League" for mutual defence. In doing so, they renounced the direct rule of the house of *Habsburg, which was then the most powerful Swabian family. In 1315 the cantons had to resist the attack of Duke Leopold of Austria. His effort to crush the Swiss ended in his defeat at the Battle of Morgarten. The victory strengthened the power of the cantons and launched the career of the Swiss infantry in Europe. Between 1332 and 1353 five more cantons, Lucerne, *Zurich, Glarus, Zug and Bern, joined the S. Its expansion led to a renewed threat from the Habsburgs. At the Battel of Sempach (1386) and at Näfels (1388) the S. defeated Leopold II of Swabia, and was relieved of Habsburg domination.

During the 15th century there were struggles with neighbours and further expansion of the cantons. Entirely autonomous, each canton pursued its own interest, with the frequent result of internecine conflict. A dispute between Zurich and the other confederates over the question of the succession in Toggenburg resulted in a civil war in 1436. Zurich allied itself with Austria, but was defeated and a peace was concluded between the cantons in 1450. The growing military power of the Swiss was expressed in the war against *Charles the Bold of Burgundy (1474-77) whose intervention in Alsace was seen as a threat to the S. The Swiss army defeated the Burgundians at Granson (2 March 1476) and at Morat (22 June 1476), and finally at the Battle of Nancy (5 January 1477), in which Charles was killed. Swiss military prestige further increased after the defeat of Emperor *Maximilian I in the *Swabian War (1499). As a result, the independence of the S. was recognized in the Treaty of Basle. The S.'s military reputation was also expressed in the important role of its mercenaries in the Italian wars. Swiss soldiers were employed by both the French and the Italian armies, and their refusal to fight against each other aided the French in the invasion of the Duchy of Milan (1499-1500). In 1511 the Swiss joined the *Holy League against France, forced the French to leave Milan and occupied northern Italy, until the invasion and the victory of *Francis I of France at Marignano (1515). In the treaty of 1516 the Swiss renounced all claims to Milan, but retained Lugano, Locarno and the Valtellina pass. Swiss mercenaries continued to serve in the French army.

Meanwhile new cantons joined the S. By 1513 Freiburg, Solothurn, *Basle, Schaffhausen and Appenzell had been admitted. The number of cantons, which was then 13, remained unchanged for nearly two centuries. Economically the S. was in difficulties. It had to import such basic commodities as corn and salt, while its chief export were the mercenaries. Economic problems, social unrest and the unique form of a loose association of largely self-governing states, made up the background of the Swiss *Reformation. The first Swiss challenge to the Catholic Church was made by Huldrych *Zwingli, who was a preacher in the Zurich Cathedral from 1518. In 1523 evangelical preaching in Zurich became compulsory, and pilgrimages, relics, images and the sale of *indulgences were prohibited. Zwingli's teachings and reforms were accepted by Schaffhausen, Glarus, Appenzell, Basle and Bern. In response the Catholic cantons Lucerne, Uri, Schwyz, Unterwalden and Zug, banded together against Zurich. In the Battle of Kappel (1531) Zurich was defeated and Zwingli killed. The Peace of Kappel, which followed, formalized the religious division of the S., which weakened it. In 1541, *Geneva, which did not belong to the S. but allied itself with the protestant cantons, adopted the Reformation. There John *Calvin became the dominant figure, and his reforms in the government and social life made the city a centre for Protestant refugees. The S. was not directly involved in the *Thirty Years' War, but it sent mercenaries to both the Catholic and the Protestant sides. In the Treaty of Westphalia (1648) it received a formal European recognition of its independence.

E. Bonjour, *A Short History of Switzerland* (1952);
W. Martin, *A History of Switzerland* (1931);
W. Oechsli, *History of Switzerland, 1499-1914* (1922);
G. Thürer, *Free and Swiss* (1970). (ND)

SWISS GUARD A corps instituted by Pope *Julius II as a permanent guard for the Vatican. It consisted of 250 men, whom the Swiss cantons of Zurich and Lucerne agreed to supply (1510). Their uniform was designed by *Michelangelo. The corps still exists.

P. Krieg, *Die päpstliche Schweizergarde* (1948).

SWISS MERCENARIES The use of mercenary troops was common everywhere during the late Middle Ages. The case of the Swiss, however, is exceptional. Between 1476 and 1477 the Swiss defeated *Charles the Bold of Burgundy in three consecutive battles, in the last of which, near Nancy, the duke was killed. These examples of massive numbers of infantry defeating the feudal cavalry revolutionized warfare even before the *arquebus was introduced on the battlefield. Carrying ten feet long pikes, the Swiss moved in formation and could deploy their compact units of up to 6,000 men to attack as well as in defence. In the last quarter of the 15th century the services of Swiss pikemen were sought by several European rulers, especially the French. The Swiss mastery of the battlefield, as the choice European infantry, continued for about 40 years, until the success of the German **Landsknechte* in the Battle of Ravenna challenged their dominance.

SYLBURG, FRIEDRICH (1536-96) German classical scholar. Born near Marburg, he spent most of his life in Heidelberg and died there. His editions of Greek and Latin authors were greatly admired at the time. They included the whole of Aristotle, Dionysius of Halicarnassus and Clement of Alexandria, and were distinguished by their critical approach.

SYPHILIS A venereal disease, formerly unknown in Europe, which claimed millions of lives during the first quarter of the 16th century. Overwhelming evidence indicates that S. was introduced to Europe by the men returning with *Columbus from his first voyage; traces of the disease have been found in skeletons of pre-Columbian American Indians. The first S. epidemic occurred in 1495, when it ravaged the French army besieging *Naples, and soon afterwards the residents of the city itself, hence the designation of S. as "the Neapolitan disease" among the French, and as "the French sickness" elsewhere. In 1530 the poet Girolamo Fracastoro wrote a Latin poem entitled *Syphilis sive morbus gallicus,* which described the disease and originated the current terminology.

C. C. Dennie, *History of Syphilis* (1962).

SYRLIN, JÖRG (c. 1425-91) German sculptor. Born in Ulm, he is known for the magnificent stalls of the cathedral of that city (1469-74). Done in late-Gothic style, they are among the best examples of 15th-century German woodcarving. The human figures in this work have powerful realist expressions.

W. Vöge, *Jörg Syrlin der Ältere und seine Bildwerke* (1950).

SZLACHTA The lesser nobility in Poland. In the 15th and 16th centuries, when parliamentarism was an increasing trend, the S. gained more privileges and influence. During the 16th century it dominated the 37 "little diets" (*sejmiki*), from which delegates were sent to the provincial and national diets. The S. had about 150 delegates in the national diet, and they constituted the lower house. From 1573 on, the lower nobility participated in the election of kings, together with the aristocracy. However, though the S. was recognized as equal to the aristocracy, the latter remained the dominant class. It possessed both power and wealth, while members of the S. were often poor.

Isabella of Portugal *by Titian (detail)*

T

TABORITES A radical group of the followers of Jan *Hus of *Bohemia, so-named after the town of Tabor, their stronghold near Prague. Composed mainly of peasants and artisans, in its early years the movement enjoyed the leadership of the noble Jan *Zizka. The T. emphasized the singing of hymns and readings from the *Bible and held ideas tinged with socialist and anarchistic notions. Their active period came to an end when they refused to comply with the religious settlement of the *compactata* (1433). In 1434 they were defeated by a combined force of *Utraquist and Catholic nobles in the Battle of Lipany.
F. G. Heymann, *John Zizka and the Hussite Revolution* (1955).
TACCA, PIETRO (1577-1640) Italian sculptor. A student of *Giambologna at Florence, he succeeded the latter as court sculptor to the *Medici. He completed his master's statues of Grand Duke Ferdinand I at Florence (1608) and those of *Philip III in Madrid (1606-13) and *Henry IV in Paris (1613), which were later destroyed. Of his own work perhaps the best pieces are the *Four Slaves* (1615-24) at Leghorn and the fountains in the Piazza della Annunziata, Florence (1629). Essentially a *Mannerist, he gradually adopted some stylistic elements from the *Baroque.
TALBOT, JOHN (1388-1453) English soldier. The younger son of a knight on the border of Wales, he had a long military career, serving in France and for some years also in Ireland. He became Earl of Shrewsbury in 1442. In 1452 he commanded the English army in France in what subsequently proved the last campaign of the *Hundred Years' War. Recovering Bordeaux and part of Gascony, T. attempted to raise the siege of Castillon, but was completely defeated by the French, who made effective use of their *artillery. He was killed in battle (17 July 1453).
TALLIS, THOMAS (?-1585) English composer and organ player. Already known as an outstanding musician towards the end of the reign of *Henry VIII, he reached the summit of his career under *Mary and *Elizabeth I, both of whom gave him their patronage. T. was the teacher of William *Byrd and, in 1575, together with the latter, received from the queen a 21-year monopoly on the publishing of music sheets in England. T. wrote vocal works for religious services, as well as composing tunes for *hymns.
TANSILLO, LUIGI (1510-68) Italian poet. Born in Venosa, he took up a military career in the service of the Spanish viceroys of Naples, fighting against the Ottoman Turks. He later became the governor of Gaeta. A prolific composer of love sonnets, T. is considered one of the best lyrical poets of 16th-century Italy. His works include *Il vendemmiatore* (1532), a bucolic poem which has become very popular because of its occasional obscenity, *Clorinda* (1547), marked by a feeling for nature, and *Lagrime di San Pietro*, a religious poem published posthumously in 1585. His 24 *Capitoli* treated his own experiences as well as social themes humourously. T. was the younger friend of the Spanish poets, *Garcilaso de la Vega and *Boscan. He had an influence upon poets outside Italy.
D. Coppola, *Profilo di Luigi Tansillo* (1939).
TARTAGLIA, NICCOLO (c. 1500-57) Italian mathematician. Born in Brescia, he taught *mathematics at Venice and Verona, in 1537 publishing his *Nova scientia*, which contained the first mathematical analysis of ballistic trajectories. In 1543 he published an Italian translation of the works of Euclid and Archimedes, and in 1556-60 came his encyclopaedic work on numbers and measures, *Trattato di numeri e misure*. Discovering certain cubic equations, T. disclosed them to Girolamo *Cardano of Milan who had them published in 1545. This breach of confidence was vehemently protested against by T., and led to a celebrated feud between the two.
TASSI, AGOSTINO (c. 1580-1644) Italian painter. Probably born in Rome, his original name was Agostino Buonamico. He received his training in Florence and was influenced by the marine pictures of Paul *Bril. T. is known for his extensive decorations at the Quirinal Palace and the Lancellotti Palace, Rome, where he originally feigned architectural settings. He also painted at the Palazzo Doria-Pamphili, Genoa, and worked as an engraver. In about 1612 he received the young Claude Lorraine (1600-82), into his household, who became his apprentice.

TASSO, BERNARDO (c. 1493-1569) Italian poet and father of Torquato *Tasso. Born in Bergamo, he was successively the servant of a number of Italian rulers, including Ferrante Sanseverino of Salerno whom he followed into exile in 1552. In his poems he imitated the classics; his *Odi* (1560) are modelled on Horace and so are his *Salmi* (1560). His most popular work was *Amadigi di Gaula* (1560), an Italian adaptation in verse of Montalvo's **Amadis de Gaula*, which he embellished with his own invented episodes. In 1587 his son, Torquato, completed and published the *Floridante.*

E. Williamson, *Bernardo Tasso* (1951).

TASSO, TORQUATO (1544-95) Italian poet. The son of the poet Bernardo *Tasso, he was born in Sorrento, and first educated by the *Jesuits in Naples. In 1554 he joined his exiled father in Rome. Following a period in Pesaro (1556-59) at the court of the duke of Urbino, he went with his father to Venice, where he made the acquaintance of artists and men of letters. In 1560 he entered the university of Padua, neglecting the study of law for the writing of poetry; in 1562, at 18, he published his first work, *Rinaldo*, a romantic epic for which he became famous. In 1565 he entered the service of Cardinal Luigi d'*Este and for the next 20 years was connected with the ruling house of *Ferrara.

T.'s first period at Ferrara was marked by the writing of a lot of court poetry and an undemanding form of life. In 1570 he accompanied his cardinal patron to France, where he met *Ronsard. In 1573 he became a success with his hedonistic pastoral drama, *Aminta*. This was performed by a famous company of actors, I. Gelosi, but published only in 1581. In the meantime he was writing his most important work, the epic poem *Gerusalemme liberata* (Jerusalem Delivered), a tribute to the Estes, dealing with the First *Crusade. This was completed by 1575 whereupon T. had his manuscript circulated among literary friends. Their criticism of the many themes of love and adventure contained in the poem made him introduce changes, eventually undermining his confidence and leading to his first attacks of insanity. He was placed under mild confinement in 1577, but escaped to his sister in Sorrento. In 1579 he returned to Ferrara, apparently cured, but soon collapsed in a paranoic outburst, and was detained at the hospital of S. Anna, where he remained for seven years. While he was there the first (incomplete) edition of the great poem was published privately in Venice in 1580 under the name of *Il Goffredo*. In 1581 the complete edition came out in Ferrara, and the work quickly gained tremendous popularity in Italy and abroad.

Released in 1586, T. went to Mantua where he published *Re Torrismondo* (1587), a tragedy about incest and betrayal. He restlessly moved from one place to another, finally settling in the monastery of S. Onofrio near Rome where he died. In his last years, tormented by remorse, he worked on a revised version of his masterpiece, expurgating all the sensuous content of the original. This appeared as *Gerusalemme conquistata*, in 1593. The author of many other poems, dialogues, letters and discourses, T.'s poetical genius and his broken life are a superb testimony to the aesthetic, moral and religious climate of *Counter-Reformation Italy.

C. P. Brand, *Torquato Tasso* (1965);
G. Getto, *Interpretazione del Tasso* (1967).

TAULER, JOHANN (c. 1300-61) German mystic. Entering the Dominican order at Strassburg in 1315, he became a famous preacher and, during the Black Death (1348-49), won popular admiration for his care for the sick. His mystical ideas are contained in his extant sermons. They emphasize humility and surrender of self to the will of God. T.'s thought influenced late 14th-century piety, especially the *Devotio Moderna. *Luther also had a high regard for his sermons.

J. M. Clark, *The Great German Mystics; Eckhardt, Tauler and Suso* (1949).

TAUSEN, HANS (1494-1561) Danish Protestant reformer. He studied in Rostock, Copenhagen, Louvain and *Wittenberg where, in 1523, he became a follower of *Luther. After being expelled from Viborg for his preaching, he approached King *Frederick I who came to his assistance, and was allowed to return to Viborg. In 1526 he came to Copenhagen and helped to draft the 43 articles presented to the diet of 1530. T.'s tolerance and his willingness to come to a compromise with the Danish Roman Catholic hierarchy brought upon him the criticism of fellow-Protestants. In 1538 he was made Professor of Theology at Roskilde, and in 1542 he became bishop of Ribe.

TAVERNER, JOHN (c. 1495-1545) English composer. A native of Lincolnshire, he became choirmaster of Cardinal College (afterwards Christ Church), Oxford. There he was accused of heresy and detained, to be subsequently pardoned by the founder of the college, Cardinal *Wolsey. He wrote a number of masses and *motets, which are among the best religious musical works of this period in England. Later in his life he served *Cromwell as an agent in the dissolution of the *monasteries.

TEBALDEO, ANTONIO (1463-1537) Italian poet. Born in *Ferrara, he was a tutor of Isabella d'*Este, later becoming secretary to Lucrezia *Borgia in Ferrara. During the pontificate of *Leo X he went to Rome where he enjoyed papal patronage and made friends with various writers and artists, including *Raphael. T. wrote many sonnets, and pastoral poems in Latin and Italian. A follower of *Petrarch, his poetry has a patriotic ring, though most of it today sounds artificial. His poems were first published without his consent in Ferrara in 1499; they were often reprinted in the 16th century.

G. de Lisa, *Un rimatore cortigiano del Quattrocento, Antonio Tebaldeo* (1928);
S. Pasquazi, *Umanesimo ferrarese* (1955).

TELESCOPE Although the effect of the magnifying lens had been known in Europe at least since the middle of the 13th century, no attempt had been made to apply this knowledge to the measurement of celestial bodies. The first T. is believed to have been made by the Dutchman Hans Lippershey, who, in 1608, sold a number of these instruments to the government of the United Provinces. Within a year his instruments reached other European countries and, in 1609, *Galileo improved upon them, initiating a new age of *astronomy. Early Ts. consisted of two lenses, placed at both ends of a metal tube about one inch-and-a-half in diameter.

H. C. King, *The History of the Telescope* (1955).

TELESIO, BERNARDINO (1508-88) Italian philosopher. Born in Cosenza, near Naples, he studied at Padua and Rome. For some time he enjoyed the support of

Pope *Paul IV, a fellow Neapolitan; after the latter's death he returned to Naples (1566) where his ideas influenced a number of the younger philosophers of southern Italy, among them *Campanella and *Bruno. T. attempted to replace the Aristotelian philosophy of matter and form with a dynamic theory of antithetical forces. His main work was *De rerum natura* (On the Nature of Things), published in two parts in Rome and Naples between 1565-87. Here he elaborated on a speculative system based on the concepts of matter and force and on an independent observation of nature.
G. Gentile, *Bernardino Telesio*, 2nd ed. (1923).

TEMPESTA, ANTONIO (1555-1630) Italian painter and engraver. Born in Florence, where he assisted *Vasari in the painting of the Palazzo Vecchio, he spent most of his career at Rome. A protegé of Pope *Gregory XIII, he decorated palaces at the Vatican and outside Rome and designed tapestries. T. is especially remembered for his almost 2,000 engravings, including many etchings on themes from the *Bible, history and mythology. He delighted in executing battle and hunting scenes, excelling particularly in the representation of horses.

TERESA OF AVILA, ST. (1515-82) Spanish mystic and religious reformer, also known as Teresa de Jesus. Born to a noble family, she was educated by Augustinian nuns and in 1533, despite the objections of her family, entered a Carmelite convent at Avila. Following an illness, which forced her for some time to abandon her vocation, she managed to return to it, but it was not until she had reached the age of 40 that she decided to lead a life of contemplation and absolute dedication to Christ. From 1557 on she began to have mystical experiences and periodic ecstatic visions, while at the same time undertaking the reform of the lax way of life the Carmelites had lapsed into, with the aim of restoring the original strictness of the order. In face of much opposition, she founded in Avila a new convent in 1563, the first of the so-called Discalced Carmelites, where poverty and strict seclusion from the outside world were maintained. In 1567 she was given permission to found more convents and, with the aid of a young Carmelite priest, *Juan de la Cruz, and others, extended her reform also to include monasteries. Her achievements roused the extreme enmity of the higher authorities of the order in Spain, but she was able to gain the support of *Philip II and later of Pope *Gregory XIII (1580). By the time of her death, there were 17 reformed houses for women and 15 for men.

Her reputation as a great mystical voice was confirmed in a series of works, including *Camino de perfección* (Way of Perfection), written in approximately 1565, an *Autobiography* and *The Interior Castle* (1577), in which she delineated the mystical techniques to enter into communion with God. These works, written in an engaging literary style and giving the accounts of her inner struggles, are held to be some of the best examples of Christian mystical writings. T. was canonized in 1622.
W. Nevin, *Therese of Avila: The Woman* (1956);
E. A. Peers, *Mother of Carmel* (1945).

TERZI, FRANCESCO (1523-91) Italian painter and engraver. Born in Bergamo, where he left two pictures on religious themes in the church of S. Francesco, he passed the most important part of his career as court painter of *Maximilian II. He executed many portraits of the imperial family. Late in his life, he settled in Rome.

TETRAPOLITAN CONFESSION (1530) A Protestant confession of faith composed by *Bucer and *Capito at the Diet of *Augsburg, and presented to *Charles V in the name of four German cities: *Strassburg, Memingen, Lindau and Constance. Like the Confession of Augsburg, which had been presented to the emperor shortly before, it attempted to minimize the doctrinal differences with Rome.

TETZEL, JOHANN (1465-1519) German preacher and promoter of the sale of *indulgences. Member of the Dominican order, T. served as prior at Glogau and in Poland, before becoming a preacher of indulgences. In 1516 he was appointed to the region of Magdeburg, charged with awarding the indulgences to those who contributed money for the rebuilding of St. Peter's in Rome. His commercial flare for this assignment and his preaching that payment of money was enough to save any soul from purgatory, stimulated the publication of Luther's 95 theses on 31 October 1517. T. answered these with his 122 antitheses (1518). The affair provoked Luther's initial public challenge of conventional Catholic practices, which he soon developed into an attack on doctrinal fundamentals.

TEUTONIC KNIGHTS A military *order of German knights which controlled the Baltic provinces, especially Prussia, from the 13th century. A product of the *Crusade experience, and originally created in 1189 in front of the walls of Acre, the order eventually dedicated its efforts to the introduction of Christianity among the heathen Prussians and Lithuanians. The 15th century, however, saw the beginning of its decline. In 1410 the knights were defeated by the Poles at Tannenberg, and had to sign the first peace of Thorn (1411) which cost them some territory and an indemnity. In 1454 a revolt against their oppressive rule took place in Prussia, signalling the renewal of war. The second peace of Thorn (1466) made the order cede West Prussia to Poland; although East Prussia with its capital of Königsberg was retained as a Polish fief, it was thus cut off territorially from the rest of Germany. Despite the efforts of succeeding grand-masters, the order continued to decline, and in 1525 Grand-Master *Albert secularized East Prussia, assuming the title of duke and converting to *Protestantism. The remaining knights who chose to remain Roman Catholic continued the order elsewhere in Germany, but it ceased having a political significance.
C. Krollmann, *The Teutonic Order in Prussia* (1938);
F. L. Carsten, *The Origins of Prussia* (1954).

THEATINES A religious order founded by Gaetano da Thiene (*Cajetan, 1480-1547), and his three companions, Bonifacio da Colle, Pado Consiglieri and Giampietro Caraffa (later *Paul IV) in Rome in 1524. Their aim was to work for church reform, making priests take religious vows to lead austere lives, thus inspiring the rest of the clergy by their example. The name T. derived from Chieti (Theate), the episcopal see of Caraffa, the first head of the order. The T. were influential in Italy and elsewhere during the early phases of the *Counter-Reformation, some of them rising in the hierarchy of the Catholic Church.

THEODORE OF GAZA (c. 1400-75) Greek scholar. A native of Salonica, he left this city shortly before its capture by the Ottoman Turks (1430), becoming the first Greek scholar of note to come West. During the visit of *Gemistos Pletho (1438-39), T. opposed the latter by defending Aristotle. He was made lecturer of Greek in Ferrara and was the teacher of the father of German humanism, Rudolph *Agricola. In 1451 he became part of the group of scholars chosen by *Nicholas V to translate the Greek classics. Besides numerous translations, he was the author of a very popular Greek grammar.

THERMES, PAUL DE LA BARTHE, SEIGNEUR DE (1482-1562) French military commander. A native of Gascony, he first distinguished himself during the siege of Naples (1528), after which he was taken prisoner at sea by Moslem pirates, but was eventually released upon payment of a ransom. In 1544 he fell prisoner again at Ceresole, and in 1550 defended Parma against the imperial army. Retiring only after he had passed the age of 75, he was at times prone to act recklessly, which brought about his defeat in his last battle at Gravelines (1558).

THIRTY-NINE ARTICLES The definitive set of religious doctrines accepted by the *Church of England during the reign of *Elizabeth. They were drafted in 1563, following closely the Forty-Two Articles of 1553, the formula of which had been adopted shortly before the return to Roman Catholicism during the reign of *Mary Tudor. Alterations, due, according to some, to the personal intervention of Queen Elizabeth, postponed final approval until 1571. According to the articles, baptism and the eucharist were the only remaining sacraments, and transubstantiation was excluded. There was a deliberate ambiguity in some of the definitions, especially with regard to *predestination. All members of the clergy were required to affirm their subscription by oath.

THIRTY YEARS' WAR, THE (1618-48) A series of wars fought out between the Roman Catholic and Protestant states of *Europe over complex religious and political issues. Kindled by the *Defenstration of Prague and a revolt of the Czechs against the *Habsburgs, the wars brought chaos and destruction to Germany and, in their final stages, involved Sweden, France, the United Provinces and Spain. The outbreak of the T. is a convenient date to divide between the *Renaissance and *Reformation periods and the world of the Enlightenment. Although at the outbreak of the war the very principle of religious coexistence was at stake, the long conflict finally broadened the settlement of *Augsburg (1555) to include Calvinists as well as Lutherans and Roman Catholics, and resulted in further affirmations of religious toleration. On the plane of international politics France succeeded Spain as the dominant European power.

C. V. Wedgwood, *The Thirty Years' War* (1938);
G. Pages, *La Guerre de Trente Ans* (1939).

THOMAS À KEMPIS (c. 1380-1471) German author of devotional writings. The son of a peasant from a village near Cologne, he was educated in Deventer at the school of the *Brethren of the Common Life and, on the advice of the head of the school, Florentius Radewyns, entered an Augustinian monastery of which his brother was prior in 1399. T. wrote biographies of the founders of the Brethren of the Common Life, Geert de *Groote and Radewyns, and other works, but his masterpiece was *The Imitation of Christ*, the most successful Christian guide to spiritual perfection. The work was circulated in manuscript at the end of the first quarter of the 15th century, and was printed in 1473. It became the first best-seller, having gone into 99 editions by the end of the century, and has remained a favourite form of devotional reading ever since.

Thomas à Kempis, *The Imitation of Christ*, trans. by Leo Sherley-Price (1952).

THOMAS, WILLIAM (?-1554) English scholar and rebel. Educated at Oxford, in 1544 he went to Italy, spending five years there. Upon his return he published his *Histoire of Italie* (1549), and a year later his *Italian Grammer with a Dictionarie for the Better Understanding of Boccace, Petrarcha and Dante*, the first work of this kind in English. He became a clerk of the privy council and gained influence over the young *Edward VI. He lost his post, however, at the accession of *Mary, and was imprisoned following the *Wyatt Rebellion in which he took part. In jail he was interrogated and tortured to find out about *Elizabeth's complicity in the plot, and tried to commit suicide. Found guilty of treason, he was hanged. T. also wrote a defence of *Henry VIII's religious reforms, and translated from the Italian.

THORN, PEACES OF Two treaties between the *Teutonic Knights and *Poland concluded in 1411 and 1466. The first peace followed the Battle of Tannenberg (1410) in which *Vladislav *Jagiello of Poland defeated the knights. This involved the transference of some territory to Poland and the payment of an indemnity, but otherwise left matters as they stood. The second peace, following a war of 13 years (1454-66), made the order give Poland approximately half of its western territory, including Elbing, Kulm, Marienburg and Pomerania. The knights thus lost their territorial continuity with Germany, while Poland gained an outlet to the Baltic Sea. Afterwards the knights, who also recognized Polish suzerainty, entered a period of complete decline.

THORPE, JOHN (c. 1563-1655) English architect. The son of a master mason, he was clerk of the Royal Works (1584-1601) and land-surveyor for the government. Contrary to what was long believed, T. did not design any building of importance. But he left behind a book of plans of many of the major houses built during the reigns of *Elizabeth and *James I which is a valuable source of architectural history.

THUANUS (Jacques Auguste de Thou; 1555-1617) French historian. The descendant of a family of jurists, he held high legal office and aided in the drafting of the Edict of *Nantes. His *Historia sui temporis* (History of His Own Time) was published in five volumes between 1604-20. Probably the best of any 16th-century French historian's accounts of the civil and religious wars, it covered the years 1546-1607 and was sympathetic towards *Henry IV, the author's patron. T., however, presented a systematic historical survey written in a highly intellectual fashion, emphasizing the relationship between politics and ecclesiastical affairs. T. was also a great collector of books and manuscripts.

S. Kinser, *The Works of J.-A. de Thou* (1966).

TIBALDI, PELLEGRINO (1527-96) Italian painter, sculptor and architect. Born at Bologna, he came to Rome in 1547, where he was influenced by the work of

The Battle of Zara *by Tintoretto, in the Doge's Palace, Venice*

*Michelangelo. In 1550 he returned to Bologna and executed his masterpiece, the decorations he did for the university treating scenes from the *Odyssey*. Later he worked at Ancona and Ferrara, in about 1564 coming under the patronage of Cardinal Carlo *Borromeo of Milan, who employed him mainly as an architect. In 1587 he went to Spain, staying for some eight years and superintending various decorative works at the *Escorial. A *Mannerist with a competent technique, he preferred to work within the confines of the style prescribed by the great masters of his age.

TILL EULENSPIEGEL A collection of German folktales, consisting mainly of pranks and humorous episodes about a clever young man of peasant origin, supposed to have lived in the first half of the 14th century. Strong in body and possessed of skill and wit behind an apparent naïvete, he delighted in outwitting the worldly-wise, thus representing the revenge of the rustic mentality over urban sophistication. Published at first in *Strassburg in 1515, although not as sometimes believed by Thomas *Murner, it has been translated into many different languages and achieved wide popularity. There have been several modern versions of the tales.

TIME OF TROUBLES, THE (1604-13) A period in *Russia of political instability and social turmoil, which began with the appearance of the first False *Dmitry in the last year of the reign of Boris *Godunov and ended with the election to the throne of Michael, the first tsar of the house of *Romanov. These nine years saw endemic stirrings of rebellion among the peasants and Cossacks and a fierce struggle for power between factions of the powerful nobles (*boyars*), which encouraged intervention on the part of *Sweden and *Poland. The most dangerous attempt was made by *Sigismund III who in 1610 occupied Moscow. A nationalist reaction then forced the Poles to withdraw (1612), although they continued to hold considerable Russian territories, including Smolensk, for a long time afterwards.

TINCTORIS, JOHANNES (c. 1435-1511) Flemish musician. Educated at the university of Louvain, he spent many years at the court of *Ferrante I, king of Naples, where he served as a tutor. His dictionary of musical terms, *Terminorum musicae diffinitorium* (1474), was dedicated to the king's daughter, Beatrice of Aragon. He later returned to Flanders; when he died he was a canon of the church of Nivelles. The composer of a number of masses and *motets, T. is also important as a theorist of early Renaissance *music. He wrote 12 treatises on the subject (1474-86), dealing with notation, types of instruments, forms of polyphony and other important themes. The best-known of his treatises is the *Liber de arte contrapuncti* (Book on the Art of Counterpoint), written in 1477, in which he formulated general rules. In the preface he ascribes the invention of counterpoint to the English and discards all the works of polyphony dating back further than 40 years as valueless.

TINO DI CAMAINO (c. 1285-1337) Italian sculptor. Born in *Siena, he was influenced by Giovanni *Pisano and was active at Pisa (1311- *c.* 18), where he executed the tomb of Emperor Henry VII at the cathedral. He then worked in Siena (1319-20), in Florence and, from 1324 until his death, in Naples. There he made several tombs for the Angevins, serving also as their court architect. His style, originally heavy and reserved, later showed an inclination towards decorativeness and grace.

W. R. Valentiner, *Tino di Camaino, a Sienese Sculptor of the 14th Century* (1935).

TINTORETTO (1518-94) The name given to the Italian painter Jacopo Robusti. Born in Venice, he derived

Susanna and the Elders *by Tintoretto (Detail)*

his pseudonym from the profession of his father, a dyer. He was trained by a number of lesser Venetian painters, but was obviously influenced by *Titian. Subsequently, he developed his own *Mannerist style, which was marked by a monumental conception of the human form and the employment of colour so as to achieve dramatic effect. Indeed, T.'s motto as reported by his 17th-century biographer, Carlo Ridolfi, was "Michelangelo's drawing and Titian's colour". T. did not become a painter of kings and princes as had Titian. He rarely left Venice, where he had a thriving business, and worked mainly for religious fraternities and customers of moderate means. His first signed picture, the *Last Supper*, dates from 1547. In 1548 he painted the *Miracle of the Slave* for the Scuola di S. Marco, a work which gave evidence of his compositional innovativeness and masterly technique and made his reputation.

Of T.'s mythological works, one of the better known is *Bacchus and Ariadne* (1578) at the Doges' Palace. His earlier *Susanna and the Elders* (1556), now in Vienna, impresses the viewer with its bright colours and with the beautiful contours of the bathing woman contrasted with the shadowy background of water and plants. His unique personal vision, however, is revealed in his religious works. From 1565 to 1587, he worked on a great series of scenes representing the life of Christ in the Scuola di S. Rocco. Here he employed unorthodox techniques that were much criticized at the time, but which endowed his paintings with a glowing illumination creating a sense of drama and tension. These effects are best seen in his final version of the *Last Supper*, painted for the Church of S. Giorgio Maggiore shortly before his death. The calm, frontal treatment of the subject has been completely discarded in favour of the depiction of a scene of dramatic gestures heightened by the presence of transparent angels and glimpses of light on a darkened background. The sum total is a true announcement of the coming of *Baroque.

E. Newton, *Jacopo Tintoretto* (1952);
H. Tietze, *Tintoretto* (1948).

TIRSO DE MOLINA (c. 1580-1648) Pseudonym of the Spanish playwright and novelist, Gabriel Tellez. Born in Madrid, according to some the illegitimate son of the duke of Osuna, he was educated at Alcalá and, in 1601, became a Mercedarian friar. He lived in Toledo between 1613 and 1614, and in Santo Domingo from 1616 to 1618. Later he resided in Madrid (1622), Salamanca (1626) and Barcelona (1632-39). T. was a friend and an admirer of *Lope de Vega, like his mentor writing hundreds of plays, eighty of which are extant. Most of these were published in five volumes between 1627 and 1636. For some time T. took part in literary controversies; when, however, in 1625 the Council of Castile condemned his plays for their bad influence, the author henceforth dedicated more of his time to his order of which he wrote a general history (1637-39). In 1645 he became a prior of a monastery in Soria where he died.

His plays include religious and biblical dramas, historical dramas and comedies. Distinguished by rapid movements and simultaneity of plots they reveal a deepening analysis of the psychology of the heroes. Among the best are those which deal with female characters, such as *La prudencia en la mujer* about the regency of a queen of Castile who defends the rights of her son. His most famous work is *El burlador de Sevilla y convidado de piedra* (The Seducer of Seville and the Guest of Stone), written before 1630. This play created the image of Don Juan, the despicable woman-chaser who deceives one victim after another in a never-ending chain of amorous conquests. Don Juan's devotion to the pursuits of pleasure is such that he fears neither God nor the dead. He is finally dragged to Hell by the statue of the commander of Ulloa, which he defiantly had invited to dinner. T. also wrote a prose collection of short stories, *Los cigarrales de Toledo* (1624) where he defended the popular theatre.

I. L. McClelland, *Tirso de Molina: Studies in Dramatic Realism* (1948);
S. Maurel, *L'universe dramatique de Tirso de Molina* (1971);
K. Vossler, *Lecciones sobre Tirso de Molina* (1965).

TISSARD, FRANCOIS (?-1508) French humanist. Born in Amboise, he studied in Paris and Orleans and went to Italy, where he devoted himself to the learning of *Greek and *Hebrew. As professor at the university of Paris he promoted the printing of the Greek classics, which he edited. In the year of his death he published the first Hebrew grammar in France, dedicated to the future *Francis I. These works were published by the printer Gilles de Gourmont.

TITIAN (Tiziano Vecelli; c. 1489-1576) Italian painter. Born in Pieve di Cadore to a poor but noble family,

The Rape of Europa *by Titian*

Mary Magdalen *by Titian*

he was apprenticed to a Venetian painter at the age of ten, eventually transferring to the shops of the old masters of his day, Gentile and later Giovanni *Bellini. T.'s great mentor was *Giorgione, another slightly older pupil of Giovanni Bellini, with whom he worked on *frescoes in the exterior of the Fondaco de' Tedeschi, now destroyed, and some of whose paintings he completed after Giorgione's early death in 1510. When T. was still very young, Giovanni Bellini's death in 1516 left him the most outstanding artist of Venice, and he immediately succeeded to the post of the official painter of the republic. His career, which was to last another 60 years, in due course saw him acclaimed as the greatest European painter of his time.

T.'s first great work was the *Assumption*, in the Frari Church, (1616-18) Venice, a monumental picture displaying a virtuoso-like technique, though without deep religious feeling. His next important painting, the *Pesaro Madonna* (1519-28) in the same church, introduced a completely new composition and iconographical setting. His growing fame brought him into contact with heads of states. In 1530 he met *Charles V in Bologna, becoming the emperor's court painter in 1533. The latter's admiration for his work was such that once, so it is said, he picked up a paint brush which T. had dropped. T. also entered the employment of Charles' son, *Philip II, whose full portrait as a young man he painted in Augsburg in 1550. For the king of Spain T. executed what he called *poesie*, that is, erotic mythological scenes. *Danaë* (1554), the best known of these, depicts the mother of Perseus as a heavy sensuous woman lying naked and half drowsing, awaiting her lover. During a visit to Rome in 1545 T. also painted a striking portrait of *Paul III. T.'s contemporaries were particularly impressed by the deeply expressive faces of his portraits, which included the memorable one of his close friend, Pietro *Aretino.

There are few drawings by T., his genius consisting in his masterful handling of oil painting. The atmospheric unity of his paintings was frequently achieved by means of variations in tone. A perfectionist who could continue to work on a single painting for months, T.'s style matured over the years, becoming freer and more dramatic. In fact, in his very last years he preferred a manner of painting which sacrificed detail to the essential and sometimes bordered on impressionism. He died of the plague in Venice at an extremely old age, though not at 99 as is traditionally believed. He was a person not entirely free of character blemishes such as greed and vanity, but he had a deep influence as an artist. Not until *Rubens would the artistic world witness a painter of his stature.

R. Pallucchini, *Tiziano*, 2 vols (1953-54);
H. Tietze, *Titian* (1950);
F. Valcanover, *All the Paintings of Titian* (1965).

TOLEDO, FRANCISCO DE (1515-82) Spanish Viceroy of Peru. The son of the Count of Oropesa, he distin-

Aretino *by Titian*

guished himself as a soldier under *Charles V, in 1568 being nominated Viceroy of Peru by *Philip II. Arriving at Lima the following year, T. undertook a two-year-long travel of inspection of the territory, reorganizing local administration and the working of the *mining industry. He introduced the *Inquisition (1570), punished Indian rebels severely and, in 1572, executed the last descendant of the Inca emperors, the young Tupac-Amaru. T. directed *Sarmiento de Gamboa to write the *Historia Indica* and is held to have been the architect of the Spanish administrative structure in South America, which continued to run efficiently until the 18th century. T. returned to Spain in 1581.

R. Levillier, *Don Francisco de Toledo, supremo organizador del Peru,* 3 vols. (1935).

TOLEDO, JUAN BAUTISTA DE (?-1567) Spanish architect. Having studied architecture in Italy, where he assisted *Michelangelo, he became architect of the Spanish viceroy of Naples and in 1559 was recalled to Spain by *Philip II. He built the façade of the Church of the Descalzas Reales in Madrid, and in 1563 began his great project, the *Escorial. His plans were later modified by his successor, Juan de *Herrera, but much in the present structure, including the quality of majestic simplicity, is due to T.'s original design.

TOLEDO, PEDRO DE (1484-1553) Spanish viceroy of *Naples. The son of the second duke of Alba, he was a page to *Ferdinand the Catholic, beginning his military career in 1512 during the conquest of Navarre. Later, he also fought in Germany and Italy, and in 1532 was appointed viceroy of Naples by *Charles V, a position he filled until his death. An energetic administrator, T. forced his authority upon the unruly Neapolitan nobility and people. He suppressed brigandage, intervened in local customs and expelled the Jews in 1540. In 1547 his institution of the *Inquisition brought about a popular rebellion; he surmounted this crisis, however, in a typically obstinate way. His power and prestige in Italy were so great that, in 1539, he married his daughter Leonora to Grand-duke *Cosimo I of Tuscany.

J. M. del Moral, *El virrey de Napoles: don Pedro de Toledo y la guerra contra el turco* (1966).

TOLOMEI, CLAUDIO (1492-1555) Italian poet. Born at Siena, he was exiled in 1526 because of his support of the *Medici, and entered the service of important political figures in Rome and Piacenza. Shortly after he had been made bishop of Padua (1549), he was recalled to Siena, given a high public office and sent as ambassador to France. He died at Rome.

T. wrote *sonnets and in his *Il Cesano* (1555) championed the usage of the Tuscan dialect. His *Versi e regole della nuova poesia toscana* (1539) attempted to apply a classical Latin metre to Italian.

P. L. Sbaragli, *Claudio Tolomei, umanista senese del Cinquecento* (1939).

TOMÁS DE JESÚS (1564-1627) Spanish mystical author. A member of the Carmelite order since 1587, he became provincial of Old Castile carrying on with the reforms begun by *Teresa of Avila. In 1607 Pope *Paul V invited him to come to Rome and work on the expansion of Roman Catholic *missions. T. then composed influential treatises, outlining his missionary ideas, which had a bearing on the founding of the Sacred Congregation of the Propagation of the Faith (1622). His best-known works, however, are the two spiritual guides, *Sobre la contemplacion divina* (1620) and *Sobre la contemplación adquirida* (1623), noted for their clarity of exposition.

TORDESILLAS, TREATY OF (7 June 1494) An agreement concluded by Spain and Portugal, awarding territorial rights and, as it were, dividing the world between them. Signed at Tordesillas, near Valladolid, Spain, the treaty fixed the line of demarcation at 370 leagues west of the Cape Verde Islands (between 48° and 49° west of Greenwich). Spain was to have exclusive rights to all *exploration and colonization west of the line and Portugal – east of it. The assumption was that Spain would thus be able to claim all the trans-Atlantic territories of the New World discovered by Christopher *Columbus. But after Pedro Alvares *Cabral's landing on the coast of Brazil (1500), it was realized that a substantial part of the South American coast fell east of the line of demarcation, and was subsequently claimed and occupied by Portugal, in addition to its eastern colonies.

F. G. Davenport, ed., *European Treaties Bearing on the History of the United States* (1917).

TORELLI, LUDOVICA (1500-69) Italian countess, founder of religious associations for women. The daughter of the duke of Guastella, she had been twice widowed by the age of 27 and, in 1529, accepted the spiritual guidance of *Battista da Crema. She cooperated with *Zaccaria, founder of the *Barnabites, and built the first convent for the order's female counterpart, the *Angeliche*. In 1538 T., under the assumed name of Paula, divested herself of her county and castles and dedicated the rest of her life to the task of bringing women closer to true religious life. In 1557 she founded a school for young noble women in Milan, entrusting it to the *Jesuits.

TORNABUONI A Florentine family which took part in the political life of the republic, usually as allies of the *Medici. Lucrezia T. (1425-82), was wife of Piero the Gouty and mother of Lorenzo the Magnificent. Members of the family later served as important churchmen, soldiers and ambassadors of the grand dukes of Tuscany.

TORQUEMADA, JUAN DE (1388-1468) Spanish cardinal and theological author, known also by his Latinized name, Turrecremata. Born in Valladolid, he joined the Dominican order in 1403 and, in 1417, went to the Council of *Constance and soon afterwards to Paris, where he completed his studies. Returning to Spain, he advanced in the hierarchy of his order and, in 1431, was called by the newly elected *Eugenius IV to Rome. In 1433 he went on a diplomatic mission to the Council of *Basle, later being active in negotiations leading to the Council of *Ferrara-Florence. He was made a cardinal in 1439, and in about 1450 completed his most important work, *Summa de Ecclesia*. Admitting the utility of general church councils in certain circumstances, T. championed the supremacy of papal authority in all spiritual matters. His interpretation of canon law and ecclesiastical institutions enjoyed wide currency at the time, and his *Meditationes,* published in 1467 in Rome, was one of the earliest printed books which combined movable type with woodblock illustrations.

P. Theews, *Jean de Turrecremata; les relations entre l'Eglise et le pouvoir civil* (1943).

Cloister of Convento de Cristo by Diogo de Torralva, at Tomar

TORQUEMADA, JUAN DE (c. 1545-1617) Spanish historian. A member of the Franciscan order, he arrived in Mexico, where he became a student of *Mendieta. his *Monarquía Indiana* was published in *Seville in 1615. Dealing with the history of the Aztecs under Spanish rule, the work was mainly a translation of Mendiata's *Historia eclesiastica indiana*. Nevertheless, it contained harsh criticism of the forced resettlement programme imposed by the Spanish administration upon the Indian communities.

TORQUEMADA, TOMAS DE (1420-98) Grand Inquisitor of the Spanish *Inquisition. The nephew of the cardinal and theologian Juan de *Torquemada (1388-1468), he joined the Dominican order, becoming a prior of a monastery in Segovia (1452). In 1474 he became confessor to Queen *Isabella, to whom he gave advice about how to deal with the *Marranos. In 1483 T. was made the head of the recently established national Inquisition of Spain. Formulating the cruel procedures which governed the work of this institution over the next 300 years, he began a harsh campaign against heretics, mainly directed at crypto-*Jews. In order that Spain would properly be able to assimilate the Marranos, T. demanded the expulsion of the Jews. This he achieved in 1492, after a public campaign in which Jews were falsely accused of practicing ritual murder. It is estimated that over 2,000 people were condemned to death by the Inquisition during T.'s tenure of office.

T. Hope, *Torquemada, Scourge of the Jews* (1939).

TORRALVA, DIOGO DE (1500-66) The major Portuguese architect of the mid-16th century. He is especially known for his Graça Church at Évora (1530-37) and his masterpiece, the cloister of the Convento de Christo at Tomar (1558). His early style was a mixture of Italian Renaissance architecture and local traditions, with the Italianate influences later gaining the upper hand.

TORRES, FRANCISCO (c. 1504-84) Spanish theologian. A graduate of the university of Salamanca, he made a name for himself as papal theologian in the Council of *Trent (1562-63), in 1566 joining the *Jesuits and becoming a professor at the order's Roman college. T. was a prolific writer who took a staunch pro-papal position on almost every issue.

TORRES NAHARRO, BARTOLOMÉ (?-1524) Spanish poet and dramatist. Born near Badajoz, he became a soldier and then priest, enduring captivity by the Moors. Later he went to Italy where he met Juan de *Encina and began to write. His collection of seven plays, *Propalladia*, was printed in Naples in 1517 with a preface containing his views on the different dramatic genres. Of these plays, *Himenea*, the best known, is held to have been the first Spanish drama revolving around a question of honour. His plays contained colourful expressions, frequent obscene passages and a truly cosmopolitan High Renaissance flavour which makes him a forerunner of the late 16th-century golden age of Spanish *drama. T. also wrote poems on such themes as national glory and love. Banned by the *Index in 1559, his works were expurgated and reissued in 1573.

J. P. W. Crawford, *Spanish Drama Before Lope de Vega* (1937).

TORRIGIANO, PIETRO (1472-1528) Italian sculptor. Born in Florence, he became known for his vile temper, and in one of his numerous brawls broke the nose of *Michelangelo. Most of his career was passed in wanderings. He worked at the *Borgia apartments in Rome (1493), in Bologna and *Siena, and in 1509 went to *Antwerp where he was briefly in the service of *Margaret of Austria. In 1510 he came to England where he executed his best-known work, the tombs of *Henry VII and his wife (1512-18). His bronzes and marbles are considered the first true example of Italian Renaissance art in England. T. visited Florence in 1519. Returning to England, he left for Spain in 1522, working in *Seville. There he was imprisoned by the *Inquisition and charged with heresy. He died in jail.

TORY, GEOFFROY (c. 1480-1533) French printer. Born in Bourges, he studied in Rome and Bologna in Italy. From 1507-15, he taught in Paris and also worked as editor for Henri *Estienne, but in 1516 revisited Rome to satisfy his passion for classical remains. Returning to France, he began to promote printing in roman letters and, in 1530, was appointed royal printer. T. wrote the *Champ fleury* (1529), where he related the letters of the alphabet to the proportions of the human body and advocated the use of punctuation marks. His *Book of Hours of 1531 was admired for the way in which its illustrations matched the text. A scholar, a poet and a translator from the *Greek, T. had a great influence on 16th-century French printing.

"Champ fleury" by Geoffroy Tory, translated by G. B. Ives (1927; rep. 1967).

The tomb of Henry VII and his wife at Westminster Abbey

TOSCANELLI, PAOLO (1397-1482) Italian humanist, mathematician, astronomer and geographer. Born in Florence, he studied medicine in Padua, returning afterwards to his native city where his friends included *Brunelleschi, *Landino and *Alberti. He corresponded with *Regiomontanus, observed and wrote on the orbits of comets and, in 1468, erected a gnomon on the cathedral of Florence, the highest ever built, which enabled him to measure the obliquity of the ecliptic. An indefatigable collector of geographic data, in 1474 T. composed the famous letter, sent to an ecclesiastical dignitary in Portugal, in which he suggested that east Asia might be reached by navigating westwards across the Atlantic. This letter, together with an accompanying map, was read by *Columbus and strengthened his belief in his project.

TOURNES, JEAN DE (1504-64) French printer. A native of Noyon, he established a printing shop at *Lyons in about 1540, becoming known for the beautiful design of his books. He published remarkable editions of *Petrarch (1550) and Vitruvius (1552) and the book of poems of Louise *Labé (1555). His son, also called Jean (1539-1615) had to leave Lyons in 1585 owing to his *Huguenot affiliation and went to *Geneva, where he carried on the firm.

TRAPEZUNTIUS, GEORGIUS (1395-1484) Greek scholar. A native of Crete, he emigrated to Venice in approximately 1430 and later became papal secretary, achieving a reputation as a champion of Aristotle and translator of Greek authors. As well as numerous works of Aristotle, including the *Rhetoric*, he also translated Plato's *Laws*.

TRAVERS, WALTER (c.1548-1643) English *Puritan author. Educated at Cambridge, he was influenced by Calvinist doctrines during a visit to *Geneva and, in 1571, refused to subscribe the *Thirty-Nine Articles. He then left England, becoming the minister of a congregation in *Antwerp, but subsequently came back. In 1584 he engaged in a controversy with Richard *Hooker, who defended the Established Church, but in 1595 was made provost of the recently founded university of Dublin, *Ireland. His reputation as a Puritan author was based on a work published in 1574, where he defended a Presbyterian form of church organization.

TRAVERSARI, AMBROGIO (c. 1386-1439) Italian humanist. A monk and later the prior of the convent of Santa Maria degli Angeli in Florence, he became an indefatigable researcher of classical texts, a promoter of the study of the *Greek Church Fathers, and one of the earliest humanists to study *Hebrew. In 1434 he discovered the works of Cornelius Nepos, shortly before his death taking part in the Council of *Ferrara-Florence, which promoted the reunification of the Eastern and Western Churches.

A. Dini Traversari, *Ambrogio Traversari e i suoi tempi* (1912).

TREMELLIUS, IMMANUEL (1510-80) Jewish scholar and convert to Protestantism. Born in *Ferrara, he studied at the university of Pavia and converted to Christianity in 1540. One year afterwards, however, Pietro Martire *Vermigli convinced him to adhere to the doctrines of *Calvin. He then left Italy for *Strassburg, and in 1547 came to England by invitation of *Cranmer, where he became lecturer of *Hebrew

The Council of Trent in session

at Cambridge. At the accession of *Mary Tudor he had to leave, and in 1561 became professor of Biblical studies at Heidelberg. Expelled in 1577, he passed his last years in Sedan, France. T. wrote Chaldean and Syriac grammars, and is especially noted for translating from Hebrew the standard Protestant Latin translation of the *Bible (1569-79).

W. Becker, *Immanuel Tremellius; ein Proselytenleben im Zeitalter der Reformation* (1890).

TRENT, COUNCIL OF (1545-63) A general council of the Roman Catholic church, which, by redefining doctrine and reorganizing the ecclesiastical system, prepared the way for the *Counter-Reformation. Although the need to pass internal reforms was widely recognized well before the rise of Protestantism, all attempts to convene a general council came to nothing because of the fear of the *papacy, that such a body might challenge its supreme authority. Finally, largely due to the insistence of *Charles V, Pope *Paul III began taking the necessary steps. In 1542, following two failures to assemble the delegates in Mantua and Vicenza, he convened the council to meet at Trent in northern Italy. After many postponements it opened there in 13 December 1545 with the participation of only 34 delegates, including three papal legates, one cardinal and four archbishops. The number of delegates later increased. At the closing session there were 255 prelates, the vast majority of them Italians. Although the discussions reflected tension between French and imperial delegates, these political divisions were upset by the preponderance of prelates loyal to Rome. Charles V's wish for the council to heal the rift with the Protestants was answered, however, by the vehemence of those rejecting compromise. The council evidently missed its opportunity to play a role in this question. By the time it had ended, the framework of the European religious and political settlement had already been determined through the Peace of *Augsburg (1555) and the Treaty of *Cateau-Cambresis (1559).

The council conducted its deliberations during three separate periods. The first period, lasting about 15 months (1545-47), was terminated because of Charles V's military victories over the *Schmalkaldic League, which made the pro-papal delegates at Trent fear that the now omnipotent emperor might force his ideas upon them. On the pretext of a plague in Trent, the council was transferred to Bologna and suspended for four years. Reconvened by *Julius III, it went into its second series of meetings in Trent (1551-52). This time a number of Protestants, delegates of German imperial cities, were present, demanding reconsideration of important dogmatic issues. But the defeat of the emperor by *Maurice of Saxony soon brought about another suspension. The council was reconvened for a third time (1562-63) only after a full decade had elapsed, and was then characterized by the contributions of *Jesuit theologians. In 1564 the decrees of the council were confirmed by Pius IV, who also ordered the publication of a summary of the doctrines, emerging from it.

With respect to dogma, the council opposed Protestant teachings on *Original Sin and *Justification by Faith, supplying definitions which hardened the Catholic position. It reaffirmed the seven Sacraments, the sanctity of the traditional Latin text of the *Bible (the Vulgate) and the validity of *Indulgences, approving many other Catholic customs and beliefs which had been contested by the *Reformation. More important, however, than its task of ensuring the passage of internal reforms, a process which was being carried on concurrently with its main objective, the council gave Roman Catholicism a solid platform that served as a barrier against dissension. In the short term it enabled Roman Catholicism during the next decades to recover its position and reconquer former territorial possessions. Subsequently, however, its doctrines proved to have a deadening effect, from which the Church has freed itself only in the present century.

H. Jedin, *A History of the Council of Trent,* 2 vols. (1957-61);

L. Christiani, *L'Eglise a l'epoque du Conseil de Trente* (1948).

TRISSINO, GIANGIORGIO (1478-1550) Italian poet and dramatist who also dabbled in music and architecture. Born in Vicenza, he left this city in 1505, spending several years in Brescia, Milan Ferrara and Florence, where he mingled with well-known statesmen and literary figures. In about 1514 he came to Rome and was well received by Pope *Leo X who sent him on diplomatic missions. *Clement VII and Paul III also gave him their favour. During the latter part of his life he stayed frequently in Vicenza, but died in Rome.

T.'s main contribution to literature was *La Sofonisba* (1515), the first modern tragedy, highly praised at the time, which dealt with an episode of the wars between Rome and Cartago and was modelled on the drama of ancient Greece. His *Il castellano della lingua italiana* was a dialogue on the merits of the Italian dialects which asserted the primacy of the Tuscan idiom. His great poetic work, *Italia liberata dai Goti* (1548), the product of long years of labour, was meant to be a national historical epic, but was later forgotten on account of its ponderousness. T. also wrote a comedy in verse, *I Simillimi* (1548) modelled on Plautus.

A. Scarpa, *Giangiorgio Trissino, poeta d'amore* (1934).

TRISTAO, NUNO (?-1446) Protuguese navigator. A protegé of *Henry the Navigator, he took part in four voyages of *exploration. In 1441 he commanded a ship to Rio de Oro and Cape Blanco. He sailed again in 1443 and in 1444 reached the area of the Senegal River. In 1446 he bypassed Cape Verde and reached the River Gambia. There he met his death by being poisoned by the venemous darts of the negroes which he and his men wanted to capture as slaves.

TRISTAN, LUIS (c. 1586-1624) Spanish painter. Born near Toledo, he became an assistant of El *Greco (1603-07), an experience which influenced his later work. One of his best paintings is the altarpiece for the church of the monastery of Yepes (1616).

TRITHEMIUS, JOHANNES (1462-1516) German humanist. Orphaned in his youth, he left his home to acquire a humanist education. In 1483 he was elected abbot of the monastery of Sponheim, which he reformed and where he collected many manuscripts. In 1506 he left his post there, following a dispute over monastic discipline, and retired to Würzburg. A friend of Conrad *Celtis and many other German humanists, T. was a historian with a patriotic flare. His *Ecclesiastical Writers* (1494) contained almost a thousand biographies, and his *Illustrious Men of Germany* (1495) described the lives of many historical figures. He also wrote about natural sciences; but his most original contribution was his *Polygraphia,* the first Renaissance treatise on cryptography, or the art of writing in secret characters, published in 1518.

K. Arnold, *Johannes Trithemius* (1971).

TRIUMPH The ancient Roman custom of honouring a victorious general with a procession, and frequently with the erection of a commemorative arch, was revived in the imagery of Renaissance poets and artists. One of the first to introduce the idea was *Petrarch in his unfinished allegorical poem *I trionfi* (c. 1350), which found many illustrators in the 15th century. Later, in his paintings and drawings, *Mantegna reconstructed the T. of Julius Caesar. *Giulio Romano depicted the T. of Scipio Africanus and *Dürer published his *Triumph of Maximilian* in a series of woodcuts. These Renaissance representations of the T. usually portrayed the chariot of the hero surrounded and followed by a swarming crowd of men, women and children. Also, the actual celebration of T.s was revived in Italy in the 15th century. Mostly these involved the construction of a temporary triumphal arch, but in at least one case, that of *Alfonso of Aragon, the celebration resulted in the marble gateway of the Castelnuovo, Naples (1443). Celebrations of T.s in the 16th century became part of the festivities organized in honour of the election of a new pope or the entry of a new ruler into his capital. In the early 17th century *Rubens designed a temporary triumphal arch of outstanding decorative merit in Antwerp. The triumphal entries of 16th-century kings frequently became the topic for engravings which were published by contemporary printers.

St. Antonio of Padua *by Cosimo Tura*

TRIVULZIO A Milanese aristocratic family which produced several important cardinals and military men. Gian Giacomo T. (1441-1518), surnamed "the Great", served under the *Sforzas until he broke with *Ludovico il Moro and joined the army of *Ferdinand of Aragon at Naples. Later, he took command of the French army of Louis XII, who gave him various noble titles. T. lost the Battle of Novara (1513), but won a great victory for the young *Francis I at *Marignano (1515). His grandson, Teodoro T. (1474-1551), also distinguished himself in the service of France. The T. assembled an impressive collection of manuscripts and early printed books.

TSCHUDI, GILG (1505-72) Swiss historian. Born in Glarus to an ancient and distinguished family, in his youth he studied under *Zwingli, and later in Basle and Paris, where he attended the classes of *Lefèvre d'Étaple. He declined to join the Reformation and, after 1530, filled many administrative posts in his native city, becoming the chief magistrate of his canton in 1558. The most important of his many historical works, *Chronicon Helveticum*, was published in Basle only in 1734. It is the first general Swiss history and covers the period 1000 to 1470.

F. Gallati, *Gilg Tschudi und die ältere Geschichte Glarus* (1938).

TUDOR, HOUSE OF The royal family which governed England between 1485 and 1603, comprising the reigns of *Henry VII, *Henry VIII and his son and daughters, *Edward VI, *Mary and *Elizabeth I. The T.s belonged to the Welsh nobility and had a rather tenuous claim to the throne. The first bearer of the name, Owen Tudor, married Catherine of Valois, widow of *Henry V clandestinely in about 1429. His son Edmond, to whom *Henry VI gave the title of Earl of Richmond, married *Margaret *Beaufort who, as the daughter of John Beaufort, had a disputed claim to being heiress of the house of *Lancaster. Edmond's posthumous son Henry, born in 1457, took possession of the throne upon his victory over *Richard III at Bosworth. The dynasty ended in 1603, after the death of Queen Elizabeth, who never had any children. The reign of the T.s was characterized by the development of the machinery of central government and a rise in the power of the monarchy.

S. T. Bindoff, *Tudor England* (1950);
G. R. Elton, *The Tudor Revolution in Government* (1953).

TUNSTALL, CUTHBERT (1474-1559) English bishop of Durham. Educated at Cambridge and in Italy, he

pe Paul III and his grandchildren *by Titian*

The Marriage at Cana *by Veronese*

The Last Supper *by Tintoretto*

Under *Edward VI, this cost him his position in the government. In 1551 he was imprisoned, and one year later deprived of his bishopric. In 1553, however, *Mary Tudor had him reinstated, giving him the task of inquiring into the question of the Protestant bishops, in which capacity he behaved with commendable restraint, taking no part in the persecutions. When Elizabeth I succeeded Mary in 1558, he refused to take the Oath of *Supremacy, and was again deprived of his bishopric.

The Coronation of the Madonna *by Cosimo Tura*

Allegorical Figure *by Cosimo Tura*

entered the service of archbishop *Warham, in 1522 becoming bishop of London. *Henry VIII, who employed him on diplomatic missions, made him bishop of Durham in 1530, electing him to the Council of Regency in his will. While acquiescing to the king's break with Rome, T. had to strive to keep the Church of England as much in line with Roman Catholicism as possible.

TURA, COSIMO (c.1431-95) Italian painter. In 1451 he became the court painter at *Ferrara where he executed works for Duke Borso d'*Este. Influenced by *Mantegna, and probably also by *Piero della Francesca, T.'s work has a sombre atmosphere, accentuated by his somewhat tortured treatment of the human figure. He later lost his position to Ercole

de' *Roberti in 1486 and died in poverty. He is considered, however, as the founder and the greatest representative of the Ferraran school which is characterized by its harsh metallic contours.
B. Nicholson, *The Painters of Ferrara* (1950);
E. Ruhmer, *Tura* (1958).

TURNÉBE, ADRIEN (1512-65) French classical scholar. A native of Normandy, he became one of the foremost French philologists of the mid-16th century and, from 1547 to his death, occupied the chair of *Greek in the *College de France. T. published a notable edition of Aeschylus (1552), Sophocles and other ancient authors. He was also famous for the daring alterations which he made in a large number of the passages of classical texts. His son, Odet de T. (1553-81), was the author of *Les Contents*, an amusing comedy of a moralizing nature.

TUSSER, THOMAS (1524-80) English poet and writer about *agriculture. Of an Essex noble family, he was educated at Eton and King's College, Cambridge, entering the service of Lord William Paget at the court as musician and singer. After ten years he left, settled in Suffolk as a farmer and wrote *A Hundreth Good Points of Husbandrie* (1557). This was later expanded to *Five Hundred Good Points of Husbandrie* (1573) and was often reprinted during the next century. T. himself, however, was not successful as a farmer. He died in London, in prison for debt.

TYARD, PONTUS DE (1512-1605) French poet. Born near Mâcon to a noble family, he studied in the Collège de Cocqueret of Paris, where he became a member of the *Pléiade. Later he joined the Church, eventually becoming a canon of the Mâcon cathedral and, in 1578, bishop of Chalon-sur-Saône, a post he filled until 1589 when he was driven away by the *League. A supporter of *Henry III, he then retired from public life. His writings, which established his name as one of the foremost Renaissance poets in France, were undertaken during his early years. Influenced by Maurice *Scève, he composed the *Erreurs amoureuses* (1549-55), dedicated to an ideal mistress and written in a Petrarchan style. Another group of poems, *Livre des vers lyriques* (1555), showed the influence of *Ronsard. T. also translated into French the *Dialoghi di amore* of Leone Ebero (Judah *Abrabanel), published in 1551. Later in his life he composed several theological works. His *Discours philosophiques* (1587), marked by *Neo-Platonism, discussed poetry, music and astrology.
K. M. Hall, *Pontus de Tyard and His "Discours philosophiques"* (1963).

TYE, CHRISTOPHER (c. 1497-1573) English composer. Educated at Cambridge and Oxford, he was choirmaster at the cathedral of Ely and wrote music for *Edward VI and *Elizabeth I. In 1560 he took orders, and was given a living near Ely. He is chiefly known for *The Actes of the Apostles, translated into Englishe Metre wyth notes to eache Chapter to synge and also to play upon the Lute* (1553).

TYNDALE, WILLIAM (c. 1494-1536) English translator of the *Bible. A student at Oxford and Cambridge (1510-15), he came under the influence of *Erasmus, one of whose works he translated into English. In 1523 he came to London seeking assistance for his projected translation of the Bible. Facing rejection, T. went to Hamburg, Germany (1524). In 1525 his English translation of the New Testament was printed at Cologne and *Worms. In England this work was virulently denounced and condemned by the ecclesiastical hierarchy, as well as by Thomas *More. T.'s next years were spent in *Antwerp, where English merchants gave him shelter. He wrote several theological treatises and continued his translation of the Bible, printing the Pentateuch (1530) and Jonah (1531). In 1535 he was arrested and charged with heresy. After spending a year in prison near Brussels, he was burnt at the stake.
J. F. Mozley, *William Tyndale* (1937).

U

UBERTI, FAZIO DEGLI (c. 1305-68) Italian poet; a minor precursor of the *Renaissance. His best-known poem, *Dittamondo,* describes an imaginary voyage through *Europe and parts of Asia and Africa. Employing a number of ancient classical works as sources it was modelled on *Dante's *Divine Comedy*.

UCCELLO, PAOLO (1397-1475) Italian painter. Born in Florence, he was given his early training in the shop which executed the first baptistry doors of *Ghiberti, in 1425 going to work in Venice, where he remained for some years. In 1436 the city of Florence commissioned him to paint the equestrian portrait of John *Hawkwood in the cathedral, where he also executed the *Four Prophets* (1443) and stained-glass windows. His most famous, though damaged *fresco, *Flood*, in S. Maria Novella, Florence, painted in about 1445, is outstanding because of its monumental realist sytle and its clear attempt to emulate the new theories on *perspective. Indeed, U.,

The Battle of San Romano *by Uccello*

a contemporary of *Masaccio and a friend of *Donatello, is said to have spent long periods trying to master perspective and foreshortening. But his other works, which include three battle scenes painted for Cosimo de' *Medici, hunting scenes and religious themes, display a taste for decoration and a regression to the style of *International Gothic. Indeed, as he grew older, U. tended more and more towards a form of painting which resembled an inoffensive dream world.

UDALL, JOHN (c. 1560-92) English *Puritan author. A graduate of Trinity College, Cambridge, he became a clergyman, and, owing to his criticism of episcopacy, was soon involved in disciplinary proceedings by the hierarchy of the *Church of England. In 1588 he published anonymously a pamphlet which was widely read and brought him under suspicion of being one of the authors of the *Marprelate Tracts (1588-89). A second pamphlet, *A Demonstration of the Truth of that Discipline which Christ Hath Prescribed for the Government of His Church,* was considered a political offence since it attacked an institution established by royal authority. Condemned to death, U. was spared at the intercession of Sir Walter *Raleigh, but died in prison. He was also the author of published sermons and a Hebrew grammar and dictionary.

UDALL, NICHOLAS (1505-56) English educator and playwright. A native of Hampshire, he was educated at Oxford, where he became a fellow of Corpus Christi College in 1524. He then found his way to the court of *Henry VIII and in 1534 became headmaster of Eton, a post he held for seven years but lost due to misconduct. Later he enjoyed the favour of *Edward VI and *Mary, and in 1554 became headmaster at Westminster. U. is the author of the first English Renaissance comedy, *Ralph Roister Doister,* written in about 1552, though only published posthumously. The comedy, modelled on the classical authors Terence and Plautus, was intended to be performed by the schoolboys in U. s care. U. also made some translations and wrote a *morality play, *Respublica* (1553).

W. L. Edgerton, *Nicholas Udall* (1965).

UDINE, GIOVANNI DA (1487-1564) Italian painter, designer of ornaments and architect. Born at Udine, he became an assistant of *Raphael, who put him in charge of the decorative works in the Vatican Loggia (1517-19) and the Villa Madama (1520). After the latter's death, he returned to his native town where he worked mainly as an architect. In his stucco decorations inspired by ancient Roman grotesque forms, he evolved a graceful ornamental style that became very popular.

UFFIZI A palace in *Florence built by Grand Duke *Cosimo I with the intention of housing the public offices. In 1565, *Vasari (1560-74) added the corridor over the Ponte Vecchio connecting the U. with the *Pitti Palace on the other side of the Arno River. Later, Bernardo Buontalenti (1536-1608) added the Loggia and Tribuna. Art treasures of the *Medici family were first moved to the U. by Grand Duke Francesco I (1574-87), a process that was continued by his successors. Gradually a collection of paintings, sculpture, drawings, engravings, armour, coins and tapestries were assembled, making it into, by far, the largest museum of Italian Renaissance art.

UGO DA CARPI (c. 1480-c. 1523) Italian painter and engraver. He is mainly known as the developer of the chiaroscuro woodcut which consists of the superimposition of several blocks in light and dark tones of the same colour to achieve a three-dimensional effect. Although this method was employed some years earlier in Germany, it was U., in about 1516, who gave it a true artistic expression.

UGOLINO DA SIENA Italian painter of the *Sienese school, active between 1317 adn 1327. A follower of *Duccio, his only surviving work is the altarpiece of the Church of S. Croce, Florence, now divided among several museums.

ULRICH (1487-1550) Duke of Württemberg. Succeeding to the duchy at the age of 11, he was declared of age in 1503, becoming one of the chief military commanders of Emperor *Maximilian I. In 1514 a peasant uprising against his oppressive rule was suppressed only after he made concessions to the estates. In 1515, when he impetuously killed a knight, Hans von Hutton, to whose wife he was attracted, caused the flight of his own wife, Sabina of Bavaria. The whole affair resulted in his being placed under the ban of the empire. In 1519, when U. supported the imperial candidacy of *Francis I of France and took over the town of Reutlingen, the *Swabian League mobilized its forces against him. He was driven away from his duchy, which was subsequently handed over to *Ferdinand of Austria, the brother of *Charles V.

In exile, U. passed some time in Switzerland where he was converted to Protestantism by *Oecolampodius and fought in the service of France. During the *Peasants' War he marched back to Germany, trying to regain his duchy by joining forces with the rebels, but had to withdraw when his mercenaries left him (1525). About that time he earned the support of *Philip of Hesse, who in 1534 helped him invade the territory of Württemberg. With the Swabian League already dissolved and the *Habsburgs at a disadvantage, U. won an easy victory and recovered the power over Württemberg, while recognizing the overlordship of Ferdinand of Austria (1535). U. quickly introduced the *Reformation and confiscated the property of the monasteries. In 1546 he joined the Protestant princes against the emperor, but was defeated by the duke of *Alba. U. maintained the duchy by fulfilling the conditions imposed by Charles V; these included a money payment and the taking of a personal oath of submission. In 1548 he was compelled to accept the *Augsburg Interim. The Emperor, however, did not accede to Ferdinand's demands for the deposition of U. because he had violated his oath of 1535. U. died at Tübingen.

UNIATE CHURCH OF POLAND In 1595 the Metropolitan of Kiev and other bishops concluded a union with the Roman Catholic Church at Brest-Litovsk, Lithuania. Approved by Pope *Clement VIII and King *Sigismund III of Poland, this union involved several millions of Ruthenians, all of the Byzantine or Greek-Orthodox rite, who, while retaining their liturgy, recognized the authority of Rome. Opposed by the Russian Orthodox Church, the U. were despised by the Roman Catholic Church of Poland and did not gain concrete benefits from their new affiliation.

UNIFORMITY, ACTS OF Four legal measures passed by the English parliament making a reformed religious service obligatory. The first act (1549) imposed upon penalty the use of the first Book of *Common Prayer.

The second (1552) enforced a revised version of the Book of Common Prayer and specified more stringent penalties. The third (1559) renewed the validity of the second act which had been nullified during the reign of *Mary Tudor. A fourth act (1662) enforced the religious settlement of the Restorarion.

UNITARIANS A radically inclined Reformation movement which denied the doctrine of the Trinity and affirmed the unipersonality of God. Although a number of Protestant theologians defended unitarian views, the most prominent role in the development of the movement was played by Faustus *Socinus, whose followers, also known as Socinians, were prevalent in Cracow, Poland. In 1605, a year after his death, they embodied their beliefs in the Cathechism of Cracow. By the mid-17th century the Polish U. had been suppressed owing to pressure applied by the *Jesuits, but the movement survived in Transylvania, in England, and later on in America.

E. M. Wilbur, *A History of Unitarianism* (1946).

UNITED PROVINCES The name given to the independent Dutch republic. Consisting of seven northern provinces of the *Netherlands, this new political entity was first formed in the Union of *Utrecht (1579), which led to a proclamation of independence from Spain (1581). Its first ruler was supposed to be Francis, duke of *Anjou, but the person who really wielded authority was *William of Orange, who had been awarded the hereditary title of count and stadtholder of *Holland and Zeeland, the two main provinces. After his death the governorship-general was briefly held by the earl of *Leicester, who commanded the English expeditionary force (1585-87). In 1588 *Maurice of Nassau, William's son and successor, became the commander-in-chief, whereas Johan van *Oldenbarnevelt took charge of the foreign affairs of the federation. The first measure of international recognition came in 1596 when alliances were established with England and France. The Twelve Years' Truce (1609) amounted to a recognition by Spain, but after its expiration the war was resumed, leading finally to a formal recognition of independence at the Treaty of Westphalia (1648).

According to the constitution of the U., each province retained its own government under a stadtholder, including complete control of its internal affairs. The task of the federal government was to organize the defence of the Provinces as a whole, under officials nominated by the Council of State. The highest organ of the federation was the Estates-General to which each of the provinces sent deputies. The republican character of the federation, however, did not hinder the growing authority of the house of Orange. Frederick Henry, who, in 1625, took over from his brother Maurice of Nassau, held five of the seven stadtholderships and supreme command of the land and sea forces, acting as a monarch in all but name. During the struggle for independence, the U. grew rich and powerful at sea. Early in the 17th century they emerged as a great commercial empire with strategic possessions in the Americas, Africa and the Far East. In spite of a conflict between *Remonstrants and Contra-Remonstrants, which reached a climax at the Synod of *Dort (1619), there was a tolerant religious climate, allowing an unprecedented flourishing of science, philosophy, art and literature.

J. L. Motley, *The Rise of the Dutch Republic*, 3 vols. (1864);
P. Geyl, *The Revolt of the Netherlands* (1932).

UNITY OF THE BROTHERS (Unitas Fratrum) A pietistic sect, known also as the Bohemian Brethren, which seceded from the *Utraquists in the second half of the 15th century. The group was first influenced by the teachings of Peter *Chelcicky, formally separating itself from the main body in 1467. The sect grew under the leadership of *Lukas of Prague, developing its own system of church government, observing the simple life, renouncing violence and recognizing the *Bible as the only religious authority. Early in the 16th century it spread over about 400 Bohemian communities. During the *Reformation a faction, led by Jan Augusta, attempted to affect an alliance with *Luther, but the project was opposed from within and a union was never achieved. Opposed to the Habsburgs in the internal struggles of Germany, the brethren felt the heavy hand of Archduke *Ferdinand. Many settled in Moravia and some went to Poland. They were given complete religious freedom in the *Majestätsbrief* of 1609, but after the Czech defeat in the Battle of the White Mountain (1620) they were exiled or forced to go underground.

P. Brock, *The Political and Social Doctrines of the Unity of Czech Brethren* (1957).

UNIVERSITIES Centres of advanced professional study in theology, law and *medicine, European universities were a product of the Middle Ages. Still, it was during the 15th and 16th centuries that they acquired some of their outstanding modern features. It was then that university education came to be regarded as a desirable experience for anybody who wanted to join the upper echelons of society. As a consequence, increasing numbers of the sons of the European aristocracy began to attend. Moreover, faculty members and students for the first time became imbued with the idealism to try to effect a change in the social and cultural values. It is not by accident, for example, that the *Reformation originated in a university town.

The oldest European university or *studium generale* was that of Salerno in Sicily, where stress was laid on the study of medicine. Salerno was followed in the 12th century by *Bologna, famous for its law school, and Paris, the mother of northern universities, where the college of theology of the Sorbonne soon attracted a student body from other countries. During the 13th century other prominent schools were established: Oxford and Cambridge in England, Salamanca in Spain and Coimbra in Portugal. Germany acquired its first university in the 14th century. Following the foundation of the first such institution beyond the Rhine, however – in Prague (1348) – other universities sprang up in Vienna (1365); Heidelberg (1386), *Cologne (1388) and Erfurt (1392). By 1400 a total of 45 *studia generalia* existed throughout Europe.

The late mediaeval university usually consisted of four faculties: The elementary faculty of arts awarded an M.A. degree, which was required for enrolment in the higher faculties of theology, law and medicine, leading to the doctorate. The government of the university, originally under the supervision of the ecclesiastical authorities, became independent. Endowments by wealthy patrons and the aid of religious orders provided the conditions necessary for the building and maintenance of colleges which became the residences of both the students and their teachers. In the largest universities, where the student body was composed of different nationalities, these various "nations" often clashed among themselves or with the residents of the town. Northern universities, organized as communities of scholars, differed from those of Italy, Spain and southern France, where students frequently hired their teachers and where teaching was oriented toward practical professional training.

The 15th century saw significant changes with respect to the universities and, from 1400 to 1500, their number increased to 78. The most outstanding development took place in Germany where, until the outbreak of the *Reformation, 12 new schools were founded, including such influential establishments as Leipzig (1409), *Basle (1456), Freiburg (1457), Ingolstadt (1472), Tübingen (1477) and *Wittenberg (1502). The impact of *humanism was of crucial importance. Although they hardly fitted into the then existing curricula of the higher faculties, lectures on classical languages and literature gradually penetrated into the elementary arts syllabus. It was then only a question of time until humanistic critical methods came to affect the study of theology. The penetration and acceptance of humanism was easier in the new German universities. Older seats of learning such as Paris and Cologne, and to a certain extent Oxford and Salamanca, resisted these trends. By the end of the 15th century, however, the influence of the new learning became unavoidable. This is perhaps best illustrated in the case of the university of Alcalá, founded in 1508, which became the headquarters of Spanish humanism. European universities enjoyed a period of expansion in the first decades of the 16th century. By now the innovative spirit of the Renaissance had also affected the more conservative disciplines of law and medicine. Bourges in France, for example, emerged as a leading centre for the study of law, whereas Padua in Italy enjoyed the ascendancy when it came to a medical training programme.

The overall effect of the Reformation and *Counter-Reformation was to usher in a period of stagnation. The former liberal attitude and cosmopolitan outlook gave away to divisions over matters of faith, and universities increasingly felt the pressure of the secular authorities. The university of Marburg, founded in 1527, was the first *Protestant school, followed by Königsberg (1544) and Jena (1558); but in the mid-16th century the total number of German university students was an estimated 3,500, about the same that it had been 50 years earlier. The Genevan Academy, founded by *Calvin in 1559, took over from the German universities as the centre of international Protestantism. In 1575, however, *William of Orange commemorated Leiden's heroic resistance against Spain by giving the city a university. In a short time it became the stronghold of Calvinism in northern Europe and, in addition, a great centre for classical studies and medical training. On the Roman Catholic side Salamanca enjoyed a period of renewed vigour, its theologians acquiring a reputation and influence which went far beyond the confines of Spain. The most outstanding Catholic university of northern Europe in the second half of the 16th century was Louvain, where Roberto *Bellarmine and Justus *Lipsius were active. The spirit of religious intransigence which came to mark most European universities in this period, however, hardly encouraged further scholarly and scientific development.

Many of the scientific achievements during the 17th century, stemmed from learned *academies of various kinds.

C. H. Haskins, *The Rise of Universities* (1923);

A print commemorating the inauguration of the University of Leiden

S. D'Irsay, *Histoire des universités*, 2 vols. (1933);
H. Rashdall, *The Universities of Europe*, 2nd ed., 3 vols. (1936).

UNIVERSITY WITS The name given to the group of young writers, graduates of the universities of Oxford and Cambridge, who enlivened the English *drama and letters of the last quarter of the 16th century. Leading irregular lives and constantly involved in polemics, the foremost of them included John *Lyly, Christopher *Marlowe, Robert *Greene and Thomas *Nash.

URBAN VII (1521-90) Pope for 13 days, 15-27 September 1590. Born Giambattista Castagna, in Rome, he studied law at Bologna and had a long ecclesiastical career before being elected to one of the briefest pontificates. U. took an active part in the third session of the Council of *Trent (1562-63). As papal nuncio to the court of *Philip II, he helped to form the Christian military alliance which defeated the Turks at *Lepanto (1571). From 1583 until his election he served as papal governor of Bologna.

URBINO Ruled since the 13th century by the family of Montefeltro, this city of the Marches, which today lies in the province of Pesaro, slowly gained in influence, till it reached its height during the rule of *Federico da Montefeltro (1444-82). U. was then promoted to become a duchy by *Sixtus IV, as a consequence of which the activity of important sculptors, painters and architects, among them Luciano *Laurana, Luca della *Robbia and *Piero della Francesca, was welcomed. *Raphael, too, was born and trained in U. The Montefeltros were succeeded in 1508 by Francesco Maria *Della Rovere, a nephew of *Julius II on the one side and of Federico da Montefeltro on the other. The rule of this new dynasty continued until 1626, when the last old and childless Della Rovere, Francesco Maria II, bequeathed the duchy to Pope Urban VIII. U. then became part of the *Papal States.

P. Rotondi, *The Ducal Palace of Urbino* (1969).

URSULINES A Roman Catholic order of women dedicated to teaching. Founded by Angela Merici in Brescia in 1535, it was approved by *Paul III in 1544. At first, members of the order lived in their own homes but, in 1572, *Gregory XIII made them a religious community, living together under vows. The order spread rapidly, especially in France. It has continued to grow until recently, being the oldest and largest women's teaching order of the Catholic Church.

UTRAQUISTS The main body of the followers of *Hus in *Bohemia, they comprised many of the nobility and formed a kind of independent Czech national church. The U. demanded Communion in both kinds (*sub utraque specie*) and, because of their demand to let the laity receive wine directly from the Eucharistic cup, were also known as Calixtines. At first rejected by the Church, in the *compacta* of 1433 the Council of Basle accepted their claim. Although *Pius II cancelled this permission in 1462, the U. continued to practice their own form of Communion. In the course of the 16th century they wavered for a while between Lutheranism and Roman Catholicism, but subsequently remained affiliated to Rome.

L. Nemec, *Church and State in Czechoslovakia* (1955).

UTRECHT, UNION OF (1579) A treaty-confederation organized by *John of Nassau, and linking seven northern provinces of the Netherlands (Holland, Zeeland, Gelderland, Utrecht, Friesland, and, later, Groningen and Overyssel). It aimed to continue the defence of their civil and religious liberties following the pro-Spanish Union of *Arras earlier that year. It was followed, in 1581, by a proclamation of complete independence from Spain.

UYTEWAEL (WTEWAEL), JOACHIM (c. 1566-1638) Dutch painter. Born in Utrecht, he worked with a number of Flemish painters before going to Italy and France. Returning in 1592, he settled in his native town where he exercised considerable influence on the development of Dutch art. Essentially a *Mannerist, U. painted many mythological pictures and biblical themes. He excelled in his dramatic exploitation of the effects of contrasting tones of shade and light.

The St. Sebaldus Reliquary *by Peter Vischer*

VACA DE CASTRO, CHRISTOBAL (c. 1492-1566) Spanish colonial governor. The son of a noble family of Leon, he filled a number of positions in the royal administration before *Charles V sent him to Peru to put an end to the war between *Pizarro and *Almagro. Arriving there after the assassination of Francisco Pizarro in 1542, he succeeded in gaining the support of enough **conquistadores* to enable him to crush the army led by Almagro's young son, Diego, who was afterwards executed as a traitor. Soon, however, V. confronted a new rebellion headed by Gonzalo *Pizarro, who refused to conform with the New Laws that had been issued in Spain concerning the tenure of **encomiendas*. V., who this time assumed a conciliatory attitude, aroused the enmity of the new viceroy, Blasco Nuñez Vela, who came to replace him and had him arrested (1544). Escaping from prison, he managed to make his way back to Spain where he was again confined for three years before being declared innocent.

VADIANUS (Joachim von Vatt; 1484-1551) Swiss humanist and reformer. Born in St. Gallen, he was educated at the university of Vienna, under Conrad *Celtis, being crowned poet laureate by *Maximilian I in 1514. In 1518 V. became city physician at St. Gallen, becoming increasingly involved with the Reformation in 1519. A follower of *Zwingli, in 1526 he became burgomaster of his native town. His commentaries on classical authors and history of the famous monastery of St. Gallen demonstrated critical judgment.

W. Näf, *Vadian und seine Stadt St. Gallen* (1944-57).

VALDES, ALFONSO DE (c. 1490-1532) Spanish author. The twin brother of Juan de Valdes, he became secretary to Emperor *Charles V, whom he represented in the negotiations with *Melanchthon at the Diet of *Augsburg in 1530. His importance as an author stems from two works: the first, *Dialogo de Lactancio y un Arcadiano* (1529), justified the imperial armies' Sack of *Rome in 1527 and violently attacked papal secular pretensions; the second, *Dialogo de Mercurio y Caron* (1530), contained many anti-clerical views and much political gossip. Both works enjoyed wide popularity in spite of papal protests.

VALDES, JUAN DE (c. 1490-1541) Spanish humanist and leader of an Italian Catholic reform movement. Born to a noble family in Cuenca, he was educated at the university of Alcala. In 1529 an anonymous publication containing strong Erasmian views was ascribed to him, provoking charges of various natures, so that he decided to go to Italy. In 1534 he settled in Naples where a circle of friends gathered around him. These included the countess Giulia *Gonzaga, Bernardino *Ochino, Peter Martyr *Vermigli, as well as other men and women of noble descent and ecclesiastics with reformist tendencies.

In his teachings, V. emphasized inward spiritual religious values rather than the manifestation of outward forms. His most famous work, *Dialogo de la lengua,* published only in the 18th century, dealt with the Spanish language. He also wrote several devotional treatises, especially the *Alfabeto cristiano,* published in 1545. His collected essays and letters, *Le cento e dieci considerazioni,* were published in Basle in 1550. Although he was frequently suspected of Lutheran tendencies, V. died a Roman Catholic. After his death, however, a number of his disciples took the road to Protestantism.

D. Ricart, *Juan de Valdes y el pensamiento religioso europeo* (1958);

J. C. Nieto, *Juan de Valdes and the Origins of the Spanish and Italian Reformation* (1970).

VALDIVIA, PEDRO DE (c. 1500-53) Spanish conqueror of Chile. A native of Estramadura, he joined the imperial army, taking part in the Battle of *Pavia (1525), before coming to the New World, where he joined in the conquest of Venezuela (1535). In 1537 he joined *Pizarro in Peru and in 1539 was commissioned by him to conquer Chile, a venture in which *Almagro had already failed. With about 150 Spaniards and 1000 Indians, he advanced south, and, in 1541, founded Santiago. In 1548 he was back in Peru, helping Pedro de la *Gasca suppress the revolt of Gonzalo *Pizarro, but afterwards returned to Chile to face an insurrection of the local Indians. In 1550 he founded Concepción in southern Chile where, in 1552, some gold deposits were found. V. met his death after he had been captured and tortured by rebels led by his former Indian servant Lautaro.

VALENCIA, MARTIN DE (c. 1473-1534) Spanish missionary. Born near Leon, he joined the Franciscan order, distinguishing himself in his zeal for reform and strict observance. Rising in the hierarchy of the Spanish branch of the order, he was chosen to lead the "Twelve Apostles to Mexico", a group that arrived at Veracruz on May 1524. During the next ten years he supervised the conversion of many thousands of Indians, communicating with his growing flock with the aid of interpreters.

S. Escalante Plancarte, *Fray Martin de Valencia* (1945).

VALENTIN, MOÏSE (1591-1632) The name given to the French painter Jean de Boulogne. Born at Coulommiers, in about 1612 he arrived in Rome where he lived until his death. His works, both in style and in subject matter, show the influence of *Caravaggio. V. is best known for tavern scenes and genre paintings of soldiers, musicians and fortune-tellers. In 1629 he was given the honour of painting *The Martyrdom of Saints Processus and Martinian* for *St. Peter's.

VALERIANO, PIERO (1477-1558) The name assumed by the Italian humanist and poet Giovanni Pietro delle Fosse. Born in Belluno, he studied classical languages in Venice and in 1509 went to Rome, where he later became a protegé of Pope *Leo X. After the Sack of *Rome (1527), he left for Florence, dying at Padua. As well as composing verse in Latin, he wrote a work on the hieroglyphics of the obelisks of Rome, published in 1552. Previously he had written the *Dialogo della volgar lingua* in which he advocated the adoption of an Italian literary language different from any of the existing regional dialects, and *De literatorum infelicitate*, describing Rome's intellectual community prior to its dispersion in 1527.

VALKENBORCH, LUCAS (c. 1530-97) AND MARTEN (1535-1612) The two most important representatives of a Flemish family of painters. Lucas was born at Malines and, after working in several towns in the Netherlands, fled to Germany on account of his Protestantism, dying at *Frankfurt. Marten, who had accompanied his brother to Germany, later worked in Venice (1602) and in Rome (1604). Both excelled in painting landscapes and small genre scenes inspired by the *Breugel tradition. Their pictures on the theme of the Tower of Babel are especially well known.

VALLA, LORENZO (1407-57) Italian humanist; the scholar who paved the way for the emergence of historical criticism. Born in Rome, he was a pupil of *Vittorino da Feltre. He perfected his superb *Latin style under Leonardo *Bruni and learned *Greek from *Aurispa. In 1431 he wrote his first work of importance, *De voluptate* (Concerning Pleasure), a dialogue between a Stoic, an Epicurean and a Christian, in which he appears to argue the case that sensual pleasure is the highest ethical standard. In the same year he was ordained priest and became professor of rhetoric at Pavia, but he soon left his appointment in order to visit Milan, Genoa, Ferrara and Mantua in the next few years. At Naples, in about 1436, he became secretary of King *Alfonso of Aragon, under whose protection he remained during the next ten years. In 1447, however, he returned to Rome, becoming a notary of the recently elected *Nicholas V in the apostolic chancery. From 1450 he was also professor of rhetoric at the university of Rome, where he died.

V's most famous work, *De falso credita et ementita Constantini Donatione declamatio* (Declamation Concerning the False Donation of Constantine), was written in 1440 while he was in Naples. Here he subjected to severe textual criticism the long suspected 8th-century fabrication which, in order to strengthen the prestige of the papacy, purported to prove that the emperor Constantine had conferred upon Pope Sylvester I (314-35) the primacy over all other Christian bishops together with supreme authority over the West. Using a variety of arguments, legal, historical, and linguistic, V. demonstrated the staggering anachronism in the style and contents of the document. The exposition, which also attacked the temporal power of the papacy brought upon him the wrath of *Eugenius IV, but the protection of King Alfonso saved him from having to stand trial. It is no wonder, therefore, that V.'s only systematic historical work, dealing with the reign of Ferdinand I of Aragon, the father of his patron, had the trappings of an official history.

Of V.'s other works, *Collatio Novi Testamenti* (Notes to the New Testament) written in 1444, was an early attempt at critical exegesis based on comparison between the Vulgate and the Greek text. In *De libero arbitrio* (On Free Will), he expressed his doubts as to whether man is able to reconcile faith and reason. In another philosophical work he ridiculed mediaeval scholasticism, and in his *De professione religiosorum* (On the Profession of the Religious), not published until the 19th century, he criticised the ideal of monastic life. His most frequently published work, written in 1444, was a Latin handbook, *De elegantiis linguae latinae*, which, after its first publication in 1471, became the standard humanist style-manual. V.'s influence as a pioneer of the historical-critical method cannot be exaggerated; *Luther was among the first to acknowledge his contribution.

C. Trinkaus, *In His Likeness and Image: Humanity and Divinity in Italian Humanist Thought* (1970).

VALOIS, HOUSE OF The ruling dynasty of France from 1328-1589. The line went back to Charles, Count of Valois, son of Philip the Bold (1270-85), whose son, Philip VI (1328-50), was the first member of the family to become king. The house continued in straight successions from father to son until *Charles VIII (1483-98). When he died a descendant of Orleans branch of the family, *Louis XII (1498-1515), mounted the throne and, upon his death, it went to *Francis I (1515-47) of the branch of Angoulême. *Henry II (1547-59) and his three sons, *Francis II (1559-60), *Charles IX (1560-74) and *Henry III (1574-89) who had no heirs, were the last kings of the dynasty, being succeeded by *Henry IV of *Bourbon.

VALTURIUS, ROBERTUS (1405-75) Italian writer. Born in Rimini, he entered the service of Sigismondo *Malatesta in approximately 1446. In 1460 he wrote *De re militari* (On the Art of War), a work divided into 12 books first published in 1472. One of the most famous Renaissance treatises on war, it was filled with many anecdotes about the military campaigns of antiquity, and also included descriptions and sketches of military weapons and instruments of war. V. is supposed to have designed Malatesta's fortresses.

Giorgione da Castel Franco Pittor Vinitiano.

E medeſimi tempi, che Fiorenza acquiſtaua tanta fama, per l'opere di Lionardo, arrecò non piccolo ornamento a Vinezia, la virtu, & eccellenza un ſuo cittadino, il quale di gran lũga paſsò i Bellini, da loro tenuti in tanto pregio, & qualunque altro fino a quel tempo haueſſe in quella città dipinto. Queſti fu Giorgio, che in Caſtel Franco in ſul Treuiſano nacque l'anno 1478. eſſendo Doge Giouan Mozenigo, fratel del Doge Piero, dalle fattezze della perſona, & da la grandezza de l'animo, chiamato poi col tempo, Giorgione. Il quale, quantunque egli fuſſe nato d'humiliſſima ſtirpe, non fu però ſe non gentile, & di buoni coſtumi in tutta ſua vita. Fu alleuato in Vinegia, & dilettoſsi continouamente de le coſe d'Amore, & piacqueli il ſuono del Liuto mirabilmen

A page from the 1568 edition of Vasari's Lives of the Artists

VANNI, ANDREA (c. 1332-1414) Italian painter. Born in *Siena, he was influenced by Simone *Martini and the brothers *Lorenzetti, and besides painting took active part in the civic life of the republic. Between about 1384-91, he worked in Naples and Sicily, before returning to Siena. His best works are those in the cathedral, and the portrait and fresco of St. Catherine in the convent of S. Domenico.

VARCHI, BENEDETTO (1503-65) Italian humanist. Born in Florence, he studied law in Pisa, becoming a notary. In 1527 he took part in the expulsion of the *Medici from Florence and, after their return (1530), spent many years in exile until he was allowed to return and given a position at court by *Cosimo I (1543). For his patron the grateful V. wrote his *Storia fiorentina*, covering the turbulent period of Florentine politics from 1527-38. Its accuracy and careful documentation is spoilt, however, by the author's adulation of Cosimo. V. also wrote poetry, lectured on *Dante and *Petrarch, championed the Tuscan dialect as an Italian literary language and wrote *drama and other types of literature.

VARIGNANA, IL (?-1534) The name given to the Italian sculptor Domenico Aimo. In 1506 he lost the contest over who could produce the best reproduction of the newly-found ancient *Laocoön* group to Jacopo *Sansovino. In 1514 he was commissioned to make the statue of Pope *Leo X, now at S. Maria d'Aracoeli, Rome. Later, he worked at Loreto and Bologna, where he completed works begun by Jacopo della *Quercia at the church of S. Petronio.

VASA, HOUSE OF The dynasty which began ruling in Sweden in 1523. During the 16th century it was represented by *Gustavus Vasa, his sons, *Eric XIV and *John III, and his grandson, *Sigismund. In 1587 the V. also came into possession of another crown, with Sigismund's election as king of Poland. The latter, however, being Roman Catholic, was subsequently deposed by Protestant Sweden and, in the early 17th century, relations between the Polish and Swedish members of the dynasty were marked by conflicts.

VASARI, GIORGIO (1511-74) Italian painter, architect and writer. Born to a well-connected family in Arezzo, in 1524 he was sent to Florence where he was trained by *Andrea del Sarto and Baccio *Bandinelli. There, too, he met *Michelangelo, for whom he felt an unbounded admiration, and earned the patronagc of the *Medici. In 1555, following a successful carreer as a painter in Florence and Rome, he was appointed architect for the Palazzo Vecchio in Florence by grand-duke *Cosimo I and, from 1560, worked on the Uffizi Palace. In 1563 he founded the Accademia del Disegno, one of the earliest *academies of art. Essentially a *Mannerist, V. enjoyed the standing of a major artist during his own lifetime.

Among his most important paintings were the great *fresco cycle in the Palazzo Vecchio treating scenes from the history of Florence, and the frescoes in the Salla della Cancelleria, Rome, depicting scenes from the life of Pope *Paul III. Of his lesser architectural works, the best known are the Palazzo dei Cavalieri in Pisa, the Loggie in Arezzo, Michelangelo's tomb in Florence and the corridor over the Ponte Vecchio connecting the Uffizi with the *Pitti Palace. His house at Arezzo has now been made into a museum to exhibit his work.

V., however, is mostly remembered for his great biographical masterpiece, *Le vite de piu eccellenti architetti, pittori et scultori italiani* (Lives of the Most Excellent Italian Architects, Painters and Sculptors), first published in 1550. One of the greatest works on art history, it presents not just a series of biographies, but a comprehensive interpretation of the development of the Italian art of the Renaissance from *Giotto to Michelangelo. V., who entertained humanist views, found inspiration in the art of classical antiquity and regarded the Middle Ages as a period of decline. Accordingly, the main connecting theme of his work is the revival of "true art" by Giotto and his Tuscan disciples, culminating in the artistic perfection of *Leonardo, *Raphael and Michelangelo, this last being the only artist to be mentioned in the first edition who was alive at the time. Though sometimes inaccurate, the biographies are eminently readable even today, and were frequently republished and translated.

E. Rud, *Vasari's Life and Lives: The First Art Historian* (1963);

P. Barocchi, *Vasari pittore* (1964).

VASCONCELOS, JORGE FERREIRA DE (c. 1515-85) Portuguese playwright and novelist. Well-educated, probably at Coimbra, he became a courtier of *John III, serving later as royal secretary and, after 1563, at the *Casa da India*. V. was the author of three long plays, intended to be read rather than acted.

Eufrosina, published in 1555 though written over ten years earlier, portrays life at the university town of Coimbra and presents a love story modelled on the famous Spanish dramatic novel *La Celestina. Ulísipo* and *Aulegrafia* were published posthumously (1618-19); the first presented love and intrigue in the middle-class setting of Lisbon, the second ridiculed the fading concepts of courtly love.

V. also wrote a novel, *Memorial da Segunda Távola Redonda* (1567), which contains a curious combination of the mediaeval ideals of *chivalry and classical mythology. It is, however, for his plays, a critical portrayal of Portuguese society, that V. is famous.

J. Subirats, *Les comedies et l'épître de Jorge Ferreira de Vasconcelos* (1976);
E. Asensio, ed., *Comedia Eufrosina* (1951).

VASILY III (1479-1533) Grand prince of Moscow from 1505. The son of *Ivan III and Sophia, niece of the last Byzantine emperor, his father preferred him to Dmitry, the grandson of an earlier marriage. V. incorporated into the Muscovite state the free area of Pskov (1510), seized Smolensk from *Lithuania (1514) and conquered Riazan (1517). During his reign there was appreciable growth in the power of the central government, although the great nobles, the *boyars*, still held important hereditary rights. Divorcing his first wife in 1525, *Ivan IV ("the Terrible") was born as a result of his second marriage.

VATABLE, FRANÇOIS (c. 1495-1547) French classical scholar. A native of Picardy, he was appointed to the recently founded *College de France in about 1530. V. is regarded as one of the greatest *Hebrew scholars of his age. His published works consist of translations and commentaries published from notes taken by his students. Some of these, which were published by Robert *Estienne, were criticised for their Protestant tendencies and disavowed by V.

VÁZQUEZ, GABRIEL (1549-1604) Spanish theologian. Joining the *Jesuits at 20, he served as professor of theology at Rome (1585-91) and at the university of Alcala where he taught until his death. V. was the rival of *Suarez, but also made himself a name as a great authority on patristic literature. His best-known work was a commentary on St. Thomas Aquinas in eight volumes.

VAZQUEZ, LORENZO (?-c. 1509) Spanish architect. Probably born in Segovia, he was the first to introduce elements of the Italian Renaissance to Spanish architecture. From 1489 on he was employed by Cardinal Pedro Gonzales de *Mendoza, first on the college of Santa Cruz in Valladolid and then in Guadalajara and elsewhere. Actually his was a transitional style, still marked by the influence of the Gothic.

VECCHIETTA (c. 1412-80) The name given to the Italian painter, sculptor and architect, Lorenzo di Pietro. Active in *Siena, he seems to have been the pupil of *Sassetta, though he was also influenced by his Florentine contemporaries, and his sculpture has a clear affinity with *Donatello's. V. is also noted for his *illumination of part of *Dante's *Divine Comedy*. V.'s paintings, mostly in Siena, are known for their expressive, naturalistic style.

G. Vigni, *Lorenzo di Pietro, detto Il Vecchietta* (1938).

VEEN, OTTO VAN (1556-1629) Flemish painter, also known as Vaenius. Born in Leiden, he came from a noble family which supported *Philip II of Spain. In 1576 he went to Italy, studying under Federico *Zuccaro for 5 years. He then returned to the Netherlands, becoming the court painter of Alessandro *Farnese in Brussels (1585) and later settling in *Antwerp (1592). Essentially a *Mannerist, he was perhaps the most influential of *Rubens' teachers. V. served also as court painter of Archduke *Albert.

VEGIO, MAFFEO (1407-58) Italian humanist. Born at Lodi, he studied at Milan and Pavia, before coming to Rome, where he joined the papal court under *Eugenius IV and *Martin V. He is largely remembered for his *De educatione liberorum* (1445-48), a treatise on education in which the synthesis is made between humanist ideas and Christian ideals. V. also wrote an additional 13th book to Vergil's *Aeneid* (1427) as well as works on *archaeology and etymology.

A. Cox Brinton, *Maphaeus Vegius and His Thirteenth Book of the Aeneid* (1930).

VELASCO, LUIS DE (c. 1511-64) Second Spanish viceroy of Mexico. Born to an ancient noble Castilian family, he had several administrative positions before coming to Mexico in 1550 to take over from Viceroy Antonio de *Mendoza. V. enforced the laws of 1542, which had put limitations upon native exploitation and liberated thousands of Indians. In 1553 he opened the university of Mexico, and in 1559 sent out an expedition to conquer Florida, a venture which failed, however. During his administration Spanish settlements penetrated further north and the rich silver mines of Zacatecas went into production. Just before his death, V. prepared the expedition of Legazpi to the *Philippines. His son, also named Luis (1539-1616), was twice viceroy of Mexico and once of Peru.

VELAZQUEZ, DIEGO DE (c. 1460-1524) Spanish *conquistador*. Born in Cuellar, he went to America with *Columbus on the latter's second voyage (1494). In due course he became a lieutenant of *Ovando in Hispaniola and, at the head of a small force of his own immediate followers, undertook the conquest of Cuba in 1511. By 1514 V. had completed the conquest, and as governor of the island founded the first settlements. In 1517 and 1518 he sent expeditions to the coasts of Mexico and, in 1519, fitted out the force which, led by his relative, Hernan *Cortes, set out to conquer the Aztec Empire. One year later, however, he sent Panfilo de *Narvaez to intercept Cortes. Owing to the failure of this mission, however, V. lost his governorship, though he regained it shortly before his death.

VELDE, ESAIAS VAN DE (1591-1630) Dutch painter. Born in Amsterdam, he was active in Haarlem and The Hague, serving also as court painter of *Maurice of Nassau. He is recognized as one of the chief contributors to the rise of the Dutch school of realist landscape painting, especially in his low-sky-views of the sea.

VÉLEZ DE GUEVARA, LUÍS (1579-1644) Spanish dramatist and novelist. Born in Ecija, near Seville, he studied at the university of Osuna, was a page of the archbishop of Seville and fought in Italy (1600-05). On his return, he became famous as a wit and was supported by various noble patrons, finally obtaining a position in the household of Philip IV. A careless spender, he was always in debt, but somehow had the courage to marry four times. V.'s 400 plays, eighty of which

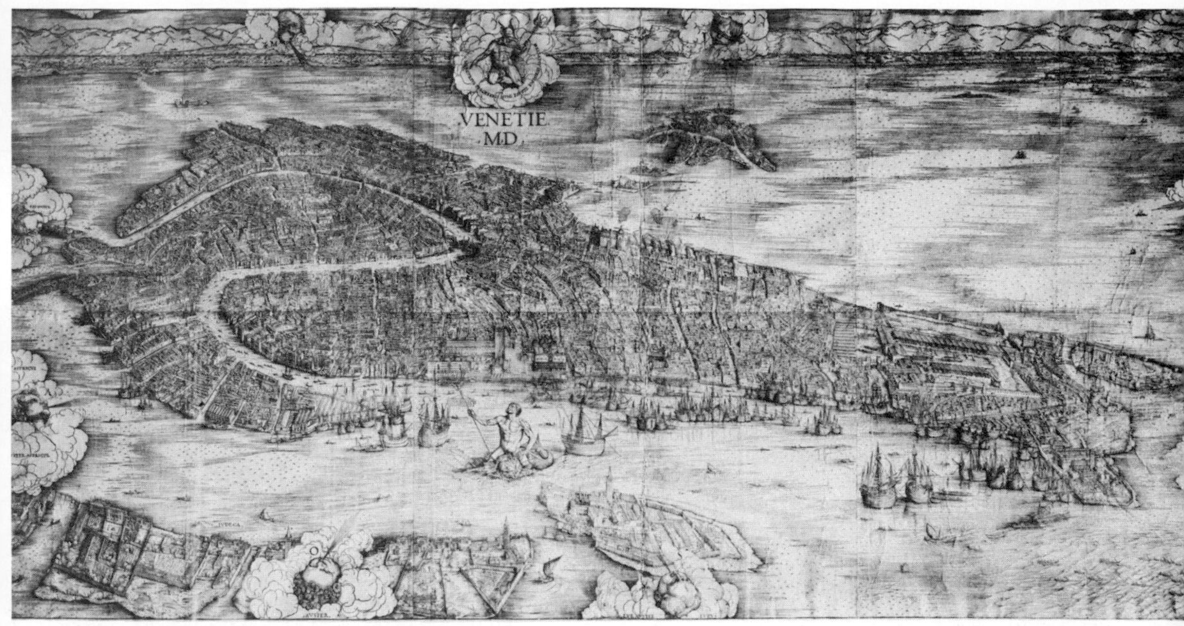

Venice, an aerial view *by Jacopo de' Barbari*

have survived, assure him a place of honour among the greatest names of the Spanish golden age of *drama. He frequently adapted from *Lope de Vega, but had his own unmistakable literary qualities, distinguished by a true poetical inspiration. His *Reinar despues de morir* dealt with the legendary love and death of Inés de Castro; *La serrana de la Vera* has a bandit-heroine who takes vengeance on her seducer. His *picaresque novel *El diabolo cojuelo* (1641), later served as a model for the French writer Lesage.
F. E. Spencer and R. Schevill, *The Dramatic Works of Luís Vélez de Guevara* (1937).

VELLERT, DIRK Flemish painter on glass, active in *Antwerp from about 1511-40. His windows, decorated with classical themes were exported and made his name famous throughout Europe. V. practised *engraving in a style inspired by *Lucas van Leyden.

VENEZIANO, ANTONIO (1543-93) Italian poet. Born at Monreale, *Sicily, he had an adventurous life. Taken captive by *Algerian corsairs (1578), he later visited Spain, where he met *Cervantes, and died in prison. His poems, especially his *Celia*, written in a Sicilian dialect, became very popular. The author of Latin epigrams as well as of some prose in the vernacular and many *canzoni*, his poetry was graceful and appealing in spite of its obvious Petrarchan derivation.

VENICE Situated on a protective lagoon at the far end of the Adriatic Sea, V. long dominated the trade of the eastern Mediterranean basin. By the early 14th century, the republic possessed many colonies, mainly in Greece and the Aegean Sea, and became engaged in a long struggle with *Genoa. The most decisive encounter, known as the War of Chioggia (1378-81), ended with the surrender of the Genoese fleet. Henceforth, V. had a free hand in the Levant, but her ascendency was soon curtailed by the rising power of the *Ottoman Turks. Successful in their first conflict with the Turks (1416), the Venetians saw their commercial stations in the Aegean plundered in their second confrontation (1425-30), and failed to give effective aid to *Constantinople when the city was besieged and captured in 1453. During the same years, however, V. accomplished a great movement of territorial expansion on the Italian mainland. In 1405 Padua, Vicenza and Verona were taken, to which were later added Brescia (1426), Bergamo (1428) and Crema (1429), seized in a war against Filippo Maria *Visconti of *Milan. These gains, confirmed by the Peace of Lodi (1454), practically established the extent of the republic until its extinction in 1797. Between 1463-79, V. conducted a long war with Sultan *Mehemmed II, losing Negroponte, the Greek island of Euboea (1470) and stations along the Adriatic coast. The peace treaty, however, allowed the Venetians to retain a quarter in Constantinople and conceded various commercial privileges. In 1489 V. acquired Cyprus, a source of further friction with the Turks.

The combined qualities of tenacity and resilience that the republic demonstrated in war were a result of its uniquely stable government. This was basically a hereditary oligarchy of some 1,500 wealthy and ancient families who controlled the Great Council. They selected various public officials and, through a complicated procedure, elected the doge, the head of government, appointed for life, whose power, however, was mainly ceremonial. Real power was vested in the Senate, which consisted of about 300 members, and alongside of whom there was a committee of ten, the *dieci*, charged with the detection and punishment of attempted treason. The committee held its deliberations in secret and acted upon anonymous denunciation. Long immune to outside influences,

V. became accessible to Renaissance culture during the last quarter of the 15th century. The new Renaissance style of *architecture replaced Venetian Gothic; *painting, led by the *Bellini brothers, emerged as a distinctive school, and *printing, introduced by German immigrants, made V. the publishing capital of Italy. The production of books indeed became an important industry. Other significant economic activities were the production of fine textiles, silks and leatherworks, and above all *shipbuilding at the state operated arsenal.

In 1508, V. became the intended victim of the League of *Cambrai, but the territorial losses incurred were soon recovered. During later phases of the *Italian Wars the republic maintained a cautious neutrality. Far from neutral, however, were relations with the Ottomans. War broke out in 1499, ending in a treaty in 1503, and again between 1537-40, when V. joined Emperor *Charles V and the papacy in a Holy League. In 1570 V. refused to comply with the demand of *Selim II to give up Cyprus and, with the aid of *Pius V and *Philip II, organized the great Christian coalition which defeated the Turks at *Lepanto (1571). In the meantime, however, Famagusta had been starved into surrender, and in 1573 the Venetians deserted their allies, acknowledged the loss of Cyprus, paid an idemnity and made a separate peace with the Turks. Afterwards, only Crete in the Aegean and a few islands in the Ionian Sea were left under Venetian jurisdiction. These were to become the target of another long war between 1645-64.

Domination of the eastern trade by the Ottomans and the opening of a sea route to the Far East, eventually sealed the fate of the republic. Also the growing importance of commercial traffic with the New World contributed to V.'s decline. Yet all this was scarcely felt during the 16th century, when Venetian culture celebrated a veritable golden age. Aldus *Manutius and his son Paulus (1512-74) and Gabriele *Giolito upheld V.'s preeminence in the field of publishing. *Aretino and *Bembo presided over a lively literary milieu, enriched by contributions by poets, novelists and historians. In painting, V. practically began to overshadow *Florence, *Giorgione, *Titian, *Tintoretto and *Veronese emerging as true heirs of the great masters of the High Renaissance. The architects *Palladio and Jacopo *Sansovino, the sculptor *Vittoria and musicians such as Giovanni *Gabrieli and Claudio *Monteverdi are further testimony of that great cultural effervescence.

W. Hazlitt, *History of the Venetian Republic,* 2 vols. (1915);
R. Cessi, *Storia della republica di Venezia,* 2 vols. (1944-46);
A. Bailly, *La Serenissime republique de Venise* (1946);
F. C. Lane, *Venice in History* (1966).

VENIER A Venetian family which supplied the republic with a number of doges as well as with military commanders and diplomats. Antonio V. was doge from 1382 to his death in 1400, presiding over *Venice's expansion in the east, including the annexation of Corfu and islands in the Aegean. Francesco V. (1490-1556) served as doge in the last two years of his life. Sebestiano V. (1496-1578) was elected duke of Candia (Crete) in 1548, became captain of Brescia in 1561 and in 1566 was made governor of Verona. In 1571, aged 75, he was made commander of the naval forces (*generale da mar*) and prepared the navy for the great victory over the Turks at *Lepanto (1573) at which he took part. In the last year of his life, V. served as doge.

VÉRARD, ANTOINE (?-1513) French printer. Probably born at Tours, he was originally director of a shop which produced *illuminated manuscripts, he turned to *printing in 1485. Based in Paris, he took great pains with the typography of his books, which carried many illustrations. V. published some 250 titles, mainly popular romances of *chivalry, devotional literature and translations of the classics.

VERGERIO, PIETRO PAOLO (1370-1444) Italian humanist. Born in Padua, he continued his studies in *Florence, where he befriended Coluccio *Salutati, and, from 1388-90, taught at Bologna. Except for returning to Florence in 1398 to study Greek under Manuel *Chrysoloras, he stayed mainly in his native town, where he taught and wrote. His most important work of those years was *De ingenuis moribus et liberalibus studiis* (1402), the first Renaissance treatise to advocate an integrated programme of *education, which remained popular during the 16th and 17th centuries. In 1406 V. went to Rome, where he served as papal secretary and later as emissary to the Council of Constance (1414-18). Then he became the secretary of Emperor Sigismund, never returning to Italy. He died in Budapest. V. also wrote on questions related to Church affairs; on *Petrarch, whose *Africa* he published; a comedy, poems and many letters which were printed posthumously. He is sometimes referred to as the founder of modern education.

W. H. Woodward, *Vittorino da Feltre and Other Humanist Educators* (1921).

VERGERIO, PIETRO PAOLO (1498-1565) Italian religious reformer. Born at Capodistria, he studied law at Padua, becoming a judge and a lawyer. In 1527, however, he joined the service of the Church as a layman and in 1533 was made papal nuncio to Germany, where he met *Luther. After being ordained, he was appointed bishop of Capodistria (1536). Afterwards his ideas tended more and more to the side of the *Reformation, and in 1549 he was forced to seek asylum in Switzerland. He became a Protestant minister, serving in several Swiss cities and in Poland, before settling at Tübingen (1553), where he wrote and translated polemical Protestant literature.

VERMEYEN, JAN CORNELISZ (c. 1500-59) Flemish painter. Born near Haarlem, he probably studied under *Mabuse and became the court painter of the regents of the Netherlands, *Margaret of Austria and Mary of Hungary. In 1535 he accompanied *Charles V to Tunis. A practitioner of the *Italianate style, V.'s work shows similarities to that of his friend van *Scorel. V. painted a considerable number of religious subjects and portraits, and also produced many engravings and designed tapestries.

VERMIGLI, PIETRO MARTIRE (1500-62) Italian Protestant reformer, known in England as Peter Martyr. Born in *Florence to a father who had been a disciple of *Savonarola, he joined the Augustinian order, becoming an abbot at Spoleto (1530) and a prior at *Naples (1533). In the next few years, however, largely through the reading of *Bucer and *Zwingly, he began to develop Protestant sympathies, and, in 1542, when

Judith *by Paolo Veronese*

threatened with investigation, fled to *Zurich, then to *Basle and *Strassburg, where he became a professor of theology. In 1547 he came to England by invitation of *Cranmer together with his friend *Ochino, and was made regius professor of divinity at Oxford. V. was frequently consulted and had an influence on the development of the English Reformation during the reign of *Edward VI. Upon the accession of *Mary (1553) he was imprisoned, but subsequently allowed to leave. He returned to Strassburg and, in 1556, moved to Zurich, where he ended his life as a professor of *Hebrew.

P. McNair, *Peter Martyr in Italy* (1967).

VERONESE, PAOLO (1528-88) Italian painter. Born in Verona, where he received his initial training, he came to Venice in about 1553, coming under the influence of *Titian and *Tintoretto, together with whom he is considered one of the foremost contributors of the 16th-century Venetian style. V. was commissioned to paint the ceilings of the Doge Palace, and some of his best canvasses are also exhibited there. In 1560 he

Young Woman *a bust by Verrocchio*

made the first of several visits to Rome, shortly after his return cooperating with the architect *Palladio, and decorating with *frescoes the latter's Villa Maser near Vicenza. In 1573, owing to the secular contents of one of his religious pictures, he was interrogated by the *Inquisition, facing his examiners with pride and defending his liberty as an artist. He is recorded to have said: "My commission was to make this picture beautiful according to my judgment." The inquisitors, however, made him change some details.

Depicter of many biblical, mythological and historical scenes, V. crowded his pictures with corpulent figures, resplendedly dressed in contemporary costumes and not lacking in grace. His idealization of Venetian society is very much in evidence in *Venice Governing the World with Justice and Peace*. He is more successful in the allegory *Rape of Europa* and in his *Finding of Moses,* where feminine beauty is harmonized with landscape in a style which is not yet consciously *Mannerist. Indeed, although he worked well into the second half of the 16th century, V. retained many of the artistic qualities of the High Renaissance.

G. Rouches, *Paul Veronese* (1950);
P. H. Osmond *Paolo Veronese* (1927).

VERRAZANO, GIOVANNI (c. 1484-1528) Italian navigator in the service of *Francis I. Born in *Florence, he spent some years in the Levant and, in 1523, undertook his first voyage of exploration to North America, leading an expedition of four French vessels. Hoping to find a northern passage to China, V. instead reached the shores of present-day South Carolina and sailed north along the coast, entering the bay of New York and reaching Maine. In a famous letter which he wrote to Francis I upon his return, he described the route and his intention of finding a passage to the East in the southern hemisphere. According to the most reliable source, he was killed and devoured by the Indians on the coast of Brazil.

VERROCCHIO, ANDREA DEL (1435-88) Italian sculptor, goldsmith and painter. Born in Florence, he was the pupil of *Donatello, whom he succeeded as the most important sculptor of the city. His two main sculptures may be compared with works of his master. V.'s *David* (*c.* 1476), a bronze statue now at the Bargello, Florence, has the same slender body, though not the look of innocence, as Donatello's. But the equestrian statue of Bartolommeo *Colleoni is much more energetic and in keeping with the Renaissance than the stern and classically inspired **Gattamelata*. This was commissioned by Venice in 1479 and occupied V. until his death. He only completed the model, which was cast after his death and placed in position in

The monument of Bartolommeo Colleoni by Verrocchio

1496, emerging as one of the greatest monumental sculptures ever made. V. also executed many small works in silver and manufactured jewellery. Of his paintings, *Tobias and the Angel* reveals a sense of sculptural elegance and attention to dress. But the picture which aroused particular interest is the *Baptism of Christ* where the left-hand angel is usually regarded as the work of *Leonardo, who was an apprentice in V.'s shop. Another pupil and later V.'s chief assistant was *Lorenzo di Credi.

VERTUE A family of late Gothic English master masons, active in the reign of *Henry VII and the early part of that *Henry VIII. Adam V. was a mason of Westminster Abbey where his sons Robert and William built Henry VII's chapel. William, who died in 1527, also worked at Windsor Castle, and designed Corpus Christi College, Oxford (1512). He also collaborated with Henry *Redman on other constructions.

VERVINS, PEACE OF (2 May 1598) A treaty signed between *Henry IV of France and *Philip II of Spain, according to which the status quo prevailing at the Treaty of *Cateau-Cambrésis (1559) was restored. France recovered all the territories along the borders of the *Netherlands, and the Spaniards were given free hand to continue their war against the Dutch. At the same time Philip surrendered the Spanish-held Netherlands to his daughter Isabella and his future son-in-law, *Albert, who were to rule as "sovereign princes".

VESALIUS, ANDREAS (1514-64) Flemish founder of modern *anatomy. The son of an imperial apothecary of Brussels, he studied at Louvain, Paris and Padua, where he was appointed lecturer of anatomy in 1537. His *Tabulae anatomicae sex* (1538), in which he established the terminology for different parts of the human organs, soon made him famous, his great masterpiece, *De humani corporis fabrica,* coming out in 1543. This contained a detailed anatomical description of the body, including particularly original sections on the muscles, the abdominal viscera and the brain, and was accompanied by outstanding illustrations, the work of Stephen de Calcar. The book won immediate acclaim and, in 1555, V. himself issued a revised edition. His fame brought about his nomination to the position of physician to *Charles V and, in 1559, he was appointed in a similar capacity to *Philip II. Dying on his way back from a pilgrimage to Jerusalem, he was buried on the island of Zante, Greece. His great contribution to anatomy was to substitute the old theories of Galen with methods of direct observation.

C. J. Singer and C. B. Rabin, *A Prelude to Modern Science* (1946);
C. D. O'Mally, *Andreas Vesalius of Brussels 1514-64* (1964).

VESPUCCI, AMERIGO (1454-1512) Italian navigator after whom the newly discovered continent of *America was called. The son of a family closely associated with the *Medici, he was born in Florence. After receiving a humanistic education, he travelled to France in 1479, in 1491 being sent to *Seville as an agent of the Medici bank. There he met *Columbus after his return from his voyage of discovery and helped outfit his second expedition.

According to a letter known as the "Letter to *Soderini", written in Lisbon in 1504 and addressed

Vesalius Conducting an Anatomical Dissection
by Stephen de Calcar

in Italian to a schoolfriend in Florence, V. made four voyages between 1497 and 1503. In 1505 this letter, of which there are also two Latin translations – *Mundus Novus* and *Quatuor Americi Navigationes* was printed in Florence. The second Latin version was published by *Waldseemüller in 1507 together with a short essay which suggested that V. should be given the honour of lending his name to the new territories across the Atlantic. In a series of three private letters addressed to the Medici (1500-02), however, V. mentions only two of his voyages. This contradiction of sources gave rise to a controversy as to exactly how many voyages V. made; according to the minimalist view, there were, in fact, only two. This, however, does not lessen V.'s stature as a navigator, nor his claim to have been the first to realize that what Columbus had discovered was actually part of a new continent.

The first voyage made by V. that has been authenticated, took place between May 1499 and June 1500, when he sailed as the navigator of an expedition under Alonso de *Ojeda. V. is believed to have discovered the mouth of the Amazon, and then continued south returning along the coast to Hispaniola in the Caribbean. Returning to Spain, he immediately proposed a voyage be made to *India; encountering a lack of enthusiasm on the part of the crown, he went to Portugal; in May 1501, he took sail from Lisbon on his second voyage, returning in July 1502. During this expedition he crossed the Atlantic from the Cape Verde Islands to the nearest coast of Brazil, then sailed to the Bay of Rio de Janeiro, discovered the estuary of Rio de la Plata, and possibly reached the coast of Patagonia further south. It was this voyage which convinced him that he was dealing with a new continent completely separated from Asia.

In 1505 V. reentered the service of Spain where, in 1508, he became chief navigator (*piloto mayor*) of the *Casa de Contratacion at Seville, a position which he held until his death. Although some of Columbus' glory accrued to him, V. was kind and friendly towards the latter, and is mentioned in a positive way in one of Columbus' last letters.

F. J. Pohl, *Amerigo Vespucci; Pilot Major* (1944);
G. Arciniegas, *Amerigo and the New World* (1955).

VESTIARIAN CONTROVERSY, THE A dispute over clerical dress in England. It began under *Edward VI, soon reaching a peak in 1550, when John *Hooper, upon his assumption of the post of bishop of Gloucester, refused to be consecrated in a surplice and rochet. In 1559 the V. flared up again, with *Puritans subsequently denouncing even the simplest vestments. Archbishop *Parker then made an effort to find common ground with the radicals on this question, publishing the Book of *Advertisements in 1566. The V. marked one of the first instances of opposition to the established *Church of England within the Protestant camp.

VETTORI, FRANCESCO (1474-1539) Florentine statesman. Rising in the ranks of the government of Florence after the expulsion of the *Medici in 1494, he became a member of the governing council (1503) and, in 1507, served as an ambassador to the imperial diet of Constance. In 1512 he changed course, was among the principal engineers of the downfall of *Soderini and attached himself to the returning Medici. V. was a close friend of *Machiavelli with whom he corresponded and whose release from prison he obtained in 1513 while serving as ambassador to Pope *Leo X. Afterwards V. was appointed ambassador to France (1515-18), later serving a second term as ambassador to Rome (1529). Of his writings, the most important is a short history of Italy from 1511-27.

R. D. Jones, *Francesco Vettori: Florentine Citizen and Medici Servant* (1972).

VETTORI, PIERO (1499-1585) Italian humanist scholar, also known as Victorius. Born in Florence to an old and noble family, while a young man he took part in the political life of the city and was a supporter of republican principles. Opposed to the *Medici, in 1530 he was forced to retire from the political life of the city but returned in 1532. In 1538 *Cosimo I gave him a lectureship in classical studies which he held until shortly before his death. V. edited works by Cicero, Terence, Sallust, Aristotle, Euripides and other classical authors. He wrote poems and letters in Latin, and corresponded with scholars in Italy and other countries. Admired as a teacher, he was acknowledged as the foremost humanist of his age. Between 1553-69 he published 38 books of *Variae lectiones* (lectures and commentaries).

R. Ridolfi and C. Roth, eds., *Lettere di Donato Giannotti a Pietro Vettori* (1932).

VICENTE, GIL (c. 1470-1536) Portuguese dramatist and poet. Although he is considered one of the greatest European playwriters of the first half of the 16th century, practically nothing is known of his life. He is usually identified with a goldsmith who in 1513 became master of the Lisbon mint. However, from 1502-36 there was hardly a year in which a play of his was not included in the court festivities. V. wrote 44 plays of which 16 are in Portuguese, 11 in Spanish and 17 in a macaronic combination of the two languages. These were first published in 1562 by his son and daughter. His reason for writing in Spanish may have been his wish to please the queen, a daughter of *Ferdinand and *Isabella.

His plays reveal some knowledge of classical *drama and the influence of Juan de *Encina. Essentially, however, he followed the patterns of the mediaeval theatre with its *morality plays and farces, and most of his poems are incorporated into his plays. V.'s religious plays included satirical comment on the clergy whom he took to task for their loose morality. Some of the best-known plays of this type are the *Auto dos Reis Magos* (1503), based on the story of the adoration of the Magi, the *Auto da Alma*, an allegory of the journey of the soul, and the three *Autos das Barcas* (1517-19). V. also directed his satire towards other social figures: physicians, penniless noblemen, *Jews, gypsies, negroes and women. In Spanish he wrote two of his best constructed plays, *Dom Duardos*, about Edward of England and **Amadis de Gaula* under the inspiration of books of *chivalry. His poetic sensibility and love of nature are best revealed in the *Tragicomédia pastoril da Serra da Estrêla.* His plays were later listed in the **Index* and a second edition that came out in 1586 was severely expurgated. He did not succeed in having any true following in Portugal, his real heirs being the Spanish dramatists of the end of the 16th century.

J. H. Parker, *Gil Vicente* (1967);
A. F. G. Bell, *Gil Vicente* (1921).

VICTORIA, TOMÁS LUÍS DE (c. 1549-1611) Spanish composer. Born in Ávila, he was brought up by his uncle, a priest, who had him trained as a choirboy. In 1565 he entered the *Jesuit Collegium Germanicum in Rome. V. was fortunate enough to get the support of well-placed patrons who recognized his talent. In 1571 he took over from *Palestrina as master of music at the Collegium Germanicum, and for the next twenty years served in different Roman churches, composing, conducting and performing religious *music. Ordained in 1575, he became close to Philip *Neri, for whose congregation of the Oratory he composed masses and *motets. In about 1592 he returned to Spain, becoming a chaplain to Empress Maria, widow of *Maximilian II, who had retired to a convent. After her death he wrote one of his greatest works, the requiem mass *Officio defunctorum* (1605). The author of some 180 compositions which became widely known during his own lifetime, V. ranks with Palestrina and *Lasso as one of the greatest masters of Renaissance vocal polyphony. His works are distinguished by a mystical fervour and by their innovative qualities.

R. Casimiri, *Il Vittoria* (1934);
R. M. Stevenson, *Spanish Cathedral Music in the Golden Age* (1961).

VIDA, MARCO GIROLAMO (1485-1566) Italian humanist poet. Born to an impoverished noble family in

Cremona, he came to Rome, where he was ordained in about 1510, becoming close to Giovanni de' Medici, soon to be elected Pope *Leo X. For the latter he wrote Latin poems on the game of chess and on the silkworm, and began writing the *Christias*, an epic poem on the life of Christ. Completed in six books and published in 1535, this was very successful. Under *Clement VII, V. became bishop of Alba (1532) later participating in some of the works of the Council of *Trent. Admired for his clear ideas and elegance of style, V. was also the author of a didactic poem on the art of poetry (1527), which dealt particularly with Vergil. Later in his long life V. wrote more on religious themes.

M. Di Cesare, *Vida's Christiad and Virgilian Epic* (1963).

VIENNA, SIEGE OF (1529) The deepest and most dangerous infiltration by the *Ottoman Turks into western Europe. In spite of the approaching winter and long lines of supply, on 21 September *Suleiman I began the siege of the *Habsburg capital of Austria. The defenders, some 20,000, were overwhelmed by a force estimated at ten times that number which, on 9 October, penetrated the walls. In the next five days the Turks made repeated attempts to capture the city by assault, all of which were checked by means of close range *artillery fire and fierce hand-to-hand combat. Fearing an attack by a German relief force and the approach of winter, Suleiman decided to withdraw.

VIETE, FRANÇOIS (1540-1603) French mathematician. A lawyer by profession, he became the councillor of Henry of Navarre, managing to decipher the secret code that the Spanish government used to pass messages. V. was the first mathematician who used letters to symbolize both known and unknown quantities, an innovation which earned him the title of being the father of modern algebra. V. wrote several mathematical works, the most important of which is *In artem analyticam isagoge* (1591), and also contributed to geometry and trigonometry.

VIGARNI, FELIPE (c.1480-1543) Spanish sculptor. Born in Langre, Burgundy, he came to Burgos, Spain in about 1498; there, at the cathedral, he executed a carved relief of *Christ Bearing the Cross*. Between 1502-04 he worked in Toledo, and in 1505 completed 14 sculptures at the university of Salamanca. His growing fame brought him commissions in Palencia (1505-09), Granada (1520-21) and, in the last years of his life, again in Toledo. A prolific and versatile artist, he also excelled as a *medallist. After 1519 he cooperated with Alonso *Berruguete, and also worked together with Diego de *Siloe. V. combined the styles of northern France with strong *Italianate influences.

VIGNOLA, GIACOMO BAROZZI DA (1507-73) Italian architect. Born near Modena, he studied painting at Bologna, and, in 1530, came to Rome where he worked under Antonio da *Sangallo. After some years

Palazzo Farnese by Vignola

he left Rome, but returned in 1546 and took a leading part in the designing of the bautiful Villa Giulia (1551-55). V. is konwn as the chief Italian Mannerist, a style of architecture in which he continued the work of *Michelangelo. He employed circular staircases and circular interior courtyards to great effect and designed the gardens of his villas. His best-known work, however, is the Church of Gesù in Rome (begun 1568) of a comparatively simple design. Characterized by the series of chapels which flank the nave, it became a model of *Baroque church architecture. In his last years (1567-73), V. was in charge of the works on *St. Peter's. He was the author of two books: the *Regole delle cinque ordini* (1562) gave an outline of the architectural orders and enjoyed an immense success as a textbook; another, published in 1583, dealt with perspective.

M. Walcher-Casotti, *Il Vignola* (1961).

VIGO, GIOVANNI DA (c. 1450-1525) Italian surgeon. After working in northern Italy, he became surgeon to Pope *Julius II (1503). His *Practica in arte chirurgia* (1514) was frequently reprinted and translated, becoming an authority on the treatment of wounds caused by firearms, until it was superseded by the new methods developed by Ambroise *Paré.

VILLEGAIGNON, NICOLAS DURAND DE (1510-71) French colonizer. Related to the grand master of the Order of St. John, he took part in *Charles V's expedition to *Algiers (1541), and was made naval commander in Britanny by *Henry II. In 1555 he left Le Havre for Brazil at the head of a group of colonizers who were mainly Protestants; near the present-day site of Rio de Janeiro, he established a settlement, which he named Fort *Coligny. In 1557 missionaries arrived, sent from Geneva by *Calvin, this, however, only caused internal disputes and, in 1560, Mem de *Sá captured and destroyed the colony. Meanwhile, in 1558, V. had returned to France where, following further dealings with Calvin, he continued to be intimate with court circles.

VILLON, FRANÇOIS (1431-63) French poet. Probably born in Paris, he took his name from his patron, Guillaume Villon, who paid for his education. While studying at the university of Paris, V. led a life of dissipation, frequently getting into trouble. In 1455 he killed a clergyman in a quarrel, and in 1457 was involved in an armed robbery. Sentenced to death, he was twice pardoned, the second time by *Louis XI himself. Following yet another sentence of imprisonment in 1462, he was banished from Paris, from which point nothing more is heard of his whereabouts.

Considered the greatest pre-Renaissance poet, V.'s violent life, including his passion for women of low birth, a sort of a complete repudiation of the ideals of courtly love, is reflected in his work. Yet his poetry has also a softer more naïve side revealed in his devotion to the Virgin and his feelings of regret and remorse. Of his writings, the best-known is the *Grand Testament*, a long poem composed in 1461. His famous *Ballade des pendus* (Ballade of the Hanged), is a touching imaginary description of his own hanging body, meant to be a lesson to those who might end with a similar fate. His poems were first published in 1489.

P. B. W. Lewis, *François Villon: A Documented Study* (1928);
I. Siciliano, *François Villon et les thèmes poétiques du moyen âge* (1934).

VINCKBOONS, DAVID (1576-1629) Dutch painter. Born at Malines, *Flanders, he came to *Holland as a boy, settling in *Amsterdam. He painted many small landscapes, usually on biblical themes, which were very popular, and also genre pictures in the tradition of *Breughel. Essentially a *Mannerist, he is, however, considered a forerunner of the 17th-century Dutch realist school.

VINDICIAE CONTRA TYRANNOS (1579) A work of political theory published in France by an anonymous author, possibly Philippe du Plessis-Mornay. It reflected the *Huguenot point-of-view and argued the right to resist royal authority on moral-religious or civil grounds. However, it was meant as an answer to concrete problems of the French *Religious Wars and should not be considered an attack on royal absolutism as such. It contained many arguments inspired by mediaeval and even feudal concepts, and failed to consider the possibility of religious pluralism and tolerance.

A Defence of Liberty Against Tyrants, edited by H. J. Lasky (1924);
W. F. Church, *Constitutional Thought in Sixteenth-Century France* (1941).

VIRET, PIERRE (1511-71) French Protestant reformer. A follower of *Farel, with whom he worked in Neuchâtel and Geneva, he played a decisive part in the introduction of Protestantism to Lausanne (1536). Like Farel, he accepted at that time the leadership of *Calvin. In the 1560s, V. went to France, where he was active in the affairs of the *Huguenots. In 1564 he published his *Instruction chrétienne,* in which he followed Calvin's ideas on civil obedience, but argued the right of moral resistance on religious grounds.

R. Linder, *The Political Ideas of Pierre Viret* (1964).

VIRGIL, POLYDORE (c. 1470-1555) Italian-English historian. Born in Urbino, in the reign of *Henry VII he went to England as a papal fiscal agent, and, impressing the king with his learning, was commissioned to write a *History of England,* which was published in Basle in 1535. Although V. was biassed in favour of his patron, Henry VII, his work was the first to present a general English history based on older chronicles, and contained valuable information on the late 15th century. V. is believed to have returned to Italy a few years before his death.

VIRGINIA The first English colony in North America. In 1584 an expedition sent by Sir Walter *Raleigh tried to establish a colony near Roanoke Island, in present North Carolina. The name V., applied to the whole area which the settlers were about to take, was derived from the Virgin Queen, *Elizabeth I. By 1589 the first venture had collapsed, and Raleigh later transferred his rights to a syndicate of merchants, headed by Sir Thomas Smith. In 1606 this V. company renewed the venture by despatching the first 144 settlers, who after several years of deprivation succeeded in developing a thriving colony based on the tobacco industry.

VISCHER A family of German sculptors in *Nuremberg. The first member of the family to have a claim to fame was Hermann the Elder, who became a citizen there in 1453. His son, Peter the Elder (*c.* 1460-1529), ex-

celled in the creation of bronze figures in a powerful realistic style. He is most famous for the reliquary shrine in the church of St. Sebald in Nuremberg, on which he worked from 1507-19, giving it the structure of a canopy. He also executed works for the *Fuggers and two statues for *Maximilian I's tomb at Innsbruck (1513). Of his three sons, Herman the Younger (1486-1517), Peter the Younger (1487-1528) and Hans (1489-1550), the second was responsible for the tomb of *Frederick the Wise in *Wittenberg. The V.s gradually came under Italian influence.
F. Kampfer, *Peter Vischer* (1960).

VISCONTI The ruling family of *Milan from 1262-1447. The V. consolidated their hold over the city with the aid of Emperor Henry VII and, by 1315, had extended their rule to Piacenza, Bergamo, Lodi, Cremona, Pavia and Novara. In 1395 Gian Galeazzo V. bought the title of duke from Emperor Wenceslas. His sons, Giovanni Maria and Filippo Maria (1412-47), succeeded him, the latter, however, leaving only an illegitimate daughter, Bianca Maria, who had married the **condottiere* Francesco *Sforza in 1441. The V. dynasty thus ended with the death of Filippo Maria and, in 1450, after a three-year interval, Sforza established the rule of his own house.
P. Pieri, *I Visconti e l'Italia del secolo XIV* (1952).

VISCONTI, FILIPPO MARIA (1392-1447) Duke of *Milan. The son of Gian Galeazzo, in 1402 he was given the countship of Pavia; until 1412, however, he was under the shade of his brother, Giovanni Maria, and of *Facino Cane. In that year these two died, V. losing no time in marrying the latter's widow and taking over the government of Milan. Proving an able administrator and an extremely clever diplomat, V. extended his rule and, by 1421, was in possession of most of the territories that had been held by his father. His victories made *Florence, *Venice and *Savoy form a coalition under his former general, Francesco Carmagnola (*c.* 1380-1432). Forced to sign a disadvantageous treaty, V. later rebuilt his position, intervening in the struggle over Naples between *Genoa and *Alfonso V of Aragon. In 1435 he ordered the Genoese to surrender Alfonso to him but then had him released.

After having executed his first wife on charges of adultery, V. had no children by his second marriage, and intended to leave the government to his natural daughter, Bianca Maria (1425-68). In 1441 she married his best general, Francesco *Sforza, but relations between V. and his son-in-law were so bad that the latter, with the loyal support of his wife, twice joined V.'s enemies. V.'s death occurred while his political fortunes were in decline.
D. Muir, *A History of Milan Under the Visconti* (1924).

VISCONTI, GIAN GALEAZZO (1351-1402) First duke of *Milan. The son of Galeazzo II (*c.* 1320-78), upon his father's death he was given the rule over Pavia, while his uncle Barnabo (1323-85) retained that of Milan. In 1385, however, V. led his uncle and his cousins into a trap, had them arrested, and later brought about the death of Barnabo by poisoning. V. thus became the only ruler of the Milanese dominions, which he soon extended by conquering Verona and Vicenza (1387) and Padua (1388). Having initially allied himself to *Venice, he subsequently had to face a coalition led by *Florence, a situation which he attempted to remedy by aligning himself with France. In 1395 he obtained the title of Duke of Milan from Emperor Wenceslas and, by 1401, following his victory over King Rupert of Germany, was the master of most of northern Italy, including Bologna, Pisa, Siena and Perugia. He died suddenly of the plague.

V. was more an effective organizer than a military leader – a schemer who masterminded plots of assassination but let his able captains do the actual fighting. V. began the building of the Milan cathedral (1386) and the Certosa di Pavia (1396), where he is buried.
E. R. Chamberlain, *The Count of Virtue; Giangaleazzo Visconti, Duke of Milan* (1965);
D. M. Bueno de Mesquita, *Giangaleazzo Visconti* (1941).

VISCONTI, GIOVANNI MARIA (1389-1412) Duke of *Milan. Upon the death of his father, Gian Galeazzo, in 1402 he succeeded to the government of Milan, at first remaining under the influence of his mother. in 1403, however, *Facino Cane became the chief aide of this 14-year-old boy, doing much to preserve the territorial gains of the previous reign. Described as a cruel person, the young V. was murdered by a group of opposing nobles.

VITELLESCHI, GIOVANNI (c. 1400-40) Italian cardinal. Born at Corneto, he first became a soldier, entering the service of the papacy under *Martin V. In 1431, he was made bishop of Recanati by Pope *Eugenius IV. In 1436 he suppressed the rebellion of the Roman nobility, which had forced the pope to flee. The grateful Eugenius then made him patriarch of Alexandria, archbishop of Florence and he also became a cardinal (1437). As ruler of Rome and ruthless commander of the papal army, V. made himself many enemies. He was finally betrayed by the commander of the castle of Sant' Angello, arrested and killed in prison.

VITELLI Italian family of Roman origins who, from merchants, became **condottieri*. Vitellozzo was the first member of the family to make an impact, dying in 1468 after a long and stormy career. His nephew Niccolo (1414-86), who had been brought up by his uncle, was the father of four sons, all of them, despite being vulgar people, were able military men. Of these, Vitellozzo found his death in Senigallia in 1502 in the notorious plot of Cesare *Borgia. The V. also contributed a number of important ecclesiastical dignitaries.

VITEZ, JANOS (c. 1408-72) Hungarian humanist. Becoming a royal secretary in 1433, in 1445 he was made bishop of Várad. V. was a loyal supporter of the *Hunyadis and took charge of the education of the future *Matthias Corvinus; the latter subsequently had him appointed chancellor of Hungary and gave him the title of count. In 1465 V. became archbishop of Esztergom. Shortly before his death he was involved in a conspiracy against the king. The first true humanist in Hungary, he was in contact with leading scholars of Italy and Germany and founded a university at Pozsony. He was the author of letters and discourses.

VITORIA, FRANCISCO DE (1486-1546) Spanish theologian. Joining the Dominican order in his youth, he studied in Burgos and, from 1506-12, attended the university of Paris. He stayed on in Paris as a lecturer of philosophy, returning to Spain in 1523, first to Valladolid and, in 1526, to the university of Salamanca. As professor of theology V. was responsible

Ottavio Grimani, *a marble bust by Alessandro Vittoria*

for substantial reforms in teaching methods. He made the *Summa Theologica* of St. Thomas Aquinas (1225-74) his basic text, stressing clarity of exposition, independence of mind and textual criticism. In his *Reflectiones*, first published in 1557, V. dealt with the question of Spain's title to America. He firmly rejected the pope's right to assign a non-Christian territory and people to the dominion of any prince, and claimed that the pope had only the power to send missionaries, though the latter might be in need of an armed force to protect them. His criticism of the methods employed by Spain in the conquest and colonization of America and his qualifications with regard to what constitutes a "just war", have earned him a reputation as one of the earliest promoters of concepts of international law. Among his pupils were Domingo *Soto and Melchor *Cano.

J. B. Scott, *Francisco de Vitoria and his Law of Nations* (1934).

VITTORIA, ALESSANDRO (1525-1608) Italian sculptor. Born in Trent, he came to Venice in 1543; entering the workshop of Jacopo *Sansovino, he added embellishments to the buildings of his master. Later, he competed with Sansovino over commissions for sculptural decorations, executed works for *Palladio and, after 1577, carried out extensive repairs on the Doge Palace. Entirely assimilated into the artistic life of Venice, V. was inspired by *Michelangelo and, like his contemporary, *Giambologna, practiced a refined form of *Mannerism. After Sansovino, he is considered the greatest Venetian sculptor in the 16th century.

L. Serra, *Alessandro Vittoria* (1923).

VITTORINO DA FELTRE (1378-1446) Italian humanist educator. Born in the town of Feltre at the foot of the Alps, he studied in Padua, to which he later returned as a teacher. In 1423 he founded his famous school in Mantua, originally for the children of the *Gonzaga family. Within a few years the school developed into the first institution of its kind to offer an integrated humanist education. It had as many as 70 students, boys and girls, including some non-Italians and a number of students from poor families. V. stressed values such as equality, mutual trust and respect for the individuality of others. He combined games and physical activity with studies, which emphasized the classical authors and the study of Greek. Among V.'s pupils were Ludovico Gonzaga and *Federico da Montefeltro. The school continued to exist for about 20 years after its founder's death.

W. H. Woodward, *Vittorino da Feltre and Other Humanist Educators* (1905).

VIVARINI The name of a family of Venetian painters. Antonio, born in about 1415 and deceased between 1476-84, worked first with his brother-in-law Giovanni d'Alemagna and, following his death (1450), with his own younger brother Bartolomeo (c. 1432-c. 99). The V. left various polyptychs with indications of changes of style. The earlier works are done in the stiff moulds reminiscent of the *International Gothic, whereas their style later reveals the obvious influence of *Mantegna and mainstream Renaissance concepts. Alvise (1446-c. 1505), son of Antonio, was trained by his uncle Bartolomeo, but soon fell under the spell of Giovanni *Bellini, whose style he imitated. He also worked in Naples (1483-85), his best work being his portraits.

VIVES, JUAN LUIS (1492-1540) Spanish humanist and social philosopher. Born in Valencia, he left Spain in 1509 and went to Paris and, in 1512, settled in Bruges, *Flanders, where there was a small Spanish colony. In 1517 he was made tutor of the young cardinal Guillaume de Croy. About that time he also taught at Louvain, and became friends with *Budé and *Erasmus. In 1523 he was invited to teach at Oxford, becoming the counselor of Queen *Catherine of Aragon. Incurring the displeasure of *Henry VIII because of his support for the Queen over the question of the royal divorce, he had to return to Bruges in 1529 and thereafter devoted his time to writing. V. was a particularly original thinker with advanced ideas on science, education and society. A sharp critic of the old scholastic methods, he advocated the inculcation of practical knowledge and skills, and wrote about the education of women, *De institutione feminae Christianae* (1529). His *De anima et vita* (1538) is considered one of the first modern works on psychology, in so far as it suggests an empirical study of the human mind. The author of many other works on philosophy, theology and matters relating to society he was certainly one of the intellectual giants of his age.

W. A. Daly, *The Educational Psychology of Juan Luis Vives* (1924);

C. G. Norena, *Juan Luis Vives* (1970);

F. Watson, *Juan Luis Vives* (1922).

VLADISLAV II (c. 1351-1434) King of Poland from 1386. *Jagiello, the son of the pagan grand prince of *Lithuania, succeeded his father in 1377. For several years he was engaged in wars with the *Teutonic order and with rivals from among his own family. Looking for allies, he agreed to have Lithuania converted to Christianity, in 1386 marrying the young Polish queen, Jadwiga, assuming the name of V. and the Polish crown at the same time. The first ruler of the Jagiello dynasty, V. increased Poland's influence over Walachia and Moldavia. In 1410 he defeated the Teutonic order at the Battle of Tannenberg, subsequently signing the Treaty of *Thorn (1411) with the knights of the order. By his third wife he had the future *Vladislav III and *Casimir IV.

VLADISLAV III (1424-44) King of Poland from 1434. Succeeding his father *Vladislav II at the age of ten, in 1440 he was also crowned king of *Hungary, having been elected to the throne by the Hungarian nobility. This brought about a conflict with the supporters of Elizabeth of Luxemburg, widow of *Albert II, who had been king of both Germany and Hungary. After the question had been settled with the aid of Pope *Eugenius IV, V. led a crusade against the *Ottoman Turks. Leading some 40,000 troops, with the help of Janos *Hunyadi he defeated *Murad II at Nish, forcing him to agree to a truce which was not to his advantage and making him give up a lot of territory (1444). Shortly afterwards, however, a new contingent of crusaders persuaded V. to break the peace treaty and renew the fight. Marching south, his army was utterly defeated at the Battle of Varna (10 November 1444) and he himself was killed.

VORSTIUS (1569-1622) The Latinized name of the German-Dutch theologian, Konrad von der Vorst. Born in *Cologne, he studied at Heidelberg and *Geneva, beginning to teach at the Academy of Steinfurt in 1596. Earning a reputation as an innovator, in 1610 he accepted an invitation to take over the Leiden position that had been vacated by the recent death of *Arminius. V. then published a work dealing with the ideas of Roberto *Bellarmine and another on the nature and attributes of God which provoked the ire of the conservative Dutch Calvinists led by *Gomar. The commotion cost V. his post at Leiden, and the Synod of *Dort later condemned him as a heretic. The author of many theological books, V. was at the time considered one of the main spokesman of the Arminians.

VOS, MARTIN DE (c. 1531-1603) Flemish painter. A student of Frans *Floris in *Antwerp, he went to Italy in 1552, visiting Rome, Florence and Venice, where he worked under *Tintoretto. Returning to Antwerp as an accomplished colourist (1558), he was commissioned to do several altarpieces and, after the death of Floris (1570), became known as the city's leading artist. Essentially a *Mannerist, V. is characterized by the somewhat elongated bodies of the people he portrayed and by his organization of light.

VOSS, GERHARD JAN (1577-1649) Dutch classical scholar and theologian. Born in Germany, for most of his career he was associated with the university of Leiden where he was educated and awarded a professorship of eloquence in 1622. In 1632, however, he left to become professor of history at Amsterdam. V. earned a reputation as a classicist with his *Rhetoric* (1606) and his text-book of Latin grammar (1607). He published two important treatises on the history of Greek and Latin literature (1623-27), an essay on poetry (1647) and works on mythology and art, and gathered an impressive collection of manuscripts. A lifelong friend of *Grotius, he was for a time suspected of sympathy with the *Remonstrants, and immediately after the Synod of *Dort temporarily lost his post at Leiden. V. also wrote on Christian theology and the early history of the Church.

VRIES, ADRIAEN DE (c. 1550-1626) Dutch sculptor. Born in The Hague, in his youth he became a pupil of *Giambologna in Florence, adopting his master's elegant *Mannerist style. He worked in Rome, Augsburg, Copenhagen, and as court sculptor to Emperor *Rudolph II, finally dying in Prague. His best works are his monumental bronze fountains, but he also produced sculptures in marble and other materials.

L. O. Larsson, *Adrian de Vries* (1967).

VRIES, HANS VREDEMANN DE (1527-c. 1604) Flemish painter and architect and designer of architectural subjects. Born in East Friesland, in his youth he was sent to *Amsterdam where he studied painting and *perspective, coming to *Antwerp in 1549. There he rose to fame because of his ornaments for the triumphal entry of the emperor, and was much sought after as a decorative painter. V. later travelled and worked in Germany, Italy and Prague, subsequently returning and settling in Antwerp. He became known epecially for his designs of palaces, courts and gardens and illusionistic structures, which were published by printers as handbooks for students. His *Architectura* (1565) and *Compertimenta* (1566) were especially influential on northern European architecture.

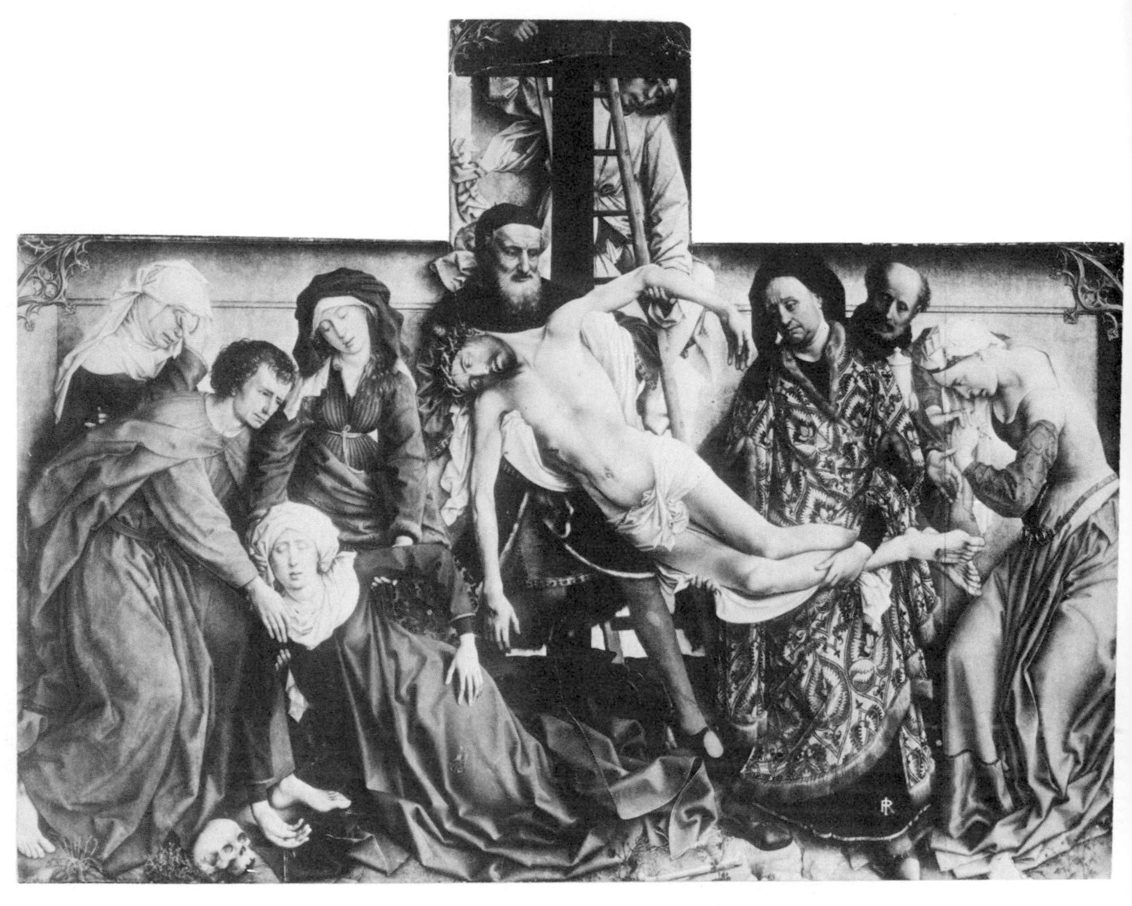

The Deposition *by Roger van der Weyden*

WALDENSIANS A mediaeval sect, also known as "Vaudois", organized by Peter Waldo at the turn of the 12th century, with the aim of returning to primitive Christianity and the simple life. In spite of numerous persecutions throughout the 13th and 14th centuries, they established communities in Piedmont, Savoy and also in Bohemia, where they later joined the followers of *Hus. *Innocent VIII issued a bull for their extermination, but when the *Reformation began the W. were still numerous and sought contact with Swiss reformers. In 1545 *Francis I organized a veritable crusade against the W. of southern France, taking toll of thousands of lives. Despite further oppressions by the secular authorities, in the valleys of the French and Italian Alps communities of W.s survived until the present century.

WALDIS, BURKARD (c. 1495-c. 1556) German author of fables. Born in Allendorf, he became a Franciscan friar, but following a visit to Rome joined the Lutheran *Reformation and settled in Riga. W. wrote *Esopus* (1548), a collection of some 400 fables adapted from the ancient Greek author to which he added many of his own. Humorous and frequently obscene, they won great popularity. W. also composed a Shrovetide play, *Der verlorene Sohn* (1527), of high literary value and in which he defended the Reformation.

WALDSEEMÜLLER, MARTIN (1470-1521) German *cartographer. Born in Baden, he studied at the University of Freiburg in Breisgau and was later associated with the educational centre of St. Die. In 1507 he published a work entitled *Cosmographiae introductio* together with a large map of the world on 12 pages, and constructed a small globe. Here, for the first time, the newly discovered territories beyond the Atlantic were referred to as *America. In 1511 he published a large map of *Europe on four pages, and in 1513 reissued his maps together with an edition of Ptolemy's *Geography*.

C. G. Herbermann, ed., *The Cosmographiae Introductio of Martin Waldseemüller in Facsimile, Followed by the Four Voyages of Amerigo Vespucci With Their Translation into English* (1907).

WALSINGHAM, SIR FRANCIS (1536-90) English statesman. A native of Kent, he was educated at Cambridge and abroad, after his return to England being recruited by William *Cecil who sent him as ambassador to France. After Cecil became chancellor, W. succeeded him as chief secretary of state (1573). W.'s most important accomplishment in this post, which he held until his death, was to bring to trial *Mary, Queen of Scots (1586), on evidence compiled by his secret agents. An indefatigable opponent of Roman Catholicism, an attitude he probably formed while witnessing the horrors of the *St. Bartholomew massacre in Paris, W. sometimes gave the *Puritans his support.

C. Read, *Mr. Secretary Walsingham and the Policy of Queen Elizabeth* (1925).

WARBECK, PERKIN (1474-99) A Flemish-born impersonator and pretender to the English throne. After spending some years in London during his youth, in 1492 he assumed the title of Richard, duke of York, younger son of *Edward IV, who had disappeared during the reign of *Richard III. For the next six years W. succeeded in deceiving several European rulers, including his would-be aunt, Duchess Margaret of Burgundy, and the kings of France and Scotland, into belief in his claim. While he never had a true popular following in England, he encouraged opposition to *Henry VII among members of the higher nobility, thus becoming a source of royal concern. Finally landing in Cornwall in September 1497, he was quickly defeated and captured. Put into custody, he was sent to the Tower in 1498, following an attempt to escape. W. was executed towards the end of the following year.

WARD, MARY (1585-1645) Founder of the "English Ladies", a Roman Catholic order for women modelled on the *Jesuits. Born in Yorkshire, in 1606 she entered the convent at St. Omer, run by English Jesuits, and in 1609 began her own congregation together with another five women. This was the first time that Jesuit rules used in colleges for young men were applied to women. The attempt was very successful enabling W. to expand her houses-schools to Liége, *Cologne, Munich and Vienna. In 1630, however, she was accused of various religious transgressions and the order was dissolved on the grounds that it allowed women excessive freedom. Later, however, she gained the reconfirmation of the order. Her last years were spent in England.

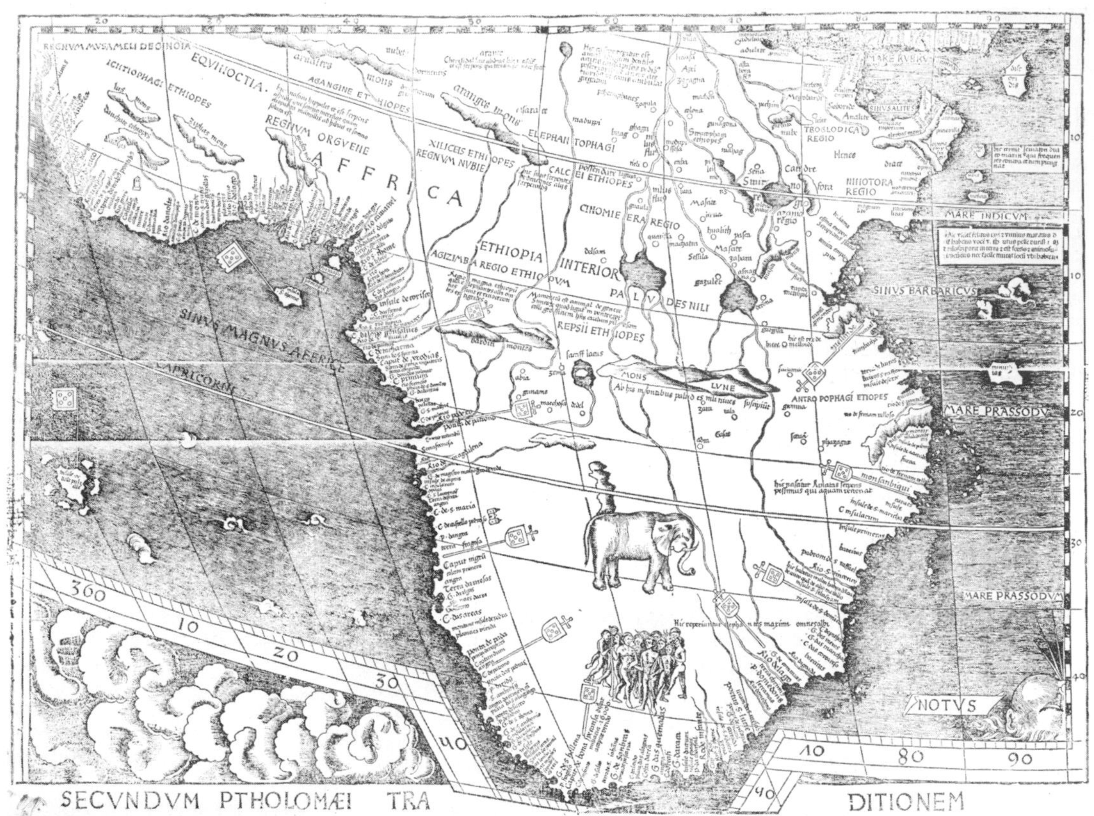

Part of Waldseemüller's map of southern Africa (1507)

WARHAM, WILLIAM (c. 1450-1532) English archbishop of Canterbury. Educated at Oxford, where he was awarded a doctor's degree, he entered on a successful administrative and legal career under *Henry VII, being employed also on diplomatic missions. In 1502 he was made bishop of London, and in 1503 lord chancellor. In the same year he became primate of England, but kept the chancellorship until 1515 when it was taken over by *Wolsey. Aferwards, relations became somewhat strained with the latter, although in 1527 he served as Wolsey's assessor to determine the legality of *Henry VIII's marriage to *Catherine of Aragon. In 1530 W. interceded with Rome in an effort to get the divorce approved, but when the king actually began to implement the seccession of the English church from Rome, W. tried to put limits to royal supremacy. Having failed to prevent a complete rupture with the papacy, he formally protested (1532), dying not long afterwards. W. was a patron of humanist scholars, especially of *Erasmus.

WARWICK, RICHARD NEVILLE, EARL OF (1428-71) English military and political leader, entitled by his contemporaries "the king-maker". The son of the earl of Salisbury, in 1449 he inherited the title of Warwick through his wife. In the alignment of factions that preceded the Wars of the *Roses, W. took the side of Richard, duke of *York. After the latter's death at Wakefield (1460), W. was defeated at St. Albans (February 1461) by the forces of *Margaret of Anjou, a battle in which he introduced the use of light firearms for the first time in England. Soon afterwards, he combined forces with *Edward IV to defeat the army of Lancaster at Towton (March 1461), becoming the right-hand man of that young monarch. Gradually, however, the King asserted his independence, making decisions contrary to the policies advocated by W., especially with regard to the latter's intention to reach an accomodation with France. In 1469 when Edward called upon W. to suppress an insurrection in Yorkshire, the latter turned against the King, took him prisoner and became for a time the real ruler of England. But early in 1470 Edward escaped, forcing W. to flee to France, where he reached an agreement with Margaret of Anjou. Invading England in September 1470, W. in his turn sent Edward fleeing to the Continent. He then formally had *Henry VI reinstated, though ruling himself for the next six months, for all practical purposes, until defeated and killed at the Battle of Barnet.

P. M. Kendall, *Warwick the Kingmaker* (1957).

WASTELL, JOHN (?-c. 1515) English architect. He is held to have been the builder of several important churches in the florid style of the Late Gothic characteristic of the reign of *Henry VII. Among these are the Abbey of Bury St. Edmonds, King's College Chapel,

Cambridge (1512-15); and the Angel Tower of Canterbury Cathedral. The cathedral of Peterborough (*c.* 1500) is also attributed to him.

WAYNFLETE, WILLIAM OF (c. 1395-1486) English prelate and Lord Chancellor. Of unknown origins, he became master of Winchester College in 1429 and, in 1442, master of Eton. In 1447 he was made bishop of Winchester, and one year afterwards founded Magdalen College, Oxford, which became the foremost college in the study of the humanities in the University. He was employed by the crown in the suppression of the *Cade's Rebellion (1450), and in 1457 was made Lord Chancellor of England. He was forced to resign from this post in 1460.

WEBSTER, JOHN (c. 1575-c. 1634) English playwright. Though little is known about his life, W. is considered one of the greatest tragedians of his times. *The White Devil*, published in 1612, presents a plot of adultery, murder and revenge, in which a married woman incites her lover, a duke, to kill her husband and his (the duke's) wife. *The Duchess of Malfi,* written in about 1613 but published only in 1623, was slightly gentler in tone. Here the duchess, a widow, secretly marries her steward, although she knows this will anger her two brothers, a duke and a cardinal. When the secret is revealed, she is imprisoned by her duke-brother, who at the end kills her. The play has a considerable psychological depth, and W. is at least partially successful in his attempt to evoke sympathy for the tormented duchess. W. also wrote a comedy, *The Devil's Law Case,* published in 1623, and collaborated with other authors, such as *Dekker, *Ford, and *Drayton.

C. Leech, *Webster: The Duchess of Malfi* (1963);
R. W. Dent, *John Webster's Borrowing* (1960).

WEDDERBURN, JAMES (c. 1495-1553) Scottish poet. The son of a merchant from Dundee, he studied at St. Andrews' University and visited France. In 1539 a tragedy and a comedy of his were performed at Dundee, causing a scandal because of their satire of Roman Catholicism. W. fled to France, where he remained until his death. His brother John (c. 1500-56), a priest, also fled from Scotland in 1540, spending two years in *Wittenberg. A second brother, Robert (c. 1510-57), also a priest, was charged with heresy and fled, returning sometime after 1546 to become vicar of Dundee. The three brothers cooperated on the writing of a compilation of satirical ballads and religious adaptations of popular songs, *The Book of Godly and Spirituall Songs*, known also as "the Dundee Psalms". The first extant edition is that of 1567 although the poems must have been written much earlier.

WEIDITZ, HANS (c. 1500-c. 36) German engraver of woodcuts. Possibly originally from *Strassburg, he was trained at the shop of *Burgkmair at *Augsburg, and later worked there, producing a large number of book illustrations on classical and scientific themes and for religious works. His prints were frequently signed, revealing a command of technique and a distinct personal style.

WEIGEL, VALENTIN (1535-88) German Protestant mystic. A Lutheran pastor of a small community near Chemnitz, W. left manuscripts containing mystical speculations and critical remarks concerning official Lutheran doctrine. Influenced by *Paracelsus, he in turn helped mould the thoughs of Jacob *Boehme. His writings were published for the first time in Halle in 1609.

W. Zeller, *Die Schriften Valentin Weigels* (1940).

WELSER A house of bankers from *Augsburg. The W.s began to rise to power in the 14th century, becoming one of the most important patrician families in the town. Later, Bartholomäus W. (1488-1561) loaned large sums to *Charles V and was rewarded with rights to exploit mines in the Caribbean and colonize Venezuela (1528). The enterprise, into which W. poured a great deal of effort and resources, did not thrive and the rights were subsequently rescinded (1546). As bankers to the emperor, the W.s were second only to the *Fuggers. Like them, they were raised to the nobility.

R. Ehrenberg, *Capital and Finance in the Age of the Renaissance* (1963).

WENCESLAS IV (1361-1419) King of *Bohemia from 1363. The son of Emperor Charles IV, he was crowned at the age of three, in 1376 being also given the title of king of the Romans. After his father's death in 1378, however, W. proved himself incapable of dealing with the internal conflicts of Germany, after 1389 residing mostly in Prague. In 1400, on his refusal to attend the German Diet, the princes had him deposed choosing Rupert, elector of the Palatinate, instead. His rule in Bohemia was also inept. He roused the German nobles against him, being deposed by his younger brother *Sigismund in 1402. Although he managed to regain his position in 1404, he had to share royal power with a council. W.'s attempts to contribute to a solution of the Great Schism likewise ended in failure. Although W. tolerated the movement led by Jan *Hus in Bohemia when the latter was condemned to death at *Constance (1415) he did nothing to save him.

WERT, GIACHES DE (1535-96) Flemish composer. Born near Antwerp, he was taken as a choirboy to Naples and, in 1561, was training in Parma under Cipriano de *Rore. In 1565 he settled in *Mantua, holding the post of *maestro di cappella* to the *Gonzagas. W. wrote *motets and other kinds of church music, but is especially important for his arrangements of *madrigals to texts by *Tasso and *Guarini.

WERVE, CLAUS DE (c. 1380-1439) Dutch sculptor. Born in Haarlem, he was the nephew of *Sluter, whom he succeeded as court sculptor to the dukes of *Burgundy (1404). W. is believed to have put the finishing touches to the tomb of Philip the Bold at Dijon, completed in 1410. He then received a commission for the tomb of *John the Fearless, but never began the work. His style was closely modelled on Sluter's realism.

WESSEL, JOHANN (1420-89) Dutch humanist and theologian, also known as Wessel Gansfort. Born in Groningen, he was educated by the *Brethren of the Common Life at Deventer, later visiting Italy where he learnt Greek. For 16 years he studied and taught in Paris, numbering Rudolf *Agricola and Johann *Reuchlin among his students. In his writing he criticized many of the deficient religious customs of his age, and thus acquired a reputation as a precursor of the *Reformation.

WETTIN, HOUSE OF A German dynasty of rulers and electors of the *Holy Roman empire. Part of the German nobility from the 11th century when members of the family first assumed the title of count, the W.s won greater influence in 1423, when Emperor *Sigismund granted Frederick I the Warlike the duchy and electorate of Saxe-Wittenberg, which became known as *Saxony.

In 1485 the dynasty was divided into the Ernestine and Albertine lines, the former retaining possession of the electorateship until it was lost to the other branch, together with a considerable amount of territory in 1547.

WEYDEN, ROGER VAN DER (Rogier de la Pasture; 1399-1464) Flemish painter. Born in Tournai, in 1427 he became an apprentice of Robert *Campin together with Jacques *Daret, joining the painters' guild as free master in 1432. In 1436 he settled in Brussels where he became the official city painter, remaining there till the end of his life. In 1450 he may have gone, however, on a pilgrimage to Rome, visiting Florence and Ferrara. A favourite painter at the court of *Philip the Good of Burgundy, during his life-time he became wealthy and acquired an international reputation.

Combining the realism of his teacher Campin together with the colour techniques of Jan van *Eyck, W. is considered the latter's successor as the greatest Flemish painter of the 15th century. W. left behind a considerable body of works, including monumentally conceived altarpieces on wood panels, and portraits and *Madonnas, which seem to have been parts of smaller diptychs. His masterpiece is the *Deposition* (1435), now at the Prado, Madrid, conveying quiet sadness and human warmth. Another large-scale work the *S. Columba Altarpiece*, now in Munich, reaffirms his ability, so much admired by contemporaries, to create a subdued emotional atmosphere.

WHITAKER, WILLIAM (1548-95) English theologian. Educated at St. Paul's School, London, and at Cambridge, he there became regius professor of divinity in 1580. W. was the principal author of the *Lambeth Articles (1593), which reflected his adherence to *Calvin's views on predestination. A fierce opponent of Roman Catholicism, he attacked the writings of Roberto *Bellarmine.

WHITECHURCH, EDWARD (?-1562) English printer. A London merchant, in about 1536 he became the associate of Richard *Grafton, with whom he financed the publication of *Coverdale's *Bible, and shortly afterwards, the Great Bible (1539). In 1543 he printed the first book of prayers of the *Church of England. An ardent Protestant, he was briefly arrested during the reign of *Henry VIII, but continued his collaboration with Grafton during the reign of *Edward VI.

WHITGIFT, JOHN (c. 1530-1604) Archbishop of Canterbury. Educated at the university of Cambridge, he was ordained in 1560. In 1563 he was appointed Lady *Margaret professor, and later Regius professor of divinity. In 1570 he was awarded the post of master of Trinity College. He became a very popular preacher and was appointed dean of Lincoln in 1573 and, three years later, bishop of Worcester. In 1583 *Elizabeth I appointed him primate of the *Church of England. Holding views that were diametrically opposed to those of his lenient predecessor *Grindal, W. took active measures against the *Puritans, whom he had already attacked in a debate with *Cartwright at Cambridge. Indeed, his name soon became synonymous with the repression of Puritanism and stern implementation of episcopal rule and ritual uniformity which characterized the latter part of Elizabeth's reign. He was also a strong opponent of Roman Catholicism. He encouraged educational reforms. In his last years, W. delegated much of his authority to Bishop *Bancroft.

P. M. Dawley, *John Whitgift and the Reformation* (1955).

WHITTINGHAM, WILLIAM (c. 1524-79) English Protestant reformer. Educated at Oxford, he left England during the reign of *Mary Tudor, finding shelter in *Frankfurt, where he befriended John *Knox. He later stayed with Knox in *Geneva, but in 1560 returned to England to be made dean of Durham (1563). An ardent Calvinist, he brought upon himself the attacks of the archbishop of York. W.'s major contribution was the Geneva *Bible (1560), a cooperative effort of which he was the moving spirit.

WICKRAM, JÖRG (1505-62) German novelist and playwright. Born in Colmar, where he spent most of his life, he was the author of several *Romane*, and is considered the father of the German novel. His early works betrayed the influence of foreign sources; his French model is still recognizable as being that in *Der Goldfaden* (1554). But *Des jungen Knaben Spiegel* (1554), which tells the story of a hard-working boy, is already dominated by a typically Protestant moralizing attitude, and his most important novel, *Von guten und bösen Nachbarn* (1556), develops further the idealization of 16th-century bourgeois existence. W. also wrote popular shrovetide plays and **Meistergesänge,* and a very readable collection of prose anecdotes, the *Rollwagenbüchlin* (1555).

WIED, HERMANN VON (1477-1552) German archbishop-elector of *Cologne and reformer. Becoming the spiritual leader of one of the most populous German dioceses (1515), for many years he adopted a negative attitude towards the *Reformation similar to that of other German bishop-princes. After 1536, however, he attempted to introduce reforms, and gradually moved toward *Protestantism. Asking the assistance of *Bucer and *Melanchthon he was opposed by his former aide, *Gropper. His plan of liturgical reforms, published in 1543, had some influence even beyond Germany, and that same year he completely threw in his lot with Lutheranism. The hostility in his own archbishopric continued, however, and *Charles V's campaigns in the area hindered the further growth of Lutheranism. W. was excommunicated in 1546 by *Paul III.

WILLAERT, ADRIAN (c. 1480-1562) Flemish composer. Born in Bruges, he studied music in Paris, later going to Italy, where he became the musical director of Alfonso I d'*Este at *Ferrara in 1522. In 1527 he was appointed choir director of St. Mark's in Venice, establishing an important music school there. W.'s experiments with polyphony anticipated later developments in counterpoint.

WILLIAM IV (1493-1550) Duke of *Bavaria from 1508. The son of Albert IV the Wise (1447-1508), who had established the unity of Bavaria, W. had to agree to divide the principality with his brother Louis. Upon the death of the latter, however, in 1545, he was able to reunite Bavaria. W. was conspicuous among the great German princes for his hostility towards the *Reformation. In 1546 he assisted *Charles V in his campaign against the Protestant princes, and in 1549 he invited the *Jesuits to the university of Ingolstadt. In return for his support, the Roman Catholic Church awarded him extensive rights in Bavaria.

WILLIAM OF CLEVES (1516-92) German duke of Cleves. He succeeded his father in 1539, taking charge of the government of an important principality on the

William of Orange

lower Rhine which included Jülich, Cleves, Berg, Mark and Guelders. At first joining the *Protestant camp, W. was soon confronted by Emperor *Charles V's claims to the duchy of Guelders. Refusing to give in, he allied himself to *Francis I of France but, following a campaign of two years (1542-44), had to surrender the territory and prohibit the activity of the reformers in his lands. His government became less effective after 1566 when he had a series of mental breakdowns. The population became divided between Roman Catholics, Lutherans and Calvinists and the ground was laid for the *Jülich-Cleves War of Succession.

WILLIAM OF ORANGE (1533-84) William I, stadholder of the *United Provinces, also known, though inappropriately, as William the Silent; the major leader of Dutch independence from Spain. The eldest son of Count William of Nassau and Juliana of Stolberg, he was born in Dillenburg, Germany, and raised as a Protestant. In 1544, however, he inherited vast territories in the *Netherlands and *Burgundy, including the principality of Orange, from his cousin René of Nassau, whereupon he agreed to reside in Brussels at the Roman Catholic court of the regent Mary of Hungary in accordance with the demand of Charles V, and was made the latter's page. In 1555 he commanded the imperial army in France, being appointed to the council of state by *Philip II and made a member of the order of the *Golden Fleece in the same year. In 1559 he took a leading part in the negotiations which ended with the Peace of *Cateau-Cambrésis, being left as governor of the northern province of the Netherlands when the king returned to Spain.

A favourite of the *Habsburgs, W.'s subsequent shift to the opposition is an aboutface not easy to explain. It became a reality, however, in 1563 when, together with Counts *Egmont and *Horn, he stayed away from the council of government, protesting against the repressive religious practices of *Granvelle, the all-powerful minister of the regent *Margaret of Parma. This shift, however, certainly had something to do with the fact that in 1561 W. had married in Dresden, as his second wife, Anna, daughter of the Lutheran *Maurice of Saxony, an event which marked a shift in his religious views. Although the pressure of the opposition led to Granvelle's removal in 1564, differences with the line of policy pursued by *Philip II could not be reconciled. Protestant agitation in the Netherlands was increasing, and W.'s brother, *Louis of Nassau, became a prominent leader of those who demanded greater tolerance. W. still took upon himself the suppression of civil strife in *Antwerp (March 1567). But in view of the absence of agreement among the other great nobles, and learning of the imminent arrival of the duke of *Alba, however, he renounced office and retired to his ancestral home in Dillenburg, thus evading the terrible fate of Egmont and Horn.

W. now undertook a war to liberate the Netherlands. In the autumn of 1568 he invaded the south with an army of German mercenaries. Suffering defeat for a time, he joined forces with the French *Huguenots, in an attempt to secure outside help. From this alliance developed the daring Dutch Sea Beggars (**Gueux*) who in 1572 established a foothold in Holland by capturing the town of Brill. This was followed by the rebels' conquest of a number of towns of the northern provinces, and late in 1572 W. arrived there from Germany, taking over the leadership of the movement as stadholder of Holland, Zeeland and Utrecht. Henceforth he resided mostly in Delft, and in October 1573, in order to identify himself completely with the rebels, became a member of the Calvinist Reformed Church.

The next years were spent in desparate fighting, in which Louis, and another brother, Henry, lost their lives. While not a great general, W. was able to put up a good resistance, and, in 1576, after a reaction against the Spaniards in the southern provinces had given the rebels an advantage, appeared as the leader of the entire Netherlands, suggesting a programme of national unity and religious toleration known as the Pacification of *Ghent. Crucial to the success of his plans was the appointment of a new ruler acceptable to all 17 provinces. Archduke *Matthias was tried, and even Don *Juan of Austria, Philip II's own half-brother, seemed to consider the plan, but was prevented from adopting it by his sudden death. Alessandro *Farnese, the new Spanish commander, succeeded, however, in undoing W.'s efforts by convincing the southern Roman Catholic provinces to sign the Union of *Arras (1579). W. was then reluctantly forced to accept the Union of *Utrecht which established the official separation of the north from Spain.

In 1581 W. published the *Apology*, a lengthy reply to a proclamation of Philip II, which had declared him a traitor and outlaw. The rebuttal contained a moving defence of his political actions, at the same time accusing the king of Spain and his people of inhuman crimes, not only in the Netherlands, but also in Spain and America. W. now began to devise a programme which would make the French duke of *Anjou succeed to the rulership of the Netherlands. In 1582, while at *Antwerp promoting this project, he was seriously wounded by an assassin; Anjou, moreover, soon proved himself to be totally unsuitable for the task alloted him. In 1583 W. married for a fourth time, on this occasion to Louise de *Coligny, daughter of the great French Huguenot leader, retiring to his father-in-law's modest house in Delft where he was shot to death by a Catholic fanatic, Balthasar Gérard.

A man of culture and eloquence, and one of the most effective statesmen of his age, W. pursued an amazing career, which saw him change from a resplendant Roman Catholic prince into a rebel and the leader of a Protestant republic. W. failed to accomplish his aim of keeping the Netherlands united, but managed to lay the foundations for the independence of the north, effectively resisting and outmanoeuvring all-powerful Spain. Married four times, W. left ten daughters and three sons. The eldest, Philip William, succeeded to the Orange title.

C. V. Wedgwood, *William the Silent* (1944);
N. Baker, *William the Silent* (1947);
P. Geyl, *The Revolt of the Netherlands, 1555-1609*, 2nd ed. (1958).

WILLIAM OF SELLING (? -1494) English humanist. A Benedictine monk, he was the first Englishman to study *Greek. In 1464 he went to Italy, attending schools in Padua, Bologna and Rome for three years. At the monastery of Christ Church, Canterbury, of which he was prior (1472-94), he attempted to develop a modest centre for the study of the humanities. He went on an embassy, back to Rome in 1485, accompanied by his young nephew, Thomas *Linacre.

WILLOUGHBY, SIR HUGH (?-1554) English explorer. He served in the war against Scotland and was knighted by *Henry VIII (1544). In 1553 he commanded a fleet of three ships sent to find a *northeastern passage to China. Off the North Cape, the ships separated. Two of them, together with W., were subsequently frozen in an inlet in which they hoped to find shelter, and all aboard perished. The third ship, however, commanded by Richard *Chancellor reached Archangel.

WIMPFELING, JACOB (1450-1528) German humanist. Born in Schlettstadt, Alsace, he was educated at the universities of Freiburg, Erfurt and Heidelberg where he eventually became rector (1481). In 1484, however, he gave up his professorship and went as a preacher to Speyer where he stayed until 1498. After returning to Heidelberg, he settled in *Strassburg in 1501, in 1515 retiring to his native town where he died. A friend of Sebastian *Brant and *Geiler von Kaiserberg, W. conserved much of the old culture and was essentially an educator who was moved by a strong sense of patriotism. His *Epitome rerum Germanicarum* (1505) was the first general history of Germany, and in other writings of his one finds warnings against France. W. also composed a play in Latin, two educational treatises, and several tracts, especially his *Apologia pro republica Christiana*, in which he pleaded for religious reform. When the *Reformation came, however, he declined to give it his support, remaining loyal to Rome.

J. Knepper, *Jakob Wimpfeling* (1902);
L. W. Spitz, *The Religious Renaissance of the German Humanists* (1963).

WIMPINA, KONRAD (c. 1465-1531) German humanist and Roman Catholic theologian. Born at Buchen in Baden, he studied at the university of Leipzig, where he became a lecturer in 1491 and rector in 1494. Ordained in 1500, he was invited to become the first rector of the new university of Frankfurt-on-the-Oder in 1505. W. was one of the first to oppose *Luther, coming to the defence of Johann *Tetzel in 1518. His *Anacephalaeosis sectarium* (1528) contained a complete refutation of Luther's doctrines, and during the Diet of Augsburg of 1530 he cooperated with others on a confutation of the *Augsburg Confession.

P. P. Albert, *Konrad Koch Wimpina von Buchen* (1931);
J. Negwer, *Konrad Wimpina, ein katholischer Theologe aus der Reformationszeit* (1909).

WINDESHEIM CANONS A monastic branch of the *Devotio Moderna, founded in Windesheim, near Zwolle, Holland, by disciples of Geert de *Groote and Florentius *Radewyns in 1387. Aspiring to a religious life more strictly regulated than that of the *Brethren of the Common Life, they took the rule of the Augustinian Canons and were approved as a separate congregation in 1395 by Boniface IX. Continually expanding throughout the 15th century, their houses were to be found in Germany and Switzerland as well as the Netherlands. They counted many scholars among their ranks, including *Thomas à Kempis and Gabriel *Biel.

WISHART, GEORGE (1513-46) Scottish Protestant preacher. Inspired by developments of the *Reformation on the Continent and at the university of Cambridge, in 1543 he returned to Scotland and began his preaching career, counting John *Knox among his followers. Early in 1546 he was arrested and, on 1 March, burnt at the stake on the orders of Cardinal *Beaton. It was believed that he had conspired to assassinate Beaton, and the cardinal's murder, three months later, was indeed prompted by his burning.

WITCHCRAFT The belief that one may invoke supernatural evil powers by entering into a pact with the devil penetrated mediaeval Christianity from a variety of sources: Biblical passages, classical mythology and popular Frankish pagan traditions. Until the 13th century, however, there were only sporadic references to witches, a number of authoritative voices actually tending to dismiss black magic as superstition and a deviation from the true faith. The change in attitude bore some relation to the rising tide of mediaeval heretic movements, which put the church on the defensive and encouraged a spirit of repression against all religious offenders, real or imaginary. In any event, particularly from the 14th century on, witches became increasingly the target of persecution. Although men could also be charged with sorcery, the vast majority of those accused of witchcraft were women. In fact, the obsession with witchcraft which lasted some 300 years saw man turning woman into a scapegoat for every kind of natural disaster and a victim of his perverse fears and aggressions. Indeed, to a large extent the case of witchcraft paralleled that of Jewish ritual murder. The number of witches tried until 1700 is estimated at between 400,000 to 2,000,000, many of whom were burned alive.

According to their detractors, witches participated in a Black Mass or Witches' Sabbath, a ceremony in honour of the devil which mocked the passion of Christ. Witches were alleged to be in the habit of riding on various animals by night in the service of the pagan goddess Diana. They were said to have intercourse with the devil in the form of a goat, to make use of corpses of newborn children in the exercise of magic rituals, to control weather, wind and diseases and to kill persons by casting spells upon them.

One of the first group trials of witches for offences of this nature was held by the *Inquisition at Toulouse in 1335. By means of torture 63 persons were found guilty, eight of whom were burned. Similar trials continued in the 15th century, particularly in Germany, the number of victims in some cases reaching into the hundreds. In 1484 Pope *Innocent VIII issued the bull, *Summis desiderantes affectibus,* which further legitimized the witch-hunting hysteria by enumerating their alleged misdemeanours. The pope also appointed two German Dominican inquisitors, Heinrich Institoris (Krämer) and Jakob Sprenger, to deal with the problem. In 1487 they published the *Malleus maleficarum* (*The Hammer of Witches*), the first printed manual on demonology and witchcraft, which outlined procedures of inquiry, torture and trial and remained the standard Renaissance and Reformation work on the subject in Roman Catholic as well as Protestant Europe. Basing itself on typically anti-feminine assumptions, it claimed among other things, that women who practiced witchcraft were driven by sexual insatiability.

The witch-baiters of the 16th century included not less a person than Martin *Luther. Among the main judicial guides of that period were those of Martin Del Rio, *Disquisitiones magicae* (1599), Nicholas Remy, *Daemonolatria* (1596), and Jean.*Bodin, *Démonomanie de sorcieres* (1580). Some voices challenging the belief in witchcraft were also heard, among them *Paracelsus and Giordano *Bruno. In his *De prestigiis daemonum* (1569), Johann Wier, a Protestant physician from Cleves, argued for greater tolerance, and in 1631 the *Jesuit Friedrich von Spee published his *Cautio criminalis,* in which he came out against the cruelty with which witches were hounded down. The burning of witches continued, however, throughout the 17th century, with many sensational cases of group trials in England, France and Germany, before coming to an end in the 18th century. The last English trial for witchcraft occurred in 1712.

C. Williams, *Witchcraft* (1941);
J. P. Russell, *Witchcraft in the Middle Ages* (1972);
G. Zilboorg, *The Medical Man and the Witch during the Renaissance* (1935);
R. H. Robbins, *The Encyclopaedia of Witchcraft and Demonology* (1959);
M. Sommers, *The History of Witchcraft and Demonology* (1956).

WITTELSBACH, HOUSE OF A German dynasty of rulers of *Bavaria. The W.s were in possession of Bavaria from the late 12th century, a branch of the family also holding the *Palatinate of the Rhine, which entailed an electorateship of the *Holy Roman empire. The dynasty went through a period of decline in the 15th century, when a lot of subdivision of territory took place. After the introduction of the principle of primogeniture, however, it made good its recovery, gaining possession of important principalities and bishoprics in northwest Germany, including *Cologne, during the second half of the 16th century.

Witches' Sabbath, *a woodcut by Hans Baldung*

WITTENBERG Situated favourably on the Elbe River, during the 15th century the town became important as the capital of *Saxony and the seat of the electors of the Ernestine branch of the *Wettin dynasty. The university, founded by *Frederick the Wise in 1502, added to the town's reputation, attracting students from abroad and counting *Luther and *Melanchthon among its professors. W. s position during the *Reformation was obviously brought about by the fact that it was the home of the chief leader of the movement. During the 30 years that followed Luther s publication of his 95 Theses (1517), W. was Protestant Europe's most important theological centre, developed a thriving printing industry and, in Lucas *Cranach, had a prominent painter and wood engraver. The decline of the town after 1547 began when it ceased being the residence of the electors of Saxony, the dignity having been transferred from the Ernestine to the Albertine branch.

WITTENBERG CONCORD An agreement arrived at in Wittenberg in May 1536, between *Luther and the fol-

St. Catherine and St. Magdalene *by Conrad Witz*

lowers of *Zwingli, represented by *Bucer. Drawn up by *Melanchthon, the document set forth a doctrinal definition of the Eucharist that tended towards the Lutheran approach. Subsequently, however, most of the followers of Zwingli in Switzerland refused their support and the union failed.

WITTENWEILER, HEINRICH Swiss poet, the author of *Der Ring,* a long satirical poem of some 10,000 verses composed in about 1400. Written in German in the tradition of the **Schwank,* the poem treats didactically themes of chivalry, love, religion and peasant life, and abound with passages excelling in the grotesque.

H. Birkhan, *Das Historische in "Ring" des Heinrich Wittenweiler* (1973);

Wittenweiler's Ring, translated by G. Fenwick (1956).

WITZ, CONRAD (c. 1400-48) Swiss painter. Born in Constance, he worked chiefly in *Basle and *Geneva. His major work is the *Heilspiegel Altarpiece,* a polyptych which included 16 panels of Biblical scenes. His Geneva altarpiece of 1444 is well known for its scene of *Christ Walking on the Water,* a very early example of the use of a recognizable landscape in a painting of a religious subject. W. was obviously influenced by Jan van *Eyck and other Flemish painters. A master of detail and of the technique of *perspective, his paintings are extremely realistic.

WOLFF, JACOB (1546-1612) German architect. Born in Bamberg, he worked in Würzburg (1601-05) and in 1607 completed the famous Pellerhaus in *Nuremberg, the most elegant German private home of this period. His son (1571-1620), who bore the same name, worked on the Nuremburg town hall; both father and son were among the earliest pioneers in Germany of Italian Renaissance architecture.

WOLGEMUT, MICHAEL (1434-1519) German engraver. A native of *Nuremberg, he is mainly known as the designer of woodcut illustrations for printed books, the two most famous being the *Schatzbehalter* (1491) and the *Liber chronicarum* (1493), both published by *Koberger. He also worked as a painter, his two altarpieces at Zwickau and Schwabach reflecting Flemish influences. W. was the godfather and master of young *Dürer.

WOLSEY, THOMAS (c. 1474-1530) English statesman and cardinal. The son of a wealthy butcher from Ipswich, he was educated at Oxford, from which he graduated at a very young age, subsequently being elected fellow of Magdalene College. W. became an ordained priest in 1498, but was obviously not interested in religion, while accumulating several benefices, he sought friendship with important people. In 1502 he became secretary to Henry Deane, archbishop of Canterbury. On the death of the latter (1503), he managed to win a post for himself as chaplain to *Henry VII (1507). Employed on

The Princely Banquet, *woodcut by Wolgemut, in the* Schatzbehälter *(1491)*

Cardinal Wolsey

diplomatic missions, he was made dean of Lincoln (1509). Under *Henry VIII W. rapidly advanced to being the young king's most important councillor. Acknowledgement of the important political role he wielded was made in 1514 when he became bishop of Lincoln and archbishop of York. In 1515 he was made a cardinal, taking over the post of lord chancellor of England from Archbishop *Warham. Later the bishoprics of Bath and Wells (1518), Durham (1523), Winchester (1528), and the abbey of St. Albans (1521) fell to his lot.

Exercising immense power and wealth, W. gave much of his attention to the direction of England's foreign policy, where he cleverly manoeuvred between the empire and France. W. was not lacking in the highest ambitions in the eccelesiastical sphere, and twice, in 1521 and 1523, pulled strings behind the scenes to gain election to the papacy. From 1518 he held the position of Legate *a latere,* or the pope's personal representative to England. In spite of the fact that he was guilty of pluralism, one of the most serious aspects of ecclesiastical corruption, W. had the temerity to enact reforms, suppressing some of the smaller monasteries and founding new schools, especially Cardinal's College, Christ Church, Oxford, of the present day, and a new grammar school at Ipswich. In the secular sphere of administration he introduced more speedy judicial processes and continued Henry VII's policy of asserting royal authority against the pretensions of the nobility.

Although he had made himself many enemies, W.'s downfall was due, primarily, to his failure to gain papal approval for a divorce of Henry VIII from *Catherine of Aragon. After some two years spent by W. negotiating with Rome, the King lost patience. In October 1529, under the Statute of Praemunire, he was arraigned for violation of the old law which forbade appeal to Rome of cases that belonged within the jurisdiction of the King's court. Condemned and stripped of the chancellorship and part of his property, he was allowed to retire to his bishopric. In November 1530, however, he was arrested on charge of high treason, dying on his way to stand trial in London.

A. F. Pollard, *Wolsey* (1929).

WORCESTER, JOHN TIPTOFT, EARL OF (1427-70) English statesman. The son of Baron John Tiptoft, he was educated at Oxford and in 1449 created earl of Worcester. In 1457 he went on a pilgrimage to the Holy Land, remaining afterwards in Italy, where he studied under famous humanists in *Ferrara, Padua, Florence and Rome. Returning to England in 1460, he was made constable of the realm of *Edward IV (1462), quickly becoming known as "the butcher of England" because of his numerous death sentences. He also served as deputy of *Ireland, where he acted in a similar harsh manner. In 1470 the rebels, who had put Edward to flight, caught up with him and he was tried and beheaded in London. W. was the first English nobleman to embody the Renaissance capacity for combining a penchant for classical studies, patronage of scholarship and book collection together with ruthless cruelty.

WORDE, WYNKYN DE (Jan van Wynkyn; ?-1535) English printer. Born in Alsace, he became the assistant of the first English printer, *Caxton with whom he worked from 1477 in the latter's Westminster printing shop. After Caxton's death in 1491 W. succeeded him, publishing over 800 titles during the following 45 years. W. was the first English printer to publish *music and the first to introduce italics. He issued many schoolbooks, including grammars by *Colet, *Erasmus and William *Lilly.

H. S. Bennet, *English Books and Readers, 1475 to 1557,* 2nd ed. (1969).

WORMS, DIET OF (1521) The most crucial German diet (*Reichstag*) of the *Reformation. *Charles V wanted to add the sanction of the secular power to the papal bull which had already condemned *Luther as heretic, but bowed to public opinion and the demand of some German princes to give the Protestant leader a hearing. Luther arrived in Worms on 16 April, and answered the questions put to him on the 17th and 18th, ending with his famous: "Here I stand. I cannot do otherwise." The Emperor, while keeping his promise of a safe-conduct, issued, on 25 May, the Edict of Worms, imposing the imperial ban on Luther, which branded him as the devil incarnate. The edict was approved the diet, but not all the princes attended, and this was later used as a pretext for disregarding it. Since the Emperor left Germany after the diet and did not return for nine years, the reformers were given considerable freedom to pursue their aims.

WOTTON, SIR HENRY (1568-1639) English diplomat, poet and art connoisseur. Educated at Winchester College and at Oxford, where he became a friend of John *Donne, from 1589 to 1594 he travelled in Germany and Italy, getting to know the languages and peoples of the two countries. In 1595 he became a close supporter of the earl of *Essex, leaving his service in 1600, just before the latter's attempted rebellion. Returning to Italy, he was employed by the grand duke of Tuscany on a mission to James VI, and when the latter succeeded

Sir Thomas Wyatt *by Holbein the Younger*

to the throne of England as *James I (1603), was made ambassador to *Venice (1604). He served for three terms in this capacity over a period of 20 years. Shortly after his return, he published *The Elements of Architecture* (1624), the first English threatise of High Renaissance architectural theory. W. is known to have been a friend of Milton's and of the biographer Isaac Walton. Of his few poems, *You meaner beauties of the night* is famous for its elegance. He is also remembered for describing an ambassador as "an honest man sent to lie abroad for the good of his country".

L. P. Smith, *Life and Letters of Sir Henry Wotton* 2 vols. (1907; reprinted 1966).

WYATT, SIR THOMAS (1503-42) English poet. Born to a noble family, he served at the court of *Henry VIII who, in 1527, sent him on a diplomatic mission to Italy. There W. was held captive for a short time by the imperial forces, but he was also able to familiarize himself with the poetry of Renaissance Italy. From 1528 to 1532 he was Marshal of Calais and between 1537 and 1539 served as ambassador to Spain. A man with a violent temper, W. was reputed to have been *Anne Boleyn's lover before, and according to his enemies also after, her marriage with the king.

W.'s works include a translation of Plutarch (published in 1528) and *Certayne Psalms,* a collection of poems published posthumously (1549). Another 40 poems attributed to him were published in 1557 in the collection of poems by various authors known as *Tottel's Miscellany* or *Songs and Sonnettes.* With *Surrey, W. is considered to have been the creator of the English sonnet in the Petrarchian style, but some of his best poems are entirely free of foreign influence and bear a deep personal tone.

P. Thompson, *Sir Thomas Wyatt and his Background* (1964);

K. Muir, *Life and Letters of Sir Thomas Wyatt* (1963).

WYATT'S REBELLION (January-February 1554) A pro-Protestant rebellion in England, sparked off by widespread discontent over *Mary's decision to wed *Philip II of Spain Thomas Wyatt (1521-54) was the son of the poet Thomas *Wyatt (1503-42), who had introduced the Italian form of the sonnet into England. In January 1554 W. led 4,000 rebels from Kent towards London even managing to win over a force sent against him. Failing, however to take possession of the city, on 7 February he surrendered. This being the most nearly-successful of the various rebellions against the *Tudors, a number of people whose presence was a menace to Mary were shortly afterwards put to death. These victims included Lady Jane *Grey, whereas *Elizabeth was committed to the Tower. Wyatt himself was executed on 11 April 1554.

WYCLIFFE, JOHN (c. 1328-84) English theologian and reformer. The son of a wealthy rural family, he studied at Oxford where he became master of Balliol College in about 1360. During the next few years he vainly looked for a substantial ecclesiastical benefice, until, in 1374, he was given the parish of Lutterworth which he retained till the end of his life. W. lectured in Oxford and was employed by the crown in its negotiations with the papacy over tribute owed to Rome by England. In 1375 and 1376 W. wrote two treatises, *De dominio divinio* (*On Divine Lordship*) and *De civili dominio* (*On Civil Lordship*). Arguing that only as long as he is in a state of grace can man have a rightful claim to property, he demanded the confiscation of the possessions of the church, since it had lost its right to dominion because of moral decay. In a further work, *De potestate Papae* (*On the Power of the Pope*), written in about 1379, he denied the divine origins of the papacy and referred to the pope as antichrist, and to his followers as "twelve daughters of a diabolical leech". W. also questioned the current belief of transubstantiation and called for a return to primitive Christianity. Regarding the *Bible as the only source of religious truth he began to translate it into English, a work later continued by his followers.

W.'s teachings, which became known outside England, were condemned by Pope Gregory XI in 1377. He himself, however, finding in John of Gaunt (1340-99), duke of Lancaster, a powerful protector, was not molested. While the higher clergy took steps to suppress his followers at Oxford, W. himself was only forbidden to lecture and allowed to die in his home parish. In 1415, however, the Council of *Constance ordered his writings to be destroyed and his bones were disinterred and burned. W.'s teachings were adopted by the *Lollards, a movement which gained adherents among the lower classes. But his link with the 16th-century *Reformation is demonstrated by the essential religious principle which he was the first to proclaim: the individual's right to seek salvation on his own, without the sacramental mediation of the established Church.

G. H. W. Parker, *The Morning Star: Wycliffe and the Dawn of the Reformation* (1965);

K. B. McFarlane, *John Wycliffe and the Beginnings of English Nonconformity* (1952).

WYKEHAM, WILLIAM OF (1324-1404) English prelate. The son of a poor peasant, he was educated at Winchester, in 1347 becoming a clerk of King Edward III. He gradually rose to a position of influence, attaining the office of lord chancellor together with the see of Winchester in 1367. More an administrator than a clergyman and a notorious pluralist, he was made to relinquish the chancellorship in 1371, for several years remaining out of office; however, in 1389 he regained the chancellorship holding it until 1391. As clerk of the Royal Works, W. supervised important architectural projects, chiefly at Windsor Castle and later in his own cathedral of Winchester. W. is best remembered, however, as the founder of New College, Oxford (1379) and Winchester School (1382), two self-governing and sovereign bodies, which served as models of 15th-century English educational institutions.

G. H. Morberg, *Life of William of Wykeham* (1893).

WYTTENBACH, THOMAS (1472-1526) Swiss humanist and reformer. Born in Biel, he studied at Tübingen and became a lecturer of biblical exegesis at the university of *Basle. An admirer of *Erasmus, he publicized his critical views on scholasticism and the monastic orders, between 1504 and 1506 having *Zwingli as a student. In 1515 he became a pastor at Biel, where, in 1523 he came out openly in favour of the *Reformation. He married shortly before his death, losing his pastorship in consequence.

St. Francis Xavier

XAVIER, ST. FRANCIS (1506-52) Spanish Jesuit missionary, known as the Apostle of *India and *Japan. The son of an aristocratic Spanish family, he belonged to the original group which gathered around *Loyola in Paris. Ordained in 1537, in 1541 he set sail from Lisbon for the East. Arriving at Goa, India, in the next following year, he first developed some highly successful missionary work on the Malabar coast, before moving on to Ceylon, *Malacca (1545) and the *Moluccas (1546). Returning to Goa, he prepared himself for his missionary work in Japan, which began in 1549. He spent two years in Japan and, while not altogether successful, laid the foundations for a Roman Catholic community which survived after he left. In 1552, despite ill health, he undertook a mission to *China. He died, however, on an island not far from the mainland, his body being later transported to Goa.

X. was known for his missionary zeal and dedication as well as for his organizational abilities. Though frequently taking advantage of the presence of the Portuguese civil authorities, he was not deterred from penetrating areas in which he had to act on his own. He was canonized in 1622.

M. Purcell, *Don Francisco: The Story of St. Francis Xavier* (1952);

A. R. McGraty, *The Fire of Francis Xavier* (1952).

XEREZ, FRANCISCO DE (1499-c. 1547) Spanish historian. Born in Andalusia, he went to the New World when he was very young and, in 1524, joined *Pizarro in his early discoveries of Peru. During the conquest of the Inca empire, he was both a soldier and a scribe (1531-33), in 1534 returning to Spain. In the same year his *Verdadera relación de la conquista del Perú* was published in Seville. Translated into Italian, and later into other languages, his book did a lot to sustain the myth of fabulous Peruvian riches.

XYLANDER, WILHELM (1532-76) German classical philologist. Born in Augsburg, he studied at the university of Heidelberg where he was professor of Greek from 1558 until his death. He edited a number of formerly unknown Latin texts, and made the first German translation of Eucid (1562).

Madonna of the Seven Sorrows *by Ysenbrandt*

Y

YÁÑEZ DE ALMEDINA, FERNANDO (c. 1480-c. 1550) Spanish painter. He collaborated with Fernando de Llanos, with whom he painted 12 panels depicting the life of the Virgin, in the cathedral of Valencia (1506-09). From the style of the paintings, one of the pair is held to have been a certain "Ferrando Spagnolo", mentioned in 1505 as one of *Leonardo's assistants in Florence. Y. enjoyed a considerable reputation in Spain. The last reference we have to him is dated 1526, when he was working in Cuenca.

YEOMEN OF THE GUARD The first permanent military force in England, established by *Henry VII at his coronation (1485). The corps, which usually did not exceed 150 men, was actually a royal bodyguard. In 1520, when *Henry VIII had the historic meeting with *Francis I at the *Field of Cloth of Gold, he was accompanied by some 600 guards wearing scarlet uniform. Eventually these became the present-day ceremonial unit.

YORK, HOUSE OF The English royal house which produced three kings: *Edward IV, *Edward V, who was never crowned, and *Richard III. York's claim to the crown was first put forward openly in 1460 by Richard, duke of York, a descendant of Edward III (1327-77) on both his father's and his mother's side. This action provided the immediate cause for the prolonged Wars of the *Roses of Yorkists and *Lancasterians, which ended only with the death of Richard III at the Battle of Bosworth (1485). Under *Henry VII, however, the Yorkist party continued to be dangerously active, thus encouraging the pretender Perkin *Warbeck, who claimed to be Richard of York, second son of Edward IV. English nobles of Yorkist blood remained under suspicion well into the reign of *Henry VIII.

YSENBRANDT, ADRIAEN (?-1551) Flemish painter. There are many gaps in the information we have on his life. Y. is alleged to have settled in *Bruges and become a pupil of Gerard *David. In 1510 he was admitted to the guild as a free master. Y. excelled in the painting of portraits and nudes but, although he seems to have been a productive artist and had an international clientèle, no picture extant can be authenticated as his on documentary evidence. He is, however, held to have been the author of several religious works, in many ways resembling the style of David. Y. was the last master of the school of Bruges.

M. J. Friedlander, *Die Antwerpener Manieristen und Adriaen Ysenbrandt* (1933).

The Conversion of St. Paul *by Taddeo Zuccari*

Z

ZABARELLA, FRANCESCO (1360-1417) Italian canonist and cardinal. A graduate of the famous legal school of Bologna, he taught canon law at Padua (1390-1409), until called to Rome to advise on settling the *Great Schism. Participating in the Council of *Pisa, he supported Pierre *D'Ailly and Jean *Gerson; on being created a cardinal by *John XXIII he worked hard at the Council of *Constance to bring about the pope's abdication so as to heal the schism (1415). Z. contended that, since the schism produced heresy, the cardinals could call a general council to deal with it. This conciliarist position later caused his *De schismate* to be listed in the *Index.

ZABARELLA, JACOPO (1533-89) Italian philosopher. Born in Padua, he became professor of logic at the local university in 1564, and remained there until his death. Z. was a champion of Aristotle, on whom he wrote several commentaries. His main contribution was in the field of logic and methodology. His collected logical treatises, *Opera logica* (1578), included essays on analytic and synthetic methodology, and in his collected essays of natural philosophy, *De rebus naturalibus* (1590), he developed theories on scientific verification and discussed the human senses, mind and intelligence. His work on logic was influential outside Italy, especially in Germany, where it was studied by Leibnitz in the 17th century. He seems to have made less impact on Italy itself.

E. F. Edwards, *The Logic of Iacopo Zabarella* (1961).

ZACCARIA, ST. ANTONIO MARIA (1502-39) Founder of the *Barnabites. A young physician, who had studied in Pavia and Padua, he worked among the poor in Cremona, where he was influenced by *Battista da Crema. Ordained priest in 1528, he became chaplain to Countess Ludovica *Torelli in Milan in 1530. The latter helped him found the Barnabite order, approved by *Clement VII in 1533. Z. was a restless preacher and conducted religious missions throughout the north of Italy. His innovations with regard to Roman Catholic religious customs and ritual impressed his audience, though rousing some opposition among the ecclesiastical authorities. After his death he became the object of a popular cult, which led to his canonization in 1897.

G. Chastel, *Saint Antoine-Marie Zaccaria, Barnabite* (1930).

ZACCONI, LUDOVICO (1555-1627) Italian musical theorist. Born in Pesaro, he studied under *Gabrieli in Venice, there becoming an Augustinian monk and choirmaster. Between 1592 and 1619 he served in Bavaria and in Austria, but ended his life in Venice. Z. was the author of *Prattica di musica,* first published in 1592, a theoretical work dealing with almost all aspects of musical composition dedicated to William V, duke of Bavaria. It is now extremely valuable as a source on late Renaissance *music. Z. was less important as a composer than as a theorist.

ZACUTO OF SALAMANCA (c. 1450-c. 1515) The name under which is known the Jewish *astronomer, mathematician and historian, Abraham ben Shmuel Zacuth. A student and afterwards a teacher at the university of Salamanca, he first acquired a reputation with his astronomical treatise *Ha-Hibbur Ha-Gadol* (1473-78), which was translated into Latin and Spanish. He contributed to further perfecting the *astrolabe, and compiled the most accurate astronomical tables of his time, which served *Columbus in his voyages. When the Jews were expelled from Spain (1492), he became astronomer and *astrologer to the court of Portugal, where he acted as Vasco da *Gama's consultant on the use of navigational instruments. In 1497, when the Jews were expelled from Portugal, he left for Tunis, Here he wrote a world history in Hebrew, *Sefer Yohasin,* which became very popular. He died in Damascus.

F. Cantera Burgos, *Abraham Zacut* (1935).

ZAINER, GÜNTHER (?-1478) German printer. Born in Reutlingen, probably he received his training as a printer in the shop of *Mentelin in Strassburg. In 1468 he became the first printer in *Augsburg. Z. was the publisher of the first illustrated best-seller, the 13th-century Jacobus de Voragine's *The Golden Legend*, a work which included 231 woodcuts (1471-72). In 1475 Z. published the first illustrated *Bible, until his death bringing out another over thirty illustrated editions of popular texts. One of these was the first printed edition of *Thomas à Kempis' *De Imitatione Christi* (1473).

ZAINER, JOHANN (?-1500) German printer. Born in Reutlingen, he was most probably the brother of Günther Z. In about 1473 he settled in Ulm where he printed some of the earliest illustrated books. In 1476 he published the first edition of Aesop's *Fables* in German. As woodcutter for his *Life of Christ* (1478), he employed Ludwig *Schongauer, who adapted engravings by his brother Martin. Some of the woodblocks were also used by Günther in nearby Augsburg.

ZAMORA, ALFONSO DE (1474-1531) Spanish *Hebrew scholar. Born a Jew, he received a rabbinical education but, in 1506, converted to Christianity and became the first professor of Hebrew at Salamanca. A master of other oriental languages as well as of Latin and Greek, he was entrusted by Cardinal *Jimenez de Cisneros with the editing of the Hebrew parts of the Complutensian Polyglot *Bible. He also was the author of a Hebrew grammar and dictionary, and wrote an open letter addressed to his former coreligionists in Rome, exhorting them to convert to Christianity.

ZAMOYSKI, JAN (1542-1605) Polish statesman. Born to a family of magnates, he was educated in France and Italy. Returning to *Poland in 1565, he became secretary to *Sigismund II, quickly advancing to become the leader of an important section of the nobility. Z. supported the election of *Henry of Valois to the Polish throne and, when the French left Poland (1574), used his influence on behalf of the election of *Stephen Bathory, whose close collaborator he remained.

Z. commanded the army in the war against Russia, and, in 1587, brought about the election of *Sigismund III. However, the king's fear of Z.'s great political influence led to a rift and, in 1592, Z. led the opposition of nobles who objected to Sigismund's negotiations with the *Habsburgs over the Polish succession. Later, Z. extended Polish influence in Moldavia and Vallachia and, in 1600, fought the Swedes in Livonia. His championship of the rights of the Polish nobility consolidated the tradition of a "republican monarchy".

ZANCHI, GIROLAMO (1516-90) Italian Protestant reformer. Born to a respected family in Alzano, north of Milan, he entered the Augustinian order and, in 1531, was sent with a friend, Count Celso Martinengo, to Lucca, where he met and was influenced by Pietro Martire *Vermigli. He began to read the writings of the leaders of the Reformation, especially those of *Bullinger and *Calvin and later preached their ideas. Forced to flee, in 1551 he went to *Strassburg, where he was appointed professor of Biblical exegesis. In 1561, however, he became party to a fierce theological controversy concerning the Eucharist and, in 1563, left to become a preacher at Chiavenna. In 1568 he was made professor of theology at the Calvinist university of Heidelberg, achieving wide fame in German Protestant circles. When Lutheranism was introduced in 1576, he moved to Neustadt-on-the-Hardt, but later resettled in Heidelberg where he died. The author of several theological and philosophical treatises, Z. was one of the few religious writers who preserved his wide intellectual perspectives in an age of increasing narrow-mindedness.

ZAPOLYA, JOHN (1487-1540) King of Hungary through friendship with the Ottoman Turks. Son of the most powerful family in the Hungarian nobility, Z. made an indirect bid for the crown already in 1505, when he moved the nobility assembled at a diet to decide that henceforth no foreign prince could be elected king of Hungary. In 1514 he brutally suppressed the peasant rebellion led by George *Dosza, an accomplishment which only enhanced his stature among the nobles. But in 1521 he was held responsible for the fortress of Belgrade's fall to the Turks, a loss which strained his relations with the young King *Louis II. In 1526 Z. neglected to march to the aid of the king who was defeated and killed by the armies of *Suleiman I at the Battle of *Mohacs. In the ensuing contest over the crown he gained the support of the national party, entering a long struggle against Archduke *Ferdinand, the brother of the emperor, who was elected by another section of the nobility. In 1528, after two years of unsuccessful campaigns, Z. was forced to ally himself to the Turks, who came to his assistance. It was, however, only in 1538 that he made peace with Ferdinand in the Treaty of Nagyvarad. Although the terms stipulated that after his death Ferdinand would inherit his part of the kingdom, Z. left his infant son *John Sigismund Zapolya as his successor, placing him under the protection of the Turks.

ZÁRATE, AUGUSTÍN DE (c. 1492-1560) Spanish historian. A royal official who served for many years as secretary of the Council of Castile, he was sent to Peru as a royal accountant in 1543. There he collected the material for his *Historia de descubrimento y conquista del Peru,* first published in Antwerp in 1555. This work, with its description of *Pizarro's exploits and the fall of the Inca empire, enjoyed a wide vogue. It was twice republished in Venice and Seville, and it was translated into the major European languages.

J. M. Cohen, ed., *The Discovery and Conquest of Peru* (1968).

ZARLINO, GIOSEFFE (1517-90) Italian musical theorist. Born at Chioggia, he became a Franciscan friar (1537) and later was ordained deacon and made maestro di cappella of St. Mark's, Venice (1565). Combining the knowledge of *music with a good classical education, Z. wrote three important treatises: *Institutioni armoniche* (1558), *Dimonstrationi armoniche* (1571) and *Sopplimenti musicali* (1588), dealing with the formation of harmony and explaining double counterpoint in canon and other musical forms.

ZASIUS, ULRICH (1461-1536) German humanist. Born at Constance, he served for a number of years as ecclesiastic notary of his native town, in 1494 becoming head of the grammar school and townclerk of Freiburg in Breisgau. In 1506 he was made professor in the law faculty of the university. An outstanding teacher, Z. attracted many students to Freiburg. Initially a supporter of *Luther, after 1523 he came out against the Reformation. He was the author of works on jurisprudence and theology.

G. Kisch, *Zasius und Reuchlin* (1961).

ZEITBLOM, BARTEL (c. 1455-c. 1518) German painter. Born at Nördlingen, he may have been a pupil of *Schongauer and, in 1482, settled in Ulm. Z. became known for his large altarpieces executed in a late Gothic style. These, however, lack true power of expression, while they do not yet embody the qualities of High Renaissance painting. Z. was very much admired by the 19th-century German Romantics.

ZELL, MATTHÄUS (1477-1548) AND KATHARINA (c. 1497-1562) German husband and wife, reformers at *Strassburg. After studying at Freiburg, Matthäus became a teacher of theology in that city in 1511; in 1518, however, he came to Strassburg as a priest and penitentiary. In 1521 he embraced the *Reformation, resisting the attacks of his bishop with the aid of the general public. Late in 1523, he married Katharina, an act defended in his *Appellatio sacerdotum maritorum* (1524). A man of simple concerns, he remained the most popular preacher of the Reformation in Strassburg. His wife became influential in her own right, caring for the many religious refugees who swelled the city. She also wrote on theological issues, defended her marriage to a priest and corresponded with *Luther, *Blaurer and other reformers.

ZELL, ULRICH (?-1507) German printer. In 1464 he became the first printer at *Cologne, which he helped to make the leading centre of publishing in north-west Germany. Many of the over 200 titles which he printed were Latin theological treatises for the use of students at Cologne's university, a stronghold of mediaeval scholasticism.

ZIMARA, MARCO ANTONIO (c. 1470-1532) Italian philosopher. The gifted child of a poor family, his uncle, a priest, paid for his education, sending him to the university of Padua. Z. taught philosophy at Padua (1501-09), Salerno (1519-23) and Naples. In 1525 he returned to Padua by invitation of the Venetian Senate. The editor of the writings of Averroes and St. Albertus Magnus, he was a dedicated champion of Aristotelianism, and wrote a number of works on the subject.

B. Nardi, *Saggi sull'Aristotelismo Padovano dal secolo XIV al XVI* (1958).

ZIZKA, JAN (c. 1376-1424) Czech military leader. Of noble extraction, he served in the Bohemian armies and he lost the use of one eye, fighting together with the Poles against the *Teutonic Knights at Tannenberg in 1410. He then returned to Prague, becoming a follower af Jan *Hus; in about 1420 he became the leader of the *Taborites, one of the most radical Hussite factions. Employing wagons as mobile fortified positions and showing great inventiveness in the use of firearms, Z. scored a number of victories over the forces of King *Sigismund, and was recognized as the most talented of the Hussite generals. He continued to command the army in spite of the fact that by 1421 he had gone completely blind. In 1423 and in the following year Z. fought the *Ultraquists, the main body of Hussite moderates of Prague and their noble supporters. His victories led to the reunification of the Hussite forces, which then invaded Moravia. Z., however, died of the plague soon afterwards.

F. G. Heymann, *John Zizka and the Hussite Revolution* (1955).

ZOPPO, MARCO (1433-78) Italian painter. Born at Cento, he completed his training in the workshop of *Squarcione in Padua, where he was influenced by *Mantegna. In 1455 he quarrelled with Squarcione and fled to Venice, later dividing his time between this city and Bologna. His works, reflecting the style of contemporary masters of northern Italy, are characterized by their sensitive contours and the transparent quality of their colouring.

ZUCCARI, FEDERICO (1542-1609) Italian painter. He was the younger brother of the *Mannerist painter Taddeo Zuccari (1529-66), who left well-known series of frescoes in the Sala Regia of the Vatican and the Villa Farnese in Caprarola. Z. executed frescoes in the dome of the cathedral of Florence, in Venice's Doge Palace and the Vatican. In 1574 he travelled to France, *Flanders and England and, between 1585-89, worked in Spain. Returning to Rome, he built his own palace, a structure known for its eccentric style, e.g. its windows, designed in the shape of a man's open mouth. In Rome, Z. founded the Academy of St. Luke (1593), of which he became the head, devoting his last years to teaching and writing about art. He codified the theory of Mannerism in his *L'idea dei scultori, pittori e architetti*, which was published in 1607. It outlined the author's concept of *disegno*, the process by which the idea pre-existing in the mind of the artist takes concrete artistic shape.

ZUMARRAGA, JUAN DE (c. 1468-1548) First Spanish archbishop of Mexico. A native of the Vizcaya region, he became a Franciscan friar, by 1520 rising to the rank of being head of the province of Concepción. Late in 1527 *Charles V appointed him first bishop of Mexico. Arriving there in the following year, Z. organized the conversion of the Indians, established parishes, and, in 1531, consecrated what was to develop into the Mexican national shrine of Our Lady of Guadalupe. As a result of his conflict with the civil authorities whom he placed under an interdict, Z. was recalled to Spain (1532), but returned to Mexico in 1534, where he dedicated a great deal of effort to the development of schools, especially for sons of the Indian nobility. He also served as inquisitor (1536-43), in this capacity encouraging the destruction of the old temples. The author of works of the catechism, which he printed in Mexico, Z. was made archbishop in 1547.

R. E. Greenleaf, *Zumarraga and the Mexican Inquisition, 1536-43* (1962).

ZURARA, GOMES EANES DE (c. 1410-74) Portuguese historian. An assistant of Fernão *Lopes, he succeeded him as royal chronicler in 1454. Z. continued Lopes' incomplete description of the reign of *John I by writing the *Crónica da tomada de Ceuta*, dealing with the conquest of the Moslem town on the shore of North Africa. His masterpiece, however, is the *Crónica do descobrimento e conquista de Guiné*, the first history to describe the Portuguese movement of overseas *exploration and a celebration of the role played by *Henry the Navigator.

E. Prestage, *The Chronicles of Fernão Lopes and Gomes Eanes de Zurara* (1928).

ZURICH The prosperous capital of the canton of the same name, Z. entered the 15th century as an independent city governed by the *guilds and holding an important membership in the *Swiss Confederation. Relations with the other city-states underwent a period of crisis during the Old Zurich War (1436-50) in which Z. was defeated. Ties with the rest of the confederation were soon improved, however, and under burgomaster Hans Waldmann, Z. led the Swiss in their successful war against *Charles the Bold of *Burgundy. Although Waldmann lost his life in a peasants' revolt in 1489, the city enjoyed a period of industrial expansion throughout the 15th century.

The history of Z. in the 16th century is intimately connected with the career of *Zwingli, the man who, in 1519, initiated the *Reformation in Switzerland, dominating the city until his death in 1531. Under *Bullinger, Z. remained a major centre of Protestantism, affording shelter to refugees from *Mary Tudor's England and to French *Huguenots. In the religious sphere the city subsequently took second place to *Calvin's *Geneva, while still retaining pre-eminence as the most important Swiss economic centre.
S. Widmer, *Zürich* (1967).

ZURITA Y CASTRO, JERONIMO DE (1512-80) Spanish historian. Born in Saragossa to a noble family of *Aragon, he was educated at Alcala and became a royal administrator. Under *Charles V he served for a time as secretary to the *Inquisition, in 1548 being appointed to the office of *historiographer of Aragon. His great masterpiece, *Anales de la corona de Aragon*, covering the history of this kingdom from the Moslem invasion in the 8th century to the death of *Ferdinand the Catholic, appeared between 1562-80. Z. was an indefatigable researcher who collected documents both in Spain and in the Spanish possessions in Italy and helped enrich the national historical archive which was established at Simancas in 1567. He is considered the first historian of Spain.

ZUTPHEN, BATTLE OF (22 September 1586) The most important, though indecisive, battle waged during the English intervention in the Netherlands. Some 6,000 English troops under the earl of *Leicester had to withdraw from the siege of Zutphen after their engagement with the Spaniards under Alessandro *Farnese. Sir Philip *Sidney's gallant death at Zutphen has imbued the battle with romance.

ZWICK, JOHANNES (c. 1496-1542) Swiss-German Protestant reformer. Born at Constance, he studied law at Freiburg, between 1518-20 completing his doctorate in civil and canon law at *Siena. At first influenced by *Luther, in 1522 he joined *Zwingli at Zurich, subsequently assuming a more or less independent orientation. After his ordination to the priesthood, he passed a stormy period as minister at Riedlingen, in 1527 becoming preacher in Constance, where he cooperated with *Blaurer. Z. is especially remembered for his educational activities and his *hymns. His influence as a leader of reforms spread to parts of southern Germany. His younger brother, Konrad, who died in 1557, was also an active reformer.

ZWICKAU PROPHETS A small group of *millenarians from the town of Zwickau in Saxony. They were inspired by the teachings of Thomas *Münzer and, after he had left for Bohemia, moved to Wittenberg (1521) where they opposed the use of sacraments, especially in infant baptism. Active in *Luther's absence, they succeeded in making a favourable impression on *Melanchthon. When Luther returned (March 1522) however, he made them leave.

ZWILLING, GABRIEL (c. 1487-1558) German reformer. Born near Annaberg, he studied in Prague and *Wittenberg, where he became a companion of *Luther in the Augustinian cloister. In 1521, when Luther was absent from Wittenberg, Z. took the lead in initiating radical reforms together with *Carlstadt and, in January 1522, caused an iconoclastic riot. Luther's return curbed his activities. Later, he served as pastor in Torgau.

ZWINGLI, HULDRYCH (1484-1531) Swiss leader of the *Reformation, theologian and statesman. Born at Wildhaus in the canton of St. Gall, the son of the village mayor, he was educated at Berne (1496-98), Vienna (1500-02) and Basle (1502-06), where he earned the degree of master of arts. Soon after, he was ordained, being appointed pastor of Glarus, where he stayed until 1516. There he continued his humanist studies, improving his *Greek and learning some *Hebrew so that he could read the early Christian fathers and classical authors in the original. As chaplain to the Swiss forces in Italy, Z. was present at their defeat at *Marignano (1515), an experience which aroused his opposition to the mercenary system of recruitment. It also contributed to his retirement from Glarus, and his transference to the shrine of Einsiedeln, where he served as preacher for about two years. In 1518 he was invited to become the priest of the principal church in *Zurich. An admirer of *Erasmus, he arrived with a thorough knowledge of patristic literature and imbued with ideas about necessary reforms. He remained in Zurich for the rest of his life.

Z.'s series of sermons on the New Testament early in 1519 marked the beginning of the Reformation in Switzerland. Always consciously jealous of the fact that *Luther had been the first to take action, he independently attacked monasticism and veneration of relics and saints, stressing the original meaning of the gospel. Enjoying the cooperation of the town-council, he was able to postpone an open confrontation with the Roman Catholic hierarchy until 1522, when Johann *Faber, vicar general of the bishop of Constance, was sent to Zurich as a result of Z.'s defense of the eating of meat during Lent, an attitude in plain contradiction to Roman Catholicism. Z. explained his position in *Architeles*, where he criticized the whole ritual structure of the Church and the authority of bishops and of the pope. In his public disputation with Faber (29 January 1523), a one-sided affair, Z. upheld his 67 theses, and declared the Scriptures the only source of religious truth. Strenghtened by a resolution drafted in his favour by the town-council, he began the abolition of any institution not specifically mentioned in the New Testament. He did away with, for instance, the old form of the Mass, pilgrimages, monastic orders, fast and clerical celibacy. In 1524 he made public his marriage to a widow, Anna Reinhardt Meyer, that actually had been contracted two years earlier. In 1525 appeared his first comprehensive work on the reforms he had instituted, *Commentarius de vera et falsa religione*. At about the same time pictures and images were removed from the churches.

The quick pace of the Reformation in Zurich soon caused Z. to face internal opposition of a more radical nature than his own. This was headed by the so-called *Anabaptists who, in 1525, began to practice adult baptism. Mobilizing the civil authorities against the dissenters, Z. reaffirmed infant baptism, threatening offenders with capital punishment by drowning. Some were indeed thus executed and, by 1527, the movement was suppressed within Zurich. Z.'s controversy with Luther persisted much longer. Entered upon in 1524 in a letter of Z.'s to a friend in which he asserted a symbolic interpretation of the Eucharist, it continued in pamphlets and letters of the two men that only

Zwingli

increased the tension between them. The Colloquy of *Marburg (1529) called by *Philip of Hesse with the intention of healing the rift, resulted in an impasse. Z. rejected any form of belief in Christ's carnal presence in the Eucharist, maintaining that the words "This is my body" had only a figurative meaning, and that the real significance of the sacrament consisted in the way God worked upon the heart of the recipient of this concrete symbol, and was conditional upon his state of belief.

During his last years Z. was increasingly preoccupied with the need to win over the other Swiss cantons for the Reformation. As a result of a major victory scored by Z. in a theological disputation at Berne early in 1528, the city allied itself with Zurich against the cantons which continued to adhere to Roman Catholicism. Their position was soon reinforced by the affiliation of Basle, St. Gall and Schaffhausen, but they failed to come to terms with the so-called Forest Cantons. War finally broke out in 1531. Zurich's small army, unprepared for the fighting, was defeated at Kappel. Z., who served as chaplain and carried the banner, was killed on the battlefield.

O. Farner, *Zwingli the Reformer* (1952);
J. Rilliet, *Zwingli: Third Man of the Reformation* (1964);

MAPS

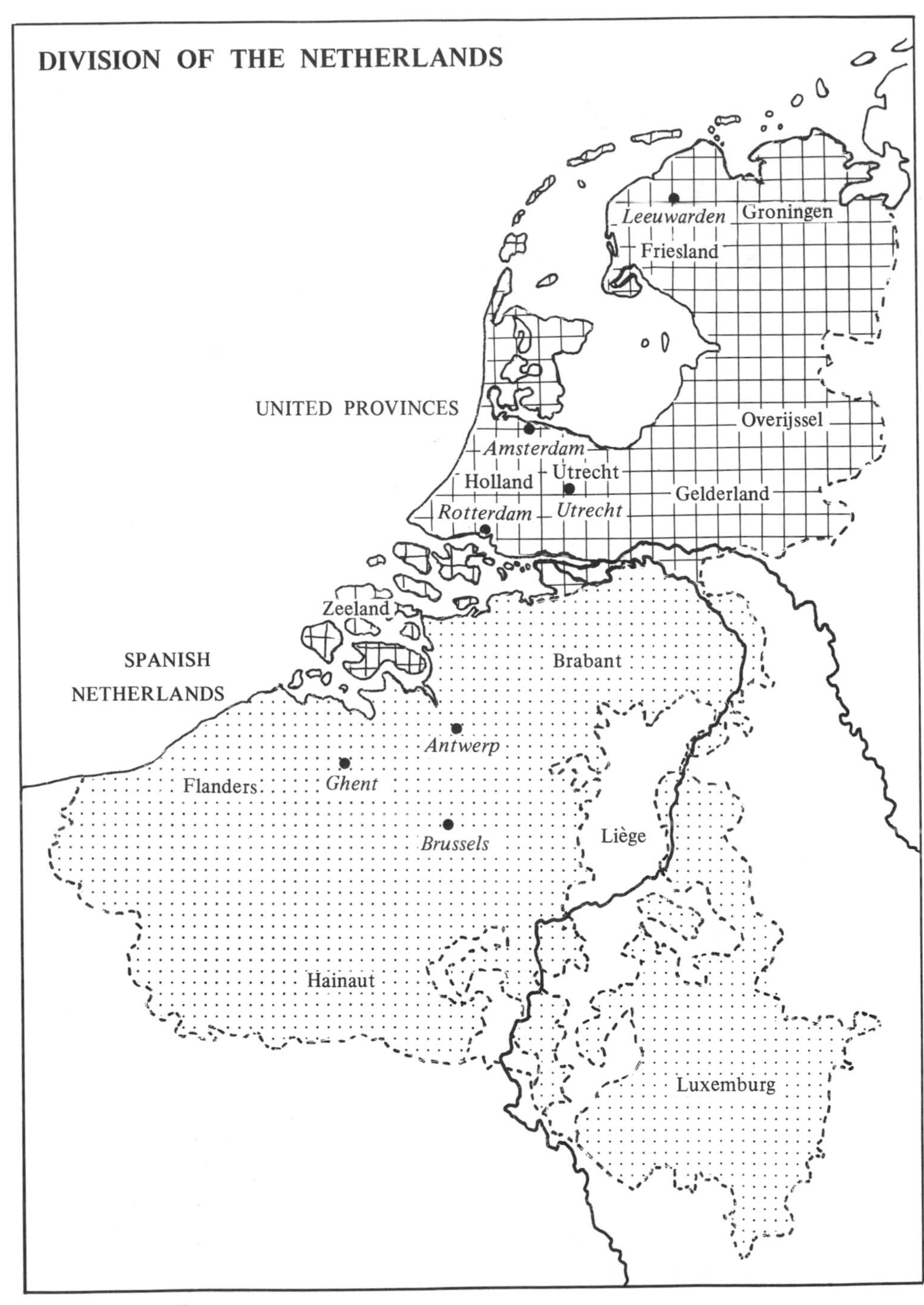

DIVISION OF THE NETHERLANDS
Leeuwarden
Groningen
Friesland
UNITED PROVINCES
Overijssel
Amsterdam
Utrecht
Holland
Gelderland
Rotterdam
Utrecht
Zeeland
SPANISH
NETHERLANDS
Brabant
Antwerp
Flanders
Ghent
Liège
Brussels
Hainaut
Luxemburg

ITALY IN THE LATE 15TH CENTURY
12
11
13
9
10
14
8
5
6
7
4
3
2
14
14
14
14
10
1
15
16
1 Naples
2 Papal States
3 Siena
4 Florence
5 Ferrara
6 Modena
7 Lucca
8 Mantua
9 Milan
10 Genoa
11 Montferrat
12 Savoy
13 Saluzzo
14 Venice
15 Sardinia
16 Sicily

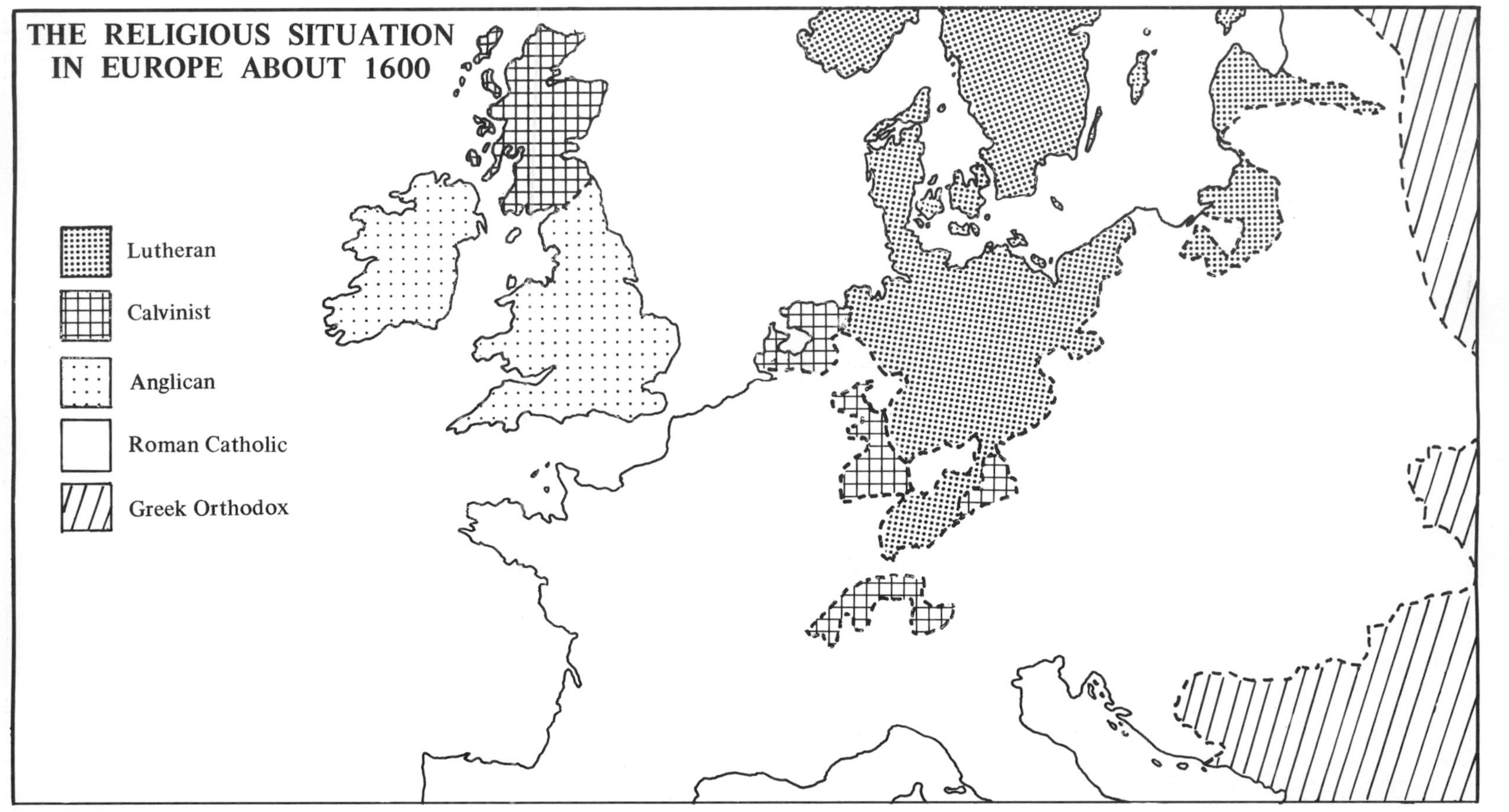
THE RELIGIOUS SITUATION
IN EUROPE ABOUT 1600
Lutheran
Calvinist
Anglican
Roman Catholic
Greek Orthodox

EUROPE IN THE MIDDLE OF THE 15TH CENTURY

EUROPE IN THE MIDDLE OF THE 16TH CENTURY
NORWAY
SCOTLAND
NORTH SEA
DENMARK
IRELAND
ENGLAND
THE NETHERLANDS
THE HOLY ROMAN E
ATLANTIC OCEAN
FRANCE
SWISS CONFEDERATION
PORTUGAL
SPAIN
MEDITERRANEAN SEA

FINLAND
LIVONIA
RUSSIA
BALTIC SEA
PRUSSIA
LITHUANIA
POLAND
MIA
UNGARY
BLACK SEA
OTTOMAN EMPIRE

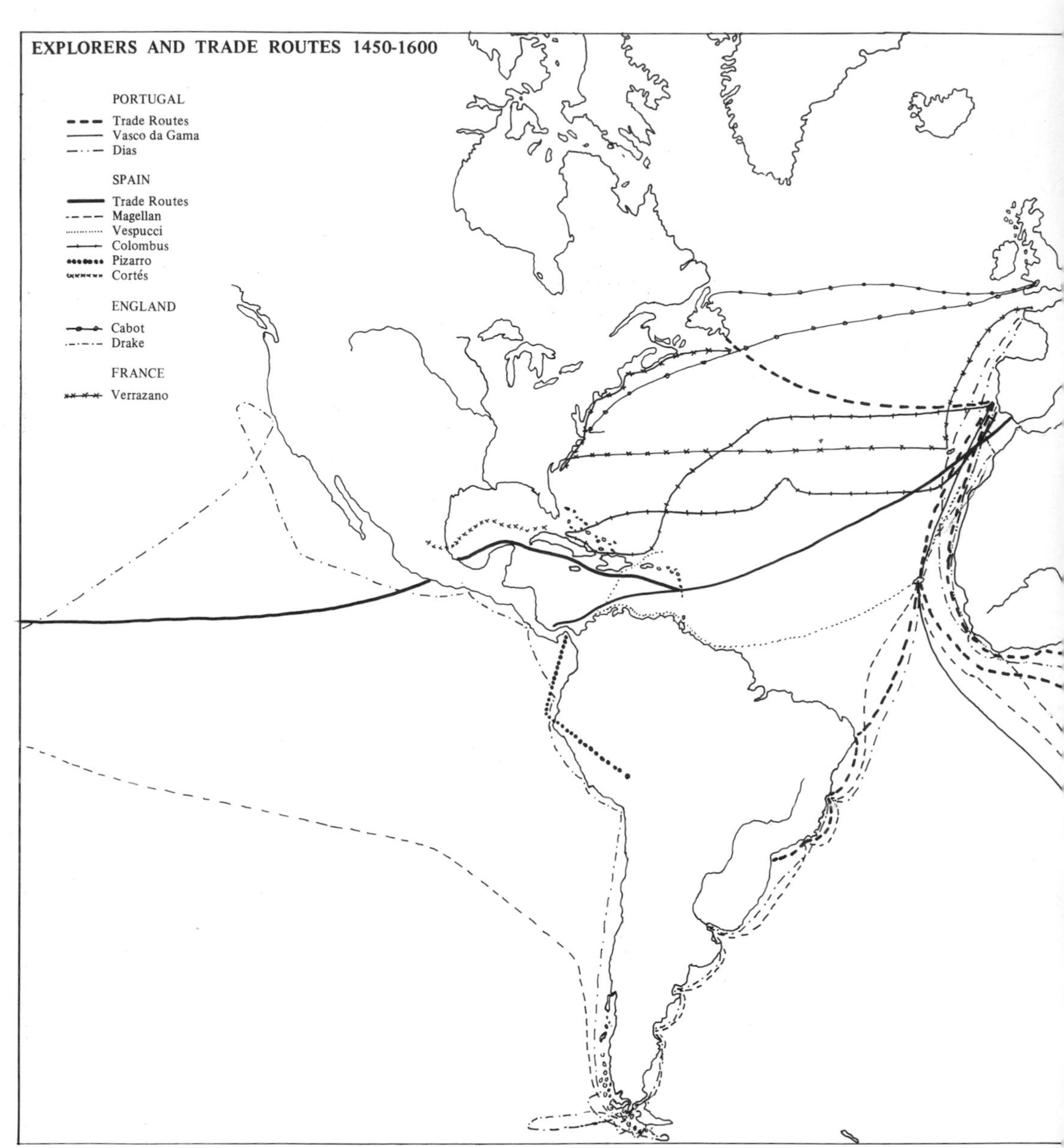
EXPLORERS AND TRADE ROUTES 1450-1600
PORTUGAL
Trade Routes
Vasco da Gama
Dias
SPAIN
Trade Routes
Magellan
Vespucci
Colombus
Pizarro
Cortés
ENGLAND
Cabot
Drake
FRANCE
Verrazano

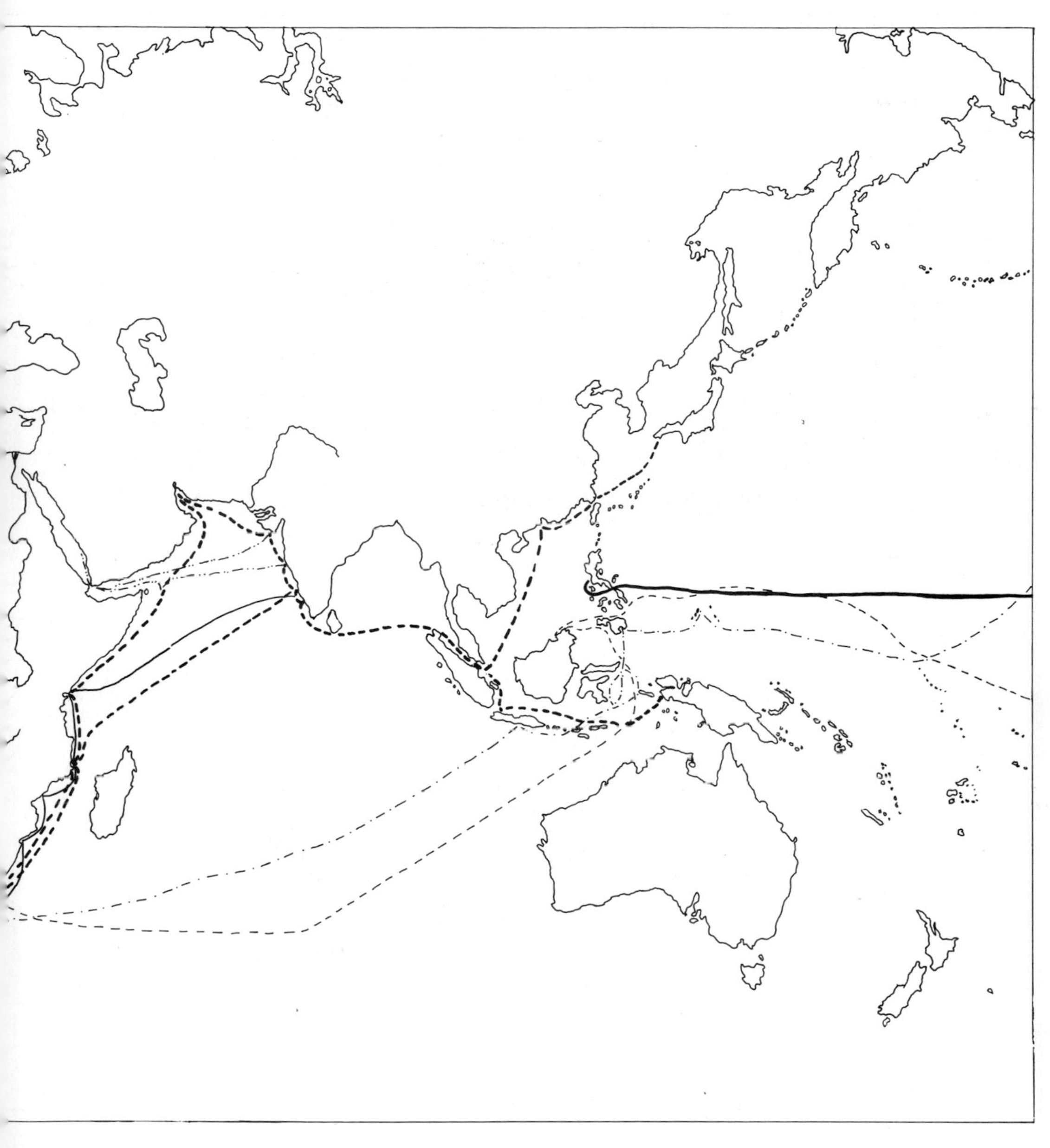

TABLES

HOLY ROMAN EMPERORS	
Wenceslas	1378-1400
Rupert	1400-1410
Sigismund	1410-1437
Albert II	1438-1439
Frederick III	1440-1493
Maximilian I	1493-1519
Charles V	1519-1556
Ferdinand I	1558-1564
Maximilian II	1564-1576
Rudolf II	1576-1612
Matthias	1612-1619

KINGS OF ENGLAND	
Henry V	1413-1422
Henry VI	1422-1461, 1470-1471
Edward IV	1461-1483
Edward V	1483
Richard III	1483-1485
Henry VII	1485-1509
Henry VIII	1509-1547
Edward VI	1547-1553
Mary	1553-1558
Elizabeth I	1558-1603
James I	1603-1625

KINGS OF FRANCE	
Charles VII	1422-1461
Louis XI	1461-1483
Charles VIII	1483-1498
Louis XII	1498-1515
Francis I	1515-1547
Henry II	1547-1559
Francis II	1559-1560
Charles IX	1560-1574
Henry III	1574-1589
Henry IV	1589-1610

KINGS OF PORTUGAL	
John I	1385-1433
Duarte I	1433-1438
Afonso V	1438-1481
John II	1481-1495
Manoel I	1495-1521
John III	1521-1557
Sebastian I	1557-1578
Cardinal Henrique	1578-1580
Philip I (Philip II of Spain)	1580-1598
Philip II (Philip III of Spain)	1598-1621

KINGS OF SCOTLAND

James I	1424-1437
James II	1437-1460
James III	1460-1488
James IV	1488-1513
James V	1513-1542
Mary	1542-1567
James VI	1567-1625

RULERS OF RUSSIA

Ivan III	1462-1505
Vasily III	1505-1533
Ivan IV	1533-1584
Fyodor I	1584-1598
Boris Godunov	1598-1605
Fyodor II	1605
Michael Romanov	1613-1645

KINGS OF SWEDEN

Eric	1412-1439
Christopher	1439-1448
Charles VIII	1448-1457, 1467-1470
Christian I	1457-1481
John	1481-1513
Christian II	1513-1523
Gustavus I	1523-1560
Eric XIV	1560-1569
John III	1569-1592
Sigismund	1592-1604
Charles IX	1604-1611
Gustavus Adolphus	1611-1632

SULTANS OF THE OTTOMAN TURKS

Orkhan	1326-1360
Murad I	1360-1389
Bayezid I	1389-1403
Mehemmed I	1413-1421
Murad II	1421-1451
Mehemmed II	1451-1481
Bayezid II	1481-1512
Selim I	1512-1520
Suleiman I	1520-1566
Selim II	1566-1574
Murad III	1574-1595
Mehemmed III	1595-1603

KINGS OF POLAND

Vladislav II	1386-1434	Sigismund I	1506-1548
Vladislav III	1434-1444	Sigismund II	1548-1572
Casimir IV	1447-1492	Henry of Valois	1573-1574
John Albert	1492-1501	Stephen Bathory	1575-1586
Alexander	1501-1506	Sigismund III	1587-1632

KINGS OF BOHEMIA

Wenceslas	1378-1419
Sigismund	1419-1437
Albert of Habsburg	1437-1439
Ladislas Posthumus	1439-1457
George of Podebrady	1458-1471
Ladislas II	1471-1516
Louis II	1516-1526
Ferdinand of Habsburg	1526-1564
Maximilian	1564-1576
Rudolf	1576-1611
Matthias	1611-1619

KINGS OF DENMARK

Eric	1412-1439
Christopher	1439-1448
Christian I	1448-1481
John	1481-1513
Christian II	1513-1523
Frederick I	1523-1533
Christian III	1534-1558
Frederick II	1558-1588
Christian IV	1588-1648

KINGS OF HUNGARY

Sigismund	1387-1437		
Albert of Habsburg	1437-1439		
Ladislas I (Vladislav III of Poland)	1440-1444		
Ladislas Posthumus	1444-1457		
Matthias Coruinus	1458-1490		
Ladislas II	1490-1516		
Louis II	1516-1526		
Ferdinand of Habsburg	1526-1564	John Zapolya	1526-1540
Maximilian	1564-1576	John Sigismund Zapolya	1540-1571
Rudolf	1576-1608		
Matthias	1608-1619		

ROMAN CATHOLIC POPES

Martin V	1417-1431	Paul III	1534-1549
Eugenius IV	1431-1447	Julius III	1550-1555
Nicholas V	1447-1455	Marcellus II	1555
Calixtus III	1455-1458	Paul IV	1555-1559
Pius II	1458-1464	Pius IV	1559-1565
Paul II	1464-1471	Pius V	1566-1572
Sixtus IV	1471-1484	Gregory XIII	1572-1585
Innocent VIII	1484-1492	Sixtus V	1585-1590
Alexander VI	1492-1503	Urban VII	1590
Pius III	1503	Gregory XIV	1590-1591
Julius II	1503-1513	Innocent IX	1591
Leo X	1513-1521	Clement VIII	1592-1605
Adrian VI	1522-1523	Leo XI	1605
Clement VII	1523-1534	Paul V	1605-1621

KINGS OF SPAIN

John II (Castile)	1406-1454	Alfonso V (Aragon)	1416-1458
Henry IV (Castile)	1454-1474	John II (Aragon)	1458-1479
Isabella (Castile)	1474-1504	Ferdinand the Catholic (Aragon)	1479-1516
Philip I (Castile)	1506		

Ferdinand the Catholic	1506-1516
Charles I (Emperor Charles V)	1516-1556
Philip II	1556-1598
Philip III	1598-1621

SELECT BIBLIOGRAPHY

GENERAL HISTORY

A. G. Dickens, *The Age of Humanism and Reformation* (1972).
J. H. Elliott, *Europe Divided, 1559-1598* (1968).
G. R. Elton, *Reformation Europe, 1517-1559* (1963).
W. K. Ferguson, *Europe in Transition, 1300-1520* (1962).
M. P. Gilmore, *The World of Humanism, 1453-1517* (1952).
V. H. H. Green, *Renaissance and Reformation: A Survey of European History Between 1450 and 1660* (1952).
J. R. Hale, *Renaissance Europe, 1480-1520* (1971).
D. Hay, ed., *The Age of the Renaissance* (1967).
History of Mankind; Cultural and Scientific Development, Vol. IV, *The Foundation of the Modern World,* edited by L. Gottschalk, L. C. MacKinney and E. H. Pritchard (1969).
H. G. Koenigsberger and G. L. Mosse, *Europe in the Sixteenth Century* (1968).
H. S. Lucas, *The Renaissance and Reformation,* 2nd ed. (1960).
E. Lucki, *History of the Renaissance,* 5 vols. (1963-65).
The New Cambridge Modern History
Vol. I, *The Renaissance, 1493-1520,* edited by G. R. Potter (1957).
Vol. II, *The Reformation, 1520-1559,* edited by G. R. Elton (1958).
Vol. III, *The Counter-Reformation and Price Revolution, 1559-1610,* edited by R. B. Wernham (1968).
M. R. O'Connell, *The Counter-Reformation, 1559-1610* (1974).
M. R. Price and D. Lindsay, eds., *A Portrait of Europe* (1975).
J. B. Ross and M. M. McLaughlin, *The Portable Renaissance Reader* (1953).
L. W. Spitz, *The Renaissance and Reformation Movements,* 2 vols. (1971).
H. Trevor-Roper, ed., *The Age of Expansion: Europe and the World, 1559-1660* (1968).
C. Wilson, *The Transformation of Europe, 1558-1648* (1976).

GOVERNMENT AND INSTITUTIONS

F. L. Carsten, *Princes and Parliaments in Germany* (1959).
H. J. Cohn, ed., *Government in Reformation Europe* (1971).
J. H. Elliott, *Imperial Spain, 1469-1716* (1963).
G. R. Elton, *The Tudor Revolution in Government* (1953).
G. Griffith, ed., *Representative Government in Western Europe in the Sixteenth Century* (1968).
H. J. Koenigsberger, *Estates and Revolutions* (1971).
J. Lynch, *Spain Under the Habsburgs,* Vol. 1 (1964).
G. Mattingly, *Renaissance Diplomacy* (1955).
C. Petrie, *Earlier Diplomatic History, 1492-1713* (1949).
J. Russell Major, *Representative Institutions in Renaissance France, 1421-1559* (1960).
J. H. Sherman, ed., *Government and Society in France, 1461-1661* (1969).

ECONOMY AND SOCIETY

P. Boissonnade, *Life and Work in Medieval Europe: The Evolution of Medieval Economy from the Fifth to the Fifteenth Centuries* (1927).
F. Braudel, *The Mediterranean and the Mediterranean World in the Age of Philip II*, 2 vols. (1973).
P. Burke, ed., *Economy and Society in Early Modern Europe* (1970).
The Cambridge Economic History of Europe
Vol. IV, *The Economy of Expanding Europe in the 16th and 17th centuries*, edited by E. E. Rich and C. H. Wilson (1967).
Vol. V., *The Economic Organization of Early Modern Europe*, edited by E. E. Rich and C. H. Wilson (1977).
R. Davies, *The Rise of the Atlantic Economies* (1973).
K. Glamann, *European Trade, 1500-1700* (1971).
A. de Maddalena, *Rural Europe, 1500-1750* (1970).
A. von Martin, *Sociology of the Renaissance* (1944).
D. C. North and R. P. Thomas, *The Rise of the Western World: A New Economic History* (1973).
B. Penrose, *Travel and Discovery in the Renaissance* (1955).
B. N. Slicher van Bath, *History of European Agriculture, 500-1850* (1963).
H. van der Wee, *The Growth of the Antwerp Market and the European Economy*, 3 vols. (1963).

RELIGION

R. Bainton, *The Reformation of the Sixteenth Century* (1952).
O. Chadwick, *The Reformation* (1964).
K. H. Dannenfeldt, *The Church of the Renaissance and Reformation* (1970).
A. G. Dickens, *The Counter Reformation* (1969).
O. Halecki, *From Florence to Brest, 1439-1596* (1958).
H. J. Hillerbrand, *The Protestant Reformation* (1968).
H. Jedin, *Ecumenical Councils of the Catholic Church: An Historical Outline* (1960).
E. G. Léonard, *A History of Protestantism*, vols. 1-2 (1965-67).
L. von Pastor, *The History of the Popes*, 40 vols. (1891-1953).
H. Trevor-Roper, *Religion, the Reformation and Social Change* (1967).
G. H. Williams, *The Radical Reformation* (1962).

PHILOSOPHY AND THE HISTORY OF IDEAS

W. J. Allen, *A History of Political Thought in the Sixteenth Century* (1928).
H. Baron, *The Crisis of the Early Italian Renaissance*, 2nd ed., 2 vols. (1966).
E. Brehier, *The History of Philosophy: The Middle Ages and the Renaissance* (1965).
N. F. Cantor and P. L. Klein, eds., *Renaissance Thought* (1969).
R. W. Carlyle and A. J. Carlyle, *A History of Mediaeval Political Theory in the West*, Vol. VI, *Political Theory from 1300 to 1600* (1936).
E. Cassirer, P. O. Kristeller and J. H. Randall, Jr., eds., *The Renaissance Philosophy of Man* (1948).
A. Chastel, *The Age of Humanism: Europe 1480-1530* (1963).
A. B. Fallico, ed., *Renaissance Philosophy* (1967).
E. Garin, *Italian Humanism, Philosophy and Civic Life in the Renaissance* (1965).
L. A. Kennedy, ed., *Renaissance Philosophy* (1973).
P. O. Kristeller, *Renaissance Thought: The Classic, Scholastic and Humanist Strains* (1961).
J. H. Randall, Jr., *The Career of Philosophy: From the Middle Ages to the Enlightenment* (1962).
R. Weiss, *The Spread of Italian Humanism* (1964).

LITERATURE, DRAMA AND MUSIC

C. T. Allmand, ed., *War, Literature and Politics in the Late Middle Ages* (1976).
F. B. Artz, *From Renaissance to Romanticism: Trends in Style in Art, Literature and Music, 1300-1830* (1962).
H. B. Brown, *Embellishing Sixteenth Century Music* (1977).
M. Bukofzer, *Music in the Baroque Era* (1947).
D. Bush, *Prefaces to Renaissance Literature* (1965).

E. K. Chambers, *The Elizabethan Stage,* 4 vols. (1924).
B. F. Dukore, *Dramatic Theory and Criticism: Greeks to Grotowski* (1974).
L. W. Forster, *The Icy Fire: Five Studies in European Petrarchism* (1969).
W. P. Friedrich, *Outline of Comparative Literature From Dante Alighieri to Eugene O'Neill* (1954).
B. Gascoigne, *World Theater: An Illustrated History* (1968).
C. Headington, *History of Western Music* (1976).
M. T. Herrick, *Tragicomedy: Its Origins and Development in Italy, France and England* (1962).
W. T. H. Jackson, *Medieval Literature* (1966).
R. A. Lanham, *The Motives of Eloquence: Literary Rhetoric in the Renaissance* (1976).
J. LaRue, ed., *Aspects of Medieval and Renaissance Music* (1966).
C. S. Lewis, *The Discarded Image: An Introduction to Medieval and Renaissance Literature* (1967).
S. M. Newton, *Renaissance Theatre Costume and the Sense of the Historic Past* (1975).
A. Nicoll, *World Drama: From Aeschylus to Anouilh* (1950).
A. M. Patterson, *Hermogenes and the Renaissance: Seven Ideas of Style* (1970).
G. Reese, *Music in the Renaissance* (1959).
N. D. Shergold, *A History of the Spanish Stage* (1967).
F. W. Sternfeld, ed., *Music From the Middle Ages to the Renaissance* (1973).
D. C. Stuart, *The Development of Dramatic Art* (1928; reprinted 1960).
W. Sypher, *Four Stages of Renaissance Style: Transformation in Art and Literature, 1400-1700* (1955).
C. J. Whitbourn, ed., *Knaves and Swindlers: Essays on the Picaresque Novel in Europe* (1974).

THE FINE ARTS

O. Benesch, *German Painting From Dürer to Holbein* (1966).
B. Berenson, *The Italian Painters of the Renaissance* (1930).
A. Blunt, *Art and Architecture in France, 1500-1700* (1953).
S. J. Feedberg, *Painting in Italy, 1500-1700* (1970).
M. J. Friedländer, *Early Netherlandish Painting From van Eyck to Breughel* (1956).
C. Gilbert, *A History of Renaissance Art* (1973).
A. Hauser, *The Social History of Art,* 2 vols. (1951).
L. H. Heydenreich and W. Lotz, *Architecture in Italy, 1400-1600* (1974).
A. M. Hind, *A History of Engraving and Etching From the Sixteenth Century to the Year 1914* (1923).
A. M. Hind, *An Introduction to the History of Woodcut,* 2 vols. (1935).
H. Hyatt Mayor, *Prints and People: A Social History of Printed Pictures* (1971).
G. Kubler and M. Soria, *Art and Architecture in Spain and Portugal and Their American Dominions, 1500-1800* (1959).
B. Lowry, *Renaissance Architecture* (1962).
L. Murray, *The High Renaissance* (1967).
P. Murray, *Architecture of the High Renaissance* (1963).
P. Murray and L. Murray, *The Art of the Renaissance* (1963).
W. Paatz, *The Arts of the Italian Renaissance: Painting, Sculpture, Architecture* (1970).
E. Panofsky, *Renaissance and Renascences in Western Art,* 2nd ed. (1965).
N. Pevsner, *An Outline of European Architecture,* 6th ed. (1960).
J. Pope-Hennessy, *Italian Renaissance Sculpture* (1971).
C. Seymour, Jr., *Sculpture in Italy, 1400-1500* (1966).
J. Sherman, *Mannerism* (1967).
A. Smart, *The Renaissance and Mannerism Outside Italy* (1972).
C. de Tolnay, *History and Technique of Old Master Drawings: A Handbook* (1943).
M. Whinney, *Early Flemish Painting* (1968).
R. Wittkower, *Architectural Principles in the Age of Humanism,* 3rd ed. (1965).

SCIENCE AND TECHNOLOGY

H. Butterfield, *The Origins of Modern Science, 1300-1800* (1949).
M. Boas Hall, *The Scientific Renaissance, 1450-1630* (1962).
E. Bruton, *Clocks and Watches, 1400-1900* (1967).
P. Butler, *The Origins of Printing in Europe* (1940).
T. F. Carter, *The Invention of Printing in China and its Spread Westward,* 2nd ed. (1955).
A. C. Crombie, *Medieval and Early Modern Science,* 2 vols. (1959).
R. J. Forbs and E. J. Dijksterhuis, *History of Science and Technology,* 2 vols. (1963).
R. H. Major, *A History of Medicine,* 2 vols. (1954).

A. Pannkock, *A History of Astronomy* (1961).
J. R. Partington, *A History of Greek Fire and Gunpowder* (1960).
G. Sarton, *Appreciation of Ancient and Medieval Science During the Renaissance* (1955).
C. Singer, E. J. Holmyard, A. R. Hall and T. Williams, eds., *A History of Technology*, Vols. II-IV (1956-58).
C. Singer, *A Short History of Scientific Ideas to 1900* (1959).
A. P. Usher, *A History of Mechanical Inventions* (1954).
L. White, Jr., *Medieval Technology and Social Change* (1962).

INDEX

INDEX OF PERSONS, TERMS AND SUBJECTS WHICH ARE NOT TITLES OF ENTRIES IN THE ENCYCLOPEDIA

E

F

G

H

I

J

ACKNOWLEDGMENTS

The Publishers wish to express their thanks to the following museums, libraries, and other institutions from whose collections works have been reproduced:

Fratelli Alinari, S.p.A., Florence 57, 73, 125, 143, 182, 185, 198, 234, 237, 260, 265, 293, 295, 307, 312, 319, 324, 326, 335, 341, 371, 392, 398, 412, 426, 427, 436, 459, 492, 505, 509, 510, 516, 531, 534, 557, 560; Ashmolean Museum, Oxford 422; B. T. Batsford Ltd., London 195, 370; Bibliothèque de l'Arsenal, Paris 40; Bibliothèque Nationale, Paris 188, 308, 513; Bodleian Library, Oxford 194; Duke of Buccleuch Collection 239, 387; By permission of the British Library 59, 60, 61, 98, 372, 433, 439, 533; British Museum, London 435; British Royal Collection, Hampton Court, Crown copyright 174, 288; British Royal Collection, Windsor Castle, Crown copyright 160, 184, 296, 523, 578; California Historical Society Museum, San Marino, California 97; Civico Museo Veneziani d'Arte e di Storia, Venice 500; Collection Pourtales, Berlin 493; Courtauld Institute, London 128; Elsevier Publishing Projects, Amsterdam 1, 11, 19, 21, 23, 24, 25, 26, 27, 28, 30, 31, 33, 35, 36, 40, 43, 44, 47, 50, 52, 56, 58, 65, 72, 74, 77, 78, 79, 80, 83, 84, 89. 91, 94, 98, 100, 106, 115, 118, 119, 122, 134, 135, 139, 144, 146, 147, 148, 154, 157, 163, 164, 165, 168, 169, 170, 178, 181, 191, 196, 205, 209, 210, 214, 215, 216, 217, 225, 226, 227, 228, 230, 235, 236, 247, 252, 253, 254, 257, 261, 268, 269, 272, 290, 296, 297, 299, 300, 304, 305, 309, 310, 311, 315, 318, 322, 323, 327, 332, 333, 337, 338, 343, 352, 356, 357, 361, 375, 376, 378, 384, 386, 389, 411, 415, 418, 421, 424, 430, 431, 444, 447, 451, 464, 465, 466, 469, 473, 479, 480, 490, 498, 503, 504, 518, 522, 542-43, 544, 545, 549, 550, 555, 568, 570, 576, 584, 589; Erzebischöfliches Museum, Cologne 303; Galleria dell'Accademia Carrara, Bergamo 69; Galleria degli Uffizi, Florence 54-55, 92, 94, 142, 162, 187, 206-207, 235, 300, 414, 476; Galleria dell'Accademia, Florence 349; Galleria dell'Accademia, Venice 12; Galleria del Prado, Madrid 108, 331, 418, 478; Galleria di Cappodimonte, Naples 541; Galleria Doria Pamphili, Rome 146; Galleria Estense, Modena 540; Gemäldegalerie, Dresden 265; Germanisches Nationalmuseum, Nuremberg 318; Gilhofer and Ranschburg, Vienna 120; Gutenberg Museum, Mainz 404; Kupfertichkabinett, Berlin 345; Kunstammlunger der Veste, Coburg 62, 179, 209, 215, 277, 310; Kunsthistorische Museum, Vienna 110, 151, 244, 283, 393, 414, 429, 532, 559; Kunstmuseum, Kupferstichkabinett, Basel 456; Kunstmuseum, Leipzig 489; By permission of the Master and Fellows of Magdalene College, Cambridge, 501; Liechtensteinische Fürstliche Sammlungen, Vienna 124; Mansell Collection, London 573; Mauritshuis, The Hague 249; Metropolitan Museum of Art, New York 220; Ivo Moretti, Rome 287, 358, 401, 402-403, 448; Musée de Grenoble, 48; Musée du Louvre, Paris 218, 291, 493; Musées Royaux d'Art, Bruxelles 151; Museo degli Argenti, Palazzo Pitti, Florence 351, 534; Museo della Basilica di S. Francesco, Assisi 113, 305, 485, 500; Museo dell'Opera della Metropolitana, Siena 155; Museo Naval, Madrid 481, 499; Museo Nazionale del Bargello, Florence 491; Museum der Bildenden Künste, Leipzig 489; Museum für Kunst und Gewerbe, Hamburg 192; Museum of Art, Philadelphia 561; Museum of Science, Mainz 321; By courtesy of the Trustees of The National Gallery, London cover, 91, 153, 270, 292, 344, 362, 397, 426, 465, 545; National Gallery of Art Washington 2, 53, 66, 100, 396, 489; National Gallery of Ireland, Dublin 171; National Gallery of Scotland, Edinburgh 483; Osterreiches Bibliothek, Vienna 45, 261; Palazzio della Farnesina, Rome 230; Rijksmuseum, Amsterdam 232, 516; John Rylands University Library, Manchester 325; Staatliche Museum, Berlin 364; Städelsches Kunstinstitut, Frankfurt 437; Stedelijke Musea, Bruges 138; Isabella Stewart Gardner Museum, Boston 533; University of Michigan, William Clements Library 452; Vatican, Rome 73, 339, 346, 350, 414; Victoria and Albert Museum, London 129, 140; Walker Art Gallery, Liverpool 363.

The Publishers have attempted to observe the legal requirements with respect to copyrights. However, in view of the large number of illustrations included in this volume, the Publishers wish to apologize in advance for any involuntary omissions or errors and invite persons or bodies concerned to write to the Publishers.